THE MĀDHAVANIDĀNA

INDIAN MEDICAL TRADITION

Edited by
Dominik Wujastyk
&
Kenneth G. Zysk

Vol. IX

THE MĀDHAVANIDĀNA

With 'Madhukośa', the Commentary by Vijayarakṣita and Śrīkaṇṭhadatta (Ch. 1-10)

Introduction, Translation and Notes by

G.J. MEULENBELD

MOTILAL BANARSIDASS PUBLISHERS
PRIVATE LIMITED • DELHI

First Indian Edition: Delhi, ***2008***
Earlier Published by E.J. Brill, Leiden, Netherlands

ISBN : 978-81-208-3330-2

MOTILAL BANARSIDASS
41 U.A. Bungalow Road, Jawahar Nagar, Delhi 110 007
8 Mahalaxmi Chamber, 22 Bhulabhai Desai Road, Mumbai 400 026
203 Royapettah High Road, Mylapore, Chennai 600 004
236, 9th Main III Block, Jayanagar, Bangalore 560 011
Sanas Plaza, 1302 Baji Rao Road, Pune 411 002
8 Camac Street, Kolkata 700 017
Ashok Rajpath, Patna 800 004
Chowk, Varanasi 221 001

PRINTED IN INDIA
BY JAINENDRA PRAKASH JAIN AT SHRI JAINENDRA PRESS,
A-45, NARAINA, PHASE-I, NEW DELHI 110 028
AND PUBLISHED BY NARENDRA PRAKASH JAIN FOR
MOTILAL BANARSIDASS PUBLISHERS PRIVATE LIMITED,
BUNGALOW ROAD, DELHI 110 007

TABLE OF CONTENTS

LIST OF ABBREVIATIONS

Ā	Ātaṅkadarpaṇa, i.e. Vācaspati's commentary on the Mādhavanidāna.
AB	Introduction to agricultural botany in India, by Chalam and Venkateswarlu.
ABORI	Annals of the Bhandarkar Oriental Research Institute.
acc.	according.
AFM	Ayurvedic Flora Medica by Mooss.
A.h.	Aṣṭāṅgahṛdayasaṃhitā.
Ainslie	Ainslie's Materia Medica.
App.	Appendix.
Arch. intern. d'hist. des sc.	Archives internationales d'histoire des sciences.
Aruṇa	Aruṇadatta.
A.s.	Aṣṭāṅgasaṃgraha.
As. Res.	Asiatick Researches.
Avk	Āyurvedīya Viśva-Kośa.
Bd.	Band, i.e. volume.
BDHM Hyderabad	Bulletin of the Department of History of Medicine, Osmania Medical College, Hyderabad (A.P.).
Bhā.pra.	Bhāvamiśra's Bhāvaprakāśa.
Bhā.pra.nigh.	Bhāvaprakāśanighaṇṭu.
Bhaṭṭ.	Bhaṭṭasvāmin's commentary on Kauṭilya's Arthaśāstra (The Pratipadapañcikā, a commentary on Arthaśāstra 2, 8, 5 to 2, 36, 47 by Bhaṭṭasvāmin, edited by K. P. Jayaswal and A. Banerji-Sastri, JBORS 11, 1925 and 12, 1926).
Bhatt.	D. C. Bhattacharyya.
Bhe.	Bheḍasaṃhitā.
Bhish	Kaviraj Kunjalal Bhishagratna's translation of the Suśrutasaṃhitā.
Bho.ku.	Raghunātha's Bhojanakutūhala.
Biswas	K. Biswas, Plants of Darjeeling and the Sikkim Himalayas.
Bor	N. L. Bor, The grasses of Burma, Ceylon, India and Pakistan.
BORI	Bhandarkar Oriental Research Institute.
Bpn	Bhāvaprakāśanighaṇṭu.
Brandis	Brandis, Indian Trees.
Bṛhad-yo.ta.	Trimallabhaṭṭa's Bṛhadyogataraṅgiṇī.
BSHM	Bulletin de la Société française d'histoire de la médecine.
BSOAS	Bulletin of the School of Oriental and African Studies.
Ca.	Carakasaṃhitā.
Cakra	Cakrapāṇidatta.
Cakradatta	Cakrapāṇidatta's Cikitsāsaṃgraha.
Calc.	Calcutta.
Candra	Candranandana.
Cat.	Catalogue.

Cat.Cat.	Aufrecht's Catalogus Catalogorum.
cf.	confer, i.e. compare.
ch.	chapter.
Chakraberty	C. Chakraberty, An interpretation of ancient Hindu medicine.
Chakravarty	T. Chakravarty's Food and drink in ancient Bengal.
Chopra	Chopra's Glossary of Indian medicinal plants.
Ci.	Cikitsāsthāna.
Ci.ka.	Tīsaṭa's Cikitsākalikā.
Class. doctr.	Filliozat, The classical doctrine of Indian medicine.
Coll.	College.
coll.	collection.
coll. Jones IO	Tawney and Thomas, Catalogue of two collections of Skt. Mss. preserved in the India Office Library.
comm.	commentary.
Comm. Vol.	Commemoration Volume.
Cooke	Cooke's Flora of Bombay.
CP	Watt, The commercial products of India.
Cult.	Culture.
Ḍa.	Ḍalhaṇa.
Dasgupta and De	Dasgupta and De, A history of Sanskrit Literature.
Dgm	Dravyaguṇamañjūṣā.
Dgv	Dravyaguṇavijñāna.
Dha. nigh.	Dhanvantarīyanighaṇṭu.
Dietz	Dietz, Analecta Medica.
Dīnānāth	Dīnānāth's Hindi commentary on the Mādhavanidāna.
Dn	Dhanvantarīyanighaṇṭu.
Dravyaguṇa	Cakrapāṇidatta's Dravyaguṇa.
Duthie	Duthie's Flora of the Upper Gangetic Plain.
Dutt; Dutt, MM; Dutt, M. M.	U. Ch. Dutt's Materia Medica.
DWH	Pharmacographia Indica, by Dymock, Warden and Hooper.
Dy	Dymock, The vegetable materia medica of Western India.
Ed., ed.	edition, editor.
esp.	especially.
f.	feminine.
fasc.	fascicle, fasciculus.
fem.	feminine.
Festschr.	Festschrift.
Filliozat	Filliozat, The classical doctrine of Indian medicine.
fr.	from (introducing a partial quotation).
Gaṇ.	Gaṇapati Śāstrī's commentary on Kauṭilya's Arthaśāstra (The Arthaśāstra of Kauṭalya with the commentary Śrīmūla of T. Ganapati Sastri, 3 parts, Trivandrum, 1924-25).
Gaṅgādhara	Gaṅgādhara's commentary on the Carakasaṃhitā.
Garbe	R. Garbe, Die Sāṃkhya-Philosophie.
Gaya	Gayadāsa.
Gesch.ind.Ph.	Frauwallner's Geschichte der indischen Philosophie.

Ghosh	J. C. Ghosh, Indigenous drugs of India.
Goudr.	Goudriaan, Kāśyapa's book of wisdom.
GSAI	Giornale della Società Asiatica Italiana.
Gul, Gul.	Carakasaṃhitā, edition and translation Gulabkunverba Ayurvedic Society.
Hā.	Hārītasaṃhitā.
Hārāṇacandra	Hārāṇacandra's commentary on the Suśrutasaṃhitā.
HB	Hoernle's edition and translation of the Bower Manuscript.
H.Ch. (Rāy)	Rāy's History of chemistry in ancient and medieval India.
He.	Hemādri.
H.I.M.	G. Mukhopādhyāya's History of Indian Medicine.
H.I.Ph.	Dasgupta's History of Indian Philosophy.
Hist.	History.
Hist. Ind. Pharm.	Srivastava's History of Indian Pharmacy.
Hist. Skt. Lit.	Keith, A history of Sanskrit literature.
HK, H.K.	Hilgenberg and Kirfel's translation of the Aṣṭāṅgahṛdayasaṃhitā.
Hoernle	Hoernle's translation of the Suśrutasaṃhitā.
Hooker	Hooker's Flora of India.
H.S.S.	Haridas Sanskrit Series.
HSu	Hoernle's translation of the Suśrutasaṃhitā.
I.	Indriyasthāna.
ibid.	ibidem.
IC	Indian Culture.
IHQ	Indian Historical Quarterly.
Imp. Gaz.	The Imperial Gazetteer of India.
Intern. Code	International Code of Botanical Nomenclature.
introd.	introduction.
instr.	instrumental (case).
IO	India Office.
I. Ph.	Radhakrishnan's Indian Philosophy.
IRM	The Wealth of India : A Dictionary of Indian Raw Materials.
JA	Journal Asiatique.
JAOS	Journal of the American Oriental Society.
JBORS	Journal of the Bihar and Orissa Research Society.
Jolly	Jolly, Medicin.
JRAS	Journal of the Royal Asiatic Society.
Ka.	Kalpasthāna.
Kā.	Kāśyapasaṃhitā.
Kauṭ.	Kauṭilīya Arthaśāstra, ed. Kangle.
Kav, Kav., Kavir., Kaviratna	Kaviratna's translation of the Carakasaṃhitā.
KB	Kirtikar and Basu, Indian medicinal plants.
Khi.	Khilasthāna.
Ki.	Kinjavadekar's edition of the Aṣṭāṅgasaṃgraha.
Krishnamachariar	Krishnamachariar's History of classical Sanskrit literature.
Kutumbiah	Kutumbiah, Ancient Indian Medicine.
L.	lexicographer.

l.c.	libro citato; loco citato.
Losch	Losch, Rājadharma.
M, M.	Madhukośa.
m.	masculine.
Mā.ni.	Mādhavanidāna.
Ma.nigh.	Madanapālanighaṇṭu.
Manson	Manson-Bahr, Manson's Tropical Diseases.
masc.	masculine.
MIO	Mitteilungen des Instituts für Orientforschung, Berlin.
M.M. (Dutt)	U. Ch. Dutt's Materia Medica.
Ms.	manuscript.
Mss.	manuscripts.
Müller	R. F. G. Müller.
Mukh.	G. Mukhopādhyāya's History of Indian Medicine.
MW., M.W.	Monier-Williams, Sanskrit-English Dictionary.
n.	neuter; note.
Na	Nighaṇṭu Ādarśa.
Nadk.	Nadkarni's Indian Materia Medica.
NAL	Nova Acta Leopoldina.
New Cat.Cat.	Raghavan's New Catalogus Catalogorum.
NF	Neue Folge.
Ni.	Nidānasthāna.
NIA	New Indian Antiquary.
Nicholson	Nicholson, A literary history of the Arabs.
Nigh.	Nighaṇṭu.
Niścala	Niścalakara.
Nobel	J. Nobel, Ein alter medizinischer Sanskrit-Text und seine Deutung.
nom. conserv.	nomen conservandum.
nom. illeg.	nomen illegitimum.
N.S.	Nouvelle Série.
N.S.-Press	Nirṇaya Sāgar Press.
N.-W. P.	North-Western Provinces.
Om Prakash, OP	Om Prakash, Food and drinks in ancient India.
p.	page.
PA	Pharmacognosy of Ayurvedic drugs, Trivandrum.
Pa.ra.	Mādhava's Paryāyaratnamālā.
Phar. Ind.	Pharmacographia Indica, by Dymock, Warden and Hooper.
Ph.gn.Ā.dr.	Pharmacognosy of Ayurvedic drugs, Trivandrum.
pl.	plural.
PO	Poona Orientalist.
Pr	Mādhava's Paryāyaratnamālā.
Purseglove	Purseglove's Tropical crops.
PW, P.W.	Petersburg Dictionary.
Rājan., Rā.nigh.	Rājanighaṇṭu.
Rā.va.nigh.	Rājavallabhanighaṇṭu.
Rn	Rājanighaṇṭu.
Roxb.	Roxburgh's Flora Indica.

S.	Série; Series.
SA	Sudhoffs Archiv für Geschichte der Medizin und der Naturwissenschaften.
Śā.	Śārīrasthāna.
Sanyal	Sanyal, Vegetable drugs of India.
Śārṅga	Śārṅgadharasaṃhitā.
Sch.	scholiast.
Seal	Seal, The positive sciences of the ancient Hindus.
Sham.	Shamasastry's translation of Kauṭilya's Arthaśāstra.
Si.	Siddhisthāna.
Sinh Jee	Sinh Jee, A short history of Aryan medical science.
Śivadāsa	Śivadāsasena.
Śkdr.	Śabdakalpadruma.
Skt.	Sanskrit.
Śrīdāsa	Śrīdāsapaṇḍita.
Śrīkaṇṭha	Śrīkaṇṭhadatta.
st.	stanza.
St. I.C.H.	Gode's Studies in Indian Cultural History.
St. I.L.H.	Gode's Studies in Indian Literary History.
Su.	Suśrutasaṃhitā.
Sū.	Sūtrasthāna.
Sudarśanaśāstrī	Sudarśanaśāstrī's Hindī commentary on the Mādhavanidāna.
Suśr.	Suśrutasaṃhitā.
t.	tome, i.e. volume.
Toḍara	Toḍara's commentary on the Nidānasthāna of the Aṣṭāṅgahṛdayasaṃhitā.
transl.	translation.
U.	Uttarasthāna; Uttaratantra.
Ullmann	Ullmann, Die Medizin im Islam.
v.	verse.
V.	Vanauṣadhicandrodaya.
Va.	Vaṅgasena.
Vā.	Vāgbhaṭa.
Vall, Vall.	Vallauri's translation of ch. 1-5 of the Mādhavanidāna.
var.	varietas, variety.
Vi.	Vimānasthāna.
Viennot	Viennot, Le culte de l'arbre dans l'Inde ancienne.
v.l.	varia lectio.
Vogel	Vogel's translation of ch. 1-5 of Vāgbhaṭa's Aṣṭāṅgahṛdayasaṃhitā.
vol.	volume.
Vśs	Vaidyakaśabdasindhu.
v.s.v.	vide sub vocabulo.
Watt CP	Watt, The commercial products of India.
Wise	Wise, Commentary on the Hindu System of Medicine.
Yādavaśarman	Vaidya Jādavjī's edition of tho Mādhavanidāna.
Yo.	Yogaratnākara.

Winternitz	Winternitz, Geschichte der indischen Literatur.
WZKM	Wiener Zeitschrift für die Kunde des Morgenlandes.
WZKSOA	Wiener Zeitschrift für die Kunde Süd- und Ostasiens.
ZDMG	Zeitschrift der Deutschen Morgenländischen Gesellschaft.

Addendum :

EI	Encyclopaedia of Islam.

INTRODUCTION

The presentation of a translation of the Mādhavanidāna and its chief commentary needs some words of introduction in order to explain why this particular treatise was selected.

Firstly I have to bring to the reader's notice that the three classical *saṃhitās* of Sanskrit medical literature are available in translations. The Carakasaṃhitā was twice translated into English (by Kaviraj Avinash Chandra Kaviratna and by a group of scholars of the Shree Gulabkunverba Ayurvedic Society); a third translation (by Ramkaran Sarma and Bhagavan Das), with extracts from Cakrapāṇidatta's commentary, is in course of preparation. The Suśrutasaṃhitā was translated into Latin (by F. Hessler) and into English (by Kaviraj Kunjalal Bhishagratna); there are also incomplete translations of this text (Sū. 1-14 by Hoernle; Sū. 1-42, 10 by Udoy Chand Dutt; Sū. 42, 10-46, 176 by Aughorechunder Chattopadhyaya). The Aṣṭāṅgahṛdayasaṃhitā was translated into German (by L. Hilgenberg and W. Kirfel); the first five chapters of both the Sanskrit original and the Tibetan version were translated into English (by C. Vogel). Among the vast mass of medical Sanskrit literature, apart from the mentioned *saṃhitās*, a restricted number of texts has been partially translated : Aṣṭāṅgasaṃgraha (BDHM Hyderabad, 1964), Bheḍasaṃhitā (Sū. 16, by Filliozat and by R. F. G. Müller), Hārītasaṃhitā (section 2, chapter 1, by Filliozat), Bhāvaprakāśa (the ophthalmological parts, by Esser), Cikitsākalikā with Candraṭa's commentary (by Jolly), Toḍara's Āyurvedasaukhya (BDHM Hyderabad, 1965) and Kalyāṇakāraka (BDHM Hyderabad, 1965), not to mention translations found in books on Indian medicine in general and articles on special subjects.

The first five chapters of the Mādhavanidāna were already translated into Italian by Vallauri (GSAI 26, 1913-14, p. 253-290).

The systematic study of the medical compendia and compilations, which were composed in increasing numbers after the age of the *saṃhitās* had passed, has scarcely begun; translations and attempts to analyze their contents are scarce. So it appeared desirable to work at a translation of the earliest and most important compendium on the section of Indian medicine that is traditionally called *nidāna*, the Rogaviniścaya by Mādhava, usually referred to as the Mādhavanidāna. Though the first work of this type to appear in the field of Sanskrit medical literature, it has remained a classic up to modern times.

Mādhava set the standard as to the order in which the diseases should be described. In this he definitely improved upon the earlier *saṃhitās*, in which a restricted number of diseases is dealt with in the section on *nidāna*, while the remaining ones are found in various other sections. Collecting his material from the *saṃhitās*, for the greater part at least, and selecting what was appropriate to the nature of his work and its scope, he organized the whole in a new way. Mādhava clearly met with success. The compendia written by subsequent authors (Vṛndakuṇḍa's Siddhayoga, Cakrapāṇidatta's Cikitsāsaṃgraha, Vaṅgasena's Cikitsāsārasaṃgraha, Bhāvamiśra's Bhāvaprakāśa, etc.) faithfully reflect the scheme of the Mādhavanidāna.

The almost complete translation of a commentary on a Sanskrit medical text hardly needs justification, because the only specimen available so far is the abbreviated rendering of the first part of Candraṭa's commentary on Tīsaṭa's Cikitsākalikā (Jolly, ZDMG 60, 1906, p. 413-468). The commentaries on Sanskrit medical texts are of great importance for a number of reasons.

The text of a Sanskrit medical treatise is not clear in many instances and may be interpreted in a number of ways. The commentaries are indispensable for a correct understanding of the way in which difficult passages were explained according to tradition. Conflicting views are often discussed by commentators and variants of the text are recorded. Quotations from and references to works which have not been preserved and works which are still extant are frequently found in commentaries. For this reason they are essential tools in establishing a relative chronology of medical authors and works. Apart from all this, the way of reasoning about medical concepts and the tendency to reconcile disagreeing traditions are interesting in themselves.

The text of the most important commentary on the Mādhavanidāna, the Madhukośa, is presented here in an almost complete translation. Only those parts of it dealing with subjects not connected with medicine, particularly discussions on grammar, have been left out. The task of rendering the commentary into English presented many problems. I have kept rather close to the peculiar style of a Sanskrit commentary, which has the disadvantage of making difficult reading, but retains the flavour of the original. On the other hand it does not obscure that it proved impossible sometimes to arrive at a full understanding of the allusions to various theories, opinions, conflicting views etc., which may have been clear in the age in which the commentary was composed, but are confusing when the sources are not referred to by name or lost to us.

Seeing that many translations of medical Sanskrit texts are unsatisfactory in certain respects, I tried to elaborate a translating technique which would render the original as consistently as possible. First of all it should make clear what is in the text and what is added by the translator. In this respect Bhishagratna's translation of the Suśrutasaṃhitā is a bad example of what a translation should be; elements from Ḍalhaṇa's commentary are incorporated in the translation without indication, a practice that results in confusing all those who cannot consult the Sanskrit text for comparison at every page. Words necessary to complete a sentence or make clear its meaning have been put between brackets in the translation here presented. There are also many versions with a tendency to overinterpretation, especially by the use of technical terms borrowed from contemporary medical science (e.g. the Gulabkunverba translation of the Carakasaṃhitā and Bhishagratna's translation of the Suśrutasaṃhitā).

Finally, it is my conviction that names of medicinal plants should remain untranslated whenever their botanical identification is doubtful, i.e. in the greater number of cases (in this respect Hilgenberg and Kirfel's translation of the Aṣṭāṅgahṛdayasaṃhitā shows much more confidence than is warranted; the Gulabkunverba translation of the Carakasaṃhitā is a particularly bad example, because it forces the reader to learn by heart the equivalents used or to consult the list of Sanskrit names with their equivalents again and again).

The most difficult problem encountered in preparing the translation of the Mādhavanidāna and the Madhukośa consisted in finding suitable English equivalents for the great number of technical Sanskrit terms. Firstly, I generally avoided the use of modern medical terms except in a few cases where they appeared adequate. Secondly, striving for a translation that would be as consistent as possible, I decided to render technical terms by a fixed equivalent whenever the range of meaning of the Sanskrit word allowed this. As a matter of fact the work went through a series of stages in order to accomplish this aim, but it proved to be a method that could be worked out. In this way it becomes easier to find out which terms are synonymous or convey a related meaning and which terms have different connotations. A better understanding of the Sanskrit technical terms used in medical texts is moreover acquired by comparing parallel passages from several texts. Those who are not versed in Sanskrit are unable to do so and will be at a loss when comparing the existing translations, which are so different from one author to another that a comparison is not possible at all. That is why I have added translations of the parallel passages in notes on the respective chapters, which has the attendant advantage that much material from hitherto untranslated texts can be presented.

The volume is provided with a series of Appendices which may increase its usefulness to those who have not made a special study of Sanskrit medical texts.

The work would have been incomplete without a concordance of the Nidāna and lists of the quotations and their sources, found in the commentary (App. 1). The printed editions are not always reliable in this respect and certainly not complete. The errors of the printed editions have been corrected; a number of hitherto unidentified passages and quotations has been traced to their sources, though gaps remain, some of which may be filled in later.

As no reliable survey of our present knowledge on the chronology of Sanskrit medical authors and works is available, I have summarized what is known to me about the authors and works referred to (App. 2). Some information on technical terms was thought to be useful, both to medical historians and Sanskritists (App. 3). The material has been largely collected from Sanskrit medical treatises and *nighaṇṭus*; the latter have so far not been much studied.

The botanical identifications of plants mentioned in Sanskrit texts is a field in which almost complete confusion reigns, a fact of which every Sanskritist is constantly aware. A preliminary survey of the identifications as found in the literature pertaining to this field seems highly desirable. The material collected only applies to plant names found in this volume (App. 4). Decisions regarding the adequacy of the identifications could not be reached in this way and require much separate study.

Identification of the syndromes described, or the clusters of symptoms enumerated, has been attempted, but proved an exceedingly difficult task (App. 5). A thorough acquaintance with the diseases prevalent in India at the present time and with the history of those diseases is absolutely required to solve the problems, and this is lacking in the present author. I have tried, however, to arrive at a first approximative evaluation of the data presented and can only hope that a great number of medical colleagues, specialized in the several branches of medicine, will endeavour to improve on these first attempts.

The translation is based on the edition of the Mādhavanidāna with the

Madhukośa and extracts from the Ātaṅkadarpaṇa by Vaidya Jādavjī Trikumjī Āchārya (fifth edition, 1955, Nirṇaya Sāgar Press, Bombay). Several other editions of the Nidāna and the Nidāna with the Madhukośa were consulted for comparison (see Bibliography). The differences proved to be of little importance, even with regard to the number of additional stanzas. Additions to Mādhava's text of the Nidāna are, as a rule, indicated as such, or have been put between brackets. Words which complete sentences and are put between brackets are by the hand of the translator. Untranslated parts of the commentaries are indicated by three dots. The editions of Sanskrit texts referred to in the notes and Appendices are those recorded in the Bibliography and, when more than one edition of a text is found there, it is the first one of the list.

I shall now give a survey of what is known about (1) Mādhava and his works, (2) the commentaries on the Mādhavanidāna, (3) Vijayarakṣita and Śrīkaṇṭhadatta, the authors of the Madhukośa, and (4) Vācaspati, the author of the Ātaṅkadarpaṇa.

MĀDHAVA(KARA).

The author of the Rogaviniścaya does not reveal his name in the text of the work, but in colophons of manuscripts of the Nidāna and its commentaries he is called Mādhava (Cat.Skt.Mss. BORI, vol. 16, part 1, nr. 149, p. 184), Śrīmādhava (l.c., nr. 151, p. 187, and nr. 153, p. 189) and Mādhavakāra (l.c., nr. 152, p. 188). In the Madhukośa his name appears as Mādhava and Mādhavakara. Śrīkaṇṭhadatta refers to him as Mādhavakāra in the introduction to the comments on chapter two of Vṛnda's Siddhayoga. Niścalakara quotes from Mādhava and Mādhavakara (Bhatt., IHQ 23, 1947, p. 146 and 153), but it is not clear from Bhattacharyya's indications whether the Nidāna is quoted in Niścalakara's Ratnaprabhā. Hemādri, who quotes, with mention of the title of the work, six times from the Rugviniścaya in his commentary on Vāgbhaṭa's Aṣṭāngahṛdayasaṃhitā, once cites it (on A.h.Sū. 8, 28) as the work of Mādhavakara, omitting its title.

Mādhava's name does appear, however, at the end of one of his other works, granted that this work, the Paryāyaratnamālā, was indeed composed by the same author; in the concluding stanzas it is disclosed that it was written by Mādhava, the physician (*bhiṣaj*). From the foregoing it is clear that we are not quite sure whether the author of the Rogaviniścaya was called Mādhava or Mādhavakara.

About Mādhava(kara)'s lineage little information is available. In a small number of manuscripts his father is mentioned by name, but there is no agreement among these sources. Mādhava is said to be a son of Indukara in the colophon of a manuscript of Vācaspati's commentary on the Nidāna (Cat.Skt.Mss. BORI, vol. 16, part 1, nr. 149, p. 184); his father's name appears as Candrakara, which may be regarded as a synonym of Indukara, in the colophon of a manuscript of the Mādhavacikitsita (l.c., nr. 143, p. 178); at the end of the printed text of Mādhava's Paryāyaratnamālā (an edition based on nine manuscripts, only one of which contains the concluding stanzas), the author says that he is a son of Indrakara (*ardhaśloka* 1756). Usually it is assumed that Indukara is the correct form of the name of Mādhava's father (see e.g. S. K. De, NIA 2, 1939-40, p. 273, footnote 4; the same in R. C. Majumdar, The history of Bengal, vol. 1, p. 315). The view, held by some, that this Indukara may be identical with Indu, the commentator on the Aṣṭāṅgasaṃgraha, is not based on evidence and certainly erroneous (see App. 2 : Indu).

It has been supposed that Mādhavakara and his father, Indukara, belonged to the Kara family, mentioned as one of the families of Bengal physicians by Bharatamallika in his Candraprabhā (Candraprabhā p. 7-9, acc. to Bhatt., IHQ 23, 1947, p. 128-129; Bharatamallika was a Bengal commentator who lived about 1800, acc. to Krishnamachariar, p. 145, footnote 1; see about Bharatamallika : N. N. Dasgupta, The Bengali commentators on the Amarakośa, IC 2, 1935-36, p. 266). The only evidence on this point is the ending -kara of the names of Mādhava and his father, and, as we have seen, there is no certainty in this regard with respect to Mādhava's name. Therefore it has rightly been pointed out (S. K. De, NIA 2, 1939-40, p. 273, footnote 4; the same in R. C. Majumdar, The history of Bengal, vol. 1, p. 315, footnote 3) that it is doubtful whether -kara really was a cognomen of Mādhava; S. K. De adds that the name of Mādhava's father, Indukara, is intelligible in itself and need not lead to the supposition of a Bengal origin; moreover he refers, as an example, to Bhānukara, the author of the Rasikajīvana, who did not belong to Bengal.

A clue with regard to his place of residence has been supplied by Mādhava himself. At the end of the Paryāyaratnamālā (*ardhaśloka* 1755) he has clearly indicated that he was an inhabitant of Śilāhrada. The problem of Mādhava's provenance can only be settled by the identification of this locality. Bhattacharyya observes (IHQ 23, 1947, p. 154) that it appears to have been a famous place at that time, at a considerable distance from Pāṭaliputra, for it is mentioned in an illustration in Vācaspatimiśra's Nyāyakaṇikā : "Someone who has obtained a favour at Pāṭaliputra will certainly not remember it without confusion at Śilāhrada" (Nyāyakaṇikā, Chowkhamba ed., p. 301, acc. to Bhatt., l.c., p. 154; Vācaspatimiśra lived about 850 acc. to Winternitz, vol. 3, p. 436-437). No more is known to me about the location of Śilāhrada.

Though it is asserted sometimes that there is no conclusive evidence to assign Mādhava to Bengal (see e.g. S. K. De, NIA 2, 1939-40, p. 273-274; S. K. De in R. C. Majumdar, The history of Bengal, vol. 1, p. 315-316), Bhattacharyya defended the view (l.c., p. 153-154) that he lived in Bengal and, in order to prove this theory, he drew attention to the Bengali synonyms of substances of vegetable, animal and mineral origin, occurring in Mādhava's Paryāyaratnamālā. N. N. Das Gupta (IC 3, 1936-37, p. 155) also claims a Bengal origin for Mādhava and pays attention to the vernacular words in the Paryāyaratnamālā, adding that the substances mentioned in it are for the greater part still known by the same names in Bengal. Many terms from the popular speech are indeed given in the work, but their relationship to terms from the contemporary Bengali language requires careful study.

Summarizing, it may be said that conclusive evidence, enabling us to assign Mādhava to Bengal, has not been produced so far. The problem may be brought nearer to its solution by a detailed study of the *deśī* words from the Paryāyaratnamālā.

With regard to the identity of Mādhava and his works, confusion was created by Hoernle in an article about the commentaries on the Suśrutasaṃhitā (JRAS, 1906, p. 283-302). He was struck by the observation that Ḍalhaṇa, in the introduction to his commentary on the Suśrutasaṃhitā, notes that he has studied the glosses (*ṭippaṇa*) of Śrīmādhava on this work before starting to write his own comments. Hoernle was puzzled by this statement because it was apparently unknown to him that references to Mādhava as a commentator are not a particularly rare occurrence. He made a link between Mādhava, the glossator, and Vṛnda, the author of the Siddhayoga, after noticing that Śrīkaṇṭhadatta, in his commentary on the Siddhayoga, repeatedly observes that Vṛnda added glosses (*ṭippaṇa*, *ṭippaṇikā*) of his own to stanzas of the Siddhayoga, taken from the Caraka- or Suśrutasaṃhitā (see e.g. Siddhayoga 12, 24cd; 22, 9-10; 39, 6cd). This led him to assume that Mādhava and Vṛnda were probably one and the same person (JRAS, 1906, p. 288-290). To give more force to this assumption he drew attention to the fact that the Siddhayoga, according to its colophons, is also called Vṛndamādhava;

the author discloses his name as Vṛnda at the end of the work, while no author's name appears in the Mādhavanidāna. Hoernle came to regard the Mādhavanidāna and Siddhayoga as the two parts of one great work by Vṛnda. The name Mādhavakara, abbreviated to Mādhava in the introduction to the Madhukośa, might in that case be forged as a poetical description, meaning 'maker of honey', in relation to the title of its commentary, Madhukośa, which means 'store of honey'.

At the present time it is clear that Hoernle's views do not reflect the real state of affairs. Mādhava wrote, apart from the Nidāna, a treatise on therapy which is different from the Siddhayoga and, moreover, he must have been active as a commentator. The works, partially extant, which are known to be his, are : (1) Rogaviniścaya, (2) Mādhavacikitsita, (3) Paryāyaratnamālā, (4) Praśnavidhāna, (5) Yogavyākhyā, (6) Dravyaguṇa, (7) one or more commentaries.

(1) The Rogaviniścaya, the title of the work as presented in its text (Nidāna 1, 2), also called Rugviniścaya (Śrīkaṇṭhadatta on Siddhayoga 1, 2; Hemādri in his commentary on the Aṣṭāṅgahṛdayasaṃhitā) and Gadaviniścaya (Siddhayoga 1, 2), which are synonyms of Rogaviniścaya, is usually referred to as the Mādhavanidāna. Śrīkaṇṭhadatta (on Siddhayoga 1, 2) also calls it Nidānasaṃgraha.

(2) Mādhavacikitsita. As already stated Hoernle was unaware of the existence of this work by Mādhava, though the description of a manuscript of its text (by R. Mitra; see below) was available at the time he wrote his studies on Indian medicine. In more recent times S. K. De (NIA 2, 1939-40, p. 273, footnote 8; the same in R. C. Majumdar, History of Bengal, vol. 1, p. 315, footnote 7) suggested that the Mādhavacikitsita is not a separate work, different from the Nidāna. He holds the view that the Cikitsā of Mādhava is either identical with the Rugviniścaya or represents a version of it. He refers to R. Mitra's Bikāner Catalogue (nr. 1413, p. 647-648) and says that the two opening verses, quoted by R. Mitra, are nothing else than the third and fourth verse of the Rugviniścaya, while the only concluding verse cited, which is too corrupt for identification, deals apparently with *viṣaroganidāna* (the origins of disease by poison), which forms the subject matter of the concluding chapter of the Rugviniścaya. S. K. De is right in observing that the manuscript, described by R. Mitra, begins in the same way as the Nidāna, but it must contain the text of the Mādhavacikitsā or part of it as well, for the concluding verse, cited by Mitra, does not occur in chapter 69 on *viṣaroganidāna* of the Rogaviniścaya, and, corrupt though it is, it

does not deal with *nidāna*, but, clearly, with *cikitsā*. S. K. De probably thought that it deals with *viṣaroganidāna* because the last word of the first line of the stanza is *viṣabheṣajam*. This term, literally meaning 'a remedy for poison', is absent from chapter 69 of the Nidāna and may, taken on its own, already point to a treatise on therapy. The second *pāda* of the verse quoted by R. Mitra reads : *nagaraṃ viṣabheṣajam*; this should be corrected into *nāgaraṃ viṣabheṣajam* (i.e. dry ginger is a remedy for poison) or *nāgaraṃ viśvabheṣajam* (both *nāgara* and *viśvabheṣaja* denote ginger); moreover, *pārada* (mercury) and *bījapūra* (a kind of citrus fruit) are mentioned in the same stanza. These indications suffice for me to disagree with S. K. De and to say that it is not open to doubt that the manuscript contains the Mādhavacikitsā, completely or partially.

Another manuscript of the Mādhavacikitsita, undoubtedly containing the text of Mādhava's treatise on therapy, is described by Har Dutt Sharma (Cat.Skt.Mss. BORI, vol. 16, part 1, nr. 143, p. 177-178). This manuscript, erroneously catalogued as being probably a manuscript of the Mādhavanidāna in Aufrecht's Catalogus Catalogorum (vol. 1, p. 449), is complete or almost complete. It is said to appear very old, consists of 102 leaves and its total number of verses is 1693. The work follows the order of diseases as presented in the Mādhavanidāna. Its colophon runs : *iti candrakarātmajavaidyarājaviracite* (read : *-viracitaṃ*) *cikitsāsūtraparibhāṣāsūtrasahitaṃ mādhavacikitsitaṃ samāptam*, i.e. : "Thus has been completed the Mādhavacikitsita, together with the Cikitsāsūtra and Paribhāṣāsūtra, composed by *vaidyarāja* Mādhava, the son of Candrakara". The meaning of Cikitsāsūtra and Paribhāṣāsūtra, connected in this way with the Cikitsita, is not clear. The manuscript may contain sections on general rules of treatment (*cikitsāsūtra*) and on definitions of technical terms (*paribhāṣā*). If this be so, they are probably found at the end of the Cikitsita, for it begins with the treatment of fever. A section on general therapeutic topics also forms part of the Siddhayoga (chapters 69-82) and a section on *paribhāṣā* is included in that on *māna* (measures), which is appended to Mādhava's Paryāyaratnamālā (1642-1754). A manuscript of a work, called Mādhavīcikitsā by Mādhavakara, which may be the Mādhavacikitsita, is present in the collection Cordier of the Bibliothèque Nationale of Paris (Filliozat, JA, t. 224, 1934, p. 159, nr. 87). No particulars about this manuscript are given, except that it consists of 81 folios, and it is not clear whether it is an independent manuscript or a copy. N. N. Das Gupta has stated (IC 3, 1936-37, p. 155) that Mādhava wrote his Cikitsā as a supplement to the Nidāna, explicitly setting down in the introduction to the work that he composed it after the Nidāna. N. N. Das Gupta refers to R. Mitra's Bikāner catalogue, which remains unintelligible to me, unless he studied the manuscript itself and read more of it than the lines quoted by Mitra, and to G. Bühler's Gujarāt catalogue (fasc. 4, p. 230; this fascicle was inaccessible to me). Mādhava's Cikitsita is quoted by Śrīkaṇṭhadatta in his commentary on the Siddhayoga, according to N. N. Das Gupta (IC 3, 1936-37, p. 155). This is confirmed by a cursory examination of the commentary. Śrīkaṇṭhadatta quotes the Mādhavacikitsita : 1) on Siddhayoga 1, 23; the quotation is, without indicating its source, introduced by *yad uktam* (i.e. as has been said) and proves to be identical to the first stanza of the Mādhavacikitsita, as presented by the Poona manuscript; 2) probably on 1, 25; Mādhava is said to be the source, but the name of the work is not mentioned; 3) in the comment on 61, 9; Mādhava is quoted, but the title of the work is omitted; it may be a quotation taken from some other work by Mādhava. Mādhava's treatise on therapy was also known to Niścalakara, who refers to it as the Mādhavasaṃgraha (Bhatt., IHQ 23, 1947, p. 146). Several quotations in the Madhukośa and Ātaṅkadarpaṇa, which I could only trace to the Siddhayoga (see App. 1), may originally have been taken from the Mādhavacikitsita; this, however, cannot be verified at the present time, because the Mādhavacikitsita has not been edited.

(3) The Paryāyaratnamālā, or, as Mādhava calls the work himself, Ratnamālā, has been critically edited by Dr. Tarapada Chowdhury (Patna, 1946). The work is a synonymous medical lexicon, written in verse; it also contains a section on homonyms and, as already stated, a section on measures (*māna*), the latter including the definition of technical terms (*paribhāṣā*); the vernacular words for the medicinal substances dealt with are added. Mādhava's Paryāyaratnamālā is, after the Dhanvantarīyanighaṇṭu, the oldest extant medical lexicon (*nighaṇṭu*). At the end of the work Mādhava mentions his name (Mādhava) and place of residence (Śilāhrada), the title of the work (Ratnamālā) and his father's name (Indrakara). Eight manuscripts are described by Chowdhury in his introduction. In addition to these, he made use of a printed edition and the material contained in the Śabdakalpadruma and Umeśacandra Gupta's Vaidyakaśabdasindhu, the authors of which often quote from the Ratnamālā and have had access to independent manuscripts. Among the eight manuscripts, which have been made use of by Chowdhury to establish a reliable text, there is only one that reaches the end (Cat.Skt.Mss. Calcutta Sanskrit College, vol. 10, nr. 51, p. 41;

Chowdhury must be in error here, for the Ms. is not described in vol. 10); according to Chowdhury it is not as correct as one would wish it to be. Another manuscript that does not break off before the end is (according to Chowdhury and Eggeling) described by R. Mitra (Notices of Sanskrit Manuscripts, vol. 10, p. 234, nr. 3150; this volume was inaccessible to me); Chowdhury says that it contains the concluding stanzas, but is probably full of omissions; Eggeling notes that Mādhavakara is given as the author in the colophon. Incomplete manuscripts are in the India Office Library (Eggeling, Cat.Skt.Mss. IO 5, nr. 2740, p. 976) and in the collection Cordier of the Bibliothèque Nationale of Paris (Filliozat, JA, t. 224, 1934, p. 159, nr. 70). Eggeling says (l.c., p. 976) that R. Mitra described another manuscript (Notices of Sanskrit Manuscripts, vol. 1, p. 111, nr. 207) that begins like Mādhava's Paryāyaratnamālā but is incomplete towards the end and in which Rājavallabha is said to be the author as well as an alternative title of the work itself (see Cat. Cat. 1, p. 330). This proves that there must be some kind of confusion with the Rājavallabhanighaṇṭu, though the latter work is quite distinct from the Paryāyaratnamālā. This manuscript, described by R. Mitra, is a source of uncertainty to S. K. De (NIA 2, 1939-40, p. 273, footnote 8; the same in R. C. Majumdar, The history of Bengal, vol. 1, p. 315, footnote 7) who hesitates to accept Mādhava as the author of the Paryāyaratnamālā. In my opinion the Ratnamālā can without much doubt be regarded as an authentic work by Mādhava, the author of the Rogaviniścaya. It is repeatedly quoted and referred to by later authors and commentators and appears to have been rather well known. Careful consideration is required, however, before quotations and references are assigned to Mādhava's medical lexicon. There is another Paryāyaratnamālā, written by Maheśvara Miśra; a manuscript of this work is in the Bibliothèque Nationale of Paris (see Cat.Skt.Mss. IO 5, p. 976; Cat.Cat. 1, p. 330). Govardhana, a prolific medical author and commentator, who is later than Mādhava, also wrote a Ratnamālā; this Govardhana is one of Niścalakara's most distinguished authorities (Bhatt., IHQ 23, 1947, p. 141). Mādhava's Ratnamālā is quoted by Vandyaghaṭīya-Sarvānanda in his commentary, called Ṭīkāsarvasva, on Amarasiṃha's Nāmaliṅgānuśāsana. This commentary was composed in 1159, as indicated by the author himself (on *kālavarga* 21; see Gaṇapati Śāstrī's introduction to the edition of the work). Mādhava is quoted at least five times (vol. 1, p. 112 : *tathā ca ratnamālā* = Ratnamālā 1324; vol. 1, p. 203 : *iti ratnamālāyāṃ mādhavaḥ* = Ratnamālā 185-186; vol. 2, p. 81 : *iti mādhavaḥ* = Ratnamālā 348; vol. 3, p. 245 : *tathā ca ślokārdhaparyāye mādhavaḥ* =

Ratnamālā 439; ibid. : *iti ślokaparyāye mādhavaḥ* = Ratnamālā 451 and 446; variants have been disregarded). Mādhava's work was known to Medinikara, who refers to the Ratnamālā and Mādhava in his Nānārthaśabdakośa, also called Medinīkośa (*upasaṃhāra* 3 and 4). Medinikara lived in the 14th century (about 1300 according to Chowdhury in his introduction to the Ratnamālā; in the 14th century according to Winternitz 3, p. 414-415; Renou and Filliozat, l'Inde Classique 2, p. 101 : 14th century; Zachariae, Die indischen Wörterbücher, p. 35-36 : towards the end of the 14th century; about 1375 : N. N. Das Gupta, IC 2, 1935-36, p. 264). Rāyamukuṭa, who wrote a commentary, called Padacandrikā, on the Amarakośa in 1431 (Aufrecht, ZDMG 28, 1874, p. 110; Zachariae, Die indischen Wörterbücher, p. 22) also quotes from Mādhava's Ratnamālā (Aufrecht, l.c., p. 115). A work with the title Ratnamālā is quoted by an author, called Kaumudīkāra, who is quoted in turn by Rāyamukuṭa (Aufrecht, l.c., p. 112). Finally, the Ratnamālā by the physician Mādhavakara is clearly referred to by Haricaraṇasena in the introductory stanzas of his Paryāyamuktāvalī, which was composed at an unknown date. From these stanzas it can be inferred that the work was based on that by Mādhava.

The Paryāyaratnamālā is probably quoted once in the Madhukośa (on 2, 10-11); the quotation is introduced by *yad uktam*, without specification of the source. The same quotation occurs in the Ātaṅkadarpaṇa (on the same passage), where it is said to be taken from a work called Abhidhāna, a very vague indication. The quoted words are identical with Paryāyaratnamālā 1506b, but may be from a different work, because it is a known fact that lexicographers often took their material from predecessors without specifying their sources. Moreover, there is a medical lexicon by an unknown author that is called Abhidhānaratnamālā (Cat.Skt.Mss. IO 5, nr. 2741 and 2742, p. 976-977).

(4) Praśnavidhāna. This work is once referred to by Vijayarakṣita (on 1, 14cd-15ab) in a discussion about the constitutions. He says that this subject is extensively dealt with in the Praśnavidhāna, which should be consulted (a variant, found in two manuscripts, reads Praśnasahasranidāna) and calls it a *suśrutaślokavārtika*, i.e. versified glosses on the Suśrutasaṃhitā, without indicating, however, that it was composed by Mādhava. The same work is twice referred to by Niścalakara, who calls it Praśnasahasravidhāna, i.e. 'Exposition on thousand questions' and instructs us about the author, Mādhava, because he once calls him *suśrutavārtikakāra*, i.e. the author of the glosses on Suśruta (see Bhatt., IHQ 23, 1947, p. 144).

(5) Yogavyākhyā is the title of a work by Mādhava, quoted twice by Niścalakara (Bhatt., l.c., p. 146). Bhattacharyya is in error when he asserts (l.c., p. 153) that Niścalakara gives the names of two new works by Mādhava, viz. the Yogavyākhyā and the Suśrutavārtika. The latter is, as we have seen, referred to by Vijayarakṣita, a fact noticed by Bhattacharyya himself (l.c., p. 144), though it is right to claim that Niścalakara is the first authority known to us who assigns the work to Mādhava. The Yogavyākhyā, however, is quoted as a work by Mādhavakara in Śrīkaṇṭhadatta's Kusumāvalī (on Siddhayoga 10, 47cd), though this may have escaped his attention and that of other scholars. The Yogavyākhyā may have been a work on medicinal compounds, to judge by Śrīkaṇṭhadatta's quotation.

(6) Dravyaguṇa. A work of this name by Mādhavakara is referred to by Śivadāsasena in his commentary on Cakrapāṇidatta's Cikitsāsaṃgraha (acc. to N. N. Das Gupta, IC 3, 1936-37, p. 155; he refers to p. 155 of the first ed. by Devendra Nath Sen, which was inaccessible to me; the reference could not be traced in the ed. by Śrījayadeva Vidyālaṃkāra, Lahore, 1928). Niścalakara also refers to it once in his Ratnaprabhā (Bhatt., IHQ 23, 1947, p. 143). An author, called Mādhavakāra, is quoted seven times by Hemādri in his commentary on the Aṣṭāṅgahṛdayasaṃhitā. Once (on A.h.Sū. 7, 40-41ab; see App. 3 : *maireya*) he quotes in this way from the Paryāyaratnamālā (a variant of *ardhaśloka* 1664), the other times probably from Mādhava's Dravyaguṇa (on A.h.Sū. 6, 75cd-78; Sū. 6, 82; Sū. 6, 97cd-98ab; Sū. 6, 99cd; Sū. 6, 137cd-138; Sū. 6, 161cd-163ab). It is not quite clear whether the text of Mādhava's Dravyaguṇa is still available in one or more manuscripts. An edition of a work, called Dravyaguṇa, by an author whose name is Mādhava, is planned by P. V. Sharma (Chowkhamba Sanskrit Series). For two reasons more information is required about the nature of this text and the identity of its author. Firstly, there is a work by a later author, also called Mādhava, which, though usually called Bhāvasvabhāva, is sometimes referred to as Dravyaguṇasaṃgraha (Cordier, Le Muséon, N.S. 4, 1903, p. 345-346). Secondly, at least one manuscript has been described of a work, called Dravyaguṇaratnamālā, by an author whose name is Mādhava (Cat.Skt.Mss. N.-W.P. 1, p. 590-591, nr. 28 : old and incorrect; not well-known; procurable with difficulty for copying). This manuscript is said to contain rules for preparing different medicines and their benefits. If its text really agrees with this description, it must be different from the Paryāyaratnamālā and from a text on Dravyaguṇa in its proper sense, but it may be the supposedly lost Yogavyākhyā.

(7) Mādhava's commentary or commentaries. Mādhavakara is once mentioned by Vijayarakṣita among a series of authors of explanatory works (Madhukośa on 1, 5d-6 : Jejjaṭa-Vāpyacandra-Mādhavakara-Kārtikakuṇḍa) in a passage that refers to Su.U. 39, 27, a stanza that was incorporated in the Mādhavanidāna by Vācaspati (see Ātaṅkadarpaṇa on 2, 6). It is unlikely that Mādhavakara should form one of this company, unless he wrote a commentary himself. Though it may be argued that he is a member of this group as the author of the Praśnavidhāna, this is improbable because that work was a metrical *vārtika*. Moreover, Śrīmādhava is mentioned as the author of a *ṭippaṇa* on the Suśrutasaṃhitā by Ḍalhaṇa in the introduction to his commentary on that work. Finally, Vācaspati quotes (on 5, 31-32 = Ca.Ci. 14, 21-22) an explanation by Mādhava that seems to be taken from a commentary in prose (the same quotation occurs in the Madhukośa where it is not attributed to Mādhava in an explicit way). So it is not unreasonable to suppose that Mādhava wrote a commentary on the Suśrutasaṃhitā, and, may be, on the Carakasaṃhitā as well.

As already remarked, there have been, apart from the author of the Rogaviniścaya, more medical authors, called Mādhava. Two works which have remained unmentioned so far are sometimes attributed to the author of the Rogaviniścaya. One of these is the Kūṭamudgara, ascribed to him in the Cat.Cat. (1, p. 449), New Cat.Cat. (vol. 4, p. 260-261) and by N. N. Das Gupta (IC 3, 1936-37, p. 155), while S. K. De notes (NIA 2, 1939-49, p. 273, footnote 8; the same in R. C. Majumdar, The history of Bengal, vol. 1, p. 315, footnote 7) that there is nothing to identify its author with the author of the Rugviniścaya. The Kūṭamudgara is a short treatise on regimen of twenty-two verses that would be unintelligible without a commentary. One manuscript has been described by Jolly (Cat.Skt.Mss. München, nr. 394, p. 62-63), who observed that the author is called Mādhava and that the anonymous commentary may be by the same person; no particulars about this Mādhava are given. Six manuscripts are at Poona (Cat.Skt.Mss. BORI, vol. 16, part 1, p. 63-68, nr. 51-56); the author of both text and commentary calls himself Mādhava, without adding any information about his lineage. Any judgment on the authorship of the treatise should be suspended until it has been thoroughly studied.

The second work that is sometimes ascribed to the author of the Rogaviniścaya is called Bhāvasvabhāva. Cordier described it as a manual of materia medica and hygiene (Le Muséon, N.S. 4, 1903,

p. 345-346). Two manuscripts were known to him (one in the collection Hodgson, catalogued by Cowell and Eggeling : Buddhist Skt.Mss., nr. 74, under the title : Dravyaguṇasaṃgraha, and another one mentioned in the lists of the Bhau Dājī Memorial). S. K. De noted (NIA 2, 1939-40, p. 273, footnote 8) that a third manuscript is described in Bühler's Gujarāt catalogue (G. Bühler, Catalogue of Skt. Mss. contained in the private libraries of Gujarāt, Kāṭhiāvād, Kachchh, Sindh and Khandeś, fasc. 4, p. 230; Cat.Cat. 1, p. 408). There is also a manuscript in the collection Cordier of the Bibliothèque Nationale of Paris (Filliozat, JA, t. 224, 1934, p. 159, nr. 79). Haraprasād Śāstrī discovered an incomplete manuscript (almost complete according to Cordier : Le Muséon, N.S. 4, 1903, p. 345) of a commentary on the Bhāvasvabhāva in Nepāl. He wrote about it : "The Bhāvasvabhāva is a well-known medical work by Mādhavadeva, perhaps the same as Mādhavakara, the author of the Nidāna. A commentary to the work, entitled Vaidyavallabhā (unknown to Aufrecht in his Cat.Cat.), by Meghadeva, the son of Ravinābha, has been acquired for Government. The work is incomplete and consists of 68 leaves; it treats of the properties of the articles of food and drink". Cordier (l.c.) added that Meghadeva imputes the composition of the work to Mādhavakara and says that his elucidations are really due to Indumatī. Cordier put forward that this Indumatī might be identical with Indu, the author of a commentary on the Aṣṭāṅgasaṃgraha. Acc. to N. N. Das Gupta (IC 3, 1936-37, p. 155) the Bhāvasvabhāva was written by a Mādhava who was later than the author of the Rogaviniścaya. In this case too we have to await more detailed studies which may throw light on the chronological position of the text.

Mādhava Upādhyāya, who wrote the medical treatise called Āyurvedaprakāśa, is without any doubt posterior to the author of the Rogaviniścaya. This Mādhava himself stated that he belonged to the Sārasvatakula of Saurāṣṭra and was a resident of Benares. The Āyurvedaprakāśa is a rather late work because it quotes from Trimallabhaṭṭa's Yogataraṅgiṇī (see App. 2 : Yogataraṅgiṇī; see about the Āyurvedaprakāśa : Cat.Skt.Mss. IO 5, nr. 2696 and 2697, p. 950-951; Cat.Skt.Mss. BORI, vol. 16, part 1, nr. 19 and 20, p. 22-25 and nr. 133 and 134, p. 157-160; R. G. Bhandarkar, Lists of Skt.Mss. in private libraries in the Bombay Presidency, part 1, p. 115, nr. 228; Śivaśarmā's introduction to the edition of the text by Gulrājśarmā Miśra). Mādhava Upādhyāya also wrote the Rasasiddhiprakāśa (Cat.Skt.Mss. BORI, vol. 16, part 1, nr. 224, p. 279-280).

A work, called Rasakaumudī, has been ascribed to Mādhava, the son of Indukara, by R. Mitra (Notices of Skt.Mss., vol. 4, p. 178, nr. 1616, acc. to N. N. Das Gupta, IC 3, 1936-37, p. 156, footnote 1) and Aufrecht (Cat.Cat. 1, p. 449). P. Rāy (History of chemistry, p. 229) places the work in the 16th or 17th century. N. N. Das Gupta (l.c., p. 156) and S. K. De (NIA 2, 1939-40, p. 273, footnote 8; the same in R. C. Majumdar, The history of Bengal, vol. 1, p. 315, footnote 7) agree that this work is of a later date than the Rogaviniścaya.

The author of the Āyurvedarasaśāstra, also attributed to Mādhava, the son of Indukara, by Aufrecht (Cat.Cat. 1, p. 449) is probably different again from the author of the Mādhavanidāna (New Cat. Cat. 2, p. 153; N. N. Das Gupta, l.c., p. 156; S. K. De, l.c., p. 273, footnote 8).

Apart from these medical authors, called Mādhava, there have been many others of the same name (see e.g. Śivaśarmā's introduction to the edition of the Āyurvedaprakāśa by Gulrājśarmā Miśra, p. 2-3). Some recent authors still confuse a great number of Mādhava's and present a very composite, but impressive, picture of Mādhava to their readers (see e.g. Jaggi's Scientists of ancient India and their achievements, p. 104-106).

Returning now to the author of the Mādhavanidāna, we are faced with the task of determining his date.

The terminus post quem has to be deduced from the sources Mādhava employed in the composition of the work. The other treatises are of no avail in elucidating the lower limit of the period in which Mādhava must have lived; the sources of the Paryāyaratnamālā have not yet been subject to research; the Mādhavacikitsita, which will undoubtedly contain much evidence supplementing that of the Nidāna, awaits study of its contents in almost all respects.

The Nidāna consists, for the greater part, of stanzas borrowed from the three classical medical *saṃhitās*, the Carakasaṃhitā, the Suśrutasaṃhitā and Vāgbhaṭa's Aṣṭāṅgahṛdayasaṃhitā, while a small number of verses has been taken from the Aṣṭāṅgasaṃgraha, attributed to Vāgbhaṭa; the remaining ones are from unidentified treatises or were composed by Mādhava himself (see App. 1). With regard to Mādhava's sources there has been some disagreement among scholars in the past, as will presently be explained.

The terminus ante quem of the Nidāna depends, firstly, on the date or Vṛnda, who explicitly refers to it, and, secondly, on the answer to the question whether a certain Indian medical treatise, known to early

Arabic authors, is identical with the Mādhavanidāna. Most scholars assent to the view that Mādhava borrowed from the Carakasaṃhitā, but it should always be specified whether this holds true with regard to the Carakasaṃhitā after its completion by Dṛḍhabala, because the latter is often assigned to a later period than Mādhava (see App. 2 : Caraka, Dṛḍhabala). It is not open to doubt that the Nidāna contains many stanzas taken from the Suśrutasaṃhitā, also from its Uttaratantra that was added later (see App. 2 : Suśruta, Nāgārjuna). Mādhava's indebtedness to the Aṣṭāṅgahṛdayasaṃhitā and Aṣṭāṅgasaṃgraha is usually admitted; the priority of the Aṣṭāṅgahṛdayasaṃhitā has only been questioned by Hoernle. If we accept that Mādhava lived when the Caraka- and Suśrutasaṃhitā had been completed and after the composition of the Aṣṭāṅgahṛdayasaṃhitā, his date cannot be earlier than about 600 (see App. 2 : Vāgbhaṭa).

Hoernle is the only scholar who has seriously investigated Mādhava's sources and has tried to fix his date, and, though his views are antiquated now, they deserve to be mentioned, because they have been influential for a considerable time. He thought that Mādhava had preceded Dṛḍhabala and adduced two arguments to sustain his thesis. The first was that Mādhava was not acquainted with the so-called *kāśmīrapāṭha* of the Carakasaṃhitā, identified by Hoernle with Dṛḍhabala's recension of the work. This argument does not bear proof, firstly because there is evidence that the *kāśmīrapāṭha* was known to Mādhava, and, secondly, because there is no certainty that the *kāśmīrapāṭha* refers to Dṛḍhabala's redaction of the Carakasaṃhitā (see App. 2 : Caraka). Hoernle's second argument was derived from the number of eye diseases described in the Carakasaṃhitā, Suśrutasaṃhitā, Aṣṭāṅgahṛdayasaṃhitā, Aṣṭāṅgasaṃgraha and Nidāna. His line of reasoning was as follows. Seventy-six eye diseases are enumerated in the Uttaratantra of the Suśrutasaṃhitā (U. 1, 28-45); their number is ninety-four in the Aṣṭāṅgasaṃgraha (see U. 20, 37), and the Aṣṭāṅgahṛdayasaṃhitā (see U. 16, 60cd-61ab) agrees with it. Mādhava, though abiding by the method of counting of the Suśrutasaṃhitā, nevertheless increases the total number to seventy-eight (see chapter 59) by adding two diseases of the eyelashes. Dṛḍhabala, attempting to reach a compromise, states the number to be ninety-six. From these data Hoernle inferred that Dṛḍhabala obtained his total of ninety-six by adopting the total of ninety-four from the Aṣṭāṅgasaṃgraha and adding to it the two new diseases set up by Madhava, from which it follows that Mādhava is anterior to Dṛḍhabala. Hoernle's interpretation of the evidence he collected is rather arbitrary and his line of reasoning is not convincing. The facts he presents are, when carefully considered, both vague and incomplete, He is right in asserting that seventy-six eye diseases are enumerated in the Suśrutasaṃhitā, but he omitted to mention that at least seventy-seven eye diseases are described; one disease, occurring in children, is added (see Su.U. 19, 8-9). Moreover, it is not clear what he meant by the two new diseases set up by Mādhava. He appears to refer to *pakṣmakopa* and *pakṣmaśāta*, but, if these two entities are really intended, he is in error. *pakṣmakopa* is not a new disease, described for the first time by Mādhava; it is already mentioned in the Suśrutasaṃhitā (U. 3, 29-30). *pakṣmaśāta*, on the other hand, may be a term borrowed by Mādhava from some unidentified treatise; Śrīkaṇṭhadatta equates it with *kṛcchronmīla*, described by Vāgbhaṭa (A.h.U. 8, 3-4); if Śrīkaṇṭhadatta is right, it is not a new disease but another name of a well-known disorder. It may be, however, that one of the two diseases meant by Hoernle is *kuñcana*; this entity was borrowed by Mādhava from 'some other treatise', as Śrīkaṇṭhadatta says (Madhukośa on 59, 96). It is inadmissible to conclude that Dṛḍhabala's number of eye diseases is a compromise between the numbers of Vāgbhaṭa and Mādhava. Therefore this piece of evidence concerning Dṛḍhabala's posteriority to Mādhava, put forward by Hoernle, can be set aside.

Hoernle was also convinced that Mādhava was later than the author of the Aṣṭāṅgasaṃgraha (called Vāgbhaṭa I by Hoernle) and earlier than the author of the Aṣṭāṅgahṛdayasaṃhitā (called Vāgbhaṭa II by Hoernle). The latter point is easily explained. As we have seen, Hoernle regarded Dṛḍhabala as posterior to Mādhava. Dṛḍhabala preceded Vāgbhaṭa II because a particular chapter from the Carakasaṃhitā (Ci. 26), redacted by Dṛḍhabala, is referred to in the Aṣṭāṅgahṛdayasaṃhitā (U. 40, 84). In addition to this, Aruṇadatta observes in his commentary on the Aṣṭāṅgahṛdayasaṃhitā that a particular stanza (Śā. 3, 62cd-63ab) was taken from a chapter of the Carakasaṃhitā (Ci. 15), which was also redacted by Dṛḍhabala. (See about Hoernle's views : JRAS, 1908, p. 1016-1018, and the Introduction to his Osteology, p. 14-16). Hoernle was right in regarding Dṛḍhabala as a predecessor of Vāgbhaṭa who composed the Aṣṭāṅgahṛdayasaṃhitā, but he was wrong in assuming Mādhava to be anterior to the latter. All the available data point to Mādhava as an author who was acquainted with Vāgbhaṭa's work. He borrowed extensively from it, especially in chapters 1, 5 and 7 (see App. 1). There is no evidence in favour of the supposition that he composed series of stanzas which were incorporated in the Aṣṭāṅgahṛdayasaṃhitā at a later date. On the contrary, Vijayarakṣita explicitly refers to Vāgbhaṭa when commenting on passages of the Nidāna which were borrowed from the Aṣṭāṅgahṛdayasaṃhitā (see Madhukośa on 1, 5d-6 and 1, 10). Moreover, Mādhava expressly states that his work was compiled from 'the words of various sages' (Nidāna 1, 2). So it may be assumed that Mādhava was later than the author of the Aṣṭāṅgahṛdayasaṃhitā, i.e. later than about 600 (see App. 2 : Vāgbhaṭa). The complicated way in which Hoernle tried to establish (JRAS, 1908, p. 1002-1028) that the author of the Aṣṭāṅgasaṃgraha was anterior to Mādhava is of no importance any more, since it can safely be admitted that the Aṣṭāṅgasaṃgraha was gradually elaborated after the Aṣṭāṅgahṛdayasaṃhitā had been written (see App. 2 : Vāgbhaṭa).

Finally we have to consider the date before which the Nidāna was composed.

In this respect it should firstly be recalled that the Mādhavanidāna is referred to by Vṛnda in his Siddhayoga. So Mādhava is earlier than Vṛnda, who lived about 800-900 (see App. 2 : Vṛndakuṇḍa). Secondly, it has already long been common knowledge that various Arabic authors mention an Indian medical treatise that may well be Mādhava's Rogaviniścaya. The older material on this subject was collected by A. Müller (Arabische Quellen zur Geschichte der indischen Medizin, ZDMG 34, 1880, p. 465-556). A number of Indian medical works is recorded by Ibn Abī Uṣaybi'a (who died in 1270, acc. to EI², vol. 3, p. 693) in the twelfth book of his History of physicians, the 'Uyūn al-anbā' fī ṭabaqāt al-aṭibbā'. The title of one of these treatises is written bdān (a variant reads ydān); this word is usually vocalized as Badān, though it is equally admissible to read Bidān. A. Müller prefers the reading bdān to ydān, but remains neutral with regard to the conjecture ndān, i.e. Nidān, proposed by Dietz in his Analecta Medica (p. 122), because the name Badān is already found in al-Rāzī's Kitāb al-ḥāwī (A. Müller, l.c., p. 475; al-Rāzī died in 925, acc. to Sezgin, Bd. III, p. 275). Uṣaybi'a observes (A. Müller, ibid.) that the signs of 404 diseases are described in the work, without indicating their treatment. This characterization points to the Mādhavanidāna and not to the Nidāna section of one of the classical *saṃhitā*s, because only a restricted number of disorders is dealt with in the latter under that heading. The Nidāna is also mentioned by the Arab historian (Ibn Wāḍiḥ) al-Ya'qūbī (M. Z. Siddiqi, Indo-Asian Culture 5, 1957, p. 279). This author, who is earlier than Uṣaybi'a and al-Rāzī (he lived in the second half of the ninth century, acc. to Nicholson, p. 349), describes the work in the same way as Uṣaybiʿa. Important new evidence came to light in 1928 with the edition of ʿAlī b. Sahl al-Ṭabarī's Firdaws al-ḥikma, i.e. Paradise of wisdom. In the so-called Indian books of this treatise several Indian medical works are mentioned : jrk, ssrd, ndān and as͟htānqhrdy, i.e. Caraka, Suśruta, Nidāna and Aṣṭāṅgahṛdaya. It is highly probable that ndān is the Mādhavanidāna, because no other famous Indian book with a similar title could have spread to the Arab world at so early a date (about 850). This reference to the Nidāna is the earliest one known in Arab literature. Because of its importance it is now expedient to give a summary of the most important facts about the work and its author. (For fuller accounts see Meyerhof's articles : ZDMG 85, 1931, p. 38-68 and Isis 16, 1931, p. 6-54; compare the introduction to the translation of the Indian books by Siggel, who disagrees with Meyerhof on a number of points; those versed in Arabic may read Siddiqi's introduction to his edition of the Firdaws al-ḥikma).

Abū'l Ḥasan ʿAlī b. Sahl Rabban al-Ṭabarī wrote his Firdaws al-ḥikma fī 'l-ṭibb in Sāmarrā in the third year of the reign of the caliph al-Mutawakkil, i.e. in 849-850. It is a work of large scope, giving a survey of the Greek, Syrian and Indian systems of medicine as known to the Muslims. Its arrangement is less methodical than in later medical works in Arabic, but it is often quoted by al-Rāzī and other writers. Particularly important is the thirtieth and last section of the Paradise of wisdom, which deals with Indian medicine. It describes succinctly in thirty-six chapters, the majority of which are rather short, the theory and general therapeutic principles of Indian medicine, while at the end a number of recipes is found. According to Meyerhof (ZDMG 85, 1931, p. 64) the translation of Sanskrit medical terms into Arabic is usually correct, which indicates that ʿAlī b. Sahl made use of the translations of Sanskrit medical works executed by order of the first ʿAbbāsid caliphs, in particular Hārūn al-Ras͟hīd (768-809) and the Barmakids. (See also M. Z. Siddiqi, Indo-Asian Culture 5, 1957, p. 374-378. Siggel holds the view that ʿAlī b. Sahl based his work on earlier translations of Indian texts into Syriac or Persian; see the introduction to his translation, p. 1102).

The Nidāna as a separate book is mentioned once in the Indian books of the Paradise of wisdom (see p. 1110 of Siggel's translation). The term Nidāna appears on two other occasions (p. 1116 and 1131 of Siggel's translation), where, however, it is not the Mādhavanidāna which is referred to, but the Nidāna section of some other treatise. No direct translation of parts of the Mādhavanidāna are traceable, nor of the Carakasaṃhitā, Suśrutasaṃhitā and Aṣṭāṅgahṛdayasaṃhitā, for ʿAlī b. Sahl only gives summaries of Indian medical doctrines.

Accepting the evidence afforded by 'Alī b. Sahl and later Arabic authors, it appears reasonable to suppose that Mādhava's date is about 700, taking into account the time needed for the work of an Indian writer to become so famous as to be translated into Arabic in Persia and to be employed as one of his chief sources by an Arabic author in 849-850.

THE COMMENTARIES ON THE MĀDHAVANIDĀNA

A great number of commentaries has been written on Mādhava's Rogaviniścaya, which proves that the work achieved considerable fame. The following are known to us :

(1) Madhukośa by Vijayarakṣita and Śrīkaṇṭhadatta. Jolly described a manuscript (Cat.Skt.Mss. München, nr. 378, p. 52-53) the text of which is partially more extensive than the printed editions and which also contains more quotations.
(2) Ātaṅkadarpaṇa by Vācaspati.
(3) Siddhāntacintāmaṇi (Cat.Cat. 2, p. 124). Eggeling, who described a manuscript of this work (Cat.Skt.Mss. IO 5, nr. 2670, p. 935-936), says that it was written by Narasiṃha Kavirāja, assistant of Rāmakṛṣṇa Bhaṭṭa and son of Nīlakaṇṭha Bhaṭṭa. Eggeling adds that the author refers to his commentary on the Carakasaṃhitā that was called Carakatattvaprakāśakaustubhaṭīkā and frequently adduces Caraka in illustration of Mādhava's precepts, whilst quotations from Suśruta are much rarer. This commentary appears to be the same as the Siddhāntacandrikā by Narasiṃha Kavirāja, son of Nīlakaṇṭha Bhaṭṭa and pupil of Rāmakṛṣna Bhaṭṭa, mentioned by Dasgupta (H.I.Ph. 2, p. 434, footnote 2), who says that the work, though based on the Madhukośa, is an excellent commentary, containing much that is both instructive and new. Dasgupta (erroneously) supposed that probably the only manuscript available was the one belonging to the library of his family; an edition was planned by him, but it never appeared. Aufrecht also recorded a manuscript of the Siddhāntacandrikā (Cat.Cat. 1, p. 527).
(4) Subodhinī; this work consists of short glosses on difficult portions of the Nidāna and was written by Vādeva (Vāsudeva ?) Māthura (Cat.Cat. 3, p. 112; Cat.Skt.Mss. München, nr. 380, p. 53-54; Cat. Skt.Mss. BORI, vol. 16, part 1, nr. 152, p. 187-188).
(5) Mādhavanidānaṭippaṇī by Bhāvamiśra (Cordier, Le Muséon, N.S. 4,

1903, p. 350); a work of the same title is also recorded, without author's name, in R. Mitra's Bikāner Catalogue (nr. 1415, p. 648-649).

(6) a commentary by Bhavānī Sahāya (Cat.Cat. 1, p. 527; Cat.Skt.Mss. N.-W.P. 1, p. 582-583, nr. 2 : Rugvinirṇayaṭīkā by Bhavāni Sahāya, a short commentary on the Rugvinirṇaya, not procurable for copying, little known, recent and incorrect).

(7) a commentary by Rāmanātha Vaidya (Cat.Cat. 1, p. 527; Cat.Skt. Mss. N.-W.P. 1, p. 582-583, nr. 5 : a short commentary on the Mādhavanidāna, not procurable for copying, little known, recent and incorrect).

(8) Vaidyamanoramā by Rāmakṛṣṇa, son of Gaurī and Nīlakaṇṭha (Cat.Cat. 3, p. 112).

(9) a commentary by Raiśarman (Cat.Cat. 3, p. 112).

(10) a commentary by Gaṇeśa Bhiṣaj (Cat.Cat. 1, p. 527).

(11) a commentary by Hāradhana (Filliozat, JA, t. 224, 1934, p. 162, nr. 152). A work, called Rugviniścayapariśiṣṭa, by Hārādhana, son of Viśārada, is recorded by Aufrecht (Cat.Cat. 2, p. 124).

(12) Śāradā by Śrīśāradācaraṇasena; this work is a relatively modern commentary in Sanskrit.

(13) Sudhālaharī by Umeśānanda Śarman; this is a modern commentary in Sanskrit.

A work, sometimes said to be a commentary on the Mādhavanidāna (Cat.Cat. 1, p. 527; R. Mitra's Bikāner catalogue, p. 652; Dasgupta, H.I.Ph. 2, p. 434), is the Nidānapradīpa by Nāganātha, the eldest son of Kṛṣṇabhaṭṭa. Eggeling observed (Cat.Skt.Mss. IO 5, nr. 2671, p. 936) that it is rather surprising that Mādhava is never once alluded to by Nāganātha, unless, indeed, the title of the work is meant to imply that the work is intended to be an exposition or paraphrase of the Mādhavanidāna. According to Jolly (Cat.Skt.Mss. München, nr. 381, p. 54-55) the Nidānapradīpa is an extensive treatise in verse on pathology and not a commentary on the Nidāna.

VIJAYARAKṢITA is the author of the first half of the Madhukośa. His share ends with the comments on chapter thirty-two. Why he did not complete his commentary is a matter of uncertainty, but probably death intervened. No other works of his hand are known. Niścalakara affords information about Vijayarakṣita's death, for he notes (in the fifth stanza of his introduction to the Ratnaprabhā, acc. to Gode, St. I.L.H. 1, p. 124, footnote 1) that he started writing his commentary after the death of Vijayarakṣita, who was his teacher. Taking into account that the Ratnaprabhā was composed between 1110 and 1120 according to Bhattacharyya (IHQ 23, 1947, p. 134), Vijayarakṣita's death must have occurred some time before that decade. If Bhattacharyya is right in stating that Niścalakara was undoubtedly a native of Bengal (l.c., p. 128-129), it may be safely assumed that Vijayarakṣita lived there too. The arguments adduced by Bhattacharyya to prove Niścalakara's Bengal origin are based on the ending -kara of his name and that of his father, on the fact that he refers to different localities of Bengal and, finally, on the local names of medicinal plants recorded in the Ratnaprabhā. Vijayarakṣita may have been in charge of an *ārogyaśālā* (hospital), for he is called *ārogyaśālīyavaidyapati* in the colophons of some old manuscripts of the Madhukośa (Cat.Skt.Mss. BORI, vol. 16, part 1, p. 178-179, nr. 144, a manuscript dated 1363; Bhatt. also refers to R. Mitra's Bikāner catalogue, p. 649).

According to N. N. Das Gupta (IC 3, 1936-37, p. 160) the term *ārogyaśālīya* is not easy to explain; he observes that it is an epithet of Śākyamuni (i.e. Buddha) and Avalokiteśvara, but adds that he does not consider this to be a proof that Vijayarakṣita openly professed Buddhism in the age he lived. N. N. Das Gupta adheres to Hoernle's date of Vijayarakṣita (about 1240), which explains his difficulties, because Buddhism had declined in Bengal at that time. Bhattacharyya (IHQ 23, 1947, p. 127-134) has contributed a great deal to the elucidation of Vijayarakṣita's date, which was erroneously fixed by Hoernle at about 1240 (Osteology, Introduction p. 17). He noticed that Niścalakara has recorded the names of some of his distinguished patients; among these there was a Buddhist monk and scholar, called Śākyarakṣita. This is only one of a whole series of references to Buddhism in the Ratnaprabhā, though Niścalakara himself professed Śaivism. Śāntideva's Bodhicaryāvatāra is referred to and Dharmakīrti is quoted; it is said that a particular medicine should be taken after paying obeisance to Khasarpaṇa, a particular manifestation of Lokeśvara, who is, in his turn, an emanation of Amitābha (see Sādhanamālā, vol. 2, Introduction, p. 152-155); Khasarpaṇa is also the name of a village in the Khāḍīmaṇḍala (Sādhanamālā, vol. 1, p. 42-43), located in lower Bengal by Bhattacharyya (l.c., p. 129). At some places Hindu and Buddhist scriptures are mentioned side by side in the Ratnaprabhā. From these data Bhattacharyya concluded that Niścalakara undoubtedly flourished when Buddhism was still reigning supreme in Bengal and certainly before the Muslim armies destroyed the Buddhist universities of Bihar. This would place Niścalakara in the last quarter of the twelfth century at the latest.

This conclusion disagrees with the date assigned by Hoernle to Niścalakara's teacher, Vijayarakṣita. Therefore Bhattacharyya argues that Hoernle's date is not correct. Firstly there is a manuscript of the Mādhavanidāna which was written in 1210; it is preserved in the Library of the Royal Asiatic Society of Bengal at Calcutta (its number is G. 4812). Though this manuscript only contains the text of the Nidāna with a line by line Newari translation, the name of the work, given in the colophon, is Śāstramadhukośa. Bhattacharyya holds the opinion that it is thus called after Vijayarakṣita's commentary. If this view is correct, Vijayarakṣita lived before 1210.

A more precise date of Niścalakara was derived by Bhattacharyya from further indications in the Ratnaprabhā. Niścala describes in a vivid and flowery way an audience given by king Rāmapāla of Bengal to the king of Kāmarūpa. Bhattacharyya says there is no doubt that the author was present on that occasion and that the panegyric epithets prove that the monarch was still alive when Niścala wrote his commentary. The date of Rāmapāla's reign is fixed by Bhattacharyya at 1078-1120 (IHQ 3, 1927, p. 571-591; Bhatt.'s method is criticized in R. C. Majumdar's History of Bengal, vol. 1, p. 180-181). His conclusion is that Niścalakara must have written his Ratnaprabhā within the decade 1110-1120. This date, which may well be correct, leads to the assumption that Vijayarakṣita may have written the first part of the Madhukośa between 1090 and 1110.

Bhattacharyya proved beyond any doubt that the way in which Hoernle determined his date of Vijayarakṣita was completely wrong (IHQ 23, 1947, p. 130-133). Hoernle held the erroneous view (Osteology, Introduction p. 17) that Vijayarakṣita controverts a certain doctrine of Aruṇadatta concerning the structure of the eye (see Madhukośa 59, 29). Now this comment on Nidāna 59, 29 was written by Śrīkaṇṭhadatta and not by Vijayarakṣita. Moreover, the interpretation rejected by Śrīkaṇṭhadatta is not ascribed to an authority called by name; this authority cannot be Aruṇadatta because the latter's comment on the corresponding passage of the Aṣṭāṅgahṛdayasaṃhitā (U. 12, 1) is very brief. In addition, Aruṇadatta is never quoted in the Madhukośa, either by Vijayarakṣita or by Śrīkaṇṭhadatta, for the simple reason that Aruṇadatta is posterior to both; the references to Aruṇadatta in Śrīkaṇṭhadatta's Kusumāvalī may be regarded as interpolations of Nārāyaṇa (see: Śrīkaṇṭhadatta). Śrīkaṇṭhadatta's note on Nidāna 59, 29 probably refers to an old interpretation, already rejected by Indu (Śaśilekhā on A.s.U. 15, 1, Trichur edition, vol. 3, p. 109, acc. to Bhatt.). Another point put to use by Hoernle to establish his date of Vijayarakṣita is a quotation from Guṇākara in the Madhukośa; with this he was also on the wrong track (see App. 2: Guṇākara). So Hoernle's date of Vijayarakṣita can be set aside.

The commentary on the first half of the Mādhavanidāna, as written by Vijayarakṣita, is not as abounding in quotations from authors and works referred to by name as Niścalakara's Ratnaprabhā evidently is. It is, however, an independent work not leaning heavily on earlier commentaries, at least as far as any judgment in these matters dares to go, because many early medical works and commentaries have not been preserved.

Śrīkaṇṭhadatta wrote the latter half of the Madhukośa, from the comments on chapter thirty-three up to the end. He was a pupil of Vijayarakṣita, as stated by himself in the introduction to his part of the commentary. Probably he completed the work of his teacher after the latter's death. Śrīkaṇṭhadatta also wrote a commentary on Vṛndakuṇḍa's Siddhayoga. Bhattacharyya (IHQ 23, 1947, p. 131) observes of this work, called Vyākhyākusumāvalī, that scholars did not generally notice that the printed text (Ānandāśrama Series Nr. 27, first ed. 1894, second ed. 1943) is really a revision by a later author, Nārāyaṇa, who collected additional notes from Ḍalhaṇa's commentary on the Suśrutasaṃhitā, etc.; quotations from Aruṇadatta, Ḍalhaṇa and Hemādri presumably belong to Nārāyaṇa's interpolations, for all these interpolated notes are quite untraceable in Niścalakara's expansive commentary on the corresponding passages from Cakrapāṇidatta's Cikitsāsaṃgraha. At the end of the printed text of the Kusumāvalī, Nārāyaṇa clearly states that he completed Śrīkaṇṭhadatta's commentary by adding to it notes from Ḍalhaṇa's commentary, etc. Jolly was led astray by Nārāyaṇa's additions to the Kusumāvalī and held that it could not have been written before the fourteenth century (Medicin, p. 7). A study devoted to this Nārāyaṇa was written by Gode (St. I.L.H. 2, p. 176-181). Nārāyaṇa states that he was a *brāhmaṇa* of *nāgaravaṃśa* stock and a son of Bhābhalla (printed text Kusumāvalī) or Bhāmalla (Gode, l.c., p. 176). The evidence collected by Gode points to Nārāyaṇa as the grandfather of Ananta who wrote a work, called Kāmasamūha, in 1457. Gode assumed that Nārāyaṇa lived about 1325-1400, but he departed from Hoernle's date of Vijayarakṣita and took that date into account, though there was no need to do so. In my opinion Nārāyaṇa may be assigned to the period 1360-1400. It is not known to me whether there exist manuscripts of the Kusumāvalī without Nārāyaṇa's interpolations. The work is not quoted or referred to by Niścalakara, though both Śrikaṇṭhadatta and Niścalakara were pupils of Vijayarakṣita.

A different author, called Śrikaṇṭha, who wrote the Amṛtavallī, is quoted by Niścalakara several times (Bhatt., IHQ 23, 1947, p. 137). Śrīkaṇṭhadatta's date is closely dependent on that of Niścalakara; as we have seen, the latter composed his Ratnaprabhā between 1110 and 1120. Śrīkaṇṭhadatta may have written his works in the same period or somewhat earlier. It is not known with certainty who was the elder of the two, but it appears reasonable to suppose that Śrīkaṇṭhadatta was the senior pupil because it was he who completed the work of his teacher. An indication pointing in the same direction may be that Śrīkaṇṭhadatta wrote a commentary on the Siddhayoga, a work still highly esteemed in his age, but soon to be replaced by Cakrapāṇidatta's Cikitsāsaṃgraha, a commentary on which was written by Niścalakara. A comparative study of the works of Śrīkaṇṭhadatta and Niścalakara may throw more light on their mutual relationschip.

Vācaspati wrote a commentary on the Mādhavanidāna called Ātaṅkadarpaṇa. In the introduction to this work the author states that his father, Pramoda, was chief physician at the court of Hammīra, and that his elder brother, Raiśarman, was one of the *paṇḍits* at the court of Muhammad Shāh (Aufrecht, Cat. Florentine Skt.Mss., nr. 345; Peterson, Sixth Report, nr. 460, p. 35-36). Hoernle (Osteology, Introduction p. 17) identified Hammīra as Amīr Muizzuddīn Muhammad, the celebrated Muhammad Ghorī, who reigned in Delhi from 1193 to 1205.

Vācaspati also observes that he has consulted the Madhukośa (Peterson, ibid.; Hoernle, ibid.), so he is later than Vijayarakṣita and Śrīkaṇṭhadatta. Hoernle assigned Vācaspati to about 1260, twenty years after the supposed date of Vijayarakṣita. The latter, however, lived much earlier, as we have seen, and an accurate determination of Vācaspati's date depends on the identification of the patrons of his father and brother. If Hoernle is right as to the identity of Hammīra, Vācaspati may have lived about 1220-1240.

The complete text of the Ātaṅkadarpaṇa has been printed, together with the Madhukośa (in the first edition of the Mādhavanidāna by Vaidya Jādavji Tricumjī Āchārya, Nirṇaya Sāgar Press, Bombay). Seeing that it often repeated the Madhukośa, only fragments of it were printed in the subsequent editions (see the Introduction to the fifth edition, 1955). I am under the impression that these fragments too are often only repetitions of what had been written by predecessors, especially Ḍalhaṇa. A thorough study of the complete text of the commentary is required to settle this point, which is not without interest, because Vācaspati may be the earliest commentator to have borrowed from Ḍalhaṇa.

CHAPTER ONE

THE FIVE CHARACTERISTICS (CONSISTING OF) THE ORIGIN, ETC. (*PAÑCANIDĀNALAKṢAṆA*)

1, 1 : Having paid homage to Śiva, who is the cause of the coming into being, continuance and absorption of the universe, who is the door to heaven and to liberation from transmigration and the refuge of the three worlds,

M :

(The *maṅgalācaraṇa* [1] is addressed to Harihara[2]). After having reflected upon the writings of the *vaidyas* [3] Bhaṭṭāra(haricandra), Jejjaṭa, Gadādhara, Vāpyacandra, Śrīcakrapāṇi(datta), Bakula, Īśvarasena, Bhoja, Īśāna, Kārtika(kuṇḍa), Sukīra and Sudhīra, and of Maitreya and Mādhava who are the foremost among them, and having studied other scientific works [4] as well, I have made this effort (of writing a commentary)... I have started (to write) this (Madhukośa, i.e.) 'Store of honey' of explanations, having collected explanations from various books, as a bee collects little bits of the juice of flowers from various trees. In the course of the commentary on (this) book also those (data on) origins (,etc.) are written down, which have been made use of by Mādhava, (but) have not been (explicitly) stated ...

1, 2 : This (book, called) 'The ascertainment of diseases', containing the secondary affections, precursory signals of death, origins and signs is, making use of the words of various sages, composed now in a succinct way on the request of accomplished physicians.[5]

1, 3 : This very (book) will enable physicians, lacking various treatises and possessing little intelligence, to discern a disorder with ease.

M :

The activity of prudent people is not (aroused) without indicating the contents (of a book), the relation (between title and contents) and (its) aim. Therefore, in order to point this out, (these) two stanzas are enunciated ...

That book by which ascertainment of, (i.e.) knowledge about, diseases (is acquired) with regard to their specificity as arising from wind, etc., as being curable or incurable, etc., is composed, (i.e.) written; 'by us' (has to be supplied) ... (The expression 'containing the secondary affections, precursory signals of death, origins and signs' points both to the contents of the book and to the relation between the title and the contents). A secondary affection is another morbid alteration, occasioned by excitement of the morbific entity which starts the disease, as Caraka declares : "An illness, added to an illness, which arises at a later time and is not in disagreement with its commencement, is called a secondary affection".[6]

A sign, inevitably pointing to death, is (called) a precursory signal of death.

An origin is a ground, bringing about the production of a disease.

A sign is a ground indicating a disease; prodrome, symptom, therapeutic diagnosis and onset are denominated by this (term). (An 'etymological' remark is added).

Although the origin also indicates a specific disease, it is denominated separately in order to substantiate the two kinds of causes as the ground of production and the ground of apprehension. The terms secondary affection, etc. will be dealt with in detail as the opportunity arises.

Mādhava says 'making use of the words of various sages' for the reason that one may ask how the activity of prudent people (can be aroused) regarding the instruction (about origins, etc.), because things are thus that the essential nature of the origin, etc. of diseases, being very subtle, is not an object of knowledge of someone who is not omniscient. With these (quoted words) the authoritativeness of the book (and) its being an expedient to (arouse) activity [7] has been stated. For sages are called those superior men, who on account of the strength of their supernatural faculties,[8] (resulting) from austerities and *yoga*, are in possession of all that knowledge which pertains to the three (divisions of) time.

Because one may reflect that, if there were already another book of this kind by someone else, this one would serve no purpose by reason of the fact that (medical) practice would be known and so the object (of the book) would already have been attained, for that reason he says '(it is composed) now'. A composition of this kind, making use of the words of various sages, is made now, for the first time, by me.

(It is made) in a succinct, (i.e.) condensed, way.

In that way the fault that it would not lead to activity in those with a restricted (range of) thinking, by being too extensive, is avoided.

'On the request of accomplished physicians' is said for this reason, that the book would be useless if one doubts whether, even when the book has been written, any physician will occupy himself with it, because (it may be regarded) to have been made by a person who has not been recognized (as an expert).

The meaning of 'request' is an entreaty with words like 'Be so kind as to make a book to render assistance to us'; or it has the sense of an order; in the latter case the author expresses his modesty.

He says 'lacking various books' because one may doubt if there will be activity of those possessing little intelligence, by reason of the profusion of the words of the sages.

This very book will enable to discern a disorder, (i.e.) a disease, in an easy way; 'it is an instrument (to discern a disorder)' should be supplied.

These words indicate its purpose to be knowledge about diseases; therapy has to be regarded as the result of this (knowledge). As has been said in the Caraka(saṃhitā) : "First of all the disease should be investigated and immediately following upon that the remedial agent; thereupon the physician should employ a therapeutical measure with which he is conversant" (Sū. 20, 20).

It is said : 'those possessing little intelligence' because one may raise the following objection : knowledge about diseases will come about only by the words of various sages; so what is the use of this book that is dependent on those (words)?

('Possessing little intelligence') means with a restricted (range of) thought, for people with a great (range of) thought are competent to study the various extensive books which are difficult to master, but those with a restricted (range of) thought (are) not (able to do so).

He says 'those lacking various books' considering that this very (book) will lead to knowledge of diseases in those who, although being of great insight, did not obtain, due to their inertia, the complete textbooks which are difficult to procure.

Ā :

... An origin is that by which an illness is ascertained, (i.e.) substantiated.

... (The words 'making use of the words of) various sages' indicate the excellence of the book. For it has been said : "First of all the best of physicians have to exert themselves in order to acquire a proper knowledge about diseases; having attained this object, therapeutical procedures can be started to (obtain) merit, fame and prosperity." [9]

1, 4 : The discernment of diseases is traditionally said to consist of five (elements) : the origin, prodromes, symptoms, and also therapeutic diagnosis and onset.

(A.h.Ni. 1, 2).[10]

M :

Considering that there are five means of (getting) knowledge about an illness one wants to understand, he mentions them ...

These five (means of getting knowledge) indicate, both dissociated and associated (with each other), an illness.

Against the view that the (mentioned means), associated (with each other, indicate the illness), it cannot be objected (that) means (are employed) to reach an aim which has already been attained, because also a set of means to acquire valid knowledge is seen. The very fire which has been acknowledged by means of inference, may certainly (also) be known by direct apprehension and verbal authority. Further, being prudent people who do not consider the origin, etc. in such a way, we cannot remain indifferent to the opinion that an illness can be substantiated by a single (means). Moreover, even when an illness has been substantiated by one (means), the other ones have necessarily to be considered because (each one) has a distinct purpose.

One can ask for example how an origin may be averted if it is not mentioned. For it has been said in the Suśruta(saṃhitā) : "That which counteracts [11] wind, etc. has been put forth extensively, but the application of therapeutical procedures, (i.e.) the aversion of the origin, (has been dealt with) in a condensed way" (U. 1, 25).[12]

Moreover a fixed determination of a disease cannot (be reached) in all cases by means of the origin in the same way as morbid pallor is determined from the consumption of earth [13] and vomiting from the consumption of flies,[14] for one (and the same) cause (gives rise) to fever, visceral swelling, etc.[15] As Caraka says : "One ground (may give rise) to several illnesess but also to a single one; many grounds (may lead) to one illness, but to many as well" (Ni. 8, 24).[16]

Moreover, Vāpyacandra says that the prodromes, etc. are enumerated in consideration of (the fact that) an illness cannot be known from the origin (as an) isolated (entity), as it may also happen sometimes that an illness is brought about by the accumulation of a morbific entity by a distant origin after it has repelled the near one.[17]

In the absence of an enumeration of the prodromes the specific therapeutical procedure which has been mentioned with regard to them cannot be adopted. For it is said in the Caraka(saṃhitā) : "When the prodromes of fever are present, a light diet or depletion (is salutary)" (fr. Ni. 1, 36).[18] And likewise (it is said) in the Suśruta(saṃhitā) that, when the prodromes of fever by wind (are present), the drinking of ghee [19] should be prescribed.[20] Moreover, knowledge about incurability would not be attained. For Caraka has said : "(The man) in whom settle down to an extraordinary degree all the described prodromes of fever falls to the share of death with fever as its harbinger; that man in whom settle down the prodromes of any other disease in the same way will certainly die as well" (I.5, 4-5).[21] Likewise (i.e. without description of the prodromes), knowledge about the specific (differences) between blood-bile and urinary disease does not arise, for Caraka has said : "In case a person will pass urine, coloured turmeric-yellow or red, but does not present the prodromes of urinary disease, one should not call it (an instance of) urinary disease, for it is an excitement of blood (and) bile" (Ci. 6, 54).

In the absence of an enumeration of the symptoms of an illness its own form as such cannot be differentiated with (its) complete (set of) specific (characteristics). Moreover, one cannot know whether it is curable or incurable. For the Caraka(saṃhitā) says about the characteristics of an easily curable (disease) : "When the grounds, prodromes and symptoms are slight, if the (constituent) subject to corruption will not possess qualities comparable (to those of the morbific entity), and if the morbific entity (dominating the disease) will not be (the same as the predominant one in) the constitution (of the patient, it is an easily curable disease)" (Sū. 10, 11).[22]

About the characteristics of a (disease), the cure of which is troublesome, Caraka says : "If the causes, prodromes and symptoms are of an intermediate force (its cure is troublesome)" (Sū. 10, 14ab).[23] Moreover (Caraka says) : "A fever by concerted action is incurable when all its characteristics are fully (developed)" (Ci. 3, 109d-110a).[24]

In the absence of the description of therapeutic diagnosis there would be no awareness of the specific (character) of an illness with miscellaneous or poorly developed characteristics. That has been said in the Caraka(saṃhitā) : "An illness with hidden signs (may be investigated) by the good or adverse effects of therapeutic diagnosis" (fr. Vi. 4, 8).

Finally, in the absence of the onset, there would not be (available) a specific therapy of an illness, even if (its) prodromes, etc. would have been acknowledged, for there would be no knowledge about the discrimination of the components [25] of each (of the morbific entities) and of strength, time, etc., (elements) which are applicable in its therapy. Therefore all the five (elements, consisting of) the origin, etc., have to be stated.

This whole series of five (elements), consisting of the grounds of production and apprehension of an illness, is expressed by the term origin. As Suśruta says : "(These are the sixteen chapters on) origins (which are called thus) on account of the detailed instruction about grounds and characteristics (they contain)" (fr. Sū. 13, 14cd).

(A lengthy exposition on the 'etymology' of the term 'origin' follows).

Ā :

... (About the statement) 'and also therapeutic diagnosis' (we remark that) the words 'and also' make clear that therapeutic diagnosis serves an end that is comparable (to that of the other elements); the same applies to the word 'and' in 'and the onset'.[26]

... One may object that, ascertainment of a disease (being accomplished) by a single one (of the mentioned elements), the enumeration of the other ones is useless. The answer is : the other ones are not useless because each (element) has a distinct purpose. Without therapeutic diagnosis there would be no awareness of the specific (character) of an illness with miscellaneous or poorly developed characteristics. As Suśruta (has said) : "A wind disease is not appeased by inunction, oleation, sudation, etc.; the morbid alteration should be discerned in that case (and) it is the blood that is corrupted in it." [27] Therapeutic diagnosis consists in that case of (the bringing about of) effusion of blood.

1, 5a-c : The origin is indicated by the synonyms (instrumental) cause (*nimitta*), ground (*hetu*), underlying factor (*āyatana*), antecedent (*pratyaya*), provenance (*utthāna*) and cause (*kāraṇa*).

(A.h.Ni. 1, 3a-c).[28]

M :

Among the (elements, consisting of) the origin, etc., the characteristics of the origin which consists of a cause are enumerated, which set apart (entities) of the same class and those of a different one ... The meaning expressed by these (synonymous) words is : origin. (Nyāyasūtra 1, 1, 15 is quoted as an example of a series of synonyms). The question may be raised : is it expressed by the accumulation (as a whole) or by each of the (synonyms) separately ? (This objector may say :) the former (alternative) is not (the correct one) because an accumulation of words which indicate one and the same meaning is not used; if the latter (alternative were the correct one), liability to inaccuracy (would arise), because *nimitta* (also) means omen, etc., *hetu* the agent effecting (a proposition [29]), *āyatana* the seat (of a morbific entity, etc.), *pratyaya* the suffixes of the present tense, etc., and *utthāna* the rising (of a star) and excretion.

(The answer is) : it is not like that, for the whole (series of words consisting of) *nimitta*, etc. does not mean omen, etc. For that very reason it is said '(the origin is indicated) by the synonyms'. They are not at all synonyms of these (words in the case that they denote other concepts), because words in a regular order and expressing the same meaning are called each other's synonyms. Something which acts as an origin can for that reason be expressed by the words *nimitta*, etc. if they are synonyms. This enumeration of synonyms occurs for the sake of common practice in science. The origin is characterized in a condensed way as the ground of production of a disease, together with the way in which this action is necessarily brought about (*itikartavyatā*). With regard to those who consider the onset as the way in which this action is necessarily brought about by a morbific entity, the expression 'together with the way in which this action is necessarily brought about' (is employed) in order to exclude (that view about) the onset, because (in their opinion) there does not exist a way in which this action is brought about which differs from that by a morbific entity. To those who consider the onset as the emersion of an illness the (following) characterization (suffices) : the origin is the ground of production of an illness. In both cases the word 'production' serves to differentiate it (i.e. the origin) from the ground of apprehension, (consisting of) the prodromes, etc.

This ground (i.e. origin) is of several kinds. With regard to it(s distinctions) it is first of all of four kinds, as Haricandra says (in his comment) on the chapter (of the Carakasaṃhitā) about the armamentarium (of a physician) [30] : "It is of four kinds according to its distinction into near and distant, subordinate and predominant (grounds)."

Near (grounds) of excitement of a morbific entity are e.g. the component parts of night, day, season and (the digestive process of) ingested food; they are not linked to accumulation, etc.

A distant (ground is indicated) e.g. (by) : "Phlegm, accumulated in the winter, brings about a phlegm disease in the spring.[31]" Or : a near (ground) of fever is the indulgence in dry (substances), a distant one is the anger of Rudra.

(A ground is) subordinate e.g. if it is too weak to bring about an illness, as Caraka says : "Or when the (specific entities, consisting of the origin, etc.) are conform, (but) very weak, a morbid alteration is not the result" (fr. Ni. 4, 4).[32]

A predominant ground is e.g. poison, etc.

Or grounds are of three kinds, distinguished into inadequate conjunction of the senses with their objects, erroneous judgment and transformation (by time).[33] Inadequate conjunction of the senses with their objects (refers to) colours, tastes, etc., subject to absence of junction, junction beyond the proper measure and junction in an improper way; erroneous judgment (denotes) improper knowledge, etc.; transformation (indicates) coldness, etc., arising from the individual nature of the seasons and subject to absence of junction, etc. "In this very case it (i.e. time) is the inner nature of demerit (as) a ground of disease" says Bhaṭṭāraharicandra, because it also brings about suffering when ripened after an interval of time. Cakra(pāṇidatta) however declares its inner nature to consist of erroneous judgment; erroneous judgment only is the root of demerit, arising from the killing of a *brāhmaṇa*, etc., brought about by improper knowledge; its relative strength need not be examined in this instance because demerit is in every respect established as a cause of disease.

(The ground) is of three kinds according to its distinction into a ground of a morbific entity, a ground of an illness and a ground of both (morbific entity and illness).

Grounds of morbific entities are e.g. the sweet (taste), etc., which is caused by accumulation, excitement and appeasement, produced in accordance with a (particular) season. The ground of a disease is e.g. the consumption of earth as a cause of morbid pallor. Though earth surely brings about excitement of a morbific entity, as said by Caraka : "Astringent (earth excites) the wind, saltish (earth) the bile, sweet (earth) phlegm" (Ci. 26, 27cd), nevertheless only morbid pallor is started by the morbific entities arising from it, and not another morbid alteration; so it is the ground of an illness. A ground of both (morbific entity and disease) is e.g. what is said about the wind-blood (disease)[34] : "(The combustive alteration arising) in someone riding on an elephant, horse or camel and in someone eating ...", etc.[35] This means that, although in this case the generation of the illness is preceded by excitement of the morbific entity, there is nevertheless causation of it, both with respect to the illness and the morbific entity. A remedy that only eliminates the illness should therefore not be employed in such a case, but (a remedy) that is opposed to both (morbific entity and illness).

And it should not be said that an illness, being an effect, ceases by reason of the very cessation of the (disturbance of the) morbific entity, which is a cause. For that reason remedial substances have a fixed faculty for each single case. For what other reason is an emetic procedure that is (the) proper (means) to eliminate phlegm not employed in (cases of) dimness of vision by phlegm? As has been said in the Suśruta(saṃhitā) : "A person with dimness of vision or visceral swelling should not be submitted to an emetic procedure, nor a person painfully oppressed by morbid pallor.[36]"

This same (ground) is of two kinds according to its distinction into a (ground) bringing about the production and a (ground) bringing about the manifestation. With regard to this (distinction) an example of (a ground) which brings about the production is the sweet taste, arising in the winter, of phlegm; an example of (a ground) which brings about the manifestation is the glowing heat of the sun in the spring, which makes this very phlegm manifest; thus says Bhaṭṭāraharicandra. Making manifest means in this case : setting in motion. (The ground) is of two kinds according to its distinction into external and internal ones. With regard to this (distinction) external (grounds) are : diet, behaviour, time, etc. With a view to these (external grounds) Tīsaṭācārya says : "From physical exercise, depletion, falling down (from something), breaking (some part of the body), decline, waking, restraint of the (natural) urges, excessive grief, coldness and excessive terror, by dry (substances), turbulent (motions), astringent, bitter and pungent (substances), the wind will become excited, (as well as) when rainclouds are arriving, when the food has been transformed (by digestion) and during the afternoon. By pungent, acid and hot (substances), by those bringing about combustive alteration, by sharp and saline (substances), by wrath, fasting, glowing heat (of the sun), sexual intercourse with women, sesame seed, linseed, thick sour milk, *surā*, verjuice, *āranāla*, etc., during the digestion of the ingested food, in the autumn and the summer, at noon and at midnight, the bile of living beings will become excited. By heavy, sweet-tasting and excessively oleaginous (substances), milk, confectionery (prepared) with sugar-cane (juice), whey, sleeping by day, flour-cakes, and (articles of food) containing a great quantity of butter (*sarpiṣprapūra*), at the time (i.e. in the season) of snow-fall, at the beginning of the day, just after the ingestion (of food) and in the spring, a general excitement of phlegm comes about.[37]"

Internal (grounds) are for example the morbific entities and the corruptible (constituents of the body).

An excited morbific entity (may be) of several kinds as well, on account of distinctions as to its being a natural one, etc. Natural ones are: phlegm in the spring, bile in the autumn and wind in the early raining season. Deviating (from their natural state) however are : bile or wind in the spring, phlegm or bile in the rainy season and phlegm or wind in the autumn. The purpose of this (distinction is the ascertainment of) easy curability, etc., according to what has been said in the Caraka-(saṃhitā) : "A natural (fever) that becomes perceptible in the spring or the autumn is, however, easily curable" (Ci. 3, 42ab), etc.

(Morbific entities) are of two kinds according to their distinction into chief and adjunctory ones. The chief one predominates, the adjunctory one is not predominant. As Caraka says : "A chief one is independent, its signs are manifest and its provenance and appeasement [38] occur in accordance with what has been said; an adjunctory one, however, shows the opposite characteristics" (fr. Vi. 6, 11). The purpose of this (distinction) is that in an illness arising by combined action the chief (morbific entity) should get a specific treatment that is not in disagreement with the adjunctory one. That has been stated in the Caraka-(saṃhitā) : "Appeasement of the secondary affection usually (results) in such a case from appeasement of the predominant one" (fr. Ci. 21, 40)[39]; a secondary affection is adjunctory.

(Morbific entities are of two kinds) according to (their distinction into those which agree with) the constitution and (those which) deviate (from it) : it is troublesome to cure a wind disease in a person whose constitution is dominated by wind, but its cure is easy in persons with a constitution dominated by phlegm or bile. As Caraka says in (his description of) the characteristics of easy curability : "In case the (constituent) subject to corruption will not possess qualities comparable (to those of the morbific entity) and in case the morbific entity (dominating the disease) will not be (the same as the predominant one in) the constitution" (Sū. 10, 11cd).

(There is another distinction) with regard to its being dragged away from its receptacle : when a morbific entity that maintains its proper measure is dragged away from its receptacle by the wind and moved to another seat, it generates, even if maintaining its proper measure, a morbid alteration. As Caraka says : "When the wind, in a condition with decline of phlegm, has carried away with itself the bile, which maintained its natural state, (has moved it) from its seat, and spreads over the limbs of the body, a cutting pain and a burning sensation of an unsteady kind arise in any place of the body, wherever (it may be affected), and in (such) a person fatigue and certainly weakness are present" (Sū. 17, 45-46). The purpose of (making) this (kind of distinction) is that the wind, (as the) sole (morbific entity) which has deviated with regard to its qualities, should be brought (back) to its own seat, and that the bile should not be diminished. Bhaṭṭāraharicandra says : "Those who do not know about this dragging away of the bile from its seat diminish the (quantity of) bile, being of the opinion that it has increased because a burning sensation is experienced; (doing thus) they produce a quite different disease with the characteristics of decline of bile and utterly ruin the patient." Others however say : as (it is known that) the bile stays in the whole body according to its distinction into a brightening (kind), etc., (it is thus that) when bile has been dragged away from its own receptacle and moved on to another subdivision of the body by the wind, a situation certainly arises in which the bile, staying in that other subdivision (of the body), is present in excess by reason of its intimate connection with the adventitious bile. On account of that (situation) a corruption (ensues) that is endowed with the very characteristics of an increase (of bile) and not a different (kind of) corruption; otherwise there would occur no burning sensation at all. For a morbific entity that maintains its own measure does not generate a morbid alteration.[40] Bhaṭṭāraharicandra however holds the following view : "Although (it may be) thus, it is nevertheless necessarily required for the sake of distinctions in therapy that a specific (type of) corruption (is recognized), consisting of the course to another seat and differing from increase and decline; otherwise, being of the opinion that there is an increase of bile, one ought to employ a purgative or bile-diminishing (procedure), which is not suitable at all in this case, for (the bile) should be brought back to its own seat. That which has been stated by Caraka : "Decline, maintenance and increase (with regard to their quantity constitute) a threefold mode of being of the morbific entities" (Sū. 17, 112ab), etc., refers to what usually occurs."

(Morbific entities are distinguished) according to their modes of being : modes of the morbific entities are the states of decline, increase, etc. As has been said in the Caraka(saṃhitā) : "Decline, maintenance and increase (with regard to their quantity constitute) a threefold mode of being of the morbific entities; (as) another threefold (mode of being) should be discerned (their moving) in an upward, downward and lateral (direction) and (as) still another threefold one (their staying) in the viscera, the branches, and in the vital points and junctures of the bones" (Sū. 17, 112-113ab).

Maintenance (with regard to their quantity means) in this (context) congruity. The characteristics of decline, etc. are in that (connection) as follows : "Increased morbific entities present the signs proper to them in accordance with their force, declined (morbific entities) lose the signs proper to them and congruous ones perform the actions proper to them" (Ca.Sū. 17, 62). The signs proper to them are their peculiarities, (as e.g.) the dryness of excited wind, etc.; actions (of excited wind are) : falling asunder (of a part of the body), piercing pain, etc. As Sudāntasena says, in agreement with the text of the Caraka(saṃhitā) : "Inflatedness, stiffness, dryness, cracking, a sensation of being bruised, turbulent movements, trembling, pricking pain, a ruined condition of the throat, prostration, fatigue, moaning, moving down (of constituents of the body), piercing pain, cutting pain, roughness, tinnitus, an incongruous (digestive) transformation, sagging (of a part of the body), confused vision, throbbing, unfastening (of parts of the body), reduction of sexual vigour, absence of (the need to) repose, a sensation of being thumped, (painful) oppression, bending (of the body in a downward direction) and bending (it) upwards, despondency, giddiness, rushing to and fro, yawning, horripilation, tossing about, convulsion, desiccation, seizing (pain), porousness, trenchant pain and cramps, a brown or ruddy colour, thirst to a high degree, numbness, disjunction and retention, and also an astringent taste, these should be known as the actions of excited wind. Blisters, acid eructations, eructation of matter that smells like smoke, confused speech, perspiration, discharges, fainting, a bad smell, rending (e.g. of the skin), (mental disturbance as in) intoxication, dispersal (of a disordered constituent), inflammatory changes, disinclination, thirst, giddiness, heat, absence of feelings of satiety, the sensation of entering into darkness, a burning sensation, the pungent, bitter and acid tastes, (all) colours except a pale one and a condition (in which parts of the body are) of a boiled aspect, (should be known to be) the actions of bile. Satiety, lassitude, heaviness, a feeling of dampness, hardness, excess of impurities, oleaginousness, absence of maturative processes, an increased presence of unctuous substances (within the body), a feeling of coldness, itching, effusion, slowness of action, swelling, excessive sleeping, the acrid and savoury tastes, a white colour and inertia, should be known to be the actions of phlegm. (In) combined action the signs of two morbific entities (are present) and (in) concerted action those of three."

The purpose of the knowledge of (these) signs is (to establish) distinctions with regard to therapy. As Suśruta says : "Declined (morbific entities) should be increased, increased ones should be diminished and congruous ones guarded.[41]"

The modes of being consisting of their moving in an upward direction, etc. are illustrated by the upwards moving (types of) blood-bile, etc. The purpose of the (distinction of these modes) is that in the upwards moving (type of) blood-bile a purgative procedure (should be employed) and in the downwards moving (type) an emetic procedure. As has been said in the Caraka(saṃhitā) : "In blood-bile an eliminative procedure is prescribed that acts in a direction contrary (to that of the disease)" (Ni. 2, 19cd). (A physician) who is not acquainted with the distinctions referring to the modes of being might apply a purgative procedure in (a case of) blood-bile moving downwards, according to the following statement : "Purgation (is the foremost) of those (procedures which) eliminate bile" (fr. Ca.Sū. 25, 40), and lead his patient to misfortune; in (cases of) fever, etc., in which the morbific entities are moving in a lateral direction, a therapy (should be employed) that is in accordance with what has been said (upon this subject). Increased morbific entities give rise to painful conditions, after taking residence sometimes in the viscera, sometimes in the branches, and sometimes in the vital points and junctures of the bones. The mode of being in which they stay in the vital points and junctures of the bones is taught to be one single entity because it leads to a state which is curable only with difficulty. The viscera (consist of) the receptacle of undigested food, etc.; the branches (consist of) blood and the subsequent elements (of the body), together with the skin, according to the meaning Caraka himself has given to this technical term.[42]

The purpose of denominating the viscera, etc. is (to establish) distinctions with regard to therapy. As has been said in the Caraka(saṃhitā) : "When the wind stays in the receptacle of undigested food or the phlegm resides in the receptacle of digested food, a sudorific procedure beginning with (the application of) dry (substances) is salutary (in the former case) and (such a procedure) beginning with (the application of) oleaginous (substances in the latter)" (Sū. 14, 9).[43] And also : "(A morbific entity) staying in the nutrient fluid and blood (brings about) continuous (fever); that one which has taken residence in the flesh (brings about) quotidian (fever)" (Su.U. 39, 67ab), etc. Moreover : "(The application of) cauterization should not be taught with regard to sores of the cords and vital points" (Ca.Ci. 25, 106ab). These morbific entities should also be known with regard to their being accompanied by or being devoid of immature matter. As has been said : "The first element (of the body), not being brought to a mature state because the heat (of the transforming fire) is of a slight force, being corrupted and staying in the receptacle of undigested food, is called immature nutrient fluid. The morbific entities and corruptible (constituents), which have come into contact with that immature matter and have been corrupted (by it), are taught to be accompanied by immature matter, and so are the diseases arising from them. Obstruction of the channels, subsidence of (bodily) force, heaviness, a confused state of the wind, inertia, absence of maturative processes, ejection of saliva, loosening of impure matter, the inability to eat and weariness are the signs of impurities accompanied by immature matter; when they are devoid of immature matter the opposite (signs are present)" (A.h.Sū. 13, 25; 27; 23cd; 24).[44] "Wind, accompanied by immature matter, will oppress the body successively by means of a confined state (of the impurities), adynamia of the (transforming) fire, lassitude, rumbling of the bowels, painful sensations, swelling and pricking pain; when excited vehemently it may wander and seize (all the limbs) simultaneously; it becomes increased by oleaginous (substances), etc., at the rising of the sun and of clouds, and at night. Devoid of immature matter it is clear, dry, not accompanied by a confined state (of the impurities) and attended by (only) slightly painful sensations; it becomes appeased by (substances) with opposite qualities, specifically by those which are oleaginous. Bile is bad-smelling, yellowish-green, brown, acid, solid and heavy, when accompanied by immature matter; it should be declared to bring about acid eructations and a burning sensation in the throat and cardiac region. In a mature state it is slightly copper-coloured, yellow, very hot, pungent as to its taste and non-solid; it should be discerned that it is odourless and bestows appetite, force and (intensity of) the maturating (fire). Phlegm, accompanied by immature matter, is turbid, ropy and grumous and remains (sticking) to the throat; (in that state) it is bad-smelling and harmful to (the feeling of) hunger and to eructation. It should be discerned to be mature when it is frothy, lumpy, pale, devoid of tough (constituents) and without any smell; being (endowed with an) unfixing (ability) it brings about an unpolluted condition of the mouth."[45]

The purpose of this (distinction) is (that) a maturation-promoting (agent should be employed) if (a morbific entity is) accompanied by immature matter and an appeasing (agent) if it is devoid of immature matter.

And these morbific entities, intimately connected with each other, are of sixty-two[46] types according to distinctions concerning more and most[47] (serious degrees of excitement), etc. Examples of those (distinctions) are not written down here because (this commentary would become too) extensive; they should be examined in Suśruta's chapter on the discrimination of the (several) distinctions with regard to the morbific entities.[48]

The mentioned distinctions with regard to grounds and morbific entities are summarized in these stanzas : "The following distinctions with regard to the ground have been described : four (types) as to its being subordinate, distant, near or predominant; three types with regard to (its subdivision into) inadequate junction of the senses with their objects, transformation (by time) and errors in judgment; also (three) with regard to (its being a) cause of a disease, a morbific entity or both; two (types with regard to the distinction of) a (ground) of manifestation and a (ground) bringing about the production and also (two) with regard to the distinction of an external and an internal (ground). Distinctions of the morbific entities (are made) with regard to their being natural or deviated, chief or adjunctory, with regard to their being correlated with (the morbific entity dominating in) the constitution or with another (morbific entity), with regard to their receptacle or their being dragged away (from it) and with regard to their mode of being." That is (all about) the origin.

1, 5d-6 : A prodrome is that by which an ailment, being about to arise, (but) not (yet) governed by the specific (characteristics of a) morbific entity, is characterized. It is an undeveloped sign on account of the slightness [49] of the illnesses (in this stage and it is) in accordance with each (particular illness).

(A.h.Ni. 1, 3d-4).[50]

M :

The prodromes are mentioned immediately after the origin because they immediately follow upon it ...

Prodromes are of two kinds : generic and specific. A generic (prodrome), generated by a state of coalescence of morbific entity and corruptible (constituent) is that by which an impending illness, (such as) fever, etc., is acknowledged as one single entity, but not its specific type with respect to (the morbific entity), wind, etc., by which it is generated. In the same way as : "Fatigue, disinclination, an altered colour (of the skin)" (Su.U. 39, 25a), etc., (should) also (be regarded) : aversion from the words of a *guru* and from children, etc.[51]

With a view to the generic (prodromes) in particular another book (states) : "Prodromes characterize the class to which an illness belongs and that it is going to come about; its nature and particular make-up are characterized by its characteristics." Parāśara says likewise : "A prodrome is called that by which an impending specific illness is characterized, but not a specific morbific entity."

Specific (prodromes) are e.g. (as follows) : in the initial (stage) of a lesion of the chest the very signs, arising from wind, etc., exist in an undeveloped condition, as has been said with regard to this very (disease) : "Its undeveloped characteristics are traditionally called its prodromes" (Ca.Ci. 11, 12cd). Moreover Suśruta says : "... are the generic (prodromes); the specific ones are : yawning to an extraordinary degree by wind, a burning sensation in the eyes by bile, the inability to eat food [52] by phlegm" (U. 39, 27). It is said in the Hārita(saṃhitā) as well : "Those are the generic prodromes of the eight fevers; from the specific (point of view the fever) arising from wind (presents) yawning and muscle pain as its chief (prodromes) and brings about disquietude in the cardiac region",[53] etc.

It may be objected that (presence) to an extraordinary degree [54] (means presence in) a developed state; the consequence of that would be that yawning, etc. are symptoms, because it is said (by Mādhava later on) : "When this very (phenomenon) has reached a developed state, it is called a symptom".[55]

The answer is : in the same way as fatigue, etc. make (one) aware of (the presence of) fever as one single entity, with the exclusion of other diseases, without however indicating specific (distinctions) as to its arising from wind, etc., from which it follows that those (prodromes) are present in an undeveloped state, (in that way) yawning, etc. make (one) aware of (the presence of) imminent wind fever, with the exclusion of fever by bile, etc.; without indicating however the specificity of symptoms, consisting of their being occasioned by the dryness, coldness, decline of the elements (of the body), covering (action) or other (particular characteristics of wind); by reason of this fact that they make (one) aware of an undeveloped wind fever, yawning, etc. are certainly in an undeveloped state; that is the explanation (given) by Jejjaṭa, Vāpyacandra, Mādhavakara,[56] Kārtikakuṇḍa, etc. Others, however, say that yawning, etc. are designated as prodromes, even when they are in a developed state and accompanied by numerous undeveloped prodromes, as (in the case of) a pile of *māṣa* beans, (in the expression) 'they walk, provided with a parasol',[57] and so on.

And it is not thus that it is not distinct from a symptom because it is present in a developed state, (for) it is said that a prodrome inevitably makes (one) aware of an impending illness and a symptom of a present one. In this (connection it is thus that) the specific prodrome remains present in the stage of the symptoms, because this (prodrome) itself (becomes) a symptom when it is well-developed. On the other side not (all the prodromes), generated by a state of coalescence of morbific entities and corruptible (constituents, and consisting of) horripilation, aversion from the words of a *guru* and from children, etc., remain inevitably present; if they would remain present, the consequence would be that all fevers are incurable. That is said to be the sense of Caraka's words : "(The man) in whom settle down to an extraordinary degree all the described prodromes of fever falls to the share of death with fever as its harbinger" (I.5, 4). Because it has been established in this way that prodromes are of two kinds, the generic prodrome is made mention of (by Mādhava).

A prodrome is that, (e.g.) fatigue, etc., by which an ailment, (i.e.) a disease, being about to arise, (i.e.) desirous of being produced on account of the complete presence of the whole (of its causes), (but) not (yet) governed by, (i.e.) not intimately connected with, the specific (characteristics of a) morbific entity, (e.g.) the special kind of shivering, etc. occasioned by wind, etc., is characterized, (i.e.) known. With the words 'it is an undeveloped sign', (etc.) the specific prodrome is made mention of. (A remark about the syntactical structure of the sentence follows).

A sign is a characteristic. Undeveloped (means) not exceedingly well-developed and the ground with respect to this is its slightness, (i.e.) minuteness, which means that it is not undeveloped by reason of its junction with a covering (agent), etc. '(It is) in accordance with each (particular illness)' means that the very symptoms of a particular illness are called its prodromes when they are in an undeveloped state.

Others, however, characterize the prodrome as follows : "That sign, which is brought about by excited morbific entities residing in their (own) seat and which makes (one) aware of an impending illness, is called a prodrome." [58] That is not very suitable, because the prodromes of kingly consumption, (consisting of) the falling down of (blades of) grass and hairs of the head, etc. and occasioned by the invisible (force),[59] are not invariably concomitant. As Caraka says : "The (phenomenon that) in (patients) with kingly consumption usually *ghūṇas*,[60] hairs of the head and (blades of) grass are falling down in foods and drinks and that the hairs of the head and the nails are growing abnormally fast (..., that is the set of prodromes ...)" (Ci. 8, 35).[61]

And this (phenomenon) does not arise from a morbific entity either because there does not exist an intimate connection between morbific entities and grass, etc., and a particular condition, not intimately connected (with a morbific entity), is regarded to be unable to act as a cause, because, by settling mutual connections in an uninterrupted series, there would arise too far-reaching consequences (and) everything would be the cause of everything.

Being of the opinion that the very competent Vāgbhaṭa has written down the words '(that) by which',[62] comprehending all the prodromes, whether arising from the invisible (force) or from a morbific entity, just because he wishes to avoid (mentioning) a morbific entity with regard to these, Mādhavakara has described the characteristics of prodromes in the very way he (i.e. Vāgbhaṭa) did.

To put it shortly the characteristic (of a prodrome) is (as follows): 'a prodrome is a sign that only makes (one) aware of an impending illness'. The word 'only' differentiates it from origin and therapeutic diagnosis and from the onset which consists of the way in which the action is brought about by a morbific entity, because the (terms) belonging to this class make (one) aware of an illness which is (either) produced (or) not (yet) produced.

For it is thus that an origin in the form of the consumption of earth makes (one) aware of an impending morbid pallor and, if it occurs as an adverse therapeutic reaction, an (actually) present specific illness; therapeutic diagnosis, applied in the stage of the prodromes, procures knowledge about an impending specific illness and, applied in the stage of the symptoms, about an (actually) present specific illness; the onset procures knowledge about an imminent specific illness by the production and excitement of the prodromes at noon, etc., and about an (actually) present specific illness by the excitement of the symptoms at noon, etc.; that is the way in which they make (one) aware of an illness, (whether it is) produced (or) not (yet) produced.

An objector may say that, when the specific (nature) of an illness that has been produced can be accurately determined after remembering the specific (nature) of its prodromes, the prodromes too make (one) aware of an (actually) present illness, as stated by Caraka with regard to the doubts about the (presence of) symptoms of blood-bile or an urinary disease: "If a person passes urine, coloured turmeric-yellow or red, but does not present the prodromes of urinary disease ..." (Ci. 6, 54ab), etc.

It is said as an answer to this (objection): can a prodrome be observed before the emersion of an illness or is this impossible? In the former (case) it verily makes (one) aware of an impending illness, in the latter there would be no production of remembering at all by want of personal experience.[63] If it is said (as an objection) that the prodromes, consisting of a condition in which the teeth, etc. are richly endowed with impure matter,[64] etc., being certainly known as to their own form by personal experience, but not having become apparent as the prodromes of urinary disease, determine, however, when the illness has been produced, in an accurate way, (if) remembered, a specific (form of) urinary disease, in that case (the answer is) : in that way the remembering of the prodromes is the cause, but not the prodromes (themselves) because these have disappeared in the stage in which the symptoms (are present).

If it be argued that the process of remembering is not a means of acquiring valid knowledge, we agree with that statement. It is, however, thus that (one) is made aware of a specific (kind of) illness by its prodromes, in co-operation with remembrance obtained from residual traces generated by previous personal experience, and not by remembrance as an isolated (process); (this occurs in the same way) as e.g. in (the process of) recognition, (where) the eye, in co-operation with remembrance procured by residual traces, makes (one) aware of a specific jar (as it was) in a former condition, (which results in the statement) : this is that jar (which I have seen before).

The same (statement) as about the process of remembering should be made concerning instruction by a trustworthy person, but this (means of acquiring valid knowledge) is excluded by the word 'sign'; the word 'impending' excludes the symptoms; the word 'sign' excludes (perception by means of) the eyes, etc., as this (perception) is not a sign because it is (of a) generic (character and also present) in the knowledge about a jar, etc.; a sign, however, is not (of a) generic (character, but characteristic of something).

And the prodromes are verily the signs of an illness though it is not (yet) present, in the same way as the coming up of specific clouds (is a sign, indicative) of rain.
That is all about the prodromes.

Ā :

... A prodrome is a sign which makes (one) aware of an impending illness. What kind of ailment? (An ailment) not (yet) governed by, (i.e.) not (yet) invested with, a specific morbific entity, (i.e.) wind, etc. The being about to arise of an illness which is not (yet) governed by a morbific entity, (i.e.) wind, etc., is impossible by reason of the absence of a cause. For as a rule it is thought impossible for an illness to arise from another source, disregarding wind, etc., because it has been said : "The origin of really all diseases (consists of) the excited impurities" (A.h.Ni. 1, 12cd). The statement that an ailment, being about to arise, is not (yet) governed by a specific morbific entity, should therefore be thought of as referring to a morbific entity the symptoms of which have not (yet) developed; thus it is said ... And these prodromes are of two kinds : generic and specific. That (prodrome), generated by a state of coalescence of morbific entities and corruptible elements (of the body), by which impending fevers, etc. are acknowledged as such, but not specific (particularities, such as) their being generated, etc. by wind, etc., is a generic one ... That (prodrome), by which the marks and location of the morbific entity, which starts an impending illness, are acknowledged, is a specific one ... In the same way as, after one has recognized by the development of smoke only that a minute spark of fire has fallen in a pile of grass, countermeasures can be taken, consisting of beating with the hands and with articles of clothing, in order to appease it, which is impossible when the fire has become blazing, in that way it is possible to appease an impending illness, after recognizing the developed specific prodromes by means of the characteristics of the morbific entity which is starting the imminent disease. For that reason a distinction (is made) between a prodrome and a symptom. Both (kinds) are observed to be sometimes of a bodily and sometimes of a mental character ...[65]

1, 7 : When this same (phenomenon, i.e. the prodrome) has reached a developed state it is called : symptom (*rūpa*), shape (*saṃsthāna*), manifestation (*vyañjana*), sign (*liṅga*), characteristic (*lakṣaṇa*), mark (*cihna*) and conformation (*ākṛti*).

(A.h.Ni. 1, 5).[66 67]

M :

Although the onset is that which immediately follows upon the (stage of the) prodromes, nevertheless the symptom is made mention of (now) for the sake of (getting) knowledge about the own form of an illness ...

'This same (phenomenon' refers to) the prodrome itself. 'A developed state' (means that it has) become perceptible. Does (the term) development (mean that the set of prodromes develops) completely or (does this occur only) fragmentarily ?

In the former case all fevers would be incurable, for Caraka has said : "(The man in whom settle down) all the prodromes" (I.5, 4a), etc.; in the latter case the consequence would be that prodromes like : "Yawning to an extraordinary degree by wind, burning of the eyes by bile" (Su.U. 39, 27bd) etc., may also become symptoms.

(The answer to this question is that) it is not like that, by reason of the fact that neither a complete nor a fragmentary (development) is assented to, but the prodromes as such are (considered to be) signs of an illness when they have developed, without having accurately determined their particularity, (i.e.) whether one or several (prodromes) are present, (in the same way) as smoke as such makes (one) aware of (the presence of) fire, without (having determined) its particularity, (i.e.) whether it arises from grass or from leaves, etc.

When it has been established to be thus, a full development of the whole (set of prodromes indicates) incurability, but otherwise curability (is present).

The consequence is not that yawning, etc. are symptoms, for these (exist) in a developed condition in an earlier (stage of the illness); (moreover), because that which from an undeveloped state has reached development, is denominated as a symptom, and because these (prodromes) cannot possibly be (called) symptoms, by reason of the fact that they are accompanied by numerous other undeveloped signs, and because prodromes and symptoms (do) not (occur) at the same time.

Īśvarasena, however, says : "The undeveloped own form of an illness is its prodrome; that which has developed is its symptom". That is not right, because the (following) alternative cannot be maintained : for thus (it has been said) : What is meant by 'own form'? Does it express 'itself as to its form' [68] or 'its own form' [69]? And (in case it expresses) its own (form), (does that point to its own) quality or (its own) effect?

(With regard to 'itself as to its form' the answer is that the term) 'own form' is not correct, first because (this would be) the contradiction of an action referring to that same thing as an object which is its subject (*svātmani kriyāvirodhaḥ* : e.g. even the best dancer cannot dance on his own shoulders, a sword cannot cut itself). For a symptom is said to be the cause of perception of an illness; if this (symptom) is said to be the very own nature of an illness, the own nature of an illness would be acknowledged from the own nature itself, and that is clearly the contradiction of an action referring to that same thing as an object which is its subject. Neither is it (its own) quality, for it is impossible (to maintain) that the black (colour) of the skin, nails, faeces, urine and eyes, etc., described by Caraka,[70] is a symptom of haemorrhoids. This black (colour) of the skin, nails, faeces, urine and eyes, etc., is not a quality of haemorrhoids at all for the (following) reasons : it does not rest on them; qualities are resting on the bearers of (those) qualities; otherwise (there would be) too far-reaching consequences (enabling one to call everything a quality). Nor is it an effect, because (in that case) the consequence would be that secondary affections, etc. would also be symptoms. If it be argued that these (secondary affections) are signs of an illness, the cure of which is difficult or which is incurable, (the answer is that) it is not thus; they are signs of incurability, etc. in itself, but not of the illness, because they have become known already (in an) earlier (stage of the illness) and have been mentioned as distinct (elements). That has been said : "This (book, called) 'The ascertainment of diseases' containing the secondary affections, precursory signals of death, origins and signs, is composed (now)" (Mā.ni. 1, 2cd). If it is said (as an objection) that a secondary affection is not the effect of an illness, but of the morbific entity which is starting an illness, as has been said in the Suśruta(saṃhitā) : "That, the root of which is this (previously produced illness) itself (*tanmūla eva*), is technically called a secondary affection" (fr.Sū. 33, 18), explained by the commentators (as follows) : "*tanmūla* is said (to mean) : that, the root of which is this, which consists of the morbific entity",[71] (the answer is that) it is not thus. As soon as an illness, by reason of improper conduct, has acquired strength by augmentation of the morbific entity which is its root, it brings about a secondary affection; therefore it has been said : 'that, the root of which is this'. For that very reason Caraka says : "Some diseases become appeased when they have become the ground of (another) disease" (Ni. 8, 21ab), etc. It may be said that really all these (meanings) are sometimes and to some degree expressed by the term 'own form'. Some are of the opinion that there is no inaccuracy (in Īśvarasena's statement) if things are thus. Nevertheless it would only be an established rule, but not a characteristic, because one quality, comprehending all symptoms, would be absent, and secondary affections would become (identical with) the own form of an illness. For that reason the characteristic of a symptom is said to be : that sign which only makes (one) aware of an illness which has (already) been produced. The word 'produced' (is made use of) in order to differentiate (a symptom) from a prodrome; the word 'only' differentiates origin, onset and therapeutic diagnosis (from the symptom), because the (latter) make (one) aware of an illness which is either produced or not (yet) produced. That has just been shown. The word 'sign' excludes the eye, etc. To those who consider the onset to consist of the emersion of an illness, the word 'sign' differentiates the (onset from a symptom); for the (onset) is (in that case) not a sign with respect to the knowledge of an illness, but a cause (of this knowledge).

The synonyms of 'symptom' are made mention of for the sake of common practice in science and in order to characterize (the symptom) in the same way as the origin.

(An objector may say) : is it not thus, that an illness is known by means of its symptoms and (knowledge about) an illness is not attained at all without symptoms, because the very agglomeration of (symptoms, consisting of) the inability to eat and so on, is (identical with) fever and (the presence of) all the eleven symptoms, (consisting of) cough and so on, is (identical with) kingly consumption ?

The answer is that it is not thus. A specific (type of) coalescence between a particular morbific entity and corruptible (constituent) is an illness in the form of fever, etc., and its effects are the inability to eat, etc. Moreover, this very inability to eat, etc., are, each one separately, symptoms and a collection of these (symptoms) is an illness, because a collection is certainly different from its constituent elements, in the same way as (this is the case with) a wood (consisting) of *khadira* trees.

Others, however, connect (this opinion) with the wish to express a distinction, even in cases where there is none, as in examples like the head of Rāhu or the body of a torso.[72] The Nyāya experts, on the other hand, do procure a distinction in those cases.[73]

(An objector may ask) on account of Caraka's words : "A morbid alteration is just suffering" (Sū. 9, 4d) : what is the position of a collection (of symptoms, consisting of) the inability to eat and so on, with regard to suffering, which is a quality of the soul ?

(The answer is) that it is not like that, because, according to the 'etymology' 'suffering is that which brings about suffering', the ground of suffering, consisting of incongruity of the elements, etc., is accepted to be the state of being an illness.

The inability to eat, etc. are certainly morbid alterations by means of their own form, but when they are substantiating another (morbid alteration), they are truly called signs. As Caraka says : "Those signs of illnesses which, for the sake of knowledge, have been mentioned in (this) summary, are also illnesses, but, when they are temporarily present, they are rightly regarded as signs and not as ailments" (Ni. 8, 40).[74]

Ā :

... The (series of) six (words), beginning with 'shape' and ending with 'conformation', consists of synonyms of 'symptom'. The same (synonyms may be applied) to 'prodrome' as well, e.g. : 'previous shape', 'previous manifestation', etc.[75]

1, 8-9 : The application of remedial agents, foods and rules of conduct, contrary to ground and illness, providing the result of that which is contrary (to ground and illness) and conducive to well-being (8), should be known as therapeutic diagnosis of an illness, which is traditionally called adequate (treatment). The opposite (of it), adverse therapeutic diagnosis, is technically called inadequate (treatment) with respect to the illness (9). (A.h.Ni. 1, 6-7).[76] [77]

M :

Therapeutic diagnosis is dealt with ... Grounds are external and internal; an illness is fever and so on. The application, (i.e.) the employment, of remedial agents, regimens of diet and behavioural rules, which are, whether dissociated or associated, contrary to ground and illness, providing, whether being dissociated or associated, the result of that which is contrary to these two, (i.e.) leading to appeasement of a disease by their special faculty, even when their peculiarities are the same as those of the origin, should be known, when conducive to well-being, as that which is called therapeutic diagnosis of an illness. Its synonym is made mention of with the words : 'this same (element) is traditionally called adequate treatment.' In the Caraka(saṃhitā) it has also been said : "For the sake of adequate (treatment, i.e.) therapeutic diagnosis" (fr.Sū. 11, 38). (The word *hi* is used to fill up a quarter of the stanza).

(About) 'conducive to well-being' (we remark that) well-being is characterized by cessation of a disease. Well-being is, for example, what is indicated in common language when people say : 'We have become happy by liberation from toil'; conducive to well-being is that which leads to well-being of that kind and brings it about uninterruptedly during a proper length of time. The purport expressed by this is that the drinking of cold water by a person with a recent fever,[78] accompanied by a burning sensation and thirst, is not (an instance of) therapeutic diagnosis, although it brings about temporary well-being.[79] In this case 'remedial agents, foods and rules of conduct' (constitute) an implicative expression; one should understand that place and time are also indicated by it. For that very reason Vṛddhavāgbhaṭa has said, after stating 'that which is contrary to the illness', etc. : "Place and time are also indicated by it" (fr. A.s.Ni. 1, 12). Also Sudāntasena says : "That which, being contrary to ground, illness, etc., is attended by well-being, and (also) places, etc. (which are contrary to the ground, etc.), should be known (to constitute) therapeutic diagnosis; when otherwise, it is adverse therapeutic diagnosis."

In a condensed way its characteristic is : "That, which is generated by remedial agents, etc., and is attended by well-being, is therapeutic diagnosis."

The words 'remedial agents', etc. mean that the well-being, generated by garlands, sandal, women, etc., is excluded. The words 'attended by' are used to differentiate from it the temporary well-being generated by something unwholesome.

Moreover, this (stanza of the Nidāna) is a proper one to illustrate (therapeutic diagnosis) by means of examples, but it is not a characteristic (of it), because (the words) 'remedial agents', etc. (on the one hand), and 'contrary to the ground', etc. (on the other), are unsuitable for a characterization by their mutually confusing character. Therefore the characteristic (of therapeutic diagnosis) is : 'therapeutic diagnosis is the ground which properly appeases the suffering arising from an illness', or : 'therapeutic diagnosis is adequate (treatment)', or again : 'therapeutic diagnosis is that which is generated by remedial agents and is attended by well-being', for regimen of diet, behavioural rules, place, time, reducing measures, etc., whether consisting of substances or not consisting of these, are stated to be remedial agents in the Caraka(saṃhitā).[80] And now (we give) examples (of the different forms of therapeutic diagnosis). (First of all) those which are contrary to the ground. A remedial agent is for instance a hot remedy, like dry ginger, etc., in (a case of) cold fever;[81] as has been said : "The best of physicians appease diseases brought about by heat by cold (measures), but diseases brought about by coldness (need) a hot drug" (Ca.Vi. 3, 41). An example of food is rice boiled in meat-broth, (prescribed) in a wind fever (arisen) from fatigue.[82] A rule concerning behaviour is for instance (the prescription of) waking during the night in a case of phlegm which has arisen from sleeping by day.[83] And now those which are contrary to the illness. A remedial agent is for instance *pāṭhā* as an obstipating agent in diarrhoea;[84] in the same way *śirīṣa* destroys poison,[85] *khadira* skin diseases [86] and *haridrā* urinary diseases.[87]

These (remedial agents) are not linked to a morbific entity, but appease the disease by their special faculty. Vāpyacandra, however, says : "That substance, which eliminates illnesses like fever, etc., is also opposed to the morbific entity (of those illnesses), but it is distinct from (a substance), opposed to a morbific entity, in the following way : that (substance), which is opposed to a morbific entity, does not necessarily eliminate an illness; emetic and reducing measures for instance, (though) being eliminative of phlegm, do not eliminate a visceral swelling by phlegm, for it has been said : "When phlegm, (though) curable by reducing measures, is the agent (which brings about) fever and visceral swelling, reducing measures (do) not (constitute an) approved (therapy), even when place, time, etc., are comparable (in such a case to those in which reducing measures are beneficial)",[88] and also : "A person with dimness of vision or visceral swelling should not be submitted to emetic procedures, nor a person oppressed by morbid pallor or abdominal disease".[89] "That which eliminates an illness, necessarily eliminates the morbific entity (of it); appeasing the illness, it also appeases the morbific entity which starts it; otherwise that disease would not be subdued at all, for its cause would remain in the same condition."

Others say that this is not very logical, for the morbific entity inheres in (the disease) or is its instrumental cause; the absence of an effect is, however, not exclusively connected with the absence of the inherent (cause) or the instrumental cause, but also with the absence of the non(-immediately) inherent cause; in the same way as the nonexistence of a jar (results) from the annihilation of the non(-immediately) inherent cause, (consisting of) its connection with the series of (component) parts,[90] in that way annihilation of a disease also (results) from the annihilation of (a non-immediately inherent cause, such as) the connection of onset and characteristics.

A morbific entity, however, ceases of its own accord or by means of another therapeutical procedure. If it is accepted that (a remedial agent) opposed to the illness necessarily brings about cessation of the morbific entity, it would be difficult to demonstrate that it is distinct from (a remedial agent) opposed to both (morbific entity and illness).

(An objector may ask) : Why is the elimination of a morbific entity by emetic procedures, etc. prescribed in a morbid alteration started by it, if a morbific entity is an instrumental cause? For abolishment of a jar does not occur in case the stick, the potter, etc. are abolished.

The answer is : as long as an effect is lasting in an instrumental cause, annihilation of the effect (results) from abolishment of the instrumental cause. Morbific entities are usually of the same kind as the light (of a lamp) that is annihilated when the wick and the oil are annihilated. Food (which is contrary to the illness consists), for example, of lentils, etc. as obstipating agents in diarrhoea.[91] Conduct (contrary to the illness) is e.g. strained evacuation in the retentive disease.[92] Vāpyacandra says that conduct, contrary to the illness, also consists of spells, the bearing of (auspicious) herbs, oblations, offerings, voluntary vows, expiatory rites, sacrifices, obedience to the *guru* and the gods, etc.

And now (those) things which are contrary to (both) ground and illness. A remedial agent (consists), for example, of the ten roots which eliminate both wind and swelling in a swelling by wind,[93] as has been said in the Caraka(saṃhitā) in the chapter about the six hundred purgative preparations, in that part of it beginning with '*pāṭalā*' until 'these ten eliminate swellings' (fr. Sū. 4, 16).[94] Food (consists), e.g., of diluted buttermilk in (cases of) *grahaṇī* (disorder) by wind or by phlegm,[95] and a thin gruel in fever arising from a cold wind,[96] for it destroys the wind by its hot potency and fever by its special faculty. As has been said in the Caraka(saṃhitā) : "They destroy fever by reason of their adequacy with respect to fever" (Ci. 3, 153c) and also in the Suśruta(saṃhitā) : "Gruel is always salutary in (case of) fever and diarrhoea" (U. 40, 158cd). Conduct is for instance waking during the night, which is (of a) dry (quality) and contrary to lassitude, in (a case of) lassitude arisen from sleeping during the day, which is (of an) oleaginous (quality).[97]

And now (those things) with the result of that which is contrary to the ground. A remedial agent is e.g. a hot poultice,[98] productive of bile, in a swelling by an inflamed sore which shows a predominance of bile.[99] Food is e.g. (such food) which brings about combustive alteration in a swelling by an inflamed sore which is in (the stage of) maturation.[100] Conduct is e.g. causing terror in (a case of) insanity by wind.[101]

And now (those things) with the results of that which is contrary to the illness. A remedial agent (consists) e.g. (of) an emetic agent, (as) *madana* fruits, etc., in (a case of) vomiting.[102] Food is e.g. milk (as) a purgative in diarrhoea.[103] Conduct is e.g. tickling (of the throat) in order to (provoke) vomiting in (a case of) vomiting.[104]

And now (those things) with the result of that which is contrary to both ground and illness. A remedial agent is e.g. an unguent (made) from *aguru*,[105] etc. in (case) someone (is) scorched by fire [106] or (the employment of) poison in (a disorder by) poison.[107] Food is e.g. an alcoholic beverage, bringing about intoxication, in an alcoholic disorder, arising from the drinking of alcoholic beverages.[108] Conduct is e.g. physical exercise, in the form of crossing a water (by swimming), in a confused state of the wind generated by physical exercise.[109]

(An objector may ask whether) it is not thus that in vomiting, arising from a great amount of phlegm and in which an emetic procedure should be employed, there would occur a disease, which remains for a long time, or is of an ineradicable character, if no emetic procedure is employed, and that the application of an emetic procedure is for that reason opposed to the morbific entity only. As has been said in the Suśruta(saṃhitā) : "An emetic procedure is said to be salutary in (cases of) vomiting which are provided with a great amount of a morbific entity" (U. 49, 16ab).[110] Also in (cases of) diarrhoea accompanied by immature (matter), there is opposedness to the ground only, because the immature (matter) flows out by means of the purgative quality of milk. In the same way there is opposedness to the ground only in cases of scorching by fire, because the blood goes to another seat, by reason of its dissolution by a hot therapeutical procedure; otherwise the blood, excited by the burning, and staying at the same seat, would begin to be subject to a maturative process. As has been said in the Suśruta(saṃhitā) : "Blood, brought to excitement by fire, becomes vehemently excited in a creature; afterwards its bile is also roused [111] by that very impetus" (Sū. 12, 17). A cold therapeutical procedure is prohibited in such a case because it is a ground of a grumous condition of the blood. As Suśruta says : "For cold water, by its natural condition, coagulates the blood to an extraordinary degree; therefore well-being is brought about by something hot, but never at all by something cold" (Sū. 12, 21); 'it coagulates' (means that) it brings about a grumous condition. In the same way a poison derived from roots, which is endowed with a downward movement as its own form, is opposed to the ground only (when it is applied) in (a disorder by) an animal poison, which is endowed with an upward movement as its own form. As has been said in the Caraka(saṃhitā) : "When it is said that poison destroys poison, the special faculty is the cause with regard to that; that which regards the movement in an upward direction or in a normal direction (i.e. downwards), is also ruled by its special faculty" (Sū. 26, 69).

The meaning of this is as follows : it has been said 'it is ruled by its special faculty' because one may ask what is the reason of this distinction regarding its (way of) movement although there are no specific kinds of being a poison. Contrary to the ground only in the same way is, in an alcoholic disorder brought about by an alcoholic beverage, the application of the same alcoholic beverage (from which the disorder has arisen), to which *mātuluṅga*, verjuice, etc. have been added, (as) prescribed by Suśruta,[112] etc.; for an (alcoholic beverage) to which other substances have been added is certainly different from the pure (beverage); or, in an alcoholic disorder with wind (as its predominant morbific entity), generated by a dry (alcoholic beverage, such as) *mādhvīka*, etc., the application of an oleaginous (alcoholic beverage, such as) *paiṣṭikā*, etc.[113] What has been said in the Suśruta(saṃhitā): "In the same way as someone oppressed by a king can obtain graciousness only from him and not from someone else, in that way someone oppressed by an alcoholic beverage can certainly obtain graciousness only from that (same beverage) and not from a different one" (U. 47, 48), (has been stated) with a view to the same class of alcoholic beverages.

Opposedness to the ground only is also present with regard to the crossing of a water in (cases of) stiffness of the thighs;[114] the heat of the body, not going outside by the coldness of the water, dissolves, as in the kiln of a potter, both fat and phlegm, which are lumped together in the interior, and by physical exercise both these (elements) are desiccated; thereupon the wind, being uncovered, resorts to its own pathway. In that way verily everything which has that result is, in accordance with its source in each particular case, comprised within (the term): opposed to the ground, etc.

The answer (to this objection) is that, even if it were thus, (things with the result of that which is contrary to a ground, an illness or both), are shown to be separate (entities) by the masters in order to substantiate subsidiary deviations of the peculiarities. That has also been stated in the Caraka(saṃhitā): "Therapeutic diagnosis is the application, attended by well-being, of remedial agents, regimens of diet and rules of conduct, which are contrary to ground and illness, or bring about the result of that which is contrary to ground and illness" (Ni. 1, 10). A deviated state of a peculiarity brings about appeasement of a disease, even when this peculiarity is the same as that of a ground.

'The opposite (of it) is adverse therapeutic diagnosis' means that the application of remedial agents, etc. is called adverse therapeutic diagnosis when it brings about suffering. Its synonym is spoken of with the words 'it is traditionally called inadequate (treatment) with respect to the illness'. By the word illness the morbific entity should be understood as well.

(An objector may ask): Does adverse therapeutic diagnosis make (one) aware of a specific illness or does it not?

If one says that it does not do so it is useless to deal with it in (the section on) the origins; if one is of the opinion that it does substantiate (a specific illness) this (view) conflicts with (the statement): 'the discernment of diseases is traditionally said to consist of five (elements)' (fr.

Mā.ni. 1, 4cd), because a number of six (elements) would be attained.

The answer is that it is not thus; yet it substantiates (a specific illness), as Caraka says: "One should investigate an illness with hidden signs by means of the good or adverse effects of therapeutic diagnosis" (fr. Vi. 4, 8). It is included in the origin because it increases a morbific entity or an illness; a number of six (elements) is not attained because adverse therapeutic diagnosis is included in the origin, as is said: "Adverse therapeutic diagnosis as made mention of in (the section on) the origin" (Mā.ni. 2, 58c).

Those are the characteristics of therapeutic diagnosis.

Ā:

... Conduct, contrary to the illness, is e.g. strained evacuation in the retentive disease; strained evacuation is the process, accompanied by noises, in which the wind, by the force of the cardiac region and the throat, is made to move in a downward direction again and again ... This therapeutic diagnosis is traditionally called adequate (treatment) with respect to the illness; the regimen of diet and conduct with the opposite qualities are inadequate with respect to the illness; as has been said in the Caraka(saṃhitā): "Those possessing knowledge about adequate (treatment) require the voluntary actions and foods to be adequate by means of their qualities, (i.e.) provided with qualities which are opposed to those of the (kind of) country (a person inhabits) and the ailments (prevalent there)" (Sū. 6, 50)...[115]

1, 10 : The coming to completion of an ailment by a morbific entity, in accordance with the (particular manner of its) corruption and the (particular manner of its) spreading, that (is called) the onset (*saṃprāpti*), emersion (*jāti*), or origination (*āgati*).

(A.h.Ni. 1, 8).[116 117]

M:

... The corruption of the morbific entities is of various kinds: it is natural or deviated from the natural (type), chief or adjunctory; (it is a corruption) of a single (morbific entity), of two or of all (the morbific entities); (it is a corruption) with all their properties, (which consist of) dryness, etc., or with a small number (of these). The coming to completion, (i.e.) the production, of an ailment, i.e. a disease, by a morbific entity corrupted by a corruption in such a way (as described above), etc., that is called the onset. 'In accordance with the (particular manner of its) spreading' (means) spreading according to the several modes of spreading of the morbific entities, distinguished into an upward, downward and lateral way of moving, etc. The two synonyms of onset are mentioned for the sake of common practice in science and in order to characterize (the onset). That which is expressed by the words emersion, etc. is the onset.

Bhaṭṭārakaharicandra says : "The words emersion and origination (indicate that) also emersion (of an illness) is a cause of knowledge because no knowledge exists about something which has not emerged." These words express that (the emersion) is not (only), like the origin, etc., a cause of knowledge as imparting knowledge, but (also) as an object of knowledge.

Others say that this is not correct because such a (view about the) onset that compares it with light, the eye, etc., is not suitable in therapeutics. Further it is not a fixed rule that only something which has emerged may be discerned, because an illness which has not (yet) emerged is knowable by means of its origin and prodromes, as (imminent) rain, etc. (are knowable) by (the arrival of) clouds, etc. Moreover, when what is expressed by the words 'it has emerged' is said to be different from the emersion, rain, etc. are indeed different from an imminent appearance (of rain). That, however, which does not emerge in any of the three (divisions of) time, cannot possibly be known. Nevertheless, the onset is not the emersion of an illness, because light, the eye, etc., would also be (elements) which have to be considered, in a similar way as in (the concept of) emersion, and (also) because, without all those (elements, i.e. light, the eye, etc.), knowledge would not exist.

Therefore Bhaṭṭārakaharicandra's view is (as follows) : "The onset is the emersion of an illness, additionally characterized by the way in which (this emersion) is brought about by a morbific entity and it is not its mere emersion." Vāgbhaṭa, who says : "In accordance with the (particular manner of its) corruption", etc., has also declared the onset to be the specified emersion of an illness. When things are thus, specific therapeutic procedures are obtained, as for instance the application of reducing measures, maturation-promoting procedures, sudation, etc. in fever, because it makes (one) aware that the receptacle of undigested food is being corrupted, the (transforming) fire damaged, etc. Although such a (concept of the) onset is reached by the very (use of the) term morbific entity, and because these morbific entities have a subsidiary function, (the onset) is nevertheless made into a separate (entity) for the very sake of specific therapy, in the same way as the prodrome is (made an entity) which is different from the symptom, although there is no specificity with regard to it as imparting knowledge. Therefore the onset is the emersion of an illness, additionally characterized by the way in which (this emersion) is brought about by a morbific entity; only that is its characteristic.

1, 11 : This (onset) is distinguished (into various forms) by means of specificities regarding number, discrimination, predominance, force and time, in a way as in this very (book) it will be said : 'there are eight (types of) fever'.

1, 12 : Discrimination is the settling of each component of the united morbific entities; the predominance of an illness will be indicated by its independence or dependence.

1, 13 : The specific force or weakness (will be determined) by the completeness of the (presence of) subdivisions of the (series consisting of the) ground, etc.; the time of an illness (will be determined) by the component parts of night, day, season and the (digestive process of the) ingested food, in accordance with the (particular) impurity (involved).

(A.h.Ni. 1, 9-11).[118 119]

M :

The distinctions which refer to the conditioning factors[120] of the (onset) are dealt with ... Because (the term) predominance is used here, non-predominance should also be noticed by reason of its correlation with the (term predominance); for that very reason it will be said in the exposition (of that term) : '(it will be indicated) by its independence or dependence'. The same explanation should be applied to (the term) force.

Number, etc. are explained with the words 'in a way as', etc. 'There are eight (types of) fever' is an exposition of (the term) number. (Fevers) are eight in number on account of the distinctions with regard to their cause, (consisting of) wind, etc. Three (fevers) arise from one (morbific entity), three from a pair (of morbific entities), one arises from concerted action and one arises adventitiously. Although there are thirteen (cases of) concerted action with increase of the morbific entities, as has been said by Caraka : "There will be six morbid alterations with an abundance of two (morbific entities) or one (morbific entity), six (cases) in which (the three morbific entities are respectively) deficiently, moderately and excessively (increased) and one (case) with a congruous (increase of the morbific entities); these are the thirteen (cases of) concerted action"[121] (Sū. 17, 41), nevertheless the (morbid alterations) by concerted action are counted here as one (entity) on account of the generic characteristic that they arise from three morbific entities. In the same way the adventitious (morbid alterations), though arising from several causes, as lust, grief, fear, etc., are taught to be one (entity) on account of the generic characteristic that they arise adventitiously. So it is said : 'there are eight (types of) fever'. Discrimination is expounded with the words 'of the (united) morbific entities'; 'united' (means that they are) intimately connected with each other; therefore the words pair and concerted action are made use of.

(About) 'the settling of each component' (we remark that) components are the dryness, etc. of the wind, etc. The accurate determination of the (degree of) excitement of the wind, etc., (i.e. whether there is excitement) by means of one, two, three, etc. or by all (the components, is called) the settling (of the components). As has been said in the Suśruta(saṃhitā): "In combined action the excited morbific entity rushes after the much excited one with all its properties or with three, two or one (of its properties)" (Sū. 21, 38).[122] Such an excitement of a morbific entity comes about on account of the diversity of the origins. The wind, e.g., which possesses dryness, coldness, lightness, clearness, etc., is increased with all its properties by the astringent taste [123] and by *kalāya* [124] which possess the same qualities; *taṇḍulīyaka* [125] (increases it) with (its components) dryness, coldness and lightness, *kāṇḍekṣu* [126] with dryness and coldness and *sīdhu* [127] with dryness. The pungent taste [128] and alcoholic beverages [129] increase in the same way the bile with all its properties; *hiṅgu* [130] (increases it) with (its components) pungentness, hotness and sharpness, *dīpyaka* [131] with sharpness and hotness, and sesame seeds [132] with (the component) hotness. In the same way phlegm is increased with all its properties by the sweet taste [133] and buffalo's milk;[134] *rājādana* fruits [135] (increase it) with (the components) oleaginousness, heaviness and sweetness, *kaśeru* [136] with coldness and heaviness and the fruits of (trees) which contain a milky juice [137] with coldness (only).

Other ways to illustrate the qualities and (likewise) the specific comments by Jejjaṭa, Gadādhara and Vāpyacandra have not been written down here because (we would) enter upon a vast subject.

Predominance is expounded with the words : '(it will be indicated) by its (relative) independence or dependence'; this means : by its being of a chief or adjunctory nature; 'of the united morbific entities' should be supplied (to 'by the independence or dependence') in this case as well; moreover 'and non-predominance' should be supplied, which is not explained because it is easily understood. So it is clear that predominance (results) from independence and non-predominance from dependence.

Force is expounded ... The force of an illness (results) from the completeness of the ground, prodromes and symptoms, its weakness from (the presence of) subdivisions, (i.e.) fragments of these (entities).

Time is expounded ... (Night and day are explained by synonyms);[138] the seasons are spring, etc.; (the digestive process of the ingested food is explained by a synonym);[139] 'by the component parts of these' (means): by fragments of these. The time of an illness (means) time as a ground of increase or deficient presence of an illness. The component parts of a season are in this case a certain number of days and nights, as Vāgbhaṭa says: "The two (periods of) seven days at the end of a season and at the beginning of (the next) one are traditionally called a seasonal juncture" (Sū. 3, 58ab). (The term) 'season component' is also employed to denote a component, in the form of a season, of time, in the form of the year; season components are not, however, as with regard to days, etc., the beginning, middle part and end of one season, because a season as a whole is spoken of as a cause.

'In accordance with the (particular) impurity (involved)' is: in accordance with the (particular) morbific entity (involved), as for instance phlegm in the beginning of the night, bile in its middle part and wind during the remaining (part); the same (applies) to the (component parts of the) day. Excitement of phlegm (occurs) in the spring, of bile in the autumn and of wind in the rainy period; in the same way excitement of phlegm (occurs) in the beginning of (the digestive process of) the ingested food, just after having ingested it, of bile in the middle part, when it is in the stage in which the maturative process is going on, and of wind in the end, when the ingested food has been properly transformed. That has been said by Vāgbhaṭa himself: "Though being pervasive, they are residing under, between and above the cardiac and umbilical regions; they belong to the end, middle part and beginning of life, day, night and (the digestive process of) the ingested food, in due order" (Sū. 1, 7cd-8ab);[140] 'they' are in this case, in due order, wind, bile and phlegm.

(An objector may ask:) Is it not thus, that Caraka, with regard to distinctions of the onset, has also mentioned the mode in the same way as the number? (He says) for instance : "Illnesses are of two modes according to their distinction into endogenous and adventitious ones" (fr. Ni. 1, 12[4]) and : "There are three modes of blood-bile" (fr. Sū. 19, 3), etc. In this connection it may be asked for which reason the mode is not mentioned here.

The answer is that the term number includes the mode, because the latter is invariably connected with number. The distinction between mode and number is as follows : a mode is a manner and it only occurs in (entities) of the same class by reason of their being accompanied by some other quality (though they, as such, are not subject to change); there exists for instance an upwards going manner in the entity (called) blood-bile, though it remains the same (conceived as an entity). Number, however, also occurs in all that which possesses distinctness; (one can say), for example : there are four jars; there are eight fevers. In this very case the mode is the manner and it cannot be applied to distinct (things); for that reason a manner, attended by a quality of the cause, is applied to illnesses which are distinct with regard to number, etc. The Nyāya experts say likewise : "(The term) mode (is made use of) when distinct entities are conceived by means of a common quality; number, however, (is applied to) everything that may be called a distinct entity";[141] the grammarians, on the other hand, explain : "A manner is provided with something common, (but) a distinction does not refer to (the occurrence of) common (qualities in the enumerated things)";[142] thus it has been written by Vāpyacandra.

(An objector may say) : Is it not thus, that the way in which a fever is known by the discrimination of each component (of the morbific entities), etc., is not the way in which (it is known) by number?

The answer is : distinctions as to the morbific entity of an illness are known by means of the distinctions concerning number; as a consequence of this, having got knowledge about fever, etc. as to their own form, the specific type should be investigated for the sake of therapy (by asking) : 'which one (out of the total number) is this fever?'; the specific type is found when that has become known; by way of such an uninterrupted series the fact arises that number is a cause. If (an illness) is just being produced and has emerged, being distinct with regard to its morbific entity, then it is suitable to inquire about it (by asking) : 'which one (out of the total number) is this one?' For which reason (is this question put forth)? For the sake of specific therapy.

That are the characteristics of the onset.

1, 14ab : Thus has been proclaimed what is meant by origin;[143] it will be taught comprehensively (later on).

(A.h.Ni. 1, 12ab).[144]

M :

The five (elements, consisting of the) origin. etc., which have been dealt with, are summarized ... The word 'thus' (points) to the completion (of the description). The word 'origin' expresses a wider notion in this case; 'that which is meant by' (denotes) that which is to be spoken of (as the origin, etc.). (A paraphrase of the stanza is given); the meaning of it is that in the whole of (this) book the origin, prodromes, etc., belonging to each particular disease, will be stated together with the specific (particulars) of each of those (diseases).

1, 14cd-15ab : The origin of really all diseases are the excited impurities (14); (the origin) of the excitement of these again is proclaimed to be the indulgence in insalutary things in several ways.

(A.h.Ni. 1, 12cd-13ab).[145]

M :

Causes of diseases are twofold : distant and near; with regard to this (distinction) disagreeing foods, etc. are distant, wind, etc. near (causes). With the words 'of (really) all', etc. is expressed that all diseases are invariably caused by these (entities, consisting of) wind, etc. As has been said in the Suśruta(saṃhitā) : "Because there is no disease without morbific entities, an experienced (physician) should treat even an illness which has not been mentioned by (making use of) the signs of the morbific entities" (Sū. 35, 19).

Although excitement of a morbific entity does not occur in the production of adventitious illnesses, nevertheless this (excitement) will necessarily come about immediately after the production, in the same way as the connection with its qualities in a (medicinal) substance which has been produced.[146] As has been said in the Caraka(saṃhitā) : "For an adventitious (disease), produced with distress at the beginning, leads to incongruity of wind, bile and phlegm later on" (fr. Sū. 20, 7).[147]

An origin is a cause. The impurities are the morbific entities because they bring about an impure condition. (An objector may ask :) What is (meant by) this condition of being a morbific entity of wind, etc. ? With regard to this (question) some say : the condition of being a morbific entity is an independent corrupting (capacity); the word independent serves to differentiate (these entities) from the corruptible (constituents, consisting of the) nutrient fluid, etc., for these, when they are corrupted by the wind, etc., bring about corruption of other corruptible (constituents). Others say with regard to this : what is this independence? Does it mean absence of linkage with another morbific entity or absence of linkage with another ground? In the first case wind only would be a morbific entity, but not phlegm and bile, which are linked to wind. As has been said : "Bile is crippled, phlegm is crippled, the impurities and the elements (of the body) are crippled; where they are carried by the wind there they go, as clouds".[148]

In the second case even wind is not a morbific entity because its corrupting (capacity) is linked to an origin, exactly like that of phlegm and bile. Therefore the characteristic is : 'being a morbific entity is being the agent of a corruption, when the condition is present of being (an entity) which starts a constitution'. 'The condition of being (an entity) which starts a constitution' (is used as) a specifying addition to exclude the nutrient fluid, blood, etc. For constitutions, (dominated) by the nutrient fluid, blood, etc., are not described in scientific treatises in a way similar to the constitutions (dominated) by wind, etc. The existence of the bodily constitutions (dominated) by wind, etc. (indicates that) the body has been started by semen and blood, corrupted by wind, etc.[149] As Caraka says : "Their bodily constitution is named in accordance with its close affixion [150] to a (particular) morbific entity" (Sū. 7, 40cd); he also says : "Those with a constitution (dominated) by wind are always ill" (Sū. 7, 40b).[151] In (his description of) the characteristics of the constitutions Suśruta has said as well : "Someone whose constitution is (dominated) by wind has fissured hands and feet, is wakeful and of an unsteady mind" (fr. Śā. 4, 64),[152] etc.

The distinction between a constitution and a disease is as follows : a constitution does not bring about much trouble when unwholesome things are indulged in, as has been stated succinctly as follows : "As an insect, arisen from poison, does not perish by poison, in that same way the body is not troubled by the constitutions, because it has arisen from these" (Su.Śā. 4, 79).[153] In a detailed way (this subject) should be examined in the glosses on the stanzas of the Suśruta(saṃhitā),[154] called Praśnavidhāna,[155] and in (other) commentaries. (The doubt may arise) whether it should exactly be thus that a morbific entity is (the agent) which starts a constitution. (This definition is) correct; rejection certainly results from the counterstatement, and the own form of a morbific entity would not have been dealt with.

Blood, of which previous commentators, Āṣāḍhadharma, Svāmidāsa, etc., admit that it has the state of a morbific entity because Suśruta,[156] etc. mention, as of wind, etc., its time of excitement, (way of) excitement, elimination, specific seats, specific signs and specific therapy, has also been differentiated (from the morbific entities by the mentioned statement), on account of the state of affairs that the contemporary (commentators) do not admit (that it is a morbific entity).

It may be argued that, in case the morbific entities are (regarded as a) cause, they would always produce diseases because they are always actually present in the body; for the reason that one may reflect in that way it is said : 'the excited (impurities)', (i.e. impurities) which have got into a deviated state.

The question may be raised whether their excitement (arises) from their own nature or from another cause. The former (alternative is) not (the right one) because the consequence would be the same as in the preceding (case), and (if their excitement would arise) from another cause one would ask what that (other cause is like); having that in mind, mention is made of the indulgence in insalutary things in several ways, (i.e.) the indulgence in several, (i.e.) various, ways, in insalutary things which are characterized by an inadequate conjunction of the senses with their objects, errors in judgment and transformation (by time).

1, 15cd : Moreover diseases occur which are functioning as the origin of diseases,

1, 16 : as for instance from the general glowing heat of fever blood-bile is roused and from blood-bile fever; from both (diseases) desiccation also arises;

1, 17 : from splenomegaly arise abdominal affections and from abdominal affections certainly swellings; from haemorrhoids arise abdominal suffering and also visceral swelling;
(from morbific factors such as sleeping by day, etc., nasal catarrh arises);

1, 18 : from nasal catarrh arises cough and from cough decline; decline also occurs as the ground of the disease (called) desiccation.

(Ca.Ni. 8, 16cd-19).[157]

M :

Caraka's words, 'functioning as the origin', etc., are adduced because there may arise doubt whether only that (which has been dealt with)[158] is an origin or another (type of origin) also occurs.

The word 'moreover' is not in its proper place. (The correct order of the words is given).

This (sentence) means that the aim, called illness, which is arrived at by an origin, (can) also (be arrived at) by a disease. By writing 'that which functions as an origin', which expresses : 'a disease bringing about a disease', (Mādhava) conveys the (following) idea : even a disease, bringing about another disease, can do so only when its force has been augmented by another origin. (The construction is : thus a disease arises which is the origin of a disease). On this very subject examples are given with the words 'as for instance', etc.

'From both (diseases)' (means) : from blood-bile and from fever.

(Because) 'suffering' is said to be that which makes one suffer, suffering is what brings about oppressing pain. According to Vāpyacandra this word 'suffering' should be added to all (the terms), (i.e.) fever and the subsequent ones, with change of the gender (as the case may require). And also visceral swelling arises from haemorrhoids. From cough arises decline; 'of the vital fluid and so on' should be supplied. This decline occurs as the ground of a disease. Because one may ask of which disease (it is the ground), it is said : of desiccation, (i.e.) kingly consumption. Some read here a different text which has been explained by Haricandra, etc. : "And desiccation also arises when decline and that which affects the chest are the ground".[150] This has the (following) meaning : decline is kingly consumption; that which affects the chest is a lesion of the chest; (a grammatical remark is made); when these are the ground, desiccation, (i.e.) decline of the elements (of the body), arises.

(An objector may raise the question whether) it is not thus, that Caraka, who has summarily described the whole origin as being threefold with the words : "Inadequate conjunction of the senses with their objects", etc. (fr. Sū. 11, 38) and who later declares that also a disease is an origin, contradicts the summarized description of the threefold origin as stated by himself.

On this (question) some reflect (as follows) : that origin which has been said to be threefold has all illnesses as its range, but this one (mentioned above) has a fixed range in each case, as a consequence of which not all diseases arise from a disease, but only some (particular) illness (arises) from some (particular) disease; that is really a fourth origin, called disease. Others however say that, even when a disease is the origin of a disease, this does not occur at all with exclusion of the threefold origin, the consequence of which is that this (mentioned) fever does not start blood-bile as long as its force is not augmented by inadequate conjunction of the senses with their objects, etc.; with regard to the production of an illness the ground is therefore only threefold, directly or indirectly.[160]

1, 19ab : First being isolated diseases, they are functioning as a ground later on.

(Ca.Ni. 8, 20ab).[161]

M:

Because (the question may be raised) whether these very diseases, which have been mentioned as the origin of another disease, generate a disease when they have been scarcely produced or immediately following upon that (production), it is said : 'they, first being', etc. These illnesses, first being isolated, (i.e.) independent, because they have not acquired a ground of augmentation, are at first only diseases because they bring about a painful condition; later on, when they have acquired a ground of augmentation, they bring about that which is the aim, (i.e.) the purpose, called generation of an illness, of a ground, (i.e.) an origin, as fever for instance (generates) blood-bile.

1, 19cd : One disease becomes appeased when it has become the ground of a disease,

1, 20 : but another one does not become appeased, though being a ground as well.

Thus the intermixtures of illnesses are regarded as being those which are the most difficult (to cure) in men.

(Ca.Ni. 8, 21-22ab).[162]

M:

The diversity of that very illness, generating a disease, is dealt with ... Thus, in the mentioned manner, intermixtures, (i.e.) assemblies of illnesses, are observed, as for instance (when) nasal catarrh does not cease and cough is produced, haemorrhoids do not cease and abdominal affection and visceral swelling occur. They are the most difficult (to cure) because they generate suffering of many kinds and, usually, are obstructive to treatment.

1, 21 : Therefore accomplished *vaidyas*, desirous of outstanding success, have to learn, exerting themselves, this very ascertainment of fever, etc. as it will be described (hereafter).

M :

With the words 'therefore', etc. is expressed that the mentioned five (elements, consisting of the) origin, etc., have necessarily to be known because they are the ground of success, characterized by cessation of the disease. (It is said) 'outstanding', (i.e.) great, success because the range (of this science covers) many (subjects). 'Ascertainment' is the origin, etc.

Now the qualities of wind, etc., as stated by Caraka, are written down in order to know, with regard to the morbid alterations which will be described, about an inherence (in a morbid alteration, the qualities of which are) congruous with the natural state, an inherence (in a morbid alteration, the qualities of which are) incongruous with the altered state, etc. : "Wind is dry, cold, light, subtle, fluctuating, clear and harsh; it is appeased by substances with contrary qualities. Bile is slightly oleaginous, hot, sharp, liquid, acid, flowing and pungent; it is quickly appeased by substances with contrary qualities. Phlegm is heavy, cold, soft, oleaginous, sweet, solid and mucilaginous; its qualities become appeased by contrary qualities" (Sū. 1, 59-61).[163]

NOTES

1 A *maṅgalācaraṇa* is an auspicious introduction in the form of a prayer for the attainment of success at the beginning of any work or composition.

2 Harihara is a combination of Viṣṇu (Hari) and Śiva (Hara), representing the union of the two deities.

3 A *vaidya* is an Āyurvedic physician.

4 This may mean that the author has also studied other sciences (e.g. grammar and logic), or it points to medical treatises not mentioned by name.

5 *sadbhiṣaj.* Cf. Ca.Sū. 9, 22-23 : "Any one of the (following characteristics) : knowledge, good sense, practical training, wide experience, accomplishment and having been educated by a good preceptor, suffices to give its owner the name of *vaidya.* But he who possesses all these auspicious qualities, (viz.) knowledge, etc., deserves to be called an accomplished *vaidya* and bestows well-being on the living beings."

6 This stanza does not occur in the Carakasaṃhitā. A variant of it is quoted, as a traditional doctrine, by Aruṇa in his comment on A.h.Sū. 1, 30. Aruṇa reads *upakrama-vighātin,* i.e. injurious to (its) treatment, instead of *upakramāvirodhin. upakrama* means (1) treatment, (2) the beginning or approach of a disease.

7 Several editions read *pravṛttyaṅgatva* instead of *pravṛttyaṅga.* The former is more correct.

8 *ṛddhi.* See Ca.Śā. 1, 140-141ab : "The entering into (other bodies), knowledge of the mind (of other persons), the accomplishment of (all one's) aims by (the force of one's) wish, seeing, hearing and remembering (of things which are beyond the reach of ordinary people), (extraordinary) beauty, also invisibility at will; these (faculties) are called the eight-fold sovereign power of the yogis."

9 I have not been able to trace this quotation to its source.

10 Cf. the latter part of A.s.Ni. 1, 7 (Ki. 1, 10) and Ca.Ni. 1, 6, which are almost identical : "One attains knowledge about it (i.e. a disease) by means of ..."

11 Su. reads *pratīghāta*, i.e. that which checks, instead of *pratīkāra*, i.e. that which counteracts.

12 Su.U. 1, 25 reads the stanza cdab; this order improves the structure.

13 See ch. 8.

14 Cf. Ca.Ci. 30, 325d : "Flies may bring about vomiting." The word *makṣikā* may denote many kinds of hymenopterous and dipterous insects; sometimes it is used to denominate several kinds of bees. In some instances it has a much more restricted sense; see: Cakra on Ca.Sū. 27, 243: "A *makṣikā* is a tawny kind of bee"; Ḍa. on Su.Sū. 45, 133 : "A *makṣikā* is a big bee of a tawny colour; others say it is a very small kind."

15 This may refer to the view that both fever and visceral swelling come about by improper diet and conduct.

16 Ca. : *vyādher ekasya cāneko bahūnāṃ bahavo 'pi ca*, which has an almost identical meaning.

17 See M. on 1, 5a-c about near and distant origins.

18 Ca. : *tatra pūrvarūpadarśane jvarādau vā hitaṃ laghvaśanam apatarpaṇaṃ vā*, i.e. "When its prodromes become visible, or in the initial stage of fever, a light diet or depletion is salutary." A light diet consists e.g. of the flesh of birds (Cakra on Ca.Ni. 1, 36).

19 ghee (*ghṛta*) : PW : über dem Feuer zerlassene und wieder gestandene Butter, Schmelzbutter; sehr oft aber ohne diese einschränkende Bestimmung : Butter, Fett überhaupt und insbesondere das flüssige Schmalz (da das *ghṛta* getrunken wird); MW : clarified butter or butter which has been boiled gently and allowed to cool; Om Prakash, p. 15, nr. 5 : solidified clarified butter.

20 Su.U. 39, 97-98a : "When the prodromes of fever are present a judicious (physician) should make (a patient) drink very clear ghee; he obtains well-being from it. This is the mode (of action in fevers) arising from wind."

21 Cakra says that 'in the same way' means : when all the prodromes are present to an extraordinary degree.

22 The complete characteristics of an easily curable disease are more elaborate; see Ca.Sū. 10, 11-13.

23 The complete characteristics are described Ca.Sū. 10, 14-16.

24 See about the characteristics of mitigable and incurable diseases Ca.Sū. 10, 17-20.

25 See Mā.ni. 1, 12.

26 A similar remark is made by Aruṇa and Śrīdāsa.

27 I have not been able to find this stanza in Su.

28 Cf. Ca.Ni. 1, 3 : "Here (i.e. in this treatise, the terms) ground, (instrumental) cause, underlying factor, agent (*kartṛ*), cause, antecedent, provenance (*samutthāna*) and origin have exactly the same meaning". Cakra says that eight synonyms are enumerated because the number eight is auspicious. As additional synonyms he mentions matrix (*yoni*), root (*mūla*), occasion (*mukha*) and original basis (*prakṛti*). A.s.Ni. 1, 9 mentions as synonyms of *nidāna* : *hetu, nimitta, āyatana, kāraka* (efficient cause), *kartṛ, kāraṇa, pratyaya, samutthāna, mūla* and *yoni*. Bhā.pra. 7, 7, 25 enumerates as synonyms : *nidāna, kāraṇa, hetu, nimitta, nibandhana* (foundation), *mūla, āyatana, pratyaya*.

29 Dīnānāth says in his Hindī comm. that in the proposition *parvato vahnimān dhūmavattvāt* (i.e. there is fire on the mountain because there is smoke on it) *dhūmavattvāt* (i.e. because there is smoke on it) is called the *prayojakaḥ kartā*.

[30] I.e. Ca.Sū. 15.

[31] Cf. Ca.Sū. 6, 22 and Su.U. 64, 32.

[32] This rather puzzling statement becomes more clear by completing the quotation fr. Ca.Ni. 4, 4 : "When these three specific (entities, consisting of) the origin, etc. (i.e. origin, morbific entity and corruptible constituent), are not conform to each other, become conform after a long time or are conform, (but) very weak, morbid alterations are not the result or only after a long time, or they are (either) attenuated or not (provided) with the whole (set of) mentioned signs."

[33] Cf. fr. Ca.Sū. 11, 42 : "Time is said to be transformation."

[34] See chapter 23.

[35] This is a partial quotation of a reading of Su.Ni. 1, 42 that differs from the printed text, but was adopted by Gayadāsa : "That combustive alteration of the food which arises in someone riding on an elephant, horse or camel, and in someone eating food that gives rise to combustive alteration, quickly alters by combustion the whole blood, and this (blood), fallen down and corrupted, accumulates in the feet." The printed text runs : "The wind, having reached excitation in someone by riding on an elephant, horse or camel and by other (comparable actions), by its own causes when indulged in (by someone), and by excessive indulgence in sharp, hot, acid and alkaline articles of food, pot-herbs, etc., and (exposure to the) glowing heat (of the sun), etc., (brings about corruption of the blood)."

[36] This a is partial quotation of a variant of Su.Ci. 33, 14, recorded by Ḍa.

[37] Cf. Cikitsākalikā 29 (text publ. by Jolly, ZDMG 60, 1906, p. 423) : "By dry, bitter, astringent and pungent (substances), abstention from eating, restraint of the (natural) urges, physical exercise, sexual intercourse, crossing (a river by swimming), fighting with someone who is strong, waking, and the eating of *śyāmā*, *nīvāra*, *kaṅgu*, etc., when rain-clouds are appearing and when the food has been digested, the wind becomes excited in the bodies of the creatures." Ci.ka. 30 is almost identical with the quotation in M. (v. l.: *paittaprakopo bhavet*). Ci.ka. 31 : "By heavy, sweet and excessively cold (substances), thick sour milk, *navānna*, dishes prepared from milk and those from sesame seed, confectionery (prepared) with sugar-cane (juice), by saline (substances), lying down to repose by day beyond the proper measure, by eating a mixed diet or incongruous (articles of food), by overeating, by *pāyasa* and (dishes) prepared from flour, in the spring and at the beginning of the day (and the night), phlegm becomes excited." Cf. Su.Sū. 21, 19-24; A.h.Ni. 1, 14-18; A.s.Ni. 1, 15-17 (Ki. 1, 26-28); Bhā.pra. 7, 41-47.

[38] Ca. : *praśama* instead of *upaśama*.

[39] Ca. : *tasya prāyaḥ pradhānapraśame praśamo bhavati*.

[40] Cf. Cakra on Ca.Sū. 17, 45-46 : "One may raise the question whether the statement 'then a burning sensation (will arise)' is appropriate to bile when it maintains its natural state, for a morbific entity, maintaining its natural state, does not bring about a morbid alteration nor does a burning sensation arise from wind as its source. The answer is : ... in that subdivision of the body where the bile is driven to by the excited wind, the bile certainly gets an increment, even when maintaining its natural state and (proper) measure, for which reason a burning sensation (by an excess of bile) is surely present in that place, considering that an intimate connection with bile to such an extent is not usual at all (there). The same explanation (is applicable) in other cases as well with regard to a morbid alteration by a morbific entity that maintains its natural state. Others, however, say that morbific entities, even when maintaining their natural state, can bring

about morbid alterations on account of an intimate connection with a corrupted morbific entity."

[41] Su.Ci. 33, 3 reads : "Declined morbific entities should be augmented, excited ones appeased, increased ones eliminated and congruous ones guarded, that is a settled doctrine." Ḍa. comments a.o. : "Excited ones, (i.e.) those which have reached the state of excitement to a slight degree, should be appeased by an appeasing method only; those which have increased pre-eminently, (i.e.) which have moved away from their seat, should be eliminated by a purificatory mode (of treatment). Master Jejjaṭa reads : increased to a high degree (*pravṛddha*), for increase is of two kinds : characterized by accumulation and by excitement. Accumulation is in this (connection) increase in the form of a compact mass and excitement is increase in the form of dissolved matter. Morbific entities which have increased in the form of dissolved matter should be eliminated by means of a purificatory procedure. Excitement is of two kinds : preceded by accumulation and not preceded by it. Those (morbific) entities which have become excited, preceded by accumulation, should be appeased by a purificatory method only."

[42] Cf. Ca.Sū. 11, 48 : "There are three pathways of disease : the branches, the vital points and junctures of the bones, and the viscera. According to this (division) the branches are the elements (of the body, to wit) blood and the subsequent ones, and the skin; that is the outer pathway of disease. Vital points are the bladder, heart, head, etc.; junctures of the bones are the places of contact between the bones, together with the cords and ropes which are attached to these (structures); that is the middle pathway of disease. The viscera again are in (this) treatise denominated by the synonyms : the great channel, the middle part of the body, the great cavity, and the receptacles of undigested and digested (food, considered as a whole); that is the inner pathway of disease." Cakra comments a.o. : "By the word skin is also understood the nutrient fluid residing in it, for it is evident that the nutrient fluid is not mentioned in order to differentiate the nutrient fluid, lastingly seated in the cardiac region, from (what is understood by) the technical term branch; this (nutrient) fluid in the cardiac region is understood (to be covered) by the term viscera. In the same manner the blood residing in liver and spleen should be understood to be indicated by the term viscera."

[43] Cakra says that, if the wind stays in the receptacle of undigested food, a sudorific procedure beginning with the application of dry substances should be employed, with regard to the seat affected; later on oleaginous substances can be employed, with regard to the wind; the receptacle of undigested food is a seat of phlegm and it has been said : "The seat should be subdued first, without doing something that disagrees with the (morbific entity) staying in that seat." See also Ca.Sū. 14, 8 : "In (disorders by) wind and phlegm, or by wind, or by phlegm, sudation is required, arranged by means of oleaginous and dry, or oleaginous, or dry (substances)."

[44] A.h. : *saṃpṛkta* (blended with) instead of *saṃyukta*; *malasaṅga* (retention of the impurities) instead of *malabheda*. Cf. A.h.Sū. 13, 26 : "Others say that immature matter only arises from morbific entities which are extraordinarily excited by their mutual coalescence, (in the same way) as a poison arises from *kodrava* grains." Ḍa. characterizes immature matter by the following quotation, found in his comment on Su.Sū. 38, 23 : "That fluid (*rasa*), which does not become altered by digestion by reason of weakness of the abdominal fire, is technically called immature matter and excites all the morbific entities in the body."

[45] This is a quotation from an unknown source. Cf. A.s.Sū. 21, 33cd-36ab : "Wind, attended by immature matter, brings about afflictedness and inflatedness and does not

circulate; bile is (in that state) bad-smelling, of a dark colour, pungent, thick and heavy, and phlegm is turbid, ropy, grumous, of a coating character and mucilaginous. When the opposite (characteristics are present wind is said to be) mature; bile, in that state, is of a coppery colour, endowed with the colour of the eyes of a peacock's tail, yellow and transparent; phlegm is transparent or lumpy, clear, frothy, pure white and of a sweet taste."

46 See ch. 2.

47 Cf. Ca.Ni. 1, 12[3] : "(Knowledge about) the predominance of the morbific entities is attained by (distinguishing) more and most (serious degrees of excitement). (The term) a more (serious degree points) to (excitement of) two (and the term) a most (serious degree) to (excitement of) three (morbific entities)."

48 Su.U. 66.

49 *alpatva* may be connected with *vyādhi* (HK) or with *liṅga* (Vall); I prefer the former construction.

50 Cf. A.s.Ni. 1, 10 (Ki. 1, 13) : "A prodrome is that by which a specific impending illness is known, but not the specific morbific entity (of that illness); it is an undeveloped symptom on account of the slightness of the illness which is (still) being about to be produced (*adhyutpatsyamāna*)." Ca.Ni. 1, 18 : "A prodrome is a characteristic that precedes the production of an illness". Bhā.pra. 7, 7, 34 : "A prodrome is that by which an impending ailment is known; it is stated to be of two kinds : generic and specific. A generic (prodrome) is not based on the specific (characteristics) of the morbific entities; a specific one will be somewhat developed and attended by the specific (characteristics)."

51 See Ca.Ni. 1, 33.

52 Su. : *nānnābhinandana*.

53 Also quoted by Cakra on Ca.Ni. 1, 8.

54 This refers to Su.U. 39, 27, quoted above.

55 Mā.ni. 1, 7ab.

56 From this one may conclude that a commentary was written by Mādhavakara.

57 The point is that it does not matter whether a pile of *māṣa* beans contains some beans of another kind; the same applies when some people without parasols are present in a crowd of people with parasols.

58 Also quoted by Cakra on Ca.Ni. 1, 8.

59 The invisible force is based on the effects of good and bad actions, performed in this life and former lives.

60 *ghuṇa* or *ghūṇa* : PW : Holzwurm; MW : a kind of insect found in timber. Fr. Su.Sū. 9, 4 it is clear that it is an insect or the larva of an insect, burrowing in wood.

61 Ca. : *makṣikāghuṇakeśānām*; *abhivardhanam*.

62 See Mā.ni. 1, 5d.

63 *anubhava*; Radhakrishnan, I.Ph. 2, p. 115 : a presentative cognition which is not a reproduction of a former state of consciousness. See Yogasūtra 1, 11 and Vaiśeṣikasūtra 9, 2, 6 about the process of remembering.

64 Cf. Su.Ni. 6, 5.

65 Ā. resembles Aruṇa's comment on A.h.Ni. 1, 4. Aruṇa says, however, that prodromes are of three kinds : of a bodily, mental, and both bodily and mental character.

66 Aruṇa comments : "When this same (phenomenon, i.e.) the prodrome, has reached a developed state, (i.e.) is based on a developed morbific entity, it is called a symptom. The word 'same' (*eva*) in 'this same (phenomenon)' makes clear that only the bodily

prodrome, described previously, should be understood here, because it is lasting. The mental prodrome and that one, which is (of a) bodily and mental (character), should not be understood, because they do not last. They do not reach a developed state because both usually disappear immediately after an illness has been produced. Therefore only the bodily prodrome of an illness, being about to arise, ought to be considered here."

[67] Cf. A.s.Ni. 1, 11 (Ki. 1, 14-15) : "A symptom, however, is clearly perceptible; other names of it are sign, conformation, characteristic, mark, shape and manifestation." Ca.Ni. 1, 9 : "A characteristic is (called) a sign; with regard to such (a characteristic the terms) sign, conformation, characteristic, mark, shape, manifestation and symptom do not differ in meaning." Cakra comments : "That which makes clear the own form of a produced illness, i.e. an illness specified by specifying marks such as wind, etc., immaturity or maturity, etc., with the exclusion of the origin, therapeutic diagnosis and onset, is a sign of that (illness). The fixed sign of each particular illness is understood by this (term), such as the general sense of glowing heat of fever; in the same way are understood by it the flux of diarrhoea, etc., the incongruous start and lapse, etc., brought about by wind, of wind fever, and the characteristics of immature and mature fever and fever of long standing, which make (one) aware of a specific illness; moreover, secondary affections are (called) characteristics because they make (one) aware that an illness has reached a state of incurability, etc. A precursory signal of death, however, is only a prodrome of death. Although the origin, etc., are also indicative of a produced illness they are nevertheless not denominated here by the word sign because separate characteristics (of these) are not taught. The synonyms ... do not differ in meaning when their aim ... is to characterize a sign, but on other occasions *liṅga*, etc., have a quite different meaning ..." Bhā.pra. 7, 7, 35ab : "A specific prodrome is traditionally called a characteristic when it has developed."

[68] *svaṃ rūpaṃ svarūpam.*

[69] *svīyaṃ rūpaṃ svarūpam.*

[70] Ca. states (Ci. 14, 11) that in haemorrhoids by wind the skin, nails, etc. are of a brown or ruddy colour; Vā. says (A.h.Ni. 7, 33; A.s.Ni. 7, 15) that the skin, nails, etc. are of a black colour in this condition. See Mā.ni. 5, 15.

[71] Ḍa. says about *tanmūla* that it means : that, the ground of which is the previously produced illness itself (*tanmūla eveti prāgutpannavyādhihetuka evety arthaḥ*). Cakra explains it by *pūrvotpannavyādhikāraṇaka*, which has the same meaning.

[72] *Rāhu* is a demon consisting of a head only; therefore it is senseless to distinguish between the demon and his head. The same explanation may be applied to 'the body of a torso'.

[73] This may refer to the Vaiśeṣika view about the relation between an aggregate as a whole and its component parts. According to the Vaiśeṣika doctrine the whole is different from its component parts. See Frauwallner, Gesch. ind. Ph. 2, p. 165-166.

[74] Cakra comments : "When the inability to eat, etc. arise as being dependent from fever, they are, because of this dependence, only signs and not ailments, for an ailment is independent and may be appeased by its own (form of) therapy; that is a settled rule in medicine."

[75] This remark is also made in the comment on Ca.Ni. 1, 9 by Cakra and that on A.h.Ni. 1, 5 by Aruṇa and Śrīdāsa.

[76] Aruṇa comments : "... Conducive to well-being is that which produces well-being; this means that it brings about well-being of the body. That application, which is conducive to well-being, should be known to be therapeutic diagnosis ... The application

of which things? ... (The application of) remedial agents, such as *harītakī*, of foods, such as red *śāli* rice, and of ways of conduct, such as specific kinds of voluntary action, performed by the organ of speach, body and mind, in the form of physical exercise, sexual intercourse, waking, studying, singing, talking, meditation, concentration, etc. ...". Aruṇa distinguishes measures which are (1) contrary to a) the ground and b) the illness, and (2) those which provide the result of that which is contrary to a) the ground and b) the illness. Measures contrary to both ground and illness and those providing the result of that which is contrary to both ground and illness are not mentioned by him. He. and Śrīdāsa distinguish four kinds of therapeutic diagnosis.

77 Cf. A.s.Ni. 1, 12 (Ki. 1, 16). Indu comments that therapeutic diagnosis is of three kinds : contrary to the ground, contrary to the illness, and providing the result of that which is (of a) contrary (nature). He supports this statement by referring to A.s.Sū. 12, 7 where it is said: "(Remedial agents) are also of three kinds: contrary to the ground, contrary to the illness and providing the result of both (preceding kinds)." A.s.Sū. 12, 7-9 provides examples of these three kinds of remedies. A.s.Sū. 12, 9 ends as follows : "A remedy of such a kind, even when it is not contrary (to ground and illness), brings about a result that is contrary to ground and illness." Cakra says in his comment on Ca.Ni. 1, 10 that therapeutic diagnosis consists of six kinds : (1) contrary to a) the ground, b) the illness and c) both ground and illness; (2) providing the result of that which is contrary to a) the ground, b) the illness and c) both ground and illness. He gives a long list of examples which are almost identical to those found in the Madhukośa.

78 A fever is called recent or fresh during the first seven days of its presence; see Bhā.pra. 8, 1, 98.

79 See about the drinking of cold water in fever: Ca.Vi. 3, 39-40; Su.U. 39, 108ab; Bhā.pra. 8. 1, 16-17 and 60-61.

80 See Ca.Sū. 11, 54.

81 Cakra idem. See about the hot quality of dry ginger e.g. Ca.Sū. 27, 296; A.h.Sū. 6, 163cd-164ab.

82 Cakra idem.

83 Cakra idem. Ca. Sū.21, 44 : sleeping by day excites phlegm and bile in all seasons with the exception of summer.

84 Cakra idem. See about the use of *pāṭhā* in diarrhoea a.o. : Ca.Ci. 13, 26-27; Su.U. 40, 34-36; A.h.Ci. 9, 26-28.

85 See Ca.Sū. 3, 28, Sū. 4, 11, Sū. 25, 40; Su.Ka. 1, 36; A.h.U. 35, 46.

86 See Ca.Sū. 4, 11, Sū. 25, 40; Su.Sū. 38, 8-9: A.h.Sū. 15, 19-20.

87 See Ca.Ci. 6, 26; Su.Sū. 38, 64-65; A.h.Ci. 12, 5.

88 I have not been able to trace this quotation.

89 Ḍa. quotes this stanza as a variant of Su.Ci. 33, 14ab.

90 *kapālamālāsaṃyoga* : this term may refer to the Vaiśeṣika view that the qualities of the component parts of a whole as a cause of the qualities of the whole are not immediately inherent (see Frauwallner, Gesch.ind.Ph. 2, p. 169); *saṃyoga* (connection) is one of the twenty-four qualities in the Vaiśeṣika system.

91 The same example is given by Cakra. Lentils are said to be constrictive; see Ca.Sū. 27, 29; Dravyaguṇa 1, 25; Ma.nigh., *dhānyavarga* (10), 42; Dha.nigh., *suvarṇādivarga* (6), 96; Bhā.pra.nigh., *dhānyavarga* 50.

92 Cakra gives the same example. See about the retentive disease ch. 27; therapy in this disease is dealt with at Ca.Ci. 26 and Su.U. 55. In his comment on Su.Sū. 7, 15 Ḍa. explains *pravāhaṇa* (strained evacuation; Hoernle : fluxing) as consisting of emetic

and purgative procedures, the bringing about of lacrimation, etc., in accordance with the number (of the procedures required) with regard to phlegm, bile, particles of (foreign) matter in the eyes (*akṣirajas*), corpora aliena, etc. See also Su.Sū. 27, 5. *pravāhaṇa* is, acc. to Gul 6, p. 305 : an effort in order to expel impure matter, etc.

93 Cakra idem.

94 Ca. : *śvayathu* instead of *śotha*. The ten plants which eliminate swelling are : *pāṭalā, agnimantha, śyonāka, bilva, kāśmarya, kaṇṭakārikā, bṛhatī, śālaparṇī, pṛśniparṇī* and *gokṣuraka*.

95 See Ca.Ci. 15, 117cd-119; Su.U. 40, 180ab; A.h.Ci. 10, 4.

96 Cakra gives as an example : a hot and fever-destroying gruel in a fever arising from coldness.

97 Cakra idem. See A.h.Sū. 7, 55ab : "Waking during the night is (of a) dry (quality), sleeping by day is (of an) oleaginous (quality)." Cf. n. 83 : sleeping by day excites phlegm which is of an oleaginous quality; waking at night excites wind which is of a dry quality.

98 See about the preparation of a poultice (*upanāha*) : Ca.Sū. 14, 35-37; Su.Ci. 32, 13; A.h.Sū. 17, 2-5; A.s.Sū. 26, 5. Cakra (on Ca.Sū. 14, 35) : "A poultice is a bandage of a diseased part (of the body, made) by taking a thick unguent and surrounding it with a (piece of a) hide, etc." Śrīdāsa (on A.h.Sū. 17, 2-3) : "A poultice is that which is wrapped up in a (piece of) hide, cloth, etc.; a poultice is a bandage in the form of a hot round mass."

99 Cakra : "A hot poultice, productive of bile, in a swelling which shows a predominance of bile and is in (the stage of) maturation." The treatment with poultices is one of the procedures called sudation. Sudation is recommended by Ca. in disorders (caused) by wind or phlegm and in those by wind and phlegm, but not in disorders with a predominance of bile (Ca.Sū. 14, 8). Su. says that sudation by means of poultices destroys wind (fr. Su.Ci. 32, 14). Vāgbhaṭa (A.h.Sū. 17, 2-4ab) describes poultices used in disorders by wind and in those by wind in combination with bile or phlegm.

100 Cakra : "Food which brings about combustive alteration in a swelling which shows a predominance of bile and is in (the stage of) maturation."

101 Cakra idem. Ca.Ci. 9, 31 : "Threatening, causing terror, offering (gifts), exhilaration, consolation, frightening and astonishing bring the mind to its natural state by loss of memory." Cf. Su.U. 62, 17-20a; A.h.U. 6, 20cd-22ab, 47-52ab.

102 Cakra idem. See Ca.Ci. 20, 34; A.h.Ci. 6, 17cd.

103 Cakra idem. See Ca.Ci. 19, 47-49, 57-58; Su.U. 40, 99cd-101; A.h.Ci. 9, 37-38.

104 Cakra idem. Cf. Aruṇa : (in a case of vomiting the bringing about of) vomiting (*udvamana*) by (introduction of) a finger, the stalk of a water-lily (*utpala*), etc. (into the throat).

105 See about the hotness of *aguru* : Ca.Sū. 26, 49; Ma.nigh., *karpūrādivarga* (3), 13; Dha.nigh., *candanādivarga* (3), 26; Rā.nigh., *candanādivarga* (12), 39; Bhā.pra.nigh., *karpūrādivarga* 21-23.

106 Cakra idem. Su.Sū. 12, 20ab : "When someone has been scorched (by fire) one should arrange a heating procedure by means of fire and (employ) a hot remedial agent."

107 See e.g. Ca.Ci. 23, 17.

108 Cakra idem.

109 Cakra idem.

110 This is a variant, not affecting the meaning, of Su.U. 49, 16ab (*vamīṣu bahudoṣāsu chardanaṃ hitam ucyate*).

111 Su. : *abhyudīryate* instead of *udīryate*.

[112] Su.U. 47, 47 : "The alcoholic beverage by which (a patient) has been brought down, the same one as he prefers to drink, *surā*, *āsava*, etc., should be given to him in the prescribed manner; in the opposite case he will necessarily reach a condition of subsidence (of his forces)." Su.U. 47, 24ab-26ab : "An alcoholic beverage, to which have been added verjuice (*cukra*), black pepper (*marica*), undried ginger (*ārdraka*), *dīpya*, *kuṣṭha* and *sauvarcala* salt, suffices to appease the wind, or, to (obtain) well-being, (one should give it), mixed with *pṛthvīka*, *dīpyaka*, dry ginger (*mahauṣadha*), *hiṅgu* and *sauvarcala* salt. One should also prepare agreeable *ṣāḍavas* and drinks (*pānaka*) with *āmrātaka*, mango fruits (*āmra*), pomegranates (*dāḍima*) and *mātuluṅga*, or one should enjoy meat broth, etc., mixed with the juice of fruits, and also the seasoned flesh of animals frequenting marshy places."

[113] A.h.Ci. 7, 12-13 : "When there is an abundance of wind in this (alcoholic disorder), one should give an alcoholic beverage made from flour (*piṣṭa*), mixed with *bījapūraka*, *vṛkṣāmla*, *kola*, pomegranates (*dāḍima*), *dīpyaka*, *yavānī*, *hapuṣā*, *ajājī*, the three irritating substances (*vyoṣa*), the three kinds of salt (i.e. *saindhava*, *biḍa* and black salt) and undried ginger (*ārdraka*), together with broached (*śūlya*) meat, vegetables (*haritaka*) and oleaginous groats (*saktu*)."
Hā. 1, 19, 10 : *paiṣṭī* annihilates wind.

[114] A.h.Ci. 21, 54cd : "(Someone suffering from stiffness of the thighs) should cross a lake with stagnant water and free from danger (or) a river against the stream."

[115] Also quoted by Aruṇa on A.h.Ni. 1, 6-7ab.

[116] Aruṇa comments : "The (process of) coming to completion of the particular ailment (which is present), (i.e.) the consummation (*niṣpatti*) (of that process), that is to say the becoming perceptible of it, in accordance with the manner in which any one of the morbific entities, wind, etc., is corrupted, (i.e.) excited, in accordance with (the manner of its) spreading, (i.e.) running through the body, (i.e.) the specific way in which it goes to take up a position (*saṃniveśa*), that (process) is taught to be the onset ..."

[117] Cf. A.s.Ni. 1, 13 (Ki. 1, 17-18) : "The onset is the illness, started in that (particular) way by a morbific entity, corrupted in that (particular way). Its synonyms are : emersion, origination, coming to completion (*nirvṛtti*) and consummation (*niṣpatti*)." Ca.Ni. 1, 11 : "Onset, emersion and origination have the same meaning with regard to an illness." Cakra comments : "Although the signs become apparent immediately after the onset, nevertheless the onset is dealt with at the end (of the series) because it is of little purpose in the examination of an illness ... With respect to it some say that it is the emersion of an illness as such, occasioned by the function of the last cause (*antyakāraṇavyāpārajanya*). Being of the opinion that, although the onset does not make (one) aware of an illness in the (same) way as the origin, etc. does, it is nevertheless not a characteristic of a not (yet) produced illness, they describe that the production leads to the perception of an illness. Others do not share this opinion. When it is different the consequence arises that some specific (peculiarity) is learnt from the onset. It is not a fixed rule that an illness is perceived only after it has been produced completely; as a consequence of this a not (yet) produced illness is indicated as an impending one by its origin and prodromes. Therefore the word onset expresses here the emersion of an illness, connected with the specific function of the morbific entity which generates the illness (*vyādhijanakadoṣavyāpāraviśeṣayukta*); for that very reason 'origination' is mentioned as a synonym. For the origination is the participation of the productive cause which extends as far as the generation of an illness (*utpādakāraṇasya vyādhijananaparyantaṃ gamanam*). The onset certainly makes (one) aware of a specific (peculiarity)

of an illness, as for instance by the onset of fever, (described in the statement) beginning with 'and, when it is excited and has entered the receptacle of undigested food' and ending with 'then it results in fever' (Ca.Ni. 1, 20), peculiarities of fever are acknowledged, consisting of the facts that it brings about corruption of the receptacle of undigested food, injury of the (transforming) fire, corruption of the nutrient fluid, etc. It should not be said that this bringing about of a corruption of the receptacle of undigested food, etc. (constitutes) a peculiarity of the morbific entities, (for) from that would result that peculiarities of causes only are understood by the term origin. As a consequence (of this reasoning) the peculiarity of the cause, consisting of a function of the morbific entity which generates the illness, is expressed by the word onset, which has been made a separate (concept) in order to make (one) aware of a specific (peculiarity) of an illness ..."

[118] Aruṇa comments : "... Discrimination is the settling of each component, (i.e.) the examination of every single part, the effect of each one having to be inferred, of the morbific entities, which have been united, (i.e.) brought about together, in one illness ... As for instance : in this illness the excited wind becomes corrupted with one quality which is present in excess, sometimes the dry, sometimes the light, sometimes the cold (quality), or sometimes with two or three qualities which are present in excess. In the same way the bile, etc. ... Such an ascertainment with regard to the (morbific entity) is (called) discrimination. As a consequence of this the ways of excitement are not comparable in all diseases. The qualities dry, etc. of wind, for instance, always lead to excitement, but sometimes there exists pre-eminence (*prakṛṣṭatva*), sometimes defectiveness (*nyūnatva*) of some quality with regard to the bringing about of excitement. That is the very ground of the infinite number of maladies and therapies ... With regard to therapeutic diagnosis, consisting of restorative measures (*saṃtarpaṇa*) or depletion, of an illness, one may also ask whether it is attended by well-being when (applied) completely or when (applied only) partially ..." He. remarks that the term number is used to indicate the special (*asādhāraṇa*) ways of production of an illness because these are not substantiated by another term. The ascertainment whether an illness arises from a couple of morbific entities or from concerted action is not covered by this concept, but is called discrimination by means of more and most (serious) degrees (of excitement).

[119] Cf. A.s.Ni. 1, 14 (Ki. 1, 19-24) : "This (onset) is distinguished by means of specificities regarding number, discrimination, predominance, force and time. With respect to these (distinctions) number is as follows : there are eight fevers, blood-bile is of three kinds, there are five (kinds of) cough. Discrimination is the settling of each component of the united morbific entities. The predominance of illnesses (is determined) from their distinction into chief and adjunctory ones or from their connection with more and most (serious) degrees (of excitement). The specific force or weakness of morbific entities (is established) by a clear ascertainment of the complete or partial (presence) of the ground, etc. The specificity of the morbific entities with regard to time is their excitement (as a condition which is) invariably connected with (periods of) time, (consisting of) season, day and night, and (the digestive process of the) food." Ca.Ni. 1, 12 : "This (onset) is distinguished by means of specificities regarding number, predominance, mode, discrimination, force and time. Number is for instance : there are eight (kinds of) fever, five (kinds of) visceral swelling, seven (kinds of) skin disease and so on. Knowledge about the predominance of morbific entities is attained by the more and most (serious) degrees (of excitement); with regard to this (distinction it is thus that) a more (serious degree

means excitement) of two and a most (serious degree excitement) of three (morbific entities). The mode is as follows : illnesses are of two modes according to their distinction into endogenous and adventitious ones, of three modes when distinguished with regard to the three morbific entities and of four modes according to their distinction into curable, incurable, mild and severe ones. Discrimination means in this context the discrimination of the force of each of the components of the united morbific entities. The specificity of illnesses with regard to the time in which they are strong is regulated by the modes of time, (consisting of) season, day and night, and (the digestive process of the) food."

120 *upādhi*. See : S. Dasgupta, H.I.Ph. 2, p. 72; O. Lacombe, L'absolu selon le védânta, passim.

121 See chapter 2 for the elaboration of this classification.

122 Ḍa. remarks that excited (*kupitaḥ*) means that the morbific entity is excited with one, two or three of its properties; much excited (*kruddhaḥ*; *prakopaṃ yātaḥ*) means that it is excited with all its properties. An excited morbific entity is (called) non-predominant or adjunctory and a much excited one predominant or chief. Ḍa. is of the opinion that a property (*bhāvaḥ*) is a quality (*guṇaḥ*), such as the dryness of wind, etc. He also gives us information about different interpretations of this term : some consider the properties to be the grounds of illnesses (and to consist of) diet, conduct, place and time; others think that the properties consist of taste, quality, potency and digestive alteration; Bhaṭṭāraharicandra and other commentators of the Carakasaṃhitā state that the properties are the qualities and actions of substances.

123 Fr. Su.Sū. 42, 8 : "With respect to that the wind is characterized by the qualities coldness, dryness, lightness, clearness and constraint; the astringent taste has the same matrix as (the wind) and increases its coldness by its (own) coldness, its dryness by its (own) dryness, its lightness by its (own) lightness, its clearness by its (own) clearness and its constraint by its own (constraint)." Cf. Ca.Sū. 26, 43 : "The astringent taste is not light." Śivadāsasena comments : "What has been said in the Suśruta(saṃhitā), (viz.) that the astringent taste increases the wind by its (own) lightness, is not a contradiction because it is light with regard to its digestion." A.h.Sū. 10, 20 : "The astringent (taste) is heavy"; Aruṇa, He. and Candra make no comment on this statement. A.s.Sū. 18, 18 : "The astringent (taste) is heavy." Bhā.pra. 6, 192-193 : "The astringent taste is light."

124 Ca.Sū. 27, 29d : "*kalāya* is productive of wind to a high degree"; Su.Sū. 46, 30d : "*kalāya* is abundantly provided with wind"; A.h.Sū. 6, 18b : "*kalāya* is productive of wind to an extraordinary degree"; Dravyaguṇa, *dhānyavarga* (1), 30 : idem; Ma.nigh., *dhānyavarga* (10), 40 : idem; Bhā.pra.nigh., *dhānyavarga* 57 : "*kalāya* is sweet as to its taste and digestion, dry and cold."

125 Ca.Sū. 27, 94cd-95ab and Su.Sū. 46, 256-258 : *taṇḍulīyaka* is dry and cold; A.h.Sū. 6, 83a-c and A.s.Sū. 7, 128 : *taṇḍulīya* is dry, cold and light; Ma.nigh., *śākavarga* (7), 41 : idem; Dha.nigh., *karavīrādivarga* (4), 117 : *taṇḍulīya* is dry and cold; Rā.nigh., *parpaṭādivarga* (5), 176 : *taṇḍulīya* is cool; Bhā.pra.nigh., *śākavarga* 12-13 : *taṇḍulīyaka* is dry, cold and light.

126 The qualities of *kāṇḍekṣu* (= *kāśa* = *kāsa*) are not very clear. Cf. Ca.Vi. 8, 144 : it belongs to the astringent group (*kaṣāyaskandha*); Ma.nigh., *abhayādivarga* (1), 337 : it is cold; Dha.nigh., *karavīrādivarga* (4), 131 : it is cold as to its potency; Rā.nigh., *śālmalyādivarga* (8), 202 : it is cool. Bhā.pra.nigh., *ikṣuvarga* 11 : it excites the wind.

127 A.h.Sū. 5, 74cd : "*sīdhu* is productive of wind and bile and destroys morbid

alterations by oleaginous substances and phlegm"; so it is dry, because the dry quality is opposed to oleaginousness. A.s.Sū. 6, 129 ab: idem. Ca.Sū. 27, 184 cd: "(The alcoholic beverage), made from boiled sugar-cane juice, is thought to destroy morbid alterations by oleaginous substances and phlegm and to be beneficial to the colour (of the skin)." *sīdhu* is generally made from sugar-cane juice, in two varieties : one made from boiled sugar-cane juice (*pakvarasa*) and the other from unboiled juice (*śītarasika*); see Aruṇa, He. and Candra on A.h.Sū. 5, 74cd-75ab and Cakra on Ca.Sū. 27, 184cd-185. Su. describes several kinds of *sīdhu*; not all of these varieties are prepared from sugar-cane juice (Su.Sū. 45, 182cd-187ab); the variety made from boiled sugar-cane juice is said to destroy wind and to be salutary in haemorrhoids by phlegm. Dravyaguṇa, *madyādivarga* 10ab: "*śīdhu* (prepared from boiled sugar-cane juice) eliminates bile and wind and destroys morbid alterations by phlegm and oleaginous substances"; *madyādivarga* 14 : "*śīdhu*, prepared from *madhūka* flowers, brings about combustive alteration, bestows (a good transforming) fire and force, is dry and astringent, destroys phlegm and excites wind and bile"; Ma.nigh., *pānīyādivarga* 8, 186-187 : "*sīdhu* prepared from boiled sugar-cane juice is productive of wind and bile and promotes the oleaginous quality; when prepared from the unboiled juice, it is attenuating (*saṃlekhana*)." Bhā.pra.nigh., *saṃdhānavarga* 25-27 : *sīdhu*, prepared from boiled sugar-cane juice, is productive of wind and bile; the variety, made from the unboiled juice, has the same qualities to a slight degree.

128 Fr. Su.Sū. 42, 8 : "Bile is characterized by the qualities hotness, sharpness, dryness, lightness and clearness; the pungent taste has the same matrix as the (bile) and increases its hotness by its (own) hotness, its sharpness by its (own) sharpness, its dryness by its (own) dryness, its lightness by its (own) lightness and its clearness by its (own) clearness." Cf. Ca.Sū. 26, 43; A.s.Sū. 18, 15; Dravyaguṇa 1, 5; Ma.nigh., *miśrakavarga* (13), 68-69ab; Bhā.pra. 6, 185-187.

129 Ca.Sū. 27, 178ab : "An alcoholic beverage is, with regard to its nature, said to be acid and hot and (also) acid as to its digestive alteration"; Ca.Ci. 24, 30 : "An alcoholic beverage is traditionally said to possess ten qualities : it is light, hot, sharp, subtle, acid, diffusive (*vyavāyin*), moving swiftly, dry, relaxation-promoting (*vikāśin*) and clear"; Su.Sū. 45, 170-171c : "All alcoholic beverages are productive of bile, are acid, appetizing, stimulating the (transforming) fire, loosening (impure matter), destroying phlegm and wind, beneficial to the cardiac region, purifying the bladder, light with regard to digestion, bringing about combustive alteration, hot, sharp, arousing the senses, relaxation-promoting and furthering the appearance of faeces and urine"; A.h.Sū. 5, 62cd-65ab : "An alcoholic beverage stimulates the (transforming) fire, is appetizing, sharp, hot, and bestows satisfaction and a well-nourished appearance; it is slightly savoury, bitter and pungent; it is acid as to its digestion and taste; it gives rise to the flowing out (of impure matter), is slightly astringent, brings about (a good condition of the) voice, health, audacity and (a good) colour (of the skin), is light, beneficial to those who suffer from loss of sleep or sleep beyond the proper measure, brings about corruption of bile and blood, is beneficial to those who are lean or gross, is dry and subtle, purifies the channels and eliminates wind and phlegm, when it is drunk in accordance with the prescriptions (*yuktyā*); otherwise it is like poison." A.s.Sū. 6, 115-117 : idem. Ma.nigh., *pānīyādivarga* (8), 165 : "An alcoholic beverage is usually productive of bile, gives rise to the flowing out (of impure matter), appetizes, stimulates the (transforming) fire, brings about combustive alteration, furthers the appearance of faeces and urine, is sharp and repels wind and phlegm." See also Dravyaguṇa, *madyādivarga* 1 and Bhā.pra.nigh., *saṃdhānavarga* 19-20.

130 Ca.Sū. 27, 299 : *hiṅgu* destroys wind and phlegm, is pungent and hot, stimulates the (transforming) fire and is light; Su.Sū. 46, 228 : it is light and hot, subdues phlegm and wind, is pungent, oleaginous and sharp; A.h.Sū. 6, 152cd-153ab : it destroys wind and phlegm, excites the bile, is pungent as to its digestion and taste, stimulates the (transforming) fire and is light; Dravyaguṇa, *lavaṇādivarga* 19 : it is sharp, pungent as to its taste, light, hot and oleaginous, stimulates the (transforming) fire and subdues phlegm and wind; Ma.nigh., *śuṇṭhyādivarga* (2), 51 : it is hot, sharp, removes phlegm and wind, and increases bile; Dha.nigh., *śatapuṣpādivarga* (2), 37 : it is hot and pungent and destroys wind and phlegm; Rā.nigh., *pippalyādivarga* (6), 61 : it is pungent and hot and repels wind and phlegm; Bhā.pra.nigh., *harītakyadivarga* 101: it is hot and sharp, removes wind and phlegm, and increases bile. The consulted sources do not conflict with the statement in the Madhukośa except with regard to the oleaginous quality of *hiṅgu*, mentioned in Su. and Dravyaguṇa.

131 Dha.nigh., *śatapuṣpādivarga* (2), 98 : *dīpyaka* = *ajamodā*; ibid., 99 : *ajamodā* is bitter and hot, subdues phlegm and wind and stimulates the (transforming) fire; Rā. nigh., *pippalyādivarga* (6), 152 : *ajamodā* is pungent, hot and dry and brings about the elimination of phlegm and wind; Ma.nigh., *śuṇṭhyādivarga* (2), 29 : *ajamodā* is pungent and sharp, stimulates the (transforming) fire, removes phlegm and wind, is hot, brings about combustive alteration and is light; Bhā.pra.nigh., *harītakyādivarga* 76 : *dīpyaka* = *ajamodā*; ibid. 79 : *ajamodā* is pungent and sharp, stimulates the (transforming) fire, removes phlegm and wind, is hot, brings about combustive alteration and is light. None of the consulted sources agrees with the statement in the Madhukośa.

132 Ca.Sū. 27, 30 : sesame seed is oleaginous, hot, sweet, bitter, astringent and pungent, destroys wind and is productive of phlegm and bile; Su.Sū. 46, 39-40ab : it is somewhat astringent, sweet, slightly bitter, constrictive, productive of bile, hot, sweet as to its digestive alteration, and oleaginous, it generates (a good transforming) fire, destroys wind and is heavy; A.h.Sū. 6, 23 : it is hot, cold on touch, heavy and pungent as to its digestion, it brings about (a good transforming) fire, phlegm and bile; A.s.Sū. 7, 34cd-35 : it is oleaginous, hot, bitter, pungent, astringent, sweet, heavy and cold on touch, it repels wind, is pungent as to its digestion and brings about (a good transforming) fire, phlegm and bile; Dravyaguṇa, *dhānyavarga* 35 = Su.Sū. 46, 39-40ab; Ma.nigh., *dhānyavarga* (10), 48-49 : it is astringent, sweet, bitter and pungent as to its taste, heavy, savoury, oleaginous, productive of phlegm and bile, cold on touch and productive of (a good transforming) fire; Dha.nigh., *suvarṇādivarga* (6), 123-124 : it is pungent, bitter, sweet and astringent as to its taste, heavy, pungent as to its digestive alteration, savoury, oleaginous and hot, it removes phlegm and bile, is cold on touch, destroys wind and bestows (a good transforming) fire; Rā.nigh., *śālyādivarga* (16), 193 : it is oleaginous, generates (a good transforming) fire, destroys wind, is heavy, somewhat hot, productive of bile, of a sweet taste accompanied by an astringent one, bitter, and pungent as to its digestive alteration; Bhā.pra.nigh., *dhānyavarga* 63-65 = Dha.nigh. 6, 123-124.

The quoted sources, except Ma.nigh. and to a less extent Rā.nigh., are in agreement with the Madhukośa with regard to the hot quality of sesame seed; its pungent taste and oleaginous quality, mentioned by some sources, may contradict the statement in the Madhukośa.

133 Fr. Su.Sū. 42, 8 : "Phlegm is characterized by the qualities sweetness, oleaginousness, heaviness, coldness and mucilaginousness; the sweet taste has the same matrix and increases its sweetness by its (own) sweetness, its oleaginousness by its (own) oleaginousness, its heaviness by its (own) heaviness, its coldness by its (own) coldness and its

mucilaginousness by its (own) mucilaginousness." Cf. Ca.Sū. 26, 43; A.h.Sū. 10, 7-9; A.s.Sū. 18, 6; Dravyaguṇa 1, 2; Ma.nigh., *miśrakavarga* (13), 65-66; Bhā.pra. 6, 175-177.

134 Ca.Sū. 27, 219 : buffalo's milk is heavier and colder than cow's milk and is not defective with regard to oleaginous constituents; Su.Sū. 45, 55cd-56ab : it is sweet, colder and more oleaginous than cow's milk, and heavy; A.h.Sū. 5, 23cd = A.s.Sū. 6, 56cd : it is heavier and colder than cow's milk and defective with regard to oleaginous substances ; Ma.nigh., *pānīyādivarga* (8), 69 : it is sweet, like cow's milk, oleaginous, heavy and cold and removes wind; Dha.nigh., *suvarṇādivarga* (6), 170 : it is sweet, annihilates wind, is productive of coldness, more oleaginous than cow's milk, and heavy; Rā.nigh., *kṣīrādivarga* (15), 219 : it is sweet (*gaulya*) as to its digestive alteration, cold and heavy, and annihilates bile; Bhā.pra.nigh., *dugdhavarga* 15 : it is sweet, oleaginous, heavy and cold to a higher degree than cow's milk.
The mucilaginous quality of phlegm is not mentioned as being present in buffalo's milk.

135 Ca.Sū. 27, 143cd-144ab : completely mature *rājādana* fruits have a savoury taste accompanied by an astringent one and are oleaginous, cold and heavy; Su.Sū. 46, 163-164 : *rājādana* fruits are cold, dry, astringent and sweet; Su.Sū. 46, 166cd : they are oleaginous, savoury, astringent and heavy; A.h.Sū. 6, 119-122ab = A.s.Sū. 7, 172-175ab : they are heavy, cold, oleaginous and savoury as to their taste and digestion; A.s.Sū. 7, 177 : they are heavy, oleaginous, savoury and astringent; Dravyaguṇa, *phalavarga* 29 : they are oleaginous, savoury, astringent and heavy; Ma.nigh., *phalādivarga* (6), 35 : they (*kṣīravṛkṣaphala*) are cold, oleaginous and heavy; Dha.nigh., *āmrādivarga* (5), 92 : *rājādana* is savoury as to its taste, acid as to its digestion and cold; ibid., 93 : *rājādanī* is sweet, heavy and very oleaginous; Bhā.pra.nigh., *āmrādiphalavarga* 86-87 : *rājādana* fruits are oleaginous, cold and heavy.
The greater part of the quoted texts is not in agreement with the Madhukośa because they make mention of a cold quality of *rājādana* fruits.

136 Ca.Sū. 27, 116cd-117ab : *kaśeruka* is heavy and cold; Su.Sū. 46, 298-299 : its tuberous root is cold, sweet and heavy; Su.Sū. 46, 304ab : it is heavy and cold; A.h.Sū. 6, 92 : it is dry, cold and heavy; A.s.Sū. 7, 137cd-138 : it is dry, cold and heavy; Dravyaguṇa, *śākavarga* 54 : it is heavy and cold; Ma.nigh., *śākavarga* (7), 90 : it is cold, savoury and heavy; Bhā.pra.nigh., *śākavarga* 112-113 : the two kinds of *kaseruka* (the big and the small one) are cold, sweet, astringent and heavy. Some of the quoted texts are in agreement with the Madhukośa; those which mention a sweet quality of *kaśeru* disagree with it.

137 Su.Sū. 46, 163-164 : the fruits of trees which contain a milky juice (*kṣīravṛkṣaphala*) are cold, dry, astringent and sweet; ibid., 165 : they are heavy, cold, astringent, sweet and somewhat acid; Ḍa. remarks that *nyagrodha, udumbara, aśvattha, plakṣa*, etc. are the trees with a milky juice; Ca.Sū. 27, 163cd-164 : the fruits of *aśvattha, udumbara, plakṣa* and *nyagrodha* are sweet, acid as to their digestion, astringent, sweet, acid and heavy; A.s.Sū. 7, 183-184ab : the seeds (*bīja*) of trees with a milky juice are astringent and sweet, dry, cold and heavy; Dravyaguṇa, *phalavarga* 32 : the fruits of trees with a milky juice (*kṣīrivṛkṣaphala*) are heavy, cold, astringent, sweet and somewhat acid; Ma.nigh., *vaṭādivarga* (5), 8 : the five trees with a milky juice are : *nyagrodha, udumbara, aśvattha, pāriśa* and *plakṣa*; Dha.nigh., *āmrādivarga* (5), 87 : *udumbara* fruits are cold and astringent, but of a sweet taste when they are ripe; Rā.nigh., *āmrādivarga* (11), 121 : *aśvattha* fruits are cold; ibid., 139 : *udumbara* fruits are extraordinarily cold, sweet when in a ripe state, but astringent when they are unripe; Bhā.pra.nigh., *vaṭādivarga* 15 : the five trees with a milky juice are : *nyagrodha, udumbara, aśvattha, pārīṣa* and

plakṣa. Ca., Su., A.s. and Dravyaguṇa disagree with the Madhukośa because they make mention of a sweet and heavy quality of the fruits of trees with a milky juice.

138 *naktaṃ rātriḥ dinam ahaḥ*.

139 *bhuktam āhāraḥ*.

140 Aruṇa remarks that, though the morbific entities are pervasive, (i.e.) wandering through the whole body, wind has its specific residence below the umbilical region, bile between the umbilical region and the cardiac region and phlegm upwards of the cardiac region. Wind belongs to the end, bile to the middle part and phlegm to the beginning of life, day, night, and (the digestive process of) the ingested food. The end of the digestive process of the ingested food is the stage in which the main part of the tastes has been disintegrated by force of their contact with the abdominal fire; the middle part is the stage of combustive alteration; the initial stage is that in which the ingested food is made sweet. He. and Candra mention in their comment the following three stages of life : old age, manhood and childhood.

141 I have not been able to trace this statement to its source.

142 I have not been able to trace this statement to its source. The original meaning may be different from the meaning it acquires in this context.

143 *nidānārtha*; HK : der Sinn der (Krankheits-)Ursache; Vall : lo sviluppo della patologia (the development of the pathology).

144 A.h. : *upadekṣyati* instead of *upadekṣyate*. Cf. A.s.Ni. 1, 14 (Ki. 1, 25); Ca.Ni. 1, 14. See about the subject of disagreeing foods : Ca.Sū. 26, 82-84; Su.Sū. 20, 13-22; A.h.Sū. 7, 29cd-45ab; A.s.Sū. 9; Bhe.Sū. 12.

145 Cf. fr. Su.Sū. 24, 8 : "The root of really all diseases (consists of) wind, bile and phlegm"; see also A.s.Sū. 22, 10.

146 See Cakra's comment on Ca.Sū. 1, 51.

147 Cf. Kā.Sū. 27, 13 : "An adventitious (disease) gives rise to trouble at the beginning and attains the morbific entities later on; an endogenous one, however, is (characterized by) accumulation (of a morbific entity) at the beginning and gives rise to trouble later on, when there is increase."

148 = Śārṅgadharasaṃhitā 1, 5, 25; Kāśirāma, the author of the Gūḍhārthadīpikā, a commentary on this *saṃhitā*, says that this stanza has been taken from another book. See also A.h.Śā. 3, 84 about the predominance of wind as a morbific entity.

149 See Su.Śā. 4, 63.

150 *anuśāyitā*; Ca. : *anuśayitā*.

151 Cf. fr. Kā.Sū., *lehādhyāya* : "Those provided with congruous 'pillars' (*sthūṇā*, i.e. *doṣa*) are healthy, but those with (a constitution dominated by) wind are always ill."

152 The full description of someone with a constitution dominated by wind is a follows (Su.Śā. 4, 64-66) : "With respect to these (constitutions) someone whose constitution is (dominated) by wind is very wakeful, averse to coldness, ugly (*durbhaga*; Ḍa. : *amanoramākāra*), thievish, wicked and not respectable; his mind is like that of a *gandharva*, his hands and feet are fissured, the hair of his beard, his nails and the hair of his head are scanty and dry, he likes to hurt (*krāthin*) and he is given to grinding his teeth (*dantakhādin*); he lacks self-control, is not abiding in his friendship, and ungrateful; he is lean and (his skin is) rough, his veins are strained, his speech is confused, he is walking fast and likes to roam about, his personality is unsteady and, when gone to sleep in an agitated state, he is walking in the sky; he is unsteady in his opinions, his eyes are (always) moving and he is sluggish with regard to the acquisition of valuable objects and goods and with regard to his friends; he speaks only little and incoherently; that is

a man whose constitution is (dominated) by wind." See about the bodily constitutions : Ca.Vi. 8, 95-100; Su.Śā. 4, 62-79; A.h.Sū. 1, 9cd-10, Śā. 3, 83-104ab; A.s.Śā. 8, 1-20; Bhe.Vi. 4, 8-27; Hā. 1, 5, 16-23; Bhā.pra. 4, 51-79.

153 Su.Śā. 4, 97cd reads : "In that same way the constitutions cannot give trouble to a mortal human being" (*tadvat prakṛtayo martyaṃ śaknuvanti na bādhitum*).

154 Suśrutaślokavārtika.

155 V.l. : Praśnasahasranidāna.

156 See e.g. Su.Sū. 21, 4 : "There is no body without phlegm, bile and wind, nor without blood, for the body is continuously sustained by these (entities)". See also Su.Sū. 21, 16; 21, 25-26.

157 Ca. presents some variants : Ni. 8, 16d = Mā.ni. 1, 15d and Ni. 8, 19d = Mā.ni. 1, 18d : *upalabhyate* instead of *upajāyate*; Ni. 8, 18 = Mā.ni. 1, 17c : *jaṭhara* instead of *jāṭhara*; Ni. 8, 19a = Mā.ni. 1, 18a : *bhavet* instead of *atho*. The sentence between brackets, which in the edition has not been numbered, is not found in Ca. Mā.ni. 1, 15cd has been incorrectly translated by Vall : la malattia che produce lo sviluppo delle cause, può nascere pure da (altra) malattia, i.e. : the disease which produces the development of the causes can also arise from (another) disease. Cf. fr. A.s.Sū. 22, 16 : "Some disease becomes the ground of some other disease; fever for instance (may become the ground) of blood-bile or blood-bile that of fever; both (may become the ground) of shortness of breath; splenomegaly (may become the ground) of abdominal affection, that (abdominal affection the ground) of swelling; haemorrhoids (may become the ground) of visceral swelling, abdominal disease, diarrhoea and the *grahaṇī* disorder, nasal catarrh that of cough and fever; both (cough and fever may become the ground) of decline, and decline that of desiccation."

158 This refers to the preceding stanza.

159 The variant referred to is *kṣayorogasya* (i.e. *kṣaya-urogasya*) instead of *kṣayo rogasya*.

160 Cakra comes to the same conclusion in his comment on Ca.Ni. 8, 16cd-19.

161 Mādhava has omitted the second half of the stanza (Ca.Ni. 8, 20cd), which runs as follows : "(Diseases) are observed, fulfilling both functions, as well as (diseases) fulfilling one function." This statement leads on to the following stanza, admitted by Mādhava (Ca.Ni. 8, 21 = Mā.ni. 1, 19cd-20ab).

162 The second half of Ca.Ni. 8, 22, omitted by Mādhava, is as follows : "Because there (has) not (been brought about) a completely pure condition by application (of a treatment) and also because they arise from each other."

163 About the qualities of wind, etc. Cakra remarks: Dryness is present in excess because wind can be cured by substances with an oleaginous quality. Although wind is called neither hot nor cold in the Vaiśeṣika philosophy, it is nevertheless said to be cold here, because a disease arisen from wind is aggravated by cold substances and appeased by hot ones. The contrary qualities which appease wind denote in this case peculiarities; taste, potency, digestive alteration and special faculty are covered by that term. It is said here that bile has an acid taste, because bile is started by water and by fiery energy; Suśruta says, however, that bile possesses a pungent taste and becomes acid by combustive alteration; the reason is that bile, according to Suśruta, only possesses a fiery nature.

CHAPTER TWO

FEVER (*JVARA*)

2, 1 : Fever, the source of which is the exhalation of Rudra,[1] whose violent wrath had been aroused by the disrespect of Dakṣa,[2] is traditionally said to be of eight kinds : it arises from one (morbific entity) separately, a pair (of morbific entities), close union (of all three morbific entities) or in an adventitious way.[3]

M :

And now fever has to be spoken of first owing to its predominance over all diseases.[4] Its predominance (arises) from (the fact) that it is the first one of all bodily diseases which has been produced, from its forcefulness, the fact that it brings about glowing heat of body, senses and *manas*, its necessary presence in birth and death [5] and its pervasion of all living beings, whether stationary or locomotive. Other morbid alterations are not like that. As has been said in the Caraka-(saṃhitā), from : "Fever has formerly been stated by you, holy one, to be the predominant disease, bringing about glowing heat of body, senses and *manas*, the firstborn of all diseases, full of force; (about the nature, etc.) of this constant enemy of living beings in their absorption and rising" (Ci. 3, 4-5ab), etc., up to : "Holy one, be so kind as to tell" (Ci. 3, 9d).[6] Moreover (it has been said) : "When fever is entering a living being, nothing whatsoever is not afflicted by glowing heat" (Ci. 3, 31cd).

In (the book of) Pālakāpya it has been said : "It is called *pākala* in elephants, *abhitāpa* in horses, *īśvara* in cattle, *jvara* in men, *pralāpa* in goats and sheep, *alasa* in camels, *hāridra* in buffalo cows, *mṛgaroga* in deer, *abhighāta* in birds, *indramada* in fish, *pakṣapāta* in flying insects, *akṣika* in beasts of prey", etc. And at another place : "Of water (it is called) *nīlikā*, of soil *ūṣara*, in a tree *koṭara*", etc.[7]

Its first production is made mention of with the words 'by the disrespect of Dakṣa'. (A paraphrase of 2, 1ab follows).

The exhalation (of Rudra) is taught to be a sign of wrath in this case; for that very reason it has been said by Suśruta : "Arisen from the fire of Rudra's anger as a source" (U. 39, 9a). The wrathful Rudra cast a glance with the third fiery eye between his eyebrows and from that (glance) a fiery arrow was formed. As Caraka says : "The Lord cast a look with the eye between his eyebrows, burnt those Asuras and emitted an arrow,[8] which was glowingly hot by the fire of wrath and which destroyed the great sacrifice" (Ci. 3, 20)... This story about the production of fever should be read, with its particulars, in the (section on) therapy of the Caraka(saṃhitā).[9]

With this (story, mentioned above), the anger of Rudra has been stated to be the distant cause; if fever were not produced by that (anger), it would be produced no more, owing to improper conduct, nowadays; thus says Bhaṭṭāraharicandra.

This tale being inapplicable with regard to therapy, other commentators explain it in another way : because anger is at the source of (fever), it becomes clear that it consists of fiery energy, for wrath is of a fiery nature. As Caraka says : "From wrath (excitement of) bile (arises)" (fr. Ci. 3, 115d).

It results from this (statement) that in every fever a therapeutical procedure should be used that is not in disagreement with bile. As has been said by Vāgbhaṭa himself : "Without bile there is no heat and without heat there is no fever; therefore one should avoid things which disagree with bile, the more so when there is an excess of bile" (Ci. 1, 16cd-17ab). For that very reason the Caraka(saṃhitā) teaches, because of its maturation-promoting character, making use of (a substance with) a bitter taste which destroys bile in a case of fresh fever, discarding (substances with) a pungent, acid and saline taste; according to what has been said (by Caraka) : "Reducing measures, sudation, time, a gruel and the bitter taste promote the maturation of morbific entities which have not been altered by digestion, in a case of fresh fever" (Ci. 3, 142cd-143ab).[10] (Time means in this case a period of eight days [11]). Others, however, say : (fever) has been shown to deserve worship because, having the anger of Rudra as its source, it is of a divine nature. As Videha says : "Or, on the other hand, fever becomes appeased at once by acts of worship".[12]

In the Harivaṃśa its actual bodily form is said to be (as follows) : "Fever has three feet, three heads, six arms and nine eyes; it has ashes for a weapon, is fierce (like Rudra) and resembles all-destroying time in the form of Yama" [13] (Harivaṃśa 2, 122, 71cd-72ab).

Fever is mentioned (by Mādhava) in a concise way, though it is manifold ... Its eight types are explained ... That has (already) been explained (in the discussion) about the onset.

2, 2 : By improper regimen of diet and conduct the morbific entities, residing in the receptacle of undigested food, after having thrown outside the visceral fire, will give rise to fever, when they follow the nutrient fluid in its course.[14]

M :

With the words 'by improper (regimen of diet)', etc. the onset is dealt with.

Impropriety of articles of food is their employment when they disagree with regard to the grounds, consisting of natural state, etc., of the employment of articles of food. As Caraka says : "In this respect there are the following eight underlying factors of the specific modalities of food, viz. natural state, getting it ready, commixture, quantity, place, time, standards about its employment and the person who enjoys the food as the eighth (item of the series)" (Vi. 1, 21).

With respect to this (series) the natural state is the junction of substances with qualities such as heaviness and lightness, belonging to their own nature, as for instance (the heaviness) of *māṣa* beans and (the lightness) of *mudga* beans.[15] Getting it ready is its preparation, as, for instance, (the preparation) of parched rice-grain, which is light, from *vrīhi* rice, which is heavy.[16] Commixture (means) close union, as, for instance, of milk and fish.[17] Quantity (means) the determination of the measure of a food substance [18] as to its components and as to its total mass.[19] Place is the region of production, occurrence, etc. of a substance.[20] Time (means time as) permanent motion and (time) in relation to stages (of life, of a disease, etc.).[21] Standards about the employment are fixed rules about the employment,[22] as for instance : one should only eat when one's food has been disintegrated.[23] He who enjoys the food is the man himself, who has been examined as to what is adequate to him, (of which kind) his constitution is, etc.[24]

Impropriety of conduct is an undertaking, etc., not in accordance with one's force.

With the words 'residing in the receptacle of undigested food' it is substantiated that the morbific entities do not start a fever without having reached the receptacle of undigested food. About the receptacle of undigested food has been said by Caraka : "The region between the navel and (the nipples of) the breast of a living being is traditionally called the receptacle of undigested food" (Vi. 2, 17ab).

'After having thrown outside the visceral fire' (means that) the visceral fire itself, hurled away by the morbific entities and got outside, becomes apparent by its heat. The visceral fire is mentioned in order to exclude the fire of the elements (of the body), etc. ...

'Following the nutrient fluid in its course' (means) : intimately connected with the nutrient fluid; (the morbific entities) necessarily produce fever after having corrupted the nutrient fluid. Jejjaṭa says : "This is the onset of bodily fevers only, but not of the adventitious ones; the latter bring about distress at first and become attended by wind, etc. afterwards."

For that very reason the onset of an adventitious (fever) is described separately in the Suśruta(saṃhitā) : "The wind of bodily beings, excited by fatigue, a lesion, or traumatic injury, will lead to a vehement fever, after having occupied the whole body" (U. 39, 80cd-81ab).[25] In this case the wind does not stay at all in the receptacle of undigested food, but wanders through the channels which carry the nutrient fluid in an upward, downward and lateral direction. In the Caraka(saṃhitā) it is also said : "In that case the wind, arising from traumatic injury and corrupting mainly the blood, brings about fever, accompanied by distress, swelling, alteration of colour and pain" (Ci. 3, 113cd-114ab).[26] It may be objected that in an adventitious fever also heat is experienced and that it has been said : "There is no heat without bile" (A.h.Ci. 1, 16c); from these (arguments it would follow that) an adventitious (fever) is a bodily (fever) as well.

That is not correct, because its production (takes place) at a later (point of) time. As has been said : "The adventitious one, bringing about distress at the beginning, is the eighth (kind of) fever; having been an isolated adventitious one for some time, it becomes attended by the morbific entities later on" (fr. Ca.Ni. 1, 30). And moreover : "An adventitious morbid alteration follows an endogenous one, and an endogenous (morbid alteration) follows, when it has extraordinarily increased, an adventitious one as well" (Ca.Sū. 19, 7ab).[27]

It may be objected that with the words 'by improper regimen of diet', etc. the onset has been stated to be one and the same and that is not correct, for the onset is a distinct (kind of) conjunction; a distinct (kind of) conjunction is founded on distinctions of its constituent elements and the constituent elements of the conjunction, (viz.) wind, etc., are in this case of various kinds; from this (reasoning it follows that) the onset will also be of various kinds, for the conjunction of wind and bile is not the same as (the conjunction) of phlegm and bile.

The answer (to this objection) is that the onset is indeed of several kinds, but these belong to one class because the corruption of the receptacle, etc. is said to be uniformly present in all cases; so the onset of an adventitious (fever) can also be distinguished by distinct (kinds of) conjunction.

Ā:

... "Food taken at the wrong time and beyond the proper quantity, as well as that food which is inadequate and incongruous, is called an improper diet".[28] A regimen of diet is improper when it disagrees with regard to place, time, constitution, etc. and when it disagrees with regard to commixture, as does (a mixture) of milk and fish. Improper conduct is an undertaking which is not in accordance with one's force. "The person who (tries to) perform an action, (though) being unable to perform it, and he who does not perform it, (though) being able to do so, are called persons with an improper conduct; one should always avoid (such) persons"...[29]

2, 3 : The disease in which obstruction (of the flow) of perspiration, a general sense of glowing heat and also a seizing (pain) in the whole body occur simultaneously, is designated as fever.

(Su.U. 39, 13cd-14ab).[30]

M:

... Obstruction (of the flow) of perspiration (means that) the warmth (of the organism) has no outlet.[31] (A grammatical remark follows). That has been said in the Caraka(saṃhitā) : "Bringing about glowing heat of body, senses and *manas*" (Ci. 3, 4a); "A deviated state of the senses should be known as a characteristic of a general sense of glowing heat" (Ci. 3, 37ab); and moreover : "A deviated state of the mind, disinclination and languor are the characteristics of a general glowing heat of the *manas*" (Ci. 3, 36cd).[32]

A seizing (pain) in the whole body is a painful sensation in the whole body.

It is said (that they occur) 'simultaneously', (i.e.) as an agglomeration, because that is the characteristic of (fever); (this is made mention of) because inaccuracy would arise in taking each of these (symptoms) separately. Obstruction (of the flow) of perspiration occurs as a prodrome of skin diseases, a general sense of glowing heat in the disease called burning and a seizing (pain) in the whole body in a wind disease affecting the whole body.

It may be objected that the (mentioned set of) characteristics is not invariably concomitant, because in bile fever perspiration appears, and in wind fever an incongruous start and lapse occur and there is erratic seizing (pain) in the whole body.[33]

Jejjaṭa, Kārtikakuṇḍa and others have answered this (objection), saying that a settlement (is made in these cases) with reference to the relation between a general rule and exceptions (to this rule). Others say that this is not logical : the relation between a general rule and exceptions (to it may be applied) to a mode, but not to a characteristic, because this (latter use) would be a case of faulty definition by limitation of the attributes (to only a portion of the disease defined) or extension of the attributes (beyond that disease which is defined); therefore perspiration means fire (in this case), according to the 'etymology' : 'one is perspiring by it'; its obstruction has an invariable concomitance with the morbific entities. Although in wind fever, owing to the fluctuating character of wind, an incongruous start and lapse occur, nevertheless there is certainly found a seizing of the whole body which has not become perceptible, because there is no cessation of the corruption by the morbific entity, starting the fever, which stays in the whole body; so inaccuracy does not occur.

In the Caraka(saṃhitā), however, the characterization of fever is : "The typical sign of fever is the general glowing heat of body and mind" (Ci. 3, 31ab).

It may be said as an objection that, on account of Caraka's words : "A bodily fever arises first in the body, a mental one in the mind" (Ci. 3, 36ab), it is not a (good) characteristic, because (fevers of) body and mind are separate from each other. That is not right, because the other symptom will necessarily arise after a very subtle interval of time, in the same way as it is the characteristic of a substance that it is provided with its qualities (after a very subtle interval of time).[34]

Ā :

... Instead of 'obstruction (of the flow) of perspiration' others read : obstruction of the (natural) urges.[35] In that case obstruction of the (natural) urges means that flatus, urine and faeces do not leave (the body). That (reading) is unsuitable because faeces, etc. are evacuated in bile fever; therefore that (reading) is a case of limitation of the attributes (to only a portion of the class defined).

2, 4-7 : Fatigue, disinclination, an altered colour (of the skin), an altered taste (in the mouth), swimming of the eyes, alternately longing for and aversion to a cold wind, glowing heat, etc. (4), yawning, muscle pain, heaviness, horripilation, inability to eat, darkness (of vision), absence of feelings of sexual pleasure, and a sense of coldness occur when a fever is about to arise (5), generally; specifically, however, excessive yawning will arise from wind, burning of the eyes from bile and inability to eat [36] from phlegm (6).

(A fever) arising from a pair (of morbific entities), however, is recognized by the combined symptoms of both (morbific entities involved);[37] union of all the signs occurs in a (fever) arising from excitement of all the morbific entities (7).

(Su.U. 39, 25-27; 28cd; 28ab).[38]

M:

The prodromes are dealt with ... Fatigue is a condition like that of someone who is fatigued. Disinclination is unsteadiness of the mind; Kārtika says it is absence of amusement. An altered colour (of the skin) is a faded condition of the limbs.

That which has been said by Vṛddhasuśruta, beginning with : "The morbific entities, corrupted by their own grounds" (Su.U. 39, 16c), up to : "And generate then, at the (periods of) time proper to them, the arrival of fever, as well as (its) increase and the colours proper to them in the skin, etc." (Su.U. 39, 18d-19ab),[39] has in view the specific prodromes, like excessive yawning, etc., because the prodromes are occasioned by a morbific entity that has entered the stage of the onset.

An altered taste (in the mouth) is the presence of a disagreeing taste in the mouth. Swimming of the eyes (means that) the eyes are filled with tears;[40] as has been said in the Caraka(saṃhitā) : "Inertia and eyes (filled) with tears" (Ci. 3, 28a). By the word 'etcetera' (4d) the undetermined longing for and aversion to water and fire are also understood; for in the Caraka(saṃhitā) it has been said : "Undetermined fondness of and aversion to fire, glowing heat, wind and water" (Ci. 3, 28cd).[41] Others, however, make it indicate water and fire, because these are provided with the same (kind of) peculiarity, (viz.) coldness and hotness, and they suppose the word 'etcetera' (to indicate) lying down to repose, etc.

Darkness (of vision means) non-perception, as when someone has entered darkness. Absence of feelings of sexual pleasure (means) absence of pleasurable sensations. The words 'and a sense of coldness' serve to point to the feeling of coldness with special emphasis, because the desire for (the warmth of) a fire is present and a sense of coldness has been acquired. It is said that by the word 'and' (5d) aversion to children, etc. are understood. (A fever) that is about to arise is an imminent fever. (Grammatical remarks are made on the word *utpatsyati*).

Ā :

... Muscle pain is a crushing sensation of the limbs ... Absence of feelings of sexual pleasure (means) absence of feelings of sensual pleasure. The word 'coldness' is mentioned once again, after its use in the sentence : 'alternately longing for and aversion to a cold (wind)', etc., in order to stress that a feeling of coldness appears ... Mādhava has written down here the generic prodromes, (as) stated by Suśruta, but not the specific prodromes. These (latter ones) are written down at this very place by us, with the words 'generally', etc.[42] The word 'generally' is connected with the preceding stanza ...

2, 8-9 : Shivering, incongruous paroxysms, complete desiccation of throat and lips, insomnia, inhibition of sneezing [43] and certainly dryness of the limbs (8), pain in head, cardiac region and limbs, an altered taste in the mouth, tightly packed faeces,[44] piercing pain, inflatedness and yawning occur in a fever arising from wind (9).[45]

(Su.U. 39, 29-30).[46]

M :

Wind, bile and phlegm are predominant (over each other) in this mentioned order as to the number and severity of the morbid alterations they bring about. As has been said in the Caraka(saṃhitā) : "There are eighty morbid alterations by wind, forty by bile and twenty by phlegm" (fr. Sū. 20, 10);[47] so the morbid alterations by wind, such as convulsions, hemiplegia,[48] etc., are severe ones. Owing to this predominance the characteristics of wind fever are mentioned first with the words 'shivering', etc. The regular order (of the morbific entities, to wit) wind, etc., should be understood in the same way, also when it occurs elsewhere.

The words 'incongruous paroxysms' (indicate) the incongruity, (i.e.) the indeterminateness with regard to time and (the appearance of) hotness, etc. in the (various) parts of the body, of the paroxysms, (i.e.) of the appearance or the increase of the fever.

Gadādhara, etc. explain (what is rendered by 'inhibition of sneezing and certainly dryness of the limbs' as meaning) : sneezing,[49] stiffness, (i.e.) rigidity of the limbs, and also dryness of these same limbs.

This is, however, considered to be an explanation based on inadvertence. In this case it is suitable to consider inhibition of sneezing as one word : sneezing-inhibition. For Vāgbhaṭa says : "Horripilation, hypersensitivity of the parts of the body and the teeth, shivering, suppression of sneezing, giddiness, confused speech, longing for warmth and moaning [50] occur in a fever by wind" (Ni. 2, 17cd-18ab). In the (section on) origins of the Caraka(saṃhitā) one also reads : "Suppression of sneezing and of eructation" (fr. Ni. 1, 21). The master (Caraka) has used the word 'suppression' in order to indicate restraint in each particular context; as for instance in the (description of the) origins of visceral swellings by wind : "Dry foods and drinks, incongruous and excessive voluntary bodily movements and suppression of the (natural) urges" (Ci. 5, 9ab), and also in (the description of) the characteristics of fever with an internal impulse : "Suppression of the morbific entity and the excremental matter" [51] (Ci. 3, 40b).

With this (exposition) has also been rejected the question of Kārtikakuṇḍa, who has his doubts about it: "How can, since sneezing is mentioned in (the description of) the characteristics of the liberation from fever, this (sneezing) be a characteristic of (fever)?'

Inflatedness is a condition, accompanied by a painful sensation, in which the abdomen is filled with wind.

The words 'pain in the head, cardiac region and limbs' (are used) to indicate a painful sensation which especially occurs in the head and cardiac region, because the latter are enumerated (separately) and the term 'limb' includes the head and the cardiac region.

Suśruta teaches that these (enumerated) symptoms are those which are usually present; by the word 'and' should be understood all the other (symptoms), mentioned by Caraka.

These very (symptoms), stated (by Caraka) in prose, are (now) described by me in verse in order to make them easily understood : "There are painful sensations of many kinds (arising) from wind, numbness of the feet, cramps of the calves, tinnitus, an astringent taste in the mouth, adynamia of the thighs, stiffness of the jaws, disjunction of the junctures and the knees, a dry cough, emesis, horripilation, hypersensitivity of the teeth, fatigue, giddiness, a ruddy colour of eyes, urine, etc., thirst, confused speech and a craving for hot things"

Ā :

Shivering (means) trembling. Incongruous paroxysms (are present) on account of deficiency and excess in the condition of the fever; moreover (they point to) the indeterminateness of the heat, etc. in the body. Inhibition of sneezing (means that) sneezing does not come about. Some, however, read (sneezing-inhibition) as two separate words; according to that opinion (the meaning is :) sneezing and stiffness, (i.e.) stiffness of the limbs. That is not correct.

(About) 'and certainly dryness of the limbs' (we remark that) the word 'and' indicates the addition of : blackness of urine, faeces and eyes. Instead of 'and certainly dryness of the limbs' others read here : 'a brown colour of the body parts, impurities and urine'...[52] 'Tightly packed faeces' (means) : a bound state of impure matter. 'Piercing pain' (indicates) a piercing abdominal pain. 'Yawning' (means) frequent yawning.

2, 10-11 : Sharp paroxysms, diarrhoea, sleep of short duration and also emesis, inflammatory changes of throat, lips, mouth and nose, perspiration (10), confused speech, a pungent taste in the mouth,[53] fainting, a burning sensation, (mental disturbance as in) intoxication, thirst, a yellow colour of faeces, urine and eyes and even giddiness occur in a fever by bile (11).

(Su.U. 39, 31-32).[54]

M :

... Diarrhoea (means in this case) the appearance of (faeces) accompanied by liquid (matter), because bile gives rise to the flowing out (of impure matter), and it is not diarrhoea in its proper sense because this (latter) is a secondary affection of fever.

Sleep of short duration (denotes) a very slight amount of sleep. For it has been said in the Suśruta(saṃhitā) : "Insomnia (arises) from wind and bile" (Śā. 4, 42a). Emesis (arises) when bile moves to the seat of phlegm. Perspiration is the arrival of warmth (in the form of sweat); restraint (of the flow) of warmth (in the form of sweat) is usually (present) in all fevers, because the channels are restrained by the morbific entities, accompanied by immature matter, but in this case it does not occur because of the sharpness of bile or the special faculty of (this) fever. Confused speech is disordered speech.

A pungent taste in the mouth (denotes) a bitter taste in the mouth, on account of the fact that in the Caraka(saṃhitā) a bitter taste in the mouth is mentioned among the forty qualified morbid alterations by bile, and on account of personal (practical) experience. Kārtika, however, also requires a pungent taste in the mouth, adducing as an example the (following) words (of Caraka) on anorexia : "One should know that a pungent, acid and hot (taste in the) mouth, an altered taste in the mouth and a foul-smelling mouth (arise) from bile, as well as a saline (taste in the) mouth" (Ca.Ci. 26, 125ab).

That is not (suitable), because in that case too (there remains) doubt. For it has been said : "Pungent may mean pungent and bitter".[55] Therefore a pungent taste in the mouth should be required, also on account of what Suśruta says : "When a person with a pungent and bitter (taste in his) mouth vomits matter which is acid, vehemently hot, yellow, accompanied by blood or yellowish-green, and he additionally suffers from a burning sensation, sucking pain, fever and desiccation of the mouth, it is the (type of) vomiting which arises from excitement of bile" (U. 49, 10).[56] Fainting is said to be non-discernment of forms, etc., the entering into darkness, loss of memory. (Mental disturbance as in) intoxication is a condition resembling intoxication, (arising) for example when one consumes betel nuts, *kodrava*, *dhattūra*, etc. Giddiness is said to be the seeing of an object turning round, as e.g. (an object) standing on a wheel; others, however, (consider it to be) the sensation of one's own body turning round.

An objector may ask why giddiness is made mention of in a morbid alteration by bile, because, being enumerated among the eighty morbid alterations by wind, it is a qualified wind disease.

The answer (to this objection) is that Jejjaṭa has reflected upon (the problem), saying : in a morbid alteration by bile giddiness is present because (bile) is attended by wind (as an adjunctory factor), for it has been said : "No disease whatever arises from (only) one morbific entity".[57] Or it should be recognized as a symptom, though unknown as to its cause, which arises from the special faculty of the coalescence between morbific entity and corruptible (constituent), as for instance the ruddy (colour), such as it is present in diarrhoea, etc., started by wind, which is colourless, and redness as it occurs in a mixture (of some substance) with turmeric powder. As to what has been said in the Suśruta(saṃhitā) : "Giddiness (arises) from *rajas*, bile and wind"

(Śā. 4, 56a), there too one should be aware of the fact that it arises only from bile which is attended by wind; otherwise giddiness would not be a qualified (disease) by wind at all. Others again (say), however, that giddiness is wrong knowledge, based on a corruption of the eyes by bile, as in statements like : 'the conch shell is yellow', etc.

The word 'and' indicates, as before, the addition of (symptoms) which have not been mentioned, such as : intense heat, red wheals, longing for coldness and inability to eat.[58]

Ā :

... Sharp paroxysms are intense paroxysms ... A pungent taste in the mouth (means) a bitter taste in the mouth; as has been said in the Abhidhāna : "Pungent may mean pungent and bitter"...[59]

2, 12 : A feeling of dampness, torpid paroxysms, inertia, a sweet taste in the mouth, a light (colour of) urine and faeces, stiffness and also a feeling of satiety,[60]

2, 13ab : heaviness, a feeling of coldness, retching,[61] horripilation, excessive sleep,

(Su.U. 39, 33ab).

additional stanza : (obstruction of the channels, slight pains, effusion, a saline taste in the mouth,[62] a non-excessive hotness of the limbs, vomiting, discharge of saliva,[63] absence of digestive alteration),[64]

(Su.U. 39, 33cd-34ab).

2, 13cd : nasal catarrh, inability to eat and cough are present in a fever arising from phlegm, and a light (colour of the) eyes as well.

(Su.U. 39, 34cd).[65]

M :

... A feeling of dampness is a condition (which seems) as if the body is covered with a wet cloth.[66] Torpid paroxysms are sluggish paroxysms.[67] The characteristics of inertia are said to be : "Want of perseverance, though one is able to act, is called inertia" (Su.Śā. 4, 52cd).[68] Stiffness is a stiff condition of the parts of the body. A feeling of satiety is the absence of relish for food in someone who is satisfied. Retching is a condition (which seems) as if vomit has come near to the throat. Inability to eat (means) here the inability to ingest food, though the relish (for food) is present; that is its distinction (from absence of the relish for food). The word 'and' (has) the same (meaning) as before; by that (word) are indicated : "And also boils on the body, a feeling of coldness, effusion, vomiting and lassitude, an increased presence of unctuous substances in the cardiac region, a relish for hot (things) and mildness of the (transforming) fire".[69]

Ā :

... A feeling of coldness (means that) a feeling of coldness has become noticeable. Retching is spitting of phlegm ... Nasal catarrh is a discharge from the nose. Obstruction of the channels (means) an obstruction of the channels which carry nutrient fluid ... Absence of digestive alteration (means) absence of digestive alteration of the food ...

2, 14-15ab : The conformation of fever by wind and bile (consists of) thirst, fainting, giddiness, a burning sensation, insomnia, a painful condition of the head, desiccation of throat and mouth, emesis, horripilation, inability to eat, darkness (of vision),[70] a cutting pain in the junctures and yawning. (Su.U. 39, 47-48ab).[71] [72]

M :

... A cutting pain in the junctures is a painful sensation, as if the junctures are cut.[73]

These signs should be understood to be based on an inherence (in a morbid alteration, the qualities of which are) incongruous with the altered state. The fact that they are based on an inherence (in a morbid alteration, the qualities of which are) incongruous with the altered state, should be understood from (the circumstance) that only some of (those signs which are mentioned) among the characteristics of fever by wind and by bile are solely written down in the text as necessarily occuring (in a fever by both wind and bile), and that (characteristics) are made mention of which differ from those (in a fever by wind and a fever by bile); as for instance in this very (fever) by wind and bile the inability to eat and horripilation,[74] in the fever by wind and phlegm, which will be described presently, perspiration and a general sense of glowing heat, in the same way in the fever by phlegm and bile a feeling of coldness and a burning sensation, which are of an unsteady kind, and moreover in a fever by concerted action eyes which are full of tears and turbid, rolling of the head, etc.

In a fever, however, based on an inherence (in a morbid alteration, the qualities of which are) congruous with the natural state, all of those very signs which arise from wind, etc. are present, or some of them (but no different ones).

It is for just this reason that Caraka in the (section on) therapy, after having described in a direct way the characteristics of fevers by a pair (of morbific entities) and by concerted action, which are based on an inherence (in a morbid alteration, the qualities of which are) incongruous with the altered state, has mentioned the characteristics of fevers by a pair (of morbific entities) and by concerted action, which are based on an inherence (in a morbid alteration, the qualities of which are) congruous with the natural state, by means of their analogy to the signs of fever by wind, etc., as they are stated in the section on origins. He says : "By means of the threefold conformation of fever, arising from (one morbific entity) separately, as proclaimed in the (section on) origins, the very characteristics of (fevers by) combined and concerted action have also been dealt with" (Ca.Ci. 3, 110cd-111ab).

In that way should be explained the characteristics of (fevers by) a pair (of morbific entities) and concerted action, which will be described (subsequently).

The meaning of (the terms) 'an inherence (in a morbid alteration, the qualities of which are) congruous with the natural state' and 'an inherence (in a morbid alteration, the qualities of which are) incongruous with the altered state' is as follows : an inherence (in a morbid alteration, the qualities of which are) congruous with the natural state, is an inherence, (i.e.) a (necessary) intimate connection, between effect and cause, which is congruous, (i.e.) corresponding to its cause, with the natural state which is its ground; this means : an effect which corresponds to its cause, as for instance the light colour of a cloth that is based on an inherence with threads of a light colour. An inherence (in a morbid alteration, the qualities of which are) incongruous with the altered state, is an inherence which is incongruous, (i.e.) not corresponding to its cause, with the altered state which is its ground, as for instance the red colour (of a cloth) arising when turmeric powder is added to it.

Ā :

... Emesis is a distinct kind of vomiting called *thugathugi* in popular speech ... In (fevers) arising from a pair (of morbific entities) and in (fevers) by concerted action, some characteristics are based on an inherence (in a morbid alteration, the qualities of which are) incongruous with the altered state, and some on an inherence (in a morbid alteration, the qualities of which are) congruous with the natural state. The characteristics of the morbific entities themselves are regarded as based on an inherence (in a morbid alteration, the qualities of which are) congruous with the natural state, but those which are different are based on an inherence (in a morbid alteration, the qualities of which are) incongruous with the altered state. (Based on) an inherence (in a morbid alteration, the qualities of which are) congruous with the natural state, are for instance in (a fever) arising from phlegm and bile the sensation that the mouth seems covered with an unctuous substance and a bitter (taste in the) mouth; inability to eat and horripilation, however, should be regarded, among the characteristics of (a fever by) wind and bile, as based on (incongruity with) the altered state; a general sense of glowing heat does not occur among the characteristics of (a fever by) wind and phlegm, (but) is observed among the characteristics of a fever by concerted action, (and so) that (symptom) is also based on (incongruity with) the altered state; rolling of the head is not observed among the characteristics of (fever by) wind, bile or phlegm, (but) is observed among the characteristics of a fever by concerted action, (and so) that (symptom) is also based on (incongruity with) the altered state. In the same way one should understand it really in all the diseases arising from a pair (of morbific entities) and concerted action.

2, 15cd : A feeling of dampness, cutting pain in the junctures, sleep aud certainly a feeling of heaviness,

(Su. U. 39, 48cd) [75]

2, 16 : a seizing (pain) in the head, nasal catarrh, cough, the appearance of perspiration, [76] a general sence of glowing heat and moderate paroxysms (constitute) the conformation of a fever by wind and phlegm.

(Su.U. 39, 49 = Ca.Ci. 3, 87). [77] [78]

M :

... Kārtika says that the appearance of perspiration on all sides without a cause (occurs) because it is based on an inherence (in a morbid alteration, the qualities of which are) incongruous with the altered state ... This is suitable as an explanation, for Hārita says :

"A seizing pain in the head, the occurrence of perspiration and cough are the signs of a fever arising from phlegm and wind". The occurrence of perspiration is the production of perspiration.

'Moderate paroxysms' are (paroxysms which are) neither exceedingly sharp nor exceedingly mild.

Ā:

A feeling of dampness is a condition (which seems) as if one is covered with a wet garment; others (say it is) the motionlessness of a patient suffering from fever.[79] A cutting pain in the junctures is a specific painful sensation in the junctures ... The appearance of perspiration is also a characteristic based on an inherence (in a morbid alteration, the qualities of which are) incongruous with the altered state, and so is a general sense of glowing heat (in this case).

2, 17 : The conformation of fever by phlegm and bile (consists of) the sensation that the mouth is covered with an unctuous substance, a bitter (taste in the) mouth,[80] lassitude, mental confusion, cough, inability to eat, thirst and alternation of a burning sensation and a feeling of coldness.

(Su.U. 39, 50).[81] [82]

M:

... The sensation that the mouth is covered with an unctuous substance and a bitter (taste in the) mouth are the condition of someone whose mouth is covered with a coating of phlegm and (made) bitter by bile. Lassitude is weariness resembling sleepiness. Mental confusion (means) fainting.

These signs are taught as being usually present. One should also be aware of the other ones, mentioned by Caraka, such as: "Inhibition (of perspiration), general perspiration and the appearance of phlegm and bile" (fr. Ca.Ci. 3, 88).[83]

Ā:

Lassitude is weariness resembling sleepiness. The characteristics of lassitude are described (by Suśruta): "Someone who does not consciously perceive [84] the sense objects, who shows heaviness, yawning, weariness, and longings as of someone afflicted by sleep, should be declared to be someone suffering from lassitude" (Śā. 4, 49).

2, 18-23 : The conformation of fever by concerted action (consists of) a burning sensation at one moment and a feeling of coldness at another one, a painful condition of the bones, junctures and head, eyes [85] which show a discharge, which are turbid, red, and also distorted, painful ears together with tinnitus, a sensation as if the throat were covered with awns, lassitude, mental confusion and confused speech, cough, shortness of breath, inability to eat, giddiness, a tongue (which looks as if) entirely burnt and is harsh to the touch, a high degree of laxity of the parts of the body, spitting of blood and bile, mixed with phlegm, rolling [86] of the head, thirst, insomnia, distress in the cardiac region, the becoming visible of perspiration, urine and faeces after a long time and in slight amounts, leanness of the limbs to a not extreme degree, persistent rumbling in the throat, the becoming visible of wheals and brown-red circular spots, muteness, inflammatory changes of the channels, heaviness of the abdomen and maturation of the morbific entities after a long time.

(Ca.Ci. 3, 103cd-109ab).[87]

M :

... (Eyes) which show a discharge are (eyes) which are full of tears. Turbid (eyes) are (eyes) of an opaque colour. (Eyes) ... which are in a contracted state are distorted (eyes);[88] Jejjaṭa says : "The meaning is : eyes which are opened wide"; others say (the meaning is : eyes) which have gone to the interior;[89] Cakra(pāṇidatta explains it as) extremely crooked (eyes).[90] (Covered) with awns (means : covered with awns) of *śūkaśimbi*, awned grain, etc.[91] (A tongue which looks as if) entirely burnt is (a tongue) of a black colour as if it has been burnt. Harsh to the touch is that which is harsh on touching it, like *gojihvā*.[92] Laxity of the parts of the body is the inability of the subdivisions (of the body) to perform their supporting function.[93] Spitting of blood or bile is (their) emission in very slight amounts from the mouth by belching.[94] Rolling of the head (means that) it is made to move hither and thither.[95] Leanness of the limbs to a not extreme degree (occurs) by means of their being filled with morbific entities.[96] Persistent (means) uninterrupted.

(The term) wheal has been mentioned in the Bhālukitantra : "Those possessing knowledge about it declare that a wheal resembles the sting of a *varaṭī*,[97] that it is itching and red, (arises) from blood, phlegm and bile, is produced in an instant and disappears as swiftly".[98]

Muteness is speaking sluggishly or not speaking at all ...[99] Maturation of the morbific entities after a long time occurs owing to the fact that the (fever by concerted action) has been started by (morbific entities) which are accompanied by immature matter to an extraordinary degree. By the word 'and' should be understood all the other (symptoms), mentioned by Vāgbhaṭa : "In the same way feelings of coldness, deep sleep by day and waking at night, either sleeping always or never at all, either intense perspiration or no perspiration, the appearance of a morbid longing for songs, dances, jests, etc." (A.h.Ni. 3, 27cd-28).[100]

These (already mentioned) characteristics of (that) fever among the thirteen (fevers) by concerted action which is started by morbific entities, which have increased to a comparable degree with regard to their own measure, have been described by Caraka. The characteristics of the twelve (fevers by concerted action) with an abundant (increase) of two (morbific entities), one (morbific entity), etc. should be examined at the same place (in the Carakasaṃhitā). Caraka says in the Kaśmīr recension (of his saṃhitā) : "Giddiness, thirst, a burning sensation, heaviness and an extreme pain in the head should be known as the signs of a fever with an abundant (increase) of wind and bile and a sluggish increase of phlegm.

A feeling of coldness, cough, inability to eat, lassitude, thirst, a burning sensation and distress in the cardiac region [101] are known as the signs in an illness with an abundant (increase) of wind and phlegm and an unimportant (increase) of bile.

Vomiting, suddenly alternating feelings of coldness and burning, thirst, mental confusion and a painful sensation in the bones are considered to be the signs in (a fever) with a sluggish (increase of) wind and an abundant (increase of) bile and phlegm. Piercing pains in junctures, bones and head, confused speech, heaviness and giddiness, thirst and a desiccated throat and mouth will occur in (a fever) with an abundant (increase of) wind, in which the other two (morbific entities) follow the wind in its course. Redness of faeces and urine, a burning sensation, perspiration, thirst, decline of force [102] and fainting will be the signs in a (fever) by three morbific entities with bile as the most important one.

Inertia, inability to eat, sickness, a burning sensation, emesis, disinclination, giddiness, lassitude and cough will indicate a (fever by) concerted action with an abundant (increase of) phlegm. Nasal catarrh, vomiting, inertia, lassitude, inability to eat and mildness of the (transforming) fire are thought to be the signs in (a fever with) a deficient (increase of) wind, a moderate one of bile and an excessive one of phlegm.

A turmeric-yellow (colour of) urine and eyes, a burning sensation, thirst, giddiness and the inability to eat are thought to be the signs in (a fever with) a deficient (increase of) wind, a moderate one of phlegm and an excessive one of bile.

Pain in the head, shivering, shortness of breath, confused speech, vomiting and anorexia are thought to be the signs in (a fever with) a deficient (increase of) bile, a moderate one of phlegm and an excessive one of wind.[103]

A feeling of coldness,[104] heaviness, lassitude, confused speech and excessive pain in head and bones are known to be the signs in (a fever with) a deficient (increase of) bile, a moderate one of wind and an excessive one of phlegm.

Loosening of faecal matter, weakness of the (transforming) fire, thirst, a burning sensation, inability to eat and giddiness are known to be the signs in (a fever with) a deficient (increase of) phlegm, a moderate one of wind and an excessive one of bile. Shortness of breath, cough, nasal catarrh, desiccation of the mouth and an extreme pain in the sides are thought to be the signs in (a fever with) a deficient (increase of) phlegm, a moderate one of bile and an excessive one of wind" [105] (Ca.Ci. 3, 91-102).[106] There is no fixed rule with regard to an altered state. For that reason there are, on account of an inherence (in a morbid alteration, the qualities of which are) incongruous with the altered state, several manners (in which these fevers present themselves). Suśruta has therefore also described the characteristics of another kind of (fever by) concerted action : "When there is neither an extreme hotness nor an extreme coldness, when consciousness is restricted, vision impaired, the lustre (of the skin) damaged,[107] the tongue harsh and the throat desiccated, when perspiration, faeces and urine are wanting and the eyes are full of tears and distorted,[108] when aversion to food is present and the voice has been damaged,[109] when (the patient) lies down, breathing with difficulty, after he has fallen down, and when confused speech follows as a secondary affection, it is called *abhinyāsa,* (which is) called *hataujas* by others. A fever by concerted action is said [110] to be difficult to cure; according to others it is incurable" (U. 39, 39-41).[111]

The characteristics of (fevers with) an abundant (increase of) one (morbific entity), etc. have also been described in the Bhālukitantra, in a different way : "The person in whom concerted action arises from excitement (of the three morbific entities) with an excess of wind and bile (shows) fever, muscle pain, thirst, desiccation of the palate, closing of the eyes, inflatedness, lassitude, inability to eat, shortness of breath, cough, giddiness and fatigue.[112] The person in whom concerted action arises from excitement (of the three morbific entities) with an excess of bile and phlegm (shows) a sensation of inner burning and feels coldness outside, lassitude troubles him, he feels pricking pain in his right side and seizing pain in his chest, head and throat, he spits out phlegm and bile, thirst and itching arise and loosening of faeces, shortness of breath and hiccup, accompanied by closing of the eyes, trouble him. These two (fevers by) concerted action are denominated *vibhu* and *phalgu*.[113]

The person in whom concerted action arises from excitement (of the three morbific entities) with an excess of phlegm and wind (shows) a cold fever, sleep, hunger, thirst, a seizing pain in the sides, heaviness of the head, inertia, stiffness of the muscles of the nape of the neck and closing of the eyes; a burning sensation occurs in his abdomen and his iliac region and bladder (feel as) consumed by fire. This (fever by) concerted action, which is very severe, should be discerned to be that one which is called *makarī*.[114]

The person in whom concerted action arises from excitement (of the three morbific entities) with an abundant (increase of) wind (shows) thirst, fever, languor, pain in the sides, decline of vision, cramp of the calves, a burning sensation, adynamia of the thighs and decline of his forces; his faeces and urine are accompanied by blood, he feels piercing pain and there is reversal (of the pattern) of sleep (and waking); his anus feels cut asunder, he feels shooting pains in his bladder, there are sensations of being stretched and cut, he hiccups and he also moans; he faints, becomes bloated and cries aloud. (This fever) is traditionally called *visphuraka*.[115]

The person in whom concerted action arises from excitement (of the three morbific entities) with an abundant (increase of) bile (shows) an increasing burning sensation and an increasing dreadful fever, externally and internally, phlegm and wind become excited when he indulges in cold (things), and thereupon hiccup, shortness of breath, closing of the eyes, *visūcikā*, cutting pain in the junctures, confused speech, heaviness and weariness rush upon him; when he has perspired, a painful condition of the umbilical region and the sides arises, increasing quickly; when he is perspiring, blood comes forth from the channels; when he is oppressed by piercing pain, thirst and a burning sensation arise to an increasing degree. This incurable (fever by) concerted action is called *śīghrakārin*. Someone into whose body this (fever) has entered, certainly dies within a day and a night.[116]

The person in whom concerted action arises from excitement (of the three morbific entities) with an abundant (increase of) phlegm (shows) a cold fever, sleep, heaviness, inertia, lassitude, vomiting, fainting, thirst, a burning sensation, a feeling of satiety, anorexia and a seizing pain in the cardiac region, spitting, a sweet (taste in the) mouth and suppression of the sense of hearing, speaking faculty and vision. When the physician proceeds to suppression of the patient's phlegm, he will bring about vehement (excitement of) bile (and) a fever accompanied by secondary affections; when, on the other hand, the bile has been suppressed, the wind becomes vehemently excited. In a person who does not take food (this fever) gives rise to trouble in fat, marrow and bones to an extreme degree; when someone with this fever takes a bath or ingests food, he will not live for more than three (days and) nights. This (fever by) concerted action, which is present in the fat (of the body), is called *kapphaṇa*. It proceeds from lust, a confused mental state, greediness and fear.[117]

When there occurs concerted action by means of morbific entities which are moderately, in a deficient way, and excessively (increased), the diseases (arising) from it are the very ones which have been mentioned (already); usually they are dependent on the strength of the morbific entities", etc.[118] It may be objected that wind, etc. are (entities) of which the qualities are disagreeing to each other; because (entities) with disagreeing qualities have joined each other, this is not a state of affairs in which one (and the same) effect can be attained, by reason of the fact that (the morbific entities) are injurious to each other, like snow and fire; how is it then possible that a morbid alteration by concerted action is produced?

The justification of the statement has in this case been given by Dṛḍhabala, who says: "The morbific entities are not injurious to each other by means of their qualities, even if these (qualities) disagree, because the morbific entities are innate and of the same nature, just as a dreadful poison (does not hurt) the serpents (producing it)" (Ca.Ci. 26, 293).[119]

But others spoil this (statement, reflecting as follows): due to the word 'innateness' there is uncertainty, because the morbific entities injure the elements (of the body), which are also innate; moreover it is, owing to the term 'being of the same nature', (a statement which is) not distinct from what is to be demonstrated, because that which is of the same nature (designates) that which is not troubling, and just that has to be demonstrated in this case with regard to the morbific entities.

The answer to this question is : the morbific entities do not injure (each other).

How can the fact that they do not injure (each other) be demonstrated ? Does (the statement) mean that they do not cause a deviation (from the natural state) or that they do not annihilate (each other) ?

The former (proposition) is not (right) because the morbific entities mutually bring about a deviation (from the natural state), as has been said in the Caraka(saṃhitā) : "When the wind desiccates the urine, which, together with semen, bile or phlegm, stays in the bladder, a stone is gradually formed, as a gall-stone in the bile of a cow" (Ci. 26, 36). And as has been said by Vāgbhaṭa : "In the case that the wind, together with phlegm and fat, after overpowering the other morbific entity (i.e. bile), which is accompanied by immature matter, accumulated to an extreme degree, reaches the thighs, it stiffens them, after filling the bones of the thighs interiorly with torpid phlegm; by that (reason) the thighs (become) stiff, cold and insensible" (Ni. 15, 48-49).[120]

Non-annihilation, however, is certainly present, because there does not exist a traditional doctrine substantiating that the elements (of the body) and the morbific entities, or the morbific entities mutually, extirpate (each other) in all respects, and (also) because this (i.e. annihilation) would lead to death; moreover (it is thus) because the morbific entities are sustainers of the body.

Therefore, with the very view of excluding an extirpation in all respects, the words of Dṛḍhabala have to be considered here. For which reason then should there be uncertainty ?

When things are thus, the example of poison is not without merit because of the fact that it brings about despondency, because poison, having an action that is respectively different from despondency, annihilates life. It is, however, not an example in an all-round way.

... The morbific entities do not injure each other because they are acknowledged as not injuring each other. In which way something is acknowledged, in that way it is defined, (in the same way) as e.g. smoke, which is an effect of fire, (is defined) as an effect of fire.

Whence therefore would there be non-distinctness from what is to be demonstrated?

Cakra(pāṇidatta), however, has explained the term 'being innate and of the same nature' as being one (and the same) ground, (in saying its meaning to be that) the morbific entities are innately, (i.e.) based on their own state of being, of the same nature.[121]

Gayadāsa, on the other hand, has stated another ground, because the two grounds mentioned by Dṛḍhabala are not to his liking: "In a (fever by) concerted action there does not occur any mutual injury of the morbific entities by their disagreeing qualities, neither by chance nor owing to their own state of being".

In this way (the problem has been explained) succinctly.

Ā:

... The throat is as if covered with awns, (i.e.) with the tips of grain, which have the form of sharp thorns; others (say it is as covered) with the stiff hairs of *kapikacchū* ... Giddiness is (a sensation) like that of someone who has mounted a wheel; others, however, (say it is) wrong knowledge concerning objects, as mistaking a pillar for a man ... (In the expression) 'inflammatory changes of the channels', (the channels are) mouth, nose, ears, etc. ...

When a (fever by) concerted action is present with an inherence (in a morbid alteration, the qualities of which are) congruous with the natural state, one should be acquainted with the characteristics of a fever (arising) from wind, etc. separately. There are six (fevers by) concerted action according to the gradation of deficiently, moderately and excessively (increased morbific entities), three with an abundant (increase of) two (morbific entities), three with an abundant (increase of) one (morbific entity) and one with a congruous (increase of the morbific entities); in that way thirteen fevers by concerted action (are counted) when there is a natural state. Suśruta, however, has not mentioned in this case the characteristics of each (of these fevers) separately, because there is an infinite number of (fevers by) concerted action, which are distinguished according to the gradations of morbific entities which are unduly increased and unduly decreased and according to the distinctions (based) on the elements (of the body), etc., which are covered (by the morbific entities); yet he has described the characteristics of one of the (fevers by) concerted action, (which arises) by means of morbific entities, excited to a (mutually) comparable degree; (he says) as follows: "Neither being extremely hot nor extremely cold ..." (fr. U. 39, 39a), etc. And in the Bhālukitantra the characteristics of (fevers) with an abundant (increase of) two morbific entities, one morbific entity, etc., are described in a different way : "Immature matter, accumulated at first by faults with regard to one's diet, injures the (transforming) fire; all the ingested food then turns into phlegm; thereupon this phlegm, corrupted by the wind and having filled the channels, will obstruct the wind; then the wind gives rise to an excited condition of the bile; having coalesced with each other in the interior (of the body), these (morbific entities) bring about in men the (fever by) concerted action which is called *prabala*".[122] Moreover (it is said) : "The person in whom concerted action arises by excitement (of the morbific entities) with an excess of wind and bile", etc.

2, 24 : When the morbific entity is in a confined condition and the (transforming) fire has been annihilated, a fever by concerted action, of which all the characteristics are fully (developed), is incurable; it is difficult to cure when it differs (from this description).

(Ca.Ci. 3, 109cd-110ab).[123]

M:

... (The term) morbific entity (denotes here) both impurity and bile, etc. Jejjaṭa, however, says (that it) only (means) impure matter, on account of the (use of the) words 'being in a confined condition'.[124]

An annihilated state of the (transforming) fire means that the food is not subject to maturation. As has been said in the Caraka(saṃhitā) : "The (transforming) fire (should be investigated) by the ability to disintegrate" (fr. Vi. 4, 8).

By (the use of) the terms incurable and difficult to cure it is shown that easy curability does not occur. For in the Caraka(saṃhitā) it has been said : "Concerted action (is the foremost) of those (diseases) which are difficult to treat" (fr. Sū. 25, 40). The same has been said by Bhāluki : "A therapist has to contend with death in a (fever by) concerted action".[125]

'Of which all the characteristics are fully (developed)' means 'of which the complete set of characteristics is very strong'.

Ā:

... Bhāluki has said : "A therapist has to contend with death in a (fever by) concerted action. The person who can subdue it, can subdue the throng of ailments. Which duty has not been fulfilled by him and which praise does not deserve the man who draws out someone drowned in the ocean of concerted action ?"[126]

Moreover, the period of time until one is delivered from or killed by a fever by concerted action has been taught in the Suśruta(saṃhitā) : "When the seventh day has arrived, the tenth or the twelfth, it becomes appeased or kills, after having become more dreadful again" (U. 39, 45cd-46ab). Bhāluki has also said : "(It lasts) as long as twice seven, ten and eleven days; these are the (time-)limits of the three morbific entities, resulting in delivery or death".[127] Moreover it has been said : "A (fever), arising from the three morbific entities with an increase of bile, phlegm and wind, kills or leaves off, owing to maturation of the elements (of the body) or the impurities, after ten, twelve or seven days".[128] It leaves off owing to maturation of the impurities or kills owing to maturation of the elements (of the body), and does so on the seventh day when an excess of wind is present, on the tenth day when an excess of bile is present and on the twelfth day when an excess of phlegm is present. The characteristics of maturation of the elements (of the body) have been described in another book (as follows) : "The person who feels a troubling sensation in his cardiac region, umbilical region or in his limbs, which are full of pain by maturation, or who, when they are mature, is afflicted by pain and fever, is called by physicians a (patient) with maturation of the elements".[129] In still another (book) it has also been said : "A fever with an excess of bile, phlegm or wind kills or leaves off after ten, twelve or seven days, after having maturated the elements or the impurities by (its) heat".

2, 25 : At the end of a fever by concerted action a very severe swelling arises at the root of the ear; only some people are released from it.

(Ca.Ci. 3, 287cd-288ab).[130]

M:

The secondary affection of fever is dealt with ...

Ā:

At the end, (i.e.) at the termination of a fever by concerted action, arises at the root, (i.e.) at the edge, of the ear of a man whose body has become emaciated by (this) concerted action, a swelling which is very severe, (i.e.) which can only be cured with the utmost trouble, accompanied by redness, pain, etc., in accordance with the specific (type of) onset and the diversity of action. Only some people are released [131] from this swelling; this means that is usually leads to death.

2, 26 :[132] Adventitious (fever) arises by means of the morbific entities from traumatic injury, magic, curses and possession; one should clearly ascertain it in accordance with the own (characteristics) of the morbific entities.[133]

2, 27-30ab : A brown (colour of the) mouth and certainly diarrhoea,[134] inability to eat food,[135] thirst and pricking pain, accompanied by fainting,[136] occur when it is brought about by poison (27).

When it arises from the smell of herbs, fainting, a painful condition of the head, emesis and sneezing are present. When it arises from (feelings of) lust there occur mental perturbation, lassitude, inertia and abstinence from food (28);[137] a painful sensation arises in the cardiac region of (such a person) and (his) limbs desiccate completely. Confused speech arises from fear, as it does from grief, and from anger arises shivering.

From magic and curses arise mental confusion and thirst (29); from possession by *bhūtas* arise disquietude, laughing, weeping and trembling.

(Su.U. 39, 76cd-80ab).[138]

M :

... Traumatic injury occurs by injuring (someone) with a cutting weapon, clod, fist, club, etc. Magic [139] is said to be performed by means of the sacrifice (called) *śyena*,[140] etc., or by a sacrificial offering accompanied by spells (recited) in the reverse order, and (a sacrificial offering) of mustard seeds [141] by means of an iron sacrificial ladle.[142] Possession is an intimate connection with lust, etc. and with *bhūtas*, as has been said in the Caraka(saṃhitā) : "The fever of persons who are possessed by lust, grief, fear and wrath should be known as a fever by possession, as well as (the fever) which arises from possession by *bhūtas*" [143] (Ci. 3, 114cd-115ab).[144] A curse is the undesirable cursing by *brāhmaṇas*, *gurus*, old people and *siddhas*.[145]

One should ascertain this adventitious fever by means of the morbific entities, in accordance with the (characteristics of its morbific entity itself). As has been said : "From lust, grief and fear the wind (becomes excited)",[146] etc. This intimate connection with the morbific entities has been examined on the occasion of the onset, when it is said to be something which occurs later on, but does not start (the disease).

(About) 'a brown colour of the mouth', etc. (we remark that) a brown colour is a black colour interspersed with white; others say that it is a dark colour.

'When it is brought about by poison' (means) : when it is brought about by the consumption, etc. of poison from vegetable origin, (for) diarrhoea occurs because poison (of vegetable origin) moves in a downward direction.

'When it arises from the smell of herbs' (means) : when it arises from smelling the intense smell of (particular) herbs. In this same (type of fevers) are included the grass fever and flower fever described by Vṛddha-suśruta with the words : "When the wind ... the fragrance and the pollen (sprung) from vigorous flowers",[147] etc.

'When it arises from lust' (means) : when it is caused by not obtaining the woman longed for.

Mental perturbation is giddiness, etc. As Vāgbhaṭa says : "From lust (arise) giddiness, inability to eat, a burning sensation and decline of shame, sleep, insight and self-control" (Ni. 2, 42cd).

'From fear' (means) : in a fever arising from fear; in the same way should be understood both 'from grief' and 'from anger'. 'From grief arises confused speech,' thus is the (syntactical) connection; confused speech is here an effect of wind, because it (occurs as) an effect of wind and of bile. (The specific type should be ascertained from the origin, for the origin is a characteristic as well). Moreover it has been said : "From lust, grief and fear the wind (becomes excited), from wrath the bile, the three impurities ..." (Ca.Ci. 3, 115cd), etc.

It may be asked as an objection how it is that shivering (can occur) in a (fever) arising from wrath when things are like that, for (shivering) is an effect of wind.

The answer is : shivering is in this case verily occasioned by wind that has been made excited by bile, according to the words : "One morbific entity may make really all of them excited", and one can observe that an angry person trembles, so it is certainly proved by eyesight; thus says Jejjaṭa. Wrath excites the wind too, as it does with regard to bile; that is a suitable (statement). As Videha says : "Wrath and grief are traditionally said to excite wind, blood and bile". (About the words) 'and from anger' (we remark that) by the word 'and' pain in the head is added. As Vāgbhaṭa says : "From wrath arise trembling and pain in the head; confused speech arises from fear and grief" (Ni. 2, 42ab).

Fevers arising from fear, etc. are dealt with separately because they are distinct as to their ground, though they are non-specific as being affections of the *manas*. The distinction is stated on account of the distinctness of the ground and on behalf of a therapy that is opposed to the ground.

(About) 'from magic', etc. (we remark that) the word 'and' in 'and thirst' adds the burning sensation, etc. (occurring) in a fever arising from magic. As has been said by Vāgbhaṭa, in agreement with the opinion of Hārīta : "When someone is being invoked by means of magic spells, his mind is afflicted by glowing heat first and his body afterwards; at last the fever of that person, who is consumed by blisters, thirst, giddiness, a burning sensation and fainting, increases daily" (Ni. 2, 44cd-45).

(About) 'from possession by *bhūta*s', etc. (we remark that) *bhūta*s are the *devagraha*s, etc., to be spoken of in (the chapter on) the origins of insanity; possession by them is an intimate connection with them ...

Ā :

... Traumatic injury (is brought about) by an iron cutting weapon, a piece of wood, etc. ... Although poison is an agent (productive) of the three morbific entities, (it brings about) a brown colour of the mouth because it gives rise to an extraordinarily great (amount of) bile ... Mental perturbation is confusion as to one's obligations. As Vāgbhaṭa says : "From lust arise giddiness, disinclination, a burning sensation and decline of shame, sleep, insight and self-control; frequent pondering and sighing are traditionally said to be signs in a fever by lust ...[148]

2, 30cd-31ab : From lust, grief and fear the wind becomes excited, from wrath bile and from possession by *bhūta*s the three impurities, the generic characteristics (of the latter) being those of the *bhūta*s.

(Ca.Ci. 3, 115cd-116ab).[149]

M :

The words '(from) lust, grief', etc. are used to show that the adventitious fevers also are attended by a morbific entity, which is a fixed one for each single case.

Due to the special faculty of *bhūtas* the three impurities become excited from possession by *bhūtas*. That which has been stated by Caraka in the section on origins : "(The fever) arising from possession, however, (is attended) by wind and bile" (fr. Ni. 1, 30) has to be considered, according to Jejjaṭa, as that which usually occurs; Cakra(pāṇidatta), on the other hand, says : "(The term) 'arising from possession' indicates (in that case a fever) arising from possession by lust, etc., but not (a fever) arising from possession by *bhūtas*".[150]

'The generic characteristics (of the latter) being those of the *bhūtas*' is explained by Jejjaṭa, etc. as follows : they being thus that their characteristics are of a generic similarity to those which are the characteristics, (i.e.) weeping, etc., of the *bhūta*, (i.e.) the *devagraha*, etc., by which, due to the (state of) possession by it, (the morbific entities) become excited. This means that the characteristics of the morbific entities are also the characteristics of the *bhūtas*.

2, 31cd-32ab : Or, on the other hand, a slight morbific entity of someone who has been released from fever, joined to something insalutary (31), brings about an irregular fever when it has reached any one of the elements (of the body).

(Su.U. 39, 66).[151]

M :

The onset of irregular fever is dealt with ... By means of a slight (morbific entity) fever is brought about when it has acquired strength after a specific (interval of) time, for it is weak (at the beginning); a strong morbific entity, however, brings about a permanent fever. 'Joined to something insalutary' (means) : joined to an insalutary diet and behaviour, etc., and increased (for that reason). 'Of someone who has been released from fever' (means) : of someone whose fever has suddenly ceased. With the word 'or' it is demonstrated that an irregular fever can also be present from the beginning. As has been said : "That one, however, which is irregular from the start".[152] 'Anyone of the elements (of the body)' (indicates) the nutrient fluid, blood, etc. 'An irregular fever' (points to) tertian fever, etc.

The generic characteristics of irregular fevers have also been described by Bhāluki : "That fever which is irregular because the time (of its duration) is indeterminate and because its coldness and hotness and also its paroxysms are irregular, is traditionally called an irregular fever".[153]

2, 32cd-33 : Continuous [154] (fever) stays in the nutrient fluid and blood; that one (occurring as a) quotidian (fever) resides in the flesh (32); (the fever) staying in the fat (appears) on the third day, but that one staying in the bones and the marrow may bring about the quartan (type), which is dreadful, fatal and an intermixture of diseases (33).

(Su.U. 39, 67-68ab).[155]

M:

The elements (of the body), which are in a fixed order objects of corruption in continuous fever, etc., are dealt with ... The term 'continuous' (fever) implies double quotidian (fever); this means that a (fever) staying in the nutrient fluid is a continuous fever and that a (fever) staying in the blood is a double quotidian one. As has been said in the Caraka(saṃhitā) : "A morbific entity, mainly residing in the element blood, (brings about) double quotidian fever" (Ci. 3, 61cd). (The word 'mainly' indicates that double quotidian fever not only resides in the blood but also in the nutrient fluid).[156] The term 'nutrient fluid' serves to specify in this case, because the nutrient fluid is necessarily an object of corruption in all fevers.

Others, however, read, in order to include double quotidian (fever) : 'The two continuous (fevers) stay in the nutrient fluid and blood'. But that is not very suitable, for in this case the words continuous and double quotidian are two different technical terms and not words denoting continuity. Because the term continuous (fever) does not denote double quotidian (fever), (the rule about) *ekaśeṣa* [157] cannot be applied; that is the (grammatical) fault (in this reading) ...[158]

'Dreadful' (means) : difficult to endure. 'Fatal' (means that it is) like Yama, because it leads to death. An intermixture of diseases is a throng of several diseases.

Ā:

... An intermixture of diseases (means that) it is productive of numerous diseases; it is conducive to other diseases because it is deep-seated and leads to vexation of long duration.

2, 34-36ab : That one which will continue without (any) lapse for seven, ten or also twelve days, is called continuous (fever) (34).

Double quotidian (fever) appears twice a day and a night, but quotidian (fever) once a day and a night (35).[159] Tertian (fever) comes forth (every) third day (and) quartan (fever every) fourth day.

(Su.U. 39, 69-71ab).[160]

M :

And now the characteristics of these (fevers) are dealt with ... These varieties should be known as being (provided) with an abundance of wind, bile and phlegm, in this mentioned due order. As has been said : "A (fever) arising from the three morbific entities with an increase of bile, phlegm or wind kills or leaves off quickly, owing to maturation of the elements or the impurities, after ten, twelve or seven days".[161] And this continuous (fever) verily arises from the three morbific entities because it is provided with twelve residences.[162] As Caraka has said : "In continuous fever the wind, etc. enter, as a fixed rule and simultaneously, upon urine and faeces in the same way as upon the elements" (Ci. 3, 56cd-57ab). (The structure and meaning of 2, 34 is explained by paraphrasing it and the remark is made that to designate a period of seven days, etc. the accusative has been used in the sense of uninterrupted contact).

Now it may be asked why it (i.e. continuous fever) is described among the irregular fevers when things are like this, for irregularity (of a fever means) that it is attending someone who has been released (from it), and that (characteristic) is not present in this case.[163]

This (reasoning) is not (correct) because also this one is of such a nature, (i.e. irregular), as Caraka says in characterizing it : "After having lapsed on the twelfth day, it yet holds on with undeveloped characteristics for a long time, being difficult to appease" (Ci. 3, 59cd-60ab).[164]

But it is not designated as such (i.e. as an irregular fever) in the (following) words of Kharanāda on continuous fever : "As to the five fevers, (i.e.) *saṃtataka* [165] (fever), etc., mentioned by me previously, four (of them), the continuous one excepted, should be known as irregular fevers",[166] because its attending someone who has been released (from fever) is of slight (importance), being conditioned by the fact that it (i.e. the release from fever) occurs only once, in the same way as the eating of (only) one grain (of rice) is designated as non-eating. It should be regarded with a view to the fact that its attending one who has been released (from fever) does not occur at all together with a recurrence as (in the case) of tertian (fever), etc. Or it serves to substantiate that the therapy mentioned in the description of irregular fever(s) should be employed in (cases of) double quotidian (fever), etc., with the exception of continuous (fever).

One should know that Haricandra with respect to the words of Caraka : "A common treatment will remove tertian and quartan (fever)" (Ci. 3, 292cd) [167] has given the following explanation : the therapy mentioned with regard to irregular fevers (should) certainly (be employed) in (cases of) tertian and quartan (fever), whereas in (cases of) other (irregular fevers) a therapy should be employed that is opposed to the morbific entity. With respect to this explanation of Haricandra one should regard it to be thus, that a common treatment should be employed in really every irregular fever, (but) specifically in tertian and quartan (fever). Otherwise (there would be) disagreement with the other treatises which have been mentioned.

'Double quotidian fever attends (one) twice a day and a night' (means) : twice a day or twice a night or once a day and once a night; twice, says Īśānadeva, because particulars are not mentioned and it is observed to be thus. 'It attends (one)' [168] (means that) it brings about a paroxysm.

'Tertian (fever) appears (every) third day' (means) : that (fever) is a tertian one which is present on the third day with reference to the day on which a paroxysm (has already appeared); with respect to quartan fever it should be expressed in the same way.

Ā :

Now, by means of the periods of time until its leaving off, the characteristics of continuous fever, which arises from one morbific entity, are made mention of ... (A paraphrase of 2, 34 follows). This (fever) is easily curable. That has been said in another book : "Continuous (fever), however, is different and has a very slight and weak cause; because it arises from one or two morbific entities it is proclaimed to be easily curable;" [169] likewise : "A fever by wind proceeds to maturation in seven (days and) nights, (a fever) by bile in ten (days and) nights and (a fever) by phlegm in twelve days (and nights)". [170] (This occurs) because they are based on an inherence (in a morbid alteration, the qualities of which are) congruous with the natural state. Is it not right to ask (as an objection) why it is described among the irregular fevers? As Kharanāda has said: "As to the five fevers, (i.e.) *saṃtataka* (fever), etc., mentioned by me previously, four (of them), the continuous one excepted, should be known as irregular fevers". Irregularity (of a fever means that) it attends one who has been released (from it); 'after having left off, it attends (one)'; that, however, is not the case here.

This (reasoning) is not (correct) because also this one is of such a nature (i.e. irregular).

With the words '(during) a day and a night' the characteristics of double quotidian fever, etc. are made mention of, with reference to (certain) time(-periods) during which they appear.

There are six (periods of) time: morning, noon, afternoon, the first part of the night, midnight and the second part of the night. The morning and first part of the night are the time(-periods) of phlegm, noon and midnight those of bile, and the afternoon and second part of the night those of wind. That (fever) which appears, (i.e.) brings about a paroxysm, twice in the six (periods of) time, consisting of morning, etc., is double quotidian (fever); (it brings about a paroxysm) once a day and once a night, twice a day or twice a night, in that way (one should regard the expression) twice, as Īśāna has said; concerning these (words of Īśāna) one should know that the (period of) time (during which it is present) may be longer or shorter on account of undue increase and undue decrease of the morbific entities and that a fixed rule does not exist.

Quotidian fever appears, (i.e.) brings about a paroxysm, once; this means that it approaches once from day to day.

Tertian (fever appears) on the third day; this has to be connected with (the word) once.

Quartan (fever appears) on the fourth day; also in this case (one has to supply) once.

These are the four irregular fevers. The due order of their production must be learnt from Vṛddhasuśruta. It is as he says: "From day to day it proceeds from (one) seat to (the subsequent) seat. Thereupon, after reaching the receptacle of undigested food, it brings about irregular fever. The morbific entity of bodily beings, who are lean and released from fever, who (indulge in) an improper diet and conduct, becomes, though very slight, increased when it is set in motion by the wind. In accordance with the number of the different seats of phlegm it brings about double quotidian, quotidian, tertian and quartan fever, together with *pralepaka* (fever)" (Su.U. 39, 53; 51; 52cd; 52ab).[171]

This has the following meaning : the five seats of phlegm are the receptacle of undigested food, the cardiac region,[172] the throat, the head and the junctures. The morbific entities, staying in these (seats), proceed, according to the number (of these seats), from (one) seat to the following one in a day and a night, reach the receptacle of undigested food and bring about a double quotidian fever, etc.

A morbific entity staying in the receptacle of undigested food brings about double quotidian (fever), no more than twice and not at all times; the consequence that it will give rise to it at all times by the fact that it has reached the receptacle of undigested food does not occur, because the production of fever depends on the time(-periods) of day and night (linked to) excitement (of a morbific entity). A morbific entity staying in the cardiac region brings about quotidian fever after it has reached the receptacle of undigested food in one day, because of its disconnectedness with regard to the morbific entity that starts a double quotidian (fever). A morbific entity staying in the throat reaches the cardiac region in one day; after it has reached the receptacle of undigested food on the following day, it starts tertian (fever). In the same way quartan fever is brought about on the fourth day by a morbific entity staying in the head, after it has reached the throat, the cardiac region and the receptacle of undigested food in three days, in regular order. The morbific entities, however, return again to their own seat on the very day of a paroxysm, because they have become light by bringing about a paroxysm.

A morbific entity staying in the junctures brings about *pralepaka* (fever); because junctures are present in the receptacle of undigested food too, it occurs at all times. Although this is not an irregular fever it has been mentioned along with the irregular (fevers), because it complies with (the rule of) the production (of these fevers) from a seat of phlegm. For in the Suśruta(saṃhitā) it has been said : "*pralepaka* (fever), however, which is not an irregular (fever), usually leads to vexation of desiccated (patients)".[173]

There is still another irregular fever, (called) reversed quartan fever.[174] In another treatise (has been said) about it : "When (the morbific entity) is staying both in the bones and the marrow, reversed quartan fever (arises); it gives rise to fever on the two middlemost days, but leaves off at the beginning and at the end". Jejjaṭa, etc. explain : not having occurred for one day at the beginning, and after having been present for two days in the middle of the (period), it does not occur during one day at the end. Another treatise says : "When (the morbific entity) is staying both in the bones and the marrow, reversed quartan fever arises; it gives rise to fever for two days out of three, and leaves off at the beginning and at the end".

2, 36cd : Some say that an irregular fever arises from possession by *bhūtas*.

(Su.U. 39, 68cd).[175]

M :

... (This) opinion of others is not prohibited and is approved of by Suśruta. For that very reason both (kinds of therapeutic measures, i.e.) those, having recourse to divine influences, (such as) *bali* offerings, etc., which are proper to the *bhūtas*, and those having recourse to natural techniques, (such as) the drinking of *kaṣāyas*, which are proper to the morbific entities, are prescribed in (cases of) irregular fever. As Caraka says : "A common treatment can remove tertian and quartan (fever); for in irregular fevers an adventitious (component) is usually (present as) an adjunctory factor" (Ci. 3, 292cd-293ab).

'Common' is explained in this case (as meaning) : having recourse to divine influences, as well as to natural techniques.[176]

2, 37-38 : Tertian (fever) may be of three kinds : (arising) from phlegm and bile it seizes the sacral region; when it is of the nature of wind and phlegm (it seizes) at the back; (arising) from wind and bile it seizes the head (37). Quartan fever shows its power in two ways : when (arising) from phlegm (it seizes) at the legs first, and at the head when it arises from wind (38).

(Ca.Ci. 3, 71-72).[177]

M :

The difference between the characteristics of tertian and quartan (fever) with respect to the morbific entities which are present in abundance are made mention of ...

'Seizing the sacral region' (means) pervading the sacral region with a painful sensation. As the sacral region is the seat of wind, bile and phlegm staying there are weak, because they are staying at the seat of another (morbific entity), and bring about a paroxysm on the third day. Jejjaṭa says that, if they were staying at their own seats, they would bring about continuous fever. One should understand it in the same way with respect to (the seizing of) the head which is a seat of phlegm and the back which is a seat of bile.

'At the back' means pervading the back with a painful sensation. (A grammatical remark is made about the use of the ablative). One should not say : how can bile and phlegm stay in the sacral region if it is a seat of phlegm ? The fixed rule about the seats of the morbific entities (applies) to them when they are in a natural state, but is not applicable when they are in an excited condition, for in the latter state they stay in the whole body. As Suśruta says : "An illness arises at that place where, on account of a deviated state of the qualities of the apertures,[178] retention occurs of the excited morbific entities moving through the body" (Sū. 24, 10).

It should be argued in the same way that in quartan (fever) too, weakness, etc. of the morbific entity arises, because it has moved to the seat of another (morbific entity).

'Power' is the ability (to give rise) to pain. It is explained to be of two kinds with the words 'at the legs', etc. (A grammatical remark follows). (It seizes at the legs) first; having got there it pervades the whole body.

'(Arising) from phlegm' [179] (means) : with an abundance of phlegm; for the five (fevers consisting of the) continuous, double quotidian, quotidian, tertian and quartan (fevers) arise from concerted action. As has been said in the Caraka(saṃhitā) : "The fivefold fever is usually seen (to arise) by concerted action; that one which is strongest in a (fever by) concerted action is proclaimed to be (its) morbific entity" (Ci. 3, 74).[180] Or, on account of the word 'usually', (one may infer that) they also arise from one and from two morbific entities.

Others, however, say : (the fevers) based on an inherence (in a morbid alteration, the qualities of which are) incongruous with the altered state, (to wit) continuous fever, etc., arise from concerted action; these very (fevers) are designated according to the morbific entity which has become perceptible. (Fevers) also exist which are based on an inherence (in a morbid alteration, the qualities of which are) congruous with the natural state, and these arise from one or from two morbific entities; thus says Jejjaṭa.

A quartan fever based on an inherence (in a morbid alteration, the qualities of which are) congruous with the natural state, is never brought about by bile on account of the own nature of the illness, (in the same way) as a *galagaṇḍa* [181] arising from bile (does not exist).

(It may be said as an objection:) is it not true that there also exists a quartan (fever) by bile? Master Hārīta says likewise: "The malady called quartan (fever) is a severe irregular fever; it desiccates all the elements (of the body) and annihilates (one's) force, colour and (transforming) fire. It may be a morbid alteration, arising from the three morbific entities, (in which) the wind stays in bones and marrow, and the bile and phlegm are excited as much according to their own nature. It brings about intense feelings of coldness and burning; it appears at the three (periods of) time; arisen from concerted action, and being irregular, it is an irregular fever. When it seizes the upper part of the body first, it is of the nature of wind; when it seizes the lower part of the body first, it is a quartan (fever) with an increase of phlegm".

Regarding this it has been said: bile is an adjunctory factor here but not (the morbific entity) starting (the disorder). For one may argue: how could this acknowledgment arise, when (its) specific seat has not been made mention of? It is just for that reason that a seat has not been stated at all, even by Hārīta, in the same way as with the words 'at the legs', etc.; that is the explanation of the commentators on the Caraka(saṃhitā).

But with this explanation one can (only) agree if signs of bile were not perceptible; they are, however, perceptible. Besides, it has been said that a bilious (quartan fever) is described in the Bheḍa(saṃhitā), with the words: "The excited wind, staying in the receptacle of undigested food, or also when staying in bones and marrow, quickly brings about excitement of phlegm, and of bile as well". Moreover, a seat has certainly been mentioned in the Nāgabhartṛtantra: "That one which seizes the upper part of the body first, is of the nature of wind; that one seizing the middle part of the body, arises from bile; the quartan fever with an increase of phlegm seizes the lower part of the body first".

Therefore one should regard it to be thus, that (a quartan fever) usually (arises) from phlegm and wind, (because) a bilious quartan fever is not dealt with by Caraka, etc., but not owing to the fact that it does not occur.[182]

The due order of the production of these (irregular fevers) must be learnt from Vṛddhasuśruta. It is as he says: "From day to day it proceeds from (one) seat to (the subsequent) seat. Thereupon, after reaching the receptacle of undigested food, it brings about irregular fever. In accordance with the number of the different seats of phlegm it brings about double quotidian, quotidian, tertian and quartan (fever), together with *pralepaka* (fever)" (Su.U. 39, 54; 52cd; 52ab).[183]

This has the following meaning: the five seats of phlegm are the receptacle of undigested food, the cardiac region, the throat, the head and the junctures. The morbific entities, staying in these (seats), according to their number, bring about double quotidian (fever), etc. A morbific entity staying in the receptacle of undigested food brings about double quotidian (fever), no more than twice (a day), and not at all times; the consequence that it (will appear) at all times when it has reached the receptacle of undigested food does not occur, because the production of fever depends on the time(-periods) of day and night, (linked to) excitement (of a morbific entity). A morbific entity staying in the cardiac region, after reaching the receptacle of undigested food, brings about quotidian fever once (a day), and not at all times, because of its disconnectedness with regard to the morbific entity that starts a double quotidian (fever). A morbific entity staying in the throat reaches the cardiac region in one day; after it has reached the receptacle of undigested food on the following (day), it starts tertian (fever). In the same way quartan (fever) is brought about by a morbific entity staying in the head, after it has reached the throat, the cardiac region and the receptacle of undigested food in three days, in regular order.

The morbific entities, however, return again to their own seat on the very day of a paroxysm, because they have become light by bringing about a paroxysm.

A morbific entity staying in the junctures brings about *pralepaka* (fever); because junctures are present in the receptacle of undigested food too, it occurs at all times. Although this one is not an irregular (fever), it has been mentioned along with the irregular (fevers), because it complies with (the rule of) the production (of these fevers) from a seat of phlegm. For in the Suśruta(saṃhitā) it has been said: "*pralepaka* (fever), however, which is not an irregular (fever), usually leads to vexation of desiccated (patients)" (U. 39, 54ab).[184]

2, 39ab : There is another and also irregular fever, the reversed quartan. (Ca.Ci. 3, 73ab).

2, 39cd : It brings about fever during two days out of three and leaves off at the beginning and at the end.[185]

M :

Mention is made of the reversed quartan (fever) ... Another book says with regard to it: "When it is staying both in bones and marrow, (there is question of) reversed quartan (fever). It brings about fever for two days out of three and it leaves off at the beginning and at the end".[186] Jejjaṭa, etc. explain this as follows : after leaving off for one day at the beginning, and being present for two days in the middle, it is absent for one day at the end. The same meaning is also pronounced by Parāśara : "When it is staying both in bones and marrow, it is reversed quartan (fever); it brings about fever for two days out of three and it leaves (one) in the beginning and at the end." The purport of the words 'out of three days', etc. is explained as follows : the first day of the three it leaves off, it brings about fever during two days, and at the end of (the period of) three days, (i.e.) on the fourth day, it leaves (one). Haricandra, however, says : after bringing about fever during two days without interruption, and after a pause of one day, it makes one feverish again; thus is reversed quartan fever. The absence (of fever on) the first day should be determined accurately (in connection with) the days on which it appears.

It is said that one should conclude that also reversed tertian fever, etc. exist as being implied in (the concept) of reversed quartan (fever). These (fevers) are as follows : reversed tertian (fever) gives rise to fever for one day in the middle, and leaves (one) at the beginning and at the end; reversed quotidian fever pervades (one) for a whole day and night, after having left off once (during this day and night); (reversed double quotidian fever leaves off twice and brings about fever during the whole (remaining part of the) day and night. The very deviated state of the morbific entity is (in these cases) a multiform ground.

Jejjaṭa, explaining the statement of Vṛddhasuśruta : "Or, when a morbific entity stays in two, three or four seats of phlegm, it brings about the irregular (fevers) called reversed (types), which are difficult to cure" (Su.U. 39, 55),[187] illustrates the reversed (types of the fevers belonging to) the group (consisting) of the quotidian, tertian and quartan ones as follows : a morbific entity, staying in the receptacle of undigested food and in the cardiac region, brings about reversed quotidian (fever), just as it has been declared to do; (a morbific entity) staying in the receptacle of undigested food, the cardiac region and the throat, (brings about) reversed tertian fever; in this (context it is thus, that) a morbific entity staying in the cardiac region, having reached the receptacle of undigested food in one day, brings about fever, together with (the morbific entity already) there; on the day this occurs, (the morbific entity) staying in the throat moves to the cardiac region, and on the following day, after reaching the receptacle of undigested food, this one brings about fever as well; in that way, after being present for two days, it is absent for one day later on; this is reversed tertian (fever). Reversed quartan (fever) is brought about by a morbific entity staying in the receptacle of undigested food, the cardiac region, the throat and the head; with respect to that one (it is thus, that) on the day the morbific entity which resides in the cardiac region brings about fever, after reaching the receptacle of undigested food, (the morbific entity) staying in the throat goes to the cardiac region, and that one staying in the head to the throat; on the following day that one staying in the cardiac region brings about fever, after reaching the receptacle of undigested food, and that one staying in the throat goes to the cardiac region; on the following day that same one staying in the cardiac region brings about fever, after reaching the receptacle of undigested food; thus, after being present for three days, it is absent during one day later on; this is reversed quartan fever. And really all these fevers are not disagreeing (with authoritative texts), because all these have indeed been taught by the sages. As has been said in the digest : "But in case two sacred traditions are conflicting, both are held to be *dharma*" [188] (Manusmṛti 2, 14ab). And irregular fevers of really various kinds are observed. This very rule has been demonstrated by Vāpyacandra with respect to the incongruity concerning skin diseases in the Caraka- and Suśruta(saṃhitā).

A distinct therapy of these (reversed fevers) has, however, not been mentioned. The same therapy as in tertian (fever), etc. (has) also (to be employed) in their reversed types.

Ā :

Reversed quartan fever is another irregular fever; it brings about fever for two days out of three, and leaves off during one day. In the same way a reversed tertian fever should also be spoken of. In the Suśruta(saṃhitā) it has been shown that the irregular fevers remain lodged in the body also when their paroxysms have become appeased; it says as follows : "And this irregular (fever) leaves the body never at all, because one is not released from languor, heaviness, (an altered taste in the mouth) and leanness; when the paroxysm has passed, however, (the fever) seems to be gone (U. 39, 63cd-64).[189] Because heaviness of the head, languor, absence of much relish for food, a sweet taste, an altered taste or on the other hand a bitter taste in the mouth arise, also when the paroxysm has passed, irregular fever definitely inhabits the body".[190]

2, 40 : Someone with a fever that is constantly of a slow kind, who is dry and swollen, becoming adynamic by it, his body being stiff, will be suffering, chiefly (afflicted by) phlegm, from *vātabalāsaka.*

(A.s.Ni. 2, 88cd-89ab).[191]

M:

Since *vātabalāsaka* which, because it is, on account of the (above-) mentioned association, a secondary affection after the model of *pralepaka,* has the same peculiarities as this (*pralepaka*), must be discussed by means of an unusual scientific treatise,[192] it is said : 'constantly', etc.

Someone who suffers from the fever called *vātabalāsaka,* is a *vātabalāsakin*; by means of that fever he becomes swollen, (i.e.) provided with swellings, and adynamic, (i.e.) prostrated; this means that it is a secondary affection of someone with swelling.

A variant reading is : 'Being swollen, one is cured with difficulty'; (swollen) 'by it' has to be supplied.

Gadādhara says : with respect to *vātabalāsaka* it is stated that it belongs to the range of (that type of) morbid pallor called *kumbha.*

(It is called) *vātabalāsaka,* because it is started by wind and by *balāsaka*; *balāsaka* is phlegm; bile should also be noticed in this case. As has been said in another book : "The excited wind, having roused both (the other) morbific entities, moves through (the body); when it stays in the head, (it gives rise to) piercing pain in the head",[193] etc. And what has been said by Suśruta : "Those possessing knowledge about it say that *pralepaka* or *vātabalāsaka* (fever arise) from an excess of phlegm" (U. 39, 58ab),[194] (should be regarded to indicate that this occurs) on account of the fact that phlegm is of a constantly clinging character; that is Jejjaṭa's opinion. And its (i.e. of *vātabalāsaka*) dryness (arises) from the fact that the oleaginousness of phlegm has been overpowered by wind and bile, or (it arises) from the special faculty of the illness.

Ā:

Of what kind is (*vātabalāsaka*)? That has been said in the Suśruta-(saṃhitā) : "Those possessing knowledge about it say that *pralepaka* or *vātabalāsaka* (fever comes about) by an excess of phlegm" (U. 39,

58ab). Elsewhere, however, it is shown (to come about) by an excess of wind. How then can it be said here that it chiefly (afflicts one) by phlegm?

On this question the answer is: because it is started by phlegm that is staying in all the junctures, and set in motion by the wind. *vātabalāsaka* is truly (that fever) of which phlegm, set in motion by immature wind, is (the morbific entity) which starts it.

2, 41 : When it covers the limbs, as it were, with an unctuous substance of warmth and heaviness, when its fever is slow and it anoints (the body) all over,[195] being accompanied by a feeling of coldness,[196] it will be *pralepaka* (fever).
(A.s.Ni. 2, 87cd-88ab).

M:

pralepaka is made mention of ... Its fever is of a slow kind and it anoints (the body) all over.[197] It anoints all over because it anoints (the body) with warmth and heaviness, i.e. it attaches (warmth and heaviness) closely (to the body). And this (fever) arises from phlegm and bile. As Suśruta has said : "*pralepaka* and *vātabalāsaka* (fever)", etc. (U. 39, 58a). And as he said on (the subject of) consumption : "Fever, a burning sensation, diarrhoea and the appearance of blood (arise) from bile" (U. 41, 12cd), for this (kind of fever) is found in consumption. Others, however, (consider) this (fever) as verily arising from the three morbific entities, on account of the fact that it is generated by consumption, which arises from the three morbific entities; phlegm and bile (only) are designated (explicitly) because they have become perceptible.

2, 42-43 : When the nutrient fluid (derived) from the food has been combustively altered [198] and phlegm and bile are established in the body, half of the body becomes cold on account of that and half of the body becomes hot (42). When in the body bile is in a corrupted state and phlegm has become established at the extremities, hotness of the body (arises) on account of that and coldness of hands and feet (43).
(A.s.Ni. 2, 92cd-94ab).

2. 44 : When in the body phlegm is in a corrupted state and bile has become established at the extremities, coldness of the

limbs (arises) on account of that and hotness of hands and feet.[199]

2, 45-47 : When in a fever phlegm and wind stay in the skin, they generate coldness at the beginning, and when these two have become appeased, bile brings about a burning sensation at the end (45).

Likewise bile brings about an extremely burning sensation at the beginning, when it stays in the skin, but when it has been appeased, the other two (morbific entities) bring about a feeling of coldness at the end (46).[200]

These two fevers, beginning respectively with a burning sensation and with a feeling of coldness, are traditionally said to arise from combined action.

That one of these two in which a burning sensation (arises) first is troublesome and most difficult to cure (47).[201]

(Su.U. 39, 59-61).[202]

M :

Specific (types of) irregular fevers are made mention of ... When the nutrient fluid (derived) from the food has been combustively altered, i.e. has become corrupted, and the likewise corrupted phlegm and bile are established in the corrupted body, this (condition becomes the) ground on account of which half of the body becomes cold by phlegm and half of it hot by bile. This (division into) halves (occurs) in the form of Ardhanārīśvara [203] or in the form of Narasiṃha,[204] because there does not exist a regulating ground with regard to respective differences in accordance with the morbific entities. About the words 'in the body',[205] etc. (we remark that) in the body (means) in the internal fire, that is to say in the viscera. 'At the extremities' (means) : in the hands and feet. The other fever is mentioned by means of the reverse of the (already) stated sense, (i.e.) with the words 'when in the body phlegm', etc.

Gadādhara says about the words 'when (phlegm and wind) stay in the skin', etc. that the word skin points to the nutrient fluid staying in the skin, by means of a figurative application of that (i.e. the skin) in which (the nutrient fluid) resides. Jejjaṭa, however, declares it (to mean) the skin itself. With a view to this same (subject) Caraka says, after enumerating oils, etc. to be used in inunction in (cases of) fever :

"By these means a fever staying in the outer pathways becomes quickly appeased" (Ci. 3, 175cd).

'When these two' [206] (points to) phlegm and wind.

'When (these two) have become appeased' means : when the paroxysm of both has become appeased, for appeasement of a morbific entity does not occur in irregular (fevers), because the paroxysms return again. As Suśruta says : "And this irregular (fever) leaves the body never at all, because one is not released from languor, heaviness and leanness; but, after its paroxysm has passed, it seems to be gone; staying in another element, it is not experienecd at all, owing to its dissolved and subtle condition" (U. 39, 63cd-65ab).[207]

'The other two' [208] are wind and phlegm.

'(These two fevers) beginning respectively with a burning sensation and with a feeling of coldness' (indicates that) one begins with a burning sensation and the other with a feeling of coldness.

Now it may be asked, because it has been said with respect to the onset that both arise from the three morbific entities, why they are declared to arise from combined action; for, according to a settled rule, combined action (refers) to two and concerted action to three (morbific entities).[209]

The answer is : a combination is an intimate connection, and such (an intimate connection) occurs both with respect to two and to many (things); thus it is said (to refer) to three (morbific entities) in this case, but it is not thus everywhere; or, combination (means) the union of the two aspects of the morbific entities, (i.e.) their *soma*-like and fiery (aspect).

In this respect bile is the adjunctory (morbific entity) in a fever, beginning with a sense of coldness, and in (that one), beginning with a burning sensation, wind and phlegm are adjunctory (entities). The purpose of this is that the chief one should be treated predominantly (with measures that are) not in disagreement with the adjunctory one(s).

Of these two fevers, beginning with a burning sensation and a sense of coldness, the fever in which a burning sensation arises first is troublesome, (i.e.) bestowing suffering. From the fact that the (fever) beginning with a burning sensation is mentioned as one that is difficult to cure, it follows that the (fever) beginning with a feeling of coldness is easily curable.

Jejjaṭa says that still more irregular fevers, (i.e.) a nightly fever, etc., should be recognized, because they are implied in the (already) mentioned irregular fevers. And in another treatise it has been said :

"In a bodily being, with decline of bile and a congruous state of wind and phlegm, fever (arises) mainly at night, but (it arises) by day in one whose phlegm is deficient".[210]

In all irregular fevers wind is necessarily present, as Vṛddhasuśruta says : "An irregular fever arises never at all without wind, for phlegm and bile are devoid of motion; wind is always the moving agent".[211] Likewise (it has) also (been said) in the Videha(tantra) : "The wind is the cause of irregular fever because it moves in an irregular way".

It is also observed that these fevers change into another (type), due to the fact that they have acquired another ground, consisting of (another) season, etc. As for instance continuous (fever), after abandoning its own form, changes into one of (the series consisting of) double quotidian (fever), etc.; likewise quartan (fever acquires) the form of tertian (fever), etc. As Caraka says : "On account of the relative strength of season, (period of) day and night, morbific entity and *manas*, and certainly owing to the force of (past) actions, fever resorts to a particular time in each case" (Ci. 3, 75). The fact of the matter is that (the term) relative strength is connected with the (series of words) beginning with season and ending with *manas*; relative strength (means) strength and weakness; the word 'action' expresses past action here; fever resorts to a particular time in each case, as mentioned with regard to double quotidian (fever), etc.; thus is the grammatical construction.

Examples of the relative strength of season and (period of) day and night are : when quartan (fever), which has been produced in summer and in which wind is predominant, reaches the rainy season, it becomes, its force having been implenished on account of that season, one of (the series) ending with tertian and beginning with double quotidian (fever), owing to undue increase. In the same way a continuous fever which has been produced in the rainy season becomes, when it has reached the autumn and its force has been unduly decreased, one of (the series) beginning with double quotidian (fever), etc., owing to (this) undue decrease. The undue increase and decrease of bile and phlegm, brought about by the seasons, should be explained in the same way.

The words 'day and night' designate a certain number of days and nights, for double quotidian (fever), etc. do not change into another (type) owing to undue increase or decrease in one day and night, but only in a certain number (of days and nights). When in the beginning of the rainy season, autumn and spring the wind, etc. start quartan fever, this same (fever), after reaching the several days forming the middle (part of the season), is transformed into one of those (fevers) of which tertian is the first one, owing to undue increase. When it reaches the last days (of the season), a continuous (fever), (started by wind when it occurs in the early rainy season), started by bile when it occurs in the autumn and started by phlegm when it occurs in the spring, is, owing to undue decrease, transformed into one of (the series) beginning with double quotidian (fever), on account of the delicateness of the morbific entity.

(An example of transformation) on account of the relative strength of the morbific entity is : when phlegm is the morbific entity which changes double quotidian (fever), etc. into another (type), and it acquires grounds (consisting of substances which are) sweet, oleaginous, etc., (consisting of) sleep by day, etc., it brings about continuous fever, etc. The same conclusion should be reached with regard to wind and bile.

(Examples of transformation) on account of the relative strength of the *manas* are : when someone suffering from continuous fever is amply provided with joy and self-confidence, due to the preponderance of the constituent *sattva*,[212] it (i.e. continuous fever) becomes one of (the series consisting of) double quotidian (fever), etc.; when someone suffering from quartan fever is overpowered by despondency, because he is chiefly provided with the constituent *tamas*, it becomes one of (the series consisting of) tertian (fever), etc., according to the traditional statement : "Despondency (is the foremost) of those (entities) which make a disease increase" (fr. Ca.Sū. 25, 40).

Others, however, explain the word *manas* (as indicating) *buddhi*, metaphorically expressing the effect in the sense of the cause.[213]

(Examples) of its (i.e. of *buddhi*) relative strength are : when someone suffering from quartan fever performs wrong deeds, disrespecting the gods, etc., on account of errors in judgment, it then becomes one of those (fevers) of which tertian is the first one; when, however, someone would be provided with a judicious *buddhi*, on account of the increase of pure *sattva*, and performs auspicious deeds, consisting of *iṣṭi*,[214] *bali* [215] oblations, etc., propitiating the gods, then his continuous fever becomes one of (the series) beginning with double quotidian (fever), etc.

(Examples of transformation caused) by the force of (past) actions are : if the actions of someone, though he is suffering from continuous fever, should be expressed by a quartan (fever), even a continuous (fever) is transformed into a quartan; and if the actions of someone entered by a quartan fever are maturing at the time of this (fever), and are stronger (than those corresponding to a quartan fever), it is transformed into a continuous (fever). And this force of (former) actions should also be recognized with regard to the relative strength of season, day and night and morbific entity, because it is taught immediately after them.[216]

Ā:

... When bile is present in the trunk in a corrupted condition and phlegm is established at the extremities in a corrupted condition, this is the ground on account of which the limbs are hot and hands and feet are cold. The other fever is made mention of by the reverse (of what has been stated before) ... (This) reverse condition should be explained in the same way as before. Thereupon the distinct (types) of continuous (fever), etc. are dealt with by (referring to) that which precedes, (i.e.) a feeling of coldness (or) a burning sensation ... When phlegm and wind are present in the skin in an excited condition, they generate, at the beginning of the fever, a feeling of coldness in the skin. These two fevers, beginning (respectively) with a burning sensation and a feeling of coldness, are traditionally said to arise from combined action; 'by the great sages' should be supplied. Which two? At the beginning of the fever phlegm and wind, being present in the skin, produce a feeling of coldness first; when these two, phlegm and wind, are in an appeased condition, bile brings about a burning sensation at the end. In the very same way bile brings about an extremely burning sensation at the beginning when it stays in the skin; when the bile has become appeased, the other two, wind and phlegm, bring about a feeling of coldness. When the paroxysm of these two, phlegm and wind, has become appeased, because the proper time has passed or because contact has been established with an opposed (entity), bile brings about a sensation of inner burning. The word 'and' (indicates the presence of) fainting, etc. When, however, bile stays in the skin, it brings about an extremely burning sensation in the skin; when (this) bile, causing a burning sensation in the skin, has become appeased, (i.e.) when its paroxysm has passed, the other two, phlegm and wind, bring about a feeling of coldness at the end. The word 'etc.' (indicates the presence of) emesis, lassitude, etc. These two are traditionally said to arise from combined action. Of these two fevers, beginning (respectively) with a burning sensation and a feeling of coldness, that one which begins with a burning sensation is troublesome, (which means that) it bestows an extreme amount of suffering; the fact that mention is made of two specifications, (to wit) 'it is troublesome and most difficult to cure' shows that it is extremely difficult to cure, and that (the fever) beginning with a feeling of coldness is easily curable. For which reason? On account of the fact that the power of a disease is (something) inconceivable.[217]

The statement that they arise from combined action is not in disagreement (with the traditional doctrine), because of its connection with the statement that one should treat (a disease) in accordance to what is above and below, without (giving) predominance (to one of the entities).

2, 48-54 : Heaviness, nausea in the cardiac region, adynamia, vomiting and anorexia are the signs with regard to a fever staying in the nutrient fluid; moreover, dejection arises in the one (suffering from it) (48).
Spitting of blood, a burning sensation, mental confusion, vomiting, agitation, confused speech, boils and thirst (are the signs) with regard to a fever that has reached the blood in men (49).
Cramp in the calves, thirst, furtherance of the appearance of urine and faeces, heat, a sensation of inner burning, tossing about and languor will occur in a fever staying in the flesh (50).
Perspiration to a vehement degree, thirst, fainting, confused speech and certainly vomiting, a bad smell, anorexia and languor, along with the inability to endure, (occur) in (a fever) staying in the fat (51).
A cutting pain in the bones, rumbling,[218] shortness of breath, emptying of the bowels, certainly vomiting, and tossing about of the limbs, these (signs occur) in a fever staying in the bones (52).
(The sensation of) entering into darkness, hiccup, cough, a sense of coldness, emesis, a sensation of inner burning, intense shortness of breath and a trenchant pain at the vital points (occur) in (a fever) staying in the marrow (53).
When the fever stays in the seat of semen one may die and (there occur) especially erections and ejaculations (54).
(Su.U. 39, 83-89ab).[219]

additional stanza : (Those fevers) which reside in the nutrient fluid and blood are curable and those which stay in flesh and fat as well; (those) which stay in bones and marrow are difficult (to cure), but (that one) which stays in the semen is incurable. (Ca.Ci. 3, 83).

M :

There are additional characteristics of the above fevers by wind, etc., in accordance with the specific elements which are subject to corruption. As has been said : "May the judicious physician tell (us) about the characteristics of fevers when they are staying in the nutrient fluid, etc., as (he told us) about those of fevers arising from wind, bile and phlegm" (Su.U. 39, 90cd-91ab). And these are mentioned on behalf of the employment of a therapy in (fevers from) wind, etc. that is not in disagreement with the elements (consisting of) the nutrient fluid, etc. For that reason they are dealt with ...

Nausea in the cardiac region is the condition (of one who is) as being about to vomit the morbific entity staying in the cardiac region, because the nutrient fluid stays in the cardiac region. The words 'staying in the nutrient fluid' (indicate) that the nutrient fluid is specifically subject to corruption in this case, because in really all fevers (the morbific entities) follow the nutrient fluid in its course.

Dejection is weariness of the mind.

About 'cramp in the calves', etc. (we remark that) the calf is a round mass of flesh of the lower leg under the knee; cramp of the calf is a cramp of it, (i.e.) a painful sensation as by painfully pressing it by means of a stick, etc.; in the same way (one should understand it) also elsewhere.

Furtherance of the appearance of urine and faeces is a condition in which urine and faeces are coming forth.

Heat (appears) externally; this serves to stress (this symptom) in a special way because this condition is usually present in all fevers. In the variant reading 'internal heat, mental confusion and tossing about' internal heat means a sensation of inner burning. Tossing about is moving the hands, etc. (to and fro). Vehement perspiration (occurs) because warmth (in the form of sweat) is the impurity of (the element) fat.[220] A bad smell of the body (originates) on account of a morbid alteration of that same (impurity).

Inability to endure is the inability to endure painful sensations; according to Kārtika (it means) an inclination to wrath.[221] Concerning the words 'a cutting pain in the bones' (we remark that) the meaning is 'as if (the bones) are cut', (i.e.) a distressing pain as in a fracture. (Words which are used in the sense of other meanings express notions conveyed by those meanings without recourse to an interpretation in the literal sense); as for instance (in the use of the words) *agnir māṇavakaḥ* (fire is meant without recourse to the literal meaning of *māṇavaka*, i.e. a youth). In the same way (the terms) cutting pain, etc. should be regarded also elsewhere.

Rumbling is grumbling; as to the variant 'contraction' : its meaning is a contraction of the bones themselves.

Entering into darkness (means) non-perception (of light) as if one has entered into darkness.

The characteristics of intense shortness of breath will be set forth in the paragraph on shortness of breath.[222]

The word vital point denotes the heart,[223] on account of its predominant position (as a vital point), says Kārtika; a sensation as if it is trenched is a trenchant pain in the vital point.

About the words 'death', etc. (in case) of (a fever) staying in the semen (we remark that) one should construct (the sentence as follows): with respect to these, (i.e.) among these fevers staying in the elements (consisting of) the nutrient fluid, etc., one may die when it stays in the seat of semen (semen and its seat).

Semen-seat (means) semen and its seat (but not the seat of semen), because semen, on account of the fact that it stays in the whole body, does not originate from a fixed seat; thus says Kārtika. (As has been said : "The best of physicians should know that semen stays in the bodies of men like clarified butter in milk and treacle in sugar-cane juice") (Su.Śā. 4, 21).[224]

The word 'especially' (indicates) the copious emission of semen and also of other (elements), (i.e.) blood, etc.; thus it is said.

Ā :

... Adynamia is languor of the parts of the body ... Although this one, because it has reached (only) one element, (viz.) the nutrient fluid, is continuous (fever) itself, it is nevertheless described here, in order to enumerate (the fevers) staying in the elements in their due order ... Mental confusion is the condition of someone who has lost his mind ... (Instead of) rumbling some read contraction; this (word) should be

connected with the words 'of the bones', because it is (placed) near (to them).

Now it is said that death (occurs) in a fever staying in the semen, but it may be rightly stated (as an objection) that death also occurs without that, for this semen stays in the whole body, and therefore (death can occur) on account of the fact that (a fever) reaches the semen also when it has overpowered the elements (consisting of) the nutrient fluid, etc. (The answer is) that it is not thus, because semen, though staying in the whole body, reaches the skin in due order by reason of the interposition of the *kalās*.

And if one argues : how can a fever, even in due order, reach the semen, (the answer is) : it reaches the semen after having passed beyond the other elements.[225] And in the Suśruta(saṃhitā) it has been said : "As a fire the fuel of which has been consumed, as poison that has destroyed the elements (of the body), thus fever, having accomplished its duty, becomes appeased after it has destroyed the body" (U. 39, 89cd-90ab). In another treatise it has also been said : ...[226]

2, 55 : In the rainy season, autumn and spring a fever is natural (when it arises) from wind, etc., in due order; when it is different it is based on a deviation (from the natural state). This (latter) one is difficult to cure, as well as that natural one which arises from wind.[227]

(A.h.Ni. 2, 50).[228]

M :

... Natural is that fever which (arises) in the rainy season, etc. from wind, etc., in due order; a (fever) by wind (is natural) in the rainy season, one by bile in the autumn and one by phlegm in the spring. (A fever) which differs from this (order) is based on a deviation, as for instance a bilious one in the rainy season, etc. That one mentioned as based on a deviation is difficult to cure; that is to say that a natural one is easily curable. As has been said : "But a natural one, arising in spring or autumn, is easily curable" (Ca.Ci. 3, 42ab).

The statement about the naturalness of (a fever) arising from wind, brought forward here by Vāgbhaṭa,[229] is not assented to by others, because it is a condition not distinguished from a deviated one on account of the fact it is curable with difficulty. Nor does Jatūkarṇa read it, because he says : "It is usually natural (arising) in spring and autumn; (when it arises) in another (season) it is based on a deviation".[230]

The answer to this question is as follows : natural condition is not a technical term serving to denote easy curability, but the meaning of the word is in accordance with its derivation, as (in the case of words like) potter, etc. For that reason for which a morbific entity, excited in accordance with the season, is spoken of as (being in) a natural condition, (a fever) arisen from it (is called) natural. Therefore Caraka and Jatūkarṇa, reflecting that (a fever) by wind, though being in a natural condition, is difficult to cure on account of the very nature of the morbific entity, like (a fever) based on a deviation, do not deal with it, because it has the same peculiarity as a (fever) based on a deviation by its being curable with difficulty, but not because a natural condition is absent; thus is the view of Vāgbhaṭa. Other diseases are curable with difficulty on account of the fact that they are based on a natural state, but fever is easily curable (when that condition exists) in consequence of the special faculty of the illness. For in another treatise (it is said) : "The characteristic of easy curability in fever is the comparability between season and morbific entity, in urinary disease comparability of the (constituent) subject to corruption and in visceral swelling (arising) from blood the presence of (blood) during a long time".[231]

2, 56-57 : The wind, having become corrupted in the rainy season, may bring about fever, attended by bile and phlegm, and bile (may bring it about) in the autumn, with phlegm as its auxiliary force (56).

By reason of the nature of these (to wit bile and phlegm), and on account of the period of emission, abstinence from food (need) not be feared in those (cases).

Phlegm (may give rise to fever) in the spring and it may be attended by wind and bile (57).

(A.h.Ni. 2, 51-52).[232]

M :

With the words 'in the rainy season', etc. mention is made of the due order of production of these same natural fevers for the sake of specific therapy.

'Corrupted' (means) excited, because (wind) has accumulated in the summer. 'Attended by bile and phlegm' (means) : with bile and phlegm, which are suitable to the time of that (season), as adjunctory factors. As has been said : "On account of the vapours, the discharges from the clouds and the acid maturative alteration of the water, the wind, etc. become excited in the rainy season, when the strength of the fire has declined" (Ca.Sū. 6, 34).[233] (A remark is made about the structure of the sentence). About the words 'bile', etc. (we remark that they) are connected with what has been said before (in the following way): 'also bile, having become corrupted in the autumn, may bring about fever'; in the same way should be supplied here: 'phlegm (may bring about fever) in the spring'. Corruption of the bile (occurs) in the autumn, because it has accumulated in the rainy season.

An auxiliary force is an adjunctory factor; its ground is its very conformity with the moisture of the rainy season. 'By reason of the nature of these', etc., (i.e.) by reason of the very state of being of bile and phlegm, abstinence from food, (i.e.) fasting, (need) not be feared in fevers which are brought about by these (morbific entities). As has been said: "Phlegm and bile tolerate intense fasting when they are liquid elements, because decline of immature matter (occurs); after that (decline of immature matter) wind does not tolerate (it) for an instant".[234]

On account of the period of emission as a ground, abstinence from food (should) not be feared. The period of emission (consists of) rainy season, autumn and winter. The living beings are in this (period) provided with accumulated strength, because the moon is strong. The period of resorption, however, (consists of) the cool season, spring and summer. The strength of living beings is in that (period) depleted, because the sun is strong. That is the explanation according to scientific doctrine.

The variant reading 'by reason of the nature of these and of the period of emission' should be arranged as follows: by reason of the nature of phlegm, wind and bile, and by reason of the nature of the period of emission.

Concerning the words 'phlegm', etc. (we remark that) wind and bile attend it, (i.e.) phlegm; the sense is that they exist in the form of adjunctory factors. The ground is here that (the season of) spring leads to excitement of wind and bile, on account of the fact that it (forms) the middle (part) of the period of resorption, and because it is of a fiery and dry character. As has been said in the Caraka(saṃhitā): "In the middle of the period of resorption it may be attended by wind and bile" (Ci. 3, 47ab). On account of the nature of phlegm and bile fasting is certainly suitable in this case, but it cannot be employed without fear, because it is the middle of the period of resorption.

For that very reason the words 'abstinence from food (need) not be feared in those (cases)' are read immediately preceding it; (if things were) otherwise, it would be read at the end of the whole (passage).

Ā:

Phlegm is the auxiliary force, (i.e.) the adjunctory factor of this bile, which has accumulated in the rainy season, has become excited in the autumn, and strives after the bringing about of bilious fever in the autumn.

An auxiliary force is that (force) which follows the (main) force; in the same way as for example another army follows some independent king, provided with an army, consisting of elephants, chariots, horses and men, who fights with his enemies, in order to augment its power, thus phlegm augments in autumn the force of the independent bile which is bringing about fever.

Candranandana, however, comments as follows: What is the reason that abstinence from food, (i.e.) fasting, is without danger in this bilious fever occurring in the autumn? By reason of their nature, (i.e.) because fevers (arising) from bile and phlegm are curable by fasting; likewise on account of the period of emission, (i.e.) due to the fact that (this period) of time is called the period of emission; in that period apprehension about a reverse result from fasting does not occur, because fever springs up from the receptacle of undigested food. And there is the (following) statement about the curability of (fevers, arising from) bile and phlegm, by fasting: "Phlegm and bile tolerate intense fasting when they are liquid, because the immature matter declines (by it); after that (decline of immature matter), wind does not tolerate (it) for an instant". Aruṇadatta, however, comments (as follows): About the words 'by reason of their nature' (we remark that) the word 'their' refers to the fever by wind and the fever by bile, arisen in the rainy season and autumn (respectively); there is no danger in abstinence from food (in the case) of such a natural fever... About the words 'and by reason of the period of emission' (we remark that the period of) time, implied by rainy season and autumn, (called) the period of emission, is of a moon-like nature'; therefore there is in a fever produced in this (period of) time no apprehension of a reverse result by fasting in such a way as there (would) be danger from abstinence from food in a fever (produced) at another time, on account of the very nature of the period of resorption and by reason of the fact that wind and bile (act as) auxiliary forces; that is the sense.[235]

2, 58ab : Appearance or even increase of all (fevers occurs) at the very (period of) time of each (of the morbific entities).

(A.h.Ni. 2, 23ab).

M :

Considering that (a particular period of) time is also a characteristic of a specific morbific entity, it is said : 'at the very (period of) time', etc. 'At the very (period of) time of each (of the morbific entities)', (i.e.) at which (period of) time excitement of wind, etc. occurs, at that (period of time) the fever arising from it appears, (i.e.) its production is brought about, or it increases; or (its sense is) : appearance of a permanent fever or increase of an irregular fever (occurs).

2, 58cd : That which has been mentioned as an origin (leads to) a reverse (result of) therapeutic diagnosis; initiation of (positive) therapeutic diagnosis (is achieved) by means of (measures) contrary (to the origin).

(A.h.Ni. 2, 23cd).

M :

Considering that therapeutic diagnosis with a positive and a reverse result are also, in the same way (as time), characteristics (of a specific morbific entity), it is said : '(by what has been mentioned as) an origin', etc.

By means of that regimen of diet, behaviour, etc., which have been mentioned as being origins, a reverse (result of) therapeutic diagnosis (is arrived at), (i.e.) suffering (arises). By means of contrary (measures, i.e.) a regimen of diet and behaviour contrary to the morbific entity, etc., initiation of (positive) therapeutic diagnosis (is achieved), (i.e.) a disposition which generates well-being (is reached).

2, 59-61ab : A sensation of excessive inner burning, thirst, confused speech, shortness of breath, giddiness, piercing pain in junctures and bones, absence of perspiration and suppression of (the evacuation of) the morbific entity and the excrements (59), these are considered to be the signs of a fever with an internal impulse.

An excessive general sense of external glowing heat and mildness of thirst, etc. (60) are the signs of (a fever) with an external impulse, along with its easy curability.

(Ca.Ci. 3, 39cd-41).[236]

M :

Among the above-mentioned fevers some are provided with an internal, some with an external impulse, by force of the onset; their characteristics are made mention of ...

A variant of shortness of breath is adynamia; that is not a suitable (reading) according to Jejjaṭa, because in the Suśruta(saṃhitā) the very (fever) with an internal impulse is described with the name deep (fever) [237] and in its (description) also shortness of breath is read. Suppression is non-appearance. About (the sentence) beginning with 'a general sense of glowing heat' (we remark that) with the word 'etc.' in '(mildness) of thirst, etc.' the above-mentioned confusion of speech, etc.[238] (should be) understood. Mildness (means) a very slight degree (of intensity).

By mentioning that (a fever with an external impulse) is easily curable it is pointed out that a fever with an internal impulse is curable with difficulty or incurable, according to the statement by Suśruta : "One should give up someone afflicted by a fever with a deep and sharp impulse" (U. 39, 93cd).[239]

Ā :

... Suppression of the morbific entity and the excrements is the non-appearance of wind and faeces ...

2, 61cd-63ab : Effusion of saliva, sickness, a polluted condition of the cardiac region, anorexia (61), lassitude, inertia, absence of digestive alteration, an altered taste in the mouth, heaviness of the limbs, annihilation of the sense of hunger, (production of) a great amount of urine, stiffness and a strong fever (62) are the signs of an immature fever.
One should not give a remedy in that case.[240]

2, 63cd : For a remedy makes the fever of someone whose morbific entity is immature flare up more strongly.

additional *pādas* : (A purifying and an appeasing remedy bring about an irregular fever).[241]

2, 64-65 : An excessive impulse of the fever, thirst, confused speech, shortness of breath, giddiness, appearance of the impurities and nausea are the characteristics of (a fever) that is in the stage of maturation (64).

Hunger, emaciation, lightness of the limbs, mildness of the fever, appearance of the morbific entity and a period of eight days are the characteristics of a fever that has become mature (65).

(Ca.Ci. 3, 136cd-138ab).[242]

M:

For the sake of specific therapy mention is made of the characteristics of an immature, maturing and mature (fever) ... (An objector may ask) : is it not a contradiction to state that 'one should not give a remedy in that case'? For Caraka has said that remedies are of two kinds : consisting of a (medicinal) substance and not consisting of such a substance.[243] With respect to this (distinction, remedies) consisting of a (medicinal) substance are a *kaṣāya*, etc., and those not consisting of a (medicinal) substance reducing measures, sudation, etc. In this case reducing measures and the *ṣaḍaṅgārdhaśṛta* [244] are employed. The answer (to this objection) is : the word remedy indicates here the preparation of medicines except for the preparation of foods and drinks, but not the group of remedial agents in a general sense.

But if one argues : how can this acknowledgment arise, (the answer is) : because one observes that in a fresh fever remedies are prescribed, although the drinking of remedies is prohibited. One should understand it to be the same in (a fever) in the stage of maturation, because, in that case too, immaturity is a really existing entity.

About the words 'hunger', etc.[245] Jejjaṭa says that these words, because they do not form a compound, (constitute), dissociated or associated, and together with the period of eight days, the characteristics of a mature (fever). Haricandra, however, is of the opinion that, even when the period of eight days is absent, maturity (is indicated) by hunger, etc. or by appearance of the morbific entity, and by a period of eight days only, when hunger, etc. are absent; both the (period of) time and the characteristics are taught out of the wish to do good to pupils.

There are two kinds of immaturity, one of the nutrient fluid and another of the morbific entity. Immaturity of the nutrient fluid is characterized by an altered taste in the mouth, etc., immaturity of the morbific entity (appears) in the form of freshness [246] (of a fever), and this (latter type) disappears in just eight days.

The ground of this (phenomenon) has been stated by Haricandra ("The impurities staying in the seven elements maturate in just seven days; therefore a fever is usually proclaimed to be mature on the eighth day", Ca.Ci. 3, 276cd-277ab); in a period of just eight days maturity (is reached), because the immature matter has been brought to maturation by the fires of the seven elements in seven days.

Immaturity of the nutrient fluid, however, can also last longer than eight days. Jejjaṭa agrees to this notion as well, because he writes in his commentary on the Caraka- and Suśruta(saṃhitā) as follows : "Immaturity in the form of fresh(ness of a fever, i.e. immaturity of the morbific entity), disappears in eight days, but immaturity of the nutrient fluid can last longer than this (period)". The purpose of this (distinction) is that no remedial agent is employed in immaturity in the form of freshness, whereas a maturation-promoting one is given in immaturity of the nutrient fluid. For that very reason Caraka says : "After six days have passed, one should give as a drink to a fever-patient, who has used light food besides the prescribed diet, a maturation-promoting or appeasing *kaṣāya*" (Ci. 3, 161ab;160cd).[247] After stating "When the fever is mild, the body is light and the impurities are moving, one should discern that the morbific entity of the fever is mature and give a remedial agent appropriate to it" (Su.U. 39, 115), Suśruta has said : "Some are of the opinion that a remedial agent should be given after seven days, others have concluded that one should give it after ten days" (U. 39, 119cd-120ab); it is taught by this that a maturation-promoting agent is not given within (a period of) seven days; that is the explanation given to it by Kārtikakuṇḍa.

Is there no contradiction between the words of Caraka : "After six days have passed (one should give) to a fever-patient" (fr. Ci. 3, 161ab) and those of Suśruta : "After seven (days and) nights", etc. (fr. U. 39, 119cd), because, after six days have passed, the seventh day is present and a *kaṣāya* is prescribed on that day?

The answer (to this objection) is : after six days have elapsed, the patient (may eat) light food besides the prescribed diet on the seventh (day) and one should give him as a drink a *kaṣāya* on the eighth (day); thus (the sentence) should be arranged according to Cakra(pāṇidatta), because there is ellipsis of the word 'eighth', in the same way as (in the term) 'rice boiled in meat broth',[248] on account of the fact that (otherwise) there would be disagreement of the above-mentioned statement by Suśruta with the (following) saying about the morbific entity : "A remedy makes the fever of someone whose morbific entity is immature flare up more strongly" (2, 63cd).

Kārtikakuṇḍa expresses the same idea in a different way as follows :

it is said 'after six days have elapsed', because of (a way of) counting with omission of the day on which the production of the fever has been brought about, in the same way as one calculates, with exclusion of the day on which a *basti* [249] has been given, the (period of) time during which (the application of a *basti* should be) avoided.[250]

In the same way should also be explained the following statement : "One should give to a patient with an immature (fever) a remedial agent in the form of a drink on the seventh day, or, having observed that (his fever) is mature, one should treat him with an appeasing (remedial agent)".[251]

This same view about the drinking of a *kaṣāya* on the seventh day, as it has been explained, deserves to be sought for according to Bhaṭṭāraharicandra, because of the disagreement of (the words of) Suśruta, etc. The author of the Candrikā has also explained it as follows : "The period of immaturity of a fever (consists of) seven days, in the same way as (it consists of) four days in diseases of the eyes; during that (period) neither maturation-promoting nor appeasing and purificatory (drugs) should be given". What Hārita has said, immediately following upon (his words about) a thin gruel, etc. : "One should apply this therapeutical procedure during six (days and) nights and on the seventh day one should drink commixtures of *kaṣāya*s which destroy the fever and are well prepared", and also the statement by Kharanāda : "Thus has been proclaimed that the precept which is salutary in a new(ly acquired) fever (is valid) for six (days and) nights; after that (period) a maturation-promoting or appeasing (remedy) is salutary", should be regarded to substantiate the (period of) eight days, in the same way as (already mentioned) above. Or, (as an alternative), these two statements refer to a fever by bile. As Suśruta says (in his statement) beginning with : "After seven (days and) nights" (U. 39, 119c), up to : "Or the remedy should be given in a bilious fever that has arisen a short time ago, as well as to someone who has recently acquired (another type of) fever when there is maturation of the morbific entity" (U. 39, 120cd-121ab).[252]

This above-mentioned drinking of a maturation-promoting *kaṣāya* after seven days should not be considered in (the case that) the immaturity has become raised to an extraordinary degree. As Vāgbhaṭa says : "Some say that a remedial agent should be given after seven days, others (say) after ten days; some (again say it should be given) to someone after he has eaten light food, but not when there is abundance of immature matter; because there is a rise of the impulse of the morbific entity [253] in a person filled by a sharp fever; or, when an extreme accumulation of the morbific entity brings about lassitude and a feeling of dampness, a remedial agent makes a fever that is not in the stage of maturation flare up more strongly" (A.h.Ci. 1, 42-44ab).[254]

It can be succinctly stated as follows : "Some therapists, who are well versed (in this matter), express the following idea : after seven days one should employ a maturation-promoting agent in a fever that is immature (but) has not become arrested (in its development); in a mature (fever) one should employ an appeasing agent, and in an immature (fever) that has become arrested (in its development) no remedial agent (at all)". The comprehensive treatment (of this subject), however, should be looked up in the paragraph about decisions concerning the *kaṣāyas*.

One should understand that the characteristics of a mature fever may also be applied to a fever of long standing with regard to a suitable therapy. As has been said in another treatise : "Up to seven days ...", etc.[255] Jatūkarṇa has said as well : "A (fever) of thirteen days' duration is (called a fever) of long standing". But what is said in another treatise : "A fever that has become attenuated after the lapse of thrice seven days, and brings about splenomegaly and adynamia of the (transforming) fire, is called a fever of long standing" should be regarded as having in view an extremely old (fever)".[256]

Ā :

... Sickness is a condition as if vomit has come near (to the throat). A polluted condition of the cardiac region (indicates) a condition as if the cardiac region is filled, (or) heavy, according to others. *kṣunnāśa* (means) that no sneezing occurs or that (the sense of) hunger has been annihilated ...[257] Others read perseverance instead of a period of eight days.[258]

2, 66ab : In strong persons with very slight morbific entities a fever is curable and not accompanied by secondary affections.

(Ca.Ci. 3, 50ab).

M :

Mention is made of the characteristics of curability of fever ... It is curable in strong men; as has been said : "Health is a condition based on strength" (Ca.Vi. 3, 29). 'In those with slight morbific entities' (means) : in those with not exceedingly strong morbific entities. The secondary affections of fever are cough, etc., as has been said in another treatise : "Cough, fainting, inability to eat, vomiting, thirst, diarrhoea, seizing of the faeces, hiccup, shortness of breath and a cutting pain in the body are the ten secondary affections of fever".[259]

2, 66cd-67ab : A fever which has arisen from many and strong grounds and which is provided with many characteristics (66) makes an end to life, as well as (a fever) which quickly annihilates the senses.

(Ca.Ci. 3, 50cd-51ab).

2, 67cd-68ab : A deep fever, lasting for a long time, is incurable when it occurs in a person whose (constituents) have declined and who is swollen, and a strong fever, making partings in the hair of the head, (is incurable) as well.

(Ca.Ci. 3, 52cd 53ab).

2, 68cd-69ab : A fever should be known as a deep one when it is accompanied by a sensation of inner burning, thirst, obstructive abdominal swelling to an extreme degree and the appearance of shortness of breath and cough.

(Su.U. 39, 92cd-93ab).

2, 69cd-70ab : A deep (fever) which is irregular from the start or lasts for a long time kills one whose (constituents) have declined and who is very dry.[260]

2, 70cd-71ab : A man whose consciousness is altered and who gasps for breath,[261] or who, fallen down, remains lying and who is tormented by coldness and feels hot inside, will die from fever.

(Su.Sū. 33, 15).

2, 71cd-72ab : Fevers kills a human being presenting horripilation, red eyes, a feeling of compression and piercing pains in the cardiac region, and certainly someone who snorts by way of his mouth.[262]

(Su.Sū. 33, 16).

2, 72cd-73ab : Fever wrecks a man who presents hiccup, shortness of breath and thirst,[263] who is mentally confused, whose eyes are moving agitatedly, who snorts continuously and whose (constituents) have declined.

(Su.Sū. 33, 17).[264]

2, 73cd-74ab : One should give up a fever-patient, the lustre of whose skin and whose senses have been damaged, whose (constituents) have declined, who is oppressed by anorexia and afflicted by deep and sharp paroxysms (of the fever).

(Su.U. 39, 93cd-94ab).

M:

The characteristics of incurable fevers are made mention of ... Is it not thus, that (a fever) which arises by means of strong and many grounds is verily (a fever) showing many characteristics? So what is the use of the term '(provided) with many characteristics'?

The answer (to this objection) is : the morbific entities, each excited in accordance with its own grounds, are the grounds of really every disease; if (these entities), dependent upon past actions, reach a specific (type of) complete (development) with the characteristics of the onset, they lead to (a state of) fever; in that way they bring about a condition with many or with few characteristics, bound up with the relative distance of the accompanying causes, consisting of (the constituents) which are subject to corruption, etc.[265] For thus it has been said in another treatise : "The excited wind, etc. are making visible in the body, on account of their junction with an element, etc., one, two, three or many morbid alterations".[266] Or, due to the fact that there is an inherence (in a morbid alteration, the qualities of which are) incongruous with the altered state, (an entity) with many grounds may be provided with (only) few characteristics, and one with few grounds with many characteristics ...

'Quickly annihilating the senses' (indicates that) this (fever), even when scarcely produced and being treated, injures the ability of the senses, characterized by the perception of colours, etc.; this (fever) is incurable, though not because it has been neglected; other diseases, however, injure the ability of the senses, and evolve towards incurability when they are neglected. Thus (a disease), though provided with many (of its) characteristics, should be understood to be treatable all the same, but only when in its initial stage.

The senses should be understood to be eleven (in number), in accordance with the Sāṃkhya doctrine,[267] and because Caraka [268] and Suśruta [269] have taught it to be thus : "Vision, hearing, smell, taste and touch are the senses of perception, the functions of hands, feet, anus, generative organs and tongue are the senses of action, the *manas* is of the nature of both (these series)". It should be considered to be thus wherever (the senses are made mention of).

Fever, occurring in a person who suffers from decline and is swollen, is another characteristic, indicative of incurability. About 'deep and lasting for a long time' (we remark that) deep (means): staying in an inner element; or deep (means) : as if it were deeply (seated), in which case one cannot possibly ascertain (whether it arises) from wind or another (morbific entity); but others say that deep means : with an internal impulse.[270] 'Lasting for a long time' (means), according to Jejjaṭa : 'attending one during a long period of time', according to Cakra(pāṇidatta) : 'resembling the long night, i.e. death', the sense being that it is incurable.[271] According to this (latter) opinion, 'lasting for a long time' should be connected with that which precedes, and 'incurable' with that which follows (in the stanza).

'Making partings in the hair of the head' (indicates a fever) which brings about, without any cause, (the appearance of) partings in the hair of the head. For in another treatise it has been said : "A person whose hair shows partings, whose brows are contracted and curved downwards, and whose eyelashes fall out, will die soon" (Su.Sū. 31, 10).[272] Among the meanings of 'deep' as explained by Jejjaṭa, etc. (the correct one) is here 'with an internal impulse' and that is the meaning approved of by Mādhavakara. For that very reason (Mādhava) writes down, immediately following upon it, the characteristics of deep (fever) according to Suśruta. That very (fever), which is described in the Caraka(saṃhitā) as (a fever) with an internal impulse, is the same as that described as a deep one in the Suśruta(saṃhitā), because (their) characteristics are comparable and a description (as) separate (fevers) does not exist.

'Accompanied by obstructive abdominal swelling' (means) accompanied by a condition in which the morbific entity is blocked.[273] (About) the stanza beginning with 'from the start' (we make the following remarks). When someone has an irregular fever from the start, (i.e.) from the production (of the fever) onwards, it is incurable. An irregular fever, however, (brought about) by improper conduct, etc. of a person with a permanent fever, or of someone abandoned by fever, is certainly curable. And this irregularity should be understood (to occur) in the form of double quotidian (fever), etc., and not at all as an irregular (fever) in a general sense, because irregularity also occurs in a fever by wind. 'Lasting a long time' [274] has already been explained. Its occurrence is no case of repetition; it has been written down because it is a statement from another treatise, and with awareness of the fact that it serves to substantiate the meaning : (lasting for an) exceedingly (long time). In the same way should be spoken about 'deep'. A variant reading of 'of someone who is very dry' is 'of someone (whose eyes are) not winking'; this means: of someone whose eyes are always opened wide.

'With an altered consciousness' (means) : with a (mental) perturbance; 'one gasps for breath' (indicates that) one is mentally confused.[275] 'Who, fallen down, remains lying' (means) : who remains lying exactly in the same position, after falling down, and who is quite unable to get up. 'Who is tormented by coldness and feels hot inside' (means) : who is tormented by coldness at the exterior (of the body) and feels hot inside, (i.e.) who has a sensation of inner burning.

'Who presents horripilation' (means) : the hairs of whose limbs stand erect. 'Who presents a feeling of compression and piercing pains in the cardiac region' is someone who feels his cardiac region as heavily pressed by an object that consists of a compact mass, like a round stone,[276] etc.; others, however, say (it means) : with various kinds of piercing pain.

About 'who snorts by way of his mouth only' (we remark that) the word 'only' excludes the nose, in order to substantiate that the open mouth (is aimed at); its sense is : someone who breathes harshly.

About 'hiccup', etc. (we remark that the meaning is) : incurability (occurs) by the agglomeration (of symptoms consisting of) hiccup, etc., and also by one of them if it is strong. 'Who is mentally confused' (indicates) someone possessed of mental confusion. 'Whose eyes are moving agitatedly' (indicates) someone whose vision is impaired or someone whose eyes move unsteadily. 'Someone who snorts continuously' (indicates) someone who incessantly breathes harshly.

About (the stanza) beginning with '(the lustre of whose skin) has been damaged' (we make the following remarks). (It points to a patient) the lustre, (i.e.) the ability, of whose vision, etc. is damaged, (i.e. whose senses) do not perceive their own objects; or (it points to a patient) the lustre, (i.e.) the brightness, (of whose skin) and whose senses are damaged.[277] Instead of 'someone troubled by anorexia', Jejjaṭa reads here the (following) variant, consisting of two parts : 'someone who is wicked and assaulted (by calamities)'. He explains this (as follows) :

someone who is wicked is someone whose inner organ [278] is corrupted, and someone assaulted (by calamities) is someone visited by the secondary affections, (consisting of) shortness of breath, etc. But the sense of the variant reading 'visited by wicked ones' is : frequented by *rākṣasas*,[279] etc.[280]

In other treatises still other (incurable fevers) should be looked up because they are implied by these (above-mentioned) characteristics of incurability. As for instance : "The person who in a dream drinks alcoholic beverages in the company of *pretas*,[281] and is dragged by a dog, leaves life, after having got a very dreadful fever.[282] The person, lacking strength and flesh, who presents a fever which occurs during the morning, and a severe dry cough, is just like a *preta* (Ca.I. 6, 10). The person, lacking strength and flesh, who presents a fever which occurs during the afternoon, and a severe cough (productive) of phlegm, is just like a *preta*.[283] The general sense of glowing heat of fever, thirst, fainting, decline of force and disjunction of the junctures suddenly arise in someone who is about to die (A.s.Śā. 11, 42cd-43ab). The person from whose face perspiration vehemently falls down at daybreak,[284] who is plagued by *lepa* fever, can recover life only with difficulty (A.s.Śā. 11, 43cd-44ab).[285] Death (occurs) in that man on whose forehead an extremely mucilaginous sweat occurs and who is ice cold; being tormented by coldness, because (this fever) is of a very mucilaginous character and brings about the flowing out (of impure matter) on all sides in a cold living being; if it, staying in the throat, does not go to the chest, the human being (suffering from it) certainly goes to the house of Yama.[286] That person will certainly die, even if (his body) is (of a) gross (frame), whose sweat flows down from the forehead, whose junctures and ligaments are slackened, and who will faint when one causes him to stand up.[287] When someone's sweat, being very copious and mucilaginous, appears from all sides, one should announce the death of that patient, suffering from coldness".[288]

The curability and incurability of fever according to the different constellations, as it has been described by means of the text : "An illness, produced in the lunar mansion of impregnation, of birth, in that called *nidhana*, *pratyara* or *vipatkara*, leads to vexation or death, but a fever, arisen in (the lunar mansion called) Aśvinī, ceases after six (days and) nights" (A.s.Ni. 1, 21-22ab),[289] etc., should be examined in (the treatises by) Hārīta [290] and Vṛddhavāgbhaṭa,[291] but has not been written down here for fear of (giving) a too detailed (exposition).

The paragraph on incurability of (fevers by) concerted action is as follows : "A fever arising from the three morbific entities, with an increase (especially) of bile, phlegm or wind, kills or leaves off quickly after ten, twelve or seven days, on account of maturation of the elements or the impurities".[292] (Such a fever does so) after seven days when it is (a fever) with an excess of wind, after ten days with an excess of bile and after twelve days with an excess of phlegm. (A fever) with an excess of wind and bile (behaves) in a way similar to (a fever) with an excess of bile, (a fever) with an excess of wind and phlegm in a way similar to one with an excess of phlegm, on account of the assimilating character of the wind. (As Caraka says : "The wind, being to a high degree of an assimilating character,[293] has both functions owing to (its) contact (with other agents); it brings about a burning sensation by its connection with fiery energy [294] and a sense of coldness because *soma* [295] is its residence" (Ci. 3, 38cd-39ab)). It kills owing to maturation of the elements, it leaves off owing to maturation of the impurities; that is the established discrimination. With respect to the discrimination between maturation of the elements and of the impurities only destiny is a ground. Maturation of the elements should be discerned by a steady increase of the disease, accompanied by decrease of strength, and by (the appearance of) urine, etc., accompanied by elements (of the body), such as semen, etc.; but when it is otherwise it is a maturation of the impurities. As has been said : "Insomnia, stiffness in the cardiac region, a constrained condition, heaviness, inability to eat, disinclination and deficiency of (bodily) force are the characteristics of maturation of the elements.[296] Alteration of the original state of the morbific entity, lightness of the fever and of the body and a pure state of the senses are the characteristics of maturation of the morbific entities".[297]

Now it may be asked how a fixed rule concerning a (period of) seven days, etc. (can be said to exist), because there are degrees of excitement, and a steady, quick and moderate power (of action) of the morbific entities.[298]

(The answer to this objection is that) it is not thus; (the rule derives) from (the fact) that the very nature of an illness is of such a kind. The very natures are diverse, in accordance with each particular disease; (e.g.) other morbid alterations are not like *agnirohiṇī*,[299] which kills in seven days. In this (connection the following statement), which is in agreement with the words of Hārīta : "It lasts as long as twice seven, nine and eleven (days); these are the (time-)limits of the three morbific entities, resulting in delivery (from fever) or death" (A.h.Ni.

2, 62cd-63ab),[300] is explained as follows : the ninth (day) is mentioned by reason of its immediate proximity to the tenth (day) and the eleventh one by reason of its immediate proximity to the twelfth (day). For that reason one should double the number everywhere, repeating the words 'with increase'.

In the same way Kārtikakuṇḍa has explained that in the following statement from the Suśruta(saṃhitā) : "After reaching the seventh, tenth or also twelfth day, having become more dreadful again, it is appeased or kills" (U. 39, 45cd-46ab), the word 'again' (expresses) doubling (of the number).[301] In the same way the statement : "A fever with an excess of bile, phlegm or wind kills or leaves off in ten, twelve or seven days, after having burnt the elements and the impurities with its heat" [302] has been explained (as providing an example of) doubling (of the number), when the words 'with an excess' are repeated here and made into an adverb. Also in (the following statement, containing) the opinion of Agniveśa : "(When caused) by wind, bile or phlegm it usually reaches its (time-)limit, (leading) to release or death, after seven, ten or twelve days" (A.h.Ni. 2, 61), doubling (of the number is said to occur) by means of the word 'usually'.

It may be asked (as an objection) how (the statement) beginning with '(as long as twice) seven (days)' should be understood (to indicate) ten, twenty, twelve and twenty-four (days).

The answer is : with respect to the word 'eleventh' the word 'one' should be repeated; in that manner one gets ninth and one, (i.e.) tenth, and eleventh and one, (i.e.) twelfth; thereupon the numbers are doubled everywhere. The word 'also' indicates an addition; (the word) seventh is understood by it, and this also indicates a double number (of days); the same way of supplying must be used with respect to the words 'ninth', etc.

A day forming the limit of (a period) exceeding twenty-four days does not exist, because a traditional text, substantiating it, does not occur.

Ā :

A fever arising from strong grounds, (i.e.) causes, and for that reason provided with many characteristics, is incurable ... 'Deep' [303] (means) : with an internal impulse, 'sharp' is : extremely difficult to endure, both externally and internally; a fever-patient, who is afflicted by both (these symptoms), who is emaciated, (i.e.) suffering from decline, should be given up because he is incurable, for fear of loss of one's possessions, knowledge and fame. Still other characteristics (of incurability) should be examined in other treatises because they are implied in these (above-mentioned) ones. As for instance ...[304] "A physician who knows his science should give up a fever-patient who is gasping for breath and sleeping, whose thin body is cold, who presents an internal combustive alteration, whose memory has gone, who snorts ...[305] and experiences piercing pain".

2, 74c-f : A burning sensation, perspiration, giddiness, thirst, trembling, loosening of faecal matter, unconsciousness, rumbling and an altered odour of the mouth (occur as) the conformation in release from fever.[306]

M:

The prodromes of release from fever are made mention of ... (A grammatical remark is made about the word for 'loosening of faecal matter'). Unconsciousness is the annihilation of consciousness. Rumbling is grumbling. As has been said : "In release from fever one vomits, rumbles and wallows" (Ca.Ci. 3, 324ab). Vāgbhaṭa says as well : "At the time of release (from fever) the morbific entity shows its strength,[307] bringing the elements into a turbulent state; panting, perspiring and rumbling from that (cause), one vomits and wallows" (A.h.Ni. 2, 76cd-77ab).[308] An altered odour is an altered odour of the body.[309]

In an imminent release from fever (this) conformation, (i.e. these) characteristics, 'occur'; (the last word) should be supplied. Because an illness does not cease without decline of the morbific entity, (an objector) may ask : how can a declined morbific entity bring about characteristics of such a kind?

The answer is : any condition shows, even when it has declined, its own ability at the time of its annihilation, as e.g. a lamp flares up especially when it is being blown out; or : a sense of burning, etc. (occur) at the (time of) departure of the morbific entity, on account of the turbulent state of the elements, which are overpowered by the morbific entity, in the same way as the tender tops of the creepers of a tree tremble when it is left by very swiftly moving monkeys.

2, 75 : Perspiration, lightness, itching of the head, inflammatory changes of the mouth, sneezing and longing for food are the characteristics of someone who has been released from fever.[310]

M:

The characteristics of release from fever are made mention of ... Perspiration is the appearance of (internal) warmth on account on the fact that the channels have burst open. Lightness (is lightness) of the body. Itching of the head (arises because) all fevers (are connected) with fiery energy; because the disagreeing (entity) has departed, phlegm, being of a *soma*-like nature, brings about, having acquired strength, its special characteristic, (to wit) itching, in its own seat, the head; it is said (that this does) not (occur) in another seat of phlegm on account of the great power of the illness. Inflammatory changes of the mouth (are produced) by bile which has been made excited by the heat of the fever; all that however, which it did not bring about formerly or elsewhere, is (produced) by the same great power of the illness.

And these characteristics, beginning with the burning sensation,[311] occur in a fever with an internal impulse arising from the three morbific entities, but not in all (fevers). As Bhāluki has proclaimed, immediately after (his description of) these (characteristics) : "These will be the characteristics in a fever arising from the three morbific entities, with an internal impulse and staying in the elements, at the time of release (from it); in another (type of fever) perspiration will appear".[312]

It may be asked (as an objection), because (the presence of) fever is directly observable as well as its absence : what is the use of studying the characteristics of it (i.e. of absence of fever)? Or, if they must be studied nevertheless, should this be done in all morbid alterations?

The answer is : (this should be done) for the sake of excluding the doubt (that) an irregular fever (is present, for) an irregular fever returns again, also when it has ceased, because the morbific entities have become dissolved in the elements; but when the characteristics of it, (i.e. of release), are present, there is no return (of fever), because it has ceased without (leaving) a remnant of the morbific entity.

In that (disease), in which such a doubt (may arise, these) characteristics are studied, but not in all cases, as e.g. in urinary diseases and in diarrhoea. In that way everything is well suited.

NOTES

1 In the Vedas Rudra is on the one hand a destructive deity who brings diseases upon men and cattle, on the other he is a beneficent deity with a healing influence. Sometimes he is identified with the god of fire. In later times the name of Rudra generally designates Śiva in his destructive aspect.

[2] See note 16.

[3] This eightfold division of fever is also found : Ca.Ni. 1, 17; Su.U. 39, 14cd-15ab; A.h.Ni. 2, 3; A.s.Ni. 2, 3 (Ki. 2, 2); Bhe.Ci. 1, 7ab; Kā.Ci., *jvaracikitsitādhyāya* 4cd; Hā. 3, 2, 40.

[4] Cf. Ca.Ni. 1, 16 : fever is the first one among the bodily diseases; Su.U. 39, 8 : fever is called the king of the army of diseases; A.h.Ni. 2, 1 : fever is the lord of diseases; Bhe.Ci. 1, 5 : fever is proclaimed to be the king of the whole army of diseases; Hā. 3, 2, 31 : fever is the king among the diseases. See also Va. 1, 134; Bhā.pra. 8, 1, 1.

[5] Cf. Ca.Ni. 1, 35 : all living beings are born and die while accompanied by fever; Ca.Ni. 1, 36 : (fever is) the great darkness at birth and death. Su.U. 39, 10 : (fever) usually enters into a bodily being at birth and death (*nidhana*); A.h.Ni. 2, 2 : fever consists of mental confusion at birth and death (*anta*).

[6] Ca.Ci. 3, 5-9 : "Holy one, be so kind as to tell me about the natural state, activity, special faculty and causes of this constant enemy of living beings in their absorption and rising, about its prodromes, basis, force, time and own characteristics, about the distinctions of its modes in detail and the conformation of the distinctions separately, about its signs when it is immature and when it is of long standing (*jīrṇa*), and the order of the therapeutical procedures together with the remedial agents, which are its marks when it leaves off and has become appeased, each of these separately, during which time, from which things and for which reason someone who has been abandoned by fever should be protected, by which causes fever returns again when it has been appeased and which therapeutical procedures appease it after returning again; (tell me) all that, for the benefit of the universe."

[7] Pālakāpya's Hastyāyurveda 1, 9 reads : "Therefore I say to you that this (disease), certainly being one and the same (entity), is (called) *jvara* in men, *abhitāpa* in horses, *khoraka* in donkeys, *īśvara* in cattle, *alasaka* in camels, *ākṣika* in beasts of prey, *pralāpaka* in goats, etc., *kaṣṇīṣa* in creeping animals, *hāridraka* in buffaloes, *mṛgaroga* in deer, *avatāpa* in birds, (*pakṣapāta*) in flying insects, *alarka* in a dog, *indramada* in fishes, *gucchaka* in bushes, *jyotiṣka* in herbs and fruit-bearing trees without clearly visible flowers, *parvaka* in garlands, *ṛṣabhaka* in lotuses, *cūrṇaka* in (good kinds of) grain (*dhānya*), *lala* in *kodrava*-grain (an inferior kind of grain), *madhūka* in potherbs, *ūṣara* in soil, *nīlikā* in water and *pākala* in elephants."

Nearest to the stanzas quoted in M. is Hā. 3, 2, 32-35 : "It is called *pātaka* in elephants, *abhitāpa* in horses, *īśvara* in cattle, *jvara* in men, *dāridra* in buffalo-cows, *mṛgaroga* in deer, *pralāpa* in goats and sheep, *alasa* in camels, *alarka* in a dog, *indramada* in fishes, *adhighāta* in birds, *aikṣita* in beasts of prey; in water it is usually called *nīlikā*, in soil *ūṣara* and in a tree *koṭarākṣa*; fever is observed everywhere."

Cakra enumerates in his comment on Ca.Ni. 1, 35 : *pākala* in elephants, *kherika* in cattle, *indrajāla* in fishes and *bhrāmaraka* in birds; Ḍa. mentions, on Su.U. 39, 9, the terms : *pākala, abhitāpa, khoraka* and *bhramaraka*. Aruṇa enumerates on A.h.Ni. 2, 2 : *pākala* in elephants, *abhitāpa* in horses, *gokarṇaka* in cattle, *makara* in birds, *alarka* in dogs, *indramada* in aquatic animals, *jyotis* in herbs, *cūrṇaka* in the classes of (good) grain, *nīlikā* in waters, *ūṣa* in soil and *jvara* in men; Candra on the same passage : "It is called *pākala* in elephants, *abhitāpa* in horses, *īśvara* in cattle, *jvara* in men, *pralāpa* in goats, etc., *alasa* in camels, *indramada* in waters, *kṣāra* in stones and *anila* in mountains;" Śrīdāsa on the same passage : it is called *pākala* in elephants, *tāpa* in horses, *alarka* in dogs, *indramada* in fishes, *jyotis* in herbs, *granthi* in trees, *upasarga* and *goraka* in cattle, *cūrṇaka* in (good kinds of) grain, *nīlikā* in water, *ūṣara* in soil and *jvara* in men; Bhe.Sū. 13, 12-14 : fever is called *indrajāla* in fishes, *pramīlaka* in birds, *citraka* in all (kinds of) grain, *dava* in roots and fruits, *phālana* in elephants and *utkarṇaka* in horses.

[8] Ca. reads *bāla* (a youth) instead of *bāṇa* (an arrow); in this version of the story the youth is called Vīrabhadra.

[9] The story of Dakṣa's sacrifice has many versions and is told in numerous Sanskrit texts. In the Carakasaṃhitā it is related as follows (Ci. 3, 15-25) : "In the second world-age the Asuras, who live upon hindrance to austerities, ran up to Śiva, in order to obstruct the austerity of the high-minded one, who performed his vow of abstention from anger during a thousand divine years. The Lord Dakṣa, seeing (this) and competent (to prevent it), remained indifferent. The Lord Dakṣa did not prepare the fixed portion of Śiva at the sacrifice, though addressed (about it) by the gods, and performed (the sacrifice) without pronouncing the stanzas of Paśupati and omitting the oblations to Śiva, which bestow success on the sacrifice. The god Rudra, who had seen Dakṣa's offence, assumed, knowing his own nature, his terrible aspect after completing his vow. The Lord cast a look with the eye between his eyebrows, burnt those Asuras and emitted from himself a youth, who was glowing with the fire of wrath and destroyed the sacrifice. Then, the sacrifice being annihilated and the celestials being distressed, the hosts of living beings, filled with a feeling of burning and full of distress, ran in confusion to the (four) quarters. The host of divine beings, together with the seven sages, praised the mighty Lord with stanzas until Śiva had assumed his benevolent aspect. The creature arisen from the fire of wrath, with ashes for a weapon, three heads and nine eyes, covered with flaming garlands, terrible to look at, short-legged and pot-bellied, seeing that Śiva was intent again on the benefit of the living beings, made an obeisance with his hands and said, for fear, to the god : 'What is my duty in your service ?' The Lord said to him who was (his own embodied) wrath: 'You will be fever in this world, (arising) at birth and death, as well as at the occasion of improper ways of conduct'."

Cf. about Dakṣa's sacrifice and its relation with the first appearance of fever : A.h.Ni. 2, 1; Bhe.Ci. 1, 1-2; Hā. 3, 2, 39-40.

[10] Cakra : a bitter taste means in this case that substances with a bitter taste should be used in the preparation of gruels and drinks; the use of drugs with a bitter taste is prohibited by Caraka in cases of fresh fever.

[11] Cakra : idem.

[12] Cf. Bhe.Ci. 1, 48-52.

[13] The bodily form of fever is also described : Hā. 3, 2, 36-37ab : "It has three feet, has ashes for a weapon, has three heads, a very big belly, is clothed in a tiger's skin, has a flaming body of the colour of that of a monkey, has tawny eyes, short legs, is loathsome (read *bībhatsa* instead of *vimatsya*) and full of force."

[14] Ca. describes the onset of fever by wind, bile and phlegm separately, as well as the agents by which wind, bile and phlegm are excited. As the descriptions of the process, set in motion by each of the morbific entities, are almost identical, one example, the onset of fever by wind, suffices; Ca.Ni. 1, 20 : "When this one (i.e. wind) is excited, it enters into the receptacle of undigested food, becomes mixed with the (transforming) heat, follows the first element, called nutrient fluid, (formed) by transformation of the (ingested) food, occludes the channels which carry the nutrient fluid and sweat, injures the (transforming) fire, throws the (transforming) heat out of the seat of the maturative process and attains the whole body; then (this process) results in fever." The same process, applied to all the morbific entities, is described in Su.U. 39, 15cd-19ab; A.h.Ni.

2, 3cd-5; A.s.Ni. 2, 4 (Ki. 2, 3). Fever is described in a different way in Bhe.Ci. 1, 9-13ab: "The wind stirs up first the (transforming) heat from the receptacle of undigested food; the phlegm, staying in the skin and got furious (*roṣam āpannaḥ*), brings about hypersensitivity (of the skin); it becomes dissolved when it has become maturated by the fiery energy, by which bile is attended, as a rain-cloud when it comes into contact (with the fiery energy of the sun); when a feeling of coldness has appeared by the appeasement (of the morbific entity), a human being gets a burning sensation again, due to bile; the fire, on the other hand, burns the bile, which has become its fuel; later on the wind, having lost its impetus and become maturated by the (transforming) heat, resorts to its own seat and enters into a normal state." Different again is the description in Hā. 3, 2, 41, the text of which is corrupt.

[15] Cf. fr. Ca.Vi. 1, 22 : "That which is the very state of being is called the natural state; this is the junction with the qualities, consisting of heaviness, etc., belonging to their own state of being, of substances, (i.e.) articles of food and remedial agents; as for instance (the qualities heavy, resp. light), of *māṣa* and *mudga* beans, of the flesh of a hog and that of the *eṇa* deer."

See about the heavy quality of *māṣa* beans : Ca.Sū. 27, 24; Su.Sū. 46, 34; A.h.Sū. 6, 21cd-22ab; A.s.Sū. 7, 31cd-32ab; Dravyaguṇa, *dhānyavarga* 26; Ma.nigh., *dhānyavarga* (10), 34; Dha.nigh., *suvarṇādivarga* (6), 86; Bhā.pra.nigh., *dhānyavarga* 41; Rā.va.nigh. 3, 29; about the light quality of *mudga* beans : Ca.Sū. 27, 23; A.h.Sū. 6, 17; A.s.Sū. 7, 24; Dravyaguṇa, *dhānyavarga* 24; Ma.nigh., *dhānyavarga* (10), 32; Dha.nigh., *suvarṇādivarga* (6), 82; Rā. nigh., *śālyādivarga* (16), 130; Bhā.pra.nigh., *dhānyavarga* 38; Rā.va.nigh. 3, 27.

See about the heavy quality of the flesh of a hog : Ca.Sū. 27, 79ab; Su.Sū. 46, 102; A.h.Sū. 6, 66; A.s.Sū. 7, 99cd-100; Dravyaguṇa, *māṃṣavarga* 13; Ma.nigh., *māṃṣavarga* (12), 23; Dha.nigh., *suvarṇādivarga* (6), 396; Rā.nigh., *siṃhādivarga* (19), 416; about the light quality of the flesh of the *eṇa* deer : Ca.Sū. 27, 46 and 59-60; Su.Sū. 46, 54; A.h.Sū. 6, 43 and 55; A.s.Sū. 7, 67cd-69ab and 86-87; Dravyaguṇa, *māṃṣavarga* 2-3; Ma.nigh., *māṃṣavarga* (12), 28-30; Dha.nigh., *suvarṇādivarga* (6), 400; Bhā.pra.nigh., *māṃsavarga* 9-14.

[16] Cf. fr. Ca.Vi. 1, 22 : "Getting it ready is the (development induced by) the preparation of natural (*svābhāvika*) substances. The imposition of another quality is called preparation. These (other) qualities are imposed by means of close contact with water and with fire, depuration, stirring, place (of storage), (maturation by) time, perfuming, saturation, etc., and by means of preservation during a long time, the kind of receptacle (and the way this receptacle is treated), etc." See also the long comment by Cakra, who discusses how it is possible that natural qualities of a substance are modified.

At Ca.Sū. 27, 338 mention is made of the fact that heavy *vrīhi* rice becomes light by preparing parched rice grain from it. See about the heaviness of *vrīhi* rice : Ca.Sū. 27, 15; Dravyaguṇa, *dhānyavarga* 14; Dha.nigh., *suvarṇādivarga* (6), 74; acc. to Su.Sū. 46, 10 and 13, and Ma.nigh., *dhānyavarga* (10), 11 and 14, *vrīhi* rice has the same qualities as *ṣaṣṭika* rice, which is light. See about the lightness of parched rice grain : Su.Sū. 46, 413; A.h.Sū. 6, 36cd-37ab; A.s.Sū. 7, 58.

[17] Cf. fr. Ca.Vi. 1, 22 : "Commixture is the close union of two or many substances; this (commixture) starts a specific (property), which is not started by each of the substances separately; as for instance the commixture of honey and butter, and of honey, fish and milk." Cakra remarks that neither honey nor butter is detrimental to health, but that their combination is fatal. The combination of milk and fish is a well-known

example of disagreeing articles of food; see e.g. Ca.Sū. 26, 82 : they are in disagreement with each other because milk is of a hot and fish of a cold potency.

[18] In the printed text *rāśihāradravyasya* should be corrected to *rāśir āhāradravyasya*.

[19] Cf. fr. Ca.Vi. 1, 22 : "Quantity (consists of) taking the whole (*sarvagraha*) and taking the components (*parigraha*); the aim (of this concept) is to ascertain the result of (taking) a proper and an improper measure. With regard to this (distinction) taking the whole (means that) a (particular) quantity (*pramāṇa*) of the whole food is taken as one mass, lumped together (*ekapiṇḍena*), and taking the components (means that) a (particular) quantity is taken from each of the substances of which the food consists (*pramāṇagrahaṇam ekaikaśyenāhāradravyāṇām*). Taking the whole is said to be taking (a part) of the whole (*sarvasya hi grahaḥ*) and taking the components is taking from the whole (*sarvataś ca grahaḥ*)."

[20] Cf. fr. Ca.Vi. 1, 22: "Place is the habitat (*sthāna*); it is said to be the (place of) production (of vegetable substances) and (of) occurrence (of animals), as well as adequacy with regard to place (i.e. with regard to the kind of country one inhabits)."

[21] Cf. fr. Ca.Vi. 1, 22 : "Time (means time as) permanent motion and (time) in relation to stages; with regard to this (distinction time) in relation to stages is linked to a morbid alteration and (time as) permanent motion to seasonal adequacy."

[22] Cf. fr. Ca.Vi. 1, 22 : "Standards about the employment are fixed rules about the employment; they are linked to the characteristics of disintegration (of the food)."

[23] Cf. fr. Ca.Vi. 1, 25 : "One should eat when (the previous meal) has been disintegrated."

[24] Cf. fr. Ca.Vi. 1, 22 : "The consumer is the person who enjoys the food; to such an extent as (the food) depends on him, it is (called) adequate with regard to the abode (*oka*)."

[25] Su. : *kṣaya* (decline) instead of *kṣata* (a lesion).

[26] Ca. : *abhighātaje* instead of *abhighātaja*; *śopha* instead of *śotha*.

[27] Ca. : *api pravṛddhaḥ* instead of *atipravṛddhaḥ*.

[28] From an unidentified source.

[29] From an unidentified source.

[30] Su.U. 39, 14ab reads : *vikārā yugapad yasmin jvaraḥ sa parikīrtitaḥ*. Cf. A.h.Ni. 2, 5-6ab : "(The impurities), giving rise to glowing heat in the whole body and making it very hot, bring about the appearance of fever; on account of the fact that (the flow through) the channels stagnates (*vibandha*), perspiration usually does not appear from these (channels)." A.s.Ni. 2, 4 (Ki. 2, 3) : "Intensifying the bodily heat to a high degree by means of their own heat, which has acquired strength because (the visceral fire) has become blended with it, inhibition of (*stambham ā-dā-*) (the function of the channels) by occluding the openings of the channels in the interior (of the body), eliminating (the appearance of) perspiration, also at the surface (of the body), and spoiling (the function of) all the senses by glowing heat, (the morbific entities) bring about the appearance of fever." Hā. 3, 2, 45-46ab : "Fatigue, rigidity, swimming of the eyes, horripilation, gurgling sounds, yawning, alteration of the colour (of the skin) and aversion (from food), accompanied by desiccation of the mouth, are the developed characteristics of fever. In (a fever by) wind there is yawning, from phlegm (arise) dejection and a feeling of affliction, from bile (arises) a sensation of glowing heat in the eyes, and in a (fever) by concerted action all (the signs are present)."

[31] *anirgama*:; Ḍa. : idem.

[32] Ca. : *manasas tāpalakṣaṇam* instead of *manaḥsaṃtāpalakṣaṇam*.

[33] *apavāda* : a special rule setting aside a general one.

[34] The same illustration is given by Cakra in his comment on Ca.Ci. 3, 31. See also his comment on Ca.Sū. 1, 51.

[35] Ḍa. makes mention of *vegoparodha* as a variant.

[36] Su. and Ā. : *nānnābhinandana* instead of *annāruci.*

[37] Su. : *dvayor dvayos tu rūpeṇa saṃsṛṣṭaṃ dvandvajaṃ viduḥ.*

[38] Cf. Ca.Ni. 1, 33 : "Its prodromes are the following : an altered taste in the mouth, heaviness of the limbs, absence of a relish for food, a disturbed state of the eyes, lachrymation, excessive sleep, disinclination, yawning, bending down (of the body), shivering' fatigue, giddiness, confused speech, waking (at night), horripilation, hypersensitivity of the teeth, (alternating states of) ability and inability to endure sounds, a cold wind and the glowing heat (of the sun), anorexia, absence of digestive alteration, weakness, muscle pain, adynamia, mental asthenia (*alpaprāṇatā*), dilatoriness, inertia, abandonment of one's usual work, refractoriness with regard to one's own affairs, indignation at the words of one's *gurus*, aversion to children, unmindfulness of one's duties, a feeling of vexation at (the wearing of) garlands, anointing (one's body) and eating, aversion from sweet articles of food and fondness of acid, saline and pungent (substances); these are the prodromes of fever which are present before (the onset of) general glowing heat; they also attend someone who is afflicted by general glowing heat;" Ca.Ci. 3, 28-29 : "Inertia, eyes which are full of tears, yawning, heaviness, weariness (read *klama* instead of *krama*), an undetermined fondness of and aversion to fire, glowing heat (of the sun), wind and water, absence of digestive alteration, an altered taste in the mouth, deficiency of (one's) strength and the colour (of one's skin), and a slight morbid deviation from the (normal) behavioural habits are the prodromes of fever;" A.h.Ni. 2, 6cd-10a : "Its prodromes are : inertia, disinclination, heaviness of the limbs, an altered taste in the mouth, inability to eat, yawning, eyes which are full of tears and in a disturbed state, muscle pain, absence of digestive alteration, mental asthenia, (the need of) much sleep, horripilation, bending down (of the body), cramp of the calves, weariness, intolerance of good advice, fondness of acid, acrid and irritant (substances), aversion to dainty articles of food as well as to children, an intense thirst, and causeless longing for and aversion to sounds, fire, a cold wind, water, shade and hotness;" A.s.Ni. 2, 5 (Ki. 2, 4) : "Its prodromes are the following : an altered taste in the mouth, absence of the relish for food, heaviness of the limbs, inertia, mental asthenia, a stumbling gait, excessive sleep, disinclination, envy, aversion to good advice, children and sweet articles of food, delight in acid, saline and pungent (substances), absence of digestive alteration, muscle pain, eyes which are disturbed and full of tears, yawning, bending down (of the body), weariness, horripilation and, without any cause, longing for and aversion to sounds, fire, water, a cold wind, shade and glowing heat (of the sun)."

[39] Su.U. 39, 16cd-19ab reads completely and with some slight variants : "The morbific entities, corrupted by the grounds proper to them, reach the receptacle of undigested food, arrive, accompanied by the heat (of the transforming fire), at (the seat of) the nutrient fluid, cover the pathway of the channels which carry the nutrient fluid and the sweat, slow down the (transforming) fire, throw the heat (of the transforming fire) out of the seat of the maturative process, pervade the whole body and generate then, at the (periods of) time proper to them, the arrival of fever or (its) increase, and the colour proper to them in the skin, etc."

[40] Cf. Ḍa. : *nayanayor aśrupūrṇatā.*

[41] See note 38.

[42] From this we must conclude that Mā.ni. 2, 6-7 did not form part of the Mādhava-

nidāna originally, but was added by Vācaspati, the author of Ā. As Vācaspati is later than Vijayarakṣita, the latter wrote no comment on it.

43 Su. : *kṣutaḥ stambhaḥ* instead of *kṣavastambhaḥ*.

44 Su. : *baddhaviṭkatā* (a bound state of the faeces) instead of *gāḍhaviṭkatā*.

45 Su.U. 39, 30cd : *jṛmbhā 'dhmānaṃ tathā śūlaṃ bhavaty anilaje jvare.*

46 Cf. Ca.Ni. 1, 21 : "Its signs are the following : an incongruous start and lapse, incongruous heat, unsteadiness of the fever's intense and attenuated condition, an approach or increase of the fever at the end of the process of disintegration (of the food), day, night or warm (season); especially roughness and a ruddy colour of the nails, eyes, face, urine, faeces and skin and a strongly developed condition (of these symptoms) (*kḷptībhāva*); painful sensations of several kinds, fluctuating and non-fluctuating, in varying subdivisions of the parts of the body, as for instance : numbness of the feet, cramp of the calves, disjunction of the knees and of all the junctures separately, adynamia of the thighs, a sensation as if the iliac region, sides, back, shoulders, arms, scapular region and chest are (respectively) broken, shattered, squeezed, pounded, severed, lacerated and bumped; a disturbed functioning (*aprasiddhi*) of the jaws, tinnitus, pricking pain in the temples, an astringent taste or an altered taste in the mouth, desiccation of mouth, palate and throat, thirst, seizing (pain) in the cardiac region, vomiting of dry matter, a dry cough, suppression of sneezing and eructation, a deterioration of the taste of (all) food, effusion, anorexia, absence of digestive alteration, despondency, yawning, bending (of parts of the body), shivering, fatigue, giddiness, confused speech, waking (at night), horripilation, hypersensitivity of the teeth, a preference for hot (things), adverse therapeutic reactions (*anupaśaya*) to those things which have been mentioned as origins and favourable therapeutic reactions (*upaśaya*) to things which are contrary (to the origins); these are the signs of a fever by wind;" A.h.Ni. 2, 10cd-18ab = A.s.Ni. 2, 6-13 (Ki. 2, 5-12) : "Incongruity of (its) arrival and departure, turbulence and mildness, painful sensations and heat, fluctuating painful sensations of varying kinds in varying parts of the body, numbness of the feet, stiffness, cramp of the calves, fatigue, a sensation as if disjunction of the junctures is arising, adynamia of the thighs, seizing (pain) of the iliac region, sensations as if the back is stamped, the abdomen is subject to pressure and the bones, especially those in the sides (of the chest), are cut, seizing (pain) in the cardiac region, pricking pain, as by a goad, in the chest, a sensation as if the shoulders are pounded, the arms cut and the scapular region pressed, inability of the jaws to masticate (*bhakṣaṇa*), yawning, tinnitus, pricking pain in the temples, a painful sensation in the head, an altered taste or an astringent taste in the mouth, non-appearance of the impurities, a dry (quality) and a ruddy (colour) of the skin, mouth, eyes, nails, urine and faeces, effusion, anorexia, absence of the desire (for food), absence of digestive alteration, absence of perspiration, waking (at night), desiccation of throat and lips, thirst, vomiting of dry matter and a dry cough, despondency, horripilation, hypersensitivity of the body-parts and the teeth, shivering, suppression of sneezing, giddiness, confused speech, longing for warmth and bending (of the body) will be present in a fever by wind;" Hā. 3, 2, 52-53 : "Shivering, incongruous paroxysms, desiccation of throat, palate and mouth, an altered taste (in the mouth), dryness of the body, a blocked state of the lateral parts of the abdomen, yawning, pain in the head, sleeplessness, a black colour of the finger-nails, confused speech, a sensation as if the limbs are broken, a man with these signs (suffers from) a fever brought about by wind."

47 These morbid alterations are enumerated at Ca.Sū. 20, 11; 20, 14; 20, 17.

[48] Ca.Sū. 20, 11 reads *pakṣavadha* instead of *pakṣāghāta*.

[49] *kṣava* (sneezing) is explained by its synonym *chikkā*.

[50] A.h. : *vināma* instead of *vilāpa*; see note 46.

[51] Gul : retention of morbid element and stools; Kav : constipation of the faults and of the stools.

[52] Ḍa. makes mention of the variant : *śyāvāṅgamalanetratā*, i.e. a brown colour of the body-parts, impurities and eyes; the latter reading is better than that found in Ā., because the term impurity (*mala*) includes urine (*mūtra*).

[53] Su. : *kaṭutā vaktre*; Ḍa. mentions as a variant : *tiktavaktratva*.

[54] Cf. Ca.Ni. 1, 24 : "Its signs are the following : approach or increase of the fever in the whole body simultaneously, specifically at the time of combustive alteration of the ingested (food), at noon, at midnight and in the autumn, a pungent (taste in the) mouth, inflammatory changes of nose, mouth, throat, lips and palate, thirst, (mental disturbance as in) intoxication, giddiness, fainting, vomiting of bile, diarrhoea, aversion to food, adynamia, deterioration (of the taste of all food), confused speech, the appearance of red wheals on the body, a yellowish-green or turmeric-yellow (colour of) nails, eyes, face, urine, faeces and skin, an extraordinarily intense condition of the heat, a burning sensation to an extraordinary degree, a preference for cold (things), adverse therapeutic reactions by those things which have been mentioned as origins and favourable therapeutic reactions by things which are contrary (to the origins); these are the signs of a fever by bile;" A.h.Ni. 2, 18cd-20 = A.s.Ni. 2, 14-16ab (Ki. 2, 13-14): "Pervasion of (all) the parts of the body (by glowing heat) at the same time, confused speech, a pungent (taste in the) mouth, inflammatory changes of nose and mouth, a desire for cold (things), giddiness, fainting, (mental disturbance as in) intoxication, disinclination, falling down of faecal matter, emesis of bilious fluid, spitting of blood, acid eructations, the appearance of red wheals, a yellow or yellowish-green (colour of the) skin, etc., perspiration, (prolonged) expirations, an altered smell and an extraordinary thirst (are present) in (a fever) arising from bile;" Hā. 3, 2, 64 : "Fainting, a burning sensation, giddiness, (mental disturbance as in) intoxication, thirst, sharp paroxysms, diarrhoea, lassitude, inertia, confused speech, emesis, inflammatory changes and glowing heat in the mouth, perspiration, shortness of breath, a pungent (taste in the mouth), a perturbed state (of mind) and hunger, these are the signs a human being is provided with in a fever by bile;" Va. 1, 233-234 : "Sharp and hot (paroxysms), a burning sensation, thirst, fainting, (mental disturbance as in) intoxication, a pungent (taste in the) mouth, giddiness, confused speech, inflammatory changes of nose, throat, lips and mouth, eyes filled with tears, a craving for cold (things), a yellow (colour of the) impurities, eyes, nails and skin, bilious eructations and diarrhoea are the characteristics of a fever by bile."

[55] This quotation is found : Paryāyaratnamālā 1506b.

[56] In translating this passage the ending of the word *sadāhacoṣajvaravaktraśoṣam* has been changed to *-aḥ*. This change is in agreement with Su.U. 49, 10, which presents a different reading, running as follows : *yo 'mlaṃ bhṛśaṃ vā kaṭutiktavaktraḥ / pītaṃ saraktaṃ haritaṃ vamed vā // sadāhacoṣajvaravaktraśoṣo / mūrcchānvitaḥ pittanimittajā sā //*, i.e. : "When a person with a pungent and bitter (taste in his) mouth vomits matter which is acid, vomits vehemently, vomits matter which is yellow, accompanied by blood or yellowish-green, this (vomiting) arises from bile as a cause if (this person) additionally suffers from a burning sensation, sucking pain, fever and desiccation of the mouth and is attended by fainting." Ḍa. interprets the beginning of the stanza as meaning : "A person who vomits matter which is vehemently acid or pungent" (*bhṛśam amlaṃ kaṭukaṃ vā yo vamet*).

[57] The source of this quotation is unknown.

[58] See note 54 (Ca.Ni. 1, 24).

[59] See note 55.

[60] This stanza is not found in Su., but is mentioned by Ḍa. as forming part of a variant of U. 39, 33-34.

[61] Su. : *utkleśa* (nausea) instead of *utkleda* (retching).

[62] Su. : *madhurāsyatā* (a sweet taste in the mouth) instead of *lavaṇāsyatā* (a saline taste in the mouth).

[63] Su. : *aṅgasāda* (adynamia of the parts of the body) instead of *lālāsrāva* (discharge of saliva).

[64] The inclusion of this additional stanza is approved of by the author of Ā.

[65] Cf. Ca.Ni. 1, 27 : "Its signs are the following : approach or increase of the fever in the whole body simultaneously, specifically just after the ingestion (of the food), in the earlier part of the day and the night or in the spring, heaviness of the limbs, absence of the relish for food, effusion of saliva, a sweet (taste in the) mouth, sickness, increased presence of unctuous substances in the cardiac region, a feeling of dampness, vomiting, a mild state of the (transforming) fire, excessive sleep, stiffness, lassitude, cough, shortness of breath, nasal catarrh, a feeling of coldness, a white (colour of the) nails, eyes, face, urine, faeces and skin, the excessive and vehement springing up of cold boils from the (various) parts of the body, a preference for hot things, adverse therapeutic reactions to those things which have been mentioned as origins and favourable therapeutic reactions to things which are contrary (to the origins); these are the signs of a fever by phlegm;" A.h.Ni. 2, 21-22 = A.s.Ni. 2, 16cd-18ab (Ki. 2, 15-16) : "In a (fever) arising from phlegm there are specifically present : inability to eat, rigidity, obstruction of the channels, slight paroxysms, effusion, a sweet (taste in the) mouth, an increased presence of unctious substances in the cardiac region, shortness of breath, nasal catarrh, sickness, vomiting, cough, stiffness, a white (colour of the) skin, etc., cold boils on the (various) parts of the body, lassitude and *udarda*;" Hā. 3, 2, 78 : "A feeling of dampness, a sweet (taste in the) mouth, rigidity, a vehement lassitude, heaviness of the limbs, inability to eat, a state of exhaustion, horripilation, a feeling of coldness, profuse perspiration, impairment of the sense of hearing, pallor of the skin of the eyes, a constrained appearance of the impurities and constrained coughing and vomiting;" Va. 1, 261-262 : "Cough, shortness of breath, nasal catarrh, effusion, inability to eat, vomiting, sleep, heaviness, sickness, a feeling of dampness, a sweet (taste in the) mouth, a feeling of coldness, horripilation, a light (colour of the) impurities, eyes, finger-nails and skin, and a relish for hot (things) are the characteristics of a fever by phlegm."

[66] Ḍa. : "It is the motionless state of a patient with fever."

[67] Ḍa. : "The paroxysms are continuously present without any change in their intensity; others, however, (say that torpid paroxysms are) those which appear in a sluggish way."

[68] Su. : *śakta* instead of *samartha*.

[69] It has not been possible to trace this quotation to its source.

[70] Su. : *tathā* instead of *tamaḥ*.

[71] Cf. Ca.Ci. 3, 85-86ab : "The conformation of fever by wind and bile (consists of) pain in the head, a cutting pain in the junctures, a burning sensation, horripilation, desiccation of throat and mouth, emesis, thirst, fainting, giddiness, inability to eat, insomnia, excessive talking, and yawning;" A.h.Ni. 2, 24 = A.s.Ni. 2, 20 (Ki. 2, 19):

"A feeling of affliction in the head, fainting, emesis, a burning sensation, mental confusion, desiccation of throat and mouth, disinclination, cutting pain in the junctures, sleeplessness, thirst, giddiness, horripilation, yawning and excessive talking (are present in a fever) from wind and bile;" Hā. 3, 2, 85 : "It will be a fever by wind and bile if there are present : thirst, fainting, vomiting, a pungent (taste in the) mouth, dryness (of the whole body), a sensation of inner burning in the body, redness of the eyes, desiccation of the throat, insomnia, shortness of breath, a painful condition of the head, cutting pain, a sensation (as if) the parts of the body are broken, horripilation and *tamaka*."

72 Alternative descriptions of the fevers by combined action, adopted by Jejjaṭa (acc. to Ḍa.), are inserted between Su.U. 39, 50 and 39, 51. The fever by wind and bile is described there as follows : "Yawning, inflatedness, (mental disturbance as in) intoxication, trembling, cutting pain in the junctures, general decline, thirst, confused speech and glowing heat will be present in a fever by wind and bile."

73 Ḍa. and He. : idem.

74 Ḍa. : idem.

75 Cf. Ca.Ci. 3, 86cd : "A feeling of coldness, heaviness, lassitude, a feeling of dampness and a painful condition of the junctures."

76 *svedāpravartana*; Ca. : idem; Su. : *pravartana* instead of *āpravartana*.

77 Cf. A.h.Ni. 2, 25 = A.s.Ni. 2, 21 (Ki. 2, 20) : "The signs of a fever, generated by phlegm and wind, are : a deficient state of the glowing heat, inability to eat, a painful condition of the junctures and the head, nasal catarrh, shortness of breath, cough, a confined state (of the impurities), a feeling of coldness, rigidity, dimness of vision, giddiness and lassitude;" Hā. 3, 2, 100 : "A feeling of coldness, shivering, a feeling (as if) the junctures are broken, vomiting, rigidity and pain in (all the) limbs, a sluggish (type of) heat, inability to eat, a confined state (of the impurities), roughness (of the body), cough, darkness (of vision), piercing pain, lassitude, rumbling (sounds) and mental inconsistency, or a feeling of dampness, yawning, inability to eat, profuse perspiration and obstruction of impure matter and urine, will be (present in) a fever by phlegm and wind."

78 The alternative description of this fever (see note 72) is : "Piercing pain, cough, nausea with (the urge to throw up) phlegm (read *kaphotkleśa* instead of *kakotkleśa*), a feeling of coldness, shivering, nasal catarrh, heaviness, inability to eat and a constrained condition (of the impurities) are present in (a fever) arising from wind and phlegm."

79 Cakra : it is a condition (as if) one is covered with a garment; Ḍa. : it is the motionlessness of a patient suffering from fever.

80 Su. : *ātiktāsyatā*, i.e. a slightly bitter (taste in the) mouth; Ḍa., however, read *liptatiktāsyatā*, for he explains the compound by *liptāsyatā tiktāsyatā ca*.

81 Cf. Ca.Ci. 3, 88-89ab : "At one moment a burning sensation and at another moment a feeling of coldness, perspiration and inhibition (of perspiration) again and again, mental confusion, cough, inability to eat, thirst, the appearance of phlegm and bile, the sensation that the mouth is covered with an unctuous substance, a bitter (taste in the) mouth and lassitude (constitute) the conformation of a fever by phlegm and bile;" A.h.Ni. 2, 26 = A.s.Ni. 2, 22 (Ki. 2, 21) : "Unsteadiness of the feeling of coldness, of the inhibition (of perspiration), of perspiration and of the burning sensation, the appearance of thirst, cough, phlegm and bile, mental confusion, lassitude, the sensation that the mouth is covered with an unctuous substance and a bitter (taste in the) mouth should be known as the symptoms of a fever by phlegm and bile;" Hā. 3, 2, 90 : "Sleep,

heaviness, cough (read *kāsa* instead of *kātsa*), pain in the junctures and in the head (read *śiroruj* instead of *śiraruj*), a state of affliction, cutting pain in the junctures and moderate paroxysms (are present) in this (fever by) phlegm, attended by bile (read *pittānvite* instead of *vātānvite*); a sensation of glowing heat in the eyes, shortness of breath, a liking for pleasant sounds (*ruciḥ śrutipathe*), desiccation (*śuṣkāvṛti*) of the throat, lassitude, mental confusion, anorexia and giddiness (are present) in a fever by phlegm and bile."

[82] The alternative description of this fever (see note 72) is : "A feeling of coldness, a burning sensation, inability to eat, inhibition (of perspiration), perspiration, mental confusion, (mental disturbance as in) intoxication, giddiness, cough, adynamia of the parts of the body and sickness are present in (a fever by) phlegm and bile."

[83] Ca. : *svedastambhaḥ* instead of *stambhaś ca saṃsvedaḥ*.

[84] Su. : *asaṃprāpti* instead of *asaṃvitti*.

[85] Ca. : *darśana* instead of *locana*.

[86] Ca. : *loṭhana* instead of *loṭana*.

[87] Cf. Su.U. 39, 35-38ab : "Insomnia, giddiness, shortness of breath, lassitude, numbness of the parts of the body, inability to eat, thirst, mental confusion, (mental disturbance as in) intoxication, stiffness, a burning sensation, a feeling of coldness, distress in the cardiac region, maturation of the morbific entities after a long time, insanity, a brown colour of the teeth, a rough and black tongue, pain arising from the junctures, the head and the bones, distorted and turbid eyes, tinnitus and pain in the ears, confused speech, inflammatory changes of the channels, rumbling, vanishment of sensibility, and the discharge of perspiration, urine and faeces in slight amounts after a long time;" A.h.Ni. 2, 27-33ab = A.s.Ni. 2, 23-29ab (Ki. 2, 22-28ab) : "(A fever) arising from all (the morbific entities is provided) with all the characteristics; in this (type of fever there are present) frequently alternating burning sensations and feelings of coldness, deep sleep by day and waking at night, either sleeping always or not at all, either an extremely intense perspiration or no perspiration at all, the appearance of a morbid longing for songs, dances, jests, etc., eyes which are filled with tears, turbid, red, distorted and provided with fluttering eyelashes, pain in the calves, sides, head, junctures and bones, giddiness, tinnitus accompanied by pain in the ears, a throat which feels as if it were covered with awns, a tongue (with an aspect as if it were) completely burnt and (which is) harsh and heavy, laxity of the parts of the body and the junctures, spitting of blood, bile and phlegm, tossing of the head and an extreme pain in it, the becoming visible of wheals and brown-red circular spots, distress in the cardiac region, retention of the impurities or their appearance either in slight or in extreme amounts, an oleaginous condition of the mouth, subsidence of (one's) force, adynamia of the voice, confused speech, maturation of the morbific entities after a long time, lassitude and a persistent rumbling in the throat;" Hā. 3, 2, 111-112 : "Enduring thirst, piercing pain, desiccation, shortness of breath, waking at night but lassitude by day, mental confusion, desiccation of the mouth, inflammatory changes of nose, tongue and lips, spitting, leanness of the body, the springing up of circular spots on the body, a brown (colour of) eyes, lips and mouth, (mental disturbance as in) intoxication, perspiration, inflatedness together with desiccation or loss of the feeling of hunger, afflication by giddiness or rolling of the head, afflictedness of the head and obstruction of the channels or emesis or being filled with gurgling sounds (*ghuraghurā*) in the throat and piercing pains; the fever called (that one caused by) concerted action, the quickly acting one among diseases, the (fever) which gives rise to extreme suffering, rules over men, horses or elephants, when they are provided with the signs mentioned above."

[88] *nirgataṃ bhugnaṃ saṃkucitatā yayos te nirbhugne.*

[89] *antaḥpraviṣṭa,* i.e. retracted.

[90] *atikuṭila*; Ḍa. : *nirbhugna* (distorted) means *kuṭila* (crooked); Aruṇa and He. : *bhugna* (distorted) means *kuṭila*; Indu : it means that the pupil (*kanīnikā*) and outer corner of the eye (*apāṅga*) are blunt (*atīkṣṇa*); Śrīdāsa : it means that the pupil and outer corner of the eye are crooked (*anārjava*).

[91] *śūkaśimbidhānya* may be interpreted as *śūkaśimbi* and *śūkadhānya* (awned grain), or as *śūkadhānya* and *śimbidhānya* (other kinds of grain, but especially pulse; the pods of the latter are only covered with hairs in a number of cases). Aruṇa : *śūka* means *kiṃśāru* (a beard of corn).

[92] Cakra : idem. *gojihvā* is the name of a plant, usually identified as Elephantopus scaber Linn., which has prickly leaves; acc. to some authorities *gojihvā* may also designate Onosma bracteatum Wall.; the stem and the upper surface of the leaves of the latter are hispid.

[93] Cakra : idem.

[94] Cakra : idem.

[95] *itas tataś cālanam*; Cakra : *itas tato nayanam.*

[96] Cakra : idem.

[97] A *varaṭī* is a kind of wasp.

[98] Also quoted by Cakra, Indu and Śrīdāsa : wheals are boils without an opening (*nirmukhāḥ piṭakāḥ*); Aruṇa on A.h.Ni. 2, 20 : wheals are boils without an opening and of a circular form; Indu on A.s.Ni. 2, 15 (Ki. 2, 14) : wheals are elevated (*sotsedha*), circular spots.

[99] Cakra : idem.

[100] A.h. : *mahāsvedo 'ti naiva vā* instead of *mahān svedo 'thavā na vā.*

[101] Ca. : *-rugvyathāḥ* (pain and a feeling of distress) instead of *-hṛdvyathāḥ* (distress in the cardiac region).

[102] Ca. : *-tṛḍ balasaṃkṣayaḥ* instead of *tṛṣṇā balakṣayaḥ.*

[103] Ca. : *liṅgaṃ syān mārutādhike* instead of *liṅgaṃ vātādhike matam.*

[104] Ca. : *śītaka* instead of *śītatā.*

[105] The two last stanzas are quoted in an inverted order.

[106] A description of the thirteen fevers by concerted action is not found in Su., nor in A.h. and A.s.

[107] Su. : *hatasvara* (the voice being damaged) instead of *hataprabha* (the lustre of the skin being damaged).

[108] Su. : *sāsro nirbhugnahṛdayaḥ* (the eyes being full of tears and the heart being distorted) instead of *sāśrunirbhugnanayana* (the eyes being full of tears and distorted).

[109] Su. : *hataprabha* instead of *hatasvara* (cf. note 107).

[110] Su. : *viduḥ* instead of *jaguḥ.*

[111] This quotation is not complete without adding Su.U. 39, 42, a stanza which is, acc. to Ḍa., omitted by some of the commentators. Su.U. 39, 42 : "As to a fever proceeding from all (the morbific entities) one should know that one, accompanied by sleep, to be *abhinyāsa,* that one with decline to be *hataujas,* and that one with complete inactivity of the limbs *saṃnyāsa.*" *hataujas* fever is described separately at Su. 39, 43-45ab; this description is, again acc. to Ḍa., not generally accepted by the commentators on Su.

Su.U. 39, 43-45ab : "(The fever) of a person whose vital fluid falls down owing to the surge of bile and wind, who wants to lie down to repose because his limbs are stiff and he feels cold, who, whether awake or sleeping, is deprived of sensibility, who is full of lassitude, talks in a confused way, shows horripilation, laxity of the parts of his body, a low degree of general glowing heat and mildly painful sensations, a competent physician should know as arising from restriction of the vital fluid." The fever by concerted action as such is also called *abhinyāsa* and *hṛtaujas* at A.h.Ni. 2, 33cd = A.s.Ni. 2, 29cd (Ki. 2, 28cd). He. remarks that this statement is sometimes interpreted in a different way : "Some say that *saṃnipāta* is a fever with an excess of wind, *abhinyāsa* with an excess of phlegm and *hṛtaujas* with an excess of bile." He. does not agree with that interpretation.

HK characterize *abhinyāsa* (p. 219) as "ein Fieber bei dem Augen und Ohren ihren Dienst versagen"; this is not an adequate description, because more functions are depressed in this fever; the quoted statement by HK is taken from the beginning of the description of *abhinyāsa* by Jolly (Medicin, p. 72). HK render *hṛtaujas* by "das die Lebenskraft raubt"; Jolly (Medicin, p. 72) says that it is "characterisiert durch Schwund der Kräfte;" the central characteristic of this fever, as described by Su., is, however, the decrease of the vital fluid. Descriptions of *abhinyāsa* fever are also found in Va., Bhā.pra. and Yo.

Va. 1, 496-500 : "The three vehemently excited morbific entities generate a very dreadful *abhinyāsa* fever in men when they invade the channel of the chest, when they are immature, confined and scybalous, and when they invade the senses of perception and the *manas*. A person (suffering from it) has stiff limbs, does not speak, is unable to make voluntary movements and has no desires, his eyes will not be able to see colours and, having reached (as objects of the other senses) smells, tastes, sensations of touch and sounds, he is not aware of them; he rolls his head again and again and finds no delight in food, he rumbles and feels pricking pain, his perception is deficient and he speaks little and inarticulately. This (fever) is called *abhinyāsa*. (A patient suffering from it) should be rejected in most cases; only some (patients) are curable;" Bhā.pra. 8, 1, 498 : "That fever, in which really all the morbific entities are very violently (excited) and strong, (and in which are present) mental confusion to an extraordinary degree, wallowing, bewilderment, vehement shortness of breath, muteness, a burning sensation, an unctuous mouth, a sluggish (transforming) fire and decline of (bodily) force, is called here from of old *abhinyāsa* by wise physicians;" Yo., p. 162 : "(Excitement of) the three morbific entities, an oleaginous condition of the mouth, sleep, bewilderment, insensibility, troubles in talking, annihilation of (one's) force and (partial) suppression of breathing, etc. is called *abhinyāsa*; (a patient suffering from it) is surely fit for death."

[112] Cf. Kā.Ka., *viśeṣakalpādhyāya* 27-28ab : "The person, in whom concerted action arises from excitement (of the three morbific entities) with an excess of wind and bile, (shows) fever, muscle pain, thirst, desiccation of the palate, closing of the eyes, inability to eat, lassitude, loosening of faecal matter, shortness of breath, cough, fatigue and giddiness;" Va. 1, 353 : "The person, in whom concerted action arises from excitement (of the three morbific entities) with an excess of wind and bile, (shows) fever, (mental disturbance as in) intoxication, thirst, desiccation of the mouth, closing of the eyes, inflatedness, inability to eat, lassitude, cough, shortness of breath, giddines and weariness; this (type of) concerted action has been denominated by the sages as *babhru*;" Va. 1, 353 = Bhā.pra. 8, 1, 455-456 (v.l. : *śrama*, fatigue, instead of *klama*, weariness; *babhra* instead of *babhru*).

[113] Cf. Kā.Ka., *viśeṣakalpādhyāya* 28cd-31ab : "The person, in whom concerted action arises from excitement (of the three morbific entities) with an excess of bile and phlegm,

(presents) a sensation of inner burning and feels coldness outside, his thirst increases, he feels pricking pain in his right side and seizing pain in his chest, head and throat, with difficulty he spits phlegm accompanied by blood, his throat (feels as) consumed by fire, and loosening of faecal matter, shortness of breath, hiccup and closing of the eyes are present to an increasing degree; these two (types of) concerted action are denominated *vidhu* and *phalgu*;" Kā.Ka., *viśeṣakalpādhyāya* 28cd-31ab = Va. 1, 354-356 (v.l. : *mukhaśoṣa*, desiccation of the mouth, instead of *uraḥśīrṣagraha*, seizing pain in chest and head; *ṣṭhīvati raktapittam*, he spits blood and bile, instead of *niṣṭhīvati kapham sāsṛk*, he spits phlegm accompanied by blood) = Bhā. pra.8, 1, 459-461 (v.l. : *ṣṭhīvati śleṣmapittam*, he spits phlegm and bile; *koṭhaś ca jāyate*, there arise wheals, instead of *kaṇṭhaś ca dūyate*, the throat feels as consumed by fire; *ṛṣibhir bhallunāmā 'yaṃ saṃnipāta udāhṛtaḥ*, this type of concerted action is denominated *bhallu* by the sages).

114 Only a fragment of the corresponding description in Kā. has been preserved, ending with : "It is a very severe (type of) concerted action." Cf. Va. 1, 357-358 : "The person, in whom concerted action arises from excitement (of the three morbific entities) with an excess of phlegm and wind, (presents) a cold fever, fainting, hunger, thirst and a seizing pain in the sides; when he is not perspiring there arise piercing pain, hiccup and shortness of breath. This (type of) concerted action is incurable and is called *śīghrakārin*; someone, into whose body it has entered, certainly dies within a day and a night;" Va. 1, 357-358 = Bhā.pra. 8, 1, 457-458 (v.l. : *pārśvanigraha* instead of *pārśvasaṃgraha*; *tandrā*, lassitude, instead of *hikkā*, hiccup).

115 Cf. Va. 1, 359-360ab : "Cough, shortness of breath, darkness (of vision), fainting, confused speech, mental confusion, shivering, a painful sensation in both sides, yawning and an astringent (taste in the) mouth should be considered as the symptoms of (the type of) concerted action in which wind is the most important (morbific entity); this (type of) concerted action, called *visphoraka*, is very severe;" Va. 1, 359-360ab = Bhā.pra. 8, 1, 449-450 (v.l. : *bhrama*, giddiness, insteadof *tamas*, darkness of vision).

116 Cf. Va. 1, 360cd-361 : "Diarrhoea, giddiness, fainting and surely inflammatory changes in the mouth, red drops on the limbs and a violent burning sensation should be considered as the symptoms of (the type of) concerted action in which bile is the most important (morbific entity); this (type of) concerted action is called *āśukārin* by physicians;" Va. 1, 360cd-361 = Bhā.pra. 8, 1, 451-452 (v.l. : *dāho 'tīva* instead of *dāhas tīvraḥ*).

117 Cf. Va. 1, 362-363 : "Rigidity, a stammering voice and also sleep at night, stiff eyes and a sweet (taste in the) mouth should be considered as the symptoms of (the type of) concerted action in which phlegm is the most important (morbific entity); this (type of) concerted action is by the sages said to be called *kampana*"; Va. 1, 362-363 = Bhā.pra. 8, 1, 453-454.

118 Descriptions of several types of fever by concerted action are met with in a number of texts :

Kā.Ka., *viśeṣakalpādhyayā* goes on, after a break in the text : "When there will be concerted action by means of (wind, bile and phlegm, which have increased respectively) to a deficient, great and moderate degree, (the patient will present) those very diseases which have been mentioned, in accordance with the strength and the residence of the morbific entities; excitement (in the form of) blood-bile, present in all the channels, arises in him and he is covered everywhere with blisters which look as if they had arisen from burning by fire; his cardiac region, abdomen, bowels, liver, spleen and *phupphusa* are subject to inflammatory changes; that which stays inside his body, both in the upper and the lower part, becomes (transformed into) purulent matter; his teeth fall out and he will die; these are the specifying (characteristics of this kind of fever);" cf. Va. 1, 378-379 : "When there will be concerted action by means of (wind, bile and phlegm, which have increased respectively) to a deficient, extreme and moderate degree, (the patient will present) those very diseases which have been mentioned, in accordance with the strength and the residence of the morbific entities; his cardiac region feels (as if it were) burning, his liver, spleen, bowels and *phupphusa* are subject to extreme inflammatory changes and purulent matter and blood come out upwards and downwards;" Va. 1, 378-379 = Bhā.pra. 8, 1, 474-475; Bhā.pra. 8, 1, 476 runs: "The teeth fall out and death (occurs) in this (fever); physicians call this (type of) concerted action *yāmya*."

Kā.Ka., *viśeṣakalpādhyāya* : "When there will be concerted action by means of (wind, bile and phlegm which have increased respectively) to a moderate, great and deficient degree, (the patient will present) those very diseases which have been mentioned, in accordance with the strength and the residence of the morbific entities; with a stiff body and stiff eyes he lies down as if he were struck; he evacuates in an extreme way and his faeces are copious, though he abstains from eating; (finally) all his channels are subject to inflammatory changes; these are the specifying (characteristics) in this (type of fever);" cf. Va. 1, 381cd-383cd : "When there will be concerted action by means of (wind, bile and phlegm which have increased respectively) to a moderate, great and deficient degree, (the patient will present) those very diseases which have been mentioned, in accordance with the strength and the residence of the morbific entities; there will be present mental confusion, confused speech, fainting, stiffness, trembling, seizing pain in the head, cough, shortness of breath, giddiness, lassitude, unconsciousness and seizing pain in the cardiac region; moreover blood flows out of the apertures (of the body); these are the specifying (characteristics); death (occurs) within three (days and) nights or there is lassitude and stiffness of the eyes;" Va. 1, 381cd-382 = Bhā.pra. 8, 1, 471-472 (v.l. : *manyāstambha*, stiffness of the muscles of the nape of the neck, instead of *stambhakampa*, stiffness and trembling; *hṛdi vyathā*, a feeling of distress in the cardiac region, instead of *hṛdi grahaḥ*, seizing pain in the cardiac region); Bhā.pra. 8, 1, 473, corresponding to Va. 1, 383a-d, runs : "Blood flows out of the apertures (of the body) and the eyes are red and stiff; these will be the specific (symptoms); death (occurs) within three days; physicians call this (type of) concerted action *pākala*."

Kā.Ka., *viśeṣakalpādhyāya* : "When there will be concerted action by means of (wind, bile and phlegm, which have increased respectively) to a great, deficient and moderate degree, (the patient will present) those very diseases which have been mentioned, in accordance with the strength and the residence of the morbific entities; (he shows) yawning, waking (at night), stretching (of the body), confused speech and pain in the head; moreover he dies from stiffness of the muscles of the nape of the neck; these are the specifying (characteristics of this fever). The names of these three (fevers) are *yāmya*, *krakaca* and *pākala*;" cf. Va. 1, 380-381ab : "By (concerted action which arises from respectively) a great, deficient and moderate (increase of) wind, bile and phlegm, the very diseases which have been mentioned (occur in a patient), in accordance with the strength and residence of the morbific entities; (the patient presents) confused speech, droopiness, complete mental confusion, trembling, fainting, disinclination and giddiness; moreover he dies from stiffness of the muscles of the nape of the neck; these are the specifying (characteristics);" Va. 1, 383ef: "The names of these three (fevers) are *yāmya*, *krakaca* and *pākala*"; Va. 1, 380-381ab = Bhā.pra. 8, 1, 477-478; Bhā.pra. 8, 1, 479 runs : "Physicians call this (type of) concerted action *krakaca*."

Va. 1, 364-368 : "When in someone concerted action springs up by means of wind, bile and phlegm, (which have increased respectively), in their due order, to a deficient, moderate and excessive degree, it oppresses (the patient) in accordance with (the degree to which) the morbific entities present themselves; (the patient presents) piercing pain to a slight degree, pricking pain in the iliac region, a burning sensation in the trunk, pain, giddiness, weariness to a vehement degree, pains in the head, mouth, muscles of the nape of the neck, cardiac region and organ of speech, states in which the eyes are closed, shortness of breath, hiccup, cough, rigidity and unconsciousness; when it has recently been produced it is sometimes curable; in this (type of) concerted action there arises, however, a very severe boil at the root of the ear, by which a living being is hardly able to stay alive; this (type of) concerted action is called *vaidārika* and is very severe; after (it has been present during) three (days and) nights the preparation of a remedial agent is useless;" Va. 1, 364-368 = Bhā.pra. 8, 1, 487-491 (v.l. : *vastiruj*, pain in the bladder, instead of *vaktraruj*, pain in the mouth).

Va. 1, 369-375 : "When there is concerted action by means of (wind, bile and phlegm, which have increased respectively) to a moderate, deficient and excessive degree, (the patient will present) those very diseases which have been mentioned, in accordance with the strength and the residence of the morbific entities; a sensation of inner burning is a specific (symptom) in this (fever) and (the patient) is unable to speak; one notices that the face is red in the very way this occurs by means of *ālaktaka*; there is no effusion of phlegm from the cardiac region, (though the patient) exerts himself to withdraw it (from that region); pricking pain is present in the side, which feels as if it were struck by an arrow, the cardiac region feels (as if someone is) digging into it; closing of the eyes, shortness of breath and hiccup increase day by day, the tongue has a burnt aspect and is harsh to the touch, the throat feels as if it were covered with awns; (the patient) is not aware of the evacuation (of faeces and urine), he rumbles like a *kapota* pigeon, he is filled with phlegm to an extreme degree, his mouth, lips and palate are desiccated, he is extremely afflicted by lassitude and sleep, the (transforming) fire and the brightness (of the body) are damaged, there is no extreme languor, abnormal movements are present (*viparītāni yacchati*) and stretching movements in many ways; (finally) matter mixed with blood is spitted out in slight amounts; this is the very severe (type of) concerted action, called *karkoṭaka*;" Va. 1, 369-375 = Bhā.pra. 8, 1, 480-486 (v.l. : *pittenākarṣita*, attracted by bile, instead of *yatnenākarṣita*, though there is exertion to withdraw it; *hatavāṅ nihatadyutiḥ*, the voice and the brightness of the body are damaged, instead of *hatavahnir hatadyutiḥ*, the transforming fire and the brightness of the body are damaged; *na ratiṃ labhate nityaṃ viparītāni cecchati*, he never finds pleasure and longs for wrong things).

Va. 1, 376-377 : "When there is concerted action by means of (wind, bile and phlegm, which have increased respectively) to a great, moderate and deficient degree, (the patient will present) those very diseases which have been mentioned, in accordance with the strength and the residence of the morbific entities; there are present confused speech, droopiness, complete mental confusion, trembling, fainting, disinclination, giddiness and also hemiplegia; these are the specific (symptoms in this fever); this very severe (type of) concerted action is called *saṃmohaka*;" Va. 1, 376-377 = Bhā.pra. 8, 1, 468-470. Kā.Ka., *viśeṣakalpādhyāya* : "Learn from me about (that type of) concerted action, which shows excitement by means of congruous morbific entities; one should observe in it all the symptoms of the three morbific entities" (= Va. 1, 384; cf. Bhā.pra. 8, 1, 462).

"(Because the morbific entities are) congruous as to their force, like three sticks, they call it that one which has three feet" (absent in Va. and Bhā.pra.).

"(All) those symptoms are present in it, which have been stated in (the chapter on) the therapy of fever; this (type of) concerted action, called *kūṭapākala*, is very severe;" cf. Va. 1, 385 : "(When) the whole of those symptoms (is present) which have been stated in (the chapter on) the therapy of fever, (when it is) provided with all those (symptoms in a) fully developed (state), it should be discerned as *kūṭapākala*" (absent in Bhā.pra.).

"*kūṭapākala* arises as a great illness which immediately kills on account of the severe illnesses (it brings about), (as one is killed) by a thunderbolt, cutting weapon and fire. Someone consumed by *kūṭapākala* is unable to hear and to see, shows no pulsating movements and does not speak, praise or blame; he is only occupied with breathing and his body and eyes are stiff; the limit of his life does not exceed three (days and) nights;" cf. Va. 1, 386-387ab : "It resembles a thunderbolt, a cutting weapon and fire, on account of the severe illnesses (it brings about); (a patient suffering from it) is only occupied with breathing and his body and eyes are stiff; it takes the life of such a person after three (days and) nights" (= Bhā.pra. 8, 1, 463-464ab).

Bhā.pra. describes two more series of thirteen fevers by concerted action. The first series is as follows : Bhā.pra. 8, 1, 493 : "The person with a fever by concerted action whose head and body are cold, who is afflicted by shortness of breath, cough, hiccup, mental confusion, trembling, confused speech, weariness, a copious amount of phlegm and wind, a burning sensation, emesis, oppressing pain in the parts of his body and morbid alteration of the voice, is said to suffer from (the fever called) *śītagātra*."

8, 1, 494: "That fever arising from the three morbific entities in which are present an extraordinary lassitude, thirst, a flux (from the bowels), an excessive shortness of breath, the painful condition (called) cough, a body afflicted by general glowing heat, itching and phlegm in the throat along with swelling, a very dark-coloured tongue, weariness, sluggishly functioning ears and a burning sensation, is called *tandrika*."

8, 1, 495 : "That fever arisen from the extraordinary (*nitānta*) fury of all the morbific entities, in which will be present trembling, a feeling of distress, falling down, a burning sensation and unconsciousness, which occur precipitately and are attended by frequent (states of) confused speech, is called *pralāpaka* on (this) earth."

8, 1, 496 : "Spitting of blood, circular spots on the body which resemble blood (as to their colour) or are black, redness of the eyes, thirst, inability to eat, emesis, shortness of breath, diarrhoea, giddiness, inflatedness, unconsciousness, falling down, hiccup and a vehement oppressing pain in the parts of the body arise as signs in the fever, generated by concerted action, (which is called) *raktaṣṭhīvin*."

8, 1, 497 : "That fever arising from all the morbific entities, which first of all presents as (its) signs a condition in which the eyes are vehemently twisted awry, a vehement degree of shortness of breath, cough and lassitude, and moreover confused speech, (mental disturbance as in) intoxication, shivering, deficient functioning of the ears and mental confusion, has been considered to be (the fever called) *bhugnanetra* by the ancient therapists."

8, 1, 498 : see note 111 about *abhinyāsa* fever.

8, 1, 499 : "That fever generated by the three morbific entities, in which the tongue is to a high degree covered by hard thorns, in which subsequently complete muteness arises, and in which are present impairment of the sense of hearing and of (bodily) force, shortness of breath, cough and a general glowing heat, is called *jihvaka* by the best ones of the ancient physicians."

8, 1, 500 : "That fever, generated by the three morbific entities, in which will be present an outstanding degree of a distressing sensation, accompanied by swelling in the junctures, a considerable amount of phlegm in the mouth, insomnia, the painful condition (called) cough and what is called the whole (set of) characteristics, is denominated *saṃdhiga* by wise (physicians)."

8, 1, 501 : "That fever, arisen by means of all the morbific entities, which is characterized by a perpetual shaking of the head, accompanied by coughing, an excessively distressing pain in all the parts of the body, together with hiccup, shortness of breath, a burning sensation and mental confusion, an extreme general glowing heat of the body, bewilderment and talking at random, has been called *antaka* by the sages."

8, 1, 502 : "That (fever), in which are present an excessive burning sensation, a violent thirst, shortness of breath, confused speech, absence of appetite, giddiness, mental confusion, oppressing pain, a distressing sensation in the muscles of the nape of the neck and in the jaws, pain in the throat and fatigue, is technically called *rugdāha*; this fever arises from the three (morbific entities)."

8, 1, 503 : "In the fever (called) *cittabhrama* a man sings, dances, laughs and talks in a confused way; his visual perception is morbidly altered, he is mentally confused and afflicted by a burning sensation, a feeling of distress, and fear."

8, 1, 504 : "In that fever, generated by the three morbific entities, which is called *karṇika*, are found a violent swelling and distressing sensation at the root of the ear, a seizing pain in the throat, deafness, shortness of breath, confused speech, profuse perspiration, mental confusion and a burning sensation."

8, 1, 505 : "That fever, (arising) from the three morbific entities, in which the complete signs consist of a (feeling as if the) throat contains hundreds of awns, an extreme shortness of breath, confused speech, inability to eat, a burning sensation, pain in the (whole) body, thirst, stiffness of the jaws, a feeling of affliction in the head and mental confusion, along with shivering, is called *kaṇṭhakubja* by the ancient therapists."

A series of thirteen fevers with the same or related names, but somewhat different as to their description and order, is found in Yo., p. 160-162 :

"That (fever by) concerted action, which presents the arising of piercing pain, brought about as a prodrome, desiccation, a condition full of many painful sensations (brought about) by wind, (a copious amount of) phlegm, glowing heat, deficiency of (one's bodily) force and waking (at night), should be called *saṃdhika*.

That one, which brings about a burning sensation, extends glowing heat over the whole body, gives rise to mental confusion and trembling of the head and covers (one) with hiccup and cough, know it to be (the fever) called *antaka*, which is avoided (as to treatment) by wise (physicians).

That (fever), which presents confused speech, glowing heat in the whole body, great mental confusion, sluggishness (of the transforming fire), fatigue, intense giddiness, painful sensations, a distressing sensation in the throat, muscles of the nape of the neck and jaws, that one which brings about an uninterrupted feeling of thirst and fills one with shortness of breath, cough and hiccup, is (called) *rugdāha*, is very difficult to cure, and kills. When somehow in men a distressing pain in the (whole) body arises, giddiness, (mental disturbance as in) intoxication, glowing heat in the whole body, a state of mental confusion and bewilderment, bewildered eyes, laughter, singing, dancing and confused speech, it is called *cittabhrama*, which is by some declared to be incurable.

When the body is like ice, when there are (present) shivering, shortness of breath and hiccup, when all parts of the body are flaccid, the voice has deteriorated (*khinnanāda*) and a ferocious glowing heat is present, accompanied by weariness, a burning sensation, coughing, vomiting and diarrhoea, it is (called) *śītagātra*, which is a ground of a hasty death on account of its special faculty.

In the malady (called) *tandrika*, there are present an intense afflictedness by lassitude, a great degree of disturbance by fever, phlegm and thirst, a dark-coloured tongue which is covered by broad and hard thorns, diarrhoea, shortness of breath, weariness, glowing heat in the whole body, pain in the ears, a vehement rigidity in the throat and (the need to) lie down to repose uninterruptedly.

When there is present a feeling of affliction in the head, a seizing pain in the throat, a burning sensation, mental confusion, trembling, fever, afflictedness by blood and wind, a seizing pain in the jaws, glowing heat, moaning and fainting, it is certainly *kaṇṭhakubja* (fever), which is difficult to cure.

That fever which by its special faculty (gives rise to) confused speech, diminishment of the sense of hearing, seizing pain in the throat, a feeling of distress in the parts of the body, shortness of breath, cough, effusion, glowing heat in the interior of the ears and oppressing pain in the cheeks, is called *karṇaka* by wise (physicians); it is difficult to cure.

The person who presents fever, decrease of (bodily) force, voidness of memory, shortness of breath, distorted eyes, mental confusion, confused speech, giddiness, trembling and swelling, (suffers from the fever called) *bhugnadṛś* and quickly leaves (this) life.

(That disease in which are present) spitting of blood, fever, emesis, thirst, mental confusion, piercing pain, diarrhoea, hiccup, inflatedness, giddiness, a burning sensation, shortness of breath, unconsciousness and a tongue which is dark-coloured, red and morbidly altered, with a form determined by the springing up of circular spots, is called *raktaṣṭhīvin* in this (world); it is a well-known fact that it destroys life.

Who (shows) trembling, confused speech, glowing heat in the whole body and oppressing pain in the head, who is full of an impetuous (*prauḍhaprabhāva*) wind, whose thoughts are distracted, who is bewildered by loss of judgment and speaks very abundantly, goes, (suffering from the fever called) *pralāpin*, quickly to the abode of the Lord of the fathers.

(The fever) characterized by perturbation by shortness of breath, cough and glowing heat in the whole body, a tongue which is covered by hard thorns, deafness, muteness and deficiency of (one's) force, is (called) *jihvaka*, which is very difficult to cure."

The last fever of this series is *abhinyāsa*; see note 111. In the Sudhālaharī-comments on Mā.ni. the same descriptions as those of Yo. are quoted as coming from the Aśvinīkumārasaṃhitā.

In Bhā.pra. there follows another series of thirteen fevers by concerted action :

8, 1, 510 : "From the openings of whose nose flows down a copious amount of viscid blood of a crimson and black colour, and who rolls his head to all sides, should be known as someone painfully oppressed by *kumbhīpāka*."

8, 1, 511 : "Who throws the parts of his own body upwards and downwards and who breathes to an extraordinary degree, should be discerned as someone visited by *proṛṇunāva*, which is (by) diverse (reasons) difficult (to cure)."

8, 1, 512 : "Perspiration, giddiness, cutting pain in the parts of the body, trembling, a burning sensation, emesis, a distressing sensation in the throat and extremely heavy limbs arise as signs in someone visited by (the fever called) *pralāpin*."

8, 1, 513 : "(Someone who shows) a sensation of inner burning and a feeling of coldness at the outside (of the body), swelling, an extreme disinclination, shortness of breath and also a body which looks as it if were burnt, is called (a patient) tormented by *antardāha* (fever)."

8, 1, 514 : "The person who neither at night nor by day obtains sleep, whose understanding is in a state of confusion and who, suffering from giddiness, feels as if he had arisen from the sky, is (called) someone with *daṇḍapāta* (fever) who feels giddy when looking in every direction."

8, 1, 515 : "The body of someone afflicted by *antaka* is everywhere covered with enlarged glands, his abdomen is filled by wind, he is continuously short of breath and he is insensible."

8, 1, 516 : "Someone afflicted by *cnīdāha* fever has sensations as if on his body, which is a vessel (full) of pain, move about a number of snakes, flying insects and *hariṇas*; he shivers and has a burning sensation."

8, 1, 517 : "The person whose body is extremely yellow, the eyes still more and the impurities more again than (the eyes), who feels a burning sensation, and an extreme coldness at the outside, should be known as someone with *hāridraka* (fever)."

8, 1, 518 : "Someone (suffering) from (the fever by) concerted action (called) *ajaghoṣa*, smells like a he-goat and has painful shoulders; the cavity of his throat is obstructed and his eyes are somewhat copper-coloured."

8, 1, 519 : "Who does not perceive the proper sense-objects, (consisting of) sounds, etc., by means of the assemblage of the senses, who laughs harshly and talks harshly in a confused way, should be known as someone afflicted by *bhūtahāsa* (fever)."

8, 1, 520 : "That fever by means of which one feels again and again, because of its paroxysms, a pressuring pain in the limbs as by an instrument, and in which one will vomit blood and bile, should be discerned as *yantrāpīḍa* (fever)."

8, 1, 521 : "In the (fever by) concerted action, (called) *saṃnyāsa* there is a flux (from one's bowels), one vomits, rumbles, and throws one's limbs in all directions during a long time, one talks in a confused way and there is a ferocious look in one's eyes."

8, 1, 522 : "In the fever (called) *saṃśoṣin*, one's body has the colour of the eyes of a peacock's tail, one's eyes possess the same colour to an extreme degree owing to the excretion of impure matter, and one's (body) shows white boils of a circular form."

119 Cakra remarks that the indeniable fact that the morbific entities do not injure each other cannot be explained; he calls it inconceivable (*acintya*) and refers for an exposition on this subject to the author of the Candrikā commentary on Su.

120 A.h.Ni. 15, 48ab : *saśleṣmamedaḥpavanam āmam atyarthasaṃcitam* instead of *saśleṣmamedaḥ pavanaḥ sāmam atyarthasaṃcitam*; 49c : *skabhnāti* instead of *stabhnāti*. This reading gives a different meaning to the stanza : "In the case that immature matter, accumulated to an extreme degree, together with phlegm, fat and wind, (reaches the thighs), it immobilizes them."

121 Cakra remarks on Ca.Ci. 26, 293 : "(As a reply to the question) 'Why don't they injure each other ?' it is said : because they are innately of the same nature; this means : because of their being of the same nature, which is based on their own state of being; being of the same nature is a state in which no injury is brought about. See also note 119.

122 Cf. fr. Kā.Ka., *viśeṣakalpādhyāya* : "On account of disagreeing food, time and the ripening of (one's) actions, the wind becomes quickly excited; afterwards it injures one's (transforming) fire. The four kinds (of food) taken by such a person with an injured bodily fire, who drinks and eats as he did before, become chiefly transformed into phlegm. The wind, carrying this phlegm away with itself, moves through the channels

of this person. Having filled and occluded all his channels, both the subtle and the gross ones, the wind reaches a restrained condition; thereupon it excites the bile of that person. This bile, set in motion by the wind and being under restraint by phlegm at all sides, brings about, due to the mutual union with regard to the places of residence, fever, sickness, inability to eat, cutting pain in the junctures, *visūcikā* and other diseases of various kinds, and squeezes (in that way) a bodily being."

[123] Cf. Su.U. 39, 41cd : "A fever by concerted action is thought to be difficult (to cure); according to others it is incurable;" Ḍa., undoubtedly under the influence of Ca.Ci. 3, 109cd-110ab, remarks that it is difficult to cure when not all its characteristics are present, and that it is incurable when all its characteristics are present, the morbific entity is in a confined condition and the (transforming) fire annihilated; A.h.Ni. 2, 34 = A.s.Ni. 2, 31cd-32ab (Ki. 2, 30) : "When the morbific entity is in a confined condition and the (transforming) fire has been annihilated, a fever by concerted action, of which all the characteristics are fully (developed), is incurable; when it is different, it will be difficult to cure or bring about bewilderment;" the term confined (*vibaddha*) is explained by Indu as : stagnant (*sthira*), by Aruṇa as : not coming forth (*apravṛttiśīla*), and by He. as : not reaching the stage of maturation (*pacyamānāvasthām agacchat*).

[124] Cakra remarks : "In this case the term morbific entity is used in the sense of impurity, because it is accompanied by the words 'being in a confined condition'." Aruṇa says that 'morbific entity' indicates here : wind, bile, phlegm, urine, faeces, etc.

[125] Also quoted by Cakra.

[126] These two stanzas occur also : Bhā.pra. 8, 1, 527-528 (in the reversed order); Va. 1, 400-401 (the two first quarters differ : "The lords among the physicians call it the crossing of a sea"); Kā.Ka., *viśeṣakalpādhyāya* (v.l. : "The physicians call it the crossing of a sea by means of a stone"). Cf. Hā. 3, 2, 152 : "What has not been performed by the *vaidya* who draws out a man who has fallen into the ocean of concerted action; which praise is not obtained on earth by a *vaidya* provided with (a sense of) duty, fame and proper conduct ?"

[127] This stanza occurs in several texts with the substitution of the period of twice ten days by a period of twice nine days : A.h.Ni. 2, 62cd-63ab = A.s.Ni. 2, 60cd-61ab (Ki. 2, 65cd-66ab) (it is quoted in both texts as the traditional doctrine of Hārīta); Bhā.pra. 8, 1, 541; Yo., p. 163; it is quoted by Ḍa. on Su.U. 39, 45cd-46ab.

[128] This stanza occurs also : Siddhayoga 1, 189; Bhā.pra. 8, 535; Yo., p. 163; it is quoted by Cakra on Ca.Ci. 3, 54cd-55ab and by Aruṇa on A.h.Ni. 2, 60-63.

[129] This stanza also occurs, with variants : Bhā.pra. 8, 1, 537. It is quoted by Ḍa. on Su.U. 39, 45cd-46ab (v.l. : *pākarujojjhita*, i.e. free from pain by maturation, instead of *pākarujānvita*, i.e. full of pain by maturation).

Bhā.pra. presents more stanzas about maturation of the elements and the impurities :

8, 1, 536 : "Insomnia, stiffness in the cardiac region, a constrained condition, heaviness, inability to eat, disinclination and deficiency of (one's) force are the characteristics of maturation of the elements."

8, 1, 538 : "If there be a distressing sensation above the umbilical and below the cardiac region, (as if these parts were) subject to pressure, one should discern it to be maturation of the element(s); when it is different, however, it is maturation of impure matter."

8, 1, 539 : "Alteration of the original state of the morbific entity, lightness of the fever and of the body and a pure state of the senses are the characteristics of maturation of the impurities."

8, 1, 540 : "The condition in which are present a continually sound functioning of the group of five senses and of the (transforming) fire, in their due order, appeasement of thirst, etc. and mildness of the fever, may be called maturation of the morbific entities. The conformation of maturation of the elements will be : an extremely painful sensation in cardiac and umbilical region, a flux (from the bowels), an intense fever, excessive shortness of breath, anorexia and disinclination."

130 This stanza occurs also : A.h.Ci. 1, 149 = A.s.Ci. 2, 115cd-116ab. Cf. Ca.Sū. 18, 27 : "Someone whose excited bile remains lodged at the root of the ear, gets at the end of a fever a swelling which is difficult to subdue (or leads) to death."

Hā. 3, 2, 153-155 : "(A fever), connected with the three (entities) wind, bile and phlegm, is (a fever) arising from the three morbific entities; such a (fever, when) also connected with blood, will be (called) a fever by concerted action. Know that a fever by concerted action does not occur without blood. One's morbific entities become appeased by maturation-promoting decoctions. Therefore, when the morbific entity has been appeased, the blood is not dissolved at all, and by means of that (blood) there arises a very severe swelling at the root of the ear."

131 Ā. : *vi-muc-* instead of *pra-muc-*.

132 Between 2, 25 and 2, 26 some editions insert five stanzas which are identical with Va. 1, 496-500 (see note 111), apart from a number of variants.

133 The source of Mā.ni. 2, 26 is unknown.

134 Su. : *dāhātīsārahṛdgrahāḥ* (a burning sensation, diarrhoea and a seizing pain in the cardiac region) instead of *tathā 'tīsāra eva ca*.

135 Su. : *abhaktaruc* instead of *bhaktāruci*.

136 Su. : *todo mūrchā balakṣayaḥ* (pricking pain, fainting and decline of force) instead of *todaś ca saha mūrchayā*.

137 Su. : *arocaka* instead of *abhojana*.

138 Cf. Ca.Ni. 1, 30 : "The eighth fever, the adventitious one, which is preceded by a distressing sensation, arises from traumatic injury, possession, magic and curses. It remains an isolated adventitious (fever) for some time and becomes attached to the morbific entities afterwards. (A fever) arising from traumatic injury becomes attached to wind, with corrupted blood as the base (of the excitement of this entity); (a fever) arising from possession becomes attached to wind and bile and (the fevers) arising from magic and curses to the concertedly acting (morbific entities);" the same subject is treated more extensively : Ca.Ci. 3, 111cd-129ab; A.h.Ni. 2, 38-45 = A.s.Ni. 2, 35cd-43ab (Ki. 2, 34-46) : "Adventitious (fever) is of four kinds : (it arises) from traumatic injury, possesssion, curses and magic. That one among these which arises from traumatic injury (is brought about) by wounds from blunt and sharp objects (*kṣataccheda*), by burning, etc. (on the one hand) and by fatigue (on the other hand). In this (type), usually, the wind, corrupting the blood, brings about fever, with a distressing sensation, swelling, alteration of colour and pain. (A fever) from possession arises from being entered by a *graha*, from herbs, poison, wrath, fear, grief and lust. When it (is caused) by a *graha*, one laughs and weeps without reason; when it arises from the smell of herbs, there occur fainting, pain in the head, emesis and sneezing; from poison arise fainting, diarrhoea, a brown (colour of the) mouth, a burning sensation and a malady of the heart; from wrath arise trembling and pain in the head; in those (fevers) arising from fear and grief, confused speech (is present); from lust arise giddiness, inability to eat, a burning sensation, and decline of shame, sleep, insight and self-control. In the series beginning with the being entered by a *graha* there is excitement (of the morbific entities) by concerted action;

in the series of three (fevers), beginning with (that one arising from) fear, there is excitement of wind, and in (the fever arising from) wrath excitement of bile. The two (fevers), however, which arise from curses and magic, are fevers by concerted action and thought to be dreadful and very difficult to endure. When someone is being invoked by magic spells, his mind is afflicted by glowing heat first and his body afterwards; at last the fever of that person, who is consumed by blisters, thirst, giddiness, a burning sensation and fainting, increases daily;" Hā. mentions (3, 2, 196-198) fevers by *bhūtas*, by curses, by lust and wrath and by the smell of herbs; Bhā.pra. adds (8, 1, 700) a fever by lust in women : "Fainting, muscle pain, thirst, quick movements of the eyes, perspiration of breasts and face and a burning sensation in the region of the heart occur in a fever by lust in women."

139 Cakra on Ca.Ni. 1, 30 : "The bringing about of fever by means of spells from the Atharva(veda), etc.;" Ḍa. : "Magic is the practice of killing (someone) by means of spells, etc."

140 See W. Caland : Altindisches Zauberritual, p. 157-158, note 1, about the *soma* sacrifice called *syena*.

141 *sarṣapa*. The sacrificial offering of mustard seeds as a form of magic is also made mention of by Ṭoḍara and Śrīdāsa. See about this form of magic : W. Caland, l.c., p.183.

142 *sruc*; PW : ein grosser Opferlöffel (nach der Vorschrift armslang mit handgrossem Kopf, der von der Rindenseite aus eingeschnitten und mit schnabelartigem Ausguss versehen ist); MW : a sort of large wooden ladle (used for pouring clarified butter on a sacrificial fire; and properly made of *palāśa* or *khadira* wood and as long as an arm, with a receptacle at the end of the size of a hand).

143 A *bhūta* is an evil spirit, able tc enter a human being and to cause insanity (see ch. 20).

144 Ca.Ci. 3, 117 deals with a different opinion about fever by possession : "Some also call the fever of a person who is possessed, because he has come into contact with a poisonous tree or wind or other things which arise from poison as a source, a fever arising from possession."

145 The *siddhas* are the "perfected"; succesful *yogins*, holy men.

146 Mā.ni. 2, 30c.

147 This is the beginning of a group of stanzas quoted by Ḍa. in his comment on Su.U. 39, 42. He informs us of the practice of some authorities of inserting these stanzas in the text of Su. Ḍa. disagrees with this practice because the fever arising from the smell of herbs includes the grass and flower fever. The complete text of the stanzas runs : "When the wind, having carried off the fragrance and pollen, (sprung) from flowers full of fiery energy (*tejasvin* instead of *ojasvin*), thwarts the *prāṇa* and *apāna* of a human being, moving along with the elements (of the body) on account of its subtlety and going towards the vital points by its fiery energy, it affects the actions, mind, force and knowledge of that (human being); the actions, etc. having been restrained, (his) friend thinks he is asleep, because there is damage to the mind when the vital fluid has become inactive; at first there arises in such a person a disease of the head as of someone who is conscious; after seeing both odourless and fragrant (things) he faints without reason; an experienced (physician) will know that this is the fever called grass and flower fever."

148 The first half of this stanza is almost identical with A.h.Ni. 2, 42cd (v.l. : *arati* instead of *aruci*); the second half is from an unidentified source.

149 Cf. A.h.Ni. 2, 43a-c (see note 138).

150 Cakra comments on Ca.Ni. 1, 30 : " '(A fever arising from possession) becomes

attached to wind and bile' (means that) some (fever becomes attached) to wind, another one to bile and another one again to wind and bile. But there are the words : (Ca.Ci. 3, 115cd-116ab is quoted). Although in (a fever arising from) possession by *bhūtas* excitement of the three morbific entities is said to occur, (one has) nevertheless (to admit) in that case predominance of wind and bile in a special way, owing to the force of these (quoted) words." Cakra comments on Ca.Ci. 3, 115cd-116ab : "Is it not thus, that it has been said in the (section on) origins : (he quotes from Ca.Ni. 1, 30) ? Why then does he say here that (a fever) arising from possession by *bhūtas* is attached to the three morbific entities ? The answer is : it is not thus; it is said there : 'it becomes attached to wind and bile' with a view to that (fever) which usually arises from possession by lust, etc."

151 Ḍa. says that Su.U. 39, 66 expresses the opinion of Agniveśa, etc. about the production of irregular fevers by means of morbific entities which have the elements (of the body) as their seats. Su.U. 39, 63cd-65 informs us, according to Ḍa., about the opinion of Bhoja, Bhāluki, Puṣkalāvata and others on the same subject : "And this irregular (fever) never leaves the body, because (the patient) is not released from his languor, heaviness and leanness. Staying in another element (of the body), it is not experienced on account of its dissolvement and subtlety; it is in a condition of decline because its fuel, consisting of the morbific entity, is present in a slight amount, as (in) a fire the fuel of which has got into decline." Compare : Su.U. 39, 56 : "Or, as pronounced by some (authorities), the ultimate ground of irregular fever is its own state of being; but usually an adventitious (factor acts as) an adjunct in an irregular fever." Cf. A.h.Ni. 2, 64-69ab = A.s.Ni. 2, 62-63ab; 70-71; 72cd-73; 65cd (ed. Ki. differs) : "The morbific entity, though being present in a slight amount, of lean persons who have been released from their illness and who indulge in an improper diet, etc., may, when it has obtained strength from another one of the corruptible (constituents), etc., bring about, together with an opponent, and being liable to decline and increase, an irregular fever. The morbific entity of these persons comes forth when it is strong, bringing about fever at its own time, and it ceases again when (it has become) weak by the force of an (entity) opposed (to it). When the morbific entity has declined, the fever, being subtle, gets dissolved in the very nutrient fluid and the other (elements of the body); on account of (this) dissolvement, it imposes leanness, alteration of colour, rigidity, etc. The whole body becomes quickly pervaded by the morbific entity because the openings of the channels, carrying the nutrient fluid, are near and exposed; it (brings about) continuous and double quotidian (fever), (but) a contrary (type) when the reverse (state of things is present). An irregular (fever shows) an irregular start, action and time (of appearance) and has a protracted course (*anuṣaṅgavat*)." Bhe.Ci. 2, 1-5 : "Some physicians proclaim that an irregular fever is of the nature of wind, some that it arises from concerted action, others that its source is bile. Others again proclaim it to arise from phlegm and yet others proclaim that *bhūtas* are its source; others, who are astrologers, (think it to come about) by means of the oppression (caused) by birth-constellations. The views of this subject and the opinions about the morbid alterations are manifold, but I shall declare, on account of its grounds, that it arises from concerted action. The excited wind, staying in the receptacle of digested food and also in the bones and the marrow, quickly brings about excitement of phlegm, and certainly also of bile. This great (disorder), which has been produced from the deep and has three seats and three characteristic features (*tantra*), will give rise to quotidian, tertian (*ekāntarita*) or quartan (fever)." Kā.Khi. 1, 4-30 : "The remedies in irregular fever have been proclaimed by you, holy man, in (the chapter about) the therapy of fever, but the cause of (this) irregularity has not (yet)

been taught. It is suitable that double quotidian (fever), etc. are said to be irregular because of their irregular appearance; (but) why is continuous fever, which does not show (any) lapse, traditionally called irregular, and what is the ground (to call) irregular the *preta* fever and that one sprung from (possession by) a *graha*?

That should be told now, in due time and according to its component parts; please tell it according to its essential nature, with its particulars and in detail. Being asked thus by his pupil, Kaśyapa said : "A regular fever is characterized by a slight ground, an external pathway, its being based on a morbid alteration (*vaikṛta*), the absence of secondary affections, its residing in (only) one (element of the body), (its being curable by) easy means, and lightness as to maturation. An irregular fever (has) the opposite (characteristics); continuous (fever) is thought (to belong to that group) on account of its sharpness; likewise (the fevers) arising from (possession by) a *preta* or *graha*, and the four (fevers which belong to this group) on account of their irregular appearance. Irregularity is said to be present in continuous (fever), etc. because (these fevers are) difficult to subdue and to grasp, are furnished with a ferocious seizing (power) and are of a severe character. In the same way I shall proclaim how irregularity, effected by time, arises in the four (fevers consisting of) double quotidian (fever), etc. The associated morbific entities, or a pair (of these entities), bring about irregular fever when they have attained the ducts which carry the nutrient fluid, and when they are in an incongruous state. When someone who is feverish, who is being released (from fever) or has just been released from it, indulges in physical exercise, heavy or inadequate food, water beyond the proper measure, foods prepared with milk (*pāyasa*), *kṛśara*, foods prepared from flour, sesame paste, thick sour milk, *mandaka*, *piṇyāka*, dishes prepared from *māṣa* beans, meat from domesticated animals and those inhabiting marshy country, and other things of a similar kind which are disagreeing and heavy, as well as (when such a person indulges in) sleeping by day, eating before the previous meal has been digested or overeating, his fever increases or an irregular fever quickly arises. The person who indulges in a *kaṣāya* when the morbific entities are not (yet) fully maturated, or, from inconsistency, (indulges) in oleaginous drinks, milk or restorative (substances), or, on account of meditation about deities or being touched by a *graha*, when he has recently been subjected to emetic or purgative procedures, to the drinking of oleaginous substances or to treatment with oleaginous enemata, indulges in the use of cold things, in heavy food and sexual intercourse, (will suffer from) a sudden excitement of the wind which, after going to the interior of the marrow in the bones, gives rise to excitement of phlegm and certainly of bile. Thereupon there arises in that person, on account of incongruity of the elements (of the body), an irregular fever, (viz.) double quotidian, quotidian, tertian or quartan (fever). It is not thus, that it does not become appeased, nor thus, that it does not become excited still more; this (kind of fever) exceeds the time (-limits) of appeasement and excitement. It does not become appeased, due to its own state of being, because it remains closely affixed (to the patient), and conditions which have become appeased due to their very state of being do not arise (again). When the impulse of the fever has become inactive, a bodily being seems to be released from it, but, nevertheless, in this stage (of the fever) he is not freed from the following signs : an altered taste, a pungent or a sweet taste, etc. in the mouth to a slight degree, a greatly diminished longing for food, languor, and heaviness of the head. Learn from me how this (fever) arises again and again. The wind, the pathway of which had been obstructed by the morbific entity that was the ground of the irregular fever, takes possession (again) of (its own) pathway at the end of the excitement of that morbific entity, carries away with itself the remainder of the morbific entity and proceeds in accordance with its seats. This remainder of the morbific entity, being dissolved in its own seat, approaches, dependent upon time and (its) force, the seat of the nutrient fluid, and generates fever again. By a specific type of therapy and due to the passing away of its own force, it declines, and it increases when it becomes connected with the same qualities (as its own). As a lamp flares up again and again owing to its own state of being, even when (the amount of) its fuel, consisting of oil, has declined, thus this same fever, after it has ceased and taken residence in its basic (seat), shows, though being appeased repeatedly, its force at (its proper) time, even when its fuel, consisting of the morbific entitiy, has declined."

152 The source of this quotation remains unidentified.

153 This stanza occurs also : Va. 1, 557; Bhā.pra. 8, 1, 722; Yo., p. 165.

154 Su. : *satata* instead of *saṃtata*.

155 Cf. Hā. 3, 2, 187-188 : "If a fever has reached the stage in which it is staying in the elements themselves, one should discern it as an irregular fever; this (irregular fever) should be known to be of four kinds. An experienced (physician) should discern (fevers with time-limits) of one (*ekāhika*), two (*dvyāhika*) and three (*tryāhika*) days, and also another fever with a time-limit (*velājvara*), which is the fourth one;" ibid., 3, 2, 195 : "A fever with a time-limit has (a limit) of one day when it stays in the nutrient fluid and also in the blood; when it stays in the flesh it will be (a fever with a time-limit) of three days, and when it resides in the bones one (with a time-limit) of four days. (A fever) staying in all the elements should be known as a fever of long standing, which brings about decline of the elements (of the body)." Compare also Va. 1, 552-553, Bhā. pra. 8, 1, 720-721 and Yo., p. 165, v. 30-32, which agree with Mā.ni.

156 Cakra remarks on Ca.Ci. 3, 61cd : "By the word 'mainly' it is shown that double quotidian fever, in addition to (residing in) the blood, resides in the elements flesh, etc. as well."

157 See Pāṇini 1, 2, 64 ff.

158 Ḍa. comments on Su.U. 39, 67-68ab : "A morbific entity staying in the nutrient fluid and blood, brings about double quotidian fever; also those who read : "A morbific entity which resides in the blood usually brings about double quotidian fever" have to accept the nutrient fluid, owing to the word 'usually', because the morbific entities bring about fever after catching hold of the nutrient fluid. Others, however, read here 'continuous' (*saṃtata*) instead of 'double quotidian' (*satata*); in that case one should know that the word 'double quotidian' has been dropped before (the word) 'continuous'. In that way they explain that it is a continuous (fever) when it stays in the nutrient fluid and a double quotidian (fever) when it stays in the blood. Some people, however, think that the word *saṃtata* is a synonym of *satata*. A continuous fever is not an irregular fever. What one (should) understand in case of its (i.e. of continuous fever) juxtaposition, by means of a variant reading and a different interpretation, is that its aim is to substantiate the irregular character, because double quotidian fever, etc. are irregular with respect to continuous (fever). With respect to what would they be irregular otherwise?"

159 Su. : *ahorātrāt* instead of *ahorātre*.

160 Cf. Ca.Ci. 3, 53cd-60ab : "The morbific entities, having spread through the channels which carry the nutrient fluid, and being heavy, invade the whole body, and bring about continuous fever after becoming immobilized. This (fever), which is very difficult to endure, becomes quickly, because it is of a quickly acting character, appeased, or it

kills (quickly), in ten, twelve or seven days. A morbific entity brings about continuous (fever) when it is comparable (as to its qualities) with the time (i.e. the season), the corruptible (constituent) and the constitution, and when it is not accompanied by an opposed (entity); for that reason it should be known to be very difficult to endure. In continuous fever the wind, etc. enter, as a fixed rule, simultaneously upon faeces and urine, in the same way as upon the elements. (This fever) becomes appeased, or kills, in a period of time, (consisting of) seven days, etc., (depending on the fact) whether it has purified or has not purified the nutrient fluid, etc. from the remnants of immature matter. When (the elements) are not completely purified or not purified at all, the places of residence of continuous (fever) are declared to be twelve (in number). After its lapse with undeveloped characteristics on the twelfth day, it still holds on for a long time, being difficult to appease." Ca.Ci. 3, 61cd-67 : "A morbific entity, mainly residing in the element blood, brings about, together with an opposed (entity), double quotidian fever, which increases and declines in accordance with (the periods of) time (suited to the morbific entity); double quotidian (fever) appears twice in a day and a night. A morbific entity generates, together with an opposed (entity), quotidian fever, (which appears) once in a day and a night, after acquiring force from one of (the entities consisting of) time (i.e. season), constitution and corruptible (constituents), and after obstructing the vessels which carry (the element) fat. A morbific entity staying in the bones or marrow will bring about (respectively) tertian or quartan (fever). Others hold a different opinion, saying that (a morbific entity) may bring about quotidian fever when it resides in the blood; following the channels of the (element) flesh, a morbific entity will generate tertian (fever), and quartan when it has taken residence in the pathway of the (element) fat. Quotidian (fever appears) every day and tertian (fever) with an interval of (one) day; that (fever) which recurs after an interval of two days is (called) quartan (fever);" A.h.Ni. 2, 58-63 = A.s.Ni. 2, 56-61 (Ki. 2, 61-66) deals with continuous fever in a way similar to Ca.Ci. 3, 53cd-60ab; A.h.Ni. 2, 60cd-70 and 71d-72c = A.s.Ni. 2, 74-75ab and 76b-77a (Ki. 2, 76-77 and 78d-79c) : "A morbific entity residing mainly in the blood brings about double quotidian fever; (it will appear) twice in a day and a night. Quotidian (fever appears) once (in a day and a night), and (the morbific entity) resides in that (fever) in the tubular vessels carrying (the element) flesh; in tertian (fever it resides) in the tubular vessels of (the element) fat ...; that is traditionally called (the fever) with an interval of one day. Quartan (fever appears) when the impurity stays in one of (the elements) fat, marrow or bone; others say it only stays in the marrow." Compare also Hā. 3, 2, 195a-d (see note 155).

161 See note 128.

162 Ca.Ci. 3, 59ab makes mention of the twelve places of residence of continuous fever (see note 160). Cakra explains that the twelve residences consist of the three morbific entities, the seven elements of the body and the two principal impurities, viz. faeces and urine.

163 See note 158 about Ḍa.'s opinion on this subject.

164 Ca. reads *avyaktalakṣaṇam* instead of *avyaktalakṣaṇaḥ*; the meaning is in that case : "When its lapse, with undeveloped characteristics, has occurred on the twelfth day," etc. Cakra remarks that the characteristics have become undeveloped because the fever has dissolved at that time.

165 *saṃtataka* is probably identical with *saṃtata*.

166 Also quoted by Cakra on Ca.Ci. 3, 74.

167 This quotation is only intelligible in conjunction with the other half of the stanza

(Ci. 3, 293ab) : "For, in an irregular fever, an adventitious (component) is usually (present as) an adjunctory factor;" Gul : "For, generally in the irregular fevers, there is seen the concomitant factor of spirit possession." Cakra's interpretation is in conformity with the latter translation; he says that a common (line of) therapy indicates that both a therapy having recourse to divine influences and one with recourse to natural techniques should be used.

168 Mā.ni. 2, 35b : *anuvartate.*

169 Also quoted by Ḍa. on Su.U. 39, 69; a closely related quotation occurs in Cakra's comment on Ca.Ci. 3, 59-60 : "Continuous (fever), however, is different and has a very slight and weak cause; it arises from one or two morbific entities; its secondary affections and characteristics are very slight; (when) the corruptible (constituent) and the constitution are not of a comparable character ..."

170 The source of this quotation remains unidentified.

171 Su. : *doṣaḥ kuryāj jvaraṃ nṛṇām* instead of *karoti viṣamajvaram.* Ḍa. says that the term morbific entity means, in this case, a single morbific entity, a pair of morbific entities or the whole group of morbific entities.

172 Replaced by chest (*uras*) in Ḍa.'s comment on Su.U. 39, 52.

173 Su. describes *pralepaka* fever along with the irregular fevers; Su.U. 39, 54ab reads : "One should know that *pralepaka* (fever), which annihilates the life of persons suffering from desiccation, is (also) of such a kind."

174 See about this fever Mā.ni. 2, 39.

175 Cf. Ca.Ci. 3, 293 ab = Su.U. 39, 56cd (see note 167).

176 This agrees with Cakra's opinion; see note 167.

177 Cf. Su.U. 39, 57ab : "Those possessing knowledge on this (subject) proclaim tertian as well as quartan (fever to arise) from an excess of wind;" Ḍa. comments : "Although in another treatise, with the words '(arising) from phlegm and bile it seizes the sacral region', it has been substantiated that tertian and quartan (fever) arise from a pair of morbific entities, (Su.) says nevertheless in his own treatise that they should be known (to arise from) an excess of wind, though there are also signs of bile and phlegm;" A.h.Ni. 2, 71 = A.s.Ni. 2, 75cd-76ab (Ki. 2, 78) : "(Tertian fever) seizes the head (when it arises) from bile and wind, the sacral region (when arising) from phlegm and bile, and (the sacral region) together with the back (when arising) from wind and phlegm; this (fever) is traditionally said to occur with an interval of one day;" A.h.Ni. 2, 72d-73ab = A.s.Ni. 2, 77b-d (Ki. 2, 79d-80ab) : "(Quartan fever) will show its power in two ways : (arising) by phlegm (it seizes) at the legs first, and at the head (when it arises) from wind;" Hā. 3, 2, 191 : "By wind and bile there will be pain in the sacral region, thighs and iliac regions, and by bile pain in the head and giddiness; the subtle (*tanu*) phlegm will bring about pain in the back; these are the threefold characteristics of tertian fever;" Hā. 3, 2, 192 = Ca.Ci. 3, 71; Hā. 3, 2, 193 : "Quartan fever should be known to be of two kinds : it is of the nature of wind or of phlegm; (when arising) from phlegm it should be known (to seize) at the legs, and when arising from wind at the head."

178 Ḍa. : the apertures (*kha*) are the channels (*srotas*).

179 Mā.ni. 2, 38c.

180 Cakra comments on Ca.Ci. 3, 74 : "With the word 'usually' it is pointed out that double quotidian (fever), etc. also arise from a pair of morbific entities, etc. Because one may ask how it is possible that a quartan fever arising from phlegm, etc. is spoken of, if things are thus, that (these fevers) are started by concerted action, it is said : 'that

one which is strongest in a (fever by) concerted action', etc. ... In (the treatise of) Jatūkarṇa it has been said, after reversed tertian and quartan (fever) have been dealt with : 'The irregular fevers, though arising from three morbific entities, are denominated according to the morbific entity which is present in excess.' Some agree that all these five fevers are irregular fevers. For irregularity means that the time (of appearance of the paroxysms) is irregular, as has been said elsewhere : 'An irregular (fever) is irregular with respect to its start, the time (of its paroxysms) and its actions, and it holds on (for a long time)' (A.h.Ni. 2, 69ab). Irregularity with respect to time is also found in continuous fever because it lapses on the twelfth day and appears again on the thirteenth day. Others, however, regard (only) the four fevers consisting of double quotidian (fever), etc., making an exception for continuous (fever), to be irregular, because continuous fever is not irregular with respect to time in the same way (as the other types). And Kharanāda has said : (the same quotation as in M. and Ā. on Mā.ni. 2, 34-36ab). Others again (are of the opinion that) only tertian and quartan (fever) are irregular, because irregular (fevers) are produced slowly. As Dāruvāha says : 'The morbific entity moves gently, in slight amounts and slowly, through the pathways of blood, etc., the openings of which are becoming more and more subtle and which are more and more distant, or it enters the body mostly while leaving some part unaffected; that is its course; therefore (irregular) fever is characterized by a discontinuous (*vichinna*) glowing heat' (= A.s.Ni. 2, 63cd-65ab) (Ki. 2, 68-69)."

181 *galagaṇḍa* is a swelling in the region of the throat, arising from wind, phlegm and fat, but never from bile; see ch. 38.

182 A quartan fever arising from bile is explicitly mentioned at Bhā.pra. 8, 1, 735ab : "That (quartan fever), however, which seizes the middle part of the body first, arises from bile."

183 See note 171.

184 Compare on the irregular fevers : Bhe.Ci. 2, 6-7 : "(Irregular fever) will corrupt marrow, bones and fat on the first day; when the second day has arrived it will corrupt flesh and blood. Thereupon it will corrupt phlegm and wind on the third day; then it reaches the bile and corrupts it on the fourth day;" Kā.Khi. 1, 31-39 : "That (fever) which, having recourse to its own ground and morbific entity, being fixed (with regard to time), inevitably shows its force, brought about by time and ground, twice a day and a night, in accordance with the morbific entity, is traditionally called double quotidian fever. Its seat is the receptacle of undigested food; that is the residence where it dwells. The seat of quotidian fever, however, is the chest. When the morbific entity has got down from the chest and attained the nutrient fluid, quotidian fever, which holds on (for a long time), arises at its proper (period of) time. The throat is the seat of tertian (fever). The morbific entity gets down from it and proceeds to the chest after a day and a night. After another day and night it takes residence, in accordance with the due order, in the element (of the body, called) nutrient fluid. Having coalesced with (the transforming) heat, it generates the completion (of the fever) on the third day. That is tertian (fever). The head is the seat of quartan (fever). It is called the fourth one. The morbific entity gets down from its seat after a day and a night and becomes lodged in the throat. From that (place) it proceeds to the chest after a day and a night again. On the third day, (lodged) in the element (of the body called) nutrient fluid, it becomes excited. This should be known as quartan (fever), which lasts for a long time and is a great fever. Arisen from a deep seat and being corrupted by the intermixture of the elements (of the body), it shows its force at (its own period of) time and becomes

dissolved in the head of a living being;" Kā.Khi. 1, 42cd-45 : "Staying for a long time, an irregular fever increases, in accordance with the (period of) time proper to each (particular type), after one, two, three or four days. Why does it not arise on the fifth or sixth day? Its seats are the receptacle of undigested food, chest, throat and head. Other seats do not exist and it does not arise in the absence of a seat. Double quotidian (fever) will be related to Agni, quotidian to Vāyu, tertian to the Viśve devāḥ and quartan to Īśāna."

185 The source of Mā.ni. 2, 39cd is unknown. A stanza, two *pādas* of which are identical with Mā.ni. 2, 39cd, is quoted by Cakra on Ca.Ci. 3, 73 with the qualification : 'thus it has been said in another treatise'. Cf. Ca.Ci. 3, 73cd : "It is brought about by each one of the three elements (= morbific entities), staying in two of the elements (of the body);" Cakra remarks that the two elements (of the body) are in this case bones and marrow; A.h.Ni. 2, 73cd-74ab = A.s.Ni. 2, 79 (Ki. 2, 81) : "When it stays both in the bones and the marrow, reversed quartan (fever) arises; it is of three kinds and brings about fever for two days, but leaves off for one day;" compare also Va. 1, 560 and Bhā.pra. 8, 1, 736-737.

186 This is a quotation from an unknown source.

187 Ḍa. comments on Su.U. 39, 55 : "A morbific entity staying in two seats of phlegm, (to wit) the chest and the receptacle of undigested food, brings about reversed quotidian (fever). How is this reversed type (of quotidian fever)? After leaving off during one (period of) time, consisting of morning, etc., of a day and a night, it is present during the whole remaining day and night. In the same way a morbific entity staying in three seats of phlegm, (to wit) the throat, chest and receptacle of undigested food, brings about reversed tertian (fever), i.e. that one which leaves off at the third day. A morbific entity staying in four seats of phlegm, (to wit) the head, throat, chest and receptacle of undigested food, brings about reversed quartan fever; that (fever) leaves off at the fourth day. A reversed (type) of double quotidian (fever) does not exist, because it is brought about by a morbific entity staying in only one seat of phlegm, or on account of the very nature of (this) illness. The term 'morbific entity' means in this case a single morbific entity, a pair or the whole (set) of morbific entities."

188 *dharma* : norm, authoritative rule.

189 Su. : *pra-muc-* instead of *vi-muc-*; *vairasya* (an altered taste in the mouth) does not occur in Su.

190 These two stanzas do not occur in Su., but are quoted by Ḍa. in his comment on Su. 39, 63cd-64 as another set of characteristics, with, as a variant, *līna* (dissolved) instead of *juṣṭa* (inhabiting).

191 A.s. : *śīta* (cold) instead of *śūnaka* (swollen); *kṛcchreṇa sidhyati* (it is cured with difficulty) instead of *tena sīdati* (one becomes adynamic by it).

192 This unusual treatise is the Aṣṭāṅgasaṃgraha.

193 The source of this quotation is unknown.

194 Su. : *kaphādhikatvena* instead of *kaphādhikatvāt*.

195 A.s. : *pralepa* instead of *vilepin*.

196 A.s. : *sa śītaḥ* instead of *saśītaḥ*.

197 The compound *mandajvaravilepin* is interpreted as a *karmadhāraya* of the type : '(an entity which) on the one hand is *mandajvara* and on the other hand also *vilepin*'.

198 A.s. : *āmāśaye yadā duṣṭe* (when the receptacle of undigested food has been corrupted) instead of *vidagdhe 'nnarase dehe* (when the nutrient fluid derived from the food has been combustively altered in the body).

199 The source of this stanza is unknown.

200 Su. : *praśānte kurutas tasmiṃś chītam ante ca tāv api* instead of *tasmin praśānte tv itarau kurutaḥ śītam antataḥ.*

201 Su .: *kṛcchrasādhyaś ca sa smṛtaḥ* instead of *kṛcchrasādhyatamaś ca saḥ.*

202 Cf. A.h.Ni. 2, 35-36ab = A.s.Ni. 2, 32-33ab (Ki. 2, 31) : "And a different (entity) is the (fever) arising from concerted action, in which the bile, separated (from wind and phlegm) and staying in the skin or the viscera, occasions a burning sensation, (manifesting itself) in the beginning or later on. In a similar way wind and phlegm (occasion) a feeling of coldness. (The fever) with a burning sensation in the beginning is the more difficult one to cure;" Kā.Khi. 1, 52-62 : "Why does, when the morbific entities are in a turbulent state, a feeling of coldness usually appear first in fever in a living being and (only) afterwards a burning sensation ? Wind is diffusive, clear, cold, dry, fluctuating and harsh; bile is fiery, hot, sharp, (present in a) slight (quantity), light and liquid. Phlegm is of the nature of *soma*, cold, heavy, oleaginous, strong and (present in a) copious (quantity); phlegm is diffusive in a sluggish way, and (its excitement) takes a long time to rise up and to cease (again). The wind is strong and is the auxiliary of phlegm because (they possess) the same quality, (i.e.) coldness; so the *soma*-like quality is traditionally said to be strong and the fiery one weak. On account of this important ground phlegm is the stronger one; for that reason a feeling of coldness appears first in fever and a burning sensation afterwards. When phlegm becomes appeased on account of transformation of its own impulse and by means of hot therapeutical procedures, bile becomes excited. Well-being will come about (in the patient) when this (bile) has been appeased by transformation and therapeutical procedures; this has been called the important ground suitable to (a fever) with a feeling of coldness at the beginning. And why arises in a living being a fever with a burning sensation at the beginning ? The same ground is said to apply to this (case) as well, on account of its very great strength. When the bile has been roused to an extreme degree, has coalesced with a slight (amount of) wind and is attended by phlegm of a slight force in the seat of the nutrient fluid, (a fever) with a burning sensation at the beginning and a feeling of coldness at the end appears in a living being, accompanied by shivering, confused speech and confusion of memory and thought. These two fevers, with a feeling of coldness or a burning sensation at the beginning, originate from combined action; of these two fevers, that one in which a burning sensation arises at the beginning, is incurable or difficult to cure;" Hā. 3, 2, 171 : "When wind and phlegm (stay) in the upper part (of one's body) and only bile moves downwards, half of the body becomes cold on account of that and hot(ness) arises in the (other) half;" ibid., 3, 2, 173 : "When blood and bile (move) upwards and both wind and phlegm (stay) in the middle part (of the body), the upper part becomes hot on account of that and the lower part cold;" ibid., 3, 2, 178 : "When bile stays at the extremities and both wind and phlegm in (the other parts of) the body, coldness of the body (arises) on account of that and hotness of hands and feet;" ibid., 3, 2, 180 : "When bile stays in the body and both wind and phlegm at the extremities, hotness arises in one's body and coldness of hands and feet;" ibid., 3, 2, 189-190 : "When coldness is present first and hotness arises later on, (an irregular fever) is proclaimed to be curable in a human being; a remedy is quickly succesful. When one acquires a burning sensation afterwards, it is a severe fever; one is not released from it quickly, and it is a fever that brings about decline of the elements (of the body)."

203 Divided into a left and a right half like Ardhanārīśvara, a form of Śiva, the left half of whose body is female, the right half being male.

[204] Divided into an upper and a lower half like Narasiṃha, the fourth incarnation of Viṣṇu; the upper half of Narasiṃha's body was that of a lion, the lower half that of a man.

[205] Mā.ni. 2, 43a.

[206] Mā.ni. 2, 45c.

[207] Ḍa. remarks on Su.U. 39, 65ab that the meaning is that the morbific entity goes from one element to another and stays there; he adds that others are of the opinion that the expression 'another element' points to the seven *kalās*.

[208] Mā.ni. 2, 46c.

[209] Ḍa. deals with this problem in his comment on Su.U. 39, 61 : he remarks that, although both fevers arise from the three morbific entities, they are said to arise from combined action here, because phlegm and wind bring about one effect or, according to others, it is thus, that phlegm and wind are designated as one (entity).

[210] This stanza is found : Siddhayoga 1, 222, with the variant *hīnapitta* (with deficiency of bile) instead of *kṣīṇapitta* (with decline of bile). Cf. A.s.Ni. 2, 90cd-92ab (Ki. 2, 95) : "If in a bodily being with a deficiency of bile and a congruous state of phlegm and wind either a sharp or a slow fever arises, it is a nightly one. When the force of the body has been absorbed by the sun and when the body is desiccated by physical exercise, a fever will occur that invariably (arises) from wind and (appears) in the first part of the night."

[211] This stanza does not occur in Su.U. 39,.

[212] In the Sāṃkhya philosophy the three constituents of *prakṛti* are *sattva*, *rajas* and *tamas*; see R. Garbe, p. 209-220. See about the personality types dominated by these constituents : Ca.Śā. 4, 36-40.

[213] In the Sāṃkhya philosophy *buddhi* evolves from *prakṛti* prior to *manas*. *manas* evolves from *ahaṃkāra* which is in its turn a product of *buddhi*. So *buddhi* and *manas* stand to each other as cause and effect. See R. Garbe, p. 244-253.

[214] An *iṣṭi* is an oblation poured into the sacrificial fire and not consisting of an animal or a part of it.

[215] A *bali* is an oblation put down or thrown down somewhere but not poured into the sacrificial fire.

[216] Compare Cakra's comment on Ca.Ci. 3, 75 : "As continuous fever can assume the form of (the) double quotidian (type), etc., thus double quotidian (fever) can assume the form of (the) continuous (type), etc.; with regard to that, it is presently said : '(on account of the relative strength of) season, (period of) day and night, etc.'... In that respect double quotidian (fever), in which wind is the most important (morbific entity) and which arises at the time of the rains, assumes the form of quotidian (fever), etc., after reaching the season opposed to it, (i.e.) the autumn. (An example) on account of the relative strength of (the period of) day and night is the reaching of a specific (period of) time; as a quartan fever, with wind (as its most important morbific entity), that has arisen during the middlemost days of the spring, assumes the form of a strong tertian (fever), after reaching the later, dry days of the spring, thus a double quotidian (fever), with phlegm (as its most important morbific entity) and arisen during the days mentioned above, assumes the form of a quotidian fever during the days which form the rest (of the season) and are opposed to phlegm. (An example) on account of the relative strength of the morbific entity : change (*parāvṛtti*) of a fever is (a) suitable (process) when it arises from indulgence in the ground of the corrupted (entity). (Examples) on account of the strength of the *manas* : someone suffering from continuous fever becomes

someone with quotidian fever, etc. when his *manas* ceases (functioning); someone suffering from quartan fever, etc. becomes someone with tertian fever, etc. when his *manas* is weak by fear, etc. (Examples) by the force of actions with regard to the change of a fever : one acquires well-being by auspicious acts because (these acts lead to) change of a fever resulting in suffering, but a fever leading to suffering arises by evil acts."

217 Su. : *sveda* (perspiration) instead of *moha* (mental confusion).

218 Su. : *kuñcana* (contraction) instead of *kūjana* (rumbling).

219 Ḍa. remarks of these stanzas that they are the reading approved of by Gayadāsa, and that he agrees with the latter, discarding the reading of this part of Su. by Jejjaṭa. Ḍa. quotes Jejjaṭa's reading : "Learn from me, my dear child, the characteristics of a fever staying in the nutrient fluid : (they consist of) heaviness, dejection, nausea, adynamia, vomiting and anorexia. Red and hot boils, thirst, spitting of blood, giddiness, a burning sensation, fainting, inability to eat, vomiting and confused speech (occur in a fever) staying in the blood. Cramp in the calves, thirst, furtherance of the appearance of urine and faeces, heat in the interior (of the body), mental confusion, tossing about and languor will occur in a fever staying in the flesh. Sharp paroxysms, thirst, fainting, vomiting, confused speech, the inability to endure (one's own) smell, languor and anorexia (occur in a fever) staying in the fat. Emptying of the bowels as well as emesis, cutting pain in the bones, rumbling, tossing about of the limbs and shortness of breath (occur) in a fever staying in the bones. Hiccup, cough, intense shortness of breath, (the sensation of) entering into darkness, a trenchant pain in the vital points, a sense of external coldness and certainly a sensation of inner burning (occur in a fever) staying in the marrow. One dies from it when it moreover slowly approaches the semen; (in that case there occur) especially erections and ejaculations." Ḍa. adds that Jejjaṭa was of the opinion that these stanzas should not be read (as forming part of Su.), because continuous (fever) pervades the whole body and double quotidian (fever), etc. (pervade) the nutrient fluid and the other elements (of the body); so there is no occasion (to assume the existence) of another (group of) fevers which reside in the nutrient fluid, etc. Cf. Ca.Ci. 3, 76-82 : "Heaviness, dejection, disquietude, adynamia, vomiting, anorexia, glowing heat at the exterior (of the body), muscle pain and yawning (occur) in (a fever) staying in the nutrient fluid. Red and hot boils, thirst, spitting of blood again and again, a burning sensation, redness, giddiness, (mental disturbance as in) intoxication and confused speech (are present) when (the fever) stays in the blood. A sensation of inner burning, thirst, mental confusion, languor, furtherance of the appearance of faeces, a bad smell and tossing about will occur in a fever staying in the flesh. Perspiration, an intense thirst, confused speech, frequent emesis, the inability to endure one's own smell, languor and anorexia (will occur) in (a fever) staying in the fat. Both emptying of the bowels and emesis, cutting pain in the bones, rumbling, tossing about and shortness of breath (occur) in a fever staying in the bones. Hiccup, shortness of breath, cough, an extreme degree of darkness before the eyes, a trenchant pain in the vital points, a sensation of coldness at the exterior and a sensation of inner burning (occur) in (a fever) staying in the marrow. When that all-pervading (fever), staying in the seat of semen, has brought about ejaculation and has annihilated the vital breath, it goes (away), accompanied by (the bodily) wind, fire and *soma*;" A.s.Ni. 2, 81-87ab (Ki. 2, 83-91) : "Nausea, heaviness, dejection, the sensation that the parts of the body break (apart), yawning, anorexia, emesis and adynamia (occur) in every fever that stays in the nutrient fluid. Spitting of blood, thirst, the appearance of red and hot boils, a burning sensation, redness, giddiness, (mental disturbance as in) intoxication and confused

speech (occur) when (the fever) resides in the blood. Thirst, languor, furtherance of the appearance of faeces, a sensation of inner burning, giddiness, darkness (of vision), a bad smell and tossing about (occur) when (the fever) stays in the flesh. Perspiration, an extreme thirst, emesis, the inability to endure one's own smell, confused speech, languor and the inability to eat (occur) when (the fever) stays in the fat. Cutting pain in the bones, the appearance of the morbific entities above and below, shortness of breath, convulsions and rumbling (occur) when (the fever) stays in the bones. A sensation of inner burning, a sense of coldness at the exterior, shortness of breath and hiccup (occur) when (the fever) stays in the marrow. Darkness of vision, a trenchant pain in the vital points, erection, the coming forth of semen and death arise when (the fever) resides in the semen. Of the (first) five (fevers) each subsequent one (in the series) is more difficult to cure and the two last ones should be given up."

220 See Ca.Ci. 15, 18-19ab.

221 Ḍa. : (it means) an inclination to wrath; some consider it as the inability to endure one's own smell.

222 See the second part of ch. 12.

223 Ḍa. : idem.

224 Su.Śā. 4, 21b : *gūḍhaś cekṣau raso yathā* (as the juice is hidden in the sugar-cane).

225 Compare this line of reasoning with the almost identical one in Ḍa.'s comment on Su.U. 39, 88cd.

226 The additional stanza, following after Mā.ni. 2, 54, is quoted with the variant *śukrasthāne na jīvati* (one certainly dies when it is present in the seat of semen). It follows from this quotation that the author of Ā. did not regard the additional stanza as forming part of the Nidāna; nor does Vijayarakṣita comment on it.

227 A.h. and A.s. : *prāyaś ca prākṛto 'nilāt* (as well as usually the natural one arising from wind).

228 Cf. Ca.Ci. 3, 48cd-49 : "A fever is taught to be natural with reference to the nature of (the period of) time (in which it occurs). (A natural fever) is usually difficult (to cure) when it arises from wind, as well as (a fever) based on a deviation (from the natural state), occurring at other (periods of) time (i.e. seasons which do not correspond with its nature). The manifest grounds of it have been shown in (the section on) the origins."

229 This refers to Mā.ni. 2, 55d, corresponding to A.h.Ni. 2, 50d.

230 Also quoted by Cakra on Ca.Ci. 3, 42.

231 This quotation has not been traced to its source.

232 Cf. Ca.Ci. 3, 42-47ab : "But a natural (fever) arising in spring or autumn is easily curable. The hot bile, increased by hot (things), becomes excited in the autumn. In the same way phlegm that has accumulated during the cold (season) is stirred up in the spring. Bile that has accumulated during the rainy season by means of the waters and herbs with an acid maturative alteration, and has become salient by the fiery energy of the sun, quickly generates fever in the autumn, with phlegm as its auxiliary force. By reason of the very nature of the period of emission abstinence from food (need) not be feared. Phlegm that has accumulated during the winter by means of the sweet waters and herbs, becomes, made glowingly hot by the sun, excited in the spring. Therefore fever arises by phlegm in the spring. In the middle of the period of resorption wind and bile may attend it."

233 Cakra remarks on Ca.Sū. 6, 34 : "By their special faculty vapours bring about excitement of the three morbific entities; discharges from clouds give rise to wind and phlegm; the acid maturative alteration of the water, brought about by the very nature

of the rainy season, gives rise to bile and phlegm. With the words 'when the strength of the fire has declined' he also points to the sluggishness of the fire which excites the morbific entities. Sluggishness of the fire again gives rise to phlegm and bile by the absence of maturation and by combustive alteration, and it gives rise to wind by decline of the elements on account of the non-production of (that) nutrient fluid which nourishes the elements. Therefore excitement of wind, etc. occurs by the sluggishness of the fire during the rainy season."

234 The implications of this quotation (= Siddhayoga 1, 146) are not clear. Cf. Ca.Ci. 3, 283cd-284ab : "In fevers which are accompanied by immature matter, which arise from phlegm or from phlegm and bile, reducing measures should be employed, as described in the chapter on reducing measures, and adapted to each particular case." Cakra remarks on this stanza : "Reducing measures should, according to these words, also be employed in a fever by wind accompanied by immature matter, for it is said elsewhere : 'Reducing measures (should) also (be employed) in (a fever) by wind accompanied by immature matter'. Reducing measures are, however, also recommended in (a fever) arising from phlegm devoid of immature matter. The words 'arising from phlegm and bile' (express that) reducing measures should be employed in (a fever) by bile, associated with phlegm, and not only in (a fever) by bile which is devoid of immature matter, for reducing measures are certainly recommended in (a fever) arising from bile accompanied by immature matter in order to promote decline of the immature matter. As has been said elsewhere : 'Reducing measures should certainly also be employed in (a fever by) bile accompanied by immature matter in order to promote maturation of the immature matter'. But what has been said (with the following words) : 'Phlegm and bile tolerate intense fasting when they are liquid elements', also refers to bile accompanied by liquid matter on account of its being accompanied by immature matter. When the liquid component of bile has declined, however, one should certainly not employ reducing measures."

235 Aruṇa comments on A.h.Ni. 2, 51-52 (= Mā.ni. 2, 56-57) : "In the early rainy season the corrupted, (i.e.) excited, wind, with bile and phlegm joined to it, brings about fever. A natural fever in the early rainy season arises predominantly from wind, bile and phlegm acting as the auxiliary forces of wind; the latter two (entities) do not bring about fever independently as in concerted action. Bile may bring about a natural fever in the autumn, thus one should supply; (this occurs) on account of the real state of affairs that bile, accumulated in the early rainy season, is in an excited condition. (Phlegm as its auxiliary force is compared with the auxiliary army of a king, as in Ā., and in identical terms. Thereupon follows that part of Aruṇa's comment, which is quoted in Ā., with almost no variants). Corrupted phlegm may bring about fever in spring-time, so (the author) continues. This phlegm again may be attended by wind and bile; this means that wind and bile are its auxiliary forces. (An objector may say :) is it not clearly thus, that phlegm is stated to be the agent in this case ?; and phlegm is of a moon-like nature; for that reason there is no danger from abstinence from food in this case. That (reasoning) is not suitable, for thus it has been said : on account of the real existence of the (following) two causes, (viz.) that in the rainy season and autumn phlegm is an auxiliary force and that the (period of) time is called period of emission, depletion of the elements is thought to be really impossible; but in the spring depletion of the elements necessarily occurs on account of the fiery character of the (period of) time and the fact that wind and bile act as auxiliary forces; therefore danger from abstinence from food should be feared in the spring. Some people, however, say that

some danger from abstinence from food should not be feared at all because fever arises from the receptacle of undigested food and in this case from phlegm."

236 Cf. A.h.Ni. 2, 48d-49 = A.s.Ni. 2, 46b-47ab (Ki. 2, 49) : "When a fever resides in the interior, the morbid alterations, present to an excessive degree, will consist of a turbulent state in the interior and seizing of the impurities. In (a fever) with an external impulse the sense of glowing heat (will be present) only at the exterior and it will be easily curable."

237 See Mā.ni. 2, 68cd-69ab = Su.U. 39, 92cd-93ab.

238 This refers to Mā.ni. 2, 59.

239 Ḍa. explains that 'deep' means : with an internal impulse, and 'sharp': very difficult to endure, with an impulse that is both external and internal.

240 Stanzas identical with Mā.ni. 2, 61cd-63ab are quoted by Ḍa. in his comment on Su.U. 39, 116cd-119ab as an alternative reading of these stanzas of Su., which is preferred by the author of the Pañjikā.

241 Mā.ni. 2, 63cd and the two additional *pāda*s are almost identical with Su.U. 39, 121cd-122ab.

242 Cf. Ca.Ci. 3, 133cd-136ab : "Inability to eat, absence of digestive alteration, heaviness of the abdomen, a polluted condition of the cardiac region, lassitude, inertia, a strong fever without lapse, non-appearance of the morbific entities, effusion of saliva, sickness, annihilation of the sense of hunger, an altered taste in the mouth, stiffness, numbness and heaviness of the limbs, (production of) a copious amount of urine, faeces (consisting of) not (completely) disintegrated (food) and the absence of languor are the characteristics of an immature fever;" Su.U. 39, 115-119ab : "(When the fever is sharp, the body is heavy and the impurities are in a confined condition, one should discern it as a fever the morbific entity of which is accompanied by immature matter; when there is a different condition it should be considered to be mature). When the fever is mild, the body is light and the impurities are moving on, one should discern the morbific entity of the fever as being mature; (then) one should give a remedial agent appropriate to it. According to some the characteristics of a mature (fever result from) alteration of the original state of a morbific entity. A cramp-like sensation in the cardiac region, lassitude, discharge of saliva, anorexia, non-appearance of the morbific entity, inertia, a confined state (of the impurities), (production of) a copious amount of urine, heaviness of the abdomen, absence of perspiration, absence of maturation of the faeces, disinclination, numbness, stiffness and heaviness of the limbs, mildness of the (transforming) fire, a polluted condition of the mouth, absence of languor and a strong fever that clings (to the patient), by means of these signs an experienced (physician) should discern a fever as being immature;" A.h.Ni. 2, 54 = A.s.Ni. 2, 52 (Ki. 2, 56) : "Sharpness of the fever and of the secondary affections, absence of languor, (production of) a copious amount of urine, non-appearance (of the morbific entities), faeces (consisting of) not (completely) disintegrated (food) and absence of hunger (constitute) the conformation of a fever accompanied by immature matter;" A.h.Ni. 2, 56ab = A.s.Ni. 2. 56ab (Ki. 2, 58): "(The presence of) a disintegrated condition (of the fever, i.e. maturity, may be concluded) from (the presence of signs which are) opposite to (those of an) immature (fever) and from fasting during seven (days and) nights;" Kā.Khi. 2, 18cd-21ab : "A confined state (of the impurities), inability to eat, thirst, fainting, cutting pain in the limbs, headache, confused speech, inertia, sickness, lassitude, a burning sensation, fatigue, giddiness, a very abundant (production of) urine, languor, faeces (consisting of food that has) not (been) digestively altered, nausea and heaviness of the viscera are

said to be the signs in an immature fever. When these (signs) have disappeared for the greater part, when the fever has become mild and (the body) has become light after eight (days and) nights, it is pointed out as a fever devoid of immature matter."

243 See Ca.Sū. 11, 54.

244 See Ca.Ci. 3, 145cd-146ab : "To appease thirst and fever one should give water that has become cold after boiling it with *musta, parpaṭaka, uśīra, candana, udīcya* and *nāgara.*" Su.U. 39, 108cd-109ab presents the same list of drugs; A.h.Ci.1, 15cd-16ab contains a list which is probably identical. This group of six drugs is called *ṣaḍaṅga*; *ardhaśṛta* means that the water has to be kept boiling till half of the original quantity remains.

245 See Mā.ni. 2, 65.

246 See Bhā.pra. 8, 1, 98 : "Thoughtful people call a fever a fresh one up to the seventh day; when it pervades one for twelve days it is said to be (of) moderate (duration); after that (period) it is called of long standing." A very similar stanza is quoted by Cakra in his comment on Ca.Ci. 3, 160cd-161ab; he adds that it is taken from the Puṣkalāvata(saṃhitā).

247 Ca. reads at the end of Ci. 3, 160d : *pāyayed bhiṣak*, instead of *pāyayet tu tam.*

248 *rasaudana*, which has the meaning of *māṃsarasaudana.*

249 A *basti* is an instrument made from the bladder of an animal with a syringe attached to it, which was used to bring medicated substances into the rectum and the urethra.

250 There are many rules concerning the application of several types of *basti*. The application of a *basti* is adduced as an example because it is sometimes given once a week.

251 This quotation is identical with Siddhayoga, 1, 81.

252 Su. : *deyaṃ syāt* instead of *bheṣajam.*

253 A.h. : *doṣavegodaye* (when there is a rise of the impulse of the morbific entity) instead of *doṣavegodayaḥ*. The former reading makes better sense.

254 Aruṇa comments on these stanzas : "... A rise of the impulse of the morbific entity is the becoming apparent, on account of the nausea (produced) by *musta, parpaṭaka*, etc., of that morbific entity called immature matter, etc. and present in abundance; or it is the rise of the morbific entities, (consisting of) wind, etc., which are abundantly immature. A remedial agent is not subject to the process of maturation in such a case because the (transforming) fire is covered by immature matter; for that reason it makes a fever flare up more strongly."

255 See note 246; according to Cakra it is quoted from Puṣkalāvata's treatise.

256 Some of the elements of this elaborate comment are also found in Cakra's explanation of Ca.Ci. 3, 137cd-138ab (= Mā.ni. 2, 65) : "In this case hunger, etc., arising from maturation of the morbific entity, are, also without the period of eight days, the characteristics of a fever started by a morbific entity devoid of immature matter. But a period of eight days, without (the presence of) hunger, etc., expresses, though maturation of the morbific entity is absent, that the fever as an illness is devoid of immature matter, which makes it suitable for the administration of a remedy. For that very reason, by means of two alternatives : 'One should give to him as a drink a maturation-promoting or an appeasing *kaṣāya*', the following statement is made : when the characteristics of maturation of the morbific entities, consisting of hunger, etc., do not appear within a period of eight days, a maturation-promoting agent should be given for the sake of maturation of the morbific entities, and when the whole collection (of symptoms),

consisting of hunger, etc., has arisen, one should give an appeasing agent because the fever is in all respects devoid of immature matter. As Kharanāda says, teaching this very (concept) of a state in which (fever) is in all respects devoid of immature matter : 'The characteristics of a fever devoid of immature matter do not consist of a period of eight days only; in a fever by concerted action the impurities (may) become mature also after a long time. The characteristics consist of the passing beyond (a period of) seven (days and) nights and (moreover) emaciation, etc. Therefore one should regard a fever to be devoid of immature matter when both these (characteristics) have been observed.' Suśruta substantiates (that a fever is) devoid of immature matter when hunger, etc. are observed, generated by maturation of the morbific entity after a period of eight days, for he shows that one should give a remedy after eight days : 'And after that one should give a remedy on account of the maturation of the morbific entity.' For that reason both hunger, etc. and a period of eight days, dissociated or associated, should be known as characteristics, on account of the argument stated above."

257 The compound *kṣunnāśa* can be interpreted as *kṣut-nāśa* or *kṣudh-nāśa.*

258 *utsāha* instead of *aṣṭāha.*

259 The ten secondary affections of fever are, from another treatise, also quoted by Cakra in his comment on Ca.Ci. 3, 50ab; the order of the affections is different and *kṛcchraviṭkatā* (difficulties at defecation) occurs instead of *viḍgraha* (seizing of the faeces). The stanza quoted in M. is also found at Va. 1, 840 and moreover at Bhā.pra. 8, 1, 840 with the variant *aṅgadāha* (a burning sensation in the body) instead of *aṅgabheda* (cutting pain in the body).

260 This stanza is taken from an unknown source.

261 Su. : *yas tāmyati visaṃjñaś ca* instead of *visaṃjñas tāmyate yas tu.*

262 Su. : *nityaṃ vaktreṇa cocchvasyāt* instead of *vaktreṇa caivocchvasiti.*

263 Su. : *pipāsārta* instead of *tṛṣāyukta.*

264 Mādhava omits Su.Sū. 33, 18 : "Fever annihilates a man whose eyes are turbid, who is breathless and extremely sleepy, and whose blood and eyes have declined."

265 Compare Cakra's comment on Ca.Ci. 3, 50cd-51ab : "Is it not thus that (a fever) arisen from many strong grounds will of course be (provided) with many characteristics ? What is then the use of the expression '(provided) with many characteristics' ? The answer (to this objection) is : just as the grounds of the morbific entities, though there exist the mentioned qualities of the morbific entities, do not bring about a disease with many characteristics, because every man has (his own) specific (transforming) fire and force, so there does not exist a condition with many characteristics when a specific onset is absent."

266 Also quoted by Cakra on Ca.Ci. 3, 50cd-51ab.

267 See about *indriya* : R. Garbe, Die Sāṃkhya-Philosophie, ed. 1894, p. 257-261; Sāṃkhyakārikā 25, 26; 25, 28 and 25, 34 (and the Sāṃkhyatattvakaumudī); Sāṃkhyasūtra 2, 18; 2, 19; 2, 23; 2, 26-29 (and the Sāṃkhyapravacanabhāṣya). See about *manas* : R. Garbe, ibid., p. 252-253; Sāṃkhyakārikā 27 (and the Sāṃkhyatattvakaumudī); Sāṃkhyasūtra 2, 26-27 (and the Sāṃkhyapravacanabhāṣya).

268 See Ca.Sū. 8, 7-8; 10-11; Ca.Śā. 1, 18-19; 25-26.

269 See Su.Śā. 1, 4-5.

270 Cakra says that 'deep' means : with an internal impulse, or : staying in a deep element.

271 Cakra says in his comment on Ca.Ci. 3, 52cd-53ab that it means : attending one for a long time or bringing about the long night, i.e. death.

272 Su. : *luṇḍanti* instead of *lunanti*; Ḍa. explains the term as meaning : incessantly moving (eyelashes). Cf. Ca.I. 8, 6 : "If, either in the brows or in (the hair of) the head of someone, many partings and whirls are clearly seen, which did not exist before and were not made (on purpose), one should announce the death (of that person)."

273 Ḍa. explains the term *anāddhatva* (a state of obstructive abdominal swelling) by *doṣapurīṣavibandha* (a confined state of the morbific entity and the faeces).

274 This refers to Mā.ni. 2, 69d.

275 Ḍa. explains it as : one faints again and again.

276 Ḍa. : idem.

277 Ḍa.'s comment is of the same character.

278 *antaḥkaraṇa*, i.e. the assembled *buddhi*, *ahaṃkāra* and *manas*; see R. Garbe, l.c., p. 253-257.

279 *rākṣasas* are a class of fiends.

280 The same variant readings and explanations are met with in Ḍa.'s comment.

281 A *preta* is the spirit of a dead person, especially before the obsequial rites have been performed.

282 Cf. A.h.Śā. 6, 40cd-41ab : "The man who, drinking an alcoholic beverage in the company of *pretas*, is dragged by a dog in his dream, is quickly carried off by death in the form of fever." A.s.Śā. 12, 18 contains the same statement in prose.

283 Cf. A.h.Śā. 5, 73 = A.s.Śā. 11, 5cd-6ab : "Someone lacking force and flesh (is killed by fever) in the morning when it is accompanied by a dry cough, and in the afternoon when it is accompanied by a cough (productive) of phlegm."

284 *gosarge*, literally : at the time the cows are let loose.

285 A.s. : *upatapta* (suffering from glowing heat) instead of *upasṛṣṭa* (plagued).

286 These statements are identical with Siddhayoga 1, 187.

287 Cf. A.h.Śā. 5, 57 and 61ab = A.s.Śā. 10, 16 and 20ab : "Someone whose sweat flows down from the forehead, whose junctures and ligaments are slackened and who will faint when one causes him to stand up, whether he be strong or weak, ... really all these (persons) should be known as falling to the share of death."

288 Signs indicating the death of a patient suffering from fever also occur : Hā. 2, 4, 6-15.

289 According to Indu and Aruṇa *nidhana*, *pratyara* and *vipatkara* are resp. the seventh, fifth and third lunar mansion from that of birth.

290 See Hā. 2, 6, 9-52.

291 See A.s.Ni. 1, 22cd-32 (Ki. 1, 34).

292 Also quoted in M. on Mā.ni. 2, 34-36ab. See note 128.

293 Ca. : *yogavāha* instead of *yogavāhin*. Cf. A.h.Ni. 2, 48 = A.s.Ni. 2, 45cd-46ab (Ki. 2, 48) : "On account of the assimilating character of wind there will be coldness when it is connected with phlegm, a burning sensation when it is connected with bile and a sensation of mixed character when it is mixed (with both entities)."

294 Fiery energy (*tejas*) corresponds with bile.

295 *soma* corresponds with phlegm.

296 = Bhā.pra. 8, 1, 536. See also note 242.

297 = Bhā.pra. 8, 1, 539. See also note 242.

298 A variant reads : on account of the quick, moderate and slow power (of action) of the morbific entities, established by their degrees of excitement, etc.

299 See ch. 55; *agnirohiṇī* is a disease with axillary inflammatory swellings.

300 Quoted by Ā. on Mā.ni. 2, 24 as originating from the Bhālukitantra (v.l. : twice ten instead of twice nine days); see note 127.

301 Ḍa.'s comment on Su.U. 39, 45cd-46ab contains elements which are similar to those occurring in M. : "On account of the quick, moderate and slow power (of action) of wind, etc. (this occurs) on the seventh day in a fever by concerted action with an excess of wind, on the tenth day when an excess of bile, and on the twelfth day when an excess of phlegm is present. It leaves off on account of maturation of the impurities or kills on account of maturation of the elements. Maturation of the impurities occurs if the actions (of the patient confer) a long life upon him; when things are different, maturation of the elements (takes place). Others think, however, that (a period of) seven days refers to *abhinyāsa* (fever), (of) ten days to *hataujas*, and (of) twelve days to *saṃnyāsa* (fever). A fatal maturation of the elements should be discerned by means of omina or precursory signals of death. The fixed periods of time resulting in delivery or death from a fever by concerted action, as proclaimed by Bhāluki (A.h.Ni. 2, 62cd-63ab is quoted), are arrived at by means of the word 'also' (*api*) in 'or also (after reaching) the twelfth day'." So Ḍa. used the word *api* instead of *punaḥ* to arrive at the doubling of the numbers.

302 The source of this quotation is unknown, though some editions indicate that it is taken from A.h.Ni. 2.

303 This refers to Mā.ni. 2, 74ab.

304 Su.Sū. 33, 18 is quoted; see note 264.

305 The printed text reads : *kupitaropamacayaḥ*, which is unintelligible.

306 Cf. Ca.Ci. 3, 324-328 : "In release from fever a man vomits while rumbling, he wallows and pants with an altered colour (of his skin), his body is wet with perspiration, he trembles, is frequently absent-minded and talks in a confused way, while his whole body is hot or cold; with an altered consciousness and afflicted by the paroxysms of the fever, he looks round as if in wrath; liquid faecal matter is discharged with great impetus, accompanied by the morbific entity and noise. An experienced (physician) should know that these are the signs of release from fever;" Su.U. 39, 321 : "At the time of release (from fever) the morbific entity shows its strength, bringing the elements into a turbulent state; owing to that (state, the patient), with a disturbed mind, behaves like someone who is dying;" Hā. 3, 2, 184 : "Giddiness, a feeling of coldness, a perturbed state of mind, trembling, loosening of faecal matter, weariness, fatigue, perspiration and garrulity are present in release from fever."

307 A.h. : *vilīyate* (it is dissolved) instead of *balīyate* (it shows its strength).

308 This quotation is not complete without adding A.h.Ni. 2, 77cd-78 : "One trembles and talks in a confused way, the parts of the body being hot and cold and the lustre (of the skin) being damaged; with an altered consciousness and afflicted by the paroxysms of the fever, one looks round as if in wrath; liquid faecal matter is emitted with great impetus, accompanied by the morbific entity and noise."

309 From this remark one can conclude that the author of M. read *vaigandhya* and not *āsyavaigandhya*.

310 Su.U. 39, 322 is closely related to this stanza : "Lightness of the head, perspiration, a somewhat pale and inflamed mouth, sneezing, and longing for food are the characteristics of someone who has been released from fever." Cf. Ca.Ci. 3, 329 : "Someone whose weariness has gone, who is free from general glowing heat and distressing sensations, whose senses are free from impurities and who possesses the *sattva* belonging to his natural disposition, should be known as a person free from fever;" A.h.Ni. 2, 79 =

A.s.Ni. 2, 97 (Ki. 2, 100) : "A light body, departed weariness, mental confusion and glowing heat, inflammatory changes in the mouth, an excellent condition of the senses, absence of distressing sensations, perspiration, sneezing, a *manas* possessed of its natural disposition, longing for food and itching of the head are the characteristics of someone whose fever has departed;" Hā. 3, 2, 185 : "Profuse perspiration, itching, (well-)nourished vessels and (the same condition) with respect to the openings, sneezing, lightness, relish for food, (an) extended (range of activity of the) senses and departure of weariness and pain (are the characteristics of someone released from fever)."

[311] See Mā.ni. 2, 74c-f.

[312] Cf. Ca.Ci. 3, 327-328 : "A strong and very recently (acquired) fever, in a person provided with a copious (amount of a) morbific entity, usually leaves off in a very severe way by maturation of the morbific entity by means of good therapeutic procedures; those slow-acting fevers, which gradually become inactive after having brought about a paroxysm by force of (their) morbific entity, (show a type of) leaving off that is not severe." Cakra remarks on these stanzas that one should know that the characteristics described in Ca.Ci. 3, 324-326 (see note 306) only occur in a fever by concerted action and not in other (types), and that, for that reason, some read here Ca.Ci. 3, 327-328.

CHAPTER THREE

DIARRHOEA (*ATĪSĀRA*)

3, 1-3 : By eating articles of food which are heavy, too oleaginous, dry, hot, liquid and gross, too cold or disagreeing, by overeating, by eating non-disintegrated and incongruous [1] articles of food (1), by oleaginous substances, etc. when overused and improperly used, by poisons, fears and grief, by drinking water and alcoholic beverages which are corrupted and drinking too much (water and alcoholic beverages), by modifications [2] with respect to adequacy and season (2), by aquatic delights, stagnation of (natural) urges and by worms as a morbific factor diarrhoea comes into being in men.

Its characteristics will be stated (presently) (3).

(Su.U. 40, 3-5).[3]

M :

Immediately after (the chapter on) fever mention is made of diarrhoea ... because (the occurrence of) diarrhoea is described in bilious fever and by reason of the fact that fever and diarrhoea are secondary affections of each other.

By the word 'heavy' is understood : heavy with respect to measure, as e.g. red rice, etc., enjoyed beyond the proper measure, and also *māṣa* beans, etc., which are heavy according to their very nature; or (it means : heavy) as to quality and maturation.[4] The word 'too' is connected with (the series of words) ending with gross.[5] 'Gross' (means) consisting of compact components, as e.g. *laḍḍuka, piṣṭaka,* etc.[6] 'Cold', (to wit) on touch and with regard to potency. 'Disagreeing' (expresses) disagreeing by way of commixture, place, time, measure, etc., as milk and fish, etc.; one should examine this (disagreement, which can be) of many kinds, in the chapter on salutary and insalutary (regimen) of the Suśruta(saṃhitā, i.e. Sū. 20), and in the chapter with the discussion between Ātreya and Bhadrakāpya of the Caraka(saṃhitā, i.e. Sū. 26). 'Overeating' is the eating of food when the meal of the previous day has not (yet) been disintegrated. For in the Caraka(saṃhitā) it has been said : "And on the other hand the ingestion of food when there is (still) a rest of the previous meal is thought to be overeating" (Ci. 15,

236cd).[7] In the same way it should be understood everywhere. Non-disintegrated (food) is uncooked [8] food.

Incongruous (eating) is eating at an improper time, etc. For in the Suśruta(saṃhitā) it has been said : "(Eating) much, a little or at an improper time should be known as incongruous eating" (Sū. 46, 508cd).[9] In the same way (it should be understood) everywhere. A variant reading of 'by incongruous (articles of food)' is 'by inadequate ones'. (The words) 'by eating articles of food' are connected with all (the terms of the series) beginning with 'disagreeing ones', etc.

(About) 'by oleaginous (substances)', etc. (we remark that) an oleaginous (substance points to) the drinking of an oleaginous (substance); those (procedures are aimed at) in which (the employment of) an oleaginous (substance) is the first (element), viz. sudation, treatment with emetics, treatment with purgatives, oleaginous enemas and corrective enemas. 'By over-use of these' (means) : in cases of (what is technically called) over-use. And this should be understood in accordance with the (technical) use of each (of these procedures), because over-use of the treatment with emetics is not related to the causation of diarrhoea. 'By improper use' (means) in cases of (what is technically called) deficient use, as wrong use of the emetic procedure, etc. does not exist; but these (procedures) do lead to diarrhoea on account of deficient use, after having brought about uneasiness of the morbific entities.[10]

(An objector may ask if) it is not thus, that wrong use of these (procedures) does exist because one observes that application of the emetic procedure sometimes brings about purging and the purgative procedure emesis ?

(The answer is that) this is not true; just that is verily called non-use (in a technical way); that is the established doctrine. As has been stated in the Caraka(saṃhitā) : "(Correct) use will be a proper activity, over-use an extreme activity and non-use no activity or a slight activity, by reason of an adverse effect" [11] (Si. 6, 31).

Poison is said to be vegetable poison in this case because (a vegetable one) moves downwards. But Kārtika says : poison (denotes) a corruptive poison [12] since diarrhoea is described among its characteristics. (About) 'by drinking water and alcoholic beverages which are corrupted and drinking too much of these' (we remark that) corrupted (denotes) : in a disordered condition; (the meaning is) : by drinking corrupted water and corrupted alcoholic beverages, and also by drinking too much of these when they are not corrupted.[13] As Caraka says : "On account of drinking corrupted alcoholic beverages and water, or drinking too much of an alcoholic beverage and water" (fr. Ci. 19, 8).[14] 'By modifications with regard to adequacy and season' (indicates) : by (acts) contrary to adequate (behaviour) and by contrarieties of the season;[15] (acts) contrary to adequate (behaviour denote) inadequate (behaviour). And by means of this (expression there arises) no case of repetition of the above-mentioned 'by inadequate ones'.[16] For in the Caraka(saṃhitā) it has been said in the chapter with the discussion between Ātreya and Bhadrakāpya : "Adequacy is of two kinds : adequacy concerning natural disposition and habitual conduct." [17]

Others say it is no case of repetition because (adequacy can be used) with respect to the distinction between regimen of diet and conduct or between foods and drinks. 'By aquatic delights' (means) by playful activities, etc. in the water. 'By stagnation of (natural) urges', i.e. of urine, faeces, etc. 'By worms ': (this is stated) because worms bring about a corrupted condition of the receptacles of digested and undigested food, or on account of the excitement of wind, etc., generated by worms. And these origins should be understood (to be related) to wind, etc. according to the source of each (of the morbific entities), and they are described for the sake of making known their being a ground of a morbific entity and illness. In the same way it should usually be regarded also elsewhere with respect to the description of specific origins.

Ā :

... 'Non-disintegrated (food)' is uncooked (food like) that which has to be masticated, etc.; according to others it is (food) that is immature, combustively altered, etc.[18] 'Grief' (as e.g.) by separation from a relative, etc. 'Corrupted water' is water in a disordered condition; (the meaning of) 'an alcoholic beverage' is well-known; drinking too much of these (is the sense of the expression).

3, 4 : After appeasing the (transforming) fire, the watery element, having increased and being mixed with faecal matter, pushed downwards by the wind, flows (out) to an extreme degree. This dreadful illness is called diarrhoea.[19] It is said to be of six kinds : (produced) by each one of the morbific entities separately, by all of them together, another one by grief and a sixth one by immature matter.

(Su.U. 40, 7ab).[20]

M :

The onset, common to all the diarrhoeas, is made mention of ... 'After appeasing' (expresses) : after having brought about appeasement (of it); (a grammatical remark of Gadādhara is quoted); it means : making the (transforming) fire sluggish. 'Increased' is corrupted. Because 'the watery element' is not a compound word one should understand it (to denote) nutrient fluid, water, urine, sweat, fat, phlegm, bile, blood, etc.[21] In the Caraka(saṃhitā) it has also been said : "(The morbific entities), making corrupted the elements of the body (consisting of) blood, etc." (fr. Ci. 19, 9). 'Pushed', (i.e.) set in motion, in a downward direction; with the words 'it flows (out) to an extreme degree' the 'etymology' (of diarrhoea) has been stated; the meaning is that diarrhoea is the flowing (out) of very liquid (matter) by way of the anus. The 'etymology' is also the characteristic by means of which it is differentiated from the *grahaṇī* disease, etc., though there is no specific (difference) as to the presence of a flowing down of liquid matter. In diarrhoea by wind, however, there is (only) a slight (flow of liquid matter) with reference to diarrhoea by phlegm and bile, but not with reference to *grahaṇī* disease. The above-mentioned six-membered state (of diarrhoea) is disassembled with the words 'by each one separately', etc.

It may be asked what has been the point of view, in stating things here in a different way from what has been done in the Caraka(saṃhitā), etc., where three (diarrhoeas occur) by each one (of the morbific entities) separately, one by concerted action and two arising from fear and grief (respectively), (arriving) thus (at) a sixfold (division).

The answer is : in the Caraka(saṃhitā two kinds of diarrhoea), (those) arising from fear and grief, are separately mentioned owing to the distinctive (features) with respect to their characteristics, appellation and effects, but a surplus of the number (of diarrhoeas) does not occur, (since) that one arising from immature matter has been included by reason of its (being a case of) concerted action, because it arises from the three morbific entities excited by non-disintegration of the food; in the Suśruta(saṃhitā), however, (two kinds of diarrhoea), (those) arising from grief and from immature matter, are described for the sake of a therapy opposed to the ground, though (these types are) not distinct from those arising from wind and concerted action (respectively), (in the same way) as for instance a (kind of) morbid pallor (is described), arising from (the ingestion of) earth, though it is not distinct with regard to its arising from wind, etc.; in the same manner (diarrhoeas) arising from fear and grief are described in the Caraka-(saṃhitā) for the sake of a therapy opposed to the ground, and in the Suśruta(saṃhitā a diarrhoea) arising from fear is (regarded to be) included in that one by wind as a single (entity) or in that one by grief, because there is no specific difference with respect to (fear and grief), since (both) are of a mental character; that is Jejjaṭa's opinion.

(An objector may ask :) is it not right that the words 'and a sixth one is said to be (brought about) by immature matter' are not appropriate in making a separate (kind of this one), because the first stage of verily all diarrhoeas should be denoted by the term 'immature', and the stage in which it has become disintegrated by the word 'mature', for which very reason the range of all diarrhoeas has been stated (as follows) : "With disregard of the due order of the immature and mature (stages) there is no salutary (therapeutic) procedure in a case of diarrhoea; for that reason one should know the characteristics of maturity and immaturity in all (types of) diarrhoea" (Su.U. 40, 24) ? [22]

(The answer is that) this is not right; (a case of diarrhoea) arising from immature matter is (a case) started by that very immature matter, and the morbific entities combine (with it) and set it in motion, but do not start it. Immature matter, being a result of corrupted food and different from the morbific entities, elements and impurities, starts an illness, in the same way as blood, etc., when it has come into combination with wind, etc. or when it has been set in motion by wind, etc. (Types of) diarrhoea, arising from a pair (of morbific entities), are not stated separately because they are reached by an inherence (in a morbid alteration, the qualities of which are) congruous with the natural state; (cases) reached by an inherence (in a morbid alteration, the qualities of which are incongruous with the altered state), do not arise on account of the nature of the illness itself. It is usually a custom of the masters that they do not enumerate (diseases by) a pair (of morbific entities) and (by) concerted action, reached by an inherence (in a morbid alteration, the qualities of which are) congruous with the natural state, but they do necessarily write down (those diseases), reached by an inherence (in a morbid alteration, the qualities of which are) incongruous with the altered state. In the same way as in the Caraka-(saṃhitā), after stating : "There are five (kinds of) visceral swelling" (fr. Sū. 19, 4), it has been said : "One should, for the sake of the preparation of remedial agents, declare that there are three other (types of) visceral swelling, having the symptoms of a combination" (Ci. 5, 16cd), in that way, having stated : "There are six (kinds of) haemorrhoids" (fr. Su.Ni. 2, 3), it has been said in the Suśruta(saṃhitā): "When the symptoms of two morbific entities [23] are observed in haemorrhoids, one should discern it as combined action, and this combined action is of six kinds" (Ni. 2, 22).[24]

Ā :[25]

3, 5 : Pricking pain in cardiac region, navel, anus, abdomen and the lateral parts of the abdomen, a sense of prostration in the limbs, restraint of the wind, retention of faeces, inflatedness and absence of digestive alteration are the harbingers when it is imminent.

(Su.U. 40, 8cd-9ab).[26]

M :

The prodromes of all diarrhoeas are dealt with ... (The term) 'pricking pain' is connected with (the whole series of words), beginning with the cardiac region. The term 'the lateral parts of the abdomen' denotes here a (particular) part of the abdomen; therefore repetition does not occur. 'Restraint of the wind' is non-appearance of wind. 'Retention of faeces' is non-appearance of faeces; this is a fixed prodrome that only applies to the stage of coalescence between morbific entity and the (constituent) subject to corruption; therefore it does not attend one in the stage in which the symptoms (are present). (If it does attend one the illness is not produced, because retention of faeces is an obstacle to it to a high degree). 'Absence of digestive alteration' (refers to) the food. 'The harbingers' are the prodromes.

3, 6 : By wind is made to flow (down) to an extreme degree faecal matter, which is of a ruddy colour, frothy and dry, which appears in small amounts and every now and then, which is immature and accompanied by pain and noise.[27] [28]

M :

(Diarrhoea) by wind is made mention of ... (About) 'ruddy' (we remark that) this (colour is present) on account of the coalescence between the morbific entity and the (constituent) subject to corruption, although wind is colourless; (it should be considered) in the same way also elsewhere. 'Frothy' (means) provided with foam; (a grammatical remark is made about the form of the word) ... The words 'accompanied by pain' (mean) : accompanied by piercing pain ...

3, 7ab : (In diarrhoea arising) from bile (the faecal matter is) yellow, swarthy or slightly red, and there are present [29] thirst, fainting, a burning sensation and inflammatory changes.

(Su.U. 40, 11ab).[30 31]

M :

(Bilious) diarrhoea is made mention of ... The words 'a burning sensation and inflammatory changes are present' (indicate) a burning sensation in the whole body, and inflammatory changes in the anal region only. For in another treatise it has been said : "(The patient is) haunted by thirst, a burning sensation, perspiration, fainting, glowing heat in the bottom [32] and inflammation of it" (fr. Ca.Ci. 19, 6).[33] The bottom is the anal region. Here also one should supply : faecal matter is made to flow (down) to an extreme degree; the same (words should) also (be supplied) in (the description of) diarrhoea by phlegm.

3, 7cd : (When it is brought about) by phlegm (the faecal matter is of a) light (colour), viscid, accompanied by phlegm, (of a) musty (smell) and cold; a man (suffering from it) presents horripilation.

(Su.U. 40, 12ab).[34 35]

M :

(Diarrhoea) by phlegm is made mention of ... It is described with the words beginning with '(of a) light (colour)' and ending with 'presenting horripilation'. '(Of a) musty (smell)' is : smelling like raw meat.

3, 8 : One should know that a diarrhoea resembling the oleaginous matter from a boar and the water of flesh and provided with all the symptoms is difficult to cure and arises from the triad of morbific entities.[36]

M :

(Diarrhoea) by concerted action is made mention of ... The oleaginous matter from a boar is the fat or marrow of a pig; the water of flesh is the water in which flesh has been rinsed; resembling those (is the meaning). Provided with all the symptoms (means) provided with the above-mentioned three (sets of) characteristics of diarrhoea by wind, etc. One should know that a diarrhoea of such a kind arises from the three morbific entities; it is difficult to cure, just because it arises from the three morbific entities.

3, 9-10 : The heat of the tears of a living being, who grieves and eats little due to this or that state of mind, enters the (transforming) fire,[37] goes to the viscera and may bring about a turbulent state of his blood. And this (blood), resembling *kākaṇantī*, may come out from below, mixed with faeces or without faeces, without a (bad) smell or (bad-)smelling.[38] The diarrhoea produced by grief is extremely difficult to treat; the *vaidya*s declare this to be a very troublesome disease.

(Su.U. 40, 13cd-15ab).[39]

M :

(Diarrhoea) arising from grief is dealt with ... 'Due to this or that state of mind' (expresses) : by the loss of (one's) property, relatives, etc. 'One who grieves' is one who feels grief. 'One who eats little' is one who takes little food, due to his very grief. It has been said that by means of this there may also occur decline of one's elements. 'Tears' (indicate here) the water in the eyes, nose, throat, etc., that has appeared to a high degree; the heat by which it is accompanied, arising from grief, the fiery energy of the body, is the heat of the tears. That (heat), after going to the viscera and entering the (transforming) fire, (i.e.) bringing it into a disturbed condition, may bring about a turbulent state of his blood on account of the fact that it has the same qualities, (viz.) hotness and liquidity. And that blood, resembling *kākaṇantī*, (i.e.) resembling *guñjā* seeds,[40] may come out from below. The variant reading 'after entering the (place of) maturation' has the same sense. Gadādhara says, however, that the word fire denotes the bile. 'And this blood may come out mixed with faeces or without it', (i.e.) with a slight amount of faeces because a small amount of food is ingested. About the alternatives 'without a (bad) smell or (bad-) smelling' Kārtika says : (they correlate with) 'not accompanied by faeces or accompanied by it'.[41] Others say that a very strong smell (arises) on account of the putrid condition of the bile, and that absence of (a bad) smell occurs when it is not very much corrupted; and it is said that it is a musty smell. The variant reading of 'it may bring about a turbulent state of the blood', (viz.) 'it may desiccate his ingested food',[42] is unsuitable because there does not exist another ground with regard to its resemblance to *kākaṇantī*. Therefore the first reading is the best one and it is explained by Jejjaṭa and all the other (commentators).

This (type of diarrhoea) has been said to arise from wind and bile.[43] 'It is extremely difficult to treat' without the removal of grief, as it is not appeased by a sole remedy. For that very reason he says : 'it is declared to be a very troublesome disease'. 'By the *vaidyas*' (i.e.) by the *brāhmaṇas*, etc. But Gadādhara says that the word 'this' (expresses that) only (a diarrhoea by grief) with such an onset is troublesome, but not the other (types) arising from grief.

Ā :

... A very (bad) smell (arises) from an extremely corrupted condition of the bile; absence of a (bad) smell occurs when it is not extremely corrupted ...

3, 11 : The morbific entities, in a dispersed state due to non-disintegrated food, bringing about a turbulent state of the viscera, the groups of the elements and the impurities, bring about a flow (of faecal matter) of various colours and of several kinds, accompanied by piercing pain; this is called the sixth one. (Su.U. 40, 15cd-16ab).[44]

M :

Immature diarrhoea is made mention of ... 'Non-disintegrated food' is food when it is in a non-disintegrated state. For that very reason Kṣārapāṇi says : "One evacuates in accordance with the food one has ingested." 'In a dispersed state' (means) that they have deviated from their (proper) pathways. 'Bringing about a turbulent state' is bringing about a corrupted condition. 'The groups of the elements' are the blood, etc. 'The impurities' are the faeces, etc. 'Of several kinds' (means) of many kinds.

Ā :

... 'In a dispersed state' (means) roused ... The word 'viscera' denotes the whole middle part of the abdomen ... The variant reading 'to a very high degree' [45] indicates the great urge ... And the word 'sixth', indicating the number, occurs here for the sake of the fixed rule that diarrhoeas caused by fear, oleaginous substances, non-disintegrated (food), *visūcikā*, haemorrhoids, disintegrated (i.e. decomposed) food, etc. should not be counted separately, because they are all included in those arising from the morbific entities.[46]

Because the occasion presents itself we write down the definition of immature matter : "The rest of the nutrient fluid (produced) from the food is called immature matter, the ground of all diseases, if it is not maturated on account of a light condition of the (transforming) fire".[47]

3, 12-13 : Faecal matter, however, that has become combined with these morbific entities, that sinks down when thrown into water, that has a vehemently bad smell and that is mucilaginous,[48] is technically called immature (12). Someone's faecal matter that presents signs contrary to these (mentioned ones), and especially if lightness is present,[49] should be designated as being mature (13).

(Su.U. 40, 17-18).[50]

M :

By reason of (their) applicability to therapy mention is made of the characteristics of immaturity and maturity of all the diarrhoeas ... 'Combined' (means) intimately connected, 'with these morbific entities', (i.e.) with the states of corruption the signs of which are those of the above-mentioned diarrhoeas by wind, etc. The states of corruption should be understood here to occur in a dissociated or an associated way, in accordance with their source in each case; it is not thus that as a consequence of this all diarrhoeas would be connected with concerted action.

'Thrown into water' (means) cast into water. 'It sinks down' (expresses that) it submerges,[51] due to the heaviness of immature matter. The word 'vehemently' is also connected with (the word) mucilaginous. 'Having a bad smell' is : of a musty smell. It is mucilaginous because it is intimately connected with immature matter. 'These (mentioned signs' consist of) the fact that it submerges in water, etc. 'Lightness' (denotes lightness) of both the viscera and the body.

By means of the word 'and' it is added that its submerging in water is a characteristic, except in cases of corruption, etc. by the coldness of phlegm. As has been said : "Immature matter submerges due to its heaviness, but mature faecal matter floats in water, except when it is extremely liquid or compact on account of corruption by the coldness of phlegm" (Siddhayoga 3, 14). Or it (viz. the word 'and') indicates that, although lightness has been established just on account of the presence of signs contrary to those of immature matter, the term lightness, used again, (serves to express) : with exclusion of corruption by phlegm, etc.

Ā :

... By the word 'and' is added : faeces corrupted by phlegm. As has been said : "Immature matter submerges due to its heaviness, but mature faecal matter floats in water, except in the case that it is extremely liquid or compact and in case of corruption by the coldness of phlegm" (Siddhayoga 3, 14).

Now one may ask : if it is right that (faecal matter) combined with phlegm submerges in water, even when mature, how then can mature diarrhoea by phlegm be known ?

The answer is : only by means of the other characteristics.[52]

3, 14-17 : A patient with a diarrhoeal flow that resembles mature *jambū* fruits or pieces of liver(-tissue), that is thin, similar to ghee, oil, muscle-fat, marrow, *veśavāra*, milk, thick sour milk (14) or water in which flesh has been washed, that is black, of a swarthy and ruddy lustre, of the colour of the eyes of a peacock's tail, oleaginous and variegated, provided with moon-like spots, dense (15), smelling like a corpse, resembling cerebral tissue, smelling agreeably, stinking or copious, and (a patient with diarrhoea) who presents thirst, a burning sensation, darkness (of vision), shortness of breath, hiccup, piercing pain in the sides and the bones (16), stupefaction, disinclination, complete mental confusion, inflammation of the folds of the anal region and confused speech should be avoided by a physician (17).[53]

3, 18 : Someone with diarrhoea whose anus is not closed, who suffers from decline, who is much inflated[54] and assaulted (by secondary affections) and whose heat has gone, though the anal region is inflamed, should be abandoned.

(Su.U. 40,21).

3, 19 : Diarrhoea will bring about the annihilation of someone afflicted by shortness of breath, piercing pain and thirst, and someone suffering from decline or oppressed by fever, especially when he is old.

(Su.Sū. 33, 19).[55]

additional stanza : One should abandon a patient with diarrhoea when one has observed swelling, piercing pain, fever, thirst, cough, shortness of breath, anorexia, vomiting, fainting and hiccup.

(Hā. 3, 3, 77).[56]

M :

The characteristics of incurability are dealt with ... 'Resembling mature *jambū* fruits' means : of a colour like that of mature *jambū* fruits, oleaginous and black. 'Resembling pieces of liver(-tissue)' means : blackish-red. 'Thin' (is) very transparent. The (series of) words, beginning with 'similar to ghee' and ending with 'similar to water in which flesh has been washed', means : being of an appearance similar to (ghee, etc.). *veśavāra* is a kind of flesh, technically defined as follows : "Flesh without bones that has been ground, to which have been added thick sour milk and a caustic, and which has been mixed with *elā* and black pepper, is traditionally called *veśavāra*." 'Black' is : resembling a collyrium. And this blackness, etc. should be understood to exclude bilious diarrhoea because it has been described in that case as being a symptom. 'Swarthy and ruddy' is : of the colour of the wings of a *cāṣa*[57] bird. 'Of the colour of the eyes of a peacock's tail' is : slightly black and dry, like the round mass of ointment (used) to rub (the body).[58] 'Variegated' is : of various colours; this (kind of faecal matter) is also oleaginous because it is connected with a liquid element consisting of oleaginous matter. 'Provided with moon-like spots' is : provided with oleaginous substances from the elements, similar to the moon-like spots on the tail-feathers of a peacock.[59] For master Karavīra has said : "One should abandon (a patient with diarrhoea when the faecal matter is) covered with moon-like spots, resembling the tail-feathers of a peacock, with streaks that are swarthy, yellow, etc., (when it) resembles *veśavāra* water, marrow and milk." That same (faecal matter) is dense because it is mixed with other elements. 'Smelling like a corpse' is bad-smelling like a dead body. 'Resembling cerebral tissue'[60] is : similar to the oleaginous matter in the interior of the head, called *ghṛtaka*. (A grammatical remark is made about the series of words beginning with thirst and ending with piercing pain). Stupefaction (means) here confusion of the *manas* and complete mental confusion (means) confusion of the senses; thus there is no repetition. The word 'and' should be understood to indicate what has been said by Caraka, viz. that a diarrhoea is incurable when it suddenly pauses.[61] ('Presenting inflammation of the folds of the anal region' is explained without the addition of anything worth mentioning).

'Someone whose anus is not closed' is someone unable to close his anus;[62] that same one when suffering from decline, (i.e.) deprived of force and tone,[63] (is referred to). 'Much inflated' is : showing a vehement inflatedness, (arisen) on account of the fact that its treatment is irreconcilable with diarrhoea, because it is (only) curable by means of a purgative procedure. The variant reading[64] 'with a bad mind' (means) with a corrupted inner organ; Jejjaṭa says (it means) : someone whose senses have not been subdued. 'Assaulted' (means) : accompanied by the secondary affections of diarrhoea, (consisting of) swelling, etc. As has been said : "One should abandon a patient with diarrhoea when one has observed swelling, piercing pain, fever, thirst, shortness of breath, cough, anorexia, vomiting, fainting and hiccup."[65] 'Whose heat has gone, though his anal region is inflamed' (expresses) that, though the bile which starts inflammation is present in the anal region, one's heat has gone, (i.e.) that one's limbs are cold or that the (transforming) fire has been annihilated.[66] (An equivalent of *atisārakin* is given, followed by a grammatical remark referring to Pāṇini 5, 2, 129). By means of the word 'especially'[67] it is indicated that diarrhoea is also incurable in a child, as Suśruta has said in the (section on) therapeutics : "This one is difficult (to cure), and incurable in children and old people" (U. 40. 13b).

Ā :

... 'Resembling a round mass[68] of liver(-tissue)', (i.e.) similar to the liver, means : blackish-red. It is similar to water mixed with *veśavāra*. 'Of the colour of the eyes of a peacock's tail' : somewhat black and dry like a round mass of the ointment used to besmear the upper part of a *mṛdaṅga*.[69] 'Oleaginous' is unctuous : (it is oleaginous) because it is accompanied by oleaginous matter from the elements. It is dense because it is mixed with components of the elements ... It is copious because it exceeds its (proper) measure.

A patient with diarrhoea who is 'assaulted', (that is to say) by the secondary affections of diarrhoea, should be abandoned. According to what has been said : "One should abandon a patient, suffering from diarrhoea, who is visited by the following secondary affections : thirst, a burning sensation, inability to eat, swelling, piercing pain in the sides, disinclination, emesis, inflammation of the anal region, confused speech, inflatedness, shortness of breath, cough, fainting, hiccup, (mental disturbance as in) intoxication, piercing pain and fever with frequent paroxysms".[70] And (according to) another (statement): "Inflammation of the junctures of fingers and toes, suppression of (the evacuation of) urine and hotness of the faecal matter lead to the death of those who suffer from diarrhoea."[71] Some read at this place two stanzas :[72] "This one is incurable in a child and an old patient, assaulted by these signs; in young adults also it may be incurable when the elements are extremely corrupted."[73] The author of the Madhukośa has made clear this (stanza),[74] because it has been collected by Mādhava.

The secondary affections of diarrhoea are made mention of with the words 'swelling', etc.; they are easily explained.

3, 20 : When in bilious (diarrhoea) substances that give rise to bile are eaten to an extreme degree and frequently, an abundant bloody diarrhoea ensues.[75]

M :

Having reflected upon the following uncertainty : 'There is also a diarrhoea arising from blood ; this (diarrhoea) contradicts the mentioned fact that there are six (diarrhoeas) because it would become the seventh one', he says, with the words '(giving rise to) bile', etc., that this is a specific stage of bilious (diarrhoea). The connection (of the words) is as follows : when, in an existing or imminent bilious diarrhoea, substances that give rise to bile are eaten to an extreme degree, (i.e.) to a high degree, and frequently, (i.e.) uninterruptedly, an abundant, (i.e.) intense, bloody diarrhoea ensues. And (also) in this case wind, etc. should be understood to be the agents, corrupting (the faecal matter) with ruddiness, blackness, paleness, etc. As has been said : "An intelligent (physician) should in that case characterize the (type of) combination by means of the signs of the morbific entities."[76] In this way redundancy concerning the group of six (diarrhoeas) should be understood as rejected with regard to diarrhoeas arising from oleaginous (substances), non-disintegrated (food), *visūcikā*, poison, haemorrhoids, worms and so on, owing to the invariable (appearance) of the signs of the morbific entities;[77] that is the opinion of Jejjaṭa.

3, 21 : The increased wind pushes downwards the accumulated phlegm [78] of someone whose food consists of insalutary things and who suddenly evacuates it, bedaubed with impure matter, in small amounts [79] and repeatedly. Those possessing knowledge about it call it *pravāhikā*.

(Su.U. 40, 138).[80]

M :

pravāhikā and diarrhoea possess common peculiarities because liquid (matter) flows (out of the anus in both conditions) and (both) are provided with the characteristics of the immature and mature (stages). It is for that reason that the onset of *pravāhikā* is mentioned in the paragraph on diarrhoea, with the words 'the (increased) wind', etc. Diarrhoea is the flowing (out) of liquid elements of various kinds, but in *pravāhikā* only phlegm flows (out); that is the distinction.

The wind pushes downwards, (i.e.) causes to fall down by way of the anus, the accumulated phlegm, bedaubed with impure matter, (i.e.) accompanied by faecal matter, of someone whose food consists of insalutary things and who suddenly evacuates, (i.e.) who makes a sudden evacuation. But in (the treatise by) Bhoja, etc. this (condition) is designated as *visraṃsin*, in (that by) Parāśara as *antargranthi* and in (that by) Hārīta as *niścāraka*, as said (by the latter) : "This (condition) should be known as being *pravāhikā*, but some call it *niścāraka*."[81]

Ā :

... (The term) *balāsa* is used here as an implicative term; one should understand it (to designate) accumulated bile or blood (as well).[82]

3, 22 : *pravāhikā* brought about by wind is accompanied by piercing pain, (arisen) from bile it is accompanied by a burning sensation, (arisen) from phlegm it is accompanied by phlegm and it is accompanied by blood when it arises from blood. These (forms of it) are thought to come about, however, by means of oleaginous and dry (substances). One should indicate that the signs, the due order (of therapeutic measures) and the immature and mature conditions of these (types of *pravāhikā*) are like those of diarrhoea.

(Su.U. 40, 139-140ab).

M :

With the words '*pravāhikā*', etc. mention is made of its symptoms, distinguished according to (the morbific entities) wind, etc.

Is it not right that it has (already) been said : 'the increased wind (pushes down) the accumulated phlegm?' Why then is '(*pravāhikā*) brought about by wind' made mention of?

The answer is : (wind) is designated because it is present in excess.

For which reason are (the types of *pravāhikā*) that arise from bile and blood mentioned as well?

The answer is that it has been said 'of someone whose food consists of insalutary things', and a disagreeing diet brings about excitement of bile and blood in that condition; and when these two (entities) as auxiliary forces of the wind show their own signs later on, it (i.e. *pravāhikā*) is designated by means of these two (entities).

(About) 'coming about by means of oleaginous and dry (substances)' (we remark that *pravāhikā*) arising from phlegm comes about by means of oleaginous (substances) and (that type) arising from wind by means of dry (substances) and, on account of the word 'however', (those types) arising from bile and blood come about by means of sharp and hot (substances). 'Signs' are the characteristics, distinguished in accordance with wind, etc. 'Due order' is the due order of therapy, with distinctions in accordance with the immature and mature conditions.

3, 23 : Who passes urine in the proper way without (passing) stools, whose wind moves, whose (transforming) fire is inflamed and whose viscera are light, is someone whose abdominal ailment has become arrested.

(Su.U. 40, 162).[83]

M :

That by which the cessation of diarrhoea is characterized is made mention of for the sake of excluding the incertitude (consisting of the problem that) cessation of diarrhoea (may be based) on non-appearance of impure matter due to a constrained condition (of the impurities) by wind or the retentive disease. The person, whose urine appears without (the simultaneous appearance of) faeces, and (in whom this occurs) in the proper way, i.e. in the way it is properly performed and not in a deficient way, (is referred to); (whose) wind goes (out), 'by way of the anus' has to be supplied. 'It has become arrested' (means) : it has ceased. 'Abdominal ailment' (means) diarrhoea, because it is the topic (of this chapter). This (stanza) describes the break-up of the onset. For in diarrhoea the onset is as follows : the liquid element, even that which is suitable to (appear as) urine, appears only by way of the anus, because really the whole of the watery element appears by way of the anus; but in the case that it appears by way of the urethra, it does so at the same time as the faeces.

Ā :

... 'Whose (transforming) fire is inflamed' (means) whose abdominal fire has increased and 'whose viscera are light' for that reason, because the maturative process (goes on) in the proper way ...

additional stanza : The origins of feverish diarrhoea will be those mentioned separately (as the origins) of fever and diarrhoea; therefore it is not appropriate to repeat them here.[84]

NOTES

[1] Su. : *asātmya* (inadequate) instead of *viṣama* (incongruous).

[2] Su. : *viṣāt, bhayāt, atipānāt* and *paryayāt* instead of the instr. pl. of the same words.

[3] Ca.Ci. 19, 4 a myth is told about the first appearance of diarrhoea in this world. Ca.Ci. 19, 5-7 enumerates the origins of diarrhoea by wind, bile and phlegm separately. Ca.Ci. 19, 8 deals with the origins and onset of diarrhoea by concerted action : "When by the eating of articles of food which are too cold, oleaginous, dry, hot, heavy, harsh, hard, incongruous, disagreeing and inadequate, by abstinence from food, by eating when the (proper) time for it has passed, by eating anything whatsoever, by drinking corrupted alcoholic and other beverages and by drinking too much of an alcoholic beverage, by the neglect of (periodical) purificatory procedures, by an incongruous effect of (therapeutic) counter-measures, by the absence of (proper) attendance (on a patient), by indulging extremely in (the heat of) a fire, (the heat of) the sun, wind and (playful activities in the) water, by lack of sleep and too much sleep, by restraint of the (natural) urges, contrariness of the season, undertakings which are not in accordance with one's force, by too much fear, grief and mental disquietude and by too much misery due to morbid alterations (like those by) worms, desiccation, fever and haemorrhoids, the (transforming) fire is subject to disorders, the three morbific entities are excited; they injure the (transforming) fire even more, enter into the receptacle of digested food and generate a diarrhoea with the signs of all the morbific entities." Cf. A.h.Ni. 8, 1cd-3a = A.s.Ni. 8, 3cd-5a (Ki. 8, 2cd-4a) : "Still more easily it arises from drinking too much water, by (eating) lean and desiccated meat, inadequate (articles of food), sesame flour, grain that has begun to sprout, by alcholic beverages, dry foods and those eaten beyond the proper measure, by haemorrhoids, erroneous application of oleaginous (substances), worms and restraint of the (natural) urges;" Hā. 3, 3, 4-5 :

"When someone eats articles of food which are oleaginous, too cold, heavy, cold or mucilaginous, by eating corrupted foods and eating beyond the proper measure, by incongruous foods, drinks and articles of diet which have to be chewed. by eating before the (previous) meal has been digested, by grief, poison and fear, by affliction from grief, by corrupted milk and by reverse conditions, weakness will arise, impure matter that has remained non-disintegrated by the eating of incongruous foods is dispersed in water, and the (transforming) fire is damaged; thereupon diarrhoea arises in a man; when the abdominal fire has been damaged, a man will get diarrhoea."

4 Ḍa. : heavy with regard to measure, quality and digestive alteration.

5 Ḍa. : idem.

6 Ḍa. : "Gross (food is) food made from flour, etc., the constituents of which are gross; although by the word 'heavy' as such (the meanings) 'oleaginous' and 'gross' are also arrived at, (these kinds of food) are nevertheless mentioned because they are grounds of diarrhoea in a special way."

7 Cakra's opinion differs from that of the author of M., for he comments on Ca.Ci. 15, 236cd : "Overeating is present when one, in addition to what has (already) been eaten during the day, eats again that very day." Su. defines the term overeating as follows (Su.Sū. 46, 509ab) : "Overeating is said to be present when one eats before (the previous meal) has been disintegrated." Cf. Kā.Khi. 5, 59ab : "A physician should know that overeating is present (when one eats) while the previously ingested (meal) has not (yet) been transformed."

8 Ḍa. : immature, combustively altered, etc.

9 Cf. Ca.Ci. 15, 236 ab : "Incongruous (eating is eating) a great or a small amount (of food, and eating it) before the proper time (of a meal), or after the proper time has passed;" Kā.Khi. 5, 60cd : "Incongruous (eating results) from violation of (the rules about) qualities and (ways of) preparation, the due order (of taking foods) and (the rules about) adequacy."

10 Ḍa. : " 'By improper use' (means) : by use in an unsuitable way; although by the very words 'by improper employment' over-use is (also) arrived at, the term over-use is (nevertheless) mentioned because this (over-use) is very specially a ground of diarrhoea."

11 Cakra says that a reverse effect is present when a purgative effect is reached by an emetic treatment or an emetic effect by a purging treatment.

12 Ḍa. : idem.

13 Ḍa. interprets the compound in a different way : "(It means) the excessive drinking of water, corrupted by way of potency, digestive alteration or contact (*sparśa*), and of corrupted alcoholic beverages, (i.e. those which are) fresh, in a disordered condition or produced at a wrong time."

14 Ca. : *praduṣṭamadyapānīyapānād atimadyapānāt*; see note 3.

15 Ḍa. : idem.

16 This refers to the variant mentioned in M. In Ḍa.'s comment a similar remark is made.

17 Ca.Sū. 26 is referred to, but the quotation does not occur in that chapter.

18 This is Ḍa.'s view; see note 8.

19 Cf. Su.U. 40, 6 : "Because the watery element, after appeasing the internal fire, mixed with excremental matter, pushed forth by the wind and having increased, flows downwards to an extreme degree, this dreadful illness is called diarrhoea;" fr. Ca.Ci. 19, 5 : "The wind gets into an excited state and the maturating (fire) is damaged. When

the fire has been damaged, the excited wind brings the urine and sweat to the faecal receptacle, liquefies the faecal matter by means of these two (substances) and (thus) makes things ready for (the appearance of) diarrhoea;" fr. Ca.Ci. 19, 6 : "The bile gets into an excited state. This excited (bile) damages the heat (of the body, i.e. the fire), by its liquidity, spreads to the faecal receptacle, loosens the faecal matter by its hotness, liquidity and ability to give rise to the flowing out (of impure matter) and (thus) makes things ready for (the appearance of) diarrhoea;" fr. Ca.Ci. 19, 7 : "Phlegm gets into an excited state. Being heavy, sweet, cold and oleaginous on account of its own nature and having become lax, it damages the fire, damages the faecal receptacle because of its *soma*-like nature, moistens the faeces and (thus) makes things ready for (the appearance of) diarrhoea;" A.h.Ni. 8, 3b-4c = A.s.Ni. 8, 5b-6c (Ki. 8, 4b-5c) : "By such things the wind becomes excited and makes the watery element fall down; after injuring the (transforming) fire by that same (watery element) and bringing into disorder the viscera which are in connection with the faecal matter, it liquefies the faeces and (thus) makes things ready for (the appearance of) diarrhoea."

[20] Ca. distinguishes the following six kinds of diarrhoea : three by one morbific entity, one by concerted action and two adventitious ones, viz. by fear and by grief; these adventitious types have the same characteristics as diarrhoea by wind because fear and grief excite the wind (Ca.Ci. 19, 5-13). A.h. and A.s. also enumerate these six types, but the two adventitious diarrhoeas are said to be, with respect to their symptoms, like a diarrhoea by wind and bile (A.h.Ni. 8, 5d-13ab = A.s.Ni. 8, 7d-15ab = Ki. 8, 6d-14ab). Kā.Sū. 27, 54 makes mention of diarrhoea among the diseases which are of six kinds. Hā. 3, 3 deals with five kinds of diarrhoea : by wind, bile, phlegm, blood and concerted action.

[21] Ḍa. : "(The watery element consists of) the liquid (constituents) of the body, (viz.) phlegm, bile, nutrient fluid, etc.; others say (that) 'the watery element' (denotes) nutrient fluid and sweat, corrupted by phlegm."

[22] Su.U. 40, 24 reads : "Because a therapeutic procedure in a case of diarrhoea (is) not (available) with disregard of the due order of the immature and mature (stages), one should know the characteristics of maturity and immaturity in all (types of) diarrhoea."

[23] Su. : *doṣadvayasya tu* instead of *vai doṣayor dvayoḥ*.

[24] The six kinds of combined action referred to are, according to Ḍa., the following : by wind and bile, wind and phlegm, bile and phlegm, wind and blood, bile and blood, and phlegm and blood.

Su.U. 40, 7cd-8ab deals with different opinions about the number of diarrhoeas to be distinguished : "Some proclaim that (diarrhoea) is of several kinds, but the king of Kāśi (= Dhanvantari) considered this view to be quite false; (according to Dhanvantari) the patient presents several stages (of development) of the morbific entities at different (periods of) time." Ḍa. remarks that Hārīta and others distinguish diarrhoeas by combined action, blood, etc.; Dhanvantari refutes this view, saying that the immature and mature types of diarrhoea are stages of this disease, and that diarrhoea by blood is a stage of (development of) diarrhoea by bile; moreover there are cases which seem to arise from combined action (*dvandvajābhāsa*), but really arise when a second morbific entity acts as an adjunctory factor. Va. describes diarrhoeas by a pair of morbific entities (2, 226-228; 233-235; 246-248); Bhā.pra. describes their treatment (8, 2, 80-83).

[25] Ā. reads *varcomiśra* instead of *śakṛnmiśra*.

[26] Cf. A.h.Ni. 8, 4d-5c = A.s.Ni. 8, 6d-7c (Ki. 8, 5d-6c) : "Its characteristics, when

it is impending, are : pricking pain in cardiac region, anal region and viscera, adynamia of the limbs, seizing of the impurities, inflatedness and absence of digestive alteration;" Kā.Sū. 25, 14 : "An altered colour of the body, disinclination, a feeling of languor with respect to the mouth, sleeplessness and cessation of the actions of wind are the prodromes of diarrhoea;" Hā. 3, 3, 30 : "A continuous feeling of restraint in the lateral parts of the abdomen, navel (*dara*), chest, umbilical region and anal region, restraint of the wind and stoppage of the faeces occur (as prodromes) in all patients with diarrhoea."

[27] The source of this stanza is unknown.

[28] The symptoms of immature and mature diarrhoea by wind are separately described at Ca.Ci. 19, 5 : "Its symptoms (are the following : by wind) is made to flow (down) to an extreme degree faecal matter which is slimy, immature, sinking down when immersed, dry, liquid, (passed) with piercing pain, smelling like raw (meat), (passed) with little noise or without noise and accompanied by a confined state of urine and wind; the wind, being confined, wanders in a lateral direction in the interior of the viscera, accompanied by noises and piercing pain; that is immature diarrhoea by wind. Or by wind (the patient) is made to pass, again and again, scybalous faeces which are mature, have been in a confined state, (are passed) in small amounts, attended by noises and piercing pain, foam, mucilaginous matter and shooting pain; he presents horripilation, he sighs, his mouth is desiccated, he experiences piercing pains in his iliac regions, thighs, sacral region, knees, back and sides and he suffers from a prolapsed anus; some call this the scybalous (type) because there is a scybalous condition of the excrements due to wind." Cf. Su.U. 40, 9cd-10ab : "(In diarrhoea) by wind (the patient presents) piercing pain, retention of urine, rumbling of the bowels, a prolapsus ani and adynamia of the iliac regions, thighs and lower legs; frothy, dry and brown excrements are passed in small amounts, accompanied by wind;" A.h.Ni. 8, 5d-7 — A.s.Ni. 8, 7d-9 (Ki. 8, 6d-8) : "When it (is brought about) by wind one passes stools in small amounts, which are slimy, attended by a profusion of noises and piercing pains, which have been in a confined condition, which are dry, frothy and transparent or scybalous and (passed) repeatedly, moreover resembling burnt treacle, accompanied by mucilaginous matter and attended by shooting pains; presenting a desiccated mouth, a prolapsus ani and horripilation, (the patient) groans loudly;" Hā. 3, 3, 31 : "Those possessing knowledge about it proclaim that the faeces will be frothy, mucilaginous, dry, (appearing) in small amounts, immature, accompanied by noises and piercing pain, and of a black colour, and that (moreover) wallowing is present in diarrhoea by wind."

[29] Su. : *ārta* instead of *upapanna*.

[30] This is the second half of Su.'s description; the first half runs (Su.U. 40, 10cd-11ab) : "(When it arises) from bile the patient's body is covered with perspiration and (the stools are) bad-smelling, hot, (emitted) with (great) impetus, resembling water in which flesh (has been washed), loosened, and extremely sharp."

[31] Cf. fr. Ca.Ci. 19, 6 : "Its symptoms are : faecal matter is made to flow (down) to an extreme degree; it is turmeric-yellow, yellowish-green, swarthy, black, tinged by blood and bile and very bad-smelling; (the patient is) haunted by thirst, a burning sensation, perspiration, fainting, piercing pain, glowing heat in the bottom and inflammation of it; thus is diarrhoea by bile;" A.h.Ni. 8, 8-9ab = A.s.Ni. 8, 10-11ab (Ki. 8, 9-10ab) : "(When it is brought about) by bile (one passes stools) which are yellow, dark-coloured, turmeric-yellow, of a colour resembling that of young grass, slightly red and very bad-smelling; one presents thirst, fainting, perspiration, a burning sen-

sation and glowing heat, and inflammation of the anal region accompanied by piercing pain;" Hā. 3, 3, 43 : "By these (origins stools are passed which are of a) ruddy (colour), yellow and extremely swarthy, accompanied by a bad smell, desiccation, fever and morbid pallor; afflictedness by giddiness, fainting, thirst and a burning sensation in the body are also characteristics of diarrhoea by bile." Compare also Va. 2, 80 and Bhā.pra. 8, 2, 45.

[32] Ca. : *bradhna* instead of *budhna*.

[33] See note 31.

[34] Su.U. 40, 12b reads : *bhaktadveṣī niḥsvanaṃ hṛṣṭaromā* (the stools appear without noise; the patient shows aversion from food and horripilation) instead of *visraṃ śītaṃ hṛṣṭaromā manuṣyaḥ* (the stools have a musty smell and are cold; a man suffering from it presents horripilation). Mādhava omits Su.U. 40, 11cd : "(When it is brought about by phlegm the patient) presents lassitude, sleep, heaviness, nausea and adynamia; even after he has defaecated he is uncertain whether still more urges (to defaecate will appear)."

[35] Cf. fr. Ca.Ci. 19, 7 : "Its symptoms are : in small amounts and frequently (faecal matter) is made to flow (down) which is oleaginous, white, mucilaginous, ropy, immature, heavy, bad-smelling, mixed with phlegm, attended by piercing pain and accompanied by *pravāhikā*; the regions of the abdomen, anus, bladder and groins are heavy; after defaecating one feels as not having voided (*kṛte 'py akṛtasaṃjñaḥ*); one presents horripilation, nausea, sleepiness, inertia, adynamia and aversion from food; thus is diarrhoea by phlegm;" A.h.Ni. 8, 9b-11c = A.s.Ni. 8, 11b-13c (Ki. 8, 10b-12c) : "(When it is brought about) by phlegm (the stools are) dense, mucilaginous, ropy, white, oleaginous, immature, mixed with phlegm, frequently (voided), heavy, bad-smelling, having been in a confined state and attended by pain; one is sleepy and inert and feels aversion from food; (the stools appear) in small amounts and accompanied by *pravāhikā*; one presents horripilation, nausea and (a feeling of) heaviness in bladder, anal region and abdomen; after defaecation one feels as not having voided;" Hā. 3, 3, 49: "By means of these (origins) phlegm, a desiccated state, loosening (of faecal matter) and inability to eat will occur; (the stools will be) viscid and have a musty smell; rigidity, horripilation, a sluggish state of the (transforming) fire and especially a sluggish urge, along with inertia, will be present; know this to be a diarrhoea arising from phlegm." Compare also Va. 2, 138 and Bhā.pra. 8, 2, 75.

[36] The source of this stanza is unknown. Cf. Ca.Ci. 19, 9 : "Moreover (the morbific entities) bring about a very protracted corruption of the elements (of the body, i.e.) blood, etc., and make apparent the diarrhoeal colours, brought about by the very nature of the elements and the morbific entities. When the elements, (i.e.) blood, etc., are extremely corrupted, stools are passed that are turmeric-yellow, yellowish-green, swarthy, madder-coloured, resembling water in which flesh has been washed, red, black, white or resembling the fat of a boar; (they are passed) attended by a painful sensation or without it; (the colours appear) in a compounded way or alternately; (the stools are) scybalous, sometimes immature and also sometimes mature; (the patient's) flesh, blood and force have not extremely declined, (his transforming) fire is sluggish and (his) mouth is without taste. Such a patient should be known to be difficult to cure. A patient, with a diarrhoea of the colours described below and provided with secondary affections, should be regarded as incurable; for instance (a patient with stools) resembling maturated blood, pieces of liver-tissue, water in which fat or flesh (has been washed), thick sour milk, ghee, marrow, oil, muscle-fat, milk and

vesavāra, (stools of an) extremely swarthy, red or black (colour), transparent like water, of the colour of the eyes of a peacock's tail, extremely oleaginous, of a yellowish-green, swarthy or yellowish-red colour, variegated, turbid, mucilaginous, ropy, immature, with moon-like spots, with an extremely fetid smell like a corpse, smelling like purulent matter, raw meat or raw fish, (with a smell) pleasing to flies, with a stinking discharge (derived) from many elements (of the body), and with a slight amount of faecal matter or no faecal matter; (a patient) suffering from a diarrhoea, attended by thirst, a burning sensation, fever, giddiness, *tamaka*, hiccup and shortness of breath, attended with much pain or no pain, someone whose anal region has become lax or inflamed, the folds of whose anal region are hanging down, whose (rectal) tube has become free (from its surrounding tissue), whose force, flesh and blood have extremely declined, who feels piercing pain in all his junctures and bones, who is full of anorexia, disinclination, confused speech and mental confusion, and someone whose morbid alteration suddenly pauses, should be known to be incurable; thus is diarrhoea by concerted action;" Su.U. 40, 12cd-13ab : "Someone showing lassitude, mental confusion, adynamia and desiccation of the mouth, being afflicted by thirst, will pass stools of several colours in (a diarrhoea) arisen from all (the morbific entities); a condition in which all the signs are present is difficult to cure, and it is incurable in children and old people;" A.h.Ni. 8, 11d = A.s.Ni. 8, 13d (Ki. 8, 12d) : "When it is of the nature of all (the morbific entities it shows) all the characteristics;" Hā. 3, 3, 60 : "(Diarrhoea by) concerted action exists in those persons who evacuate (stools) which resemble the muscle-fat of a boar, sesame grains, water in which flesh has been washed and mature *jambū* fruits."

37 Su. : *bāṣpavegaḥ paktim āvidhya* (the urge of the tears, having pierced the place of maturation) instead of *bāṣpoṣmā vai vahnim āviśya* (the heat of the tears, having entered the fire).

38 Su.U. 40, 14cd, corresponding to Mā.ni. 3, 10ab, reads : *varcomiśraṃ niḥpurīṣaṃ sagandhaṃ nirgandhaṃ vā sāryate tena kṛcchrāt* (it is made to flow out with difficulty, mixed with, etc.).

39 Cf. A.h.Ni. 8, 12-13ab = A.s.Ni. 8, 14-15ab (Ki. 8, 13-14ab) : "When the mind has been brought into a turbulent state by fear, the wind, together with the bile, may liquefy the faeces; thereupon may be made to flow (down faecal matter, flowing) quickly, that is hot, liquid and floating (in water); with respect to its signs it is said to be congruous with (diarrhoea) by wind and bile; (diarrhoea) from grief is of the same kind." See also note 20.

40 Ḍa. : idem.

41 This is also Ḍa.'s interpretation.

42 As an alternative reading of Su.U. 40, 13d-14, Ḍa. quotes : "The fiery energy (of grief), having desiccated the ingested food, goes, seized by the (transforming) heat, to the viscera and sets in motion the extremely hot blood, which resembles *guñjā* seeds, and makes it flow out from below, accompanied by excremental matter or not accompanied by it, with (a bad) smell or without smell; that is diarrhoea."

43 This is Vāgbhaṭa's opinion; see note 20.

44 Su.U. 40, 15cd-16ab presents a slightly different text : "The entirely corrupted morbific entities, assaulted by non-disintegrated, immature matter, giving rise to a turbulent state of the viscera, which contain the residue (of the food), bring about in a living being a flow (of faecal matter) of various colours and of several kinds, (emitted) with difficulty; this is called the sixth (type)." Ḍa. mentions in his comment the variant *dhātusaṃghān malāṃś ca*, adopted by Mādhava. Cakra quotes, in his comment on Ca.Ci. 19, 12-13, Mādhava's reading *annājīrṇāt pradrutāḥ*.

[45] *bhūyasā* instead of *naikaśaḥ* (of several kinds).

[46] This refers to Su.U. 40, 23 : "(A diarrhoea) caused by oleaginous substances and non-disintegrated (food), accompanied by many piercing pains and *pravāhikā*, caused by *visūcikā*, caused by other disorders of the process of disintegration (of the food), and arisen from poison, haemorrhoids or worms, is provided with the characteristics of (that) morbific entity (which is excited) in each particular case."

[47] Cf. Yo., p. 220, *atisāranidāna* 15-16 : "The element, (derived from) non-maturated food, is technically called immature matter when it stays in the receptacle of undigested food and no digestive alteration has been brought about in it on account of the weakness of the bodily fire. The first element is called immature nutrient fluid when no digestive alteration has been brought about in it on account of the slight force of the (transforming) heat and when it stays in a corrupted state in the receptacle of undigested food." The first one of these stanzas is quoted by Cakra on Ca.Ci. 8, 20 with the variant *ādya āhāradhātuḥ* (the first element derived from the food).

[48] Su. : *vichinna* (appearing with interruptions) instead of *picchila* (mucilaginous); Ḍa. makes mention of *picchila* as a variant.

[49] Su. : *lāghavaṃ ca manuṣyasya* (and lightness of the human being, i.e. the patient) instead of *lāghavaṃ ca viśeṣeṇa* (and especially lightness). As a variant Ḍa. mentions : *lāghavaṃ ca purīṣasya* (and lightness of the faecal matter).

[50] Cf. A.h.Ni. 8, 13cd-15ab = A.s.Ni. 8, 15cd-17ab (Ki. 8, 14cd-16ab) : "Stated succinctly, diarrhoea is of two kinds : accompanied by immature matter or devoid of it, accompanied by blood or devoid of it. In the first case among these (alternatives), the faecal matter submerges by its heaviness (if thrown) into water, it is bad-smelling, and the patient presents (abdominal) distension, a constrained condition (of the impurities), a feeling of affliction, and effusion. (If) the opposite (symptoms are present, it is a diarrhoea) devoid of immature matter. Mature (faecal matter, in a diarrhoea arisen) from phlegm, also submerges (when thrown into water)." Compare also a quotation from Kṣārapāṇi, occurring in Cakra's comment on Ca.Ci. 19, 7 : "A diarrhoea by wind, accompanied by immature matter, is attended by piercing pain, (the stools are) frothy, thin and brown, (appear) with noise, (are) bad-smelling, have been in a confined state and (appear) little by little; one should state that a diarrhoea, accompanied by immature matter, is of the same kind if bile or phlegm (are excited)."

[51] Ḍa. : it sinks (*bruḍati*).

[52] Ḍa. comments in a very similar way.

[53] The source of these stanzas is unknown.

[54] Su. : *durādhmāta* (badly inflated) instead of *dūrādhmāta* (much inflated).

[55] Compare with Mā.ni. 3, 14-19 : the second half of Ca.Ci. 19, 9 (see note 36); Su.U. 40, 19-20 : "If a discharge (of faecal matter) is present of the colour of butter, fat, water in which *vesavāra* (has been washed), oil, marrow, milk or *kṣaudra* honey, of the colour of madder, similar to cerebral tissue, of a musty smell, (of a) cold (quality), smelling like a corpse, resembling a collyrium or provided with streaks, with moon-like spots spread over it, resembling pus or mud, and (of a) hot (quality), it may kill one, as well as (when it is provided) with (signs indicating) refractoriness (to treatment); numerous additional affections will kill (a patient) who is subject to decline;" A.h.Śā. 5, 80cd-84 = A.s.Śā. 11, 13-17ab : "Diarrhoea (kills if it is) comparable to a round mass of liver-tissue, water in which flesh has been washed, (if it is) of a colour comparable to that of the eyes of a peacock's tail, (comparable) to oil, ghee, milk, thick sour milk, marrow, muscle-fat, *āsava*, cerebral tissue, ink, pus, water in which *vesavāra* (has been washed), or *mākṣika* honey,

(if it is) extremely red, oleaginous, foul-smelling, transparent, dense, painful, (if it is) variegated, discharging the elements (of the body), (if it is) devoid of faecal matter or accompanied by it to an extreme degree, (if it is) ropy, visited by flies, provided with streaks with moon-like spots, (if it is) accompanied by thirst, shortness of breath (A.s. : cough), fever, vomiting, a burning sensation, obstructive abdominal swelling and *pravāhikā*, brings about the evacuation of food (in a person) whose anal folds have withered, whose (rectal) tube has become free (from its surrounding tissue), who feels piercing pains in his junctures and bones, whose anus has prolapsed and whose force has declined;" Hā. 2, 4, 19-20 : "When in a person at first only diarrhoea is observed and afterwards shortness of breath and desiccation, he will quickly die. Diarrhoea will annihilate a man afflicted by shortness of breath, piercing pain and thirst, subject to decline and oppressed by fever, especially if he is old. A person with diarrhoea and swelling, who moreover presents anorexia and piercing pain, will quickly die, though many (therapeutic) counteractions (are employed);" Hā. 3, 3, 75-78 : "One should avoid (treating) someone with a diarrhoeal flow smelling like garlic, a corpse, or pus, someone whose flow is dense, resembling the water of sesame paste, mature *jambū* (fruits), ghee, honey, milk or oil, (of a) swarthy (colour like) *śaivāla*, accompanied by dense matter and of the colour of thick sour milk. A good physician should, without being seen, completely shun (a patient with diarrhoea accompanied by) giddines and (mental disturbance as in) intoxication, haemorrhoids, piercing pain, fainting, combustive alteration, shortness of breath and an extreme alteration of colour, (a patient who is) afflicted by vomiting, fainting and thirst, who is outstandingly bewildered and who shows happiness and afflictedness by swelling and fever. He should abandon a patient with diarrhoea after having observed swelling, piercing pain, fever, thirst, shortness of breath, cough, anorexia, vomiting, fainting and hiccup. He should abandon a patient with diarrhoea after having observed swelling and inflatedness, hiccup, vomiting and anorexia and also when seeing him afflicted by morbid pallor."

56 This stanza occurs also : Va. 2, 308; Bhā.pra. 8, 2, 127; Yo., p. 220, *atisāranidāna* 21.

57 *cāṣa* : PW : der blaue Holzhäher, Coracias indica; MW : the blue jay.

58 Cakra says that *mecaka* means : oleaginous and black, Aruṇa : of a swarthy colour.

59 Ḍa. : (covered with) moon-like spots which resemble the tail-feathers of a peacock.

60 Ḍa. : "Cerebral tissue is the marrow of the head, the appearance of which is like the four oleaginous substances (i.e. ghee, oil, muscle-fat and marrow) in a half-dissolved state."

61 See Ca.Ci. 19, 9 (note 36).

62 Ḍa. : someone whose anus is not contracted.

63 Ḍa. : deprived of perseverance, tone and force.

64 Ḍa. mentions two variants : *sadā 'dhmātam* (continuously inflated) and *durātmānam* (with a bad mind).

65 This stanza is identical with the additional one following upon Mā.ni. 3, 19. It is also quoted by Ḍa. on Su.U. 40, 20.

66 Ḍa. : whose heat has got outside and has been annihilated.

67 This refers to Mā.ni. 3, 19c.

68 Ā. reads *piṇḍa* instead of *khaṇḍa*.

69 A *mṛdaṅga* is a kind of drum.

70 This is a quotation from an unknown source.

71 This stanza, with some variants, also occurs : Va. 2, 309 and Bhā.pra. 8, 2, 128.

72 The first stanza quoted is identical with Mā.ni. 3, 19.

73 This stanza occurs also : Bhā.pra. 8, 2, 130 and Yo., p. 220, *atisāranidāna* 18cd-19.

74 This refers to Mā.ni. 3, 19.

75 The source of this stanza is unknown. Cf. Ca.Ci. 19, 69-70 : "But in someone with a bilious diarrhoea who, having abandoned this therapeutic procedure, indulges in bile-provoking foods and drinks, the very strong bile may bring about a bloody diarrhoea; it will quickly bring about a corruption of the blood and (give rise to) thirst, piercing pain, combustive alteration and a severe inflammation of the anal region;" Su.U. 40, 116-117ab : "The corrupted bile of someone who, suffering from a bilious diarrhoea, indulges too much in bile-provoking (substances), may be quickly conducive to a bloody diarrhoea, fever, piercing pain, thirst, a burning sensation and a severe inflammation of the anal region;" A.h.Ci. 9, 82-83a : "The bile of someone, suffering from a bilious diarrhoea, who would indulge in bile-provoking (substances), brings about a bloody diarrhoea, accompanied by thirst, fever and a severe inflammation of the anal region;" fr. A.s.Ci. 11, 23 : "The extremely increased bile of someone suffering from a bilious diarrhoea, who indulges in bile-provoking (substances), brings about a bloody diarrhoea, thirst, a burning sensation, mental confusion, fever, piercing pain and inflammation of the anus;" fr. Bhe.Ci. 10 : "It has been observed that a bilious diarrhoea, residing in a deep seat, that makes blood flow (down) to a high degree, is a diarrhoea arising from blood;" Hā. 3, 3, 54 : "The condition of a person who at defaecation evacuates pure blood to a high degree, (accompanied by) desiccation and a burning sensation, should be known as bloody diarrhoea by *vaidyas* with a great understanding."

76 This quotation also occurs : Yo., p. 220, *atisāranidāna* 22ef.

77 Compare Ā. on Mā.ni. 3, 11 and note 46.

78 *balāsa.*

79 Su. : *pravāhamāṇasya muhuḥ* (of someone who suddenly evacuates again and again) instead of *pravāhato 'lpam* (of someone who suddenly evacuates in small amounts).

80 Cf. Su.Ci. 34, 18.

81 In his comment on A.h.Ci. 9, 17 Aruṇa makes mention of *nistānikā* as a synonym of *pravāhikā*; from an unknown source he quotes the following definition : "That which, without faecal matter and resembling foam, appears by (the action of) the wind after blood and faeces have been discharged, is called *pravāhikā*." Śivadāsa quotes, in his comment on the same passage, Parāśara : "When someone repeatedly evacuates frothy matter without (an admixture of) faeces, (the condition) is called *pravāhikā*; some call it *niścārika*."

82 Ḍa. : idem.

83 Su.U. 40, 162 = A.h.Ci. 9, 124 = A.s.Ci. 11, 30. A.h. and A.s. read : *pavano vā pravartate* instead of *samyag vāyuś ca gacchati*; *śāntas tasyodarāmayaḥ* instead of *sthitas tasyodarāmayaḥ*.

84 Feverish diarrhoea is treated separately in later medical works, such as Siddhayoga, Cakradatta, Va., Bhā.pra. and Yo.

CHAPTER FOUR

THE *GRAHAṆĪ* DISEASE (*GRAHAṆĪROGA*)

4, 1 : Even when diarrhoea has ceased, the (transforming) fire of someone whose fire is sluggish and who eats insalutary things, being brought into a still more corrupted state, may bring about a great corruption of the *grahaṇī*.

(Su.U. 40, 167).[1]

M :

Immediately after diarrhoea the *grahaṇī* disease (is described) because (both) have the same peculiarity, (consisting of) a flowing (out) of liquid (matter), and because (both) attend each other.

Its onset is made mention of ... The word 'even' informs (us) about the fact that the *grahaṇī* disease may arise due to its own ground, even in the absence of diarrhoea. Others, however, explain that the word 'even' indicates (that it may occur) also in the case that the diarrhoea has not ceased.[2] The words 'of someone whose fire is sluggish' express that even the eating of insalutary things does not bring about a morbid alteration in a person whose fire is inflamed. For in the Suśruta(saṃhitā) it has been said : "Disagreeing (articles of food) will be inoperative in a person with an inflamed fire" (fr. Sū. 20, 22).[3] 'Still more' (means) : again,[4] or to an extreme degree. (The expression) 'more corrupted' (is used) because it has been made corrupted already previously in diarrhoea. 'It may bring about a great corruption' (means) : it may bring about a complete corruption. This means that insalutary (foods) have to be avoided by someone whose diarrhoea has ceased, until he has acquired a strong (transforming) fire. For that very reason Suśruta says : "Therefore one should avoid (insalutary foods) in diarrhoea in the same way as when one has been purged, until one's natural condition (has been regained) with respect to the morbific entities and the vital breath" (U. 40, 168).

Ā :

... What is this (organ) called *grahaṇī* ? "There are three (*kalās*), (those) of flesh, blood and fat (respectively), a fourth one of liver and spleen, moreover a fifth one of the bowels; a sixth one is thought to be that holding the (transforming) fire; a seventh one is that holding the semen; these are the seven *kalās* according to tradition" (Śārṅgadharasaṃhitā 1, 5, 6-7ab) ...

4, 2-3 : This (*grahaṇī*), being corrupted by the extremely intensified [5] morbific entities, by one of them separately [6] or by all of them together, releases the ingested food repeatedly in a quite immature state (2) or in a mature state, accompanied by pain, foul-smelling, at one moment being bound, at another moment being liquid. People who know the Āyurveda call it the *grahaṇī* disease (3).

(Su.U. 40, 171-172).[7] [8]

M :

Preceded by the onset, the generic characteristics (of the *grahaṇī* disease) are made mention of ... 'Intensified' (means) : extremely increased. (A remark is made about the meanings of *mūrchā*).[9] The variant reading 'surged' [10] has that very meaning. (A paraphrase of 4, 2cd and the beginning of 4, 3 follows; some grammatical remarks are made). 'Accompanied by pain' (means) : accompanied by piercing pain. 'Foul-smelling' (means) : with a bad smell. (The excremental matter) is at one moment bound by (the action of) wind, at another moment liquid by (the action of) bile. (The term) *grahaṇī* disease (means) a disease (brought about) by the *grahaṇī*. And the *grahaṇī* is the basis of the (transforming) fire. As Caraka says : "The *grahaṇī* is thought to be the basis of the fire because it seizes the (ingested) food;[11] it (is present) above the umbilical region and is furthered by the support [12] (consisting of) the strength of the fire. It sustains the immature food and emits it downwards [13] when it is mature" (Ci. 15, 56-57ab). Moreover, the following has been said in the Suśruta(saṃhitā) : "That one, which is proclaimed to be the sixth *kalā*, called the bile-holding one, staying between the receptacles of digested and undigested food, is proclaimed to be the *grahaṇī*" (U. 40, 169). A *kalā* is a boundary between the receptacles of the elements; the meaning of 'staying between the receptacles of digested and undigested food' means that it consists of the receptacle of the food that is subject to the process of maturation.

Ā :

... It releases (the ingested food) 'repeatedly', (i.e.) many times. It is also corrupted by bile, as fire (is corrupted) by heated water; for that reason the term 'morbific entity' is used in the plural ...

4, 4 : Its prodromes are the following ones : thirst, inertia, decline of force, combustive alteration of the food, maturation (of it) after a long time and heaviness of the body.

(Ca.Ci. 15, 55).[14]

M :

The prodromes are dealt with ... 'Combustive alteration of the food'... (occurs) because of the sluggish state of the (transforming) fire, and for that very reason maturation of that same food (takes place) after a long time. 'Heaviness of the body' (is present) on account of the fact that it is (filled) with immature matter.

4, 5-10 : Excited by pungent, bitter, astringent, extremely dry and completely corrupted [15] foods, by a restricted diet, abstinence from food, too much travelling, suppression of (natural) urges and sexual intercourse (5), the wind brings about maladies, after having covered the (transforming) fire.[16]

(Such) a person suffers when his food maturates, he shows a maturation of a fermentative type, harshness of the body (6), desiccation of throat and mouth, absence of hunger,[17] thirst, dimness of vision, tinnitus, frequently occurring pain in the sides, thighs, groins and neck, *visūcikā* (7), oppressing pain in the cardiac region, leanness, weakness, an altered taste, shooting pain, an eager longing for (food of) all tastes and asthenia of the *manas* (8).

When (the food) has been disintegrated and when it is being disintegrated, inflatedness (occurs); when one has ingested (food), one gets relief.

Such a man is uncertain (whether) a visceral swelling by wind (is developing), a disease of the cardiac region or a (disorder of the) spleen (9); he may, after a long time and accompanied by suffering, again and again emit excrements that are liquid, desiccated, thin, immature, accompanied by noises and frothy, and he is tormented by cough and shortness of breath, (when the *grahaṇī* disease arises) from wind (10).

(Ca.Ci. 15, 59-64).[18]

M :

With the words 'pungent, bitter', etc., the symptoms of *grahaṇī* (disease) by wind arc dcalt with, preceded by (its) origins and onset. 'Completely corrupted foods' are foods which disagree by way of commixture, etc. A variant reading of 'by completely corrupted foods' is 'by foods which are cold,[19] etc.' A restricted diet is the eating of slight amounts of food. The variant reading *pramṛta* should be understood (to mean) the taking of food when the (proper) time has passed. 'Abstinence from food' is fasting. The wind, excited by these causes, having brought about a complete corruption of the fire, gives rise to diseases. Reflecting : 'Which maladies does it bring about ?' he says : '(such) a person, when his food', etc. 'A maturation of a fermentative type' is an acid maturation; this occurs on account of the combustive alteration of the food, generated by the sluggishness of the (transforming) fire. 'Harshness of the body' is a scabrous state of the body due to the desiccation by wind of the oleaginous substance staying in the skin. 'Dimness of vision' is a sluggish state of the visual organ.[20]

'Pain' is oppressing pain; this (word) is connected with the (series of) words beginning with 'the sides'. '*visūcikā*' is the appearance of immature food above and below. 'Alteration of taste' is a condition in which the taste in the mouth is disagreeing. 'Shooting pain' is an oppressing pain in the anal region as if it were being cut to pieces. 'An eager longing' is a desire, for (food of) all tastes, (i.e.) sweet (foods), etc. ; (a grammatical remark is made) ; and this occurs by means of a corrupted condition of the inner organ, brought about by wind, or by means of the great power of the illness. 'Asthenia of the *manas*' is prostration. To 'inflatedness (occurs), when it has been disintegrated and when it is being disintegrated,' should be supplied '(when) the food (has been disintegrated)'. (About) 'such a man is uncertain whether a visceral swelling by wind (is developing), a disease of the cardiac region or a (disorder of the) spleen' (we remark that) he suspects these (disorders) because (*grahaṇī* disease) is accompanied by oppressing pains, like those occurring in visceral swelling by wind, etc.[21] '(He may emit excrements which are) liquid, desiccated' (means that the excrements are) sometimes liquid, sometimes desiccated. 'Thin' (means) in slight amounts.

Ā :

The word 'extremely' is connected with pungent, bitter and astringent ... The groin is the juncture between hip and thigh[22] ... 'Asthenia of the *manas*' is languor of the *manas* ...[23]

4, 11-12 : By means of pungent and non-disintegrated[24] (substances), by those which bring about combustive alteration, by acid, by caustic (substances), etc., the bile, being present in abundance, damages, overwhelming [25] it, the (transforming) fire, as hot water (extinguishes) a fire (11).

(In such a case the patient), being of a yellow complexion, is made to flow (faecal matter) that is non-disintegrated, of a swarthy and yellow colour and liquid, while he is tormented by foul-smelling and acid eructations, a burning sensation in cardiac region and throat, inability to eat and thirst (12).

(Ca.Ci. 15, 65-66) [26]

M:

The symptoms of *grahaṇī* disease by bile are dealt with, preceded by (its) origins and onset ... '(Substances) bringing about combustive alteration', (i.e.) generating combustive alteration, are *vaṃśa* shoots,[27] etc. Caustic (substances) are made from *apamarga*,[28] etc.; caustics are also *yavakṣāra*,[29] etc., and moreover substances to which a caustic has been added; a sauce, prepared with alkaline water, is eaten in Kāmarūpa,[30] etc. The word 'etcetera' denotes saline, sharp and hot substances; the bile, increased by these (substances), overwhelming, (i.e.) overpowering, the fire, damages it. He says: 'as hot water (extinguishes) a fire', for the very reason that one may ask: 'Is it not right that bile is of a fiery nature or fire itself, and that it increases bile for that reason? So why does it damage (the fire)?' (The answer is): just as water, even when it is provided with the quality 'hot', destroys fire, in that way bile, (though) consisting of heat, yet damages the (transforming) fire when its liquid component has increased.[31]

To '(in such a case) the patient being of a yellow complexion is made to flow (down)' should be supplied 'excremental matter'.

4, 13-16: Having become excited on account of the enjoyment of food that is heavy, extremely oleaginous, cold, etc., on account of taking too much food and of sleeping when one has scarcely ingested one's meal, phlegm damages the (transforming) fire (13).

Suffering accompanies the maturation of the food of such a man; there are present sickness, vomiting, anorexia, a condition of the mouth (in which it seems covered) with a liniment, a sweet (taste in the) mouth, cough, spitting and nasal catarrh (14).

(The patient) has the impression that his cardiac region is in a grumous condition and that his abdomen is torpid and heavy; there occur corrupted and sweet eructations, and adynamia; libidinous feelings towards women are absent (15).

There appear excrements which are loosened, combined with immature matter and phlegm, and heavy; even (a patient) who is not lean is weak and inert, if it is of the nature of phlegm (16).

(Ca.Ci. 15, 67-70).[32]

M:

Mention is made of the symptoms of *grahaṇī* disease by phlegm, preceded by (its) origins, etc. ... The word 'etcetera' denotes (foods that are) mucilaginous, sweet, etc. 'On account of taking too much food' is : on account of the taking of food beyond the (proper) measure.

Is it not a disagreeing statement to say : 'It damages the (transforming) fire on account of sleeping when one has scarcely ingested one's meal?'; sleeping should be understood here in the sense of sleeping by day, on account of the fact that sleeping at night is a ground of soundness; sleeping by day, however, animates the abdominal fire by closure of the channels; for that very reason it is said : "Sleeping by day is prescribed to persons with diarrhoea and disorders of the process of disintegration (of the food)".[33]

The answer (to this objection) is : sleeping by day damages the (transforming) fire by an exceedingly great increase of phlegm in persons who have ingested a meal, but animates it in persons who have not ingested a meal. As has been said : "One may cause to sleep by day, according to inclination, people who abstain from food".[34]

'A condition of the mouth (in which it seems covered) with a liniment, and a sweet (taste in the) mouth', (i.e.) a condition in which the mouth (seems covered) with an unctuous substance, and in which it is sweet, (occur) by means of phlegm itself'. 'In a grumous condition' is : as filled with a dense liquid.[35] 'An abdomen which is torpid' is an abdomen (the contents of which are) confined, in the sense of devoid of movement, or torpid (means) stiff. 'Heavy' is rigid. 'Corrupted' is morbidly altered. 'Sweet eructations' are (eructations which are) secondarily characterized by sweetness. 'Adynamia' is adynamia of the (transforming) fire. 'Absence of libidinous feelings towards women' is the non-existence of lasciviousness with respect to women. (Excrements which are) loosened, and combined with immature matter and phlegm; that is the sense of the compound. 'Weakness' is inability.

Ā :

... 'Adynamia' (is adynamia) of the parts of the body. 'Loosened' is : torn asunder; 'heavy excrements' are (excrements which are) a little bound.

4, 17 : When the grounds and signs, which have been declared to be those of wind, etc. separately, are present together, one should declare in the same way that it is (a case of excitement of) the three morbific entities. (Now) I shall tell about the remedy of these (conditions).[36]

(Ca.Ci. 15, 72).[37]

Four additional stanzas : (When) rumbling in the bowels, inertia, weakness and adynamia (occur), (when) one releases liquid, cold, dense or oleaginous faeces, accompanied by a painful sensation in the iliac regions (1), (when) immature, copious (faeces), together with mucilaginous matter, (are released), accompanied by noises and a mildly painful sensation, during half a lunar month, a (whole) lunar month, ten days or also permanently (2), (when) by day excitement is present and it becomes appeased at night, it may be (the disorder), difficult to discern and difficult to treat, attending one for a long time (3), which (is brought about) by immature wind and is called *saṃgrahagrahaṇī*.

(When) in a sleeping person piercing pains in the sides (occur), and the sound of water trickling from a water-bucket, it is called *ghaṭīyantra*,[38] an incurable malady of the *grahaṇī* (4).[39]

M :

Out of the desire to benefit pupils, the characteristics of *grahaṇī* disease, arising from the three morbific entities, are made mention of ... by means of analogy, though it is easily to be understood because it is a condition with an inherence (in the morbid alteration, the qualities of which are) congruous with the natural state.

'(Now) I shall tell about the remedy of these (conditions)' is written down to comply with the full (extent of the) stanza. Because the fire, residing in the *grahaṇī*, is also corrupted by a corruption of the *grahaṇī*, sluggishness, etc. of the (transforming) fire are also called morbid alterations of the *grahaṇī*. As has been said in the Caraka(saṃhitā) : "The four types of the (transforming) fire, which have been previously taught in the *rogānīka* (chapter),[40] are also considered by us to be faults of the *grahaṇī*, with exception of the congruous (condition of the) fire" (Ci. 15, 71). Also elsewhere it has been said "The three (types of the transforming) fire, (to wit) the incongruous one, etc., which have been mentioned in the (chapter on the) division of the body,[41] may also be (called) faults of the *grahaṇī*; the congruous (type), however, is the cause of a sound state" (A.h.Ni. 7, 29cd-30ab).

4, 18-19 : One should know that in this case, as in that of diarrhoea, the morbific entity is provided with immature matter or devoid of it (18).

Accompanied by whatever signs a morbid alteration of the *grahaṇī* will be incurable, accompanied by those very ones a diarrhoeic malady is incurable. Verily, having struck the body of an old man, a morbid alteration of the *grahaṇī* never turns back (19).[42]

additional stanza : *Grahaṇī* (disease), when it has been set in motion, should be discerned as being curable in a child, difficult (to cure) in young adults, but incurable in old people; that is the opinion of Dhanvantari.[43]

M :

(Just) as in diarrhoea an immature condition is known by means of the submerging in water, etc. (of faecal matter), and a condition devoid of immaturity by means of the contrary (signs), in that same way (these conditions) should be known in this (disease) as well. (4, 19ab is paraphrased).

NOTES

1 Cf. A.h.Ni. 8, 15cd-16ab = A.s.Ni. 8, 17cd-18ab (Ki. 8, 16cd-17ab) : "Regarding diarrhoeas (one can say that) in a person who does not exert himself very much (to curb the disease) the *grahaṇī* malady may arise, and (also) in other persons by the

indulgence in (foods and drinks) that extinguish the (transforming) fire." Compare also Hā. 3, 3, 79-80.

[2] Ḍa. is of this opinion.

[3] Su.Sū. 20, 22 reads : "Owing to their adequacy (by habitual use, acc. to Cakra) or their small amount, disagreeing (articles of food) will be inoperative in a person with an inflamed fire, a youth, and in persons who are strong from (eating) oleaginous (foods) and from physical exercise."

[4] This is Ḍa.'s opinion.

[5] Su. : *ucchrita* (surged) instead of *mūrchita* (intensified).

[6] Su. : *ekaśaḥ* instead of *ekaikaśaḥ*.

[7] Ca. acknowledges four kinds of *grahaṇī* disease, viz. arising from one of the morbific entities separately and by concerted action (Ci. 15, 58; 15, 72). Kā. mentions it among the diseases which are of four kinds (Sū. 27, 51-52). Hā. describes the same four types as Ca. and Su. (Hā. 3, 3, 81), but presents also the statement : "The *grahaṇī* malady arises not at all by means of one morbific entity" (3, 3, 82ab).

[8] Cf. A.h.Ni. 8, 16cd-19ab = A.s.Ni. 8, 18cd-21ab (Ki. 8, 17cd-20ab) : "That diarrhoea, which brings about an extreme flowing (down) of faecal matter, accompanied by immature matter or not accompanied by it, after (the food) has been disintegrated, acts quickly from its own nature on account of the extreme flow (caused by it). A slowly acting *grahaṇī* disorder, (arising) from an accumulation (of the morbific entities), makes one evacuate (stools) accompanied by immature matter, or (ingested) food when the food has not been disintegrated, but mature (faecal matter) or no (flow) at all when (the food) has been disintegrated; (it makes one evacuate stools which are), without any reason, at one moment bound and at another moment flabby. It arises in four ways, by one morbific entity separately or from concerted action."

[9] *mūrchā* may mean mental confusion (*moha*) or surge (*samucchrāya*).

[10] See note 5.

[11] The term *grahaṇī* is connected with the verbal root *grah-* which means : to seize.

[12] Ca. : *upastabdhopabṛṃhita* (supported and furthered) instead of *upastambhopabṛṃhita* (furthered by the support).

[13] Ca. : *sṛjati pārśvataḥ* (it emits it laterally) instead of *sṛjati cāpy adhaḥ* (it emits it downwards).

Cakra remarks that the left side is aimed at, because the *grahaṇī* and the rectum (*guda*) have their residence at the left side of the body.

[14] Cf. Su.U. 40, 173 : "At its production (there occur) combustive alteration of the (ingested) food, adynamia, inertia, thirst, weariness, decline of (bodily) force, inability to eat, cough, buzzing in the ears and rumbling of the bowels;" A.h.Ni. 8, 19cd-20 = A.s.Ni. 8, 21cd-22 (Ki. 8, 20cd-21) : "Its prodromes are adynamia, maturation after a long time, acid eructations, effusion (of saliva), an altered taste in the mouth, inability to eat, thirst, weariness, giddiness, obstructive abdominal swelling, vomiting, buzzing in the ears and rumbling of the bowels."

[15] Ca. : *śītala* (cold) instead of *saṃduṣṭa* (completely corrupted).

[16] Ca. : *karoti kupito mandam agniṃ saṃchādya mārutaḥ* (the excited wind, having covered the fire, makes it sluggish).

[17] Ca. : hunger instead of absence of hunger.

[18] Cf. Su.U. 40, 174-177 : "When it has arisen, one may get swollen feet and hands, and become lean; one may present pain in the junctures, fickleness, thirst, vomiting, fever, anorexia and a burning sensation; one may eructate matter that is fermented,

bitter, acid, smelling like blood, smoke or raw meat, and one is painfully oppressed by effusion (of saliva), an altered sense of taste in the mouth, *tamaka* and inability to eat. (One may recognize it) by means of excessive piercing pains in anus, cardiac region, sides, abdomen and head (when it arises) from wind, by means of a burning sensation (in these regions when it arises) from bile, and by (sensations of) heaviness (when it arises) from phlegm; (when it arises) from the three morbific entities (one may recognize it) by means of the three (sets of) characteristics; (it may be recognized) by the colours of the morbific entities, which are present in the nails and in the same way in the faeces, urine, eyes and face. A human being may be uncertain (in such a case whether a disease of) the cardiac region (is developing), morbid pallor, an abdominal disease, visceral swelling, haemorrhoids or (a disorder of) the spleen;" A.h.Ni. 8, 21 = A.s.Ni. 8, 23 (Ki. 8, 22) : "The generic characteristics are leanness, eructation of matter that smells like smoke, *tamaka*, fever, fainting, pain in the head, a constrained condition (of the impurities) and swelling of hands and feet;" A.h.Ni. 8, 22-25ab = A.s.Ni. 8, 24-27ab (Ki. 8, 23-26ab) : "When it (arises) from wind (there are present) desiccation of the palate, dimness of vision, tinnitus, repeatedly occurring pains in the sides, thighs, groins and neck, *visūcikā*, an eager longing for (food of) all tastes, hunger, thirst and shooting pain. When (the food) has been disintegrated and when it is being disintegrated, inflatedness (occurs); when one has ingested (food), one enjoys relief. One is uncertain whether a wind disease (is developing), a disease of the cardiac region, visceral swelling, haemorrhoids, (a disorder of the) spleen or morbid pallor. Attended by pain in the anus, shortness of breath and cough, one emits after a long time and with difficulty, again and again, excremental matter that is liquid, desiccated, thin, immature, accompanied by noises, and frothy;" Hā. 3, 3, 88 : "In *grahaṇī* disease by excitement of wind there will be emission of diversely (coloured) excremental matter, accompanied by noises and of an extremely dry (kind); swelling and flatus will be present, as well as afflictedness by shortness of breath; the discharge will be thin and flabby."

19 See note 15.

20 The visual organ (*dṛṣṭi*) is thought to be of a fiery nature; hence the same terms are applied to it as to the (transforming) fire.

21 Cakra makes a similar remark.

22 *vaṅkṣaṇaḥ sakthyūrvoḥ saṃdhiḥ*. Cf. Rā.nigh., *varga* 18, 45 : *śroṇisakthnoḥ saṃdhis tu vaṅkṣaṇaḥ*, i.e. : the groin is the juncture between pelvic region and thigh.

23 Ā. reads at Mā.ni. 4, 96 *svāsthyaṃ samaśnute* (one enjoys relief) instead of *svāsthyam upaiti ca* (and one gets relief); the former reading is also found in A.h. and A.s.

24 *ajīrṇa*; it may also mean : by taking food when the previous meal has not yet been digested.

25 *ā-plu-*, caus., literally : to inundate. Cakra : *draveṇārdrīkaraṇa*, i.e. : making it wet by (its) liquid (component).

26 Cf. A.h.Ni. 8, 25cd-26ab = A.s.Ni. 8, 27cd-28ab (Ki. 8, 26cd-27ab), only differing from Ca.Ci. 15, 66 in replacing *so ' jīrṇam* by *pittena*; Hā. 3, 3, 89: "When someone, suffering from combustive alteration, being withered, feeling pain, and afflicted by thirst, emits impure matter that is bad-smelling, (of a) yellow, ruddy, swarthy or black (colour) and (of a) mixed (type), it is a *grahaṇī* disease arising from bile."

27 *vaṃśa* shoots give rise to combustive alteration acc. to Bhā.pra.nigh., *guḍūcyādivarga* 155.

28 The ashes of the *apāmārga* plant, as a constituent of a caustic, are made mention of : Su.Sū. 11, 11; A.h.Sū. 30, 10; A.s.Sū. 39, 10.

29 Acc. to Dutt, M.M., p. 87, it is prepared by reducing to ashes the green spikes of barley (*yava*); chemically it is carbonate of potash with some impurities.

30 Kāmarūpa : the east part of Bengal and the west part of Assam.

31 A similar line of reasoning is found in Cakra's comment on Ca.Ci. 15, 65-66.

32 Cf. A.h.Ni. 8, 26cd-29a = A.s.Ni. 8, 28cd-31a (Ki. 8, 27cd-30a), enumerating almost the same series of symptoms (only a sweet taste in the mouth and inertia are omitted); Hā. 3, 3, 90 : "(In *grahaṇī* disease by phlegm) there will be present sickness, vomiting, shortness of breath, swelling, cough, rigidity, a feeling of coldness, an altered taste in the mouth, heaviness of the limbs, anorexia, and seizing of the temples and the faeces."

33 See Ca.Sū. 21, 39-41 and Bhā.pra. 5, 217-218 about the conditions in which sleep by day is thought to be beneficial.

34 This statement is found in the last part of Bhā.pra. 5, 218.

35 Aruṇa : feeling like a lumpy mass.

36 Ca. : *bheṣajaṃ śṛṇvataḥ param* instead of *teṣāṃ vakṣyāmi bheṣajam.*

37 Cf. A.h.Ni. 8, 29b = A.s.Ni. 8, 31b (Ki. 8, 30b) : "In (a *grahaṇī* disease) arising from all (the morbific entities there exists) an intermixture of all (their symptoms);" Hā. 3, 3, 91 : "When all three (morbific entities) are excited together, there will be the enumerated marks, a sweet (taste in the) mouth, a burning sensation, fainting, shortness of breath and rigidity; that is the *grahaṇī* malady by concerted action."

38 *ghaṭīyantra* : PW : das Brunnenrad mit dem Stricke und dem Wassereimer; MW : the buckets of a well or any machine for raising water.

39 The additional stanzas are, with a number of variants, also found at Va. 3, 142-144 (with the exception of the four last *pādas*); Bhā.pra. 8, 4, 20-24; Yo., p. 241, *grahaṇīnidāna* 21-24ab and 25cd-26ab.

40 Ca.Vi. 6.

41 A.h.Śā. 3.

42 The source of these stanzas is unknown.

43 The source of this stanza is unknown.

CHAPTER FIVE

HAEMORRHOIDS (*ARŚAS*)

5, 1 : One should know that haemorrhoids (occur) in the triad of anal folds and are of six kinds : (they are brought about) by each of the morbific entities separately, by the associated (morbific entities), (they arise) from blood and they (are) innate.[1]

M :

Haemorrhoids are made mention of ... immediately after *grahaṇī* disease because diarrhoea, *grahaṇī* disease and haemorrhoids attend each other.

The etymology of 'haemorrhoid' is said to be : it crushes, (i.e.) it harms, the vital breaths like a foe [2] (Pāṇini 6, 3, 109 is referred to).

'Innate (ones)' are (those which have) arisen together with the body, on account of the fact that the germinal part which starts the anal folds has been brought into a corrupted condition.[3] Those arising from a pair of morbific entities have not been counted separately in this case, since they are reached by an inherence (in a morbid alteration, the qualities of which are) congruous with the natural state. For it has been said in the Suśruta(saṃhitā) : "When in (a case of) haemorrhoids the symptoms of two morbific entities are observed, one should discern it as (a case of) combined action; and this combined action is of six kinds" (Ni. 2, 22). The sixfold condition of combined action (means) here (that there exist) three (kinds of) combined action by means of couples consisting of wind, etc., and three other ones by means of the same (morbific entities) when they are connected with blood. That one arising from concerted action has been counted as a separate (item) in the numeration, considering it to be reached by an inherence (in a morbid alteration, the qualities of which are) incongruous with the altered state, because it is connected with incurability, which is not observed in those arising from one single morbific entity.

(About) the triad of anal folds (we remark that) the anal area measures four digits and a half; the three folds, which are components of it, established one above the other, resembling the convolutions of a conch-shell, are called *pravāhaṇī*, *visarjanī* and *saṃvaraṇī*. In this (area) the anal lip is half a digit (in measure). Suśruta has pointed out that the first fold upwards of it occurs at a distance of one digit. Moreover, it has been said in (the treatise by) Bhoja : "The anal lip is called (that part measuring) one barley grain and a half from the edges of the hair(y region); it is known that the first fold is at one digit from the anal lip; the two other ones are proclaimed (to occur) at distances of one digit and a half each."

This means that the second and third one are found at a distance of one digit and a half (each).[4]

Ā :

... 'Innate' means : arising from (one's) lineage ...

5, 2 : The morbific entities, after having made skin, flesh and fat completely corrupted, bring about sprout-like growths of flesh of diverse conformations in the (area of the) *apāna*, etc. These are called haemorrhoids.

(A.h.Ni. 7, 2).[5]

M :

The very form of haemorrhoids is dealt with, preceded by the onset. The words 'skin and flesh' include the blood, residing in skin and flesh, in accordance with the bringing about of a discharge of blood, as it has been taught in the (section on) therapeutics.[6] The (area of the) *apāna* is the anal region; by the word 'etc.' the nose, etc. are understood. The specialists in internal medicine, however, require (that) the term haemorrhoids (be applied only) to those (sprout-like growths) which arise from the anal region, although an excess of flesh (also occurs) in those arising from the nose, etc. (They require it) because there does not exist in those (latter ones) an onset as described with the words 'the fivefold wind', etc., and there do not occur prodromes as described with the words 'a constrained condition', etc.[7] As Caraka says (in the statement) beginning with 'the penis' up to 'properly designated as an excess of flesh' (fr. Ca.Ci. 14, 6).[8] Suśruta, however, has employed the term haemorrhoids with respect to these (growths at other places of the body), by reason of the common peculiarity of consisting of sprout-like growths of flesh and of being curable by means of a cutting instrument, caustic or cauterization, in the same way as the oleaginous substance from *sarṣapa*, etc. is designated as oil. This very view is shared by Vāgbhaṭa, who reiterates (the opinion of) Suśruta.

Ā :

... By the word 'etc.' the nose, ears, eyes, penis, navel and so on are designated. The characteristics of these (sprout-like growths of flesh at the mentioned places of the body) are described in the Suśruta-(saṃhitā).[9]

5, 3-4 : Astringent, pungent and bitter (substances), dry, cold and light (substances), taking a restricted or a slight amount of food, a sharp alcoholic beverage, indulgence in sexual intercourse (3), reducing measures, a cold place and time, performance of physical exercise, grief and exposure to wind and the glowing heat (of the sun) are thought to be grounds of haemorrhoids by wind (4).

(Ca.Ci. 14, 12-13).[10]

M :

Mention is made of the origin of haemorrhoids by wind ... Eating a restricted (amount of food) is (eating) a very slight (amount), (eating) a slight (amount) is (eating an amount) the measure of which is deficient. Jejjaṭa, however, says that (a) restricted (diet means) : taking food when the (proper) time has passed. If *pramṛta* (instead of *pramita*) is read, it is said (to denote) grain, etc., the power of which has been annihilated.

Others say that a restricted (diet) is the habitual use (of foods) with one (particular) taste. That is not a very suitable application (of this term). Does it mean (the habitual use) of pungent (substances), etc., which bring about excitement of wind, or of sweet ones, etc., which bring about excitement of phlegm ?

The first (alternative is) not (the right one) because pungent (substances), etc. have (already) been enumerated in this very (stanza); as to the second (alternative), however, (it should be noticed that) the habitual use of sweet (foods), etc. verily brings about appeasement of wind and, (moreover), it has been stated that weakness (arises) from the habitual use (of foods) with one (single) taste, but no increase of wind. Thus should be reflected about it.

'Sharp' is added to 'alcoholic beverage' as a specification, because mild alcoholic beverages, such as *paiṣṭika*, etc., appease the wind.[11] 'A cold place' is a marshy place; 'a cold time' is the winter, etc. 'Glowing heat' is hot(ness); glowing heat (of the sun), though provided with the quality 'hot', brings about excitement of wind because (its) dryness is (distinctly) perceptible.[12]

5, 5-6 : Pungent, acid, saline and hot (substances),[13] physical exercise, the radiance of fire and of the glowingly hot (sun), a place and time which are not cool, wrath, alcoholic beverages, envy (5) and all drinks, foods and remedies that give rise to combustive alteration, that are sharp or hot [14] should be discerned to be grounds of haemorrhoids with an abundance of bile with respect to excitement (of the morbific entity) (6).

(Ca.Ci. 14, 15-16).[15]

M :

Haemorrhoids by bile are made mention of ... About 'a place and time which are not cool' (we remark that) a hot place is a desert and (hot) times are autumn and summer. 'Envy' is aversion to the good fortune of others; it is a specific kind of wrath. By the words 'of (haemorrhoids) with an abundance of bile' (it is established that) all haemorrhoids arise by three morbific entities, but are designated by means of that one which is (present) in excess, as Caraka has shown. As that same (Caraka) says : "Certainly haemorrhoids do not arise without the three morbific entities, acting concertedly; the specific type of haemorrhoids, however, is designated in accordance with the specific morbific entity (which is prevalent)" (Ci. 14, 23).[16]

5, 7-8 : Sweet, oleaginous and cold (substances) and those which are saline, acid and heavy, want of physical exercise, sleeping by day, finding pleasure in the ease of lying and sitting down (7), indulgence in the east wind,[17] a cold place and time and unmindfulness, these are declared to be causes of haemorrhoids by phlegm (8).

(Ca.Ci. 14, 18-19).[18]

M :

Mention is made of the origins of haemorrhoids by phlegm ... 'Finding pleasure in the ease of lying and sitting down' is the being attached to a comfortable couch and seat ...

5, 9ab : One should discern those (haemorrhoids) with an abundance of a pair (of morbific entities) by the combination of the grounds and characteristics (of both morbific entities involved).

(Ca.Ci. 14, 20ab).

M:

The origins, etc. of haemorrhoids by a pair (of morbific entities) are made mention of. 'By the combination of the grounds and characteristics', (i.e.) by means of the assembly of the origins and the assembly of the characteristics of a dyad of morbific entities, one should discern those arising from a pair (of morbific entities).

5, 9cd : The whole of the (series of mentioned) grounds (forms the ground) of (haemorrhoids by) the three morbific entities; (their) characteristics are the same as those of innate ones.[19]

(Ca.Ci. 14, 20cd).

M:

The origin of haemorrhoids arising from the three morbific entities is dealt with ... 'The whole of the (series of mentioned) grounds' (means) : the grounds which have been stated to be those of haemorrhoids by wind, etc. separately, are those of (haemorrhoids) arising from the three morbific entities ... Their characteristics are similar to those of innate (ones) ... But to the variant reading 'there is agreement with the characteristics of innate ones' should be supplied : the whole of the grounds of the three morbific entities is in agreement with, (i.e.) is accompanied by, the characteristics existing in innate haemorrhoids.

The characteristics of innate haemorrhoids are not mentioned in this summary and have to be remembered from another treatise. They have been stated by Suśruta as follows : "They are difficult to be seen, rough, (of a) ruddy (colour), pale and severe, facing the interior; someone assaulted by them is lean and ingests a slight (amount of food); vessels are stretched over his whole body, he has few offspring, his semen has undergone decline, his voice is debilitated, he is inclined to wrath, his (transforming) fire is (of) slight (intensity), his nose, head, eyes and ears are diseased and he is continually painfully oppressed by rumbling of the bowels, (abdominal) distension, an increased presence of unctuous substances in the cardiac region, anorexia and so on" (fr. Ni. 2, 25).[20] And in the Caraka(saṃhitā) more numerous characteristics have been stated with the words "Some are minute", etc. (fr. Ci. 14, 7).[21] Is it not right to say that the announcement of a specific (type), with the words 'those arising from the three morbific entities', is based on an inconclusive argumentation, because verily all diseases arise from the three morbific entities, according to what has been said : "A substance with (only) one taste does not exist nor a disease arising from (only) one morbific entity; they are defined by means of that one of the tastes and morbific entities which is present in excess?" [22] That is not right. According to the statement : "Wind, bile and phlegm are coursing through the whole body" (fr. Ca.Sū. 20, 9), there occurs necessarily, when one (constituent) element, etc. has been corrupted by a morbific entity, some kind of corruption with respect to the other morbific entity residing in it, owing to the intimate connection (that exists) between a corrupted (constituent) and a morbific entity. Moreover it is thus, that the wind, when it has become increased on account of its own causes, supplies, owing to its coldness, force to phlegm which is cold and, owing to its lightness, to bile which consists of fiery energy; bile (supplies force) to wind owing to its pungency, and to phlegm owing to its liquidity; phlegm (supplies force) to wind owing to its coldness, and to bile owing to its liquidity. For that very reason it has been said : "No disease whatever arises from one (single) morbific entity." [23] With this very view (in mind) it has been said : "One excited morbific entity will bring about excitement of really all of them." [24] In that case in which all three (morbific entities) are excited on account of their own causes, the designation '(arising from) three morbific entities' (is used); that is the settled doctrine. (It should be used) in the same way everywhere.

5, 10-15 : Sprout-like growths of the anal region are, when provided with much wind, desiccated, accompanied by a tingling sensation,[25] shrunken, (of a) brownish-ruddy (colour), stiff, clear,[26] rough, harsh (10), not resembling each other, twisted awry and sharp; their head (tip) is cracked, they resemble the fruits of *bimbī*, *kharjūra*, *karkandhū* and *kārpāsī* (11); some are like the flowers of *kadamba*, some are similar to *siddhārthaka*. They (give rise to) an excessively distressing sensation in the head, sides, shoulder-blades, iliac region, thighs, groins, etc. (12), bestow sneezing, eructation, a constrained condition, a seizing (pain) in the cardiac region and anorexia, and are conducive to cough, shortness of breath, incongruity of the (transforming) fire, tinnitus and giddiness (13).

> Someone afflicted by these is made to evacuate scybalous (faeces), in small amounts, accompanied by noise and by *pravāhikā*, followed by pain, by frothy and mucilaginous matter and (faeces) which have been confined (14). One's skin, nails, faeces, urine, eyes and mouth become black, and afterwards there arise visceral swelling, splenomegaly, abdominal disease and *aṣṭhīlā* (15).
>
> (A.h.Ni. 7, 28cd-34ab).[27]

M:

The origins have been mentioned previously; mention is made now of the characteristics of haemorrhoids according to the distinctions with regard to wind, etc. Among these the characteristics of haemorrhoids by wind are stated first ...

'Sprout-like growths of the anal region' are fleshy excrescences in the anal region, having the form of sprouts; these very ones are haemorrhoids. 'Provided with much wind' (means): with an abundance of wind. 'Desiccated' (means): deprived of a discharge. 'A tingling sensation' is a specific kind of painful sensation.[28] 'Shrunken' (means that they are) not plump.[29] (They are) 'stiff' on account of (their) hardness.[30] (They are) 'clear', (i.e.) non-mucilaginous, feeling like dust when they are touched. (They are) 'rough', (i.e.) scabrous, feeling like *gojihvā* to the touch.[31] (They are) 'harsh', (i.e.) like the fruits of *karkoṭa*, covered with many subtle thorns.[32] To (the description of) these varieties should be added the word 'some' that is mentioned subsequently. (The words) 'not resembling each other' (mean that) their forms are distinct from one another. 'Twisted awry' (denotes that they are) like a bow, a piece of wood, etc.[33] 'Sharp' (means): with subtle tips.[34] 'They resemble fruits' is connected with the series beginning with *bimbī*; one should know that the resemblance to *bimbī*, etc. concerns (their) conformation.

The fruits of *bimbī* resemble lips[35] and are called in common language *telākucā*;[36] *kārpāsī* is *vanakārpāsī*.[37] 'Like *kadamba* flowers' (means that they are) gross and provided with several subtle tops.[38] 'Similar to *siddhārthaka*' (means that they occur) in the form of subtle pustules.[39] 'A seizing (pain) in the cardiac region' is a painful sensation as if it the heart has been seized.[40] 'Scybalous (faeces)' are knotted (faeces), which are like stones. 'Pain' is piercing pain (in this case).[41] 'Mucilaginous matter' is the mucilaginous liquid part. 'One is made to evacuate' (means): one is made to pass excrements. The word 'black' is connected with each of (the words of the series) beginning with 'skin' and ending with 'mouth'. With the words 'visceral swelling', etc. mention is made of their secondary affections. '*aṣṭhīlā*' is a specific kind of wind disease.

Ā :

A tingling sensation is a specific kind of painful sensation, as when one is besmeared with *sarṣapa* paste; that is its explanation ... The variant reading 'incongruous' (means) : depressed and elevated.[42] 'Twisted awry' is : crooked like a bow. 'Sharp' is : with subtle tips as *darbha* sprouts. 'Having cracked heads (tips)' are those of which the head (tip) is like the filament of a lotus; this means that their upper part is torn asunder ... '*karkandhu*' (denotes) *kola* and *badarī*.[43] Some are gross like *kadamba* flowers, some are subtle like *sarṣapa* (seeds) ... 'A constrained condition' is the seizing of impure matter ... '*pravāhikā*' is *pravāhikā* by wind ... An '*aṣṭhīlā*' is like a stony globular mass in the part (of the abdomen) under the navel; it is a specific kind of wind disease.

5, 16-18 : Those of which bile is the most important (morbific entity) have an upper part which is (of a) swarthy (colour); they have a red, yellow and dark lustre, discharge thin blood, have a musty smell, are thin, soft and slack (16), resemble the tongue of a parrot, a piece of liver and the mouth of a leech, bestow a burning sensation, inflammation, fever, perspiration, thirst, fainting, inability to eat and mental confusion (17), and are accompanied by heat; (in their presence) the excrements are liquid, swarthy, hot, yellow, red and immature; their middle part is like that of a barley grain; (when they are present) skin, nails, etc. are yellowish-green, yellow and turmeric-yellow (18).

(A.h.Ni. 7, 34cd-37ab).[44]

M :

The characteristics of haemorrhoids by bile are made mention of ... 'The upper parts of which are of a swarthy colour' (means) : the tips of which are (of a) swarthy (colour). They discharge thin, (i.e.) not dense,[45] blood. They have a musty smell, (i.e.) smell like raw meat. (They are) thin, (i.e.) very small.[46] (They are) soft, (i.e.) tender.[47]

(They are) slack, (i.e.) they usually hang down.[48] 'Their middle part is like that of a barley grain' (means that they are) gross with respect to their middle part, like barley grains.[49] Yellowish-green is the colour of leaves; yellow is the hue of orpiment;[50] turmeric-yellow is the colour of turmeric. From the word 'etc.' [51] should be understood (that) faeces, urine, eyes and mouth (are included).[52]

Ā:

... They make one evacuate excrements which are liquid, swarthy, hot, yellowish-red and immature. 'Their middle part is like that of barley grain' (means) : their middle part is gross like a barley grain and they are subtle at the extremities ...

5, 19-23 : Those with an abundance of phlegm are provided with big roots, are dense, mildly painful and white; they are raised,[53] stout, oleaginous, stiff, round, heavy and solid (19).

They are mucilaginous, torpid, smooth, richly endowed with itching and they like to be touched; they are like the kernel of a *karīra* and a *panasa* and also resemble the dugs of a cow (20).

They bring about obstructive swelling of the inguinal region and a drawing pain [54] in anus, bladder and navel; they are accompanied by shortness of breath, cough, sickness, effusion, inability to eat and nasal catarrh (21).

They bring about urinary disease, strangury,[55] rigidity of the head and cool fever; there occur impotence, mildness of the (transforming) fire and vomiting; they bestow (one with) morbid alterations which abound in immaturity (22).

They are attended by faeces which are like muscle-fat and abundantly [56] provided with phlegm; they are accompanied by *pravāhikā*, do not discharge and do not burst open; (when they are present) one's skin, etc. are pale and oleaginous (23).

(A.h. Ni. 7, 37cd - 42ab)[57]

M:

The characteristics of haemorrhoids by phlegm are dealt with ... 'With big roots' (means) : plunging far into their site of foundation.[58] 'Dense' (means) : the component parts of which are without interstices. 'Raised' (means) : having come forth lengthwise.[59] 'Stout' (means) : gross with respect to their circumference.[60]

'Stiff' (means) : not bent. 'Round' (means) : circular as to their circumference. '(They are) heavy' (means that) they make the anal region full, as if a heavy substance has come to press upon it. 'Solid' (means) : not dangling.[61] 'Smooth' (means) : polished like a gem. 'Richly endowed with itching' (means) : amply provided with it; 'they like to be touched' (denotes that) someone having haemorrhoids is soothed when they are touched for the sake of the disappearance of the itching. ('They are like the kernel of a *karīra* and a *panasa*' means that) they resemble the kernels of a *karīra*, (i.e.) a tree growing in the desert, and of a *panasa*, (i.e.) a thorny fruit, or *karīra* (means) *vaṃśa* sprout and the meaning is that they resemble these (sprouts) and the kernels of a *panasa*.[62] ... 'Bringing about obstructive swelling of the inguinal region' means that they are bringing about in both inguinal regions, because of (their) proximity to the anal region, an inability to set in motion, etc. 'They bring about a drawing pain in anus, bladder and navel' (means that) they bring about an oppressing pain, which gives the sensation that one is pulling [63] at (these parts), in the anus, etc. 'Effusion' is (effusion) of the mouth or of the anus; 'difficulty' [64] (means) strangury; 'rigidity of the head' (denotes) torpidity of the head; 'bringing about cool fever' (refers to) cold fever. 'Impotence' is the absence of perseverance (in sexual activity) with regard to women; 'mildness of the (transforming) fire' (means that) it is sluggish; 'vomiting' is emesis. 'They bestow (one with) morbid alterations which are full of immaturity' (means that) they bestow one with diseases which are amply provided with immaturity, (i.e.) diarrhoea, *grahaṇī* disease, etc. The variant reading 'present in a copious quantity' [65] has the same meaning, because the two terms 'present in abundance' and 'present in a copious quantity' have the sense of 'present in a very great quantity'... To 'they do not discharge' has to be supplied : 'moisture, blood, etc.' 'They do not burst open' (means that) they are not torn asunder, though they are subject to pressure by the tightly packed faeces.

5, 24ab : Those which possess the nature of all (the morbific entities) are said to be provided with all the characteristics and (this applies) as well (to) the innate ones.[66]

M :

(Gives only a paraphrase of these two *pāda*s).

5, 24cd-27ab : When provided with an abundance of blood cuneate growths in the anal region possess the conformation of (those by) bile (24), are similar to offshoots of a *vaṭa* (tree) and resemble *guñjā* (seeds) and red coral. Subject to pressure from the tightly packed faeces,[67] they suddenly discharge extremely corrupted and hot blood; because it is coming forth to an extreme amount, (such a person), with the hue of a frog, is painfully oppressed by sufferings, arising from the decline of blood (26); (his) colour, force and perseverance are deficient, (his) vital energy is damaged and (his) senses are turbid.

(A.h.Ni. 7, 43-45).[68]

M:

Mention is made of the characteristics of haemorrhoids (arising) from blood ... (A grammatical remark is made about the form of the compound *gudekīla* with reference to Pāṇini 6, 3, 9). 'Possessing the conformation of (those by) bile' (means that) they are provided with the characteristics of haemorrhoids by bile ...[69] 'Subject to pressure from the tightly packed faeces', (i.e.) held by the firm (mass of) faecal matter acting as a mechanical contrivance,[70] they discharge 'corrupted',[71] (i.e.) turbid, and hot blood. Because 'it', (i.e.) blood, 'is coming forth to an extreme amount', (i.e.) on account of its extreme decline, (such a person is provided) 'with the hue of a frog', (i.e.) with the hue of the frog which appears in the rainy season, (i.e.) with a yellow skin; '(such) a person' has to be supplied. (He is oppressed) 'by sufferings', (i.e.) by diseases, 'arising from the decline of blood', (i.e. those which have been) mentioned by Suśruta : "Roughness of the skin, asking for acid and cold (things) and flaccidity of the vessels" (fr. Sū. 15, 9).[72] 'Force' is grossness (of the body); 'perseverance' (refers to) sexual pleasure. 'One whose vital energy is damaged' is someone with a damaged ability (of performance).[73] 'One whose senses are turbid' is someone with turbid eyes or someone with a disturbance [74] of all his senses.

Ā:

... (They resemble) as to their conformation *guñjā* (seeds), (i.e.) red *guñjā* [75] (seeds) ...

Two additional *pādas* : With respect to these there are two adjunctory (morbific entities) : phlegm and wind.

(Ca.Ci. 14, 170cd).[76]

5, 27cd-30 : If the faeces are brown, hard and dry and the downwards moving wind does not come forth (27), if the blood from the haemorrhoids is thin, of a ruddy colour and frothy, if there are found piercing pain in the iliac region, thighs and anal region and weakness to an excessive degree (28), the adjunctory (factor) is wind, and also if the ground promotes dryness.

If the faeces are flabby, white, yellow, oleaginous, heavy and cold (29), if the blood from the haemorrhoids is dense, ropy, pale and mucilaginous, if the anal region is provided with mucilaginous matter and is torpid, and if the cause is of a heavy and oleaginous (quality), wise men should discern phlegm to be the adjunctory (factor) of the haemorrhoids (arising) from blood (30).

(Ca.Ci. 14, 171-174).[77]

M :

Mention is made now of the characteristics of these same haemorrhoids by blood, according to the distinctions of blood as an origin with respect to wind, etc. ... The word *viṣ* can also be of the neutral gender just because it has been taught to be so. But in the Kaśmīr text of the Caraka(saṃhitā) it is used as a female noun in the same passage.

'The downwards moving wind does not come forth' by way of the anus because it moves in the reverse direction... 'In that case wind is the adjunctory (factor)' because only blood which has been corrupted by wind, etc. acts as a starting factor, and not blood as an isolated (element), on account of the non-existence of a morbific entity (in the latter case). Phlegm as an adjunctory (factor) is (also) mentioned...

If it is asked why bile is not said to be an adjunctory (factor), the answer is : because blood and bile are usually provided with the same signs. And it has been said previously : "Cuneate growths in the anal region with an abundance of blood are provided with the conformation of (those by) bile" (Mā.ni. 5, 24cd).

Ā :

... 'Thin' (means) : in slight amounts... 'Ropy' (means) : in the form of threads... 'Torpid' (means) : devoid of movement...

5, 31-32 : A constrained condition of the food, weakness and certainly distension of the lateral parts of the abdomen, leanness, copious eructations, adynamia of the thighs, the appearance of slight amounts of faeces (31), and uncertainty (as to the existence) of a *grahaṇī* disorder, morbid pallor and abdominal disease, are taught to be the prodromes leading to the development of haemorrhoids (32).

(Ca.Ci. 14, 21-22).[78] [79]

M:

Mention is made of the prodromes... 'A constrained condition of the food' (means that) the food, after it has become constrained, enters into a state of disintegration; food that has become constrained remains lodged in the receptacle of undigested food, owing to the altered qualities of the wind.[80] 'Weakness' is a deficient state of one's ability (of performance).

The variant reading *aṅga* (instead of *anna*) (changes the meaning of the first quarter into) : a constrained condition of the impure matter and weakness of the body.

Although the prodromes should be stated immediately after the origins, nevertheless in this case the prodromes (are stated) immediately after the origins and characteristics. The origins and signs are mentioned previously in order to substantiate that they belong to the several parts of therapeutics, or (it is thus that) those things, which necessarily should be stated, can be mentioned according to one's inclination. One should also regard it to be thus in other cases of violation (of the rule).[81]

'Distension of the lateral parts of the abdomen' (means) a murmuring sound according to Cakra(pāṇidatta); according to Guṇākara it is *tanatanī*;[82] according to Gadādhara it is a state of turbulence, preceded by a painful condition; in the (paragraph on the) characteristics of increase of faecal matter he [83] explained : 'distension (means) inflatedness'.[84] But this (latter explanation) is not (correct) because in all the (descriptions of the) prodromes of visceral swelling both distension and inflatedness are mentioned.[85] 'Copious eructations' (occur) by reason of the upward motion of the wind, which has become restrained below. 'Adynamia of the thighs' is prostration with regard to the legs. There is uncertainty (as to the existence) of morbid pallor, connected with a *grahaṇī* disorder, and of abdominal disease, because the characteristics (of these diseases) are observed. The variant reading *grahaṇīdoṣapāṇḍvartiḥ* (means that) there may be the affliction, (i.e.) the oppressing pain, of a *grahaṇī* disorder and morbid pallor. 'Leading to the development of' (means) with the production of (haemorrhoids) as (their) aim.

Ā :

... Mādhava has said about the characteristics of increase of faecal matter: distension (means) inflatedness...

5, 33-34 : The wind which is of five kinds, the bile, the phlegm and the triad of anal folds, all (these) become excited without exception when haemorrhoids arise (33). For that reason haemorrhoids bring about sufferings and many illnesses, (for that reason) they spoil the whole body by glowing heat and are usually very difficult (to cure) (34).

(Ca.Ci. 14, 24-25).

M :

Because one may ask in what way a corruption of the whole body, consisting of leanness, blackness of the skin, etc., (can arise) owing to the production of haemorrhoids by way of a corruption of the anal region, it is said : 'the wind which is of five kinds', etc.

(The wind) 'which is of five kinds', (i.e.) the very forms of which are five (in number), according to the distinction of *prāṇa*, *apāna*, *samāna*, *udāna* and *vyāna*. Their seats are (as follows) : "*prāṇa* has its seat in the cardiac, *apāna* in the anal and *samāna* in the umbilical region; *udāna* will stay in the region of the throat and *vyāna* in the whole body." [86] 'Being of five kinds' should, by change of gender, in the same way be applied to bile as well, for bile is distinguished into *ālocaka*, *rañjaka*, *sādhaka*, *pācaka* and *bhrājaka*. *ālocaka* (resides) in the eyes, *rañjaka* in liver and spleen, *sādhaka* in the heart, *pācaka* between the receptacles of digested and undigested food and *bhrājaka* in the skin. Phlegm also is in the same way of five kinds, (residing) in the cardiac region, receptacle of undigested food, tongue, head and junctures, in due order, according to (its) distinction into *avalambaka*, *kledaka*, *bodhaka*, *tarpaka* and *śleṣmaka*. As Gautama says : "Phlegm is of five kinds, (which are distinguished) by means of the own actions of *kledaka* (phlegm), etc.; that (kind) which stays in the chest is (called) *avalambaka* because it has an upholding function in all the dwelling-places of phlegm; that (kind of) phlegm, however, which resides in the receptacle of undigested food is (called) *kledaka* because it moistens the compact food-mass; that (kind) which stays in the tongue is (called) *bodhaka* because it makes one perceive taste; that (kind) which has its seat in the head is (called) *tarpaka* because it satiates the eyes; that (kind) which is (called) *śleṣmaka*, because it makes (things) adhere in the proper way, stays in the junctures." And excitement of the triad of anal folds (indicates) a morbidly altered state and a condition in which one's own effects, (consisting of) evacuation, etc., cannot be brought about. The variant reading 'in the triad of anal folds' is not suitable by reason of the non-existence of *prāṇa* and *udāna* and of a gathering-place in that (region), and because a corruption of the folds has not been attained.

'All (these) without exception' are these very mentioned (entities), the winds, etc. 'For that reason', etc., they bring about many illnesses, (i.e.) secondary affections, (like) sluggishness of the abdominal fire, etc. 'They are usually very difficult (to cure)' (means), on account of (the use of) the word 'usually', that they are also incurable (or) easily curable.

Ā:

... The five kinds of wind are stated to be as follows: "The wind which circulates in the mouth is called *prāṇa* and sustains the body; it makes the food enter the interior (of the body) and is verily an upholder of the vital breaths. When it is excited, it brings about maladies (like) hiccup, shortness of breath, etc. By means of the uppermost wind called *udāna*, which moves upwards, (actions like) speaking, singing, etc. come forth; when excited, it brings about maladies residing in the region of the body above the collar-bones. The (wind called) *samāna* courses through the receptacles of undigested and digested food and assists the (transforming) fire; it maturates the food and dissociates the products arising from it; when corrupted, it brings about visceral swelling, adynamia of the (transforming) fire and diarrhoea. The *apāna* resides in the receptacle of digested food and drags wind, urine and faeces, semen, foetus and menstrual discharge downwards at the (proper) time; when it is excited, it brings about dreadful diseases residing in bladder and anal region. The *vyāna* flows through the whole body; it strives to carry the nutrient fluid all through (the body), brings about the discharging of perspiration and blood, and brings about the five kinds of movement; when excited, it brings about diseases which usually reside in the whole body. Seminal disorders and urinary diseases arise from excitement of *vyāna* and *apāna*. These (winds), being excited simultaneously, will undubitably cut (up) the body" (Su.Ni. 1, 13-21ab).[87] Thus is the fivefold wind. "(Wind) consists of the constituent *rajas*, it is subtle, cold, dry and light." [88] This condition of being of five kinds should in the same way be applied to bile, according to the distinction of *ālocaka*, *rañjaka*, *sādhaka*, *pācaka* and *bhrājaka*. "*pācaka* and *bhrājaka*, *rañjaka* and *ālocaka* and (also) *sādhaka* are the five names of bile in due order." [89] "The bile (called) *pācaka* stays in its own receptacle, has the form of fire and has the measure of a sesame grain. (The bile called) *bhrājaka* bestows beauty (to the skin) and is that which maturates unguents, ointments, etc. *rañjaka* (stays) in liver and spleen; it will lead the nutrient fluid to (the state of) blood. *ālocaka* stays in the eyes; it makes one (able to) see colours. *sādhaka* will stay in the heart and it brings about intelligence and judgment. Bile is hot, liquid, yellow and swarthy; its most important constituent is *sattva*; its state should be known as pungent and bitter and, when combustively altered, it leads to acidity." [90] In the same way phlegm is of five kinds as well : "Chest, throat, head, junctures,[91] receptacle of undigested food, nutrient fluid, fat, nose and tongue are the seats of phlegm, (but) the chest (is its seat) in a very special way." [92] Thus it has been established that the three morbific entities are of five kinds.[93]

5, 35-37 : Haemorrhoids which have arisen in the outer fold and are provided with an abundance of one morbific entity are easily curable, as well as those which have not been produced a long time ago (35).

Those arising from a pair (of morbific entities) and those which reside in the second fold are said to be difficult to cure, as well as those which have (already) existed for a whole year (36).

The innate ones, those with three morbific entities and those which arise with the inner fold as their residence, should be taught to be incurable (37).

(Ca.Ci. 14, 31; 30; 28).[94]

M :

Mention is made of the curability, etc. of the mentioned haemorrhoids by wind, etc. ... 'Those which have not been produced a long time ago' (are haemorrhoids) with a duration not exceeding a year.[95] 'Those which have (already) existed for a whole year' are those with a duration exceeding a year. Those, however, which arise in the outer fold and are provided with an abundance of two morbific entities are difficult (to cure), and those arising from three morbific entities are (only) mitigable; thus it has been said. In the same way (those arising) in the second fold and provided with an abundance of one morbific entity are difficult (to cure); provided with an abundance of two morbific entities they are mitigable, and provided with an abundance of three morbific entities incurable. In the same way (those arising) in the third fold are mitigable when provided with one morbific entity; the remaining ones, (arising in the third fold), are incurable. Those, which are mitigable or to be rejected (as to treatment), are certainly incurable, though there are distinctions concerning (the number of) morbific entities and (the location of the) fold (involved). As Caraka has said : "An incurable (disease) does not become curable, but a curable one can become incurable" (Ni. 8, 35ab).

Ā :

... 'Difficult to cure' means : mitigable...

5, 38 : These (haemorrhoids) can be mitigated, when a remnant of vitality has been left (in a patient) who is provided with the four basic elements (of treatment) and whose bodily fire is inflamed; when (conditions are) different they should be rejected.

(Ca.Ci. 14, 29).

M :

There are two kinds of incurable (diseases) according to the distinction of mitigable ones and those which should be rejected. With regard to this (distinction) mitigable (haemorrhoids) are present if a remnant of vitality has been left and if the requirements concerning the four basic elements are fulfilled; (if conditions are) different (the case) should be rejected. To 'someone provided with the four basic elements' should be supplied : 'a patient with haemorrhoids'. (A grammatical remark is made, supported by a quotation from Cakrapāṇidatta's commentary on this stanza).

Ā :

Mention is made of the existence of two kinds of incurable (disorders) by means of the distinction of mitigable ones and those which should be rejected. If a remnant of vitality has been left, these haemorrhoids can be mitigated if the four basic elements are present; 'in the diseased one' should be supplied. In a diseased one of which kind? In someone with an inflamed bodily fire. And of which kind further? In someone provided with the four basic elements. 'When (conditions are) different', (i.e.) when the opposite (conditions) are present, 'they should be rejected', (i.e.) they are incurable. The four basic elements are as follows : the diseased one, the physician, (his) attendant and the remedial agent. When the diseased one acts according to the words of the physician, is rich and has subdued his senses, when the *vaidya* is competent in theory and practice, devoid of greediness and intent upon the truth and his duty, when the attendant is trustworthy, well-born, devoid of inertia and compliant regarding the wishes of the patient, and when the remedial agent is fresh(ly prepared) and endowed with taste, potency, etc., (the requirements are fulfilled). This has been said : "The *vaidya*, the person plagued by an illness, the remedy and the attendant, these are the basic elements of therapy, the grounds for successful accomplishment of (therapeutic) action. The physician who has thoroughly learnt the purport of (his) science, who has been trained in the practice of it (by seeing his master perform the therapeutic procedures), who has himself performed (the therapeutic procedures), who possesses manual skill, who is honest and valiant, and whose implements and remedies are of a good quality, who possesses presence of mind and wisdom, acts with determination, is adroit and intent upon the truth and his duty, (that one) is said to be a basic element. A diseased one who possesses vitality and *sattva*, who is curable, furnished with (therapeutic) substances, who is also self-possessed, acting according to the words of the *vaidya* and religious, is said to be a basic element.[96] A remedy which originated from a commended place and has been dug out at a commended day, which is in a slight quantity [97] of a great potency [98] and possesses (the right) smell, colour and taste, which strikes down the morbific entities, does not bring about languor and no morbid alteration in a contrary case, and when given after close inspection and at (the right) time, is called a basic element. An attendant who is affectionate, who does not dislike (the patient), who is strong and intent upon the protection of the ill one, who acts according to the words of the *vaidya* and who is indefatigable is traditionally called a basic element" (Su.Sū. 34, 15cd-16ab, 19cd-24).[99] This is the fulfilment (of the requirements) with respect to the four basic elements. And this (fulfilment) is possible when a remnant of vitality has been left (in the patient).

5, 39-40 : A sufferer from haemorrhoids, in whom swelling of hands, feet, face, umbilical region, anal region and testicles, and piercing pain in the cardiac region and the sides occur, is incurable (39).

Piercing pain in the cardiac region and the sides, complete mental confusion, vomiting, a painful condition of the body, fever, thirst and inflammation of the anal region will kill a patient with haemorrhoids (40).

(Ca.Ci. 14, 26-27).

5, 41 : Haemorrhoids wreck [100] someone who is afflicted by thirst, anorexia and piercing pain, who has discharged an extreme amount of blood, and who shows swelling and diarrhoea.

(Su.Sū. 33, 10).[101]

M :

Mention is made of incurability owing to (the occurrence) of secondary affections... Swelling of the hands, feet, etc., when occurring assembled together, is a characteristic of incurability. Piercing pain in the cardiac region and the sides, complete mental confusion, etc., are in this respect, whether dissociated or associated, (characteristics of incurability).

Ā :

... Incurability of haemorrhoids from blood is made mention of with the words 'thirst', etc. ...

5, 42 : All those occurring on the penis, etc. will be mentioned in the respective (chapters dealing with the diseases of these organs); those arising in the umbilical region possess the form of the mouth of an earthworm, are mucilaginous and soft.

(A.h.Ni. 7, 56).[102]

M :

... 'They possess the form of the mouth of an earthworm' (means that) they resemble the mouth of a *kiñculaka*.[103]

Ā :

With the words 'on the penis', etc. mention is made of the fact that polypous growths also occur at other seats. These are designated by the term polypous growth because they are sprout-like growths, in the same way as the designation (sesame) oil (is used) with regard to the oleaginous matter from *sarṣapa* (seeds), etc. ...

5, 43 : The *vyāna*, after having seized the phlegm, brings about a polypous growth at the outside of the skin, which resembles a peg, and is solid and harsh; it is known as a wart.

(A.h.Ni. 7, 57).[104]

M :

Mention is made of the onset of warts... Kārtikakunda and others say : "And these (warts) only occur in the region of the anal lip and not elsewhere."

Ā :

... 'At the outside of the skin' means : at some distance from the anal lip, because haemorrhoids as such arise at that place.[105]

5, 44 : (When it arises) from wind (there occur) pricking pain and roughness, (when it arises) from bile a dark colour of the mouth,[106] (when it arises) from pghlem (there are found) in it oleaginousness, a knotty condition and the same colour (as that of the skin).

(A.h.Ni. 7, 58).[107]

M :

Mention is made of the characteristics of these very ones distinguished according to wind, etc... 'The same colour' (indicates that) its colour is the same as that of the body.

Ā :

... From wind (arise) pricking pain, (i.e.) a specific kind of oppressing pain, and roughness. From bile (arises) 'a dark colour', (i.e.) a slightly black colour of the mouth. From phlegm (arise) oleaginousness, a condition resembling that of a knot and equality of colour, (i.e.) the same colour as that of the body.[108]

The excited morbific entities, having brought about a corrupted condition of the flesh and blood of the penis, bring about itching sensations; thereupon (they give rise to) an itching condition with lesions.[109] "In these lesions may occur, arising from the flesh, excrescences which discharge blood; these (excrescences) bring about annihilation of the penis and they destroy the virility speedily"... 'Virility' is the semen. "And in the vulvar region also these corrupted (morbific entities) generate (growths), which have the conformation of the mouth of an earthworm, which are bad-smelling, very delicate and mucilaginous;" 'sprout-like growths of flesh' should be supplied. From the word 'and' (it follows that one should supply) : they destroy the menstrual discharge from the vagina. "By means of these same morbific entities, which have gone upwards, a polypous growth of the ear arises. (In this condition there are found) deafness, an extremely ferocious piercing pain and a continuous foul-smelling condition of the ears. (In those polypous growths) arising at the eyes (there occur) a watery discharge and also a painful sensation; in polypous growths which obstruct the eyelids tears are continuously absent. In those arising at the nose there will occur nasal catarrh, respiratory difficulties, a distressing sensation in the head, sneezing, a foul smell and a nasal speech. In polypous growths of the mouth, which arise at one particular place, (viz.) the throat, lip or the middle part of the palate, a stammering speech, non-perception of taste and ailments of the mouth will arise." [110]

NOTES

[1] Ca. divides haemorrhoids first into two classes : those which are innate and those which arise at a later time in life (Ci. 14, 5). The latter are distinguished into those arising from wind, bile, phlegm, a combination of (two) morbific entities and concerted action (Ci. 14, 11-20). At Ci. 14, 23 it is said, however, that haemorrhoids never occur without excitement of all three morbific entities and that their type is determined in accordance with the morbific entity which is prevalent. Haemorrhoids arising from blood are not made mention of in the *nidāna* section of Ci. 14, but do appear in the section on therapy, though in an ambiguous phrasing; Ci. 14, 38cd : "(Haemorrhoids, which are) discharging, and (those, which are) wet, are possessed of an abundance of blood and bile." Su. agrees with Mā.ni. 5, 1. Su.Ni. 2, 3 : "There are six (kinds of) haemorrhoids, (those) by wind, bile, phlegm, blood and concerted action and (those which are) innate." Ḍa. observes : "... Is it not thus, that by means of the very words '(those) by wind, bile, phlegm, blood and concerted action and (those which are) innate' a number of six (kinds of haemorrhoids) has been obtained? So why is (their) number taught by the word 'six'? The answer is : (it is done) in order to avoid that haemorrhoids generated by two morbific entities are included in counting (the types). Although wind, etc., when having blood as a basis, are the starting agents of bloody haemorrhoids, nevertheless the words '(those) arising from blood' are used, metaphorically, in the same way as something burnt by means of a fire with ghee as its basis is said to be burnt by means of ghee." Gayadāsa comments : "... Is it not thus, that the accurate determination of a number of six (kinds of haemorrhoids) is contradictory on account of the fact that it has also

been shown that there is a number of six (kinds of) haemorrhoids by a combination (of two morbific entities) ? That has been stated (as follows) : "When in (a case of) haemorrhoids the symptoms of two morbific entities are observed, one should discern it as (a case of) combined action; combined action is traditionally said to be of six kinds" (Ni. 2, 22). The answer is that the meaning has been explained as follows : in those cases in which concerted or combined action occurs with an inherence (in the morbid alteration, the qualities of which are) congruous with the natural state, the number is not made redundant according to the consideration : 'an aggregate is not different from its component parts', because (cases of) combined action, the signs of which are those of each single morbific entity as a (constituent) element, (i.e. those of) wind, etc., are included in (the syndromes by) wind, etc. solely, as one (category) with respect to (their) therapy. That has been stated in the Caraka(saṃhitā) : after saying "There are five (kinds of) visceral swelling, (to wit those) arising from wind, bile, phlegm, concerted action and blood" (fr. Sū. 19, 4), it is said on the other hand : "One should point out, however, that the other visceral swellings, the signs of which are (of a) combined (character), are three (in number), for the sake of the preparation of medicinal agents" (Ci. 5, 16). If, according to the words : 'an aggregate is not different from its component parts', the inclusion of those arising from combined action in those arising from a single morbific entity, (to wit) wind, etc., does not occur, the statement 'there are five (kinds of) visceral swelling' disagrees with the accurate determination of a number of five (types). On the other hand others say : (it occurs) on account of the tracing back of the word 'concerted action' to its derivation ... That (is) not (correct), because it has been demonstrated in the Caraka(saṃhitā), etc., that haemorrhoids by combined action (do exist)." (Compare this reasoning with the similar one in Cakra's comment on Ca.Ci. 5, 16).

Su.Ni. 2, 4 mentions haemorrhoids by one and two morbific entities, by the associated ones and by morbific entities accompanied by blood. Gayadāsa comments on this statement : "... Some do not read 'by two morbific entities'. Blood is separately mentioned for the sake of its predominance. That has been said in (the chapter on) the questions about inflammatory swellings : "By these very ones with blood as the fourth one ..." (fr. Sū. 21, 3), as it has been said previously : the morbific entities are also, when abiding in their own (natural) condition, (constituent) elements, in accordance with the consideration that they support (the body); as Caraka says : "A morbid alteration is an incongruous state of the (constituent) elements" and an incongruous state of the (constituent) elements means an incongruous state of morbific entities, elements (of the body) and impurities. (Constituent) elements, which are not abiding in their (normal) condition, on account of increase or decline, are morbific entities ..."

Cf A.h.Ni. 7, 3ab : "(They are), succinctly stated, of two kinds, according to the distinction of innate ones and those arising (at a) later (time);" Ni. 7, 9ab : "The others (which are not innate) are of six kinds : (they arise) from (one) morbific entity separately, combined action, accumulation (of the three morbific entities) and blood;" A.s.Ni. 7, 4 (Ki. 7, 3) agrees with A.h.Ni. 7, 3ab and A.s.Ni. 7, 9 (Ki. 7, 8) agrees with A.h.Ni. 7, 9ab; Bhe.Ci. 18, 1 : "The haemorrhoids of bodily beings are of six kinds : (they arise) from wind, bile and phlegm, and also from concerted action, (there are) innate ones and (they arise) from blood;" Ci. 18, 7 : "The three morbific entities, wind, bile and phlegm, excited in that way, singly, collectively or pairwise, or by means of blood...;" Kā.Sū. 27, 50 makes mention of haemorrhoids among those diseases which are of six kinds; Hā. 3, 11, 2-3ab : "They arise by means of all three morbific entities, (i.e.) by wind, bile, phlegm, etc.; with respect to concerted action there will be a fourth (kind); a fifth one has its source in blood and the sixth one should be known to be the innate (type); the condition of haemorrhoids is of six kinds."

[2] Cf. A.h.Ni. 7, 2a-c : "They are called haemorrhoids because they, being cuneate growths of flesh, cut up living beings like a foe;" A.s.Ni. 7, 3 (Ki. 7, 2) contains a similar statement.

[3] Cf. fr. Ca.Ci. 14, 5 : "In this respect the support of innate haemorrhoids is the germ (of a human being) when it has been spoilt by heat by the germinal part of the anal folds." A.h.Ni. 7, 6 and A.s.Ni. 7, 7 (Ki. 7, 6) contain a similar statement.

See about the term 'germinal part' (*bījabhāga*) e.g. Ca.Śā. 4, 30-31 and Cakra's comment on it. Succinctly stated, a germinal part is a particular part of the embryo, either derived from the father or from the mother. A particular part of the paternal component leads e.g. to the formation of the bones of the embryo, a particular part of the maternal component to the formation of the upper and lower anal region (see Ca.Śā. 3, 6).

[4] Cf. fr. Ca.Ci. 14, 6 : "The field (of occurrence) of all haemorrhoids (is as follows) : (their) field (of occurrence consists of) the three anal folds, which have three intervening parts, (and are present) in the space occupied by the anal region, which covers four digits and a half." Cakra remarks that there are three parts of one digit and a half each; the anal lip is included in the measure of four digits and a half; the outer fold is at a distance of half a digit and is not included. Su.Ni. 2, 5-7 : "(The part, measuring) four digits and a half and attached to the gross bowel, is called anal region. Three folds are present in it, with intervening distances of one digit and a half, and they are called *pravāhaṇī*, *visarjanī* and *saṃvaraṇī*. They are extended over a distance of four digits, and all have a lateral elevation (into the lumen) of one digit. They resemble the convolutions of a conch-shell and are situated one above the other. They are proclaimed to be of a colour like that of the palate of an elephant. The anal lip is proclaimed (to be at a distance of) one barley grain and a half from the edges of the hair(y region). The first fold, however, is found at a distance of one digit from the anal lip." Ḍa. comments : "The gross bowel, (i.e.) the iliac bowel, is commonly known as the anal bowel ... The two upper folds, resembling the convolutions of a conch-shell, (measure) each, together with the intervening space, one digit and a half, but the first fold (measures), without an intervening space, one digit in elevation ... A digit measures three grains of barley." Gayadāsa comments: "... A digit is three grains of barley ..." Bhāluki says: "... Upwards of the row of hairs of the fold (of the skin) is the anal lip, at a distance of one barley grain and a half; upwards of this (lip) is the first (anal fold), at a distance of one digit; the second one is at a distance of one digit and a half and the third one is (at) the very same (distance from the second) ..." A.h.Ni. 7, 3c-5 : "The anal region is connected with the gross bowel and measures four digits and a half. There are three folds in it at (a distance of) one digit and a half; the inner(most) of these is the *pravāhiṇī*, the middle one is the *visarjanī* and the outer one the *saṃvaraṇī*; at (a distance of) one digit from it, at the outside, is the anal lip, measuring one barleycorn and a half; further down are the hairs." A.s.Ni. 7, 6 (Ki. 7, 4-6) : "The anal region is attached to the gross bowel and (measures) four digits and a half. In it (are found) the three previously mentioned muscles, technically called (anal) folds, (at a distance of) one digit and a half. They are (called) *pravāhiṇī*, *visarjanī* and *saṃvaraṇī*. It is said that the anal lip (is at a distance of) one barley corn and a half from the edges of the hair(y region). The first fold, however, (is present) at one digit from the anal lip." Hā. 3, 11, 20 : "Within the anal area with its three folds, at the outside and in the inner (parts), one should discern (to be present) the three seats of haemorrhoids."

[5] Cf. fr. A.s.Ni. 7, 3 (Ki. 7, 2) : "These are cuneate growths of flesh, residing in the anus, on the penis, etc., of very many kinds and with very many secondary affections;" A.s.Ni. 7, 5 (Ki. 7, 3) : "And the basis of all (kinds consists of) fat, flesh and skin;" fr. Ca.Ci. 14, 6 : "The basis of all (kinds of) haemorrhoids (consists of) fat, flesh and skin."

[6] See Ca.Ci. 14, 24 = Mā.ni. 5, 33.

[7] See Ca.Ci. 14, 21 = Mā.ni. 5, 31.

[8] Fr. Ca.Ci. 14, 6 : "Some, however, teach that the area (of occurrence) of haemorrhoids, (i.e. polypous growths), is even larger, (and also consists of) the penis, birth-channel, throat, palate, mouth, nose, eyes, ears, eyelids and skin. That is (said) on account of these being areas in which an excess of flesh (may be present). But, in this treatise, 'haemorrhoids' is the technical term denoting those (polypous growths) which arise from the anal folds."

[9] *taila* means, sensu stricto, sesame oil (*tilataila*), but it is often used to denote any kind of vegetable oil.

[10] Su. only enumerates the generic origins of haemorrhoids : Su.Ni. 2, 4 : "In this (connection), the morbific entities of persons, who are not self-possessed, excited by those (causes) which have been stated as bringing about excitement of a particular morbific entity, by disagreeing foods, overeating, attachment to women, sitting in a squatting posture, riding, restraint of the (natural) urges and other specific (causes), (excited) separately, in a number of two, the whole (set of morbific entities being excited), or being accompanied by blood, expand in the (previously) described way, attain the predominant ducts, move downwards, reach the anal region, give rise to corruption of the anal folds and generate fleshy excrescences, especially in persons with a sluggish (transforming) fire. These tuber-like growths increase in size by (repeated) contact with grass, wood, stones, clods, clothes, etc., and cold water; they are called haemorrhoids." A.h. and A.s. present the same scheme : A.h.Ni. 7, 10-15c : "The ground of excitement of the morbific entities has been stated previously. When by that (ground) adynamia of the (transforming) fire has been brought about and impure matter has accumulated to an extreme degree, (it occurs that) the wind (called) *apāna*, having become excited from sexual intercourse beyond the proper measure, from jolts when riding, sitting on an uneven or hard (surface), sitting in a squatting posture, scrubbing with the tube of a *basti*, a stone or clod, scrubbing against the surface of the earth and against clothes, from coming into contact with extremely cold water, from evacuating stools persistently and to an extreme degree, restraining the urge to pass flatus, urine and faeces and rousing these (urges), from fever, visceral swelling, diarrhoea, (the disease by) immature matter, *grahaṇī* disease, swelling and morbid pallor, from reducing procedures, and incongruous movements, moreover in women from the descent of an immature foetus and pressure by the increase in size of the foetus and from other (causes) of such a kind, deposits impure matter in the anal folds; in these (folds), the form of which has been destroyed, haemorrhoids arise." A.s.Ni. 7, 10 (Ki. 7, 10) presents a closely related text. Bhe.Ci. 18, 3-11 describes the origins of haemorrhoids as follows : "In those who indulge in (substances) which bring about combustive alteration, and in (substances which are) heavy and dry, who frequent marshy places and water, who enjoy thick sour milk, milk, treacle and meat, on account of the use of defective vehicles and corrupted waters, in those who constantly eat before the previous meal has been digested, on account of restraint of the (natural) urges, evacuating to an extreme degree, indulgence in sexual intercourse beyond the proper measure, attachment to corrupted drinks, oppressing pain by hard (objects) and (riding on) the back (of an animal), on account of overuse of

the corrective enema and erroneous application of *bastis*, errors with respect to the drinking of oleaginous substances, addiction to alcoholic beverages and on account of decline, thus being excited, the three morbific entities, wind, bile and phlegm, residing in the anal region, quickly bring about, each one separately or all of them together, combined into a pair or (accompanied) by blood, an effluxion from the anal region. At that place cuneate growths shoot forth resembling very small *sarṣapa* (seeds), similar to (grains of) barley, *mudga* (beans) etc., *niṣpāva* (beans), *karkandhu* and *badara* (fruits), or of the size of the thumb, copper-coloured and resembling the dugs of a cow. When these cuneate growths have arisen in the anal region, they immobilize it vehemently, obstructing the mouth of the channels or clipping their roots. On account of the obstruction of these channels, the morbific entities which are seated in the upper region, after having been roused and having corrupted them one by one, make people ill owing to disease." Hā. describes the origins of haemorrhoids in a very corrupt passage (3, 11, 4-6).

11 See Hā. 1, 19, 10 : "*paiṣṭī* annihilates wind."

12 Cakra's comment contains a similar statement.

13 *kaṭūṣṇalavaṇakṣāra* (pungent, hot, saline and caustic) instead of *kaṭvamlalavaṇoṣṇa* (pungent, acid, saline and hot). Cakra mentions as a variant : *kaṭvamlalavaṇakṣāra* (pungent, acid, saline and caustic). Cakra remarks that the term 'hot' denotes hot on touch when it occurs the first time, and hot with regard to potency when it occurs for the second time.

15 Cf. Hā. 3, 11, 7 : "By indulgence in pungent, acid, saline and hot (substances), those bringing about combustive alteration and those which are heavy, by wind, water, fatigue, oppressing pain from physical exercise, and by faults regarding riding and sexual intercourse, haemorrhoids arising from bile (will occur)."

16 Ca. : *kalpyate* instead of *kathyate*.

17 See about the qualities and actions of the east wind e.g. Su.Sū. 20, 23-24, Hā. 1, 5, 25 and Bhā.pra. 5, 206-207.

18 Cf. Hā. 3, 11, 8 : "From want of physical exercise and the perpetual practice of it, from cold (substances) and the indulgence in winds coming from the woods, from inconsistency and very acid (substances), by oily and by mucilaginous (substances), haemorrhoids arise on account of the phlegm disease (caused by the mentioned factors)."

19 Ca. : *sahajair lakṣaṇaiḥ samam* (there is agreement with the characteristics of innate ones) instead of *sahajair lakṣaṇaṃ samam* (their characteristics are the same as those of innate ones).

20 Su. : *paruṣāṇi pāṃsūni* (they are rough and of the colour of dust) instead of *paruṣāruṇapāṇḍūni* (they are rough, of a ruddy colour and pale); *alpāgniprāṇaḥ param alasaś ca* (his transforming fire and vital breath are of slight intensity and he is above all things inert) instead of *alpāgniḥ* (his transforming fire is of slight intensity).

21 Cf. Ca.Ci. 14, 7 : "In this (connection), some innate haemorrhoids are minute and some large, some are long and some short, some are round and some projecting unevenly, some are crooked internally and some externally, some are twisted together and some are facing the interior; their colours are those of the morbific entities attending each (type);" Ca.Ci. 14, 8 : "Someone who is injured by these (innate) haemorrhoids is from his birth onwards extremely lean, the colour (of his skin) is altered, he is debilitated, dejected, provided with a very great amount of confined wind, urine and faeces, provided with (urinary) gravel and stones; to a variable degree his excrements are confined, let loose, mature, immature, desiccated or loosened; now and then he evacuates faecal matter that is white, pale, yellowish-green, yellow, red, ruddy, thin, viscid, mucilaginous,

melling like a corpse or like raw meat; he is attended by very abundant shooting pains in the region of the navel, bladder and groins; he suffers from piercing pain in the anal region, *pravāhikā*, horripilation, urinary diseases, a prolonged constrained condition (of the impurities), rumbling of the bowels, the retentive disease and an increased presence of unctuous substances in the cardiac region and the senses; he suffers from eructation of very abundant (quantities of) matter that has been in a confined condition and from bitter and acid eructations, he is very weak, his (transforming) fire is very weak, he has a slight amount of semen, is inclined to wrath, is of a character that is difficult to be dealt with, is haunted by cough, shortness of breath, *tamaka*, thirst, sickness, vomiting, anorexia, absence of digestive alteration, nasal catarrh and sneezing; there is dimness of vision and piercing pain in the head, his voice is debilitated, hoarse, adynamic, impeded and decrepit, his ears are diseased, his hands, feet, face and region around the eyes are swollen, he is feverish, suffers from muscle pain and piercing pain in all the junctures and bones; now and then he suffers from seizing pain in the sides, lateral parts of the abdomen, bladder, cardiac region, back and sacral region; he is chiefly occupied with deep thought and, above all things, he is inert. The *apāna* wind of (such) a person, surrounded by haemorrhoids from birth onwards, mounts again because its pathway has been checked, and brings about excitement of *samāna*, *vyāna*, *prāṇa*, *udāna*, bile and phlegm. All these (entities, i.e.) the five winds, bile and phlegm, being excited, overrun a person with (innate) haemorrhoids and generate additionally these (mentioned) morbid alterations. Thus have been described the innate haemorrhoids;" A.h.Ni. 7, 8 : "The innate ones are specifically dry and difficult to see; they face the interior, are pale and accompanied by severe secondary affections;" A.s.Ni. 7, 8 (Ki. 7, 7) : "The innate ones are specifically difficult to see, rough, pale, big and severe, facing the interior and accompanied by many strong secondary affections."

22 This quotation has not been traced to its source.

23 See the preceding quotation from an unknown source.

24 The source of this quotation is unknown.

25 A.h. : *cimicimā* instead of *cimacimā*.

26 A.h. : *viṣama* (uneven) instead of *viśada* (clear).

27 A.s.Ni. 7, 15 is closely related to A.h.Ni. 7, 28cd-34ab. Cf. Ca.Ci. 14, 11 : "These are their specific (characteristics) : one should know that haemorrhoids with an abundance of wind are desiccated, hard, rough, dry and brown, endowed with sharp tips, twisted awry, provided with fissured heads, projecting unevenly, and making one haunted by piercing pain, convulsions, pricking pain, twitching, tingling and hypersensitivity; oleaginous and hot (substances) are therapeutically efficient; they are accompanied by a very strong *pravāhikā*, inflatedness, seizing pain of penis, testicles, bladder, groins and cardiac region, muscle pain, tachycardia and a persistent confinement of wind, urine and excrements, and bringing about piercing pain in thighs, iliac region, back, sacral region, sides, lateral parts of the abdomen and bladder, glowing heat in the head, sneezing, eructation, nasal catarrh, cough, retentive disease, stretching (of the body), desiccation, swelling, fainting, anorexia, alteration of taste in the mouth, dimness of vision, itching, piercing pain in nose, ears and temples and an injured voice, in a man whose nails, eyes, mouth, skin, urine and faeces are brownish ruddy and rough;" Su.Ni. 2, 10 : "In this respect (those arising) from wind are completely desiccated, (of a) ruddy (colour) or of an altered colour; their middle part is uneven; their tips have the conformation of a *kadamba* flower or a *tuṇḍikerī* (fruit), are tubular, bud-shaped or formed like a needle; someone assaulted by these is made to evacuate compact (faecal matter),

accompanied by piercing pain. He experiences painful sensations in the iliac region, back, sides, penis, anal region and umbilical region. Caused by these very (haemorrhoids, there arise) visceral swelling, *aṣṭhīlā*, splenomegaly and abdominal disease. (Such) a man's skin, nails, eyes, teeth, mouth, urine and faeces become black;" Bhe.Ci. 18, 15-18 : "The characteristics of haemorrhoids by wind (are as follows) : the faeces are black, dry and somewhat frothy; the faeces of such a person are permanently tightly packed and are loosened again and again (at other times); there is a (morbid) seizing of thighs, back and iliac region, and one is always very weak without a reason; a cutting pain in the junctures arises, piercing pain in the ears, thirst and giddiness. By increase of the haemorrhoids there is also increase of the wind and (the affection of) the abdomen; cuneate growths and inflatedness appear later on, to an increasing degree; when the *grahaṇī* has been corrupted, alteration of colour is added, and piercing pains (arise) in the cardiac region, sides and viscera. (These are the symptoms) by haemorrhoids arising from wind."

28 Toḍara : it is the specific kind of painful sensation (which arises when one is) besmeared with *sarṣapa* (paste); Śrīdāsa : it is the sensation (as if) minute living beings are crawling about (on one's skin). Ḍa. says, explaining the term *cumucumāyana*, occurring Su.Ni. 1, 25 : it is a painful sensation like that (occurring) when the body is besmeared with *sarṣapa* paste.

29 Toḍara : they are not plump, (i.e. like) scabs.

30 Toḍara : (they are stiff), like pegs, on account of their hardness.

31 Aruṇa : they are comparable, on touching them, to the leaves of potherbs, etc.

32 Toḍara : they are hard, similar to a stone, etc. to the touch, like a *karkoṭikā* fruit.

33 Aruṇa : they are like the curved end of a bow, etc.; Śrīdāsa : they are of a crooked form.

34 Aruṇa : they are like *darbha* sprouts.

35 *oṣṭhopamaphalā* is used as a synonym of *bimbī*.

36 Nadk. 1, p. 33 : *bimbī* is called *tala-kucha* in Bengali; Bhā.pra.nigh., p. 674 : *bimbī* is called *telā kucā* in Bengali.

37 The wild (*vana*) cotton tree is meant.

38 See Ph.gn.Ā.dr., S. 1, Nr. 5, p. 46 : the flowers of the *kadamba* tree are arranged in large solitary globular peduncled heads; they have conspicuously long exserted white stigmas (see pl. XI).

39 Śrīdāsa : subtle sprout-like growths of the form of *sarṣapa*.

40 Toḍara reads *hṛdrava* and explains it by *hṛdroga* (disease of the heart). Śrīdāsa reads *hṛddrava* and comments : *hṛddrava* is moisture (*kleda*) in the cardiac region; it is like a discharge of the cardiac region; it is a specific kind of painful sensation.

41 This refers to Mā.ni. 5, 14c.

42 Śrīdāsa : idem.

43 *kola* and *badarī* are species of Zizyphus with resp. big and small fruits.

44 A.s.Ni. 7, 16 (Ki. 7, 16) reads : "Those with an abundance of bile have swarthy tips, are (of a) red, somewhat yellow and black (colour), soft and flaccid; one cannot endure that they are touched; they have a musty smell, are thin, discharge thin blood, are accompanied by a burning sensation and inflammation, bring about fever, mental confusion and inability to eat, resemble liver(-tissue), and are similar to a parrot's tongue and the mouth of a leech; their middle part is like that of a grain of barley and they are moist; (when they are present), the excrements are loosened and yellow, and they impart a turmeric-yellow colour to the skin, nails, etc." Cf. Ca.Ci. 14, 14 : "One should

know that haemorrhoids with an abundance of bile are soft, flaccid and very delicate, intolerant of touch, (of a) red, yellow, swarthy and black (colour), amply provided with perspiration and moisture, of a musty smell, discharging thin, yellow and red (matter), carrying (off) blood, and accompanied by a burning sensation, itching, piercing pain, pricking pain and inflammation; cold (substances) are therapeutically efficient; (when they are present) the excrements are loosened and (of a) yellow and yellowish-green (colour); yellow and musty-smelling urine and faeces are present in very great quantities; they bring about thirst, fever, *tamaka*, complete mental confusion and aversion from food in a person whose nails, eyes, skin, urine and faeces are yellow;" Su.Ni. 2, 11: "(Arising) from bile their tips are (of a) swarthy (colour), they are thin, (tend to) spread, have a yellow appearance, resemble liver(-tissue) and have the form of a parrot's tongue; their middle part is like that of a grain of barley, they resemble the mouth of a leech and are moist. Someone assaulted by these (haemorrhoids) is made to let flow (faecal matter) accompanied by a burning sensation and blood. Fever, a burning sensation, thirst and fainting are present in him as secondary affections. (Such) a man's skin, nails, eyes, teeth, mouth, urine and faeces are (of a) yellow colour;" Bhe.Ci. 18, 19-20: "The characteristics of haemorrhoids by bile are (as follows): accompaniment by fever, boils, thirst, a sharp impulse, accompanied by blood, hotness, liquidity and accompaniment by a burning sensation are observed in haemorrhoids by bile; a pale colour is present and a yellow complexion is observed; the anal region is extremely burning and inflammation of it arises;" Hā. 3, 11, 10: "When in someone a burning sensation and giddiness occur, or when one's body is feverish and thirsty, when fainting and inability to eat are present, or when one's eyes, teeth, mouth and skin are yellow and when loosening of faecal matter occurs, these (should be known to be) the characteristics of haemorrhoids arisen by bile."

45 Aruṇa: thin means transparent.

46 Aruṇa: thin means not dense, as the sprout-like growths by phlegm in the anal region.

47 Aruṇa: they are soft like the flowers of *śirīṣa*, etc.

48 Aruṇa: they are slack, (i.e.) like steamed meat. Śrīdāsa: slack means flaccid, decomposed.

49 Aruṇa: their middle parts having the shape of that of a grain of barley; Ḍa.: the middle parts of which are large and round, their roots and tips being thin; Gayadāsa: the middle parts of which are large and round.

50 *haritāla*: orpiment, As_2S_3.

51 This refers to Mā.ni. 5, 18d.

52 The author of M. does not explain the following terms, elucidated by Gayadāsa: resembling the tongue of a parrot: with the thin tip of the tongue of a parrot; resembling the mouth of a leech: their upper part having a subtle cavity, because it is split.

53 A.h.: *ucchūna* (swollen up) instead of *utsanna* (raised).

54 A.h.: *vikartin* (cutting asunder) instead of *vikarṣin* (drawing).

55 *kṛcchra* = *mūtrakṛcchra* (strangury).

56 A.h.: *prājya* (copious) instead of *prāya* (abundant).

57 Cf. A.s.Ni. 7, 17 (Ki. 7, 17): "Those with an abundance of phlegm are provided with big roots, are solid, oleaginous, pale, round and stout, heavy, stiff, smooth and mucilaginous, very numb, tolerant of touch and formed like a *karīra*, *panasa* kernel and the dugs of a cow; they give rise to a very high degree of excessive evacuation, *pravāhikā*, obstructive swelling of the inguinal regions, shooting pain in the umbilical region, sickness and effusion together with shortness of breath, nasal catarrh, inability to eat,

vomiting, strangury, urinary disease, cold fever, swelling, heaviness of the head, an increased presence of unctuous substances in the sense (organs), mildness of the (transforming) fire, impotence and morbid alterations by immature matter; they do not burst open, do not discharge, are amply endowed with itching, bring about evacuation of impure matter that is accompanied by phlegm and resembles muscle-fat, and give rise to a light colour of skin, nails. etc.;" Ca.Ci. 14, 17 : "In this respect those which are sizable, stout, smooth, tolerant of being touched, oleaginous, white, pale and mucilaginous, stiff, haevy, torpid, very numb, solid by being swollen, amply endowed with itching, persistently discharging much tawny, white, red and mucilaginous (matter), accompanied by urine and faeces which are heavy, mucilaginous and white, associated with therapeutic efficiency of dry and hot (substances), accompanied by *pravāhikā*, an extreme degree of evacuation, obstructive swelling of the inguinal regions, bringing about shooting pain, sickness, ptyalism, cough, anorexia, nasal catarrh, heaviness, vomiting, strangury, desiccation, swelling, morbid pallor, cold fever, (bladder-)stones and gravel, an increased presence of unctuous substances in the cardiac region and the sense (organs), a sweet taste in the mouth and urinary disease, attending one for a long time, bringing about an extreme degree of mildness of the (transforming) fire and of impotence, giving rise to very strong morbid alterations by immature matter, and occurring in a person with a light colour of nails, eyes, mouth, skin, urine and faeces, (these) should be known to be haemorrhoids with an abundance of phlegm;" Su.Ni. 2, 12 : "Those arising from phlegm are white, have big roots, are solid, round, oleaginous, pale and formed like a *karīra*, *panasa* kernel and the dugs of a cow; they do not burst open, have no discharge and are amply endowed with itching. Someone assaulted by these is made to let flow to an extreme degree (faecal matter), accompanied by phlegm, in great amounts, resembling water in which flesh has been washed. He gets, caused by these very things, swelling, cold fever, anorexia, absence of digestive alteration and heaviness of the head; (such) a man's skin, nails, eyes, teeth, mouth, urine and faeces assume a light colour;" Bhe.Ci. 18, 21-24ab : "The characteristics of haemorrhoids by phlegm are (as follows) : in haemorrhoids, dominated by phlegm, the faeces are mucilaginous, of a light colour, floating, and accompanied by phlegm; they appear little by little, attended by a painful sensation. One stays for a long time in a sitting posture and is made to evacuate without a sound. The penis and testicles feel crushed, as well as the bladder, and certainly the anal region. One is not purged of mature (faecal matter); inability to eat and absence of digestive alteration enter (such) a person, as well as swelling, especially of the region around the eyes. These are said to be the symptoms of haemorrhoids arising from phlegm;" Hā. 3, 11, 11: "When there is sleepiness, rigidity, denseness, mild pain, swelling, piercing pain, extreme visceral swelling and a breaking sensation (*bhaṅguraka*) of the anal region, a confined state of the faeces, pricking pain, inability to eat and a sluggish way of moving, a physician should know that the haemorrhoids certainly arise from phlegm."

58 Gayadāsa adds that haemorrhoids arising from bile have thin roots.

59 The variant *ucchūna* (swollen up; see note 53) is explained by Toḍara as meaning : having become perceptible by means of their length, or swollen.

60 Toḍara says : stout (*pīvara*) or gross as to their circumference.

61 Gayadāsa and Ḍa. : hard.

62 Ḍa. : "A *karīra* is a particular kind of tree which is very numerous in desert country; a *panasa* has fruits with a thorny exterior and is called *kaṭahala* in common language; (the haemorrhoids) resemble the fruits of this (tree). (*kaṭahal* is a Hindī word for *panasa*). Śrīdāsa : a *karīra* is a *vaṃśa* sprout.

[63] Toḍara explains *vikartin* (see note 54) by *chedin* (bringing about a trenchant pain) and makes mention of the variant *vikarṣin*, explained, as in M., by : the sensation that one pulls at (the mentioned parts). Śrīdāsa says that *vikarta* is a particular kind of piercing pain giving rise to the sensation of being cut asunder.

[64] *kṛcchra*, which is a shortened form of *mūtrakṛcchra* in this case.

[65] *prājya* instead of *prāya* (5, 23a).

[66] The source of these two *pāda*s is unknown. Cf. A.h.Ni. 7, 42cd : "(Arising) from combined action they possess combined signs; (arising) from accumulation (of the three morbific entities) they possess the whole of the characteristics;" A.s.Ni. 7, 18 (Ki. 7, 18) : "One should divide those arising from combined and concerted action (into the appropriate types) according to the (particular) intermixture of characteristics;" Su.Ni. 2, 14 : "Those arising from concerted action are provided with the characteristics of all the morbific entities;" Bhe.Ci. 18, 24cd-26a : "The characteristics of haemorrhoids by concerted action are (as follows) : one should know (that haemorrhoids) arising from concerted action (are provided) with the characteristics of all (the morbific entities). The evacuated (stools) of such a person are (accompanied by) compact blood, of a musty smell, loosened or mixed with bile, (they appear) after a long time or are sometimes retained; release of effluent matter occurs;" Hā. 3, 11, 12 : "Piercing pain, obstructive abdominal swelling, inability to eat, cough, sickness, (*ruciḥ*), pricking pain and rigidity of the shoulders (are present) when the haemorrhoids arise from all (the morbific entities)."

[67] A.h. : *gāḍhaviṭpratipīḍita* instead of *gāḍhaviṭkaprapīḍita*; this does not affect the meaning.

[68] Cf. A.s.Ni. 7, 19 (Ki. 7, 19) : "But those with an abundance of blood are like offshoots of a *vaṭa* (tree), red coral and *kākaṇantikā*, and their characteristics are like those (of haemorrhoids) by bile. Moreover, subject to pressure from the tightly packed faeces, they let suddenly flow out extremely corrupted hot blood. With regard to the coming forth of this (blood) to an extreme amount there occur secondary affections (arising) from the decline of blood;" Su.Ni. 2, 13 : "Those arising from blood are similar to offshoots of a *nyagrodha* (= *vaṭa*) tree, red coral and the seeds of *kākaṇantikā*, and their characteristics are those of (haemorrhoids) by bile. When they are subject to pressure from tightly packed faeces, they let suddenly flow out extremely corrupted blood to great amounts. With respect to the coming forth of this (blood) to extreme amounts there occur the same secondary affections as those arising from overuse of bleeding (procedures);" Bhe.Ci. 18, 26b-27 : "Haemorrhoids, (arising) from blood, (release) blood; they carry (off) blood in a stream, as a (blood-)vessel that remains pierced; they repeatedly release blood, like a menstruating woman (does);" Hā. 3, 11, 16 : "(When they are) accompanied by a burning sensation and pains, (when they are of a) brown (colour), (when) itching is present, desiccation arises and blood is continuously discharged, these (people, attended) by itching, are afflicted by haemorrhoids of the nature of blood."

[69] Aruṇa and Śrīdāsa : idem. Gayadāsa and Ḍa. explain that, though remaining unmentioned, the symptoms of wind and phlegm, acting as adjunctory factors, should be added.

[70] Toḍara : idem.

[71] Gayadāsa explains 'extremely corrupted' by : being of a black colour, etc., brought about by the corrupting activity of the morbific entities which are present as adjunctory factors.

[72] Ḍa. comments on this passage from Su.Sū. 15, 9 : "In (a state of) decline of blood

one desires (substances with) an acid taste, because there is an increase of wind and acid substances are opposed to wind; in the same way one asks for cold (substances) because, on account of the liquidity of blood, there is an increase of fiery energy in (a state of) decline of blood; some say : because blood is of the nature of *agni* and *soma* one asks for acid and cold (substances), the qualities of which are comparable to it, (i.e.) to blood." Cakra comments : "Asking for acid and cold (substances) occurs because blood is of the nature of *soma* and *agni*, by their being its own matrices; flaccidity of the vessels occurs because the blood which fills them is present to a slight amount." Cf. Ca.Sū. 17, 65ab: "In (a state of) decline of blood the skin is rough, cracked, withered and dry;" A.h.Sū. 11, 17cd : "In (a state of) decline of blood there occur fondness of acid and cool (substances), flaccidity of the vessels and dryness."

[73] Toḍara : idem; Śrīdāsa : one whose fiery energy has been annihilated.

[74] Toḍara : someone with weak senses or with a disturbance of all the senses; Śrīdāsa : someone whose senses are not acute.

[75] Su. and A.s. make mention of *kākaṇantikā* instead of *guñjā*. Ḍa. says : "*kākaṇantikā* is *guñjā*; others say it is *kākādanī*." Bhā.pra.nigh., *guḍūcyādivarga* 125, mentions a white and red variety of *guñjā*. The red variety is also called *kākaṇantī* and *kākādanī* (ibid., 125-126).

[76] These additional *pāda*s are not explained in M. and Ā.

[77] Cf. A.h.Ci. 8, 94cd-97 : "And after one has observed that wind or phlegm are present as an adjunctory factor in (cases of) haemorrhoids (arising) from blood, one should employ an ice-cold oleaginous or dry (substance). If the faeces are brown, harsh and dry and the wind does not come out from below, if there occurs piercing pain in the iliac region, thighs and anal region and the ground promotes dryness, wind is present as the adjunctory factor, (but) it is phlegm if the faeces are slack, white, yellow, heavy and oleaginous, the anal region is provided with mucilaginous matter and torpid, and the ground is of an oleaginous and heavy (quality). One should discern (the adjunctory factor) in each particular case by means of the characteristics of the blood."

[78] Cf. Su.Ni. 2, 8 : "When they are imminent, however, the prodromes are : absence of the desire for food, maturation of the food with difficulty, acid eructations, a general burning sensation, a constrained condition (of impure matter), thirst, adynamia of the thighs, (abdominal) distension, leanness, copious eructations, swelling of the eyes, rumbling of the bowels, the sensation that the anal region is cut to pieces, uncertainty (about the presence) of morbid pallor, a *grahaṇī* disorder and desiccation, cough, shortness of breath, deficiency of (one's bodily) force, giddiness, lassitude, sleep and weakness of the senses;" A.h.Ni. 7, 15cd-20 : "Its prodromes are : a sluggish state of the (transforming) fire, a constrained condition (of the impurities), adynamia of the thighs, cramps of the calves, giddiness, adynamia of the body, swelling of the eyes, and loosening of faecal matter or seizing of it; the wind, present in very great quantities and being in a confused state, usually coursing (in the region) under the navel, comes out with difficulty, accompanied by pain, by the sensation of being cut into pieces, and by noises; (there occur) rumbling of the bowels, (abdominal) distension and emaciation; many eructations (occur), urine (appears) in great and faeces in slight amounts, (there occur) absence of longing for food, eructation of matter that smells like smoke, acid eructations, piercing pain in head, back and chest, inertia, discoloration, lassitude, weakness of the senses, (liability to) wrath, a type of behaviour that is difficult to deal with, and uncertainty about (the presence of) a *grahaṇī* disorder, morbid pallor, visceral swelling and abdominal disease. These very (signs) increase when the haemorrhoids have arisen."

79 Some treatises describe the generic characteristics of haemorrhoids : Bhe.Ci. 18, 12-14 : "The generic characteristics of haemorrhoids are : loosening of faecal matter, alteration of colour, piercing pain, diarrhoea (*nirvāhikā*), a sensation of being torn asunder (*avadāra*), thirst, a burning sensation in the anal region and back, (mental disturbance as in) intoxication, fever, inability to eat, absence of digestive alteration, decline of the body and of (bodily) force, pallor, cutting pain in the junctures, swelling of the *haṭṭas* of the eyes, languor, abandonment of sexual intercourse, anal prolapse and seizing pain in the anal region are the common symptoms of haemorrhoids. The separate (symptoms) of each type will be described (presently);" Kā.Sū. 25, 25 : "A bound and mature state of the faeces, or faeces accompanied by blood, in someone with a lean body, the sensation that the anal region is subject to downward pressure, itching and pricking pain should be considered as characteristics in (cases of) haemorrhoids."

80 Cakra : a constrained condition of the food is a condition in which it does not move on.

81 Confirmed by Cakra's comment on Ca.Ci. 14, 21.

82 The sense of this word is unknown.

83 Possibly Mādhava is meant and a commentary written by him is alluded to, or Gadādhara is the commentator referred to.

84 Ḍa. : distension (*āṭopa*) means inflatedness; Śrīdāsa : *āṭopa* is twitching, downwards of the umbilical region; Hārāṇacandra : it is a murmuring sound accompanied by a painful sensation.

85 Not confirmed by Ca.Ni. 3, 15; Su.U. 42, 8cd-9; A.h.Ni. 12; A.h.Ci. 14; Bhe.Ni. 3; Kā.Sū. 25; Hā. 3, 4.

86 This is a quotation from an unknown source.

87 Su. presents a number of variants which do not affect the meaning. Cf. Ca.Ci. 28, 6-11; A.h.Sū. 12, 4-9; A.s.Sū. 20, 4; Bhe.Sū. 16.

88 This is a quotation from an unknown source. Cf. Su.Ni. 1, 7cd-8ab where it is said a.o. that wind consists of two constituents (*dviguṇa*), but is amply provided with (the constituent) *rajas*.

89 This is a quotation from an unknown source.

90 This is a quotation from an unknown source.

91 The terms *saṃdhi* and *parvan*, which usually are synonymous, are both used in this case. Possibly *saṃdhi* denotes here the junctures of the eye and *parvan* the other kinds of junctures in the body.

92 This is a quotation from an unknown source.

93 Cf. Su.Sū. 21, 10; 21, 12-14; A.h.Sū. 12, 10-18ab; A.s.Sū. 20, 5-6; Bhe.Śā. 4, 1-17.

94 Cf. Su.Ni. 2, 16 : "A foremost physician should counteract (haemorrhoids) seated in the outer and middlemost fold; in (cases of haemorrhoids) springing up from the inner fold he should employ a therapeutical procedure after having rejected (any hope of cure);" Su.Ni. 2, 23-26 : "Those, which are provided with the three morbific entities and with slight signs, should be taught to be mitigable; those, which arise from a pair (of morbific entities) and reside in the second fold, are said to be difficult to cure, as well as those which have (already) existed for a whole year; those arising from concerted action and the innate ones should, however, be avoided. If all the (anal) folds are assaulted by haemorrhoids, the *apāna* wind, checked by these (growths), turns back; for that reason it batters, after coming into contact with the *vyāna*, the light (= fire) of bodily beings;" A.h.Ni. 7, 53 = A.s.Ni. 7, 27 : "The innate ones, those with three morbific entities and those which are seated in the innermost fold are incurable; they may

be mitigated by (a strong transforming) fire and by (bodily) force;" A.h.Ni. 7, 54-55 = A.s.Ni. 7, 28-29 = Ca.Ci. 14, 30-31 = Mā.ni. 5, 36 and 35.

95 Aruṇa : arisen within (the span of) a year; Śrīdāsa : produced recently. Gayadāsa remarks that haemorrhoids are curable when they have not been present for a period exceeding a year.

96 Su. : a diseased one who is religious and abides by the words of the *vaidya*.

97 Su. : *yuktamātra* (in the suitable quantity) instead of *alpamātra* (in a slight quantity). Cakra reads *alpamātra*.

98 Su. : *manaskānta* (agreeable to the mind) instead of *mahāvīrya* (of a great potency).

99 Cf. Ca.Sū. 9, 6-9; A.h.Sū. 1, 28-29 = A.s.Sū. 2, 23-24; Kā.Sū. 26, 4-7.

100 Su. : *arśovyādhir vināśayet* (the haemorrhoidal illness may annihilate) instead of *arśāṃsi kṣapayanti hi* (haemorrhoids wreck).

101 Cf. A.h.Śā. 5, 79cd-80ab = A.s.Śā. 11, 12 : "Haemorrhoids (will kill) someone with swelling of the hands, feet, umbilical region, anal region, testicles and mouth and a patient with a painful condition of the cardiac region, sides and limbs, vomiting, inflammation of the anus and fever;" Hā. 3, 11, 24-26 : "Swelling and desiccation of hands, feet and face, of the umbilical region and penis or of the anal region, fever, shortness of breath, *tamaka*, vomiting, mental confusion, piercing pain in the cardiac region and the sides, leanness, inability to eat, a confined state (of the impurities) and diarrhoea as additional affections, these are the twelve (disorders) which arise as secondary affections of haemorrhoids. Persons without secondary affections are curable, incurable are persons with many secondary affections. Someone afflicted by piercing pain, anorexia and thirst, someone who has evacuated an extreme amount of blood and someone afflicted by piercing pain, swelling and diarrhoea will certainly not live when suffering from haemorrhoids."

102 Cf. fr. Su.Ni. 2, 17 : "When (the morbific entities) have attained the umbilical region, they generate very delicate, bad-smelling and mucilaginous shoot-like growths, which resemble the mouth of an earthworm."

103 *kiñculaka* as a synonym of *gaṇḍūpada* is also given by Aruṇa.

104 Cf. Su.Ni. 2, 18 : "The excited *vyāna*, after seizing the phlegm, causes the coming forth of solid, peg-like polypous growths at the exterior; these polypous growths are called warts."

105 Aruṇa : 'at the outside of the skin' (means) : in the outer region; Toḍara : at the very place of the anal lip and not elsewhere; Śrīdāsa : in the outer region, and according to Indu : outside of the anal region. Gayadāsa : " 'At the outside' (means) : at the outside of the skin; according to some (it means) : outside of the anal lip; but others say (it means) : outside of the anal lip and also elsewhere, because the *vyāna* has the whole of the skin as its basis, has not been mentioned previously with regard to haemorrhoids brought about by morbific entities which have gone downwards, and because (the warts) have been started by morbific entities which have moved laterally, (a conclusion arrived at) by the fact that haemorrhoids brought about by morbific entities which have moved from below in an upward direction have been mentioned previously." Ḍa. : " 'At the outside' (means) : outside of the anal lip; others, however, say that by the words 'at the outside' (it is indicated that they may) also (occur) elsewhere."

106 A.h. and A.s. : *asitaraktatā* (a dark and red colour) instead of *asitavaktratā* (a dark colour of the mouth).

107 Cf. Su.Ni. 2, 19-20 : "With respect to these cuneate growths there arises pricking pain (when they arise) by wind; it should be taught that the colour belonging to it

and a knotty condition (arise) by phlegm, and that dryness, blackness, smoothness and a pronounced harshness arise from bile and blood; (these are) the characteristics of warts."

108 Aruṇa : a colour comparable to the natural one of the body; Ḍa. : the same colour as that of phlegm.

109 Cf. fr. Su.Ni. 2, 17 : "The excited morbific entities which have attained the penis generate itching, after having brought about corruption of the flesh and blood; from this itching lesions additionally arise."

110 Compare this series of stanzas, quoted from an unknown source, with the version in prose from Su.Ni. 2, 17 : "And in those lesions (of the penis) there arise, from the corrupted flesh, excrescences with a mucilaginous and bloody discharge, resembling the hairs of a brush, and (localized) at the inside (of the prepuce and at the surface of the glans penis), or on the upper part (i.e. the outside of the prepuce); these growths annihilate the penis and destroy the virility. Having attained the vulvar and vaginal region, (the morbific entities) generate very delicate, bad-smelling shoot-like growths with a mucilaginous and bloody discharge and the form of a mushroom; they injure the vulvar and vaginal region and the menstrual discharge ... These same (morbific entities), having gone upwards, give rise to the additional coming forth of polypous growths at the ears, eyes, nose and mouth. With respect to these (polypous growths) there occur in those arising at the ears deafness, piercing pain and a foul smell from the ears, in those arising at the eyes obstruction of the eyelids, a painful sensation, a discharge and annihilation of vision, in those arising at the nose an extreme degree of nasal catarrh, sneezing, respiratory difficulties, a foul smell from the nose, nasal speech and suffering (from pain) in the head, and in those arising in the mouth and any one of (the following places) : throat, lips or palate, there occur a stammering speech, non-perception of taste and diseases of the mouth."

CHAPTER SIX

SLUGGISHNESS OF THE (TRANSFORMING) FIRE (*AGNIMĀNDYA*), DISORDERS OF THE PROCESS OF DISINTEGRATION (OF THE FOOD) (*AJĪRṆA*), *VISŪCIKĀ*, INTESTINAL INERTIA (*ALASAKA*) AND RETARDATION OF EVACUATION (*VILAMBIKĀ*)

6, 1 : Sluggish, sharp, incongruous and congruous, of four types is the abdominal fire, owing to excess of phlegm, bile and wind and owing to a congruous state of these.[1]

M :

On account of the fact that sluggishness of the fire, etc. are effects of haemorrhoids, mention is made of these (conditions) ... The sluggish (fire) is mentioned first because it is difficult to subdue. 'Owing to excess of phlegm, bile and wind' should be connected with 'sluggish', etc., in due order. 'Owing to a congruous state of these' (means) owing to a congruous state of phlegm, etc. 'Congruous' means : not morbidly altered, its ground being a congruous state of the elements. This absence of a morbid alteration is included in the subject 'morbid alteration' in order to indicate that knowledge about morbid alterations is directly connected with knowledge about natural states. The abdominal (fire is expressly denoted) to differentiate it from the fire of the elements (of the body) and that of the gross elements.[2]

6, 2 : An incongruous fire brings about diseases arising from wind, a sharp one (diseases) arising from bile as a cause and a sluggish one morbid alterations with phlegm as a source.

(Su.Sū. 35, 25).

6, 3-4 : In a person with a congruous fire a congruous quantity of eaten (food) is digestively altered in a proper way; even a very slight (quantity, however, is) not at all (digestively altered) in a person with a sluggish fire; but in a bodily being with an incongruous fire (3) (the eaten food) is sometimes properly maturated and sometimes not digestively altered. Someone, in whom the eaten quantity (of food), even when it is beyond the proper measure, is easily digestively altered, should be known as a person with a sharp fire. A person with a congruous fire is said to be the foremost (among them) (4).[3]

M :

Mention is made of the symptoms of these (types of fire) by the application of an unusual treatise...[4]

'(An incongruous fire brings about) diseases arising from wind', (i.e.) any one of the eighty qualified [5] wind (diseases) and of the unqualified[6] ones, (consisting of) fever, diarrhoea, etc.; in the same way (a sharp fire brings about) any one of the forty qualified bile (diseases), burning, sucking pain,[7] etc.; in the same way (a sluggish fire brings about) any one of the twenty qualified phlegm (diseases), inertia, etc. All these morbid alterations should be looked for in the Caraka(saṃhitā), in the very chapter on the great diseases.[8]

'A congruous quantity' (is) an adjusted quantity of food. 'The (eaten) quantity (of food), when it is beyond the proper measure' is an implicative expression; this (expression) should be understood to characterize eating before the previous meal has been digested, and eating heavy food, etc. as well. As has been said elsewhere : "That fire is the most excellent one, by which a quantity (of food) beyond the proper measure is maturated, even in a person whose previous meal has not yet been digested, and heavy food of someone who eats though he sleeps by day."[9] The word 'sharp' includes the person with an incinerating fire, (for) only an extremely sharp fire is called incinerating. As has been said in the Caraka(saṃhitā) : "In a man whose phlegm has declined, the bile, being excited and following the wind (in its course), renders, by its own heat, force to the fire in the seat of the fire. Thereupon the fire, together with the wind, having acquired force, may give rise to a general painful condition of the body. Having overpowered the food, it quickly maturates it again and again on account of its sharpness.[10] Then, after maturating the food, it also maturates the elements (of the body, consisting of) blood, etc. Thereupon it leads a man to weakness, disorders and death. After ingesting food, one becomes appeased; having scarcely disintegrated it, one becomes breathless. Illnesses like thirst, cough,[11] a burning sensation, fainting, etc. find their source in an extremely (sharp) fire" (Ci. 15, 217cd-221ab).[12]

6, 5 : The disorders of the process of disintegration (of the food consist of) the immature, combustively altered and constrained (type, arising) by means of the three (morbific entities), phlegm, bile and wind. Some require a fourth (type), due to a remnant of the *rasa*.

(Su.Sū. 46, 499).[13]

6, 6 : Some say there is a fifth (type of) disorder of the process of disintegration (of the food), devoid of a morbific entity, and (in which) maturation (of the food occurs) on the (following) day, and a sixth one that is of a natural kind and occurring daily.[14]

M :

Mention is made of the disorders of the process of disintegration (of the food) because a sluggish state of the fire and disorders of the process of disintegration (of the food) are causally related to each other...

'By means of the three (morbific entities)', (i.e.) every single one (of the morbific entities), phlegm, etc., in accordance with their number (in this series). (About) 'due to a remnant of the *rasa*' (we remark) : a remnant of the *rasa* is the remnant (set apart) for the *rasa*, (a grammatical remark follows), as e.g. the wood (set apart) for the sacrificial post (is called) the sacrificial post-wood; or, as Jejjaṭa holds : "By the word *rasa* the food which possesses taste is intended by means of an elliptical expression; by this word *rasa* the food which possesses taste is designated; the remnant of it, which is characterized by the absence of transformation, is the remnant of the *rasa*." [15]

(An objector may ask :) Is it not true that, if things are like that, there is no distinction between the latter and the immature, combustively altered and constrained (types), because it necessarily occurs in the form of any one of these, and that, moreover, there must occur acid eructations, etc., which are the signs of these, and that, accordingly, when an unpolluted condition exists with regard to the eructations, the consequence arises that the characteristics of the disorder of the process of disintegration (of the food, arising) from a remnant of the *rasa*, will not come forth? For it has been said in the Suśruta-(saṃhitā) : "When no desire for food arises, though there exists an unpolluted condition with regard to the eructations, and when one's cardiac region feels heavy, it is proclaimed to be the fourth disorder of the process of disintegration (of the food), accompanied by effusion, (arising) by means of the remnant of the *rasa*" (Sū. 46, 503). Also, Nāgārjuna says in the Ārogyamañjarī : "Absence of the desire for food, etc., even when an unpolluted condition has been reached with respect to the eructations, oleaginousness of the mouth, a painful condition of the junctures and heaviness of the head, these are the characteristics of the *rasa* of the sluggish (type of the) disorder of the process of disintegration (of the food). When it has increased extremely, there may also occur sickness, fever, fainting, etc., giving rise to a turmoil of all ailments."

Thus it is not; on account of the extremely slight amount of the remnant of the food, though necessarily occurring in the form of the combustively altered (type), etc., the consequence is not that eructations, which correspond to it, arise, as in the case of the desire to ingest food at an improper time. As Suśruta says : "When a very small amount of immature matter, confined by the morbific entities and in a dissolved [16] condition, does not cover the path of the fiery energy,[17] there occurs, even in a disorder of the process of disintegration, the desire to ingest food; this (desire) kills, as a poison, the person with a sluggish *buddhi*" (Sū. 46, 51).[18] The characteristics of a remnant of the *rasa*, arising from non-maturation of the food, have also been stated in another treatise : "Disorders of the process of disintegration (of the food) may be of four kinds, (of) the immature, combustively altered and constrained (type), and also (of the type arising from) a remnant of the *rasa*; they arise from incomplete maturation of the food." Gadādhara, however, says : "A remnant of the *rasa* is a remnant with regard to the *rasa*; it is a remnant with regard to the *rasa* generated from the food, a component part of the food which has entered it additionally, and is not perceptible, like the water which is present in milk." [19]

But what then is the distinction between (the disorder from) a remnant of the *rasa* and the immature type, etc. of the disorder of the process of disintegration ?

The answer is : the triad, consisting of the immature type, etc., arises from the food, but (the disorder from) a remnant of the *rasa* arises from the *rasa* of the food, and designations according to (the morbific entities), wind, etc., are not made in the latter because the signs of wind, etc. are of a slight kind; distinctions are made according to ground, characteristics and therapy.

(About the term) 'disorder of the process of disintegration'... (we remark that) disintegrated (means) maturated; non-disintegrated is the opposite (term), in the same way as black (non-white) (is the opposite of white). All disorders of the process of disintegration arise from the three morbific entities; it is explained that the designation of one (particular) morbific entity is made by means of the signs of that single morbific entity, which has unduly increased. For that reason the causation of disorders of the process of disintegration has been stated to relate to the three morbific entities, with the words "From the drinking of an extreme amount of water", etc.[20] Excitement of the triad of morbific entities also occurs on account of disorders of the process of disintegration. As has been said in the Suśruta(saṃhitā) : "From disorders of the process of disintegration a strong agitation of the wind, etc. may arise."[21]

(About) 'some (say there is) a fifth (type of) disorder of the process of disintegration', etc. (we remark that) 'devoid of a morbific entity' (means): not causing a corruption (consisting of) inflatedness, etc. (About) '(in which) maturation (of the food occurs) on the (following) day' (we remark that) food is maturated in a day and a night according to the general rule; in case it is maturated, however, on the following day, on account of a morbid factor, (consisting of) inadequacy with respect to the measure and time (of the meal), etc., it is (called that type in which) maturation (of the food occurs) on the (following) day. It is distinguished from the former types by the fact that it does not bring about inflatedness, etc., though maturation (occurs) with violation of the time(-limit). The purpose of the (separate) denomination of this (type) is that attention be paid to the time of maturation, because ingestion of food is prohibited in a nocturnal disorder of the process of disintegration.

(About 'a sixth one that is) of a natural kind and occurring daily' (we remark that) 'of a natural kind' (indicates that) it does not give rise to a morbid alteration. What is aimed at is the following : is the ingested food at this very moment disintegrated or not? It is not disintegrated at all because there is no rise of hunger, thirst, excretion of impurities, etc., which are characteristics of disintegration. Therefore non-disintegration is present, and this does not bring about inflatedness, etc.; so it is distinct from the former (types). And the purpose of its (separate) denomination is the employment, for the sake of maturation, of lying down on the left side, and other ways of (prescribed) conduct. For it has been said in the Suśruta(saṃhitā) : "After having ingested one's meal[22] and having walked a hundred feet, one should lie down on the left side; one who has ingested his meal should indulge in sounds, colours, tastes, sensations of touch and smells which are agreeable to one's mind; by means of that (conduct) the food remains in the right condition" (Sū. 46, 487cd-488).[23] And in this case food is not prohibited, being prescribed by (medical) science.

In the Caraka(saṃhitā), however, from : "The signs of this disorder of the process of disintegration" (Ci. 15, 45a), up to : "It is a dreadful food-poison" (Ci. 15, 46d),[24] the (type of) disorder of the process of disintegration, called food-poison, is described. And it is explained that this is the very disorder of the process of disintegration (arising) from a remnant of the *rasa*, combined with bile, etc. Therefore (the disorder arising from) a remnant of the *rasa* has not been described separately (in the Carakasaṃhitā), being included in it (i.e. : in the food-poison type).

Ā :

A remnant of the *rasa* is the non-maturated *rasa* which has been left behind...

6, 7-8 : From the drinking of an extreme amount of water, the eating of incongruous (articles of food), restraint (of the natural urges) and from inversion (of the pattern) of sleep, adequate food, though one ingests it at the proper time and though it is light, does not maturate (7). Food indulged in by someone who is overwhelmed [25] by jealousy, fear or wrath, someone who is greedy, oppressed by pain [26] or dejection, and someone who is full of aversion does not reach complete maturation [27] in a proper way (8).

(Su.Sū. 46, 500-501).[28]

6, 9 : Though eaten in measure and being wholesome, food is not disintegrated by (people given to) anxiety, grief, fear, wrath, suffering, lying down to repose and waking at night.

(Ca.Vi. 2, 9).

M :

Mention is made of the causes of disorders of the process of disintegration... 'Restraint' (is) restraint of the natural urges. 'Inversion (of the pattern) of sleep' (means) sleeping by day, etc. By the word '*api*' [29] should be understood as well : (food) provided with the qualities oleaginousness, heat, etc. Some read the stanza, beginning with 'overwhelmed by jealousy, fear or wrath'; (this stanza) should be understood to indicate the range of disorders of the process of disintegration (caused) by a morbific factor of a mental character.

Ā:

... After having made mention of the bodily causes, mention is made of the mental causes, of which *rajas* and *tamas* are the morbific factors... Jealousy is the inability to tolerate the good fortune of others. Fear is feeling terror for other people. Wrath is characterized by the malicious assailing of other people... Dejection is a condition in which one does not move about... Aversion is displeasure.[30]

6, 10-13ab : In the immature type (there occur) heaviness, retching, and swelling of the cheeks and the prominent part of the eyes; eructations appear, which are in accordance with what has been ingested, and which are not combustively altered (10).

In the combustively altered type (there occur) giddiness, thirst, fainting, and the several kinds of painful conditions arising from bile; eructations accompanied by (a smell like) smoke and by (an) acid (taste) arise, perspiration and a burning sensation (11).

In the constrained type (there occur) piercing pain, inflatedness, and the several kinds of painful sensations by wind; impure matter and wind do not come forth; stiffness, mental confusion and painful oppression of the limbs (arise) (12).

In the type arising from a remnant of the *rasa* (there arise) aversion to food, and a polluted condition and heaviness of the cardiac region.

(Ā.s.Sū. 11, 55; 57; 56; 60ab).[31]

M:

Mention is made of the characteristics of the described disorders of the process of disintegration... Owing to the special faculty (of this disorder) there occurs swelling of the cheeks [32] and of the prominent part of the eyes, (i.e.) the eye-balls. 'Eructations which are in accordance with what has been ingested' (are eructations which are) sweet, etc. 'Not combustively altered', (i.e.) not acid, for it has been shown (that) acidity (arises) in the second (stage of the) maturative process. 'The several kinds of painful conditions arising from bile', (i.e.) burning, sucking pain, etc... 'The several kinds of painful sensations by wind' assume the form of pricking pain, cutting pain, etc. 'Painful oppression of the limbs' (is) the painful sensation of wind, accompanied by immature matter, etc.

Ā :

... 'Heaviness' (is heaviness) of the abdomen and of the limbs. 'Retching' is a condition as that in which vomit has come near to (the throat)... (Su.Sū. 46, 502a is quoted) : this very (statement) is only a description of the very nature of food, brought into a corrupted state by phlegm. The effects of phlegm, (to wit) heaviness, oleaginousness, itching and so on, should also be considered... (Su.Sū. 46, 502b is quoted)... (Su.Sū. 46, 502cd is quoted). In this constrained type the several kinds of painful sensations by wind occur, which assume the form of pricking pain, cutting pain, etc.; yawning, muscle pain, pain in the head, etc. should also be taken into consideration... 'A polluted condition' is heaviness, together with effusion (of saliva). (Su.Sū. 46, 503 is quoted).

6, 13c-f : The secondary affections (of disorders of the process of disintegration) are fainting, confused speech, emesis, effusion (of saliva), adynamia and giddiness; one may also die from a disorder of the process of disintegration.

(Su.Sū. 46, 504).

M :

Mention is made of the secondary affections...[33] In a disorder of the process of disintegration death may occur when (the disorder) has increased to an extreme degree.

6, 14 : Those people who, being not self-possessed, ingest, like animals, food which is not in accordance with the proper measure, get a disorder of the process of disintegration, which is the root of an array of diseases.[34]

M :

Mention is made of the fact that, among the described causes of disorders of the process of disintegration, the (most) specific cause is the ingestion (of a quantity of food) beyond the proper measure... 'People who are not self-possessed' are persons with a corrupted *manas*, desirous of temporary well-being by reason of their cupidity. For that very reason it is said : 'like animals'. (A disorder of the process of disintegration) is the root, (i.e.) the cause, of an array, (i.e.) a multitude, of diseases, *visūcī*, etc.

6, 15 : From the disorders of the process of disintegration which have been set in motion, (to wit those of) the immature, constrained and combustively altered type, may arise *visūcī*, intestinal inertia and also retardation of evacuation.

(Su.U. 56, 3).

M :

Mention is made of *visūcī*, etc., immediately after (the description of) the disorders of the process of disintegration, because the latter (disorders) are the source of the former... Kārtikakuṇḍa says: "In the three (disorders, to wit) those of the immature, constrained and combustively altered types, *visūcī*, intestinal inertia and retardation of evacuation arise in accordance with their number (in this series)." Bakulakara says that this is not correct. For retardation of evacuation arises from the combustively altered type, if there is agreement with its number (in the series), but it will be described (as arising) from phlegm and wind. Therefore it is suitable (to assume that) the production of *visūcī*, etc. is brought about by the three types of disorder of the process of disintegration, in accordance with their source. For it has been said : "A strong agitation of wind, etc. may arise from a disorder of the process of disintegration." [35]

6, 16-17 : (The disorder) of someone in whom the wind stagnates, pricking the limbs as with needles, (that disorder, arising) by means of a disorder of the process of disintegration, is called *visūcī* [36] by the *vaidya*s (16).
It is not acquired by those with a restricted diet who know the traditional doctrines.
Confused persons who have not subdued their minds and are cupidous with regard to eating [37] acquire it (17).

(Su.U. 56, 4-5).[38]

M :

Mention is made of the 'etymology' of *visūcī*... The 'etymology' of *visūcī* is as follows : "The wind, owing to its copiousness, pricks as with needles." Disregarding the pricking pain as by needles, other distinct kinds of painful sensations of several kinds also occur, as in morbid pallor. As has been said in another treatise : "Owing to the vehement excitement of wind, etc., it cuts [39] the limbs by distinct kinds [40] of painful sensations of several types, as by needles; that is why it is called *visūcikā*" (A.h.Sū. 8, 7cd-8ab).

'Those knowing the traditional doctrines' are those possessing knowledge of Āyurveda. 'Those who are confused' are those who are unacquainted with knowledge about it. 'Those who have not subdued their minds' are persons who have not subdued their senses. 'Those who are cupidous with regard to eating' are persons who ingest, like animals, food that is not in accordance with the proper measure.

Ā :

... 'Confused persons', (i.e.) those who are unacquainted with what should be eaten and should not be eaten, get it. (About 'persons who are cupidous with regard to eating' we remark that) others read 'persons with a turbid receptacle', (i.e.) persons with a corrupted receptacle of undigested food; and this corruption of the receptacle of undigested food occurs because corrupted matter and food are blended, and because of excitement of the wind and the other (morbific entities).

6, 18 : Fainting, diarrhoea, emesis, thirst, piercing pain, giddiness, cramp, yawning, a burning sensation, alteration of colour, trembling and pains in the cardiac region occur in it (i.e. in *visūcī*), together with a cutting pain in the head.

(Su.U. 56, 6).[41]

M :

Mention is made of the characteristics of *visūcī*... A cutting pain in the head is a piercing pain in the head. Emesis and diarrhoea, occurring together, are in this case a characteristic. In the Suśruta(saṃhitā) the downwards moving type is included in (the disorder called) immature diarrhoea, and the upwards moving type in vomiting. In the Caraka(saṃhitā), however, one reads : "One should know to be *visūcī* that one, in which the morbific factor consisting of immature matter has come forth upwards and downwards, and the symptoms of which correspond to those which have been described" (Ca.Vi. 2, 11).[42] From this it follows that there exist an upwards moving type of *visūcī*, and also a downwards moving type, because the immature type of diarrhoea has not been described in the Caraka(saṃhitā). It is explained that the word 'and' [43] indicates that a type that moves along both pathways exists as well. One should consider the upwards moving type to be distinct from the types of vomiting which arise from the three morbific entities, because non-maturated food is vomited in it.

6, 19-20 : (In the case) that the lateral parts of the abdomen become extremely swollen by obstruction, (in the case) that one becomes breathless [44] and moaning,[45] (if) the restrained wind moves about upwards [46] of the lateral parts of the abdomen (19), and (if) one presents extreme [47] restraint of wind and excrements, one is declared to be suffering from intestinal inertia, (if) thirst and eructations are present as well (20).[48]
(Su.U. 56, 7-8).[49]

M :

Mention is made of intestinal inertia... (The lateral parts of the abdomen) 'become swollen by obstruction' (i.e.) become inflated, because it will be stated presently that the impure matter is constrained. 'One becomes breathless', (i.e.) one becomes confused;[50] 'one moans', (i.e.) one makes the loud sound of someone who is afflicted. (The wind) 'being restrained', (i.e.) its downward course or (its motion) in the lateral parts of the abdomen having been checked by the non-disintegrated matter, moves upwards of (these parts), (i.e.) it goes upwards, to the cardiac region, throat, etc. It is technically called intestinal inertia because the (matter which constitutes its) morbific factor is solid. As has been said in another treatise : "The food advances neither upwards nor downwards, and is not digestively altered;[51] because it stays in the receptacle of undigested food in an inert condition, this (disorder) is traditionally called intestinal inertia" (A.h.Sū. 8, 6cd-7ab).

6, 21 : When the ingested food, corrupted by phlegm and wind, comes forth neither upwards nor downwards in someone, the knowers of science of olden times declare it to be retardation of evacuation, which is extremely difficult to treat.
(Su.U. 56, 9).[52]

M :

Mention is made of retardation of evacuation... 'Extremely difficult to treat' means that one should reject, (i.e.) avoid, (a patient suffering from it).

What is the distinction between intestinal inertia and retardation of evacuation? We may ask this question, because both (diseases) are comparable regarding the great strength of wind and phlegm and by reason of the fact that habitually (immature matter) does not come forth, neither along the upward nor the downward (path). The answer is that in intestinal inertia violent piercing pains occur (and not in retardation of evacuation), as has been said (A.h.Sū. 8, 10cd-11 is quoted).[53]

Ā :

... Instead of 'corrupted' (ingested food) some read : dissolved. This very retardation of evacuation is described with the name 'stick-like (type of) intestinal inertia' in another treatise : "For in intestinal inertia the corrupted morbific entities bring about intense piercing pain and the other (symptoms), vomiting and diarrhoea excepted; they restrain (the flow through) the channels and they stiffen, of their own accord, the whole body like a stick. This stick-like (type of) intestinal inertia quickly brings about the annihilation of the human body." [54] [55]

6, 22 : At what particular place the immature matter stays, at that very place it may specifically give rise to a painful condition by means of hosts of morbid alterations, the characteristics of which are those of the morbific entity that has spread over the body, and those which arise from immature matter.[56]

(Su.U. 56, 10).

M :

After noticing *visūcī*, etc., which have arisen from a disorder of the process of disintegration, mention is made of another effect of immature matter that is being generated from a disorder of the process of disintegration... 'Immature matter' is the agent; at what particular place it may stay, at that very place it may specifically give rise to a painful condition; by this (statement) it is indicated that it brings about a slightly painful condition at another place as well. By the use of *yatra*, a word of the class called *sarvanāman*,[57] it is shown that immature matter has a variable seat, like excited wind and the other (morbific entities).

By means of what does it give rise to a painful condition ? By means of hosts, (i.e.) multitudes, of morbid alterations. Of what kind are these ? The characteristics of these are those of the morbific entity, excited by its own cause, by which the body is overspread, (i.e.) pervaded; these characteristics are pricking pain (by wind), a burning sensation (by bile), heaviness (by phlegm), etc. Not only by these hosts of morbid alterations, but also by those arising from immature matter, (i.e.)

absence of maturation, intestinal inertia, etc. (it may give rise to a painful condition). It is said that by means of this stanza Suśruta has included the disease, described in other treatises, called immature wind,[58] because its characteristics are the same.

Ā :

Immature matter is that which has not been properly transformed, according to what has been said : "That which is not digestively altered and has not been subject to the process of commixture, which is bad-smelling, copious, mucilaginous and bringing about adynamia of all the limbs, is called immature matter." [59]

At what particular place the immature matter, which is the agent of the setting in motion and attraction of the wind, stays, (i.e.) remains established on account of the alteration of its qualities, at that very place it may specifically give rise to a painful condition, (i.e.) it may painfully oppress. On account of the fact that desiccation, inflammatory swellings, abcesses and other diseases, by means of sluggishness of the fires of the elements of the body and the gross elements, have their source in immature matter, its being a source of production has been declared to be such as has been said (in the following statement) : "Seven fires of the elements of the body and five of the gross elements make, together with the abdominal fire, thirteen fires." [60] At what particular place of one of the elements of the body the fire is sluggish, at that very place may occur, with immature matter as its source, the production of boils, etc.[61]

6, 23 : That man whose teeth, lips and nails are brown, whose consciousness is restricted, who is tormented by emesis,[62] whose eyes have receded to the interior, whose voice is in a debilitated condition and all the junctures of whom have become detached, will go to the place of no return.

(Su.U. 56, 11).

M :

Mention is made of the characteristics (indicating) incurability of *visūcī* and intestinal inertia... Jejjaṭa says that retardation of evacuation is incurable by its very symptoms.

'Someone whose consciousness is restricted' is someone who is mentally confused.[63] 'Someone whose eyes have receded to the interior' is someone whose eye-balls have entered into the interior of their cavities.[64] 'Someone, all the junctures of whom have become detached', is someone, of whom all the joints and junctures of the bones have become slackened. '(He will go) to the place of no return' (means that) he will die.

6, 24 : An unpolluted condition of the eructations, perseverance, excretion accompanied by the (corresponding) urge and adjusted to whatever (food one has ingested), lightness, hunger and thirst are the characteristics of someone whose food has been disintegrated.

(A.s.Sū. 11, 69cd-70ab).[65]

6, 25 : Insomnia, disinclination, trembling, dysuria and an altered state of consciousness, those are the five dreadful and severe secondary affections with respect to *visūcī*.

6, 26 : A disorder of the process of disintegration usually arises in men owing to incongruity of the food. The closely united mass of diseases, the root of which is that (incongruity), becomes annihilated by annihilation of that (incongruity).

6, 27 : The generic characteristics of a disorder of the process of disintegration are : languor, heaviness, a constrained condition, giddiness, a confused state of the wind and either a confined state (of the impurities) or (their) coming forth.[66]

M :

Mention is made of the characteristics of someone whose food has been disintegrated, by way of (their) correlation with (those in) a disorder of the process of disintegration... 'An unpolluted condition of the eructations' (indicates that they are) deprived of a smell like smoke, an acid taste, etc. 'Perseverance' is strength of body and mind. 'Excretion' is the coming forth of impure matter and urine... 'Adjusted to whatever (food one has ingested)' (means) corresponding to the food one has enjoyed. 'Lightness' is (lightness) of the body, specifically of the viscera.[67]

NOTES

[1] Cf. fr. Ca.Vi. 6, 12 : "There are four specific types with regard to the bodily fires, distinguished according to (their) force, namely the sharp, sluggish, congruous and in-

congruous (types);" fr. Su.Sū. 35, 24 : "The fire, mentioned previously, maturates the food. It is of four types : there is one (type) when it is not attained by a morbific entity, and there are three types when it has entered into a morbidly altered state : (an) incongruous (state) by wind, (a) sharp (one) by bile and (a) sluggish (one) by phlegm; the fourth (type) is the congruous one due to a congruous state of all (the morbific entities);" A.h.Śā. 3, 73-74ab (A.h.Śā. 3, 73 = A.s.Śā. 6, 80; A.h.Śā. 3, 74ab corresponds to the beginning of A.s.Śā. 6, 70) : "The fire is congruous when the *samāna* stays in its (own) seat, and incongruous when it deviates from its pathway; it is sharp when (the *samāna*) is intensified by bile, and sluggish when (the *samāna*) is oppressed by phlegm. The fire is congruous, incongruous, sharp and sluggish, in that way it is fourfold;" Hā. 3, 6, 1 : "Ātreya said : the fire is proclaimed to be of four kinds : congruous, incongruous and sharp; the opposite of the (latter) is the sluggish (type). Hear now (from me their) marks."

[2] See about the fires of the five gross elements : Ca.Ci. 15, 13-14 = A.h.Śā. 3, 59-60; A.s.Śā. 6, 59.

[3] Cf. fr. Ca.Vi. 6, 12 : "The sharp fire is able to endure all kinds of improper regimen; the sluggish (type), however, has the opposite characteristics; the congruous (fire) enters into a morbidly altered state by an improper regimen, but remains in its natural state when the proper regimen is observed; the incongruous fire has characteristics opposite to those of the congruous (type);" fr. Su.Sū. 35, 24 : "That (fire), which properly maturates the food (when it has been) enjoyed in agreement with (the proper) time, is congruous by means of congruous morbific entities. That (fire), which sometimes maturates in a proper way and sometimes (only) after bringing about inflatedness, piercing pain, the retentive disease, diarrhoea, abdominal disease, heaviness, rumbling of the bowels and excessive evacuation, is incongruous. That (fire), which quickly maturates even a considerable (amount of) enjoyed food, is (called) sharp. That same (type) is technically defined as an extreme (type of) fire when it increases (in intensity); very quickly it maturates again and again even considerable (amounts of) enjoyed food and, at the end of the maturative process, it generates desiccation of the throat, palate and lips, a burning sensation and a general sense of glowing heat. That (fire), however, which maturates even a slight (amount of) enjoyed (food) after a long time, having brought about heaviness of abdomen and head, cough, shortness of breath, effusion (of saliva), vomiting and adynamia of the limbs, is sluggish;" A.s.Śā. 3, 74cd-76 : "(The fire) which will properly maturate food, ingested in the proper way, is (called) congruous. An incongruous (fire) will quickly maturate improperly (ingested food), or properly (ingested food) slowly. A sharp (fire) will quickly maturate even improperly (ingested) food. A sluggish (fire), however, will slowly maturate even the food which has been enjoyed in the proper way, after bringing about desiccation of the mouth, (abdominal) distension, rumbling of the bowels, inflatedness and heaviness;" A.s.Śā. 6, 70 presents in prose a somewhat extended version of A.h.Śā. 3, 74cd-76; fr. Bhe.Vi. 3 : "The internal fires (are as follows). A person (who has presented the signs of immature matter), whose ingested food is digestively altered, is deprived of his force and colour, (if) he enjoys articles of food in addition. When the ingested food, though being a of slight (amount) and a light (quality), is disintegrated with difficulty, and force and colour are not acquired, (such a person) is called someone with a weak fire. One whose ingested food is sometimes maturated and sometimes not digestively altered, whether it be heavy or light, is called someone with an incongruous fire. Someone, in whom a limited (amount of) food comes to be maturated, or (an amount of) ingested food beyond the proper measure, should be known as a man with a congruous fire, whose bile, phlegm and wind

are congruous. A man constitutionally dominated by wind and bile has a sharp fire; someone dominated by wind has an incongruous fire, and from phlegm a man acquires a sluggish fire. Someone whose fire is congruous and who is equanimous, will enjoy a long life;" Hā. 3, 6, 2-7 : "From a congruous state of wind, bile and phlegm a congruous fire arises. An incongruous fire arises when an incongruous state has been reached by these (morbific entities). A sharp abdominal fire arises by means of excess of bile. By excess of wind and phlegm arises (the fire) called sluggish. (The fire) is called congruous when it causes maturation of an ingested accumulated mass of food which is in a natural state; it is devoid of a morbific entity and makes all the elements (of the body) increase. The incongruous (fire) sometimes causes maturation of the food, and does not bring about digestive alteration at other times; or, (increased) by wind, it also brings about *viṣūcikā*. When one eats excessively, owing to one's constitution, and yet does not obtain satiety, and when one's eyes are burning and (of a) yellow (colour, the fire) is sharp; it brings about decline of (bodily) force. When one is unable to ingest (food), and phlegm is present in excess, one is said to have a sluggish fire, and is thought to be liable to visceral swelling and abdominal disease."

[4] It is not clear which treatise has been employed : the source of Mā.ni. 6, 3-4 is unknown.

[5] *nānātmaja*; this term, occurring Ca.Sū. 20, 10, is explained by Cakra : "(Qualified diseases are those) which are generated by wind, etc., without being blended with another morbific entity."

[6] *sāmānyaja*; this term is also explained by Cakra in his comment on Ca.Sū. 20, 10: "(Unqualified diseases are those) which are generated by wind, etc., by each single one (of the morbific entities) and by the assembled ones."

[7] Ca.Sū. 20, 14 reads *ploṣa* (scorching) instead of *coṣa* (sucking pain).

[8] These diseases are enumerated : Ca.Sū. 20, 10-11; 14; 17. See also Kā.Sū. 27, 20-29ab; 34-37; 41-43.

[9] This stanza also occurs : Bhā.pra. 8, 6, 7.

[10] Cf. Ca.Ci. 15, 218cd-219ab: "Thereupon the fire, together with the wind, having acquired strength in a body that has become dry, surrounds the food, and quickly maturates it again and again, on account of its sharpness."

[11] Ca. reads *śvāsa* (shortness of breath) instead of *kāsa* (cough).

[12] In order to understand the full purport of these stanzas it is useful to add the two subsequent ones : Ca.Ci. 15, 221cd-223ab : "This extreme (type of) fire should be appeased by heavy, oleaginous, cold, sweet and slimy foods and drinks, as an inflamed fire (is extinguished) by water. Again and again, one should offer to such a person articles of food, even when the previous meal has not yet been digested, lest (the fire), devoid of fuel, after reaching the inner (elements), should make that man perish." Cf. A.h.Ci. 10, 81-83ab = A.s.Ci. 13, 27 : "When, in a state of decline of phlegm, the bile, increased in its own seat and following the wind (in its course), brings about an increase of the fire, then this fire, together with the wind, having quickly maturated the food and all the elements (of the body), and bringing the vital fluid into a condensed state, causes death. Such a person may feel relief when he has ingested food, but gasps for breath when (the food) has been disintegrated. Thirst, coughing, a burning sensation, fainting and other illnesses find their source in the extreme (type of the) abdominal fire;" Hā. 3, 6, 10cd-11 : "When both wind and phlegm have declined and the bile is violent, when the ingestion of food procures a pleasurable sensation, (but the food), being scarcely ingested, is disintegrated, that abdominal fire which is called incinerating arises." Com-

pare also : Va. 5, 29-30; Bhā.pra. 8, 6, 9-10 and Yo., p. 267, *bhasmakalakṣaṇa* 1-4.

[13] Cf. fr. Kā.Sū. 24 : "The disorder of the process of disintegration (of the food) is of four kinds : the immature and combustively altered (types), that (type) which is accompanied by phlegm, and also that (arising) from a remnant of the *rasa*. I shall proclaim its characteristics."

[14] This stanza derives from an unknown source; there are no parallels in Ca., Su., A.h. and A.s.

[15] Ḍa. comments : "The remnant of the *rasa* is the *rasa* left over from the maturated food itself; it is not designated as a morbific principle, because it has been corrupted (only) by a slight (amount of a) morbific entity." Hārāṇacandra remarks : "The remnant of the *rasa* is the remnant of the food that possesses taste, the component (of it) which has remained, by not being properly transformed."

[16] Ḍa. : dissolved (means) dissolved at one side (i.e. in one lateral part of the chest), by the wind staying there.

[17] Ḍa. : the path of the fiery energy is the pathway of the abdominal fire.

[18] Cf. A.s.Sū. 11, 71 : "If, in a person with an abundance of bile, the food, wrapped up by the morbific entities and in a dissolved condition, does not cover the fire, a corrupt desire to ingest food, which (desire), like poison, kills persons with a sluggish *buddhi*, may arise from that (condition)."

[19] Cf. A.h.Sū. 8, 29ab : "Absence of the desire for food and distress in the cardiac region, though the eructations have become unpolluted, (arise) from a remnant of the *rasa*." Introducing this statement Aruṇa says : "Even if the food has been disintegrated, the *rasa*, which is the essential constituent of the food, may sometimes remain non-disintegrated." Aruṇa comments : "By means of these words (it is indicated that) the meaning of this remnant of the *rasa* is quite different from a disorder of the process of disintegration; from this it follows that the *rasa*, which is the ground of the blood, etc., is not properly maturated." He. comments : "The word *rasa* characterizes the quantity of (ingested) food which is the ground of the *rasa*; non-disintegratedness of the immature *rasa* as an element (of the body) does not occur, for this (element) is indicated by the word *rasa*, just when it is immature, and by the word blood when it is mature."

[20] See Mā.ni. 6, 7.

[21] This is a quotation that has not been traced in the Suśrutasaṃhitā.

[22] Su. : *tataḥ* (thereupon) instead of *bhuktvā* (having ingested one's meal).

[23] Su.Sū. 46, 487ab reads : "After having ingested one's food, one should sit down like a king, until the weariness by (the ingestion of) the food has gone."

[24] Ca.Ci. 15, 44-47 : "(By...) the fire is corrupted; when in a corrupted state, it does not maturate the food, even if it is light. Being not maturated, (the food) gets into a fermented state and acquires the form of a poison. The signs of this disorder of the process of disintegration are : a constrained condition, adynamia, a painful condition of the head, fainting, giddiness, seizing pain in the back and iliac region, yawning, muscle pain, thirst, fever, vomiting, (excessive) evacuation, anorexia and absence of digestive alteration. It is a dreadful food-poison. When it is being combined with bile it generates a burning sensation, thirst, ailments of the mouth, acid and bilious eructations, and other maladies which arise from bile."

[25] Su. : *parikṣata* (hurt) instead of *paripluta* (overwhelmed).

[26] Su. : *śuc* (grief) instead of *ruc* (pain).

[27] Su. : *pariṇāma* (transformation) instead of *paripāka* (complete maturation).

[28] Cf. Ca.Ci. 15, 42-43 : "(The fire is corrupted) by abstinence from food, eating when

the previous meal has not yet been disintegrated, eating too much, eating incongruous articles of food, by the ingestion of (foods which are) inadequate, heavy, cold, extremely dry or completely corrupted, by the erroneous application of purgative, emetic and oleaginous (substances), by the miseries of illness, incongruity with respect to place, (period of) time and season, and by restraint of the (natural) urges;" A.s.Sū. 11, 21 : "For thus (it has been said) : (Foodstuffs, which are) heavy, dry, desiccated, cold, disagreeable, bringing about a constrained condition or combustive alteration, defiled or disagreeing, an extreme amount of water, drinks in general or liquid substances, (foodstuffs which are ingested) at an improper time, or foods and drinks which are enjoyed by someone who is distressed by lust, wrath, greed, jealousy, shame, grief, disquietude, fear or hunger, all these things bring about corruption of the immature matter;" Bhe.Sū. 10, 1-3ab : "Then he said : The bodily fire of a creature is appeased by oil, ground foodstuffs, *kṛśara* and foods prepared with milk, by disagreeing foods, overeating (read : *adhyaśana*), raw meat, lotus-roots and dried potherbs, by shame, grief, wrath, lust, jealousy, greed, disquietude (read : *udvega*), fear, and other similar (states of mind), or by waking at night and lying down to repose."

29 Mā.ni. 6, 7c : *laghu cāpi* (and though it is light).

30 The same series of explanations is found in Ḍa.'s comment on Su.Sū. 46, 501.

31 Cf. Su.Sū. 46, 502 : "(Ingested) food, which has become sweet, is technically called immature; when it has become acid and is somewhat digestively altered, it is technically called combustively altered; when there are vehement pricking and piercing pains, and the wind has become barred and obstructed (in its course, it is technically called) constrained;" A.h.Sū. 8, 25-26 : "The disorder of the process of disintegration (is said to be of the) immature (type when it arises) from phlegm; in this (type there are present) swelling of the eyes and cheeks, eructations as immediately after the ingestion of food, effusion (of saliva), nausea and heaviness. The constrained (type, arising) from wind, brings about piercing pain, confinement (of the impurities), inflatedness and adynamia. The combustively altered (type, arising) from bile, is accompanied by thirst, mental confusion, giddiness, acid eructations and a burning sensation."

32 *gaṇḍa* (cheek) is explained by its synonym *kapola*.

33 Ḍa. explains *upadravāḥ* (secondary affections) in this case by : additional effects, which are generated by the special faculty of the illness, and are generic characteristics of it.

34 The source of this stanza is unknown.

35 Ḍa. remarks : "The reason of the fact that no mention has been made here of the fourth (type of) disorder of the process of disintegration, (to wit the type arising from) a remnant of the *rasa*, is that its nature is not such as to start *visūcī*, etc., because it is based on non-transformation (of the food) and has been mentioned by one author only."

36 Su. : *ucyate tu visūcikā* instead of *visūcīti nigadyate*.

37 Su. : *kaluṣāśaya* (with a turbid, i.e. corrupted, receptacle) instead of *aśanalolupa* (cupidous with regard to eating).

38 Cf. A.h.Sū. 8, 4-8ab : "Also (food, enjoyed) beyond the proper measure, quickly excites all the morbific entities. For, in a man who has not subdued his mind, the wind and the other (morbific entities), being oppressed and simultaneously excited by this immature, corrupted food, bring about, after having entered it, intestinal inertia when they make it constrained, and *visūcikā* when they make it move, quite unexpectedly, along the lower and upper pathway. The food advances neither upwards nor downwards

and is not maturated, because it stays in an inert condition in the receptacle of undigested food; therefore this (disorder) is traditionally called intestinal inertia. When, owing to a vehement excitement of wind, etc., the limbs are pierced by bursts of painful sensations of several kinds, as by needles, it is called *visūcikā*;" A.s.Sū. 11, 12-15 corresponds to A.h.Sū. 8, 4-8ab.

[39] A.h. : *bhid-* (to cut) instead of *vyadh-* (to pierce).

[40] A.h. : *udbheda* instead of *bheda*.

[41] Cf. fr. Ca.Vi. 2, 7 : "In such a person (with *visūcikā* or intestinal inertia), wind brings about piercing pain, obstructive abdominal swelling, muscle pain, desiccation of the mouth, fainting, giddiness, incongruity of the fire, seizing pain in the sides, back and iliac region, and contraction and stiffening of the vessels. Bile (brings about) fever, diarrhoea, a sensation of inner burning, thirst, (mental disturbance as in) intoxication, giddiness and confused speech. Phlegm (brings about) vomiting, anorexia, absence of digestive alteration, cold fever, inertia and heaviness of the limbs;" A.h.Sū. 8, 8cd-9 : "In this (*visūcikā*) there occur by wind piercing pain, giddiness, obstructive abdominal swelling, trembling, stiffness, etc., by bile fever, diarrhoea, a sensation of inner burning, thirst, loss of consciousness, etc., by phlegm vomiting, heaviness of the limbs, impeded speech, spitting, etc.;" A.s.Sū. 11, 16 : "In this (disorder) wind brings about piercing pain, obstructive abdominal swelling, muscle pain, desiccation of the mouth, confused speech, trembling, fainting, giddiness, yawning, cramp, an extremely painful condition of the entrance of the eye (*akṣipraveśa*), head and cardiac region, and contraction and stiffening of the vessels. Bile (brings about) fever, diarrhoea, a sensation of inner burning, alteration of colour, thirst, (mental disturbance as in) intoxication, giddiness and confused speech. Phlegm (brings about) vomiting, anorexia, effusion (of saliva), adynamia of the body, absence of digestive alteration, cold fever and heaviness of the limbs;" fr. Bhe.Ci. 11 (the chapter on the therapy of *viṣūcī*) : "In such a person occur cough, fever, fainting, aversion to food, alteration of colour, languor, absence of digestive alteration, effusion of phlegm and closing of the eyes. Then (there arise) injury of the chest to an extreme degree, heart disease, (obstructive abdominal swelling) and deficient (functioning of the) limbs; this is the severe (disorder called) intestinal inertia. Nausea, shivering, vomiting, combustive alteration, cramp, fever, shortness of breath, inflatedness and loosening of the faeces are characteristics (caused) by food one feels aversion from. (There may also occur) effusion of phlegm, cough, yawning and seizing of the cardiac region, and moreover shortness of breath and cough, attended by a painful condition of the sides and the head. The prodromes of *viṣūcī* are perspiration, coldness of the body, eructation, heaviness of the viscera and seizing of urine, wind and faeces. These are proclaimed to be the characteristics of the five kinds of erroneous employment of food."

[42] The order of the words differs in Ca.Vi. 2, 11. It is preceded by the statement (Ca.Vi. 2, 10) : "The physicians explain that this disease, the morbific factor of which consists of immature matter, is of two kinds : *visūcikā* and intestinal inertia."

[43] *ūrdhvaṃ cādhaś ca.*

[44] Su. : *pratāmyati* instead of *pratāmyet.*

[45] Su. : *vikūjati* instead of *parikūjati.*

[46] Su. : *viparidhāvati* (it moves about) instead of *upari dhāvati* (it moves about upwards of...).

[47] Su. : *kukṣau yasya bhṛśaṃ bhavet* (if one presents a vehement ... in the lateral parts of the abdomen) instead of *yasyātyarthaṃ bhaved api* (if one presents an extreme...).

[48] Su. : *tṛṣṇodgārāvarodhakau* (restraint of thirst and eructation) instead of *tṛṣṇodgārau ca yasya tu* (who presents thirst and eructation as well).

[49] Cf. Kā.Sū. 25, 27-28 : "(The child) that cannot sustain its head, that feels a cutting pain, yawns again and again, does not drink very much milk at the breast, vomits knotty matter, and presents despondency, inflatedness and inability to eat, a child presenting that set of symptoms should be known to suffer from intestinal inertia."

[50] Ḍa. : one enters as it were into darkness.

[51] A.h. : *na ca pacyate* (it is not maturated) instead of *na vipacyate* (it is not digestively altered).

[52] Cf. fr. Ca.Vi. 2, 12 : "We shall teach (about the subject of) intestinal inertia : Of someone who is weak, whose fire is slight, who has (a) copious (amount of) phlegm, who restrains the urge (to pass) wind, urine and faeces, who indulges in foods that are solid, heavy, copious, dry, cold and desiccated, the food and drink of such a person, subject to pressure by wind, its pathway being encompassed by phlegm, being in an extremely dissolved state, cannot proceed outwards by reason of its inertia. Thereupon it shows, to an extreme degree, the signs of the disease, the morbific factor of which consists of immature matter, except vomiting and diarrhoea. The extremely corrupted morbific entities, their pathways being blocked by the corrupted immature matter, move in a lateral direction, and stiffen his whole body sometimes like a stick. For that reason it is called the stick-like (type of) intestinal inertia, which is incurable. The disease, the morbific factor of which consists of immature matter, when occurring in someone who habitually practises the eating of incongruous foods, overeating and eating before the previous meal has been digested, is called the poison consisting of immature matter by the physicians, because its signs are like those of poison. This (disorder) is most incurable by reason of its rapid action and because the treatments (of immature matter and of poison) are irreconcilable;" Cakra observes that in the above statements the specific ground, usually resulting in intestinal inertia, is made mention of, but that one should know that its generic ground consists of eating food beyond the proper measure; wind and phlegm are the predominant morbific entities of intestinal inertia, but bile is also present, bringing about its own symptoms; A.h.Sū. 8, 10-14 : "Specifically in a weak person with a slight fire, who restrains his (natural) urges, the food, oppressed by the wind, obstructed in the interior by phlegm, being inert, brought into a turbulent state by the morbific entities, and being stagnant like a corpus alienum, brings about intense piercing pain and the other (symptoms), with the exception of vomiting and diarrhoea. That is intestinal inertia. In the case that the extremely corrupted morbific entities, the apertures (of the channels) being blocked by the corrupted immature matter, move in a lateral direction, and stiffen the whole body like a stick, it is called the stick-like (type of) intestinal inertia. One should abandon (a patient with) this quick-acting (disease). The very dreadful disease, the morbific factor of which consists of immature matter, with the characteristics of poison, (occurring) in someone who habitually practises the eating of incongruous foods, overeating and eating before the previous meal has been digested, should be avoided (with regard to treatment); (this disease) is technically called 'poison' because, assuming the form of poison, it acts quickly, and because the treatments (of poison and of immature matter) are irreconcilable;" A.s.Sū. 11, 17-19 corresponds to A.h.Sū. 8, 10-14 and is even closer to Ca. than A.h.; A.h.Sū. 8, 28 = A.s.Sū. 11, 59 : "From immature matter itself, when present in a very great amount and in a dissolved condition, retardation of evacuation may arise, attended by phlegm and wind; its signs are those of immature matter and it is cured in the same way."

53 See preceding note.

54 These stanzas also occur : Va. 5, 155.

55 Ḍa. comments on Su.U. 56, 9 : "Though retardation of evacuation arises from the combustively altered (type of) disorder of the process of disintegration, when the combustively altered matter is present in a copious amount, and though corruption of the bile arises from the combustively altered (type of) the process of disintegration and not a corruption of wind and phlegm, nevertheless corruption of the other two (morbific entities) comes about by corruption of the bile. In the same way it should be known that in *visūcī* and intestinal inertia, which have sprung up from a non-specified kind of the immature type, when it occurs to a high degree, and which are also provided with an excess of phlegm and wind, the other (morbific entity) is really present."

56 Su. : *doṣeṇa yenāvatataṃ svaliṅgais taṃ lakṣayed āmasamudbhavaiś ca* (one should characterize the morbific entity that has spread over the body by its own signs and by those arising from immature matter).

57 The words of the class called *sarvanāman* are the pronominalia and their derivatives, etc.

58 See ch. 25.

59 This is a quotation from an unknown source.

60 This is a quotation from an unknown source.

61 Ḍa. comments on Su.U. 56, 10 : "... What is the purpose of this mentioning of the seat of immature matter ? Is it mentioned because a morbidly altered morbific entity will give rise to a painful condition at the very place where it comes to be seated ? That is true, but not in all cases, because one can see, for instance in *gaṇḍamālā*, etc., that the morbific entity, though staying in the globular mass (of flesh of the shoulders), is an agent (bringing about) a morbid alteration in the throat, etc. Instruction about the place painfully oppressed by immature matter has been given in this case to make therapy easy. That is to say that the *vaidya* should recognize the very place where the immature matter will bring about a particular painful condition. By means of what hosts of morbid alterations ? By those arising from immature matter, (i.e.) stiffness, heaviness, etc. Brahmadeva, however, explains (as follows) : he should recognize the morbific factor, arising from immature matter and attended by any one of the morbific entities, wind, etc., by its own signs, (i.e.) by the signs of any one of the morbific entities, wind, etc. Others read and explain (this stanza) differently. (But) that has been excluded (in this comment)..."

62 Su. : *chardi* instead of *vami*.

63 Ḍa. : someone who is sluggish with regard to sensibility.

64 Ḍa. : someone whose vision has suffered decline.

65 Cf. A.h.Sū. 8, 55c-j : "When faeces and urine have been emitted, the cardiac region is completely free from impure matter, the morbific entities are following their own paths, the eructations are unpolluted, hunger is approaching, the wind flows in its normal way, the (bodily) fire is preponderant (again), and the body, its senses being clear (again), is completely light, one should employ food, prescribed in accordance with the fixed rules, for that is thought to be the proper time."

66 Cf. A.h.Sū. 8, 30cd-31ab, the contents of which are identical with Mā.ni. 6, 27. Cf. fr. Kā.Sū. 24 : "Despondency, heaviness, lassitude, effusion of phlegm, disinclination, giddiness and interruption of the rules to preserve health, these are the characteristics of a disorder of the process of disintegration."

67 Mā.ni. 6, 25-27 is not commented upon by the author of M.

CHAPTER SEVEN

WORMS (*KRIMI*)

7, 1-2a : Worms are proclaimed to be of two kinds, as they are distinguished into external and internal ones.
They are of four kinds according to their distinction into those born out of external impure matter, out of phlegm, blood and faeces (1).
They are of twenty kinds (distinguished) according to their names.

(A.h.Ni. 14, 42cd-43c).[1]

M:

Mention is made of the origins of (the disorders by) worms, immediately after the disorders of the process of disintegration, because the latter ones are the source of the former... Regarding these (worms), there are external ones, which find their source in external impure matter, (consisting of) the unctuous substance (produced) by the skin, and internal ones, which find their source in the receptacle of undigested food, etc.; these (worms) are said to be of two kinds if distinguished according to their location, and of four kinds if distinguished according to their cause... External impure matter is said to be perspiration, etc., with which the body is daubed.[2] ... These same (worms) are of four kinds, and, when distinguished according to their names, of twenty kinds. Surpassing (the number of) twenty are the extremely subtle worms which are innate and have been mentioned by Caraka,[3] but these are not described in the paragraph on diseases (by worms), because they do not bring about morbid alterations.[4] Those worms which are of twenty kinds, however, are said to be (related to) diseases, because they generate fever, piercing pain, etc., by means of excitement of the morbific entities.

Ā :

Some are external, arising from the hair of the head, garments, etc., (viz.) lice, nits, etc., and others are internal. The source of the internal ones is immature matter, etc... Some of these specific names are related (to each other), others are unrelated; they have been taught by the early masters for the sake of common practice. Their names are (as follows) : the two (kinds of worms), springing up from external impure matter, are the lice and the nits; thep laces of their residence are the hairs of the head and the garments. Those arising from phlegm are (called) *antrāda*, *udarāveṣṭa*, *hṛdayāda*, *mahāguda*, *curu*, *darbha-kusuma* and *sugandha*; in that way there are seven (kinds); their place of residence is the receptacle of undigested food. Those arising from blood are (called) *keśāda*, *lomavidhvaṃsa*, *romadvīpa*, *uḍumbara*, *saurasa* and *mātṛ*; in that way there are six (kinds); they are seated in the blood-carrying vessels. There are five (kinds of worms) springing up from faecal matter : (their names are) *kakeruka*, *makeruka*, *sausurāda*, *saśūla* and *leliha*; their place of residence is the receptacle of digested food. Thus there are twenty (kinds of worms).[5]

7, 2b-3 : Among these the external ones arise from impure matter;[6] their size, shape and colour are like those of a sesame seed; their places of residence are the hairs of the head and the clothes (2).

They are of two kinds, possessing many feet or subtle (as to their size), and their names are lice and nits. They bring about wheals, boils, itching and nodules. (3).

(A.h.Ni. 14, 43d-45ab).[7]

M :

The external ones, which have been mentioned, are expounded... Like sesame seeds are their size, (i.e.) their measure, their shape, (i.e.) their conformation, and their colour, (i.e.) they are white and black...[8] Those possessing many feet are lice and those which are subtle are nits.[9]

Ā :

... A wheal is a distinct kind of *udarda*.[10] Boils are well known... Nodules have the form of boils and are hard.

7, 4 : Someone who ingests food when his previous meal has not yet been digested, who permanently (eats) sweet and acid (substances), is fond of liquid (substances), ingests (dishes made from) flour and from treacle, who abstains from physical exercise and lies down to repose by day, and someone who ingests disagreeing food, acquires worms.[11]

M :

Mention is made of their origin...

Ā :

... (Dishes made from) flour are flour cakes, covered with powdered wheat, etc.

7, 5-6ab : Those (worms) arising from faecal matter develop by (consuming) *māsa* beans, (foods made from) flour, acid [12] and saline [13] (substances), treacle and potherbs,[14] those arising from phlegm by (consuming) meat, fish,[15] treacle, milk, thick sour milk and verjuice (5),[16] and those springing up from blood by (consuming) disagreeing (foods), by eating when the previous meal has not yet been digested, by (consuming) potherbs, etc.

(Su.U. 54, 17-18ab).[17]

M :

Mention is made of specific origins with regard to specific (groups of) worms...

Ā :

... By means of these causes are born (those worms) which arise from faecal matter; 'in the receptacle of digested food' has to be supplied... Verjuice is the juice of the sugar-cane, which has become acid after an interval of time. Those (arising from phlegm develop) in the receptacle of undigested food... (Consuming) potherbs is the consumption of immature, yellowish-green *caṇaka* and other potherbs.

7, 6cd-7ab : Fever, alteration of colour, piercing pain, disease of the cardiac region, adynamia, giddiness (6), aversion to food and diarrhoea are the characteristics of the development of worms.

(Su.U. 54, 18cd-19ab).

M :

Mention is made of the characteristics of internal worms...

Ā :

Alteration of colour (indicates) a dark and yellow colour of the (skin of the) body. Piercing pain (arises) in the receptacles of undigested and digested food. A disease of the cardiac region is a morbid alteration of the cardiac region, (viz.) sickness, etc...

7, 7cd-11ab : Those, which have arisen from phlegm in the receptacle of undigested food, crawl, when they have grown up, in every direction (7).

Some resemble a broad *bradhna*, others an earthworm, (some) *dhānya* sprouts, which have grown out; (some) are thin and long, (others) minute (8), (some) are white and (others) have a copper-coloured shine.

These (mentioned ones) are of seven kinds as to their names; (they are called) *antrāda*,[18] *udarāveṣṭa*,[19] *hṛdayāda*,[20] *mahāguda*,[21] *curu*,[22] *darbhakusuma* [23] and *sugandha*.[24]

And these (worms) bring about sickness, a discharge from the mouth, absence of digestive alteration, anorexia (10), fainting, vomiting, fever, obstructive abdominal swelling, leanness, sneezing and nasal catarrh.

(A.h.Ni. 14, 47-50).[25]

M :

Mention is made of those arising from phlegm... Those which are caused by phlegm, crawl, when they have grown up, in every direction, (i.e.) upwards and downwards. Those arising from faecal matter, etc., should be looked at in the same way. A *bradhna* is a thong made from leather,[26] in common language called *bradhnī*.[27] (*dhānya* sprouts), which have grown out, are (such sprouts), which have formed excrescences. (Some worms are) thin as to their circumference and long as to their extension, (others are) minute, (i.e.) of a very slight (size) with regard to both (circumference and extension)... And these (seven) specific names, some of them being related, others unrelated, have been taught by the early masters for the sake of common practice. Thus it should be understood as well with regard to (those worms) to be mentioned presently.

Ā :

... (Some) resemble, with regard to their form, a broad *bradhna*, (i.e.) their form is that of a part of a spread-out skin; others resemble an earthworm, (i.e.) their form is that of a *bhūmilatā*...[28]

7, 11cd-12 : The minute creatures, arising from blood, seated in the vessels carrying blood (11), are footless, round and copper-coloured; some are invisible owing to their subtlety. There are six (kinds of these worms, called) *keśāda*,[29] *romavidhvaṃsa*,[30] *romadvīpa*,[31] *udumbara*,[32] *saurasa*[33] and *mātṛ*;[34] [35] their action is the same as that of skin diseases (12).

(A.h.Ni. 14, 51-52).[36]

M :

Mention is made of those arising from blood... 'Those, arising from the blood-carrying-vessel-seat-blood', (means either) those which are seated in the vessels carrying blood and arise from blood, or those which arise from the blood seated in the vessels carrying blood... 'Their action is the same as that of skin diseases' (means that) their effect is just the same as that of skin diseases, that is to say that they generate skin diseases; for it has been said in the Suśruta(saṃhitā) : "All (kinds of) skin diseases are taught[37] to be accompanied by wind, bile, phlegm and worms" (fr. Ni. 5, 6).

Ā :

... 'Their action is the same as that of skin diseases' means that their result is the same as that of skin diseases, or that they have, together with skin diseases, one and the same action, (i.e. that they bring about) hypersensitivity, itching, pricking pain, etc., destruction of the hair of the head, face and body, etc., and consumption of the skin, vessels, cords, flesh and cartilages.[38]

7, 13-16 : Those springing up from faecal matter arise in the receptacle of digested food. When they have grown up they will spread downwards. When they turn into the direction of the receptacle of undigested food (13) the eructations and expirations of the person (afflicted) will be consistent with the smell of faeces.

(These worms) are broad, round, thin or gross, and (of a) brown, yellow, white or black (colour) (14).

These five (kinds of) worms are called *kakeruka*, *makeruka*, *sausurāda*,[39] *saśūla*[40] and *leliha*.[41]

They generate (15), when deviating from their normal pathway,[42] loosening of faecal matter, piercing pain, a constrained condition, leanness, roughness, pallor, horripilation, adynamia of the fire and itching of the anus (16). (A.h.Ni. 14, 53-56).[43]

M :

Mention is made of those (worms) arising from faecal matter... 'They are spreading downwards'... (means that) it is their habit to come forth out of the anal region... The eructations and expirations of the diseased one are consistent with the smell of faeces, (i.e.) are provided with the smell of faeces. The rest is easily understood.

Ā :

... They will spread downwards and not upwards. They are broad, (i.e.) long..., they are thin, (i.e.) slight (regarding their size), or gross, (i.e.) raised; 'as to their form' has to be supplied. ... Loosening of faecal matter is the coming forth of viscid impure matter;[44] piercing pain (occurs) in the receptacle of digested food; a constrained condition is (a constrained condition) of impure matter; roughness is a scabrous condition of the (skin of the) body...[45]

NOTES

[1] Cf. fr. Ca.Vi. 7, 8 : "Thereupon Agniveśa asked the venerable Ātreya, embracing his feet, about the specific way of springing up, seat, shape, colour, name, special faculty and therapy of all the worms having their residence in man (read *puruṣa* instead of *purīṣa*);" Ca.Vi. 7, 9 : "And the venerable Ātreya said to him : on this very subject, Agniveśa, (it may be said that) worms are of twenty kinds, (as) previously taught (Sū. 19, 4), with their division into various kinds, and with the exception of those which are innate. These (twenty kinds of worms) again, divided according to their nature, are of four kinds, namely those arising from faecal matter, phlegm, blood and (external) impure matter;" Su.U. 54, 7 : "The source of the twenty classes of worms is said to be threefold, (viz.) faecal matter, phlegm and blood. I shall tell about these at length;" Hā. 3, 5, 1-2 : "Ātreya said : Worms are proclaimed to be of two kinds; those having their source in the exterior and those having their source in the interior (of the body). The externally (residing) lice will be well known, the internal ones are *kiñcakas*. The external (group) will be of seven kinds, the (group) arising from the interior of six kinds. I shall describe their source, with reference to the external and internal ones, (residing) in men."

[2] Toḍara explains external impure matter by : that which is called perspiration and with which the body is daubed, and Śrīdāsa by : the impure matter of the hairs of the head, the garments, etc., at the exterior of the body.

[3] See note 1 : Ca.Vi. 7, 9.

[4] This statement is also found in Cakra's comment on Ca.Vi. 7, 9.

[5] The names of the twenty kinds of worms occur in the actual text of the Nidāna. It is not clear why the author of Ā. enumerates them at this place.

The names of the twenty kinds of worms, according to Ca., are : fr. Ca.Sū. 19, 4 : There are twenty classes of worms : the two kinds arising from external impure matter are lice and nits (*pipīlikā*; Cakra : = *likhyā*); the six (kinds) arising from blood (are called) : *keśāda, lomāda, lomadvīpa, saurasa, audumbara* and *jantumātṛ*; the seven (kinds) arising from phlegm (are called) *antradā, udarāveṣṭa, hṛdayāda, curu, darbhapuṣpa, saugandhika* and *mahāguda*: the five (kinds) arising from faecal matter (are called) *kakeruka, makeruka, leliha, saśūlaka* and *sausurāda*." Bhe. states the names of the twenty kinds of worms at Sū. 26, 31-33 (read 32a as follows : *romāntrādāhitāś caiva*) : "Those arising from marrow, from membranous coverings, those formed like a *lambā* (a kind of cucumber; or : *lambarūpaka*, i.e. pendulous), those with many forms, those crawling about, those spreading, those derived from one's family, those arising from the eyes, those eating the body-hair (*romāda*), those eating the bowels (*antrāda*), the insalutary, the troublesome and the severe ones, those arising from the head, from the teeth and from phlegm, those residing in the faecal matter, the red and the black (*kālaka*) ones, and those (called) *śatamātṛka*, these twenty one should know to be the classes of worms (occurring) in bodily beings." Hā. 3, 5, 3-17 presents a different classification : "Owing to dryness, an extreme amount of impure matter, perspiration, anxiety and grief, sharp lice occur, which have arisen from phlegm and from the elements. (Some of these) lice are black, others are white and a third (type) stays in the skin; (this third type) is subtle, extremely hideous and dry, it resembles the skin (and is called) *carmayūkikā*. The fourth (type) is called *bindukī*; it is round and its source is the urine. The fifth (type) may be (called) *matkuṇā* and brings about external secondary affections. The louse dwelling on the head is white and is called *śironivāsinī*. The *carmayūkā* is (also) present on the subtle skin of the eyes, and the *yaṣṭikā* on the hairs (of the body). By means of dry food, foods (prepared) from wheat and barley, (foods prepared from) flour, treacle, wrong use of milk, by lying down to repose by day, (dishes) accompanied by mucilaginous (substances), by warmth and by indulging in glowing heat and water, by these (factors) arises, in the receptacles of impure matter, the flock of worms, bringing about morbid alterations in the viscera. They are taught to be of six kinds. I shall tell about their characteristics. They spread, like serpents, through the organs which contain impure matter, in (that part of) the visceral cavity in which phlegm (resides). Some are (called) *pṛthumuṇḍa* ('broad and bald'), others resemble an earthworm (*kiñcuka*), some resemble the sprouts of grain, some are subtle, some are minute; (others) are known as *sūcīmukha* ('with a mouth like a needle') and these bring about adynamia of the bowels. I shall tell about their characteristics and therapy. Listen to me. Fever, or disease of the heart together with piercing pain, emesis, moistening of the cardiac region, giddiness, suppression of the appetite, alteration of colour, diarrhoea accompanied by frothy matter, growling (sounds) in the abdomen, a sluggish state of the fire, thirst and a yellow colour of the eyes arise in someone oppressed by *kiñcukas*. A feeling of pricking pain in the bowels as by needles, or a bloody diarrhoea, in other cases (the sensation) that the liver is eaten away or a vehement haematemesis, moisture in the mouth, inability to eat, rigidity, a sluggish state of the fire, shivering, hunger, thirst and fever should be known to be the painful conditions (caused) by the worms (called) *sūcīmukha*. And now I shall tell about the characteristics of those (which resemble) the sprouts of grain. These worms, staying in the receptacle of impure matter, eat this impure matter vehemently. By those (worms) there arise abscesses in the body and a cutting pain, roughness, leanness, a painful condition of the body and weariness of the heart." Śārṅgadharasaṃhitā 1, 7, 14-17 also enumerates twenty kinds of worms, called : *yūkā, likṣā, hṛdayodaka, antrāda, udarāveṣṭa, cyuru, mahāguha, sugandha, darbhakusuma, mātṛ, saurasa, lomavidhvaṃsa, romadvīpa, udumbara, keśāda, makeruka, leliha,s alūna, sausurāda* and *kakeruka*. It adds (1, 7, 18) : "There is another one, arisen from phlegm and blood, and traditionally called *snāyuka*. Other worms again, (occurring) in inflamed sores, are disproportioned and have an external matrix."

[6] A.h. : *amṛjodbhava* (arising from non-cleansing) instead of *malodbhava* (arising from impure matter). Aruṇa explains *amṛjodbhava* by : produced by external impure matter; Candranandana says : arising from non-cleansing (means that they) spring up from pollution, (i.e.) they arise when one does not cleanse oneself by means of bathing, etc.; Śrīdāsa explains the term as : the ground of which is non-cleansing.

[7] Cf. Ca.Vi. 7, 10 : "This impure matter (may be) external and internal. Those which have arisen from external impure matter are called (worms) arising from impure matter. Their way of springing up (consists of) the abstention from cleansing; their seats are the hair of the head, the face and the body, the eyelashes and the clothes. As to their shape they are minute, they possess the conformation of sesame seeds and have many feet. They are of a black or light colour. They are called lice and nits. Their special faculty consists of the generation of itching, and the bringing about of a state resulting in wheals and pustules. The therapy consists of the removal of these (lice and nits), a procedure injurious to the impure matter, and the non-indulgence in conditions bringing about (the accumulation of) impure matter."

[8] Toḍara : idem.

[9] Toḍara : idem.

[10] See ch. 50.

[11] In his comment on Su.U. 54, 3-6, Ḍa. quotes this stanza as a variant; the third and fourth *pāda* of the quotation run as follows: *vyāyāmajātāni ca varjyamānaḥ svapnādivān vai labhate krimīn* (a man who abstains from all kinds of physical exercise and who is addicted to sleep, etc., acquires worms). Cf. Su.U. 54, 3-6 : "By eating before the previous meal has been digested, overeating, eating inadequate, disagreeing and impure (foods), by want of physical exercise, sleeping by day, by heavy, too oleaginous and cold (foods), *māṣa* beans, ground food, *vidala, bisa, śālū* and *kaseruka*, vegetables of which the leaves are used (*parṇaśāka*), *surā*, verjuice, thick sour milk, milk, treacle, sugar-cane, sesame paste, the flesh of animals living in marshy places, *piṇyāka, pṛthuka*, etc., and by dainty, acid and (very) liquid drinks, phlegm and bile become excited. This brings about (the development of) worms of many forms with different places of residence. It is traditionally said that the procreation of those arising from phlegm and faecal matter usually (occurs) in the receptacles of undigested and digested food, and of those arising from blood in the ducts."

[12] Su. : *piṣṭānna* (food prepared from flour) instead of *piṣṭāmla* (food prepared from flour and acid substances).

[13] Su. : *vidala* instead of *lavaṇa* (saline substances).

[14] Su. : *parṇaśāka* (vegetables of which the leaves are used) instead of *guḍaśāka* (treacle and potherbs).

[15] Su. : *māṣa* (*māṣa* beans) instead of *matsya* (fish).

[16] Su. : *taila* (oil) instead of *śukta* (verjuice).

[17] Cf. A.h.Ni. 14, 45cd-46 = A.s.Ni. 14, 48-49ab : "Those which arise in the interior have the same ground as skin diseases; those among these (interior ones) which arise

from phlegm (develop) abundantly by (consuming) sweet foods, treacle, milk, thick sour milk, groats and freshly prepared boiled rice, and those which arise from faecal matter by (consuming) *dhānya* (i.e. grain and pulse), vegetables of which the leaves are used, *ulaka*, etc., which (substances) give rise to a great amount of faeces."

18 *antrāda*, i.e. bowel-eater; this is the worm resembling a broad *bradhna*; it may be a tapeworm.

19 *udarāveṣṭa* (*udārāveṣṭa* is a misprint), i.e. throttling the abdomen (Jolly, HK : Bauchwürger; PW : Bandwurm, MW : tapeworm); it resembles an earthworm, so it may be a round-worm and not a tapeworm.

20 *hṛdayāda*, i.e. eater of the heart or the cardiac region; these worms resemble *dhānya* sprouts which have grown out.

21 *mahāguda*, i.e. having a big anus or anal region (Jolly : Langschwanz); they are thin and long. A.h. and A.s. read : *mahākuha*, the meaning of which is not clear.

22 *curu*; these worms are minute. A.h. and A.s. read : *kuru*. The meaning of these words is not clear.

23 *darbhakusuma*, i.e. *darbha* flower; these worms are white (the inflorescence of *darbha*, Imperata cylindrica Beauv., is a dense, fluffy, silver-white panicle).

24 *sugandha*, i.e. fragrant; this worm has a copper-coloured shine.

25 Cf. Ca.Vi. 7, 12 : "Those, arising from phlegm, spring up by (the ingestion of) milk, treacle, sesame, fish, flesh of animals living in marshy places, food made from flour, *paramānna*, *kusumbha* and oleaginous substances, by eating before the previous meal has been digested, and by the ingestion of foul-smelling, moist, adulterated, disagreeing and inadequate food. Their seat is the receptacle of undigested food. When growing up they spread upwards, downwards or in both directions. There are specific (differences) as to their shape and colour : some are white and shaped like a broad *bradhna*, some are round with regard to their circumference, with the conformation of an earthworm, white and with a copper-coloured shine, others are minute, long, with the conformation of a thread, and white. The names of these three kinds of worms caused by phlegm are : *antradā*, *udarāda* ('belly-eater'), *hṛdayacara* ('wanderer in the heart or cardiac region'), *curu*, *darbhapuṣpa*, *saugandhika* and *mahāguda*. Their special faculty is (to bring about) sickness, a discharge from the mouth, anorexia, absence of digestive alteration, fever, fainting, vomiting, leanness and roughness;" Su.U. 54, 12-14 : "(The worms called) *darbhapuṣpa*, *mahāpuṣpa* ('large flower'), *pralūna* (the 'cut off'), *cipiṭa* ('the flat one'), *pipīlikā* (ant or nit) and *dāruṇa* ('the severe one') arise from excitement of phlegm. They are covered with hair (on the whole of their body), covered with hair on their head, possess tails, are provided with circular spots of a brown colour, possess the form of *dhānya* sprouts which have grown out, and are of a light colour and thin. They eat the marrow, eat the eyes by licking them up, ingest the palate and the ears, and bring about diseases of the head and cardiac region, emesis and nasal catarrh."

26 *carmalatā*; Cakra and Toḍara : idem.

27 Toḍara : *vādhī*.

28 *bhūmilatā* : = *gaṇḍūpada* (see Cakra on Ca.Ci. 8, 151 and Pr 803); a *gaṇḍūpada* is an earthworm.

29 *keśāda*, i.e. eater of the hair of the head.

30 *romavidhvaṃsa*, i.e. destroying the body-hair.

31 *romadvīpa*, i.e. bringing about a condition in which areas of body-hair are left, or : endowed with islands of hairs (Jolly : Zerstörer der Haarwurzeln, HK : Haarinsel).

32 *udumbara,* i.e. resembling the fruit of an *udumbara* tree, or : connected with the skin disease called after this fruit (HK : Feige).

33 *saurasa*; the meaning of this word is not clear.

34 *mātṛ*, i.e. mother.

35 Aruṇa makes mention of the variant : *sahajā rasamātaraḥ* (the innate ones and those of which the nutrient fluid is the mother) instead of *sahasaurasamātaraḥ* (together with those called *saurasa* and *mātṛ*).

36 Cf. Ca.Vi. 7, 11 : "Those arising from blood spring up from the same (source) as the skin diseases. They are seated in the ducts carrying the blood. As to their form they are minute, round and without feet; some are invisible owing to their subtlety; their colour is that of copper. Their names are *keśāda, lomāda, lomadvīpa, saurasa, auḍumbara* and *jantumātṛ* ('mother of creatures'). Their special faculty (consists of) the destruction of the hair of the head and face, the nails, the body-hair and the eyelashes. When they stay in inflamed sores, (they give rise to) hypersensitivity, itching, pricking pain and a creeping sensation, and when they have increased extremely, they consume the skin, vessels, cords, flesh and cartilages. Their therapy is the same as that of skin diseases; we shall teach it on a later occasion;" Su.U. 54, 15-16 : "(The worms) which find their source in blood should be known as *keśāda, romāda* ('eater of the body-hair'), *nakhāda* ('eater of the nails'), *dantāda* ('eater of the teeth'), *kikkiśa, kuṣṭhaja* ('arising from skin diseases') and *parisarpa* ('that one which crawls about'). These (worms) are slightly red, black, oleaginous (or : glossy) and broad. They usually generate morbid alterations arising from blood as their basis."

37 Su. : *ca bhavanti* instead of *copadiśyante.*

38 The latter alternative has been adopted by Aruṇa.

39 The meaning of *kakeruka, makeruka* and *sausvrāda* is not clear.

40 *saśūla,* i.e. accompanied by piercing pain, or : endowed with a pointed dart. A.h. : *sulūna*; a variant is : *salūna*; the meaning of these words is not clear (*lūna* means : cut off).

41 *leliha,* i.e. constantly licking.

42 A.h. : *vinirgamāt* (by coming out, i.e. out of the anus) instead of *vimārgagāḥ* (deviating from their normal pathway).

43 Cf. Ca.Vi. 7, 13 : "The way of springing up of (the worms) arising from faecal matter is comparable to that of those arising from phlegm. Their seat is the receptacle of digested food. When they are growing up, they spread downwards. At that time at which they will turn into the direction of the receptacle of undigested food in someone, there will occur in that person at that time eructations and expirations, smelling of faeces. As to their specific shapes and colours some are subtle (in size), and round with regard to their circumference, white and long, resembling a woollen thread; others again are gross and round with regard to their circumference, and (of a) brown, swarthy, yellowish-green or yellow (colour). Their names are *kakeruka, makeruka, leliha, saśūlaka* and *sausurāda.* Their special faculty is that (their presence) results in loosening of faecal matter, leanness, roughness and horripilation. These same ones bring about a pricking sensation at the opening of the anus, generate an itching sensation and remain sitting round the opening of the anus. These same ones, when they have become hypersensitive, leave (their seat) and come out (of the opening of the anus,) transgressing their limit. These are the specific ways of springing up of worms arising from phlegm and from faecal matter;" Su.U. 54, 8-11 : "The seven (kinds of worms) arising from faecal matter should be known (to be called) *ajava, vijava, kipya, cipya, gaṇḍūpada* ('earthworm'), *curu* and *dvimukha* ('having two mouths or faces'). These are white, subtle, bring about

a pricking sensation in the anal region, and return to attack; others among these are provided with tails and are broad. (The worms) arising from faecal matter bring about piercing pain, sluggishness of the fire, pallor, a constrained condition (of impure matter), decline of force, effusion (of saliva), inability to eat, diseases of the cardiac region and loosening of faecal matter. (Those called) *gaṇḍūpada* are red, long, bring about itching of the anal region on falling out (of the anal opening), piercing pain, (abdominal) distension, loosening of faecal matter and destruction of the maturative process."

44 Ḍa.: a liquid condition of the faeces.

45 Su. adds (U. 54, 19cd-20ab): "The first thirteen (kinds of) worms are said to be visible; (the series) beginning with *keśāda*, (consisting of the seven kinds arising from blood), is invisible; the first two (of that series) should be avoided (with respect to treatment)."

CHAPTER EIGHT

MORBID PALLOR (*PĀṆḌUROGA*), JAUNDICE (*KĀMALĀ*), *KUMBHAKĀMALĀ* AND *HALĪMAKA*

8, 1 : There are traditionally said to be five (kinds of) morbid pallor : three (kinds) by wind, bile and phlegm (separately), a fourth (kind) by concerted action and a fifth (kind) by the consumption of earth.

(Ca.Ci. 16, 3).[1]

M :

Subtle worms, arising from faecal matter, generate pallor; for that reason mention is made of morbid pallor, immediately after the (chapter on) worms... A disease, additionally characterized by pallor, is (called) morbid pallor.[2] "What has been said in the chapter (called) 'On the eight abdominal diseases' of the Caraka(saṃhitā), (viz.) "There are five (kinds of) morbid pallor" (fr. Sū. 19, 4[4]), and also the very words of Caraka again : "There are traditionally said to be five (kinds) of morbid pallor" (Ci. 16, 3a), indicate the curability of all the five (kinds of morbid pallor), but not, as in the five (kinds of) insanity, the incurability of that kind caused by concerted action"; thus says Jejjaṭa. "(It is said) in order to exclude a deficient number;" thus says Cakra(pāṇidatta).[3]

Now it may be objected that (the type) arising from (the eating of) earth, does not occur in the Suśruta(saṃhitā), and also that (the eating of) earth generates morbid pallor just by way of excitement of the morbific entities, as has been said : "Astringent (earth brings about excitement of) wind, salt-containing (earth excitement of) bile, and sweet (earth excitement of) phlegm" (Ca.Ci. 16, 27cd); moreover the consequence would be that the number of diseases would be endless, if the distinctions with regard to origins were applied to the distinction of diseases; and also (it is thus, that the type of morbid pallor) arising from wind is occasioned by wind, excited by the several origins (of its excitement, consisting of substances which are) dry, cold and so on.

The answer (to this objection) is: also in the absence of specificity with regard to the morbific entity from which it arises, mention is made (of a disease as a) separate (entity) in order to substantiate the specificity of its symptoms and therapy, as in enlargement (of the genitals) by urine and by the bowels;[4] Suśruta, however, has not made it (into a) separate (entity) in the final paragraphs,[5] with a view to abstaining from diffusiveness. (Its) therapy, however, is in agreement with the therapy of the morbific entities.[6]

8, 2 : The morbific entities of someone who indulges in physical exercise,[7] acid (substances), saline (substances), intoxicating beverages, earth, sleeping by day and extremely sharp (substances), after bringing about a corrupted condition [8] of the blood, convey pallor to the skin.[9]

(Su.U. 44, 3).[10]

M :

Mention is made of the onset...[11] 'Blood' is an implicative expression, by which Dṛḍhabala describes skin and flesh as liable to corruption also.[12] Hārīta says that the nutrient fluid is also (liable to corruption).

Ā :

With the words 'sexual intercourse',[13] etc. mention is made of the origins of morbid pallor. From 'extremely (frequent)', (i.e.) outstandingly (frequent) sexual intercourse, etc. ...[14] 'Sexual intercourse' (means) indulgence in (sexual intercourse) with women; others read 'physical exercise'. Because the plural of the word 'saline (substance)' (is used), caustic (substances) are also understood. 'Sharp (substances)' are *rājikā*, etc.[15]

8, 3 : A cracked skin, spitting out (saliva), adynamia of the limbs, the consumption of earth, swelling of the prominent part of the eyes, a yellow colour of faeces and urine and absence of digestive alteration are its harbingers, when it is imminent.

(Su.U. 44, 5).[16]

M :

Mention is made of the prodromes... 'A cracked skin' is a condition in which the skin is somewhat torn asunder. 'The consumption of earth' is the desire to consume earth.[17] 'Swelling of the prominent part of the eyes' is swelling of the eye-balls... 'Harbingers' are prodromes.

Ā :

Others read 'bursting open of the skin, spitting out (saliva) and adynamia of the limbs'; this (reading) has exactly the same meaning. 'Spitting out (saliva)' (occurs) by way of the mouth; it is called *thuga-thugī* [18] in common language.

8, 4 : The skin, urine, eyes, etc. have a dry, black and ruddy hue in morbid pallor by wind, and there occur pricking pain, trembling, obstructive abdominal swelling, giddiness, etc.[19]

M :

Mention is made of the characteristics of that kind (which arises) from wind... The black and ruddy hue do not surpass the pallor in this case; otherwise it would not be a case of morbid pallor. As has been said in the Suśruta(saṃhitā) : "Just by reason of the fact that in all these (diseases) a pale condition is present in excess, (they are called cases of) morbid pallor" (U. 44, 4cd). By the word 'etcetera' should be understood that cutting pain, piercing pain, etc. (are also present).

8, 5 : Someone whose urine, faeces and eyes are yellow, who is attended by a burning sensation, thirst and fever, whose faeces are loosened, and who has an extremely yellow hue, is a man with a morbid pallor by bile.[20]

M :

Mention is made of the characteristics of that kind (which arises) from bile... Is it not right to object that it is not suitable to speak of someone with morbid pallor from bile, on account of the very fact that morbid pallor is an effect of bile ?

The answer (to this question) is : it is called 'arising from bile' because it is occasioned by a very strong bile, which is not intimately connected with (one of) the other two morbific entities, in the same way as (one speaks of) blood-bile by bile.[21]

Ā :

'Someone whose faeces are loosened' is someone whose impure matter is somewhat liquid.

8, 6 : Someone with morbid pallor from phlegm presents effusion of phlegm, swelling, lassitude, inertia, an extreme degree of heaviness and a light colour of skin, urine, eyes and face.[22]

M :

Mention is made of the characteristics of that kind (which arises) from phlegm... Someone with morbid pallor from phlegm is additionally characterized by the light colour of his skin, urine, eyes and face.

8, 7 : Someone with morbid pallor by the three morbific entities, who is (moreover) attended by fever, anorexia, sickness, vomiting, thirst and weariness, who suffers from decline and whose senses have been damaged, should be abandoned.[23]

M :

It should be understood that (morbid pallor) by concerted action presents the very mentioned characteristics of (those kinds) arising from wind and the other (morbific entities), because there is an inherence (in the morbid alteration, the qualities of which are) congruous with the natural state. For it has been said in the Caraka(saṃhitā) : "Of someone who indulges in all (kinds of) food, all the morbific entities, having become corrupted, bring about morbid pallor, arising from the three morbific entities, provided with the signs of (each of the) three (morbific entities), and very difficult to endure" (Ci. 16, 26). Mention is made of the fact that this very (type) is incurable if it is accompanied by secondary affections.[24] 'Someone whose senses have been damaged' is someone whose senses are unable to grasp their own objects.

Ā :

Morbid pallor arising from the three morbific entities should be abandoned, which means that it is incurable if it is accompanied by these secondary affections.

8, 8-10 : In someone, who habitually eats earth, any one of the impurities becomes excited.
Astringent (earth) brings about excitement of the wind, salt-containing (earth excites) bile, and sweet (earth) phlegm (8).
On account of its dryness earth brings about dryness of the nutrient fluid and the other (elements of the body), and of the ingested food.
Being not digestively altered at all, it fills the channels and restrains them (9).
After damaging the strength of the senses, the fiery energy,

potency and vital fluid, it brings about morbid pallor that quickly annihilates (one's) force, colour and fire (10).

(Ca.Ci. 16, 27-29).[25]

M :

The onset of (morbid pallor) arising from (the eating of) earth is made mention of... 'Any one of the impurities' (denotes) wind and the other (morbific entities). 'Salt-containing' (earth designates earth) containing a caustic substance...[26] 'On account of its dryness', (i.e.) on account of the raised quality of dryness, belonging to its natural state. 'Being not digestively altered at all', (i.e.) not having reached maturation at all by the visceral fire and the fires of the elements (of the body);[27] 'it fills and restrains the channels', (i.e. those channels) carrying the nutrient fluid and the other (elements of the body). 'The strength of the senses' is the ability (of the senses) to grasp their own objects. 'Fiery energy' is brightness according to Jejjaṭa, and heat according to Cakra(pāṇidatta). 'Potency' (indicates here) the ability (to perform one's functions). 'Vital fluid' is 'that which, being the essential constituent of all the elements (of the body), stays in the heart', according to Parāśara, and it is 'the desire of overpowering others' according to Jejjaṭa.

Ā :

... 'Impure matter' (denotes) wind and the other (morbific entities)... The ground with respect to the excitation of the three morbific entities by earth is shown with the words 'astringent (earth)', etc. ... 'Salt-containing (earth)' is (earth) containing a caustic substance. ... 'Being not digestively altered at all' on account of the fact that the dry quality is raised, in agreement with its own nature. 'Force' is aptitude with (regard to the functions of) the body.

8, 11 : The prominent part of the eyes, the cheeks and the superciliary region (of a person, suffering from it), are swollen, the feet, umbilical region and penis are swollen, there are worms in the viscera, and one may be made to let flow down impure matter, accompanied by blood and attended by phlegm.

(Ca.Ci. 16, 30).[28]

M :

The characteristics of (morbid pallor) arising from earth are made mention of... Jejjaṭa says : "When in any (kind of) morbid pallor the viscera will contain worms, then the characteristics of this (condition will be present)." Others say that these are the characteristics of only this (kind of morbid pallor by earth), by reason of the fact that they are described immediately following upon the (description of the onset of morbid pallor) arising from earth.[29] In the (treatise by) Videha, however, one reads : "The patient suffering from morbid pallor from the eating of earth will be oppressed by lassitude and inertia; he will be attended by shortness of breath, cough, desiccation, haemorrhoids, adynamia and inability to eat; his feet, face and hands will be swollen, his body will be lean and his fire feeble."

8, 12-14ab : Morbid pallor which has been produced a long time ago and, owing to the length of time (elapsed), has become harsh, is not curable, and (when it occurs in) someone among those who are swollen,[30] who sees (all) things (endowed with a) yellow (colour, it is incurable as well) (12). Someone whose faeces are bound and of a slight amount, who is made to let flow (down faecal matter), accompanied by yellowish-green (matter) and phlegm, and someone who is dejected, whose body is (as) covered with a white plaster to an extreme degree and who is afflicted by vomiting, fainting and thirst (13), (a person of these two classes) will die, as well as someone suffering from morbid pallor who, on account of decline of the blood, acquires a white (colour).

(Ca.Ci. 16, 31-33ab).

8, 14c-f : Someone suffering from morbid pallor, whose teeth and nails will be pale, whose eyes will be pale and who sees the aggregates (of matter endowed with a) pale (colour), becomes annihilated.

(Su.U. 33, 23).

8, 15a-f : Someone suffering from morbid pallor whose extremities are swollen, whereas his trunk is deficient (in bulk), and someone whose extremities are shrunken, whereas his trunk is swollen, and someone whose anal region, penis and testicles are swollen, who is breathless and almost unconscious,[31] should be avoided by (a physician) wanting fame, as well as someone oppressed by diarrhoea and fever.

(Su.U. 44, 39-40).[32]

M:

The characteristics of incurability are made mention of... 'Morbid pallor which has been produced a long time ago and, owing to the length of time (elapsed), has become harsh, (i.e.) has become hard, is not curable; and someone suffering from morbid pallor which has not been produced a long time ago, who is among those swollen or who sees (all) things (endowed with a) yellow (colour), is not curable; that is another characteristic of incurability'. Thus is the construction of (this passage as applied by) Jejjaṭa. Cakra(pāṇidatta), however, says : '(Someone whose morbid pallor) has been produced a long time ago and (who) has become harsh, (i.e.) in whom all the elements (of the body) have become extremely dry, is not curable; and with the (passage), beginning with '(someone among those who), on account of the length of time (elapsed, are swollen)', another characteristic of incurability (is stated)'.[33] A variant of 'someone among those who are swollen' is : a swollen man.[34] The variant 'and someone with a swollen body who sees (all) things (endowed with a) yellow (colour)' is easy to understand.

The words beginning with '(someone whose faeces are) bound' (indicate) another (set of) characteristics of incurability. Also in this state, in which (the faeces) are accompanied by phlegm, their condition of being bound, of a slight amount and yellowish-green (arises) from the special faculty of the illness. A variant reads 'frequent (stools)' instead of 'bound and of a slight amount'. (A grammatical remark follows).

Another (set of) characteristics of incurability (is stated) by the words 'someone who is dejected', etc. 'Dejected' (is) languid. 'Someone whose body is (as) covered with a white plaster' means : someone whose body is as besmeared with a (substance of a) white colour. 'Such a person will die', (i.e.) is annihilated as it were; this means that he is incurable.

Another (characteristic of incurability) is made mention of by the words '(on account of decline of) the blood', etc. Another (set of) characteristics of incurability (again) is made mention of by the words 'someone whose teeth are pale', etc. 'Someone who sees the aggregates (of matter endowed with a) pale (colour)' (means that) one sees the bile, which has gone out (of the body) along with the rays from the eyes, lumped together.

Another (set of) characteristics of incurability is made mention of by the words '(someone who is swollen) at the extremities', etc. Someone whose 'extremities', i.e. whose arms, legs and head are swollen...;

'whose trunk is deficient (in bulk)', i.e. the middle part of whose body is weak.

Another (set of) characteristics of incurability is made mention of by (stating) the opposite condition... 'Shrunken' is weak. 'Almost unconscious' (means) well-nigh dead. Such a person suffering from morbid pallor should be avoided by a *vaidya* who wants fame.

'Someone suffering from *pālaki*' occurs as a variant of 'someone suffering from morbid pallor' in this stanza from the Suśruta(saṃhitā); the former (reading) is also suitable; if one reads (the stanza) in the (former) way, the characteristics of someone suffering from *pālaki*, which is a specific stage of morbid pallor, may be (regarded to be) stated as well. For in the Suśruta(saṃhitā) it has been said : "There exist, along with jaundice and the morbid pallor (called) *pālaki*, (the type) with the appellation *kumbha*, and *lāghavaka*, (also) called *alasa*" (U. 44, 6ab).[35] With this same intention someone versed in (this subject) has written : "Someone whose extremities are swollen and whose trunk is lean, someone who is (characterized by) the opposite (symptoms), someone whose anal region and penis are swollen and someone who is afflicted by fever and diarrhoea, is almost a dead person and suffers from *pālaki*." [36]

8, 16-18 : When someone suffering from morbid pallor indulges in bile-provoking (substances) to an extreme degree, the bile burns the blood and flesh of this person and favours the development of (further) disease (16).
Such a person's eyes, skin, nails and face are vehemently (coloured) turmeric-yellow, his faeces and urine are reddish-yellow,[37] he has the colour of a frog, his senses are in a damaged state (17) and he is made miserable by a burning sensation, absence of digestive alteration, weakness, adynamia and inability to eat. This (condition), provided with a great amount of bile, (is called) jaundice; it is thought to reside in the viscera or the branches (of the bodily system) (18).

(Ca.Ci. 16, 34-36).[38]

M :

Referring to the (fact that it is a particular) stage of morbid pallor, mention is made of jaundice... '(The bile) burns (the blood and flesh)' (means that it) corrupts (the blood and the flesh) completely. '(It favours the development) of disease' in the form of jaundice. 'He has the colour of a frog' (indicates that) he has the colour of the frog which appears in the early rainy season. 'It resides in the viscera or the branches (of the bodily system)' (means that) there is one (kind) residing in the viscera and another one residing in the branches (of the bodily system); the branches are blood and the other elements (of the body). Jaundice is an independent (disease), in the same way as consumption is an independent (disease), which also occurs in neglected (cases of) cough; thus it is said.[39]

Ā:

... 'Bile-provoking (substances)' are those which generate bile. ... The faeces and urine of such a person are red and yellow or, according to another reading, the faeces and eyes are red and yellow...

8, 19ab : Having become harsh after an interval of time, it will be difficult (to cure) and is called *kumbhakāmalā*.

(Ca.Ci. 16, 37ab).[40]

M:

Mention is made of another stage of this (disease, called) *kumbhakāmalā*... 'Having become harsh' should be explained as in the preceding instance...[41] '*kumbha*' [42] (indicates) the viscera because these possess the same peculiarity (as a jar, to wit) a porous interior; jaundice which resides there is (called) *kumbhakāmalā*; this means that it is (that type) residing in the viscera.[43]

Ā:

... 'Having become harsh' (means that) it has become hard.

8, 19cd-21ab : A human being, suffering from jaundice, quickly perishes when his faeces and urine are blackish-yellow, when he is vehemently swollen, his eyes, face, vomit, faeces and urine are red, and when he gasps for breath; when he is attended by a burning sensation, inability to eat, thirst, obstructive abdominal swelling, lassitude and (mental) confusion, and when his (transforming) fire and consciousness are annihilated.

(Ca.Ci. 16, 37cd-39ab).[44]

M :

Mention is made of the characteristics of incurability of jaundice... (The stanza) beginning with '(when)... (are) blackish(-yellow)' and ending with '(when) he gasps for breath', (describes) one (set of) characteristics (pointing) at incurability. 'He gasps for breath' (means that) he is (mentally) confused. (The stanza) beginning with '(attended by) a burning sensation' and ending with 'one perishes', (describes) another (set of) characteristics (pointing) at incurability; thus says Jejjaṭa.

Ā :

The vomit is also red...

8, 21cd-22ab : Someone suffering from *kumbhakāmalā*, who is oppressed by vomiting, anorexia, sickness, fever and weariness, who is afflicted by shortness of breath and cough, and whose faeces are loosened, (will) be annihilated.

M :

The characteristics of an incurable patient suffering from *kumbhakāmalā* are made mention of...

Ā :

Weariness is fatigue occurring without any exertion...

8, 22cd-23 : When, however, of someone suffering from morbid pallor, the colour will be yellowish-green, brown or yellow, and (there will be present) decline both of force and perseverance, lassitude, sluggishness of the (transforming) fire, a mild fever, absence of sexual feelings towards women, muscle pain, a burning sensation,[45] thirst, inability to eat and giddiness, one should know (the disease) of this person to be *halīmaka*, which (arises) from wind and bile. (Ca.Ci. 16, 132cd-134ab).[46]

Additional stanza : The person who presents a general sense of glowing heat, a loosened state of the excrements, a yellow colour of the exterior and the interior and pallor of the eyes, will be (someone provided with) the characteristics of *pānakī*.[47]

M :

Mention is made of *halīmaka* with reference to (its being) a stage of morbid pallor. When in a person, suffering from morbid pallor, presenting a yellowish-green colour, etc., these (mentioned) secondary affections occur, one should know (the disease) of that person to be *halīmaka*, arising from excitement of wind and bile. 'Yellowish-green' (means) : of the colour of potherbs. 'Brown' (means) : of a swarthy colour. ... 'Absence of sexual feelings towards women' is the absence of lasciviousness with regard to women. 'Muscle pain' is a crushing pain in the body. The characteristics of the specific stages of morbid pallor, (called) *lāghavaka*, *alasaka*, etc., should be remembered (as described) in the Suśruta(saṃhitā), etc.

NOTES

1 Cf. Su.U. 44, 4ab : "Morbid pallor is declared to be of four kinds, (arising) by (one morbific entity) separately and by the associated morbific entities simultaneously." Ḍa. remarks that some read 4a as follows : "Morbid pallor is of eight kinds;" according to that opinion morbid pallor by the consumption of earth, the two kinds of jaundice and *halīmaka* are counted as separate entities. Ḍa. adds that in another treatise it is said : "It may arise by means of wind, bile and phlegm; its source may (consist of) the three morbific entities and of the consumption of earth; there are two (kinds of) jaundice and one (kind of) *halīmaka*; in that way morbid pallor is of eight kinds in this world." (This stanza is, with some insignificant variants, also quoted by Cakra in his comment on Ca.Ci. 16, 34-39ab). Cf. A.h.Ni. 13, 7cd = A.s.Ni. 13, 9cd : "This (disease) is of five kinds, (viz. arising) by means of each morbific entity separately, by the associated (morbific entities) and from the eating of earth;" Hā. 3, 8, 1-2 : "Ātreya said : Listen, (my) son, I shall tell about morbid pallor, the great malady. Verily, there are five (kinds of) morbid pallor; these arise in human beings in this world. They are caused by wind, bile, phlegm and concerted action; a fifth (kind) is said to promote dryness. I shall tell about their source." Kā.Sū. 27, 53-54 makes mention of morbid pallor among those diseases which are of five kinds.

2 Cf. Cakra's comment on Ca.Ci. 16, 1-2 : "A disease, additionally characterized by a pale colour as the predominant one among the yellowish-green and other colours that will be mentioned, is (called) morbid pallor; for it has been said in the Suśruta(saṃhitā) : 'it is (called) morbid pallor for this very reason that a pale condition is present in excess in all these (morbid states)' (U. 44, 4cd)." See also A.h.Ni. 13, 3-4ab = A.s.Ni. 13, 5-6ab (Ki. 13, 4-5ab).

3 I have not been able to find this statement in Cakra's commentary on Ca.

4 See ch. 37.

5 I.e. in the Uttaratantra.

6 Cf. Aruṇa's comment on A.h.Ni. 13, 7cd : "One may object that it should not be stated that there is a separate (kind of) morbid pallor, (arising) from the eating of earth, because that (kind) which arises from wind, etc. separately, comprises the former (kind); for earth renders wind, etc. excited, as (substances which are) bitter, irritant, etc. do, and excitement of wind, etc. brings about morbid pallor; therefore it is not suitable to teach that a separate (kind caused) by (the eating of) earth exists. (As a reply) to this (objection) we say : those grounds of excitement of wind, etc., different from (the eating

of) earth, which are liable to assemble in contriving to bring about morbid pallor, turn away after contriving to bring about morbid pallor by means of (bringing into) existence the very symptoms of (these) grounds; earth, however, except (when treated) by sharp depurants, remains in the body as long as the morbid pallor. This is, with regard to morbid pallor by earth, the specific difference from the other grounds of excitement of wind, etc. Therefore it is right to speak about morbid pallor by earth (as a) separate (entity)." Ḍa remarks on Su.U. 44, 4ab : "Although (that kind of) morbid pallor which arises from earth is made mention of as a fifth (kind) in another treatise, it is nevertheless in this (treatise regarded to be) comprised by that very (kind) which arises from the three morbific entities, and (those kinds called) jaundice, etc., which will be mentioned (later on), are synonyms of morbid pallor itself; for that reason (there are said to be) only four (kinds) in this treatise."

[7] Su. : *vyavāya* (sexual intercourse) instead of *vyāyāma* (physical exercise).

[8] Su. : *vidūṣya* instead of *pradūṣya.*

[9] Su. : *kurvanti doṣās tvaci pāṇḍubhāvam* (the morbific entities bring about a pale condition with regard to the skin) instead of *doṣās tvacam pāṇḍuratāṃ nayanti* (the morbific entities convey pallor to the skin).

[10] Cf. Ca.Ci. 16, 4-6 : "In someone whose morbific entities, with bile as the predominant one, become excited in the elements (of the body), flaccidity of (these) elements and heaviness arise. Thereupon the colour, force, oleaginous matter and all the other qualifying constituents of the vital fluid reach an extreme state of decline, on account of the corruption of the corruptible constituents by the morbific entities. Such a man, possessing a slight amount of blood and fat, being devoid of the essential constituents (of the elements) and his senses being flaccid, is subject to alteration of the colour (of his skin). Listen to the grounds of this (condition), together with its characteristics;" Ca.Ci. 16, 7-12a : "When, roused by caustic, acid, saline and extremely hot (substances), by the ingestion of disagreeing and inadequate foods, the indulgence in *niṣpāva, māṣa* beans, *piṇyāka* and sesame oil, by sleeping by day, by physical exercise and sexual intercourse in a condition in which the food has been combustively altered, by incongruity of (therapeutic) counteractions and of the season, by restraining the (natural) urges and by a mind hurt by lust, anxiety, fear, wrath and grief, the bile which remains in the cardiac region reaches, hurled by the strong wind, the ten ducts, attains the whole body and becomes resident in the space between skin and flesh; it brings about corruption of phlegm, wind, blood, skin and flesh; this (bile) brings about pale, turmeric-yellow and yellowish-green colours of many kinds in the skin. This (condition) is called morbid pallor;" A.h.Ni. 13, 1-7ab = A.s.Ni. 13, 3-9ab (Ki. 13, 2-8ab) : "When, in a condition in which the impurities (= morbific entities) with bile as the predominant one are excited by means of those things leading to their excitement which have been made mention of, the bile residing in the cardiac region has been hurled by the strong wind and has reached the ten ducts, it pervades the whole body, brings about corruption of phlegm, skin, blood and flesh and resides in the space between the skin and the flesh; (then) this (bile) brings about manifold colours, pale, turmeric-yellow and yellowish-green, in the skin. By reason of the fact that pallor is present in excess among these (colours), this (condition) is called morbid pallor. With this (disease) there will occur heaviness and flaccidity of the elements (of the body) and decline of the qualities of the vital fluid. For these reasons (such) a man will possess a slight amount of blood and fat, he will be devoid of the essential constituents (of the elements) and his senses will be slack; together with the sensation that his limbs are squeezed and accompanied by

tachycardia, there occurs swelling of the region around his eyes, he suffers from adynamia, is liable to anger, spits out (saliva), speaks little and feels aversion to food and to coolness; his body-hair is withered, his fire is damaged and his hips are adynamic; he suffers from fever, shortness of breath, buzzing in the ears, giddiness and fatigue;" Hā. 3, 8, 3-5 : "This morbid pallor arises in a human being who makes long travels, is oppressed by fever, discharges blood, and is oppressed by inflamed sores; it arises from anxiety, exertion and restraint; it arises in someone indulging in caustic and acid (substances) and in *kalya* and *maireya*; it arises from lack of physical exercise, from sexual intercourse, extreme fatigue, insomnia, too much sleep and sleep by day, by these ways of conduct, and by the consumption of earth. A condition in which one's body has become flaccid by travelling or by being oppressed by disease, the indulgence in saline, pungent and astringent (substances), acid (substances), earth and the perpetual and excessive indulgence in extremely juicy (substances, these things) lead to desiccation of the blood, and by way of that (condition) morbid pallor (arises)."

11 Ḍa.'s remark is more correct : "Mention is made of (both) the grounds and the onset of morbid pallor."

12 The same remark is made by the author of Ā., who adds that Dṛḍhabala says so because Hārīta has declared it to be thus.

13 Ā. reads *vyavāya* (sexual intercourse) instead of *vyāyāma* (physical exercise), in agreement with Su.

14 Ā. connects *atīva* with all the preceding terms; Ḍa. connects it with *tīkṣṇa* (sharp) only.

15 Ḍa. remarks on Su.U. 44, 3 : "Sexual intercourse excites all the morbific entities, but others are of the opinion that it excites (only) wind and bile...; acid and saline (substances) give rise to bile and phlegm; earth excites all the morbific entities because it is of various kinds...; sleep by day excites the three morbific entities; a sharp (substance) excites the bile...; with regard to (the words) 'extremely sharp (substances)' the words 'and so on' should be considered to have been elided; flour, milk, *māṣa* beans, sesame seeds, etc. should be understood by these words."

16 Cf. Ca.Ci. 16, 12b-d : "Its signs, when it is imminent, are : cardiac palpitations, dryness, absence of perspiration and fatigue;" A.h.Ni. 13, 8-9a = A.s.Ni. 13, 10-11a (Ki. 13, 9-10a) : "Its prodromes are : cardiac palpitations, dryness of the skin, inability to eat, a yellow colour of the urine, absence of perspiration, a slight amount of fire, adynamia and fatigue;" Hā. 3, 8, 6 : "It gives rise to swelling of the region around the eyes, the body becomes pale, the urine is yellow, (the patient spits out (saliva) and his skin is torn asunder; (these signs) arise as its harbingers."

17 Ḍa. : idem.

18 Ḍa. : spitting out (saliva) is making (the sound) *thūt*.

19 Mādhava omits the generic characteristics of morbid pallor. These are described : Ca.Ci. 16, 13-16 : "When it has completely arisen, every (patient) suffering from whatever type of the disease), will present buzzing in the ears, a damaged state of the (transforming) fire, weakness, adynamia, aversion to food, oppression by fatigue and giddiness, piercing pain in the limbs, fever, shortness of breath, heaviness and inability to eat; his limbs feel as squeezed, subject to pressure and pounded; the region around his eyes is swollen, (his skin is of a) yellowish-green (colour), his body-hair is withered and the lustre (of his skin) damaged, he is liable to anger, feels aversion to coolness, is sleepy, spits out (saliva) and speaks little; there occur cramps in the calves and a painful

condition and adynamia of the iliac region, thighs and feet when he mounts an object and exerts himself (in other ways). The specific (grounds and symptoms) of it will be stated (now);" Kā.Sū. 25, 34 : "In morbid pallor there are present swelling at all sides around the navel, (a) white (colour of the) eyes, nails and mouth, adynamia of the (transforming) fire and swelling of the region around the eyes." Compare also A.h.Ni. 13, 5-7ab and its parallels (see note 10). Generic symptoms are not dealt with by Su. and Hā.

Compare with Mā.ni. 8, 4 : Ca.Ci. 16, 17-18 : "By means of foods and practices which are wind-provoking the excited wind generates blackness and pallor, a dry and ruddy condition of the body, muscle pain, a painful condition, pricking pain, trembling, pain in the sides and the head, desiccation of the excrements, an altered taste in the mouth, swelling, obstructive abdominal swelling and decline of (bodily) force;" Su.U. 44, 7 : "One should determine that morbid pallor (has been brought about) in a human being by wind if his eyes are black, black vessels cover his body as tied on to it, his faeces, urine, nails and face are of that (same) colour and he presents yet other (symptoms), as well as the secondary affections belonging to this (disorder);" A.h.Ni. 13, 9-10ab = A.s.Ni. 13, 11-12ab (Ki. 13, 10-11ab) : "With respect to this (morbid pallor) there are present, (when it arises) from wind, a painful condition of the limbs, pricking pain, trembling, a black, dry and ruddy condition of the vessels, nails, faeces, urine and eyes, swelling, obstructive abdominal swelling, an altered taste in the mouth, desiccation of the faeces and a painful condition of the sides and the head;" Hā. 3, 8, 7 : "(If there are present) pricking pain, roughness, heaviness of the head and a yellow colour of skin, urine, eyes and nails, know that (condition) of a human being to be of the nature of wind; provided with (these) signs is morbid pallor by wind."

20 Cf. Ca.Ci. 16, 19-22 : "When bile, in a person whose constitution is dominated by bile, has accumulated (and become excited) by its own excitants as they have been made mention of, and has corrupted the blood and the subsequent (elements, a condition is present) which favours the development of morbid pallor. The man (suffering from it has a) yellow (colour) or a yellowish-green hue, is attended by fever and a burning sensation, afflicted by fainting (brought about) by thirst, and by thirst, and his urine and faeces are yellow. He perspires, loves cold (things), is not delighted by food and has a pungent taste in his mouth; neither hot nor acid (substances) are therapeutically efficient in his case; there arise in him acid eructations and combustive alteration, after the food has been combustively altered; he presents a bad smell, loosened faeces, weakness and darkness (of vision);" Su.U. 44, 8 : "One should determine that morbid pallor in a human being (is brought about) by bile if his eyes are yellow, yellow vessels cover (his body) as tied on (to it), his faeces, urine, nails and face are of that (same) colour and he presents still other symptoms, as well as the secondary affections belonging to this (disorder);" A.h.Ni. 13, 10cd-11c = A.s.Ni. 13, 12cd-13c (Ki. 13, 11cd-12c) : "A condition in which the vessels, etc. are endowed with a yellowish-green or yellow hue, fever, darkness (of vision), thirst, perspiration, fainting, a desire for cold (things), a bad smell, a pungent taste in the mouth, loosening of faeces, acid eructations and a burning sensation (arise) from bile;" Hā. 3, 8, 8 : "Morbid pallor by bile brings about immaturity and yellowness; it carries (with it) in (this) world desiccation and a pungent taste in the mouth; there are (also) present swelling, thirst, a sluggish fever, mental confusion and a yellow skin."

21 The same argument is found in Cakra's comment on Ca.Ci. 16, 19-22; Cakra adds : "For this very reason, to show the extremely great strength of the bile, the constitution

dominated by bile is spoken of as a cause, and the constitutions dominated by wind and phlegm are not made mention of in such a way."

22 Cf. Ca.Ci. 16, 23-25 : "When phlegm has increased by means of phlegm-provoking (substances), it brings about morbid pallor in the way described above. Morbid pallor by phlegm (consists of) heaviness, lassitude, vomiting, a white hue, effusion, horripilation, adynamia, fainting, giddiness, weariness, shortness of breath, cough, inertia, inability to eat, seizing of the organ of speech and the voice, a light colour of urine, eyes and excrements, a craving for pungent, dry and hot (substances), swelling and a sweet taste in the mouth;" Su.U. 44, 9 : "One should determine that morbid pallor in a human being (is brought about) by phlegm if his eyes are of a light colour, vessels of a light colour cover (his body) as tied on to it, his faeces, urine, nails and face are of that (same) colour and he presents still other (symptoms) as well as the secondary affections belonging to this (disorder);" A.h.Ni. 13, 11d-12c = A.s.Ni. 13, 13d-14c (Ki. 13, 12d-13c) : "A light colour of the vessels, etc., lassitude, a saline taste in the mouth, horripilation, decline of the voice, cough and vomiting;" Hā. 3, 8, 9 : "When lassitude and swelling accompanied by coughing up of phlegm, inertia, perspiration and heaviness arise in someone, this morbid alteration productive of (morbid) pallor (should be known to be) of the nature of phlegm."

23 Ca.Ci. 16, 26 : "In someone who indulges in all (kinds of) food, all the morbific entities, having become corrupted, bring about morbid pallor arising from the three morbific entities, provided with the signs of (each of) the three morbific entities and very difficult to endure;" Su.U. 44, 10a : "One should determine (that) the whole (of the three sets of characteristics is present) in (morbid pallor) with the nature of all (three morbific entities);" A.h.Ni. 13, 12cd = A.s.Ni. 13, 14cd (Ki. 13, 13cd) : "From accumulation (i.e. concerted action) (a morbid pallor arises) with mixed signs, which is extremely difficult to endure;" Hā. 3, 8, 10 : "When there are present lassitude, inertia, swelling, emesis, cough, sickness, desiccation, loosening of faeces, rough eyes, fever, afflictedness by hunger, mental confusion and thirst, and when it is observed that a man becomes weary in a short time, *vaidyas* with an acute intelligence should keep far away from (such a patient with) morbid pallor springing up from concerted action."

24 Cf. Su.U. 44, 13 (describing the secondary affections of all kinds of morbid pallor, jaundice and *halīmaka* included) : "The secondary affections with regard to these (disorders) are : inability to eat, thirst, vomiting, fever, a painful condition of the head, adynamia of the fire, swelling, weakness of the throat, fainting, weariness and oppression of the cardiac region."

25 Compare A.h.Ni. 13, 13-14c = A.s.Ni. 13, 15-16c (Ki. 13, 14-15c), closely agreeing with Ca. Cf. Hā. 3, 8, 11-14 : "(My) son, listen (to me) : by the consumption of earth the great and very serious malady (called) morbid pallor may occur, which brings about decline of the elements (of the body). On account of this consumption of earth the channels become filled with earth, because the impure matter has been scattered. Therefore, (the channels) do not make the blood turn round and do not satiate the body with nutrient fluid. This earth quickly excites (the morbific entities) in a man owing to a caustic (quality), an astringent (taste), and owing to the drinking of (substances with a) sweet (taste). This earth brings about excited states of phlegm (of a) sweet (origin), and does not give rise to anything salutary when it is eaten. The three (morbific entities), wind, etc., bringing injury to the brightness (of one's skin) and strength, destroy one's prospect of remaining alive, when they have become morbidly altered; infirmity of one's body

arises in that way in morbid pallor, and the abdominal fire is eliminated by the consumption of earth."

[26] Cakra : with a caustic after-taste.

[27] Cakra : completely maintaining its own form; Aruṇa : earth is not subject to the maturative process on account of its heaviness, or *a-* (in : *apakva*) means here : somewhat (maturated).

[28] Cf. A.h.Ni. 13, 14cd-15ab = A.s.Ni. 13, 16cd-17ab (Ki. 13, 15cd-16ab) : "Owing to this (morbid pallor) a man, with swollen umbilical region, feet, mouth and penis, releases loosened faecal matter that contains worms and is accompanied by blood and phlegm."

[29] According to Cakra, Aruṇa and Śrīdāsa the characteristics of morbid pallor arising from the eating of earth are described.

[30] Ca. : *śūno nā yaś ca* instead of *śūnānāṃ yo vā*.

[31] Su. : *muṣkaśūnaṃ pratāmyamānaṃ ca visaṃjñakalpam* instead of *muṣkayoś ca śūnaṃ pratāmyantam asaṃjñakalpam*.

[32] Cf. A.h.Śā. 5, 91cd = A.s.Śā. 11, 24ab : "Morbid pallor, when it is accompanied by swelling, (kills) one whose eyes, nails and vision (i.e. visible objects) are yellow;" Hā. 2, 4, 23-24 : "A human being whose teeth and nails are pale, whose eyes are pale, and certainly a sufferer from morbid pallor who (sees) the aggregates (of matter endowed with a) pale (colour), is annihilated. Someone whose skin and eyes are pale, or someone whose urine becomes pale, and certainly someone who (sees) the aggregates (of matter endowed with a) pale (colour) is annihilated."

[33] The printed text of Cakra's comment runs : "Having become harsh (means) : being extremely dry; by the (passage), beginning with '(on account of the length of) time', another characteristic of incurability (is expressed)."

[34] See note 30.

[35] A variant of *lāghavaka* is : *lāgharaka*. Ḍa. remarks that the names mentioned at U. 44, 6ab are synonyms of morbid pallor itself.

[36] This is a quotation from an unknown source.

[37] This may also be translated : red or yellow; another possible meaning is : the faeces are red and the urine is yellow.

[38] Cf. Su.U. 44, 10-11b : "Now I shall tell about the signs of jaundice : the bile of a person, who, when an ailment is (already) present, eats acid food inconsiderately and unwholesome (foods in general), specifically brings about pallor of the face and, set in motion by the other (morbific entities), lassitude and decline of (one's) force;" A.h.Ni. 13, 15cd-17 = A.s.Ni. 13, 17cd-19 (Ki. 13, 16cd-18) : "The bile of that person, suffering from morbid pallor, who indulges in bile-provoking (substances), may conduce, after burning the blood and the flesh, to jaundice, residing in the viscera or the branches (of the bodily system). By this (disease) one's eyes, urine, skin, nails, face and faeces become turmeric-yellow; one presents a burning sensation, absence of digestive alteration and thirst, one is provided with the hue of a frog and one's senses are weak. This (disease) may also occur in the absence of morbid pallor in a person with an abundance of bile;" Kā.Sū. 25, 35 : "The eyes, nails, face, faeces and urine of someone tormented by jaundice are yellow. In both (morbid pallor and jaundice the patient is) devoid of perseverance and his (transforming) fire, blood and eagerness (for food) are annihilated."

[39] Cakra comments on Ca.Ci. 16, 34-36 (= Mā.ni. 8, 16-18) : "According to the words 'someone suffering from morbid pallor', etc., stages of this same morbid pallor, occurring in the form of jaundice, etc., are produced by specific grounds. For that very reason it

has been said in the Hārīta(saṃhitā) that jaundice, etc. are also certainly states of morbid pallor; it says : "(It occurs) by wind, bile and phlegm, its source consists of the three morbific entities and the consumption of earth; there are two (kinds of) jaundice and there is also *halīmaka*; according to this (division) morbid pallor is traditionally said to be of eight kinds." Another (kind of) jaundice, described by Suśruta, is (a) distinct (entity); a separate ground of jaundice is stated with the words... (Su.U. 44, 10cd-11ab is quoted; see preceding note). And Vāgbhaṭa says... (A.h.Ni. 13, 17cd is quoted; see preceding note). According to this (statement jaundice) may occur both in the presence and in the absence of morbid pallor; in the same way as boils occur in urinary disorders, dependent on (these) urinary disorders, and as well in the absence of a urinary disorder, in that way jaundice occurs in someone suffering from morbid pallor, and (as a) separate (entity) as well. That (kind of jaundice), which resides in the viscera and the branches (of the bodily system) and is provided with a great amount of bile, is preceded by morbid pallor, but that (kind), which only resides in the branches and should be designated as provided with a slight amount of bile, also occurs independently; thus some say. For that reason its grounds and signs will be stated separately, with the words '(by) dry and cold (substances)' (Ci. 16, 125c), in the remaining part of the chapter." Very important with respect to these statements by Cakra is Ca.Ci. 16, 124cd-128ab (= A.h.Ci. 16, 45-48 = A.s.Ci. 18, 29-31) : "When someone suffering from jaundice emits excrements which resemble ground sesame seeds, one should subdue this (condition) by means of phlegm-eliminating (procedures because) the pathway of bile has been obstructed by phlegm. The wind, coalesced with phlegm and grown powerful by dry, heavy and dainty (substances), by physical exercises and by suppression of the (natural) urges, will hurl the bile from its seat. Then a man's eyes, urine and skin will be turmeric-yellow, his excrements will be white, he will present (abdominal) distension and a constrained condition (of the impurities); heaviness of the cardiac region, weakness, a condition in which the (transforming) fire is of a slight amount, affliction of the sides (of the chest), hiccup, shortness of breath, inability to eat and fever will gradually cling to him, when the bile, being of a slight amount, resides in the branches (of the bodily system)."

40 Cf. Su.U. 44, 11cd : "A distinct (kind) of this (jaundice) is that one with the appellation *kumbha*; a great (degree of) swelling and a cutting pain in the junctures (are present) in it;" A.h.Ni. 13, 18ab = A.s.Ni. 13, 20ab (Ki. 13, 19ab) : "By neglect (it becomes) richly endowed with swelling; this (disease), which is difficult (to cure, is called) *kumbhakāmalā*."

41 Cakra says it means : having become indurate.

42 *kumbha* means a jar. Another explanation of the name *kumbhakāmalā* may be that in this disease the belly is swollen to a great degree, like a pot; so the term may mean : pot-bellied jaundice.

43 Cakra : *kumbhakāmalā* is the technical term (denoting), by means of a distinction in accordance with its stage, (that kind of) jaundice, which stays in the viscera, (for) *kumbha* (means) viscera.

44 Cf. Hā. 2, 4, 38 : "That man afflicted by jaundice and (or) morbid pallor, who presents swelling, shortness of breath, thirst and piercing pain, perishes."

45 Ca. : *śvāsa* (shortness of breath) instead of *dāha* (a burning sensation).

46 Cf. Su.U. 44, 12 : "(When this jaundice with the appellation *kumbha* is) attended by fever, muscle pain, giddiness, adynamia, lassitude and decline, it is (called) *lāgharaka*, which has (also) the name *alasa*. (When) it is (accompanied by) a yellowish-green, yellow or swarthy (colour), those possessing knowledge about it call it *halīmaka*;" A.h.Ni. 13,

18cd-20a = A.s.Ni. 13, 20cd-22a (Ki. 13, 19cd-21a) : "When there comes to be present a yellowish-green, brown or yellow colour in morbid pallor (arising) from wind and bile, (and moreover) giddiness, thirst, absence of sexual feelings towards women, a mild fever, lassitude and subsidence of one's force and (transforming) fire, this (disorder) is declared (to be called) *loḍhara, halīmaka* and *alasa*."

[47] A closely related stanza is quoted by Ḍa. in his comment on Su.U. 44, 12 : "A general sense of glowing heat, a loosened state of the excrements, a yellow colour of the exterior and the interior, pallor and disease of the eyes may be said to be the characteristics of *pānakī*;" the same stanza is quoted by Cakra in his comment on Ca.Ci. 16, 132cd-133 (*pīnatā*, i.e. plumpness, instead of *pītatā*, i.e. a yellow colour).

CHAPTER NINE

BLOOD-BILE (*RAKTAPITTA*)

9, 1 : (When) by extreme indulgence in warmth, physical exercise, grief, travelling and sexual intercourse, by sharp, hot, caustic, saline, acid and certainly by pungent (substances),[1]

9, 2 : the bile has become combustively altered, it quickly combustively alters, by means of its own qualities, the blood. Thereupon blood comes forth, upwards, downwards or in both (directions).

(Su.U. 45, 4cd-5ab).[2]

9, 3 : Being excited, it comes forth from the nose, eyes, ears and mouth upwards, from the penis, vagina and anus downwards, and from all the pores (of the skin) in which the hairs are seated.

(A.h.Ni. 3, 7cd-8ab).[3]

M :

Blood-bile is made mention of, immediately after morbid pallor, on account of the fact that the former is, like the latter, occasioned by bile... 'Sharp' (means) possessed of a sharp potency, (like) *marica*, etc.; 'hot' (means) the glowing heat of a fire; 'caustic' (substances are) *yavakṣāra*, etc., and those made from *ghaṇṭāpāṭali*, etc.; 'combustively altered' is : excited. 'By means of its own qualities', (i.e.) by those (qualities) mentioned in the statement : "Bile is sharp, liquid, foul-smelling," etc. (Su.Sū. 21, 11a). 'It alters combustively', (i.e.) it brings about excitement by means of the very qualities of itself, according to the saying : "Its combustive alteration (is of the same character) as that of bile" (Su.Sū. 21, 17d). 'Thereupon (blood) comes forth', (i.e.) bile and blood in the form of elements flow out, and not only blood, because (otherwise) the designation (of it as) blood-bile would be irrelevant. And when blood corrupted by bile is called blood-bile, one may (also) cling to the designation (of it as) bile-blood; by way of this (reasoning) Suśruta has said that its explanation is : both blood and bile, in agreement with the compounds of the *dvandva* (type).

Now it may be objected that it has been said in the Caraka(saṃhitā) : "Bile that has reached redness is (called) blood-bile;" by way of this (reasoning) its explanation has been said to be : both blood and this (red) bile, in agreement with the compounds of the *karmadhāraya* (type); a triad of causes has been stated with respect to this, with the words : "On account of its commixture with and corrupting of blood and its generic similarity with it as to smell and colour, bile is called blood-bile (in this case) by thoughtful (physicians)" (Ca.Ci. 4, 9).

How is it possible that there is no contradiction if things are like that?

(The answer is) : There is no contradiction in it, because in this case also blood is coming forth; for when the blood, being corrupted and depositing its redness in the bile, combines with (the latter), blood itself comes forth as well; in this way the same meaning as that mentioned above (is reached).

By way of this (reasoning) there is no fault in both ways of stating the explanation (of the term blood-bile) : blood-bile (means) both blood and bile, (and) blood-bile (means) both blood and this (red) bile.[4]

Ā :

... 'Hot' (means) made glowingly hot by fire, or a substance (provided) with the quality hot. 'Caustic (substances)' are *yavakṣāra*, etc., and those made from *apāmārga*, etc... (When it is) extremely excited (it comes forth) from both pathways, the upper and lower one, and from all the holes (of the skin) in which the hairs (are seated).

9, 4 : Adynamia, a state of craving for cold (substances), (a smell of) smoking (matter) in the throat, emesis and an exhalation smelling of iron are present when it is imminent.

(Su.U. 45, 7cd-8ab).[5]

M :

... '(A smell of) smoking (matter) in the throat' is the acknowledgment that smoke as it were comes out of the throat.

Ā :

... 'An exhalation smelling of iron' (means that there is) a smell with regard to one's breath as of iron, (the fire for which) is being blown.

9, 5ab : Attended by phlegm it is viscid, somewhat pale, somewhat oleaginous, and mucilaginous.

(Ca.Ci. 4, 11ab).

M:

... 'Viscid' is dense...

9, 5cd : (Arisen) from wind it is (of a) brown and ruddy (colour), attended by some foam, thin and dry.

(Ca.Ci. 4, 11cd).

M:

... 'Thin' is not dense.

9, 6-7ab : Blood-bile has a yellowish-red hue, is black, resembles the urine of a cow, has a hue as that of the eyes of a peacock's tail, of *āgāradhūma* [6] and of a collyrium, (when arisen) by bile (6).

(Arisen) from a combination (of morbific entities) it has combined signs; it has the signs of the three (morbific entities when arisen) from concerted action.

(Ca.Ci. 4, 12-13ab).[7]

M:

Mention is made of that (kind arisen) from bile... 'With a yellowish-red hue' is : with the colour of a *kvātha* (made) from *vaṭa*, etc.

... 'The colour of the eyes of a peacock's tail' (indicates) a colour as that of a polished black gem; thus Jejjaṭa and others say; this means : unctuous and black. 'With the hue of a collyrium' (means) with the hue and colour of the collyrium (called) *sauvīra*.[8]

Is it not right to ask why (a particular kind of) blood-bile (arising) from bile is made mention of, if really every (kind of) blood-bile is started by corrupted bile?

The answer (to this question) is : this is right, but it is designated as (arisen) from bile when bile, staying in its own seat and starting blood-bile, is taken hold of by bile that is lodged in another seat, or when bile alone, not being closely connected with another morbific entity, is the starting (agent).

To this it may be objected that (a kind of blood-bile arising) from bile alone does not arise at all, because he (i.e. Mādhava) will say (presently) : "(That one) going upwards is combined with phlegm and (that one) going downwards is attended by wind" (9, 7ab); a pathway of that (kind, arisen from bile), has not been defined.

The answer (to this objection) is : when (blood-bile) has become combined with phlegm or wind, which have become perceptible (by increase) due to their own causes, and which are bringing about their own characteristics, it is designated as (arising) from phlegm, etc., but not (in the case that it has become combined) by means of a relationship to phlegm or wind which is attended by a relationship with regard to its pathway. For that kind which is going upwards is necessarily attended by phlegm as an adjunctory factor by reason of the great power of the relationship regarding the pathway, and that kind which is going downwards (is attended) by wind. And phlegm and wind do not bring about their characteristics in that case, (in the same way) as in the following instance : though bile brings about fever in the autumn, attended by the adjunctory factor phlegm which is attended by the great power of the season, that (type of) fever, being of a natural kind, is nevertheless (called) bilious, as has been said : "And bile may bring about (fever) in the autumn, with phlegm as its auxiliary force" (A.h.Ni. 2, 51cd).

By way of this (reasoning it is thus, that) that (kind of blood-bile) which is accompanied by the signs of one morbific entity is attended by one morbific entity; in the same way it should be understood with regard to (those kinds) accompanied by the signs of two or three morbific entities. Therefore both that kind going upwards and that one going downwards (may be endowed) with the signs of one, two or three morbific entities. By means of this (reasoning), (viz.) that the pathway of (blood-bile arising) from bile has not been shown, that which was said (as an objection) is excluded.[9]

Ā :

'The colour of the eyes of a peacock's tail' is like the colour of the black colouring-stuff used in dyeing garments, made shining by means of a gem coloured with black streaks; thus Jejjaṭa and others say; this means : unctuous and black...

9, 7c-f : The upwards going (type) is combined with phlegm, the downwards going one attended by wind, and that one (using) both pathways attended [10] by both phlegm and wind.

(Ca.Ci. 4, 24).[11]

M :

Mention is made of its distinctive pathways according to its specific (kinds of) combination...

Ā :

... In this (statement) a (specific) pathway of the (type) by bile is not shown by reason of the very predominance of blood-bile in (this) disease.

9, 8ab : (That type going) upwards is curable, the downwards (going type) is mitigable, and (that type) going simultaneously (in both directions) is incurable.

(Su.U. 45, 7ab).[12]

M :

Mention is made of its curability, etc. according to its distinctive pathways... (With regard to the words) '(that type going) upwards is curable' (we remark that substances with) an astringent and bitter taste, which eliminate phlegm and bile, can be applied, because the upwards going (blood-bile) is closely connected with phlegm and wind; as the predominant (means) in eliminating the bile, however, purgative procedures should be applied. In the downwards going (type), however, (substances with) only one (taste, viz.) a sweet (taste), appease the wind and the bile, and emetic procedures only disagree with the impulse (of the downward motion) because they are acting in a contrary direction, but they do not eliminate the bile. And (that kind going) along both pathways is incurable for the very reason that the (two kinds of) treatment are irreconcilable. As has been said in the Caraka-(saṃhitā) : "That (kind of) blood-bile which reaches the upper (pathway) is curable because of the fact that purgative procedures can be applied [13] and because there are many remedies; purgative procedures, however, are the superior remedial agents for subduing the bile" (Ni. 2, 12-13ab), etc.[14]

9, 8cd-9ab : Blood-bile may be curable when it (affects only) one pathway, (occurs) in a strong person, its impetus is not extreme, has sprung up recently, (comes about) in a favourable (period of) time and is devoid of secondary affections.

(Ca.Ci. 4, 22).[15]

M :

The ground of curability is made mention of... (With the words) '(affecting only) one pathway' the upward going (type) is intended because the downward going (type) is (merely) mitigable. ... 'In a favourable (period of) time' (means) in the winter and the cool season...

9, 9cd-10 : (Blood-bile), attended by one morbific entity, is said to be curable, and that one with two morbific entities mitigable (9); that one with three morbific entities will be incurable, as well as (blood-bile) with an extreme impetus, occurring in a person with a sluggish (transforming) fire, someone whose body has undergone decline due to illnesses, someone who has increased (in size by swelling) and someone who does not take food (10).

(Ca.Ci. 4, 13cd-14).[16]

M :

Mention is made of (its) curability, etc. by way of the distinctions (made) according to the morbific entities (attending it)... The disagreements between curability and incurability, according as there are made distinctions concerning the pathways or the morbific entities, should be explained in the same way as (the disagreements between) curability and incurability according to the distinctions concerning the morbific entities and the folds (of the anal region) in (the case of) haemorrhoids.

... 'In a person who does not take food', i.e. by reason of the inability to eat, etc., or due to the absence of food.

9, 11 : Weakness, shortness of breath, cough, fever, emesis and (mental disturbance as in) intoxication, pallor,[17] a burning sensation and fainting, a dreadful combustive alteration of the ingested (food),[18] lack of self-control and a constantly present unequalled oppressing pain in the cardiac region, thirst, loosening (of the contents) of the viscera,[19] a sensation of glowing heat [20] in the head, a condition in which foul-smelling matter is spitted out, aversion to food and absence of digestive alteration, as well as a deviated state [21] (of blood-bile), may occur (as) additional affections in blood-bile.

(Su.U. 45, 9).[22]

M :

... 'Weakness' is, according to Gayadāsa, absence of ability and stoutness. (A grammatical remark follows)... (With regard to) 'a strained (feeling in the) head' as a variant (of 'a sensation of glowing heat in the head' we remark that a) strained (feeling means a sensation) as when (the head) is being stretched; Kārtika(kuṇḍa) says (it means that) one has a painful sensation spread out over (the whole of) the head; the variant 'a strained condition of the vessels' (means that the surface of) the body is covered by vessels [23]... These are the additional, (i.e.) the secondary, affections of blood-bile; a deviated state of it may occur as well; thus (this part of the sentence) should be construed.[24] And this (deviated state) may occur in the form of (blood-bile), to be mentioned presently, with the hue of water in which flesh has been rinsed, etc. The variant '(all these conditions may arise) owing to additional affections of blood-bile' is easy to understand.

Ā:

... 'A condition in which foul-smelling matter is spitted out' is the eructation of bilious matter.

9, 12 : If it has the hue of water in which flesh has been rinsed, if it is like stinking [25] matter or muddy water, if it resembles fat, purulent matter, blood or liver-tissue, or if it has the hue of a ripe *jambū* fruit, in case it is (of a) very black or swarthy (colour), or smelling like a decayed corpse, and in the case that the mentioned morbid alterations are present, (all) these (cases of) blood-bile should be avoided, as well as that (case in which it) shines forth like the bow of the Lord of the gods. (Su.U. 45, 10).[26]

9, 13 : That (kind of) blood-bile by which a human being, when suffering injury from it, will see the objects of vision, and also the atmosphere, (endowed with a) red (colour), is without any doubt incurable. (Ca.Ni. 2, 26).

9, 14 : A person suffering from blood-bile who will vomit blood many times, whose eyes are red, whose eructations are red and who sees (the visible objects endowed with a) red (colour) will die.[27] (Su.Sū. 33, 24).[28]

M:

The characteristics of incurability are made mention of... 'Resembling muddy water', i.e. (resembling) turbid water, or (it means) resembling mud and resembling water...[29] 'Having the hue of a ripe *jambū* fruit' (means) : in an oleaginous way black. 'Black' (means) endowed with the hue of a collyrium. 'Swarthy' (means) similar to the (colour of the) wings of a *cāṣa* (bird).

Is it not right to state that in (blood-bile arising) from bile the presence of a black colour has been described and not at all that this (condition) is incurable?

It is not thus, because in this case the specified character (of its blackness has been expressed) by the words '(present) to an extreme degree': "it indicates in this case blackness present to a small degree" says Jejjaṭa; or one should construe (this passage as follows): that blackness which has the hue of a ripe *jambū* fruit. 'The mentioned morbid alterations' are shortness of breath, cough, etc.[30] 'Like the bow of the Lord of the gods' [31] (means: endowed) with various colours. ... 'One will see even the atmosphere as a visible object', (i.e.) one sees, though it is invisible, the atmosphere as a visible object; thus (this passage) should be construed, because the eyes have suffered injury from blood-bile; or (it means) one sees visible objects, (viz.) a jar, a cloth, etc., and (also) the atmosphere, (endowed with a) red (colour).[32]... 'Someone whose eructations are red and who sees (the visible objects endowed with a) red (colour)' may also mean: someone who sees that his eructations are red.[33]

NOTES

1 Cf. Su.U. 45, 3-4ab: "Owing to wrath, grief, fear, exertion, disagreeing food, glowing heat (of the sun) and (the heat of a) fire, and when someone permanently practises (the eating of) pungent, acid, saline, caustic, sharp and hot (substances) and those bringing about an extreme combustive alteration, the nutrient fluid is corrupted and excites the bile."

2 Cf. Ca.Ni. 2, 1-5: "And now we shall expound the origins of blood-bile; thus said the venerable Ātreya. We shall expound that condition in which the bile acquires the technical appellation blood-bile. When a creature ingests food, which mainly consists of *yavaka, uddālaka* or *koradūṣa*, and also (when ingesting) other kinds of food, (viz. those which are) violently hot and sharp, (all these when they are used) in combination with a soup (made from) *niṣpāva, māṣa* beans, *kulattha* or with a caustic substance, or food prepared by pouring upon it thick sour milk, whey, buttermilk diluted with an equal part of water (*udaśvit*), buttermilk to which no water has been added (*kaṭvara*), acid (buttermilk) or fermented rice-water (*kāñjika*), or flesh of a boar, buffalo, sheep, fish or cow in combination with *piṇyāka, piṇḍālu* and dried potherbs or relishes (prepared) from *mūlaka, sarṣapa, laśuna, karañja, śigru, madhuśigru*, (*khaḍayūṣa*), *bhūstṛṇa, sumukha, surasa, kuṭheraka, gaṇḍīra, kālamālaka, parṇāsa, kṣavaka* and *phaṇijjhaka*, or postprandial potions mainly consisting of *surā, sauvīra, tuṣodaka, maireya, medaka* and *madhūlaka*, verjuice and (other) acid (postprandial potions prepared) from *kuvala* or *badara* (fruits), or (dishes eaten) at the end (of a meal) which chiefly consist of articles

of food made from flour, or when one, being hot with glowing heat, drinks unboiled milk beyond the (proper) measure or beyond the (proper) time-limit, or when one eats *rauhiṇīka* or a *kāṇa* pigeon dressed with *sarṣapa* oil or a caustic substance, or when one, being hot with glowing heat, drinks milk together with *kulattha*, *piṇyāka*, *jambu* and *lakuca* (fruits) which have been boiled, or together with dishes prepared with verjuice, when one behaves in such a manner, one's bile enters into a state of excitement and one's blood exceeds its own measure. When this (blood) has exceeded its measure, the excited bile spreads through the body, approaches the openings, which are heavy with the effluxion of blood, of the blood-carrying channels originating from the liver and the spleen, and (the bile) may become checked; this same (bile) corrupts the blood. On account of (this) combination, (this) bringing about of a corrupt condition of the blood, and the fact that its smell and colour are consistent with those of blood, (this condition of the) bile is called blood-bile;" Ca.Ci. 4, 5-10 : "One who knows its grounds and characteristics should speedily treat the great malady which has a great impetus and acts as quickly as fire, (viz.) blood-bile. Its grounds, (consisting of) hot, sharp, acid, pungent and saline (substances), as well as warmth and combustive alteration of the food, have already been shown. The bile, made very uneasy by these grounds, attains the blood and, after attaining it, increases; it corrupts this (blood) because (blood) is its matrix. By means of the heat of this (bile), liquid (parts of the) element(s of the body) effuse from one perspiring element after another; by means of this (process the bile) increases considerably. This bile, on account of its commixture with and corrupting of the blood and the generic similarity of its smell and colour to that of blood, is called blood-bile by thoughtful (physicians);" A.h.Ni. 3, 1-4ab = A.s.Ni. 3, 3-6ab (Ki. 3, 2-5ab) : "By violently hot, sharp, pungent, acid, saline (substances), etc., by those bringing about combustive alteration, by extreme indulgence in *kodrava*, *uddālaka* and foods accompanied by these, by (these and other) bile-provoking (substances) excited, the liquid bile and the blood, having coalesced, acquire a mutually comparable form and pervade the body. The bile is (in this case), owing to the morbidly altered state of the blood (it has caused), its combination with and corruption of the blood and its conformity with it as to smell and colour, designated together with the blood. It springs up from the seat of blood, (i.e.) the spleen and the liver;" Bhe.Ci. 3, 2-4ab : "Owing to food that is extremely acid and saline, owing to continuous indulgence in the glowing heat (of the sun), owing to fasting, giddiness, terror, eating of disagreeing (foods), etc., indulgence in sesame, *piṇyāka*, potherbs, (food) prepared from flour, all (kinds of) bile-provoking (substances), fish, etc., the bile, coursing upwards and downwards, comes forth (as) blood-bile;" Hā. 3, 10, 1-2 : "By an extreme degree of warmth, owing to indulgence in sharp, hot, pungent, caustic or acid (substances), indulgence in the drinking of intoxicating beverages, etc., on account of too much physical exercise, by cold (substances) and on account of indulgence (in the eating of) dried potherbs, by (all) these (factors) the bile is excited and coalesces with the blood;" Hā. 3, 10, 6ab-8 : "The blood becomes excited by those very (origins) by which bile is excited. As long as a state of excitement is present in the viscera, the wind tears asunder vehemently. The (wind called) *prāṇa* conveys in an upward direction, the (wind called) *apāna* sets in motion (towards) the region of the *apāna* (i.e. the anal region); in the middle (part of the body the wind called) *samāna* brings about an excited state of blood-bile. Thus the bile becomes excited along with the blood, (both) simultaneously."

3 Cf. Ca.Ni. 2, 8 : "It has two pathways, (one) upwards and (one) downwards. It finds

egress through the ears, nose, eyes and mouth when it reaches, on account of its combination with phlegm in a body with a copious (amount of) phlegm, the upper (pathway); it finds egress through the pathways of urine and faeces when it reaches, on account of its combination with wind in a body with a copious (amount of) wind, the lower (pathway); in a body with a copious (amount of both) phlegm and wind it reaches, on account of its combination with phlegm and wind, both pathways; reaching both these pathways it finds egress through really all the apertures of the body mentioned above;" Su.U. 45, 5cd-6 : "From the receptacle of undigested food it may go upwards, from the receptacle of digested food downwards. When both (these receptacles) are combustively altered it proceeds to both (the upper and lower) part. Some proclaim that the blood comes forth from the spleen and the liver."

4 In his comment on Ca.Ni. 2, 5 Cakra makes mention of three explanations of the term blood-bile : a) blood-bile is bile joined to blood (*raktayuktaṃ pittam*); b) it is bile with regard to blood as the object of corruption (*rakte dūṣye pittam*); c) it is bile possessed of blood (*raktavat pittam*).

5 Cf. Ca.Ni. 2, 6 : "The following prodromes occur in it : absence of the relish for food, combustive alteration of the ingested (food), eructations with the smell of fermented matter and with an acid taste, a repeatedly approaching (urge to) vomit, loathing for that which has been vomited, inarticulateness of the voice, adynamia of the limbs, a general burning sensation, a sensation as if smoke is coming out of the mouth, a sensation as if the mouth is smelling of iron, blood, fish or raw meat, a red, yellowish-green or turmeric-yellow condition of the component parts of the body, of the faeces, urine, sweat and saliva, of the secretions of the nose (*siṅghāṇaka*), the impure matter of mouth and ears, the secretions of the eyes (*piḍakolikā*) and (the impure matter of) boils, a painful sensation of the (whole) body and the repeated vision of red, swarthy, yellow, brown and resplendent forms in one's dreams; these are the prodromes of blood-bile;" A.h.Ni. 3, 4cd-7ab = A.s.Ni. 3, 6cd-9ab (Ki. 3, 6-8) : "Heaviness of the head, inability to eat, a desire for cold (substances), the eructation of matter smelling like smoke and of acid matter, vomiting, loathing for that which has been vomited, cough, shortness of breath, giddiness, weariness, a smell of iron, blood, fish and raw meat in the mouth, decline of the voice, a red, turmeric-yellow and yellowish-green colour of the eyes, etc., the inability to distinguish swarthy, red and yellow colours and the seeing of (objects endowed with) these colours in one's dreams occur in it when it is imminent."

6 PW and MW : name of a plant; Kaviratna : domestic soot; Gul : smoke; the term probably designates soot.

7 Cf. Su.U. 45, 8cd : "The number (of types of blood-bile) and (the intensity of) the surge of the morbific entities in it are known by means of the characteristics of blood (that has gone) out of the body." (This refers to Su.Sū. 14, 21 : "Corrupted by wind, (blood is) frothy, ruddy, black, rough, thin, quickly coursing and non-coagulating; corrupted by bile it is swarthy, yellow, yellowish-green, brown, musty-smelling, undesirable to ants and flies and non-coagulating; corrupted by phlegm it resembles *gairika*-water, is oleaginous, cold, thick, mucilaginous, slowly discharging and endowed with the lustre of flesh and muscles; corrupted by concerted action it is provided with the characteristics of all (the morbific entities), resembles fermented rice-water (*kāñjika*) and is especially bad-smelling; (corrupted) by a combination (of two morbific entities) it is provided with the signs of two morbific entities"); A.h.Ni. 3, 16ab = A.s.Ni. 3, 18ab (Ki. 3, 17ab) : "In this (disease) one should characterize the morbific entity attending it as if (one were dealing with a case of) blood (coming out) of a vessel;" Bhe.Ci. 3, 4cd-7 :

"One voids from the nose, ears, eyes, mouth, anus and penis (bile) accompanied by blood that is bitter and also acid. (If) fallen on the ground, it is not consumed by ants or flies, because it is bitter. Desiccated bile is characterized (by the following symptoms) : one's throat feels intensely burning and (as) consumed by fire and one's palate desiccates. (When blood-bile occurs) in the lower half (of the trunk), it is characterized by these (following) symptoms : there is a smell (like that) of iron in one's mouth and (the smell of) smoking matter in one's throat;" Hā. 3, 10, 20 (a corrupt stanza that may be rendered as follows) : "(If blood-bile is) ruddy and frothy, (it arises) from wind; (if it is) extremely black by bile, yellow or endowed with the hue of *kusumbhaka* (i.e. carmine-coloured), intelligent (physicians) proclaim (that) it (has arisen) by bile; (if it is) viscid, arising with an extremely pale colour and dense, (it arises) by phlegm."

[8] *sauvīra* : stibnite = antimony trisulphide, Sb_2S_3, or : galena = lead sulphide, PbS. See C. Vogel : A.h., p. 85.

[9] Cf. Cakra's comment on Ca.Ci. 4, 11-13ab : " 'With a yellowish-red hue' means : pale red. 'The colour of the eyes of a peacock's tail' is the colour of black garments, etc., made shining by means of *gandhaka* (used) together with its core-wood. Now the question may be raised whether (a kind of blood-bile arising) from phlegm does exist, as it is said that blood-bile (consists of) bile as such. This question is answered in the following way : bile as such accomplishes (the appearance of) blood-bile with regard to its generic onset, as wind does in every kind of visceral swelling, and in the same way as bile is the starting agent in every kind of fever. In that very case in which it brings about blood-bile, when accompanied by an abundant amount of phlegm giving rise to its own characteristics, (in that case) it is, after dismissing the bile that has effected the stage of the generic onset, designated as (arising) by means of phlegm giving rise to its own characteristics, (consisting of) viscidness, etc...; in the same way as in visceral swelling by phlegm (the visceral swelling) is designated as (arising) by means of phlegm, after it has discarded the wind by means of which it has arrived at (the stage of) the generic onset; in the same way as in fever by phlegm (this fever) is designated as (arising) by means of phlegm that gives rise to its specific characteristics, disregarding the invariably present cause of all fevers; the same explanation is also suitable in blood-bile by wind. That (kind of) blood-bile which is generated by a strong bile merely, deprived of phlegm and wind and endowed with the characteristics of blood-bile by bile, is called blood-bile (arising) from bile. The designation (of a disease) with respect to its morbific entity comes about by means of its characteristics and by nothing else. Therefore blood-bile is designated as arising from whatever morbific entity, of which the characteristics, generated by (the morbific entity), accompany it. In blood-bile by bile the bile is, compared with blood-bile by phlegm, etc., extremely abundant, and that is why bile brings about its own characteristics in that one case only and not in other cases. And also the following statement : blood-bile, brought about by bile only, has no (particular) pathway because it has been substantiated that blood(-bile) by wind moves downwards and (blood-bile) started by phlegm upwards; (that statement) is not correct for this reason, that (blood-bile) by bile also possesses an upward and downward way of moving; moreover, (blood-bile) by bile, when moving upwards, is accompanied by phlegm on account of the great power of the pathway, and that (type) which moves downwards is attended by wind on account of its relationship with a seat of wind. And a morbific entity, attended by (another morbific entity) by reason of its relationship with a (particular) pathway, is not at all (designated as) an adjunctory (morbific entity) because it brings about its own characteristics; therefore that one, (by which

it is attended), is not referred to with the words : "(Blood-bile), attended by one morbific entity, is curable" (Ca.Ci. 4, 13c), even in blood-bile by bile. Because an independent morbific entity with developed signs is a chief one and (a morbific entity) with the opposite (characteristics) an adjunctory one, for that reason the designation of (cases of) blood-bile as (arising) by wind, etc. comes about by means of the chief morbific entity bringing about its mentioned characteristics, and not by means of the adjunctory one attending it on account of its relationship with a (particular) pathway and not bringing about its own characteristics. Others, however, say : 'When bile has accumulated at another place and blood-bile comes into contact with it at a later (point of) time, blood-bile by bile occurs."

10 Ca. : *anubadhyate* instead of *anuvartate*.

11 Cakra remarks that the statement of Ca.Ci. 4, 24 does not represent an obligatory connection that is always present, but only a usually occurring one. He deduces this from the preceding stanza by applying the word *prāyaḥ* (usually) that is found in it to the following stanza as well. The preceding stanza (4, 23) runs : "Oleaginous and hot (substances), and those which are hot and dry, cause blood-bile; the latter (substances) will usually (cause blood-bile) of the (type) moving downwards and the former (blood-bile) of the (type) moving upwards."

12 Cf. Ca.Ni. 2, 12ab : "That (kind of) blood-bile which reaches the upper (pathway) is curable;" Ca.Ni. 2, 15ab : "It has been determined that blood(-bile which goes to) the lower part (of the trunk) is (only) mitigable;" Ca.Ni. 2, 18 : "(That kind of) blood-bile, which reaches both pathways, should be known to be incurable, by the very cause stated before." Statements with the same purport occur : A.h.Ni. 3, 8a; 3, 11a; 3, 13ab; A.s.Ni. 3, 10a; 3, 13a (Ki. 3, 12a); 3, 15ab (Ki. 3, 14ab); Bhe.Ci. 3, 8; Hā. 3, 10, 9-12.

13 Ca. : *yogitva* instead of *yogyatva*.

14 M. disagrees with Ca.Ni. 2. Ca. says that substances with a sweet taste should be applied in blood-bile going upwards (Ni. 2, 14). There exists, however, a variant agreeing with M. Cakra remarks that astringent and bitter (substances) can be used because they are opposed to bile and phlegm, and that sweet (substances) are suitable after subduing phlegm by fasting, etc. Ca.Ni. 2, 17 mentions that in blood-bile going downwards (substances with) an astringent and bitter taste lead to misapplication (*ayogāvaha*); Cakra comments that the implication of this statement is that sweet substances should be used, for astringent and bitter ones are excluded by Ca. himself, and acid, saline and pungent substances are disagreeing in this case. Cf. A.h.Ni. 3, 10 = A.s.Ni. 3, 12 (Ki. 3, 11) and A.h.Ni. 3, 12cd = A.s.Ni. 3, 14cd (Ki. 3, 13cd).

15 Cf. A.h.Ci. 2, 1 = A.s.Ci. 3, 3 : "One may cure blood-bile when it goes upwards, (occurs) in a strong person, is without impetus, attended by one morbific entity, (of) recent (origin), (occurring) at a favourable (period of) time and devoid of secondary affections;" Hā. 3, 10, 13 (read : *ekamārgo balavato nātivegena cotthitaḥ*) : "Blood-bile which (affects) one pathway, (occurs) in a strong person, has sprung up without an extreme impetus and is devoid of secondary affections, may even be cured easily."

16 Cf. A.h.Ci. 2, 2-3ab = A.s.Ci. 3, 4-5ab : "One may mitigate blood(-bile) going downwards, and that (type) attended by a dyad of morbific entities; that (kind) which from (one) pathway (goes) to another, in which (blood-bile) has come forth to an extreme degree, that (kind occurring) in a person with a sluggish (transforming) fire, that (kind attended) by three morbific entities, and that one which (moves along) two paths, should be abandoned, (being unsuitable for treatment);" Hā. 3, 10, 14 : "Blood-bile is said to be curable when it is attended by one morbific entity, and mitigable when (attend-

ed) by two morbific entities; it is incurable in those with three (excited) morbific entities."

[17] Su. : *tandritā* (lassitude) instead of *pāṇḍutā* (pallor).

[18] Su. : *bhukte cānne vidāhaḥ* (combustive alteration when the food has been ingested) instead of *bhukte ghoro vidāhaḥ* (a dreadful combustive alteration of the ingested food).

[19] Su. : *kaṇṭhasya bhedaḥ* (a cutting pain in the throat, or : loosening of matter residing in the throat) instead of *koṣṭhasya bhedaḥ* (loosening of the contents of the viscera).

[20] Su. : *davana* (a burning sensation) instead of *tapana* (a sensation of glowing heat).

[21] Su. : *viratir api rate* (as well as absence of pleasure in someone engaged in sexual activity).

[22] Cf. Ca.Ni. 2, 7 : "Its secondary affections are weakness, anorexia, absence of digestive alteration, shortness of breath, cough, fever, diarrhoea, swelling, desiccation, morbid pallor and inarticulateness of the voice;" Hā. 3, 10, 16-17ab : "A skin that is deteriorated by disease (read : *rogakṣīṇā chaviḥ*), a deficient and weak state of the body without bewilderment (*avikale hīnadaurbalyakāye*), a sluggish fire, sneezing, pallor, a burning sensation, desiccation, thirst, vomiting, shortness of breath, lack of self-control, aversion to food, mental confusion, oppressing pain in the cardiac region and giddiness may come about by additional affections of blood-bile. These eighteen (disorders) are proclaimed to be the secondary affections with regard to blood-bile." (One item is missing in this series).

[23] This variant is also made mention of by Ḍa.

[24] The reading : 'a deviated state may occur as well' is recorded by Ḍa. as a variant and explained as meaning : a deviated state consisting of flexion of the body; this explanation refers to another variant recorded by Ḍa. : 'bending down (i.e. flexion) of the body may occur as well'.

[25] Su. : *kvathita* (boiled) instead of *kuthita* (stinking).

[26] Cf. Ca.Ci. 4, 18-20 : "That (kind of) blood(-bile) which comes forth along both pathways to an extreme degree, which has a smell comparable to that of a corpse, and which is extremely black, that (kind) which occurs in combination with phlegm and wind and moreover sticks to the throat (and does not come forth), that (kind) which is infested by all the mentioned secondary affections, and that (kind) which, occurring in a person who has suffered decline and is coughing, is infested by a turmeric-yellow, swarthy, yellowish-green or coppery colour, is incurable."

[27] Su.Sū. 33, 24cd reads : *raktānāṃ ca diśāṃ draṣṭā raktapittī vinaśyati* (a person suffering from blood-bile who sees the quarters endowed with a red colour is annihilated).

[28] Compare about characteristics of incurability of blood-bile : Ca.Ni. 2, 14-15 : "That blood-bile which is black, swarthy or resembling the bow of Śakra is incurable and also that (type) which colours the clothes. That blood(-bile) which is vehemently foul-smelling, coming forth in an extreme amount and accompanied by all the secondary affections, and that (type) which (occurs) in a person with decline of his force and flesh, are incurable;" A.h.Śā. 5, 74-76ab = A.s.Śā. 11, 6cd-8 : "Blood-bile (kills a patient if it is) very red, black or similar to Indra's bow, (if it) shows the (visible) forms (as endowed with a) coppery, turmeric-yellow, yellowish-green or red (colour), (if it) has poured forth from the pores (of the skin) in which the hairs are seated and (remains) sticking to the throat, mouth or cardiac region, (if it) does not colour clothes, is foul-smelling, endowed with an extreme impetus, present to an intense degree, and (if it), having increased, occurs in someone with pallor, fever, vomiting, cough, swelling or diarrhoea;" Hā. 2, 4, 32 : "Someone suffering from blood-bile who voids red urine and red faecal matter, and whose eyes or whose tongue and lips are red, or who vomits blood, is annihilated."

29 Ḍa. chooses the first alternative.

30 Ḍa. remarks that these should be present to an intense degree.

31 The bow of the Lord of the gods (i.e. Indra = Śakra) is the rainbow.

32 Cakra gives the latter explanation.

33 Ḍa. makes mention of the reading adopted by Mādhava (compare note 27); he says it means that the eructations are red and that one sees all objects red, because the morbific entities have reached the marrow. Two other variants are recorded by Ḍa. : *lohitotkaradarśin* (one who sees the multitude of objects red) and : *lohitākāradarśin* (one who sees the visible forms red).

CHAPTER TEN

KINGLY CONSUMPTION (*RĀJAYAKṢMAN*) AND DECLINE FROM A LESION (OF THE CHEST) (*KṢATAKṢĪṆA*)

10, 1 : From the restraint of (natural) urges and certainly from a state of decline, from rashness and from incongruous eating, from (this) tetrad of grounds the malady (called) consumption arises, which is (endowed) with the three morbific entities.[1]

M :

The origins of consumption (are made mention of), immediately following upon (the description of) blood-bile, because it has been said : the appearance of blood occurs among the symptoms of kingly consumption (arising) from bile.[2]

The fourfold distant cause, being applicable in therapy, is discussed... '(Natural) urge' (indicates) here (only the urge to pass) flatus, urine and faeces, and not all (the urges, to wit those) of yawning, etc., which are stated in (the chapter) on the non-restraint of the (natural) urges.[3] As has been said in the Caraka(saṃhitā) : "When someone, out of shamefulness, disdain or fear, suppresses the urge (to pass) flatus, urine and faeces when it has arrived..." (Ci. 8, 20), etc. 'From a state of decline'... ; by this (term) the grounds of decline of the elements (of the body) are understood, (consisting of) sexual intercourse beyond the proper measure, abstinence from food, jealousy, despondency, etc. (About) 'from rashness' (we remark that) rashness, (consisting of acts like) the contest with a strong man, etc., is a cause (of consumption), because it is a ground of a lesion of the chest. (About) 'from incongruous eating' (we remark that) it is the employment (of foods) different from the twelve kinds of food set forth by Suśruta,[4] by reason of the fact that this (incongruous eating) quickly obstructs the channels. For it has been said in the Caraka(saṃhitā) : "In those who use a mixed diet, consisting of foods and drinks of many kinds, in an incongruous way, the wind and the other (morbific entities), (having become) incongruous, generate dreadful ailments.[5] Having obstructed the channels of the elements (of the body), got into an incongruous state by reason of the incongruity (of the food), the morbific entities favour the development of disease and so do not nourish the elements (of the body)" (Ci. 8, 28-29).[6]

'(Endowed) with the three morbific entities' (indicates that) it arises, being of only one kind, from the three morbific entities assembled together, and (that) it is not of several kinds on account of distinctions among its causes. As Suśruta says : "Because desiccation is thought of as being of only one kind, (viz.) that one with the nature of concerted action, the signs of the morbific entities settle down in it, according to the (degree of) preponderancy (of each morbific entity)" (U. 41, 7cd-8ab).

And (what is the answer) if it be argued, since it is true that restraint of the (natural) urges, etc. excites the wind : how is it possible that consumption, which is generated by this (restraint, etc.), is (said to be endowed) with the three morbific entities ?

(In case of this objection) the answer is : it is said that by the very excitement of wind excitement of phlegm and bile (occurs) as well, by means of corruption of the (transforming) fire. By (the use of) the words 'from (this) tetrad of grounds' it is shown that, though the grounds are innumerable, they are comprised in the mentioned tetrad.

It was Suśruta who made the association between the various words, (consisting of) desiccation, etc., by which it is expressed. (He did so) in the following (stanzas) : "It is denominated desiccation on account of the complete desiccation of the nutrient fluid and the other (elements); wise people call it decline because it brings about decline of the actions;[7] owing to the fact that this ailment (once) occurred in the moon, who is a king, some thoughtful (physicians) call it the king's consumption" (U. 41, 4-5). In Vāgbhaṭa('s treatise), however, it has been said : "King-consumption is the king of consumptions." [8] (A grammatical remark follows).

Ā :

'Decline' is decline of the elements (of the body), which arises from several causes, (consisting of) sexual intercourse, abstinence from food, discharge of blood, fasting, etc. (About) 'from incongruous eating' (we remark that) it has been said : "(Eating) copiously, little or at an improper time, that should be known to be incongruous eating" (Su.Sū. 46, 508cd).

10, 2 : When the trails of the nutrient fluid have been obstructed by the morbific entities, with phlegm as their predominant one, or also when the semen has gone into a state of decline in a person who has indulged in sexual intercourse to an extreme degree, all the elements (of the body) go into a state of decline in an uninterrupted series; thereupon a man is subject to desiccation.

(Su.U. 41, 9cd-10).[9]

M :

(Its) specific onset is described in order to show that consumption does not arise solely from the group of states of decline of the elements, but also from obstruction, etc. of the channels which carry the nutrient fluid, etc... When it would not be thus, the declined state of the elements itself (would constitute) the disease, and not consumption.

(With respect to the words : 'by the morbific entities with phlegm as their predominant one') it may be said that the triad of morbific entities is pointed to by the term 'the morbific entities'; because phlegm is comprised in it as a specified (component, the question may be raised) why this same phlegm should be expressed (again) by another word.

The reply (to this question) is : it is (a case) of analysis by means of the members composing it; it is a collection in the sense of a compound, in the same way as something consisting of many trees is (called) a wood. The extensive justification of (this) statement should be looked for in Jejjaṭa('s commentary) on the Suśruta(saṃhitā). The predominance of phlegm should be understood (to be indicated) by the sluggishness of the fire, etc., which suffers disorder by the wind that is excited by the restraint of the (natural) urges, etc.

'The trails of the nutrient fluid' are the ducts carrying the nutrient fluid; in this case the word 'etcetera' should be considered to have been elided. Therefore, obstruction of the channels carrying blood, etc., should also be understood (as aimed at). Or, since the nutrient fluid is the cause (of the production) of blood, etc., the very corruption of the nutrient fluid (is conducive) to corruption of the blood, etc.; thus says Kārtika(kuṇḍa). On this (subject) the following has been pointed out : because the nutrient fluid, which stays in the cardiac region, remains lodged in that same (seat) on account of the obstruction of (its) pathway and becomes morbidly altered, it flows out by way of the mouth. As Caraka says : "When the channels are obstructed, the nutrient fluid, staying in its own seat, becomes combustively altered, and it comes forth in many forms (from the) upper (pathway) by the impulse of coughing" (Ci. 8, 43). By this (statement) a process of decline is shown that occurs in the normal way, because, since there is decline of the nutrient fluid as an element (of the body), which acts as a causative agent, a process of decline of blood and the subsequent (elements), which are products of the nutrient fluid, is going on, due to the absence of (a) nourishing (factor).

In order to show the reverse process of decline it is said 'or also in a person who has indulged in sexual intercourse to an extreme degree'. When the semen has undergone decline, the elements (of the body), constituting an uninterrrupted series, (i.e.) being contiguous with each other, are subject to decline : when for instance the semen has declined, the marrow declines, when the marrow has declined, the bones are subject to decline, (and) in that way each (element) that precedes (in the series).

And if one objects, asking how it is possible that decline occurs of elements that act as causative agents, owing to decline of semen that is a product ?

(In that case) the answer is (as follows) : due to the decline of semen the wind is excited. As has been said: "Excitement of the wind occurs from decline of the elements (of the body) and (from obstruction) by covering (its) pathway" (Ca.Ci. 28, 59ab). This wind desiccates the marrow, due to its vicinity, and in the same way each preceding element in its turn. The generation of effects in cases of immediate proximity has been shown, as for example in the desiccation of a piece of wet soil by placing it near to a ball of iron made glowing hot by fire.

To the same effect are Suśruta's words in (his) thesis on the circulation of the nutrient fluid : "By an extreme increase each (element) preceding (in the series) increases the next one (of the series); therefore it is salutary to diminish elements which have increased to an extreme degree" (Sū. 15, 18).

10, 3-4 : Shortness of breath, muscle pain,[10] a discharge of phlegm, desiccation of the palate, emesis, adynamia of the (transforming) fire, (mental disturbance as in) intoxication, nasal catarrh, cough [11] and sleep occur when desiccation is imminent; a creature in this state has also eyes of a light colour, is devoted to meat and lascivious (3).

In his dreams such a person is carried by a crow, parrot, porcupine, peacock, vulture, monkey or lizard;[12] he may see (in his dreams) rivers devoid of water, and trees that are desiccated and tormented by wind, smoke and fire (4).

(Su.U. 41, 29-30).[13]

M :

The prodromes are dealt with... 'A discharge (of phlegm), is spitting out (phlegm)... 'A lascivious one' is a person desirous of sexual intercourse with a woman; this occurs by means of the great power of the illness and is due to a fault of the *manas*. The being carried in one's dreams by a crow, etc. is in itself a prodrome as well. 'A porcupine' is (an animal ordinarily) called *śarāru*... 'Tormented' (means) overpowered. From (the use of) the word 'and' (it follows that) the falling down of leaves of grass and hairs of the head (in one's food) should (also) be noted. As has been said in the Caraka(saṃhitā)...[14] In this (quotation) 'beasts of prey' are tigers, etc.

Ā :

... 'A porcupine' is (an animal) mimicking a *godhā* :[15] it is a *vajra-śakalī*, generally called *sellaka*.[16] A lizard is a *saraṭa*; those living in the east call it a *girgiṭ*...[17]

10, 5 : Glowing heat of the scapular region and sides, glowing heat of hands and feet and fever in the whole body are the characteristics of the kingly consumption.

(Ca.Ci. 18, 52).

M :

(Kingly consumption), endowed with three symptoms, is dealt with... 'The scapular region' is the upper part of the arm. 'Glowing heat (of the scapular region and sides)' is one symptom; the same should be stated about 'glowing heat (of hands and feet)'. As to '(glowing heat) of hands and feet' the Kaśmīrians [18] read 'glowing heat of (the aggregation consisting of) feet and hands',[19] because they are of the opinion that (these feet and hands) constitute one entity, on account of their being a part (of the body) of a living being; (another) variant is '(glowing heat) relative to hands and feet'.[20]

This triad of (symptoms) has been made mention of by Caraka as usually occurring; therefore it should be understood that some other triad (may occur) as well among the eleven symptoms.[21] Likewise Bhoja (says) : "Cough, fever and blood-bile (are present) in the kingly consumption with three symptoms." Others, however, say: when fever occurs in kingly consumption it is (that type) of which it is a characteristic. Jejjaṭa, however, has expounded that all three symptoms are required.

Additional stanza :[22] Aversion to food, fever, shortness of breath, cough, the becoming visible of blood and inarticulateness of the voice arise in kingly consumption as (a set of) six symptoms.[23]

(Su.U. 41, 11).[24]

10, 6-7 : Inarticulateness of the voice, piercing pain and a contracted state [25] of the scapular region and the sides should be discerned (to arise) from wind; fever, a burning sensation, diarrhoea and the arrival of blood from bile (6); and fullness of the head, absence of the wish to eat, cough and a ruined condition of the throat from excitement of phlegm (7).

(Su.U. 41, 12-13).[26]

M :

The eleven symptoms of kingly consumption, (arisen) from the three morbific entities, being separate (entities), arise according to the power of the illness, and not all (the symptoms) by all the morbific entities together, as the signs of fever by concerted action. ... A contracted state of the scapular region and the sides should be counted as one (symptom)... 'A ruined condition of the throat' (means) inarticulateness of the voice; Kārtika(kuṇḍa) says (it means) expectoration.

Ā :

... Instead of 'a contracted state' others read 'a sensation of plucking'...[27]

10, 8-9 : (A physician) who strives after completely stainless fame [28] should refrain from (treating) a creature tormented by desiccation and attended by these (mentioned) eleven signs or by (the following) six ones : cough, diarrhoea, affliction of the sides, inarticulateness of the voice, inability to eat and fever;[29] or one painfully oppressed by (the following) three : cough, shortness of breath [30] and an ailment regarding the blood.

(Su.U. 41, 14-15).

10, 10 : One should refrain from (treating) someone who is provided with the signs, with half (of them) or three (of them), in the case that decline of flesh and force (is present in him); he should be treated, however, even if all the symptoms are present, when (his condition is) otherwise.

(Ca.Ci. 8, 47).[31]

10, 11 : Someone suffering from consumption should be given up when he is subject to decline (though) being a great eater, when he is oppressed by diarrhoea, and certainly when his testicles and abdomen are swollen.

(Su.U. 41, 31).

10, 12 : A human being is killed by consumption in this world when his eyes are (of a) light (colour), when he feels aversion from food, is oppressed by the expiratory (type of) shortness of breath,[32] or passes a great amount of urine with difficulty.

(Su.Sū. 33, 20).[33]

M:

The characteristics of incurability are made mention of... '(Attended) by these eleven (signs' means attended) by (the series of signs) beginning with inarticulateness of the voice and ending with a ruined condition of the throat. (About 'attended) by the six (signs' we remark that) the six signs have been described by Suśruta : "Aversion to food, fever, shortness of breath, cough, the becoming visible of blood and inarticulateness of the voice arise in kingly consumption as (a set of) six symptoms" (U. 41, 11).[34] 'Cough, diarrhoea, affliction of the sides, inarticulateness of the voice, inability to eat and fever', however, are the six symptoms as written down by Mādhava from some (other) treatise.[35]

And these eleven, six or three symptoms are described because they are the usually occurring ones, many other symptoms being excluded; a set of eleven and six (symptoms) would indeed also arise in case of the joint occurrence of other symptoms; for that reason, after describing the eleven symptoms in (the section on) origins, Caraka has written down (these) eleven symptoms in the (section on) therapeutics as well, (in stating) the fourfold counteractions regarding (the consumptions) arising from the tetrad of causes (consisting of) restraint of the (natural) urges, etc. : "Cough, glowing heat of the scapular region, an altered state of the voice, fever, a painful condition of the sides and the head, vomiting of blood and phlegm, shortness of breath, seizing of the excremental matter [36] and inability to eat, these eleven symptoms (occur) in consumption, and (also) the six following ones : cough, fever, piercing pain in the sides, seizing of the voice and of the excremental matter [37] and inability to eat" (Ci. 8, 45-46). By the word eleven it is indicated that all the eleven symptoms are present in the fully developed (form of) consumption.

(To) 'one should refrain (from treating)' should be supplied : 'when there is a state of decline of force and flesh'. Likewise it is said by Caraka : "A man whose illness is (caused) by wind, a man with epilepsy, a skin disease, *bradhna*,[38] long-lasting fever, visceral swelling, diabetes mellitus and kingly consumption, these (persons) are not fit for treatment on account of the decline of (their) force and flesh; a physician should abstain from (treating) them even if (their) morbid alterations are very slight" (I. 9, 8-9).[39]

About '(someone who is provided) with all (the signs)', etc. it may be rightly asked, since all the symptoms are eleven (in number) and the half of eleven is five and a half, which of the (many) symptoms is present in the state of half (a symptom) or of what kind (this symptom) is.

The answer (to this question) is : as there is no such thing as the coming into being of the half of one (particular) symptom, only (a set of) six symptoms can be understood (to constitute the intended) half (number), on account of the fact that (this number) holds the best position with regard to five or six symptoms (considered) as half (the number of eleven).[40]

... 'When (the condition is) otherwise' (means) : when decline of force and flesh is absent.

'When one is subject to decline (though) being a great eater' is (in itself) one characteristic of incurability, as it constitutes a precursory signal of death. 'Being oppressed by diarrhoea' is the second (characteristic of incurability), because it has been stated that a person with consumption is someone whose life is dependent on (his) impure matter (as a resource).[41] 'The testicles and abdomen being swollen' (constitutes) the third (characteristic of incurability) because, swelling of the testicles being curable by means of purgative procedures, treatment disagrees (in this case). 'A light (colour of the) eyes', etc. are one by one characteristics of incurability.

Ā :

Mention is made of the incurable (type of) kingly consumption with many symptoms...[42] The signs of decline of flesh and force have been stated by Suśruta as follows : "When decline of flesh occurs, there are present a desiccated state of the bones,[43] cheeks,[44] sexual organs, thighs, chest, armpits, calves, abdomen and neck, dryness,[45] adynamia of the limbs and flaccidity of the ducts" (fr. Sū. 15, 9). Force is vital energy;[46] "Fainting, decline of flesh, mental confusion, confused speech and especially absence of knowledge, together with the previously stated [47] signs, and death, (occur) in a state of decline of force" (Sū. 15, 27cd-28ab). Others read : 'in case decline of flesh and force (is present)'... (About) 'oppressed by diarrhoea' (we remark that) it has been said : "The force of men is dependent on impure matter, but life is dependent on semen; therefore one should exert oneself to protect the impure matter and semen of a person with consumption..."[48]

10, 13 : One may treat a man deprived of fever as an adjunctory (disease), strong, able to endure therapeutic procedures, self-possessed, (endowed) with an inflamed (transforming) fire and not lean.[49]

M :

The condition that may be treated is made mention of... By (the words 'someone who is) not lean' it is pointed out that treatment is administered even to someone who would have been rejected on account of his young age. As has been said elsewhere : "If a human being lives longer than a thousand days, being (of a) tender (age) and oppressed by desiccation, he has been treated by good physicians." [50]

10, 14 : Hear about those who are desiccated by sexual intercourse, grief, old age, physical exercise and travelling, and those persons with (a type of) desiccation that is technically called after the inflamed sore and lesion of the chest (giving rise to it), (together) with (their) characteristics.[51]

M :

It is said '(desiccated by) sexual intercourse', etc. in order to exclude the group of states of desiccation of the elements (of the body), generated by sexual intercourse, etc., from the condition (called) kingly consumption. As has been said in the Suśruta(saṃhitā) : "According to (the view of) some (authorities, the condition called) desiccation has distinctions in that way, (i.e.) according to (its particular) cause; in this (case, however,) the associated signs of the morbific entities do not crop up; therefore these (conditions) should be known to be just (conditions of) decline, (arising) one by one from decline of an element (of the body)" [52] (U. 41, 26cd-27). (A grammatical remark by Kārtikakuṇḍa is quoted).

10, 15 : Someone desiccated by sexual intercourse is assaulted by the signs of decline of semen, and, his body being (of a) pale (colour), his elements go into a state of decline one after another.

(Su.U. 41, 17).

M :

The characteristics of someone desiccated by sexual intercourse are dealt with... Suśruta stated the signs of decline of semen in the following way : "In a state of decline of semen there are present a painful sensation in penis and testicles, impotence in sexual intercourse or ejaculation after a long time, and the appearance of a slight amount of red-coloured semen when ejaculating" (fr. Sū. 15, 9).[53]

10, 16ab : Someone desiccated by grief is immersed in deep thought and there is laxity of his body; moreover he is in such a condition (as someone desiccated by sexual intercourse).

(Su.U. 41, 18ab).

M :

The characteristics of someone desiccated by grief are dealt with... 'Moreover he is in such a condition' (means that) he is provided with the signs of desiccation by (loss of) semen, with the exclusion of the characteristics of decline of semen. As has been said in the Suśruta-(saṃhitā) : "He is secondarily characterized [54] by (these signs), excepting those morbid alterations which are brought about by decline of semen" (U. 41, 18cd).

Ā :

... 'Immersed in deep thought' is given up to anxiety...

10, 16cd-18ab : Someone desiccated by old age is lean, his potency, thinking, force and senses are of a sluggish character (16); he is trembling and unable to eat; his damaged voice is (like the sound of) a broken brazen vessel;

he spits without (producing) phlegm; he is oppressed by heaviness and disinclination (17); his mouth, nose and eyes show a discharge and his impurities and skin are desiccated,[55] (respectively) dry.

(Su.U. 41, 19-20).

M:

The characteristics of someone desiccated by old age are dealt with ... His voice is like (the sound of) a broken, (i.e.) cracked, brazen vessel, struck with a stick, etc. 'He spits without (producing) phlegm' (means that) there is no coming forth of phlegm, though he exerts himself to eliminate it...

10, 18cd-19ab : Someone desiccated by travelling (shows) laxity of his body; his skin is parched and rough (18); the subdivisions of the limbs (of his body) are numb and his *kloman*, throat and mouth [56] are desiccated.

(Su.U. 41, 21).

M:

The characteristics of someone desiccated by travelling are dealt with ... 'His skin is parched' (means that) the colour (of his skin looks) roasted. '(His limbs are) numb' (means that he is) insensitive to touch. The *kloman* is the seat of thirst in the cardiac region; a variant of *kloman* is 'palate'.

Ā:

... 'Numb' is : insensitive to touch, unfit to perform its function. ... Though, in agreement with what has been taught, the person with desiccation from physical exercise ought to be described immediately following on (the description of) the person with desiccation from old age, and not (that) one with desiccation from travelling, nevertheless the person with desiccation from travelling is described here first, on account of the analogy of the characteristics of a person with desiccation from travelling with those of a person with desiccation from physical exercise.

If it is thus, what is then the reason that the characteristics of a person with desiccation from physical exercise are not transferred by analogy to (those of) a person with desiccation from travelling?

It is truly for this reason that in a person with desiccation from physical exercise the signs of a person with a lesion of the chest are additionally and actually present.[57]

And if it is asked as an objection why it is that in the enumeration (of the types of desiccation) [58] the person with desiccation from travelling itself is not spoken of prior (to that one with desiccation from physical exercise, it is answered that) it is because this agrees with the metre.

10, 19c-f : A person with desiccation from physical exercise is attended by these same (characteristics) to a high degree, and moreover provided with the signs brought about by a lesion of the chest, without a lesion (actually being present). (Su.U. 41, 22).

M :

The characteristics of a person with desiccation from physical exercise are made mention of... 'By these (same characteristics' points to) the characteristics of a person with desiccation from travelling, (consisting of) laxity of the body, etc., because of the generic similarity to travelling of everything that can be called physical exercise. 'To a high degree' (indicates) : to an extreme degree. This means that the characteristics are present (to a) slight (degree) in desiccation from travelling and (to a) great (degree) in that (kind) arising from physical exercise. The (variant) reading : 'provided with the signs brought about by a lesion of the chest, the lesion (itself) being excluded (from them)' is easy to understand. Gadādhara, however, reads : "Also (that type of desiccation) brought about by a lesion of the chest is provided with (these) signs, the lesion being absent." He explains (this as follows) : that (type of) desiccation brought about by a lesion of the chest, the grounds of which are physical exercise, toil, study, running, riding, etc., is also provided to a high degree with the same characteristics as those of desiccation by travelling, (while) the lesion, (i.e.) the effect of the lesion, is absent. The effect of the lesion (described) by Suśruta (in the statement) beginning with : "In such a person with a lesion of the chest, blood, pus and phlegm come (out)" (U. 41, 42cd) and ending with : "The colour (of the skin) and the voice of (such) a man are indistinct" (U. 41, 26b), these very characteristics are additionally present in a lesion of the chest. The intended meaning is that the same characteristics, present to a high degree in desiccation brought about by physical exercise, toil, etc., which are causes of a lesion of the chest, are also present in (desiccation brought about by) travelling, just because this belongs to the group of causes of a lesion of the chest.

Or (it is possible that) 'without a lesion (actually being present' means) : without a sore; that (kind of) desiccation which is brought about by toil, study, etc. beyond the proper measure, (constituting) instrumental causes of lesions of the chest, is also attended by these very signs of desiccation from too much travelling; thus is the relationship, (established) by means of what has been put forward. The characteristics of (that kind of a lesion of the chest) which is accompanied by a sore will be stated (shortly).

10, 20 : In a person with a sore, desiccation may come into being from decline of blood, painful sensations, and certainly from a limited intake of food; this (type) is thought [59] to be incurable to the highest degree.

(Su.U. 41, 23).

M :

The person with desiccation from a sore is made mention of by (describing) the triad of causes (leading to this condition)... 'Painful sensations' (refer in this case to) painful sensations from a sore; these (painful sensations) bring about desiccation on account of the turbulent state of the mind, which is full of fear and grief, and due to the very excitement of the wind (as a result of this). (A grammatical remark follows). ... Or (it is thus that) the term 'incurable to the highest degree' expresses, with reference to (the term) mitigable, (a type of desiccation that) should be rejected (as unfit for treatment), because a mitigable (type) also (belongs to the) incurable (group).

If this is not true, the question may rightly be asked whether this is not contradicted by what has been said by Suśruta in the section on therapy: "To those with desiccation (caused) by a sore who are lean, the roborant mode (of treatment) should be applied" (Ci. 1, 30d and 31b).[60]

The answer (to this question) is : (a person with) a very strong (degree of) desiccation should be rejected, but when (desiccation is) not (present to an) extremely strong (degree), a (particular) therapeutic method should be fixed.

The author of the commentary (called) Candrikā reads, however : 'it is mitigable (or) incurable to the highest degree', instead of : 'it is traditionally said [61] to be incurable to the highest degree', because the roborant mode (of treatment) is dealt with in the (section on) therapy.

Ā :

... 'From decline of blood' (means) : from an extreme discharge of blood.

10, 21-29ab : In someone extremely exerting himself with the bow, lifting up heavy loads, fighting with strong(er) men, falling from a rugged (or) high (place) (21),[62] (trying to catch and) check a bull or horse that is running away and should be tamed or another (animal), (trying to) kill enemies by hurling rocks, pieces of wood, stones or missiles (22), or reading with an extremely loud voice, covering a long distance by running, crossing great rivers [63] (by swimming), or running (keeping pace) with horses (23), making long jumps in an inconsidering way, or dancing with quick motions,[64] or vehemently injured by other formidable actions (24), a lesion of the chest having developed, a powerful illness is stirred up, as well as in someone who is extremely attached to women, or who eats dry (articles of food), a slight amount (of food) or a restricted amount (of food) (25).

The chest (of such a person seems to be) broken asunder to an extreme degree, (seems to be) cut and becomes painful everywhere;[65] thereupon a feeling of pressure arises in the sides, the body becomes subject to desiccation, and shivering arises (26).

Gradually (such a person) is deprived of his potency, force, colour, appetite and (transforming) fire, moreover (there arise) fever, distressing sensations, dejection of the mind, loosening of faecal matter and destruction of the (transforming) fire (27).

In such a repeatedly coughing person phlegm, accompanied by blood, comes forth,[66] which is corrupted, brown, very bad-smelling, yellow, globose and copious (28).

Such a person with a lesion (of the chest) is subject to an extreme decline; (this occurs), moreover, due to decline of the semen and the vital fluid.

(Ca.Ci. 11, 4-12ab).[67]

M :

Lesions of the chest, together with their origins, are made mention of in the paragraph on desiccation, because the source of a lesion of the chest is the very origin from which desiccation (arises, to wit) inconsiderate actions, etc., and because the source of desiccation (may) also (consist) of a lesion of the chest... 'In someone who stretches (his body)', as a variant of 'in someone exerting himself', (means) : in someone whose cardiac region is being expanded.

'That should be tamed', (i.e.) that deserves to be tamed, refers to that same (already mentioned) strong bull, etc. 'Or another animal' (means) : an elephant, camel, etc. 'In someone (trying to catch and) check' (means) : in someone (trying to) restrain. 'A rock' is a rock (of an) oblong (shape); 'a stone' is a piece of (flat) rock (of) a different (shape); a missile is a specific kind of missile weapon, or a specific kind of (contrivance), provided with an extreme force, to set rocks, etc. in motion. 'In someone (trying to) kill enemies' (means) : in someone beating down (his) foes. ... To 'in someone crossing great rivers' should be supplied : 'with one's arms'. ... 'Or in someone injured by other formidable actions' (points to) wrestling, etc.; instead of 'formidable' others read : valiant (actions), (i.e.) by foes. Among these causes some should be understood to bring about exertion of the whole body, some of the chest especially. 'Illness (is stirred up', i.e. the illness) with the characteristics of a lesion of the chest; or 'illness' (may denote) the wind, according to the (following) tradition : "The morbific entities may also be denominated by the term illness", thus says Jejjaṭa.[6] 'The chest (seems to be) broken asunder', (i.e.) feels broken as it were; '(seems to be) cut', (i.e.) feels as torn asunder, as if divided into two parts; the variant '(the chest) is combustively altered' is unsuitable by reason of the absence of a cause and because the commentators have not expounded it. 'Potency' is power; 'force' is stoutness of the flesh(y parts of the body). The variant 'loosening of faecal matter on account of the very destruction of the (transforming) fire' means that loosening of faecal matter comes into being, destruction of the (transforming) fire being its ground; it is said that the word '(the) very (destruction)' expresses that loosening of faecal matter by destruction of the fire also occurs in the absence of the great power of the illness. 'Corrupted' (means) subject to disorder; this very (term) is explained with the words 'brown', etc. 'Globose' (means) : specifically composed of globules; Jejjaṭa says (it means) confined. 'Such' a man 'with a lesion', (i.e.) with a lesion of the chest, 'is subject to decline', (i.e.) acquires desiccation of the elements (of the body). He is subject to decline, not only from the lesion as such, but even more so from decline of the semen and vital fluid by indulgence in (sexual intercourse with) women, etc. ...

10, 29cd : Its undeveloped characteristics are traditionally called the prodromes.

(Ca.Ci. 11, 12cd).

M :

Mentioin is made of the prodromes...

Ā :

The undeveloped characteristics, (i.e. the characteristics) which have not (yet) become manifest, of it, (i.e.) of (this) lesion (of the chest, are traditionally called the prodromes).

10, 30 : A painful condition of the chest, vomiting of blood and a specific (kind of) cough (occur) in someone with a lesion (of the chest); in someone subject to decline, the urine is accompanied by blood and there is seizing (pain) of the sides, back and iliac region.

(Ca.Ci. 11, 13).

M :

(Those) characteristics are made mention of which are not common to persons suffering from a lesion (of the chest) and from decline ... 'A specific (kind of) cough' (occurs); this specificity has been said to (consist of) its being accompanied by phlegm which is corrupted, brown, etc.; or 'a specific (kind of' means that cough is present) to a raised degree. ... 'The urine is accompanied by blood' (means that) the urine is somewhat red.

Ā :

... 'A specific (kind of cough)' means an excessive cough with regard to that (kind which arises) in someone subject to decline. In decline of semen and vital fluid, however, (the passing of) urine accompanied by blood, etc. (appear as) secondary affections...

10, 31 : In someone with (a) slight (number of) signs, with an inflamed (transforming) fire, in someone who is strong, and when it is (of) recent (origin), it is curable; when it has been (already) present during a full year, it is mitigable; one should, however, abstain from (treating) someone with all the signs. (Ca.Ci. 11, 14).[69]

M:

Mention is made of the characteristics of curability of these two (affections).

NOTES

[1] Cf. Ca.Ni. 6, 3 : "There are four underlying factors with respect to desiccation, namely rashness, restraint (of the natural urges), a state of decline and incongruous eating;" Ca.Ni. 6, 4-11 presents an elaborate description of these four underlying factors; Ca.Ni. 6, 12 : "By indulging in these four underlying factors in desiccation, wind, bile and phlegm enter into a state of excitement. These (three morbific entities) desiccate the body by means of various secondary affections. The physicians call this (disease) kingly consumption because it is the most troublesome of all diseases, or it is called kingly consumption because it occurred for the first time to the venerable Soma, the king of the constellations;" Ca.Ci. 8, 3-10 deals with the mythic origin of kingly consumption; Ca.Ci. 8, 13 : "Undertakings which are not in agreement with one's force, restraint of the (natural) urges and decline should be known to be the causes of consumption, together with incongruous eating as the fourth one;" the topic of the four causes and the symptoms they produce is elaborated in the subsequent stanzas (Ca.Ci. 8, 14-32); Su.U. 41, 8cd-9ab : "From decline, checking of the (natural) urges, rough acts (causing injury), and incongruous eating, (desiccation) arises in a being with a body pervaded by the excited morbific entities;" A.h.Ni. 5, 4 = A.s.Ni. 5, 6 (Ki. 5, 5) : "Rashness, restraint of the (natural) urges, decline of semen, vital fluid and oleaginous matter, and abandoning of the precepts regarding foods and drinks are its four grounds;" Bhe. Ni. 2 recognizes four grounds as well : rashness, restraint (of the natural urges), sexual intercourse beyond the proper measure and incongruous food; Hā. 3, 9, 104cd-106 : "Consumption arises by means of four grounds. Listen now (to me, proceeding to expound these). This great malady arises in a man by means of a diseased condition of the body, (occurring when it is) painfully oppressed by physical exercise, (travelling in) a vehicle and sexual intercourse; (it springs up) from the body when it is painfully oppressed by inflamed sores and when it is subject to decline, (moreover) from wrath, extreme grief, fear and reducing measures, (as well as) from the absence of (any) fasting. The (disease) called kingly consumption, which deprives man of his force, arises from old age, straining a bow and its spring by all means, carrying extremely (heavy) burdens and (injuries from) striking, jumping and binding (activities); it may arise from fighting, by blowing (a fire) from too great a distance, by force of the eating of bad foods, by anxiety and excessive sexual intercourse."

[2] See Mā.ni. 10, 6d.

[3] I.e. Ca.Sū. 7.

[4] Su.U. 64, 56 : "Henceforth we shall set forth the twelve kinds of food. These (consist of those which are) cold, hot, oleaginous, dry, liquid and desiccated, (those which are)

taken once a day, twice a day, together with a remedial agent and those taken in smaller quantities (than other foods), those which appease the morbific entities and (those which are taken) for the sake of subsistence."

[5] Ca. : *janayanty āmayān ghorān viṣamān mārutādayaḥ* (the wind, etc. generate dreadful incongruous ailments).

[6] Ca.Ci. 8, 29 reads : "Having got into an incongruous state by reason of the incongruity (of the food) and so obstructing the channels of the blood and the other (elements of the body), they favour the development of disease and do not nourish the elements at all."

[7] Ḍa. : 'action' means therapy, or it is bodily, vocal and mental action.

[8] Cf. A.h.Ni. 5, 2cd = A.s.Ni. 5, 4cd (Ki. 5, 3cd) : "Since it is both a king and a consumption it is called king-consumption."

[9] Cf. Ca.Ci. 8, 39-40 : "The bodily elements reach a state of maturation by means of their own heat in each of them and (each) element gets nourishment from the (preceding) element (in the series) by way of the (appropriate set of) channel(s). Due to obstruction of the channels, decline of blood and the subsequent (elements) and depletion of the heat of the elements, the kingly consumption comes forth;" A.h.Ni. 5, 5-6 = A.s.Ni. 5, 7-8 (Ki. 5, 6-7) : "The wind, roused by these (grounds), having roused bile and phlegm (in its turn) everywhere, enters the junctures of the body, and, exerting pressure on those (junctures) and on the vessels, obstructing the openings of the channels or distending them to an extreme degree, it moves about upwards, downwards and laterally and generates the maladies that correspond to each (of the three ways in which it moves)."

[10] Su. : *aṅgasāda* (adynamia of the body) instead of *aṅgamarda* (muscle pain).

[11] Su. : *pāṇḍu* (paleness) instead of *kāsa* (cough).

[12] *kṛkalāsaka*; this word may also mean a chameleon.

[13] Cf. Ca.Ni. 6, 13 : "The following prodromes occur in it : nasal catarrh, frequent sneezing, effusion of phlegm, a sweet taste in the mouth, absence of the relish for food, droopiness at the time of meals, the seeing of faults in circumstances where there are none or (only) slight (faults) with regard to the dishes (in which the food is served), the water, (solid) food, soup, flour-cakes, relishes and the waiters, sickness (just) after one has eaten, and also bringing up again and again during the intervals of a meal, swelling of face and feet, looking with extreme attention at (one's) hands, an extremely white hue of the eyes, the desire to know the size of (one's) arms, lustfulness towards women, the seeing of loathsome (appearances) in (one's) body, frequent dreaming about water reservoirs devoid of water, deserted villages, towns, cities and (formerly) inhabited countries, desiccated, burnt and broken forests, (dreaming about) touching a lizard, peacock, monkey, parrot, snake, crow or owl, mounting or riding (in a vehicle drawn by) dogs, camels, donkeys or boars, and mounting a pile of hairs, bones, ashes, chaff or charcoal, (these are the prodromes of desiccation);" Ca.Ci. 8, 33-38ab : "The prodromes (consist of) nasal catarrh, weakness, seeing faults even in circumstances where there are none, seeing loathsome (appearances) in (one's) body, disdain even when eating, a general decline of strength and flesh, fondness for women, intoxicating beverages and meat, fondness of covering (the body with clothes), (the phenomenon that) flies, *ghuṇas*, hairs of the head and leaves of grass frequently fall into (one's) foods and drinks, (rapid) growth of the hair of the head and the nails, being overpowered by birds, flying insects and beasts of prey, the (act of) mounting a pile of hairs, bones or ashes in (one's) dream and seeing water receptacles, rocks, forests and heavenly bodies which are drying up, subject to decline or falling; these should be known to be the prodromes of the kingly

consumption of many forms;" A.h.Ni. 5, 7-13ab = A.s.Ni. 5, 9-15ab (Ki. 5, 8-13) : "When it is imminent its symptoms (i.e. prodromes) are : nasal catarrh, violent sneezing, effusion (of phlegm), a sweet taste in the mouth, adynamia of the (transforming) fire and of the body, seeing cooking-vessels, drinking-vessels, foods, drinks, etc. in a defiled condition though they are clean, (the phenomenon that) flies, leaves of grass, hairs of the head, etc. frequently fall into (one's) foods and drinks, sickness, vomiting, absence of appetite even when eating, decline of (bodily) force, looking with attention at (one's) hands, swelling of feet and mouth, an extremely white colour of the eyes, the desire to know the size of (one's) arms, seeing loathsome (appearances) in (one's) body, fondness for women, intoxicating beverages and meat, disdain, covering the head, and an extremely (rapid) growth of the nails and the hairs of the head; in one's dreams one may be overpowered by flying insects, lizards, snakes, monkeys, beasts of prey and birds, one may mount a pile of hairs, bones, chaff, ashes, etc. and one may see deserted villages and countries, water that is drying up, heavenly bodies and mountains that are falling and trees that are on fire;" fr. Bhe.Ci. 4 : "In (their) dreams they constantly see desiccated and burnt trees; flies and hairs of the head fall in his food; especially the hairs of his head are growing (fast); covering (of the body with clothes) is habitually practised; (the patient) is liable to irritation, springing up from his fondness of solitude; he is full of disgust, impatient, fond of women, provided with weak senses and deprived of the suitable shade (of his skin); desiccation of the palate, a discharge of various (colours), nasal catarrh, inarticulateness of the voice and a painful condition of the head arise in him; his thighs perspire extremely and his force and colour are deficient; there is a sensation of complete fullness in the head; hands and feet become desiccated; inability to eat and absence of digestive alteration are present; fainting, shortness of breath and a mild fever occur; he suffers from a lesion of the chest, and spits out, while coughing, (matter that is) accompanied by blood; these prodromes are proclaimed (to be present) in persons with consumption."

14 Ca.Ci. 8, 33-36ab is quoted (see note 13) with the variants : *ativardhana* instead of *abhivardhana* and *abhigharṣaṇa* (rubbing, friction) instead of *abhidharṣaṇa* (overpowering).

15 See about the *godhā* the article by Lüders : "Von indischen Tieren", ZDMG 96, 1942, p. 23 ff.

16 Ḍa. : "A porcupine (*śallakī*) is (an animal) mimicking a *godhā*; it is a *vajraśakala*, in common language well known (as) a *śallaka*."

17 Ḍa. : "A lizard is a *kṛkaṇṭaka*; those living in the east call it a *girgiṭ*;" Indu : a lizard is a *śaraḍa*; Śrīdāsa : a lizard is a *saraṭa*. *saraṭa* : PW : Eidechse, Chamäleon; MW : lizard, chameleon.

18 I.e. those holding on the Kaśmīr recension of the Carakasaṃhitā.

19 *tāpaḥ pādakarasya ca* instead of *saṃtāpaḥ karapādayoḥ*.

20 *karapādika*.

21 See Ca.Ni. 6, 14 : "Thereupon its eleven symptoms come into being, which are : fullness of the head, cough, shortness of breath, inarticulateness of the voice, vomiting of phlegm, spitting of blood, a painful condition of the sides, squeezing pain in the scapular region, fever, diarrhoea and anorexia." Cf. A.h.Ni. 5, 13cd-15ab = A.s.Ni. 5, 15cd-17ab (Ki. 5, 14-15) : "Nasal catarrh, shortness of breath, cough, pain in the scapular region, the head and the organ of speech and inability to eat come into being (when) the morbific entity (is present) in the upper (part of the body), descent of faecal matter or desiccation of it (when it is present) in the lower (part), vomiting (when it is present)

in the viscera, pain in the sides (when) it stays in the lateral (channels) and fever (when) it is present in the junctures. These eleven symptoms arise in a person with kingly consumption."

22 This additional stanza is approved of in Ā., but not in M.

23 Su. : *ṣaḍrūpe rājayakṣmaṇi* (in kingly consumption with six symptoms) instead of *ṣaḍrūpaṃ rājayakṣmaṇi* (as a set of six symptoms in kingly consumption).

24 Ḍa. remarks that this type of desiccation is started by morbific entities of moderate strength.

25 Su. : *saṃloca* (a sensation of plucking) instead of *saṃkoca* (a contracted state); Ḍa. makes mention of *saṃkoca* as a variant.

26 Cf. A.h.Ni. 5, 16cd-18 = A.s.Ni. 5, 18cd-20 (Ki. 5, 17-19) : "In this (consumption arise) from wind : piercing pain in head and sides, a squeezing sensation in the (whole) body and (especially) in the scapular region, a ruined condition of the throat and a failing voice; from bile (arise) : a burning sensation in the feet, scapular region and hands, diarrhoea, vomiting of blood, a (bad-)smelling mouth, fever and (mental disturbance as in) intoxication; from phlegm (arise) : anorexia, vomiting, cough, heaviness of the (whole) body and (especially) of the head, effusion (of phlegm), nasal catarrh, shortness of breath, exhaustion of the voice and a slight (activity of the transforming) fire."

27 See note 25.

28 Su. : *suvipulaṃ yaśaḥ* (very great fame) instead of *suvimalam yaśaḥ* (completely stainless fame).

29 Compare the six symptoms enumerated Ca.Ci. 8, 46cd : "Cough, fever, piercing pain in the sides, a malady concerning the voice and the excremental matter, and inability to eat."

30 Su. : *jvarakāsa* (fever and cough) instead of *kāsaśvāsa* (cough and shortness of breath).

31 Cf. Ca.Ni. 6, 15-16; A.h.Ni. 5, 23 — A.s.Ni. 5, 25 (Ki. 5, 22).

32 *ūrdhvaśvāsa*; see ch. 12.

33 Cf. Ca.I. 5, 7-8 : "Desiccation leads to death in a person who is deprived of his force, whose nasal catarrh is increasing and who is attached to women. A person who in his dreams travels to the south by means of dogs, camels or donkeys, will leave life after meeting with consumption;" Ca.I. 9, 7 : "Glowing heat of the scapular region, hiccup, vomiting of blood, obstructive abdominal swelling and piercing pain in the sides lead to the end (of life) in a person with consumption;" A.h.Śā. 5, 77ab = A.s.Śā. 11, 9cd : "Consumption (kills) someone who presents a painful condition of the sides, obstructive abdominal swelling, vomiting of blood and glowing heat of the scapular region;" Hā. 2, 4, 25 = Su.Sū. 33, 20 = Mā.ni. 10, 12; Hā. 2, 4, 26 : "Someone, suffering from kingly consumption, is annihilated if deficiency of the elements (of the body) comes to be present, if he is oppressed by swelling and shortness of breath, eats a great amount of food and is full of disgust;" fr. Bhe.Ci. 4 : "One should not treat (a patient) with desiccation if the secondary affections have surged, if he is silent, overrun by the prodromes, and if decline of his force and flesh are present. It is thought that he should not be rejected at all if he presents a small (number of) secondary affections, (if these) secondary affections have sprung up a short time ago, (if) he is provided with the substances (constituting the elements of the body) and (if) he is in the vigorous period of his life."

34 This is the additional stanza inserted between Mā.ni. 10, 5 and 6.

35 It is clear from Ḍa.'s comment that his text did not contain Su.U. 41, 14cd-15ab; he remarks that it is read in a different way in other treatises.

[36] Ca. : *varcogada* (a malady concerning the excremental matter) instead of *varcograha* (seizing of the excremental matter).

[37] Ca. : *svaravarcogada* instead of *svaravarcograha.*

[38] The term *bradhna* occurs in a quotation found in M. on Mā.ni. 37, 9-10; it is a kind of swelling of the groins.

[39] Ca. reads : "Persons with a wind illness, epilepsy, a skin disease, swelling, abdominal disease, visceral swelling, diabetes mellitus and kingly consumption, these are not fit for treatment if decline of force and flesh is present; a physician should also abstain from (treating) these (persons) in the case that other morbid alterations are present."

[40] Cakra also holds the opinion that six is the intended number.

[41] See e.g. Ca.Ci. 8, 42 and A.h.Ci. 5, 73cd-74ab.

[42] Ā. omits Mā.ni. 10, 8cd-9ab.

[43] Su. : *sphic* (buttock) instead of *asthi* (bone).

[44] Su. adds *oṣṭha* (lip).

[45] Su. : *raukṣyatodau* (dryness and pricking pain) instead of *rūkṣatā* (dryness).

[46] See Su.Sū. 15, 19.

[47] See Su.Sū. 15, 25-27ab.

[48] This stanza occurs : Siddhayoga 10, 81.

[49] The second half of this stanza is closely related to Su.U. 41, 32ab : "One may treat (a patient) who is self-possessed, whose (transforming) fire is inflamed, who is not lean and who (has acquired the disease) recently."

[50] This stanza is identical to Siddhayoga 10, 86; the same stanza occurs : Va. 10, 15; Bhā.pra. 8, 11, 17; Yo. p. 313.

[51] This stanza is related to Su.U. 41, 16: "Others say there are (types of) desiccation (arising) from sexual intercourse, grief, old age, physical exercise, fasting and the oppressing conditions consisting of an inflamed sore and a lesion of the chest." Cf. Hā. 3, 9, 107-111 : "On account of decline (arisen) from a lesion (of the chest), or on account of fatigue, a sudden accident (*upaplava*), extreme attachment to sexual intercourse and extreme indulgence in dry (articles of food), the body declines and a mild fever arises. At the end of (this) fever swelling occurs and an extreme (amount of) impure matter, faecal matter and urine (appears), diarrhoea comes into being and too much of the consumed food remains (? *bhakṣaṇenātiśeṣate*); by coughing one spits out excessively and a violent desiccation is brought about; an extreme craving for women occurs and aversion to looking after one's business. One should discern (this) malady as kingly consumption; a curable (type of it) does not occur. If the feet (of a patient) are numb, if he considers a mouthful (of food) to be much and if his voice is shrill, kingly consumption does not resolve itself;" Bhe.Ni. 2 describes the symptoms of the various kinds of decline according to their origin; Bhe.Ci. 4 states that the symptoms of consumption are said to be six or eleven in number, but they are not enumerated.

[52] Su. : *pratyekaṃ dhātusaṃjñitāḥ* (one by one technically called after the element of the body) instead of *pratyekaṃ dhātusaṃkṣayāt* (arising one by one from decline of an element).

[53] Cf. Ca.Sū. 17, 69 : "Weakness, desiccation of the mouth, pallor, adynamia, fatigue, impotence and non-emission of semen are the characteristics of someone whose semen is in a state of decline;" A.h.Sū. 11, 20: "When the semen (is in a state of decline), semen or even blood may be ejaculated after a long time, an extremely pricking pain is present in the testicles and it is as if smoking matter comes out of the penis;" fr. A.s.Sū. 19, 10 : "Semen, (when in a state of decline, oppresses painfully) by means of fatigue, weakness,

desiccation of the mouth, dimness of vision, pallor of the body, adynamia, impotence, pricking pain in the testicles, a condition (as if) smoking matter is coming out of the penis and ejaculation after a long time, or ejaculation (of semen) accompanied by blood."

[54] Su. : *abhilakṣita* (characterized) instead of *upalakṣita* (secondarily characterized).

[55] Su. *supta* (numb) instead of *śuṣka* (desiccated). Ḍa. remarks that the qualifications numb and dry refer to the lustre (of the skin) and that the qualification dry refers to the impurities.

[56] *ānana*, by Ḍa. explained as oral cavity (*mukhakuhara*).

[57] The same reasoning is found in Ḍa.'s comment on Su.U. 41, 21.

[58] This refers to Mā.ni. 10, 14ab.

[59] Su. : *smṛta* (traditionally said) instead of *mata* (thought).

[60] Su.Ci. 1, 30cd-31ab reads : "To those with desiccation (caused) by a sore, who present secondary affections and who are dry and lean, the drinking of oleaginous substances, prepared with remedial agents that are adequate to each particular case, is prescribed."

[61] From this it is clear that the author of M. read *smṛta* (in agreement with Su.) instead of *mata* (see note 59).

[62] Ca. : *patato viṣamoccebhyo balibhiḥ saha yudhyataḥ* instead of *yudhyamānasya balibhiḥ patato viṣamoccataḥ*.

[63] Ca. : *mahānadīm* (a great river) instead of *mahānadīḥ* (great rivers).

[64] Ca. : *atipranṛtyataḥ* (when dancing beyond the proper measure) instead of *api pranṛtyataḥ* (also when dancing).

[65] Ca. : *uro virujyate tasya bhidyate 'tha vibhajyate* instead of *uro vibhajyate 'tyartham bhidyate 'tha virujyate*.

[66] Ca. : *kāsamānasya ca śleṣmā saraktaḥ saṃpravartate* instead of *kāsamānasya cābhīkṣṇaṃ kaphaḥ sāsṛk pravartate*.

[67] Cf. Su.U. 41, 23-26ab : "In someone whose chest has been torn asunder by physical exercise, (lifting up heavy) loads, study, traumatic injury, sexual intercourse beyond the proper measure and by other actions requiring (exertion of) the chest, blood, pus and phlegm come (forth) when a lesion of the chest (has developed). While coughing, (such a person) will vomit matter that is (of a) yellow, red, dark or ruddy (colour). (Such) a man experiences an extreme glowing heat in his whole chest, and gasps for breath because of this (sensation of) being (internally) consumed by fire; his mouth and breath are bad-smelling and the colour (of his skin) and his voice are indistinct;" A.h.Ni. 3, 27cd-32ab = A.s.Ni. 3, 33-37 (Ki. 3, 31-35) : "When there has developed an internal lesion of the chest by fighting and other inconsiderate actions of that kind, indulged in beyond one's force, the wind, attended by the bile, (grown) strong and excited, gives rise to coughing. By means of this (coughing) one may spit out phlegm, accompanied by blood and (of a) yellow or brown (colour), desiccated, globose, stinking and copious, by way of a painful throat and chest that feel (as if) cut asunder, (as if) being pricked with sharp needles and in which one feels a piercing pain. Cutting pain in the junctures, fever, shortness of breath, thirst, an altered state of the voice and trembling occur (in such a person); he makes sounds like the cooing of a pigeon and experiences a piercing pain in his sides; thereupon, one is gradually deprived of one's potency, appetite, maturating (fire), force and colour; in a person presenting (this kind of) decline, the urine may be mixed with blood and there may occur a seizing pain in the back and iliac region;" Kā.Sū. 25, 37-38 : "When (a child), every time it has drunk at the breast, breathes by way of the mouth, when there is a discharge from its nostrils, its forehead is glowingly

hot, it repeatedly touches its (nose-)channels, when it sneezes and coughs, (these signs refer) to nasal catarrh; when an injury of the chest is present, the same (signs) may occur, and murmurs in the chest additionally;" fr. Kā., *uroghātacikitsitādhyāya* : "The morbific entities, excited by their own causes, give rise to the fourfold injury of the chest in those who indulge in inconsistency, overeating, etc. (In this disease are present :) cold fever, nasal catarrh, a sensation as if the throat were covered with awns, expectoration, a sluggish... (the text breaks off). Injury of the chest is an illness arising from the three morbific entities, of which bile and phlegm are the most important ones (in this case). Therefore the wet-nurse should permanently apply (therapeutical measures) damaging to bile and phlegm."

68 Cakra remarks : " 'Illness' (denotes) the illness, the characteristics of which will (shortly) be stated, (viz.) that one called decline from a lesion (of the chest); others say that the term illness indicates the lesion (of the chest) as such, according to the saying : 'the term illness is also applied to the morbific entities', etc."

69 Cf. Su.U. 41, 32ab (see note 49); Hā. 3, 9, 115-118 : "(Someone suffering from consumption) may remain alive for four months or, if he is excessively strong, for six months; he (may) live a thousand days with (the help of) excellent counter-measures. Longer than a thousand (days) does not endure the life of a man with kingly consumption whose vital breaths, vital fluid and potency are gone, who is subject to decline and whose senses are bewildered. When there comes no (new) surge (of the symptoms, however), it is a mitigable disease and one is released. If it increases in case of exertion and coughing also comes to arise, it is an extremely severe (kind of) kingly consumption, that eliminates the vital breaths of a person (suffering from it) within three months, six months or three years."

APPENDIX ONE

A. A CONCORDANCE OF MĀDHAVANIDĀNA CH. 1-10 AND ITS SOURCES

1, 1.
1, 2.
1, 3.
1, 4 — A.h.Ni. 1, 2.
1, 5 — A.h.Ni. 1, 3.
1, 6 — A.h.Ni. 1, 4.
1, 7 — A.h.Ni. 1, 5.
1, 8 — A.h.Ni. 1, 6.
1, 9 — A.h.Ni. 1, 7.
1, 10 — A.h.Ni. 1, 8.
1, 11 — A.h.Ni. 1, 9.
1, 12 — A.h.Ni. 1, 10.
1, 13 — A.h.Ni. 1, 11.
1, 14 — A.h.Ni. 1, 12.
1, 15ab — A.h.Ni. 1, 13ab.
1, 15cd — Ca.Ni. 8, 16cd.
1, 16 — Ca.Ni. 8, 17.
1, 17 — Ca.Ni. 8, 18.
2 add. *pādas*
1, 18 — Ca.Ni. 8, 19.
1, 19ab — Ca.Ni. 8, 20ab.
1, 19cd — Ca.Ni. 8, 21ab.
1, 20 — Ca.Ni. 8, 21cd-22ab.
1, 21.

2, 1.
2, 2.
2, 3ab — Su.U. 39, 13cd.
2, 3cd — related to Su.U. 39, 14ab.
2, 4 — Su.U. 39, 25.
2, 5 — Su.U. 39, 26.
2, 6 — Su.U. 39, 27.
2, 7ab — related to Su.U. 39, 28cd.
2, 7cd — Su.U. 39, 28ab.
2, 8 — Su.U. 39, 29.
2, 9 — Su.U. 39, 30.
2, 10 — Su.U. 39, 31.
2, 11 — Su.U. 39, 32.
2, 12 — variant of Su.U. 39, 33 recorded by Ḍa.
2, 13ab — Su.U. 39, 33ab.
add. stanza — Su.U. 39, 33cd-34ab.
2, 13cd — Su.U. 39, 34cd.
2, 14 — Su.U. 39, 47.
2, 15 — Su.U. 39, 48.
2, 16 — Su.U. 39, 49 — Ca.Ci. 3, 87.
2, 17 — Su.U. 39, 50.
2, 18 — Ca.Ci. 3, 103cd-104ab.
2, 19 — Ca.Ci. 3, 104cd-105ab.
2, 20 — Ca.Ci. 3, 105cd-106ab.
2, 21 — Ca.Ci. 3, 106cd-107ab.
2, 22 — Ca.Ci. 3, 107cd-108ab.
2, 23 — Ca.Ci. 3, 108cd-109ab.
2, 24 — Ca.Ci. 3, 109cd-110ab.
2, 25 — Ca.Ci. 3, 287cd-288ab — A.h.Ci. 1, 149.
2, 26.
2, 27 — Su.U. 39, 76cd-77ab.
2, 28 — Su.U. 39, 77cd-78ab.
2, 29 — Su.U. 39, 78cd-79ab; 79cd.
2, 30ab — Su.U. 39, 80ab.
2, 30cd — Ca.Ci. 3, 115cd.
2, 31ab — Ca.Ci. 3, 116ab.
2, 31cd — Su.U. 39, 66ab.
2, 32 — Su.U. 39, 66cd-67ab.
2, 33 — Su.U. 39, 67cd-68ab.
2, 34 — Su.U. 39, 69.
2, 35 — Su.U. 39, 70.
2, 36ab — Su.U. 39, 71ab.
2, 36cd — Su.U. 39, 68cd.
2, 37 — Ca.Ci. 3, 71.
2, 38 — Ca.Ci. 3, 72.
2, 39ab — Ca.Ci. 3, 73ab.
2, 39cd — quoted by Cakra on Ca.Ci. 3, 73.
2, 40 — A.s.Ni. 2, 88cd-89ab.
2, 41 — A.s.Ni. 2, 87cd-88ab.
2, 42 — A.s.Ni. 2, 92cd-93ab.
2, 43 — A.s.Ni. 2, 93cd-94ab.
2, 44.

2, 45 — Su.U. 39, 59.
2, 46 — Su.U. 39, 60.
2, 47 — Su.U. 39, 61.
2, 48 — Su.U. 39, 83.
2, 49 — Su.U. 39, 84.
2, 50 — Su.U. 39, 85.
2, 51 — Su.U. 39, 86.
2, 52 — Su.U. 39, 87.
2, 53 — Su.U. 39, 88a-d.
2, 54 — Su.U. 39, 88ef-89ab.
add. stanza — Ca.Ci. 3, 83.
2, 55 — A.h.Ni. 2, 50.
2, 56 — A.h.Ni. 2, 51.
2, 57 — A.h.Ni. 2, 52.
2, 58 — A.h.Ni. 2, 23.
2, 59 — Ca.Ci. 3, 39cd-40ab.
2, 60 — Ca.Ci. 3, 40cd-41ab.
2, 61ab — Ca.Ci. 3, 41cd.
2, 61cd-2, 63ab — part of a variant of Su.U. 39, 116cd-119ab, recorded by Ḍa.
2, 63cd — Su.U. 39, 121cd.
2 add. *pādas* — Su.U. 39, 122ab.
2, 64 — Ca.Ci. 3, 136cd-137ab.
2, 65 — Ca.Ci. 3, 137cd-138ab.
2, 66 — Ca.Ci. 3, 50.
2, 67ab — Ca.Ci. 3, 51ab.
2, 67cd — Ca.Ci. 3, 52cd.
2, 68ab — Ca.Ci. 3, 53ab.
2, 68cd — Su.U. 39, 92cd.
2, 69ab — Su.U. 39, 93ab.
2, 69cd.
2, 70ab.
2, 70cd — Su.Sū. 33, 15ab.
2, 71 — Su.Sū. 33, 15cd-16ab.
2, 72 — Su.Sū. 33, 16cd-17ab
2, 73ab — Su.Sū. 33, 17cd.
2, 73cd — Su.U. 39, 93cd.
2, 74ab — Su.U. 39, 94ab.
2, 74c-f.
2, 75 — related to Su.U. 39, 322.

3, 1 — Su.U. 40, 3.
3, 2 — Su.U. 40, 4.
3, 3 — Su.U. 40, 5.
3, 4a-d — related to Su.U. 40, 6.
3, 4ef — Su.U. 40, 7ab.
3, 5 — Su.U. 40, 8cd-9ab.
3, 6.
3, 7ab — Su.U. 40, 11ab.
3, 7cd — related to Su.U. 40, 12ab.
3, 8.
3, 9 — Su.U. 40, 13cd-14ab.
3, 10 — Su.U. 40, 14cd-15ab.
3. 11 — related to Su.U. 40, 15cd-16ab.
3, 12 — Su.U. 40, 17.
3, 13 — Su.U. 40, 18.
3, 14.
3, 15.
3, 16.
3, 17.
3, 18 — Su.U. 40, 21.
3, 19 — Su.Sū. 33, 19.
add. stanza — Hā. 3, 3, 77.
3, 20.
3, 21 — Su.U. 40, 138.
3, 22a-f — Su.U. 40, 139-140ab.
3, 23 — Su.U. 40, 162 — A.h.Ci. 9, 124 — A.s.Ci. 11, 30.
add. stanza.

4, 1 — Su.U. 40, 167.
4, 2 — Su.U. 40, 171.
4, 3 — Su.U. 40, 172.
4, 4 — Ca.Ci. 15, 55.
4, 5 — Ca.Ci. 15, 59.
4, 6 — Ca.Ci. 15, 60.
4, 7 — Ca.Ci. 15, 61.
4, 8 — Ca.Ci. 15, 62.
4, 9 — Ca.Ci. 15, 63.
4, 10 — Ca.Ci. 15, 64.
4, 11 — Ca.Ci. 15, 65.
4, 12 — Ca.Ci. 15, 66.
4, 13 — Ca.Ci. 15, 67.
4, 14 — Ca.Ci. 15, 68.
4, 15 — Ca.Ci. 15, 69.
4, 16 — Ca.Ci. 15, 70.
4, 17 — Ca.Ci. 15, 72.
4 add. stanzas.
4, 18.
4, 19.
add. stanza.

5, 1.
5, 2 — A.h.Ni. 7, 2.
5, 3 — Ca.Ci. 14, 12.

5, 4 — Ca.Ci. 14, 13.
5, 5 — Ca.Ci. 14, 15.
5, 6 — Ca.Ci. 14, 16.
5, 7 — Ca.Ci. 14, 18.
5, 8 — Ca.Ci. 14, 19.
5, 9 — Ca.Ci. 14, 20.
5, 10 — A.h.Ni. 7, 28cd-29ab.
5, 11 — A.h.Ni. 7, 29cd-30ab.
5, 12 — A.h.Ni. 7, 30cd-31ab.
5, 13 — A.h.Ni. 7, 31cd-32ab.
5, 14 — A.h.Ni. 7, 32cd-33ab.
5, 15 — A.h.Ni. 7, 33cd-34ab.
5, 16 — A.h.Ni. 7, 34cd-35ab.
5, 17 — A.h.Ni. 7, 35cd-36ab.
5, 18 — A.h.Ni. 7, 36cd-37ab.
5, 19 — A.h.Ni. 7, 37cd-38ab.
5, 20 — A.h.Ni. 7, 38cd-39ab.
5, 21 — A.h.Ni. 7, 39cd-40ab.
5, 22 — A.h.Ni. 7, 40cd-41ab.
5, 23 — A.h.Ni. 7, 41cd-42ab.
5, 24ab.
5, 24cd — A.h.Ni. 7, 43ab.
5, 25 — A.h.Ni. 7, 43cd-44ab.
5, 26 — A.h.Ni. 7, 44cd-45ab.
5, 27ab — A.h.Ni. 7, 45cd.
2 add. *pādas* — Ca.Ci. 14, 170cd.
5, 27cd — Ca.Ci. 14, 171ab.
5, 28 — Ca.Ci. 14, 171cd-172ab.
5, 29 — Ca.Ci. 14, 172cd-173ab.
5, 30a-f — Ca.Ci. 14, 173cd-174.
5, 31 — Ca.Ci. 14, 21.
5, 32 — Ca.Ci. 14, 22.
5, 33 — Ca.Ci. 14, 24.
5, 34 — Ca.Ci. 14, 25.
5, 35 — Ca.Ci. 14, 31.
5, 36 — Ca.Ci. 14, 30.
5, 37 — Ca.Ci. 14, 28.
5, 38 — Ca.Ci. 14, 29.
5, 39 — Ca.Ci. 14, 26.
5, 40 — Ca.Ci. 14, 27.
5, 41 — Su.Sū. 33, 10.
5, 42 — A.h.Ni. 7, 56.
5, 43 — A.h.Ni. 7, 57.
5, 44 — A.h.Ni. 7, 58.

6, 1.
6, 2 — Su.Sū. 35, 25.
6, 3.
6, 4.
6, 5 — Su.Sū. 46, 499.
6, 6.
6, 7 — Su.Sū. 46, 500.
6, 8 — Su.Sū. 46, 501.
6, 9 — Ca.Vi. 2, 9.
6, 10 — A.s.Sū. 11, 55.
6, 11 — A.s.Sū. 11, 57.
6, 12 — A.s.Sū. 11, 56.
6, 13ab — A.s.Sū. 11, 60ab.
6, 13c-f — Su.Sū. 46, 504.
6, 14.
6, 15 — Su.U. 56, 3.
6, 16 — Su.U. 56, 4.
6, 17 — Su.U. 56, 5.
6, 18 — Su.U. 56, 6.
6, 19 — Su.U. 56, 7.
6, 20 — Su.U. 56, 8.
6, 21 — Su.U. 56, 9.
6, 22 — Su.U. 56, 10.
6, 23 — Su.U. 56, 11.
6, 24 — A.s.Sū. 11, 69cd-70ab.
6, 25.
6, 26.
6, 27 — related to A.h.Sū. 8, 30cd-31ab.

7, 1 — A.h.Ni. 14, 42cd-43ab.
7, 2 — A.h.Ni. 14, 43cd-44ab.
7, 3 — A.h.Ni. 14, 44cd-45ab.
7, 4 — related to a variant of Su.U. 54, 3-6, recorded by Ḍa.
7, 5 — Su.U. 54, 17.
7, 6 — Su.U. 54, 18.
7, 7ab — Su.U. 54, 19ab.
7, 7cd — A.h.Ni. 14, 47ab.
7, 8 — A.h.Ni. 14, 47cd-48ab.
7, 9 — A.h.Ni. 14, 48cd-49ab.
7, 10 — A.h.Ni. 14, 49cd-50ab.
7, 11 — A.h.Ni. 14, 50cd-51ab.
7, 12a-f — A.h.Ni. 14, 51cd-52.
7, 13 — A.h.Ni. 14, 53.
7, 14 — A.h.Ni. 14, 54.
7, 15 — A.h.Ni. 14, 55.
7, 16 — A.h.Ni. 14, 56.

8, 1 — Ca.Ci. 16, 3.
8, 2 — Su.U. 44, 3.

8, 3 — Su.U. 44, 5.
8, 4.
8, 5.
8, 6.
8, 7.
8, 8 — Ca.Ci. 16, 27.
8, 9 — Ca.Ci. 16, 28.
8, 10 — Ca.Ci. 16, 29.
8, 11 — Ca.Ci. 16, 30.
8, 12 — Ca.Ci. 16, 31.
8, 13 — Ca.Ci. 16, 32.
8, 14ab — Ca.Ci. 16, 33ab.
8, 14c-f — Su.Sū. 33, 23.
8, 15a-f — Su.U. 44, 39-40.
8, 16 — Ca.Ci. 16, 34.
8, 17 — Ca.Ci. 16, 35.
8, 18 — Ca.Ci. 16, 36.
8, 19 — Ca.Ci. 16, 37.
8, 20 — Ca.Ci. 16, 38.
8, 21ab — Ca.Ci. 16, 39ab.
8, 21cd.
8, 22ab.
8, 22cd — Ca.Ci. 16, 132cd.
8, 23a-f — Ca.Ci. 16, 133-134ab.
add. stanza — related to stanza quoted by Ḍa. in comm. on Su.U. 44, 12.

9, 1.
9, 2 — Su.U. 45, 4cdab.
9, 3 — A.h.Ni. 3, 7cd-8ab.
9, 4 — Su.U. 45, 7cd-8ab.
9, 5 — Ca.Ci. 4, 11.
9, 6 — Ca.Ci. 4, 12.
9, 7ab — Ca.Ci. 4, 13ab.
9, 7c-f — Ca.Ci. 4, 24.
9, 8ab — Su.U. 45, 7ab.
9, 8cd — Ca.Ci. 4, 22ab.
9, 9ab — Ca.Ci. 4, 22cd.
9, 9cd — Ca.Ci. 4, 13cd.
9, 10 — Ca.Ci. 4, 14.
9, 11 — Su.U. 45, 9.
9, 12 — Su.U. 45, 10.
9, 13 — Ca.Ni. 2, 26.
9, 14 — Su.Sū. 33, 24.

10, 1.
10, 2a-f — Su.U. 41, 9cd-10.
10, 3 — Su.U. 41, 29.
10, 4 — Su.U. 41, 30.
10, 5 — Ca.Ci. 18, 52.
add. stanza — Su.U. 41, 11.
10, 6 — Su.U. 41, 12.
10, 7 — Su.U. 41, 13.
10, 8 — Su.U. 41, 14.
10, 9 — Su.U. 41, 15.
10, 10 — Ca.Ci. 8, 47.
10, 11 — Su.U. 31, 41.
10, 12 — Su.Sū. 33, 20.
10, 13ab.
10, 13cd — Su.U. 41, 32ab.
10, 14 — related to Su.U. 41, 16.
10, 15 — Su.U. 41, 17.
10, 16ab — Su.U. 41, 18ab.
10, 16cd — Su.U. 41, 19ab.
10, 17 — Su.U. 41, 19cd-20ab.
10, 18 — Su.U. 41, 20cd-21ab.
10, 19a-f — Su.U. 41, 21cd-22.
10, 20 — Su.U. 41, 23.
10, 21 — Ca.Ci. 11, 4.
10, 22 — Ca.Ci. 11, 5.
10, 23 — Ca.Ci. 11, 6.
10, 24 — Ca.Ci. 11, 7.
10, 25 — Ca.Ci. 11, 8.
10, 26 — Ca.Ci. 11, 9.
10, 27 — Ca.Ci. 11, 10.
10, 28 — Ca.Ci. 11, 11.
10, 29 — Ca.Ci. 11, 12.
10, 30 — Ca.Ci. 11, 13.
10, 31 — Ca.Ci. 11, 14.

B. A SYSTEMATIC ARRANGEMENT OF THE SOURCES OF MĀDHAVANIDĀNA CH. 1-10 AND THE CORRESPONDING STANZAS OF THE NIDĀNA

Carakasaṃhitā :

Ca.Ni.

2, 26 — 9, 13.

8, 16cd — 1, 15cd.
8, 17 — 1, 16.
8, 18 — 1, 17.
8, 19 — 1, 18.

8, 20ab — 1, 19ab.
8, 21ab — 1, 19cd.
8, 21cd-22ab — 1, 20.
Ca.Vi.
2, 9 — 6, 9.
Ca.Ci.
3, 39cd-40ab — 2, 59.
3, 40cd-41ab — 2, 60.
3, 41cd — 2, 61ab.
3, 50 — 2, 66.
3, 51ab — 2, 67ab.
3, 52cd — 2, 67cd.
3, 53ab — 2, 68ab.
3, 71 — 2, 37.
3, 72 — 2, 38.
3, 73ab — 2, 39ab.
3, 83 — add. stanza between 2, 54 and 2, 55.
3, 87 — 2, 10.
3, 103cd-104ab — 2, 18.
3, 104cd-105ab — 2, 19.
3, 105cd-106ab — 2, 20.
3, 106cd-107ab — 2, 21.
3, 107cd-108ab — 2, 22.
3, 108cd-109ab — 2, 23.
3, 109cd-110ab — 2, 24.
3, 115cd — 2, 30cd.
3, 116ab — 2, 31ab.
3, 136cd-137ab — 2, 64.
3, 137cd-138ab — 2, 65.
3, 287cd-288ab — 2, 25.
4, 11 — 9, 5.
4, 12 — 9, 6.
4, 13ab — 9, 7ab.
4, 13cd — 9, 9cd.
4, 14 — 9, 10.
4, 22ab — 9, 8cd.
4, 22cd — 9, 9ab.
4, 24 — 9, 7c-f.
8, 47 — 10, 10.
11, 4 — 10, 21.
11, 5 — 10, 22.
11, 6 — 10, 23.
11, 7 — 10, 24.
11, 8 — 10, 25.
11, 9 — 10, 26.
11, 10 — 10, 27.
11, 11 — 10, 28.
11, 12 — 10, 29.
11, 13 — 10, 30.
11, 14 — 10, 31.
14, 12 — 5, 3.
14, 13 — 5, 4.
14, 15 — 5, 5.
14, 16 — 5, 6.
14, 18 — 5, 7.
14, 19 — 5, 8.
14, 20 — 5, 9.
14, 21 — 5, 31.
14, 22 — 5, 32.
14, 24 — 5, 33.
14, 25 — 5, 34.
14, 26 — 5, 39.
14, 27 — 5, 40.
14, 28 — 5, 37.
14, 29 — 5, 38.
14, 30 — 5, 36.
14, 31 — 5, 35.
14, 170cd — 2 add. *pāda*s between 5, 27ab and 5, 27cd.
14, 171ab — 5, 27cd.
14, 171cd-172ab — 5, 28.
14, 172cd-173ab — 5, 29.
14, 173cd-174 — 5, 30a-f.
15, 55 — 4, 4.
15, 59 — 4, 5.
15, 60 — 4, 6.
15, 61 — 4, 7.
15, 62 — 4, 8.
15, 63 — 4, 9.
15, 64 — 4, 10.
15, 65 — 4, 11.
15, 66 — 4, 12.
15, 67 — 4, 13.
15, 68 — 4, 14.
15, 69 — 4, 15.
15, 70 — 4, 16.
15, 72 — 4, 17.
16, 3 — 8, 1.
16, 27 — 8, 8.
16, 28 — 8, 9.
16, 29 — 8, 10.
16, 30 — 8, 11.
16, 31 — 8, 12.
16, 32 — 8, 13.
16, 33ab — 8, 14ab.

16, 34 — 8, 16.
16, 35 — 8, 17.
16, 36 — 8, 18.
16, 37 — 8, 19.
16, 38 — 8, 20.
16, 39ab — 8, 21ab.
16, 132cd — 8, 22cd.
16, 133-134ab — 8, 23a-f.
18, 52 — 10, 5.

Suśrutasaṃhitā :

Su.Sū.
33, 10 — 5, 41.
33, 15ab — 2, 70cd.
33, 15cd-16ab — 2, 71.
33, 16cd-17ab — 2, 72.
33, 17cd — 2, 73ab.
33, 19 — 3, 19.
33, 20 — 10, 12.
33, 23 — 8, 14c-f.
33, 24 — 9, 14.
35, 25 — 6, 2.
46, 499 — 6, 5.
46, 500 — 6, 7.
46, 501 — 6, 8.
46, 504 — 6, 13c-f.
Su.U.
39, 13cd — 2, 3ab.
39, 25 — 2, 4.
39, 26 — 2, 5.
39, 27 — 2, 6.
39, 28ab — 2, 7cd.
39, 29 — 2, 8.
39, 30 — 2, 9.
39, 31 — 2, 10.
39, 32 — 2, 11.
39, 33ab — 2, 13ab.
39, 33cd-34ab — add. stanza between 2, 13ab and 2, 13cd.
39, 34cd — 2, 13cd.
39, 47 — 2, 14.
39, 48 — 2, 15.
39, 49 — 2, 16.
39, 50 — 2, 17.
39, 59 — 2, 45.
39, 60 — 2, 46.
39, 61 — 2, 47.
39, 66ab — 2, 31cd.
39, 66cd-67ab — 2, 32.
39, 67cd-68ab — 2, 33.
39, 68cd — 2, 36cd.
39, 69 — 2, 34.
39, 70 — 2, 35.
39, 71ab — 2, 36ab.
39, 76cd-77ab — 2, 27.
39, 77cd-78ab — 2, 28.
39, 78cd-79ab + 39, 79cd — 2, 29.
39, 80ab — 2, 30ab.
39, 83 — 2, 48.
39, 84 — 2. 49.
39, 85 — 2, 50.
39, 86 — 2, 51.
39, 87 — 2, 52.
39, 88a-d — 2, 53.
39, 88ef-89ab — 2, 54.
39, 92cd — 2, 68cd.
39, 93ab — 2, 69ab.
39, 93cd — 2, 73cd.
39, 94ab — 2, 74ab.
39, 121cd — 2, 63cd.
39, 122ab — 2 add. *pādas* between 2, 63 and 2, 64.
40, 3 — 3, 1.
40, 4 — 3, 2.
40, 5 — 3, 3.
40, 7ab — 3, 4ef.
40, 8cd-9ab — 3, 5.
40, 11ab — 3, 7ab.
40, 13cd-14ab — 3, 9.
40, 14cd-15ab — 3, 10.
40, 17 — 3, 12.
40, 18 — 3, 13.
40, 21 — 3, 18.
40, 138 — 3, 21.
40, 139-140ab — 3, 22a-f.
40, 162 — 3, 23.
40, 167 — 4, 1.
40, 171 — 4, 2.
40, 172 — 4, 3.
41, 9cd-10 — 10, 2a-f.
41, 11 — add. stanza between 10, 5 and 10, 6.
41, 12 — 10, 6.
41, 13 — 10, 7.

41, 14 — 10, 8.
41, 15 — 10, 9.
41, 17 — 10, 15.
41, 18ab — 10, 16ab.
41, 19ab — 10, 16cd.
41, 19cd-20ab — 10, 17.
41, 20cd-21ab — 10, 18.
41, 21cd-22 — 10, 19a-f.
41, 23 — 10, 20.
41, 29 — 10, 3.
41, 30 — 10, 4.
41, 31 — 10, 11.
41, 32ab — 10, 13cd.
44, 3 — 8, 2.
44, 5 — 8, 3.
44, 39-40 — 8, 15a-f.
45, 4ab — 9, 2cd.
45, 4cd — 9, 2ab.
45, 7ab — 9, 8ab.
46, 7cd-8ab — 9, 4.
45, 9 — 9, 11.
45, 10 — 9, 12.
54, 17 — 7, 5.
54, 18 — 7, 6.
54, 19ab — 7, 7ab.
56, 3 — 6, 15.
56, 4 — 6, 16.
56, 5 — 6, 17.
56, 6 — 6, 18.
56, 7 — 6, 19.
56, 8 — 6, 20.
56, 9 — 6, 21.
56, 10 — 6, 22.
56, 11 — 6, 23.
39, 14ab — related to 2, 3cd.
39, 28cd — related to 2, 7ab.
39, 322 — related to 2, 75.
40, 6 — related to 3, 4a-d.
40, 12ab — related to 3, 7cd.
40, 15cd-16ab — related to 3, 11.
41, 16 — related to 10, 14.

Aṣṭāṅgahṛdayasaṃhitā :

A.h.Ni.

1, 2 — 1, 4.
1, 3 — 1, 5.
1, 4 — 1, 6.
1, 5 — 1, 7.
1, 6 — 1, 8.
1, 7 — 1, 9.
1, 8 — 1, 10.
1, 9 — 1, 11.
1, 10 — 1, 12.
1, 11 — 1, 13.
1, 12 — 1, 14.
1, 13ab — 1, 15ab.
2, 50 — 2, 55.
2, 51 — 2, 56.
2, 52 — 2, 57.
2, 53 — 2, 58.
3, 7cd-8ab — 9, 3.
7, 2 — 5, 2.
7, 28cd-29ab — 5, 10.
7, 29cd-30ab — 5, 11.
7, 30cd-31ab — 5, 12.
7, 31cd-32ab — 5, 13.
7, 32cd-33ab — 5, 14.
7, 33cd-34ab — 5, 15.
7, 34cd-35ab — 5, 16.
7, 35cd-36ab — 5, 17.
7, 36cd-37ab — 5, 18.
7, 37cd-38ab — 5, 19.
7, 38cd-39ab — 5, 20.
7, 39cd-40ab — 5, 21.
7, 40cd-41ab — 5, 22.
7, 41cd-42ab — 5, 23.
7, 43ab — 5, 24cd.
7, 43cd-44ab — 5, 25.
7, 44cd-45ab — 5, 26.
7, 45cd — 5, 27ab.
7, 56 — 5, 42.
7, 57 — 5, 43.
7, 58 — 5, 44.
14, 42cd-43ab — 7, 1.
14, 43cd-44ab — 7, 2.
14, 44cd-45ab — 7, 3.
14, 47ab — 7, 7cd.
14, 47cd-48ab — 7, 8.
14, 48cd-49ab — 7, 9.
14, 49cd-50ab — 7, 10.
14, 50cd-51ab — 7, 11.
14, 51cd-52 — 7, 12a-f.
14, 53 — 7, 13.
14, 54 — 7, 14.
14, 55 — 7, 15.
14, 56 — 7, 16.

A.h.Ci.
1, 149 — 2, 25.
9, 124 — 3, 23.
A.h.Sū.
8, 30cd-31ab — related to 6, 27.

Aṣṭāṅgasaṃgraha :

A.s.Sū.
11, 55 — 6, 10.
11, 56 — 6, 12.
11, 57 — 6, 11.
11, 60ab — 6, 13ab.
11, 69cd-70ab — 6, 24.
A.s.Ni.
2, 87cd-88ab — 2, 41.
2, 88cd-89ab — 2, 40.
2, 92cd-93ab — 2, 42.
2, 93cd-94ab — 2, 43.
A.s.Ci.
11, 30 — 3, 23.

A concordance of stanzas from the Aṣṭāṅgahṛdayasaṃhitā which are also found in the Aṣṭāṅgasaṃgraha

A.h.Ni.	2, 50	=	A.s.Ni.	2, 47cd-48ab (Ki. 2, 50-51ab).
	2, 51	=		2, 49 (Ki. 2, 52-53ab).
	2, 52	=		2, 50 (Ki. 2, 53cd-54).
	2, 53	=		2, 51 (Ki. 2, 55).
	3, 7cd-8ab	=		3, 9cd-10ab (Ki. 3, 9).
	7, 56	=		7, 30 (Ki. 7, 30).
	7, 57	=		7, 31 (Ki. 7, 31).
	7, 58	=		7, 32 (Ki. 7, 32).
	14, 42cd-43ab	=		14, 45 (Ki. 14, 43).
	14, 43cd-44ab	=		14, 46 (Ki. 14, 44).
	14, 44cd-45ab	=		14, 47 (Ki. 14, 45).
	14, 47ab	=		14, 49cd (Ki. 14, 47cd).
	14, 47cd-48ab	=		14, 50 (Ki. 14, 48).
	14, 48cd-49ab	=		14, 51 (Ki. 14, 49).
	14, 49cd-50ab	=		14, 52 (Ki. 14, 50).
	14, 50cd-51ab	=		14, 53 (Ki. 14, 51).
	14, 51cd-52	=		14, 54-55ab (Ki. 14, 52-53ab).
	14, 53	=		14, 55cd-56ab (Ki. 14, 56cd-57ab).
	14, 54	=		14, 56cd-57ab (Ki. : not numbered).
	14, 55	=		14, 57cd-58ab (Ki. : not numbered).
	14, 56	=		14, 58c-f (Ki. : not numbered).
A.h.Ci.	1, 149	=	A.s.Ci.	2, 115cd-116ab.
	9, 124	=		11, 30.

Hārītasaṃhitā

Hā. 3, 3, 77 — add. stanza between 3, 19 and 3, 20.

Other sources (Cakrapāṇidatta and Ḍalhaṇa)

1) variant of Su.U. 39, 33, recorded by Ḍa. : 2, 12.
2) quotation by Cakra on Ca.Ci. 3, 73 : 2, 39cd.
3) part of a variant of Su.U. 39, 116cd-119ab, recorded by Ḍa. : 2, 61cd-63ab.
4) variant of Su.U. 54, 3-6, recorded by Ḍa. : related to 7, 4.
5) stanza quoted by Ḍa. on Su.U. 44, 12 : related to add. stanza after 8, 23.

From unknown sources or composed by Mādhava

1, 1.
1, 2.
1, 3.
2 add. *pādas* between 1, 17 and 1, 18.
1, 21.
2, 1.
2, 2.
2, 26.
2, 44.
2, 69cd.
2, 70ab.
2, 74c-f.
3, 6.
3, 8.
3, 14.
3, 15.
3, 16.
3, 17.
3, 20.
add. stanza after 3, 23.
4 add. stanzas between 4, 17 and 4, 18.
4, 18.
4, 19.
add. stanza after 4, 19.
5, 1.
5, 24ab.
6, 1.
6, 3.
6, 4.
6, 6.
6, 14.
6, 25.
6, 26.
8, 4.
8, 5.
8, 6.
8, 7.
8, 21cd.
8, 22ab.
9, 1.
10, 1.
10, 13ab.

C. A SURVEY OF THE QUOTATIONS AND REFERENCES IN M. AND Ā. ON CH. 1-10 OF THE MĀDHAVANIDĀNA

1, 1

1, 2-3 M. Caraka : quotation not traceable in the Carakasaṃhitā.
Caraka : Sū. 20, 20.
Ā. *uktaṃ ca* : quotation from an unknown source.

1, 4 M. Suśruta : U. 1, 25.
Caraka : Ni. 8, 24.
Vāpyacandra.
Caraka : fr. Ni. 1, 36.
Suśruta : reference to U. 39, 97-98a.
Caraka : I. 5, 4-5.
Caraka : Ci. 6, 54.
Caraka : Sū. 10, 11.
Caraka : Sū. 10, 14ab.
tathā (Caraka) : Ci. 3, 109d-110a.
Caraka : fr. Vi. 4, 8.
Suśruta : fr. Sū. 13, 11cd.
Ā. Suśruta : quotation not traced in the Suśrutasaṃhitā.

1, 5 a-c M. (Nyāyasūtra 1, 1, 15).
Haricandra.
yathā : quotation related to Su.U. 64, 32.
Caraka : fr. Ni. 4, 4.
Bhaṭṭāraharicandra.
Cakra.
Caraka : Ci. 26, 27cd.
yathā : partial quotation of a variant of Su.Ni. 1, 42, differing from the printed text but, acc. to Ḍa., adopted by Gayadāsa.
Suśruta : partial quotation of a variant of Su.Ci. 33, 14, recorded by Ḍa.
Bhaṭṭāraharicandra.
Tīsaṭācārya : Cikitsākalikā 29-31 (many variants; see note 37).
Caraka : Ci. 3, 42ab.
Caraka : fr. Vi. 6, 11.
Caraka : fr. Ci. 21, 40.
Caraka : Sū. 10, 11cd.
Caraka : Sū. 17, 45-46.
Bhaṭṭāraharicandra.
Bhaṭṭāraharicandra.
Caraka : Sū. 17, 112ab.
Caraka : Sū. 17, 112-113ab.
yathā : Ca.Sū. 17, 62.
Sudāntasena (*carakapāṭhasaṃvādin*).
Suśruta : quotation related to Ci. 33, 3.
Caraka : Ni. 2, 19cd.
iti vacanam : fr. Ca.Sū. 25, 40.
Caraka (*carakakṛtaivaitā saṃjñāḥ*) : reference to Sū. 11, 48.
Caraka : Sū. 14, 9.
tathā : Su.U. 39, 67ab.
tathā : Ca.Ci. 25, 106ab.
yad uktam : A.h.Sū. 13, 25; 27; 23cd; 24; followed by a quotation from an unknown source.
Suśruta (*sauśrutadoṣabhedavikalpādhyāya*, i.e. U. 66).

1, 5d-6 M. *yathā* : Su.U. 39, 25a = Mā.ni. 2, 4a.
tathā : reference to Ca.Ni. 1, 33.
tantrāntara : quotation from an unknown source.
Parāśara.
yad uktam : Ca.Ci. 11, 12cd = Mā.ni. 10, 29cd.
Suśruta : U. 39, 27.
Hārīta.
Mādhava : 1, 7ab.
Jejjaṭa.
Vāpyacandra.
Mādhavakara.
Kārtikakuṇḍa.
Caraka : I. 5, 4.

Caraka : Ci. 8, 35.
Vāgbhaṭa : reference to A.h.Ni. 1, 3d = Mā.ni. 1, 5d.
Caraka : Ci. 6, 54ab.
Ā. *tathā hi* : A.h.Ni. 1, 12cd.

1, 7 M. Caraka : I. 5, 4a.
iti : Su.U. 39, 27bc = Mā.ni. 2, 66bc.
Īśvarasena.
Caraka : reference, disagreeing with Ca.Ci. 14, 11, to the symptoms of haemorrhoids by wind.
tad uktam : Mā.ni. 1, 2cd.
Suśruta : fr. Sū. 33, 18.
ṭīkākṛtaḥ.
Caraka : Ni. 8, 21ab.
naiyāyikāḥ.
Caraka : Sū. 9, 4d.
Caraka : Ni. 8, 40.

1, 8-9 M. Caraka : fr. Sū. 11, 38.
Vṛddhavāgbhaṭa : fr. A.s.Ni. 1, 12.
Sudāntasena.
Caraka : reference to Sū. 11, 54.
yad uktam : Ca.Vi. 3, 41.
Vāpyacandra.
uktaṃ hi : quotation from an unknown source.
tathā : variant of Su.Ci. 33, 14ab, recorded by Ḍa.
Vāpyacandra.
Caraka : fr. Sū. 4, 16.
Caraka : Ci. 3, 153c.
Suśruta : U. 40, 158cd.
Suśruta : U. 49, 16ab.
Suśruta : Sū. 12, 17.
Suśruta : Sū. 12, 21.
Caraka : Sū. 26, 69.
Suśruta : reference to Su.U. 47.
Suśruta : U. 47, 48.
Caraka : Ni. 1, 10.
iti : fr. Mā.ni. 1, 4cd.
Caraka : fr. Vi. 4, 8.
vakṣyati ca : Mā.ni. 2, 58c.
Ā. Caraka : Sū. 6, 50.

1, 10 M. Bhaṭṭāraharicandra.
Bhaṭṭāraharicandra.
Vāgbhaṭa : fr. A.h.Ni. 1, 8a = fr. Mā.ni. 1, 10a.

1, 11-13 M. Caraka : Sū. 17, 41.
Suśruta : Sū. 21, 38.

		Jejjaṭa.
		Gadādhara.
		Vāpyacandra.
		Vāgbhaṭa : A.h.Sū. 3, 58ab.
		Vāgbhaṭa : A.h.Sū. 1, 7cd-8ab.
		Caraka : fr. Ni. 1, 12; fr. Sū. 19, 3.
		nyāyavidaḥ : quotation from an unknown source.
		vaiyākaraṇāḥ : quotation from an unknown source.
		Vāpyacandra.
1, 14cd-15ab	M.	Suśruta : Sū. 35, 19.
		Caraka : fr. Sū. 20, 7.
		yad uktam : Śārṅgadharasaṃhitā 1, 5, 25.
		Caraka : Sū. 7, 40cd.
		tathā : Ca.Sū. 7, 40b.
		Suśruta : fr. Śā. 4, 64.
		yad uktam : Su.Śā. 4, 79.
		Praśnavidhāna (Suśrutaślokavārtika).
		ṭīkāḥ.
		Āṣāḍhadharma.
		Svāmidāsa.
		Suśruta : reference to Sū. 21.
		adhunātanāḥ.
1, 15cd-18	M.	Vāpyacandra.
		Haricandra.
		Caraka : fr. Sū. 11, 38.
1, 21	M.	Caraka : Sū. 1, 59-61.
2, 1	M.	Caraka : Ci. 3, 4-5ab; Ci. 3, 9d (*ityādi yāvat ... iti*).
		tathā : Ca.Ci. 3, 31cd.
		Pālakāpya (see note 7).
		Suśruta : U. 39, 9a.
		Caraka : Ci. 3, 20.
		Caraka : reference to Ci. 3.
		Bhaṭṭārakaharicandra.
		anye ṭīkākṛtaḥ.
		Caraka : fr. Ci. 3, 115d.
		Vāgbhaṭa : A.h.Ci. 1, 16cd-17ab.
		Caraka : Ci. 3, 142cd-143ab.
		Videha.
		Harivaṃśa : II, 122, 71cd-72ab.
2, 2	M.	Caraka : Vi. 1, 21.
		Caraka : Vi. 2, 17ab.
		Jejjaṭa.
		Suśruta : U. 39, 80cd-81ab.
		Caraka : Ci. 3, 113cd-114ab.

ity uktam : A.h.Ci. 1, 16c.
yad uktam : fr. Ca.Ni. 1, 30.
tathā : Ca.Sū. 19, 7ab.
Ā. *iti* : quotation from an unknown source.
iti : quotation from an unknown source.

2, 3 M. Caraka : Ci. 3, 4a; Ci. 3, 37ab.
tathā : Ca.Ci. 3, 36cd.
Jejjaṭa.
Kārtikakuṇḍa.
Caraka : Ci. 3, 31ab.
Caraka : Ci. 3, 36ab.

2, 4-7 M. Kārtika.
Vṛddhasuśruta : Su.U. 39, 16c; Su.U. 39, 18d-19ab (*ity ārabhya ... iti samprāptau*).
Caraka : Ci. 3, 28a.
Caraka : Ci. 3, 28cd.
Ā. Mādhava.
Suśruta : reference to U. 39, 25-26 = Mā.ni. 2, 4-5.

2, 8-9 Caraka : fr. Sū. 20, 10.
Gadādhara.
Vāgbhaṭa : A.h.Ni. 2, 17cd-18ab.
Caraka : fr. Ni. 1, 21.
ācārya (i.e. Caraka) : Ca.Ci. 5, 9ab.
tathā : Ca.Ci. 3, 40b.
Kārtikakuṇḍa.
Suśruta.
Caraka : reference to Ni. 1, 21.

2, 10-11 Suśruta : Śā. 4, 42a.
Caraka : reference to Sū. 20, 14.
Kārtika.
iti vacanam : Ca.Ci. 26, 125ab = Mā.ni. 14, 2ab.
yad uktam : Paryāyaratnamālā 1506b.
Suśruta : U. 49, 10.
Jejjaṭa.
iti vacanam : unidentified quotation.
Suśruta : Śā. 4, 56a.
Ā. Abhidhāna : Paryāyaratnamālā 1506b.

2, 12-13 M. *ity āhuḥ* : Su.Śā. 4, 52cd.
iti : unidentified quotation.

2, 14-15ab M. Caraka : Ci. 3, 110cd-111ab.

2, 15cd-16 M. Kārtika.
Hārīta.

2, 17 M. Caraka : fr. Ci. 3, 88.
Ā. *āha* : Su.Śā. 4, 49.

2, 18-23 M. Jejjaṭa.
Cakra.
Bhālukitantra.
Vāgbhaṭa : A.h.Ni. 3, 27cd-28.
Caraka : reference to Ci. 3, 103cd-109ab = Mā.ni. 2, 18-23.
tatraiva : reference to Ca.Ci. 3, 90-102.
kāśmīrapāṭhe carakaḥ : Ca.Ci. 3, 91-102.
Suśruta : U. 39, 39-41.
Bhālukitantra.
Dṛḍhabala : Ca.Ci. 26, 293.
Caraka : Ci. 26, 36.
Vāgbhaṭa : A.h.Ni. 15, 48-49.
Dṛḍhabala.
Cakra.
Gayadāsa.
Dṛḍhabala.
Ā. Suśruta : fr. U. 39, 39a.
Bhālukitantra.
tathā : Bhālukitantra.

2, 24 M. Jejjaṭa.
Caraka : fr. Vi. 4, 8.
Caraka : fr. Sū. 25, 40.
Bhāluki.
Ā. Bhāluki.
Suśruta : U. 39, 45cd-46ab.
Bhāluki.
uktaṃ ca : Siddhayoga 1, 189.
tantrāntara : quotation from an unknown source.
tantrāntara : quotation from an unknown source.

2, 26-30ab M. Caraka : Ci. 3, 114cd-115ab.
yad uktam : Ca.Ci. 3, 115c = Mā.ni. 2, 30c.
Vṛddhasuśruta : see note 147.
Vāgbhaṭa : A.h.Ni. 2, 42cd.
uktaṃ ca : Ca.Ci. 3, 115cd = Mā.ni. 2, 30cd.
iti vacanam : unidentified quotation.
Jejjaṭa.
Videha.
Vāgbhaṭa : A.h.Ni. 2, 42ab.
Vāgbhaṭa (*hārītārthānuvādin*) : A.h.Ni. 2, 44cd-45.
Ā. Vāgbhaṭa : quotation, partially almost identical with A.h.Ni. 2, 42cd; the second half of the stanza remains unidentified.

2, 30cd-31ab M. Caraka : fr. Ni. 1, 30.
Jejjaṭa.
Cakra.
Jejjaṭa.

2, 31cd-32ab M. *yad uktam* : unidentified quotation.
Bhāluki.

2, 32cd-33 M. Caraka : Ci. 3, 61cd.

2, 34-36ab M. *yathoktam* : Siddhayoga 1, 189.
Caraka : Ci. 3, 56cd-57ab.
Caraka : Ci. 3, 59cd-60ab.
Kharanāda.
Haricandra.
Caraka : Ci. 3, 292cd.
Īśānadeva.
Ā. *tantrāntara* : quotation from an unknown source.
tathā ca : quotation from an unknown source.
Kharanāda.
Īśāna.
Vṛddhasuśruta : Su.U. 39, 53; 51; 52cd; 52ab.
Suśruta : quotation, disagreeing with U. 39, 54ab.
tantrāntara : unidentified quotation.
Jejjaṭa.
tantrāntara : unidentified quotation.

2, 36cd M. Suśruta : reference to U. 39, 68cd = Mā.ni. 2, 36cd.
Caraka : Ci. 3, 292cd-293ab.

2, 37-38 M. Jejjaṭa.
Suśruta : Sū. 24, 10.
Caraka : Ci. 3, 74.
Jejjaṭa.
Hārīta.
carakaṭīkākṛtaḥ.
Bheḍa.
Nāgabhartṛtantra.
Caraka.
Vṛddhasuśruta : Su.U. 39, 54; 52cd; 52ab.
Suśruta : quotation, disagreeing with U. 39, 54ab.

2, 39 M. *tantrāntara* : unidentified quotation.
Jejjaṭa.
Parāśara.
Haricandra.
Jejjaṭa.
Vṛddhasuśruta : Su.U. 39, 55.

		smṛtiśāstra : Manu, 2, 14ab.
		Caraka : reference to Ni. 5, 4.
		Suśruta : reference to Ni. 5, 5.
		Vāpyacandra.
	Ā.	Suśruta : U. 39, 63cd-64, followed by an unidentified quotation (see note 190).
2, 40	M.	Gadādhara.
		tantrāntara : quotation from an unknown source.
		Suśruta : U. 39, 58ab.
		Jejjaṭa.
	Ā.	Suśruta : U. 39, 58 ab.
		anyatra : reference to an unknown source.
2, 41	M.	Suśruta : U. 39, 58a.
		tathā : Su.U. 41, 12cd.
2, 42-47	M.	Gadādhara.
		Jejjaṭa.
		Caraka : Ci. 3, 175cd.
		Suśruta : U. 39, 63cd-65ab.
		Jejjaṭa.
		tantrāntara : Siddhayoga 1, 222.
		Vṛddhasuśruta : unidentified quotation.
		Videha.
		Caraka : Ci. 3, 75.
		āgama : fr. Ca.Sū. 25, 40.
	Ā.	*iti* : quotation from an unknown source.
2, 48-54	M.	*yad uktam* : Su.U. 39, 90cd-91ab.
		Kārtika.
		Kārtika.
		Kārtika.
		(*yad uktam* : Su.Śā. 4, 21).
	Ā.	Suśruta : U. 39, 89cd-90ab.
		granthāntara : Ca.Ci. 3, 83.
2, 55	M.	*yad uktam* : Ca.Ci. 3, 42ab.
		Vāgbhaṭa : reference to A.h.Ni. 2, 50 = Mā.ni. 2, 55.
		Jatūkarṇa.
		Caraka : reference to Ci. 3, 42ab.
		Jatūkarṇa.
		Vāgbhaṭa : reference to A.h.Ni. 2, 50 = Mā.ni. 2, 55.
		tantrāntara : quotation from an unknown source.
2, 56-57	M.	*yad uktam* : Ca. Sū. 6, 34.
		yad uktam : Siddhayoga 1, 146.
		Caraka : Ci. 3, 47ab.

	Ā.	Candranandana.
		vacanam : quotation from an unknown source.
		Aruṇadatta.
2, 59-61ab	M.	Jejjaṭa.
		Suśruta : reference to Su.U. 39, 92cd-93ab = Mā.ni. 2, 68cd-69ab.
		Suśruta : U. 39, 93cd.
2, 61cd-65	M.	Caraka : reference to Sū. 11, 54.
		Jejjaṭa.
		Haricandra.
		Haricandra.
		(*iti* : Ca.Ci. 3, 276cd-277ab).
		Jejjaṭa (*carakasuśrutaṭīkā*).
		Caraka : Ci. 3, 161ab; 160cd.
		Suśruta : Su.U. 39, 115; 39, 119cd-120ab.
		Kārtikakuṇḍa.
		Caraka : fr. Ci. 3, 161ab.
		Suśruta : fr. U. 39, 119cd.
		Cakra.
		iti : closely related to Su.U. 39, 121cd = Mā.ni. 2, 63cd.
		Kārtikakuṇḍa.
		iti vacanam : Siddhayoga 1, 81.
		Bhaṭṭāraharicandra.
		Suśruta : reference to U. 39, 119cd.
		Candrikākāra.
		Hārīta.
		Kharanāda.
		Suśruta : fr. U. 39, 119c; U. 39, 120cd-121ab (*ity ārabhya yāvat ... iti*).
		Vāgbhaṭa : A.h.Ci. 1, 42-44ab.
		tantrāntara : quoted, acc. to Cakra on Ca.Ci. 3, 160cd-161ab, from the Puṣkalāvatatantra.
		Jatūkarṇa.
		tantrāntara : quotation from an unknown source.
2, 66ab	M.	*yad uktam* : fr. Ca.Vi. 3, 29.
		tantrāntara : quotation from an unknown source.
2, 66cd-74ab	M.	*tantrāntara* : quotation from an unknown source.
		sāṃkhyasiddhānta.
		Caraka : reference to Sū. 8 and Śā. 1.
		Suśruta : reference to Śā. 1.
		quotation from an unknown source.
		Jejjaṭa.
		Cakra.
		tantrāntara : Su.Sū. 31, 10.
		Jejjaṭa.
		Mādhavakara.

Suśruta : reference to U. 39, 92cd-93ab = Mā.ni. 2, 68cd-69ab.
Caraka : reference to Ca.Ci. 3, 39cd-40 = Mā.ni. 2, 59-60ab.
Suśruta : reference to U. 39, 92cd-93ab = Mā.ni. 2, 68cd-69ab.
tantrāntara : reference to Mā.ni. 2, 69cd-70ab, which derives from an unknown source.
Jejjaṭa.
tantrāntarāḥ : 1) related to A.h.Śā. 6, 40cd-41ab.
2) Ca.I. 6, 10.
3) related to A.h.Śā. 5, 73.
4) A.s.Śā. 11, 42cd-43ab.
5) A.s.Śā. 11, 43cd-44ab.
6) Siddhayoga 1, 187.
7) related to A.h.Śā. 5, 57; 5, 61ab.
8) quotation from an unknown source.
Hārīta.
Vṛddhavāgbhaṭa : A.s.Ni. 1, 21-22ab.
yathā : Siddhayoga 1, 189.
(Caraka : Ci. 3, 38cd-39ab).
yad uktam : quotation from an unknown source.
iti : A.h.Ni. 2, 62cd-63ab.
Hārīta.
Kārtikakuṇḍa.
Suśruta : U. 39, 45cd-46ab.
iti : quotation from an unknown source.
iti : A.h.Ni. 2, 61.
Agniveśa.

Ā. *tantrāntarāḥ* : Su.Sū. 33, 18, followed by a quotation from an unknown source.

2, 74c-f M. *yad uktam* : Ca.Ci. 3, 324ab.
Vāgbhaṭa : A.h.Ni. 2, 76cd-77ab.

2, 75 M. Bhāluki.

3, 1-3 M. Suśruta : reference to *hitāhitīyādhyāya*, i.e. Sū. 20.
Caraka : reference to *ātreyabhadrakāpyīyādhyāya*, i.e. Sū. 26.
Caraka : Ci. 15, 236cd.
Suśruta : Sū. 46, 508cd.
Caraka : Si. 6, 31.
Kārtika.
Caraka : fr. Ci. 19, 8.
Caraka : reference to Sū. 26 acc. to the ed., but the quotation cannot be traced there.

3, 4 M. (Gadādhara).
Caraka : fr. Ci. 19, 9.
Caraka : reference to Ci. 19, 5-13.
Caraka : reference to Ci. 19, 11-12.

Suśruta : reference to U. 40, 7ab = Mā.ni. 3, 4ef.
Jejjaṭa.
iti : Su.U. 40, 24.
ācāryāḥ.
Caraka : fr. Sū. 19, 4; Ci. 5, 16cd (*ity abhidhāya ... iti*).
Suśruta : fr. Ni. 2, 3; Ni. 2, 22 (*ity abhidhāya ... iti*).

3, 7ab M. *tantrāntara* : fr. Ca.Ci. 19, 6.

3, 9-10 M. Gadādhara.
Kārtika.
Jejjaṭa.
Gadādhara.

3, 11 M. Kṣārapāṇi.
Ā. *iti* : quotation from an unknown source.

3, 12-13 M. *yad uktam* : Siddhayoga 3, 14.
Ā. *yad uktam* : Siddhayoga 3, 14.

3, 14-19 M. *iti* : quotation from an unknown source.
Karavīrācārya.
Caraka : reference to Ca.Ci. 19, 9.
Jejjaṭa.
yad uktam : quotation, identical with Hā. 3, 3, 77.
(*iti* : Pāṇini 5, 2, 129).
Suśruta : U. 40, 13b.
Ā. *yad āhuḥ* : quotation from an unknown source.
anyac ca : quotation from an unknown source.
kecana paṭhanti : quotation from an unknown source.

3, 20 M. *yad uktam* : quotation from an unknown source.
Jejjaṭa.

3, 21 M. Bhoja.
Parāśara.
Hārīta.

4, 1 M. Suśruta : fr. Sū. 20, 22.
Suśruta : U. 40, 168.
Ā. quotation : Śārṅgadharasaṃhitā 1, 5, 6-7ab.

4, 2-3 M. Caraka : Ci. 15, 56-57ab.
Suśruta : U. 40, 169.

4, 13-16 M. *ata evāha* : quotation from an unknown source.
yad uktam : quotation from an unknown source.

4, 17	M.	Caraka : Ci. 15, 71. *anyatra* : A.h.Ni. 7, 29cd-30ab.
5, 1	M.	(reference to Pāṇini 6, 3, 109). Suśruta : Ni. 2, 22. Suśruta : reference to Ni. 2, 7. Bhoja.
5, 2	M.	*kāyacikitsakāḥ*. Caraka : fr. Ci. 14, 6 (*ity ārabhya yāvat ... iti*). Suśruta : reference to Ni. 2, 17. Vāgbhaṭa (*suśrutānuvādin*) : reference to A.h.Ni. 7, 56.
	Ā.	Suśruta : reference to Ni. 2, 17.
5, 3-4	M.	Jejjaṭa.
5, 5-6	M.	Caraka : Ci. 14, 23.
5, 9cd	M.	Suśruta : fr. Ni. 2, 25. Caraka : fr. Ci. 14, 7. *yad uktam* : quotation from an unknown source. *iti vacanam* : fr. Ca.Sū. 20, 9. *ata evoktam* : referring to the preceding quotation from Ca.Sū. 20, 9. *iti* : quotation from an unknown source.
5, 24cd-27ab	M.	(reference to Pāṇini 6, 3, 9). Suśruta : fr. Sū. 15, 9.
5, 27cd-30	M.	*kāśmīrāḥ* (*kāśmīrās tu carake*). *uktaṃ ca pūrvam* : Mā.ni. 5, 24cd.
5, 31-32	M.	Cakra. Guṇākara. Gadādhara.
	Ā.	Mādhava.
5, 33-34	M.	*iti* : quotation from an unknown source. Gautama.
	Ā.	*evaṃ kathyate* : Su.Ni. 1, 13-21ab. *iti* : quotation from an unknown source. *iti* : quotation from an unknown source. *iti* : quotation from an unknown source.
5, 35-37	M.	Caraka : Ni. 8, 35ab.
5, 38	M.	(Cakra).
	Ā.	*tad uktam* : Su.Sū. 34, 15cd-16ab; 19cd-24.

5, 43	M.	Kārtikakuṇḍa.
5, 44	Ā.	*iti* : quotation from an unknown source. *iti* : quotation from an unknown source. *iti* : quotation from an unknown source.
6, 2-4	M.	Caraka : reference to Sū. 20. *yad uktam anyatra* : quotation from an unknown source. Caraka : Ci. 15, 217cd-221ab.
6, 5-6	M.	Jejjaṭa. Suśruta : Sū. 46, 503. Nāgārjuna's Ārogyamañjarī. Suśruta : Sū. 46, 513. *tantrāntara* : quotation from an unknown source. Gadādhara. *iti* : fr. Mā.ni. 6, 7a. Suśruta : quotation, untraceable in the Suśrutasaṃhitā. Suśruta : Sū. 46, 487cd-488. Caraka : Ci. 15, 45a; Ci. 15, 46d (*ityādinā ... ityantena*).
6, 10-13ab	Ā.	Suśruta : Sū. 46, 502a. Suśruta : Sū. 46, 502b. Suśruta : Sū. 46, 502cd. Suśruta : Sū. 46, 503.
6, 15	M.	Kārtikakuṇḍa. Bakulakara. *uktaṃ hi* : unidentified quotation, elsewhere said to be taken from Suśruta.
6, 16-17	M.	*tantrāntara* : A.h.Sū. 8, 7cd-8ab.
6, 18	M.	Suśruta. Caraka : Ca.Vi. 2, 11. Caraka.
6, 19-20	M.	*tantrāntara* : A.h.Sū. 8, 6cd-7ab.
6, 21	M.	*tantrāntara* : A.h.Sū. 8, 10cd-11.
	Ā.	*tantrāntara* : quotation from an unknown source.
6, 22	M.	*tantrāntara* : reference to an unknown source. Suśruta : reference to U. 56, 10 = Mā.ni. 6, 22.
	Ā.	*tatha cā* : quotation from an unknown source. *yad uktam* : quotation from an unknown source.
6, 23	M.	Jejjaṭa.

7, 1-2a	M.	Caraka : reference to Vi. 7, 9.
	Ā.	*pūrvācāryāḥ.*
7, 7cd-11ab	M.	*pūrvācāryāḥ.*
7, 11cd-12	M.	Suśruta : fr. Ni. 5, 6.
8, 1	M.	Caraka : fr. Sū. 19, 4. Caraka : Ci. 16, 3a. Jejjaṭa. Cakra. Suśruta. *yad uktam* : Ca.Ci. 16, 27cd = Mā.ni. 8, 8cd. Suśruta (*parādhikaraṇeṣu*, i.e. in the Uttaratantra).
8, 2	M.	Dṛḍhabala. Hārīta.
8, 4	M.	Suśruta : U. 44, 4cd.
8, 7	M.	Caraka : Ci. 16, 26.
8, 8-10	M.	Jejjaṭa. Cakra. Parāśara. Jejjaṭa.
8, 11	M.	Jejjaṭa. Videha.
8, 12-15	M.	Jejjaṭa. Cakra. Suśruta (*sauśrutaśloka*) : reference to U. 44, 39-40 = Mā.ni. 8, 15. Suśruta : U. 44, 6ab. *kaścid abhiyukto likhitavān* : quotation from an unknown source.
8, 19cd-21ab	M.	Jejjaṭa.
,8 22cd-23	M.	Suśruta : reference to U. 44, 6ab.
9, 1-3	M.	*iti* : Su.Sū. 21, 11a. *ity uktiḥ* : Su.Sū. 21, 17d. Suśruta. Caraka : quotation, untraceable in the Carakasaṃhitā. *yad āha* : Ca.Ci. 4, 9.
9, 6-7ab	M.	Jejjaṭa. *yad vakṣyati* : Mā.ni. 9, 7ab.

		yad uktam : A.h.Ni. 2, 51cd = Mā.ni. 2, 56cd.
	Ā.	Jejjaṭa.
9, 8ab	M.	Caraka : Ni. 2, 12-13ab.
9, 11	M.	Gayadāsa. Kārtika.
9, 12-14	M.	Jejjaṭa.
10, 1	M.	*iti* : Mā.ni. 10, 6d. Caraka : Ci. 8, 20. Suśruta : reference to U. 64, 56. Caraka : Ci. 8, 28-29. Suśruta : U. 41, 7cd-8ab. Suśruta : U. 41, 4-5. Vāgbhaṭa : quotation, untraceable in A.h. and A.s.
	Ā.	*iti* : Su.Sū. 46, 508cd.
10, 2	M.	Jejjaṭa (*suśrute jejjaṭe*) (comm. on the Suśrutasaṃhitā). Kārtika. Caraka : Ci. 8, 43. *yad uktam* : Ca.Ci. 28, 59ab. Suśruta : Sū. 15, 18.
10, 3-4	M.	Caraka : Ci. 8, 33-36ab.
10, 5	M.	*kāśmirāḥ*. Caraka. Bhoja. Jejjaṭa.
10, 6-7	M.	Kārtika.
10, 8-12	M.	Suśruta : U. 41, 11. Mādhava : reference to 10, 8cd. Caraka : Ci. 8, 45-46. Caraka : I. 9, 8-9.
	Ā.	Suśruta : fr. Sū. 15, 9. *iti* : Su.Sū. 15, 27cd-28ab. *uktaṃ ca* : Siddhayoga 10, 81.
10, 13	M.	*yad uktam anyatra* : Siddhayoga 10, 86.
10, 14	M.	Suśruta : U. 41, 26cd-27. (Kārtika).
10, 15	M.	Suśruta : fr. Sū. 15, 9.

10, 16ab	M.	Suśruta : U. 41, 18cd.
10, 19c-f	M.	Gadādhara. Suśruta : U. 41, 42cd; U. 41, 26b (*ity ārabhya ... ity antam*).
10, 20	M.	Suśruta : Ci. 1, 30d and 31b. Candrikākāra.
10, 21-29ab	M.	*āgama* : quotation from an unknown source. Jejjaṭa. *ṭīkākārāḥ*. Jejjaṭa.

D.

(1) *The authors and works quoted or referred to in M. and Ā. on ch. 1-10 of the Mādhava-nidāna, arranged according to the Sanskrit alphabet, and with the exception of Ca., Su., A.h. and A.s., which are dealt with separately*

Agniveśa : M. on 2, 66cd-74ab.
Abhidhāna (= Paryāyaratnamālā) : M. on 2, 10-11 : *yad uktam*; Ā. on 2, 10-11.
(Aruṇadatta : Ā. on 2, 56-57).
Āṣāḍhadharma : M. on 1, 14cd-15ab.
Īśāna : M. on 1, 1; Ā. on 2, 34-36ab.
Īśānadeva : M. on 2, 34-36ab.
Īśvarasena : M. on 1, 1; 1, 7.
Karavīrācārya : M. on 3, 14-19.
Kārtika : M. on 1, 1; 2, 4-7; 2, 10-11; 2, 15cd-16; 2, 48-54 (three times); 3, 1-3; 3, 9-10; 9, 11; 10, 2; (10, 14).
Kārtikakuṇḍa : M. on 1, 5d-6; 2, 3; 2, 8-9; 2, 61d-65 (twice); 2, 66cd-74ab; 5, 43; 6, 15.
Kāśmīrapāṭha : M. on 2, 18-23 (*kāśmīrapāṭhe carakaḥ* : = Ca.Ci. 3, 91-102).
Kāśmīrāḥ : M. on 5, 27cd-30 (*kāśmīrās tu carake*).
Kṣārapāṇi : M. on 3, 11.
Kharanāda : M. and Ā. on 2, 34-36ab; M. on 2, 61cd-65.
Gadādhara : M. on 1, 1; 1, 11-13; 2, 8-9; 2, 40; 2, 42-47; (3, 4); 3, 9-10 (twice); 5, 31-32; 6, 5-6; 10, 19c-f.
Gayadāsa : M. on 2, 18-23; 9, 11.
Guṇākara : M. on 5, 31-32.
Gautama : M. on 5, 33-34.
Cakra : M. on 2, 18-23 (twice); 2, 30cd-31ab; 2, 61cd-65; 2, 66cd-74ab; 5, 31-32; 8, 1; 8, 8-10.
Cakrapāṇi : M. on 1, 1.
(Candranandana : Ā. on 2, 56-57).
Candrikākāra : M. on 2, 61cd-65; 10, 20.
Jatūkarṇa : M. on 2, 55 (twice); 2, 61cd-65.
Jejjaṭa : M. on 1, 1; 1, 5d-6; 1, 11-13; 2, 2; 2, 3; 2, 10-11; 2, 18-23; 2, 24; 2, 26-30ab; 2, 30cd-31ab (twice); Ā. on 2, 34-36ab; M. on 2, 37-38 (twice); 2, 39 (twice); 2, 40; 2, 42-47 (twice); 2, 59-61ab; 2, 61cd-65 (twice; second time : *carakasuśrutaṭīkāyām*);

2, 66cd-74ab (three times); 3, 4; 3, 9-10; 3, 14-19; 3, 20; 5, 3-4; 6, 5-6; 6, 23; 8, 1; 8, 8-10 (twice); 8, 11; 8, 12-15; 8, 19cd-21ab; 9, 6-7ab; Ā. on 9, 6-7ab; M. on 9, 12-14; 10, 2 (*suśrute jejjaṭe*); 10, 21-29ab (twice).

Tīsaṭācārya('s Cikitsākalikā) : M. on 1, 5a-c.

Dṛḍhabala : M. on 2, 18-23 (three times); 8, 2.

Nāgabbhartṛtantra : M. on 2, 37-38.

Nāgārjuna's Ārogyamañjarī : M. on 6, 5-6.

(Nyāyasūtra : M. on 1, 5a-c : *yathā*).

Parāśara : M. on 1, 5d-6; 2, 39; 3, 21; 8, 8-10.

Pālakāpya : M. on 2, 1.

Praśnavidhāna (Suśrutaślokavārtika) : M. on 1, 14cd-15ab.

Bakula : M. on 1, 1.

Bakulakara : M. on 6, 15.

Bhaṭṭāra(haricandra) : M. on 1, 1.

Bhaṭṭāraharicandra : M. on 1, 5a-c (four times); 1, 10 (twice); 2, 1; 2, 61cd-65.
(see also : Haricandra)

Bhāluki : M. on 2, 24; Ā. on 2, 24 (twice); M. on 2, 31cd-32ab; M. on 2, 75.

Bhālukitantra : M. on 2, 18-23 (twice); Ā. on 2, 18-23.

Bheḍa : M. on 2, 37-38.

Bhoja : M. on 1, 1; 3, 21; 5, 1.

Mādhava : M. on 1, 1; 1, 5d-6; Ā. on 2, 4-7; Ā. on 5, 31-32; M. on 10, 8-12.

Mādhavakara : M. on 1, 5d-6; 2, 66cd-74 ab.

Maitreya : M. on 1, 1.

Vāpyacandra : M. on 1, 1; 1, 4; 1, 5d-6; 1, 8-9 (twice); 1, 11-13 (twice); 1, 15cd-18; 2, 39.

Videha : M. on 2, 1; 2, 26-30ab; 2, 42-47; 8, 11.

Vṛddhavāgbhaṭa : M. on 1, 8-9; 2, 66cd-74ab.
(see : Vāgbhaṭa)

Vṛddhasuśruta : M. on 2, 4-7; 2, 26-30ab; Ā. on 2, 34-36ab; M. on 2, 37-38; 2, 39; 2, 42-47.
(see : Suśruta)

Sukīra : M. on 1, 1.

Sudāntasena : M. on 1, 5a-c; 1, 8-9.

Sudhīra : M. on 1, 1.

Svāmidāsa : M. on 1, 14cd-15ab.

Haricandra : M. on 1, 5a-c; 1, 15cd-18; 2, 34-36ab; 2, 39; 2, 61cd-65 (twice).

Harivaṃśa : M. on 2, 1.

Hārīta : M. on 1, 5d-6; 2, 15cd-16; 2, 37-38; 2, 61cd-65; 2, 66cd-74ab (twice); 3, 21; 8, 2.

(2) *Various sources*

adhunātanāḥ : M. on 1, 14cd-15ab.

anyatra : Ā. on 2, 40; M. on 4, 17 (= A.h.Ni. 7, 29cd-30ab); M. on 10, 13 (= Siddhayoga 10, 86).

āgama : M. on 2, 42-47 (= fr. Ca.Sū. 25, 40); 10, 21-29ab.

ācārya (i.e. Caraka) : M. on 2, 8-9 (= Ca.Ci. 5, 9ab).

ācāryāḥ : M. on 3, 4.

kāyacikitsakāḥ : M. on 5, 2.

granthāntara : Ā. on 2, 48-54 (= Ca.Ci. 3, 83).

carakaṭīkākṛtaḥ : M. on 2, 37-38.
ṭīkāḥ : M. on 1, 14cd-15ab.
ṭīkākāraḥ : M. on 10, 21-29ab.
ṭīkākṛtaḥ : M. on 1, 7.
ṭīkākṛtaḥ, anye : M. on 2, 1.
tantrāntara : M. on 1, 1; 2, 24 (twice); Ā. on 2, 34-36ab (three times); M. on 2, 39; 2, 40; 2, 42-47 (= Siddhayoga 1, 222); 2,55; 2, 61cd-65 (acc. to Cakra on Ca.Ci. 3, 160cd-161ab, this is a quotation from the Pauṣkalāvatatantra); 2, 61cd-65; 2, 66ab; 2, 66cd-74ab; 2, 66cd-74ab (= Su.Sū. 31, 10); 2, 66cd-74ab (reference to Mā.ni. 2, 69cd-70ab, which derives from an unknown source); 2, 66cd-74ab (1 : related to A.h.Śā. 6, 40cd-41ab; 2 : = Ca.I. 6, 10; 3 : related to A.h.Śā. 5, 73; 4 : = A.s.Śā. 11, 42cd-43ab; 5 : = A.s.Śā. 11, 43cd-44ab; 6 : = Siddhayoga 1, 187; 7 : related to A.s.Śā. 5, 57 and 5, 61ab; 8 : from an unknown source); Ā. on 2, 66cd-74ab (= Su.Sū. 33, 18, followed by a quotation from an unknown source); M. on 3, 7ab (= fr. Ca.Ci. 19, 6); 6, 5-6; 6, 16-17 (= A.h.Sū. 8, 7cd-8ab); 6, 19-20 (= A.h.Sū. 8, 6cd-7ab); 6, 21 (= A.h.Sū. 8, 10cd-11); Ā. on 6, 21; M. on 6, 22.
naiyāyikāḥ : M. on 1, 7.
nyāyavidaḥ : M. on 1, 11-13.
pūrvācāryāḥ : Ā. on 7, 1-2a; M. on 7, 7cd-11ab.
vaiyākaraṇāḥ : M. on 1, 11-13.
sāṃkhyasiddhānta : M. on 2, 66cd-74ab.
smṛtiśāstra : M. on 2, 39 (= Manusmṛti 2, 14ab).

(3)

Caraka in M. and Ā. :

Sū. 1, 59-61 : M. on 1, 21.
fr. Sū. 4, 16 : M. on 1, 8-9.
Sū. 6, 34 : M. on 2, 56-57 : *yad uktam.*
Sū. 6, 50 : Ā. on 1, 8-9.
Sū. 7, 40b : M. on 1, 14cd-15ab : *tathā.*
Sū. 7, 40cd : M. on 1, 14cd-15ab.
Sū. 8 : referred to : M. on 2, 66cd-74ab.
Sū. 9, 4d : M. on 1, 7.
Sū. 10, 11 : M. on 1, 4.
Sū. 10, 11cd : M. on 1, 5a-c.
Sū. 10, 14ab : M. on 1, 4.
fr. Sū. 11, 38 : M. on 1, 8-9 and 1, 15cd-18.
Sū. 11, 48 : referred to : M. on 1, 5a-c.
Sū. 11, 54 : referred to : M. on 1, 8-9 and 2, 61cd-65.
Sū. 14, 9 : M. on 1, 5a-c.
Sū. 17, 41 : M. on 1, 11-13.
Sū. 17, 45-46 : M. on 1, 5a-c.
Sū. 17, 62 : M. on 1, 5a-c : *yathā.*
Sū. 17, 112ab : M. on 1, 5a-c.
Sū. 17, 112-113ab : M. on 1, 5a-c.
fr. Sū. 19, 3 : M. on 1, 11-13.

fr. Sū. 19, 4 : M. on 3, 4; M. on 8, 1.
fr. Sū. 19, 7ab : M. on 2, 2 : *tathā*.
Sū. 20 : referred to : M. on 6, 2-4.
fr. Sū. 20, 7 : M. on 1, 14cd-15ab.
fr. Sū. 20, 9 : M. on 5, 9cd : *iti vacanam*; reference to the same passage : M. on 5, 9cd : *ata evoktam*.
fr. Sū. 20, 10 : M. on 2, 8-9.
Sū. 20, 14 : referred to : M. on 2, 10-11.
Sū. 20, 20 : M. on 1, 2-3.
fr. Sū. 25, 40 : M. on 1, 5a-c : *iti vacanam*; M. on 2, 24; M. on 2, 42-47 : *ity āgamaḥ*.
Sū. 26 : referred to : M. on 3, 1-3.
Sū. 26 : M. on 3, 1-3; quotation referred to Sū. 26 by the ed. of the text, but not traceable there.
Sū. 26, 29 : M. on 1, 8-9.
Ni. 1, 10 : M. on 1, 8-9.
fr. Ni. 1, 12 : M. on 1, 11-13.
fr. Ni. 1, 21 : M. on 2, 8-9.
Ni. 1, 21 : referred to : M. on 2, 8-9.
fr. Ni. 1, 30 : M. on 2, 2 : *yad uktam*; M. on 2, 30cd-31ab.
Ni. 1, 33 : referred to : M. on 1, 5d-6 : *tathā*.
fr. Ni. 1, 36 : M. on 1, 4.
Ni. 2, 12-13ab : M. on 9, 8ab.
Ni. 2, 19cd : M. on 1, 5a-c.
fr. Ni. 4, 4 : M. on 1, 5a-c.
Ni. 5, 4 : referred to : M. on 2, 39.
Ni. 8, 21ab : M. on 1, 7.
Ni. 8, 24 : M. on 1, 4.
Ni. 8, 35ab : M. on 5, 35-37.
Ni. 8, 40 : M. on 1, 7.
Vi. 1, 21 : M. on 2, 2.
Vi. 2, 11 : M. on 6, 18.
Vi. 2, 17ab : M. on 2, 2.
fr. Vi. 3, 29 : M. on 2, 66ab : *yad uktam*.
Vi. 3, 41 : M. on 1, 8-9 : *yad uktam*.
fr. Vi. 4, 8 : M. on 1, 4; M. on 1, 8-9; M. on 2, 24.
fr. Vi. 6, 11 : M. on 1, 5a-c.
Vi. 7, 9 : referred to : M. on 7, 1-2a.
Śā. 1 : referred to : M. on 2, 66cd-74ab.
I. 5, 4a : M. on 1, 7.
I. 5, 4 : M. on 1, 5d-6.
I. 5, 4-5 : M. on 1, 4.
I. 6, 10 : M. on 2, 66cd-74ab : *tantrāntara*.
I. 9, 8-9 : M. on 10, 8-12.
Ci. 3 : referred to : M. on 2, 1.
Ci. 3, 4a : M. on 2, 3.
Ci. 3, 4-5ab : M. on 2, 1.
Ci. 3, 9d : M. on 2, 1.
Ci. 3, 20 : M. on 2, 1.

Ci. 3, 28a : M. on 2, 4-7.
Ci. 3, 28cd : M. on 2, 4-7.
Ci. 3, 31ab : M. on 2, 3.
Ci. 3, 31cd : M. on 2, 1 : *tathā.*
Ci. 3, 36ab : M. on 2, 3.
Ci. 3, 36cd : M. on 2, 3 : *tathā.*
Ci. 3, 37ab : M. on 2, 3.
Ci. 3, 38cd-39ab : M. on 2, 66cd-74ab.
Ci. 3, 39cd-40 : referred to ; = Mā.ni. 2, 59-60ab; M. on 2, 66cd-74ab.
Ci. 3, 40b : M. on 2, 8-9 : *tathā.*
Ci. 3, 42ab : M. on 1, 5a-c; M. on 2, 55 : *yad uktam*; reference to the same passage : M. on 2, 55.
Ci. 3, 47ab : M. on 2, 56-57.
Ci. 3, 56cd-57ab : M. on 2, 34-36ab.
Ci. 3, 59cd-60ab : M. on 2, 34-36ab.
Ci. 3, 61cd : M. on 2, 32cd-33.
Ci. 3, 74 : M. on 2, 37-38.
Ci. 3, 75 : M. on 2, 42-47.
Ci. 3, 83 : Ā. on 2, 48-54 : *granthāntara.*
fr. Ci. 3, 88 : M. on 2, 17.
Ci. 3, 90-102 : referred to : M. on 2, 18-23 : *tatraiva.*
Ci. 3, 91-102 : M. on 2, 18-23 : *kāśmīrapāṭhe carakaḥ.*
Ci. 3, 103cd-190ab : referred to ; = Mā.ni. 2, 18-23; M. on 2, 18-23.
Ci. 3, 109cd-110a : M. on 1, 4 : *tathā.*
Ci. 3, 110cd-111ab : M. on 2, 14-15ab.
Ci. 3, 113cd-114ab : M. on 2, 2.
Ci. 3, 114cd-115ab : M. on 2, 26-30ab.
Ci. 3, 115c : = Mā.ni. 2, 30c; M. on 2, 26-30ab : *yad uktam.*
fr. Ci. 3, 115d : M. on 2, 1.
Ci. 3, 142cd-143ab : M. on 2. 1.
Ci. 3, 153c : M. on 1, 8-9.
Ci. 3, 161ab and 160cd : M. on 2, 61cd-65.
fr. Ci. 3, 161ab : M. on 2, 61cd-65.
Ci. 3, 175cd : M. on 2, 42-47.
[Ci. 3, 276cd-277ab : M. on 2, 61cd-65 : *iti*].
Ci. 3, 292cd : M. on 2, 34-36ab.
Ci. 3, 292cd-293ab : M. on 2, 36cd.
Ci. 3, 324ab : M. on 2, 74c-f.
Ci. 4, 9 : M. on 9, 1-3 : *yad āha.*
Ci. 5, 9ab : M. on 2, 8-9 : ... *ācāryeṇa nirdiṣṭaḥ yathā* ...
Ci. 5, 16cd : M. on 3, 4.
Ci. 6, 54ab : M. on 1, 5d-6.
Ci. 6, 54 : M. on 1, 4.
Ci. 8, 20 : M. on 10, 1.
Ci. 8, 28-29 : M. on 10. 1,
Ci. 8, 33-36ab : M. on 10, 3-4.
Ci. 8, 35 : M. on 1, 5d-6.
Ci. 8, 43 : M. on 10, 2.

Ci. 8, 45-46; M. on 10, 8-12.
Ci. 8, 52 : referred to : = Mā.ni. 10, 5; M. on 10, 5.
Ci. 11, 12cd : = Mā.ni. 10, 29cd; M. on 1, 5d-6 : *yad uktam.*
fr. Ci. 14, 6 : M. on 5, 2.
fr. Ci. 14, 7 : M. on 5, 9cd.
Ci. 14, 11 : disagreeing reference; M. on 1, 7.
Ci. 14, 23 : M. on 5, 5-6.
Ci. 15, 45a : M. on 6, 5-6.
Ci. 15, 46d : M. on 6, 5-6.
Ci. 15, 56-57ab : M. on 4, 2-3.
Ci. 15, 71 : M. on 4, 17.
Ci. 15, 217cd-221ab : M. on 6, 2-4.
Ci. 16, 3a : M. on 8, 1.
Ci. 16, 26 : M. on 8, 7.
Ci. 16, 27cd : = Mā.ni. 8, 8cd; M. on 8, 1 : *yad uktam.*
Ci. 19, 5-13 : referred to : M. on 3, 4.
fr. Ci. 19, 6 : M. on 3, 7ab : *tantrāntara.*
fr. Ci. 19, 8 : M. on 3, 1-3.
fr. Ci. 19, 9 : M. on 3, 4.
Ci. 19, 9 : referred to : M. on 3, 14-19.
Ci. 19, 11-12 : referred to : M. on 3, 4.
fr. Ci. 21, 40 : M. on 1, 5a-c.
Ci. 25, 106ab : M. on 1, 5a-c : *tathā.*
Ci. 26, 27cd : M. on 1, 5a-c.
Ci. 26, 36 : M. on 2, 18-23.
Ci. 26, 125ab : = Mā.ni. 14, 2ab; M. on 2, 10-11 : *iti vacanam.*
Ci. 26, 293 : M. on 2, 18-23 : *uktaṃ dṛḍhabalena.*
Ci. 28, 59ab : M. on 10, 2 : *yad uktam.*
Si. 6, 31 : M. on 3, 1-3.
untraceable quotation in M. on 1, 2-3.
untraceable quotation in M. on 9, 1-3.
Caraka : M. on 6, 18 : reference to the absence of a particular disease in Ca.

Suśruta in M. and Ā. :

Sū. 12, 17 : M. on 1, 8-9.
Sū. 12, 21 : M. on 1, 8-9.
fr. Sū. 13, 14cd : M. on 1, 4.
fr. Sū. 15, 9 : M. on 5, 24cd-27ab; M. on 10, 15; Ā. on 10, 8-12.
Sū. 15, 18 : M. on 10, 2.
Sū. 15, 27cd-28ab : Ā. on 10, 8-12 : *iti.*
Sū. 20 : referred to : M. on 3, 1-3.
fr. Sū. 20, 22 : M. on 4, 1.
Sū. 21 : referred to : M. on 1, 14cd-15ab.
Sū. 21, 11a : M. on 9, 1-3 : *iti.*
Sū. 21, 17d : M. on 9, 1-3 : *ity uktiḥ.*
Sū. 21, 38 : M. on 1, 11-13.
Sū. 24, 10 : M. on 2, 37-38.

Sū. 31, 10 : M. on 2, 66cd-74 ab : *tantrāntara.*
fr. Sū. 33, 18 : M. on 1, 7.
Sū. 33, 18 : Ā. on 2, 66cd-74ab : *tantrāntara.*
Sū. 34, 15cd-16ab : Ā. on 5, 38 : *tad uktam.*
Sū. 34, 19cd-24 : Ā. on 5, 38 : *tad uktam.*
Sū. 35, 19 : M. on 1, 14cd-15 ab.
Sū. 46, 487cd-488 : M. on 6, 5-6.
Sū. 46, 502a : Ā. on 6, 10-13ab.
Sū. 46, 502b : Ā. on 6, 10-13ab.
Sū. 46, 502cd : Ā. on 6, 10-13ab.
Sū. 46, 503 : M. on 6, 5-6; Ā. on 6, 10-13ab.
Sū. 46, 508cd : M. on 1, 1-3; Ā. on 10, 1.
Sū. 46, 513 : M. on 6, 5-6.
Ni. 1, 13-21ab : Ā. on 5, 33-34 : *evaṃ kathyate.*
Ni. 1, 42 : M. on 1, 5a-c : *yathā*, partial quotation of a variant recorded by Ḍa.
fr. Ni. 2, 3 : M, on 3, 4.
Ni. 2, 7 : referred to : M. on 5, 1.
Ni. 2, 17 : referred to : M. and Ā. on 5, 2.
Ni. 2, 22 : M. on 3, 4; M. on 5, 1.
fr. Ni. 2, 25 : M. on 5, 9cd.
Ni. 5, 5 : referred to : M. on 2, 39.
fr. Ni. 5, 6 : M. on 7, 11cd-12.
Śā. 1 : referred to : M. on 2, 66cd-74ab.
[Śā. 4, 21 : M. on 2, 48-54 : *yad uktam*].
Śā. 4, 42a : M. on 2, 10-11.
Śā. 4, 49 : Ā. on 2, 17 : *āha.*
Śā. 4, 52cd : M. on 2, 12-13 : *ity āhuḥ.*
Śā. 4, 56a : M. on 2, 10-11.
fr. Śā. 4, 64 : M. on 1, 14cd-15ab.
Śā. 4, 79 : M. on 1, 14cd-15ab : *yad uktam.*
Ci. 1, 30d and 31b : M. on 10, 20.
Ci. 33, 3 : quotation related to; M. on 1, 5a-c.
Ci. 33, 14ab : variant, recorded by Ḍa.; M. on 1, 8-8 : *tathā.*
Ci. 33, 14 : partial quotation of a variant recorded by Ḍa.; M. on 1, 5a-c.
Su.U. : referred to : M. on 8, 1.
U. 1, 25 : M. on 1, 4.
U. 39, 9a : M. on 2, 1.
U. 39, 16c : M. on 2, 4-7 : vṛddhasuśruta.
U. 39, 18cd-19ab : M. on 2, 4-7 : vṛddhasuśruta.
U. 39, 25a : = Mā.ni. 2, 4a; M. on 1, 5d-6 : *yathā.*
U. 39, 25-26 : = Mā.ni. 2, 4-5; referred to : M. on 2, 4-7.
U. 39, 27 : M. on 1, 5d-6.
U. 39, 27bc : = Mā.ni. 2, 6bc; M. on 1, 7 : *iti.*
U. 39, 29-30 : = Mā.ni. 2, 8-9; referred to : M. on 2, 8-9.
fr. U. 39, 39a : Ā. on 2, 18-23.
U. 39, 39-41 : M. on 2, 18-23.
U. 39, 42 : quotation by Ḍa. on; M. on 2, 26-30ab : vṛddhasuśruta.
U. 39, 45cd-46ab : Ā. on 2, 24; M. on 2, 66cd-74ab.

U. 39, 53; 39, 51; 39, 52cdab : Ā. on 2, 34-36ab : vṛddhasuśruta.
U. 39, 54; 39, 52cdab : M. on 2, 37-38 : vṛddhasuśruta.
U. 39, 54ab : disagreeing quotation; Ā. on 2, 34-36ab; M. on 2, 37-38.
U. 39, 55 : M. on 2, 39.
U. 39, 58a : M. on 2, 41.
U. 39, 58ab : M. and Ā. on 2, 40.
U. 39, 63cd-64 : Ā. on 2, 39.
U. 39, 63cd-65ab : M. on 2, 42-47.
U. 39, 67ab : M. on 1, 5a-c : *tathā*.
U. 39, 68cd : = Mā.ni. 2, 36cd; referred to : M. on 2, 36cd.
U. 39, 80cd-81ab : M. on 2, 2.
U. 39, 89cd-90ab : Ā. on 2, 48-54.
U. 39, 90cd-91ab : M. on 2, 48-54 : *yad uktam*.
U. 39, 92cd-93ab : = Mā.ni. 2, 68cd-69ab ; referred to : M. on 2, 59-61ab and twice in M. on 2, 66cd-74ab.
U. 39, 93cd : M. on 2, 59-61ab.
U. 39, 97-98a : referred to : M. on 1, 4.
U. 39, 115 : M. on 2, 61cd-65.
U. 39, 119c : M. on 2, 61cd-65.
U. 39, 119cd : referred to : M. on 2, 61cd-65.
fr. U. 39, 119cd : M. on 2, 61cd-65.
U. 39, 119cd-120ab : M. on 2, 61cd-65.
U. 39, 120cd-121ab : M. on 2, 61cd-65.
U. 39, 121cd : = Mā.ni. 2, 63cd; M. on 2, 61cd-65 : *iti*, closely related quotation.
U. 40, 7ab : = Mā.ni. 3, 4ef; referred to : M. on 3, 4.
U. 40, 13b : M. on 3, 14-19.
U. 40, 158cd : M. on 1, 8-9.
U. 40, 168 : M. on 4, 1.
U. 40, 169 : M. on 4, 2-3.
U. 41, 4-5 : M. on 10, 1.
U. 41, 7cd-8ab : M. on 10, 1.
U. 41, 11 : M. on 10, 8-12.
U. 41, 12cd : M. on 2, 41 : *tathā*.
U. 41, 26b : M. on 10, 19c-f.
U. 41, 26cd-27 : M. on 10, 14.
U. 41, 42cd : M. on 10, 19c-f.
U. 44, 4cd : M. on 8, 4.
U. 44, 6ab : M. on 8, 12-15; referred to : M. on 8, 22cd-23.
U. 44, 39-40 : = Mā.ni. 8, 15; referred to : M. on 8, 12-15.
U. 47 : referred to : M. on 1, 8-9.
U. 47, 48 : M. on 1, 8-9.
U. 49, 10 : M. on 2, 10-11.
U. 49, 16ab : M. on 1, 8-9.
U. 56, 10 : = Mā.ni. 6, 22; referred to : M. on 6, 22.
U. 64, 32 : related quotation; M. on 1, 5a-c : *yathā*.
U. 64, 56 : referred to : M. on 10, 1.
U. 66 : referred to : M. on 1, 5a-c.
Suśruta : M. on 6, 18 (reference to particular concepts in Su.); M. on 8, 1 (reference to

the absence of a particular type of morbid pallor in Su.); M. on 9, 1-3 (reference to a particular concept in Su.).
Vṛddhasuśruta : unidentified quotation : M. on 2, 42-47.
untraced quotation from Suśruta : Ā. on 1, 4; M. on 6, 5-6.

Vāgbhaṭa in M. and Ā. :

Aṣṭāṅgahṛdayasaṃhitā :

Sū. 1, 7cd-8ab : M. on 1, 11-13.
Sū. 3, 58ab : M. on 1, 11-13.
Sū. 8, 6cd-7ab : M. on 6, 19-20 : *tantrāntara.*
Sū. 8, 7cd-8ab : M. on 6, 16-17 : *tantrāntara.*
Sū. 8, 10cd-11 : M. on 6, 21 : *tantrāntara.*
Sū. 13, 23cd : M. on 1, 5a-c : *yad uktam.*
Sū. 13, 24 : idem.
Sū. 13, 25 : idem.
Sū. 13, 27 : idem.
Śā. 5, 57 : related quotation; M. on 2, 66cd-74ab : *tantrāntara.*
Śā. 5, 61ab : idem.
Śā. 5, 73 : idem.
Śā. 6, 40cd-41ab : idem.
Ci. 1, 16cd-17ab : M. on 2, 1.
Ci. 1, 16c : M. on 2, 2 : *ity uktam.*
Ni. 1, 3d : = Mā.ni. 1, 5d; referred to : M. on 1, 5d-6.
fr. Ni. 1, 8a : = Mā.ni. 1, 10a; M. on 1, 10.
Ni. 1, 12cd : Ā. on 1, 5d-6 : *tathā.*
Ni. 2, 17cd-18ab : M. on 2, 8-9.
Ni. 2, 42ab : M. on 2, 26-30ab.
Ni. 2, 42cd : M. and Ā. on 2, 26-30ab.
Ni. 2, 44cd-45 : M. on 2, 26-30ab.
Ni. 2, 50 : = Mā.ni. 2, 55; twice referred to : M. on 2, 55.
Ni. 2, 51cd : = Mā.ni. 2, 56cd; M. on 9, 6-7ab : *yad uktam.*
Ni. 2, 61 : M. on 2, 66cd-74ab : *iti.*
Ni. 2, 62cd-63ab : M. on 2, 66cd-74ab : *iti.*
Ni. 2, 76cd-77ab : M. on 2, 74c-f.
Ni. 3, 27cd-28 : M. on 2, 18-23.
Ni. 7, 29cd-30ab : M. on 4, 17 : *anyatra.*
Ni. 7, 56 : referred to : M. on 5, 2.
Ni. 15, 48-49 : M. on 2, 18-23.

Aṣṭāṅgasaṃgraha :

Śā. 11, 42cd-43ab : M. on 2, 66cd-74ab.
Śā. 11, 43cd-44ab : idem.
fr. Ni. 1, 12 : M. on 1, 8-9 : vṛddhavāgbhaṭa.
Ni. 1, 21-22ab : M. on 2, 66cd-74ab : vṛddhavāgbhaṭa.
Vāgbhaṭa : M. on 10, 1 (untraceable quotation).

Śārṅgadharasaṃhitā in M. and Ā. :

1, 5, 6-7ab : Ā. on 4, 1.

1, 5, 25 : M. on 1, 14cd-15ab : *yad uktam*; the stanza is taken from another book acc. to Kāśirāma's comm. on Śārṅga).

Siddhayoga in M. and Ā. (The stanzas listed below may be from the Siddhayoga or from some other treatise, e.g. the Mādhavacikitsita) :

1, 81 : M. on 2, 61cd-65 : *iti vacanam.*
1, 146 : M. on 2, 56-57 : *yad uktam.*
1, 187 : M. on 2, 66cd-74ab : *tantrāntara.*
1, 189 : Ā. on 2, 24 : *uktaṃ ca*; M. on 2, 34-36ab : *yathoktam*; M. on 2, 66cd-74ab : *yathā.*
1, 222 : M. on 2, 42-47 : *tantrāntara.*
3, 14 : M. and Ā. on 3, 12-13 : *yad uktam.*
10, 81 : Ā. on 10, 8-12 : *uktaṃ ca.*
10, 86 : M. on 10, 13 : *yad uktam anyatra.*

Unidentified quotations :

1, 2-3 M.
vyādher upari yo vyādhir bhavaty uttarakālajaḥ / upakramāvirodhī ca sa upadrava ucyate //

Ā.
rogajñānārtham ovādau yatnaḥ kāryo bhiṣagvaraiḥ / sati tasmin kriyārambhaḥ puṇyāya yaśase śriyai //

1, 4 Ā.
abhyaṅgasnehasvedādyair vātarogo na śāmyati / vikāras tatra vijñeyo duṣṭam astrāsti śoṇitam //

1, 5a-c M.
hemante nicitaḥ śleṣmā vasante kapharogakṛt /
(related to Su.U. 64, 32 :
hemante nicitaḥ śleṣmā śaityāc chītaśarīriṇām / auṣṇyād vasante kupitaḥ kurute ca gadān bahūn//).

vāyuḥ sāmo vibandhāgnisādatandrāntrakūjanaiḥ / vedanāśothanistodaiḥ kramaśo 'ṅgāni pīḍayet // vicared yugapac cāpi gṛhṇāti kupito bhṛśam / snehādyair vṛddhim āpnoti sūryameghodaye niśi // nirāmo viśado rūkṣo nirvibandho 'lpavedanaḥ / viparītaguṇaiḥ śāntiṃ snigdhair yāti viśeṣataḥ // durgandhaṃ haritaṃ śyāvaṃ pittam amlaṃ sthiraṃ guru / amlikākaṇṭhahṛddāhakaraṃ sāmaṃ vinirdiśet // ātāmraṃ pītam atyuṣṇaṃ rase kaṭukam asthiram / pakvaṃ vigandhaṃ vijñeyaṃ rucipaktṛbalapradam // āvilas tantulaḥ styānaḥ kaṇṭhadeśe 'vatiṣṭhate / sāmo balāso durgandhaḥ kṣududgāravighātakṛt // phenavān piṇḍitaḥ pāṇḍur niḥsāro 'gandha eva ca / pakvaḥ sa eva vijñeyaś chedavān vaktraśuddhikṛt //

1, 5d-6 M.
vyādher jātir bubhūṣā ca pūrvarūpeṇa lakṣyate / bhāvaḥ kimātmakatvaṃ ca lakṣyate lakṣaṇena hi //

1, 8-9 M.
kaphe laṅghanasādhye tu kartari jvaragulmayoḥ / tulye 'pi deśakālādau laṅghanaṃ na ca sammatam //

1, 11-13 M.
nyāyavido bruvate : samānena dharmeṇa parigraho bhedānāṃ yatra kriyate sa vidhiḥ saṃkhyā tu bhedamātram.
vaiyākaraṇā api vyācakṣate : anvayavān prakāraḥ niranvayo bhedaḥ.

2, 2 Ā.
akāle cātimātraṃ ca hy asātmyaṃ yac ca bhojanam / viṣamaṃ cāpi yad bhuktaṃ mithyāhāraḥ sa ucyate //

aśaktaḥ kurute karma śaktimān na karoti yaḥ / mithyāvihāra ity uktaḥ sadā taṃ parivarjayet //

2, 10-11 M.
na rogo 'py ekadoṣajaḥ.

2, 12-13 M.
tathā 'ṅge pīḍakāḥ śītaṃ prasekaś charditandrike / hṛdupalepa uṣṇābhilā-ṣitā vahnimārdavam //

2, 24 Ā.
saṃbādhyamāno hṛdi nābhideśe gātreṣu vā pākarujānviteṣu / pakveṣu vā teṣu rujājvarārtaḥ sa dhātupākī kathito bhiṣagbhiḥ //

daśadvādaśasaptāhaiḥ pittaśleṣmānilādhikaḥ / paktvoṣmaṇā dhātumalān hanti muñcati vā jvaraḥ //

2, 26-30ab M.
ekaḥ prakupito doṣaḥ sarvān eva prakopayet /
Ā. ... (A.h.Ni. 2, 42cd);
dhyānaniḥśvāsabahulaṃ liṅgaṃ kāmajvare smṛtam /

2, 31cd-32ab M.
ārambhād viṣamo yas tu.

2, 34-36ab Ā. saṃtatajvara eva anyaḥ svalpadurbalakāraṇaḥ / ekadoṣo dvidoṣo vā sukhasādhyaḥ prakīrtitaḥ //

vātikaḥ saptarātreṇa daśarātreṇa paittikaḥ / ślaiṣmiko dvādaśāhena jvaraḥ pākaṃ pragacchati //

asthimajjobhayagate cāturthikaviparyayaḥ / madhye 'hanī jvarayati hy ādāv ante ca muñcati //
asthimajjobhayagate cāturthakaviparyayaḥ / tryahād dvyahaṃ jvarayati hy ādāv ante vimuñcati //

2, 40 M.
vāyuḥ prakupito doṣāv udīryobhau vidhāvati / sa śiraḥsthaḥ śiraḥśūlam.

2, 42-47 M.
Vṛddhasuśruta :
narte 'nilād vai viṣamajvaraḥ samupajāyate / kaphapitte hi niśceṣṭe ceṣṭayaty anilaḥ sadā //
Ā. iti :
anu uparyadhaś cāprādhānyena cikitsyate.

2, 55 M. tantrāntara :
jvare tulyartudoṣatvaṃ pramehe tulyadūṣyatā / raktagulme purāṇatvaṃ sukhasādhyasya lakṣaṇam //
Ā. vacanam :
kaphapitte dravatvāc ca sahete laṅghanaṃ mahat / āmakṣayād ūrdhvam api vāyur na sahate kṣaṇam //
(compare Śrīkaṇṭhadatta's comm. on Siddhayoga 1, 31 : yad uktam).

2, 61cd-65 M. tantrāntara :
trisaptāhe vyatīte tu jvaro yas tanutāṃ gataḥ / plīhāgnisādaṃ kurute sa jīrṇajvara ucyate //

2, 66ab M. tantrāntara :
kāso mūrchā 'ruciś chardis tṛṣṇātisāraviḍgrahāḥ / hikkāśvāsāṅgabhedāś ca jvarasyopadravā daśa //

2, 66cd-74ab M. tantrāntara :
ekaṃ dvau trīn bahūn vā 'pi dehe dhātvādiyogataḥ / darśayanti vikārāṃs te kupitāḥ pavanādayaḥ //

cakṣuḥ śrotraṃ ghrāṇaṃ rasanaṃ sparśanaṃ ceti buddhīndriyāṇi hastapādagudopasthajihvāḥ karmendriyāṇi ubhayātmakaṃ manaḥ.

yasya svedo 'tibahulaḥ picchilo yāti sarvataḥ / rogiṇaḥ śītagātrasya tadā maraṇam ādiśet //
(compare Śrīkaṇṭhadatta's comm. on Siddhayoga 1, 187).

yad uktam :
nidrānāśo hṛdi stambho viṣṭambho gauravāruci / aratir balahāniś ca dhātūnāṃ pākalakṣaṇam //

iti :
daśadvādaśasaptāhaiḥ pittaślesmānilādhikaḥ / dagdhoṣmaṇā dhātumalān hanti muñcati vā jvaraḥ //

Ā. tantrāntara:
yas tāmyati svapiti śītalagātrayaṣṭir antarvidāhasahitaḥ smaraṇād apetaḥ/ socchvāsavān kupitaropamacayaḥ saśūlas taṃ varjayed bhiṣag iha jvaritaṃ vidhijñaḥ //

3, 1-3 M. Caraka (the ed. of the text refers to Ca.Sū. 26, but the quotation is untraceable there):
dvividhaṃ hi sātmyaṃ prakṛtisātmyam abhyāsasātmyaṃ ca.

3, 11 Ā. iti:
āhārasya rasaḥ śeṣo yo na pakvo 'gnilāghavāt / sa hetuḥ sarvarogāṇām āma ity abhidhīyate //

3, 14-19 M. iti:
nirasthipiśitaṃ piṣṭaṃ dadhikṣārasamanvitam / elāmaricasaṃyuktaṃ veśavāra iti smṛtam //

Ā. yad āhuḥ:
tṛṣṇā dāho 'ruciḥ śothaḥ pārśvaśūlo 'ratir vamiḥ / gudapākaḥ pralāpaś ca hy ādhmānaṃ śvāsakāsakau // mūrcchā hikkā madaḥ śūlaṃ bahuvego jvaras tathā / etair upadravair juṣṭam atisāriṇam utsṛjet //
anyac ca:
hastapādāṅgulīsaṃdhiprapāko mūtranigrahaḥ / purīṣasyoṣṇatā caiva maraṇāyātisāriṇām //

kecana paṭhanti:
śvāsaśūlapipāsārtaṃ kṣīṇaṃ jvaranipīḍitam / viśeṣeṇa naraṃ vṛddham atīsāro vināśayet //
bāle vṛddhe tv asādhyo 'yaṃ liṅgair etair upadrutaḥ / api yūnām asādhyaḥ syād atiduṣṭeṣu dhātuṣu //

3, 20 M. yad uktam:
doṣaliṅgena matimān saṃsargaṃ tatra lakṣayet /

4, 13-16 M. ata evāha:
atīsāriṇām ajīrṇināṃ ca divāsvāpo vihitaḥ /
yad uktam:
narān niraśanān kāmaṃ divā svāpayet /

5, 9cd M. yad uktam:
dravyam ekarasaṃ nāsti na rogo 'py ekadoṣajaḥ / yo 'dhikas tena nirdeśaḥ kriyate rasadoṣayoḥ //
iti:
ekaḥ prakupito doṣaḥ sarvān eva prakopayet /

5, 33-34 M. iti:
hṛdi prāṇo gude 'pānaḥ samāno nābhisaṃsthitaḥ / udānaḥ kaṇṭhadeśe syād vyānaḥ sarvaśarīragaḥ //

Ā. iti :
rajoguṇamayaḥ sūkṣmaḥ śīto rūkṣo laghuś calaḥ /
iti :
pācakaṃ bhrājakaṃ caiva rañjakālocake tathā / sādhakaṃ ceti pañcaiva pittanāmāny anukramāt // svāśaye pācakaṃ pittam agnirūpaṃ tilonmitam / bhrājakaṃ kāntidaṃ yat tu lepābhyaṅgādipācakam // rañjakaṃ tu yakṛtplīhnos tad rasaṃ śoṇitaṃ nayet / ālocakaṃ sthitaṃ netre rūpadarśanakāri tat // sādhakaṃ hṛdaye tiṣṭhen medhāprajñākaraṃ ca tat / pittam uṣṇaṃ dravaṃ pītaṃ nīlaṃ sattvaguṇottaram / kaṭutiktarasaṃ jñeyaṃ vidagdhaṃ cāmlatāṃ vrajet //
iti :
uraḥkaṇṭhaḥśiraḥsaṃdhiparvāṇy āmāśayo rasaḥ / medo ghrāṇaṃ ca jihvā ca kaphasthānam uro bhṛśam //

5, 44 Ā. iti :
tasmin kṣate prarohāḥ syur māṃsajāḥ rudhirasravāḥ / vināśayanti śephaṃ te ghnanti puṃstvaṃ ca satvaram //
iti :
tathā yonau ca te duṣṭā gaṇḍūpadamukhākṛtīn / durgandhān sukumārāṃś ca picchilān janayanti hi //
iti :
tair evordhvagatadoṣaiḥ karṇajārśas tu jāyate / bādhiryaṃ śūlam atyugraṃ satataṃ karṇapūtitā // netrajeṣu jalasrāvo vedanā cāpy adarśanam / aśrūṇāṃ jāyate vartmāvarodho arśaḥsu saṃtatam // ghrāṇajeṣu pratiśyāyaḥ kṛcchrocchvāsaḥ śirovyathā / kṣavathuḥ pūtivaktraṃ ca vākyaṃ syāt sānunāsikam // mukhārśaḥsu ca kaṇṭhauṣṭhatālumadhyaikajanmasu / syād dhi gadgadavākyatvaṃ rasājñānaṃ mukhāmayāḥ //

6, 2-4 M. yad uktam anyatra :
atimātram ajīrṇe 'pi guru cānnam athāśnataḥ / divā 'pi svapato yasya pacate so 'gnir uttamaḥ //

6, 5-6 M. tantrāntara :
āmaṃ vidagdhaṃ viṣṭabdhaṃ rasaśeṣam athāpi ca / caturvidham ajīrṇaṃ syād āhārāparipākataḥ //
yad uktaṃ suśrute :
ajīrṇāt pavanādīnāṃ vibhramo balavān bhavet /

6, 15 M. uktaṃ hi :
ajīrṇāt pavanādīnāṃ vibhramo balavān bhavet /

6, 22 Ā. tathā ca :
avipakvam asaṃyuktaṃ durgandhaṃ bahu picchilam / sādanaṃ sarvagātrāṇām āmam ity abhidhīyate //
yad uktam :
dhātūnāṃ sapta saptānāṃ bhūtānāṃ pañca pāvakāḥ / trayodaśa bhavanty evaṃ saha jāṭharavahninā //

8, 12-15	M. kaścid abhiyukto likhitavān : ante śūnaḥ kṛśo madhye 'nyathā ca gudaśephasi / śūno jvarātisārārto mṛtakalpas tu pālakī //
9, 1-3	M. Caraka : rāgaparipräptaṃ pittaṃ raktapittam.
10, 1	M. Vāgbhaṭa : yakṣmaṇāṃ rājā rājayakṣmā.
10, 21-29ab	M. āgama : doṣā api vyādhiśabdaṃ labhante.

APPENDIX TWO

The Sanskrit medical authors and works quoted and referred to in M., Ā., the notes and the appendices.

AGNIVEŚA was one of the six disciples of Ātreya Punarvasu; each of them wrote a treatise (*tantra*) on *kāyacikitsā* (internal medicine) (Ca.Sū. 1, 30-33). The Agniveśatantra has not been preserved in its original form, but the Carakasaṃhitā is the form it acquired after its redaction by Caraka (and Dṛḍhabala). An Agniveśasaṃhitā is mentioned in some Ms. catalogues, but this must be the Carakasaṃhitā (see New Cat.Cat. 1, p. 36). Puzzling is a Nidānasthāna ascribed to Agniveśa (see Cat. Skt. Mss. N.-W. P. 1, p. 586-587). A text called Añjananidāna is ascribed to Agniveśa, but certainly written by a later author. Mukhopādhyāya states (H.I.M. 3, p. 520) that Śrīkaṇṭhadatta, in his Vyākhyākusumāvalī on the Siddhayoga, quotes stanzas from the Agniveśatantra which are not found in the Carakasaṃhitā (these stanzas are reproduced on p. 521). Agniveśa is once referred to in M. (on 2, 66cd-74ab); this is really a reference to A.h.Ni. 2, 61-62a, where Agniveśa's opinion on a certain subject, in contrast to that of Hārīta, is reported.

ARUṆADATTA was a son of Mṛgāṅkadatta, as indicated in the colophons of his comm. on A.h. This comm., called Sarvāṅgasundarī or Sarvāṅgasundarā, extends over the whole of A.h. and has been printed. From a remark by Ḍa. on Su.Ka. 1, 30 it is clear that Aruṇadatta also wrote a comm. on A.s. (see Bhatt., IHQ 23, 1947, p. 131-132 and Vogel, Introd. A.h., p. 12); this comm. on A.s. has not been preserved. Moreover, mention is made of a comm. on Su. by Aruṇadatta (see Cat. Skt. Mss. N.-W. P. 1, p. 594-595 : Suśrutaṭīkā by Aruṇadatta; cannot be procured for copying; old and apparently correct). It is uncertain whether the medical author Aruṇadatta is the same as an author of that name who is quoted as a lexicographer and grammarian. The earliest work in which the latter is cited is Vardhamāna's autocomm. on the Gaṇaratnamahodadhi, a work dated 1140 (Cat.Cat. 1, p. 30; Gode, St.I.L.H. 1, p. 185; Vogel, Introd. A.h., p. 13). This Aruṇadatta is also quoted in Sarvānandavandyaghaṭīya's Ṭīkāsarvasva on the Amarakośa, dated 1159 acc. to N.N. Das Gupta (IC 3, 1936-1937, p.

159-160), but dated 1180 acc. to Bhatt. (ABORI 28, 1947, p. 119; Bhatt. refers to p. 34-36 of the Introd. to Puruṣottamadeva's Paribhāṣāvṛtti, Rajshahi, 1946); moreover in Ujjvaladatta's Vṛtti on the Uṇādisūtras of Pāṇini (New Cat.Cat. 2, p. 287), dated about 1250 (Gode, Introd. A.h., p. 8 : assigned by Aufrecht to circa 1250), and finally in Rāyamukuṭa's comm. on the Amarakośa, dated 1431 (R.G. Bhandarkar, Report on the search for Skt. Mss. in the Bombay presidency during the year 1883-4, p. 467).

In his article in IHQ Bhatt. remarks that the first and the second Aruṇadatta may be identical; in his article in ABORI he states that they are evidently identical, without adducing arguments to prove his point. No other author made such a definite statement in this matter. Acc. to Cordier (JA, t. 17, 1901, p. 186-187) Aruṇadatta may be identical with a commentator on A.h., called Hāṭakāṅka (a fragmentary Ms. of a comm. on A.h.Ni., said to be by Hāṭakāṅka, is described in Burnell's Index to the Skt. Mss. in the Palace at Tanjore, p. 65 (5,384); an incomplete Ms., probably a copy of the Tanjore Ms., is in the coll. Cordier of the Bibliothèque Nationale at Paris : see Filliozat, JA, t. 224, 1934, p. 156, nr. 8; see about other Mss. : New Cat.Cat. 1, p. 465), the comm. of which shows a close analogy to that of Aruṇadatta. This suggestion of Cordier cannot be correct because Aruṇa and Hāṭakāṅka are frequently quoted as different authors in Śrīdāsapaṇḍita's comm. on A.h.

Aruṇadatta's date was determined by Hoernle (Osteology, Introd. p. 17) to be about 1220. This date was regarded as the correct one for a long time, but Bhatt. has proved (IHQ 23, 1947, p. 130 ff.; see also Vogel, Introd. A.h., p. 13, footnote 1) that Hoernle's method in fixing the date was wrong. The earliest writer to quote from Aruṇadatta is Ḍalhaṇa (on Su.Ka. 1, 30). Ḍalhaṇa is generally assigned to about 1200, so Aruṇa must be earlier. Vijayarakṣita, Śrīkaṇṭhadatta and Niścalakara do not quote him, so his date may be somewhere between the dates of these authors and 1200. Bhatt. fixes Aruṇadatta's date (assuming that the first and second Aruṇadatta are identical) at about 1150 (IHQ 23, 1947, p. 132). If both authors are indeed identical, the date is somewhat earlier : 1100-1120. Acc. to Bhatt. (ABORI 28, 1947, p. 119) Niścalakara was probably an elder contemporary of Aruṇadatta. N.N. Das Gupta says (IC 3, 1936-1937, p. 159 ff.) that Aruṇadatta was a Bengali, but he offers no proof to give force to that statement. In Bhatt.'s opinion (IHQ 23, 1947, p. 132) Aruṇadatta lived in the north, because he remarks that the practice of fellatio, current in the south, is not approved of. Acc. to Bhatt. again (ibid.), Aruṇadatta indulges in advanced grammatical polemics and has interesting notes on prosody and rhetoric from hitherto unknown sources. So it is not improbable that Bhatt. is right in assuming that the first and the second Aruṇadatta are identical.

Cordier remarks (JA, t. 28, 1901, p. 154) that Aruṇa's most important source was the comm. of Candranandana; this statement may be right as there is indeed much affinity between the two comm.

Aruṇadatta is quoted once in Ā. (on 2, 56-57), but this passage is probably a later interpolation and has been put between brackets by the ed. of the text. The quotations from Aruṇadatta in Śrīkaṇṭha's comm. on the Siddhayoga are probably additions by Nārāyaṇa, a late writer (after Ḍalhaṇa and Hemādri), who revised Śrīkaṇṭha's comm., as indicated in the colophon on p. 665 of the ed. of the work in the Ānandāśrama Series.

AŚVINĪKUMĀRASAṂHITĀ. Acc. to the New Cat.Cat. (1, p. 441) a work called Dhāturatnamālā forms part of the Aśvinīkumārasaṃhitā. Another part of it, called Saṃnipātakalikā or Saṃnipātārṇava, is known in some Mss. There seems to exist a comm. on the latter work by Māṇikya, son of Padmanābha (New Cat.Cat. 1, p. 441). Acc. to Cordier (Le Muséon, N.S. 4, 1903, p. 349-350) the Saṃnipātārṇava and Dhāturatnamālā are said to form part of the Aśvinīsaṃhitā, which is probably identical with the Aśvinīkumārasaṃhitā. A Ms. of the Dhāturatnamālā from the Aśvinīkumārasaṃhitā is described in Cat. Skt. Mss. BORI, vol. 16, part 1, p. 133-134. A Ms. containing the *saṃnipāta* chapter of the Aśvinīsaṃhitā is described in Cat. Skt. Mss. Madras, vol. 23, nr. 13069, p. 8787. Acc. to Bhatt. (IHQ 23, 1947, p. 136) Niścalakara remarks that Cakrapāṇidatta borrowed from the Aśvinīkumārasaṃhitā. Acc. to Gode (St.I.L.H. 1, p. 133) Candraṭa quotes from the Aśvinīsaṃhitā in his Yogaratnasamuccaya. The work must be rather old and should not be said to be a relatively late compilation, as Hoernle thought it to be (JRAS, 1909, p. 861).

ĀLAMBĀYANA must have been the author of a treatise of toxicology (*agadatantra*), as appears from quotations by commentators. The quotations have been partially collected by Mukhopādhyāya (H.I.M. 3, p. 760).

ĀṢĀḌHADHARMA, referred to by Vijayarakṣita on 1, 14cd-15ab as one of the early commentators (*pūrvaṭīkākāra*), must be the same as

Āṣāḍhavarman, referred to as one of the early commentators (*pūrvaṭīkākṛt*) by Cakra on Ca.Ci. 3, 217. In both cases he is mentioned together with Svāmidāsa (Cakra puts him after Svāmidāsa and Vijayarakṣita mentions Āṣāḍhadharma first). Āṣāḍhavarman and Svāmidāsa undoubtedly belong to the group of the earliest commentators on Ca., because they are quoted by Jejjaṭa. Cakra's quotations from Āṣāḍhavarman clearly indicate that the latter commented on the whole of Ca., after it had been completed by Dṛḍhabala. In the Introd. to the Lahore ed. of Ca. Āṣāḍhavarman and the author of the comm. called Parihāravārtika are classified as two different commentators on Ca. on p. 22, but on p. 26 the Parihāravārtika is said to have been written by Āṣāḍhavarman. Cakra mentions the Parihāravārtika twice; in Cakra's comment on Ca.Ci. 23, 137-139 both Āṣāḍhavarman and the Parihāravārtika are quoted in such a context that indeed it may be true that Āṣāḍhavarman's comm. on Ca. was called Parihāravārtika.

INDU was the author of a comm. on A.s., called Śaśilekhā. This comm. has been preserved and printed for the greater part (from imperfect Mss.). It is often quoted by Niścalakara as Indumatī (Bhatt., IHQ 23, 1947, p. 138-139). Indu also wrote a comm., called Śaśilekhā, on A.h. (Gode, St.I.L.H. 1, p. 157, footnote; Gode is not quite sure about it, but there seems to be no doubt, because the colophons of the Madras Ms. are clear; see Gode about the particulars; a second Ms. of Indu's comm. on A.h. may be present in the Adyar Library, see Gode, l.c., p. 154, footnote, and the Index of Skt. Mss. in the Adyar Library, p. 9, nr. 55). It is not impossible that the commentator Indu is identical with the author of a Nighaṇṭu, also called Indu, who is frequently quoted by Kṣīrasvāmin in his comm. on the Amarakośa (see Vogel, Introd. A.h., p. 15; N.N. Das Gupta, IC 3, p. 154; Gode, St.I.L.H. 1, p. 159-160). Some are of the opinion that Indu, the commentator (and possibly the author of a Nighaṇṭu), is identical with Indukara, the father of Mādhavakara (N.N. Das Gupta, IC 3, p. 154 : not improbable; refuted by Bhatt., IHQ 23, 1947, p. 139, because Indu, the commentator, belonged to Kaśmīr, and Indukara, the father of Mādhavakara, to Eastern India; Vogel, Introd. A.h., p. 14 : based on very shaky evidence). It is almost beyond doubt that Indu was a native of Kaśmīr (see Bhatt., IHQ 23, 1947, p. 131; Gode, St.I.L.H. 1, p. 158 : Indu gives terms current in Kaśmīr for particular plants; Vogel, Introd. A.h., p. 13). It is difficult to make definite statements about Indu's date. If Indu, the commentator, is identical with the author of the

Nighaṇṭu, he is earlier than 1050 (see Vogel, Introd. A.h., p. 15). In any case he must have lived before Niścalakara, whose Ratnaprabhā was written between 1110 and 1120, and after Bhaṭṭāraharicandra, who is quoted by him (see Vogel, Introd. A.h., p. 14; Gode, St.I.L.H. 1, p. 160-161). A more precise statement would be possible if Indu, the commentator, were identical with the father of Mādhavakara; this is, however, very improbable.

Tradition makes Indu the pupil of Vāgbhaṭa, but there is no reliable evidence to support the tradition (see Vogel, Introd. A.h., p. 13-14 and Vogel's footnotes). In my opinion it is even very improbable because Indu himself observes that there were already some commentaries on A.s. before he started writing the Śaśilekhā (see Gode, St. I.L.H. 1, p. 155, footnote); at least one generation of commentators on A.s. must have preceded him; so he cannot have been a direct pupil of Vāgbhaṭa. It is clear, however, that Indu was acquainted with both A.s. and A.h. (because he wrote a comm. on both texts; A.h. is quoted in the comm. on A.s., see Gode : St.I.L.H. 1, p. 156). The unsatisfactory conclusion is that Indu lived before 1050 and after the composition of A.h. and A.s. There is still one point to be mentioned. Acc. to Rudrapāraśava (the ed. of A.s. with Indu's comm.) Indu quotes from the Kāśikāvṛtti on Pāṇini, composed about 650 (see Gode, St.I.L.H. 1, p. 155-156). If correct, this fact is not of much avail in fixing Indu's date, because the A.h. was composed about 600 and A.s. was elaborated after that date.

ĪŚĀNA(DEVA) was a commentator on Ca. (Bhatt., IHQ 23, 1947, p. 139), quoted by Vijayarakṣita, Śrīkaṇṭhadatta (on the Siddhayoga), Vācaspati, Niścalakara and Nāganātha (in his Nidānapradīpa : Jolly, Cat.Skt.Mss. München, nr. 381, p. 54-55; see Introd., Comm. on the Nidāna, about Nāganātha). The full name, Īśānadeva, is used once by Vijayarakṣita and also only once by Niścalakara, suggesting (acc. to Bhatt., l.c.) that Deva was probably his family title. From the quotation in M. and Ā. on 2, 34-36ab nothing definite can be deduced about the nature of Īśānadeva's work.

ĪŚVARASENA is quoted by Vijayarakṣita, Śrīkaṇṭhadatta (on Siddhayoga 81, 52), Niścalakara (see Bhatt., IHQ 23, 1947, p. 139) and Cakra. The latter quotes him on Ca.Ci. 15, 92-93 and mentions him (as a commentator on Ca.) on Ca.Si. 1, 20-22ab. From Cakra's remarks on Ca.Si. 1, 20-22ab may be concluded that Īśvarasena lived after Dṛḍhabala. He may have been later than Jejjaṭa because he is not quoted by the latter; moreover, Cakra's list of commentators (in the comm. on Ca.Si. 1, 20-22ab) impresses as being arranged in a chronological order : the commentator, called Saindhava (who is already quoted by Jejjaṭa) precedes Jejjaṭa and Īśvarasena is mentioned after Jejjaṭa. If Bhatt. (IHQ 23, 1947, p. 139) is right in assuming that a particular list of authors, given by Niścala, is put in a chronological order (see also : Gadādhara), Īśvarasena was later than Vāgbhaṭa and Ravigupta (author of the Siddhasāra) and anterior to Gadādhara.

KARAVĪRA was one of the seven disciples of Dhanvantari; he is called Karavīra or Karavīrya (Su.Sū. 1, 3). Each of these seven disciples is supposed to have written his own treatise on surgery. Karavīra is quoted once in M. on ch. 1-10; he is also quoted in Ā. (New Cat.Cat. 3, p. 177) and by Niścalakara (Bhatt., IHQ 23, 1947, p. 139).

KĀRTIKAKUṆḌA, often called Kārtika, was a famous commentator on Su. He is quoted once in Cakra's Bhānumatī on Su.Sū. (Bhatt., IHQ 23, 1947, p. 140); he is often and respectfully quoted by Vijayarakṣita, Niścalakara (Bhatt., ibid.) and Ḍa. Acc. to Śrīkaṇṭhadatta (Kusumāvalī on Siddhayoga 12, 22-24) he preceded Vṛndakuṇḍa, the author of the Siddhayoga. This view is refuted by Hoernle (JRAS, 1906, p. 287) on insufficient grounds. Bhatt. (l.c.) is of the opinion that both Kārtikakuṇḍa and Vṛndakuṇḍa, as their common family title proves, belonged to a *vaidya* family of Bengal.

It is interesting to notice that Kārtikakuṇḍa is very often quoted by Ḍa., but only on Su.U. Vijayarakṣita also quotes him on passages from Su.U., except once (on 5, 43). From Ḍa.'s quotations and remarks Kārtikakuṇḍa appears as a person with an independent mind and many views of his own, often discarding stanzas from Su.U. or reading them in a different way. From Śrīkaṇṭhadatta's comm. on Siddhayoga 12, 22-24 and 59, 30 it is evident that Kārtikakuṇḍa sometimes adopted certain views on the authority of Vṛddhakāśyapa and other old medical writers. Hoernle tried to establish (JRAS, 1906, p. 286-288) that Kārtikakuṇḍa is identical with Bhāskara, mentioned in the introduction to Ḍa.'s comm. on Su. as the author of a *pañjikā* on Su. Hoernle thought he might be right because Kārtikakuṇḍa is not mentioned in Ḍa.'s introduction and Bhāskara is not quoted by Ḍa. Hoernle was certainly wrong because Ḍa. states that both Gayadāsa and Bhāskara wrote a *pañjikā* on Su., and, though Bhāskara is indeed never quoted by Ḍa., the latter frequently quotes the two authors of a *pañjikā* (*pañjikākārau*) and the Bṛhat- and Laghupañjikā, both separately and together.

About Kārtikakuṇḍa's date I offer as a hypothesis to be verified that it may be in the range between Mādhavakara and Vṛndakuṇḍa, if Śrīkaṇṭhadatta's remark on Siddhayoga 12, 22-24 is to be trusted, and assuming that the series of commentators mentioned by Vijayarakṣita on 1, 5d-6 is put in a chronological order (see : Vāpyacandra). (See also about Kārtikakuṇḍa : Gode, IC 13, 1947, p. 199-208).

KĀŚYAPASAṂHITĀ, also called Vṛddhajīvakīyatantra and ascribed to Vṛddhajīvaka, is an old medical work, which has been partially preserved in a single Ms., discovered by Haraprasād Śāstrī in Kāṭhmāṇḍū aṭ the end of 1898 (see H. Śāstrī's Report on the search of Skt. Mss. during the years 1895-1900, p. 9). Cordier corrected Haraprasād Śāstrī's statements about the Ms. (Le Muséon, N.S. 4, 1903, p. 322-323). A fragment of the work has been preserved in a Chinese translation (see P.C. Bagchi, IC 9, p. 53-64). The Kāśyapasaṃhitā has been edited, with a long introduction in Sanskrit, by Paṇḍit Hemarāja Śarmā. The Kalpasthāna of the work has been revised by someone called Vātsya (see the colophon of the Kalpasthāna). Quotations from Kāśyapa occur in many commentaries; an author called Vṛddhakāśyapa is also quoted by commentators. The quotations found in Madhukośa, Kusumāvalī and Nibandhasaṃgraha have been collected by Mukhopādhyāya (H.I.M. 1, p. 182). Acc. to the latter (l.c., p. 186-187) the Ms. of the Kāśyapasaṃhitā is described by Burnell (in : A classified index to the Skt.Mss. in the Palace at Tanjore, London, 1879-1880, p. 70, Nr. 41); this is, however, an erroneous assertion for the work described by Burnell, though called Kāśyapasaṃhitā, is a completely different medical treatise of Tantric inspiration. A Ms. of a work called Kāśyapīyaroganidāna is described by S. Kuppuswami Sastri (Cat.Skt. Mss. Madras, vol. 26, nr. 13112). The Kāśyapasaṃhitā is a text that especially deals with children's diseases. It is a remarkable fact that quotations from the Bhālukitantra, met with in commentaries, are sometimes very close to passages found in the Kāśyapasaṃhitā.

KṢĀRAPĀṆI was one of the six disciples of Ātreya Punarvasu; each of them wrote his own treatise on *kāyacikitsā* (Ca.Sū. 1, 30-33). Kṣārapāṇi's treatise was called Kṣārapāṇitantra, and not *kāyacikitsātantra*, as is asserted in the New Cat.Cat. (5, p. 150). An (incomplete) list of quotations from the Kṣārapāṇitantra has been collected by Mukhopādhyāya (H.I.M. 3, p. 561-564), who states that Kṣārapāṇi is quoted by Śrīkaṇṭhadatta, Śivadāsasena, Candraṭa and Cakrapāṇidatta. To this list should be added : Jejjaṭa, Vijayarakṣita, Niścalakara, Aruṇadatta, Ḍalhaṇa, Hemādri and Śrīdāsapaṇḍita. A very long quotation (in verse) from Kṣārapāṇi's treatise is found in Candraṭa's comm. on Tīsaṭa's Cikitsākalikā (Mukh., H.I.M. 3, p. 562-564).

KHARANĀDA. The medical treatise by Kharanāda was known from quotations only until the year 1938. During excavations at Navapura near Gilgit in the summer of 1938 a fragment of a comm. on this work was found by M. S. Kaul Shastri (see his Report on the Gilgit excavation in 1938, Quarterly Journal of the Mythic Society, vol. 30, p. 1-12). The comm. is called Khāraṇādanyāsa and relates to a chapter on pregnancy from Kharanāda's treatise (the chapter is called *khuṇḍikāgarbhāvakrānti*; cf. the title of Ca.Śā. 3). Kaul Shastri dates the Ms. fragment between the seventh and ninth century. Gode says in an article about this fragment of the Khāraṇādanyāsa (St.I.L.H. 1, p. 126-131) that he is inclined to fix 650 A.D. as the terminus before which Kharanāda may have composed his work and about 850 A.D. as the terminus before which the comm. was composed. A short time before Kaul Shastri's Report was published Gode had written an article on the references to Kharanāda's treatise (St.I.L.H. 1, p. 112-125). In that article he concluded that Kharanāda's treatise had been composed before 1150 A.D. Judging by the quotations no more could be said at that time, acc. to Gode, though Kharanāda is also quoted by Jejjaṭa, which leads to the conclusion that Kharanāda lived before 600. The date of composition of the Kharanādasaṃhitā is pushed back to a still earlier date by the fact that Haricandra quotes it (see : Haricandra). In the same article Gode stated that Kharanāda's treatise had assumed so much importance in the 13th century that Keśava wrote his Siddhamantra to harmonize the mutually conflicting views of Caraka, Suśruta and Kharanāda, as stated by Keśava himself. From Gode's study of quotations from Kharanāda's treatise it became clear that Kharanāda and an author called Khāraṇādi are identical and that the names Kharanāda and Khāraṇādi were current in Bengal and Mahārāṣṭra respectively.

The two quotations from Kharanāda in M. and Ā. are not found among the collection of quotations from Hemādri's Āyurvedarasāyana and Vopadeva's Siddhamantraprakāśa (a comm. on the Siddhamantra by Keśava, the father of Vopadeva) in Gode's first article. (See about Kharanāda also : Haricandra).

GADĀDHARA. Acc. to Bhatt. (IHQ 23, 1947, p. 140) there are two medical authors of this name. This statement is not correct, for it is quite unknown whether the second Gadādhara, mentioned as the father of Vaṅgasena, ever wrote a medical work. Bhatt. is right, however, in distinguishing two persons called Gadādhara, mentioned in medical treatises.

1) A medical author Gadādhara is quoted or mentioned eleven times in M. Judging by these quotations he seems to have been a commentator on Su. Gadādhara is also quoted by Niścalakara who gives some interesting details about him: "Gadādhara was of the Dāsa family and preceded Cakrapāṇidatta, as clearly indicated by Niścalakara; the latter calls him once *antaraṅgagadādharadāsa*, which may mean that he was a court physician" (Bhatt., IHQ 23, 1947, p. 140). Stanzas ascribed to Vaidya Gadādhara are quoted in the Saduktikarṇāmṛta of Śrīdharadāsa, composed in 1205 (N.N. Das Gupta, IC 3, p. 159). Bhatt. is sure that Gadādhara wrote a treatise called Vaidyaprasāraka; as a proof of this he quotes from Ms. P of the Ratnaprabhā : *vaidyaprasārake gadādharādayas tu* (l.c.), which is not convincing, but he says elsewhere (IHQ 23, 1947, p. 148) that the Vaidyaprasāraka by Gadādhara is often quoted by Niścalakara. A work, called Vaidyaprasāraka, is repeatedly quoted in Śrīkaṇṭhadatta's comm. on the Siddhayoga (e.g. on 9, 51; 11, 28; 37, 59); Gadādhara is quoted in the same comm. (e.g. on 41, 51; 46, 4), but Śrīkaṇṭha nowhere indicates that the Vaidyaprasāraka was written by Gadādhara. The Ms. of an anonymous medical work, called Bṛhadvaidyaprasāraka, is in the Coll. Cordier in Paris (Cordier, Le Muséon, N.S. 4, 1903, p. 341; Filliozat, JA, t. 224, 1934, p. 162, nr. 161). Gadādhara is not quoted by Cakra (on Ca.), Ḍa., Aruṇa and He.; nor does Gayadāsa quote him on Su.Ni. If the names of authors who wrote a comm. on Su. and who are mentioned by Vijayarakṣita on 1, 5d-6 and 1, 11-13 are really put in a chronological order, Gadādhara preceded Vāpyacandra and lived after Jejjaṭa (see : Vāpyacandra). Bhatt. assumes (IHQ 23, 1947, p. 139) that a particular list of authors, given by Niścala, is in a chronological order; if this statement is correct, Gadādhara was later than Vāgbhaṭa, Ravigupta (author of the Siddhasāra) and Īśvarasena and anterior to Govardhana (author of a Ratnamālā and later than Mādhavakara), Cakrapāṇidatta and Bakula.

2) Another Gadādhara, who was not of the Dāsa family (Bhatt., IHQ 23, 1947, p. 140), was the father of Vaṅgasena. If my hypothesis about Gadādhara 1) is correct, the father of Vaṅgasena is indeed a different person, for Vaṅgasena's date is after that of Mādhavakara.

GAYADĀSA, also called Gayin, wrote a comm. on Su., called Nyāyacandrikāpañjikā, which covered the whole of Su. as the numerous quotations show (Hoernle, JRAS, 1906, p. 293). Part of it has been preserved; the comm. on the Nidānasthāna has been printed; the comm. on the Śārīrasthāna is extant, for the greater part, in a Ms. of the Cambridge University Library (Add. nr. 2491; see about this Ms. : Jolly, ZDMG 58, 1904, p. 114-116 and Hoernle, JRAS, 1906, p. 294). It is assumed that Gayadāsa was also the author of a comm. on Ca. (Bhatt., IHQ 23, 1947, p. 141; Renou et Filliozat, l'Inde Classique 2, p. 159), but this comm. is not extant. Gayadāsa is quoted twice in M.; the quotation in M. on 2, 18-23 may refer to Gayadāsa's comm. on Ca.; the quotation on 9, 11 refers to the comm. on Su. Gayadāsa is one of Ḍa.'s chief authorities, often quoted by him. Ḍa. refers once to the Nyāyacandrikā (on Su.Sū. 27, 26). In the introd. to his comm. Ḍa. mentions Gayadāsa and Bhāskara as authors of a *pañjikā* on Su. and often quotes and refers to *pañjikākāra* (in the singular or dual), *bṛhatpañjikā*, *mahāpañjikā* and *laghupañjikā*, without further specifications. It is not clear which of these *pañjikā*s designates the comm. by Gayadāsa. Moreover Ḍa. quotes (once, on U. 49, 19) a *candrikākāra* on Su. Bhatt. (IHQ 23, 1947, p. 141) assumes that a comm. called Candrikā, often quoted by Niścalakara, is the famous comm. on Su. by Gayadāsa, but he does not even try to give evidence of this identity. Bhatt. (l.c., p. 154) quotes an interesting passage from Niścalakara, which proves that Gayadāsa was the court physician of a king of Bengal (*ity etad gauḍeśvarāntaraṅgaśrīgayadāsena darśitam*). Cordier (Le Muséon, N.S. 4, 1903, p. 333) had already noticed that at the end of a Ms. of Gayadāsa's comm. on Su.Ni. the latter is called an *antaraṅga* (see about this term : Cakrapāṇidatta). At the end of the printed text the term *antaraṅga* does not occur.

For a long time it was difficult to determine Gayadāsa's date. Jolly stated (ZDMG 58, 1904, p. 116) : earlier than Ḍa. Hoernle remarked (Osteology, Introd. p. 16) : not later than 11th century, and (ibid.; JRAS, 1906, p. 291) : Cakrapāṇidatta and Gayadāsa may have been contemporaries. It is possible to say something more about it now. Important in narrowing the limits of the time in which Gayadāsa must have lived is the fact that Jejjaṭa is quoted by him. Moreover, Gayadāsa is referred to once by Cakrapāṇidatta, acc. to Bhatt. (IHQ 23, 1947, p. 154). Bhatt. (ibid.) arrived at the conclusion that Gayadāsa can be placed about 1000 A.D. in the reign of one of the greatest Pāla kings : Mahīpāla I (c. 988-1038 acc. to Majumdar, History of Bengal I, p. 136). It is, however, not clear at all that Cakra (on Ca.Ci. 26, 293) refers to Gayadāsa; he only speaks about a *candrikākṛt* on Su. Therefore the problem remains whether Gayadāsa and Cakrapāṇidatta were contemporaries or not. It is not without importance that Gayadāsa is quoted by Vijayarakṣita, for the latter preceded Ḍalhaṇa. So Gayadāsa's date is somewhere between those of Jejjaṭa and Vijayarakṣita.

GUṆĀKARA. The author of this name, quoted once in M. (on 5, 31-32), has played an important part in Hoernle's efforts to fix the chronology of a number of medical authors. Hoernle writes (Osteology, Introd. p. 17) : "Vijayarakṣita quotes Guṇākara who wrote the Yogaratnamālā in 1239 A.D." This fact established, in Hoernle's opinion, the lower limit for Vijayarakṣita's date. In footnote 3 on p. 17 of Hoernle's Osteology it is made clear that the information about Guṇākara was obtained by letter from Cordier. With regard to the date of Guṇākara Hoernle refers the reader to Peterson's Report, 1886-1892, p. XXVI. Cordier possessed a manuscript of the Yogaratnamālā, also called Āścaryaratnamālā (see Cat.Cat. 1, p. 283), ascribed to Siddha Nāgārjuna, with a comm. by Guṇākara (this Ms. is now in the Coll. Cordier of the Bibliothèque Nationale in Paris; see Filliozat, JA, t. 224, 1934, p. 160, nr. 95). The commentary was written in 1239-1240 by the Jaina scholar Guṇākara (Cat.Cat. 1, p. 155; Bhatt., IHQ 23, 1947, p. 132-133). The Yogaratnamālā is a work on magical rites, incantations and sorcery and it is very improbable that Vijayarakṣita quotes from a commentary on a work of such a kind. Moreover, Guṇākara is quoted, together with Cakrapāṇidatta and Gadādhara, in order to explain a medical technical term. Bhatt. (IHQ 23, 1947, p. 132-133) has contributed a great deal to the elucidation of the problem. The three quotations to explain the term *āṭopa* which are found in M. on 5, 31-32 were traced by him in Niścalakara's Ratnaprabhā, where they serve the same purpose (the third quotation, taken from Gadādhara acc. to M., is said to be from a work, called Candrikā, in Niścalakara's comm.). In Niścalakara's comm. another quotation from Guṇākara occurs, again pointing to him as a medical author. Moreover, Bhatt. failed to find both quotations in two Mss. of Guṇākara's comm. on the Yogaratnamālā. It is clear now that Hoernle was wrong and that Guṇākara, quoted by Vijayarakṣita and Niścalakara, is not the Jaina scholar but a medical author, who probably wrote a comm. on Ca. Guṇākara, the medical author, is moreover quoted in Nāganātha's Nidānapradīpa (New Cat.Cat. 6, p. 58) and in Gopāladāsa's Cikitsāmṛta (New Cat.Cat. 6, p. 58; Bhatt., IHQ 24, 1948, p. 322).

GAUTAMA. A sage, called Gautama, is mentioned: Ca.Sū. 1, 8; Ca.Ci. 14, 3; Ca.Si. 11, 4, but the author Gautama, quoted in M., must have been a different person. A medical author, called Gautama, is quoted in A.s. (Sū. 8, 125; the passage is quoted from A.s. by Hemādri in his comm. on A.h.Sū. 7, 22cd-26). An author, called Gotama, is quoted by Gayadāsa on Su.Śā. (Hoernle, JRAS, 1906, p. 302). Other quotations are not known to me.

CAKRAPĀṆIDATTA, often called Cakrapāṇi or Cakra, wrote the following works: 1) a comm. on Ca., called Āyurvedadīpikā or Carakatātparyaṭīkā, which has been preserved and repeatedly printed; 2) a comm. on Su., called Bhānumatī; this work has been partially (on Su.Sū.) preserved and printed; acc. to Cordier (Le Muséon, N.S. 4, 1903, p. 332) a complete Ms. of the Bhānumatī forms part of a private collection in Benares; from quotations in other comm., especially Niścalakara's Ratnaprabhā, it is clear that Cakra's Bhānumatī covered the whole of Su.; 3) Cikitsāsaṃgraha, a well-known and often printed treatise on therapy; Niścalakara and Śivadāsasena wrote a comm. on it; 4) Dravyaguṇasaṃgraha, a short work on materia medica, which has been printed; Niścalakara and Śivadāsasena wrote a comm. on this work too; 5) Śabdacandrikā; this work has not yet been printed; Mss. of it are in the IO Library and the Oxford University Library; acc. to Jolly (Medicin, p. 6) it is a collection of pharmaceutical and botanical terms with their explanations; 6) Sarvasārasaṃgraha (Jolly, Medicin, p. 6); this work too has not been printed; N.N. Das Gupta (IC 3, p. 156-157) observes that this work may be by a later author, also called Cakrapāṇidatta; 7) Vyagradaridraśubhaṃkara, also known as Śubhaṃkara; this work is quoted in Niścala's Ratnaprabhā and was written before the Cikitsāsaṃgraha (acc. to Bhatt., IHQ 23, 1947, p. 148); it is also referred to, as Vyagradīnaśubhaṃkara, in Gopāladāsa's Cikitsāmṛta (Bhatt., IHQ 24, 1948, p. 318); 8) Muktāvalī, mentioned in the New Cat.Cat. (6, p. 284) as a medical lexicon.

Cakra has given us information about his person at the end of the Āyurvedadīpikā and Cikitsāsaṃgraha. He was a son of Nārāyaṇa who was the superintendent of the kitchen (*rasavatyadhikārin*) and a minister of the king of Bengal (*gauḍa*). His elder brother, Bhānu, was a court physician (*antaraṅga*). Cakra was born from a family of *vaidyas*, bearing as a family name Lodhravalī; this name is mentioned as one of the eight aristocratic *vaidya* families of Bengal by Bharatamallika in his Candraprabhā (p. 8, acc. to Bhatt., IHQ 23, 1947, p. 128, footnote 6). Bhatt. (l.c., p. 134-135) rejects the current reading of the colophon of Cakra's Cikitsāsaṃgraha and favours a variant (warranted by some Mss.; he refers to Peterson's Ulwar Cat., p. 154), in which Cakra states that he himself was the superintendent of the kitchen and a minister of the king of Bengal. Bhatt. adduces as arguments that the variant is stylistically faultless and that Niścala was removed by some length of time even from Cakra's disciples, whose views are sometimes criticized by Niścala.

Cakra's teacher was Naradatta and the Āyurvedadīpikā is based on Naradatta's interpretation of Ca. (see Introd. Āyurvedadīpikā). Vṛnda's Siddhayoga was the chief source of Cakra's Cikitsāsaṃgraha (as indicated by Cakra himself: Jolly, Medicin, p. 6). Niścala carefully records whether Cakra's formulas are found in the Siddhayoga or absent from it. In Cakra's time the Siddhayoga must have been the most popular compendium on therapy in Bengal (see Cikitsāsaṃgraha, *susthādhikāra* 16).

There is no doubt that Cakra was a native of Bengal. He is said to have been a resident of the Vīrabhūma district of Bengal (*vaṅga*) (see Gul 1, p. 117; the statement is supported by a quotation from an author called Jayadeva; no particulars about the latter are given). Śivadāsasena observes (on Cakra's Cikitsāsaṃgraha, *susthādhikāra* 16) that Nārāyaṇa, Cakra's father, was a minister of king Nayapāla of Bengal (1038-1055 acc. to Bhatt., l.c. p. 134, and Majumdar, History of Bengal I, p. 144; 1040-1070 acc. to Gul 1, p. 117). Cakrapāṇidatta's date is usually fixed at about 1060 (Cordier, JA, t. 17, 1901, p. 182; Hoernle, Osteology, Introd. p. 16), but Bhatt., being of the opinion that Cakra himself was a minister of king Nayapāla, says that it can now be definitely stated that Cakrapāṇi wrote his Cikitsāsaṃgraha in the decade 1040-1050 (l.c., p. 135). Bhatt.'s arguments, referred to above, are weak. I am of the opinion that the period in which Cakra wrote his works should be fixed at about 1060-1075.

The meaning of the term *antaraṅga* has been the subject of a study by N.N. Das Gupta (IC 1, p. 684-686). The word *antaraṅga* is repeatedly used, a.o. by Cakrapāṇidatta (whose elder brother was an *antaraṅga*), Niścalakara and Śivadāsasena. Bhatt. translates *antaraṅga* as royal physician (IHQ 23, 1947, p. 135). Śivadāsasena observes (on Cakra's Cikitsāsaṃgraha, *susthādhikāra* 16) that the term designates a learned physician of good family. See about the possible meanings and the development of the use of the term N.N. Das Gupta's article.

CANDRANANDANA was the son of Ratinandana (Vogel, Introd. A.h., p. 15) or Ravinandana (New Cat.Cat. 6, p. 355; Cordier, JA, t. 17, 1901, p. 185) and a native of Kaśmīr (Vogel, Introd. A.h., p. 15). He wrote a comm. on A.h., called Padārthacandrikā, on the instance of Śakunadeva (see Introd. Padārthacandrikā; New Cat.Cat. 1, p. 464). This comm. has been preserved, at least almost completely (see Introd. A.h., *sūcīpatraṃ saptamam*, about two Mss., covering together the whole of the work, some stanzas of the last chapter excepted) and has been printed partially (on Sūtrasthāna). The complete text of the comm. is available in a Tibetan translation.

There is also a medical lexicographer called Candranandana, who is frequently quoted in Kṣīrasvāmin's comm. on the Amarakośa, esp. in that part dealing with the *vanauṣadhivarga* (Vogel, Introd. A.h., p. 16, footnote 2; Gode, St.I.L.H. 1, p. 160). A Ms. of the work of this Candranandana, called Guṇanighaṇṭu, is in the coll. Cordier in Paris (Filliozat, JA, t. 224, 1934, p. 157, nr. 31). Acc. to Cordier (JA, t. 17, 1901, p. 185) the work is called Gaṇanighaṇṭu (New Cat.Cat. 6, p. 356 indicates : Oṣadhinighaṇṭu or Gaṇanighaṇṭu) and is a small vocabulary of materia medica in 33 sections (*gaṇa*), mainly drawn from A.h. (Cordier calls this work Guṇanighaṇṭu in his article in Le Muséon, N.S. 4, 1903, p. 350). The identity of these two authors, called Candranandana, is accepted by Cordier (l.c.), Bhatt. (ABORI 28, 1947, p. 119), Gode (St.I.L.H. 1, p. 160) and Bāpālāl G. Vaidya (Introd. Nighaṇṭu Ādarśa, p. 37); Vogel (Introd. A.h., p. 16) has his doubts about this question. New Cat.Cat. mentions also (6, p. 356) a work by Candranandana called Madanādinighaṇṭu.

About Candranandana's date opinions differ. He may be identical with the physician Candrābhinandana who is said to have assisted Vairocana in translating the four Tantras (rGyud bźi, the classic of Tibetan medicine) into Tibetan at the time of the Tibetan king Khri-sroṅ-ldeḫu-btsan (755-797) (Vogel, Introd. A.h., p. 15-16; see also p. 16, footnote 1); this identity is a matter of doubt. Bhatt. (ABORI 28,

1947, p. 119) says that Candranandana lived in the middle of the 11th century at the latest, because he is identical with the lexicographer of the same name quoted by Kṣīrasvāmin. Cordier was of the opinion that Candranandana was a contemporary of king Abhimanyu II of Kaśmīr (Cordier, Catalogue 3, p. 472, acc. to Vogel, Introd. A.h., p. 15, footnote 8). Candranandana must in any case have lived before the date of the translation of his comm. on A.h. into Tibetan. This translation was made by Rin-chen-bzaṅ-po between 1013 and 1055.

The quotation from Candranandana in Ā. on 2, 56-57 is probably a later interpolation and has been put between brackets by the ed. of the text.

CANDRIKĀKĀRA. This authority, quoted in commentaries under the name of Candrikākāra, has often been identified as Gayadāsa, who wrote the comm. called Nyāyacandrikāpañjikā on Su. (see a.o. : Bhatt., IHQ 23, 1947, p. 141). Cordier supposed (Le Muséon, N.S. 4, 1903, p. 331) that a comm., called Carakacandrikā, might be Gayadāsa's comm. on Ca.

One has to be careful in identifying the Candrikākāra or Candrikākṛt and his comm., for Cakrapāṇidatta refers to a comm. called Candrikā, once clearly as a comm. on Ca. (Cakra on Ca.Sū. 27, 129) and speaks also about a Candrikākṛt on Su. (Cakra on Ca.Ci. 26, 293). Ḍa. once refers to a Candrikākāra as a commentator on Su. (Ḍa. on Su.U. 49, 19), who does not agree with Cakra's comment on the stanza; I think that it is very improbable that Ḍa. refers to Gayadāsa in this way, for he always quotes the latter either under his name or as Pañjikākāra and (probably) as the author of the Bṛhatpañjikā. Moreover, the Candrikā which is quoted by Aruṇadatta, is acc. to Cordier (JA, t. 17, p. 185) Candranandana's Padārthacandrikā. So the Candrikākāra, mentioned twice by Vijayarakṣita in M. on ch. 1-10, may not be Gayadāsa, but some other commentator. The Candrikākāra, quoted in M. on 2, 61cd-65, may be the author of a comm. on Su., but this is not quite clear; the Candrikākāra quoted in M. on 10, 20 is, however, evidently a commentator on Su.

CARAKA made a revision of the Agniveśatantra; the revised text became known as the Carakasaṃhitā (see the colophons of Ca.). Some scholars made rather definite statements about Caraka's date. On the authority of the Chinese version of the Sūtrālaṃkāra, translated from Sanskrit into Chinese in the 5th century, S. Lévi (JA, t. 8, 1896, p.

480-482) argued that he was the physician of king Kaniṣka. Jolly was in doubt about this identification (WZKM 11, 1897, p. 164-166) and so was Müller (JRAS, 1932, p. 803-808). Filliozat (in : Renou et Filliozat, l'Inde Classique 2, p. 150) observes, however, that there is nothing to invalidate this tradition; he goes on to assert that, even if the tradition proves to be incorrect, this will not substantially alter the state of affairs as to Caraka's date, because the tradition that he lived during Kaniṣka's reign established itself at an early date; so Caraka probably lived during the first century of our era. Hoernle was of the opinion (JRAS, 1909, p. 857-893) that the Carakasaṃhitā, in its original form, is anterior to the Nāvanītaka (which forms part of the Bower Ms.) because at least twenty-five formulae found in the Nāvanītaka are identical with formulae occurring in the printed editions of the Carakasaṃhitā and exclusively in those portions of it, which are attributed to Caraka himself and not to Dṛḍhabala. Caraka's name, however, is nowhere mentioned in the Bower Ms. Hoernle fixed Caraka's date as lying between that of Kaniṣka and that of the Bower Ms., which he dated in the second half of the 4th century. The Nāvanītaka, contained in the Bower Ms., must have been composed some centuries before the date of the Ms. (see Hoernle's article in JRAS, 1909). Hoernle thought it might have been written in the 2nd or 3rd century. So Caraka's date would fall between that of Kaniṣka and the 2nd or 3rd century. Müller (JRAS, 1932, p. 809-810) disagrees with Hoernle and says that the formulae found in both Nāvanītaka and Carakasaṃhitā do not prove that the latter already existed when the Nāvanītaka was composed. He is of the opinion that the Carakasaṃhitā was redacted in a number of stages about the middle of the period 500-1000, but before 700. Mukhopādhyāya (H.I.M. 3, p. 610-613) is convinced that the Carakasaṃhitā is a book of great antiquity, because Patañjali (unspecified by Mukh.), who flourished in the 2nd century B.C., wrote a comm. on it (he refers to a quotation found in Nāgeśa Bhaṭṭa's Laghumañjūṣā) and for other reasons too (l.c., p. 611-613). The arguments used by Mukhopādhyāya to prove the great antiquity of Caraka are repeated by Srivastava (Hist.Ind.Pharm., p. 44-47). (See also Hariprapanna, Rasayogasāgara, Introd. p. 71-84). Rāy (Hist.Chem., p. 60) tries to prove that Caraka should be placed in the early Buddhistic era. In my opinion the best solution is to assume that Caraka's redaction of the Agniveśatantra already existed or was made in the first two or three centuries of our era.

Many commentators, among whom Vijayarakṣita, refer to and quote from a text called the *kāśmīrapāṭha* of the Carakasaṃhitā. Vijayarakṣita's reference (on 5, 27c) to the *kāśmīrāḥ* who read Ca.Ci. 14, 171a differently, was discussed by Hoernle (JRAS, 1909, p. 890-891), who thought that the Kaśmīr recension of Ca., referred to by Vijayarakṣita, should with good reason be ascribed to Dṛḍhabala, and the original form of the verse, adopted by Mādhavakara, to Caraka. Acc. to Hoernle this implied that the Kaśmīr recension was not known to Mādhava and that Dṛḍhabala was posterior to Mādhava. I do not see why it should be thus, for the printed editions of Ca., which contain Dṛḍhabala's recension. read the verse in the same way as Mādhavakara. The other quotation by Vijayarakṣita from the *kāśmīrapāṭha* of Ca. is identical with that in the printed recension of Dṛḍhabala. Hoernle also deals with the Kaśmīr recension of Ca. in his Osteology (Introd. p. 3) : "The early commentators of the eleventh and thirteenth centuries (e.g. Cakrapāṇidatta and Vijayarakṣita) often refer to a Kashmirian recension (*kāśmīrapāṭha*) when commenting on passages of the earlier portion of the compendium, i.e. the portion written by Caraka himself. The probability is that in all these cases the reference is to Dṛḍhabala's revision of Caraka's work; for in references to the concluding portion of the compendium, Dṛḍhabala, as a rule, is quoted by name as its author." Mukhopādhyāya (H.I.M. 3, p. 637) disagrees with Hoernle, drawing attention to the fact that Hoernle regards both Caraka and Dṛḍhabala as Kashmirians, so that it is natural for commentators to refer to Caraka's edition of the earlier part of the work as the Kaśmīr recension. He further observes that this theory is based upon a conjecture because nothing is known about Caraka's birthplace and that the Kaśmīr recension may have been the work of a Kashmirian physician, whose name is lost to us and who may have been a different individual, neither Caraka nor Dṛḍhabala.

I tend to assume that Hoernle is wrong. Cakrapāṇidatta refers to the *kāśmīrāḥ* (on Ca.Ci. 3, 117 and 119; Ci. 25, 41) and the *kāśmīra(pāṭha)* (on Ca.Ci. 13, 112cd-113ab) in such a way that the impression is created that not Dṛḍhabala's recension is referred to (Cakra's remarks on Ci. 3, 117 and 119 refer to passages incorporated in the text, read by the *kāśmīrāḥ* and adopted by Cakra; his remark on Ci. 25, 41 concerns a variant, adopted by the *kāśmīrāḥ*, but not read by Cakra; also on Ci. 13, 112cd-113ab Cakra records a variant found in the *kāśmīrāḥ*). All these remarks may point to a Kaśmīr school of interpreters of Ca., who adopted their own readings and variants of Ca. This is not improbable because a number of schools of interpreters of

Ca. may have existed, as appears from Jejjaṭa's comm. on Ca., mentioning the *kāśmīrasaindhavabhiṣajaḥ*, *vaiṣṇavāḥ*, *paitāmahāḥ* (and also the *gauḍa* recension acc. to Bhatt., IHQ 23, 1947, p. 153). It is for these reasons that I consider it probable that a *kāśmīrapāṭha* of Ca. has existed that had nothing to do with Dṛḍhabala. In the Introd. to the Lahore ed. of Ca. (p. 23, nr. 12) mention is made of a Ms. of Ca. that is said to follow the *kāśmīrapāṭha*, but no particulars about it are given.

JATŪKARṆA was one of the six disciples of Ātreya Punarvasu. He wrote his own treatise on *kāyacikitsā* (Ca.Sū. 1, 30-33). From quotations by various commentators it is clear that there must indeed have existed a Jatūkarṇasaṃhitā. The quotations in M. also point to this. Mukhopādhyāya (H.I.M. 3, p. 547-550) collected the quotations from the Madhukośa, Śrīkaṇṭhadatta's Vyākhyākusumāvalī on the Siddhayoga, Ḍa.'s comm. on Su. and Śivadāsasena's Tattvacandrikā on Ca. Jatūkarṇa is also quoted by Jejjaṭa (his name is written there Jātukarṇa), Cakrapāṇidatta (on Ca.), Aruṇadatta (who writes his name Jātūkarṇa), Niścalakara, and in the Kairalī comm. on A.h.U.; Niścalakara quotes Jatūkarṇa very often in his Ratnaprabhā (Bhatt., IHQ 23, 1947, p. 142). In Niścala's time the Jatūkarṇasaṃhitā must still have been available, for he consulted three old copies of it (Bhatt., l.c., p. 127). Jolly says (Medicin, p. 125) that acc. to Cordier (in : Origines, évolution et décadence de la médecine indienne, Annales d'hygiène et de médecine coloniales, 1901, p. 77-89) fragments of Jatūkarṇa's work have been discovered in Nepal (I have not been able to verify this statement).

JEJJAṬA. The orthography of the name of this author varies : Jajjaṭa (in the colophons of the preserved parts of his comm. on Ca.), Jarjaṭa (A.s., ed. Trichur; see Bhatt., ABORI 28, 1947, p. 112, note 1), Jejjaṭa (M.; Ā.; Gayadāsa on Su.Ni.; Cakra on Ca.; often in Ḍa.; He.; etc.), Jejjhaṭa (sometimes in Ḍa.), Jejjaḍa (Ms. A of Niścalakara's Ratnaprabhā; see Bhatt., IHQ, 23, 1947, p. 142), Jaijjaṭa (Su. with Ḍa.'s comm., ed. by Jīvānanda Vidyāsāgara, 1889, acc. to Hoernle, JRAS, 1906, p. 285; Jolly, ZDMG 60, 1906, p. 414), Jaijjhaṭa (Jolly, ZDMG 58, 1904, p. 114, referring to Roth in ZDMG 48, 1894, p. 139, who reviews the third ed. of Su. by Jīvānanda Vidyāsāgara; Roth, however, writes Jaijhaṭa) and Jaiyyaṭa (Dasgupta, H.I.Ph. 2, p. 427). Jaḍa, quoted five times in the Ms. of Gayadāsa's comm. on Su.Śā., is identical with Jejjaṭa (Jolly, ZDMG 58, 1904, p. 116 : Jaḍa may be the same as

Jejjaṭa; Jolly, ZDMG 60, 1906, p. 413-414 : "The supposition of this identity, simultaneously put forward by Cordier and by me, proves to be right"; in a study of the Ms. of Gayadāsa's comm. on Su.Śā. Hoernle arrived at the same conclusion : JRAS, 1906, p. 301).

Jejjaṭa wrote a commentary on both Ca. and Su. (see M. on 2, 61cd-65 and on 10, 2; the comm. on Su. is referred to by Ḍa. in the introduction to his comm. on Su.). Gayadāsa ascribes also a *tantra* (textbook) to him (see Hoernle, JRAS, 1906, p. 301). His comm. on Su. must have been the oldest comm. on this text, but has not been preserved. The only one to whom it seems to have been accessible in recent times is Rudrapāraśava, the editor of A.s. with Indu's comm. (Trichur, 1913-1926), who filled up a lacuna in Indu's Śaśilekhā with the text of the Nirantarapadī comm. on Su. by Jarjaṭa (vol. 2, p. 298) and who printed many notes from Jarjaṭa's comm. in the second and third volume of his ed. of A.s. (see Bhatt., ABORI 28, 1947, p. 112, note 1). The name of Jejjaṭa's comm. on Su. was known to Dasgupta, who writes (H.I.Ph., 2, p. 428) that it went by the name of Bṛhallaghupañjikā. Dasgupta, however, is wrong. (It is possible that Dasgupta copied Cordier who also held the opinion that Jejjaṭa's comm. on Su. was called Bṛhallaghupañjikā; see : Le Muséon, N.S. 4, 1903, p. 334). In Ḍa.'s comm. on Su. the Bṛhatpañjikā and Laghupañjikā are clearly referred to as two separate works (Ḍa. on Su.Sū. 45, 157) and, moreover, as the works of two authors with an opinion on a particular point that differs from that of Jejjaṭa (Ḍa. on the same passage). Jejjaṭa's comm. on Su. was consulted by Candraṭa before he started writing his Suśrutapāṭhaśuddhi (as indicated by Candraṭa himself at the end of this text; see Introd. Ca., p. 13). It seems to have been available at least up to the time of Vijayarakṣita and Ḍa., who quote from it; even Hemādri refers to it in his introd. to the Āyurvedarasāyana.

Jejjaṭa's comm. on Ca., in a revised version by Haridatta, has been partly preserved in a single manuscript, kept in the Government Oriental Manuscripts Library at Madras. It has been printed, together with Cakra's comm. on Ca. (Lahore, 1940, 2 vols.), and is called Nirantarapadavyākhyā. The extant fragments extend from Ca.Ci. 13, 32 to Ci. 5, 73; from Ci. 23, 161 to Ka. 1, 4 and from Si. 3 to Si. 7, 31. It is evident from the quotations in Jejjaṭa's comm. that a number of commentators on Ca. preceded him.

Jejjaṭa mentions in his comm. on Ca. that he was a pupil of Vāgbhaṭa. His date depends on the identity and date of this Vāgbhaṭa. It is often silently assumed that the latter is the well-known medical author who wrote the A.h.; this assumption is not contradicted by the dates of both authors. There are, however, divergent opinions about the time in which Jejjaṭa lived : Haridattaśarman (ed. of Jejjaṭa's comm. on Ca.) : sixth century (Introd. p. 20), Gul (1, p. 116) : ninth century; Bhattacharyya (IHQ 23, 1947, p. 153) : about 875-900. Only Hoernle noticed (JRAS, 1906, p. 292) that Jejjaṭa's comm. on Ca. was known to Vṛndakuṇḍa who mentions it : Siddhayoga 39, 33 (*carake prāha jaijjaṭaḥ*). So Jejjaṭa must have preceded Vṛndakuṇḍa. Hoernle's conclusion is that this would refer Jejjaṭa to the seventh century at the latest. If my hypothesis on the enumeration in a chronological list of some authors by Vijayarakṣita on 1, 5d-6 and 1, 11-13 is correct (see : Vāpyacandra), Jejjaṭa lived before Gadādhara. He is anterior to Gayadāsa because the latter quotes him.

In the Gul ed. of Ca. (1, p. 117) it is said : "Jejjaṭa may have been a Kashmirian as is suggested by the ending -ṭa of his name, common among Kashmirians (e.g. Kaiyaṭa, Mammaṭa). More probably he was an inhabitant of Sindh, because he studied under Vāgbhaṭa, though he may have travelled from Kashmir to Sindh in order to study under Vāgbhaṭa." (Vāgbhaṭa, the author of the A.h., was indeed an inhabitant of Sindh; see : Vāgbhaṭa). Haridattaśarman (Introd. Ca. with Jejjaṭa's comm., p. 20) observes : "Some say that Jajjaṭa is identical with the father of Kaiyaṭa; in the introduction to his comm. on the Mahābhāṣya Kaiyaṭa says that he is a son of Jaiyaṭa. Others are of the opinion that Jajjaṭa and Jaiyaṭa are different persons." The identity of Jejjaṭa with this Jaiyaṭa is rejected by Gul (1, p. 116).

I think that Jejjaṭa's date may be : about 600 (the age in which Vāgbhaṭa lived), because he quotes Dṛḍhabala; moreover, Jejjaṭa quotes Bhaṭṭāraharicandra who lived before 600; Jejjaṭa preceded Vāpyacandra, who preceded Mādhavakara; so Jejjaṭa must have lived before 700.

ḌALHAṆA wrote a comm. on Su., called Nibandhasaṃgraha, which has been preserved and repeatedly printed. In the introd. he states that he was a favourite of king Sahapāla and gives as his genealogy that he was a son of Bharatapāla, son of Jayapāla, son of Govinda; Govinda and Jayapāla are described as physicians; his family's home was in the neighbourhood of Mathurā. Acc. to Hoernle (JRAS, 1906, p. 290) he had his home in the north-west; acc. to Filliozat (in Renou et Filliozat, l'Inde Classique 2, p. 159) he was a Kashmirian.

Ḍa.'s date must be : about 1200; Cakrapāṇidatta is quoted once by Ḍa. (on U. 49, 19); Ḍa. quotes from Śrīpati's Jyotiṣaratnamālā (on Śā. 1, 11; see : Bhatt., IHQ 23, 1947, p. 132); Śrīpati wrote another work, the Siddhāntaśekhara, about 1040 (see Introd. to Śrīpati's Gaṇitatilaka, p. 62-63, ed. H. R. Kāpadīā, Gaekwad's Oriental Series, vol. 58). Ḍa. is quoted by Hemādri once (on A.h.Sū. 7, 40). (See also Introduction : Vācaspati). Ḍalhaṇa is not quoted in the Madhukośa, nor by Niścalakara, which may indicate that the proposed date is correct. He is repeatedly quoted in the Kusumāvalī, but these quotations were added by Nārāyaṇa, the reviser of that comm. (see : Śrīkaṇṭhadatta).

TĪSAṬA was a son of Vāgbhaṭa (see Cat.Skt.Mss. BORI, vol. 16, part 1, p. 86-87) and the father of Candraṭa. He is the author of the Cikitsākalikā, also called Yogamālā (Cat.Skt.Mss. BORI, vol. 16, part 1, p. 84-85). Tīsaṭa is quoted by Vijayarakṣita and must be prior to the latter. It is of more importance, however, that Cakrapāṇidatta borrowed from the Cikitsākalikā as Niścalakara observes (Bhatt., ABORI 28, 1947, p. 124-125). So Tīsaṭa cannot have lived later than the 10th century, though Filliozat (in Renou et Filliozat, l'Inde Classique 2, p. 160) places him in the 11th century. Bhatt. (ABORI 28, 1947, p. 125) assigns Tīsaṭa and Candraṭa to the first half of the tenth century. The Cikitsākalikā has been printed; Jolly has translated and published the first part of it (ZDMG 60, 1906, p. 413-468).

Tīsaṭa's son, Candraṭa, wrote a comm. on the work of his father; two versions of this comm. are known, one much more elaborate than the other (see Jolly, l.c.). The comm. has also been partially translated by Jolly (ibid.). Besides the comm. on the Cikitsākalikā Candraṭa wrote a revised version of Su., called Suśrutapāṭhaśuddhi. The importance of this work was already noticed by Hoernle (JRAS, 1906, p. 293). Moreover Candraṭa wrote a work called Yogaratnasamuccaya in which many of his sources are specified, which is of importance for the chronology of the authors and works quoted and referred to by Candraṭa (the authors and works quoted by Candraṭa in the Yogaratnasamuccaya have been studied by Gode : St.I.L.H. 1, p. 132-137). Apart from the already enumerated works of Candraṭa the New Cat. Cat. mentions (6, p. 354) a Candraṭasāroddhāra and a comm. by Candraṭa, called Vaidyatriṃśaṭṭīkā.

TOḌARA(MALLA) was a famous minister of the emperor Akbar (1556-

1605). Under his inspiration an encyclopaedic work, called Toḍarānanda, was written. The medical part of this work is called Āyurvedasaukhya. Acc. to Gode (St.I.L.H. 1, p. 295) the Toḍarānanda was composed between 1563 and 1589 (Toḍara died in 1589). Aufrecht notices (Cat.Cat. 1, p. 214) that Toḍaramalla, minister of Akbar and author of the Toḍarānanda, was a son of Bhagavatīdāsa. Jolly describes (Cat.Skt.Mss. München, nr. 373, p. 49-50) a Ms. of Toḍaramallavaidya Kānhaprabhu's comm. on A.h.Ni., called Nidānacintāmaṇi (which is different from the Āyurvedasaukhya), in which it is stated that the author was the son of Mahāvaidya Beīṃdevaprabhu and Sāmāmbikā. See about Toḍara and his medical works : BDHM Hyderabad 3, 1965, p. 151-160 and 210-219.

DĀRUVĀHA is an old medical authority, already quoted by Jejjaṭa. He is mentioned twice in the Kāśyapasaṃhitā (Sū. 25, 3; Sū. 27, 3).

DṚḌHABALA was a son of Kapilabala (Ca.Ci. 30, 290) and was born in Pañcanadapura (Ca.Si. 12, 39); an author on *kāyacikitsā*, called Kapilabala, is quoted by Cakra on Ca.Sū. 7, 45-50. Pañcanada is mentioned in Kalhaṇa's Rājataraṅgiṇī (*taraṅga* 4, 248); it is said to be situated near the confluence of the rivers Vitastā and Sindhu (Introd. Ca., p. 11). Acc. to M. A. Stein it is a place called nowadays Pañcyanor; so Dṛḍhabala would have been a Kashmirian (Introd. Ca., p. 11). Jolly (Medicin, p. 11), however, says that Dṛḍhabala was born in the Pañjāb (*pañcanada*). Hoernle (Osteology, Introd. p. 2-3 and footnote p. 3) remarks : "There are several places called Pañcanada; anciently one of them appears to have existed in Kaśmīr, near the confluence of the rivers Jhelam (Vitastā) and Sindhu; its place is indicated by the modern village of Pantzinōr, which lies close to what was the original site of that confluence, before its removal to its present site, in the latter half of the ninth century, in the reign of king Avantivarman; it is this Kashmirian Pañcanada, which was probably the home of Dṛḍhabala. (See Dr. Stein's transl. of the Rājataraṅgiṇī, ch. 4, 248 and ch. 5, 66ff. The usual identification of Pañcanada with the Pañjāb is untenable, for Dṛḍhabala clearly indicates a locality, *pura*, not a country, as his home)." (See also the remainder of Hoernle's footnote on p. 3 about Cordier's erroneous identification of Pañcanadapura). Filliozat (in Renou et Filliozat, l'Inde Classique 2, p. 150) holds the view that Dṛḍhabala was a native of Kaśmīr. Dasgupta (H.I.Ph. 2, p. 426) is in doubt whether Dṛḍhabala was born in Kaśmīr or in the Pañjāb. (See also Mukhopādhyāya, H.I.M. 3, p. 622-624; Gul 1, p. 96-99).

Dṛḍhabala completed Caraka's revision of the Agniveśatantra, as clearly indicated in the text of Ca. Dṛḍhabala states (Ca.Ci. 30, 289-290) that he has written the last seventeen chapters of the Cikitsāsthāna and the whole of the Kalpa- and Siddhisthāna. Dṛḍhabala also says that he has made use of many treatises to complete Caraka's work. Cakra comments on this passage and observes that the treatises referred to are those of Suśruta, Videha, etc. It has long been a problem which are the seventeen chapters of Ca.Ci. redacted by Dṛḍhabala, because his name appears in only some of the colophons. His statement that he has written the last seventeen chapters does not solve the puzzle, because there are two ways of arrangement of the chapters of Ca.Ci. (see e.g. Hoernle, JRAS, 1908, p. 999-1001; Mukhopādhyāya 3, p. 624-626; Gul 1, p. 101-103). The authors of the Gul ed. of Ca., after studying the subject (Gul 1, p. 103-105), concluded that the authorship of only seven chapters out of the thirty of Ca.Ci. remains doubtful. Twenty-three chapters can definitely be assigned, either to Caraka (1-8; 14, 19 and 21, because they are quoted in the Nāvanītaka of the Bower Ms., which is anterior to Dṛḍhabala; 24 and 25, because ascribed to Caraka by Jejjaṭa), or to Dṛḍhabala (26, 27 and 28 are ascribed to Dṛḍhabala by Vijayarakṣita; 15 is ascribed to him by Aruṇadatta; 16, 17, 22 and 23 are quoted by Vijayarakṣita and ascribed to Dṛḍhabala; 29 and 30 are the last chapters in both orders of arrangement and have been redacted by Dṛḍhabala as stated in the colophons). (The order of the chapters is that of the ed. Gul and the ed. Nirṇaya Sāgar Press. See also the treatment of the problem by Hoernle, JRAS, 1908, p. 1001-1027 and by Mukhopādhyāya, H.I.M. 3, p. 626-629). Dṛḍhabala not only wrote the mentioned portions of the Carakasaṃhitā but probably revised the whole, though it is very difficult to determine what he added to the text of Caraka or what was changed by him (see about this question : Hoernle, JRAS, 1908, p. 1001-1002; Mukhopādhyāya, H.I.M. 3, p. 633-636; Gul 1, p. 105-106).

Dṛḍhabala's date has often been discussed. Filliozat (in Renou et Filliozat, l'Inde Classique 2, p. 150) is very cautious, saying that his date is uncertain, but that he is anterior to Cakrapāṇidatta because the latter quotes him. Hoernle, basing his statements on a rather complicated, but not convincing reasoning (see his Osteology, p. 14-16, and his article in JRAS, 1908, p. 997-1028), arrives at the conclusion that Dṛḍhabala is posterior to the authors of A.s., Mādhavanidāna and Siddhayoga, because he incorporated portions of these texts in the Carakasaṃhitā. The author of A.h., however, is posterior to Dṛḍhabala acc. to Hoernle (Osteology, Introd. p. 14-15; JRAS, 1908, p. 1016-1018). Dṛḍhabala should be dated, acc. to Hoernle (Osteology, Introd. p. 16), between Mādhava (7th or 8th century) and the author of A.h. (8th or 9th century). Many scholars argue that Dṛḍhabala must have lived in the 8th or 9th century (Dasgupta, H.I.Ph. 2, p. 426; Jaggi, p. 71; Müller, SA 30, 1937, p. 54; Kutumbiah, Introd. p. 29). Mukhopādhyāya has examined Hoernle's arguments regarding Dṛḍhabala's date and seems to disagree with him, being of the opinion that Dṛḍhabala preceded Mādhavakara (H.I.M. 3, p. 630-633). I agree with Mukhopādhyāya that Vijayarakṣita's comment on Mādhavanidāna 22, 14 indicates that Mādhavakara was acquainted with Dṛḍhabala's work. Hoernle's objection (Osteology, Introd. p. 14, footnote 1) that it was Vijayarakṣita's aim to make an exegetical and not a chronological statement does not convince me at all. This leads to the important conclusion that Dṛḍhabala must have preceded Mādhavakara.

Another point of value in determining Dṛḍhabala's date is the fact, which was unknown to Hoernle, that Dṛḍhabala is quoted by Jejjaṭa (dated by Hoernle as living in the seventh century at the latest), who preceded Vṛndakuṇḍa and, in my opinion, was anterior to Gadādhara and Gayadāsa. The editors of the Gul ed. of Ca. agree with Hoernle that Vāgbhaṭa, the author of A.h., must have lived after Dṛḍhabala, because prose portions of Ca., redacted by Dṛḍhabala, appear in a closely related versified form in A.h. (Gul 1, p. 100). The same editors (Gul 1, p. 100) state that Vāgbhaṭa, the author of A.h., cannot have lived later than the 4th century, because quotations from him are found in the Kāndarpika chapter of Varāhamihira (Bṛhatsaṃhitā, adhyāya 76; ed. and transl. Subrahmanya Sastri, p. 600-602) who lived in the 5th century and because Bhaṭṭāraharicandra, who flourished during the reign of king Sāhasāṅka (375-413), was a contemporary of Vāgbhaṭa. They also hold the opinion that the lack of evidence of any reference to Dṛḍhabala in the Nāvanītaka, composed in the first part of the 4th century, provides the upper limit to Dṛḍhabala's date. Their conclusion is that Dṛḍhabala can be put fairly somewhere between the end of the third and the beginning of the fourth century. Their argument regarding Bhaṭṭāraharicandra's date is open to doubt and it is unknown to me whether A.h. is quoted by Varāhamihira, but Varāhamihira's date is later, because his son wrote an astrological treatise dated about 600 (Winternitz 3, p. 571). In my opinion Dṛḍhabala's date may be about 500 or earlier, because he preceded Mādhavakara, Vāgbhaṭa, Jejjaṭa and Āṣāḍhavarman.

DHANVANTARINIGHAṆṬU. This work is acc. to Zachariae (Die indischen Wörterbücher, p. 38) older than the Amarakośa. Gode (St.I.L.H. 1, p. 160) notices that it is quoted in Kṣīrasvāmin's comm. on the Amarakośa (Kṣīrasvāmin's date is acc. to Zachariae, l.c., p. 21 : 11th century; acc. to Vogel, Introd. A.h., p. 15 : second half 11th century). Acc. to T. Chowdhury (Introd. Paryāyaratnamālā p. 9) the Dhanvantarinighaṇṭu was utilized by Maṅkha (who wrote his Śrīkaṇṭhacarita between 1135 and 1145 acc. to Winternitz 3, p. 53).

The work is the oldest medical Nighaṇṭu that has been preserved. Two recensions of it are known, comprising seven and nine chapters respectively (Cult. and Hist. of the Ind. P. 4, p. 198). Amara may have used some older version of the work than that which is extant; one Ms. is known in which it is stated that the original work of Dhanvantari has been revised by someone called Kāśyapa (Hist. and Cult. of the Ind. P. 4, p. 198, referring to : Devasthali, Descr. Cat. of Skt. and Prkt. Mss. in the Libr. of the Univ. of Bombay, p. 113, no. 278).

NĀGABHARTṚTANTRA. From the quotation in M. on 2, 37-38 it is clear that this is the name of a medical treatise. It is quoted by Niścalakara as Nāgabhartṛtantra, Nāgabhaṭṭatantra or Nāgatantra (Bhatt., IHQ 23, 1947, p. 143). Nāgabhartṛ is quoted once by Nāganātha in his Nidānapradīpa (Jolly, Cat.Skt.Mss. München, nr. 381, p. 54-55).

NĀGĀRJUNA. There are many problems about medical works attributed to Nāgārjuna. A long series of works, among which also non-medical treatises, is ascribed to him (see Cat.Cat. 1, p. 283; 2, p. 61; 3, p. 61). Su.U. is said to have been revised (*pratisaṃskṛta*) by Nāgārjuna (Ḍa. mentions a reviser of Su. in his comm. on Sū. 1, 1; Cakra refers to a reviser in his Bhānumatī, but does not mention his name; see also Dasgupta, H.I.Ph. 2, p. 425 and Cordier, Le Muséon, N.S. 4, 1903, p. 332). Gayadāsa quotes Nāgārjuna twice on Su.Ni.; the first quotation is a variant of a stanza of Su.U., as read by Nāgārjuna, the second quotation is said to be taken from a treatise called Nāgārjunīya, which appears to be a work in verse related to Su. There seems to have been a school of interpreters of Su., who were called *nāgārjunīyāḥ* and who adopted particular readings of Su., rejected by others. (See Cordier, Le Muséon, N.S. 4, 1903, p. 333, about the *nāgārjunīyāḥ*, mentioned in Bhaṭṭa Narahari's comm. on A.h., called Vāgbhaṭakhaṇḍanamaṇḍana). The tradition that Su. was revised and completed (by writing its Uttaratantra) by Nāgārjuna is accepted by Filliozat (Renou et Filliozat, l'Inde Classique 2, p. 157) who says that this reviser may be identical with the author of the Yogaśataka, which is usually ascribed to Nāgārjuna. Filliozat is of the opinion that the Yogaśataka is the medical compendium referred to by I-Tsing (see : A record of the Buddhist religion, etc. by I-Tsing, transl. Takakusu, p. 128); I-Tsing stayed in India from 672 to about 688 (Vogel, Introd. A.h., p. 8); acc. to Filliozat's hypothesis this Nāgārjuna would have lived in the sixth century. Hoernle (Osteology, Introd. p. 9) still supposed that Nāgārjuna, the reviser of Su., might be the well-known Buddhist patriarch of that name, who is said to have been a contemporary of king Kaniṣka. Another possibility mentioned by Filliozat (Renou et Filliozat, l'Inde Classique 2, p. 157) is that Nāgārjuna, the reviser of Su., may be the Nāgārjuna who lived at Daihak near Somnāth a hundred years before the age of al-Bīrūnī (see Sachau's transl. of al-Bīrūnī 1, p. 189 : this Nāgārjuna was an authority on *rasāyana*, i.e. the art of preserving youth and acquiring a long, healthy life); in this case Nāgārjuna would have lived in the tenth century. The Nāgārjuna mentioned by Vijayarakṣita as the author of a work called Ārogyamañjarī may be the Nāgārjuna mentioned by al-Bīrūnī, though this cannot be proved (a work, called Ārogyamañjarī, is referred to in Gopāladāsa's Cikitsāmṛta; see Bhatt., IHQ 24, 1948, p. 318). In any case it seems probable that there was more than one author called Nāgārjuna and that several works were attributed to an author of this name in later times. Niścalakara often quotes Nāgārjuna (Bhatt., IHQ 23, 1947, p. 143) and mentions two of his works by name : the Yogamañjarī (Bhatt., l.c., p. 146) and the Vārtāmālā (Bhatt., l.c., p. 148).

See about Nāgārjuna : Filliozat, Class. doctr., p. 12-14; Rāy, Hist. Chem., p. 116-118; Srivastava, Hist. Ind. Pharm., p. 83-90; Mukhopādhyāya, H.I.M. 3, p. 822-843.

NIŚCALAKARA. This author must be treated here on account of the great importance of his still unedited commentaries, which contain data throwing light on a great number of points which would have remained obscure without Niścala's information. Niścalakara wrote commentaries on Cakrapāṇidatta's Cikitsāsaṃgraha and Dravyaguṇasaṃgraha. The first comm. is called Ratnaprabhā. It has been studied carefully by

D. C. Bhattacharyya (New light on Vaidyaka literature, IHQ 23, 1947, p. 123-155). Bhatt. remarks (l.c., p. 125) that Niścalakara as a commentator forms a class by himself, because he refers almost all his quotations to their sources. Bhatt. holds the view that Niścalakara was of Bengal origin. His father was called Sadānandakara. The Kara family is mentioned as one of the *vaidya* families of Bengal in Bharatamallika's Candraprabhā (p. 7-9; Bhatt., l.c., p. 129). From several indications it is clear that Niścala flourished at a time in which Buddhism was still reigning supreme in Bengal. This would place Niścala in the last quarter of the 12th century at the latest. Moreover, Niścala has recorded an important clue to his date. He describes an audience given by king Rāmapāla to the king of Kāmarūpa. The panegyric epithets in this description indicate that this king, who had a long reign of at least 42 years, was still alive when Niścala wrote his comm. Bhatt. fixes Rāmapāla's reign at 1078-1120 (Bhatt. is criticized by Majumdar: History of Bengal I, p. 180-181) and is of the opinion that Niścala's Ratnaprabhā was written in the decade 1110-1120. Niścalakara himself remarks that he wrote the Ratnaprabhā after the death of his teacher, Vijayarakṣita, who was in charge of the royal hospital (*ārogyaśālā*); Niścala was in charge of the royal harem.

Niścala's date enables us to fix the dates of many authors and works more accurately than before Bhattacharyya's study of the Ratnaprabhā. This applies particularly to the dates of Niścala's teacher, Vijayarakṣita, and another pupil of the latter, Śrīkaṇṭhadatta.

PARĀŚARA was one of the six disciples of Ātreya Punarvasu. He wrote his own treatise on *kāyacikitsā* (Ca.Sū. 1, 30-33). Jolly says (Medicin, p. 125) that acc. to Cordier (in : Origines, évolution et décadence de la médecine indienne, in : Annales d'hygiène et de médecine coloniales, 1901, p. 82 and 84) fragments of Parāśara's work have been found in Nepal. Parāśara's treatise is referred to and quoted by Vāgbhaṭa (A.s. Sū. 17, 19-20) and by many commentators. A short text, called Takravidhi (Ms. coll. Cordier, Paris; see: Filliozat, JA, t. 224, 1934, p. 158, nr. 48) and a Takrakalpa (the same text as the Takravidhi ?, Ms. Bikaner nr. 1438), are ascribed to Parāśara. An important text, called Vṛkṣāyurveda, is also attributed to Parāśara (see G. P. Majumdar, Arch. int. d'hist. des sciences 4, 1951, p. 104-112), as well as a text on husbandry, called Kṛṣipaddhati (Cat.Skt.Mss. IO 5, nr. 1274; Aufrecht's Cat.Skt.Mss. Cambridge, nr. R.15.87).

PĀLAKĀPYA. To this author is ascribed the Hastyāyurveda (ed. Ānandāśrama Sanskrit Series, nr. 26, Poona, 1894). Haraprasād Śāstrī has tried to assign a very early date to the work of Pālakāpya : 5th or 6th century B.C. (JBORS 5, 1919, p. 307-313). The work is quoted in Kṣīrasvāmin's comm. on the Amarakośa; so it cannot be later than the 11th century (see S. K. De's article about Pālakāpya in the D.R. Bhandarkar Volume, publ. by the Indian Research Institute, Calcutta, 1940, p. 73-75); an analysis of the contents of Pālakāpya's treatise has been given by Mukhopādhyāya, H.I.M. 2, p. 402-423.

PAUṢKALĀVATA was one of the six disciples of Dhanvantari; each of them wrote a surgical treatise (Su.Sū. 1, 3). Jolly (Medicin, p. 125) states that acc. to Cordier (Origines, évolution et décadence de la médecine indienne, in : Annales d'hygiène et de médecine coloniales, 1901, p. 82 and 84) fragments of his treatise have been discovered.

BAKULA or Bakulakara is probably identical with Vakulakara, one of the chief authorities of Niścalakara and profusely quoted in the latter's Ratnaprabhā. Niścala devotes a flowery panegyric to Vakulakara, which should prove (acc. to Bhatt., IHQ 23, 1947, p. 147) that Vakula was a close connection of Niścala and may have been the uncle of the latter once referred to in the Ratnaprabhā. Vakula's work was called Sāroccaya (Bhatt., l.c., p. 149). He was later than (Bhatt., l.c., p. 147) or more or less a contemporary of Cakrapāṇidatta, and a Bengali (Bhatt., l.c., p. 155). Vakula is mentioned as a commentator on Ca. by Mukhopādhyāya (H.I.M. 3, p. 615) and in the Introd. to Ca. with Jejjaṭa's comm. (p. 22). Vijayarakṣita refers to him in M. on 6, 15 as an author who does not agree with Kārtikakuṇḍa's interpretation of a passage from Su.U., which indicates that he was a commentator on Su. and that his date is after that of Kārtikakuṇḍa. A long passage from a work in verse by Bakula is quoted by Śrīkaṇṭhadatta on Siddhayoga 20, 24-27 and said to be inspired by Jejjaṭa's comments.

BRAHMADEVA is mentioned as a *ṭippaṇakāra* (writer of glosses) on Su. by Ḍa. in the introd. to his comm. He is repeatedly quoted in the Kusumāvalī and by Ḍa. and once by Hemādri (on A.h.Sū. 7, 40, about *maireya*). The quotations have been collected and studied by Gode (St.I.L.H. 1, p. 191-194), who assigns him to the period between 900 and 1100. Hoernle supposed that Brahmadeva might be posterior to Gayadāsa, because Ḍa. observes in his comment on Su.Sū. 18, 45 that Brahmadeva follows Gayadāsa's opinion, who says that the stanza should be rejected as not belonging to the text of Su. Hoernle may well be right on this point. It has not been stressed, as far as I know, that Brahmadeva is mentioned by Cakra (on Ca.Ci. 3, 217) as an early commentator on Ca. (he is the last one of the series of early commentators on Ca. enumerated by Cakra : Bhāsadatta-Svāmidāsa-Āṣāḍhavarman-Brahmadeva). His date must at least be earlier than that of Cakrapāṇidatta. To Gode it was a problem that the quotations from Brahmadeva's comm. on the Siddhayoga as occurring in the Kusumāvalī might not form part of the original version of Śrīkaṇṭhadatta's work, but could have been added later by Nārāyaṇa Bhiṣaj, the reviser of the Kusumāvalī. For that reason he had to date Brahmadeva between 900 and 1100. If all the references to Brahmadeva as a commentator on Ca., Su. and the Siddhayoga apply to one and the same person, his date should be between those of Vṛndakuṇḍa and Cakrapāṇidatta.

BHĀLUKI is said to have written a treatise on surgery (*śalyatantra*) (Gul 1, p. 145). He is already quoted by Jejjaṭa, but his work has not survived. Quotations from it are frequent in the works of many commentators. In Srīkaṇṭhadatta's time his work must still have been available, for Śrīkaṇṭha informs us (on Siddhayoga 1, 151) that a particular recipe is to to be found in the Siddhisthāna of the Bhālukitantra.

BHĀVAMIŚRA is the author of the Bhāvaprakāśa, of which the Bhāvaprakāśanighaṇṭu forms an integral part. Bhāvamiśra was the son of Miśralaṭakana, as indicated in the colophons of the work. Jolly observes (Medicin, p. 2-3) that Bhāvamiśra is said to have been a famous physician in Benares. He also notes (ibid.) that a good Ms. of the Bhāvaprakāśa is present in Tübingen and dated 1558-1559 (he refers to Garbe's Verz. no. 153). In his opinion the work cannot be much older than this Ms., because syphilis (*phiraṅgaroga*) and the drug used to treat it (*cobacīnī*) are made mention of in the Bhāvaprakāśa and both disease and drug were imported into India by the Portuguese about 1535. Later authors agree with Jolly as to the date of the work. Another treatise by Bhāvamiśra, dealing with materia medica, is called Guṇaratnamālā (Jolly, Medicin, p. 3; Eggeling, Cat.Skt.Mss. IO 5, p. 981; Filliozat, JA, t. 224, 1934, p. 157, nr. 32). Cordier mentions (Le Muséon, N.S. 4, 1903, p. 350) a Mādhavanidānaṭippaṇī by Bhāvamiśra.

BHEḌA- or BHELASAṂHITĀ. This old text has fragmentarily been preserved in a single Ms. described by Burnell in : A classified index to the Skt. Mss. in the Palace at Tanjore, p. 63, nr. 2 (10,773). The text of this Ms. is mutilated and contains many scribe's errors (it has been edited twice in an unsatisfactory way). A fragment of the Bheḍasaṃhitā was found in Tuyoq in East-Turkestan by von Le Coq; it has been studied by Lüders (Medizinische Sanskrittexte aus Turkistan, in : Aus Indiens Kultur, Festschrift für R. Garbe, 1927, p. 148-162 = H. Lüders, Philologica indica, Göttingen 1940, p. 579). The fragment of this paper Ms. dates probably from the 9th century. A second fragment from a different Ms., found at the same place, may or may not belong to the Bheḍasaṃhitā (Lüders, l.c.). The Bheḍasaṃhitā is in many respects similar to Ca., though much more concise. There are, however, also so many dissimilarities that it is clear that Bheḍa represents a separate branch of the school of Ātreya, to which both Ca. and Bheḍa belong (see Filliozat in Renou et Filliozat, l'Inde Classique 2, p. 151). Filliozat (ibid.) is of the opinion that the Bheḍasaṃhitā may be older than Ca. Barua (IC 3, p. 190-194) dates it in the early Buddhist period. Burnell was of the opinion that Bheḍa was a native of Gandhāra because that country is repeatedly mentioned in the treatise (Mukhopādhyāya, H.I.M. 3, p. 528). Many quotations from Bheḍa have been collected by Mukhopādhyāya (l.c., p. 529-534).

BHOJA. There is much confusion about the identity of one or more medical authors called Bhoja, Bhojadeva or Bhojarāja. Medical commentators distinguish between Bhoja and Vṛddhabhoja (e.g. Ḍa.). A series of medical works is ascribed to Bhoja : Āyurvedasarvasva, Cārucaryā, Rājamārtaṇḍa, Rājamṛgāṅka and Viśrāntavidyāvinoda (Cat.Cat. 1, p. 41 and 2, p. 95; Cordier, JA, t. 28, 1901, p. 180). Bāpālāl G. Vaidya mentions a Bhojarājanighaṇṭu (Introd. Nighaṇṭu Ādarśa 1, p. 37). Filliozat says (in : Renou et Filliozat, l'Inde Classique 2, p. 159) that Bhoja was a commentator on Su. Hoernle had already noticed (JRAS, 1906, p. 286) that Bhoja is frequently quoted by Ḍa., by Gayadāsa and by Cakrapāṇidatta in his Bhānumatī in connection with Su.'s views, and that his work does not appear to have been a comm. on Su., but rather an independent textbook, for Ḍa. once describes it as a *saṃhitā* and Gayadāsa once as a *tantra.* Acc. to Hoernle he may well have been the famous king Bhoja of Dhārā (1018-1063 acc. to Krishnamachariar). Cordier (JA, t. 28, 1901, p. 180) thought it not improbable that at the court of this king medical works were composed which appeared under his name. Jolly (ZDMG 58, 1904, p. 116) cautiously remarked that the medical author Bhoja might well be different from the famous king of that name, because a renowned physician, called Bhoja, already appears in Buddhist texts. Bhatt. (IHQ 23, 1947, p. 145-146) writes that it has hitherto been overlooked by all scholars that there were three medical authorities of the name of Bhoja : 1) an ancient *ācārya*, pupil of Divodāsa and a class-fellow of Suśruta (referred to and quoted in Cakra's Bhānumatī and by Ḍa.); he is sometimes referred to as Vṛddhabhoja (e.g. in Candraṭa's comm. on the Cikitsākalikā, Lahore ed., p. 200); 2) an earlier king Bhoja, cited already by Jejjaṭa and quoted by Candraṭa; this cannot be Bhoja of Dhārā, because Candraṭa predeced Bhoja of Dhārā; acc. to Bhatt. this king Bhoja is evidently identical with the Paramāra king Bhoja of Citor who reigned in 665; 3) Bhoja, the author of the Rājamārtaṇḍa. See also about kings called Bhoja and works attributed to authors called Bhoja : Introd. by E. D. Kulkarni to Śālihotra of Bhoja, p. 17-20.

I feel unable to disentangle the problems about Bhoja. From the quotations in M. it seems probable that he wrote a treatise that was, at least in part, composed in verse.

MADANAPĀLANIGHAṆṬU, also called Madanavinodanighaṇṭu or shortly Madanavinoda, is a work attributed to Madanapāla, a king to whom many works are ascribed (see Cat.Cat. 1, p. 425). The work was composed in 1374, as indicated at the end of some of the Mss. (see R. Roth, Madanapāla, in : Indische Studien 14, 1876, p. 398-401; Eggeling, Cat.Skt.Mss. IO 5, p. 977-979). It is also recorded in some Mss. that Madanapāla ruled at Kāṣṭhā (sometimes written Kāṭhā), a town situated on the Yamunā to the north of Delhi (see Roth and Eggeling about the details and the genealogy of this king). Not only in the time of Roth, but also at the present time, this king Madanapāla is confused with an earlier namesake of his (see e.g. Krishnamachariar, p. 849 : "The inscriptions of this king are dated 1104-1109").

YOGATARAṄGIṆĪ. This work is a compilation of which two versions exist : the Bṛhad- and Laghuyogataraṅgiṇī. It was written by Trimallabhaṭṭa, as stated in the introductory stanzas of the work. The author was a son of Vallabha, grandson of Siṅgaṇa Bhaṭṭa, a Telugu *brāhmaṇa* residing at Benares, and brother of Rāma and Gopa (Cat.Skt.Mss. IO 5, p. 956). Sinh Jee (A short history of Aryan medical science, second ed., London, 1927, p. 215) was of the opinion that the work had been written in 1751. Jolly (Medicin, p. 2-3) remarks that the work must be much older, because one Ms. dates from 1663 at the latest and there exists a Ms., dated 1498, of another work by Trimallabhaṭṭa. Gode (St.I.L.H. 1, p. 295) quotes H. D. Velankar (Cat. of BBRAS Mss. 1, p. 59) on the subject of Trimallabhaṭṭa's date : "Trimalla quotes the Vīrasiṃhāvaloka (written in 1383) in his Yogataraṅgiṇī and a Ms. of his Dravyaguṇaśataślokī is dated 1499; Trimalla's date, therefore, falls between 1383 and 1499."

YOGARATNĀKARA. The author of this medical compilation is unknown; Sinh Jee (A short history of Aryan medical science, second ed., London, 1927, p. 215) says, however, that it is a work by Nayanaśekhara, a Jain priest, who wrote it in 1633. The oldest known Ms. dates from 1746 (Jolly, Medicin, p. 2). The Yogaratnākara quotes a work called Nirṇayasindhu, composed in 1611 (Jolly, ibid.) or 1612 (Gode, Bhāratīya Vidyā 4, 1943, p. 154-156) by Kamalākarabhaṭṭa. The date of composition of the Yogaratnākara must therefore lie somewhere between 1611 and 1746. Gode (l.c.) was of the opinion that the work was written between about 1650 and 1725, because it contains some stanzas on the properties of tobacco, which, acc. to him, was first seen in India at the Bījāpūr court about 1605; the incorporation of tobacco in an Indian medical treatise must in Gode's opinion have required about forty years; moreover, the proposed date is in harmony with the fact that the Yogaratnākara refers to the works called Vaidyajīvana and Vaidyavilāsa, written by Lolimbarāja, who flourished towards the end of the 16th century (Gode, l.c.; see also Gode's article : Lolimbarāja and his works, St.I.L.H. 2, p. 79-96). Katre (Bhāratīya Vidyā 12, 1951, p. 59-61) has proved, however, that the Vaidyavilāsa, quoted in the Yogaratnākara, is not a work by Lolimbarāja but by Raghunātha Paṇḍita and was composed in 1697. The conclusion is therefore that the Yogaratnākara was written between 1697 and 1746. A problem with the Yogaratnākara is that there are more works bearing the same title. Niścalakara quotes from the Yogaratnākara by Bhavyadatta, who is one of Niścala's chief authorities (Bhatt., IHQ 23, 1947, p. 146 and 148).

RAGHUNĀTHA SŪRI was the author of the Bhojanakutūhala, a treatise about dietetics. He also wrote works of a non-medical nature. He lived in the 17th century, was a friend of Rāmdās and enjoyed the patronage of queen Dīpā Bāi, the wife of Ekoji Bhosala of Tanjore. See about

Raghunātha and his works : Introd. to Bhojanakutūhala, vol. 1, by Mahādeva Śāstrī; Gode wrote several articles about this author and his Bhojanakutūhala : St.I.L.H. 2, p. 380-390, 391-403, 404-415 and 425-434. The Bhojanakutūhala was composed between 1650 and 1685 acc. to Gode (St.I.L.H. 2, p. 425-434).

RĀJANIGHAṆṬU, also called Nighaṇṭurāja and Abhidhānacūḍāmaṇi, is a work by Narahari, also called Narahara, Nṛhari and Narasiṃha (Cat.Skt.Mss. IO 5, p. 977), pupil of Śrīkaṇṭha and son of Īśvarasūri, an inhabitant of Kaśmīr. In the introduction to his work the author states that he has consulted the Dhanvantarīyanighaṇṭu, Madananighaṇṭu, Halāyudha and various other works, but that he follows the opinions of the Dhanvantarīyanighaṇṭu (see Cat.Skt.Mss. Madras, vol. 23, nr. 13254, p. 8928-8930 and Cat. Calc. Skt. Coll., nr. 69 and 70). It is clear that the work is later than the Madanapālanighaṇṭu, dated 1374; this fact was already known to Aufrecht (ZDMG 41, 1887, p. 487-488). Acc. to Filliozat (Renou et Filliozat, l'Inde Classique 2, p. 162) it dates from the 14th century; Gode (St.I.L.H. 1, p. 388) dates it : about 1450. Acc. to Garbe (Die indischen Mineralien, pref. p. 6), Keith (Hist. Skt. Lit., p. 512) and Dutt Sharma (Cat.Skt.Mss. BORI, vol. 16, part 1, p. 291) the work was composed about 1235-1250, which cannot be correct. Garbe's argument for this date was that the author refers to his patron, called Nṛsiṃha; Garbe identified this Nṛsiṃha with king Siṃhadeva of Kaśmīr who reigned from 1235-1250. T. Chowdhury (Introd. Paryāyaratnamālā) assumes that the work was written about 1400, which may be correct.

RĀJAVALLABHANIGHAṆṬU, also called Rājavallabhadravyaguṇa. This work has been ascribed, erroneously, to an author called Nārāyaṇa or Nārāyaṇadāsa (Cat.Skt.Mss. IO 5, p. 961-962; Jolly, Medicin, p. 2; Cat.Cat. 1, p. 263). It is really a work written by Rājavallabha, an author of unknown date, and has been revised by Nārāyaṇadāsa, who lived about 1760 (acc. to Umeśacandra Gupta, Vaidyakaśabdasindhu, Preface). The fact that the work has been revised by Nārāyaṇadāsa is clearly indicated in the introduction and colophon of some Mss. (see Cat.Skt.Mss.Calc. Skt. Coll. 9, nr. 67, p. 56 ff.). There are considerable differences among the various Mss. and editions of the work (see the descr. of the enlarged version in the Cat.Skt.Mss. IO 5, nr. 2718, p. 962 and of Ms. no. 24 of the coll. Jones of IO). Acc. to Bāpālāl G.

Vaidya (Introd. Nighaṇṭu Ādarśa 1, p. 37) internal evidence leads to the conclusion that the author hailed from Bengal.

VAṄGASENA is the author of a medical treatise called Cikitsāsārasaṃgraha, sometimes called Cikitsāmahārṇava or Cikitsātattvasaṃgraha (Cat.Skt.Mss. BORI, vol. 16, part 1, nr. 82, p. 99-100). This work is often quoted as Vaṅgasena, Vaṅgasenasaṃgraha or Vaṅgadatta. Aufrecht (Cat.Cat. 2, p. 130) considers the Cikitsāmahārṇava by Vaṅgasena as distinct from the Cikitsāsārasaṃgraha. Vaṅgasena describes the diseases (and their therapy) in the order introduced by Mādhavakara and must have lived after the latter, as has already often been noticed (Cat.Skt.Mss. IO 5, p. 951; Jolly, Medicin, p. 5). Vaṅgasena adheres to Mādhavakara's arrangement of diseases even more closely than Vṛndakuṇḍa. Jolly was of the opinion (Medicin, p. 5) that variants found in Vaṅgasena's text are sometimes better than Mādhavakara's readings. Vaṅgasena was the son of Gadādhara, who had moved from Kāñjikā to another place of residence that is not specified (Va. 1, 4). This Gadādhara is considered by some to be identical with Gadādhara, the commentator on Su. (N.N. Das Gupta, IC 3, p. 159 : not improbable; refuted by Bhatt., IHQ 23, 1947, p. 140; see : Gadādhara). N. N. Das Gupta says (IC 3, p. 159), without adducing data supporting his statement, that the original place of residence of Vaṅgasena's parents, Kāñjikā, may be the same as Kañjivillī in Rāḍha (Western Bengal). Jolly supposed already (Medicin, p. 5), like N. N. Das Gupta later, that Vaṅgasena might hail from Bengal (on account of his name, acc. to Jolly; on account of his name, original place of residence and from internal evidence, acc. to N. N. Das Gupta).

Vaṅgasena's Cikitsāsārasaṃgraha is, as indicated at the end of the treatise (Ed. Veṅkaṭeśvar Press, p. 1100), a revision of what was called before Vaṅgasena's birth the Agastisaṃhitā (an author called Agastya is quoted by Cakra on Ca.Sū. 1, 62-63ab; more than 200 medical works in Tamiḻ are attributed to Agastya : see Renou et Filliozat, l'Inde Classique 2, p. 162-163). A comm. on Vaṅgasena's work, written by Vaidyanātha, is mentioned by Aufrecht (Cat.Cat. 1, p. 548).

The date of Vaṅgasena has been studied by Jolly (Medicin, p. 5 : he may have been a contemporary of the Sena dynasty of Bengal); N. N. Das Gupta (IC 3, p. 159) : 13th century; Gode (St.I.L.H. 1, p. 325) : 12th century at the latest. Bhatt. discovered (IHQ 23, 1947, p. 147) that Niścalakara quotes the Vaṅgasenasaṃgraha. So his date must fall between those of Vṛndakuṇḍa and Niścalakara. A Ms. of Vaṅgasena's work, dated 1276, is in the Cambridge University Library (see Cat.Skt.Mss. IO 5, p. 952) and a Ms. dated 1320 in the BOR Institute (Cat.Skt.Mss. BORI, vol. 16, part 1, nr. 78, p. 94-95).

VĀGBHAṬA. Three works are ascribed to Vāgbhaṭa : the Aṣṭāṅgahṛdayasaṃhitā, the Aṣṭāṅgasaṃgraha and the Rasaratnasamuccaya. The last work of these three is certainly not by the same author as the other two works (see Vogel, Introd. A.h., p. 1, and Cordier, JA, t. 18, 1901, p. 148-150; Bhatt. has traced a quotation from Rasavāgbhaṭa in Candraṭa's Yogaratnasamuccaya, see ABORI 28, 1947, p. 122).

It has long been a problem whether both other works have been written by one author. Commentators often refer to the author of A.h. as Vāgbhaṭa and to the author of A.s. as Vṛddhavāgbhaṭa, which led to the assumption that A.s. is older than A.h. The questions whether there have been one or two Vāgbhaṭa's and which of the two works is older have often been discussed. The date to be assigned to the composition of the texts has also been a favourite topic in articles and books on the history of Indian medicine. The discussions on these problems have recently been reviewed and summarized by C. Vogel (Introd. A.h., p. 1-10) and there is no need to repeat his work. His conclusion is in agreement with that reached by Hilgenberg and Kirfel in the introduction to their translation of A.h. into German : A.h. is older than A.s. and the process by which A.h. has been transformed into A.s. must have been a gradual one. This last point is confirmed by Bhatt.'s study of Niścalakara's Ratnaprabhā (ABORI 28, 1947, p. 112-127; IHQ 23, 1947, p. 123-155). Niścalakara frequently quotes from a work called Madhyavāgbhaṭa, the text of which is intermediate between A.h. and A.s., but not all the quotations from it can be traced either to A.h. or to A.s. Bhatt. says (ABORI 28, 1947, p. 113) that the existence of this Madhyavāgbhaṭa became known to scholars for the first time with the publication of Śivadāsasena's comm. on A.h., called Tattvabodha; Śivadāsasena quotes from Madhyavāgbhaṭa as well as from Vṛddhavāgbhaṭa (identical with A.s. acc. to Śivadāsasena) and Svalpavāgbhaṭa (identical with A.h. acc. to Śivadāsasena; Bhatt., ABORI 28, 1947, p. 113). It was unknown to Bhatt., as rightly stressed by Vogel (Introd. A.h., p. 5, footnote 3), that Cordier already knew about the existence of a text intermediate between A.s. and A.h. (JA, t. 18, 1901, p. 150-151; this text has been partially published as Bābhaṭa in Calcutta in 1873). Both Cordier and Bhatt. regarded the existence of the Madhyavāgbhaṭa as a proof that A.h. had gradually grown out of A.s.

About Vāgbhaṭa's life we only know what he has said himself (A.s.U. 50, 132-133) : he was a son of Siṃhagupta (in some Mss. : Saṅghagupta), who was a physician, and a grandson of Vāgbhaṭa; his teacher was called Avalokita and he was born in Sindh. If Vāgbhaṭa, the author of A.h., is identical with the teacher of Jejjaṭa, something more may be said about his birthplace. In two colophons of the fragments of Jejjaṭa's comm. on Ca. (not his comm. on Su., as erroneously stated by Vogel, Introd. A.h., p. 8, footnote 2) Jejjaṭa calls his teacher Vāhaṭa (Vāgbhaṭa's name is always spelled in this way by Jejjaṭa and by Indu) Mahājahnupati. Bhatt. observes (ABORI 28, 1947, p. 122) about this appelllation that it indicates that Vāgbhaṭa was the chief of a small kingdom in Sindh, which may be identical with Majhanda in the Karachi district, about 50 miles north of Hyderabad in Sindh (see Bhatt., l.c., and Vogel, Introd. A.h., p. 8, footnote 2).

About Vāgbhaṭa's date much has been written. When we assume that there has been only one Vāgbhaṭa, the author of A.h., the problem is not too complicated. Many scholars have connected Vāgbhaṭa with a person about whom I-Tsing (a Chinese pilgrim who stayed in India from 672 to about 682) states that he lately summarized the eight sections of medical science and made them into one bundle (see Vogel, Introd. A.h., p. 8-9 and his references to the literature on the subject; see also J. Nobel, JAOS, suppl. nr. 11, 1951, about I-Tsing's medical knowledge). I think Vogel is right in adopting the view that the person alluded to by I-Tsing must be Vāgbhaṭa, which implicates me in disagreement with Filliozat, who is of the opinion that I-Tsing most probably refers to Nāgārjuna, the author of the Yogaśataka. I-Tsing enables us to determine the date of composition of Vāgbhaṭa's A.h. at about 600.

There are some other points worthy of consideration with regard to Vāgbhaṭa's date. Filliozat observes (in : Renou et Filliozat, l'Inde Classique 2, p. 158) that A.h. reproduces stanzas from the Yogaśataka. Fragments of a Ms. of the Yogaśataka have been found in Central Asia; the date of this Ms. has been fixed as the 7th century or somewhat later (Filliozat, l.c., p. 157). This implies that the text of the Yogaśataka must be older; it may date from the period between 500 and 600 or earlier; so Vāgbhaṭa may quote from it. Another point is that the A.h., as to the arrangement of its sections, follows Su. as a model; A.h. contains an Uttarasthāna, as Su. has its Uttaratantra;

moreover, there are so many similarities between the contents of Su.U. and A.h.U. that A.h.U. must be later than Su.U. (Filliozat, l.c., p. 158; Hoernle, Osteology, Introd. p. 14). A third point is that Vāgbhaṭa must be later than Dṛḍhabala (Hoernle, Osteology, Introd. p. 14-15; Hoernle, JRAS 1908, p. 1016-1018). Some stanzas of A.h. are taken from that part of Ca. which has been redacted by Dṛḍhabala (see e.g. Aruṇadatta's comment on A.h.Śā. 3, 62cd-63ab). In my opinion Dṛḍhabala's date is about 500 or earlier, so Vāgbhaṭa may indeed have borrowed from him. A fourth point is that Mādhavakara has borrowed from A.h.; Mādhavakara has to be dated about 700, which again leads to the conclusion that the date of composition of A.h. may be about 600. This date is further corroborated by the date of translation of a lost medical Sanskrit work into Tibetan; this work, usually called rGyud bźi in Tibetan, sometimes agrees rather closely with A.h. and was translated during the reign of the Tibetan king Khri-sroṅ-ldeḫu-btsan (755-797 acc. to Vogel, Introd. A.h., p. 16, footnote 1; 728-786 acc. to Filliozat in l'Inde Classique 2, p. 158). With regard to the date of Vāgbhaṭa, it is of great importance that the A.h. is mentioned by ʿAlī b. Sahl Rabban al-Ṭabarī, a Persian physician who wrote a medical treatise, called Firdaws al-ḥikma (Paradise of wisdom) in 849-850 (A.h. is written: as͟htānqhrdy; see Siggel: Die indischen Bücher aus dem Paradies der Weisheit; Vogel, Introd. A.h., p. 10 and footnote 1 on p. 10 with references). The fact that the A.h. was so famous in Persia at that time warrants the assumption that it had been written long before ʿAlī b. Sahl. All the available evidence points to about 600 as the probable date of composition of the A.h.

The A.s. must have evolved gradually after the A.h. had been written. It is not known at what date the A.s. was completed. The only thing which can be said with certainty is that the A.s. was complete in Indu's time.

VĀPYACANDRA, whose name is also written Bāṣpacandra, was a famous commentator on Ca., quoted by Vijayarakṣita, Śrīkaṇṭhadatta, Niścalakara and Hemādri.

From the quotations in M. it is clear that he commented on Ca. He may also have written a comm. on Su.; M. on 1, 5d-6 points in that direction; moreover, he is mentioned there in a series of names of commentators on Su. : Jejjaṭa-Vāpyacandra-Mādhavakara-Kārtikakuṇḍa. The latter series, particularly on account of Mādhavakara's position in it, may be in chronological order as well as the series of authors of a comm. on Su., enumerated in M. on 1, 11-13 : Jejjaṭa-Gadādhara-Vāpyacandra. There are no data contradicting the supposition of an enumeration in chronological order. If this hypothesis is correct, Vāpyacandra must have preceded Mādhavakara and have lived after Jejjaṭa and Gadādhara. It may be that this assumption is confirmed by the list of authors mentioned by Vijayarakṣita in the introduction to the Madhukośa; the first six names are probably arranged in the correct chronological order : Bhaṭṭāra(haricandra)-Jejjaṭa-Gadādhara-Vāpyacandra-Cakrapāṇi-Bakula. This argument is weakened, however, by the series of authors which follows in the same introduction; among these Īśvarasena is put after Cakrapāṇi and Bakula, though he preceded Cakra (see : Īśvarasena). The order may have been influenced by the metre of the stanza (*vasantatilakā*), or a second list begins with Īśvarasena.

VIDEHA is the same as Nimi or Nemi, the lord of Videha (Videha is Tirhut in the eastern part of Bihar : Hoernle, Osteology, Introd. p. 8; Müller, JRAS, 1933, p. 323). The lord of Videha is credited with a *śālākyatantra* (on eye diseases and diseases of the ears, nose and mouth) in Su. (U. 1, 5) and identified as Nimi by Ḍa. (who says that the passage does not refer to other authors of a *śālākyatantra*, such as Karāla and Bhadraśaunaka); Ḍa. remarks that some identify the lord of Videha as the famous king Janaka of Videha, but that this is refuted by the author of the Bṛhatpañjikā (probably Gayadāsa) and that he refutes it too on the authority of the latter. Nimi, the king of Videha, is also mentioned in Ca.Sū. 26, 5; A.h. mentions Nimi : U. 11, 27; U. 13, 16; U. 13, 100 and U. 30, 31. Quotations from Nimi, Videha and Mahāvideha were collected by Mukhopādhyāya (H.I.M. 2, p. 339-350; the quotations are drawn from Madhukośa, Kusumāvalī, Nibandhasaṃgraha, Tattvacandrikā and Bhāvaprakāśa; Videha is moreover quoted by Cakra on Ca., Gayadāsa on Su.Ni., Niścalakara and Hemādri; Vṛddhavideha is quoted once by Niścalakara; Nimi is quoted by Aruṇadatta). Vijayarakṣita's quotations from Videha seem to indicate that his work did not deal with eye diseases only, but was of a broader scope.

VṚNDAKUṆḌA wrote the Siddhayoga, a treatise on therapy, also called Vṛndamādhava. The author calls himself Vṛnda and his work Siddhayoga. Śrīkaṇṭhadatta calls the author Vṛnda in the colophons, but in the introd. to the comm. Vṛndakuṇṭha (Ānandāśrama ed.). The treatise is called Vṛndamādhava and Siddhayoga in the colophons of the comm. The work follows the Rugviniścaya (by Mādhavakara) in its arrangement as stated by Vṛnda himself (1, 2), though he devotes a separate chapter to *jvarātisāra* (fever-diarrhoea), which is omitted by Mādhavakara. Hoernle was of the opinion that Mādhavakara was the author of the Siddhayoga and that it was clear that the Rugviniścaya was only the first part of a larger work, the second of which is the Siddhayoga (JRAS, 1906, p. 288-290). Hoernle was wrong. It is known to us now that Mādhavakara wrote a therapeutic treatise, the Mādhavacikitsita, which is different from the Siddhayoga by which it was superseded, as the latter was by Cakrapāṇidatta's treatise. Cakrapāṇidatta's Cikitsāsaṃgraha was modelled upon the Siddhayoga. The model of the Siddhayoga may have been the Mādhavacikitsita, but the Mādhavacikitsita has not yet been sufficiently studied to be certain about this point. Vṛndakuṇḍa (more often called Vṛnda) is frequently quoted by Niścalakara (Bhatt., IHQ 23, 1947, p. 148).

The Siddhayoga must still have been a very popular work in Cakrapāṇidatta's time as appears from a stanza at the end of the Cikitsāsaṃgraha (*susthādhikāra* 16), but I do not see that it proves that Vṛnda belonged to Bengal as Bhatt. states (IHQ 23, 1947, p. 154). Another piece of evidence, however, clearly indicates that Vṛndakuṇḍa was an inhabitant of Eastern Bengal : Bhatt. (IHQ 23, 1947, p. 155) quotes a stanza from Bharatamallika's Candraprabhā in which it is said that Vṛndakuṇḍa, who wrote a medical treatise, was a resident of Eastern Bengal (*vaṅgabhūmikṛtāśraya*). Regarding Vṛnda's date Jolly remarked (Medicin, p. 7) that the Siddhayoga must have been written at least a century before Cakrapāṇidatta, because it had probably become an authoritative work in Cakra's time; he added that Vṛnda is later than Vāgbhaṭa (quoted Siddhayoga 1, 27) and Mādhava (because the Rugviniścaya is mentioned). Hoernle assigned to Vṛnda the same date as that of Mādhava (7th or 8th century) because he thought that both authors were identical (Osteology, Introd. p. 16). Acc. to Bhatt. (IHQ 23, 1947, p. 153; ABORI 28, 1947, p. 125) the date to be assigned to Vṛndakuṇḍa is 975-1000. In my opinion this date must be lowered to about 800-900, because Bhatt.'s date of Mādhava is wrong (see : Introd., Mādhavakara); moreover there is the fact that Brahmadeva, referred to as an early commentator by Cakra, wrote a comm. on the Siddhayoga, which makes it probable that the gap between Vṛndakuṇḍa and Cakrapāṇidatta is wider than assumed by Bhatt. Acc. to M. Z. Siddiqi (Indo-Asian Culture 5, 1957, p. 279) the Siddhayoga is mentioned by the Arabian historian (Ibn Wāḍiḥ) al Ya'qūbī, who lived in the second half of the 9th century (Nicholson, p. 349), but this is doubtful in my opinion because Ya'qūbī writes about an Indian medical treatise called Sindhshan (Siddiqi's transcription), which should literally mean 'purity of success' or 'elixir of success' (ṣafw al-nujḥ, transcribed by Siddiqi as safwun najh; Ullmann, p. 105 : ṣafwat an-nuǧḥ); Sindhshan may be a reflection of the Sanskrit term Siddhisthāna, but if ṣafwat an-nuǧḥ may mean 'elixir of success' it is possible that Ya'qūbī indeed refers to the Siddhayoga and that its date of composition should be fixed at about 800. (See about the work called sindh(ī)s̲h̲ān by Arab authors : Dietz, p. 118; Stenzler, ZDMG 11, 1857, p. 327; Ullmann, Die Medizin im Islam, p. 105).

VOPADEVA was a contemporary and protégé of Hemādri and a paṇḍit to Mahādeva, a king of the Yādava dynasty of Devagiri. He was a pupil of Dhaneśa and a son of Keśava, the author of the medical work called Siddhamantra. Vopadeva was a prolific author; his medical works are the following : 1) Śataślokī, with the autocomm. Śataślokīcandrakalā, 2) Siddhamantraprakāśa, a comm. on the Siddhamantra, written by his father Keśava, 3) a comm. on the Śārṅgadharasaṃhitā, called Gūḍhārthadīpikā, 4) Hṛdayadīpanighaṇṭu (Cat.Cat. 1, p. 616). In the Siddhamantraprakāśa Vopadeva states that his father learnt Āyurveda from Bhāskara and that his grandfather was called Mahādeva. Keśava says that he was honoured by Siṃharāja. This Siṃharāja is identical with Siṃghaṇa or Siṃhaṇa II of the later Yādavas of Devagiri, who ruled from 1210 to 1247 (See Gode, St.I.L.H. 1, p. 116-118). Keśava's Siddhamantra will have been written during the reign of this king. Vopadeva's works have therefore to be dated in the latter half of the 13th century.

ŚĀRṄGADHARASAṂHITĀ. This work has been written by Śārṅgadhara, the son of Dāmodara (as indicated in the colophons). As there exists a comm. by Vopadeva on the work, it must have been composed before Vopadeva's time (Jolly, Medicin, p. 4). Filliozat observes (Renou et Filliozat, l'Inde Classique 2, p. 160) that the work is usually regarded as dating from the 13th century, but that it may date from the 11th century. Acc. to Dutt (M.M., Preface p. 14) the Śārṅgadharasaṃhitā is the oldest work containing a detailed account of the calcination and preparation of various metals. Acc. to Jivanram who published a critical edition of the work (Bombay, 1891), Śārṅgadhara used Vṛndakuṇḍa's Siddhayoga in the composition of his *saṃhitā*. Acc. to Burnell (see Preface Vaidyakaśabdasindhu) the author of the Śārṅgadharasaṃhitā is posterior to Maheśvara, who wrote the Viśvaprakāśa (dated 1111). His date must lie between those of Vṛndakuṇḍa and Vopadeva. A difficulty with Śārṅgadhara is that there are various authors of this name. Another Śārṅgadhara, son of Devarāja, was the author of a medical work called Triśatī, Vaidyavallabha or Jvaratriśatī (Cat.Skt. Mss. IO 5, nr. 2713, p. 960). This author was a Baḍa-nagara Gujarātī *brāhmaṇa* (Cat.Skt.Mss. BORI, vol. 16, part 1, p. 112). Moreover a Śārṅgadhara, son of Dāmodara, grandson of Rāghava and great-grandson of Hammīra Bhūpati of the Śākambharī country, composed an anthology, called Śārṅgadharapaddhati, in 1363 (Krishnamachariar, p. 386). Some identify the latter with the author of the Śārṅgadharasaṃhitā (e.g. Paraśurāma Śāstrī, ed. of the Śārṅgadharasaṃhitā, and Umeśacandra Gupta, author of the Vaidyakaśabdasindhu).

Besides Vopadeva there are three more authors of a comm. on the Śārṅgadharasaṃhitā : 1) Āḍhamalla, who wrote the comm. called Dīpikā; Āḍhamalla was, acc. to the introd. to his comm., a royal physician to Jaitrasiṃha at Hastīkāntapurī and a descendant of the author Śārṅgadhara, who lived in Hammīrapura in the country called Śākambharī; he even claims to descend from Cakrapāṇidatta. 2) Kāśirāma, who wrote the comm. called Gūḍhārthadīpikā; at the end of the work he says that he has composed it in the reign of Shāh Salīm (i.e. Jahāṅgīr, 1605-1627). 3) Rudrabhaṭṭa, the son of the *vaidya* Konerībhaṭṭa; he wrote a comm., called Āyurvedadīpikā, that closely resembles Āḍhamalla's comm. (see Śārṅgadharasaṃhitā, Introd. by Paraśurāma Śāstrī, p. 7-8).

Śivadāsasena was the son of Anantasena, son of Uddharaṇa, son of Lakṣmīdharasena, son of Kākutsthasena, son of Sāhisena, who lived at the court of king Śikhareśvara. This information is given by Śivadāsasena himself at the end of his commentary on Cakrapāṇidatta's Cikitsāsaṃgraha. At the end of his comm. on Cakra's Dravyaguṇasaṃgraha he says that his father was a royal physician to Bārbak Shāh. Bārbak Shāh, Sultan of Bengal, reigned from 1457 to 1474 (Introd. Ca. p. 16, referring to Stuart's History of Bengal) or from 1459 to 1476 (Bhatt., IHQ 23, 1947, p. 125). Śivadāsasena's father lived at Mālañcikā, as stated at the end of the comm. on Cakra's Cikitsāsaṃgraha. From other indications in the same comm. it may be concluded that

Mālañcikā was a village in the Pavanāmaṇḍala of Varendra, a part of Bengal (see Introd. Ca. p. 16, footnote 2).

Śivadāsasena wrote four commentaries : 1) the Tattvapradīpikā on Ca. (there is a Ms. of this work, containing the comm. on Sū. 1-27, in the library of the Asiatic Society at Bombay, see Introd. Ca., p. 17; acc. to the Introd. to the Lahore ed. of Ca. there exists elsewhere a Ms. containing the comm. from the beginning up to Ci. 27); 2) the Tattvabodha on A.h.U. (which has been printed); 3) the Tattvacandrikā on Cakrapāṇidatta's Cikitsāsaṃgraha (printed) and 4) a comm. on Cakrapāṇidatta's Dravyaguṇasaṃgraha (printed). Śivadāsasena's commentaries on the works of Cakrapāṇidatta are abridgments of those by Niścalakara on the same works (Bhatt., IHQ 23, 1947, p. 125) as acknowledged by Śivadāsasena himself at the beginning of his comm. Śivadāsasena must have written his works about 1500. A Ms. of his comm. on A.h.U. is dated 1526 (see Introd. Ca. p. 16, footnote 3).

ŚRĪDĀSAPAṆḌITA is the author of a comm. on A.h., called Hṛdayabodhikā (in certain Mss. it is referred to as Hṛdayabodhinī). The author was a native of Kerala and gives the Malayālam equivalents of technical terms. His teacher was called Vāsudeva, as indicated in the introduction of the comm. Another pupil of the same teacher also wrote a comm. on A.h., called Vyākhyāsāra. Śrīdāsa often quotes from the latter. The Vyākhyāsāra and Hṛdayabodhikā are closely followed by a Malayālam comm. on A.h., called Alpabuddhiprabodhana and written by Śrīkaṇṭha. The ed. of part 2 of Śrīdāsa's comm., Narayana Pillai, identifies this Śrīkaṇṭha with the teacher of Rāghava, author of a comm. on the Yuddhiṣṭhiravijaya. Rāghava was the teacher of Śaṅkara, author of the Śrīkṛṣṇavijaya. Rāghava is mentioned in a *kāvya* dated from the 15th century and Śaṅkara is referred to by an author flourishing in the beginning of the 15th century; Śrīkaṇṭha may have lived in the latter half of the 14th century. It may be tentatively accepted that Śrīdāsapaṇḍita flourished earlier than 1300. (Extracted from the Introd. by P. K. Narayana Pillai to part 2 of A.h. with Śrīdāsapaṇḍita's comm.).

SUKĪRA is mentioned by Vijayarakṣita in his Introduction to the Madhukośa. He is once quoted by Ḍa. (acc. to the Introd., p. 25 of the N.S. Press ed., 1938; on the page indicated the name Sukīra does not occur and I could not find the name elsewhere in Ḍa.'s comm. on Su.).

SUDĀNTASENA is twice quoted by Vijayarakṣita in M. The quotations point to his being the author of a work in verse that closely followed Ca. He is repeatedly quoted by Niścalakara (Bhatt., IHQ 23, 1947, p. 149).

SUDHĪRA is mentioned by Vijayarakṣita in his introduction to the Madhukośa. He is quoted several times by Ḍa. (a.o. on Su.Ci. 1, 27ab; Ci. 1, 72cd; Ci. 1, 74cd-75ab). From Ḍa.'s quotations it may be concluded that he was a commentator on Su. Acc. to Haridattaśarman (Introd. p. 22 of the Lahore ed. of Ca. with Jejjaṭa's comm.) he was a commentator on Ca., but there is no evidence to support this statement.

SUŚRUTA. The original text of the Suśrutasaṃhitā, before its revision and completion (by adding the Uttaratantra) by a *pratisaṃskartṛ* (supposed to be Nāgārjuna), must be very old, because Suśruta is already mentioned and quoted in the Bower Ms., dated between the 4th and the 6th centuries (see Filliozat in : Renou et Filliozat, l'Inde Classique 2, p. 147 and p. 675-676; Hoernle thought that the date of the Bower Ms. was 350-375). Some Indian authors ascribe a very early date to Suśruta. Rāy (Hist. Chem., p. 61) says he was, acc. to a Buddhist Jātaka (no particulars are given), a teacher in the University of Kāśī in Buddha's times. Srivastava (Hist. Ind. Pharm., p. 57) dates him somewhere between 1000 and 600 B.C. and notes that Kātyāyana, who lived in the 4th century B.C., is said to have written about Suśruta in his Vārtikas (Winternitz 3, p. 390 says that, as a working hypothesis, it may be assumed that Kātyāyana, the author of the Vārtikas on Pāṇini's grammar, may have lived in the 3rd century B.C.). Mukhopādhyāya (H.I.M. 3, p. 576) says that the latest limit which we can assign to Suśruta is 600 B.C.; he also refers to Kātyāyana's Vārtikas, in which it is said : *suśrutena proktaṃ sauśrutam*. (See about the opinions of a series of scholars : Mukhopādhyāya, l.c., p. 578-579). It is clear that no more can be said than that the original Suśrutasaṃhitā must have been composed in the first three centuries of our era at the latest.

A difficult problem is presented by the revision of the text. There must have been a reviser, because Cakrapāṇidatta and Ḍalhaṇa refer to him (Ḍalhaṇa calls him Nāgārjuna; see Nāgārjuna). This reviser not only added the Uttaratantra, but also made slight changes in the remainder of the text, which is proved by the fact that the Uttaratantra is referred to Su.Sū. 3, 3 and in other passages. The original text dealt with surgery as its special object; the Uttaratantra deals with what is called *śālākya* (eye diseases and ophthalmic surgery, diseases of the ears, nose and mouth) and internal medicine, called *kāyacikitsā*. About the date of the revision nothing definite is known. Filliozat says (Renou et Filliozat, l'Inde Classique 2, p. 147) that, if the reviser is indeed Nāgārjuna and identical with the author of the Yogaśataka, his date is the 6th century, and, if he is the Nāgārjuna who lived a hundred years before al-Bīrūnī, his date is the 10th century. Mukhopādhyāya (H.I.M. 3, p. 574 and 581) thinks that Nāgārjuna may be the celebrated Buddhist chemist, who is said to have been a contemporary of king Sātavāhana (l.c., p. 574) and of king Kaniṣka who lived in the first century B.C. (l.c., p. 581).

I think that the reviser of the Suśrutasaṃhitā may have lived before Dṛḍhabala, i.e. before 500, because Cakrapāṇidatta says (see : Dṛḍhabala) that the redactor of the Carakasaṃhitā made use of the works of Suśruta and Videha, which means that chapters on *kāyacikitsā* from Su.U. were employed by Dṛḍhabala; the latter wrote a.o. the chapter of the Carakasaṃhitā on *pāṇḍuroga* (morbid pallor) and this subject is dealt with in Su.U. If this be true, the problem remains where the reviser of Su. found his material. Another point is whether Cakra's remark is trustworthy. Moreover it is probable that Dṛḍhabala did not create whole chapters anew, but that the Agniveśatantra was still extant, completely or partially; the revision of this work, started by Caraka, was completed by Dṛḍhabala.

Another point to be considered in relation to the Suśrutasaṃhitā is a text called Vṛddhasuśruta by commentators. It has been assumed (Hoernle, Osteology, Introd. p. 5 and JRAS, 1909, p. 879; Mukhopādhyāya, H.I.M. 3, p. 572) that the work referred to as Vṛddhasuśruta is the Suśrutasaṃhitā before it had been revised. This, however, cannot be true, because four quotations from Vṛddhasuśruta in M. and Ā. (see list of quotations from Suśruta) are found in the Uttaratantra. Other quotations from Vṛddhasuśruta, however, are untraceable in the Suśrutasaṃhitā as it has come down to us. Many of the quotations from Vṛddhasuśruta and the Sauśrutatantra have been collected by Mukhopādhyāya (H.I.M. 3, p. 583-587). The problems concerning Vṛddhasuśruta and the work called Sauśrutatantra by commentators have not been studied sufficiently and need further elucidation.

SVĀMIDĀSA. This author is referred to in M. on 1, 14cd-15ab as one of the early commentators (*pūrvaṭīkākāra*). He is also mentioned as such by Cakra on Ca.Ci. 3, 217. Vijayarakṣita mentions Svāmidāsa after Āṣāḍhadharma, Cakrapāṇidatta puts him before Āṣāḍhavarman; therefore it is not clear whether one of the two lists (Cakra : Bhāsadatta-Svāmidāsa-Āṣāḍhavarman-Brahmadeva; Vijayarakṣita : Āṣāḍhadharma-Svāmidāsa) is in correct chronological order. Svāmidāsa is certainly one of the group of early commentators on Ca. because he is quoted by Jejjaṭa.

HARICANDRA or Bhaṭṭārakaharicandra, sometimes only indicated by his title of distinction, Bhaṭṭāra, was an early commentator on Ca. He is already quoted by Jejjaṭa as a good commentator (Gul 1, p. 114; Introd. Ca., p. 12; Introd. Ca., Lahore ed., p. 26). There is also a reference to him in a Ms. containing part of a comm. on A.s. (Indu's comm. on that work ?) : "The ignorant one who attempts to understand Caraka's thought without (consulting) Haricandra's commentary, is (like) a man who wants to drink up (read *pātum* instead of *vātum*) the ocean" (Cat.Skt.Mss. Madras, vol. 23, nr. 13071, p. 8789). Indu refers to Bhaṭṭārakaharicandra several times; these references by Indu show that he had not much respect for Haricandra's views (Gode, St.I.L.H. 1, p. 161). Candraṭa praises Haricandra in the beginning of his comm. on Tīsaṭa's Cikitsākalikā : "As there exist the commentaries of Haricandra and of the very intelligent Jejjaṭa, it is presumptuous for another man to comment on the Āyurveda" (Jolly, ZDMG 60, 1906, p. 426; Jolly's reading of the stanza is somewhat different; Gul 1, p. 113; Introd. Ca., p. 13; Introd. Ca., Lahore ed., p. 19). Cakrapāṇidatta remarks (on Ca.Sū. 7, 46) that Vāgbhaṭa follows Haricandra's opinion on a particular point. Maheśvara writes about him in the Viśvaprakāśakośa 1, 5 (composed in 1111 acc. to Winternitz 3, p. 413): "He whose name was Haricandra, whose behaviour was as agreeable as the moon, held in a wholly unrivalled way the position of an irreproachable court physician to king Sāhasāṅka and adorned the treatise of Caraka with his own commentary" (Introd. Ca., p. 13; Introd. Ca., Lahore ed., p. 19; Gul 1, p. 114). Haricandra was one of Maheśvara's ancestors (Krishnamachariar, p. 146-147). An author, also called Haricandra but probably a different person, is mentioned by Bāṇa (Harṣacarita 1, 12) as an important prose writer. This same Haricandra is referred to in Vākpati's Gaüḍavaha (stanza nr. 800). It is said that he wrote a romance called Mālatī (Krishnamachariar, p. 146). He is also referred to in the Saduktikarṇāmṛta by Śrīdharadāsa (compiled in 1260 acc. to Dasgupta and De, in 1205 acc. to Krishnamachariar; see Banerji's ed. of the work, stanza nr. 2130) and in the Subhāṣitāvalī by Vallabhadeva (written between 1417 and 1467 acc. to Krishnamachariar, p. 387). A third author, called Haricandra, was a Jain poet of the Digambara sect and a son of Ārdradeva and Rādhā (Krishnamachariar, p. 146-147). Finally, a poet, called Haricandra and living at the court of Bhillama III of Devagiri, composed an inscription in 1205 (Krishnamachariar, ibid.).

A small portion of Haricandra's comm. on Ca., called Carakanyāsa, has been preserved in a single Ms. (see its description in the Cat.Skt. Mss. Madras, vol. 23, nr. 13092, p. 8801-8802). The fragment contains the comm. on Ca.Sū. 3 (acc. to Gul 1, p. 115 it contains the comm. on Ca.Sū. 1-3 and 5). This very important fragment of the oldest comm. on Ca. known to us has not yet been edited. Acc. to Bhatt. (IHQ 23, 1947, p. 149-150) Haricandra also wrote a revised version of the Kharanādasaṃhitā (he refers to a remark by Indu in the Śaśilekhā : ed. Trichur, vol. 2, p. 368 and p. 372). Bhatt. is of the opinion that Haricandra wrote a *saṃhitā* of his own, quoted by Niścala, which cannot be identical with the Kharanādasaṃhitā from which Niścala quotes separately. Moreover, a passage from Niścala's Ratnaprabhā proves that Haricandra himself quotes from Kharanāda. Acc. to Bhatt. a recipe, couched in an elegant verse, taken by Niścala from Haricandra, must be quoted from Haricandra's own *saṃhitā*; at the end of it a poetic address to a king is found, which proves, acc. to Bhatt. again, that Haricandra wrote his *saṃhitā* for his patron, king Sāhasāṅka.

Haricandra's date cannot be established with certainty. It is only clear that he lived before Jejjaṭa, Indu, Candraṭa, etc. Many scholars who have written on the subject assume that the medical author Haricandra is identical with the author of the same name, referred to in the Harṣacarita and by Vākpati (see Gul 1, p. 112-115; Introd. Ca., p. 13; Introd. Ca., Lahore ed., p. 19; Bhatt., IHQ 23, 1947, p. 149-150); others deny the identity or have their doubt about it (see references in Krishnamachariar, p. 146). There is no evidence to prove the identity, nor any evidence disproving it. With regard to Haricandra's date this problem is of little importance. Haricandra lived before Jejjaṭa and after the composition of the Kharanādasaṃhitā. It follows from these data that he lived before 600. Crucial in fixing his date more precisely is the identity of king Sāhasāṅka. The identity of this king, however, cannot be determined with any certainty. The editors of the Gul ed. of Ca., however, remark without adducing any proofs to support their statements : "The date of king Sāhasāṅka has been fairly well established as 375-413. King Sāhasāṅka is very often identified with Vikrama, i.e. Candragupta II, but this identification is not justified. Vikrama was the predecessor of Sāhasāṅka and Haricandra is not mentioned among the 'nine gems' of Vikrama's court. Thus Haricandra's date is the 5th century". Though this reasoning has its weak points, the date assigned to Haricandra is not unreasonable. In my opinion his date is before 600 and it may be said that he probably lived between 400 and 600. It is not clear whether Haricandra wrote his comm. before the Carakasaṃhitā had been completed by Dṛḍhabala. The quotations from Haricandra in M. refer to parts of Ca., which are due to Caraka himself. In order to establish Haricandra's date with regard to that of Dṛḍhabala all the quotations from Haricandra and the references to him should be collected and studied. A cursory examination of Cakra's comm. on Ca. shows that Haricandra is referred to only once in that part of Ca. which has been redacted by Dṛḍhabala (on Ca.Si. 12, 41cd-45ab); this reference gives the impression that Haricandra commented on the whole of Ca.; if this is correct, he is later than Dṛḍhabala.

HĀRĪTA. To Hārīta is ascribed the Hārītasaṃhitā, also called Ātreyasaṃhitā or Ātreyabhāṣitaṃ Hārītottaram. Hārīta says that he is a disciple of Ātreya, but the work as it has come down to us seems to be of a much later date than the other medical *saṃhitās*. Cordier had not much respect for the work (Le Muséon, N.S. 4, 1903, p. 348-349) and regarded it as a relatively late text of an apocryphal nature, though he admitted that parts of it might be old. He was of the opinion (JA, t. 18, 1901, p. 180) that it must have been composed somewhat earlier than the Mādhavanidāna and that its *pariśiṣṭādhyāya* has been added later at an indeterminate date. Filliozat observes (Renou et Filliozat, l'Inde Classique 2, p. 151) that the text as it has been preserved is a revision of a relatively late date, but he stresses (JA, t. 225, 1934, p. 127, footnote) that the work is of more importance than Cordier ascribed to it. The work is composed in verse on a plan different from that of Ca. and Su. Quotations from Hārīta occur in many commentaries, but can be traced only partially to the text printed as the Hārītasaṃhitā (see : Mukhopādhyāya, H.I.M. 3, p. 811). A long series of quotations has been collected by Mukhopādhyāya (H.I.M. 3, p. 551-555), acc. to whom an author called Vṛddhahārīta is quoted in the Toḍarānanda (l.c., p. 556).

HEMĀDRI wrote a comm. on A.h., called Āyurvedarasāyana, which has been partially preserved (see about the Mss. : A.h., ed. Kuṇṭe, *sūcīpatraṃ saptamam*). Hemādri was a son of Kāmadeva, son of Vāsudeva, son of Vāmana (Cat.Cat. 1, p. 768). He lived during the reign of two Yādava kings of Devagiri : Mahādeva (1261-1271 acc. to Hist. and Cult. of the Ind. P. 5, p. 335; 1260-1271 acc. to Cat.Cat. 1, p. 768 and Vogel, Introd. A.h., p. 16) and Rāmacandra (1271-1309 acc. to Cat.Cat.; Gode, St.I.L.H. 1, p. 112; Krishnamachariar, p. 120; Vogel, Introd. A.h., p. 16). Hemādri was a prolific author and many works of his hand are known. In the Caturvargacintāmaṇi he states to be in charge of the state records of Mahādeva (Vogel, Introd. A.h., p. 16). In the introd. to his Āyurvedarasāyana he mentions the Caturvargacintāmaṇi; from this introd. and a contemporary inscription he appears to have been the archivist and chief minister of Rāmacandra (Vogel, Introd. A.h., p. 16; Gode, St.I.L.H. 1, p. 186-190). From these data it may be concluded that Hemādri wrote his Āyurvedarasāyana during the reign of Rāmacandra.

APPENDIX THREE

TECHNICAL TERMS

aṃsa — (upper) scapular region.

See on the interpretation of *aṃsa* and terms connected with it : Dasgupta, H.I.Ph. 2, p. 286, n. 4 and p. 287, n. 2; Hariprapanna, Rasayogasāgara, *upodghāta* p. 81-82 and 138; Hoernle, Osteology, p. 133-141.

agni — (transforming) fire.

There are thirteen fires in the human body (Ca.Ci. 15, 38cd; A.h.Śā. 3, 70cd). Chief of all is the abdominal fire; the others are dependent on it and subject to increase or decline when the abdominal fire increases or declines (Ca.Ci. 15, 39). Each of the five gross elements (earth, water, fire, wind and space) is provided with its own fire, which has a maturative effect on the constituent of the ingested food belonging to it (Ca.Ci. 15, 13 — A.h.Śā. 3, 59; Su.Sū. 46, 526; A.s.Śā. 6, 59), following upon the separation of these constituents by the abdominal fire (Cakra on Ca.Ci. 15, 13) or by the wind (A.s.Śā. 6, 59). Subsequently, the earthy constituent of the food replenishes the earthy constituents of the body, etc. (Ca.Ci. 15, 14 = A.h.Śā. 3, 60; A.s.Śā. 6, 59). Moreover, there are the seven fires of the elements of the body. Each element is transformed into the subsequent element of the series by its own fire and the seventh element, semen, is transformed into an embryo (Ca.Ci. 15, 15-16; A.h.Śā. 3, 62-63ab; A.s.Śā. 6, 64-66) or into the vital fluid (A.s.Śā. 6, 66). See : Bhish 1, Introd. p. 48-50; Kirfel, Die fünf Elemente; Kutumbiah, p. 41 and 53; Müller, Grundlagen, p. 50-52, Zur Feuerwertung, SA 37, 1953, p. 312-319.

aṅga — part of the body.

The body is divided into six (chief) parts : (1) the head (and neck), (2) the trunk (*antarādhi* or *madhya*), (3) and (4) the two arms, (5) and (6) the two legs (Ca.Śā. 7, 5; Su.Śā. 5, 3; A.h.Śā. 3, 1; A.s.Śā. 5, 3). See : Müller, Wörterheft, p. 75, nr. 4.

aṅgula — digit.

See : Müller, Wörterheft, p. 75, nr. 5.

añjana — collyrium.

añjana usually denotes a substance applied to the eyelids as a cosmetic or medicine. It is often said to consist of antimony (MW; PW). Really two different substances are used for the purpose : antimony trisulphide (Sb_2S_3) or stibnite, and lead sulphide (PbS) or galena. The two substances are often confused, as Watt observes (CP, p. 72) : "Antimony sulphide (stibnite) is employed by the ladies as a cosmetic, but much of the antimony sold for that purpose is really galena, which is often confused with antimony;" see about galena : Watt CP, p. 707. Vogel (A.h., p. 85, n. 1) had two samples of stibnite, bought in Indian bazaars, analysed in Germany; they turned out to consist of galena.

añjana is also confused sometimes with *rasāñjana* acc. to Dutt, who writes (MM, p. 108, footnote) : "Galena or the sulphide of lead ore is sometimes called *rasāñjana* in Sanskrit and some physicians in Bengal use the lead ore or *rasāñjana* whenever this term occurs in a prescription. In the Upper Provinces, however, *rasāñjana* is invariably translated as *rasot* in the vernacular. This, no doubt, is the correct practice. The mistake on the part of the Bengali physicians probably occurred from their not being acquainted with *rasot*, which is the produce of plants indigenous to the Himalayan range;" Dutt, MM, p. 108 : "*rasāñjana* is prepared by boiling together equal parts of a decoction of *dāruharidrā* and milk, till reduced to the consistence of an extract." Nadk. says about antimony sulphide (2, p. 13, nr. 8) : "It is a tersulphide of antimony purified by fusion and reduced to a black powder. The powder is used as an application to the eyelids and eye-brows especially by women in Upper India;" about galena he observes (2, p. 87, nr. 33) : "It is obtained from the mountains of Sauvīra, a country along the Indus, whence it derives its name (*sauvīrāñjana*). The sulphide of lead is of glimmering lustre and is an ore of lead, occurs in cubic masses destitute of rays and is tabular in its crystalline arrangement. *sroto'ñjana* or white *surmā* is produced in the bed of the Yamunā and other rivers. It is, like the black *surmā* or *sauvīrāñjana*, used as a collyrium for the eyes, but is considered inferior to the black *surmā* or galena." Five kinds of *añjana* are distinguished in the Rasaratnasamuccaya (3, 101-112; ed. H.S.S.), a text referred to in Vśs and dealt with by Rāy (H.Ch., p. 175) : (1) *sauvīrāñjana*, which is smoke-coloured;

Rāy : "It is mostly galena or sulphide of lead, though it is usually translated as sulphide of antimony; it is said to be obtained from the mountains of Sauvīra, a country along the Indus, whence it derives its name;" Hindī comm. : stibnite; (2) *rasāñjana*, said to be endowed with a yellow hue; Rāy : the extract of the wood of Berberis asiatica (*dāruharidrā*); Hindī comm. : yellow oxide of mercury (HgO); (3) *sroto'ñjana*, said to be astringent; Rāy : "Evidently stibnite or the native sulphide of antimony; the word literally means 'produced from a river', especially from the Yamunā;" Hindī comm. : antimony sulphide; (4) *puṣpāñjana*, said to be white; Rāy : unidentifiable; Hindī comm. : zinc oxide (ZnO); (5) *nīlāñjana*; Rāy : undoubtedly stibnite (this may be incorrect; compare Rāy, p. 151 : Rasendracūḍāmaṇi : lead is prepared from *nīlāñjana*; Hindī comm. : lead sulphide.

Garbe (Ind. Mineralien) makes the following observations : (1) *sauvīrāñjana* (p. 54) : this is antimony sulphide; possibly the name was transferred later to lead sulphate, because *sauvīrāñjana* is already said to be white in Bhā.pra.; the series of synonyms in Rn (*varga* 13, 214) points to a substance of a black colour, i.e. antimony sulphide, which is of a greyish colour and in its natural state greyish black and easy to pulverize; (2) *rasāñjana* (p. 57-58) : the description in Rn (*varga* 13, 221-223) enables us to identify this substance with certainty as prepared from slags of brass; the name was transferred later to a decoction of the roots of Curcuma; acc. to the Amarakośa (followed by PW) *rasāñjana* is copper sulphate (*tuttha*), prepared by adding a decoction of Curcuma (*dārvikā*); (Garbe is in error here, because *dārvikā* is a synonym of *dāruharidra* and not of *haridrā*); (3) *sroto'ñjana* (p. 58-59) : this substance can only be identical with pure antimony on account of the synonyms *sauvīrasāra* and *kapotasāra* (Rn, *varga* 13, 226); Garbe points to the erroneous observations in Dutt (MM, p. 74): "*sroto'ñjana* is described as of a white colour and is said to be produced in the bed of the Yamunā and other rivers. It is called *saffed surmā* in the vernacular, and the article supplied under this name is calcareous or Iceland spar;" (4) *puspāñjana* (p. 56) : the synonyms *rītika*, *rītikusuma* and *rītipuṣpa* (Rn, *varga* 13, 224) point to the chief ingredient as brass; the only possibility left is to explain *puṣpāñjana* as a collyrium prepared from calx of brass, in agreement with PW; in Bhā.pra. this *añjana* is no longer mentioned and it must already have been out of use for centuries; Dutt (MM, p. 74) is unable to identify the substance and says : "I have not met with any person who could identify or supply the drug;" (5) *nīlāñjana* (p. 54-55) : antimony sulphide. See also : Ainslie 1, p. 495-498; DWH 1, p. 65-67 (about *rasāñjana* and *rasot*); IRM 1, p. 85-86.

anupāna — postprandial potion.

The term *anupāna* is used in two senses : (1) a fluid drunk in combination with a remedial agent or after the taking of a medicinal substance; (2) a fluid drunk after eating a dish during a meal and at the conclusion of a meal. See about the rules in relation to an *anupāna* : Ca.Sū. 27, 319-328 and Cakra's comment; see also Ḍa. on Su.Sū. 46, 419 and 438 and the article in Vśs.

apatarpaṇa — depletion.

Ca.Vi. 3, 43-44 : *apatarpaṇa* is of three kinds : (1) *laṅghana*, reducing measures, used in disorders in which the morbific entities are of slight strength; (2) *laṅghanapācana*, reducing and maturation-promoting measures, used when the morbific entities are of moderate strength; (3) *doṣāvasecana*, measures bringing about the effusion of the morbific entities, resorted to when the morbific entities are present in copious amounts. A.h.Sū. 14, 1cd-4cd : *apatarpaṇa* is synonymous with *laṅghana*; *laṅghana* is that which promotes lightness of the body; *laṅghana* is of two kinds : (1) *śamana*, (2) *śodhana* (the latter term corresponds to *doṣāvasecana*). See Kutumbiah, p. 141.

apūpa — flour-cake.

OP (p. 8, 19, 36, 284) : a round, sweet cake of barley meal or rice flour, baked in clarified butter on a slow fire; honey was added to sweeten it. Vśs quotes from the Vaidyanighaṇṭu : "*apūpa*s are made from finely ground wheat, mixed with treacle and squeezed (after the addition) of water; they are of a circular shape and (should be) baked in ghee." Ca. mentions *apūpa*s of barley flour (Sū. 27, 265) and also makes use of the terms *pūpa* (Sū. 27, 267), *pūpaka* (Sū. 27, 269) and *pūpalikā* (Sū. 27, 267); Ca. describes *pūpa*s of wheat flour (Sū. 27, 272) and *pūpaka*s made with milk and sugar-cane juice (Sū. 27, 269). Cakra says (on Sū. 27, 267) that a *pūpalikā* is called *cāpaḍikā* (in common language) and quotes a recipe for its preparation from (the treatise on cooking by) Nala. The preparation of aphrodisiac *pūpa*s and *pūpalikā*s is described Ca.Ci. 2[2], 10-12 (Kav p. 1080, footnote : those cakes that have conical ends with the middle portion thicker are called *pūpalikā*s;

OP, p. 290 : *pūpalikās* are small cakes of rice or wheat-flour, fried in ghee, with ghee-filled inside and coated with treacle and saffron. A.h. distinguishes (Sū. 6, 42) five types of *apūpa* according to different ways of baking. He. remarks that *apūpas* are thin and flat and prepared from flour. Ma.nigh. describes the way *pūpālikās* are made (*varga* 11, 51) and gives the recipe for two varieties of *pūpaka* (*varga* 11, 73-74).

amla

The term *amla* has several meanings when used as a noun :

m. : (1) vinegar (MW ; PW) ; (2) Oxalis corniculata Linn. (MW ; PW) ; (3) = *amlavetasa* (PW ; Śkdr) ; (4) = *phalāmla* ; (5) = *amlīkā* (HK).

n : (1) = *dhānyāmla* = *kāñjika* (Vśs ; Cakra on Ca.Ci. 29, 151) ; (2) = *takra* (PW ; Śkdr ; Cakra on Ca.Ni. 2, 4) ; (3) = *ghola* (Vśs) ; (4) = *phalāmla* ; (5) the fruit of *amlavetasa* (Vśs) ; (6) the fruit of the *badara* tree (Vśs) ; (7) = *barbaracandana* (Vśs).

Kauṭ. 2, 15, 18-19 (text p. 64 ; transl. Kangle p. 142 ; transl. J. J. Meyer p. 141 ; transl. Sham. p. 101) distinguishes *dravāmla*, i.e. *dadhi*, *dhānyāmla*, etc., and *phalāmla*, i.e. *vṛkṣāmla*, *karamarda*, *āmra*, *vidalāmalaka* (i.e. *vidala* and *āmalaka*), *mātuluṅga*, *kola*, *badara*, *sauvīraka*, *parūṣaka*, etc. There is a group, called 'the four acids' (*caturamla*), mentioned at Ca.Ci. 15, 111 ; Cakra observes that it consists of (1) *vṛkṣāmla*, (2) *amlavetasa*, (3) *dāḍima*, (4) *badara*, but acc. to others of (1) *kapittha*, (2) *cukrikā*, (3) *vṛkṣāmla*, (4) *dāḍima*, and that, in another treatise, it is said to be composed of (1) *vṛkṣāmla*, (2) *mātuluṅgāmla*, (3) *badarāmla*, (4) *amlavetasa*. See about the 'five acids' : Dn, *varga* 7, 57 ; Rn, *varga* 22, 28. See about the '*phalāmla*-pentad' : Dn, *varga* 7, 53 ; Rn *varga* 22, 24.

ariṣṭa, m.

HB, p. 86, n. 52 : a medicated spirituous liquor, prepared from honey and treacle with the addition of (unboiled) medicinal drugs, the whole being steeped in water and allowed to ferment. OP, p. 298 : a tincture of medicines in which solid ingredients predominate. Vśs quotes from the Atrisaṃhitā : "By steeping properly (medicinal) substances of several kinds in *surā*, making them float in it for seven days and straining the fluid through a cloth, (a beverage is prepared) that is called *ariṣṭa* by physicians." Bpn, *saṃdhānavarga* 21 : "That intoxicating beverage will be an *ariṣṭaka*, which is prepared with the water in which remedial agents have been boiled." Cakra on Ca.Sū. 27, 182 :

"An *ariṣṭa* is prepared with a decoction of remedial agents, honey, etc." Ḍa. on Su.Sū. 45, 197 : "The solid ingredients (*dravya*) predominate in an *ariṣṭa*." He. on A.h.Sū. 5, 70cd-71 : "An *ariṣṭa* is the same (as an *āsava*, but it is prepared) with remedial agents which have been boiled." A great number of *ariṣṭas* is described : Śārṅga 2, 10, 44-92.

ariṣṭa, *riṣṭa*, n. — a precursory signal of death.

Ca.I. 2, 5 : "A precursory signal of death, once arisen, never disappears, except in death, and death does not occur without a precursory signal as its harbinger." Su.Sū. 30, 3 : "If someone presents a deviation from the natural state of his body or mind this is, briefly stated, (called) a precursory signal of death." A.h.Śā. 5, 1-2ab : "A precursory signal of death is a sure sign (indicative) of imminent death, in the same way as a flower (is such a sign) with regard to (the appearance of) a fruit, smoke with regard to fire and the rising of clouds with regard to rain. Death does not occur without a precursory signal and life is impossible when such a signal has been observed." A.s.Śā. 9, 3 : "In both healthy and sick people who crave for another body, morbific entities, having got beyond the reach of remedial agents and pervading the whole body, indicate the decline of life, as compact clouds (indicate) rain, and generate suddenly an overthrow of the natural state; that is, briefly stated, said to be a precursory signal of death." A great number of *ariṣṭas* is described : Ca.I.; Su.Sū. 29-33; A.h.Śā. 5 and 6; A.s.Śā. 9-12; Bhe.I.; Kā.I.; Hā. 2, 3-5. See : Filliozat, Appendix : Accadian, Greek and Indian medical prognostics; Jolly, Medicin, p. 23-24; Kutumbiah, p. 99-106; Sinh Jee, p. 164-175.

alpaprāṇatā — mental asthenia.

This term is explained by Cakra on Ca.Ni. 1, 33 as deficiency of mental strength and by Aruṇa on A.h.Ni. 2, 7 as (the presence of) little (bodily) strength.

asātmyendriyārthasaṃyoga — inadequate conjunction of the senses with their objects.

Ca.Sū. 1, 54 : "Summarized, the threefold ground of illnesses which have two residences (i.e. body and mind) consists of improper junction, absence of junction and excessive junction with time, the mind (*buddhi*) and the objects of the senses." Ca.Sū. 11, 43 : "Thus there are three grounds of morbid alterations, to wit inadequate conjunction of the senses with their objects, errors in judgment and transformation (by time); each of these (grounds) has three varieties; in connection with a congruous junction they are grounds of a natural state (i.e. health)." Cf. A.h.Sū. 12, 34cd-43b; A.s.Sū. 22, 11-13. Examples are given : Ca.Sū. 11, 37; 11, 39; 11, 42; A.h.Sū. 12, 36-38ab; 12, 39; 12, 40-42. See : Dasgupta, H.I.Ph. 2, p. 320-321; Kutumbiah, p. 76-77.

asthi—bone.

There are said to be three hundred and sixty bones in the human body. See about the bones : Ca.Śā. 7, 6; Su.Śā. 5, 18-23; A.h.Śā. 3, 16; A.s.Śā. 5, 68-72; Bhe.Śā. 7, 2. Another system of classification with a total number of three hundred bones is mentioned : Su.Śā. 5, 18; A.h.Śā. 3, 16. The classification and the total number of bones in Kā. (*śarīravicayaśārīrādhyāya*) deviates from the other systems. See : Chakraberty, p. 6-17; Hariprapanna, Rasayogasāgara, *upodghāta* p. 170-178; Hoernle, Osteology; Kutumbiah, p. 6-18.

āgāradhūma

This term occurs Ca.Ci. 23, 51, Si. 7, 25 and Si. 9, 58, but is not explained by Cakra. Its synonym *gṛhadhūma* is found Ca.Sū. 3, 5, Ci. 7, 87 (*gṛhād dhūmaḥ*), Ci. 23, 41, Ci. 23, 197, Ci. 23, 198, Ci. 26, 194 and Ci. 29, 149. The synonym *veśmadhūma* occurs once in Ca. : Ci. 26, 14. Kav and Gul translate : domestic soot, resp. kitchen soot, which is probably correct. If these terms denoted a particular plant (PW : Name einer Pflanze, MW : name of a plant, = *dhundhumāra*), Cakra would have given a synonym in his commentary. Hoernle also was of the opinion that the term means soot. See HB, p. 19, n. 56 : "*gṛhadhūma*, lit. 'house-smoke', is soot. The Petersburg and other Sanskrit dictionaries make it to be the name of a plant. I do not know on what authority. At Su.Ka. 1, 58 it is said to be *dhūma āgārasaṃbhavaḥ*, i.e. 'smoke produced in a house', that is, the soot deposited in the cobwebs over the hearth or fireplace of a house. It is a substance often prescribed by Kavirāja. In Bengali it is called *jhūl* and in Sanskrit commentaries it is generally rendered by *alandhuka*, e.g. in Cakradatta, p. 661 (*strīrogacikitsā* 7), comm. (Śivadāsa) : *gṛhadhūmam alandhukaḥ*. The latter is a wrong form of the Sanskrit *alandhūma*, 'thick smoke' or soot."

ādāna — period of resorption.

visarga — period of emission.

See Ca.Sū. 6, 4-8; Su.Sū. 6, 7-8; A.h.Sū. 3, 2-7ab; A.s.Sū. 4, 5-8; Kā.Khi. 7, 5-12; Hā. 1, 4, 21-31; Bhā.pra. 5, 329-339.

ādāna is that half of the year in which the sun moves to the north, *visarga* the other half in which it moves tò the south. *ādāna* consists of the cool season, spring and summer, *visarga* of the rainy season, autumn and winter. During *visarga* the moon is strong and during *ādāna* the sun. In the period of *ādāna* the oleaginous constituents of the earth are resorbed by the sun, leading to a predominance of dry qualities and the dry (i.e. bitter, astringent and pungent) tastes, which bring about weakness. In the period of *visarga* there is predominance of the non-dry (i.e. acid, saline and sweet) tastes, which increase the strength of men.

ānāha — obstructive abdominal swelling.

This term has often been translated erroneously : Gul : constipation, distension; HSu, and HB, p. 125, n. 242: habitual constipation, constipation; MW : suppression of urine, constipation; Vogel : constipation; more adequate is PW : Verstopfung des Leibes; the sense is too broad in MW : epistasis (= acc. to Butterworths Medical Dictionary : suppression of a secretion or discharge) and HK : Verstopfung.

ānāha is defined : Su.U. 56, 20cd-21ab = Mā.ni. 27, 17 = Bhā.pra. 8, 31, 19 : "Gradually accumulated immature or faecal matter, greatly confined by the wind which has deviated from its (normal) qualities, (constitutes), when it does not come forth in its normal way, the morbid alteration called obstructive abdominal swelling." Defined in this way, *ānāha* means an obstruction of the bowels, either on a high or on a low level. Obstruction on a high level (*āmodbhava*) is called *pratyānāha* : Śārṅga 1, 7, 49. The characteristics of *ānāha* are described by Vāgbhaṭa as follows : A.h.Ni. 11, 60 = A.s.Ni. 11, 49 (Ki. 11, 48) : "A vehement abdominal inflatedness, with a very ferocious pain, accompanied by distension and (arisen) by obstruction of the wind (in its) upward and downward (course), that (condition) is declared to be obstructive abdominal swelling." Sometimes the term is used in a broader sense : Ḍa. on Su.Sū. 26, 10 explains it as : obstruction of wind, urine, faeces, etc.

āranāla, n. (m., acc. to Rn, *varga* 15, 294).

A sour gruel made from the fermentation of boiled rice (Dutt, MM, p. 12; HK, p. 299, footnote; MW; PW). Dn, *varga* 6, 249 and Rn, *varga* 15, 294 : *āranāla* = *kāñjika*. Bpn, *saṃdhānavarga* 10 : "Made with unboiled, husked wheat grains, or with boiled (grains), it will be *āranāla* when fermentation has occurred; in qualities it is like *sauvīra*" (the same stanza is found : Bho.ku. 1, p. 124).

ālakta(ka)

Acc. to Watt (CP, p. 1053) *ālakta* is washed lac (*lākṣā*); acc. to Dutt (MM, p. 277) *ālakta* is the fluid lac-dye obtained by dissolving the crushed stick-lac (see Watt CP, p. 1060, about stick-lac) in water. Lac is the product of a very small hemipterous insect, *Tachardia lacca* Kerr (synonyms : *Certeria lacca*, *Coccus lacca*), feeding chiefly on Butea monosperma Kuntze (*palāśa*); this tree is often called *lākṣātaru* or shortly *lākṣā*. Cotton coloured with lac and pressed into flat circular pieces is used in painting the hands and feet of Hindu women. See : Ainslie 1, p. 188-191; Dutt, MM, p. 277; Mārg, vol. 19, no. 3, 1966, p. 4-15; Nadk. 2, p. 148-150; Watt CP, p. 1053-1066.

āsava

PW : Liquor, häufig ein mit Zucker oder Lauge gemischter Trank; ein berauschendes Getränk überh.; Rum. MW : rum, spirit distilled from sugar or molasses, spirituous liquor in general. Dutt, MM, p. 274 : vinous or fermented liquor from sugar or molasses; rum. HB, p. 86, n. 52 : a medicated spirituous liquor, prepared from honey and treacle with the addition of (a decoction of) medicinal drugs, the whole being steeped in water and allowed to ferment. Vśs : an intoxicating beverage prepared with unboiled drugs. Bpn, *saṃdhānavarga* 28 and Śārṅga 2, 10, 2ab : "The intoxicating beverage, prepared with unboiled remedial agents and water, is (called) *āsava*." Ḍa. on Su.Sū. 45, 197 and 45, 420 : the liquid (ingredients) predominate in an *āsava*. Ca. employs the term *āsava* in a very broad sense, including *surā*, *maireya*, *dhānyāmla*, etc. Ca.Sū. 25, 49 mentions eight sources for the preparation of an *āsava* : grain, fruits, roots, core-wood (of a number of trees), flowers, joints (of the stalks of plants), leaves and barks; eighty-four varieties are enumerated among the innumerable medicated *āsavas* which may be prepared. See about the way in which a medicated *āsava* is prepared : Su.Sū. 44, 28-30. Kauṭ. 2, 25, 19 (text p. 79; transl. Kangle p. 177; transl. J. J. Meyer p. 186; transl. Sham. p. 132) : an *āsava* is prepared with one *tulā* of *kapittha*, 5 *tulās* of *phāṇita* (inspissated sugar-cane juice) and one *prastha* of *madhu* (honey or the juice of grapes); Kauṭ. 2, 25, 29 (text p. 79; transl. Kangle p. 178; transl. J. J. Meyer p. 186; transl. Sham. p. 133) : the requisite quantity (of spices) to be added (*saṃbhāra*) to an *āsava* (consists of) one *karṣa* of *coca*, *citraka*, *vilaṅga* and *gajapippalī* and two *karṣas* of *kramuka*, *madhuka*, *mustā* and *lodhra*.

iṇḍarikā

Is probably identical with *iḍarikā*. OP, p. 206 : *iḍarikā* is a preparation of fermented fine flour of *māṣa* made into small circular balls. See P. K. Gode : Studies in the history of Indian dietetics — History of the dishes iḍli and dośe (Ind. Linguistics 16, 1955, p. 226-231).

indriya — sense(-organ).

See about the senses in Indian medicine : Müller : Sinneslehre altindischer Medizin; Manas und der Geist altindischer Medizin; Eigenwertungen, p. 102-106; Wörterheft, p. 85-86, nr. 42; Ueber indische Bewertungen der Sinne.

utkleśa — nausea.

PW : das Heraustreten der drei Flüssigkeiten (*doṣa*) des Leibes aus ihrem normalen Stande. MW : disorder or corruption of the humors (of the body); sickness, nausea. HK : Mattigkeit. Kav : nausea, throwing up; the stage before vomiting, a tendency to sickness. Gul : nausea, retching. Vśs : a condition as if vomiting of the morbific entity, staying in the body, is near at hand. The term is defined Su.Śā. 4, 53 : "When someone feels uneasy, the (ingested) food will not come out, effusion (of saliva) and spitting have been set in motion and the cardiac region is painfully oppressed, one may define this (condition) as nausea." Ḍa. on Su.Sū. 46, 128 and U. 40, 11 : it is the making of the sound *thūt*. Aruṇa on A.h.Sū. 8, 25 : it is the moving away of the morbific entities from their seat; He. on the same passage : it is the moving of the morbific entities from their seat or the moving upwards of phlegm.

udaśvit

PW : zwei Theile Buttermilch mit einem Theile Wasser. MW : a mixture consisting of equal parts of water and buttermilk. Dutt, MM, p. 283 : butter-milk mixed with half its bulk of water. Kav p. 538 : butter-milk mixed with an equal proportion of water. Vśs : *takra,* half of which consists of water. See : *takra.*

upadrava — secondary affection.

PW : Symptom (sowohl eine hinzukommende Krankheitserscheinung als Krankheitszufall überhaupt). MW : a supervenient disease or one brought on whilst a person labours under another. Bhish : sympathetic disease, morbid affliction, unfavourable symptom. Filliozat (Fragm. koutch.) : maladie intercurrente. Gul : complication, sequela, affliction. HK : Folge-erscheinung. HSu : troublesome disease. Jolly : schlimmer Zufall. Vall : complicazione. Vogel : sequela. It is very difficult to find an adequate term to render the sense of *upadrava.* Translations like 'complication, intercurrent disease and supervenient disease' are inadequate because an *upadrava* is a secondary development of the primary morbific process. The term is explained in the following passages : Ca.Ci. 21, 40 : "A secondary affection is a disease in itself, (of a) major or minor (character), arising at a later time than the (originally present) disease and dependent on (that) disease. It is technically called a secondary affection as it arises after a disease. In such a case the (original) illness is predominant and the secondary affection has the (same) qualities as that illness. It usually becomes appeased when the predominant (illness) is appeased. It is, however, more painfully oppressing because, as it is produced later on, the body is (already) being vexed by illness. Therefore a secondary affection should be attacked promptly." Cakra comments : "... (The words) 'arising at a later time than the disease', (which mean) : arising during the middle course of the disease, differentiate (a secondary affection) from a sign that is produced together with the disease. Although there are signs which sometimes arise at a later time than the disease, these (are) not (signs said to) arise at a later time than the illness, strictly speaking, as they usually arise together with the disease; therefore they are not of the nature of secondary affections. (The words) 'dependent on (that) disease' (mean that their) cause is comparable to that of the disease because they are occasioned by excitement of the morbific entity starting the disease ... 'A disease in itself' designates the secondary affection dealt with by the word disease, separately from the illness which is its root. In this way it is differentiated from (that) stage of an illness which arises at a later time ... A stage of an illness has the very form of the illness which is the root (of the secondary affection) because it is something which necessarily occurs, but a secondary affection does not necessarily occur. Although some illnesses, started by morbific entities with a great force, already join secondary affections at their production, and the term secondary affection does not refer to (a disease that is) simultaneously produced, those maladies which arise as secondary affections are in that case nevertheless called secondary affections and rightly so, though produced together with (the predominant disease). In the true sense of the word, however, (those diseases which) arise simultaneously do not present the characteristics of secondary affections, but (only) those which arise in such a case as an intermixture (of diseases) ..." Fr. Su.Sū. 35, 18 : "The illness, arising at a later time, which is added to a previously produced illness, is a superinduced one (*aupasargika*); such an (illness), the root of which is that (previously produced illness) itself, is technically called a secondary affection." A.h.Sū. 12, 60d : "Those (dependent diseases) which arise later on are secondary affections." Kā.Sū. 27, 57cd-58a : "That malady which arises later, by the (same) cause as that one arisen previously, is called a secondary affection." Hā. 3, 2, 17 : "That illness which is added to an illness is called a secondary affection; those people who have a secondary affection are to die, those without it will live."

ulaka

Variants : *uluka* and *okula* (see also *darbha*, App. 4).
PW : *okula* : Kuchen von Waizenmehl, Rājan. im Śkdr. MW : *ula* : half-ripe pulses fried over a small fire, Nigh.; *okula* : wheat fried lightly, L. Śkdr. : *okula* is made from heated, immature wheat. The word *ulaka* occurs A.h.Ni. 14, 46 = A.s.Ni. 14, 49 (Ki. 14, 47 : *okula*). HK translated : Schweiss (= sweat). Aruṇa : "*ulaka* is a synonym of *sveda* (perspiration); others read *uluka* and this is explained as *śimbīdhānya* which is in a yellowish-green state." Candra (reading *okula*) : "Wheat, barley, etc., softened by steaming (*svedita*) and for the greater part burnt, are called *okula*." Indu (reading *okula*) : "*okula* has been mentioned (in the paragraphs) on prepared foods; (it consists of) crops remaining on their stalks (*kāṇḍastha*), which are immature and have been roasted." Toḍara : "*ulaka* is a synonym of *sveda* (perspiration);

others say it means salt." Śrīdāsa, after quoting Aruṇa and speaking about the reading *okula* adopted by Indu, adds the opinion of Hāṭaka : *okula* is steamed *śimbīdhānya* still in the pods (*kośastha*), and the opinion of the author of the Pāṭhya commentary : *okula* is a particular kind of confectionery (*bhakṣya*) made from immature barley, or it is potherb-water (*śākodaka*). In Aruṇa's comment on A.h.Sū. 6, 41 it is said that *olaka* arises from *śimbi* that is still yellowish-green.

ṛtu — season.

See HSu, p. 34-46, n. 80 : "From Su.Sū. 6, it may be seen that there are two divergent systems of arranging the seasons, a civil and a medical system. The following table renders these two systems clear.

The civil arrangement of the seasons :

Season :	Months :	Months :
(1) *śiśira*	*māgha* = *tapas*	15th January-15th February
(cool season)	*phālguna* = *tapasya*	15th February-15th March
(2) *vasanta*	*caitra* = *madhu*	15th March-15th April
(spring)	*vaiśākha* = *mādhava*	15th April-15th May
(3) *grīṣma*	*jyeṣṭha* = *śuci*	15th May-15th June
(summer)	*āṣāḍha* = *śukra*	15th June-15th July
(4) *varṣāḥ*	*śrāvaṇa* = *nabhas*	15th July-15th August
(rainy season)	*bhādrapada* = *nabhasya*	15th August-15th September
(5) *śarad*	*āśvina* = *īṣa*	15th September-15th October
(autumn)	*kārtika* = *ūrja*	15th October-15th November
(6) *hemanta*	*mārgaśīrṣa* = *sahas*	15th November-15th December
(winter)	*pauṣa* = *sahasya*	15th December-15th January.

The medical arrangement of the seasons :

(1) *vasanta*	*phālguna*	15th February-15th March
	caitra	15th March-15th April
(2) *grīṣma*	*vaiśākha*	15th April-15th May
	jyeṣṭha	15th May-15th June
(3) *prāvṛṣ*	*āṣāḍha*	15th June-15th July
(early rainy season)	*śrāvaṇa*	15th July-15th August

(4) *varṣāḥ*	*bhādrapada*	15th August-15th September
	āśvina	15th September-15th October
(5) *śarad*	*kārtika*	15th October-15th November
	mārgaśīrṣa	15th November-15th December
(6) *hemanta*	*pauṣa*	15th December-15th January
	māgha	15th January-15th February.

It will be noticed that in these two systems the seasons overlap one another and that while the civil system omits the season of *prāvṛṣ*, the medical omits the season of *śiśira*. Usually, in medical texts also, the civil system is followed." See also : Jolly, Medicin, p. 38-39; Kutumbiah, p. 132-133; Müller, Wörterheft, p. 87-88, nr. 49; Sinh Jee, p. 80-83.

eṇa

See also : *hariṇa*.

PW : eine Antilopenart (schwarz und mit kurzen Beinen). MW : a species of deer or antelope (described as being of a black colour with beautiful eyes and short legs). Kav, p. 169 : the black antelope. Nadk. 2, p. 143 : Antilope cervicapra Linn. Vśs : = *hariṇa*: a particular kind of black deer. Bpn, *māṃsavarga* 10 : it is of a black colour. Rn, *varga* 19, 417 : it is also called *pṛṣata* (spotted antelope). Ma.nigh., *varga* 12, 29 : it is of a black colour. Cakra on Ca.Sū. 5, 5 : *eṇa* is the spotted antelope (*kṛṣṇasāra*). Ḍa. on Su.Sū. 20, 5 : it is the black deer (*kṛṣṇamṛga*). Ḍa. on Su.Sū. 46, 54 : it is the black *hariṇa*. Candra on A.h.Sū. 6, 43 : it is of a black colour and also called *kamala*. He. on A.h.Sū. 6, 43 : it is of a black colour.

It is clear that *eṇa* is usually regarded as a black antelope; only Cakra and Rn consider it a spotted antelope. The animal called *eṇa* is probably the male of *Antilope cervicapra* (Linnaeus, 1758), the black buck or Indian antelope. It is an elegant animal of a striking colour and with beautifully spiralled horns. The coat of the males begins to turn black when they are three years old. The darkening of the coat varies in intensity; it may remain a dark brown colour, especially in southern India..Besides *Antilope cervicapra* two other antelopes occur in India : the nilgai or blue bull, *Boselaphus tragocamelus* (Pallas, 1766) and the four-horned antelope, *Tetracerus quadricornis* (Blainville, 1816). See : Prater, The book of Indian animals, p. 270-273.

ojas — vital fluid.

ojas is described : Ca.Sū. 17, 74-75; Su.Sū. 15, 19; A.h.Sū. 11, 37-39ab; A.s.Sū. 19, 34ab-37; Kā.Sū. 27, 25; Bhā.pra. 3, 181-186. Ca.Sū. 17, 74-75 : "That pure (substance) which stays in the heart and is (of a) slightly red (colour), tinged with yellow, is called the vital fluid of the body; by its annihilation a man is annihilated. The vital fluid arises first in the body of bodily beings; it arises with the colour of ghee, the taste of honey and the smell of parched grain." See about *ojas* : Bhish 1, Introd. p. 53-57; Filliozat, p. 166-168 (Fr. ed. p. 135-137); Filliozat, Kumāratantra, p. 29, n. 2; Hariprapanna, Rasayogasāgara, *upodghāta* p. 114-121; Kutumbiah, p. 47; Müller, Die Herzlehre, p. 289-292, Ueber begriffliche Bewertungen, p. 401-405. See about the meaning of *ojas* in old texts : J. Gonda, Ancient-Indian ojas.

kaṭvara

PW : Molken (*dadhisara*); Buttermilch mit Wasser (*takra*). MW : buttermilk mixed with water. Vśs : butter-milk; *dadhisneha*; *dadhisara*; *takra*. Śkdr : *dadhisara* acc. to the Ratnamālā; *vyañjana* acc. to the Uṇādikośa; *takra* acc. to Cakrapāṇidatta's Saṃgraha : "Diluted buttermilk (*takra*), made from thick sour milk (*dadhi*) together with its fatty constituents (*sāra*), is called *kaṭvara*." Cakra on Ca.Ni. 2, 4 : "*kaṭvara* is undiluted buttermilk (*nirjalaṃ takram*) or acid buttermilk." Ḍa. on Su.Sū. 46, 451 : "*kaṭvara* is diluted buttermilk (*takra*); others, however, say : *sauvīrāmla*, exceedingly acid (buttermilk) and *kāñjika* are known as *kaṭvara*; others (say) it is its lower portion or diluted buttermilk which has become exceedingly acid; others again say it is buttermilk from thick sour milk together with its fatty constituents (*sasnehaṃ dadhijaṃ takram*)."

kaṇḍarā — rope, large cord (large nerve trunk ?, ligament ?).

There are sixteen 'ropes' in the human body. See about these : Su.Śā. 5, 11; A.h.Śā. 3, 14; A.s.Śā. 5, 61 and 5, 83. See : Chakraberty, p. 29-30; Dasgupta, H.I.Ph. 2, p. 352; Kutumbiah, p. 22-23.

kapota — pigeon.

PW : Taube. MW : a dove, pigeon, (esp.) the spotty-necked pigeon. Ḍa. on Su.Sū. 46, 67 : the *kapota* lives in the forest and is called *pāṇḍuka* in common language; it is of various kinds; the *pārāvata* pigeon has its home in houses and temples; He. on A.h.Sū. 6, 47 : it is (called) *pāṇḍuka* and *aṅgāracūḍaka*. See Ainslie 1, p. 313-314. See also : *pārāvata*.

Many kinds of pigeons occur in India (see : Handbook of the birds of India and Pakistan, vol. 3). It is not clear at all whether *kapota* designates a particular species or group of species but the term *pāṇḍuka* seems to exclude the green pigeons of the genus *Treron*. The spotty-necked pigeon mentioned by MW may be : a) *Columba elphinstonii* (Sykes, 1833) (Handbook 3, p. 132-133) : it has a grey head and a conspicuous black-and-white 'chessboard' on the hind-neck; b) *Columba hodgsonii* Vigors, 1832 (Handbook 3, p. 131-132) : head and neck grey, the latter speckled with blackish behind; c) *Columba pulchricollis* Blyth, 1846 (Handbook 3, p. 134-135) : it has a conspicuous buff collar, broad, stippled and blackish at the back. Ḍa.'s comment excludes the pigeons called *pārāvata*. The term *aṅgāracūḍaka*, used by He. and meaning : with a crest of the colour of charcoal, does not fit any description in the Handbook.

kapha — phlegm.

The five kinds of phlegm are described : Su.Sū. 21, 12-14; A.h.Sū. 12, 15-18ab; A.s.Sū. 20, 6; Bhā.pra. 3, 127-132. See : Bhish 1, Introd. p. 46-47; Gul 1, p. 565-567 and 569; Kirfel, Die fünf Elemente; Kutumbiah, p. 68-70; Sinh Jee, p. 89-90.

kalā

PW : Bezeichnung der Substrate der Elemente des menschlichen Leibes. MW : a term for the seven substrata of the elements of the human body. Vśs : cellular tissue and fascia of the body. The seven *kalā*s are described : Su.Śā. 4, 5-20. Su.Śā. 4, 5-7 : "Verily, there are also seven *kalā*s which are the boundaries between the receptacles of the elements. As the core of a piece of wood becomes visible when it is cut, thus the element becomes visible when the fleshy parts (of the body) are cut. One should know that these parts, (consisting of) the *kalā*s, are covered by cords; a membranous covering is spread over the whole of them and they are enveloped by phlegm." The seven *kalā*s hold resp. flesh, blood, fat, phlegm, faecal matter, bile and semen. A description of the seven *kalā*s, resembling that in Su., occurs : A.s.Śā. 5, 34-41. The term *kalā* is also defined at A. h.Śā. 3, 9cd-10c: "The moist parts between the receptacles of the elements, each (part) digestively altered by its own heat (i.e. the fire of the element within the receptacle) and covered by phlegm, cords and membranes, as the core (is hidden) in wood, is called *kalā*. They are seven (in number)." In Aruṇa's comment on this passage a description of the seven *kalā*s is quoted from an unknown source. The same quotation is found in Śrīdāsa's very extensive comment, in which are moreover quoted the opinions of Indu and Hāṭaka about the subject. Compare Bhā.pra. 3, 219-222 and Śārṅga 1, 5, 6-7ab. A second meaning of *kalā* is : layer of the skin. See : Dasgupta, H.I.Ph. 2, p. 317; Hariprapanna, Rasayogasāgara, *upodghāta* p. 164-168; Jolly, Medicin, p. 43; Kutumbiah, p. 6; Müller, Wörterheft, p. 90-91, nr. 59, Die vermeintlichen "Temperamente", Janus 51, 1964, p. 184-185.

kalya

PW : an intoxicating beverage; MW : spirituous liquor; Vśs : = *surā*. Ma.nigh., *varga* 8, 164 : *kalya* is a synonym of *madya*. The term *kalya* may be related to Tamil *kaḷ(ḷu)* : toddy (Burrow, Collected papers, p. 185).

kaṣāya

This term is often, but in many cases erroneously, translated by decoction. It has a very broad sense in Ca. Five kinds of *kaṣāya* are enumerated at Ca.Sū. 4, 7 : (1) *svarasa* : the juice pressed out from a medicinal plant by mechanical means; (2) *kalka* : the paste made by rubbing a medicinal plant; (3) *śṛta* : a decoction sensu proprio, made by boiling medicinal plants or parts of these with water over a fire; (4) *śīta* : a cold infusion made by crushing a medicinal plant and keeping it in boiled water for a night; (5) *phāṇṭa* : a hot infusion, made by pouring hot water on a crushed drug. These five *kaṣāya*s are mentioned by Ḍa. in his comment on Su.Sū. 37, 12. They are also described at A.h.Ka. 6, 8-11. At A.s.Ka. 8, 9-13 they appear with partially different names : (1) *niryāsa* (= *svarasa*), (2) *kalka*, (3) *niryūha* (= *śṛta*), (4) *śīta*, (5) *phāṇṭa*. In the Kāśyapasaṃhitā seven kinds of medicinal preparations are described which correspond to seven types of *kaṣāya*. They are enumerated at Khi. 3, 35-43ab : (1) *cūrṇa* : a powder, (2) *śītakaṣāya* : prepared by pouring cold water on a crushed drug, (3) *svarasa*, (4) *abhiṣava*, which seems to correspond to a *śīta* in Ca., (5) *phāṇṭa*: made by having the water boil once, (6) *kalka*, (7) *kvātha* (= *śṛta*). The five *kaṣāya*s are also enumerated at Śārṅga 2, 1, 1 : (1) *svarasa*, (2) *kalka*,

(3) *kvātha* (= *śṛta*), (4) *hima* (= *śīta*), (5) *phāṇṭaka*. See about their preparation : Śārṅga 2, 1, 2; 2, 5, 1-2; 2, 2, 1-2; 2, 4, 1-2ab; 2, 3, 1-2. See also : Bhā.pra. 7, 2, 1-8; 7, 2, 10-13; 7, 2, 27-36 and Yo. p. 101-104.

kāñjika — fermented rice-water.

PW : saurer Reisschleim. MW : sour gruel, water of boiled rice in a state of spontaneous fermentation. Dutt, MM, p. 12 : "*kāñjika* is a sour liquid produced from the acetous fermentation of powdered paddy. Two seers of powdered paddy grown in the rainy season are steeped in eight seers of water and laid aside in an earthen pot for fifteen days and upwards, when the mixture undergoes acetous fermentation. The resulting fluid is called *kāñjika* or *dhānyāmla*, that is, the acid produced from paddy. *kāñjika* is a clear transparent fluid with an acid taste and vinous smell." Vśs : sour gruel, the water of boiled rice in a state of spontaneous fermentation; Caraka (says) : "After putting into a vessel quickly ripening rice (*āśudhānya*) which has been pounded, (as well as) young radishes (*bālamūla*) which have been cut into pieces, to the measure of one *prastha* (= 1/4 of an *āḍhaka*) and throwing one *āḍhaka* of water into that vessel, one should keep the mixture until it has become acid; (then) it is known as *kāñjika*, which is everywhere honoured;" Atrisaṃhitā 11 : "After taking one *tulā* of *ṣaṣṭika* grains that have been boiled and distributing them properly, throwing them into a *droṇa* (a sort of wooden vessel) full of water, one should keep this (mixture), carefully covered, for seven (days and) nights; one should remove from it all the (rice-)paste; (the resulting fluid) is called *kāñjika* (or) *āranāla*." *kāñjika* was not only prepared from rice, but also from *jūrṇāhva* and *kodrava* (Ḍa. on Su.Sū. 45, 214). *dhānyāmla* is usually synonymous with *kāñjika* (Ḍa. on Su.Sū. 45, 214; He. on A.h.Sū. 5, 79), but sometimes the two are distinguished : Bpn, *saṃdhānavarga* (1 : *kāñjika* is, by fermentation, prepared from the scum of boiled grain; 12 : *dhānyāmla* is prepared from powdered *śāli* rice, *kodrava*, etc.); Bho.ku. 1 (p. 123 : *kāñjika*; p. 125 : *dhānyāmla*) : idem. Compare Śārṅga 2, 10-12ab. See : Ainslie 1, p. 461-463.

kāṇakapota

Ḍa. on Su.Sū. 46, 69 : it is a pigeon of a pale colour living in the woods; others say it is a pigeon of a ruddy colour. He. on A.h.Sū. 6, 60 : a distinct kind of pigeon; it is small and of a ruddy colour. Many species of the genus *Streptopelia* may be described as small pigeons of a ruddy colour (see : Handbook of the birds of India and Pakistan, vol. 3, p. 140-157).

kiñculaka — an earthworm.

The term *kiñcaka*, occurring once (Hā. 3, 5, 1), may be a printing error. Variants of *kiñculaka* are : *kiñcilika* and *kiñculuka* (PW ; MW).

kiṇva

PW : Hefe überh. oder ein best. Gährungsstoff, insbes. der zur Bereitung von geistigen Getränken angewendete. MW : ferment, drug or seed used to produce fermentation in the manufacture of spirits from sugar, bassia, etc.

The preparation of *kiṇva* is described : Kauṭ. 2, 25, 26 (text p. 79; transl. Kangle p. 178; transl. J. J. Meyer p. 187; transl. Sham. p. 133) : "One *droṇa* of the paste of unboiled or boiled *māṣa* beans and a third part more (or : three quarters more) of rice constitute, with the addition of one *karṣa* of *moraṭa*, etc., *kiṇva*."

kīṭa

This term, often translated by worm or insect (PW ; MW), designates many kinds of animals of small or moderate size, chiefly arthropods and their larvae. See about their names and classification : Su.Ka. 3, 5 and Su.Ka. 8. Acc. to Seal (p. 194) the term *kīṭa* designates butterflies and moths.

kṛkalāsa — lizard.

kṛkalāsa is usually translated by lizard or chameleon (PW ; MW). Vśs says the word means : (1) *saraṭa*, (2) *gṛhagodhikā*. The *nighaṇṭu*s and commentators give us a confused mass of synonyms and not much actual information about these animals : Pr 508 : *śaya*, *kṛkalāsī*, *śaraṭa* and *kṛkalāśaka* (are synonyms); (the vernacular term is) *kāṃkalāsa*; ibid., 610 : a *gṛhagodhikā* is a *jyeṣṭhī*, (called in the vernacular) *ṭikṭiki*. Ca.Ci. 23, 156, Cakra : it is said that a *gṛhagodhikā* is a *jyeṣṭhā*, but others say it is a *saraṭa*. Su.Sū. 29, 37, Ḍa. : a *kṛkalāsa* is called *kaṇṭikāyā* in common language; those living in the East call it *girigiṭ*. Su.Ka. 8, 24cd-25ab, Ḍa. (quoting from Ālambāyana) : "A *kṛkalāsa* is traditionally said to live on trees and to have poison in its teeth; that one, the hue of which is like that of the moon, is a different (kind);

(the animal called) *trikaṇṭaka* is a particular type of the latter." The terms *gṛhagodhikā*, *jyeṣṭhā* and *jyeṣṭhī* designate small house-lizards, called gecko (Lüders, ZDMG, Bd. 96, 1942, p. 56 : a *jyaiṣṭhī* is a kind of gecko; ibid., p. 35, n. 6 : *ṭikṭikī* is the Bengal name of the gecko). Acc. to Ainslie (2, p. 276-278) *saraṭa* is also a name for a gecko. Among the Geckonidae several species belonging to the genus *Hemidactylus* are found in houses; besides the small house geckoes found commonly in India, a larger species, often a foot long, *Gecko gecko gecko* (Linnaeus, 1758) = *Gecko verticillatus*, enters human habitations (Imp. Gaz., 1909, vol. 1, p. 268). Acc. to Platts' Dictionary the *girgiṭ* is the tree-lizard, a species of chameleon (commonly called by Europeans 'the blood-sucker', on account of the redness of its throat). Lüders, referring to this animal (l.c., p. 33, n. 2) says : very frequent is in India *Calotes versicolor* called blood-sucker by the Singhalese, and often called a chameleon on account of its change of colour. *Calotes versicolor* is, acc. to the Imp. Gaz. (1909, vol. 1, p. 268-269). the commonest agamoid lizard, found all over India and known as the 'bloodsucker' in southern India; males of this lizard assume brilliant colours in the breeding season, red and black predominating. The correct name of this animal is *Calotes versicolor* (Daudin, 1802).

kṛśara = *kṛsara*; m., m.pl., f. (-*ā*).

PW : ein Gericht aus Reis und Sesamkörnern. MW : a dish consisting of sesamum and grain (mixture of rice and peas with a few spices). OP, p. 287 : a dish prepared with sesamum and rice cooked in milk; in Ḍa.'s time it was a dish prepared with sesamum, rice and *māṣa* (beans). Hoernle remarks about *kṛsarā* (Bower Ms., p. 149, n. 352): "*kṛsarā*, in the vernacular *khicaṛī* or *khicuṛī* or *khiciṛī*, is a well-known Indian dish; its modern mode of preparation is to boil rice and *dāl* (i.e. 'split pulses') with *garm masālā* (i.e. 'warm spices', such as ginger, pepper, etc.) and salt, and then to grease it with ghee or 'clarified butter'; this practice agrees with the description in Bpn, *kṛtānnavarga* 9 : "Rice together with *dāli*, mixed with salt, fresh ginger and asafoetida, and boiled in water, is called *kṛsarā* by those who know"; there appears to have been, however, another kind of dish, under the same name, which was made with *tila* or 'sesame seeds' instead of *dāl*; it is mentioned in the Chandoga Pariśiṣṭa : "Sesame seed and rice, boiled together, are what is called *kṛsara*"; similarly in Kullūka Bhaṭṭa's commentary to Manu 5, 7 : "Rice boiled with sesame seed is *kṛsara*";

this variety of *khicaṛī* is unknown at the present day as an article of food, so far as I can ascertain; both are mentioned as varieties of *kṛsarā* (fem.) in Śārṅga 2, 2, 138-139, but according to the medical vocabulary Āyurvedārtha Candrikā the *tila* variety is *kṛsara* (masc.), while the *dāl* variety is *kṛsarā* (fem.)." Bpn, *kṛtānnavarga* 9 : "Rice, mixed with *dāli*, to which salt, fresh ginger (*ārdraka*) and *hiṅgu* have been added, and cooked in water, is called *kṛśarā* by wise men." Bṛhad-yo.ta., *taraṅga* 16, 64cd-67ab describes two varieties of *kṛśarā* : one prepared with husked rice and *māṣa* beans (four parts of rice to one part of beans), cooked in water, with addition of *hiṅgu*, *ārdraka* and salt, the other prepared in the same way with rice and *mudga* beans. Ḍa. on Su.Sū. 20, 13 and 46, 346 and He. on A.h.Sū. 7, 38 : it is a gruel prepared with sesame, rice and *māṣa* beans.

kopa

See *caya*.

koṣṭhāṅgāni — the viscera.

Ca. distinguishes (Śā. 7, 10) : (1) *nābhi* (navel), (2) *hṛdaya* (heart), (3) *kloman* (see below), (4) *yakṛt* (liver), (5) *plīhan* (spleen), (6) *vṛkkau* (the kidneys), (7) *basti* (bladder), (8) *purīṣādhāra* (colon sigmoides), (9) *āmāśaya* (receptacle of undigested food), (10) *pakvāśaya* (receptacle of digested food), (11) *uttaraguda* (upper part of the rectum), (12) *adhara-guḍa* (lower part of the rectum), (13) *kṣudrāntra* (small intestine), (14) *sthūlāntra* (gross intestine), (15) *vapāvahana* (omentum). A.h. distinguishes (Śā. 3, 12) : (1) *hṛdaya*, (2) *kloman*, (3) *phupphusa* (see below), (4) *yakṛt*, (5) *plīhan*, (6) *unduka* (see below), (7) *vṛkkau*, (8) *nābhi*, (9) *ḍimbha* (see below), (10) *antra* (intestine), (11) *basti*. Bhe.Śā. 7, 4 presents the same list as Ca. with the omission of *pakvāśaya*. Kā. distinguishes (Śā., *śarīravicayaśārīrādhyāya*): (1) *nābhi*, (2) *plīhan*, (3) *yakṛt*, (4) *kloman*, (5) *hṛd* (heart), (6) *vṛkkau*, (7) *guda*, (8) *basti*, (9) *kṣudrāntra*, (10) *sthūla(-antra)*, (11) *āmāśaya*, (12) *pakvāśaya*, (13) *vapā* (omentum).

kloman : PW, MW, HK and Jolly : the right lung; Bhish : pancreas ?; Filliozat, p. 148 (Fr. ed. p. 123) : probably lungs, sometimes right lung, more often totality of lungs (singular) or lungs (and their lobes) (plural); Gul : pharynx; Hariprapanna, Rasayogasāgara, *upodghāta* p. 143 : gall bladder, but acc. to Gaṇanāthasena's Pratyakṣaśārīra 2, 178 : trachea; Kav : the part that joins the throat with the thorax, *kloman* sometimes indicates the bladder; Kutumbiah, p. 30 : the lungs; Seal : gall bladder; Vśs : bladder, the seat of thirst.

The *kloman* lies in the right half of the trunk (Su.Śā. 4, 31; He. on A.h.Sū. 12, 3; Aruṇa and Śrīdāsa on A.h.Śā. 3, 12). A synonym of it is *tilaka* (Ḍa. on Su.Śā. 4, 31). He. (on A.h.Sū. 12, 3) calls it a small fleshy organ (*māṃsagranthi*), the root of the channels carrying water. Cakra (on Ca.Śā. 7, 10) calls it the seat of thirst. Gaya (on Su.Ni. 1, 23) remarks that it is in the receptacle of undigested food and that thirst arises when the *kloman* is desiccated by the wind. Aruṇa says (on A.h.Śā. 3, 12) that the *samāna* blows into it and that it is of a slightly raised (*ucchrita*) appearance.

phupphusa = *phusphusa* : about the *phupphusa* nothing more can be said than that it is situated in the left half of the trunk (Su.Śā. 4, 31; Aruṇa and Śrīdāsa on A.h.Śā. 3, 12). It is often identified as the left lung.

uṇḍuka, unduka : PW : ein Theil des Leibes (Bauchfell ?); MW and HK : the stomach; Dasgupta, H.I.Ph. 2, p. 318 : a gland in the colon ?; Hariprapanna : descending colon, pelvic colon; Vśs : receptacle of impure matter.

ḍimba, ḍimbha : HK : Darm; Vśs : bladder (*mūtrāśaya*), uterus (*garbhāśaya*); Śrīdāsa on A.h.Śā. 3, 12 : that which contains faecal matter.

See about the viscera : Kutumbiah, p. 30-31; Müller : Zu altindischen Anschauungen von den Eingeweiden des Leibes, SA 28, 1935, p. 229-263. See about *kloman* and *phupphusa* : Dasgupta, H.I.Ph. 2, p. 288, n. 1; Hariprapanna, Rasayogasāgara, *upodghāta* p. 96-101; Karambelkar, Atharvaveda and Āyurveda, p. 90-92; Müller : Kannten die altindischen Aertze die Lunge ?, SA 39, 1955, p. 134-144, and Wörterheft, p. 93, nr. 69 and p. 118, nr. 138.

kṣaya — decline.

Several types of decline are distinguished and described, together with their characteristics. Ca.Sū. 17, 64-73 : the characteristics of decline of the elements of the body, the vital fluid and the impurities. Su.Sū. 15 : the characteristics of decline of the elements (15, 9), of the impurities (15, 11), of the additional elements (*upadhātu*) (15, 12) and of the vital fluid (15, 24). A.h.Sū. 11, 15-22 : decline of the morbific entities, the elements of the body and the impurities. A.s.Sū. 19 : decline of the morbific entities (19, 9), the elements (19, 10), the impurities

(19, 11) and the vital fluid (19, 38-39). Bhā.pra. 7, 7, 78-92 : decline of the morbific entities, the elements, the vital fluid and the impurities. See : Kutumbiah, p. 82-83.

kṣāra — a caustic.

See about different kinds of *kṣāra* : Su.Sū. 46, 322-325; Dravyaguṇa, *lavaṇavarga* 10-11; Dn, *varga* 2, 17-24; Rn, *varga* 6, 24-32; Ma.nigh., *śuṇṭhyādivarga* (2), 62-66; Bpn, *harītakyādivarga* 252-256. See also IRM 1, p. 52-56 and Rāy, H.Ch., p. 62-65. Su. distinguishes : (1) *yavakṣāra*, made from the awns of barley acc. to Ḍa.; see about its preparation and composition : Dutt, MM, p. 87; Nadk. 2, p. 88-93; Watt CP, p. 48-57. (2) *svarjikākṣāra* (often called *sarjikākṣāra*); see about its preparation and composition : Ainslie 1, p. 395-398; Dutt, MM, p. 88; DWH 3, p. 141-142; Nadk. 2, p. 101-103: Watt CP, p. 48-57 and 112-114. (3) *ūṣakṣāra*, prepared from salt-containing sand acc. to Ḍa.; see Watt CP, p. 48-57. (4) *pākimakṣāra*, prepared from the ashes of certain trees and plants; see Su.Sū. 11; Dutt, MM, p. 21-22; Watt CP, p. 48-57. (5) *ṭaṅkanakṣāra* : borax; see Ainslie 1, p. 44-46; Dutt, MM, p. 81-82; IRM 1, p. 207; Nadk. 2, p. 103-107; Watt CP, p. 171-173.

khaḍayūṣa

PW : *khaḍa* : ein aus Buttermilch u.s.w. bereitetes saures Getränk. MW and Kav : *khaḍa* : buttermilk boiled with acid vegetables and spices. Vśs : it is made with 8 *tola*s of *takra*, 24 *tola*s of water and 2 *tola*s of *kapittha*, etc., which should be boiled together till a quarter (of the original quantity of fluid) remains; another (recipe) is : one should mix together the fluid of a *yūṣa* of *mudga* beans, *takra*, *dhānya*, *jīraka* and *saindhava* salt. Cakra on Ca.Sū. 13, 23 : a *khaḍa* is a *yūṣa* to which the young shoots of potherbs have been added. Cakra on Ca.Ni. 2, 1-5 : it is called *rāgakarpūra*. Ḍa. on Su.Sū. 46, 376ab : "There are two kinds of *khaḍa*, (made) with *takra* and *śamīdhānya*, or with *takra* and potherbs, for thus it has been said: '(Made) with *śamīdhānya* to which *takra* has been added, they are ... *khaḍas*;' made with *takra* and potherbs (it is prepared as follows) : 'It is a *khaḍayūṣa* when well boiled together with *kapittha*, *takra*, *cāṅgerī*, *marica*, *ajāji* and *citraka*, but *kāmbalika* is another (dish), prepared with *dadhyamla*, salt, fatty substances, sesame and *māṣa* beans.' Prepared with *takrāmla* it is a *kāmbalika*. Jejjhaṭa, however, is of the opinion that a *khaḍa* is a sauce, prepared with *dadhi*, *māṣa* beans, potherbs and fatty substances. Nala's opinion is as follows : a wise man should husk sesame grains, grind them and keep them in milk for three days, strain (the mixture) through a cloth, boil (the remaining paste) in ghee mixed with fresh ginger and add to it *marica*, *ajāji* and *sāmudra* salt; thus it will be a sesame *khaḍa*."

guḍa — treacle.

See : *śarkarā*.

guṇa — quality.

There are five series of qualities (Ca.Sū. 1, 49). The first series consists of the objects of the senses : sound, touch, colour, taste and smell. The second series consists of twenty qualities, arranged as ten pairs of opposites (Ca.Śā. 6, 10 and Cakra on Ca.Sū. 1, 49) : *guru* (heavy) — *laghu* (light); *śīta* (cold) — *uṣṇa* (hot); *snigdha* (oleaginous) — *rūkṣa* (dry); *manda* (sluggish) — *tīkṣṇa* (sharp); *sthira* (solid) — *sara* (flowing); *mṛdu* (soft) — *kaṭhina* (hard); *viśada* (clear) — *picchila* (mucilaginous); *ślakṣṇa* (smooth) — *khara* (harsh); *sthūla* (gross) — *sūkṣma* (subtle); *sāndra* (viscid) — *drava* (liquid). Su. enumerates twenty-four qualities (Sū. 46, 514-525ab), though it is said that they are twenty in number : *śīta-uṣṇa*; *snigdha-rūkṣa*; *picchila-viśada*; *tīkṣṇa-mṛdu*; *guru-laghu*; *drava-sāndra*; *śuṣka* (desiccated)-*ślakṣṇa*; *karkaśa* (scrabous)-*viśada*; *sugandha* (fragrant)-*durgandha* (bad-smelling); *sara-manda*; *vyavāyin* (diffusive)-*vikāsin* (relaxation-promoting); *āśukārin* (quickly acting)-*sūkṣma*. The third series is summarily designated as *buddhi* (thought) (Ca.Sū. 1, 49); acc. to Cakra this term implies special types of *buddhi*, such as *smṛti* (remembrance), *cetanā* (consciousness), *dhṛti* (self-control), *ahaṃkāra*, etc. The fourth series (Ca.Sū. 1, 49) is that ending with *prayatna* (exertion); it consists of *icchā* (desire), *dveṣa* (aversion), *sukha* (well-being), *duḥkha* (suffering) and *prayatna* (exertion) (see Ca.Śā. 1, 72ab). The fifth series is that beginning with *para*; the items of this series are enumerated at Ca.Sū. 26, 29-30ab : *paratva* (superiority), *aparatva* (inferiority), *yukti* (proper application), *saṃkhyā* (number), *saṃyoga* (commixture), *vibhāga* (disunion), *pṛthaktva* (separate existence), *parimāṇa* (measure), *saṃskāra* (preparation) and *abhyāsa* (habituation). These ten terms are explained in the subsequent stanzas and extensively commented upon by Cakra. See : Dasgupta, H.I.Ph. 2,

p. 360 and 369-371; Gul 1, p. 466-469; Kutumbiah, p. 37-38 and 113-114; Müller, Wörterheft, p. 95-96, nr. 76.

gairika

Dutt, MM, p. 96-97 : red and yellow ochre; red ochre is a silicate of alumina coloured with oxide of iron; Nadk. 2, p. 7-11 : kaolinum, a native white aluminium silicate; p. 95 : a clay found in lead and iron ore and containing an excess of oxide of iron over any other clay; there are two varieties : bole (yellow) and red ochre; the red ochre contains more iron than the bole; Rāy, H.Ch., p. 201 : haematite, which is red and often hard, and limonite, which is yellow or brown; both occur in the form of ochres.

Ochre is a native earth coloured with hydrated iron oxide; it is of two kinds, one having a clayey basis, while the other is a chalky earth. Haematite is ferric oxide (Fe_2O_3); much of it occurs in a fine-grained earthy form (red ochre); limonite, or brown iron ochre, is a natural hydrated ferric oxide ($Fe_2O_3 . H_2O$), impure and with a variable water content.

godhā

A *godhā* is a varan and not an iguana, nor an alligator. PW describes it correctly as a large kind of lizard (eine grosse Eidechsenart). MW is wrong in saying that it is an iguana (either the gosamp or the alligator); neither the iguana nor the alligator is found in India, and the animal called *gosāṃp* is a varan. The *godhā* has been rightly identified as a varan by Hoernle; he writes (Bower Ms., p. 154, n. 374) : "*godhā* or 'Monitor' is a name applied to several large species of lizard of the genus *Varanus*, called by the Natives of India *gosāṃp*, and by Europeans miscalled 'iguana'. They are looked upon as especially choice food by the people who eat them. They are not any species of *Lacerta*, which does not occur in India. So I am informed by Dr. Alcock, Superintendent of the Indian Museum." In an important article by H. Lüders (Von indischen Tieren, ZDMG 96, 1942, p. 23-81) much attention has been given to the *godhā* (p. 23-50). Lüders proves that the *godhā* must be a varan. He says that four species of the genus *Varanus* occur in India : *Varanus monitor*, two smaller species : *Varanus griseus* and *flavescens*, and *Varanus salvator*, the largest species, nowadays only found in N.E. India and Ceylon; *Varanus griseus* may be the *śvetagodhā* and *Varanus flavescens* the *kapilagodhā*, both mentioned by Varāhamihira (Bṛhatsaṃhitā 54, 13 and 69); *Varanus salvator* is probably the *jalajagodhā*, because it is often found in trees along rivers and escapes into the water when alarmed; the other species are called *sthalajagodhā*. The names of the varans mentioned by Lüders are, acc. to Mertens (R. Mertens, Die Familie der Warane, 1942) : *Varanus* (subgenus *Indovaranus* Mertens, 1942) *bengalensis* (Daudin, 1802); *V.* (subgenus *Psammosaurus* Fitzinger, 1826) *griseus* (Daudin, 1803); *V.* (subgenus *Empagusia* Gray, 1838) *flavescens* (Hardwicke et Gray, 1827); *V. salvator* (Laurenti, 1768). In my opinion it is not clearly established that *V. griseus* is the *śvetagodhā*: *V. griseus* is only found at the periphery of the Indian peninsula and moreover *V. bengalensis* may be of a yellow colour (its colour varies between yellow and almost black); *V. flavescens* may be the *kapilagodhā*, but its colour (yellowish) is not characteristic of the species. Much confusion about the *godhā* is found among the commentators on medical texts. Cakra (on Ca.Sū. 27, 38) says that a *gaṇḍaka* is a particular kind of *godhā*, but Lüders (l.c., p. 56, n. 3) is of the opinion that *gaṇḍaka* designates the rhinoceros. Ḍa. says (on Su.Sū. 46, 109) that the *godhā*, as well as the *ghaḍiyāla*, is a particular kind of *kumbhīra*; Lüders (l.c., p. 70) is of the opinion that *kumbhīra* always designates a crocodile, of which there are three kinds in India : *Crocodilus palustris palustris* Lesson, 1831, *Crocodilus porosus porosus* Schneider, 1801, and *Gavialis gangeticus* (Gmelin, 1789); the latter is called *ghaṛiyāl* (l.c., p. 35 and p. 70). See about synonyms of *godhā* : Dn, *varga* 6, 39; Rn, *varga* 19, 17; Ma.nigh., *varga* 12, 109. See also : Ainslie 2, p. 263-264. See about varans : R. Mertens, Die Familie der Warane (Varanidae), 1942; Liste der Warane Asiens und der Indo-Australischen Inselwelt mit systematischen Bemerkungen, 1959; J. Rotter, Die Warane, 1963. (*Varanus monitor* is a nomen rejiciendum).

graha

See : Filliozat, Kumāratantra; Müller, Wörterheft, p. 96-97, nr. 79.

grāhin — seizing.

PW : adstringirend, verstopfend. MW : astringent, obstructing, constipating. Gul : astringent. Kav : operating as an inspissant which dries up the fluids of the body. Vogel : constipating. Va. 96, 11 = Śārṅga 1, 4, 11cd-12ab = Bhā.pra. 6, 221 : "That which stimulates the (transforming) fire, promotes maturation and desiccates the liquids (of the body) by its hotness, is (called) *grāhin*, such as dried ginger (*śuṇṭhī*), *jīraka* and *gajapippalī*." Candra on A.h.Sū. 5, 29cd : that which makes loosened faeces, etc. lumpy (is called *grāhin*).

ghūṇa

See ch. 1, n. 60. Pr 820 : a *ghuṇa* is a wood-eating worm.

ghṛta — ghee.

See ch. 1, n. 19. *ghṛta, ājya, sarpis* and *havis* are synonyms acc. to Pr 836; Dn, *varga* 6, 144; Rn, *varga* 15, 202; Ma.nigh., *varga* 8, 127; Bpn, *ghṛtavarga* 1. In ancient times the enumerated terms were not synonymous; see J. Gonda, The savayajñas, p. 199-200.

ghṛtapūra

(The term *sarpiṣprapūra*, found in the quotation from Tīsaṭa's Cikitsākalikā in M. on Mā.ni. 1, 5a-c, is probably a synonym of *ghṛtapūra*). PW : Butterkuchen. MW : a sweetmeat (composed of flour, milk, coconut and ghee). OP, p. 286 : a cake prepared with fine wheat flour mixed with milk and fried in ghee; it is then coated with sugar; it is also called *haviṣpūra*. OP, p. 145, n. 2 (quotation from Śrīkaṇṭhadatta's comm. on the Siddhayoga) : a *haviṣpūra*, called *ghevara* in common language, is made by squeezing fine wheat-flour (*godhūmapaṭaśuddhikā*) with milk, frying it in a copious amount of ghee and adding white sugar to it. Ḍa. on Su.Sū. 46, 293 : wheat-flour, squeezed with milk, coconut and white sugar, plunged into ghee and fried, is the best kind of *ghṛtapūra*; in common language it is called *ghevara*. Ma.nigh., *varga* 11, 62cd-63 : powdered wheat, squeezed with milk, strained, provided with a copious amount of ghee and thereupon mixed with white sugar, is taught to be a *ghṛtapūra* when *karpūra* and *marica* are added to it. Vśs (after giving a recipe similar to that of Ḍa.) : another way (to prepare it) is as follows : take finely powdered wheat and add very clear ghee to it to such an amount that (the flour) will lump together; then one should squeeze it in milk; when it has become a soft mass one should pour ghee into the vessel; when it has been well moistened, making much noise, and has become hot, one should pour off (the fluid); the *ghṛtapūra* will then rise until it has filled the vessel; whatever part of it assumes a coppery colour should be immersed in a paste of candied sugar. Bṛhad-yo.ta. describes various kinds of *ghṛtapūra* (*taraṅga* 16, 201-207). Bpn gives the recipe to make a *pūrikā* (*kṛtānnavarga* 48-50).

cāturjāta

Consists of *elā*, *tvac*, *patra* and *nāgakeśara* (the latter is also called *kesara* or *nāgapuṣpa*); see A.h.Sū. 6, 160; Pr 1690-1691; Dn, *varga* 7, 11; Cikitsākalikā 60 (quoted by He. on A.h.Sū. 6, 160).

caya

I.e. accumulation, and (*pra*)*kopa*, i.e. excitement, of a morbific entity are distinguished as different forms of *vṛddhi*, i.e. increase, of a morbific entity. A.s.Sū. 20, 8 : increase is of two kinds : accumulation and excitement. Ḍa. on Su.Sū. 21, 18 : accumulation is increase in a compact form (*saṃhatirūpa*), excitement is increase in a dissolved form (*vilayanarūpa*). The stages of the process of excitement are described more fully : Su.Sū. 21. See : Dasgupta, H.I.Ph. 2, p. 335, n. 3; Gul 1, p. 572-582; Kutumbiah, p. 71 and 85.

cāṣa

PW : der blaue Holzhäher, Coracias indica. MW : the blue jay. Bhish : the blue jay; acc. to some : a kingfisher. Cakra on Ca.Sū. 27, 36 : = *kanakavāyasa* (variant : *kānanacaṭaka*). Ḍa. on Su.Sū. 29, 29 : = *karaṭāsa*. Ḍa. on Su.Sū. 46, 74 : a *cāṣa* has wings of the colour of sapphire and is called *karaṭāśana* in common language. Aruṇa on A.h.Sū. 6, 49 : = *kikīdivi*.

The bird, designated in PW as *Coracias indica*, is called now *Coracias benghalensis indica* Linnaeus, 1766. Probably *cāṣa* is *C. benghalensis* (Linnaeus, 1758); two subspecies of this bird are common in northern, resp. southern India : *C. benghalensis benghalensis* Linnaeus, 1758 and *C. b. indica* Linnaeus, 1766. It is a striking Oxford-and-Cambridge blue bird with rufous-brown coloured breast and pale blue abdomen and vent; in flight the dark and pale blue portions of the wings flash as brilliant bands (see : Handbook of the birds of India and Pakistan 4, p. 116-119); the subspecies *C. b. affinis* Horsfield, 1839, found in eastern India, is darker and deeper coloured than *benghalensis* or *indica* (see : Handbook 4, p. 119-120). See about the many species of kingfishers found in India : Handbook 4, p. 68-98.

cukra

See *śukta*. Ḍa. on Su.Sū. 42, 11 and 45, 210 : *cukra* = *śukta*.

chedana — unfixing.

PW : vernichtend, entfernend. MW : removing the humors of the body. Kav : cutting away and removing by force (adherent phlegm and other humours). Vśs : annihilating phlegm, etc. Va. 96, 9 = Śārṅga 1, 4, 9cd-10ab = Bhā.pra. 6, 223 : "That which extirpates by force adherent morbific entities, phlegm, etc., is (called) *chedana.*" Ḍa. on Su.Sū. 45, 166 : loosening lumps of phlegm, etc.

chedin — cutting up.

PW : vernichtend, entfernend. MW : removing. Vogel : dissolvent (of lumps). Vśs : bringing about disjunction. Ḍa. on Su.Sū. 45, 134 : cutting up fat, enlarged glands, etc. A.h.Sū. 5, 51, Aruṇa : that which by its sharpness cuts up, (i.e.) disassembles, constituents which are present in the body in a lumped condition, is called *chedin*; Candra : that which unfixes; He. : that which brings about disjunction of phlegm, etc., present in a compact state, is (called) *chedin.*

jatru — collar-bone (clavicle).

See on this term and the problems concerning its interpretation : Filliozat, p. 142, n. 2, and p. 149 (Fr. ed. p. 119, n. 1 and p. 123-124); Hoernle, JRAS, 1906, p. 922-941, Osteology, p. 159-168.

jalaukas — leech.

Leeches and their medicinal employment are described : Su.Sū. 13; A.h.Sū. 26, 35-45; A.s.Sū. 35. See Ainslie 1, p. 191-193; Dutt, MM, p. 276-277; Nadk. 2, p. 167-170.

takra — diluted buttermilk.

PW : Buttermilch zur Hälfte mit Wasser gemischt (nach den Lexicogr. drei Theile Buttermilch mit einem Theile Wasser). MW : buttermilk mixed with (a third part of) water. Dutt, MM, p. 283 : buttermilk with one fourth part of water. OP, p. 174 : curds (*dadhi*) when mixed with water in the ratio of 3 : 1. Su.Sū. 45, 85 : "That which is obtained when the fatty constituents (*sneha*) have been separated by churning, etc., half of it consisting of water and being neither too thick nor too thin, is (called) *takra*; it is sweet, acid and astringent (*tuvara*) as to its taste; that, however, which is produced by churning and (still) contains the fatty constituents while no water is added, is called *ghola*." A.h.Sū. 5, 33cd-34, He. : thick sour milk, when churned, is (called) *takra*; it is of two kinds : diluted or not diluted; when diluted it is of two kinds (again) : containing the fatty constituents or not containing these. Hā. 1, 8, 60ab : it is *udaśvit* when half of it consists of water, and *takra* when it contains one fourth of water. Dravyaguṇa, *kṣīravarga* 30 : together with its fatty constituents (*sara*) and with no water added, it is *ghola*; *takra* contains one fourth of water; when half of it consists of water, it is *udaśvit*; *mathita* is devoid of the essential (= fatty) constituents (*sāra*). Dn, *varga* 6, 211-212 : with twice the amount of water it is *śvetapayas*; when half of it consists of water, it is *udaśvita*; it is *takra* when it is divided into three parts (i.e. when three parts of buttermilk are mixed with one part of water) and it is traditionally called *mathita* when it is not mixed; the watery upper part of *takra* is called *udaśvit*. Ma.nigh., *varga* 8, 110-112ab : (synonyms of buttermilk are) *daṇḍāhata*, *kālaśeya*, *gorasa* and *viloḍita*; together with its fatty constituents (read *sara* instead of *rasa*) and with no water added, it is *ghola*; *mathita* is devoid of fatty constituents; when water is present to the same amount it is *śveta*, but when half of it consists of water it is *udaśvit*; when one fourth consists of water it is *takra*, but others say (it is *takra*) when half of it is water. Bpn, *takravarga* 1-2 : (there are five varieties of buttermilk) : *ghola*, *mathita*, *takra*, *udaśvit* and *chacchikā*; (the whole product), together with its fatty constituents (*sara*) and with no water added, is (called) *ghola*; it is (called) *mathita*, however, when the fatty constituents are absent and when no water is added; it is called *takra* when one fourth of it consists of water, and it is *udaśvit* when half of it is water; it is *chacchikā* when it is deficient as to its essential constituents (*sāra*), when it is very clear and contains an abundant quantity of water. Bho.ku. 1, p. 143 : it has been said by Suṣeṇa that *takra* is of four kinds : *ghola*, *mathita*, *udasvit* and *takra*; *ghola* contains the fatty constituents and is devoid of (an added quantity of) water; *mathita* is devoid of the fatty constituents; when one fourth of it consists of water, it is *udasvit* and when half of it is water, it is (called) *takra*. Bṛhad-yo.ta., *taraṅga* 23, 4cd-7ab : the foremost among the sages, Suśruta and so on, have proclaimed that *takra* is of four kinds : *ghola*, *mathita*, *udaśvit* and *takra*; *ghola* contains the fatty constituents while no water is added, *mathita* is devoid of the fatty constituents, but no water is added to it; *takra* is said to contain one fourth part of water and, as to *udaśvit*, half of it consists of water; Divodāsa, etc. have said that *takra* consists of equal amounts of water and buttermilk and the same (authorities) are of the opinion that *udaśvit* contains one fourth part of water.

Many sources (Hā. 1, 8, 54; Dn, *varga* 6, 214-215; Rn, *varga* 15, 267; Ma.nigh., *varga* 8, 119-120; Bṛhad-yo.ta., *taraṅga* 23, 10-11) distinguish three kinds of *takra* : with all the ghee removed, half of it removed and no ghee removed at all (*samuddhṛtaghṛta, ardhoddhṛtaghṛta, anuddhṛtaghṛta*). The only term corresponding to 'buttermilk' is *mathita*.

tamas

See : *sattva*.

tarpaṇa — satiating (agent).

PW : sättigend. MW : satiating, refreshing. Bhish : a pleasing tonic, a soothing measure. Gul : nourishing. HB, p. 17, n. 43 : *tarpaṇa* are of two kinds : a soothing medicine, or emollient, for external, and a refreshing drink or sherbet for internal application. Kav : that which soothes and promotes nourishment. Vogel : refreshing, satiating. Cakra on Ca.Ci. 4, 30 : *tarpaṇa* is food which satiates. A.h.Sū. 5, 1, Aruṇa : that which eliminates weariness; Candra : that which destroys weariness; He. : that which generates satiety.

tāḍana — a sensation of being thumped.

Ḍa. on Su.Sū. 22, 11 : it means (a sensation) as if one were struck with sticks, etc.

tuṣodaka

PW : saurer Reis- oder Gerstenschleim. MW : sour rice- or barley-gruel. Dutt, MM, p. 12 : other grains besides paddy are sometimes used for acetous fermentation; when the husks of fried *māṣakalāya* (pulse of Phaseolus roxburghii) and barley are boiled together for acetous fermentation, the acid is called *tuṣāmbu* (= *tuṣodaka*). OP, p. 184, n. 4 : a sour gruel prepared with unhusked cereals. Vśs : when fried *māṣa* pods (*māṣatuṣa*) and boiled barley grains, to which powdered (drugs) have been added, are slightly boiled (together) in water, (the fluid) arising from it (after fermentation) is (called) *tuṣodaka*. Śārṅga 2, 10, 11ab : *tuṣāmbu* is the product of fermentation of unboiled grains of barley which have been broken into pieces. Bpn, *saṃdhānavarga* 6 :

tuṣodaka is made with unhusked barley grains which have been broken into pieces. Su.Sū. 44, 40cd-44ab contains the description of the way in which a medicinal *tuṣodaka* is prepared. See also Kav, p. 1982. Compare : *kāñjika*, App. 3 and *māṣakalāya*, App. 4.

tṛpti — a feeling of satiety.

Cakra on Ca.Sū. 4, 8 : a feeling of satiety is that morbid alteration by phlegm, by which one gets the feeling of being satisfied.

triphalā

This term usually designates the fruits of a) *āmalakī*, b) *vibhītakī*, c) *harītakī* (see Dn, *varga* 7, 1 ; Rn, *varga* 22, 1).

dadhi — thick sour milk.

PW : saure Milch ; MW : coagulated milk, thick sour milk (differing from curds in not having the whey separated from it). Dutt, MM, p. 283 : *dadhi* or curdled milk is prepared by adding some acid or a little curdled milk as a ferment to milk previously boiled ; in the course of twelve hours the whole of the milk thus acted upon is changed into a more or less thick, acidulous, jelly-like mass. Cakra on Ca.Sū. 27, 228 distinguishes three kinds of *dadhi* : *mandaka*, i.e. milk already subject to the process of alteration but not yet coagulated ; *jāta*, when it has just coagulated and is of a sweet and somewhat acid taste ; *sujāta*, when it is of a manifestly acid taste. Aruṇa on A.h.Sū. 5, 29cd distinguishes three varieties of *dadhi* : *mandajāta* (= *mandaka*), when the acid taste has not yet become manifest, *samyagjāta*, when the acid taste is manifest, and *atijāta*, when the acid taste has become excessive. Ma.nigh., *varga* 8, 88 enumerates four kinds of *dadhi* : thickened (*styāna*), completely thickened, somewhat thickened milk and *mandaka*. Bpn, *dadhivarga* 3-9 distinguishes five kinds of *dadhi* : *manda*, when the (acid) taste has not yet become manifest and the milk has only somewhat coagulated ; *svādu*, when it has coagulated, is of a sweet (*svādu*) taste and not yet manifestly acid ; *svādvamla*, when it is viscid and sweet, with an astringent after-taste ; *amla*, when the sweet taste has disappeared and the acid taste has become manifest, and *atyamla*, when it has become excessively acid. Bho-ku. 1, p. 135 enumerates the same five varieties as Bpn and so does Bṛhad-yo.ta., *taraṅga* 22, 3-9. The fatty constituents of *dadhi* are called *dadhisāra* or *dadhisneha*.

The upper, dense part of *dadhi* is called *sara* (Cakra on Ca.Sū. 27, 228; Ḍa. on Su.Sū. 45, 78cd-79ab; Aruṇa on A.h.Sū. 5, 29cd-33ab; Bpn, *dadhivarga* 20). *dadhi* should not be translated by curds, for curds are called *gālita(dadhi)*.

dāli

PW : gespaltene Hülsenfrucht. Rn, *varga* 16, 17 : *caṇaka* (chickpeas), etc. are called *dāli* when they have burst open. Bpn, *kṛtānnavarga* 7 : *śamīdhānya* that has burst is called *dāli* or *dālī*.

dīpana — stimulating the (transforming) fire.

PW : das Feuer der Verdauung anzündend, reizend. MW : digestive, stimulating. Dutt, MM, p. 5 : promoting the appetite, but not aiding in digesting undigested food. Gul : digestive, digestive-stimulant, stimulating (the digestive fire). Kav : promoting, increasing the appetite without helping the digestion of undigested food. Va. 96, 1ab = Śārṅga 1, 4, 1ab = Bhā.pra. 6, 212 : "That which will not maturate immature matter, but gives rise to (an increase of the transforming) fire, is (called) *dīpana*."

deśa — place (kind of country).

Three kinds of country are distinguished : *ānūpa* (marshy country), *jāṅgala* (an arid country, sparingly grown with trees and plants, though not unfertile) and *sādhāraṇa* (occupying a middle position, being neither too dry nor too wet). See about these types of country and their characteristics : Ca.Vi. 3, 47-48; Ca.Ka. 1, 8; Su.Sū. 35, 42-43; A.h.Sū. 1, 23-24ab; A.s.Sū. 1, 46-47ab; Hā. 1, 4, 2-7; Dravyaguṇa, *guṇakarmavidhi* 24; Rn, *pariśiṣṭa, varga* 1, 1-7; Bhā.pra. 5, 1-8. The patient himself is also called *deśa*, as the field of action of the physician. See : Jolly, Medicin, p. 39; Kutumbiah, p. 91; Sinh Jee, p. 56-57.

doṣa — morbific entity.

See about the meaning of the term *doṣa* and the doctrine of the three morbific entities (*tridoṣa*) in Indian medicine : Dasgupta, H.I.Ph. 2, p. 325-339; Gul 1, p. 551-560; Hariprapanna, Rasayogasāgara, *upodghāta* p. 40-72; Jolly, Medicin, p. 39-40; Kutumbiah, p. 57-75; Müller, Ueber *pitta* oder Galle, p. 77-84, Ueber die *tridoṣa*-Lehre, SA 32, 1939,

p. 290-314, Grundlagen, p. 63-70, Eigenwertungen, p. 72-76 and 78-91, Wörterheft, p. 105, no. 104; Nobel.

doṣasthāna — the seat of a morbific entity.

The seats of the morbific entities are described : Ca.Sū. 20, 8; Su.Sū. 21, 6-7; A.h.Sū. 12, 1-3; A.s.Sū. 20, 3; Kā.Sū. 27, 7cd-12; Bhā.pra. 3, 109; 3, 122; 3, 128. See : Kutumbiah, p. 67.

dhamanī — duct.

There are twenty-four ducts in the human body acc. to Su.Śā. 9, 3-10, A.h.Śā. 3, 39-40ab and A.s.Śā. 6, 28-33, but their number is two hundred acc. to Ca.Śā. 7, 14 and Kā.Śā. See : Dasgupta, H.I.Ph. 2, p. 344-352; Kav p. 470, note; Filliozat, p. 160-162 (Fr. ed. p. 130-132); Kutumbiah, p. 23-30 and 49-50; Müller, Wörterheft, p. 106, nr. 106; Seal, p. 208-218.

dhātu — element (of the body).

Seven elements of the body are distinguished : *rasa* (nutrient fluid), *rakta* (blood), *māṃsa* (flesh), *medas* (fat), *asthi* (bone), *majjā* (marrow) and *śukra* (semen). These elements are transformed into each other in the order given. During the process of transformation they are separated into a pure portion (*prasāda*) and waste matter (*kiṭṭa*). Each element has its own type of waste matter (see *mala*). Both *prasāda* and *kiṭṭa* may be called *dhātu* when they maintain their proper measure and serve to maintain a healthy state. Moreover, there is the essential part of the food (*āhārarasa*), which is also separated into a pure portion and waste matter, both called *dhātu* when present in their proper measure. Impure matter (*mala*) is a synonym of waste matter (*kiṭṭa*) and styled *maladhātu* when present in a congruous measure. The three morbific entities (*doṣa*) are called *dhātu* when they are in a balanced state. See about *dhātu* : Ca.Sū. 28, 4; Ca.Ci. 15, 15-35; Su.Sū. 14, 3-20; Su.Sū. 15; Su.Sū. 16, 3-6; Su.Sū. 21, 3-4; A.h.Sū. 1, 13; A.s.Sū. 1, 31. Besides the mentioned (chief) elements (of the body), a series of seven additional elements (*upadhātu*) is discerned. This series consists of : milk (*stanya*), the menstrual discharge (*rajas*), muscle-fat (*vasā*), sweat, teeth, the hair and the vital fluid (*ojas*). Milk is the *upadhātu* of the nutrient fluid, the menstrual discharge that of blood, etc. See : Śārṅga 1, 5, 16-17 and Bhā.pra. 3, 210-212. See about *dhātu* : Dasgupta,

H.I.Ph. 2, p. 319-320 and 322-324; Gul 1, p. 551-558; Jolly, Medicin, p. 41-42; Kutumbiah, p. 34-36, 40-43 and 57-61; Müller, Vom Körperaufbau, p. 310-317, Ueber indische Vorstellungen von der Verdauung, p. 203-223, Wörterheft, p. 106-107, nr. 107, Dhātu, PHMA, Heft 7, 1961, p. 3-23, Ueber verschiedene Ergebnisse, p. 106-107; Nobel; Sinh Jee, p. 91-96.

dhānya — grain and pulse.

dhānya is divided into a number of categories; there are several systems of classification : Ca.Sū. 27 : (1) *śūkadhānya* : awned grain, (2) *śamīdhānya* : pulse; Su.Sū. 46 : (1) *śāli* (i.e. *śāli*, *ṣaṣṭika* and *vrīhi*), (2) *kudhānya* (every kind of grain and pulse, except rice); A.h.Sū. 6 and A.s.Sū. 7 : (1) *śūkadhānya*, (2) *śimbīdhānya* (= *śamīdhānya*); Rn, *pariśiṣṭa*, *varga* 16 : (1) *śūkadhānya*, (2) *śimbīdhānya*, (3) *tṛṇadhānya* (grass-like kinds of grain, considered to be of an inferior quality); Ma.nigh., *dhānyavarga* (10), 2-3ab : (1) *śāli* (*raktaśālyādi*), (2) *vrīhi* (*ṣaṣṭikādi*), (3) *vaidala* (*mudgādi*), (4) *tṛṇadhānyaka* = *kṣudradhānya* = *kudhānya* , (5) *śūkadhānya* (*yavādi*); Bpn, *dhānyavarga* : (1) *śāli*, (2) *vrīhi*, (3) *śūkadhānya*, (4) *śimbīdhānya*, (5) *kṣudradhānya* = *kudhānya* = *tṛṇadhānya*.

navānna

Freshly prepared *anna*, i.e. usually boiled rice, but Bho.ku. 1, p. 28 six kinds of *anna* are distinguished. Acc. to T. N. Chakravarti (Bhāratīya Vidyā 12, 1951, p. 9) *navānna* may also mean uncooked new rice.

nāḍī — tubular vessel.

See : Dasgupta, H.I.Ph. 2, p. 344-352; Filliozat, p. 158-159 (Fr. ed. p. 129-130); Karambelkar, p. 94-98; Kutumbiah, p. 27-28.

pataṅga

Flying insect; acc. to PW particularly a moth; acc. to Seal (p. 194) the term designates grasshoppers and locusts.

paramānna

PW : die schönste Speise, Reis in Milch gekocht. MW : "best food", rice boiled in milk with sugar. Gul : milk pudding. Kav : cakes of diverse varieties. OP, p. 289 : it was prepared by boiling four parts (in weight) of rice with twelve parts of milk; six parts of clarified butter and three parts of treacle were added to it (Aṅgavijjā p. 220; Bho.ku. p. 28). Synonyms of *paramānna* are usually : *kṣīrikā, kṣaireyī* and *pāyasa* (Bho.ku., however, distinguishes between *kṣīrikā* and *paramānna*). Bpn, *kṛtānnavarga* 15-16ab : one should boil rice, smeared over with ghee, in pure milk, reduced to half (the original amount) by boiling; when ready, it is called *kṣīrikā*; it is best when white sugar and melted butter are added (= Bho.ku. 1, p. 30). Bho.ku. 1, p. 28 : *paramānna* is traditionally said (to be prepared) with thrice as much milk as rice, ghee (*jīvanīyaka*) to half the amount of the milk and powdered treacle to half the amount of the ghee. Bṛhad-yo.ta., *taraṅga* 16, 38-39 : one should boil eight parts of rice of good quality in milk, reduced to half (its original amount) by boiling; this is traditionally called *paramānna*, when it is neither too thin nor too thick. Ḍa. on Su.Sū. 20, 13 and 46, 425 : rice boiled in milk.

When rice is replaced by pulse the resulting dish is called *avarānna* (Ḍa. on Su.Sū. 46, 491). See about *avarānna* : Gode, St.I.L.H. 3, p. 153-160.

pariṇāma — transformation (by time).

See : *asātmyendriyārthasaṃyoga.*

palala — sesame paste.

palala is a sweetmeat made of ground sesame and sugar; the word also designates sesame paste (PW; MW; Vśs; Rn, *pariśiṣṭa, varga* 16, 5; Ma.nigh., *varga* 11, 141; Bpn, *kṛtānnavarga* 182).

pācana — maturation-promoting.

PW : Verdauung befördernd. MW : digestive. Dutt, MM, p. 5 and Kav : assisting in digesting undigested food, but not increasing the appetite. Gul : digestive, helping the digestion (of food). Va. 96, 1cd = Śārṅga 1, 4, 1cd = Bhā.pra. 6, 213ab : "That which maturates immature matter without giving rise to (increase of the transforming) fire is (called) *pācana*."

pānaka

PW : Trank, Getränk, Tränkchen. MW : drink, beverage, potion.

Kav p. 1951 : *pānaka* is prepared with sugar and water and the juice of Citrus acida. OP : syrup (many kinds of *pānaka* are described : p. 301-303). Vśs : a drink made with savoury (*miṣṭa*) substances, such as crude sugar (*matsyaṇḍikā*); sugar-cane liquor (*pakvarasa*) to which a restricted amount of sugar and the (acid) juice of the *nimbū*(fruit) have been added or some other acid (fruit)juice. Bṛhad-yo.ta., *taraṅga* 16, 12-13ab (closely related to Ma.nigh., *varga* 11, 42-43ab, which reads, erroneously, *arūṣa* instead of *parūṣa*) : water (to which the juice) of grapes, *amlikā*, *parūṣa*, etc. (has been added), mixed with sugar and prepared with *marīca* (black pepper), *ārdraka* (fresh ginger), *karpūra*, *cāturjāta*, etc., is (called) *pānaka*; it is of two kinds (and) distinguished into acid and non-acid (varieties).

pārāvata

PW : Turteltaube. MW : turtle-dove, pigeon. Dn, *varga* 6, 56-59 : the *pārāvata* is a pigeon (*kapotaka*) with red eyes and of a swarthy colour; it is traditionally called *gṛhasvāmin*, *varāroha* and *ghurghurāga*; the domestic pigeon is the white *pārāvata*; the aquatic pigeon is called *jalapārāvata* or *kopin*; another (kind of) pigeon is of an ashy colour, makes the sound *ghūghū* and has smoke-coloured eyes. Rn, *varga* 19, 28-29 : the *pārāvata* makes a low and sweet sound and has ruddy eyes; it is called *madanakākurava* and *kāmin*; the domestic pigeon has red eyes and is called *madanamohanavāc*, *vilāsin* and *kaṇṭhīrava*; the *pārāvata* from another country is called *kāmuka* and *ghullusārava*; the *jalapārāvata* is called *kāmin* and *galarava*. Ma.nigh., *māṃsavarga* 56ab : the *pārāvata* is called *kalarava* (making a low, sweet sound), *mañjughoṣa* and *madotkaṭa*. In my opinion *pārāvata* may designate the blue rock pigeon, *Columba livia neglecta* Hume, 1873, the Indian blue rock pigeon, *C. livia intermedia* Strickland, 1844 and the Eastern stock pigeon, *Columba eversmanni* Bonaparte, 1856 (see : Handbook of the birds of India and Pakistan 3, p. 124-129). It is not clear why PW and MW indicate that it is a turtle-dove. See also : *kapota* and *kāṇakapota*.

piṇyāka

PW, MW and HK : oil-cake. Vśs : the waste matter remaining after the oil has been pressed out of sesame seeds (*tailakiṭṭa*). In agreement with Vśs are : Rn, *varga* 16, 6; Bpn, *kṛtānnavarga* 183ab; Ḍa. on Su.U. 54, 5; Aruṇa on A.h.Sū. 6, 40; He. on A.h.Sū. 6, 34. Ḍa. on Su.Sū. 46, 294 mentions, besides sesame seeds, linseed and mustard seed as a source of *piṇyāka* and Candra on A.h.Sū. 6, 40 linseed (read *kṣauma* instead of *kṣauḍa*). Synonyms of *piṇyāka* are *khala* (Rn), *khali* (Bpn) and *khalī* (Ḍa. on Su.U. 54, 5; Ḍa. adds that it is called *pītā* in common language.

pitta — bile.

The five kinds of bile are described : Su.Sū. 21, 10; A.h.Sū. 12, 10-14; A.s.Sū. 20, 5; Bhā.pra. 3, 121-125. Compare Bhe.Śā. 4, 1-9 and 10-17. See : Bhish 1, Introd. p. 43-46; Gul 1, p. 564-565 and 568-569; Kutumbiah, p. 68-69; Müller, Ueber *pitta* oder Galle, Janus 38, 1934, p. 77-106, Wörterheft, p. 112-113, nr. 123; Sinh Jee, p. 88-89.

piṣṭaka — cake, sweetmeat.

PW : Backwerk, Kuchen. MW : a cake or anything made of flour, pastry. OP, p. 290 : probably cakes made of powdered rice. Chakravarty, p. 6, 7, 45 and 48 : many types of boiled and fried cakes, popularly known in Bengal as *piṭhā*; all kinds of cooked and specially prepared cakes (see the description of the bridal banquet on the occasion of Damayantī's marriage in the Naiṣadhacarita). Śkdr : a product made of ground (rice) grain, etc.; a flour-cake (*pūpa*, *apūpa*, acc. to Amara). Vśs : sesame paste; a particular substance which has to be masticated, made of (rice) grain, etc., reduced to powder. Rn, *pariśiṣṭa, varga* 16, 5 : = *palala*.

piṣṭānna — farinaceous food.

Ḍa. on Su.Sū. 46, 424 : rice-flour (*taṇḍulapiṣṭa*); Ḍa. on Su.U. 54, 4 : rice-flour, etc.

piṣṭikā

PW and MW : a sort of grit. Bpn, *kṛtānnavarga* 40, describes a special kind of *piṣṭaka*, called *piṣṭikā* : "*dāli* that has been deposited in water and the pods (*kañcuka*) of which are afterwards removed is, when thoroughly ground on a stone, called *piṣṭikā* by wise people."

pūga(*phala*) — betel-nut.

The betel-nut is the seed of the palm Areca catechu Linn. It contains a mixture of alkaloids; the principal ones, chemically closely related, are arecaidine, arecoline, gavacine and guvacoline. Arecoline is a parasympathicomimetic substance, which is transformed for the greater part, during the process of chewing, into arecaidine; the betel-nut is chewed because of the stimulating properties of arecaidine, which is almost without parasympathicomimetic action. See : Ainslie 2, p. 268-271; Chopra, Indigenous drugs, p. 280-282; Dutt, MM, p. 250-251; DWH 3, p. 522-532; IRM 1, p. 110-114; Nadk. 1, nr. 219; R. Schmidt, Beiträge zur Flora Sancritica IV : Arekanusz und Betelpfeffer, ZDMG 67, 1913, p. 653-659; Steinegger und Hänsel, Lehrbuch der Pharmakognosie auf phytochemischer Grundlage, 1968, p. 254-256; Tawney-Penzer, The ocean of story, vol. 8, app. 2 : The romance of betel-chewing; Watt CP, p. 83-91.

pūpa(ka)

See : *apūpa.*

pūpălikā

See *apūpa.*

pṛthuka

PW : breitgedrücktes Korn. MW : rice or grain flattened; rice scalded with hot water and then dried over a fire and ground in a mortar. Dutt, MM, p. 270 : paddy is moistened and lightly fried; it is then flattened and husked. Kav p. 50 : in this country, paddy unhusked is boiled, and while still soft, is flattened by pressure; it is then exposed to the sun and dried; p. 377 : *pṛthukā* is ordinarily known by the name of *chidā*; paddy is first boiled, it is then fried a little and flattened with the aid of the husking apparatus; sometimes, again, unripe paddy is brought from the fields and then flattened into *chidā*. OP, p. 290 : rice seeds when moist are slightly parched and flattened by the strokes of a pestle. Vśs : roasted rice or grain. Pr 850 : *pṛthukas* are *cipiṭas*, commonly called *ciṛā*; 1576 : *pṛthuka* = *cipiṭa*. Rn, *pariśiṣṭa, varga* 16, 11ab : (grains of) *vrīhi* rice, half-ripe and heated, are traditionally called *pṛthukas*. Ma.nigh., *varga* 11, 108ab : ripe, wet (grains of) *vrīhi* rice, properly pressed, are known as *pṛthukas*. Bpn, *kṛtānnavarga* 176 : (grains of) *śāli* rice, unhusked, wet, roasted (but) not burst open, and then bruised, are said to be *cipiṭas* and are also traditionally called *pṛthukas* (= Bho.ku. 1, p. 24, with some variants). Cakra on Ca.Sū.

5, 9 : *pṛthuka*s are called *cippiṭa*s in common language; Cakra on Ca.Sū. 27, 273 : *pṛthuka*s are *cipiṭa*s. Ḍa. on Su.Sū. 46, 415 : wet *śāli* rice grains, mildly roasted and partially flattened by strokes with a pestle, are called *pṛthuka*s; Ḍa. on Su.U. 54, 5 : *pṛthuka*s are *cipiṭaka*s. A.h.Sū. 6, 37, Aruṇa : yellowish-green grains, devoid of chaff, roasted and struck with a pestle, are technically called *pṛthuka*s or *cipiṭa*s; Candra : (idem), (but) some say *pṛthuka*s consist of roasted rice; He. : roasted grains (of rice) that has not been dried are (called) *pṛthuka*s.

peyā — thin gruel.

PW : Reisschleim, Reiswasser. MW : rice gruel or any drink mixed with a small quantity of boiled rice. Cakra on Ca.Sū. 27, 250 : a thin gruel is a gruel (*yavāgū*) with a great amount of liquid and a thick gruel (*vilepī*) contains a small quantity of liquid. Ḍa. on Su.Sū. 46, 341cd-342ab : a thin gruel is the same as a gruel; it contains a small quantity of liquid; its upper part is called scum (*maṇḍa*). Su.Sū. 46, 344cd-345ab : "A scum is free from residues (*siktha*) and a gruel contains the residues; it is a thick gruel when it contains a great amount of residual substances and a gruel when it contains a small quantity of liquid." Ḍa. adds that a thick gruel consists of the dense residue and has therefore to be eaten by licking. Because the descriptions mentioned are not very clear, Ḍa. quotes another opinion on the subject : "Solid food (*anna*) should be boiled with five times as much of water, a gruel with six, a scum with fourteen and a thick gruel with four times as much of water." Aruṇa on A.h.Sū. 7, 26cd : a scum, etc. should be understood to be prepared with parched grain (*lājāḥ*), but not, as boiled rice (*odana*), with unparched grain (*taṇḍulāḥ*); as the sage says : "A scum, boiled with parched grain, *amla* and *dāḍima*, to which long pepper and dried ginger have been added, will stimulate the fire and also normalize the wind (Ca.Sū. 27, 256cd and 251cd);" then Aruṇa quotes Su.Sū. 344cd-345ab, gives the recipe for a thin gruel from an unidentified source and also the definition of a scum and a thin gruel according to others. He. remarks on the same passage : the liquid part without a residue is a scum; when it contains the residue it is a gruel; this (latter) is of two kinds : with a small amount of residual substances it is a thin gruel and with a great amount a thick gruel; residues without any liquid are (called) solid food. Śārṅga 2, 2, 152 : "One should boil four *pala*s of a (medicinal) substance in sixty-four *pala*s of water and prepare a dense gruel by boiling it till half of the original quantity remains;" 2, 2, 166cd : "A *vilepī* contains a dense residue and is prepared with four times the amount of water;" 2, 2, 167cd-168a : "Wise men consider a *peyā* to be prepared with fourteen parts of water; it chiefly consists of liquid and contains a very small amount of residue;" 2, 2, 170cd : "A *maṇḍa* contains no residual substances and is prepared with fourteen parts of water." See also : Pr 1642 (*yavāgū*), 1643 (*vilepī*), 1644 (*peyā*), 1645 (*maṇḍa*); Rn, *pariśiṣṭa*, *varga* 20, 52-53; Ma.nigh., *varga* 11, 9ab (*yavāgū*), 9cd (*vilepī*), 10ab (*peyā*), 10cd (*maṇḍa*); Bho.ku. 1, p. 26 and 27; Bṛhad-yo.ta., *taraṅga* 16, 21cd (*yavāgū*), 22cd (*vilepī*), 24ab (*peyā*), 25cd (*maṇḍa*). Compare Dutt, MM, p. 269. Hoernle remarks about gruels (Bower Ms., p. 151, n. 361) : "*yavāgū* properly means a 'gruel made of rice', but it may also be used occasionally of gruels made of other cereals. It is, as a rule, taken warm. There are three kinds : *maṇḍa* or 'liquid', *peyā* or 'drinkable', and *vilepī* or 'viscous', with fourteen, six and four parts of water respectively to one part of rice. The quantity of rice should be one-fourth of that which a person usually consumes for his meal; and for the purpose of a gruel the rice should be crushed. The medicaments added to a gruel may be in the form of either a paste or a decoction, and thence gruels are called *kalkasādhya* and *kvāthasādhya* respectively. When in paste, they should be mixed with the rice, and the whole boiled together; when used in decoction, this should be made first, and afterwards rice put in in the proportions above noted."

peśī — muscle.

The male body counts two hundred muscles, the female twenty more acc. to A.h.Śā. 3, 17cd-18ab and A.s.Śā. 5, 86-91. There are four hundred muscles acc. to Ca.Śā. 7, 14, and their number is five hundred in men and twenty more in women acc. to Su.Śā. 5, 37-41. See: Chakraberty, p. 19-27; Kutumbiah, p. 18-23; Müller, Wörterheft, p. 155, nr. 129.

paiṣṭikā

See *paiṣṭī*.

paiṣṭī

MW : spirituous liquor distilled from rice or other grain. Dutt, MM, p. 273 : spirit distilled from different sorts of grain. OP, p. 299 : *surā* prepared from rice or barley meal. Vśs : an acid, intoxicating beverage prepared from different kinds of grain; it is the least intoxicating among the alcoholic drinks. Rn, *varga* 14, 305-306 (the same statement: Bho.ku. 1, p. 168) : there are three kinds of intoxicating beverage : *gauḍī*, *mādhvī* and *paiṣṭī*; *paiṣṭī* is made from different sorts of grain and the least intoxicating of the three.

prakṛti — constitution.

See : Gul 1, p. 544-551 and 602-610; Kutumbiah, p. 63-66; Müller, Die vermeintlichen "Temperamente" in den indischen wundärztlichen Lehren, Janus 51, 1964, p. 184-192; Sinh Jee, p. 90-91.

prakṛtisamasamavāya

See about this term Ca.Vi. 1, 10 and Cakra's commentary.

prakopa — excitement.

See *caya*.

prajñāparādha — errors in judgment.

See : *asātmyendriyārthasaṃyoga*. See also : Dasgupta, H.I.Ph. 2, p. 415-418; K. Krishnamoorthy, The conception of personality in the Carakasaṃhitā and the concept of *prajñāparādha*, PO 15, 1950, p. 65-89.

prabhā — lustre (of the skin).

Ca.I. 7, 14-15 describes three qualities of the skin : a) *chāyā*, the shade, which depends on the other two qualities and is of five kinds, viz. related to space, air, fire, water or earth; b) *varṇa*, the colour; c) *prabhā*, the lustre, originating from the fiery element and of seven kinds : red, yellow, white, brown, yellowish-green, pale and black. Ca.I. 7, 16 characterizes these qualities as follows : "The shade overcomes the colour, but the lustre reveals it; the shade is noticed when near, but the lustre reveals itself from a distance." Hoernle, Bower Ms., p. 174, n. 472 writes about *chāyā* as follows : "The word *chāyā* has several meanings. In its widest sense it signifies the general appearance of a person, in point of figure, size, colour and lustre; and any morbid or unnatural change in these respects is an indication of approaching death. The 'reflection' of one's appearance with regard to *saṃsthāna* or 'figure' and *pramāṇa* or 'size' as cast in sunshine, water or a mirror, is called *praticchāyā*. *chāyā*, in a narrower sense, is distinguished from it as the appearance of a person in point of *varṇa* or 'colour', and *prabhā* or 'lustre'. Thirdly, *chāyā* signifies the mere *varṇa* or 'colour' (as different in kind : viz., red, yellow, white, blue, green, fallow and black, altogether seven), as distinguished from its *prabhā* or 'light' or 'lustre'. The presence of 'colour' can be recognised from a distance by its 'light', but whether it is of this or that variety (red, yellow, etc.) can only be distinguished when near. Finally, *chāyā* is used in the sense of 'morbid appearance' just as *tṛṣṇā*, 'thirst', has also the sense of 'morbid thirst'."

prabhāva — special faculty.

This concept is treated Ca.Sū. 26, 67-73ab : "When one characteristically observes (in a medicinal substance) a generic similarity of taste, potency and digestive alteration and yet specificity of (its) actions, one traditionally calls this its special faculty. (For example) : *citraka* is regarded to be pungent (in taste), pungent with regard to its digestive alteration, of a hot potency (and useful in treating diarrhoea); *dantī* is the same (as to the enumerated qualities), but it purges a human being by its special faculty. Poison is said to kill poison; (its) special faculty is the cause of that (action); the action (of stimulating movement) in an upward direction and in the natural direction (i.e. downwards) is ruled over by the special faculty. The manifold action of gems (and herbs) which should be worn (on the body) is brought about by their special faculty; special faculty is said to be inconceivable (*acintya*). Thus have been duly illustrated digestive alteration, potency and also special faculty. One (medicinal) substance performs (one) action by its taste and another one by its potency, another (medicinal) substance (does so) by its quality, digestive alteration and special faculty. When taste, etc. are in a congruous state with regard to their force, (the due order of their) inborn force (*naisargikaṃ balam*) is (as follows) : digestive alteration displaces taste, potency (displaces) both (taste and digestive alteration) and the special faculty displaces (all of) these." Cakra comments : "... That effect, which cannot accurately be determined by (considering it) as an effect of taste, etc., is pointed out as being brought about by the special faculty. For that very reason it has been stated that the special faculty is said to be inconceivable; this means that it is inconceivable as an effect of taste, potency and digestive alteration. He (i.e. Caraka) gives many examples because this very (concept) is difficult to understand ..."

A.h.Sū. 9, 25 and A.s.Sū. 17, 25cd-26ab are identical with Ca.Sū. 26, 27cd-33ab. A.h.Sū. 9, 26-27ab = A.s.Sū. 17, 45-46ab : "The specific action which occurs when taste, etc. are in a congruous state, arises from the special faculty. Though *dantī* is comparable to *citraka* as to taste, etc., it has a purgative action; the same applies to *mṛdvīkā* (grapes), (when compared) with *madhuka* (liquorice), and ghee is, (compared) with milk, a stimulant of the (transforming) fire;" Aruṇa comments : "The special faculty of a substance is its very nature, outstanding above qualities such as taste, potency, digestive alteration, etc." See also Śārṅga 1, 2, 21cd-23ab = Bhā.pra. 1, 6, 246cd-248. The term *prabhāva* is also used in a more general sense, designating the power (*śakti*) of a medicinal substance and of an illness (see Ca.Vi. 1, 12-24 and Cakra's comment). See : Dasgupta, H.I.Ph. 2, p. 362-366; Kutumbiah, p. 114-116; Sinh Jee, p. 116-117.

pramāṇa — a means of acquiring valid knowledge.

Ca.Vi. 8 describes four means of acquiring valid knowledge : (1) direct apprehension (*pratyakṣa*) : 8, 39; (2) inference (*anumāna*): 8, 40; (3) comparison (*aupamya*) : 8, 42; (4) trustworthy tradition (*etihya*) : 8, 41. See : Dasgupta, H.I.Ph. 2, p. 373-377; Gul 1, p. 459-463; Kutumbiah, Gener. Introd. p. 24-25, and p. 93-95.

phalāmla

See also *amla*. Vśs : the group of fruits characterized by an acid taste. Cakra on Ca.Ka. 1, 12 : the juice of *dāḍima*, etc. Ḍa. on Su.Sū. 46, 420 : *bījapūra*, etc.

babhru

PW and MW : a kind of large ichneumon; any ichneumon. Vśs : = *nakula* (ichneumon). Kohl (Asiatica, Festschr. Weller, 1954, p. 374) : *nakula* = *Herpestes griseus* or *Mungo mungo*. [Both *Herpestes griseus* and *Mungos mungo* are obsolete names : *Herpestes edwardsi lanka* (Wroughton, 1915) = *H. griseus* Kelaart, 1852; *H. edwardsi edwardsi* (Geoffroy, 1818) = *Mungos mungo ellioti* Wroughton, 1915; *H.*

edwardsi nyula (Hodgson, 1836) = *Mungos mungo moerens* Wroughton, 1915; *H. edwardsi ferrugineus* Blanford, 1874 = *Mungos mungo pallens* Ryley, 1914]. Cakra on Ca.Sū. 27, 35 : it is an exceedingly hairy dog (*kukkura*) in Parvatopakaṇṭha; acc. to others it is a large *nakula*; Cakra on Ca.Sū. 30, 77 : a large *nakula*. A.h.Sū. 6, 48, Aruṇa : = *jāhaka*, acc. to others = *nakula*; Candra : = *nakula*; He. : = *acchabhalla*.

It is generally assumed that *babhru* and *nakula* designate Indian species of *Herpestes* (mongoose) and there is no reason to doubt this. Six species of *Herpestes* are found in India : *Herpestes edwardsi* (Geoffroy, 1818), *H. auropunctatus* (Hodgson, 1836), *H. vitticollis* Bennett, 1835, *H. fuscus* Waterhouse, 1838, *H. urva* (Hodgson, 1836), and *H. smithi* Gray, 1837. The largest species is *H. vitticollis*. Very common are the rather large common mongoose, *H. edwardsi*, and the much smaller small Indian mongoose, *H. auropunctatus* (see Prater, The book of Indian animals, p. 96-105).

basti

An instrument, made from the bladder of an animal, with a syringe attached to it, used to bring medicated substances into the rectum, urethra and vagina. Dutt, MM, p. 17 : "A tube with a membranous bag tied to its end. The bag was recommended to be made of the bladder of some animal, such as a bull, goat, etc. It was filled with the fluid to be injected and tied to one end of a tube, about eight inches long and with a tapering rounded extremity for introduction into the rectum. Injections into the urethra and vagina were thrown in by similar contrivances, the tubes being adapted in length and thickness to the passages for which they were intended." The term *basti* also designates the fluid content of the instrument. There are two kinds of *basti*, distinguished with respect to the kind of fluid used : (1) *anuvāsana*, also called *snehabasti* : an oleaginous enema; only oleaginous substances are used for it; (2) *āsthāpana*, also called *nirūha* : a corrective enema; other liquids, besides oleaginous substances, may be used for it; there are two kinds of *āsthāpana* : a) *basti* in a restricted sense, designating a clyster per anum, b) *uttarabasti*, designating a fluid brought into the urethra. See about the application of *basti*s, their classification and the rules about their use : Ca.Si. 3-5; Su.Ci. 35-38; A.h.Sū. 19; A.s.Sū. 28; Bhe.Si. 5-8; Ka.Si. 2; Kā.Si. 5-8; Kā.Khi. 8; Hā. 4, 3. See : HB, p. 105, n. 142; Jolly, Medicin, p. 26-27.

bisa — mṛṇāla

See also *śālū(ka)*. There is much confusion about the exact meaning of these terms, as is clearly visible from the material collected: PW : *bisa* : Wurzelschoss, Untergrundstengel des Lotus; die jungen Wurzelschosse des Nelumbium und einiger Nymphaeen (namentlich N. edulis) [N. lotus Linn. = N. edulis DC.] so wie die im Boden befindlichen Theile des Stengels werden mit Vorliebe gegessen (Roxb.), und scheinen schon in frühester Zeit als Leckerbissen gegolten zu haben; *mṛṇāla* : die essbare röhrige an den Knoten mit Fasern besetzte Wurzel der Lotusarten. MW : *bisa* : a shoot or sucker, the film or fibre of the water-lily or lotus, also the stalk itself or that part of it which is underground (eaten as a delicacy); *mṛṇāla* : the edible fibrous root of some kinds of lotus, a lotus-fibre, fibre attached to the stalk of a water-lily. Bhish : *bisa* : bulb of the lotus plant; *mṛṇāla* : the upper stem of the lotus plant; vol. 1, p. 525, footnote : certain authorities aver that the inner lining or membranous fibres of a lotus-stem are called *bisa*, the outer covering being known as *mṛṇāla*. Dutt, MM, p. 110 : *mṛṇāla* is the leaf-stalk of Nymphaea lotus Linn., N. stellata Willd. and N. rubra Roxb. HB, p. 166, n. 435 : *bisa* is the root-stalk or scape, i.e. that part of the stalk which is embedded in the ground down to the roots; hence *bisagranthi* is the same as *padmamūla*, i.e. properly, the knots of the underground stalk; it is opposed to *mṛṇāla*, the above-ground, or leaf-stalk. HK : *bisa* : grobe Lotusstengel; *mṛṇāla* : Blattstengel von *kamala* = *padma*, feine Lotusstengel. See also : Bosch, De gouden kiem, p. 9; id., The golden germ, p. 23 ff.

Besides *bisa* and *mṛṇāla* the following terms are used to designate parts of a lotus or water-lily : (*padma-*, etc.) *kanda*, *tantu*, *nāla* and *mūla*, moreover *śālū(ka)* and *bisāṇḍa*.

Pr 676 : *mṛṇāla* = *padmamūla*; 677 : *bisa* = *padmakanda*; 678 : *nāla* is (the stalk) to which the flowers, etc. are attached (*puṣpādibandhana*). Dn, *varga* 4, 161 and Rn, *varga* 10, 258 : *bisa*, *mṛṇāla* and *padmanāla* are synonyms. Rn, *varga* 10, 258 : *padmatantu* = *bisa*. Ma.nigh., *varga* 3, 83 : *bisa* = *mṛṇāla*; *padmādimūla* = *śālūka*. Su.Sū. 46, 464 enumerates *mṛṇāla*, *bisa* and *śālūka* as three separate items; Ḍa. observes : *mṛṇāla* = *padmanāla*, *bisa* = *bhisāṇḍaka*, *śālūka* is well known. Ḍa. comments on Su.Sū. 46, 298 : *bisa* is the root (*mūla*) of *padma*, but others say that it is the gross stalk (*sthūlapadmanāla*); *mṛṇāla* is the gross offshoot of the root of *padma* (*padmamūlāt sthūlaprarohaḥ*), but others say that it is the fine stalk (*sūkṣmaṃ nālam*); Ḍa. on Su.U. 54,

14 : *bisa* = *bisāṇḍaka*. A.h.Sū. 6, 91, Aruṇa and Candra : *mṛṇāla* is of two kinds, fine and gross; the fine one is (called) *mṛṇāla* (in its proper sense), the gross one *bisa*; He. : *mṛṇāla* is the fine and *bisa* the gross root of *kamala*. It is difficult to determine the meaning of the mentioned terms with certainty and the commentators are of little help on account of their disagreeing opinions. Nevertheless there are some terms which may be assigned to a part of a particular type of plant with some degree of accuracy. The genus Nymphaea possesses creeping rootstocks; the rootstock of N. lotus Linn. is tuberous, short, erect and roundish, that of N. stellata Willd. is ovoid, short and acute; Nelumbium speciosum Willd., however, has a slender, elongated, much-branched and creeping rhizome, sending out roots at the nodes (see Cooke 1, p. 26-28; Duthie 1, p. 33-35; Hooker 1, p. 114-115). From these data we may infer that *padmakanda*, *bisāṇḍaka* and *bhisāṇḍaka* designate the rootstock of species of Nymphaea. It may be that *bisa* refers to the rootstock of Nymphaea and *mṛṇāla* to the slender rhizome of Nelumbium, but this is not certain; another possibility is that *bisa* designates the gross and *mṛṇāla* the fine parts of the rhizome of Nelumbium, or *mṛṇāla* is a term for the roots sent out from the nodes of the rhizome, and this does not exhaust the number of possible interpretations. *nāla* probably means the stalk of the leaves and flowers of Nymphaea and Nelumbium. Acc. to Rau (Asiatica, Festschrift Weller, 1954, p. 511) Indian poets distinguished species of Nymphaea from Nelumbium.

buddhi

See about *buddhi* in Indian medicine : Dasgupta, H.I.Ph. 2, p. 340-342; Müller, Manas und der Geist altindischer Medizin, NAL, NF, vol. 15, nr. 108, 1952, p. 269-305; Wörterheft, p. 119-120, nr. 143.

bṛṃhaṇa — roborant.

PW : feist machend, kräftigend, nährend. MW : making big or fat or strong, nourishing. Gul : nourishing, roborant. HB : a medicine to promote bulk. Kav : promoting nutrition and bulk, increasing corpulency. Vogel : nutritious, nourishing. Rn, *pariśiṣṭa*, *varga* 20, 78 : that which bestows a well-nourished appearance, that which makes one well-fed and bestows plumpness (to the body). Ca.Sū. 22, 10ab : "That which generates bulkiness of the body is (called) *bṛṃhaṇa*" (compare the similar statement in A.h.Sū. 14, 2). Ḍa. on Su.Sū. 45, 112 : it is (called) *bṛṃhaṇa*, because it, as an agent nourishing the elements, leads to robustness of the body; Ḍa. on Su.Sū. 46, 102 : bringing about increase of the body; Ḍa. on Su.Sū. 46, 411 : bringing about (increase of the element) flesh.

bṛṃhaṇa is opposed to *lekhana* (Ḍa. on Su.Sū. 45, 112 and 46, 411); acc. to A.h.Sū. 14, 1-2 it is synonymous with *saṃtarpaṇa* and the opposite of *apatarpaṇa* = *laṅghana*. See : Kutumbiah, p. 138-139.

bhūta

See : Filliozat, Kumāratantra (esp. p. 24-28); Müller, Wörterheft, p. 121, nr. 147.

bhedana — loosening (impure matter).

PW : Stockungen oder Anhäufungen der Excretionen des Körpers lösend. MW : loosening (the faeces), cathartic, purgative. Gul : disruptive, loosening, laxative. Kav p. 345 and 451 : purging the intestines without producing watery motions. Va. 96, 5 = Śārṅga 1, 4, 5cd-6ab = Bhā.pra. 6, 217 : "That which bound or not bound impure matter, etc., lumped together by (the action of) the morbific entities, loosens and makes it move downwards, is (called) *bhedana*."

bhramara

See also : *madhu*. A large black bee, probably *Apis dorsata* Fabr. (see Watt CP, p. 123-124). Su.Ka. 8, 8cd-12ab : a *bhramara* is one of the twenty-four *kīṭas* which are of a fiery nature.

makara

PW : 1) ein best. Meerthier (das auch an's Land kommen soll), vielleicht Delphin.
2) ein best. Insect oder ein anderes kleines Thier.

MW : 1) a kind of sea-monster (sometimes confounded with the crocodile, shark, dolphin, etc.).
2) a partic. species of insect or other small animal.

Bhish : a dolphin, shark or a shark with a proboscis; alligator ? (vol. 2, p. 695). Kohl (Asiatica, Festschr. Weller, 1954, p. 366-368) suggests that a *makara* may be a dugong, i.e. a sea-cow, *Dugong dugon* (Statius Müller, 1776) (see : Prater, The book of Indian animals, p. 315-316). Ḍa. on Su.Ka. 3, 5 : some say a *makara* is an aquatic animal, others (say that it is) a *kīṭa*, enumerated as being of the fiery type (and called) *makara* because it has the form of a *makara*, others again say that it is a *karkaṭavṛścika* (i.e. a kind of scorpion ?). Su.Ka. 8, 8cd-12ab : a *makara* is one of the twenty-four *kīṭas* of a fiery nature. The aquatic animal called *makara* may be *Crocodilus porosus porosus* Schneider, 1801 (J. Ph. Vogel, BSOAS 20, 1957, p. 561-564).

makṣikā

See ch. 1, n. 14 and *madhu*. Su.Ka. 8, 35 enumerates six kinds of *makṣikā*.

maṇḍa — scum.

See : *peyā*.

maṇḍūka — frog.

Frogs belong to the class of animals called *bileśaya*, i.e. living in hollows (Ca.Sū. 25, 39), or *bhūmiśaya*, i.e. living on the ground (Ca.Sū. 27, 38). Different kinds of frogs are distinguished (Su.Ka. 8, 31 ; Rn, *varga* 19, 497). Synonyms of *maṇḍūka* are enumerated : Pr 764 ; Dn, *varga* 6, 486 ; Rn, *varga* 19, 496.

matkuṇa

This word probably means : a bug. Rn, *varga* 19, 12 enumerates as synonyms of *matkuṇa* : *raktapāyin* (blood-drinking), *raktāṅga* (having a red body) and *mañcakāśrayin* (having a couch for its residence).

madirā

PW : ein geistiges Getränk. MW : spirituous liquor, any inebriating drink, wine. HB : distilled liquor. Kav : wine. OP, p. 299 : cream of *surā*. Cakra on Ca.Sū. 27, 180 : *madirā* is the scum (*maṇḍa*) of *surā*. Pr 1656 : *madirā* = *prasannā*. Dutt, MM, p. 274 : *prasannā* is the clear upper portion of *surā*, but acc. to some it is liquor distilled from rice with the addition of medicinal herbs. The method of preparation of *prasannā* is described : Kauṭ. 2, 25, 18 (text p. 79 ; transl. Kangle p. 177 ; transl. J. J. Meyer p. 186 ; transl. Sham. p. 132).

madya — intoxicating beverage.

Dutt, MM, p. 273 : all fermented and distilled liquors causing intoxication are called *madya* or *madirā* in Sanskrit. OP, p. 75 : strong liquors are called *madya*. See the article *madya* in Vś. Su.Sū. 45, 170, Ḍa. : intoxicating beverages are of three types, (i.e.) prepared from flour, grapes or treacle; Su.Sū. 46, 120 : in *madya* the solid and the fluid ingredients are present to an equal degree. A.h.Sū. 5, 62, He. : *madya* is a fermented liquid prepared from grapes, etc. See : P. Aalto : Madyam apeyam, Comm. Vol. J. Nobel, 1959, p. 17-37.

madhu — honey.

Several varieties of honey are distinguished : Ca.Sū. 27, 243-244 : "*mākṣika, bhrāmara, kṣaudra* and *pauttika* are the (four) classes of honey; *mākṣika* is the best of these and *bhrāmara* is especially heavy; *mākṣika* has the colour of (sesame) oil, *pauttika* that of ghee, *kṣaudra* is monkey-coloured and *bhrāmara* is said to be white." Cakra remarks : *makṣikā*s are tawny (bees); *bhramara*s are well known; *kṣaudra* is made by small (*kṣudra*) *makṣikās*; *puttikās* are large, tawny *makṣikās*. Su.Sū. 45, 133 : "The eight classes of honey are : *pauttika, bhrāmara, kṣaudra, mākṣika, chātra, ārghya, auddālaka* and *dāla*." Ḍa. remarks : (1) *puttikā*s are large, tawny *makṣikās*; others say that *puttikā*s are *makṣikā*s of a black colour that resemble *maṣaka*s (a *maśaka* is a stinging gnat or fly); (2) *bhramara*s are well known; (3) *kṣudrā*s are completely tawny, very small *makṣikās*; (4) *makṣikā*s (in a restricted sense) are large and of a tawny colour; others say that they are exceedingly small; (5) that (kind of honey) which is made (in a nest) of the form of a parasol (or : mushroom, *chatraka*) by (*makṣikā*s) of a yellow and tawny colour, called *baga* in common language, in the forests of the Himālaya and in those of Mālava, is called *chātra*; (6) that (honey) which is produced from the flowers of the *madhūka* trees in Jaratkārvāśrama ('Jaratkāru's hermitage', the name of a locality), is *ārghya* honey, called *śvetaka* (white) by the people of Mālava; others say that *ārghya* is produced by (*makṣikā*s) called *arghā*, which have sharp mouth-parts (*tīkṣṇatuṇḍa*), are of a yellow colour and resemble *ṣaṭpada*s ('six-footed' animals); (7) the *uddālaka*s are very small, monkey-coloured *kīṭa*s which usually accumulate honey (called *auddālaka*) in termitaries; (8) *dāla* : a *dala* is a petal (*patra*) and (the honey) which is present on (these petals) is (called) *dāla*, but others say that completely tawny, very small *makṣikās*, usually living in the hollows of trees, are called *dalas*. A.s.Sū. 6-98 distinguishes the same four varieties of honey as Ca.; A.h. does not mention them. Dravyaguṇa, *aikṣavādivarga* 18-19 = Ca.Sū. 27, 243-244. Dn, *varga* 6, 234-236 : "*mākṣika, bhrāmara, kṣaudra, pauttika, chātraka, arghya, auddālaka* and *dāla* are the eight classes of honey; *mākṣika* is of the colour of (sesame) oil, *kṣaudra* is monkey-coloured, *pauttika* is of the colour of ghee and *bhrāmara* is said to be white; (the honey) called *chātra* is slightly yellow, that (kind) called *arghya* tawny, *auddāla* resembles gold and *dāla* is said to be pale red (*pāṭala*)." Rn, *varga* 14, 272-282ab = Bho.ku. 1, p. 165 : "That honey which is produced by large, monkey-coloured bees of the forest (*vanamakṣikā*), feeding on the juice of various flowers, is called *mākṣika*. That honey which is produced by *bhramaras*, which have the hue of a round lump (*gola*) of glossy (*snigdha*) *añjana* and are wholly devoted to the nectar of flowers, is called *bhrāmara*. That honey which is produced by very small, tawny *makṣikās*, generally known as *kṣudrās*, is called *kṣaudra*. The honey produced by the tawny *makṣikās* which arise from food and are known as *puttikās*, is called *pauttika* by wise men. The honey produced by those bees (*saraghā*) of a yellow and tawny colour, which make a nest (*paṭala*) of the form of a parasol (or : mushroom), is called *chātraka*. The honey made by *makṣikās* with sharp mouth-parts, which resemble *ṣaṭpadas*, is called *arghya*, because it is valuable. The honey produced in the interior of termitaries by tawny *kīṭas* which make the earth burst and are called *auddālas*, is said to be *auddālaka*. The honey accumulated in the interior of the cavities of trees by very small *makṣikās* which look like pieces of sapphire (*indranīladala*), is called *dāla*. Thus has been told, in due order, the production of this (honey) of eight varieties. *mākṣika* is of the colour of (sesame) oil, *bhrāmara* is said to be white, *kṣaudra* has a tawny colour, *pauttika* resembles ghee, *chātra* is slightly yellow, *arghya* is tawny, *auddāla* resembles gold and *dāla* is slightly yellow." See also Hā. 1, 18, 1 and 8; Bpn, *madhuvarga* 6-24; Rā.va.nigh., *pariccheda* 3, 333-338; Bṛhad-yo.ta., *taraṅga* 29, 1-3. See about Indian bees and their honey : Ainslie 1, p. 172-174; Dutt, MM, p. 278-279; IRM 1, p. 166-172; Nadk. 2, p. 191-193; Watt CP, p. 123-129. Acc. to Watt (CP, p. 124) there are three kinds of honey-bees in India : (1) *Apis dorsata* Fabr.; this is probably the *bhramara*; (2) *Apis indica* Fabr., a smaller species; one of its names is *ṣaṭpada*; (3) *Apis florea* Fabr., the smallest species, about the size of the domestic fly.

madhūlaka

Cakra on Ca.Sū. 27, 170 : *madhūlaka* (m.) is a distinct kind of wheat; the intoxicating beverage made from it is (called) *madhūlaka* (n.); others, however, call it *medaka*. Ḍa. on Su.Sū. 45, 179 : *madhūlaka* (m.) is a very small kind of wheat, called *piśikā* in Madhyadeśa, or it is the grass called *markaṭahasta*; the ferment made from its seeds is (called) *madhūlaka* (n.); Jejjhaṭa says it is the intoxicating beverage made from *madhūka* flowers, when not completely fermented.

manas

See about *manas* in Indian medicine : Dasgupta, H.I.Ph. 2, p. 340-342 and 366-373; Müller, Vom *manas* (Geist) und seinen Krankheiten in der altindischen Medizin, Janus 39, 1935, p. 74-93, Manas und der Geist altindischer Medizin, NAL, NF, vol. 15, nr. 108, 1952, p. 269-305, Wörterheft, p. 122, nr. 151.

marman — vital point.

The vital points are one hundred and seven in number. See about these : Ca.Śā. 7, 14; Su.Śā. 6; A.h.Śā. 4; A.s.Śā. 7. Ca. distinguishes three principal vital points, called *mahāmarman* : head, heart and bladder (Ci. 26, 1-3), but also enumerates six principal vital points (Śā. 7, 9). A.s. makes mention of seven principal vital points (Śā. 5, 59-60). Kā. remarks (*śārīrasthāna*) that head, heart and bladder are the three principal vital points. See : Dasgupta, H.I.Ph. 2, p. 352; Filliozat, p. 163-164 (Fr. ed. p. 133-134); Kutumbiah, p. 146-155.

mala — impurity.

The impurities are described : Ca.Sū. 28, 4 : the ingested food is separated into a pure portion (*prasāda*) which is called *rasa*, and waste matter (*kiṭṭa*); the *rasa* of the food (*āhārarasa*) is transformed into the element *rasa* (the nutrient fluid), and so on (see : *dhātu*); the *āhārarasa*, the element *rasa* and each of the subsequent elements have their own form of waste matter (*kiṭṭa*), called impure matter (*mala*); these impurities consist of : sweat, urine, faeces, flatus (*vāta*), bile, phlegm, the impurities of the ears, eyes, nose, mouth, pores of the hairs and generative organs, the hairs of the head, the beard, the body-hair, the nails, etc. Ca.Ci. 15, 18-19ab : the waste matter of the food consists of faeces and urine, that of the nutrient fluid is phlegm, of blood it is bile, of flesh it is the particular impurities (*svamala*, i.e. those of the ears, eyes, nose, mouth and generative organs), of fat it is sweat, of the bones it consists of the hair of the head and the body-hair, of marrow it consists of the fatty substance of the eyes and the skin. Ca.Śā. 6, 17 : impure constituents of the body are those which bring trouble to the body; they consist of : the excretions (*upadeha*) which come out of the various openings of the body, elements which have become putrescent (*paripakva*, i.e. overripe), excited wind, bile and phlegm and all the other constituents present in the body, of whatever kind they may be, that injure it; all those (constituents) are designated as impure matter. Su.Sū. 46, 528a and 529 : faeces and urine are the impurities (derived) from the food; the impurities of the elements (of the body) are, in due order, phlegm, bile, the impure matter of the openings (of the body), sweat, nails and body-hair, and (finally) the impure matter of the eyes and the fatty substance of the skin. (Su.Sū. 46, 529 = Śārṅga 1, 5, 15 = Bha.pra. 3, 209). A.h.Śā. 3, 61cd and 63cd-64ab : the transparent part of the waste matter of the food is urine, the dense part consists of faeces; the impurities of the elements (of the body) are, in their due order, phlegm, bile, the impurities of the openings (of the body), sweat, nails and body-hair, the fatty matter of the excretions of the eyes and the skin and (finally) the vital fluid (as the impurity of the element semen). A.s.Śā. 6, 65-66 : the transparent part of the waste matter of the food is urine, the dense part consists of faeces; the impure matter of the nutrient fluid consists of phlegm and *lasīkā* (serous fluid), of blood it is bile, of flesh it consists of the impurities of the ears, eyes, nose, mouth, pores of the hair and generative organs, of fat it is sweat, of the bones it consists of the hairs of the head, the body-hair and the nails, of marrow it consists of the impure matter of the eyes and the fatty substance of the skin; the essential part of semen is the vital fluid; because (semen) is very pure, it has no impure matter; others say that the essential part of semen is the germ (of the embryo).

Another series of impurities is enumerated : Śārṅga 1, 5, 13-14 : the following impurities arise from the seven elements (of the body), in their due order : the water of the tongue, eyes and cheeks (arises from the nutrient fluid), the colouring bile (from the blood), the impure matter in the ears (arises from flesh), the impure matter of the tongue, teeth, armpits, penis, etc. (from fat), nails (arise from the bones), the impure matter of the eyes and the oleaginous matter in the mouth (arise from marrow) and pustules (*piṇḍikā*) (arise from semen). Different again is the enumeration found Manusmṛti 5, 135. The term *mala* may also designate an excited morbific entity; see e.g. Śārṅga 1, 5, 23. Rather often it occurs that 'the impurities' in a more restricted sense designate : flatus, urine and faeces. See about *mala* : Dasgupta, H.I.Ph. 2, p. 327; Gul 1, p. 551-558; Kutumbiah, p. 43-44; 58-60; Müller, Wörterheft, p. 123, nr. 154.

mastu

= *dadhimaṇḍa* = *dravadadhi*.

PW : saurer Rahm (*dadhimaṇḍa* : das Obere von saurer Milch); nach einigen Erklärern : Molken. MW : sour cream; the watery part of curds, whey. Dutt and Gul : whey. HK : saurer Rahm. Kav : barm of curds. Pr 844, Bpn, *dadhivarga* 20 and Bṛhad-yo.ta., *taraṅga* 22, 21 : *mastu* is the scum (*maṇḍa*) of thick sour milk. Dn, *varga* 6, 200 and Bho.ku. 1, p. 142 : *mastu* is the lower, watery part of thick sour milk. Cakra on Ca.Sū. 27, 228 and Ca.Ni. 2, 4 : *mastu* = *dadhimaṇḍa*. Ḍa. on Su.Sū. 45, 90cd : *mastuka* = *maṇḍa* : the transparent part of thick sour milk when in the stage called *sujāta*. Aruṇa on A.h.Sū. 5, 29cd-33ab : the lower portion of thick sour milk in the stages called *sujāta* and *atyamla*. He. on A.h.Sū. 5, 35ab : the liquid part of thick sour milk when it is *sujāta*.

mahābhūta — gross element.

See about the gross elements in Indian medicine : Kutumbiah, p. 36-37, 58, 64-65, 116-118; Müller, Grundlagen, p. 58-60, Manas und der Geist altindischer Medizin, p. 269-305, Eigenwertungen, p. 98-102, Wörterheft, p. 124, nr. 156, Ueber verschiedene Ergebnisse, p. 105-106; Seal, p. 56-61.

mādhvīka

PW and MW : a kind of intoxicating drink. Vśs : (1) an *āsava* made from honey; (2) an intoxicating beverage prepared from *madhūka* flowers; (3) an intoxicating beverage in general; (4) an intoxicating beverage made from grapes. Pr 1661 : an intoxicating beverage made from honey. Cakra on Ca.Sū. 27, 188 : an *āsava* in which honey is the predominant ingredient.

māñjiṣṭha — madder-coloured.

The roots of *mañjiṣṭhā* (see App. 4) contain a dye, alizarin, formerly much employed by the Indians. See Watt CP, p. 926-927.

mṛṇāla

See : *bisa*.

medaka

PW and MW : spirituous liquor used for distillation. Dutt, MM, p. 274 : the liquor distilled from rice receives different names according to its consistence; the clear transparent fluid which floats on the top is called *prasannā*; that below it, is called *kādambarī*; *jagala* is a thicker fluid than *kādambarī*; *medaka* is the thickest and weakest of all. Pr 1662 : *medaka* = *jagala*. Ma.nigh., *varga* 8, 171cd-172ab : *prasannā* is the scum of *surā*; *kādambarī* is more dense than (*prasannā*); the portion lower than (*kādambarī*) is called *jaṅgala* (= *jagala*) and *medaka* is more dense than *jagala* (compare Śārṅga 2, 10, 5-6; see : *surā*). Cakra on Ca.Sū. 25, 49 : *medaka* is *śvetasurā*, called *jagala*. Aruṇa on A.h.Sū. 5, 68 : *medaka* is the lower part of *jagala*, and *jagala* is the dense, lower part of *vāruṇī*. Kauṭ. 2, 25, 17 (text p. 79; transl. Kangle p. 177; transl. J. J. Meyer, p. 186-187; transl. Sham. p. 132-133) : *medaka* is prepared with one *droṇa* of water, half an *āḍhaka* of rice and three *prasthas* of *kiṇva*; Kauṭ. 2, 25, 27 : the formula for the requisite spices (*saṃbhāra*) to be added to *medaka* is : five *karṣas* of each of (the following items) : *pāṭhā*, *lodhra*, *tejovatī*, *elāvāluka*, *madhuka*, *madhurasā*, *priyaṅgu*, *dāruharidrā*, *marica* and *pippalī*.

maireya

PW : ein aus Zucker und andern Stoffen bereitetes berauschendes Getränk. MW : a kind of intoxicating drink (acc. to Suśr., Sch. a combination of *surā* and *āsava*). Dutt, MM, p. 274 : a sort of spirituous liquor from the blossoms of Lythrum fruticosum with sugar, etc. Vśs : a particular kind of *surā*, prepared by fermentation of a mixture consisting of *dhātakī* flowers, treacle and *dhānyāmla*; or it is made by mixing *surā* and *āsava* which have been prepared separately, and having this mixture ferment again, adding honey to it (afterwards). Pr 1664 : *maireya* is made from *dhātakī* flowers, treacle and *dhānyāmla*. See also Ma.nigh., *varga* 8, 178-181. Ca.Sū. 27, 187, Cakra : the mixture of both *āsava* and *surā*, put in one vessel, should be known (after it has fermented again) as *maireya*, which is related to both (these drinks). Su.Sū. 45, 170, Ḍa. : mention is made of that *āsava* which has a threefold matrix and is called *maireya*; *maireya*, taken in that sense, arises when *surā* and *āsava*, prepared separately and mixed together, are made to ferment again; *surā* is prepared from flour (*surā paiṣṭī*); *āsava* from treacle and honey should be added (to *maireya*); in that way it has a threefold matrix; or, there are two kinds of *maireya*, (i.e.) in the case that (it is prepared) by fermentation of a mixture of *paiṣṭī*, *madhvāsava* (an *āsava* prepared from honey) and treacle.

A.h.Sū. 5, 75cd, Aruṇa : *maireya* is prepared from *kodrava* grain. A.h.Sū. 7, 40, Aruṇa : *maireya* is an *āsava* prepared from *kharjūra*. He. : according to Candranandana *maireya* is *dhānyāsava*, according to Aruṇadatta and Indu it is *kharjūrāsava*; Mādhavakāra says : it is prepared by fermentation of a mixture, consisting of *dhātakī* flowers, treacle, *dhātrī* and *akṣa*; Jejjaṭa and Brahmadeva say : the mixture of both *āsava* and *surā*, (put) in one vessel, should be known (after it has fermented again) as *maireya*, which is related to both (these drinks); Ḍalhaṇa says : *maireya* has a threefold matrix and (is prepared) from *paiṣṭī*, *guḍāsava* and honey, or from *paiṣṭī*, *madhvāsava* and treacle; all these statements are authoritative, for all these persons are trustworthy. Kauṭ. 2, 25, 22-23 (text p. 79; transl. Kangle p. 178; transl. J. J. Meyer p. 186-187; transl. Sham. p. 132-133) : *maireya* is prepared from a fermented decoction (*kvāthābhiṣuta*) of *meṣaśṛṅgī* and *tvac*, with the addition of treacle and also, as requisite spices, *pippalī* and *marica*, or with the addition of *triphalā*.

yavāgū

See : *peyā*.

yūkā — louse.

Rn, *pariśiṣṭa*, *varga* 19, 31-32ab : a *yūkā* is a *kīṭa* of the hair of the head, arises from sweat and has six feet; a *pakṣmajā* is a louse of the eyelashes, is very small and also has six feet; a white louse (*śvetayūkā*) arises from the body and its clothes; a nit (*likṣā*) is (also called) *yūkāṇḍa* (the egg of a louse) and *vastraka*.

yūṣa.

PW : Fleischbrühe, Brühe überh. MW : the water in which pulse of various kinds has been boiled. Kav p. 375-376 : 'unprepared soup' means such soup as has been prepared with only oil or ghee and salt, but in which no spices occur; 'prepared soup' is that in which occur oil or ghee, salt, and also spices of every kind. OP, p. 137, n. 6 : *yūṣa* was generally a soup of pulses prepared with spices (*kṛtayūṣa*) or without them (*akṛtayūṣa*); the Kāśyapasaṃhitā mentions twenty-four varieties of *yūṣa*; the most common were those prepared with *mudga* and *kulattha*; OP, p. 294-295 : a soup generally prepared by cooking cereals and pulses with buttermilk. Vśs : a *yūṣa* is the thin fluid prepared by boiling roasted pieces of *mudga* beans in one *pala* of water, clarifying (the fluid by straining) and cleansing it of fragments of the beans; a *yūṣa* is the watery fluid obtained by boiling *vaidala* in four times their quantity of water and pressing out (the fluid, separating the pulse from it); a *yūṣa* is prepared by boiling roasted and husked *vaidala* in four times their quantity of water and pressing out the watery fluid. Ma.nigh., *varga* 11, 19ab : a *yūṣa* is made with *vaidala*, (boiled) in eighteen parts of water; 11, 26 : a *yūṣa* is called *kṛta* when boiled in water with salt and an oleaginous substance is added to it; it is called *akṛta* when prepared without both (these substances). Su.Sū. 46, 379 : "Any *yūṣa*, prepared without oleaginous substances, salt and spices (*kaṭukāḥ*), should be called *akṛta*, and a *yūṣa* is *kṛta*, when it is prepared with an oleaginous substance, salt and spices." A.h.Sū. 3, 45, He. : a *yūṣa* is a decoction of *dhānya*. Many kinds of *yūṣa* are described : Su.Sū. 46, 367-375; Kā.Khi. 4, 14cd-67; Hā. 1, 13, 1-13; Dravyaguṇa, *kṛtānnavarga* 33-40; Ma.nigh., *varga* 11, 19cd-27; Bṛhad-yo-ta., *taraṅga* 16, 33-43.

rajas

See : *sattva*.

rasa — taste.

Six tastes are distinguished in classical Indian medicine : *madhura* (sweet), *amla* (acid), *lavaṇa* (saline), *kaṭu* (pungent), *tikta* (bitter) and *kaṣāya* (astringent). See about the tastes, their combinations, actions, etc. : Ca.Sū. 26; Su.Sū. 42; Su.U. 63; A.h.Sū. 10; A.s.Sū. 18; Bhe.Sū. 12; Bhe.Vi. 1; Kā.Khi. 6; Bhā.pra. 6, 170-194. See on the subject of the tastes : Dasgupta, H.I.Ph. 2, p. 357-360; Jolly, Medicin, p. 25-26; Kutumbiah, p. 37, 114-115, 118-119; Lüders, Medizinische Sanskrittexte aus Turkistan; Müller, Grundlagen, p. 52-54, Grundsätze, p. 36-49, Eigenwertungen, p. 66-72, Vorstellungen von der Verdauung, p. 198-203, Wörterheft, p. 129, nr. 173; Nobel; Sinh Jee, p. 101-103.

rasaudana — rice boiled in meat broth.

About boiled rice (*odana*), the various ways it may be prepared and mixed with other ingredients and the qualities of these dishes see : Ca.Sū. 27, 257cd-260ab, Su.Sū. 46, 346-347; A.h.Sū. 6, 30cd-31; Bpn, *kṛtānnavarga* 4-6.

roga — disease.

See : *vyādhi.*

rocana — appetizing.

Aruṇa and Candra on A.h.Sū. 5, 30: *rocana* is that which, like *ghṛta-pūra,* etc., gives appetite (*rocate*), but does not destroy (the disorder called) inability to eat (*aruci*); *rociṣṇu* means : acting as an appetizer, and is applied to substances which, at the end of a meal, give appetite again to persons who were already satisfied; there are also substances, like *paṭola* leaves, which are not appetizing but yet destroy *aruci* (*arucighna*).

laṅghana — reducing measures.

PW : Fasten. MW : fasting, starving system. Gul : lightening therapy, starvation. Kav p. 399 : anything that lightens or attenuates (the aggravated humours). Ca.Sū. 22, 9ab : "Everything that brings about lightness of the body is traditionally called *laṅghana.*" Ca.Sū. 22, 18 : "Reducing measures consist of the four types of purificatory procedure, (being subject to) thirst, (exposure to) the wind and the heat (of the sun), maturation-promoting measures, fasting and physical exercise." See also : *apatarpaṇa.* See : Kutumbiah, p. 138-141.

laḍḍuka

PW : eine Art Gebäck; it is made of coarsely ground gram or other pulse, or of corn-flour, mixed with sugar and spices, and fried in ghee or oil; several varieties of it are distinguished, Molesw. MW : see PW. OP, p. 288 : *laḍḍuka* is the same as *modaka* (sweet balls prepared with the flour of rice or some pulse and sugar). Chakravarty, p. 6-7 : sweets or sweet cakes of round shape or *laḍḍuka* which are commonly known as '*lāṛu*' (in Bengal); ibid., p. 45 : the word '*laḍḍuka*' seems also to have been used in ancient Bengal to denote a special kind of sweetmeat of a round shape or a variety of confectionary usually having a round shape. Vśs : a particular kind of sweetmeat (*miṣṭānna*). Śkdr : a particular kind of *piṣṭaka*. Śabdacandrikā (by Cakrapāṇidatta), quoted in Śkdr and Vśs : *laḍḍuka* is a powdered (substance) boiled in (sesame) oil on a fire. Su.Sū. 46, 396, Ḍa. : *modaka* (a small, round sweetmeat, or any kind of sweetmeat) = *laḍḍuka*. Several varieties of *laḍḍuka* are described : Bṛhad-yo.ta., *taraṅga* 16, 156-175.

lavaṇa — salt.

Several kinds of salt are distinguished :

(1) *saindhava*, rock-salt; it is found in deposits in Sindh and the Pañjāb (Watt CP, p. 963-965).

(2) *sauvarcala*, sonchal salt; acc. to Nadk. (2 p. 100), who quotes N. N. Sen Gupta on this subject, it is a dark coloured salt made by dissolving common salt in a solution of crude soda and evaporating it; acc. to Rāy, p. 228-229, it is saltpetre; acc. to Cakra on Ca.Sū. 27, 303 and Ḍa. on Su.Sū. 46, 313 it is also called black salt (*kālalavaṇa*); Dn, *varga* 7, 67 calls it *rucaka*.

(3) *biḍa* or *viḍa*; this is an artificially prepared black salt; see Nadk. 2, p. 98-99 about the methods of preparing it; Ḍa. remarks on Su.Sū. 46, 313 that it is an artificially prepared salt, made by heating (and evaporating a solution consisting of) a mixture of the paste of (the plant called) *prasāraṇī* and common table-salt (*bhaktalavaṇa*).

(4) *audbhida*; Nadk. 2, p. 100-101 : it is a saline efflorescence on reh lands (see Watt CP, p. 51); acc. to Cakra on Ca.Sū. 27, 303 it is called *utkārikā*; Ḍa. says on Su.Sū. 46, 313 that it is made by evaporating, either by the heat of the sun or by fire, an alkaline water that comes out of the earth (this may refer to subsoil brine and brine-springs; see about these Watt CP, p. 965-967).

(5) *sāmudra(ka)*, sun-dried sea salt; Cakra remarks on Ca.Sū. 27, 304 that it is made on the shores of the southern sea (see Watt CP, p. 969, about Madras salt).

(6) *romaka*; this is the salt from the Sambar lake near Ajmer; it is also called *śākambharīya*; Ḍa. remarks on Su.Sū. 46, 313 that it comes from the *śākambharī* region and that others say its origin is the *rumā* lake.

(7) *pāṃśuja*; Nadk. 2, p. 101 : salt manufactured from saline earth; Cakra says on Ca.Sū. 27, 304 that it originates from the eastern sea; Aruṇa remarks on A.h.Sū. 6, 149, where it is called *pāṃsūttha*, that it

is a rock-salt (*śilālavaṇa*), but He. says it is manufactured from an alkaline earth (*kṣāramṛttikā*).

(8) *kṛṣṇa*, black salt; it is mentioned as a separate kind : A.h.Sū. 6, 148 and Dravyaguṇa, *lavaṇādivarga* 5; acc. to Ca. and Ḍa. black salt (*kālalavaṇa*) is *sauvarcala* (see : *sauvarcala*); Pr 446 : *kṛṣṇalavaṇa* = *sauvarcala.*

(9) *guḍikāhvaya*; mentioned as a separate kind : Dravyaguṇa, *lavaṇādivarga* 8; see about it Nadk. 2, p. 101.

See about salts : Ca.Sū. 27, 300-304; Su.Sū. 46, 313; A.h.Sū. 6, 143-149; Dravyaguṇa, *lavaṇādivarga* 1-8; Ma.nigh., *varga* 2, 54-59; Bpn, *harītakyādivarga* 241-250. See also : Ainslie 1, p. 372-373; Dutt, MM, p. 23, 84-86 and 88-91; Nadk. 2, p. 90-93, 97-101 and 108-114; Rāy, H.Ch., p. 204-205 and 228-229; Watt CP, p. 112-114 and 963-971.

lāja, m. pl. — parched grain.

PW : geröstetes Korn. MW : fried or parched grain (esp. rice grain). Dutt, MM, p. 270 : *lājā* is paddy fried in a sand bath; the husks open out and the rice swells into a light spongy body. Śārṅga 2, 2, 174cd, Āḍhamalla : roasted *śāli* rice or other kinds of roasted grain; Kāśirāma on the same passage : old *śāli* rice, when roasted, or similar kinds of grain. Rn, *pariśiṣṭa, varga* 16, 8 : every kind of roasted *vrīhi* rice is called *lāja* (the same statement occurs Bho.ku. 1, p. 22). Ma.nigh., *varga* 11, 106 : mention is made of *lāja* of roasted *śāli* rice, etc. and of roasted barley. Bpn, *kṛtānnavarga* 174 : the grains of any kind of *dhānya* that produces (grain, and not pulse) are, when unhusked, roasted and burst open, called *lāja* by thoughtful people (the same statement is found Bho.ku. 1, p. 22).

lekhana — attenuating.

PW : in Fluss bringend. MW : attenuating. Bhish : liquefying, attenuating. Dutt, MM, p. 6 : *lekhana* or attenuants remove bad humours and altered constituents of the body by thinning them gradually and thus clearing the system of them. Gul : depletive. Kav p. 364 : operating as an attenuant by removing bad humours. Su.Sū. 45, 112, Ḍa. : eliminating fat; acc. to Ḍa. on Su.Sū. 45, 112 and 46, 411 *lekhana* is the opposite of *bṛṃhaṇa.* Va. 96, 10 = Śārṅga 1, 4, 10cd-11ab = Bhā.pra. 6, 224 : "That which desiccates the elements (of the body) or the impurities and scrapes them away is called *lekhana.*"

varaṭī — a kind of wasp.

Su.Ka. 8, 8cd-12ab : it is one of the twenty-four *kīṭas* which are of a fiery nature. Pr 804 : a synonym of *varaṭī* is *gandholī*.

vāta — wind.

= *vāyu*, etc. The five kinds of wind are described : Ca.Ci. 28, 6-11; Su.Ni. 1, 12-19; A.h.Sū. 12, 4-9; A.s.Sū. 20, 4; Bhā.pra. 3, 108-119. Compare also Bhe.Sū. 16. See : Bhish 1, Introd. p. 41-42; G. W. Brown, Prāṇa and apāna, JAOS 39, 1919, p. 104-112; A. H. Ewing, The Hindu conception of the functions of breath, JAOS 22, 1901, p. 249-308; Filliozat, p. 170-185 and 196-228 (Fr. ed. p. 139-152 and 161-190); Gul 1, p. 561-564 and 567-568; Kutumbiah, p. 51 and 68-69; Müller, Grundlagen, p. 57-58, Grundsätze, p. 49-61, Wörterheft, p. 77, nr. 11 (*anila*), p. 117, nr. 135 (*prāṇa*), p. 118, nr. 136 (*prāṇāyatanāni*), p. 134, nr. 187 (*vāta*), p. 145, nr. 225 (*samīraṇa*), Eine Wind-lehre der Bhela-saṃhitā, WZKSOA 6, 1962, p. 29-39; Sinh Jee, p. 86-88.

vāruṇī

PW : Branntwein. MW : a partic. kind of spirit (prepared from hog-weed mixed with the juice of the date or palm and distilled), any spirituous liquor. Dutt, MM, p. 273 : the fermented juice of the palm and date trees. HB, p. 80, n. 18 : *vāruṇī* is the liquor made by fermenting the sap of the palmyra and date palms (the *tāla* or Borassus flabelliformis, and the *kharjūra* or Phoenix sylvestris), commonly called 'palm-wine'; it is mentioned in the Vāruṇī Jātaka (I, 120) as a kind of spirits, dearer than *surā*, or spirits of rice. OP, p. 301 : a strong liquor prepared by fermenting the juices of palm fruit and dates. Śārṅga 2, 10, 7ab : *vāruṇī* is the fermented juice of *tāla* and *kharjūra* (see also Āḍhamalla's remarks). Ma.nigh., *varga* 8, 170 : *vāruṇī* is thought to be prepared with *punarnavā* and ground *śāli* rice. Bpn, *saṃdhānavarga* 24 : *vāruṇī* is said to be prepared with ground *punarnavā* and *śāli* rice; the (liquor) prepared by fermentation of the juice of *tāla* and *kharjūra* is also (called) *vāruṇī*. A.h.Sū. 5, 68, Candra : the upper, transparent (part, i.e. the) scum of *surā* is called *vāruṇī* or *prasannā*; the traditional doctrine is as follows : "*prasannā* is known as *vāruṇī*, as *parisrut* (is known as) *madirā*; the dense (part of) *surā* is called *kādambarī* and the portion lower (than *kādambarī*) is called *jagala*." He. on the same passage : *vāruṇī* is *śvetasurā*; this (*śvetasurā*) is made with *śāli* rice flour to which the root of the white *punarnavā* and other roots have been added; some say that *vāruṇī* is (the) transparent (part of) *surā*, but that is not correct.

vikāśin, vikāsin — relaxation-promoting.

PW : den Zusammenhang aufhebend, lösend (daher lähmend). MW : dissolving, relaxing, paralysing. Dutt, MM, p. 7 : drying the humours, depressing the system and causing relaxation of the joints. Kav p. 1628 : drying up the humours, depressing the system, and causing relaxation of the joints; p. 1914 : the action of a substance called *vikāśin* lasts as long as it is under the process of digestion; p. 1976-77 : causing secretion of the filthy matter; p. 1984 : that which dissolves the compact or current material of the joints; a quick solvent that causes much secretion of the body elements. Ca.Sū. 26, 43, Cakra : unfixing moist matter. Su.Sū. 45, 112 and 45, 171, Ḍa. : detaching the structures which connect (the parts of) junctures. Su.Sū. 46, 523cd : "(A substance is called) *vikāsin* when it, permeating (the whole body) in the same way (as a substance called *vyavāyin*), detaches the structures connecting the elements (*dhātubandhāḥ*);" Ḍa. : (a substance with) the quality (called) *vikāsin* permeates, i.e. spreads, in the same way, i.e. pervading the whole body while remaining immature, (and) detaches the structures connecting the elements, i.e. brings about flaccidity of the elements; others, however, say that *vikāsin* is a particular (type of the quality) 'sharp', but Gayī (i.e. Gayadāsa) does not agree with that (interpretation). Va. 96, 20 = Śārṅga 1, 4, 20cd-21ab = Bhā.pra. 6, 231 : "(A substance) is called *vikāśin* when it brings about flaccidity of the structures which connect (the parts of) junctures and desiccates the vital fluid (withdrawing it) from the elements."

vikṛtiviṣamasamavāya

See about this term Ca.Vi. 1, 10 and Cakra's commentary.

vidala

PW and MW : split peas. Śkdr : split (*dvidhākṛta*) *kalāya*, etc.; it is called *dāli* in common language. Vśs : = *dālī*. Su.Sū. 46, 348, Ḍa. : *vidala* is a subdivision (*avayava*) of *śamīdhānya*. Su.U. 54, 5, Ḍa. : *vidala* is *makuṣṭha*, etc. Hā. 1, 15, 17-18 : the foods, called *vidala*, consist of barley, wheat, *caṇaka*, *māṣa* beans, *mudga* beans, *āḍhakī*, *makuṣṭaka, kulattha, masūra, tripuṭa, niṣpāvaka* and *kalāya*. See also : *vaidala*. See Gode's article about *avarānna* : St.I.L.H. 3, p. 153-160.

vidāhin — giving rise to combustive alteration.

PW : hitzig, brennend. MW : burning, scorching, hot. Gul : irritant. HB : heating. Jolly : brennend. Kav p. 1502 : causing a burning sensation in the stomach or the chest. Su.Sū. 45, 158, Ḍa. : those foods and drinks are called *vidāhin* which, owing to their own nature or their heaviness, are maturated by the abdominal fire only after a long time and therefore bring about excitement of bile, which is of a combustively altering action. Su.Sū. 45, 198, Ḍa. : people well-versed in traditional doctrine say : "A substance is said to be *vidāhin* when it is not maturated by contact with the abdominal fire, remains in the middlemost stage of (digestive) maturation for a long time, is subject to combustive alteration, brings about (excitement of) bile and is not disintegrated rapidly either on account of its heaviness or its own nature;" others say that *vidāhin* means : bringing about sensations of glowing heat of several kinds. Aruṇa's comment on A.h.Sū. 5, 45 contains the same statement as quoted by Ḍa. on Su.Sū. 45, 198, but with a variant giving a better sense (*gacchan* instead of *agacchan*) : a substance is said to be *vidāhin* when, being subject to maturation by contact with the abdominal fire, it remains ..., etc.; He. remarks on A.h.Sū. 5, 45 : though all foods and drinks give rise to combustive alteration, because the stage in which they are combustively altered does necessarily occur, nevertheless those (foods and drinks) are called *vidāhin* which remain in that stage for a long time. Bhā.pra. 6, 236 : "A substance is *vidāhin* when it brings about acid eructations and thirst, generates a burning sensation in the cardiac region and reaches maturation only after a long time."

vidruma — red coral.

See about *vidruma*, its synonyms, varieties and qualities : Pr 768; Dn, *varga* 6, 64-68; Rn, *varga* 13, 73-77; Ma.nigh., *varga* 4, 49; Bpn, *dhātvādivarga* 186. See also : Ainslie 1, p. 89-91; Dutt, MM, p. 93-94; IRM 2, p. 323-326; Nadk. 2, p. 156-158; Watt CP, p. 989-990.

vipāka — digestive alteration.

There are divergent opinions on the subject of *vipāka* : Ca.Sū. 26, 57cd-58 : "Usually it is thus that substances with a pungent, bitter and astringent taste become pungent by digestive alteration, acid substances (remain) acid, savoury substances become sweet and saline ones sweet as well." Cakra points to the word 'usually', because there are exceptions to these rules; he defines *vipāka* as that quality which is produced at the time of completion of the contact of the ingested food with the abdominal fire. A.h.Sū. 9, 20-21 agrees with Ca.Sū. 26, 57cd-58 : "Usually savoury and acrid (*paṭu*, = *lavaṇa*) substances become sweet by digestive alteration, acid substances (remain) acid, and bitter, irritant (*ūṣaṇa*, = *kaṭu*) and astringent ones become pungent;" *vipāka* is defined (Sū. 9, 20) as follows : "When, owing to the contact with the abdominal fire, another taste arises at the end of the transformation of the tastes, one traditionally calls this digestive alteration." A.s.Sū. 17, 17-20 agrees with A.h. and Ca., but adds that three degrees of the transformed tastes should be distinguished : slight, moderate and preponderant; moreover it mentions the divergent view of Parāśara who was of the opinion that acid substances are acid after digestive alteration, pungent substances pungent and the remaining four (sweet, bitter, astringent and saline substances) sweet. Su. differs from Ca., A.h. and A.s.; Su.Sū. 40, 10-12 : "Some say that digestive alteration is (the) predominant (quality of a substance). Why (do they say so)? Because there is a proper and improper digestive alteration. All ingested substances generate, when properly or improperly altered by digestion, a quality or a fault (*doṣa*). Others say with regard to this (subject) that digestion (occurs) with regard to the tastes. Some want it to be of three kinds : sweet, acid and pungent. That, however, is not suitable because there is, on account of the qualities of the gross elements, no acid digestive alteration different from that of immature matter; for bile, when combustively altered, reaches an acid condition, because of its fiery nature. If it would be thus, (that there is an acid digestive alteration), there would also be a saline digestive alteration, for phlegm, when combustively altered, reaches a saline condition. Some say that a sweet (substance) is sweet (after digestive alteration), an acid one acid and so on ... Others say that weak (tastes) come under the control of strong ones (during the process of digestive alteration). An established doctrine does not arise in that way and therefore the question remains unsettled. According to traditional doctrine there are only two kinds of digestive alteration : a sweet and a pungent one. Of these, that one called sweet is heavy and that one called pungent, light. In this respect (the five gross elements, i.e.) earth, water, fire, air and space, are (regarded as) composed of two groups on account of similarities of their qualities (and characteristics of) heaviness or lightness; earth and water are heavy, the remaining ones light. Therefore digestion is only of two kinds. (The following stanzas) pertain to this (subject) : "With regard to substances in which, when being digested, the qualities of water and earth appear in excess, the digestion is said to be sweet; with regard to substances in which, when being digested, the qualities of fire, air and space appear in excess, the digestion is said to be pungent." See also : Śārṅga 1, 2, 19-21ab; Bhā.pra. 6, 241-244. See : Dasgupta, H.I.Ph. 2, p. 362-366; Kutumbiah, p. 40 and 114-116; Sinh Jee, p. 114-116.

vibandha — a confined state (of the impurities).

PW : Stockung, Verstopfung (des Leibes). MW : obstruction, constipation. Gul : constipation, stasis. HB : obstruction of any of the canals of the body, esp. (1) of the bowels, retention of discharges, (2) of the wind-pipe. HK : Verhaltung (der Ausscheidungen), Verstopfung. Kav : suppression of stools and urine, constipation. A.h.Sū. 5, 68, Aruṇa and Candra : *vibandha* is (that condition in which) the morbific entities, etc. are not conveyed (outwards) because there is an increase of unctuous substances in the channels; He. : it is restraint of the wind.

vilepī — thick gruel.

See : *peyā*.

viṣṭambha — a constrained condition (of the impurities).

PW : Stopfung, Obstruction. MW : obstruction of the urine or faeces, ischury, constipation. Gul : intestinal stasis. Vogel : constipation. Su.Sū. 45, 59cd-60ab, Ḍa. : borborygmi (*guḍaguḍāśabda*); Su.Sū. 45, 79cd-80ab, Ḍa. : *viṣṭambha* is the not coming forth of impure matter, accompanied by wind, pricking pain and piercing pain, (but) others say it means borborygmi. Rn, *pariśiṣṭa*, *varga* 20, 12 : *viṣṭambha* = *vibandha* = *ānāha* : restraint of the impurities.

visarga — period of emission.

See : *ādāna*.

vīrya — potency.

Potency is described : Ca.Sū. 26, 62-65 : "Some say that potency is of eight kinds : soft, sharp, heavy, light, oleaginous, dry, hot and cold; others consider it to be of two kinds : cold and hot. Potency is that by which an action is brought about; nothing at all is achieved without potency, for every action is brought about by potency." Su.Sū. 40, 5 : "Others say that potency is (the) predominant (quality). Why (do they say so)? Because the consummation of the action of remedial agents is controlled by it. According to this (opinion) the actions of remedial agents ... occur owing to the predominance of potency. This potency is of two kinds : hot and cold, because the universe is of the nature of *agni* and *soma*. Some say that (potency) is of eight kinds : cold, hot, oleaginous, dry, clear, mucilaginous, soft and sharp. These potencies bring about their own actions after having overpowered taste by their own force and the excellence of the quality." A.h.Sū. 9, 12cd-18ab : "Some say that potency (may be) heavy, oleaginous, cold, soft, light, dry, hot and sharp; in that way it is thought to be of eight kinds. Caraka says however : potency is that by which an action is brought about; nothing at all is achieved without potency, for every action is brought about by potency. That which is called potency is described by him as being in conformity with this meaning only when applied to (the qualities) heavy, etc., which are essential ones in the whole of the qualities, displaying great power, and by reason of the fact that they are the foremost to be designated and the very first to be perceived. On these grounds that (which is called *vīrya*) is declared not to refer to taste, etc., because (the latter) are of an opposite nature, though (the qualities heavy, etc.) are present in them. Others say that potency is of two kinds only, hot and cold, and that even a substance of a manifold nature surpasses never at all the two great forces (called) *agni* and *soma*, as the universe (never surpasses) that which is manifest and not manifest." See about *vīrya* also : A.s.Sū. 17, 11-16; Śārṅga 1, 2, 17cd-18; Bhā.pra. 6, 238. See : Dasgupta, H.I.Ph. 2, p. 361-366; Kutumbiah, p. 38 and 114-116; Müller, Ueber begriffliche Bewertungen, p. 399-401; Sinh Jee, p. 113-114.

vṛddhi — increase.

See : *caya*.

veśavāra, vesavāra.

PW : eine als Zuspeise gebrauchte teigartige Masse aus zerriebenen Stoffen, Mehl oder Fleisch, mit Gewürzen bereitet; a condiment con-

sisting of splitpease, coriander seed, turmeric, peppers etc., fried together, Molesw. MW : a partic. condiment or kind of seasoning (consisting of ground coriander, mustard, pepper, ginger, spice, etc.). HB, p. 97, n. 110 : spiced mince-meat. Kav p. 377 : a kind of food made of rice or barley or wheat and flesh and spices of diverse kinds. OP, p. 297 : stuffing. Pr 1682-1683 : well-steamed and ground meat, to which treacle, melted butter, *kaṇā* and *ūṣaṇa* have been added, is (called) *vesavāra*; ibid., 1698-1699 : meat without bones, ground and steamed, mixed with treacle, ghee, *kṛṣṇā* and *marica* (black pepper), is traditionally called *vesavāra*. Dn, *varga* 7, 30 : *dhānyaka*, *ajāji* and *dāḍima*, together with dried ginger, black pepper and long pepper, to which roots of long pepper have been added, is traditionally called *vesavāra*. Rn, *varga* 22, 15 : *ajājī*, black pepper, dried ginger, *granthi* (= *pippalīmūla*, root of long pepper), *dhānya*, *niśāhvaya* (= *haridrā*, turmeric), long pepper and *marica* are thought to be the *vesavāra* group (of spices). Ma.nigh., *varga* 11, 128-129 : well-steamed meat without bones, afterwards ground on a stone and mixed with *vyoṣa*, etc., should be boiled again after ghee has been added; this (dish) is called *vesavāra*; also called *vesavāra* is another (variety), made with paste of steamed *mudga* beans, etc.; a *vesavāra*, to which have been added *haridrā*, *vyoṣa*, *sindhūttha* (= *saindhava* salt), *hiṅgu*, *dhānyaka*, *dāḍima* and *ajāji*, is called *saurabha* ('the fragrant' *vesavāra*); ibid., *varga* 11, 131 : broth (made of ground meat) mixed with *vesavāra* is called *khāniṣka*. Bpn, *kṛtānnavarga* 80-84 : one should put ghee in a cooking-vessel or sesame oil when one has no ghee; thereupon one should fry *hiṅgu* and *haridrā* in it; one should take the flesh of a goat, etc., without bones, cut into pieces, washed and strained and fry it slowly in the ghee; one should add a suitable quantity of water and salt and boil (the whole again); when it has boiled one should grind (the meat) together with the water and throw out (of the cooking-vessel this) *vesavāra*. The substances (i.e. spices, used) in a *vesavāra* are, shortly stated, pieces of *nāgavallī*, *taṇḍulas*, *lavaṅgas* and black peppers; (the dish) prepared in this way is traditionally called *śuddhamāṃsa*. The same recipe is found : Bho.ku. 1, p. 51. Bho.ku. adds : according to Haimana a *vesavāra* is an *upaskara*; the substances (used) in it (as spices) are enumerated in the Nighaṇṭu : *ajājī*, black pepper, dried ginger, *granthi*, *dhānya*, *niśāhvaya*, long pepper and *dāḍima* are thought to be the *vesavāra* group (of species) (cf. Rn, *varga* 22, 15); the Hṛdayadīpa says : well-steamed and ground meat, mixed with treacle, ghee and *vyoṣa*, is called *vesavāra*. Bṛhadyo.ta., *taraṅga* 90, 103 : meat without bones, ground and steamed, mixed with treacle and ghee and after the addition of *kṛṣṇā* and *marica*, is called *vesavāra*. Su.Sū. 46, 364cd-365 : "Flesh without bones, well-steamed and afterwards ground on a stone, to which have been added long pepper, dried ginger, black pepper, treacle and ghee, should be cooked properly together; this is traditionally called *vesavāra*." This recipe is quoted by Cakra on Ca.Sū. 27, 269 from a *sūdaśāstra* (a work on cooking). Gaṅgādhara quotes in his commentary, called Jalpakalpataru, on Ca.Sū. 27, 269 the following recipes : "Flesh without bones, ground and steamed, to which have been added treacle and ghee and which has been mixed with *kaṇā* and black pepper, is traditionally called *vesavāra*; when *mudga* beans, etc. are steamed and ground in the same way, adding treacle, and mixing them with *kaṇā* and black pepper, it is another (kind of) *vesavāra*." Su.Sū. 46, 399cd-400ab distinguishes between *vesavāra* made with *mudga* beans, etc. and that made with meat. Su.U. 40, 19, Ḍa. : *vesavāra* = *khāniska*. A.h.Sū. 6, 41 also distinguishes between the common type of *vesavāra*, made with meat, and the variety made with *mudga* beans, etc.; Aruṇa comments : *vesavāra* is pounded meat, prepared with dried ginger, *dhānyaka*, *ajāji*, *hiṅgu*, ghee, etc.; those (varieties of) *vesavāra* wich are made with *iṇḍarikā* substances, etc., cut into very small pieces, are well known in common language as *pūraṇa* (Candra reads *mudgavaṭaka*, i.e. a round cake of ground *mudga* beans, instead of *iṇḍarikādravya*; an *iṇḍarikā* is also a small kind of cake); He. comments : *vesavāra* is steamed and ground meat, mixed with treacle, *jīraka*, etc.; the other variety is prepared, acc. to He., by taking *mudga*, *caṇaka*, etc. instead of meat.

vaidala

PW : Hülsenfrucht. MW : any leguminous vegetable or grain. Bpn, *dhānyavarga* 36 : *vaidala* = *śimbīdhānya*. Su.Sū. 46, 27, Ḍa. : *vaidala* consists of *mudga*, *vanamudga*, *kalāya*, *makuṣṭha*, *masūra*, *maṅgalya*, *caṇaka*, *satīna*, *tripuṭaka*, *hareṇu*, *āḍhakī*, etc. See also : *vidala*.

vyañjana — sauce, seasoning.

PW : Brühe. MW : anything used in cooking or preparing food, seasoning, sauce, condiment. HK : zusätzliche Speise. OP : condiment, seasoning (see esp. p. 77, n. 11 and p. 218-219). Vśs : soups, potherbs, savoury foods (*miṣṭānna*), etc. Pr 1497 : *vyañjana* also means soup, etc. Rn, *pariśiṣṭa*, *varga* 20, 54 : *vyañjana* consists of soups, potherbs, etc., it is savoury food, traditionally called *temana*. Su.Sū. 46, 350,

Ḍa. : one kind of *vyañjana* consists of steamed potherbs, pressed out and prepared with an oleaginous substance.

vyavāyin — diffusive.

PW : eindringend. MW : pervading, diffusive. Dutt, MM, p. 7 : affecting the entire system. Gul : diffusive. Kav p. 1811 : producing effect when it has been assimilated by the system; p. 1914 : pervading and penetrating the system, its effect being rather of a permanent character. Va. 96, 19 = Śārṅga 1, 4, 19cd-20ab = Bhā.pra. 6, 230 : "That (substance) which pervades the whole body first and reaches maturation afterwards, is called *vyavāyin*." Su.Sū. 45, 112, Ḍa. : (a substance which), when not having been transformed at all, pervades the (whole) body and is maturated (afterwards); Su.Sū. 46, 318, Ḍa. : (a substance which), being not maturated at all, pervades the whole body and afterwards, still staying in the body, reaches a maturated state. Su.Sū. 46, 523ab : "(A substance is called) *vyavāyin*, when it, after pervading the whole body, reaches maturation;" Ḍa. : it pervades, being not maturated at all, the whole body and reaches maturation afterwards, like alcoholic beverages and poison ...; others say it designates a particular type of (the quality) 'giving rise to the flowing out (of impure matter)' (*sara*), but Gayī (i.e. Gayadāsa) does not agree with that (interpretation).

vyādhi — illness.

The following synonyms are used to designate disease : *ātaṅka*, *ābādha*, *āmaya*, *gada*, *jvara*, *duḥkha*, *pāpman*, *yakṣman*, *roga*, *vikāra* and *vyādhi* (see Ca.Ni. 1, 5; Ca.Ci. 3, 11; A.h.Ni. 1, 1). Acc. to Filliozat (Kumāratantra, p. 73, n. 3) *roga* means pain, not illness, and *vyādhi* corresponds to disease. Filliozat observes that *roga* and *vyādhi* are clearly distinguished in medical treatises; *roga* points to a local lesion and *vyādhi* to a general affection; the sense of *roga* is near to morbid symptom and that of *vyādhi* to syndrome. In the Madhukośa, however, and in many medical texts and commentaries, *roga* and *vyādhi* are used as synonyms, as well as *ātaṅka*, *āmaya* and *gada*. Sometimes *roga* is a synonym of *ruj* or *rujā* and means pain; the latter two terms may also occur denoting disease; *vikāra* is often used in a broader sense than *roga* and *vyādhi* and refers to a morbid process in such cases. See also : Müller, Wörterheft, p. 131, nr. 178 (*roga*) and p. 137-138, nr. 198 (*vyādhi*).

vyoṣa

The term *vyoṣa* designates the triad of irritating substances : black pepper, long pepper and dried ginger. Synonyms of *vyoṣa* are : *kaṭutraya, kaṭutrika, trikaṭu(ka), tryūṣaṇa.* See e.g. : Pr 1687; Dn, *varga* 7, 6; Rn, *varga* 12, 4; Ma.nigh., *varga* 2, 15; A.h.Sū. 6, 164, Aruṇa, Candra and He.

vrīhi

MW : rice ripening in the rainy season. Vśs : rice sown in the early rainy period and ripening quickly. Dutt, MM, p. 269 : *vrīhi* ripens in the rainy season. OP, p. 35 : the ordinary variety of rice; it was grown in autumn; p. 133 : rice ripening in autumn. Chakravarty, p. 12 : paddy becoming ripe in early autumn (acc. to Aniruddha Bhaṭṭa's Hāralatā : *śaratpakvadhānyaṃ vrīhiḥ*). Rn, *varga* 16, 80 : *vrīhi* arises from the waters of the rainy season. Bpn, *dhānyavarga* 17 : *vrīhi* belongs to the rainy season and is white after husking. Ca.Sū. 27, 8-12, Cakra : *vrīhi* belongs to the autumn. Su.Sū. 46, 4, Ḍa. : *vrīhi* belongs to the rainy season, (but) others say it (is that rice which) is white after husking. Kauṭ. 2, 24, 12 (text p. 77; transl. Kangle p. 172; transl. J. J. Meyer p. 179; transl. Sham. p. 128) : both *śāli* and *vrīhi* rice belong to the class of seeds called *pūrvavāpa* (to be sown first, i.e. at the beginning of the rainy season).

śamana — appeasing (agent).

Dutt, MM, p. 5 : medicines which rectify the deranged state of the humours and calm their excited action, without promoting the excretions. Śārṅga 1, 4, 2cd-3ab : "That which has no purifying action on morbific entities which have increased (*uddhata*) and does not hurt those which are congruous, (but) makes congruous those which are incongruous, is (called) *śamana.*" (Compare Va. 96, 2, the reading of which is not clear). Bhā.pra. 6, 214 : "That which has no purifying action on congruous morbific entities nor rouses them, (but) makes congruous those which are incongruous, is (called) *śamana.*" Su.Sū. 39, 7, Ḍa. : *saṃśamana* is that which completely appeases corrupted morbific entities without eliminating them, and does not rouse them when they are not corrupted; Ḍa. quotes the statement found Bhā.pra. 6, 214 (variant : *kruddha* instead of *viṣama*). See : Kutumbiah, p. 140-141.

śarkarā — (ground) sugar.

śarkarā is one of the products of the sugar-cane, which are called, as a group, *ikṣuvikāra* or *ikṣuvikṛti*. Several of these substances are distinguished :

1) the juice, divided into two or more varieties : a) obtained by chewing, b) obtained by mechanical pressure, c) obtained by mechanical pressure, but having stood for a time (*paryuṣita*) (only Bhā.pra.), d) the boiled juice (Su.; Dravyaguṇa; Bhā.pra.)

2) the inspissated juice (*phāṇita*; Bpn, *ikṣuvarga* 21 : sugar-cane juice which by boiling has become somewhat inspissated but is still liquid to a considerable degree); *phāṇita* is called *kṣudraguḍa* in Ca. (Sū. 27, 239); *kṣudraguḍa(ka)* as a synonym of *phāṇita* is mentioned : Ḍa. on Su.Sū. 45, 159, Aruṇa on A.h.Sū. 5, 47 and Ma.nigh., *varga* 9, 13.

3) treacle (*guḍa*); there are differences of opinion about *guḍa*; usually it means sugar-cane juice that has become very thick by boiling (Ḍa. on Su.Sū. 45, 159), but Bpn, *ikṣuvarga* 24-25 says : sugar-cane juice which has become firm like a clod of clay by boiling it a long time is called *guḍa*, but in Gauḍadeśa *guḍa* is called *matsyaṇḍī*; several varieties of *guḍa* are distinguished : Ca.Sū. 27, 239 : a) sugar-cane juice boiled down to one fourth, b) one third, c) half of its original quantity, d) washed *guḍa*; Su.Sū. 45, 160-161 : purified (pure white) and not purified (of a dark colour); A.h.Sū. 5, 47cd-48 : a) washed, b) not washed, c) old and d) fresh; Dravyaguṇa, *aikṣavādivarga* 7-9 : a) washed, b) not washed, c) somewhat old; Bpn, *ikṣuvarga* 26-27 : a) old and b) fresh.

4) crude sugar (*matsyaṇḍikā, matsyaṇḍī*); Bpn, *ikṣuvarga* 22-23 describes it differently : sugar-cane juice which has become thick by boiling and contains only a small quantity of liquid is called *matsyaṇḍī*, because it flows slowly (*mandaṃ yat syandate*).

5) candied sugar (*khaṇḍa*).

6) ground sugar (*śarkarā*, also called *śvetā, sitā, sitopalā*; Bpn, *ikṣuvarga* 30 : *śarkarā* or *sitā* is very white and looks like gravel). Sugar was, as well as from the sugar-cane, also obtained from honey (*madhujā*) and from *yāsa* (also called *yavāsa*, equated by the commentators with the plant called *durālabhā*) (Cakra on Ca.Sū. 27, 241; He. on A.h.Sū. 5, 50ab); some sources mention a kind of sugar obtained from flowers (Ma.nigh., *varga* 9, 13; Bpn, *ikṣuvarga* 31). See about these products of the sugar-cane and other kinds of sugar : Ca.Sū. 27, 237-242; Su.Sū. 45, 157-167; A.h.Sū. 5, 44-53; Dravyaguṇa, *aikṣavādivarga* 1-14;

Ma.nigh., *varga* 9, 10-20; Bpn, *ikṣuvarga* 16-32. See also : Ainslie 1, p. 407-411; Dutt, MM, p. 266-267; Nadk. 1, p. 1083-1084; Watt CP, p. 951-953.

śallaki

śallaki, śallakī, śallaka and *śalyaka* mean : porcupine. PW remarks (s.v. *śalyaka*) that it is a porcupine distinguished from another type called *śvāvidh*. Not all the texts, however, maintain this distinction : Ma.nigh., *varga* 12, 40 says that a *śallaka* is also called *śvāvidh*; Bpn, *māṃsavarga* 51 does not distinguish them either. The commentators and *nighaṇṭus* are not of much help in identifying this animal; usually only one or more synonyms are enumerated : Ca.Sū. 27, 38, Cakra : a *śallaka* is a *mahāśakalin*, called *śalaka* (in common language). Su.Sū. 46, 78, Ḍa. : a *śalyaka* is a *vajraśakala*, called *sālā* in common language. Pr 802 : a *śalūka* (variants : *śallaka, sallaka*) is (also called)*śalalin* and *śalin*. Rn, *pariśiṣṭa, varga* 19, 3 : a *śalyaka* is (also called) *śalyamṛga* and *vajraśukti*. Ma.nigh., *varga* 12, 40 : a *śallaka* is (also called) *śalalin, śvāvidh, medhā, sūcinī* and *kharā*. Bpn, *māṃsavarga* 51 : a *sedhā* is (also called) *śalyaka* and *śvāvidh*. Only Ḍa. (on Su.Sū. 46, 78) makes a remark about the form of the animal and says that it resembles a large *godhā*. Acc. to Seal (p. 191) *śallaka* means a porcupine and *śvāvidh* a hedgehog. Acc. to Gul a porcupine is called *śvāvidh* (vol. 6, Animals and birds, p. 78, nr. 110) and a hedgehog *kūrcikā* (p. 66, nr. 60). Three species of porcupine are found in India; the most common species is *Hystrix indica* Kerr, 1792; *H. hodgsoni* (Gray, 1847) is found only in the central and eastern Himālayas, Assam and lower Bengal; the third species, *Atherurus macrourus* (Linnaeus, 1758), found in lower Bengal and Assam, is an uncommon animal (see : Prater, The book of Indian animals, p. 215-217; Fauna of India, Mammalia, second ed., vol. 3, Rodentia, part 1, p. 288-313). The most common hedgehogs of northern India are *Hemiechinus auritus* (Gmelin, 1770) and *Paraechinus micropus* (Blyth, 1846) (see : Prater, p. 166-167). The *śallaki*, resembling a large *godhā* acc. to Ḍa., cannot be a porcupine or hedgehog; it may be tentatively identified as the Indian pangolin, *Manis crassicaudata* Gray, 1827 (see : Prater, p. 301-303).

śāka — potherb.

A.h.Sū. 6, 72, He: : *śāka* consists of a particular class of plants (*udbhidavayava*), prepared with an oleaginous substance, etc. Potherbs are divided into : a) four kinds : leaves, flowers, fruits and tubers (Hā. 1, 16, 1; Ma.nigh., *varga* 7, 2); b) six kinds : leaves, flowers, fruits, stalks, tubers and mushrooms (*saṃsvedaja, bhūsvedaja*) (Dravyaguṇa, *śākavarga* 2 = Bpn, *śākavarga* 1 = Rā.va.nigh., *pariccheda* 3, 43 = Bṛhad-yo.ta., *taraṅga* 32, 1); c) ten kinds : roots, leaves, shoots (*karīra*), tops (of plants) (*agra*), fruits, joints (of stalks) (*kāṇḍa*), parasitical plants (mushrooms ?, *adhirūḍhaka*), rinds (*tvac*), flowers and (seed-)capsules (? *kavaca*) (Bho.ku. 1, p. 58).

Kauṭ, 2, 15, 21 (text p. 64; transl. Kangle p. 142; transl. J. J. Meyer p. 142; transl. Sham. p. 101) interprets *śāka* in a different way : "The *śāka* group consists of dried fish and meat, tubers, roots, fruits, potherbs, etc." See about the term *saṃsvedaja* : Bpn, *śākavarga* 119. See about (*pari*)*śuṣkamāṃsa* : OP, p. 296.

śākhā — 'branch'.

See ch. 1, n. 42.

śāli

Dutt, MM, p. 269 : rice reaped in the cold season. Kav p. 50 : *śāli* is red paddy, i.e. the paddy that is gathered at the end of autumn; p. 273 : *śāli* paddy is that which grows in a damp soil or a field covered with water. OP, p. 35 : a fine variety of rice, grown in winter; p. 133 : rice ripening in winter. Chakravarty, p. 11, n. 3 : *śāli* is a better type of rice produced from paddy which grows in later autumn; p. 12 : paddy ripening during later autumn (acc. to Aniruddha Bhaṭṭa's Hāralatā : *haimantikaṃ śaliḥ*); it is naturally white (acc. to the Hāralatā). Vśs : winter-rice; "*śāli* is said to be white when it is still unhusked and to belong to (the season of) winter." Bpn, *dhānyavarga* 3 : *śāli* is white when still unhusked and belongs to (the season of) winter. Ca.Sū. 27, 8-12, Cakra : winter-rice. Su.Sū. 46, 4, Ḍa. : *śāli* is white when still unhusked and belongs to (the season of) winter; others say that it is white, both unhusked and husked, and that it belongs to (the season of) winter. Kauṭ. 2, 24, 12 (text p. 77; transl. Kangle p. 172; transl. J. J. Meyer p. 179; transl. Sham. p. 128) : both *śāli* and *vrīhi* rice belong to the class of seeds called *pūrvavāpa* (to be sown first, i.e. at the beginning of the rainy season.)

śālū̆(*ka*)

PW : eine essbare Lotuswurzel. MW : the esculent root of different kinds of lotus. Gul : lotus rhizome, lotus bulb. HK : Lotuswurzel. Kav : the esculent root of Nymphaea lotus; the bulbous root of the lotus and other plants of the same species. Pr 675 : *śālūka* is the bulbous rootstock of *utpala*. Dn, *varga* 4, 163 and Rn, *varga* 10, 260 : *śālūka* = *padmamūla* = *padmakanda*. Ma.nigh., *varga* 3, 83 : *śālūka* is the root of *padma*, etc. Bpn, *śākavarga* 115-116 : *śālūka* is the bulbous rootstock of *padma*, etc. Ḍa. on Su.U. 54, 4 : *śālū* is the bulbous rootstock of *padma*. A.h.Sū. 6, 71, Aruṇa and Candra : *śālūka* means : the roots of *padma*; He. : it is the bulbous rootstock of *padma*. In my opinion *śālūka* probably designates the bulbous rootstock (*kanda*) of species of Nymphaea; see : *bisa*.

śukta = *cukra* — verjuice.

PW : jedes durch Fermentation mit Pflanzenstoffen gewonnene saure Getränk, saurer Reisschleim u.s.w. MW : anything fermented or become sour, any sour liquor or gruel (esp. a kind of acid beverage prepared from roots and fruits). Dutt, MM, p. 12 : a mixture called *śukta* or *cukra* is thus prepared : take of treacle one part, honey two parts, *kāñjika* four parts and whey eight parts, mix together in a clean earthen pot, and bury the pot in a heap of paddy for three days. OP : vinegar; p. 92 : vinegar was prepared from sugar-cane juice, *guḍa*, honey, inspissated juice of sugar-cane, rose-apple and jackfruits; a decoction of *meṣaśṛṅgī* and pepper was poured into it; fruits such as cucumber, pieces of sugar-cane, mango and *āmalaka* were preserved in vinegar (see Kauṭ. 2, 15). Kauṭ. 2, 15, 17 (text p. 63; transl. Kangle p. 141; transl. J. J. Meyer p. 141; transl. Sham. p. 101) : anyone (of the following articles), sugar-cane juice, treacle, honey, inspissated sugar-cane juice, (the juice of) *jambu* fruits or of *panasa* fruits, to which a decoction of *meṣaśṛṅgī* and long pepper has been added, subjected to fermentation (*abhiṣuta*) during one month, six months or a year, either mixed with *cirbhiṭa*, *ervāruka*, joints of the sugar-cane, mango fruits or *āmalaka*, or pure (without the mentioned additions), constitutes the *śukta* group. Su.Sū. 45, 210, Ḍa. : *śukta* is also called *cukra*, as has been said : "The whey, etc., which, together with treacle, *kṣaudra* honey or *kāñjika*, has been put in a clean vessel (and kept) in a heap of grain for three days, is called *śukta* or *cukra*" (= Pr 1652-1653); it is, together with sugar-cane juice, *madhūka* flowers, *pīlu*, etc., (but) without anything astringent, subjected to fermentation; others say that the fermented juice of tubers, etc. is also (called) *śukta*. Su.Sū.

45, 212, Ḍa. : "Any intoxicating beverage with five tastes is called *śukta* when it has become acid after an interval of time, the other tastes having become unnoticeable." A.h.Sū. 5, 76-77ab, He. : *śukta* is a fermented mixture, consisting of tubers, etc., for it has been said : "*śukta* is called a liquid in which tubers, roots, fruits, etc., together with oleaginous substances and salt, are subjected to fermentation" (= Śārṅga 2, 10, 7cd-8ab = Bpn, *saṃdhānavarga* 14). About varieties of *śukta* see Su.Sū. 45, 212 (and Ḍa.'s comment), A.h.Sū. 5, 77cd, Dravyaguṇa, *madyādivarga* 27 and Śārṅga 2, 10, 8cd-10. See Watt CP, p. 1108-1112.

śodhana — purifying (agent).

Dutt, MM, p. 5 : medicines which remove collections of bad humours and discharge them by the excretions. Va. 96, 8 = Śārṅga 1, 4, 8cd-9ab = Bhā.pra. 6, 220 : "That which an accumulation of impure matter moves away from its seat in an upward or downward direction, is an agent that purifies the body." A.h.Sū. 5, 52, Aruṇa : *śodhana* is that which sets in motion purulent and mucilaginous matter; He. : it is that which eliminates corrupted, purulent matter, etc. See : Kutumbiah, p. 140-141.

śyena — a bird of prey.

Synonyms are enumerated : Dn, *varga* 6, 65; Rn, *varga* 19, 34; Ma.nigh., *varga* 12, 83.

ṣaṣṭika

PW : in sechzig Tagen reifender Reis. MW : a kind of rice of quick growth (ripening in about sixty days). Dutt, MM, p. 269 : rice grown in the hot weather in low lands; it is reaped within sixty days of its sowing. HB, p. 113, n. 187 : a white variety of rice which ripens in sixty days from the sowing, between *jyeṣṭha* (May-June) and *śrāvaṇa* (July-August). Kav p. 50 : it is called *āśudhānya,* i.e. the paddy which grows on comparatively higher soil and is gathered in September; it ripens in a very short time. Vśs : a kind of *śāli* ripening in sixty days. Ca.Sū. 27, 8-12, Cakra : it belongs to (the season of) summer. Su.Sū. 46, Ḍa. : it belongs to (the season of) summer, but others say it usually ripens during (the latter period of the sky's) pregnancy. A.h.Sū. 6, 8ab, He. : it is that kind of *vrīhi* which ripens in sixty days.

ṣāḍava

PW : Zuckerwerk mit Früchten u.s.w. (die richtige Form ist *khāṇḍava*). MW : confectionery, sweetmeats. Bhish : a preparation with a variety of articles of sweet, acid and saline tastes. HB : a kind of compound powder, prepared with a condiment, or confectionery, of various drugs. OP, p. 120 : a preparation of juices from fruits such as pomegranates and raisins was called *ṣāḍava* if the juices were reduced to a thick consistency. Ca.Sū. 27, 281, Cakra : a *ṣāḍava* is made with sweet and acid substances. Su.Sū. 46, 378, Ḍa. : the characteristics of a *ṣāḍava* (*khāḍava*) are said to be: "A *khāḍava* (is a preparation) in which the acid and sweet tastes are clearly perceptible, the astringent, saline and irritant (= pungent) tastes are not clearly perceptible, the bitter taste is absent and to which *kola*, *kapittha*, etc. have been added to support (the predominant tastes);" Su.Sū. 46, 383, Ḍa. : *ṣāḍava*s are of various kinds and arise from combinations of (substances with a) sweet, acid and saline taste; Su.U. 47, 25, Ḍa. : a *ṣāḍava* is a particular kind of *yūṣa*; it should be prepared with boiled *āmrātaka*, etc., to which sugar-cane products have been added; the mode of preparation of a *ṣāḍava* (has been described) in another treatise : 'the boiled fruits of the mango tree, to which a sugar-cane product, ghee, dried ginger and sesame seeds have been added, should be known as a thick *ṣāḍava*'. Ma.nigh., *varga* 11, 37ab : *khāṇḍava* arises from the combination of (substances with a) taste that is sweet, acid, etc.

saṃśamana

See : *śamana*.

saṃśodhana

See : *śodhana*.

saktu — groats.

PW and MW : coarsely ground meal; grit, groats, esp. of barley-meal. Dutt, MM, p. 270 : powder of parched barley. Gul : roasted corn-flour. HB : powdered parched grain. Kav : fried rice, reduced to powder. Ca.Sū. 27, 263-264 mentions *saktu* (in a restricted sense) and *saktu*, made of *śāli*. Ḍa. on Su.Sū. 46, 411 and 414 : *saktu* is made of barley and of *lāja*. He. on A.h.Sū. 6, 38cd : *saktu* is roasted, husked barley, reduced to powder. Ma.nigh., *varga* 11, 98 : fresh, husked and roasted barley, reduced to powder, is (called) *saktu*. Bpn, *kṛtānnavarga* 165 : *saktu* is grain, roasted in a frying-pan and ground with a pestle (*yantra*); ibid., 166-170 : *saktu* of barley, *caṇaka* and *śāli* rice is described. Bṛhad-yo.ta., *taraṅga* 16, 29cd-35 : *saktu* is made of barley, *caṇaka* and *lāja*, with grains that are husked, roasted and ground.

saṃgrāhin — constrictive.

See : *grāhin* and *bhedin*.

sattva

sattva, *rajas* and *tamas* are the three constituents of *prakṛti* in the Sāṃkhya philosophy. See about the relation between the Sāṃkhya system and the use of Sāṃkhya terms in medical texts : Dasgupta, H.I.Ph. 1, p. 213-217. See about *sattva*, *rajas* and *tamas* in Indian medicine : Gul 1, p. 464-465; Müller, Ueber pitta oder Galle, p. 102-106, Eigenwertungen, p. 91-94 and 113-115, Wörterheft, p. 102-103, nr. 97 (*tamas*), p. 128-129, nr. 171 (*rajas*) and p. 144-145, nr. 222 (*sattva*), Die vermeintlichen "Temperamente", Janus 51, 1964, p. 184-192.

saṃtarpaṇa — restorative measures.

See : *bṛṃhaṇa*.

saṃdhi — juncture.

The number of junctures in the human body is said to be two hundred and ten : Su.Śā. 5, 24-28; A.h.Śā. 3, 16cd-17ab; A.s.Śā. 5, 73-77. Ca., however, adheres to a number of two hundred : Śā. 7, 14. If the junctures of cords, muscles and vessels are also counted, the total number is two thousand, acc. to A.s.Śā. 5, 78. In A.h. it is remarked that a number of two thousand is approved of by the son of Atri. See : Chakraberty, p. 17-19; Müller, Wörterheft, p. 145, nr. 223.

samavāya — inherence.

See about inherence Ca.Sū. 1, 50 and Cakra's commentary. See also : Dasgupta, H.I.Ph. 2, p. 371.

samitā

PW and MW : wheat-flour. Bpn, *kṛtānnavarga* 21 : pure white, washed grains of wheat, which are bruised and then dried, besprinkled, ground with a pestle and strained, are traditionally called *samitā*. Ḍa. on Su.Sū. 46, 398cd-399ab : *samitā* is powdered wheat. Pr 854 : *kaṇikā* and *rajas* are synonyms of *samitā*.

sirā — vessel.

There are seven hundred vessels in the human body. See about these : Ca.Śā. 7, 14; Su.Śā. 7; A.h.Śā. 3, 19cd-38; A.s.Śā. 6, 1-27. See : Chakraberty, p. 35-38; Dasgupta, H.I.Ph. 2, p. 344-352; Filliozat, p. 162-163 (Fr. ed. p. 132-133); Kutumbiah, p. 23-29 and 48-50; Müller, Wörterheft, p. 146, nr. 229; Seal, p. 208-216.

sīdhu, śīdhu.

See ch. 1, n. 127 about *sīdhu* prepared from boiled and unboiled sugar-cane juice. Other kinds of *sīdhu* are also described : a) *ākṣika* (Su.Sū. 45, 186), made, acc. to Ḍa., from a decoction of *vibhītaka* (= *akṣa*) and treacle, and prepared by adding *dhātakī* flowers, etc. b) *gauḍa* (Su.Sū. 45, 182; Dravyaguṇa, *madyādivarga* 12), perfect in its kind, and made, acc. to Ḍa., from boiled sugar-cane juice, with *dhātakī* (flowers), etc.; when it is ready after an interval of time and some treacle and ghee are added to it, it is of a perfect quality. c) *jāmbava* (Su.Sū. 45, 187; Dravyaguṇa, *madyādivarga* 15), prepared, acc. to Ḍa., from the juice of *jambū* fruits, a decoction of *tumbaru*, treacle, *dhātakī* (flowers), etc. d) *madhūkapuṣpottha* (Su.Sū. 45, 191; Dravyaguṇa, *madyādivarga* 14), prepared from *madhūka* flowers; some say, acc. to Ḍa., that treacle should be added, others are of the opinion this should not be done. e) *śārkara* (Su.Sū. 45, 183; Dravyaguṇa, *madyādivarga* 13), made, acc. to Ḍa., from refined sugar (*guḍaśarkarā*) or candied sugar (*khaṇḍaśarkarā*).

surā

The term *surā* has a very broad sense in Ca. (see Ca.Sū. 27, 179-195) and is applied to an alcoholic beverage together with its scum (*maṇḍa*); the scum of *surā* is called *madirā* (see Cakra's comment); several beverages, called *sīdhu* in Su., are included in Ca.'s concept of *surā*; Ca. mentions separately (Sū. 27, 190) a variety of *surā* made from barley. Ḍa. remarks (on Su.Sū. 45, 175cd-176ab) that *surā* is of a red colour and somewhat turbid from the paste of ground *kiṇva* (ferment). The varieties of *surā*, mentioned in Su., are : a) *śvetā* (Sū. 45, 176-cd-177ab); Ḍa. : *śvetasurā* arises from the roots of *śvetapunarnavā*, etc., ground rice and *kiṇva*, and is well known as *katolī*. b) *prasannā* (Sū. 45, 177cd-178ab); Ḍa. : it is the scum, i.e. the upper transparent portion of *surā*. c) *surā* made from barley (Sū. 45, 178cd-179a). d) *madhūlaka* (Sū. 45, 179b) (vide s.v.). e) *ākṣikī* (Sū. 45, 179cd); Ḍa. : made with the bark of *akṣa*, i.e. *vibhītaka*. f) *kohala* (Sū. 45, 180ab); Ḍa. : made from *saktu* of barley, and called *kauhalikā* in common language. g) *jagala* (Sū. 45, 180cd-181ab); Ḍa. : the lowest portion of an intoxicating beverage, consisting of residual substances which are (usually) thrown away. h) *bakkasa* (Sū. 45, 181cd-182ab); Ḍa. : it is, like *jagala*, the non-liquid part, consisting only of *kiṇva* and drugs.

He. remarks (on A.h.Sū. 5, 67) that *surā* is made with ground *śāli* rice. The varieties of *surā*, mentioned in A.h. are : a) *śvetasurā* (Sū. 5, 68); He. describes it in the same way as Ḍa., but adds that it is called *vāruṇī*. b) *vaibhītakī surā* (Sū. 5, 69) (= *ākṣikī*); He. : it is made with the bark of *vibhītaka*, added to ground *śāli* rice. c) *yavasurā* (Sū. 5, 70ab); He. : made from ground barley.

The Dravyaguṇa mentions in its *madyādivarga* : *śvetasurā* (3), *prasannā* (4), *yavasurā* (5), *valkalīsurā* (= *ākṣikī*) (6), *kohola* (= *kohala* in Su.) (7), *jagala* (8) and *vakkasa* (= *bakkasa* in Su.) (9). Ma.nigh., *varga* 8, 169 : *surā* is thought to be made from ground *śāli* and *ṣaṣṭika* rice, etc. Mention is made of the following varieties : a) *vāruṇī* (8, 170-171ab), made from *punarnavā* with ground *śāli* rice; b) *prasannā* (8, 171cd); c) *kādambarī* (8, 171cd); d) *jaṅgala* (= *jagala*) (8, 172ab); e) *medaka* (8, 172ab); f) *pakvaśa*(= *bakkasa*) (8, 172cd); g) *kiṇvaka* (8, 172cd). Bpn, *saṃdhānavarga* 23ab : the intoxicating beverage, traditionally called *surā*, is made from ground *śāli* and *ṣaṣṭika* rice, etc.; ibid., 24a-d : when it is prepared from ground *punarnavā* and *śāli* rice it is traditionally called *vāruṇī*; it is also called *vāruṇī* when (it is prepared) with the fermented juice of *tāla* or *kharjūra*. Śārṅga 2, 10, 5-6 : that which arises from fermentation of well-boiled rice (*paripakvānna*) is said to be *surā*, the scum of *surā* is (called) *prasannā* and *kādambarī* is that portion (of *surā*) which is more dense than (*prasannā*); the (portion) lower than (*kādambarī*) should be known as *jagala* and *medaka* is more dense than *jagala*; *vakkasa* is (*surā*) without the essential constituents and 'the seed of *surā*' (*surābīja*, i.e. that substance which makes the liquid ferment) is called *kiṇvaka*. Kauṭ. 2, 25, 32 (text p. 79; transl. Kangle p. 178-179; transl. J. J. Meyer p. 188; transl. Sham. p. 133) describes a kind of *surā*, called *sahakārasurā*, which is manufactured with mango fruits (*sahakāra*); three varieties of it are distinguished; in the same chapter *śvetasurā* is described, but the way it is prepared differs from that given by Ḍa. and He. See also : Aalto : Madyam apeyam, Comm. Vol. J. Nobel, 1959, p. 17-37; Ainslie 1, p. 451-453.

surāsava

PW : ein durch Maischen unreifer Fruchtkörner gewonnener Branntwein. MW : beer or spirituous liquor produced by the fermentation of unripe corn. Ca.Sū. 27, 187, Cakra : (an *āsava*) in (the manufacture of) which *surā* takes the place of water; a similar remark is made by Ḍa. in his comment on Su.Sū. 45, 187cd-188ab.

soma and *agni*

Phlegm (*kapha*) is often said to be of the nature of *soma* (*saumya*) and bile (*pitta*) of the nature of *agni* (*āgneya*). See e.g. Ca.Sū. 12, 11-12; A.h.Śā. 3, 90 and 96. See moreover on this subject : Kirfel, Die fünf Elemente; Kutumbiah, p. 64; Müller, Wörterheft, p. 82, nr. 30 and p. 148, nr. 236.

sauvīra — a partic. type of collyrium.

See : *añjana*.

sauvīra

PW : saurer Gersten-, Reis-, oder Weizenschleim. MW : sour gruel. Dutt, MM, p. 12 : other grains besides paddy are sometimes used for acetous fermentation (see : *kāñjika*); if the husked grains of barley are boiled and steeped in water, the resulting acid liquor is called *sauvīra*. HK : saurer Gerstenschleim. OP, p. 181, n. 4 : sour gruel prepared with husked cereals. Dn, *varga* 6, 251 : *sauvīra* is made from barley and wheat. Rn, *varga* 15, 297 : *sauvīra* is made from wheat. Ma.nigh., *varga* 8, 204cd : *sauvīraka* is made from unboiled or boiled, husked grains of barley. Bpn, *saṃdhānavarga* 8 : *sauvīra* is made from unboiled or boiled, husked grains of barley, and also from wheat according to some authorities (the same statement occurs Bho.ku. 1, p. 124). Śārṅga 2, 10, 11cd : *sauvīra* is the product of fermentation of husked and boiled grains of barley. Ca.Sū. 25, 49, Cakra : *sauvīra* is prepared with husked barley. The preparation of *sauvīraka* (= *sauvīra*) is described in detail : Su.Sū. 44, 35-40ab.

stambhana — obstipating (agent).

PW : stopfend. MW : a styptic or astringent. Dutt, MM, p. 6 : *stambhana* or constipators are medicines which from their drying, astringent and cooling qualities, and from their easy digestibility, increase the air and retain the secretions. Bhish : a constipator. Gul : astringent, styptic. HB : a styptic medicine. Ca.Sū. 22, 12ab : "*stambhana* is that which immobilizes what is moving and stabilizes that which is fluctuating." Va. 96, 12 = Śārṅga 1, 4, 12cd-13ab = Bhā.pra. 6, 222 : "That which on account of its dry, cold, astringent and easily maturating (qualities), brings about (an increase of) wind, is (called) *stambhana*." Su.Sū. 42, 10, Ḍa. : *stambhana* is that which immobilizes the limbs, or that which makes firm what is soft. A.h.Sū. 5, 29cd, Aruṇa : it is the opposite of *bhedin* and a synonym of *grāhin*; He. : it is the same as *grāhin*.

snāyu = *snāva* — cord.

There are nine hundred cords in the human body. See about these : Ca.Śā. 7, 14; Su.Śā. 5, 29-36; A.h.Śā. 3, 17; A.s.Śā. 5, 79-85. See : Chakraberty, p. 33-34; Dasgupta, H.I.Ph. 2, p. 352; Müller, Wörterheft, p. 149, nr. 239.

srotas — channel.

Ca. uses the term *srotas* in a very broad sense, including *sirā*, *dhamanī*, *nāḍī*, etc. (see Vi. 5, 9). This view is made mention of : A.s.Śā. 6, 50. Su.Śā. 5, 10 : there are nine channels, opening outwards, in men : the ears, the eyes, the mouth, the nostrils, the anus and the urethra; in women there are three more : (the openings) of the nipples of the breasts and the vagina. For another meaning of the term *srotas* in Su. see : Śā. 9, 12. A.h. distinguishes two classes of channels : a) the first class consists of the two nostrils, ears and eyes, the anus, mouth and urethra; in women there are three more : the nipples of the breasts and the vagina; b) the thirteen innner channels, which are the abodes of life, and carry the breath, the elements of the body, the impurities, water and food (Śā. 3, 40cd-42ab). The latter are of the same colour as the element (they carry); they are round, gross or minute, of an elongated form and like ramifications (of a plant) (Śā. 3, 43). A.s. says that the channels are innumerable (Śā. 5, 95), but enumerates also the two classes of channels, mentioned in A.h. (Śā. 6, 34-47). Kā. (Śā.) distinguishes two classes of channels : subtle and gross ones; the gross channels are nine in number : two below and seven above; subtle channels are the navel and the pores of the hairs. See : Chakraberty, p. 65-68; Dasgupta, H.I.Ph. 2, p. 344-352; Hariprapanna, Rasayogasāgara, *upodghāta* p. 168-169; Müller, Wörterheft, p. 149-150, nr. 240; Seal, p. 208-216.

sveda — sudation.

There are several methods of sudation. These are described : Ca.Sū. 14; Su.Ci. 32; A.h.Sū. 17; A.s.Sū. 26; Bhe.Sū. 23; Kā.Sū. 23; Hā. 4, 4. See also : Dutt, MM, p. 19-20; Jolly, Medicin, p. 27-28; Kutumbiah, p. 128.

haṭṭa

This word may be related to *haḍḍa*, which is a synonym of *asthi* acc. to Dn, *varga* 6, 369. Acc. to Dn again, *ekārthāni* nr. 18 (p. 435), *haṭṭavilāsinī* is a synonym of *nakha* (nail).

hariṇa

PW : Gazelle (*Antilope cervicapra*, Molesw.). MW : deer, antelope. Bhish : a red deer, a spotted deer. HK : Gazelle. Kav p. 169 : the common variety of the spotted deer. Acc. to many sources a *hariṇa* is a deer of a coppery colour (Cakra on Ca.Sū. 27, 46 and Ca.Ci. 3, 191; Su.Sū. 46, 57b; Ḍa. on Su.Sū. 20, 5; He. on A.h.Sū. 6, 43).

The term *hariṇa* is applied to a number of different species of deer; Cakra on Ca.Sū. 27, 46 : *pṛṣata* = *citrahariṇa*, *mṛgamātṛkā* = *hariṇajāti*, *kuraṅga* = *hariṇabheda*, *gokarṇa* = *hariṇaviśeṣa*, *ṛṣya* = *nīlāṇḍo hariṇaḥ*, *cāruṣka* = *hariṇabheda*, etc.; see also Cakra on Ca.Sū. 5, 5. The term *hariṇa* may be used to designate the female of *Antilope cervicapra* (Linnaeus, 1758) (see : *eṇa*), but it is often loosely applied to animals of related species (Antilopinae and Cervidae). The animals mentioned by Cakra are identified as follows : a) *pṛṣata* : the spotted deer or chital, *Axis axis* (Erxleben, 1777) = *Cervus axis* Erxleben, 1777 (Gul, vol. 6, Animals and birds, p. 55, nr. 19); PW : die gesprenkelte Gazelle; MW : the spotted antelope; Bhish : the porcine deer ?;

b) *mṛgamātṛkā*: the hog deer, *Axis porcinus* (Zimmermann, 1780) (Gul, p. 75, nr. 95); MW : a kind of red-coloured hare-like deer; c) *kuraṅga* : this may be *Muntiacus muntjak* (Zimmermann, 1780) = *Cervus muntjak* Zimmermann, 1780; d) *gokarṇa*; PW and MW: *Antilope picta* (Pallas, 1766), i.e. *Boselaphus tragocamelus* (Pallas, 1766); the mule deer (Gul, p. 53, nr. 12); the nilgai or blue bull, *Boselaphus tragocamelus* (Pallas, 1766) (Kohl, Asiatica, Festschr. Weller, 1954, p. 370); e) *ṛṣya*; PW : the buck of a species of antelope; MW : the painted or white-footed antelope; the musk deer, *Moschus moschiferus* Linnaeus, 1758 (Gul, p. 64, nr. 51); f) *cāruṣka* : the Indian gazelle, *Gazella gazella* (Pallas, 1766) (Gul, p. 54, nr. 14).

harita(ka) — vegetables.

The term *harita(ka)* is usually rendered by : (green) vegetable, (green) potherb. (PW; MW; HB; Kav). It designates, however, a restricted group of vegetables and potherbs : Cakra on Ca.Sū. 8, 20 : *haritaka* is fresh ginger (*ārdraka*), etc.; Ḍa. on Su.Sū. 19, 16: the group, called *haritaka*, consists of *kuṭhera, śigru, surasa, sumukha, āsuri, bhūstṛṇa, mūlaka* and *cukrikā*; A.h.Sū. 7, 32, Aruṇa and Candra : *haritaka* consists of *mūlaka, kuṭhera,* etc.; He. : (it consists of) that series of potherbs, which begins with *mūlaka* and is enumerated in the section on potherbs.

haritāla — orpiment (As_2S_3).

See about this substance : Ainslie 1, p. 499-504; Dutt, MM, p. 41-44; Garbe, Ind. Mineral., p. 48; IRM 1, p. 118-119; Nadk. 2, p. 20-23; Watt CP, p. 92-93. See about its synonyms and properties : Pr 434; Dn, *varga* 7, 119-127; Rn, *varga* 13, 58-60; Ma.nigh., *varga* 4, 27; Bpn, *dhātvādivarga* 127-131.

haridrā — turmeric.

Turmeric is the rhizome of Curcuma longa Linn.; the powder made from the rhizome is of a yellow colour; it is used in dyeing, in medicine and as a constituent of condiments. The yellow colour arises from curcumin (diferuloyl methane) and other related pigments, some of which have been isolated and chemically characterized. See : Chopra, Indigenous drugs, p. 325-327; Steinegger und Hänsel, Lehrbuch der Pharmakognosie, p. 403.

APPENDIX FOUR

SANSKRIT NAMES OF PLANTS AND THEIR BOTANICAL EQUIVALENTS

Introduction

Except in a rather restricted number of cases the botanical identification of plants mentioned in Sanskrit texts has always presented many problems. The number of disagreeing identifications, and above all the number of botanical names met with in the literature, has shown a steady increase in the course of time. This situation makes it expedient to collect the data scattered in the more important books on the subject and to arrange them systematically. The collection of references in this glossary, dealing with all the plants mentioned in the translation, notes and Appendices may be useful to others, the more so because many books on the subject have no adequate index; moreover, a great number of printing errors, inaccurate transcriptions of Sanskrit terms, etc., are frequent obstacles, diminishing the reliability of no small number of works. The omission of author's names after scientific names of plants is a very common occurrence and this unhappy practice, adopted in the Sanskrit-English dictionary of Monier-Williams, often leads to confusion, as will appear from the glossary.

The botanical names in this glossary have been checked, without any exception, by help of the Index Kewensis, the only work containing all the names of phanerogamous plants, and the nomenclature and synonymy have been set up in agreement with it. The name given by the Index Kewensis as the valid one has been put first, followed by the synonyms. There are, however, some exceptions to this general scheme. Deviations from the Index Kewensis occur whenever prescribed by the International Code (ed. 1972) in its list of nomina conservanda; names of species found in that list have been adopted. These changes are indicated by a reference to the International Code.

Names put between square brackets are not found in the Index; in the majority of cases this means that they are invalid or erroneous, but there are exceptions. Invalid names are usually those between square brackets when followed by a single author's name after the Latin name. When two author's names occur, the first one being put between round brackets, the name of the plant may be valid or invalid. I refrained from decisions regarding the validity of this type of names, prescribed by the International Code, by reason of my insufficient knowledge of botanical taxonomy and the complicated chronological problems which beset the field of nomenclature. In many cases, however, I tried to supply the synonyms necessary to construct the names in the way prescribed by the Code or to check those put between square brackets.

Names of varieties have been put between square brackets too when not recorded in the Index; for the greater part they are not found in the latter; whenever possible, i.e. whenever the botanical literature was accessible to me, I referred to botanical works in which the particular variety is described.

akṣa

(1) = *vibhītaka* (Avk; Bpn, p. 9; Dgv, nr. 149; Dn 1, 212; Gul; HB; HK; KB 2, p. 1017-1020; MW; Pr 220; PW; Rn 11, 322-323; V 6, p. 160; Vśs);

(2) a) = *rudrākṣa* (Avk; Vśs);
b) the seed of *rudrākṣa* (MW; PW);

(3) a) = *indrākṣa* (Vśs : = the tuberous root of the creeper called *ṛṣabhaka*);
b) =*ṛṣabhaka* (Avk; Vśs); *ṛṣabhaka* is an unidentifiable plant, but Vśs identifies it as CARPOPOGON PRURIENS; see : *kapikacchū*;

(4) = *devaśirīṣa* (Vśs, unidentified).

agaru (sometimes considered to be a synonym of *aguru*)

(1) a) Chopra : [COMMIPHORA ROXBURGHII (ARN.) ENGL.] = [C. AGALLOCHA (WIGHT ET ARN.) ENGL.] = BALSAMODENDRUM ROXBURGHII ARN. = AMYRIS COMMIPHORA ROXB.;
b) KB 1, p. 528-529 : COMMIPHORA AGALLOCHA ENGL. = BALSAMODENDRUM ROXBURGHII ARN. = AMYRIS COMMIPHORA ROXB.; the Index Kewensis disagrees with Chopra and KB and distinguishes:
a) COMMIPHORA MUKUL ENGL. = C. ROXBURGHII ENGL. = BALSAMODENDRUM ROXBURGHII STOCKS = B. WIGHTII ARN.;
b) COMMIPHORA ROXBURGHII ALSTON = C. AGALLOCHA ENGL. = BALSAMODENDRUM AGALLOCHA WIGHT ET ARN. = B. COMMI-

PHORA ROYLE = B. ROXBURGHII ARN. = AMYRIS COMMIPHORA ROXB.; the confusion in the nomenclature is due to the fact that Chopra identifies C. ROXBURGHII ENGL. with C. AGALLOCHA ENGL., distinguished as two species in the Index Kewensis, and that he considers C. MUKUL ENGL. as a separate species, synonymous with B. MUKUL HOOK. EX STOCKS, while C. MUKUL ENGL. is a synonym of C. ROXBURGHII ENGL. in the Index Kewensis; Hooker describes (1, p. 529) : a) BALSAMODENDRON MUKUL HOOK. EX STOCKS = B. ROXBURGHII STOCKS = (?) B. WIGHTII ARN., and b) B. ROXBURGHII ARN. = AMYRIS COMMIPHORA ROXB. = (?) AMYRIS AGALLOCHA ROXB.; Cooke describes (1, p. 212-213) COMMIPHORA MUKUL ENGL. = BALSAMODENDRON MUKUL HOOK. EX STOCKS = B. ROXBURGHII STOCKS (NON ARNOTT); Duthie (1, p. 139-140) agrees with Cooke;

(2) AQUILARIA AGALLOCHA ROXB. (Chopra; IRM 1, p. 89-90; KB 3, p. 2171-2172; Nadk. 1, nr. 208; Watt CP, p. 72-74);

(3) AMYRIS AGALLOCHA ROXB. (MW; PW); acc. to HK this is a synonym of AQUILARIA AGALLOCHA ROXB., but the Index Kewensis regards it as a separate species;

(4) SAPIUM SEBIFERUM ROXB. (KB 3, p. 2284);

(5) EXCOECARIA AGALLOCHA LINN. (Chopra; KB 3, p. 2285-2286);

(6) DYSOXYLUM MALABARICUM BEDD. EX C.DC. (Avk; Nadk. 1, nr. 902).

aguru

(1) AQUILARIA AGALLOCHA ROXB. (Ainslie 1, p. 479; Avk; Bpn, p. 194; Dgv, nr. 272; DWH 3, p. 217-224; Dy, p. 674-677; Gul; HB; HK; Kav; MW; PW; Roxb., p. 377; V 1, p. 6; Vśs; Watt CP, p. 72-74; Wise) = ALOËXYLUM AGALLOCHUM LOUR. = ALOËXYLUM VERUM LOUR.;

(2) AMYRIS AGALLOCHA ROXB. (HK); see : *agaru*;

(3) a) AQUILARIA MALACCENSIS LAM. [Intern. Code] (Avk; DWH 3, p. 217-224) = AQUILARIA OVATA CAV.;

b) A. OVATA (Avk; PW);

c) [A. OVATA LINN.] (Ainslie 1, p. 479);

(4) DALBERGIA SISSOO ROXB. (Avk : = *śiṃśapā*; IRM 3, p. 7-11; KB 1, p. 818-819; PW : = *aguruśiṃśapā* = *śiṃśapā*; Vśs : = *kapilaśiṃśapā* = *śiṃśapā*);

(5) D. LATIFOLIA ROXB. (Avk).

agnimantha

(1) PREMNA INTEGRIFOLIA LINN. (Ainslie 2, p. 210-211; Avk; Bpn, p. 281-282 : *bṛhadagnimantha*; Chopra, Ind. drugs; Dutt; DWH 3, p. 66-68; HK; KB 3, p. 1927-1928; Nadk. 1, nr. 2025; V 1, p. 79) = P. SPINOSA ROXB. (Avk; Dutt; HK; Kav; MW; Nadk. 1, nr. 2025; PW; Wise) = P. SERRATIFOLIA LINN. (Avk; Dy, p. 604; Kav; KB 3, p. 1927-1928; Nadk. 1, nr. 2025; PA 1, 2, p. 32-38; Vśs);

(2) P. LONGIFOLIA (PW : ?); the Index Kewensis mentions two species of this name, both occurring in India : a) P. LONGIFOLIA ROXB., b) P. BENGALENSIS C. B. CLARKE = P. LONGIFOLIA WALL.;

(3) P. LATIFOLIA ROXB. (PA 1, 2, p. 32 : used as a substitute);

(4) P. CORIACEA C. B. CLARKE (PA 1, 2, p. 32 : used as a substitute);

(5) CLERODENDRUM PHLOMOIDES LINN.F. (Avk; Bpn, p. 281-282 : *kṣudrāgnimantha*; Gul; IRM 2, p. 232; KB 3, p. 1947-1948; Nadk. 1, nr. 618) [= C. PHLOMIDIS LINN.F.] (IRM 2, p. 232); see about the spelling of this name : Flora Pavagadh, p. 187;

(6) C. INERME GAERTN. (Avk; DWH 3, p. 76-79 : = *kṣudrāgnimantha* acc. to some; Nadk. 1, nr. 616 : *kṣudrāgnimantha*);

(7) C. NEREIFOLIUM WALL. (Nadk. 1, nr. 616 : *kṣudrāgnimantha*) = C. INERME R.BR.

aṅkola = *aṅkoṭa*

ALANGIUM DECAPETALUM LAM. [Intern. Code] (AFM 1, p. 16-19; Avk; Nadk. 1, nr. 88) = A. HEXAPETALUM LAM. (Dutt; HK; Kav; MW; Nadk. 1, nr. 88; PW; Vśs) = A. LAMARCKII THW. (AFM 1, p. 16-19; Avk; Bpn, p. 365; Chopra; Dutt; DWH 2, p. 164-166; Gul; IRM 1, p. 42; Kav; KB 2, p. 1237-1239; Nadk. 1, nr. 88; V 1, p. 8) [= A. LAMARCKII LINN.] (HK) = A. TOMENTOSUM LAM. (Avk; Nadk. 1, nr. 88) = A. SALVIIFOLIUM WANGERIN (AFM 1, p. 16-19) [= A. SALVIIFOLIUM (Linn.f.) Wangerin] (Chopra; IRM 1, p. 42) = GREWIA SALVIFOLIA LINN.F.

ajamodā

(1) APIUM GRAVEOLENS LINN. (Avk; Bpn, p. 27; Chopra; Gul; KB 2, p. 1199-1201; Na 1, nr. 250; Nadk. 1, nr. 205; V 1, p. 15);

(2) a) [TRACHYSPERMUM ROXBURGHIANUM (DC.) Sprague] (Chopra) = CARUM ROXBURGHIANUM BENTH. ET HOOK.F. (Chopra);

b) TRACHYSPERMUM INVOLUCRATUM H. WOLFF = T. ROXBURGHIANUM H. WOLFF = CARUM ROXBURGHIANUM BENTH. ET

Hook.f. (Avk; Dutt; Dy, p. 378; HK; Nadk. 1, nr. 484 and 2065; V 1, p. 15; Watt CP, p. 285) = Apium involucratum Roxb. ex Flem. (Avk; Dutt; HK; Kav; MW; PW; Vśs) = Ptychotis roxburghiana DC. (Avk; Nadk. 1, nr. 2065) = Pimpinella involucrata Wight et Arn. (Avk; HSu; Kav; Vśs);

(3) a) [Trachyspermum ammi (Linn.) Sprague] (Chopra) = Carum copticum Benth. et Hook.f. (Chopra); Index Kewensis : Trachyspermum ammi Sprague = Sison ammi Linn.;

b) Trachyspermum copticum (Linn.) Link [Intern. Code] = Carum copticum Benth. et Hook.f. (Avk; DWH 2, p. 116-119; KB 2, p. 1204-1206; Nadk. 1, nr. 482 and 2065) = C. ajowan Benth. et Hook.f. (Nadk. 1, nr. 479) = Ptychotis ajowan DC. (Avk; DWH 2, p. 117; Nadk. 1, nr. 2065) = P. coptica DC. (Nadk. 1, nr. 2065)= Ammi copticum Linn. (Avk; Nadk. 1, nr. 2065) = Ligusticum ajawain Roxb. ex Flem. (Avk) = L. ajowan Royle (MW; PW; Vśs);

(4) Carum carvi Linn. (PW);

(5) C. petroselinum Benth. et Hook.f. = Apium petroselinum Linn. (Avk).

ajājī

(1) Cuminum cyminum Linn. (Ainslie 1, p. 100-101; Avk, = *sthūlajīraka*; Bpn, p. 30-33; Dgv, nr. 176; HB; HK, = *jīraka*; Kav; KB 2, p. 1227-1228; MW; Na 1, nr. 246 : *śuklājājī*; Nadk. 1, nr. 741; Vśs : = *jīraka*; Watt CP, p. 442-443);

(2) Nigella sativa Linn. (Avk : *kālājājī*; Kav, = *kṛṣṇajīraka*; KB 1, p. 11-12 : *kālājājī* = *kṛṣṇajīraka* = *sthūlajīraka*; Na 1, nr. 5, = *sthūlajīraka*; Vśs : = *kṛṣṇajīraka*) = N. indica Roxb. ex Flem. (Avk; KB 1, p. 11-12; MW; PW : = *kṛṣṇajīraka*; Vśs);

(3) Carum carvi Linn. (KB 2, p. 1201-1203 : *kṛṣṇājājī*; Na 1, nr. 247, = *kṛṣṇajīraka*);

(4) Ficus hispida Linn.f. (KB 3, p. 2322-2324; Vśs) = F. oppositifolia Willd. (Avk; MW; PW : = *kākoḍumbarikā*; Vśs).

atasī

Linum usitatissimum Linn.

apāmārga

(1) Achyranthes aspera Linn. (AFM 1, p. 4-6; Ainslie 2, p. 221-

222; Avk : *śvetāpāmārga*; Bpn, p. 414; Chopra; Dgv, nr. 259; Dutt; DWH 2, p. 65 and 3, p. 135-138; Dy, p. 651-652; Ghosh; Gul; HB; HK; IRM 1, p. 24; Kav; KB 3, p. 2066-2068; MW; Nadk. 1, nr. 33; PA 1, 6, p. 54-64; PW; Sanyal; V 1, p. 45; Vśs) = A. OBTUSIFOLIA LAM. (AFM 1, p. 4; Avk) [= A. HEPTAPETALUM ROXB.] (HK) = A. INDICA MILL. [= A. INDICA ROXB.] (Avk);

(2) A. BIDENTATA BLUME (Avk; Chopra; Dutt; KB 3, p. 2069; Vśs) = A. ASPERA WALL.;

(3) [A. SPICATA BURM.] (Avk);

(4) CYATHULA GENICULATA LOUR. [Intern. Code : Cyathula is a nom. conserv.] = C. PROSTRATA BLUME (PA 1, 6, p. 54, footnote : *kṣudrāpāmārga*) = DESMOCHAETA PROSTRATA DC. = PUPALIA PROSTRATA R.BR.

amlavetasa

(1) RUMEX VESICARIUS LINN. (Avk; Dutt : = *cukra*; HB; HK; Kav; KB 3, p. 2114-2115; MW; PW; V 1, p. 66-67; Vśs; Wise);

(2) R. CRISPUS LINN. (Avk; Chopra; Nadk. 1, nr. 2171);

(3) RHEUM WEBBIANUM ROYLE (Nadk. 1, nr. 2113 and 2118) = RH. AUSTRALE D. DON (Nadk. 1, nr. 2113) = RH. EMODI WALL. (Nadk. 1, nr. 2113);

(4) RH. ACUMINATUM HOOK.F. ET THOMS. (Nadk. 1, nr. 2112 and 2113);

(5) RH. MOORCROFTIANUM ROYLE (Nadk. 1, nr. 2113 and 2114);

(6) RH. OFFICINALE BAILL. (Nadk. 1, nr. 2113 and 2116);

(7) RH. SPICIFORME ROYLE (Nadk. 1, nr. 2113);

(8) GARCINIA PEDUNCULATA ROXB. (Na 1, nr. 49);

(9) CALAMUS VIMINALIS WILLD. = C. FASCICULATUS ROXB. (Kav, p. 281); Bpn (p. 581-582) gives no botanical name of *amlavetasa*, because there are many different opinions.

amlikā

(1) TAMARINDUS INDICA LINN. (Ainslie 1, p. 425-428; Avk; Bpn, p. 581; Dgv, nr. 120; Dutt; DWH 1, p. 532-536; Dy, p. 270-272; Gul; HK : *amlīkā*; Kav; KB 2, p. 887-890; MW; Na 1, nr. 178; Nadk. 1, nr. 2434; PW; Roxb., p. 530; Sanyal; V 1, p. 145; Vśs);

(2) OXALIS CORNICULATA LINN. (Ainslie 2, p. 324-326; Chopra; MW; Nadk. 1, nr. 1777) = O. MONADELPHA ROXB. EX WIGHT ET ARN. (Vśs, = *cāṅgerī*) = O. PUSILLA SALISB. (PW, — *kṣudrāmlikā* = *cāṅgerī*);

(3) RUMEX DENTATUS LINN. (V 1, p. 63);

(4) MANGIFERA INDICA LINN. (Vśs);
(5) SPONDIAS MANGIFERA WILLD. (Vśs, = *mācikā* = *āmrātaka*);
(6) PHYLLANTHUS NIRURI LINN. (KB 3, p. 2225-2227);
(7) = *palāśīlatā* (PW; Vśs); acc. to KB 1, p. 788-789 and Nadk. 1, nr. 397 *palāśīlatā* is BUTEA SUPERBA ROXB.;
(8) Kav (footnote p. 352): "Cakra says (on Ca.Sū. 27, 121) that it is a little shrub growing in Kāmarūpa and its neighbourhood; Gaṅgādhara believes that *amlikā* is otherwise called *amlārdraka*, a sour variety of ginger; the plant is difficult to identify."

amlīkā

(1) TAMARINDUS INDICA LINN. (HK);
(2) OXALIS CORNICULATA LINN. (MW);
(3) = *amlikā* (PW).

arjaka

(1) OCIMUM GRATISSIMUM LINN. (MW; PW; V 1, p. 78);
(2) O. BASILICUM LINN. (Avk; Bpn, p. 511-512);
(3) O. SANCTUM LINN. (KB 3, p. 1965-1968) = O. VILLOSUM ROXB. (Roxb., p. 462);
(4) O. CANUM SIMS (Chopra; KB 3, p. 1960-1961, = *kṣudratulasī*) = O. AMERICANUM LINN. (Chopra);
(5) ORTHOSIPHON GRANDIFLORUS BOLDINGH EX HEYNE (Bpn, p. 511-512).

aśvattha

FICUS RELIGIOSA LINN. = UROSTIGMA RELIGIOSUM GASP.

āḍhakī

CAJANUS CAJAN (LINN.) MILLSP. [Intern. Code] (Chopra; IRM 2, p. 6-11) = C. INDICUS SPRENG. (Avk; Bpn, p. 647; Chopra; Dutt; DWH 1, p. 489; Gul; HK; IRM 2, p. 6; Kav; KB 1, p. 809-811; MW; Na 1, nr. 135; Nadk. 1, nr. 409; PW; V 1, p. 82; Vśs; Watt CP, p. 196) = C. BICOLOR DC. (Avk) = C. FLAVUS DC. (Avk) = CAJAN CAJAN MILLSP. = CYTISUS CAJAN LINN. (Avk; Dutt; HK; Kav; V 1, p. 82; Vśs); there are two varieties of this plant, var. flavus DC. (corolla yellow) and var. bicolor DC. (corolla veined with red), both cultivated in India; these varieties have been looked upon as species by some authors; see Watt CP, p. 196-197 and Purseglove 1, p. 237.

āmalaka = *āmalakī*

(1) PHYLLANTHUS EMBLICA LINN. = EMBLICA OFFICINALIS GAERTN.; (2) JUSTICIA GENDARUSSA BURM.F. = GENDARUSSA VULGARIS NEES (MW); (3) ADHATODA VASICA NEES (KB 3, p. 1899-1902; Vśs) = JUSTICIA ADHATODA LINN. = GENDARUSSA ADHATODA STEUD. (PW); (4) = *padmakāṣṭha* (Vśs).

āmra

MANGIFERA INDICA LINN. = M. DOMESTICA GAERTN. (Nadk. 1, nr. 1547) = M. MONTANA HEYNE EX WIGHT ET ARN. (Nadk. 1, nr. 1547).

āmrātaka

(1) SPONDIAS MANGIFERA WILLD. (Avk; Bpn, p. 551; Chopra; Dutt; DWH 1, p. 395-396; Gul; HB; HK; KB 1, p. 673-675; MW; Na 1, nr. 120; Nadk. 1, nr. 2367; PW; Roxb., p. 387; Sanyal; V 1, p. 116; Vśs) = S. PINNATA KURZ (Chopra; KB 1, p. 673-675) [= S. MANGIFERA PERS.] (Kav) [= S. EKMINUT] (Nadk. 1, nr. 2367) = MANGIFERA PINNATA LINN.F. (KB 1, p. 673-675);
(2) = *rājāmra*, a kind of MANGIFERA INDICA LINN. (Vśs);
(3) BUCHANANIA LATIFOLIA ROXB. = SPONDIAS ELLIPTICA ROTTB. EX HOOK.F. (Avk).

ārdraka

ZINGIBER OFFICINALE ROSC. (Avk; Bpn, p. 14; Chopra; Dgv, nr. 309; Dutt; DWH 3, p. 420-425; Gul; HB; HK; KB 4, p. 2435-2438; Nadk. 1, nr. 2658; PA 1, 9, p. 102-117; Roxb., p. 16; V 1, p. 33; Vśs) = Z. MISSIONIS WALL. (PA 1, 9, p. 114) [= CURCUMA LONGIFOLIA WALL. CAT.] (PA 1, 9, p. 114) = AMOMUM ANGUSTIFOLIUM SALISB. = A. ZINGIBER LINN. (Ainslie 1, p. 152-153; V 1, p. 33) [= A. ZINGIBER ROSC.] (PA 1, 9, p. 114).

āsurī

= *rājikā* (Bpn, *dhānyavarga* 72; Dgm, p. 115; Dn, *varga* 4, 60; KB 1, p. 168-170; MW; Pr 243; PW; Rn, *varga* 16, 90; V 9, p. 1).

ikṣu — sugar-cane

SACCHARUM OFFICINARUM LINN.

ikṣvāku = *kaṭutumbī* = *tiktatumbī*

(1) a) LAGENARIA SICERARIA STANDLEY = L. VULGARIS SERINGE (Avk; Bpn, p. 671; Dgv, nr. 165; DWH 2, p. 63 : the bitter variety; Gul; KB 2, p. 1116-1119; Nadk. 1, nr. 1419; V 2, p. 28) = CUCURBITA LAGENARIA LINN. (Avk; Kav; KB 2, p. 1116-1119; Nadk. 1, nr. 1419; V 2, p. 28) = C. SICERARIA MOLINA;

b) the wild variety of a) (MW; PW; Roxb., p. 700; Vśs);

(2) CUCURBITA PEPO LINN. (Nadk. 1, nr. 1419);

(3) CITRULLUS COLOCYNTHIS SCHRAD. (MW; PW).

indrayava

= the seeds of *kuṭaja*.

utpala

(1) NYMPHAEA STELLATA WILLD. (Chopra; Dutt; Gul; HK; KB 1, p. 113-115; Na 1, nr. 18; Nadk. 1, nr. 1726) = N. CYANEA ROXB. (HK; PW) = N. CAERULEA SAVIGN. (Kav; MW) [= N. STELLATA LINN.] (Kav) = CASTALIA STELLATA BLUME (KB 1, p. 113-115);

(2) N. LOTUS LINN. (Nadk. 1, nr. 1726) [= N. LOTUS HOOK.F. ET THOMS.] (KB 1, p. 112-113) = N. RUBRA ROXB. EX SALISB. (KB 1, p. 112-113) = N. RUBRA (Nadk. 1, nr. 1726; PW);

(3) N. ODORATA [SOLAND. IN] AIT. (Ainslie 2, p. 381);

(4) COSTUS SPECIOSUS SM. (MW; PW, = *kuṣṭha*; Vśs : = *kuṣṭha*);

(5) SAUSSUREA LAPPA C. B. CLARKE (Nadk. 1, nr. 2239, = *kuṣṭha*);

(6) = *padmakāṣṭha* (Vśs);

(7) BOMBAX CEIBA LINN. = B. MALABARICUM DC. = B. HEPTAPHYLLUM CAV. (Vśs).

udīcya = *udīcī*

(1) = *bālā* (HK; Kav; KB 1, p. 323-324);

(2) = *hrīvera* (KB 1, p. 323-324 : = *bālā* = *hrīvera*; Vśs);

(3) a kind of perfume (MW; PW); the term *udīcya*, though occurring thirteen times in Ca., is not explained by Cakra.

udumbara

(1) FICUS RACEMOSA WALL. = F. RACEMOSA (Nadk. 1, nr. 1041) [= F. RACEMOSA LINN.] (acc. to Chopra, but the Index Kewensis indicates

that this is not a synonym of F. RACEMOSA WALL., but may be a synonym of F. HISPIDA LINN.F.) = F. GLOMERATA ROXB. (AFM 1, p. 71-74; Avk; Bpn, p. 516; Chopra; Dgv, nr. 287; Dutt; DWH 3, p. 340; Ghosh; Gul; HB; HK; Kav; KB 3, p. 2327-2329; MW; Nadk. 1, nr. 1041; PA 1, 3, p. 93-99; PW; Roxb., p. 646; V 3, p. 122; Vśs) = F. CHITTAGONGA MIQ. (AFM 1, p. 71) = COVELLIA GLOMERATA MIQ. (Dutt; HK; Kav);

(2) F. INFECTORIA ROXB. = F. RACEMOSA WILLD. (Ainslie 2, p. 30-31);

(3) F. GIBBOSA BLUME (Chopra; KB 3, p. 2311-2312; Nadk. 1, nr. 1040) = F. TUBERCULATA ROXB. (KB 3, p. 2311-2312; Nadk. 1, nr. 1040);

(4) F. CARICA LINN. (Ainslie 1, p. 131-132; Ghosh).

uddāla(*ka*)

(1) PASPALUM SCROBICULATUM LINN. (Bpn, p. 654; KB 4, p. 2705-2706) = P. FRUMENTACEUM ROTTL. EX ROEM. ET SCHULT. (HK; MW; PW);

(2) a) CORDIA MYXA (Bpn, p. 571-572; MW; PW; V 9, p. 32; Vśs);
b) C. LATIFOLIA (Avk; MW; PW; Vśs);
c) C. OBLIQUA (V 9, p. 32); these names are insufficient to determine which species of Cordia is meant, for the Index Kewensis records (for the greater part in agreement with Hooker's Flora of India):
a) C. MYXA LINN. = C. DICHOTOMA FORST.F. = C. LATIFOLIA WALL.;
b) C. OBLIQUA WILLD. = C. LATIFOLIA ROXB. = C. MYXA THW.;
c) C. MYXA FORSK.;

(3) CORDIA WALLICHII G. DON (IRM 2, p. 347; KB 3, p. 1677-1678) [= C. OBLIQUA WILLD. VAR. WALLICHII C. B. CLARKE] (IRM 2, p. 347; KB 3, p. 1677-1678); see Hooker 4, p. 137;

(4) BAUHINIA VARIEGATA LINN. (Dgv, nr. 121, = *kovidāra*; KB 2, p. 898-900);

(5) B. ACUMINATA LINN. (Kav, p. 620 : acc. to Gaṅgādhara).

umā

= *atasī*.

uśīra is the root of

(1) [VETIVERIA ZIZANIOIDES (LINN.) NASH] (Bpn, p. 239; Chopra) =

V. ZIZANIOIDES NASH (Dgv, nr. 344; Gul; Nadk. 1, nr. 2583; V 3, p. 44-45) = V. ZIZANIOIDES STAPF (KB 4, p. 2671-2673; Watt CP, p. 1106) = V. ODORATA VIREY (Nadk. 1, nr. 2582; Watt CP, p. 1106) = PHALARIS ZIZANIOIDES LINN. = ANDROPOGON MURICATUS RETZ. (Avk; Bpn, p. 239; Chopra; Dutt; DWH 3, p. 571-573; Gul; HB; HK; Kav; KB 4, p. 2671-2673; MW; Nadk, 1. nr. 180; PW; V 3, p. 44-45; Vśs; Watt CP, p. 1106; Wise) = A. SQUARROSUS LINN.F. (Nadk. 1, nr. 180; Watt CP, p. 1106) [= A. SQUARROSUS COOKE (NON LINN.F.)] (KB 4, p. 2671-2673) = ANATHERUM MURICATUM BEAUV. (Watt CP, p. 1106);

(2) ANDROPOGON LANIGER (Avk : *śvetośīra*); the Index Kewensis records two species :

a) A. IWARANCUSA ROXB. = A. LANIGER DESF.;

b) SPODIOPOGON ANGUSTIFOLIUS TRIN. = S. LANIGER NEES EX STEUD. = A. LANIGER MUNRO.

ūṣaṇa

(1) = *marica* (Bpn; Dgv; Dn; MW; Pr; Rn);

(2) = *pippalī* (PW, = *uṣaṇā*);

(3) = the root of *pippalī* (*pippalīmūla*) (Bpn; Dn; Rn);

(4) = *cavika* (PW, = *uṣaṇā*);

(5) = *śuṇṭhī* (Bpn; PW, = *uṣaṇā*);

(6) = *citraka* (Bpn; KB 2, p. 1466-1469).

ervāru(*ka*)

(1) [CUCUMIS MELO LINN. VAR. MOMORDICA DUTHIE ET FULLER] (Chopra; HK; KB 2, p. 1142; Watt CP, p. 438-439); see Duthie 1, p. 340-342; = C. MOMORDICA ROXB. (Avk; Chopra; HK; Kav; KB 2, p. 1142; Nadk. 1, nr. 729);

(2) [C. MELO LINN. VAR. UTILISSIMUS DUTHIE ET FULLER] (KB 2, p. 1143); see Duthie 1, p. 340-342; = C. UTILISSIMUS ROXB. (Avk; Bpn, p. 671; Gul; HB; HSu; KB 2, p. 1143; MW; PW; Vśs).

elavālu(*ka*)

Much confusion exists concerning this substance as will become apparent from the material collected :

(1) Bpn, *karpūrādivarga* 120 : it is also called *kapitthatvac* (the bark of *kapittha*). Acc. to the Hindī comm. (p. 262-263) the substance is described somewhere in Bhā.pra. as resembling *kaṅkola* and smelling like *kuṣṭha*. In the same comm. three different identifications are made

mention of : a) PRUNUS CERASUS LINN., b) GISEKIA PHARNACIOIDES LINN., c) MUKIA SCABRELLA ARN. (Index Kewensis : MELOTHRIA MADERASPATANA COGN. = MUKIA SCABRELLA ARN. = MUKIA MADERASPATANA M. ROEM).

(2) DWH 2, p. 105-107 : GISEKIA PHARNACIOIDES LINN.; p. 105 : "This plant is called in Sanskrit *vāluka* and *elavāluka* on account of the number of large raphides contained in the leaves, and which give them the appearance of being full of sand (*vālu*)." (Raphides are minute intracellular crystals, usually of an acicular form).

(3) Gul : cherry tree (PRUNUS CERASUS LINN.).

(4) HB, p. 21 : GISEKIA PHARNACIOIDES LINN.; ibid., footnote 70 : "*elavālu* is mentioned Su.Sū. 38, 14, where Ḍa.'s comm. explains it as a reddish powder (*harivāluka*), resembling that of the seeds of the *kṛṣṇagandhā* (*kṛṣṇagandhikaphala*). The latter is a name of the horse-radish tree or *śigru* or *śobhāñjana*;" ibid., p. 91, footnote 74 : "In the Phar. Ind. (= DWH) 2, p. 105, it is wrongly identified with *vāluka*; the seeds, supplied to me by a native druggist, seem to be simply those of chickweed."

(5) HK : quotes the identifications of PW and Hoernle.

(6) Kav, p. 37 : a kind of red powder made of some seeds obtainable of every native druggist, not identified; p. 294 : a fragrant powder of a bark sold under that name; it is believed to come from the Spice Islands; p. 642 : Gaṅgādhara takes it as implying *tejavala*, a kind of wood apparently dry but juicy within; it is brought from Nepal.

(7) KB 2, p. 1187-1188 : GISEKIA PHARNACIOIDES LINN.

(8) MW : the fragrant bark of FERONIA ELEPHANTUM (*kapitthatvac*); a granular substance (apparently a vegetable of a reddish-brown colour, used as a drug and perfume).

(9) PW : the fragrant bark of FERONIA ELEPHANTUM (*kapitthatvac*), used medicinally.

(10) V 7, p. 67 : GISEKIA PHARNACIOIDES.

(11) Vśs : name of a perfume; a red powder sold under that name; the seed of some plant.

(12) Ḍa. on Su.Sū. 38, 14 (printed ed., different from Hoernle's text) : "a reddish powder (*harivāluka*), resembling the black, fragrant *kaṭphala*;" *kaṭphala* is usually identified as MYRICA NAGI THUNB.

elā

Two kinds of *elā* are distinguished : 1) *sūkṣmailā* or *kṣudrailā*, the small cardamom, and 2) *sthūlailā* or *bṛhadelā*, the large cardamom.

(1) ELETTARIA CARDAMOMUM MATON (Avk; Bpn, p. 222-223; Chopra; Dgv, nr. 308; Dutt; DWH 3, p. 428-436; Gul; HB; HK; IRM 3, p. 149-160; KB 4, p. 2442-2444; Nadk. 1, nr. 924; V 1, p. 147; Vśs; Watt CP, p. 511-517) = E. MAJOR SM. (Avk) = E. REPENS BAILL. (Avk; Nadk. 1, nr. 924) = ALPINIA CARDAMOMUM ROXB. (KB 4, p. 2442-2444);

(2) AMOMUM SUBULATUM ROXB. (Bpn, p. 221; Chopra; Dgv, nr. 308; Dutt; DWH 3, p. 436; HK; KB 4, p. 2432-2433; Nadk. 1, nr. 154; V 1, p. 148; Vśs; Watt CP, p. 65);

(3) A. AMARUM F. P. SMITH (Nadk. 1, nr. 150);

(4) A. XANTHIOIDES WALL. (Dy, p. 788-789);

(5) A. KEPULAGA SPRAGUE ET BURKILL (Bpn, p. 224 : used as a substitute) = A. CARDAMOMUM ROXB. (NON LINN.) (Roxb., p. 24 : *elā*);

(6) A. AROMATICUM ROXB. (Bpn, p. 222 : used as a substitute).

elāvāluka

This term occurs Kauṭ. 2, 25, 27 (text p. 79; transl. Kangle p. 178; transl. J. J. Meyer p. 187; transl. Sham. p. 133). Sham. renders it by SOLANUM MELONGENA, without any comment. J. J. Meyer takes it as the fragrant bark of FERONIA ELEPHANTUM (*elavāluka*), but remarks that the reading *elāvāluka* makes it probable that one should translate : *elā* and *vāluka* (i.e. *harivāluka*, the fragrant bark of *kapittha*); Kangle translates : cardamum, *vāluka*. Acc. to Vśs *elāvāluka* is a synonym of *elavāluka*.

oṣṭhopamaphalā

= *bimbī*.

kakkola

(1) PIPER CUBEBA LINN.F. (Gul);

(2) possibly the fruit of COCCULUS INDICUS (Avk; Vśs); Index Kewensis : COCCULUS INDICUS ROYLE = ANAMIRTA PANICULATA COLEBR.?;

(3) a species of plant bearing a berry, the inner side of which is waxy and aromatic (Kav; MW);

(4) a rutaceous berry, apparently that of LUVUNGA SCANDENS BUCH.-HAM. (DWH 1, p. 268).

kaṅkola

(1) PIPER CUBEBA LINN.F. (Bpn, p. 258-259; Dgv, nr. 267; DWH 3, p. 180-183; HK; MW; PW; V 2, p. 66);

(2) a particular substance sold under that name (Vśs).

kaṅgu

(1) SETARIA ITALICA BEAUV. (Avk; Chopra; Dutt; DWH 3, p. 619; HK; KB 4, p. 2718-2719; Nadk. 1, nr. 2291; V 2, p. 113; Watt CP, p. 988-989) = PANICUM ITALICUM LINN. (Ainslie 1, p. 226-227; Avk; Chopra; Dutt; Gul; HK; Nadk. 1, nr. 1793; PW; Roxb., p. 101-102; Vśs; Watt CP, p. 988-989);

(2) PANICUM FRUMENTACEUM (Nadk. 1, nr. 1791); Nadk. considers P. FRUM. as a synonym of SETARIA ITALICA BEAUV., but this is not confirmed by the Index Kewensis, which distinguishes two species: P. COLONUM LINN. = P. FRUMENTACEUM ROXB., and SORHGUM VULGARE PERS. = P. FRUMENTACEUM SALISB.; Hooker (7, p. 30-32) regards P. FRUMENTACEUM ROXB. as a synonym of P. CRUS-GALLI LINN. VAR. FRUMENTACEUM and describes P. COLONUM LINN. as a separate species; Cooke (3, p. 446-447) says that P. FRUMENTACEUM ROXB. is a synonym of P. STAGNINUM RETZ. VAR. FRUMENTACEA TRIM.;

(3) PAPAVER DUBIUM (Bpn, p. 653); the Index Kewensis mentions two plants of this name: P. DUBIUM LINN., and P. DUBIUM TENORE = P. PINNATIFIDUM MORIS.; it may be that P. D. LINN. is meant, because this species is also described in the Flora Iranica.

kaṭukā

(1) PICRORRHIZA KURROA ROYLE EX BENTH. (Bpn, p. 70; Chopra) = P. KURROA ROYLE (DWH 2, p. 459; Dy, p. 577-578) = [P. KURROA BENTH.] (Dutt; HK; KB 3, p. 1825-1826; Nadk. 1, nr. 1907) = P. KURROA (Avk; Dgv, nr. 235; HB; Sanyal; Vśs);

(2) = *kaṭvī* (PW: name of several plants);

(3) = *kaṭurohiṇī* (PW);

(4) = *tāmbūlī* (PW; acc. to PW: ARECA CATECHU LINN., but acc. to PA 1, 9, p. 71: PIPER BETLE LINN.);

(5) RUELLIA LONGIFOLIA (PW: = *kulikavṛkṣa*); the Index Kewensis enumerates five species of this name; the genus Ruellia consists of herbs and undershrubs (Hooker 4, p. 411), not of trees; the species meant by PW may be R. LONGIFOLIA T. ANDERS., described by Hooker (4, p. 412);

(6) = *kaṭutumbī* (Vśs);
(7) a tree with a fragrant fruit (PW);
(8) a) = *kṣudracuñcu* (Vśs); *cuñcu* is identified as [MARSILEA DENTATA];
b) = *kṣudracañcu* : CORCHORUS ANTICHORUS RAEUSCH. = C. DEPRESSUS STOCKS (KB 1, p. 402-403) = ANTICHORUS DEPRESSUS LINN. (KB 1, p. 402-403);
(9) = *pītarohiṇī* = *pītakaṭukī* (Vśs; acc. to PW : GMELINA ARBOREA ROXB.);
(10) = *latākastūrī* (Vśs, = HIBISCUS ABELMOSCHUS LINN.);
(11) COCCINIA INDICA WIGHT ET ARN. (Avk; KB 2, p. 1151-1154) = MOMORDICA MONADELPHA ROXB. (Avk; KB 2, p. 1151-1154);
(12) STRYCHNOS BEDDOMEI C. B. CLARKE (DWH 2, p. 502-505);
(13) S. CINNAMOMIFOLIA THW. (DWH 2, p. 502-505);
(14) S. COLUBRINA LINN. (DWH 2, p. 502-505);
(15) S. LAURINA WALL. (DWH 2, p. 502-505);
(16) S. RHEEDEI C. B. CLARKE (DWH 2, p. 502-505).

kaṭukī

(1) PICRORRHIZA KURROA ROYLE EX BENTH. (Avk; Dutt; DWH 3, p. 10-13; Dy, p. 510-511; HK; V 2, p. 147);
(2) = *kaṭukā* (Vśs);
(3) = *kaṭurohiṇī* (Avk; PW);
(4) GENTIANA KURROO ROYLE (see DWH 2, p. 510; Nadk. 1, nr. 1112);
(5) LUFFA ACUTANGULA ROXB. = L. AMARA ROXB. (Nadk. 1, nr. 1516) = L. FOETIDA CAV. (Nadk. 1, nr. 1516) = L. PLUKENETIANA SER. (Nadk. 1, nr. 1516).

kaṭutumbī

= *ikṣvāku*.

kaṭurohiṇī

(1) PICRORRHIZA KURROA ROYLE EX BENTH. (Avk; Bpn, p. 70; Dgv, nr. 235; Dutt; DWH 3, p. 10-13; Dy, p. 577-578; Gul; HK; Kav; KB 3, p. 1825-1826; Nadk. 1, nr. 1907; Sanyal);
(2) HELLEBORUS NIGER LINN. (Ainslie 1, p. 164-167; MW; Nadk. 1, nr. 1907; PW);
(3) H. VIRIDIS LINN. (Nadk. 1, nr. 1907);
(4) = *kaṭukā* (Vśs).

kaṇā

(1) PIPER LONGUM LINN. (Bpn; Dgv; Dutt; DWH 3, p. 176; MW; PW; V 6, p. 120; Vśs);

(2) a) = *jīraka* (Bpn; Vśs);
b) cumin seed (MW; PW);

(3) = *vanajīraka* (see *jīraka*) (Avk; KB 2, p. 1325-1327).

kaṇṭakārikā

(1) SOLANUM XANTHOCARPUM SCHRAD. ET WENDL. (Avk; Bpn, p. 289-292; Chopra; Dutt; DWH 2, p. 557-559; Dy, p. 636-637; Gul; HK; Kav; KB 3, p. 1759-1762; Nadk. 1, nr. 2338; PA 1, 4, p. 93; Sanyal; Vśs) = S. JACQUINI WILLD. (Ainslie 2, p. 90-91; Avk; Dutt; HK; Kav; MW; Nadk. 1, nr. 2330; PA 1, 4, p. 93; PW; Roxb., p. 191; Sanyal; Vśs; Wise) = S. DIFFUSUM ROXB. (Nadk. 1, nr. 2330) = S. VIRGINIANUM JACQ. (Nadk. 1, nr. 2330);

(2) S. INDICUM LINN. (KB 3, p. 1755-1757);

(3) S. FEROX LINN. (DWH 2, p. 560 : incorrectly used; KB 3, p. 1754-1755 and V 3, p. 70 : *śvetakaṇṭakārikā*);

(4) S. TRILOBATUM LINN. (DWH 2, p. 559-560 : used as a substitute);

(5) S. TORVUM SW. (DWH 2, p. 560 : incorrectly used);

(6) S. VERBASCIFOLIUM LINN. (DWH 2, p. 560 : incorrectly used).

kadamba

(1) ANTHOCEPHALUS INDICUS A. RICH. (Chopra; PA 1, 5, p. 45) = A. CADAMBA MIQ. (Avk; Bpn, p. 496; Chopra; DWH 2, p. 169-171; Gul; IRM 1, p. 83; KB 2, p. 1251-1252; Nadk. 1, nr. 204; PA 1, 5, p. 45) [= A. CADAMBA BENTH. ET HOOK.] (Dutt; HK) = A. CADAMBA (Ghosh; HB; Kav; Na 1, nr. 263; Sanyal; V 2, p. 42; Vśs) = A. MORINDAEFOLIUS KORTH. (PA 1, 5, p. 45) = NAUCLEA CADAMBA ROXB. (Avk; Chopra; Dutt; HK; Kav; KB 2, p. 1251-1252; MW; PA 1, 5, p. 45; PW; Vśs) = SARCOCEPHALUS CADAMBA KURZ (Avk; PA 1, 5, p. 45; Sanyal);

(2) MITRAGYNA PARVIFOLIA KORTH. (Bpn, p. 495 : *dhārākadamba*) = NAUCLEA PARVIFOLIA ROXB. = STEPHEGYNE PARVIFOLIA KORTH.;

(3) [ADINA CORDIFOLIA (ROXB.) BENTH. ET HOOK.F.] (Chopra : *dhārākadamba*) = A. CORDIFOLIA BENTH. ET HOOK.F. (Avk : *dhūlikadamba*; Bpn, p. 495 : *dhūlikadamba*; DWH 2, p. 171-172 : *dhārākadamba*; KB 2, p. 1253-1254 : *dhārākadamba, dhūlikadamba*; Sanyal : *dhārākadamba*;

V 5, p. 108 : *dhārākadamba, mahākadamba, nīpa*) = NAUCLEA CORDIFOLIA ROXB. (Avk : *dhārākadamba*; KB 2, p. 1253-1254);

(4) CORALLOCARPUS EPIGAEUS BENTH. ET HOOK.F. = BRYONIA EPIGAEA ROTTL. (Nadk. 1, nr. 385);

(5) ANDROPOGON CARICOSUS LINN. = A. SERRATUS RETZ. (MW; PW);

(6) CURCUMA LONGA LINN. (MW);

(7) a) = *sarṣapa* (KB 1, p. 165-166 and 170-171; Vśs);
b) white mustard (PW).

kapikacchū

MUCUNA PRURITA HOOK. (Chopra; KB 1, p. 778-780; MW; Nadk. 1, nr. 1663; PA 1, 5, p. 4; PW) = M. PRURIENS DC. (Dutt; DWH 1, p. 447-450; HK; PA 1, 5, p. 4) [= M. PRURIENS BAK. (non DC.)] (Bpn, p. 357; Chopra; KB 1, p. 778-780; Nadk. 1, nr. 1663) = M. PRURIENS (Avk; Dgv, nr. 111; Na 1, nr. 166; V 3, p. 20-21; Vśs) = M. UTILIS WALL. (PA 1, 5, p. 14; acc. to Hooker 2, p. 187 this is a cultivated variety with a velvety pod) = CARPOPOGON PRURIENS ROXB. (Avk; Dutt; HK; Nadk. 1, nr. 1663; PA 1, 5, p. 14; Roxb., p. 553; Vśs) = DOLICHOS PRURIENS LINN. (Ainslie 1, p. 92-94; Nadk. 1, nr. 1663).

kapittha

(1) FERONIA ELEPHANTUM CORR. (AFM 1, p. 68-71; Ainslie 2, p. 82-83 : *bhūkapittha*; Bpn, p. 560; Chopra; Dgv, nr. 73; Dutt; Gul; HB; HK; KB 1, p. 496-498; MW; Na 1, nr. 89; Nadk. 1, nr. 1021; PW; Roxb., p. 374; Sanyal; V 2, p. 90; Vśs) = F. LIMONIA SWINGLE [= F. LIMONIA (LINN.) SWINGLE] (Chopra) = SCHINUS LIMONIA LINN. = LIMONIA ACIDISSIMA LINN. = CRATAEVA VALLANGA KOEN. EX WIGHT ET ARN. (Nadk. 1, nr. 1021) [= ANISIPHALINS RUMPHII] (Nadk. 1, nr. 1021);

(2) FICUS RELIGIOSA LINN. (Vśs : = *aśvattha*);

(3) GISEKIA PHARNACIOIDES LINN. (V 6, p. 67; see : *elavāluka*).

kamala

(1) NELUMBIUM SPECIOSUM WILLD. (Bpn, p. 480; Dgv, nr. 80; Dutt; Gul; HB; HK; Kav; KB 1, p. 116-120; V 2, p. 70; Vśs) [= N. SPECIOSUM WIGHT] (DWH 1, p. 70-73) = N. NUCIFERUM GAERTN. = NELUMBO NUCIFERA GAERTN. (KB 1, p. 116-120; Na 1, nr. 18) = NYMPHAEA NELUMBO LINN. (Vśs);

(2) NYMPHAEA LOTUS LINN. [= N. LOTUS HOOK.F. ET THOMS.] (KB 1, p. 112-113) = N. RUBRA ROXB. EX SALISB. (KB 1, p. 112-113); N. LOTUS LINN. is a species different from N. LOTUS HOOK.F. ET THOMS. acc. to KB 1, p. 112, but the names are synonyms acc. to Hooker (1, p. 114);

(3) = *padmakāṣṭha* (Vśs);

(4) = *kuṅkuma* (Vśs, CROCUS SATIVUS LINN.).

karañja

(1) PONGAMIA PINNATA (LINN.) PIERRE [Intern. Code] [= P. PINNATA (LINN.) MERRILL] (Chopra) = P. PINNATA MERRILL = P. GLABRA VENT. [Intern. Code : nom. illeg.] (Avk; Bpn, p. 350; Chopra; Dgv, nr. 110; Dutt; DWH 1, p. 468-470; Gul; HB; HK; KB 1, p. 830-832; MW; Na 1, nr. 142; Nadk. 1, nr. 2003; PA 1, 4, p. 8; PW; Sanyal; V 2, p. 72; Vśs) = GALEDUPA INDICA LAM. (Avk; Dutt; HK; Nadk. 1, nr. 2003; Roxb., p. 538; Vśs) = G. ARBOREA ROXB. (Wise) = DALBERGIA ARBOREA WILLD. (Ainslie 2, p. 332-333) = CYTISUS PINNATUS LINN.;

(2) HOLOPTELEA INTEGRIFOLIA PLANCH. (KB 3, p. 2293-2294; PA 1, 4, p. 8) = ULMUS INTEGRIFOLIA ROXB. (KB 3, p. 2293);

(3) CAESALPINIA JAYABO MAZA = C. BONDUC ROXB. (Avk : *pūtikarañja*; Nadk. 1, nr. 402 : *pūtikarañja, latākarañja*) = GUILANDINA BONDUC LINN.;

(4) CAESALPINIA CRISTA LINN. (Bpn, p. 352 : *pūtikarañja*; Chopra; Dgv, nr. 118; IRM 2, p. 3-4 : *pūtikarañja*; KB 2, p. 842-845);

(5) C. BONDUCELLA FLEMING (Avk : *pūtikarañja*; *latākarañja*; Bpn, p. 352; Chopra; Dutt; Ghosh; IRM 2, p. 3-4 : *pūtikarañja*; KB 2, p. 842-845; Sanyal; Vśs; Watt CP, p. 190-191) = GUILANDINA BONDUCELLA LINN. (Avk : *latākarañja*; HK; Vśs); some authors regard 4) and 5) as synonyms, but Hooker and the Index Kewensis distinguish the two species, though they are very near to each other; see Hooker 2, p. 254-255;

(6) CLERODENDRUM SIPHONANTHUS [R. Br. in] Ait. = OVIEDA VERTICILLATUM ROXB. EX D. DON (Avk : *karañjaviśeṣa* = *aṅgāravallarī*);

(7) = *kapittha* (Vśs);

(8) = *bhṛṅgarāja* (Vśs), variously identified, but chiefly as

a) ECLIPTA ALBA (LINN.) HASSK. [Intern. Code] = E. ERECTA LINN. [Intern. Code : nom. illeg.]

b) WEDELIA CALENDULACEA LESS.

karamarda(ka)

(1) CARISSA CARANDAS LINN. [Intern. Code] (Avk; Bpn, p. 565; Dutt; DWH 2, p. 419-420; Dy, p. 507-508; Gul; HK; IRM 2, p. 82; Kav; KB 2, p. 1546-1548; MW; Nadk. 1, nr. 449 and 477; PW; V 2, p. 83) = C. CONGESTA WIGHT (Dutt; HK; Kav); [Flora Pavagadh, p. 136 : C. CONGESTA WIGHT = C. CARANDAS GRAHAM (*pro parte*) (NON LINN.) = C. CARANDAS VAR. CONGESTA BEDD.]; see also Hooker 3, p. 630-631;

(2) C. DIFFUSA (Avk; Nadk. 1, nr. 450); the Index Kewensis mentions only C. DIFFUSA RIDLEY, a species from the Malayan peninsula, but Hooker describes vol. 3, p. 631 a species from India : C. SPINARUM DC. = C. DIFFUSA ROXB.; see Roxb., p. 231-232 : C. DIFFUSA ROXB., *karamaḍikā*;

(3) CAPPARIS CARANDAS BURM.F. (Avk; Nadk. 1, nr. 449 and 477);

(4) FLACOURTIA CATAPHRACTA ROXB. EX WILLD. (Vśs : = *pānīyāmalaka*) [= F. JANGOMAS (LOUR.) RAEUSCH.] [Chopra] = F. JANGOMAS RAEUSCH. = F. JANGOMAS STEUD. = STIGMAROTA JANGOMAS LOUR.

karīra

(1) CAPPARIS APHYLLA ROTH (Avk; Bpn, p. 541; Chopra; Dgm, p. 151-152; Dgv, nr. 32; Dutt; DWH 1, p. 131-132; Dy, p. 64; Gul; HK; IRM 2, p. 67; Kav; KB 1, p. 197-199; MW; Nadk. 1, nr. 448; PW; V 2, p. 79; Vśs) = C. DECIDUA EDGEW. (Chopra; IRM 2, p. 67; KB 1, p. 197-199; Na 1, nr. 32; V 2, p. 79) = C. SODADA R. BR. (Dutt; HK) = SODADA DECIDUA FORSK. (KB 1, p. 197-199);

(2) C. SPINOSA LINN. (Dgm, p. 151-152; Nadk. 1, nr. 448);

(3) [unguis odoratus] (Losch : = *marujadruma*; *marujadruma* is acc. to PW a tree related to *khadira*); see Dietz, p. 57, about unguis odoratus;

(4) [CADABA APHYLLA ROTH] (Avk); the Index Kewensis mentions only : CADABA JUNCEA HARV. = C. APHYLLA (THUNB.) WILLD.

karkandhū

(1) ZIZYPHUS JUJUBA LAM. (Bpn, p. 563-564; HB; HK : the variety with small fruits; MW; PW : the variety with a large type of fruit, fructu oblongo acc. to Voigt; Vśs) = Z. SORORIA ROEM. ET SCHULT. (Nadk. 1, nr. 2667);

(2) Z. OENOPLIA MILL. (Kav; KB 1, p. 595-596; V 8, p. 8) = Z.

NAPECA ROXB. (Roxb., p. 206) = RHAMNUS OENOPLIA LINN. (KB 1, p. 595);

(3) Z. ROTUNDIFOLIA LAM. = Z. NUMMULARIA WIGHT ET ARN. (Dgv, nr. 84; Gul); Cakra remarks on Ca.Sū. 25, 49 and Ca.Si. 3, 8 that *karkandhu* designates the very small *śṛgālabadarī*; *śṛgālabadarī* :

a) = 1), acc. to KB 1, p. 589-591,
b) = 2), acc. to KB 1, p. 595-596 and Roxb., p. 206.

karkoṭa

(1) a) MOMORDICA COCHINCHINENSIS SPRENG. (Avk; HK) = MURICIA COCHINCHINENSIS LOUR. (Avk);
b) a creeper with an edible fruit (Vśs);
c) the fruit of *karkoṭī* (He. on A.h.Sū. 6, 76);
(2) a) a particular poisonous fruit (PW);
b) the poisonous fruit of *parpaṭaka* (Vśs);
(3) AEGLE MARMELOS (LINN.) CORREA [Intern. Code] (Vśs);
(4) SACCHARUM OFFICINARUM LINN. (Vśs).

karkoṭaka

(1) MOMORDICA COCHINCHINENSIS SPRENG. (Avk) = M. MIXTA ROXB. (Kav; MW; PW) = M. DIOICA WALL. = MURICIA COCHINCHINENSIS LOUR. (Avk);

(2) a) MOMORDICA DIOICA ROXB. (Gul);
b) M. DIOICA (ROXB.? WALL.?) (Dgv, nr. 169; Na 1, nr. 232);
c) a creeper with an edible fruit (Vśs);
(3) the poisonous fruit of *parpaṭaka* (Vśs);
(4) AEGLE MARMELOS (LINN.) CORREA [Intern. Code] (MW; PW; Vśs);
(5) SACCHARUM OFFICINARUM LINN. (KB 4, p. 2662-2664; MW; PW; Vśs).

karkoṭikā

(1) MOMORDICA COCHINCHINENSIS SPRENG. (Avk) = M. MIXTA ROXB. (MW; PW) = MURICIA COCHINCHINENSIS LOUR. (Avk);

(2) BENINCASA CERIFERA SAVI (KB 2, p. 1127-1128; Vśs) = B. HISPIDA COGN. [= B. HISPIDA (THUNB.) COGN.] (KB 2, p. 1127-1128);

(3) = *karkoṭaka* (Vśs).

karpūra

(1) Cinnamomum camphora T. Nees et Eberm. (Avk; Bpn, p. 173-176; Chopra; Dutt; DWH 3, p. 199-203); Dy, p. 665; HK; KB 3, p. 2152-2153; Nadk. 1, nr. 433; Vśs);

(2) C. zeylanicum (see *tvac*) (Avk);

(3) Dryobalanops aromatica Gaertn.f. (Avk; DWH 1, p. 197-201; Gul; Nadk. 1, nr. 899) = D. camphora Colebr. (Ainslie 1, p. 48-51; Bpn, p. 173-176; Nadk. 1, nr. 900);

(4) Blumea balsamifera (Linn.) DC. [Intern. Code] (Avk; Bpn, p. 174);

(5) B. densiflora DC. (Avk; Bpn, p. 174) = B. grandis DC. (Avk);

(6) B. lacera DC. (Avk; Bpn, p. 174);

(7) B. malcolmii Hook.f. (Avk; Bpn, p. 174);

(8) Ocimum kilimandscharicum Guerke (Bpn, p. 174);

(9) Limnophila gratioloides R.Br. [Intern. Code] (Bpn, p. 174);

(10) the tuber of Curcuma zedoaria (Bergius) Rosc. (Vśs) = C. zerumbet Roxb. = Amomum zedoaria Bergius.

kalāya

(1) Pisum sativum Linn. (Bpn, p. 648; Dutt; HK; Kav; KB 1, p. 772-773; V 8, p. 12; Vśs);

(2) P. arvense Linn. (Nadk. 1, nr. 1939);

(3) Lathyrus sativus Linn. (Gul; Na 1, nr. 139). MW : a) a kind of pea or pulse, b) a kind of plant with dark-coloured flowers; PW : a) a kind of pea, b) another plant; Vśs : name of various leguminous seeds; Bpn, *dhānyavarga* 57-58 : a) *kalāya* = *vartula* = *satīna* = *hareṇuka* : Pisum sativum Linn. b) *kalāya* = *tripuṭa* = *khaṇḍika* : Lathyrus sativus Linn.; Cakra on Ca.Sū. 27, 28 : a) *kalāya* = *vartulakalāya* = *hareṇu* : Pisum sativum Linn. b) *kalāya* = *tripuṭakalāya* = *khaṇḍikā* : Lathyrus sativus Linn.

kaśeru(ka) = *kaseru(ka)*

(1) Scirpus kysoor Roxb. (Avk; Chopra; Dgv, nr. 338; Dutt; Gul; HK; Kav; KB 4, p. 2646; Nadk. 1, nr. 2255; PW; V 2, p. 100; Vśs);

(2) S. grossus Linn.f. (Bpn, p. 684; Chopra; KB 4, p. 2644-2645; Nadk. 1, nr. 2254);

(3) Cyperus rotundus Linn. (KB 4, p. 2638-2640);

(4) C. esculentus Linn. (Chopra; KB 4, p. 2640-2641; V 2, p. 100);

(5) EUONYMUS TINGENS WALL. (Wise); some sources (Bpn, *śākavarga* 112-113; Cakra on Ca.Sū. 27, 116cd-117ab) distinguish two kinds of *kaśeru(ka)* : *rājakaśeru(ka)* and *ciṃcoḍakā*; the latter is also called *ciṃcoḍa, ciñcoṭa(ka)* or *cicoḍha. rājakaśeru(ka)* :

1) CYPERUS ROTUNDUS LINN. (MW; PW);

2) C. SCARIOSUS R.BR. = C. PERTENUIS ROXB. (MW; PW; Vśs);

3) SCIRPUS TUBEROSUS (Avk; Nadk. 1, nr. 2256);

the Index Kewensis distinguishes two species of this name :

a) ELEOCHARIS TUBEROSA SCHULT. = S. TUBEROSUS ROXB.;

b) S. MARITIMUS LINN. = S. TUBEROSUS DESF.;

ciṃcoḍakā : 1) S. ARTICULATUS LINN. (Avk; Chopra; Nadk. 1, nr. 2253);

2) C. ESCULENTUS LINN. (Bpn, p. 684);

3) [MARSILEA DENTATA] (Vśs).

kākaṇantī = *kākaṇantikā*

(1) ABRUS PRECATORIUS LINN.;

(2) = *muñja* (HK).

kākatinduka

(1) DIOSPYROS TOMENTOSA ROXB. (Avk; Dutt; HK; KB 2, p. 1504-1505; Nadk. 1, nr. 852; PW; Vśs);

(2) D. MELANOXYLON ROXB. (Bpn, p. 531-532; Dutt; HK; KB 2, p. 1504-1505; V 2, p. 110); Kirtikar and Basu consider 1) and 2) as synonyms, but the Index Kewensis and Hooker describe 1) and 2) as separate species; see Hooker 3, p. 564;

(3) STRYCHNOS NUX-VOMICA LINN. (Bpn, p. 561-562; Dgv, nr. 218; KB 3, p. 1645-1647);

(4) CAPPARIS SEPIARIA LINN. (KB 1, p. 199-200) = C. INCANESCENS DC. (KB 1, p. 199-200).

kākādanī

(1) ABRUS PRECATORIUS LINN. (KB 1, p. 764-767);

a) the white variety (MW; PW; Vśs);

b) the red variety (Vśs);

(2) CAPPARIS SEPIARIA LINN. (Avk; Chopra; Dgm, p. 160; Dutt; DWH 1, p. 131-132; HK; KB 1, p. 199-200; MW; Na 1, nr. 35; Nadk. 1, nr. 453) = C. INCANESCENS DC. (KB 1, p. 199-200);

(3) C. SPINOSA LINN. (Avk; Dgm, p. 157; Nadk. 1, nr. 454; V 2, p. 65);

(4) ARDISIA HUMILIS VAHL = A. SOLANACEA ROXB. (Vśs);

(5) ZIZYPHUS JUJUBA LAM. (PW : = *gṛdhranakhī*; *gṛdhranakhī* designates CAPPARIS SEPIARIA LINN. acc. to KB);

(6) HYGROPHILA SPINOSA T. ANDERS. = ASTERACANTHA LONGIFOLIA NEES (PW : = *gṛdhranakhī*);

(7) NARDOSTACHYS JATAMANSI DC. (PW : = *hiṃsrā*);

(8) the red variety of SOLANUM NIGRUM LINN. (Vśs : = *raktakākamācī*);

(9) FICUS HISPIDA LINN.F. = F. OPPOSITIFOLIA WILLD. (Wise);

(10) = *kākatinduka* (Vśs).

kāṇḍekṣu

(1) HYGROPHILA SPINOSA T. ANDERS. (Kav; KB 3, p. 1864-1865; Vśs) = ASTERACANTHA LONGIFOLIA NEES (KB 3, p. 1864-1865; MW; PW) = RUELLIA LONGIFOLIA ROXB. (Kav; Vśs);

(2) SACCHARUM SPONTANEUM LINN. (HB; Kav; MW; PW; Vśs);

(3) a particular type or particular types of sugar-cane (Gul : big sugar-cane; Kav, p. 293 : a variety of sugar-cane that yields less juice and is much harder; Vśs : white sugar-cane, dark sugar-cane).

kārpāsī

(1) GOSSYPIUM HERBACEUM LINN. (Ainslie 2, p. 282-284; Avk; Bpn, p. 374; Chopra; Dgv, nr. 45; Dutt; Dy, p. 109-112; Gul; KB 1, p. 344-346; Na 1, nr. 55; Nadk. 1, nr. 1145; Roxb., p. 520; Sanyal; V 2, p. 43; Vśs; Watt CP, p. 575-576) = G. HIRSUTUM LINN. (Vśs; Wise) = G. INDICUM LAM. (Nadk. 1, nr. 1147) = G. RELIGIOSUM LINN. (Avk);

(2) G. ARBOREUM LINN. (Avk);

(3) [G. STOCKSII MAST. VAR. HERBACEUM LINN.] (Avk; DWH 1, p. 224-228); see Hooker 1, p. 346-347.

kālamāla(ka) = *kālamālā*

(1) OCIMUM SANCTUM LINN. (HK; MW);

a) the type with dark leaves (PW);

b) the black variety (Kav, p. 647);

(2) *kṣudratulasī* with dark leaves (Vśs); Cakra on Su.Sū. 38, 18 : = *parṇāsa* with dark flowers; Ḍa. on Su.Sū. 38, 18 : = *kṛṣṇamallikā*, commonly called *barbarikā*; Ḍa. on Su.Sū. 46, 221 : = *barbarikā*.

kāśa = *kāsa*

SACCHARUM SPONTANEUM LINN. (Bpn, p. 380; Gul; HB; HK; Kav; KB 4, p. 2668-2669; Nadk. 1, nr. 2185; MW; PW; Vśs).

kāśmarya = *kāśmarī*

(1) GMELINA ARBOREA ROXB. (AFM 1, p. 74-77; KB 3, p. 1932-1934; PA 1, 2, p. 63-74; PW) [= G. ARBOREA LINN.] (Bpn, p. 277; Dutt; DWH 3, p. 70-72; Gul; HK; Nadk. 1, nr. 1137) = G. ARBOREA (Kav; MW; V 2, p. 68);

(2) G. ASIATICA LINN. (PA 1, 2, p. 63 : occasionally used as a substitute);

(3) MYRICA NAGI THUNB. (Vśs : = *kāyaphala* = *kaṭphala*).

kuṭaja

(1) HOLARRHENA ANTIDYSENTERICA WALL. (Bpn, p. 347; Chopra; Dgv, nr. 210 : *śvetakuṭaja*; Dutt; DWH 2, p. 391-397; Dy, p. 497-500; Ghosh; Gul; HK; Kav; KB 2, p. 1570-1573; Na 1, nr. 323; Nadk. 1, nr. 1236; PA 1, 4, p. 45-60; Sanyal; V 1, p. 135; Vśs; Watt CP, p. 640) = H. CODAGA G. DON (PA 1, 4, p. 45) = ECHITES ANTIDYSENTERICA ROXB. EX FLEM. (Dutt; HK; Kav; Nadk. 1, nr. 905; PA 1, 4, p. 45; Vśs; Wise) = WRIGHTIA ANTIDYSENTERICA J. GRAH. (HK; Nadk. 1, nr. 2628; PA 1, 4, p. 45) = W. ANTIDYSENTERICA R.BR. (PW) = W. ANTIDYSENTERICA (MW; Vśs) = NERIUM ANTIDYSENTERICUM LINN. (Ainslie 1, p. 88-89 and 2, p. 461-463) = CHONEMORPHA ANTIDYSENTERICA G. DON (Nadk. 1, nr. 1236);

(2) WRIGHTIA TINCTORIA R. BR. (Avk; Chopra : *śvetakuṭaja*; Dgv, nr. 210 : *asitakuṭaja*; DWH 2, p. 397-398 : used as a substitute; KB 2, p. 1581-1583 : *śvetakuṭaja*; Nadk. 1, nr. 2629 : *asitakuṭaja*; PA 1, 4, p. 45; V 1, p. 139 : *śvetakuṭaja*) = W. ROTHII G. DON (Nadk. 1, nr. 2629);

(3) W. TOMENTOSA ROEM. ET SCHULT. (see DWH 2, p. 394; PA 1, 4, p. 45);

(4) HOLARRHENA PUBESCENS WALL. (see DWH 2, p. 397; Nadk. 1, nr. 1236);

(5) CLEISTANTHUS COLLINUS BENTH. ET HOOK.F. (KB 3, p. 2215-2216) = CLUYTIA COLLINA ROXB. (KB 3, p. 2215-2216).

kuṭhera(ka)

(1) OCIMUM BASILICUM LINN. (Avk; Bpn, p. 511-512);

(2) O. SANCTUM LINN. (KB 3, p. 1967; MW ?);
(3) O. GRATISSIMUM LINN. (MW ?);
(4) O. CANUM SIMS (KB 3, p. 1961);
(5) a) CEDRELA TOONA ROXB. EX ROTTL. (MW);
b) = *nandīvṛkṣa* (PW; Vśs); PW : the white variety of *tulasī*; Vśs : the white variety of *kṣudratulasī* (see *tulasī*).

Ḍa. on Su.Sū. 38, 18 : *arjaka* is called *śvetakuṭheraka* when it has minute leaves and is odourless; Ḍa. on Su.Sū. 46, 221 : *kuṭheraka* is a variety of *barbarikā*; Aruṇa on A.h.Sū. 6, 106 : = *vaikuṇṭhaka*; He. on A.h.Sū. 6, 106 : = *kālamālā*; Dn, *varga* 4, 54 : = *arjaka* = *vaikuṇṭha*; Rn, *varga* 10, 84-85 : = *arjaka* = *kṣudratulasī* (see *tulasī*).

kumbhī(vṛkṣa)

(1) CAREYA ARBOREA ROXB. (Chopra; DWH 2, p. 19-20; IRM 2, p. 76; Na 1, nr. 216; Nadk. 1, nr. 475; V 2, p. 18);
(2) STEREOSPERMUM SUAVEOLENS DC. (KB 3, p. 1848-1849) = BIGNONIA SUAVEOLENS ROXB. (MW; PW; Vśs);
(3) LEUCAS LAVANDULAEFOLIA SM. = L. LINIFOLIA SPRENG. (KB 3, p. 2020-2021; PW : = *droṇapuṣpī*);
(4) LEUCAS CAPITATA DESF. = L. CEPHALOTES SPRENG. (PW : = *droṇapuṣpī*);
(5) MYRICA NAGI THUNB. (KB 3, p. 2350-2351; Nadk. 1, nr. 1673) = M. SAPIDA WALL. (MW; Nadk. 1, nr. 1673; Vśs);
(6) M. CERIFERA LINN. (Nadk. 1, nr. 1673);
(7) BALIOSPERMUM AXILLARE BLUME = B. MONTANUM MUELL. ARG. (KB 3, p. 2278-2279; Vśs) = CROTON POLYANDRUS ROXB. (MW; Vśs);
(8) BOSWELLIA SERRATA ROXB. EX COLEBR. (KB 1, p. 521-523);
(9) COMMIPHORA MUKUL ENGL. (KB 1, p. 526-528 [= BALSAMODENDRUM MUKUL HOOK. EX STOCKS] (KB 1, p. 526-528; Vśs) = B. ROXBURGHII STOCKS (KB 1, p. 526-528) (see about the nomenclature : *agaru*);
(10) = *pṛśniparṇī* (Vśs).

kulattha

(1) DOLICHOS BIFLORUS LINN. (AFM 1, p. 64-66; Avk; Bpn, p. 649; Chopra; Dutt; DWH 1, p. 489; Ghosh; Gul; HK; IRM 3, p. 101-104; Kav; KB 1, p. 805-806; Roxb., p. 563; Vśs; Watt CP, p. 503-504; Wise) [= D. BIFLORUS LINN. VAR. UNIFLORUS LAM.] (Nadk. 1, nr. 864)

= D. UNIFLORUS LAM. (AFM 1, p. 64-66; Dutt; HK; Kav; MW; Nadk. 1, nr. 864; Vśs; Watt CP, p. 503-504); see Hooker 2, p. 210;
(2) CASSIA ABSUS LINN. (KB 2, p. 873-874).

kuvala

(1) ZIZYPHUS JUJUBA LAM. (MW; PW; Vśs);
(2) Z. SATIVA GAERTN. (Gul);
(3) a jujube with large fruits (Kav; Vśs; Cakra on Ca.Sū. 25, 49 : *kuvala* is a gross *badarī*);
(4) a) a water-lily (MW; PW);
b) = *padma* (Vśs);
c) = *utpala* (Vśs).

kuṣṭha

(1) SAUSSUREA LAPPA C. B. CLARKE (Bpn, p. 91; Chopra; Dgv, nr. 191; Dutt; DWH 2, p. 296-303; Dy, p. 449-456; Gul; HK; KB 2, p. 1420-1423; Na 1, nr. 280; Nadk. 1, nr. 2239; V 3, p. 15; Watt CP, p. 980) = APLOTAXIS LAPPA DECNE. (Nadk. 1, nr. 2239) = AUCKLANDIA COSTUS FALCONER (Nadk. 1, nr. 2239);
(2) SAUSSUREA HYPOLEUCA SPRENG. EX DC. (Nadk. 1, nr. 2239 : used as a substitute) = S. AURICULATA (DC.) Sch. Bip. (HSu; Kav; MW; Nadk. 1, nr. 2239; Vśs) = APLOTAXIS AURICULATA DC. (Avk; Dutt; HK; Kav; Nadk. 1, nr. 2239; Vśs);
(3) COSTUS SPECIOSUS SM. (Ainslie 1, p. 35-37 and 2, p. 164-165; KB 4, p. 2440-2442; MW; PW; Wise) = C. ARABICUS LINN. (same sources, except Wise).

kusumbha(ka)

CARTHAMUS TINCTORIUS LINN.

kṛṣṇā

(1) PIPER LONGUM LINN. (Ainslie 1, p. 308; Bpn, p. 15; Dutt; HK; MW; PW; V 6, p. 120; Vśs);
(2) = *kṛṣṇajīraka* (Avk; KB 2, p. 1201-1203; MW; PW; Vśs);
(3) a) = *indrayava* = the seeds of *kuṭaja* (Vśs);
b) = *kuṭaja* (Vśs);
(4) = *kaṭukā* (Vśs);

(5) = *kākolī* (MW; PW; Vśs); *kākolī* is an unidentifiable plant;
(6) = *kṛṣṇatulasī* (see *tulasī*) (Vśs);
(7) = *kṛṣṇanirguṇḍī* : VITEX NEGUNDO LINN. (Vśs);
(8) = *kṛṣṇasārivā* (see *śyāmā*)(MW and PW : a sort of *sārivā*; Vśs);
(9) = *gāmbhārī* = *kāśmarī* = *kāśmarya* (see *kāśmarya*) (MW; PW; Vśs);
(10) = *jaṭāmāṃsī* : NARDOSTACHYS JATAMANSI DC. (Vśs);
(11) = *dūrvā* : CYNODON DACTYLON (LINN.) PERS. [Intern. Code] (Vśs);
(12) VITIS VINIFERA LINN. (MW; PW; Vśs);
(13) = *nīlapunarnavā* (see *punarnavā*) (MW; PW; Vśs);
(14) = *nīlī* (MW; PW; Vśs);
(15) = *paṭola* (Vśs);
(16) = *marica* (Vśs);
(17) = *rājasarṣapa* (see *sarṣapa*) (MW; PW; Vśs);
(18) = *vanakulattha* (Vśs) : unidentified;
(19) = *śirīṣa* (Vśs);
(20) = *somarājī* : a) VERNONIA ANTHELMINTICA WILLD., b) = *bākucī* : PSORALEA CORYLIFOLIA LINN. (MW; PW; Vśs).

keśara = *kesara*

(1) = *nāgakeśara* (Bpn, p. 229-232; Gul; HK; Kav; KB 1, p. 274-276; MW; PW; V 5, p. 122-123; Vśs);
(2) = *bakula* (DWH 2, p. 362-364; KB 2, p. 1494-1496; MW; PW; Sanyal; V 8, p. 93; Vśs);
(3) = *punnāga* (Dgm, p. 235-236; KB 1, p. 269-270; MW; PW; Vśs);
(4) = *hiṅgu* (KB 2, p. 1216-1218; MW; PW; Vśs);
(5) = *mātuluṅga* (Vśs);
(6) CROCUS SATIVUS LINN. (Avk; Chopra; IRM 2, p. 370-372; KB 4, p. 2462-2464);
(7) MALLOTUS PHILIPPINENSIS MUELL. ARG. (KB 3, p. 2267-2270).

kodrava

PASPALUM SCROBICULATUM LINN.; Nadk. 1, nr. 1817, p. 924 : the new grain is said to be powerfully narcotic and is eaten only by the poor who prepare it in various ways and from use are able to use it with impunity; Watt, CP, p. 869 : the grain cannot be considered a wholesome article of diet, and in some seasons contains a poisonous narcotic principle.

koradūṣa

= *kodrava*.

kola

(1) Zizyphus jujuba Lam.;
(2) Z. oenoplia Mill. (Nadk. 1, nr. 2662);
(3) [Z. laccifera] (Nadk. 1, nr. 2662);
(4) = *marica* (Vśs);
(5) = *cavya* (Vśs);
(6) = *kroḍa* = *vārāhīkanda* (Vśs);
(7) = *citraka* (Vśs);
(8) = *kakkola* (Vśs);
(9) = *aṅkola* (Vśs);
(10) = *gajapippalī* (Vśs);
(11) = *pippalī* (Vśs);
(12) = *kulattha* (Vśs);
(13) = *bahuvāra* : a species of Cordia (Vśs).

kramuka

(1) Areca catechu Linn. (Ainslie 2, p. 268-271; Dutt; DWH 3, p. 522-532; Dy, p. 802-804; HK; Kav; KB 4, p. 2547-2549; MW; Nadk. 1, nr. 219; PW; Vśs; Watt CP, p. 83-91) = A. faufel Gaertn. (MW);
(2) Morus indica Linn. (KB 3, p. 2306-2307; MW; PW; Vśs);
(3) a) = *paṭṭikālodhra* : Symplocos crataegoides Buch.-Ham. ex D. Don (Bpn, p. 128-130; Gul; KB 2, p. 1510-1511; MW; PW; V 9, p. 42; Vśs) = S. paniculata Wall. ex D. Don;
b) = *raktalodhra* (see *lodhra*) (Vśs);
(4) Cedrus libani Barrel = Pinus deodara Roxb. (Vśs).;
(5) = *bhadramustaka* (MW; PW; Vśs);
(6) = *pāriṣāśvattha* (Vśs, unidentified);
(7) the fruit of *kārpāsī* (MW; PW).

kṣavaka

(1) Achyranthes aspera Linn. (HB; HK; MW; PW);
(2) Centipeda orbicularis Lour. (Gul; KB 2, p. 1388-1389) = C. minima A. Br. et Aschers = Artemisia sternutatoria Roxb. (KB 2, p. 1388-1389) = Myriogyne minuta Less. = Dichrocephala schmidii Wight (KB 2, p. 1388-1389);

(3) [MYRIOGYNE LANUGINOSA] (Kav);

(4) = *rājikā* (MW; PW);

(5) = *bhūtāṅkuśa* (MW; PW);

(6) a particular plant eaten as a vegetable (MW; PW);

(7) Ḍa. on Su.Sū. 38, 10 : *kṣavaka* has a form like *phaṇijjhaka* and is well known as *cihvariyāka* in Pāriyātra.

khadira

(1) ACACIA CATECHU WILLD. (Ainslie 1, p. 63-66; Avk; Bpn, p. 525; Chopra; DWH 1, p. 557-559; Dy, p. 283-285; Gul; IRM 1, p. 9-13; KB 2, p. 926-928; MW; Nadk. 1, nr. 13; PW; Sanyal; V 3, p. 53; Vśs) [= A. CATECHU LINN.] (Dutt; HK; Kav) = A. POLYACANTHA WILLD. (Nadk. 1, nr. 13) = A. WALLICHIANA DC. (Nadk. 1, nr. 13) = MIMOSA CATECHU LINN.F. (Dutt; HK; Kav; Vśs);

(2) ACACIA SUNDRA DC. = A. SUMA BUCH.-HAM. EX WALL. (Nadk. 1, nr. 13);

(3) A. SUMA KURZ EX BRANDIS (Nadk. 1, nr. 13); 2) and 3) are synonyms acc. to Chopra, IRM (1, p. 20) and Nadk.;

(4) A. PENNATA WILLD. (KB 2, p. 934-935 : *ballikhadira*) = A. FERRUGINEA ROTTL. (Ainslie 2, p. 477);

(5) A. FERRUGINEA DC. (KB 2, p. 928-929, = *somavalkala*);

(6) A. SENEGAL WILLD. (Chopra : *śvetakhadira*; KB 2, p. 929-930 : *śvetakhadira*).

kharapatra

(1) MAJORANA HORTENSIS MOENCH. [Intern. Code] = ORIGANUM MAJORANA LINN. (KB. 3, p. 1985-1986);

(2) = *maruvaka* (MW; PW; Vśs);

(3) a) a kind of OCIMUM (MW; PW);
b) *tulasī* with small leaves (Vśs);
c) *tāmratulasī* (Vśs, unidentified);

(4) a variety of *kuśa* grass (see *darbha*) (MW);

(5) a) = *yāvanāla* (Vśs);
b) = *yāvanālaśara* (PW);
c) a kind of cane (MW);

(6) TECTONA GRANDIS LINN.F. (KB 3, p. 1924-1926; MW; PW; Vśs : = *śākavṛkṣa*);

(7) = *bhūrjavṛkṣa* : BETULA UTILIS D. DON = B. BHOJPATTRA WALL. (Vśs);

(8) STREBLUS ASPER LOUR. = TROPHIS ASPERA RETZ. (MW);

(9) NYCTANTHES ARBOR-TRISTIS LINN. (KB 2, p. 1526-1528 : *khara-patraka*).

kharjūra

(1) PHOENIX SYLVESTRIS ROXB. (Avk; Bpn, p. 574-576; Chopra; Dutt; DWH 3, p. 520; Dy, p. 801; HK; Kav; KB 4, p. 2563-2565; MW; Nadk. 1, nr. 1881; PW; Roxb., p. 723; V 3, p. 33; Watt CP, p. 885-886);

(2) PH. DACTYLIFERA LINN. (Avk; Bpn, p. 574-576; Chopra; Dgv, nr. 331; Gul; KB 4, p. 2561-2563; Nadk. 1, nr. 1878; V 3, p. 32), usually distinguished as *piṇḍakharjūra*.

gajapippalī

(1) SCINDAPSUS OFFICINALIS SCHOTT = POTHOS OFFICINALIS ROXB.

(2) LITSEA POLYANTHA JUSS. (KB 3, p. 2160-2161);

(3) L. SEBIFERA PERS. = TETRANTHERA APETALA ROXB. (Roxb., p. 734) = TOMEX SEBIFERA WILLD. (Roxb., p. 734).

gaṇḍīra

(1) a) a particular plant eaten as a vegetable (PW; Vśs);
b) a kind of potherb described as growing in watery ground (Kav; MW), but acc. to some a species of cucumber (MW);

(2) RUBIA CORDIFOLIA LINN. (HB; Vśs);

(3) EUPHORBIA NERIIFOLIA LINN. (DWH 3, p. 253-257; Vśs);

(4) E. ANTIQUORUM LINN. (DWH 3, p. 253-257; Vśs);

(5) SOLANUM VERBASCIFOLIUM LINN. (KB 3, p. 1753-1754);

(6) S. PUBESCENS WILLD. (Roxb., p. 189);

(7) = *kaṭuśaraṇa* (Vśs, unidentified);

(8) = *śamaṭha* (Cakra on Ca.Sū. 27, 106; unidentified); Cakra on Ca.Sū. 27, 171 : "*gaṇḍīra* is of two kinds : red and white; the red type has been described as a pungent potherb, the white type grows in water;" Ḍa. on Su.Ci. 4, 32 : "*gaṇḍīra* is of two kinds : terrestrial and aquatic; the terrestrial type is a vegetable, the aquatic type is *jala-pippalīgaṇḍīra*" (see *jalapippalī*).

gandhaka

MORINGA OLEIFERA LAM. = M. PTERYGOSPERMA GAERTN. (KB 1, p. 677-682; MW; PW; Vśs).

gandhapatra

(1) a) MAJORANA HORTENSIS MOENCH. [Intern. Code] = ORIGANUM MAJORANA LINN. (KB 3, p. 1985-1986);
b) = *maruvaka* (PW; Vśs);
(2) a) the white type of *tulasī* (PW; Vśs);
b) = *barbara* (PW; Vśs);
(3) = *bilva* (PW; Vśs);
(4) = *nāgaraṅga* : CITRUS AURANTIUM LINN. (PW; Vśs); see Watt CP, p. 320-321.
(5) = *tejapatra* (see *patra*) (Vśs);
(6) the leaves of *prasāraṇī* (Vśs);
(7) a partic. kind of *sugandhapatrā* = *rudrajaṭā* (Vśs; Nadk. 1, nr. 229 : *rudrajaṭā* = ARISTOLOCHIA INDICA LINN.).

guñjā

ABRUS PRECATORIUS LINN. = A. MINOR DESV. (Nadk. 1, nr. 6) = A. PAUCIFLORUS DESV. (Nadk. 1, nr. 6) = GLYCINE ABRUS LINN.

guḍūcī

(1) [TINOSPORA CORDIFOLIA (WILLD.) MIERS] (Bpn, p. 269-270; Chopra) = T. CORDIFOLIA MIERS (Avk; Dgm, p. 25; Dgv, nr. 14; Dutt; DWH 1, p. 54-56; Gul; HB; HK; Kav; KB 1, p. 77-80; Na 1, nr. 12; Nadk. 1, nr. 2472; PA 1, 7, p. 13-27; Sanyal; V 3, p. 86; Vśs) = MENISPERMUM CORDIFOLIUM WILLD. (Dutt; HK; Kav; KB 1, p. 77-80; Nadk. 1, nr. 2472; PA 1, 7, p. 13-27; Vśs) [= M. CORDIFOLIUM RUSSELL] (Ainslie 2, p. 377-378) = M. GLABRUM BURM.F. (PA 1, 7, p. 13-27) = COCCULUS CORDIFOLIUS DC. (HK; MW; Nadk. 1, nr. 2472; PA 1, 7, p. 13-27; PW);
(2) TINOSPORA CRISPA MIERS (DWH 1, p. 64 : known by the same vernacular names as T. CORDIFOLIA; PA 1, 7, p. 32, footnote : used sometimes as a substitute) = MENISPERMUM CRISPUM LINN.;
(3) T. MALABARICA MIERS (PA 1, 7, p. 32, footnote : used sometimes as a substitute) = MENISPERMUM MALABARICUM LAM.;
(4) T. TOMENTOSA MIERS (PA 1, 7, p. 32, footnote : used sometimes

as a substitute; PA considers 3) and 4) as synonyms) = MENISPERMUM TOMENTOSUM ROXB.

gokṣura(ka)

(1) TRIBULUS TERRESTRIS LINN. (Avk; Bpn, p. 292-293; Chopra; Dgv, nr. 60; Dutt; DWH 1, p. 243-245; Dy, p. 119-120; Ghosh; Gul; HB; HK; Kav; KB 1, p. 420-423; Na 1, nr. 83; Nadk. 1, nr. 2496; PA 1, 2, p. 75-79; Sanyal; V 3, p. 128) = T. LANUGINOSUS LINN. (Dutt; HK; Kav; MW; Nadk. 1, nr. 2496) [= T. ZEYLANICUS] (Nadk. 1, nr. 2496);

(2) T. ALATUS DELILE (Bpn, p. 292-293 : may be used as a substitute);

(3) PEDALIUM MUREX LINN. (Bpn, p. 292-293 : *bṛhadgokṣura*; KB 3, p. 1856-1857; PA 1, 2, p. 75, footnote : considered by some as a large form of *gokṣura*);

(4) HYGROPHILA SPINOSA T. ANDERS. = ASTERACANTHA LONGIFOLIA NEES (MW; PW);

(5) BARLERIA LONGIFLORA LINN.F. (KB 3, p. 1882).

gojihvā

(1) ELEPHANTOPUS SCABER LINN. (Avk; Bpn, p. 471-472; Chopra; Dutt; DWH 2, p. 243-244; Dy, p. 423; Gul; HK; IRM 3, p. 149; Kav; KB 2, p. 1328-1330; MW; Na 1, nr. 290; Nadk. 1, nr. 923; PW : acc. to Wilson; Sanyal; Vśs);

(2) ONOSMA BRACTEATUM WALL. (Bpn, p. 471-472; Dgv, nr. 222);

(3) LEUCAS ASPERA LINK = PHLOMIS ESCULENTA ROXB. (MW; PW : possibly, acc. to Colebr.);

(4) PREMNA ESCULENTA ROXB. (MW; PW : acc. to Haught. *gojiā* designates, in Beng., P.E. ROXB.);

(5) a species of HIERACIUM (MW; PW : acc. to Haught.);

(6) POLYTOCA BARBATA STAPF = CHIONACHNE BARBATA R. BR. = COIX BARBATA ROXB. (MW; PW : = *gavedhukā*, but, acc. to KB 4, p. 2655-2656, *gavedhukā* designates COIX LACHRYMA-JOBI LINN.);

(7) = *dārvikā* (PW; unidentified, but probably = *dārvī*).

granthi

(1) the root of PIPER LONGUM LINN. (MW);

(2) CYNODON DACTYLON (LINN.) PERS. [Intern. Code] (DWH 3, p. 577; Nadk. 1, nr. 772);

(3) CYPERUS ROTUNDUS LINN. (KB 4, p. 2638-2640);

(4) = *granthiparṇa* (MW; PW; Vśs);
(5) = *piṇḍālu* (MW; PW; Vśs);
(6) = *bhadramustā* (MW; PW; Vśs);
(7) = *hitāvalī* (MW; PW; unidentified).

granthiparṇa

(1) Polygonum aviculare Linn. (Bpn, p. 252);
(2) Artemisia vulgaris Linn. (KB 2, p. 1395-1397);
(3) a particular fragrant plant (MW; PW);
(4) = *coraka* (MW; PW; Vśs).

ghaṇṭāpāṭali = *ghaṇṭāpāṭalaka* = *muṣkaka* = *mokṣaka* = *kṣāraśreṣṭha*

(1) Schrebera swietenioides Roxb. [Intern. Code] (Avk; Bpn, p. 544; Chopra; KB 2, p. 1531-1532; MW; Na 1, nr. 318; Vśs);
(2) Elaeodendron glaucum Pers. (Bpn, p. 544 : = *kṛṣṇamokṣaka* ?) = E. paniculatum Wight et Arn.;
(3) Stereospermum suaveolens DC. (HSu) = Bignonia suaveolens Roxb. (MW; PW).

caṇaka

Cicer arietinum Linn.; see about *caṇaka* : Gode, St.I.C.H. 1, p. 193-217; p. 218-232; p. 233-239; p. 240-244; p. 245-255.

candana

(1) Santalum album Linn. = S. myrtifolium Roxb. = Sirium myrtifolium Linn.;
(2) *raktacandana* : Pterocarpus santalinus Linn.f.;
(3) *raktacandana* : Caesalpinia sappan Linn. (Watt CP, p. 976);
(4) *pītacandana* : Berberis asiatica Roxb. ex DC. (KB 1, p. 105-106);
(5) Crocus sativus Linn. (KB 4, p. 2462-2464).

cavika

= *cavya*.

cavya

Piper chaba Hunter.

cāṅgerī

(1) Oxalis corniculata Linn. (AFM 1, p. 100-102; Avk; Bpn, p. 663; Dgv, nr. 62; Dutt; DWH 1, p. 246-247; Dy, p. 121-122; Gul; HB; HK; Kav; KB 1, p. 437-438; Na 1, nr. 85; Nadk. 1, nr. 1777) = O. monadelpha Roxb. ex Wight et Arn. (Avk; Vśs) = O. procumbens Steud. ex A. Rich. (Avk) = O. pusilla Salisb. (PW);

(2) Rumex dentatus Linn. (Chopra; Nadk. 1, nr. 2172);

(3) Rumex scutatus Linn. (Avk; Nadk. 1, nr. 2175);

(4) [R. corniculata] (Avk);

(5) = *nimbuka* (see *nimbū*) (Vśs);

(6) Beta vulgaris Linn. = B. bengalensis Roxb. (Vśs, = *pālaṅka*).

citraka

(1) Plumbago zeylanica Linn. (Ainslie 2, p. 77-79; Avk; Bpn, p. 21-24; Chopra; Dgv, nr. 200 : *śvetacitraka*; Dutt; DWH 2, p. 329-340; Dy, p. 620-622; Gul; HB; HK; Kav; KB 2, p. 1466-1469; MW; Nadk. 1, nr. 1967; PA 1, 4, p. 34-44; PW; Roxb., p. 155; Sanyal; V 4, p. 21; Vśs; Wise);

(2) *raktacitraka* : P. indica Linn. (Chopra) = P. rosea Linn. (Bpn, p. 21-24; Chopra; Dgv, nr. 200; Dutt; DWH 2, p. 329-340; KB 2, p. 1469-1470; Nadk. 1, nr. 1966; PA 1, 4, p. 34-44; Sanyal) = P. coccinea Boiss. (Dy, p. 620-622; PA 1, 4, p. 34-44);

(3) P. capensis Thunb. (Avk : *kṛṣṇacitraka*; Bpn, p. 21-24);

(4) Ricinus communis Linn. (KB 3, p. 2274-2277; MW; PW; Vśs);

(5) Pterospermum suberifolium Lam. (KB 1, p. 373-374; V 8, p. 72; Vśs);

(6) Amorphophallus campanulatus Blume ex Decne. = Arum campanulatum Roxb. (Vśs); see about *citraka* : HB, p. 171, footnote 463.

cirbhiṭa

(1) a) [Cucumis melo Linn. var. momordica Duthie et Fuller] (KB 2, p. 1142 : *kṣetracirbhiṭa*) = C. momordica Roxb. (Bpn, p. 555; KB 2, p. 1142 : *kṣetracirbhiṭa*);

b) a variety of C. melo Linn. (Kav);

c) C. melo Linn. (Avk) = C. dudaim Linn. (Avk) = C. madraspatanus Roxb. (Avk);

(2) C. TRIGONUS ROXB. (KB 2, p. 1139-1140) = C. PSEUDOCOLOCYNTHIS ROYLE (KB 2, p. 1139-1140);

(3) CUCUMIS ANGUINUS (Nadk. 1, nr. 726); the Index Kewensis indicates two species of this name : a) TRIÇHOSANTHES ANGUINA LINN. = C. ANGUINUS LINN.; b) C. PROPHETARUM LINN. = C. ANGUINUS T. ANDERS.;

(4) CARICA PAPAYA LINN. (KB 2, p. 1097-2000).

cukrikā = *cukra*

(1) RUMEX VESICARIUS LINN. (Ainslie 1, p. 398-400; Bpn, p. 663; Chopra; Dgv, nr. 260; DWH 3, p. 157-158; Dy, p. 658-659; Gul; HK; Nadk. 1, nr. 2176; PW);

(2) RUMEX ACETOSELLA LINN. (Nadk. 1, nr. 2170);

(3) OXALIS CORNICULATA LINN. (Ainslie 2, p. 324-326; Avk; Bpn, p. 663 : = *cāṅgerī*; KB 1, p. 437-438 : = *cāṅgerī* = *amlaloṇikā*; Vśs : = *amlaloṇikā*) = O. PUSILLA SALISB. (Roxb., p. 389);

(4) = *amlavetasa* (PW; Vśs);

(5) = *vṛkṣāmla* (PW; Vśs);

(6) = *phalāmla* (KB 1, p. 262-263);

(7) = *cukravāstūka* (Vśs, unidentified); Vśs : *vāstūka* is CHENOPODIUM ALBUM LINN.;

(8) = *amlapālaṅka* (Vśs, unidentified);

(9) TAMARINDUS INDICA LINN. (KB 2, p. 887-890; PW; Vśs).

coca

(1) = *tvac*, *tvacā* (Bpn, p. 224-225; Dgv, nr. 270; HK; MW; Nadk. 1, nr. 579; PW; Vśs);

(2) = *patra* (Vśs);

(3) banana (MW; PW; Vśs);

(4) coco-nut (MW; PW; Vśs);

(5) the fruit of BORASSUS FLABELLIFER LINN. (*tāla*) (MW; PW; Vśs);

(6) the fruit of ARTOCARPUS INTEGRIFOLIA LINN.F. (*panasa*) (Aruṇa on A.h.Sū. 3, 31);

(7) a clove, i.e. the dried flower bud of SYZYGIUM AROMATICUM (LINN.) MERR. ET L. M. PERRY (*lavaṅga*) (Vśs);

(8) = *dvīpakharjūra* (Vśs), = a) *mahāpārevata* (Vśs, unidentified), b) *dvīpāntarakharjūra* (Vśs, unidentified).

coraka

(1) Trigonella corniculata Linn. (HB; MW; PW);

(2) Chrysopogon aciculatus Trin. (HK) = Andropogon aciculatus Retz. (HK; Kav);

(3) Angelica glauca Edgew. (Bpn, p. 254-255; Gul);

(4) Gynandropsis gynandra Merr. (KB 1, p. 187-189) = G. pentaphylla DC. (KB 1, p. 187-189) = Cleome pentaphylla Linn. (KB 1, p. 187-189);

(5) = *caṇḍālaka* (Cakra on Ca.Ci. 9, 45; unidentified);

(6) = *granthiparṇa* (Aruṇa and He. on A.h.Sū. 15, 43).

jambīra

(1) a) Ocimum canum Sims (KB 3, p. 1960-1961);
b) a kind of Ocimum (MW; PW);

(2) Majorana hortensis Moench. [Intern. Code] = Origanum majorana Linn. (KB 3, p. 1985-1986);

(3) Citrus medica Linn. (Vśs) = C. acida Pers. (Vśs).

jambŭ

(1) [Syzygium cumini (Linn.) Skeels] (Chopra) = S. cumini Skeels = S. jambolanum DC. (AFM 1, p. 119-122; Kav; Nadk. 1, nr. 2424; PA 1, 5, p. 51-62; Sanyal; Vśs) [= S. jambolana Wight et Arn.] (Dutt; HK) = S. caryophyllifolium DC. (PA 1, 5, p. 55) = Eugenia jambolana Lam. (Avk : *rājajambū*; AFM 1, p. 119-122; Bpn, p. 562-563 : *rājajambū*; Chopra; Dutt; DWH 2, p. 25-29; Dy, p. 333-334; HK; Kav; KB 2, p. 1052-1054; MW; Nadk. 1, nr. 967; PA 1, 5, p. 51-62; PW; Roxb., p. 398; Sanyal; V 4, p. 85; Vśs; Watt CP, p. 526) [= E. jambolana Lam. var. caryophyllifolia] (PA 1, 5, p. 55; see Hooker 2, p. 499) = E. caryophyllifolia Lam. (KB 2, p. 1052-1054; PA 1, 5, p. 55) = E. frondosa Wall. (PA 1, 5, p. 55) = E. obtusifolia Roxb. (PA 1, 5, p. 55) = Calyptranthes jambolana Willd. (PA 1, 5, p. 55) = C. capitellata Buch.-Ham. ex Wall. (PA 1, 5, p. 55) = C. caryophyllifolia Willd. (Ainslie 2, p. 232-233 : *kākajambu*) = Myrtus cumini Linn.;

(2) Syzygium fruticosum DC. = Eugenia fruticosa Roxb. (Na 1, nr. 211 : *bhūmijambū*; Nadk. 1, nr. 967);

(3) Jambosa jambos (Linn.) Millsp. [Intern. Code] = J. vulgaris DC. (KB 2, p. 1049-1051) [= Syzygium jambos (Linn.) Alst.] (Cho-

pra) = Eugenia jambos Linn. (Chopra; Gul; KB 2, p. 1049-1051; Nadk. 1, nr. 968; V 3, p. 109 : *rājajambū*);

(4) Syzygium caryophyllaeum Gaertn. [Intern. Code] (PA 1, 5, p. 61-62 : considered by some *vaidyas* of Kerala to be the small variety of *jambu*) = Eugenia caryophyllaea Wight (PA 1, 5, p. 61) = Calyptranthes caryophyllata Pers. (PA 1, 5, p. 61) = Myrtus caryophyllata Linn. (PA 1, 5, p. 61);

(5) Syzygium operculatum Gamble = Eugenia operculata Roxb. (KB 2, p. 1051-1052 : *jalajambuka, bhūmijambu*) = E. cerasoides Roxb. (KB 2, p. 1051-1052);

(6) Syzygium rubicundum Wight et Arn. = Eugenia rubicunda Wight (Na 1, nr. 211 : *kāka-, vanajambū*);

(7) Premna herbacea Roxb. (Bpn, p. 562-563 : *kṣudrajambū*; Chopra : *bhūmijambū*; Nadk. 1, nr. 2024 : *bhūmijambukā*);

(8) Ardisia humilis Vahl = A. solanacea Roxb. (Avk : *bhūjambū, kākajambū*);

(9) = *nāgadamanī* (MW; PW; Vśs).

jalapippalī

(1) Lippia nodiflora Michx. (Avk; Bpn, p. 470; KB 3, p. 1916-1917); [Flora Iranica : Phyla nodiflora (Linn.) Greene = Verbena nodiflora Linn. = Lippia nodiflora (Linn.) Rich. in Michx.];

(2) Commelina salicifolia Roxb. (KB 4, p. 2536-2537); it may be that *toyapippalī* is not a synonym of *jalapippalī*, but a different plant: *toyapippalī* : Sapium sebiferum Roxb. (Chopra; KB 3, p. 2284; Nadk. 1, nr. 2222); it is not clear whether *jalapippalīgaṇḍīra* (see *gaṇḍīra*) is identical with *jalapippalī*.

jīraka

(1) Cuminum cyminum Linn. (*śveta-* or *śuklajīraka*) (Avk; Bpn, p. 31-32; Chopra; Dgv, nr. 176; Dutt; DWH 2, p. 113-115; Dy, p. 369-370); Gul; HK; IRM 2, p. 396-398; KB 2, p. 1227-1228; Na 1, nr. 246; Nadk. 1, nr. 741; Roxb., p. 271; Sanyal; V 4, p. 101; Vśs; Watt CP, p. 442-443);

(2) Carum carvi Linn. (*kṛṣṇajīraka*) (Bpn, p. 31-32; Dgv, nr. 177; DWH 2, p. 119-121; KB 2, p. 1201-1203; Na 1, nr. 247; Sanyal; V 4, p. 102);

(3) Nigella sativa Linn. (*kṛṣṇajīraka* : Ainslie 1, p. 128; Avk; Chopra; Dutt; DWH 1, p. 28-29; HK; KB 1, p. 11-12; Nadk. 1, nr.

1716; Vśs; Wise; *araṇyajīraka* : Nadk. 1, nr. 1716; *sthūlajīraka* : Dgm, p. 13; KB 1, p. 11-12; V 2, p. 88) =N. INDICA ROXB. EX FLEM. (Avk; KB 1, p. 11-12; MW : *kṛṣṇajīraka*; Nadk. 1, nr. 1716; PW : *kṛṣṇajīraka*; Wise);

(4) VERNONIA ANTHELMINTICA WILLD. (Ainslie 2, p. 54-55 : *kānanajīraka*; Avk : *vanajīraka*; Bpn, p. 31-32 : *araṇyajīraka*; KB 2, p. 1325-1327 : *vanajīraka*; Nadk. 1, nr. 2577 : *aṭavijīraka*; V 2, p. 132 : *araṇyajīraka*) [= CENTRATHERUM ANTHELMINTICUM (WILLD.) KUNTZE] (Na 1, nr. 279 : *araṇyajīraka*) [= C. ANTHELMINTICUM O. KUNTZE] (KB 2, p. 1325-1327) = SERRATULA ANTHELMINTICA ROXB. (Avk; Nadk. 1, nr. 2577) = ASCARICIDA INDICA CASS. (Nadk. 1, nr. 2577) [= CONYZA ASCARADIA] (Nadk. 1, nr. 2577) = CONYZA ANTHELMINTICA LINN.;

(5) PANICUM MILIACEUM LINN. (MW).

jūrṇāhvā, jūrṇāhvaya

[SORGHUM VULGARE (LINN.) PERS. VAR. SACCHARATUM BOERL.] = S. VULGARE PERS. = ANDROPOGON BICOLOR ROXB. (MW) = A. SACCHARATUS ROXB. (PW); Dn, *varga* 6, 108 : = *yāvanāla*; Pr 697 and Rn, *varga* 16, 169 : = *devadhānya*.

jyotiṣmatī

(1) CELASTRUS PANICULATUS WILLD. (Avk : *mahājyotiṣmatī*; Bpn, p. 90; Dgv, nr. 83; DWH 1, p. 343-345; Gul; IRM 2, p. 112-113; KB 1, p. 574-577; Na 1, nr. 107; V 2, p. 6);

(2) CARDIOSPERMUM HALICACABUM LINN. (Avk; Dutt; DWH 1, p. 366-367; Dy, p. 187-188; HK; Kav; KB 1, p. 623-625; MW; Na 1, nr. 107 : acc. to some; Nadk. 1, nr. 473; Roxb., p. 335; V 2, p. 45; Vśs).

tagara

(1) ERVATAMIA DIVARICATA BURKILL (W. Rau) = TABERNAEMONTANA CORONARIA WILLD. (KB 2, p. 1577-1578) [= T. CORONARIA R. BR.] = T. CORONARIA (HB; Vśs) (see Bpn, p. 200; Dutt; DWH 2, p. 413-414; HK; Nadk. 1, nr. 2425) = NERIUM DIVARICATUM LINN.;

(2) ERVATAMIA CORONARIA STAPF (KB 2, p. 1577-1578 : = 1);

(3) ERVATAMIA HEYNEANA COOKE = TABERNAEMONTANA HEYNEANA WALL. (see DWH 2, p. 413; Nadk. 1, nr. 2425);

(4) T. DICHOTOMA ROXB. (see DWH 2, p. 413);

(5) VALERIANA WALLICHII DC. (Bpn, p. 199; Dgv, nr. 188; DWH 2,

p. 238-240; KB 2, p. 1311-1312; Na 1, nr. 277; Nadk. 1, nr. 2558) [= V. BRUNONIANA C. B. CLARKE] (Nadk. 1, nr. 2558);

(6) V. LESCHENAULTII DC. (Nadk. 1, nr. 2558) = V. BRUNONIANA WIGHT ET ARN.;

taṇḍula

(1) ORYZA SATIVA LINN.;

(2) EMBELIA RIBES BURM.F. (Bpn, p. 52; KB 2, p. 1478-1480; MW; PW);

(3) = *taṇḍulīya* (KB 3, p. 2057-2059; MW; PW).

taṇḍulīya(ka)

(1) AMARANTHUS POLYGAMUS LINN. (Dutt; Gul; HK) = A. POLYGONOIDES ROXB. (MW; PW) = AMBLOGYNA POLYGONOIDES DALZ. ET GIBS. (Vśs);

(2) AMARANTHUS SPINOSUS LINN. (Avk; Bpn, p. 660; Chopra; Dutt; DWH 3, p. 138; Dy, p. 652; HK : acc. to some; IRM 1, p. 67; KB 3, p. 2057-2059; Vśs);

(3) A. VIRIDIS LINN. (Chopra; KB 3, p. 2061-2062; Nadk. 1, nr. 146);

(4) [A. GANGETICUS LINN. VAR. TRISTIS PRAIN] (KB 3, p. 2060-2061) = A. GANGETICUS LINN. = A. TRICOLOR LINN. = A. TRISTIS LINN.;

(5) A. BLITUM LINN. (V 5, p. 10) = A. GANGETICUS WALL.;

(6) GARCINIA XANTHOCHYMUS HOOK.F. EX T. ANDERS. = XANTHOCHYMUS PICTORIUS ROXB. (HSu);

(7) COMMELINA BENGHALENSIS LINN. (KB 4, p. 2536).

tāla

BORASSUS FLABELLIFER LINN. = B. FLABELLIFORMIS MURR.

tila

(1) SESAMUM INDICUM DC. = S. ORIENTALE LINN. = S. LUTEUM RETZ. (Nadk. 1, nr. 2285);

(2) S. TRIFOLIATUM MILL. (Nadk. 1, nr. 2285).

tīkṣṇagandha

(1) MAJORANA HORTENSIS MOENCH. [Intern. Code] (MW);

(2) a) = *phaṇijjhaka* (PW; Vśs);

b) = *gandhatulasī* (Vśs, unidentified; probably OCIMUM SANCTUM LINN., see KB 3, p. 1965-1968);

c) the dark type of *arjaka* (Vśs);

(3) MORINGA PTERYGOSPERMA GAERTN. (= *tīkṣṇagandhaka*; Bpn, p. 339-340; MW; PW; Vśs);

(4) = *palāṇḍu* : Allium cepa Linn. (Vśs);

(5) = *bhairavīvacā* (Vśs, unidentified; *vacā* is usually identified as ACORUS CALAMUS LINN.);

(6) = *kṣavaka* (Vśs);

(7) = *kṛṣṇaśigru* = *śigru* (Vśs);

(8) = *elā* (Vśs).

tuṇḍikerī

(1) = *kārpāsī* (Dgv, nr. 45; KB 1, p. 344-346; MW; Na 1, nr. 55; PW);

(2) = *tuṇḍikeśī* = *bimbī* : COCCINIA INDICA WIGHT ET ARN. (Dgv, nr. 167; DWH 2, p. 86; KB 2, p. 1151-1154; MW; PW).

tumbaru = *tumburu*

(1) ZANTHOXYLUM ALATUM ROXB. (Avk; Bpn, p. 56; Chopra; Dgv, nr. 95; Dutt; DWH 1, p. 255-260; Gul; HB; HK; Kav; KB 1, p. 460-461; Na 1, nr. 95; Nadk. 1, nr. 2644; V 5, p. 39; Vśs) = Z. HOSTILE WALL. (Dutt; HK; Kav; Vśs);

(2) Z. BUDRUNGA WALL. (DWH 1, p. 255-260);

(3) Z. RHETSA DC. (Bpn, p. 57; Dgv, nr. 95; DWH 1, p. 255-260; V 5, p. 26); Chopra, DWH and KB 1, p. 464 : 2) = 3); see Hooker 1, p. 495-496; the Index Kewensis distinguishes the two species;

(4) Z. ACANTHOPODIUM DC. (Bpn, p. 56; DWH 1, p. 255-260);

(5) Z. OXYPHYLLUM EDGEW. (DWH 1, p. 255-260);

(6) Z. HAMILTONIANUM WALL. (DWH 1, p. 255-260);

(7) CORIANDRUM SATIVUM LINN. (KB 2, p. 1225-1227; MW; PW; V 5, p. 104); see HB, p. 87, footnote 59;

(8) the fruit of DIOSPYROS EMBRYOPTERIS PERS. [= D. EMBRYOPTERIS LINN.] (MW; PW) = D. PEREGRINA GUERKE = EMBRYOPTERIS PEREGRINA GAERTN.;

(9) DIOSPYROS MELANOXYLON ROXB. (Nadk. 1, nr. 849);

(10) EXCOECARIA AGALLOCHA LINN. (Avk).

tulasī

(1) Ocimum sanctum Linn. (Avk : *kṛṣṇatulasī*; Bpn, p. 509; Dgv, nr. 250; Dutt; DWH 3, p. 86-88; HK; KB 3, p. 1965-1968; Nadk. 1, nr. 1741; V 5, p. 32; Vśs) = O. hirsutum Benth. (Avk; Nadk. 1, nr. 1741) = O. tomentosum Lam. (Avk; Nadk. 1, nr. 1741);

(2) O. basilicum Linn. (Avk : *śuklatulasī*; Vśs) = O. album Linn. (Ainslie 2, p. 91-92 : *viśvatulasī*; Avk);

(3) O. gratissimum Linn. (Avk : *vanatulasī, rāmatulasī*; Chopra : *vṛddhatulasī*; KB 3, p. 1964-1965 : *rāmatulasī*);

(4) O. canum Sims (KB 3, p. 1960-1961 : *kṣudratulasī*) = O. americanum Linn. (KB 3, p. 1960-1961);

(5) Ocimum viride Willd. (Nadk. 1, nr. 1741);

(6) Orthosiphon stamineus Benth. (Avk) = Ocimum grandiflorum Blume (Avk).

tejovatī

(1) = *jyotiṣmatī* (HK);

(2) = *mahājyotiṣmatī* (see *jyotiṣmatī*) (MW; PW; Vśs);

(3) Piper chaba Hunter (KB 3, p. 2130-2131; MW; PW; Vśs);

(4) Piper nigrum Linn. (Vśs);

(5) Scindapsus officinalis Schott (MW; PW; Vśs) = Pothos officinalis Roxb. (Vśs; Wise);

(6) Acorus calamus Linn. (Vśs);

(7) Zanthoxylum alatum Roxb. (Bpn, p. 89 : *tejavatī*; Dgv, nr. 74);

(8) Z. rhetsa DC. (KB 1, p. 464-465 : *tejavatī*; Na 1, nr. 94);

(9) Z. budrunga Wall. (KB 1, p. 464-465 : *tejavatī*) = Fagara budrunga Roxb. (KB 1, p. 464-465);

(10) = *tejovalkala* (Vśs, unidentified);

(11) *jīvantī* with yellow flowers (*svarṇajīvantī*) (Vśs); a great number of plants is called *jīvantī*.

tripuṭa

(1) = *tripuṭakalāya* : Lathyrus sativus Linn. (Bpn, p. 649; Dutt : *tripuṭī*; DWH 1, p. 489-491; KB 1, p. 770-771; Na 1, nr. 139; Nadk. 1, nr. 1439);

(2) = *satīna* : Pisum sativum Linn. (KB 1, p. 772-773; PW);

(3) = *gokṣura* (PW; Vśs);

(4) Ipomoea turpethum R. Br. (DWH 2, p. 527-530; Nadk. 1, nr. 1339).

tvac(ǎ)

(1) a) CINNAMOMUM ZEYLANICUM NEES (Avk); many sources identify *tvac* with C. ZEYLANICUM BREYN, the name used by Hooker, see vol. 5, p. 131-132; C. ZEYLANICUM BREYN includes both C. ZEYLANICUM NEES and C. ZEYLANICUM BLUME, which are distinguished as separate species in the Index Kewensis; = LAURUS CINNAMOMUM LINN. (Roxb., p. 336-337) = L. CASSIA LINN. (Ainslie 1, p. 58-59; Roxb., p. 337); Roxb. distinguishes L. CINNAMOMUM from L. CASSIA, but these names are synonyms acc. to the Index Kewensis;

b) C. ZEYLANICUM BREYN (Dutt; Gul; HK; KB 3, p. 2149-2150);

c) C. ZEYLANICUM (Dgv, nr. 270; HK; Kav; Nadk. 1, nr. 579);

(2) CINNAMOMUM ZEYLANICUM BLUME (Bpn, p. 226);

(3) C. CASSIA BLUME (Bpn, p. 224-225; DWH 3, p. 203-208; Nadk. 1, nr. 579) = C. AROMATICUM NEES (Nadk. 1, nr. 579);

(4) C. MACROCARPUM HOOK.F. (KB 3, p. 2151);

(5) C. SAIGONICUM FARWELL (Nadk. 1, nr. 579);

(6) [C. LAURUS] (Nadk. 1, nr. 579).

dantī

(1) BALIOSPERMUM AXILLARE BLUME = B. MONTANUM MUELL. ARG. = CROTON POLYANDRUS ROXB. = JATROPHA MONTANA WILLD.;

(2) CROTON TIGLIUM LINN. (Avk : *kṣudradantī*, *laghudantī*; KB 3, p. 2256-2257);

(3) JATROPHA CURCAS LINN. (V 5, p. 59 : *bṛhaddantī*);

(4) J. MULTIFIDA LINN. (V 5, p. 59 : *bṛhaddantī*).

darbha

(1) IMPERATA ARUNDINACEA CYRILL. (Dutt; HK) = I. CYLINDRICA BEAUV. (Dutt; HK; Vśs, = *uluka*) = SACCHARUM CYLINDRICUM LAM. (HSu; Kav; MW; Vśs, = *uluka*) = DESMOSTACHYA BIPINNATA STAPF (Chopra; Dgv, nr. 342; IRM 3, p. 43, = *kuśa*; KB 4, p. 2688-2689, = *kuśa*; V 3, p. 14) = ERAGROSTIS CYNOSUROIDES BEAUV. (Avk, = *kuśa*; Chopra, = *kuśa*; DWH 3, p. 575-577, = *kuśa*; IRM 3, p. 43; KB 4, p. 2688-2689; V 3, p. 14; Vśs, = *kuśa*) = BRIZA BIPINNATA LINN. = UNIOLA BIPINNATA LINN. = POA CYNOSUROIDES RETZ. (Avk; Dy, p. 854; Gul; Roxb., p. 112, = *kuśa*; Vśs; Wise);

(2) CYNODON DACTYLON (LINN.) PERS. [Intern. Code] (Viennot) = PANICUM DACTYLON LINN. (Goudr.);

(3) SACCHARUM SPONTANEUM LINN. (Vśs : = *kāśa*). Many authors equate *darbha* with *kuśa*, but Ḍa. (on Su.Sū. 38, 75) distinguishes them clearly : "*kuśa* is short and soft and has leaves with the form of a needle; *darbha* has leaves which are broad, long and rough."

dāḍima

PUNICA GRANATUM LINN.

dāruharidrā

(1) BERBERIS ARISTATA DC. (AFM 1, p. 60; Avk; Bpn, p. 119; Chopra; Dgm, p. 44; Dgv, nr. 17; Dutt; DWH 1, p. 64-68; Dy, p. 35-37; Ghosh; Gul; HK; IRM 1, p. 178; KB 1, p. 102-103; Nadk. 1, nr. 335; PA 1, 2, p. 15; V 5, p. 65) [= B. ARISTATA VAR. FLORIBUNDA HOOK.F. ET THOMS.] (KB 1, p. 102-103) = B. CORIARIA ROYLE EX LINDL. (KB 1, p. 102-103) = B. CHITRIA D. DON (Dgm, p. 44);

(2) B. ASIATICA ROXB. EX DC. (Avk; Bpn, p. 119; Dgm, p. 44-45; Dutt; DWH 1, p. 64-68; Dy, p. 35-37; HB; Kav; KB 1, p. 105-106; Na 1, nr. 16; PA 1, 2, p. 15; Sanyal; Vśs);

(3) B. LYCIUM ROYLE (Bpn, p. 119; Dgm, p. 44-45; DWH 1, p. 64-68; Dy, p. 35-37);

(4) B. VULGARIS LINN. (Avk; Dgm, p. 44-45; PA 1, 2, p. 15);

(5) B. CORIACEA BRANDIS EX GAMBLE (Dgm, p. 44-45);

(6) B. NEPALENSIS (Dgm, p. 44-45); the Index Kewensis indicates two species : a) B. NEPALENSIS SPRENG.; b) B. VULGARIS LINN. = B. NEPALENSIS HORT. EX C. KOCH;

(7) [COSCINIUM FENESTRATUM (GAERTN.) COLEBR.] (Chopra; IRM 2, p. 360; KB 1, p. 84-86) = C. FENESTRATUM COLEBR. (AFM 1, p. 60; Bpn, p. 121-122 : used as a substitute; Nadk. 1, nr. 685; PA 1, 2, p. 15; V 5, p. 71; Vśs) = MENISPERMUM FENESTRATUM GAERTN. (KB 1, p. 84-86; PA 1, 2, p. 15);

(8) CURCUMA AROMATICA SALISB. (MW) (usually called *vanaharidrā*);

(9) C. XANTHORRHIZA ROXB. (MW);

(10) MORINDA UMBELLATA LINN. (KB 2, p. 1296-1297).

dārvī

= *dāruharidrā*.

dīpya(ka)

(1) APIUM GRAVEOLENS LINN. (Avk; Bpn, p. 27; KB 2, p. 1199-1201);

(2) TRACHYSPERMUM ROXBURGHIANUM H. WOLFF = CARUM ROXBURGHIANUM BENTH. ET HOOK.F. (Avk; Dgv, nr. 179; Nadk. 1, nr. 2065) = APIUM INVOLUCRATUM ROXB. EX FLEM. (Avk; MW; PW; Vśs) = PTYCHOTIS ROXBURGHIANA DC. (Avk) = PIMPINELLA INVOLUCRATA WIGHT ET ARN. (Avk);

(3) TRACHYSPERMUM COPTICUM (LINN.) LINK [Intern. Code] = CARUM COPTICUM BENTH. ET HOOK.F. (Avk; Dgv, nr. 178; Gul; KB 2, p. 1204-1206; Na 1, nr. 249; Nadk. 1, nr. 2065; V 1, p. 17; Vśs) = C. AJOWAN BENTH. ET HOOK.F. (Avk) = PTYCHOTIS AJOWAN DC. (Avk; MW; Na 1, nr. 249; Nadk. 1, nr. 2065; PW) = AMMI COPTICUM LINN. (Avk) = LIGUSTICUM AJAWAIN ROXB. EX FLEM. (Avk);

(4) CUMINUM CYMINUM LINN. (HK; KB 2, p. 1227-1228; Vśs);

(5) CARUM PETROSELINUM BENTH. ET HOOK.F. (Avk) = APIUM PETROSELINUM LINN. (Avk);

(6) CELOSIA ARGENTEA LINN. = C. CRISTATA LINN. (MW; PW; Vśs : = *mayūraśikhā*);

(7) ARISTOLOCHIA INDICA LINN. (Vśs : = *rudrajaṭā* = *īśvarī*);

(8) PLUMBAGO INDICA LINN. = P. ROSEA LINN. (Vśs : = *raktacitraka*);

(9) CROCUS SATIVUS LINN. (Vśs : = *kuṅkuma*);

(10) HYOSCYAMUS NIGER LINN. (KB 3, p. 1794-1796);

(11) = *nimbū* (Vśs);

(12) = *tagara* (Vśs).

durālabhā

= *yavāsa*.

devadhānya

(1) [SORGHUM VULGARE (LINN.) PERS. VAR. SACCHARATUM BOERL.] = S. VULGARE PERS. = S. SACCHARATUM MOENCH. (DWH 3, p. 621) = S. CERNUUM WILLD. (MW) = ANDROPOGON SACCHARATUS ROXB. (Chopra; MW; PW; Roxb., p. 91) = A. SORGHUM ROXB. (PW) = A. SORGHUM BROT. (MW) = HOLCUS SACCHARATUM LINN. (MW); see about sorghum : Gode, St.I.C.H. 1, p. 266-282;

(2) ZEA MAYS LINN. (Vśs).

drākṣā

VITIS VINIFERA LINN.

dhattūra

(1) DATURA STRAMONIUM LINN. (Bpn, p. 317-320; Chopra; DWH 2, p. 584-624; KB 3, p. 1784-1787; V 5, p. 93-94 : *kṛṣṇadhattūra*) = D. TATULA LINN. (Bpn, p. 317-320; Chopra);

(2) D. METEL LINN. (Bpn, p. 317-320 : *kṛṣṇadhattūra*; Chopra : *dhustūra*; Dutt : *dhustūra*; DWH 2, p. 585-624; KB 3, p. 1791-1792 : *dhustūra*; Vśs; Wise);

(3) D. FASTUOSA LINN. (AFM 1, p. 61-64; Ainslie 1, p. 442 : *kṛṣṇa-*; Chopra; Dgv, nr. 232 : *kṛṣṇa-*; Dutt : *dhustūra*; DWH 2, p. 585-624; Dy, p. 626-629; HK; KB 3, p. 1788-1789 : *kṛṣṇa-*; Nadk. 1, nr. 797 : *kṛṣṇa-*; PW : *kṛṣṇa-*; V 5, p. 93-94 : *kṛṣṇa-*; Vśs) = D. ALBA NEES (Dgv, nr. 232 : *śveta-*; Dy, p. 626-629; HK; KB 3, p. 1790-1791 : *śveta-*; MW; Nadk. 1, nr. 796 : *dhustūra*; PW; V 5, p. 101 : *śveta-*; Vśs) [= D. FASTUOSA LINN. VAR. ALBA C. B. CLARKE] (AFM 1, p. 61-64 : *śveta-*; HK : *śveta-*; KB 3, p. 1790-1791 : *śveta-*) (see Hooker 4, p. 243) = D. INNOXIA MILL. (Bpn, p. 317-320) = D. NILHUMMATU DUN. (Nadk. 1, nr. 796); there is no agreement about the nomenclature of the species of Datura : Hooker considers D. METEL LINN. and D. FASTUOSA LINN. as separate species (vol. 4, p. 242-243), as well as Cooke (vol. 2, p. 343-344), but a different classification is found in Chopra : a) D. INNOXIA MILL. is a separate species, b) D. METEL LINN. = D. FASTUOSA LINN. = D. ALBA NEES, and in IRM vol. 3, p. 14-15 : a) D. INNOXIA MILL. = D. METEL AUCTT. (NON LINN.), b) D. METEL LINN. = D. FASTUOSA LINN. = D. ALBA NEES = D. FASTUOSA VAR. ALBA (NEES) C. B. CLARKE; IRM 3, p. 16-19 : the names *dhattūra* and *dhustūra* are applied to representatives of the genus Datura irrespective of the species.

dhātakī

(1) WOODFORDIA FLORIBUNDA SALISB. = W. FRUTICOSA KURZ = W. TOMENTOSA BEDD. = GRISLEA TOMENTOSA BUCH.-HAM. = LYTHRUM FRUTICOSUM LINN.;

(2) CALYCOPTERIS FLORIBUNDA LAM. (IRM 2, p. 23 : *śvetadhātakī*) = C. NUTANS KURZ (IRM 2, p. 23);

(3) ANOGEISSUS LATIFOLIA WALL. (Avk).

dhātrī

(1) = *āmalaka* : PHYLLANTHUS EMBLICA LINN.;

(2) = *dhātakī* : WOODFORDIA FLORIBUNDA SALISB. = W. FRUTICOSA KURZ (KB 2, p. 1074-1076) = GRISLEA TOMENTOSA BUCH.-HAM. (Roxb., p. 317).

dhānyaka

CORIANDRUM SATIVUM LINN. (Ainslie 1, p. 91-92; Bpn, p. 34; Dgv, nr. 180; Dutt; Gul; HB; HK; Kav; KB 2, p. 1225-1227; MW; Na 1, nr. 257; Nadk. 1, nr. 679 : PA 1, 9, p. 128-136; PW; Roxb., p. 272).

nandīvṛkṣa

(1) CEDRELA TOONA ROXB. EX ROTTL. (Chopra; Dutt; DWH 1, p. 339; HK; IRM 2, p. 104-106; KB 1, p. 562-564; MW; Nadk. 1, nr. 515; PW) = TOONA CILIATA M. ROEM. (IRM 2, p. 104);

(2) ERVATAMIA CORONARIA STAPF (IRM 3, p. 192-193; KB 2, p. 1577-1578);

(3) [ERVATAMIA DIVARICATA (LINN.) ALSTON] (IRM 3, p. 192);

(4) ERVATAMIA HEYNEANA COOKE = TABERNAEMONTANA HEYNEANA WALL. (see DWH 2, p. 413; Nadk. 1, nr. 2425);

(5) ERVATAMIA DIVARICATA BURKILL = TABERNAEMONTANA CORONARIA WILLD. (KB 2, p. 1577-1578 : = E. CORONARIA STAPF) = [T. CORONARIA R. BR.] (Ainslie 2, p. 257-258; IRM 3, p. 192: = E. CORONARIA STAPF; Nadk. 1, nr. 2425) = T. DIVARICATA R. BR. EX ROEM. ET SCHULT. = NERIUM CORONARIUM JACQ. (Ainslie 2, p. 257-258) = N. DIVARICATUM LINN.;

(6) TABERNAEMONTANA DICHOTOMA ROXB. (see DWH 2, p. 413);

(7) THESPESIA POPULNEA (LINN.) SOLAND. EX CORREA [Intern.Code] (Vśs : = *gardabhāṇḍa*) = TH. POPULNEOIDES KOSTEL. (PW);

(8) STEREOSPERMUM SUAVEOLENS DC. = BIGNONIA SUAVEOLENS ROXB. (MW; PW);

(9) FICUS BENGHALENSIS LINN. (HSu);

(10) F. RETUSA LINN. (Bpn, p. 515);

(11) = *sthālī* (PW; acc. to PW : F. BENJAMINA or F. INDICA); the Index Kewensis records : a) F. TSIELA ROXB. = F. INDICA WILLD. = F. BENJAMINA WALL., b) F. RETUSA LINN. = F. INDICA HEYNE EX ROTH = F. BENJAMINA WILLD., c) F. BENJAMINA LINN.; F. BENGHALENSIS LINN. = F. INDICA LINN.;

(12) a kind of FICUS RELIGIOSA LINN. (*aśvattha*) with branches and leaves facing downwards (Vśs);

(13) a kind of fragrant tree, well known in Kāṅkana (Vśs);

(14) = *gǎmbhārī* = *kāśmarī* = *kāśmarya* (Vśs);

(15) = *meṣaśṛṅgī* (PW; Vśs).

nāgakeśara = *nāgakesara*

(1) MESUA FERREA LINN. (Avk; Bpn, p. 229-232; Chopra; Dgm, p. 226; Dgv, nr. 38; Dutt; DWH 1, p. 170-172; HK; Kav; KB 1, p. 274-276; Na 1, nr. 43; Nadk. 1, nr. 1595; Roxb., p. 437; Sanyal; Vśs) = M. COROMANDELINA WIGHT (Dgm, p. 226; KB 1, p. 274-276; Nadk. 1, nr. 1595) = M. PEDUNCULATA WIGHT (KB 1, p. 274-276) = M. ROXBURGHII WIGHT (Dgm, p. 226; HK; MW; Nadk. 1, nr. 1595; PW) = M. SPECIOSA CHOISY (KB 1, p. 274-276);

(2) OCHROCARPUS LONGIFOLIUS BENTH. ET HOOK.F. EX T. ANDERS. (Bpn, p. 229-232; DWH 1, p. 172-173; KB 1, p. 269-270; Na 1, nr. 44; Nadk. 1, nr. 1731);

(3) CALOPHYLLUM INOPHYLLUM LINN. (Bpn, p. 229-232);

(4) = *nāgadamanī* (Vśs);

(5) the immature fruit of CINNAMOMUM CASSIA BLUME (DWH 3, p. 210; Dy, p. 670);

(6) the immature fruit of C. INERS REINW. EX BLUME (DWH 3, p. 210; Dy, p. 670);

(7) the buds of C. ZEYLANICUM NEES = LAURUS CASSIA LINN. (Ainslie 1, p. 60).

nāgadamanī

(1) ARTEMISIA VULGARIS LINN. (Chopra; DWH 2, p. 285-286; KB 2, p. 1395-1397; MW; Nadk. 1, nr. 244; V 2, p. 128; Vśs) = A. INDICA WILLD. (Chopra; Vśs);

(2) CRINUM ASIATICUM LINN. (Chopra; see DWH 2, p. 285; IRM 2, p. 367; KB 4, p. 2471-2472) = C. TOXICARIUM ROXB. (KB 4, p. 2471-2472);

(3) ALPINIA NUTANS ROSC. (MW) = A. SPECIOSA K. SCHUM.;

(4) PUPALIA LAPPACEA MOQ. (Bpn, p. 473);

(5) = *jambū* (PW);

(6) = *jāmbavatī* (PW, unidentified);

(7) = *vṛkkā* (PW, unidentified).

nāgapuṣpa

= *nāgakeśara*.

nāgara : dried ginger

See : *ārdraka*.

nāgaramusta

Cyperus scariosus R. Br. (Bpn, p. 243-244; Chopra; Dutt; DWH 3, p. 554-555; KB 4, p. 2637-2638; Nadk. 1, nr. 783; V 5, p. 120) = C. pertenuis Roxb. (Avk; Dutt; Dy, p. 845-846; Vśs).

nāgavallī

(1) Piper betle Linn. (Avk; Bpn, p. 272; Dgv, nr. 265; Dutt; DWH 3, p. 183-192; MW; Nadk. 1, nr. 1925; PW; Vśs; Watt CP, p. 891-896) = Chavica betle Miq. (Avk; Dutt; Nadk. 1, nr. 1925; Vśs); see R. Schmidt, Beiträge zur Flora Sanscritica IV, Arekanusz und Betelpfeffer, ZDMG 67, 1913, p. 653-659;

(2) Mussaenda frondosa Linn. (Avk; DWH 2, p. 202-204; Nadk. 1, nr. 1671) = M. flavescens Buch.-Ham. (Nadk. 1, nr. 1671);

(3) M. frondosa (V 7, p. 91); the Index Kewensis distinguishes three species : a) M. frondosa Linn., b) M. pubescens Ait. = M. frondosa Lour., c) M. roxburghii Hook.f. = M. frondosa Roxb. = M. frondosa Wall.;

(4) M. glabrata Hutchinson ex Gamble (KB 2, p. 1270-1271; V 7, p. 91) = M. frondosa var. glabrata Hook.f. (KB 2, p. 1270-1271); see Hooker 3, p. 89-90.

nimbū(ka)

(1) a) Citrus medica Linn. = C. acida Pers. (Ainslie 1, p. 193-194; Bpn, p. 580; Dgv, nr. 68; MW; Na 1, nr. 96);

b) [C. medica Linn. var. acida] (Dutt; KB 1, p. 489-490; Vśs; Watt CP, p. 326); see Cooke 1, p. 200-201; Duthie 1, p. 131-132; Hooker 1, p. 514-515;

(2) [C. limon (Linn.) Burm.f.] (Chopra: *mahānimbu*); see Purseglove 2, p. 502-504; = [C. medica Linn. var. limonum] (Chopra); see Cooke 1, p. 200-201; Duthie 1, p. 131; Hooker 1, p. 514-515; Watt CP, p. 325-326;

(3) CITRUS AURANTIUM LINN. = C. BERGAMIA RISSO (KB 1, p. 494-495) = [C. AURANTIUM LINN. VAR. BERGAMIA] (KB 1, p. 494-495); see Hooker 1, p. 515; see about *nimbū* : H. W. Glidden, The lemon in Asia and Europe, JAOS 57, 1937, p. 381-396.

niśāhvaya

= *haridrā*.

niṣpāva(ka)

(1) VIGNA SINENSIS SAVI EX HASSK. = DOLICHOS SINENSIS LINN. (Dutt; HK; Kav; MW; Nadk. 1, nr. 867; PW) = D. CYLINDRICUS MOENCH. (Nadk. 1, nr. 867); Dutt and HK consider, in agreement with Hooker (2, p. 205-206), D. SINENSIS LINN. as a synonym of VIGNA CATIANG ENDL.; the latter is not recorded in the Index Kewensis; see about the nomenclature Purseglove 1, p. 322;

(2) VIGNA CATJANG WALP. (KB 1, p. 800-802; Vśs : = *rājamāṣa*); see Cooke 1, p. 404-405; Duthie 1, p. 209 and Purseglove 1, p. 322;

(3) DOLICHOS LABLAB LINN. (Gul; KB 1, p. 806-807; Na 1, nr. 151; V 7, p. 100) = LABLAB VULGARIS SAVI (Bpn, p. 646); see Watt CP, p. 508-510;

(4) PHASEOLUS MUNGO LINN. = PH. RADIATUS LINN. (Avk : *śvetaniṣpāva*; Vśs).

nīlī = *nīlikā* = *nīlinī* = *nīlā*

(1) INDIGOFERA TINCTORIA LINN. (Avk; Bpn, p. 406; Chopra; Dgv, nr. 101; Dutt; DWH 1, p. 406-411; Dy, p. 213-215; Gul; HK; KB 1, p. 712-714; MW; Na 1, nr. 154; Nadk. 1, nr. 1309; PA 1, 4, p. 61-71; PW; Roxb., p. 585; V 6, p. 23; Wise) = I. INDICA LAM. (Nadk. 1, nr. 1309) = I. SUMATRANA GAERTN. (Nadk. 1, nr. 1309; PA 1, 4, p. 61, considered as a separate species) [= I. ARRECTA] (Nadk. 1, nr. 1309);

(2) a) I. ANIL LINN. (Ainslie 1, p. 178-180);
b) I. ANIL (Nadk. 1, nr. 1309); the Index Kewensis records two species : a) I. ANIL LINN.; b) I. PAUCIFOLIA DELILE = I. ANIL SM. EX WIGHT ET ARN.;

(3) I. PAUCIFOLIA DELILE (KB 1, p. 711-712 and V 4, p. 112 : *nīlā*);

(4) a) I. ARGENTEA LINN. (Nadk. 1, nr. 1297) = I. CAERULEA ROXB. (Nadk. 1, nr. 1297);
b) I. ARGENTEA (Avk); the Index Kewensis distinguishes two

species of this name : a) I. ARGENTEA LINN., b) I. PAUCIFOLIA DELILE = I. ARGENTEA ROXB.;

(5) I. OBLONGIFOLIA FORSK. (KB 1, p. 711-712 : *nīlā*);

(6) I. ANGUSTIFOLIA (Nadk. 1, nr. 1293); the Index Kewensis records three species : a) I. ANGUSTIFOLIA LINN., b) I. HIRSUTA LINN. = I. ANGUSTIFOLIA BLANCO, c) I. STRICTA LINN. = I. ANGUSTIFOLIA CURT.

nīvāra

(1) a) the wild variety of rice (Dutt; HK; MW; PW; Vśs);
b) ORYZA SATIVA LINN. (KB 4, p. 2651-2653);

(2) HYGRORYZA ARISTATA NEES (DWH 3, p. 620; Gul; KB 4, p. 2653-2654);

(3) SETARIA ITALICA BEAUV. = PANICUM ITALICUM LINN. (Bpn, p. 655).

nyagrodha

(1) = *vaṭa*;

(2) = *śamī* (MW; PW).

paṭola

(1) TRICHOSANTHES DIOICA ROXB. (Avk; Bpn, p. 674; Chopra; Dgv, nr. 166; Dutt; DWH 2, p. 72-74; Dy, p. 343-344; Ghosh; Gul; HB; HK; Kav; KB 2, p. 1110-1111; MW; Nadk. 1, nr. 2508; PA 1, 7, p. 38-49; V 6, p. 36; Vśs);

(2) T. CUCUMERINA LINN. (Avk; Bpn, p. 674; Chopra; DWH 2, p. 72-74; Dy, p. 343-344; KB 2, p. 1112-1114; Na 1, nr. 227; Nadk. 1, nr. 2506; PA 1, 7, p. 38-49; Sanyal) = T. LACINIOSA KLEIN EX WILLD. (Ainslie 2, p. 296-297; PA 1, 7, p. 38) = T. LOBATA ROXB. (PA 1, 7, p. 38) = T. PILOSA BUCH.-HAM. EX WALL. (PA 1, 7, p. 38);

(3) T. CORDATA ROXB. (PA 1, 7, p. 38) = T. PALMATA WALL.;

(4) T. NERVIFOLIA LINN. (KB 2, p. 1111);

(5) T. BRACTEATA VOIGT (PA 1, 7, p. 38);

(6) T. PUBERA BLUME = T. PALMATA ROXB. (PA 1, 7, p. 38); acc. to PA 1, 7, p. 38 T. BRACTEATA VOIGT is a synonym of T. PALMATA ROXB.; this is not confirmed by the Index Kewensis.

patra

(1) CINNAMOMUM TAMALA T. NEES ET EBERM. (Bpn, p. 228 : = *tamāla*-

patra; IRM 2, p. 178-179 : = *tejapatra*) [= C. TAMALA NEES] (Dutt : *tejapatra*; HK : = *tejapatra*; Kav; KB 3, p. 2146-2147; Nadk. 1, nr. 581) = C. ALBIFLORUM NEES (KB 3, p. 2146-2147) = LAURUS CASSIA ROXB. (Dutt and HK : *tejapatra*; Kav; MW : = *tamālapatra* = *tejapatra* = *tejaḥpatra*; PW; Vśs : = *tejapatra*);

(2) C. INERS REINW. EX BLUME (Gul; Nadk. 1, nr. 581 : *tejapatra* = *tamālapatra*) = C. NITIDUM HOOK. (Nadk. 1, nr. 581) = C. EUCALYPTOIDES NEES (Nadk. 1, nr. 581);

(3) C. MACROCARPUM HOOK.F. (Chopra : *tejapatra*);

(4) C. ZEYLANICUM BLUME (Chopra : *tamālapatra*; HB);

(5) [C. ZEYLANICUM BREYN] (IRM 2, p. 179-183: *tamālapatra*; KB 3, p. 2149-2150);

(6) C. LIGNEUM LUKMANOFF (?) (Nadk. 1, nr. 581 : C. LIGNEA);

(7) GARCINIA XANTHOCHYMUS HOOK.F. EX T. ANDERS. = XANTHOCHYMUS PICTORIUS ROXB. (MW : *tamālapatra*).

padma

(1) = *kamala*;

(2) EURYALE FEROX SALISB. (KB 1, p. 115-116) = ANNESLEA SPINOSA ANDR. (KB 1, p. 115-116);

(3) SALVADORA PERSICA LINN. (Vśs);

(4) = *padmakāṣṭha* (PW; Vśs);

(5) = *dhustūra* (see *dhattūra*) (Vśs);

(6) = *puṣkaramūla* (often identified as the root of IRIS GERMANICA LINN.) (Vśs);

(7) = *guggulu* (the gum of COMMIPHORA MUKUL ENGL.) (MW; PW); see about *padma* 1) : W. Rau, Lotusblumen, in Festschrift F. Weller, 1954, p. 505-513, 2): R. Schmidt, Beiträge zur Flora Sanscritica III, Der Lotus in der Sanskrit-Literatur, ZDMG 67, 1913, p. 462-470.

padmakāṣṭha

(1) PRUNUS PUDDUM ROXB. EX WALL. (DWH 1, p. 567; Kav; KB 2, p. 959-960; V 6, p. 33) = P. CERASOIDES D. DON (Kav; KB 2, p. 959-960; V 6, p. 33) = CERASUS PUDDUM WALL. (MW; PW).

panasa

(1) ARTOCARPUS INTEGRIFOLIA LINN.F. (Avk; Chopra; Dutt; DWH 3, p. 355; Gul; HK; IRM 1, p. 125; KB 3, p. 2336-2338; MW; Nadk. 1,

nr. 249; PW; Roxb., p. 633; Watt CP, p. 94) = A. HETEROPHYLLA LAM. (Chopra; IRM 1, p. 125) [= A. INTEGRA (THUNB.) MERRILL] (IRM 1, p. 125-126) = A. INTEGRA MERRILL = RADERMACHIA INTEGRA THUNB.;

(2) [ANTIARIS TOXICARIA (PERS.) LESCH.] (Bpn, p. 553) = A. TOXICARIA LESCH. = IPO TOXICARIA PERS.

parūṣa(ka)

(1) GREWIA ASIATICA LINN. (Avk; Bpn, p. 570; Chopra; Dgv, nr. 56; Dutt; DWH 1, p. 238; Gul; HB; HK; Kav; KB 1, p. 388-389; MW; Na 1, nr. 75; Nadk. 1, nr. 1158; PW; Vśs) = G. ELASTICA ROYLE (Nadk. 1, nr. 1158) = G. VESTITA WALL. (Nadk. 1, nr. 1158 : G. ELASTICA VAR. G. VESTITA) (see Hooker 1, p. 386-387 about G. ASIATICA LINN. VAR. VESTITA WALL) [= G. ABUTILISSIMA VENT.] (HK); HK probably made an error; the Index Kewensis indicates : G. ASIATICA WALL. *partim* = G. ABUTILIFOLIA VENT. EX JUSS.; see Hooker 1, p. 390;

(2) CARAPA MOLUCCENSIS LAM. = XYLOCARPUS GRANATUM KOEN. (MW; PW; Vśs).

parṇāsa

(1) a) OCIMUM SANCTUM LINN. (DWH 3, p. 86-88; KB 3, p. 1965-1968; Roxb., p. 463; Sanyal);
b) a kind of basilicum (MW; PW);
c) a kind of *tulasī* (Vśs);
d) *kṣudratulasī* with dark leaves (see *tulasī*) (Vśs);

(2) = *pārasīkayamānī* (see : *yamānī*) (Vśs);

(3) CEDRELA TOONA ROXB. EX ROTTL. (MW).

parpaṭa(ka)

(1) OLDENLANDIA CORYMBOSA LINN. (Avk : *kṣetraparpaṭa*; Bpn, p. 325-328; Chopra; Dgm, p. 110; Dgv, nr. 182; Dutt; DWH 2, p. 197-199 : *kṣetraparpaṭa*; Dy, p. 403-404; HK; KB 2, p. 1263-1264; Nadk. 1, nr. 1746; Sanyal; Vśs) = O. BIFLORA ROXB. (Avk : *kṣetraparpaṭa*; Dgm, p. 110 : *kṣetraparpaṭa*; DWH 2, p. 198; Dy, p. 403-404; Kav; Nadk. 1, nr. 1746; Roxb., p. 142 : *kṣetraparpaṭi*; Vśs; Wise) = O. HERBACEA DC. (Avk; Dgm, p. 110; Dgv, nr. 23; Dutt; DWH 2, p. 198; Dy, p. 403-404; HK; Kav; Na 1, nr. 22; Nadk. 1, nr. 1746;

Sanyal) = O. RAMOSA ROXB. (KB 2, p. 1263-1264) = HEDYOTIS BURMANNIANA R. BR. (Dgm, p. 110; MW; PW);

(2) OLDENLANDIA BIFLORA LINN. (?) (Chopra : *khet papra*);

(3) O. UMBELLATA LINN. (Ainslie 2, p. 101-102 : *kṣetraparpaṭī*);

(4) a) FUMARIA PARVIFLORA LAM. (Chopra; Dgm, p. 109; Dgv, nr. 23; Na 1, nr. 22; Nadk. 1, nr. 1080; V 6, p. 110);

b) [F. PARVIFLORA LAM. VAR. PERSICA PUGSLEY] (KB 1, p. 138-140);

(5) F. INDICA PUGSLEY (Bpn, p. 325-328; Dgm, p. 110);

(6) F. OFFICINALIS LINN. (Dgm, p. 109; Dgv, nr. 23; Nadk. 1, nr. 1080);

(7) RUNGIA REPENS NEES (Chopra; Dgv, nr. 23; Gul; KB 3, p. 1907-1908; Na 1, nr. 22);

(8) R. PARVIFLORA NEES (Dgm, p. 110) = R. REPENS T. ANDERS. (Dgm, p. 110);

(9) MOLLUGO PENTAPHYLLA LINN. (MW; PW) = M. STRICTA LINN. (Bpn, p. 325-328; V 4, p. 106);

(10) M. CERVIANA SER. = PHARNACEUM CERVIANA LINN. (Ainslie 2, p. 345);

(11) GLOSSOCARDIA LINEARIFOLIA CASS. (Bpn, p. 325-328) = G. BOSVALLIA DC. (Dgm, p. 109);

(12) JUSTICIA PROCUMBENS LINN. (Bpn, p. 325-328; Dgm, p. 110);

(13) POLYCARPAEA CORYMBOSA LAM. (Bpn, p. 325-328; Dgm, p. 109 and p. 203-204 : used as a substitute);

(14) PODOPHYLLUM EMODI WALL. (DWH 1, p. 69-70; Sanyal);

(15) = *kumbhīvṛkṣa*.

palāśa

(1) BUTEA MONOSPERMA (LAM.) TAUB. [Intern. Code] = [B. MONOSPERMA (LAM.) KUNTZE] (Chopra; IRM 1, p. 251-252) = B. MONOSPERMA KUNTZE (AFM 1, p. 39-42; KB 1, p. 785-788) = B. MONOSPERMA TAUB. = B. MONOSPERMA (Dgv, nr. 97; Na 1, nr. 130; V 4, p. 118) = B. FRONDOSA ROXB. (AFM 1, p. 39-42; Dutt; DWH 1, p. 454-458; Dy, p. 231-234; Ghosh; Gul; HK; Roxb., p. 540; Sanyal) [= B. FRONDOSA KOENIG EX ROXB.] (Bpn, p. 536; Chopra; IRM 1, p. 251-252; KB 1, p. 785-788) [= B. FRONDOSA ROXB. ET KOENIG] (Nadk. 1, nr. 395) = B. FRONDOSA (Kav; MW; PW; V 4, p. 118; Vśs); (BUTEA FRONDOSA ROXB. EX WILLD. is, acc. to the Intern. Code, a nomen illeg.); = ERYTHRINA MONOSPERMA LAM. (AFM 1, p. 39-42; Avk) = PLASO MONOSPERMA KUNTZE;

(2) ERYTHRINA INDICA LAM. (KB 1, p. 781-784; V 6, p. 42);
(3) CINNAMOMUM TAMALA T. NEES ET EBERM. [= C. TAMALA NEES] (KB 3, p. 2146-2147);
(4) CURCUMA ZEDOARIA ROSC. (HK; MW; PW; Vśs);
(5) IPOMOEA DIGITATA LINN. = I. PANICULATA R. BR. (Vśs);
(6) THESPESIA POPULNEA (LINN.) SOLAND. EX CORREA [Intern. Code] (Bpn, p. 514-515; Vśs).

pāṭalā

(1) STEREOSPERMUM SUAVEOLENS DC. (Avk; Bpn, p. 279-281; Dgv, nr. 238; Dutt; DWH 3, p. 20-22; Dy, p. 546; HK; Kav; KB 3, p. 1848-1849; Nadk. 1, nr. 2376; PA 1, 2, p. 49-62; V 6, p. 40; Vśs) = BIGNONIA SUAVEOLENS ROXB. (Avk; Dutt; Dy, p. 546; HK; Kav; MW; Nadk. 1, nr. 2376; PW; Vśs; Wise) = SPATHODEA SUAVEOLENS BENTH. ET HOOK.F.;
(2) STEREOSPERMUM TETRAGONUM DC. (PA 1, 2, p. 49-62; V 6, p. 40);
(3) S. CHELONOIDES DC. (Bpn, p. 279-281; DWH 3, 22-23; Gul; Vśs);
(4) [S. CHELONOIDES C. B. CLARKE] (PA 1, 2, p. 49-62);
(5) S. XYLOCARPUM BENTH. ET HOOK.F. (PA 1, 2, p. 49-62) = BIGNONIA XYLOCARPA ROXB. (PA 1, 2, p. 49-62) = SPATHODEA XYLOCARPA T. ANDERS. EX BRAND. (PA 1, 2, p. 49-62) = RADERMACHERA XYLOCARPA K. SCHUM. (PA 1, 2, p. 49-62);
(6) = *raktalodhra* (see : *lodhra*) (MW; PW).

pāṭhā

(1) CISSAMPELOS PAREIRA LINN. (Avk; Bpn, p. 395; Chopra; Dgm, p. 34-35; Dgv, nr. 15 : *laghupāṭhā*; DWH 1, p. 53-54; Dy, p. 29-30; KB 1, p. 95-98 : *pāṭhā, laghupāṭhā*; Na 1, nr. 15 : *laghupāṭhā*; Nadk. 1, nr. 592: *laghupāṭhā*; V 2, p. 134) = C. HERNANDIFOLIA WALL. [= C. CAAPEBA ROXB.] (KB 1, p. 95-98) = C. CAAPEBA LINN. [= C. TRIANDRA ROXB.] (KB 1, p. 95-98) = C. TETRANDRA ROXB. = C. CONVOLVULACEA WILLD. (KB 1, p. 95-98); unclear are : [C. HERNANDIFOLIA LINN.] (Dutt) and C. HERNANDIFOLIA (Avk; Kav; Vśs);
(2) STEPHANIA HERNANDIFOLIA WALP. (Avk; Bpn, p. 395 : used as a substitute; Dgm, p. 34-35; Dutt; HK; Kav; KB 1, p. 92-93; Vśs) = S. DISCOLOR SPRENG. (DWH 1, p. 54 : known by the same native names as CISSAMPELOS PAREIRA LINN., but it seems that the true name of this plant is *vanatiktikā*) = CISSAMPELOS HERNANDIFOLIA WILLD. (HK; KB 1, p. 92-93) = C. HEXANDRA ROXB. (KB 1, p. 92-93; V 6, p. 29;

Wise) = Clypea discolor Blume = C. hernandifolia Wight et Arn. (HK; KB 1, p. 92-93; MW; PW);

(3) Cyclea peltata Hook.f. et Thoms. (Bpn, p. 395 : used as a substitute; Dgv, nr. 15 : *rājapāṭhā*; Gul; Na 1, nr. 15).

pārīśa, pārīṣa

(1) Thespesia populnea (Linn.) Soland. ex Correa [Intern. Code] (Bpn, p. 514-515; Chopra; Dutt; KB 1, p. 340-343; MW; Na 1, nr. 61; Nadk. 1, nr. 2465; Sanyal; V 6, p. 63; Vśs) = Hibiscus populneus Linn. (Chopra; Dutt; Nadk. 1, nr. 1224; Vśs : = *gardabhāṇḍa*);

(2) Ficus arnottiana Miq. (Bpn, p. 514-515 : acc. to some, but incorrect);

(3) F. rumphii Blume (Bpn, p. 514-515 : acc. to some, but incorrect);

(4) F. infectoria Roxb. (Vśs : = *plakṣa*);

(5) = *hrasvaplakṣa* (Vśs : unidentified).

piṇḍālu

(1) a) Dioscorea alata Linn. (Chopra; Nadk. 1, nr. 838; V 3, p. 37);
b) D. globosa Roxb. (Chopra; Dutt; DWH 3, p. 551; Gul; HK; Kav; KB 4, p. 2490; MW; Nadk. 1, nr. 838; V 3, p. 37);
c) D. atropurpurea Roxb. (Chopra);
d) D. purpurea Roxb. (Chopra);
e) D. rubella Roxb. (Chopra);

Watt (CP, p. 492-493) observes : "Roxburgh (see Flora Indica, p. 726-728) assigned four or five types of tubers to separate specific positions, chiefly on account of their shape and colour. He, however, admitted that he would be quite prepared to accept all these races as belonging to the same species." Hooker (Flora of India 6, p. 296-297) described D. alata Linn. as a species and considered b, c, d and e as "imperfectly known and indeterminable species;" Prain and Burkill (see Watt, l.c.) have recorded Roxburgh's four forms (b, c, d and e) under D. alata Linn. and have formed varietal positions for each; the Index Kewensis gives the five forms, mentioned as a-e, as separate species; see also the article : Dioscorea, IRM 3, p. 67-76;

f) [D. alata Linn. var. globosa Prain] (KB 4, p. 2490);

(2) Ipomoea batatas Poir. (KB 3, p. 1719-1720; V 9, p. 50) = Convolvulus batatas Linn. (Avk) = Batatas edulis Choisy (Bpn, p. 679-680; MW; PW);

(3) Randia uliginosa DC. (DWH 2, p. 207; KB 2, p. 1272-1273;

V 6, p. 89) = Gardenia uliginosa Retz. (KB 2, p. 1272-1273) = Posoqueria uliginosa (Willd.) Roxb. (KB 2, p. 1272-1273);

(4) Tinospora cordifolia Miers = Cocculus cordifolius DC. (PW : = *kandaguḍūcī*; Vśs : = *kandaguḍūcī*; identical with *guḍūcī*).

pippalī

Piper longum Linn.

pīlu

(1) Salvadora persica Linn. (Avk; Chopra : *bṛhatpīlu*; Dgv, nr. 209; Dutt; DWH 2, p. 380-384; Gul; HB; HK; Kav; KB 2, p. 1537-1539; MW; Nadk. 1, nr. 2203; PW; Vśs) = S. indica Wight (Chopra; Dutt; HK; Kav; KB 2, p. 1537-1539; Vśs) = S. wightiana Planch. ex Thw. (Nadk. 1, nr. 2203) = S. oleoides Decne. (Bpn, p. 577; Chopra; DWH 2, p. 380-384; KB 2, p. 1539-1540; Vśs); acc. to the Index Kewensis S. persica Linn. = S. oleoides Decne.; Chopra considers them to be two separate species; so do Kirtikar and Basu; Hooker says in his Flora of India 3, p. 620, that S. oleoides Decne. is closely allied to S. persica Linn., but well distinguished by Brandis (see Brandis' Indian Trees, p. 453): the Flora Iranica also regards S. persica and S. oleoides as separate species;

(2) Careya arborea Roxb. (KB 2, p. 1061-1063; MW; PW).

punarnavā

(1) Boerhaavia repens Linn. (Chopra; Dgm, p. 210; DWH 3, p. 130-132; Gul; HK; IRM 1, p. 199; Nadk. 1, nr. 363; PA 1, 5, p. 9-26; Sanyal) = B. diffusa Linn. (Ainslie 2, p. 205-207; Avk; Bpn, p. 421 : *śvetapunarnavā*; Chopra; Dgv, nr. 258; Dutt; Dy, p. 655-656; HB; HK; IRM 1, p. 199; Kav; KB 3, p. 2045-2048; Nadk 1, nr. 363; PA 1, 5, p. 9-26; V 6, p. 125; Vśs; Wise) [= B. procumbens Roxb.] (KB 3, p. 2045-2048; Nadk. 1, nr. 363; PA 1, 5, p. 9-26; Roxb., p. 49) [= B. erecta Banks ex Roxb.] (HK); unclear are :

a) B. procumbens, mentioned by Dutt, Nadk. (1, nr. 363) and Vśs, which may be the plant designated as B. procumbens Roxb. by some authors, or another species: B. procumbens Banks ex Roxb.;
b) B. erecta, mentioned by Dutt, Nadk. (1, nr. 363) and Vśs, which may be B. erecta Ell., a synonym of B. repens Linn., or a different species : B. erecta Linn. = B. diandra Burm.f.;

c) B. DIANDRA, mentioned by Vśs, which may be B. DIANDRA LINN. = B. HIRSUTA LINN., or B. DIANDRA BURM.F. (see b);

(2) B. VERTICILLATA POIR. (Dgm, p. 210) = B. REPANDA ROXB. (Ainslie 2, p. 207);

(3) B. REPANDA WILLD. (PA 1, 5, p. 9-26);

(4) B. ALATA (Wise); the Index Kewensis records only B. ALATA S. WATS., an American species;

(5) B. PROCUMBENS BANKS EX ROXB. (HK ?);

(6) TRIANTHEMA PORTULACASTRUM LINN. (Bpn, p. 421 : *raktapunarnavā*; Chopra : *punarnavī*; KB 2, p. 1180-1181 : *śvetapunarnavā*; PA 1, 5, p. 9-26) = T. MONOGYNA LINN. (Chopra : *punarnavī*; Dgm, p. 210; DWH 2, p. 102-103 : *śvetapunarnavā*; Ghosh : *śvetapunarnavā*; KB 2, p. 1180-1181; Nadk. 1, nr. 2491; PA 1, 5, p. 9-26; Sanyal) = T. OBCORDATA ROXB. (Nadk. 1, nr. 2491; PA 1, 5, p. 9-26);

(7) T. PENTANDRA LINN. (Nadk. 1, nr. 2491) = T. OBCORDATA WALL.;

(8) T. DECANDRA LINN. (Chopra : *punarnavī*; Dgm, p. 210; KB 2, p. 1182 : *punarnavī*; PA 1, 5, p. 9-26);

(9) T. CRYSTALLINA VAHL (Dgm, p. 210).

punnāga

(1) CALOPHYLLUM INOPHYLLUM LINN. (Dgv, nr. 40; Dgm, p. 235-236; Dutt; DWH 1, p. 173-176; HK; IRM 2, p. 18-19; KB 1, p. 270-271; MW; Na 1, nr. 45; Nadk. 1, nr. 425; V 6, p. 124; Vśs);

(2) C. TOMENTOSUM WIGHT (Dgm, p. 235-236);

(3) C. WIGHTIANUM WALL. (Dgm, p. 235-236);

(4) C. APETALUM WILLD. (Dgm, p. 235-236) = C. INOPHYLLUM ?;

(5) OCHROCARPUS LONGIFOLIUS BENTH. ET HOOK.F. EX T. ANDERS. (DWH 1, p. 172-173; KB 1, p. 269-270; Nadk. 1, nr. 731);

(6) [CALLITRIS INOPHYLLUM LINN.] (Nadk. 1, nr. 422);

(7) MALLOTUS PHILIPPINENSIS MUELL. ARG. (KB 3, p. 2267-2270) = ROTTLERA TINCTORIA ROXB. (KB 3, p. 2267; MW; PW; Roxb., p. 737);

(8) nutmeg, i.e. the seed of MYRISTICA FRAGRANS HOUTT. (*jātīphala*) (MW; PW; Vśs);

(9) white lotus (MW; PW; Vśs : *śvetapadma*).

pṛthvīkā

(1) ELETTARIA CARDAMOMUM MATON (KB 4, p. 2442-2444; MW; PW; Vśs);

(2) AMOMUM SUBULATUM ROXB. (Gul; MW; PW; Vśs);

(3) NIGELLA SATIVA LINN. (Avk; Dgm, p. 13; Dgv, nr. 9; Kav; KB 1, p. 11-12; Na 1, nr. 5) = N. INDICA ROXB. EX FLEM. (Avk; KB 1, p. 11-12; MW; PW);

(4) CARUM CARVI LINN. (Bpn, p. 30-32);

(5) BALANITES ROXBURGHII PLANCH. (HK : = *hiṅgupatrī*);

(6) B. AEGYPTIACA (LINN.) DELILE [Intern. Code] (HK : = *hiṅgupatrī*);

(7) GARDENIA GUMMIFERA LINN.F. (HK : = *hiṅgupatrī*);

(8) a kind of grass (Vśs : = *hiṅgupatrī*);

(9) = *śvetapunarnavā* (see : *punarnavā*) (Vśs);

(10) CLEOME VISCOSA LINN. (Vśs) = POLANISIA ICOSANDRA WIGHT ET ARN. (Vśs);

(11) CALOTROPIS GIGANTEA [DRYAND. IN] AIT. (Vśs).

pṛśniparṇī

(1) URARIA LAGOPOIDES DC. (Avk; Bpn, p. 287; Chopra; Dutt; DWH 1, p. 426-428; Dy, p. 221-222; HK; Kav; KB 1, p. 750-751; Nadk. 1, nr. 2542; PA 1, 2, p. 96; Sanyal; V 6, p. 109-110; Vśs) [= U. LAGOPODIOIDES MERR.] (PA 1, 2, p. 96) = DOODIA LAGOPODIOIDES ROXB. (Avk; Dutt; HK; Kav);

(2) U. LAGOPUS DC. = U. LAGOPODIOIDES WALL. (HK, considered as a synonym of U. LAGOPOIDES DC., which is incorrect; see also Hooker 2, p. 156);

unclear is : U. LAGOPODIOIDES (MW);

incorrect is : [DOODIA LAGOPOIDES] (Nadk. 1, nr. 2542);

(3) URARIA PICTA DESV. (Bpn, p. 287; Gul; Nadk. 1, nr. 2542; PA 1, 2, p. 96; V 6, p. 110) = DOODIA PICTA ROXB. = HEDYSARUM PICTUM JACQ.;

(4) DESMODIUM GANGETICUM DC. (PA 1, 2, p. 96-104) [= D. COLLINUM ROXB.] (PA 1, 2, p. 96) = HEDYSARUM COLLINUM ROXB. = H. GANGETICUM LINN.;

(5) DESMODIUM LATIFOLIUM DC. (PA 1, 2, p. 96 : alternate source of *pṛśniparṇī*) = D. COLLINUM WALL. = HEDYSARUM LATIFOLIUM ROXB.;

(6) [HEMIONITIS CORDIFOLIA ROXB.] (Avk; MW; PW; Vśs); this plant is not recorded in the Index Kewensis, but has been described by Roxburgh (Flora Indica, p. 756).

prasāraṇī = *prasāriṇī*

(1) PAEDERIA FOETIDA LINN. (Avk; Bpn, p. 424-425; Chopra; DWH

2, p. 228-230; Dy, p. 400-401; Ghosh; KB 2, p. 1297-1299; MW; Nadk. 1, nr. 1781; PW; Sanyal; Vśs) = APOCYNUM FOETIDUM BURM.F. (DWH 2, p. 229; Nadk. 1, nr. 1781) [= CONVOLVULUS FOETIDUS] (Nadk. 1, nr. 1781);

(2) CONVOLVULUS ARVENSIS LINN. (Bpn, p. 424-425 : acc. to some; KB 3, p. 1735-1736; V 10, p. 64);

(3) IPOMOEA TRIDENTATA ROTH (Avk; Chopra; KB 3, p. 1734; Nadk. 1, nr. 1338) = MERREMIA TRIDENTATA HALLIER.F. (Bpn, p. 424-425 : used in Kerala; Chopra; KB 3, p. 1734);

(4) LEPTADENIA SPARTIUM WIGHT (Bpn, p. 424-425 : used in Rājasthān);

(5) MIMOSA PUDICA LINN. (KB 2, p. 915-917; Vśs);

(6) = *devadhānya* (Vśs).

priyaṅgu

(1) SETARIA ITALICA BEAUV. (Avk; Gul; HK; KB 4, p. 2718-2719; MW; PW; Vśs) = PANICUM ITALICUM LINN. (Avk; Roxb., p. 101; Wise);

(2) AGLAIA ROXBURGHIANA MIQ. (Avk; Bpn, p. 248-251; Chopra; Dutt; DWH 1, p. 342-343; Gul; HK; Kav; Na 1, nr. 201; Nadk. 1, nr. 81);

(3) A. ODORATA LOUR. [Intern. Code] (HK; MW);

(4) A. DIEPENHORSTII MIQ. = A. ODORATISSIMA BLUME (KB 1, p. 550-551; V 6, p. 99) = A. ROXBURGHIANA HIERN (KB 1, p. 550-551) = MILUCA ROXBURGHIANA WIGHT ET ARN. (KB 1, p. 550-551);

(5) PRUNUS MAHALEB LINN. (Avk; Bpn, p. 248-251; Chopra ?; Dgv, nr. 144; Nadk. 1, nr. 2041; V 3, p. 69);

(6) CALLICARPA MACROPHYLLA VAHL (Bpn, p. 248-251);

(7) WOODFORDIA FLORIBUNDA SALISB. = W. FRUTICOSA KURZ (Vśs);

(8) MIMOSA RUBICAULIS LAM. (Vśs : = *rāla*);

(9) PIPER LONGUM LINN. (MW; PW);

(10) a) BRASSICA JUNCEA COSS. = SINAPIS RAMOSA ROXB. EX FLEM. (MW; PW);
b) = *kṛṣṇasarṣapa* (see : *sarṣapa*) (Vśs);
c) = *rājikā* (Vśs);

(11) = *kaṭukī* (PW; Vśs);

(12) = *śyāmā* (Vśs);

(13) PAPAVER DUBIUM LINN. (Bpn, p. 653).

plakṣa

(1) Ficus infectoria Roxb. (Bpn, p. 518; Chopra; Dutt; HK; KB 3, p. 2319-2321; Nadk. 1, nr. 1044; V 6, p. 103) = F. lacor Buch.-Ham. (Chopra; Dgv, nr. 286; KB 3, p. 2319-2321);

(2) F. tsjakela Burm.f. (DWH 3, p. 340; Nadk. 1, nr. 1044; Roxb., p. 643) = F. tjakela Miq. = F. infectoria Willd. (Kav; PW; Roxb., p. 643); unclear are MW and Vśs : F. infectoria (Roxb. ?; Willd. ?);

(3) F. arnottiana Miq. (Chopra; KB 3, p. 2331; Nadk. 1, nr. 1032);

(4) F. talboti King (Chopra; Nadk. 1, nr. 1051; PA 1, 4, p. 105-112);

(5) F. tsiela Roxb. (Gul; KB 3, p. 2333; PA 1, 4, p. 105-112; V 6, p. 58);

(6) F. retusa Linn. (PA 1, 3, p. 100-109);

(7) F. rumphii Blume (Avk);

(8) F. religiosa Linn. (MW; PW; Vśs);

(9) Thespesia populnea (Linn.) Soland. ex Correa [Intern. Code] [= Th. populneoides Wall.] (MW; PW) = Hibiscus populneus Linn. (Vśs).

phaṇijjhaka = *phaṇijja(ka)*

(1) a) Majorana hortensis Moench. [Intern. Code] = Origanum majorana Linn. (Bpn, p. 510; HB; KB 3, p. 1985-1986; MW; PW; V 8, p. 39);
b) Dn, *varga* 4, 52 : = *marubaka* = *kharapatra* = *jambīra*;
Rn, *varga* 10, 80 : = *marubaka* = *kharapatra* = *gandhapatra*;
Ḍa. on Su.Sū. 38, 18 : = *marubaka* = *tīkṣṇagandha*;
c) = *madhurajambīra* (see *jambīra*) (Vśs);
(2) a) a species of Ocimum (Kav);
b) a kind of *tulasī* with small leaves (Vśs);
c) fragrant *tulasī* (Vśs);
(3) Pogostemon parviflorus Benth. (V 6, p. 41);
(4) Piper nigrum Linn. (HK : = *marica,* but *marica* is also a name of Majorana hortensis Moench.);
(5) = *palāśa* (Vśs).

phalāmla

(1) Rumex vesicarius Linn. (KB 3, p. 2114-2115; MW; PW; Vśs : = *amlavetasa*);

(2) Tamarindus indica Linn. (MW; PW);

(3) Hibiscus cannabinus Linn. (KB 1, p. 327-329; Nadk. 1, nr. 1218);

(4) Garcinia indica Choisy (KB 1, p. 262-264) = G. purpurea Roxb. (KB 1, p. 262-264). See also *phalāmla*, App. 3.

bakula

Mimusops elengi Linn.; M. elengi without an author's name designates M. elengi Linn. or two other species:
a) Sideroxylon tomentosum Roxb. = M. elengi Wight;
b) Labramia bojeri A.DC. = M. elengi Sieber ex A.DC.

badara

(1) Zizyphus jujuba Lam. (Ainslie 2, p. 94-96; Avk; Bpn, p. 563-564; Chopra; Dutt, = *kola*; DWH 1, p. 350; Gul; HK, = *kola*; KB 1, p. 589-591; MW; Nadk. 1, nr. 2662; PW; V 7, p. 97; Vśs: = *ghoṇṭābadara*; Wise);

(2) Z. sativa Gaertn. (DWH 1, p. 350; Na 1, nr. 110 : *rājabadara*; V 1, p. 163 : *sauvīrabadara*) = Z. vulgaris Lam. (same sources);

(3) Z. oenoplia Mill. (Nadk. 1, nr. 2662) = Z. scandens Roxb. (Wise);

(4) Z. rotundifolia Lam. = Z. nummularia Wight et Arn. (*bhūbadarī* : Chopra; KB 1, p. 592-593; V 4, p. 109) = Z. microphylla Roxb. (KB 1, p. 592); incorrect is [Z. laccifera] (Nadk. 1, nr. 2662);

(5) = *kārpāsī* (KB 1, p. 344-346; PW; Vśs);

(6) = *kapikacchu* (KB 1, p. 778-780; PW; Vśs);

(7) = *devasarṣapa* (MW : a tree; PW : a kind of mustard); see Vśs about a number of different identifications of *devasarṣapa*.

badarī

= *badara*.

barbara

(1) Ocimum basilicum Linn. (Dutt; KB 3, p. 1963; Sanyal) [= O. pilosum Linn.] (Dutt) = O. pilosum Willd.;

(2) O. gratissimum Linn. (DWH 3, p. 85-86; Sanyal);

(3) a) a kind of Ocimum (PW);

b) the dark type of *arjaka* (Vśs);

c) *vaijayantītulasī* (Vśs, unidentified);

d) = *barbarīka* = *ajagandhikā* : a kind of Ocimum (PW);

(4) CLERODENDRUM SERRATUM SPRENG. (KB 3, p. 1948-1949);

(5) C. SIPHONANTHUS [R. BR. IN] AIT. (MW; PW);

(6) GYNANDROPSIS PENTAPHYLLA DC. = CLEOME PENTAPHYLLA LINN. (MW; PW);

(7) CLEOME VISCOSA LINN. (KB 1, p. 183-185);

(8) ACACIA ARABICA WILLD. (Nadk. 1, nr. 12) = MIMOSA ARABICA LAM. (Roxb., p. 421);

(9) A. FERRUGINEA DC. (Nadk. 1, nr. 12);

(10) A. LEUCOPHLOEA WILLD. (KB 2, p. 924-925 : *śvetabarbara*);

(11) = *pītacandana* (see *candana*) (PW; Vśs);

(12) a partic. fragrant plant (MW);

(13) [unguis odoratus] (MW; PW : = *vyāghranakha* : a) possibly *ὄνυξ* of Dioscorides, unguis odoratus; see Dietz, p. 57; b) EUPHORBIA ANTIQUORUM LINN. — TITHYMALUS ANTIQUORUM MOENCH.).

barbaracandana

Dn, *varga* 3, 9 : *barbarika* is a white, odourless type of *candana*; Rn, *varga*, 12, 17: *barbaraka*, (also called) white *barbaraka*, is (a kind of *candana* that is) fragrant; a synonym (see Dn and Rn) is *barbarottha*, explained in PW as white sandalwood.

barbarikā

Is not recorded in the dictionaries; see *vanabarbarikā*.

barbarī

(1) a) OCIMUM BASILICUM LINN. (Avk; Bpn, p. 511-512; KB 3, p. 1961-1964) [= O. BASILICUM VAR. THYRSIFLORA BENTH.] (Avk); see Hooker 4, p. 608;

b) a kind of Ocimum, = *barbara* (MW; PW);

c) Bpn, p. 511 : = *parṇāsa*; three types are distinguished : a) black : *kuṭheraka*, b) white : *arjaka*, c) with leaves like *vaṭa* : *vaṭapatra*;

(2) ORTHOSIPHON GRANDIFLORUS BOLDINGH EX HEYNE (Bpn, p. 511-512).

bālā

(1) Pavonia odorata Willd. (Avk; Dutt; DWH 1, p. 224; HK; KB 1, p. 323-324; Nadk. 1, nr. 1822; V 6, p. 28);

(2) Hibiscus tortuosus (Wise); there are two plants of this name in the Index Kewensis :

a) H. tiliaceus Linn. = H. tortuosus Roxb.;

b) H. tortuosus Wall. ex Prain;

(3) Elettaria cardamomum Maton (MW; PW; Vśs);

(4) Cocos nucifera Linn. (Vśs);

(5) Barleria cristata Linn. (Vśs, = *nīlajhiṇṭī*);

(6) B. prionitis Linn. (Vśs, = *nīlajhiṇṭī*);

(7) = *yūthī* (Vśs); a number of species of Jasminum is called *yūthī*; see KB 2 : a) J. humile Linn. = J. bignoniaceum Wall.;

b) J. officinale Linn.;

c) J. auriculatum Vahl;

(8) = *haridrā* (Vśs);

(9) = *pāṭhā* (Vśs);

(10) = *āmrātaka* (Vśs);

(11) = *kumārī* (Vśs); a number of species of Aloë, but esp. A. vera Linn. = A. indica Royle, is called *kumārī* or *ghṛtakumārī*.

bimbī

Coccinia indica Wight et Arn. (Avk; Bpn, p. 674; Chopra; Dgv, nr. 167; Gul; HK; IRM 2, p. 257; Kav; KB 2, p. 1151-1154; Nadk. 1, nr. 534; Sanyal; V 2, p. 45) [= C. cordifolia (Linn.) Cogn.] (Chopra; IRM 2, p. 257) = C. cordifolia Cogn. (Nadk. 1, nr. 534) = Cephalandra indica Naud. (Avk; Chopra; DWH 2, p. 86-89; Dy, p. 351; Ghosh; HK; IRM 2, p. 257; KB 2, p. 1151-1154; Na 1, nr. 236; Nadk. 1, nr. 534; Sanyal; V 2, p. 45) = Momordica monadelpha Roxb. (Avk; HK; Kav; KB 2, p. 1151-1154; MW; Nadk. 1, nr. 534; PW; Roxb., p. 696; Vśs; Wise) = Bryonia cordifolia Linn.

bilva

Aegle marmelos (Linn.) Correa [Intern. Code].

bījapūra(ka)

(1) a) Citrus medica Linn. (Chopra; Dgv, nr. 66; Gul; HK; MW; Na 1, nr. 88; PW; V 6, p. 21) = C. acida Pers. (Bpn, p. 578) = C. limonum Risso (Avk; Nadk. 1, nr. 603);

b) [C. MEDICA LINN. VAR. MEDICA] (Chopra; KB 1, p. 486-487; Watt CP, p. 325);
c) [C. MEDICA LINN. VAR. ACIDA] (KB 1, p. 489-490);
d) [C. ACIDA ROXB. VAR. 7] (Dutt, p. 127; DWH 1, p. 269); see about the varieties of C. MEDICA LINN. : Cooke 1, p. 200-201; Duthie 1, p. 131-132; Hooker 1, p. 514-515; see about the varieties of C. ACIDA ROXB. : Roxburgh, Flora Indica, p. 589.

(2) PUNICA GRANATUM LINN. (KB 2, p. 1084-1087).

bṛhatī

(1) SOLANUM INDICUM LINN. (Ainslie 2, p. 207-208; Bpn, p. 288-289; Dgv, nr. 229; Dutt; DWH 2, p. 555-557; Dy, p. 637-638; Ghosh; Gul; HK; Kav; KB 3, p. 1755-1757; Nadk. 1, nr. 2329; PA 1, 4, p. 78-104; PW; Vśs);

(2) S. XANTHOCARPUM SCHRAD. ET WENDL. (KB 3, p. 1759-1762; PA 1, 4, p. 78-104; Vśs : = *kaṇṭakārī*);

(3) S. MELONGENA LINN. (Bpn, p. 288-289; PA 1, 4, p. 78-104; Vśs : = *vārtākī*; Wise) = S. LONGUM ROXB. (PA 1, 4, p. 78-104) = S. ESCULENTUM DUN. (Vśs);

(4) S. TORVUM SWARTZ (Bpn, p. 288-289 : *śvetabṛhatī*; PA 1, 4, p. 78-104 : used as an adulterant of S. MELONGENA LINN.);

(5) [S. INSANUM WILLD.] (PA 1, 4, p. 78-104) (see Roxb., p. 191) [= S. MELONGENA LINN. VAR. INSANUM PRAIN] (PA 1, 4, p. 78-104);

(6) S. ACULEATISSIMUM JACQ. (PA 1, 4, p. 78-104 : recently introduced, used as a substitute of S. XANTHOCARPUM).

bhadramustā

(1) CYPERUS ROTUNDUS LINN. (Dgv, nr. 337; HB; HK; Kav; KB 4, p. 2638-2640; Nadk. 1, nr. 782);

(2) C. SCARIOSUS R.BR. (Bpn, p. 243-244) = C. PERTENUIS ROXB. (Avk; HB, p. 18, footnote 51);

(3) [C. TUBEROSUS ROTH] (Gul); the Index Kewensis enumerates :
a) C. ROTUNDUS LINN. = C. TUBEROSUS ROXB.;
b) C. ESCULENTUS LINN. = C. TUBEROSUS PURSH;
c) C. STOLONIFERUS RETZ. = C. TUBEROSUS BOJ. HORT. MAURIT.;
d) C. TUBEROSUS ROTTB.;
e) MARISCUS MICROCEPHALUS J. ET C. PRESL = C. TUBEROSUS WILLD. EX KUNTH.

bhūtāṅkuśa

(1) CROTON OBLONGIFOLIUS ROXB. (Chopra; KB 3, p. 2254-2255; Nadk. 1, nr. 717; V 3, p. 141);

(2) ANISOMELES MALABARICA R. BR. EX SIMS (Nadk. 1, nr. 196; Vśs);

(3) A. OVATA R. BR. = A. DISTICHA HEYNE EX ROTH (Nadk. 1, nr. 196);

(4) [A. FRUTICOSA] (Nadk. 1, nr. 196);

(5) = *kṣavaka* (PW; Vśs);

(6) = *apāmārga* (Vśs);

(7) = *rājikā* (Vśs);

(8) = *gokṣura* (PW);

(9) = *krūra* = *raktakaravīra* (PW : NERIUM ODORUM RUBRO-SIMPLEX); the correct name of N. ODORUM is N. ODORUM [SOLAND. IN] AIT.; acc. to Bpn, p. 314-316, *raktakaravīra* is THEVETIA NEREIFOLIA JUSS. EX STEUD.;

(10) = *tīkṣṇa* (PW : name of a number of plants).

bhūstṛṇa

(1) [CYMBOPOGON CITRATUS (DC.) STAPF] (Chopra) = C. CITRATUS STAPF (Bpn, p. 383-384; IRM 2, p. 412-414; KB 4, p. 2681-2683; Nadk. 1, nr. 767) = ANDROPOGON CITRATUS DC. (Bpn, p. 383-384; Chopra; Dy, p. 852; IRM 2, p. 412-414; KB 4, p. 2681-2683; Nadk. 1, nr. 173; V 1, p. 14);

(2) CYMBOPOGON SCHOENANTHUS SPRENG. (Nadk. 1, nr. 767; Watt CP, p. 461) = C. MARTINIANUS SCHULT. = ANDROPOGON SCHOENANTHUS LINN. (Avk; Dutt; DWH 3, p. 557-562; HK; Kav; MW; Nadk. 1, nr. 173 and nr. 186; PW; Roxb., p. 92; Vśs) = A. IWARANCUSA BOISS. = A. AROMATICUS SIEBER EX SCHULT. (Avk) = A. CALAMUS-AROMATICUS ROYLE (Avk; Nadk. 1, nr. 177) = A. PACHMODES TRIN. (Nadk. 1, nr. 177);

(3) CYMBOPOGON IWARANCUSA SCHULT. (Bpn, p. 384; Watt CP, p. 461-462) = ANDROPOGON IVARANCUSA ROXB. [= A. IWARANCUSA JONES] [Chopra];

(4) CYMBOPOGON MARTINII (ROXB.) WATSON = C. MARTINI STAPF = ANDROPOGON MARTINI ROXB. (Avk; Nadk. 1, nr. 177);

(5) CYMBOPOGON FLEXUOSUS STAPF (Nadk. 1, nr. 767) = ANDROPOGON FLEXUOSUS NEES EX STEUD. = A. NARDUS LINN.; the Index Kewensis prefers to keep these species in the genus Andropogon, but I follow the Flora Iranica and Bor in this case.

makuṣṭaka

See : *makuṣṭha(ka)*.

makuṣṭha(ka)

PHASEOLUS ACONITIFOLIUS JACQ. (Bpn, p. 646; Chopra; Dutt; DWH 1, p. 488; Gul; HK; KB 1, p. 798-799; MW; Na 1, nr. 149; Nadk. 1, nr. 1860; V 8, p. 102; Vśs).

maṅgalya

(1) LENS ESCULENTA MOENCH. [Intern. Code] = ERVUM LENS LINN. (Vśs) = CICER LENS WILLD. (MW; Vśs) = VICIA LENS COSS. ET GERM. (Vśs);

(2) AEGLE MARMELOS (LINN.) CORREA [Intern. Code] (KB 1, p. 499-502; MW; PW; Vśs);

(3) FICUS RELIGIOSA LINN. (KB 3, p. 2317-2319; MW; PW; Vśs);

(4) F. HETEROPHYLLA LINN.F. (MW; PW : = *trāyamāṇa*);

(5) COCOS NUCIFERA LINN. (KB 4, p. 2581-2585; MW; PW; Vśs);

(6) FERONIA ELEPHANTUM CORR. (KB 1, p. 496-498; MW; PW; Vśs);

(7) CROCUS SATIVUS LINN. (Nadk. 1, nr. 701);

(8) SAPINDUS TRIFOLIATUS LINN. (Bpn, p. 530; KB 1, p. 632-635; V 1, p. 85) = S. LAURIFOLIUS VAHL (KB 1, p. 632);

(9) SAPINDUS MUKOROSSI GAERTN. (Bpn, p. 529; V 1, p. 85) = S. DETERGENS ROXB.;

(10) DENDROBIUM MACRAEI LINDL. (DWH 3, p. 389-390; KB 4, p. 2401-2402; Nadk. 1, nr. 812);

(11) D. PLICATILE LINDL. = DESMOTRICHUM FIMBRIATUM BL. (KB 4, p. 2401-2402); acc. to Hooker (vol. 5, p. 714), followed by Chopra and KB, DENDROBIUM MACRAEI LINDL. and DESMOTRICHUM FIMBRIATUM BL. are synonyms;

(12) = *jīvaka* (MW; PW; Vśs, = PENTAPTERA TOMENTOSA ROXB., i.e. TERMINALIA TOMENTOSA WIGHT ET ARN.);

(13) = *rīṭhākarañja* (PW; Vśs, unidentified);

(14) = *jalamadhūka* (Vśs, unidentified; synonyms are enumerated in PW, a.o. *pataṅga* : CAESALPINIA SAPPAN LINN.).

mañjiṣṭhā

(1) RUBIA CORDIFOLIA LINN. = R. MUNJISTA ROXB. (Dutt; HK; Nadk. 1, nr. 2162) — R. SECUNDA MOON (Nadk. 1, nr. 2162);

(2) R. SIKKIMENSIS KURZ (used in Assam acc. to Watt CP, p. 927).

madana

(1) RANDIA DUMETORUM LAM. (Avk; Bpn, p. 77; Chopra; Dgv, nr. 183; Dutt; DWH 2, p. 204-207; Dy, p. 406-408; Gul; HK; Kav; KB 2, p. 1273-1276; Na 1, nr. 265; Nadk. 1, nr. 2091; PA 1, 9, p. 37-47; Sanyal; V 8, p. 86; Vśs) = R. LONGISPINA DC. (PA 1, 9, p. 43; Vśs) = GARDENIA DUMETORUM RETZ. (PA 1, 9, p. 43) = POSOQUERIA DUMETORUM (WILLD.) WILLD. EX ROXB. (Dutt; HK; Vśs);

(2) certain other species of Randia (PA 1, 9, p. 43, footnote);

(3) ARTABOTRYS ODORATISSIMUS R.BR. (PA 1, 9, p. 46 : used in certain parts of Kerala) = A. HAMATUS BLUME (PA 1, 9, p. 46) = UVARIA ODORATISSIMA ROXB. (PA 1, 9, p. 46) = UNONA ODORATISSIMA STEUD. (PA 1, 9, p. 46) = UNONA HAMATA BLUME (PA 1, 9, p. 46);

(4) VANGUERIA SPINOSA ROXB. (MW; PW; Wise);

(5) PTEROSPERMUM SUBERIFOLIUM LAM. (Vśs, = *mucukunda*);

(6) DATURA STRAMONIUM LINN. (KB 3, p. 1784-1787);

(7) D. METEL LINN. (Wise);

(8) D. FASTUOSA LINN. (KB 3, p. 1788-1790) = D. ALBA NEES (KB 3, p. 1790-1791);

(9) ACACIA CATECHU WILLD. (MW; PW; Vśs) = MIMOSA CATECHU LINN.F. (Vśs; Wise);

(10) PHASEOLUS MUNGO LINN. = PH. RADIATUS LINN. (MW; PW; Vśs);

(11) MIMUSOPS ELENGI LINN. (PW; Vśs, = *bakula*);

(12) ALANGIUM DECAPETALUM LAM. [Intern. Code] = A. HEXAPETALUM ROXB. (PW; Vśs, = *aṅkola*) = A. LAMARCKII THW. (KB 2, p. 1237-1239);

(13) HOLARRHENA ANTIDYSENTERICA WALL. (Vśs. = *kuṭaja*);

(14) = *kośāmra* (Vśs, a wild mango-tree; *kośāmra* is MANGIFERA SYLVATICA ROXB. acc. to HK);

(15) LUFFA ACUTANGULA ROXB. (Vśs, = *kośātakī*);

(16) L. AEGYPTIACA MILL. = L. PENTANDRA ROXB. (Vśs, = *kośātakī*);

(17) PINUS ROXBURGHII SARG. = P. LONGIFOLIA ROXB. EX LAMBERT (Vśs, = *sarala*);

(18) JASMINUM MULTIFLORUM ANDR. (Vśs, = *kunda*);

(19) ARTEMISIA VULGARIS LINN. = A. INDICA WILLD. (Vśs, = *damanaka*);

(20) A. SCOPARIA WALDST. ET KIT. (Vśs, = *damanaka*);

(21) A. SIVERSIANA EHRH. EX WILLD. (KB 2, p. 1400-1401: *madanaka* = *damanaka*).

madhuka

(1) a) GLYCYRRHIZA GLABRA LINN. = G. GLANDULIFERA WALDST. ET KIT. (Nadk. 1, nr. 1136);

b) [G. GLABRA LINN. VAR. GLANDULIFERA] (KB 1, p. 727-729);

(2) CYNOMETRA RAMIFLORA LINN. = C. MIMOSOIDES WALL. (KB 2, p. 880-881; V 8, p. 37) [= C. RAMIFLORA LINN. VAR. MIMOSIOIDES BAKER] (KB 2, p. 880-881); see Hooker 2, p. 267 : C. R. LINN. VAR. MIMOSOIDES WALL.;

(3) MADHUCA LATIFOLIA MACBRIDE = BASSIA LATIFOLIA ROXB. (MW; PW; Vśs);

(4) SARACA INDICA LINN. = JONESIA ASOCA ROXB. (MW; PW);

(5) = *vallīyaṣṭimadhuka* (Vśs, unidentified; compare PW);

(6) = *jīvaka* (Vśs : TERMINALIA TOMENTOSA WIGHT ET ARN.).

madhurasā

(1) VITIS VINIFERA LINN. (Bpn, p. 573; KB 1, p. 607-609; MW; PW; V 1, p. 11; Vśs);

(2) GMELINA ARBOREA ROXB. (MW; PW; Vśs);

(3) GLYCYRRHIZA GLABRA LINN. (Vśs);

(4) EUPHORBIA HYPERICIFOLIA LINN. (Vśs, = *dugdhikā*);

(5) OXYSTELMA ESCULENTUM R.BR. (Vśs, = *dugdhikā*);

(6) BORASSUS FLABELLIFER LINN. (KB 4, p. 2571-2575; V 5, p. 8);

(7) = *mūrvā* (Bpn, p. 433; DWH 3, p. 493; HB; HK; MW; PW; V 8, p. 81; Vśs);

(8) = *prasāraṇī* (Vśs);

(9) = *śatapuṣpā* (Vśs); various identifications, but chiefly : ANETHUM SOWA KURZ.

madhūka

(1) [MADHUCA INDICA J. F. GMEL.] (Chopra) [= M. LATIFOLIA (ROXB.) MACBRIDE] (Chopra) = MADHUCA LATIFOLIA MACBRIDE = BASSIA LATIFOLIA ROXB. (Avk; Bpn, p. 569; Chopra; Dgv, nr. 202; Dutt; DWH 2, p. 354-362; Dy, p. 476-479; Gul; HK; Kav; KB 2, p. 1488-1490; MW; Na 1, nr. 307; Nadk. 1, nr. 320; PW; Roxb., p. 411; V 8, p. 42; Vśs; Wise);

(2) [MADHUCA LONGIFOLIA (LINN.) MACBRIDE] (Chopra) = M. LONGIFOLIA MACBRIDE = BASSIA LONGIFOLIA LINN. (Ainslie 2, p. 99-101; Bpn, p. 569; Chopra; DWH 2, p. 354-362; KB 2, p. 1490-1491; Nadk. 1, nr. 321);

(3) Diploknema butyracea H. J. Lam (IRM 3, p. 88-89) = Madhuca butyracea Macbride (IRM 3, p. 88-89) = Bassia butyracea Roxb. (DWH 2, p. 354-362);

(4) Glycyrrhiza glabra Linn. (MW; PW).

madhūlikā

(1) a) = *mūrvā* (Vśs);

b) Clematis triloba Heyne ex Roth (KB 1, p. 4-5, = *mūrvā*);

(2) Glycyrrhiza glabra Linn. (Vśs, = *yaṣṭimadhu*);

(3) = *jalayaṣṭi* (Vśs, = *vallīyaṣṭimadhu*; unidentified);

(4) = *markaṭahastatṛṇa* (Vśs, unidentified);

(5) a small kind of wheat (Vśs).

marica

(1) Piper nigrum Linn. [= P. nigrum Linn. var. trioicum Cav.] (PA 1, 9, p. 64) (see Hooker 5, p. 90-91 : P. nigrum var. trioicum C. DC.) = P. trioicum Roxb. (DWH 3, p. 175; PA 1, 9, p. 64) (see Roxb., p. 51 and Hooker 5, p. 90-91) = P. malabarense C. DC. (PA 1, 9, p. 64) = P. baccatum C. DC. (PA 1, 9, p. 64) = Muldera multinervis Miq. (PA 1, 9, p. 64);

(2) Majorana hortensis Moench. [Intern. Code] = Origanum majorana Linn. (KB 3, p. 1985-1986; MW; PW, = *maruva*; Vśs, = *maruva*);

(3) Strychnos potatorum Linn.f. (MW; Vśs, = *kataka*);

(4) a) Capsicum frutescens Linn. (KB 3, p. 1770-1771 : *raktamarica*) [= C. minimum Willd.] (KB 3, p. 1770-1771);

b) = *kumarica* (Vśs : capsicum);

(5) C. minimum Roxb. (KB 3, p. 1773);

(6) = *kakkola* (MW; PW; Vśs).

marīca

(1) = *marica* (Dgv, nr. 266; MW; PW; Vśs);

(2) = *marubaka* (MW; PW; Vśs);

(3) Strychnos potatorum Linn.f. (MW; Vśs).

marubaka = *maruva(ka)*

(1) Majorana hortensis Moench. [Intern. Code] (Chopra : *maru*) = Origanum majorana Linn. (Avk; Bpn, p. 510; Chopra; Dgv, nr. 251; DWH 3, p. 108-109; Gul; KB 3, p. 1985-1986; V 8, p. 39);

(2) OCIMUM BASILICUM LINN. = O. CARYOPHYLLATUM ROXB. (Avk; HSu) = O. MINIMUM LINN. (Avk);

(3) VANGUERIA SPINOSA ROXB. (MW; PW);

(4) CLERODENDRUM PHLOMOIDES LINN.F. (MW; PW: = *tilaka*);

(5) RANDIA DUMETORUM LAM. (KB 2, p. 1273-1276; Vśs);

(6) = *nāgadamanī* (Vśs);

(7) = *kharapatra* (PW);

(8) a kind of *jambīra* (Vśs).

markaṭahastatṛṇa

= *madhūlikā* (Cakra on Ca.Vi. 8, 139).

masūra

LENS ESCULENTA MOENCH. [Intern. Code] = L. CULINARIS MEDIC. = ERVUM LENS LINN. = CICER LENS WILLD.

mahauṣadha

= dried ginger; see *ārdraka*.

mātuluṅga

Is considered as a synonym of *bījapūra*, but acc. to Gul it is CITRUS DECUMANA MURR.; acc. to KB 1, p. 488-489 it may also designate [CITRUS MEDICA LINN. VAR. LIMONUM].

māṣa

PHASEOLUS MUNGO LINN. (Gul) [= PH. MUNGO LINN. VAR. RADIATUS LINN.] (Dutt; DWH 1, p. 488; HK) (see Hooker 2, p. 203) = PH. RADIATUS LINN. (Chopra; KB 1, p. 795-796; Nadk. 1, nr. 1869) [= PH. RADIATUS ROXB.] (PW) [= PH. RADIATUS WILLD.] (Roxb., p. 557) = PH. RADIATUS (Bpn, p. 645; Kav; MW; Na 1, nr. 132; V 1, p. 160; Vśs) = PH. ROXBURGHII WIGHT ET ARN. (Avk; Dutt; HK; Kav; Nadk. 1, nr. 1869; Vśs).

See about the nomenclature: Cooke 1, p. 403; Duthie 1, p. 207-208; Flora Pavagadh, p. 78-79; Hooker 2, p. 203; Purseglove 1, p. 284-310 (Phaseolus).

māṣakalāya

= *māṣavrīhi* (Vśs, unidentified).

muñja

(1) SACCHARUM ARUNDINACEUM RETZ. (Chopra; HK; KB 4, p. 2665-2666; V 9, p. 92) = S. CILIARE ANDERSS. (KB 4, p. 2666-2668) = S. MUNJA ROXB. (Bpn, p. 380; Chopra; Dutt; HK; MW; PW) = S. MOONJA ROYLE; S.A. RETZ and S.M. ROXB. are regarded as distinct species by Chopra and KB; see, however, Hooker 7, p. 119-120;

(2) S. SARA ROXB. (MW; Vśs).

mudga

PHASEOLUS MUNGO LINN. (the greater part of the sources) [= PH. MUNGO WILLD.] (Roxb., p. 556) = PH. RADIATUS LINN. (Gul) [= PH. MUNGO LINN. VAR. ROXBURGHII PRAIN] (KB 1, p. 797-798); see *māṣa* for references to literature on the nomenclature.

mustă

(See also *nāgaramusta* and *bhadramustă*.)

(1) CYPERUS ROTUNDUS LINN. (Avk; Bpn, p. 243; Chopra; Dgv, nr. 337; Dutt; DWH 3, p. 552-553; Ghosh; HB; HK; IRM 2, p. 424-425; Kav; KB 4, p. 2638-2640; MW; Nadk. 1, nr. 782; PW; Roxb., p. 66; V 8, p. 98; Vśs; Watt CP, p. 465-466; Wise) = C. HEXASTACHYOS ROTTB. [= C. HEXASTYCHOS LINN.] (Vśs);

(2) C. SCARIOSUS R. BR. = C. PERTENUIS ROXB. (Avk; Nadk. 1, nr. 781; Vśs);

(3) [C. JUNCIFOLIUS ROTTL.] (Ainslie 2, p. 162-164; Wise);

(4) KYLLINGA MONOCEPHALA ROTTB. (KB 4, p. 2634-2635).

mūrvā

(1) SANSEVIERIA ROXBURGHIANA SCHULT.F. (Avk; Bpn, p. 435-437; Dutt; HK; Kav; MW; Nadk. 1, nr. 2216; PA 1, 2, p. 1-14; PW; Vśs) = S. ZEYLANICA ROXB.;

(2) S. ZEYLANICA WILLD. (Avk; Dutt; DWH 3, p. 493-495; HK; Kav; Nadk. 1, nr. 2216; PA 1, 2, p. 1-14; Roxb., p. 294; Vśs; Wise); many sources regard 1) and 2) as synonyms, which is not confirmed by the Index Kewensis; see Hooker 6, p. 270-271 about the differences between the two species; unclear : [S. ZEYLANICA THUNB.] (Ainslie 2, p. 192-193);

(3) CLEMATIS TRILOBA HEYNE EX ROTH (Gul; IRM 2, p. 231; KB 1, p. 4-5; PA 1, 2, p. 1-14);

(4) CLEMATIS GOURIANA ROXB. (Bpn, p. 435-437);
(5) CHONEMORPHA MACROPHYLLA G. DON (PA 1, 2, p. 1-14);
(6) MARSDENIA TENACISSIMA WIGHT ET ARN. (Bpn, p. 435-437);
(7) BAUHINIA VAHLII WIGHT ET ARN. (Bpn, p. 435-437);
(8) MAERUA OVALIFOLIA CAMBESS. = M. ARENARIA HOOK.F. ET THOMS. (Bpn, p. 435-437);
(9) HELICTERES ISORA LINN. (Bpn, p. 435-437).

mūlaka

(1) RAPHANUS SATIVUS LINN.;
(2) = *uśīra* (Vśs);
(3) = the root of *śigru* (Vśs);
(4) = *kālaśāka* : CORCHORUS CAPSULARIS LINN. (PW);
(5) a sort of yam (i.e. a species of DIOSCOREA) (MW).

mṛdvīkā

grapes, i.e. the fruits of VITIS VINIFERA LINN.

meṣaśṛṅgī = *ajaśṛṅgī*

(1) GYMNEMA SYLVESTRE R. BR. (Avk; Bpn, p. 443; Chopra; Dutt; DWH 2, p. 450-455; Dy, p. 521-523; HK; KB 3, p. 1625-1627; MW; Nadk. 1, nr. 1173; Sanyal; V 3, p. 96) = ASCLEPIAS GEMINATA ROXB. (Avk; Dutt; HB; HK; Nadk. 1, nr. 1173; Wise);

(2) LANNEA GRANDIS ENGL. [Intern. Code : Lannea is a nom. conserv.] (KB 1, p. 664-666) = ODINA WODIER ROXB. (Avk; HK: ?; KB 1, p. 664-666; Nadk. 1, nr. 1742) [= O. PINNATA ROTTL.] (HK) (The Index Kewensis has its doubts about the identity) [= O. PENNATA LINN.] (PW) [= O. PINNATA] (MW) = RHUS ODINA BUCH.-HAM. EX WALL. (Nadk. 1, nr. 1742) = HABERLIA GRANDIS DENNST. (KB 1, p. 664-666) [= CALENUM GRANDE O. KUNTZE] (KB 1, p. 664-666) = CALESIUM GRANDE KUNTZE;

(3) HELICTERES ISORA LINN. (Avk; DWH 1, p. 231-233, = *mṛgaśṛṅga*; Gul);

(4) RHUS SUCCEDANEA LINN. (Avk; Vśs : = *karkaṭaśṛṅga*) = RH. ACUMINATA DC. (Avk; Vśs);

(5) PISTACIA KHINJUK STOCKS = P. INTEGERRIMA STEW. EX BRANDIS (Avk).

moraṭa

(1) Alangium decapetalum Lam. [Intern. Code] = A. hexapetalum Roxb. (MW; PW; Kauṭ., transl. J. J. Meyer p. 187, note 3 and transl. Sham. p. 133);

(2) = *mūrvā* (HK; KB 1, p. 4-5);

(3) a tree known as *latākarāḍa* (Vśs); Pr 376: = *pīluparnī*, called *latā kaḍāra* in the vernacular; KB 1, p. 4-5 : *pīluparṇī* = *mūrvā* : Clematis triloba Heyne ex Roth;

(4) a partic. plant with a sweet milky juice (MW; PW);

(5) the root of Saccharum officinarum Linn. (MW; PW);

(6) a kind of Acacia catechu Willd. (Vśs);

(7) Cedrus libani Barrel = C. deodara Loud. (Vśs, = *aṅkolla* = *devadāru*);

(8) = *muraṅgī* (Candra on A.h.Sū. 15, 24; Vśs : *muraṅgī* = *kṛṣṇa-śigru* = *śigru*).

moraṭā

(1) = *mūrvā* (DWH 3, p. 493; MW; PW);

(2) Heliotropium indicum Linn. (Kauṭ., transl. J. J. Meyer p. 187, note 3 : acc. to Bhaṭṭ.);

(3) Helianthus annuus Linn. = H. indicus Linn. (ibid., acc. to Gaṇ.);

(4) Alangium decapetalum Lam. [Intern. Code] = A. hexapetalum Roxb. (Kauṭ., transl. Sham. p. 133).

yava

(1) Hordeum vulgare Linn. = H. sativum Pers. = H. hexastichon Linn. = H. distichon Linn.;

(2) = *indrayava* (Bpn, p. 642).

yavaka

(1) = *yava*;

(2) a) wild barley (Gul);

b) a smaller variety of barley (Kav);

(3) a partic. kind of rice (Ca.Sū. 27, 12; Cakra on Ca.Ni. 2, 4; Aruṇa on A.h.Sū. 6, 6).

yavānī = *yamānī*; see also *vanayamānī*

(1) Trachyspermum copticum (Linn.) Link [Intern. Code] = Carum copticum Benth. et Hook.f. (Avk; Dutt; DWH 2, p. 116-119; Dy, p. 365-367; Ghosh; Gul; HK; KB 2, p. 1204-1206; Nadk. 1, nr. 482; Sanyal; Vśs) = C. ajowan Benth. et Hook.f. (Avk) = Ptychotis ajowan DC. (Avk; Dutt; DWH 2, p. 117; Dy, p. 365-367; HK; Kav; MW; Nadk. 1, nr. 482; PW) [= Ligusticum ajowan Roxb.] (Avk; HK; Kav; Roxb., p. 271) = L. ajawain Roxb. ex Flem. = L. ajowan Royle = Ammi copticum Linn. (Avk; Vśs);

(2) Trachyspermum involucratum H. Wolff = Carum roxburghianum Benth. et Hook.f. (Avk) = Apium involucratum Roxb. ex Flem. (Avk) (see *ajamodā*);

(3) Carum petroselinum Benth. et Hook.f. (Avk);

(4) Hyoscyamus niger Linn. (Avk; KB 3, p. 1794-1796; Nadk. 1, nr. 1273) (often called *pārasīkayamānī* or *khorāsānīyamānī*; Avk; DWH 2, p. 626-632; Dy, p. 629-632; MW; V 1, p. 19; Vśs);

(5) H. albus Linn. (Dy, p. 629-632);

(6) H. reticulatus Linn. (Avk; DWH 2, p. 626-632) [= H. reticularis] (Avk);

(7) H. muticus Linn. (DWH 2, p. 626-632).

yăvanāla; see also *devadhānya*

(1) [Sorghum vulgare (Linn.) Pers. var. saccharatum Boerl.] = S. vulgare Pers. (AB 1, p. 354; DWH 3, p. 618-619; KB 4, p. 2723-2724; Watt CP, p. 1031-1043) = Andropogon sorghum Brot. (KB 4, p. 2723-2724) = A. bicolor Roxb. (MW; PW);

(2) Zea mays Linn. (Chopra; KB 4, p. 2659-2661; Nadk. 1, nr. 2653; Vśs).

yavāsa = *yāsa* = *dhanvayavāsa* = *dhanvayāsa* = *durālabhā*

(1) Alhagi camelorum Fisch. (Avk; Bpn, p. 411-412; DWH 1, p. 417-420; KB 1, p. 743-744; PA 1, 6, p. 97-116) [= A. pseudalhagi (Bieb.) Desv.] (Chopra) = A. pseudalhagi Desv.;

(2) a) A. maurorum Desv. (Avk; Dutt; DWH 1, p. 417-420; Dy, p. 218-220; Gul; HB; HK; Nadk. 1, nr. 97 and 1191) [= A. maurorum Baker] (Chopra; KB 1, p. 743-744; PA 1, 6, p. 97-116) [= A. maurorum Tournef.] (Avk; PW) = A. maurorum (Kav; MW; Sanyal; V 4, p. 81; Vśs) =

HEDYSARUM ALHAGI LINN. (Dutt; HK; Nadk. 1, nr. 1191; PA 1, 6, p. 97-116);

b) H. ALHAGI (Kav; Vśs) [= H. ALHAGI WILLD.] (Roxb., p. 574) [= H. MAURORUM DC.] (Kav); the name HEDYSARUM ALHAGI is insufficient to determine the species : the Index Kewensis records :

a) H. ALHAGI LINN., a synonym of A. MAURORUM DESV.;

b) H. ALHAGI LERCH. = A. CAMELORUM FISCH.;

c) H. ALHAGI FORSK. = A. CAMELORUM FISCH.;

d) H. ALHAGI SIBTH. ET SM. = A. GRAECORUM BOISS.;

(3) FAGONIA CRETICA LINN. (Bpn, p. 411-412; Dgv, nr. 61; Gul; KB 1. p. 426-428; Na 1, nr. 84; Nadk. 1, nr. 1011; PA 1, 6, p. 97-116) = F. BRUGUIERI DC. (KB 1, p. 426-428; Nadk. 1, nr. 1011) = F. MYSORENSIS HEYNE EX ROTH (KB 1, p. 426-428; Nadk. 1, nr. 1011; PA 1, 6, p. 97-116) [= F. CRETICA LINN. VAR. ARABICA LINN.] (PA 1, 6, p. 97-116) [= F. CRETICA VAR. ARABICA T. ANDERS.] (KB 1, p. 426-428); see Duthie 1, p. 120 and Hooker 1, p. 425 about the nomenclature;

(4) TRAGIA INVOLUCRATA LINN. (KB 3, p. 2280-2281; PA 1, 6, p. 97-116) = T. HISPIDA WILLD. (PA 1, 6, p. 97-116);

(5) T. BICOLOR MIQ. (PA 1, 6, p. 97-116) = T. MIQUELIANA MUELL. ARG. [= T. MIQUELIANA VAR. BICOLOR] (PA 1, 6, p. 97-116); see Hooker 5, p. 465;

(6) GOSSYPIUM HERBACEUM LINN. (Vśs);

(7) = *spṛkkā* (Vśs).

rājādana = *rājādanī*

(1) MANILKARA HEXANDRA DUBARD [Intern. Code : Manilkara is a nom. conserv.] = MIMUSOPS HEXANDRA ROXB. (Avk; Bpn, p. 567; Chopra; Dutt; DWH 2, p. 364-365; Dy, p. 482; Gul; HK; Kav; KB 2, p. 1496-1497; Nadk. 1, nr. 1624; PW; Vśs) = MIMUSOPS INDICA A. DC. (Dutt; HK; Kav; Nadk. 1, nr. 1624) = M. KAUKI WALL.;

(2) MANILKARA KAUKI (LINN.) DUBARD [Intern. Code] = MIMUSOPS KAUKI LINN. (MW; PW);

(3) ALSTONIA VENENATA R. BR. (Avk; Chopra; Nadk. 1, nr. 122);

(4) BUTEA MONOSPERMA KUNTZE = B. FRONDOSA ROXB. (MW; PW; Vśs);

(5) BUCHANANIA LATIFOLIA ROXB. (KB 1, p. 659-662; MW; PW; Vśs : = *pītaśāla*);

(6) B. LANZAN SPRENG. (KB 1, p. 659-662, considered as a synonym

of B. LATIFOLIA); see about the nomenclature Cooke 1, p. 293-295; Brandis (Indian Trees, p. 205) regards 5) and 6) as synonyms;

(7) the seeds of *nīpa* (Vśs); *nīpa* is the large type of *kadamba* acc. to HK; Chopra and KB 2, p. 1057-1058 : BARRINGTONIA RACEMOSA ROXB.; PW : = *dhārā-*, *dhūlīkadamba*; acc. to MW and PW *nīpa* has more meanings; see also Meyer, Trilogie 3, p. 67, note 4;

(8) = *kṣīriṇīvṛkṣa* (Vśs); *kṣīriṇīvṛkṣa* usually designates the two mentioned species of MANILKARA.

rājikā

(1) BRASSICA JUNCEA COSS. (Nadk. 1, nr. 378) [= B. JUNCEA HOOK.F. ET THOMS.] (Dutt; Dy, p. 59 : probably; HK; KB 1, p. 166-167) (see Hooker 1, p. 157) = B. JUNCEA (Avk; Bpn, p. 652; Dgm, p. 115; Dgv, nr. 24; DWH 1, p. 122-129; V 9, p. 1-2; Vśs) [= B. JUNCEA HOOK.F. ET THOMS. SUBSP. B. RUGOSA VAR. 1 AGRESTIS and VAR. 3 CUNEIFOLIA PRAIN] (KB 1, p. 166-167) (see Watt CP, p. 182-183) = SINAPIS JUNCEA LINN. (Nadk. 1, nr. 2307; Vśs) = S. RAMOSA ROXB. EX FLEM. (Ainslie 1, p. 230-232; Dutt; HK; MW; Nadk. 1, nr. 2307; PW) = S. CHINENSIS LINN. (Ainslie 1, p. 230-232) [= S. CHINENSIS LINN. VAR. INTEGRIFOLIA STOCKS] (KB 1, p. 166-167) = S. CUNEIFOLIA ROXB. (KB 1, p. 166-167; Nadk. 1, nr. 2307) = S. RUGOSA ROXB. (Nadk. 1, nr. 2307);

(2) [BRASSICA INTEGRIFOLIA (WEST) O. E. SCHULZ] (Chopra; KB 1, p. 166-167, considered as a synonym of B. JUNCEA HOOK.F. ET THOMS.) = B. INTEGRIFOLIA O. E SCHULZ = B. INTEGRIFOLIA (Na 1, nr. 23; V 9, p. 1-2);

(3) B. NIGRA KOCH (Avk; Bpn, p. 652 : *kṛṣṇarājikā*; KB 1, p. 168-170; Vśs) = SINAPIS NIGRA LINN. (KB 1, p. 168-170; Nadk. 1, nr. 2307);

(4) [BRASSICA CAMPESTRIS LINN. VAR. RAPA (LINN.) HARTM.] (KB 1, p. 165-166) (see Hooker 1, p. 156) = B. CAMPESTRIS LINN. = B. RAPA LINN. (KB 1, p. 165-166);

(5) ERUCA SATIVA MILLER (V 4, p. 115);

(6) ELEUSINE CORACANA GAERTN. (AB 1, p. 403; Chopra; IRM 3, p. 160-166; KB 4, p. 2692-2693; Nadk. 1, nr. 927; V 8, p. 9; Watt CP, p. 517-521) = CYNOSURUS CORACANUS LINN. (Ainslie 1, p. 245-246);

(7) ELEUSINE INDICA GAERTN. (Nadk. 1, nr. 927);

(8) ELEUSINE AEGYPTIACA DESF. = DACTYLOCTENIUM AEGYPTIUM BEAUV. (V 8, p. 9);

(9) = *kṛṣṇoḍumbara* = *kākoḍumbarikā* : FICUS HISPIDA LINN.F. (Vśs). See about the Indian species and varieties of Brassica: D. Prain,

A note on the mustards cultivated in Bengal, 1898; Watt CP, p. 174-183.

rudrākṣa

(1) Elaeocarpus ganitrus Roxb.;
(2) E. tuberculatus Roxb. (Nadk. 1, nr. 921).

rohiṇī

(1) a) Picrorrhiza kurroa Royle ex Benth. (Bpn, p. 69 and HB : = *kaṭurohiṇī*; Kav);
b) = *kaṭuṃbharā* (PW) (Bpn, *harītakyādivarga* 151 : *kaṭaṃbharā* or *kaṭuṃbharā* is a synonym of *kaṭurohiṇī*);
(2) Helleborus niger Linn. (MW; PW : = *kaṭurohiṇī*);
(3) Terminalia chebula Retz. (= *harītakī* : Bpn, p. 7; DWH 2, p. 1; HB; HK; KB 2, p. 1020-1023; PW);
(4) Myrica nagi Thunb. (HK, = *kaṭphala*; KB 3, p. 2350-2351);
(5) Soymida febrifuga Juss. (Avk; Chopra; Dgv, nr. 82, = *māṃsarohiṇī*; Gul; KB 1, p. 559-560; Na 1, nr. 106, = *māṃsarohiṇī*; Nadk. 1, nr. 2349; V 9, p. 20) = Swietenia febrifuga Roxb. (KB 1, p. 559-560; Nadk. 1, nr. 2349) = S. rubra Wight ex Wall. (Nadk. 1, nr. 2349);
(6) Amoora rohituka Wight et Arn. (Avk, *rohitaka*, *rohiṇī*; Dgv, nr. 81 : *rohītaka*; Dutt; DWH 1, p. 341-342, *rohitaka*, *rohiṇī*; Gul : *rohitaka*; HK; IRM 1, p. 86-87 : *rohitaka*; KB 1, p. 551-553 ; *rohitaka*) = A. polystachya Wight et Arn. [= A. polystachya Hook.f. et Jacks.] (KB 1, p. 551-553) = Aphanamixis rohituka Pierre [= Aph. polystachya Blatter, *nov. comb.*] (KB 1, p. 551-553) [= Aph. polystachya (Wall.) R. N. Parker] (Chopra : *rohitaka*; IRM 1, p. 86-87); (acc. to the Index Kewensis this is a synonym of Aglaia polystachya; the latter plant is described in Roxburgh's Flora Indica, ed. 1824, acc. to KB); = Andersonia rohituka Roxb. (KB 1, p. 551-553; Roxb., p. 311 : *rohitaka*);
(7) Loranthus longiflorus Desr. (V 6, p. 163) = Dendrophthoë falcata Blume;
(8) ? Tecoma undulata G. Don (KB 3, p. 1841-1842 : *rohitaka*) = Tecomella undulata Seem. (Bpn, p. 527 : *rohitaka*);
(9) Rubia cordifolia Linn. (KB 2, p. 1303-1305; PW);
(10) Gmelina arborea Roxb. [= G. arborea Linn.] (MW; PW);
(11) Acacia arabica Willd. (MW; PW : = *somavalka*).

rauhiṇīka

Cakra on Ca.Ni. 2, 4 : = the potherb called *rohiṇī*.

lakuca

ARTOCARPUS LAKOOCHA ROXB.

lambā

= *ikṣvāku* (Ca.Ka. 3, 3cd-4ab).

lavaṅga

(1) SYZYGIUM AROMATICUM (LINN.) MERRILL ET PERRY (Bpn, p. 219; Chopra) = EUGENIA CARYOPHYLLATA THUNB. (Watt CP, p. 526-530) [= E. CARYOPHYLLATA WILLD.] (Nadk. 1, nr. 965; Roxb., p. 401); see Hooker 2, p. 506; [= E. CARYOPHYLLATA LINN.] (Ainslie 1, p. 75-77) = E. CARYOPHYLLATA (Nadk. 1, nr. 1682) [= E. AROMATICA KUNTZE] (Bpn, p. 219; Chopra) = E. AROMATICA BAILL. = CARYOPHYLLUS AROMATICUS LINN. (Avk; Bpn, p. 219; Dgv, nr. 151; Dutt; DWH 2, p. 20-23; Gul; HB; HK; Kav; Na 1, nr. 213; Nadk. 1, nr. 485; Vśs);

(2) EUGENIA CARYOPHYLLUS (SPRENG.) BULLOCK ET S. G. HARRISON = E. CARYOPHYLLAEA WIGHT = MYRTUS CARYOPHYLLUS SPRENG. (Nadk. 1, nr. 1682).

laśuna

ALLIUM SATIVUM LINN.; see R. Bedi : Garlic, in P. K. Gode Comm. Vol., 1960, p. 9-18; J. Jolly : Der Knoblauch in der indischen Medizin, in : Festgruss an R. von Roth, 1893, p. 18-20.

lodhra

(1) SYMPLOCOS RACEMOSA ROXB.;

(2) S. THEIFOLIA (Nadk. 1, nr. 2420); the Index Kewensis records :

a) S. THEIFOLIA HAYATA = S. ADINANDRIFOLIA VAR. THEIFOLIA HAYATA;

b) S. THEAEFOLIA D. DON;

(3) S. CRATAEGOIDES BUCH.-HAM. EX D. DON (see Bpn, p. 130; Chopra; Dgv, nr. 204; KB 2, p. 1510-1511; PA 1, 3, p. 65-71; V 9, p.

42 : *paṭṭikālodhra, valkalodhra*) = S. PANICULATA WALL. EX D. DON (Chopra);

(4) S. SPICATA ROXB. (PA 1, 3, p. 65-76);

(5) DESMODIUM PULCHELLUM BENTH. (PA 1, 3, p. 75-76) = HEDYSARUM PULCHELLUM LINN. (PA 1, 3, p. 75) = DICERMA PULCHELLUM DC. (PA 1, 3, p. 75, footnote : "This plant has been equated as *lodhra* by Rama Rao in his 'Flowering plants of Travancore' and Sir R. N. Chopra in his 'Indigenous drugs of India'; it is, however, very doubtful whether this plant is used as the source of *lodhra* anywhere in Travancore-Cochin or in India").

vaṃśa

(1) BAMBUSA BAMBOS DRUCE (Chopra) = B. ARUNDINACEA WILLD. (Bpn, p. 376; Chopra; Gul; IRM 1, p. 153-154) [= B. ARUNDINACEA RETZ.] (Dutt; DWH 3, p. 586-592; HK; Kav; KB 4, p. 2724-2727; Nadk. 1, nr. 307) = B. ARUNDINACEA (Dgv, nr. 341; Vśs) = ARUNDO BAMBOS LINN.; B. ARUNDINACEA is a name of three distinct species :

a) see 1);

b) B. ORIENTALIS NEES = B. ARUNDINACEA WIGHT EX STEUD.;

c) B. VULGARIS SCHRAD. = B. ARUNDINACEA AIT.;

acc. to Nadk. (1, nr. 307) *vaṃśa* also designates : B. SPINOSA, APUS and ORIENTALIS; B. APUS and B. ORIENTALIS are distinct from B. BAMBOS DRUCE; B. SPINOSA may be meant as a synonym of B. BAMBOS DRUCE or as the name of a distinct species :

a) B. BAMBOS DRUCE = B. SPINOSA NEES = B. SPINOSA BUCH.-HAM.;

b) B. SPINOSA ROXB.;

(2) ? B. SPINOSA ROXB., (Nadk. 1, nr. 307);

(3) B. APUS SCHULT.F. (Nadk. 1, nr. 307);

(4) B. ORIENTALIS NEES (Nadk. 1, nr. 307);

(5) DENDROCALAMUS STRICTUS NEES (IRM 3, p. 33-34; KB 4, p. 2728-2729; V 7, p. 54);

(6) SACCHARUM OFFICINARUM LINN. (KB 4, p. 2662-2664; MW; PW; Vśs);

(7) SHOREA ROBUSTA GAERTN.F. (KB 1, p. 288-290; MW; PW; Vśs).

vaṭa

FICUS BENGHALENSIS LINN. = F. INDICA LINN. (Ainslie 2, p. 10-11) [= F. INDICA ROXB.] (Dutt; HK; Roxb., p. 639) = F. INDICA (MW;

Nadk. 1, nr. 1034; PW; Vśs) = UROSTIGMA BENGALENSE GASP. (KB 3, p. 2312-2314); see Hooker 5, p. 499-500 about the nomenclature.

vanakārpāsī

(1) HIBISCUS VITIFOLIUS LINN. (Avk; Dutt; Kav and Vśs, = *bhāradvājī*) = H. TRUNCATUS ROXB. (Avk);

(2) THESPESIA MACROPHYLLA BLUME = TH. LAMPAS DALZ. ET GIBS. (Avk; Bpn, p. 375) = HIBISCUS LAMPAS CAV. (Avk);

(3) GOSSYPIUM NIGRUM BUCH.-HAM. (Avk); this is an obsolete name, which covers two species acc. to the Index Kewensis :

a) G. BARBADENSE LINN.;

b) G. ARBOREUM LINN.

vanakodrava = *kodrava*

vanabarbarikā

(1) OCIMUM GRATISSIMUM LINN. (KB 3, p. 1964-1965);

(2) O. BASILICUM LINN. = O. PILOSUM WILLD. (MW);

(3) = *kuṭhera* (PW).

vanamudga

(1) PHASEOLUS TRILOBUS AIT. (Avk; KB 1, p. 794-795; Nadk. 1, nr. 1870, = *mudgaparṇī*);

(2) PH. ACONITIFOLIUS JACQ. (Bpn, p. 646 and KB 1, p. 798-799, = *makuṣṭha*; MW; Vśs, = *makuṣṭhaka*) = PH. TRILOBUS WALL.; unclear are MW and PW : PH. TRILOBUS.

(3) PH. ADENANTHUS G. F. W. MEYER (Chopra and KB 1, p. 799-800 : *araṇyamudga*) = PH. ROSTRATUS WALL. (KB 1, p. 799-800).

vanayamānī

(1) SESELI INDICUM WIGHT ET ARN. (Avk; Chopra; Dutt; Kav; KB 2, p. 1209-1210; Nadk. 1, nr. 2289; V 1, p. 21; Vśs) = CNIDIUM DIFFUSUM DC. (Kav; MW) = LIGUSTICUM DIFFUSUM ROXB. EX SM. (KB 2, p. 1209-1210; Vśs).

vārāhīkanda

(1) TACCA INTEGRIFOLIA KER-GAWL = T. ASPERA ROXB. (Bpn, p. 386-387; Chopra; DWH 3, p. 549-550; KB 4, p. 2476-2477);

(2) a) Diosorea bulbifera Linn. (Bpn, p. 386-387; KB 4, p. 2483-2489) [= D. sativa Thunb.] (KB 4, p. 2483-2489);
b) Dioscorea (MW; PW; Vśs);

(3) = *śuklabhūmikuṣmāṇḍa* (Vśs = *vidārīkanda* : Ipomoea digitata Linn. = I. paniculata R. Br.);

(4) = *priyaṅgu* (Vśs);

(5) = *vṛddhadāraka* (Vśs : a) Gmelina asiatica Linn.; b) Rourea santaloides Wight et Arn.);

(6) *varāhakrāntā* (Vśs) : Mimosa pudica Linn. (acc. to Dutt and Nadk. 1, nr. 1618).

viḍaṅga

(1) Embelia ribes Burm.f. (Avk; Bpn, p. 52; Chopra; Dgv, nr. 201; Dutt; DWH 2, p. 349-354; HB; HK; IRM 3, p. 167-168; Kav; KB 2, p. 1478-1480; MW; Na 1, nr. 306; Nadk. 1, nr. 929; PW; Sanyal; V 7, p. 55; Vśs) = E. glandulifera Wight (Avk; Dutt; HK; Kav; Nadk. 1, nr. 929);

(2) E. tsjeriam-cottam A. DC. (Bpn, p. 52; Nadk. 1, nr. 931) [= E. robusta C. B. Clarke (Fl. Br. Ind.), non Roxb.] (Sanyal);

(3) E. robusta Roxb. (Avk); see Hooker 3, p. 515.

vidalāmalaka

This term occurs Kauṭ. 2, 15, 18 (text p. 74; transl. Kangle p. 142; transl. J. J. Meyer p. 141; transl. Sham. p. 101); (see App. 3: *amla*). Sham. is of the opinion that it is a synonym of *āmalaka*; J. J. Meyer (p. 141, footnote 7) is unsure about the meaning of the word; he seems to prefer to take the word as a compound and remarks that *vidala* (acc. to the dictionaries) designates Bauhinia variegata, but acc. to Gaṇ. the pomegranate (*dāḍima*). In my opinion the word *vidalāmalaka* is a compound and the first member is *vidala* or *vidalā*.

vidala : (1) Bauhinia variegata Linn. (MW; Vśs : = *raktakāñcana*);
(2) B. purpurea Linn. (Vśs : = *raktakāñcana*);
(3) the seeds of Punica granatum Linn. (Vśs).

vidalā : (1) Ipomoea turpethum R. Br. (MW; Vśs);
(2) = *sātalā* (Vśs; variously identified, but acc. to Vśs. Euphorbia neriifolia Linn.);
(3) the bark of Punica granatum Linn. (MW).

The best solution is to read *vidala* and to take it in the sense of *dāḍima* (Punica granatum Linn.) because the pomegranate is usually enumerated as one of the fruits called *phalāmla*. (Kangle also translates : pomegranate).

vibhītaka

TERMINALIA BELLERICA ROXB. = T. BELIRICA WALL. = T. PUNCTATA ROTH = MYROBALANUS BELLIRICA GAERTN.

vilaṅga

This plant is mentioned Kauṭ. 2, 25, 29 (text p. 79; transl. Kangle p. 178; transl. J. J. Meyer p. 186; transl. Sham. p. 132); see App. 3 : *āsava*. Sham. does not translate the term. J. J. Meyer remarks (p. 188, note 1) that it may denote a climbing plant, that it is a synonym of *viḍaṅga* (EMBELIA RIBES) acc. to Stein and that it is a synonym of *amoghā* acc. to Gaṇ.

amoghā : 1) STEREOSPERMUM SUAVEOLENS DC. (Vśs) = BIGNONIA SUAVEOLENS ROXB. (MW ;Vśs);
2) TERMINALIA CHEBULA RETZ. (DWH 2, p. 1; Vśs: = *harītakī*);
3) T. CITRINA ROXB. EX FLEM. (MW, = *harītakī*);
4) ERYCIBE PANICULATA ROXB. (MW);
5) = *padmabheda* (Vśs, unidentified);
6) EMBELIA RIBES BURM.F. (Bpn, p. 52, = *viḍaṅga*);
7) PHYLLANTHUS EMBLICA LINN. (Cakra on Ca.Sū. 4, 18 : = *āmalakī*).

vṛkṣāmla

(1) SPONDIAS PINNATA KURZ = S. MANGIFERA WILLD. (HK; MW; PW; Vśs : = *āmrātaka*);
(2) GARCINIA INDICA CHOISY (Avk; Bpn, p. 582; Dgm, p. 241; Dgv, nr. 41; Gul; KB 1, p. 262-263; Na 1, nr. 46) = G. PURPUREA ROXB. (Avk; Dgm, p. 241; KB 1, p. 262-263);
(3) G. PEDUNCULATA ROXB.; G. DON (Dgm, p. 241);
(4) G. XANTHOCHYMUS HOOK.F. EX T. ANDERS. (Dgm, p. 241);
(5) the fruit of TAMARINDUS INDICA LINN. (Kav; MW; Vśs);
(6) OXALIS CORNICULATA LINN. (Kav; Vśs : = *amlaloṇī*);
(7) = *amlavetasa* (Vśs);
(8) RHUS PARVIFLORA ROXB. (Dgm, p. 242).

vaikuṇṭha

(1) Anisomeles malabarica R. Br. ex Sims (Chopra; KB 3, p. 2011-2012; V 4, p. 70);

(2) a) a kind of Ocimum (MW);
b) = *arjaka* (Rn, *varga* 23, 6; Vśs);
c) = *kuṭhera* (HK).

śamī

(1) Acacia sundra DC. = A. suma Buch.-Ham. ex Wall. (Kav; KB 2, p. 935-936) = Mimosa suma Roxb. (? Index Kewensis) (Chopra; Dutt; HK; Kav; KB 2, p. 935-936; MW; Nadk. 1, nr. 1622; PW);

(2) A. suma Kurz ex Brandis (Dutt and HK, considered as a synonym of M. suma Roxb.; Chopra : 1 = 2) = A. sundra Roxb.; unclear are : Avk and Nadk. 1, nr. 1622 : A. suma;

(3) Prosopis spicigera Linn. (Avk; Bpn, p. 545-546; Chopra; Dgv, nr. 129; Gul; KB 2, p. 910-912; MW; Na 1, nr. 188; Nadk. 1, nr. 2032; PW; V 4, p. 47; Vśs);

(4) = *somarājī* (Vśs : Vernonia anthelmintica Willd.).

śālaparṇī

Desmodium gangeticum DC. (Bpn, p. 285; Chopra; Dutt; DWH 1, p. 428-429; Dy, p. 222; Gul; HK; IRM 3, p. 41; Kav; MW; Nadk. 1, nr. 1192; PW; Sanyal; V 9, p. 58; Vśs) = Hedysarum gangeticum Linn. (Avk; Chopra; Dutt; HK; Kav; Nadk. 1, nr. 1192; PW; Vśs; Wise).

śālmalī

(1) Bombax ceiba Linn. (Chopra; Goudr.; KB 1, p. 354-357; Na 1, nr. 66); (I deviate from the Index Kewensis in this case; see Biswas 1, p. 186 : the name adopted acc. to priority is B. ceiba Linn.) = Bombax malabaricum DC. (Avk; Bpn, p. 537; Chopra; Dgv, nr. 48; Dutt; DWH 1, p. 215-218; Ghosh; Gul; HB; HK; Kav; KB 1, p. 354-357; Nadk. 1, nr. 364 : *raktaśālmalī*; Sanyal; V 10, p. 31; Vśs) = B. heptaphyllum Cav. (Dutt; HK; Kav; MW; Nadk. 1, nr. 364) = B. heptaphyllum Roxb. (KB 1, p. 354-357) = Salmalia malabarica Schott et Endl. (Chopra; HK; MW; PW; Vśs) = Gossampinus malabarica Merrill; see about the nomenclature : A. Robyns, Contribution à l'étude monographique du genre Bombax s.l., in : Taxon 10, 1961, p.

156-160; A. Robyns : Essai de monographie du genre Bombax s.l., Bruxelles, 1963;

(2) CEIBA PENTANDRA GAERTN. (Bpn, p. 518-519 : *kūṭaśālmali*; IRM 2, p. 110-112; KB 1, p. 358-360) = BOMBAX PENTANDRUM LINN. (KB 1, p. 358-360; Nadk. 1, nr. 947) = ERIODENDRON ANFRACTUOSUM DC. (*śvetaśālmalī* : Avk; Bpn, p. 518-519; IRM 2, p. 110-112; KB 1, p. 358-360; Nadk. 1, nr. 947) = E. PENTANDRUM KURZ (KB 1, p. 358-360) = GOSSAMPINUS RUMPHII SCHOTT ET ENDL.

śigru = *śobhāñjana*

(1) MORINGA PTERYGOSPERMA GAERTN. (AFM 1, p. 91-93; Avk; Bpn, p. 339-340; Chopra; Dgv, nr. 95; Dutt; DWH 1, p. 396-399; Dy, p. 206-208; Gul; HB; HK; Kav; KB 1, p. 677-682; MW; Na 1, nr. 129; Nadk. 1, nr. 1656; PA 1, 4, p. 19-33; PW; V 9, p. 100; Vśs) = M. OLEIFERA LAM. (AFM 1, p. 91-93; Chopra; KB 1, p. 677-682; Na 1, nr. 129; Nadk. 1, nr. 1656; PA 1, 4, p. 19-33) = HYPERANTHERA MORINGA VAHL (Ainslie 1, p. 175-177; HK) [= H. MORINGA WILLD.] (Dutt; Kav; Roxb., p. 360) = H. MORINGA (Nadk. 1, nr. 1656; Vśs; Wise);

(2) MORINGA MORINGA (LINN.) MILLSP. = GUILANDINA MORINGA LINN. (Avk; Nadk. 1, nr. 1656);

(3) MORINGA CONCANENSIS NIMMO EX DALZ. ET GIBS. (see Bpn, p. 340; Chopra : *śvetaśigru*; Dgv, nr. 95; KB 1, p. 682-683 : *tiktaśigru*, *madhuśigru*, *śvetaśigru*; Na 1, nr. 129 : *kaṭuśigru*; Nadk. 1, nr. 1655 : used as a substitute; PA 1, 4, p. 19 : *madhuśigru*; V 10, p. 1).

śirīṣa

(1) ALBIZZIA LEBBEK BENTH. (AFM 1, p. 19-25; Avk: *pītaśirīṣa*; Bpn, p. 518; Chopra; Dgv, nr. 132; Dutt; DWH 1, p. 561-563; Gul; HB; HK; IRM 1, p. 43; Kav; KB 2, p. 936-939; Na 1, nr. 187; Nadk. 1, nr. 91 : *pītaśirīṣa*; PA 1, 3, p. 1-20; V 10, p. 10; Vśs; Watt CP, p. 45) = MIMOSA SIRISSA ROXB. (AFM 1, p. 19; Dutt; HK; Roxb., p. 417; Vśs) = ACACIA SIRISSA BUCH.-HAM. (HK; MW; PW; Wise) = A. LEBBECK WILLD. (Vśs) = A. SPECIOSA WILLD. (AFM 1, p. 19; Avk; Nadk. 1, nr. 17);

(2) ALBIZZIA ODORATISSIMA BENTH. (Bpn, p. 518 : *kālaśirīṣa*; DWH 1, p. 561-563; KB 2, p. 939-940; PA 1, 3, p. 16-20; V 10, p. 12 : *pītaśirīṣa*) = MIMOSA ODORATISSIMA LINN.F. [= M. ODORATISSIMA ROXB.] (PA 1, 3, p. 16-20) = ACACIA ODORATISSIMA WILLD.;

(3) ALBIZZIA AMARA BOIVIN (Avk and Chopra : *kṛṣṇaśirīṣa*; DWH 1, p. 561-563; KB 2, p. 941-942 and Nadk. 1, nr. 89 : *kṛṣṇaśirīṣa*; PA 1, 3, p. 1) = MIMOSA AMARA ROXB. (KB 2, p. 941-942);

(4) ALBIZZIA PROCERA BENTH. (Avk and Bpn, p. 518 : *śvetaśirīṣa*; PA 1, 3, p. 1) = MIMOSA PROCERA ROXB.;

(5) ALBIZZIA MARGINATA MERRILL (PA 1, 3, p. 1-10) = MIMOSA MARGINATA LINDL.;

(6) A. STIPULATA BOIV. (AFM 1, p. 19-25; PA 1, 3, p. 1-10) = A. MARGINATA BUCH.-HAM. EX WALL.;

PA regards 5) and 6) as synonyms;

(7) A. JULIBRISSIN DURAZZ. (Avk : *raktaśirīṣa*) = MIMOSA KALKORA ROXB. (Avk).

śuṇṭhī : dried ginger

See : *ārdraka*.

śūkaśimbī = *kapikacchū*

śaivāla

(1) VALLISNERIA SPIRALIS LINN. (Bpn, p. 486-487; Dutt; Gul; HK; V 2, p. 105) [= BLYXA OCTANDRA RICH.] (Dutt; HK) [= B. SAIVALA SKUD.] (HK);

(2) BLYXA OCTANDRA PLANCH. EX THW. (MW and PW : B. OCTANDRA);

(3) B. ROXBURGHII RICH. = VALLISNERIA OCTANDRA ROXB. (Wise) = [V. OCTANDRA WILLD.] (Roxb., p. 711, who refers to Jones, As. Res. 4, p. 275; see Hooker 5, p. 660-661);

(4) B. GRIFFITHII PLANCH. (Hooker 5, p. 661, who refers to Jones, As. Res. 4, p. 275);

(5) ? B. SAIVALA STEUD. (meant by HK ? : B. SAIVALA SKUD.);

(6) CERATOPHYLLUM DEMERSUM LINN. (Bpn, p. 486-487; Chopra; KB 3, p. 2371-2372, = *jalanīlī*) = C. VERTICILLATUM ROXB. (KB 3, p. 2371-2372);

(7) EICHHORNIA SPECIOSA KUNTH = E. CRASSIPES SOLMS (Bpn, p. 486-487);

(8) PISTIA STRATIOTES LINN. (Bpn, p. 486-487);

(9) = *jalanīlī* (Vśs, unidentified; see 6); it designates green algae acc. to G. P. Majumdar in The history of botany etc., Arch. intern. d'hist. des sc. 4, 1951, p. 105);

(10) = *padmakāṣṭha* (MW; PW);
(11) = *badara* (Vśs);
(12) moss (Gul; Kav).

śyāmā

(1) PANICUM COLONUM LINN. = P. FRUMENTACEUM ROXB. (Chopra; IRM 3, p. 125-126; KB 4, p. 2715) [= ECHINOCHLOA COLONA LINK VAR. FRUMENTACEA BLATTER ET MCCANN] (KB 4, p. 2715);
(2) P. CRUS-GALLI LINN. = ECHINOCHLOA FRUMENTACEA LINK (IRM 3, p. 125-126, considered as a synonym of P. FRUMENTACEUM ROXB.);
(3) SETARIA ITALICA BEAUV. = PANICUM ITALICUM LINN. (MW; PW);
(4) = *śyāmalatā* = *kṛṣṇasārivā* : ICHNOCARPUS FRUTESCENS R. BR. (DWH 2, p. 423-424; Kav; KB 2, p. 1591-1592; MW; PW) = ECHITES FRUTESCENS ROXB. (Kav; Roxb., p. 245);
(5) = *sārivā* : HEMIDESMUS INDICUS R. BR. (KB 3, p. 1596-1598; MW; PW);
(6) a) IPOMOEA TURPETHUM R. BR. (DWH 2, p. 527-530; HK; KB 3, p. 1730-1732; Vśs) = CONVOLVULUS TURPETHUM LINN. (HK; Kav; Vśs);
b) = *pālindhī*, an Ipomoea with dark flowers (PW);
(7) = *śiṃśapā* : DALBERGIA SISSOO ROXB. (Bpn, p. 522; KB 1, p. 818-819; PW; Vśs);
(8) AGLAIA ROXBURGHIANA MIQ. (Vśs : = *priyaṅgu*);
(9) A. DIEPENHORSTII MIQ. = A. ODORATISSIMA BLUME (KB 1, p. 550-551 : *śyāmā* = *gundrā* = *priyaṅgu*);
(10) = *gundrā*, name of several plants (MW; PW; Vśs);
(11) a dark type of *punarnavā* (*nīlapunarnavā*) (PW; Vśs);
(12) = *dūrvā* : CYNODON DACTYLON (LINN.) PERS. [Intern. Code] (KB 4, p. 2689-2691; PW; Vśs);
(13) = *nīlī* (KB 1, p. 712-714);
(14) HIBISCUS ABELMOSCHUS LINN. (PW : = *kastūrī*; Vśs : = *latākastūrī*);
(15) CRINUM ZEYLANICUM LINN. = AMARYLLIS ZEYLANICA LINN. (PW : = *kastūrī*);
(16) ROUREA SANTALOIDES WIGHT ET ARN. (KB 1, p. 684-685 and Vśs : *śyāmā* = *vṛddhadāraka*);
(17) GMELINA ASIATICA LINN. (Vśs : = *vṛddhadāraka*);
(18) ARGYREIA SPECIOSA SWEET (KB 3, p. 1707-1708 : *vṛddhadāraka*);
(19) = *somalatā* (PW):

a) Ruta graveolens Linn. (KB 1, p. 453-455; PW);
b) Sarcostemma brevistigma Wight et Arn. (KB 3, p. 1622-1623);

(20) = *vandā* : name of a great number of plants (PW; Vśs);
(21) = *kākajaṅghā* (Vśs; variously identified, but acc. to KB 1, p. 620-621 and Vśs : Leea hirta Banks ex Roxb.);
(22) = *vaṭapatrī* (PW, unidentified);
(23) = *ajaśṛṅgī* = *meṣaśṛṅgī* (Vśs);
(24) = *balā* : name of a number of plants (Vśs);
(25) = *śvāsā* (Vśs, unidentified);
(26) = *trikā* (Vśs, unidentified);
(27) = *bākucī* = *vākucī*, usually identified as Psoralea corylifolia Linn. (Vśs);
(28) = *kokilā* = *kākolī*, an unidentifiable plant (Vśs);
(29) = *guggulu* : Commiphora mukul Engl. (Vśs); see about the nomenclature : *agaru*;
(30) = *guḍūcī* (PW; Vśs : = *chinnā* = *guḍūcī*);
(31) = *harītakī* (Vśs);
(32) = *haridrā* (PW; Vśs);
(33) = *pippalī* (PW; Vśs);
(34) = *tulasī* (PW; Vśs);
(35) = the seeds of *padma* (PW; Vśs).

śyonāka

(1) Oroxylum indicum Vent. (Avk; Bpn, p. 284; Chopra; Dgv, nr. 237; Dutt; DWH 3, p. 15-20; HK; KB 3, p. 1839-1841; Nadk. 1, nr. 1770; PA 1, 2, p. 39-48; V 1, p. 80; Vśs) = Calosanthes indica Blume (Avk; Gul; HK; Kav; KB 3, p. 1839; Nadk. 1, nr. 1770; PA 1, 2, p. 41; Vśs) = Bignonia indica Linn. (Avk; Dutt; HK; Kav; MW; Nadk. 1, nr. 1770; PW; Roxb., p. 495; Vśs; Wise);
(2) = *lodhra* (Vśs).

satīna = *satīlā*

(1) Pisum sativum Linn. (Avk; Bpn, p. 648; Chopra; Dutt; DWH 1, p. 489; HK; KB 1, p. 772-773; Vśs);
(2) P. arvense Linn. (HK; MW; PW).

sarṣapa

(1) Brassica campestris Linn. (Bpn, p. 651; Dgm, p. 121; Gul;

HK; V 9, p. 97 : *gaurasarṣapa*; Vśs) [= B. CAMPESTRIS LINN. VAR. RAPA (LINN.) HARTM.] (Chopra : *kālasarṣapa*; KB 1, p. 165-166 : *kālasarṣapa*; Nadk. 1, nr. 376 : *raktasarṣapa*) (see Hooker 1, p. 156) [= B. CAMPESTRIS LINN. VAR. SARSON PRAIN] (Nadk. 1, nr. 376 : *raktasarṣapa*) (see Watt CP, p. 175-177) = B. RAPA LINN. (KB 1, p. 165-166) = SINAPIS GLAUCA ROXB. (HK; Nadk. 1, nr. 2306 : *raktasarṣapa*) = S. DICHOTOMA ROXB. EX FLEM. (Ainslie 1, p. 231; Avk; Nadk. 1, nr. 2306; Vśs; Wise);

(2) BRASSICA JUNCEA COSS. [= B. JUNCEA HOOK.F. ET THOMS.] (Dutt : *rājasarṣapa*; HK, = *rājikā*) (see Hooker 1, p. 157) = B. JUNCEA (Avk : *gaurasarṣapa*; Sanyal; Vśs, = *rājikā*) = SINAPIS JUNCEA LINN. (Avk; Nadk. 1, nr. 2307 : *rājasarṣapa* = *rājikā*; Vśs) = S. RAMOSA ROXB. EX FLEM. (Avk; Dutt; HK; Nadk. 1, nr. 2307) = S. CUNEIFOLIA ROXB. (Nadk. 1, nr. 2307) = S. RUGOSA ROXB. (Nadk. 1, nr. 2307);

(3) BRASSICA NIGRA KOCH (KB 1, p. 168-170 : *kṛṣṇa-*, *raktasarṣapa*; Nadk. 1, nr. 379) [= B. NIGRA LINN.] (Na 1, nr. 25) = B. NIGRA (Dgm, p. 121; Dgv, nr. 25; Nadk. 1, nr. 2307 : *rājasarṣapa* = *rājikā*; Vśs : *kṛṣṇasarṣapa*) = SINAPIS NIGRA LINN. (KB 1, p. 168-170) = S. ERYSIMOIDES ROXB. (KB 1, p. 168-170);

(4) ERUCA SATIVA MILLER [= E. SATIVA LAM.] (Avk; KB 1, p. 170-171) = E. SATIVA GARS. (KB 1, p. 170-171);

(5) PANICUM COLONUM LINN. (Wise).

sahakāra

A fragrant mango-tree, = *āmra*.

siddhārtha(ka)

(1) BRASSICA CAMPESTRIS LINN. (DWH 1, p. 122-129; Dy, p. 58; HK) [= B. CAMPESTRIS LINN. VAR. RAPA (LINN.) HARTM.] (KB 1, p. 165-166) (see Hooker 1, p. 156) = B. RAPA LINN. (KB 1, p. 165-166) = SINAPIS GLAUCA ROXB. (Dutt; HK);

(2) [BRASSICA ALBA RABENH.] (Nadk. 1, nr. 374) ? = B. ALBA BOISS. [? = B. ALBA HOOK.F. ET THOMS.] (see Hooker 1, p. 157; Watt CP, p. 176);

(3) B. NIGRA KOCH [= B. NIGRA LINN.] (Na 1, nr. 25) = SINAPIS NIGRA LINN.;

(4) BRASSICA JUNCEA COSS. = B. JUNCEA (HB);

(5) ERUCA SATIVA MILLER = E. SATIVA GARS. (KB 1, p. 170-171).

sumukha

(1) a) OCIMUM BASILICUM LINN. (HK) = O. ALBUM LINN. (HK);
b) [O. BASILICUM PILOSUM] (MW; PW);
(2) O. GRATISSIMUM LINN. (KB 3, p. 1965);
(3) a) a wild Ocimum (PW);
b) = *barbara* (PW);
c) a dark kind of *barbara* (Vśs);
d) = *vanabarbarī* (Vśs);
e) = *vanabarbarikā* (Ḍa. on Su.Sū. 38, 18 and Sū. 46, 221; Rn, *varga* 10, 88);
(4) = *kṣudratulasī* with white leaves (see *tulasī*) (Vśs);
(5) a kind of *parṇāsa* (Cakra on Ca.Sū. 27, 173);
(6) = *kaṭupatraka*: acc. to PW and Vśs: a) = *sitārjaka* (see *arjaka*), b) = *parpaṭa*;
(Aruṇa on A.h.Sū. 6, 106; Dn, *varga* 4, 57);
(7) = *rājikā* (Vśs; Ḍa. on Su.Sū. 38, 18).

surasa

(1) OCIMUM BASILICUM LINN. (KB 3, p. 1963; MW; PW);
(2) O. SANCTUM LINN. (KB 3, p. 1967; Vśs);
(3) = *parṇāsa* (Vśs);
(4) VITEX TRIFOLIA LINN. (Chopra; KB 3, p. 1936-1937; Vśs : = *sindhuvāra*; Wise);
(5) V. NEGUNDO LINN. (KB 3, p. 1937-1940; MW; PW);
(6) CYMBOPOGON SCHOENANTHUS SPRENG. = ANDROPOGON SCHOENANTHUS LINN. (= *bhūstṛṇa*) (DWH 3, p. 557; MW; PW);
(7) a) = *gandhatṛṇa* (MW; PW);
b) = *sugandhatṛṇa* (Vśs);
c) a fragrant kind of *bhūtṛṇa* = *bhūstṛṇa* (Vśs); this may be CYMBOPOGON CITRATUS STAPF (see *bhūstṛṇa*);
(8) = *surabhimallikā* (PW); this may be some species of Jasminum;
(9) the resin of CEIBA PENTANDRA GAERTN. (*śvetaśālmalī*) = GOSSAMPINUS RUMPHII SCHOTT ET ENDL. (MW; PW);
(10) the resin of BOMBAX CEIBA LINN. (*śālmalī*) (Vśs : = *mocarasa* = *śālmalīveṣṭa*;
(11) = *kaṇaguggulu* (Vśs) = a) *śvetajīraka* (see *jīraka*) (Vśs); b) a partic. kind of *guggulu* (Vśs);
guggulu usually designates the gum of COMMIPHORA MUKUL ENGL.;

(12) CINNAMOMUM TAMALA T. NEES ET EBERM. (KB 3, p. 2146-2147);

(13) [C. ZEYLANICUM BREYN] (see *tvac*) (KB 3, p. 2149-2150);

(14) Cassia-bark (MW; PW);

(15) myrrh (MW; PW).

sauvīra(ka)

See *karkandhŭ, kola, badara.*

(1) ZIZYPHUS SATIVA GAERTN. (Dgv, nr. 84, = *rājakola* = *rāja-badara*; V 1, p. 163) = Z. VULGARIS LAM. (Dgv, nr. 84; V 1, p. 163);

(2) a) = *kola* (HK);

b) = *bṛhadbadara* (Vśs);

J. J. Meyer, transl. Kauṭ., p. 141, note 8 : Gaṇ. explains that *kola* is the small, *badara* the large and *sauvīraka* the sweet jujube. Ḍa. on Su.Sū. 46, 139 : *badara* is large, *kola* is of a moderate size and *karkandhu* is small; *sauvīra* is the largest (among the jujube-fruits) and is, both ripe and unripe, sweet.

spṛkkā

(1) TRIGONELLA CORNICULATA LINN. (Dutt; HB; HK; MW; PW);

(2) MELILOTUS OFFICINALIS LAM. (Gul) = TRIFOLIUM OFFICINALE LINN. (Bpn, p. 265 : acc. to some);

(3) ANISOMELES MALABARICA R. BR. EX SIMS (Bpn, p. 265 : acc. to others);

(4) [MARSILEA QUADRIFOLIATA LINN.] (Bpn, p. 265);

(5) MIMOSA PUDICA LINN. (KB 2, p. 915-917; PW; Vśs).

hapuṣā

(1) a) black stalks like those of black pepper, possessed of an aromatic smell (Dutt; HK; Kav);

b) name of a partic. substance, said to be of a long form and black colour, and smelling like raw meat or fish; it is of two kinds (MW);

c) a partic. plant of two kinds, smelling like fish; the fruits of one kind resemble those of the *aśvattha* (PW);

d) *hapuṣā* : an article of trade that is of a black colour and of a long form like the stalks of black pepper (*marīca*) (Vśs); *havuṣā* : a fruit of that name; it is of two kinds; one is like a fish and of a musty smell; the other resembles *aśvattha* fruits and smells like fish; their qualities are the same (Vśs);

(2) JUNIPERUS COMMUNIS LINN. (Bpn, p. 50-51; Chopra; Dgv, nr. 302; Gul; KB 3, p. 2380-2382; Nadk. 1, nr. 1383);

(3) TAMARIX GALLICA LINN. (Bpn, p. 51 : acc. to some);

(4) FLUGGEA LEUCOPYRUS WILLD. (Bpn, p. 51 : acc. to some);

(5) SPHAERANTHUS INDICUS LINN. (AFM 1, p. 115-119) [= S. HIRTUS BURM.] (ibid.) = S. HIRTUS WILLD. = S. MOLLIS ROXB. (ibid.);

(6) S. AFRICANUS LINN. (ibid. : *śvetahapuṣā*);

(7) PIPER NIGRUM LINN. (Nadk. 1, nr. 1929);

(8) THEVETIA NEREIFOLIA JUSS. EX STEUD. (Nadk. 1, nr. 2466) = CERBERA THEVETIA LAM. (ibid.);

(9) NERIUM ODORUM [SOLAND. IN] AIT. (Nadk. 1, nr. 2466).

haridrā

(1) CURCUMA LONGA LINN. (AFM 1, p. 59-60; Ainslie 1, p. 454-455; Bpn, p. 114; Chopra; DWH 3, p. 407-414; IRM 2, p. 402-405; KB 4, p. 2423-2426; Nadk. 1, nr. 750; PW; Watt CP, p. 445-449) [= C. LONGA ROXB.] (Dutt; Dy, p. 764-768; Gul; HK; Roxb., p. 11) = C. LONGA (Avk; Dgv, nr. 304; MW; V 10, p. 58; Vśs);

(2) C. AROMATICA SALISB. (*vanaharidrā*) (Avk; Bpn, p. 117; Chopra; Dgv, nr. 310; Dutt; DWH 3, p. 396-398; KB 4, p. 2419-2420; Nadk. 1, nr. 748; Vśs) = C. ZEDOARIA ROXB. (Dutt; Vśs);

(3) C. AMADA ROXB. (Avk : *āmraharidrā*; *karpūraharidrā* : Chopra; IRM 2, p. 401; KB 4, p. 2422-2423; Nadk. 1, nr. 746) [= C. MATICO] (Nadk. 1, nr. 746);

(4) ZINGIBER ZERUMBET ROSC. EX SM. (KB 4, p. 2438-2439 : *karpūraharidrā*);

(5) HEDYCHIUM SPICATUM SM. (Avk; KB 4, p. 2430-2431 : *amlaharidrā*);

(6) = *dāruharidrā*.

harītakī

(1) TERMINALIA CHEBULA RETZ. (Ainslie 2, p. 128-129; Avk; Bpn, p. 7; Chopra; Dgv, nr. 148; Dutt; DWH 2, p. 1-5; Dy, p. 317-320; Gul; HB; HK; Kav; KB 2, p. 1020-1023; MW; Na 1, nr. 206; Nadk. 1, nr. 2451; PA 1, 7, p. 92-105; PW; Sanyal; V 10, p. 50; Vśs) [= T. CHEBULA WILLD.] (Ainslie 1, p. 237-239; Roxb., p. 381) = T. RETICULATA ROTH (PA 1, 7, p. 102) = T. ARATA BUCH.-HAM. EX G. DON (PA 1, 7, p. 102) = T. TOMENTELLA KURZ (PA 1, 7, p. 102) [= T.

MYROBALANUS CITRINA KOEN.] (PA 1, 7, p. 102) [= MELANOXYLON CADIKAMARUM KOEN.] (PA 1, 7, p. 102) = MYROBALANUS CHEBULA GAERTN.;

(2) T. CITRINA ROXB. EX FLEM. (Bpn, p. 7) = MYROBALANUS CITRINA GAERTN.; see about the varieties of *harītakī* : HB, part 2, v. 923-925 and p. 166-167, footnote 441; PA 1, 7, p. 98-99.

hareṇu

(1) a) PISUM SATIVUM LINN. (Ainslie 1, p. 297-299; Bpn, p. 648; Gul; KB 1, p. 772-773; V 8, p. 12; Vśs : = *kalāya*);
b) MW and PW : a kind of pea which is slightly globular;
(2) a) PIPER AURANTIACUM WALL. (= *reṇukā*) (Dutt; HB; HK; Kav);
b) a partic. drug (MW; PW);
(3) = *bṛhaccaṇaka* (see *caṇaka*) (Vśs);
(4) = *parpaṭaka* (Vśs).

hiṅgu

(1) FERULA ASA-FOETIDA LINN. (Ainslie 1, p. 20; Dutt; Gul; HK; Kav; MW; Nadk. 1, nr. 1023; PW; Vśs) = SCORODOSMA FOETIDUM BUNGE (Dy, p. 385-389);

(2) F. FOETIDA REGEL (Avk; Bpn, p. 41; Chopra; DWH 2, p. 147-152 : used as a substitute; Nadk. 1, nr. 1023; Sanyal; Watt CP, p. 534-535) = F. SCORODOSMA BENTLEY ET TRIM. (Nadk. 1, nr. 1023);

(3) F. ALLIACEA BOISS. (Bpn, p. 41; Chopra; Dutt; DWH 2, p. 141-147; Dy, p. 381-385; HK; Nadk. 1, nr. 1022; Vśs; Watt CP, p. 534);

(4) F. NARTHEX BOISS. (Bpn, p. 41; Chopra; Dgv, nr. 172; Dy, p. 385-389; KB 2, p. 1216-1218; Nadk. 1, nr. 1023; V 10, p. 64) = NARTHEX ASAFOETIDA FALC. (KB 2, p. 1216-1218; V 10, p. 64);

(5) GARDENIA LUCIDA ROXB. (KB 2, p. 1278-1279 : *nāḍīhiṅgu*, *hiṅgunāḍikā*);

(6) MELIA AZADIRACHTA LINN. = AZADIRACHTA INDICA A. JUSS. (KB 1, p. 536-541).

hrīvera

(1) PAVONIA ODORATA WILLD. (Avk; Bpn, p. 237; Chopra; Dutt; DWH 1, p. 224; Dy, p. 109; HB; HK; Kav; KB 1, p. 323-324; MW : acc. to some; Nadk. 1, nr. 1822; Vśs);

(2) a kind of ANDROPOGON (MW; PW).

APPENDIX FIVE

Medical annotations

The interpretation of Āyurvedic Sanskrit texts from a medical point of view is a field that has been neglected by non-Indian scholars. Many Indian authors, on the other hand, readily equate disorders described in the Sanskrit texts with syndromes and diseases recognized in modern medicine. As I shall point out, many of these identifications are doubtful.

As soon as one makes any attempt to connect the clusters of symptoms enumerated in the Sanskrit texts with entities called syndromes and diseases in Western medicine, a great number of problems emerges. First of all it may be useful to stress that the course of a disease is thought of in Indian medicine as a continuous process of development. A disease is something that gradually is made manifest. Prodromes (*pūrvarūpa*) develop into full-fledged symptoms (*rūpa*). Secondary affections (*upadrava*) are consequences of the basic morbid process. At the end of this process recovery takes place or fatal signs (*ariṣṭa*) appear, foreboding death. The stages of this evolutionary process are delineated. Each stage is characterized by a cluster of signs. In many cases the enumeration of these signs occurs in the form of verses, more easy to remember than statements in prose. These verses, however, do not allow free presentation of the characteristics, in accordance with their importance; so it is inadmissible to regard the sign heading the list as the central one. Secondly one should always remember that the listed signs depend on the morbific entity (*doṣa*) or group of morbific entities which is thought to be involved. Each of these is provided with a fixed set of qualities and effects. Analysis of the groups of symptoms may therefore proceed from within, by determining which of the components of the morbific entity or entities have been selected in a particular disease. In order to achieve this aim the Indian medical system must be mastered. In addition, the medical texts must be studied comparatively, because the order of the symptoms, their number and the terms which are employed vary from one treatise to another.

If one proceeds in this way the problem remains as to what extent empirical considerations and actual observations were important in delimiting diseases and establishing their symptoms and course. On reading the texts one cannot help receiving the impression that the diseases distinguished and the symptoms enumerated are not based only on theoretical considerations, but also on observation of facts. In many cases, however, it is difficult to ascertain which signs may have been met with in patients and which are stated for the sake of theory. To this general rule there is one exception. It is repeatedly observed by commentators that one or more of the symptoms of a particular disease does not fit into the theoretical frame, but is nevertheless present. Such a symptom is called *vikṛtiviṣamasamavāyārabdha* (see Madhukośa on 2, 14-15ab); this difficult term expresses that the symptom referred to cannot be explained theoretically as an effect of one of the morbific entities involved. This type of symptoms may be considered to have been really observed.

It seems therefore legitimate to try to find out how far the described syndromes correspond to real diseases which may have been encountered by the ancient Indian physicians. In the annotations which follow I make a first attempt in this direction. It should be borne in mind, however, that it is only possible to put forward a number of suggestions, because I have no personal experience in the field of tropical medicine.

Chapter 2

In Indian medicine fever is regarded as the principal disease and is dealt with first. It is designated as *jvara* in medical treatises; the corresponding term in older texts (Atharvaveda) is *takman*. (See about *takman* : Filliozat, The classical doctrine, p. 119-121; Grohmann, Indische Studien 9, p. 381-423; Karambelkar, The Atharva-Veda and the Āyur-Veda, p. 278-291; Müller, Der takman des Atharva-veda, Artibus Asiae 6, 1937, p. 230-242; id., Wörterheft, nr. 94, p. 101-102; see about *jvara* several publications by Müller : Grundlagen, p. 72-73; Eigenwertungen, p. 27-29; Wörterheft, nr. 92, p. 100-101; Ueber verschiedene Ergebnisse, p. 111-112).

The concept of fever is broad and includes fever arising from the smell of herbs (2, 28), emotional states (2, 28-29), magic (2, 29) and possession by evil spirits (2, 30). The set of its prodromes (2, 4-5) resembles the symptoms encountered when the body temperature is rising. The general signs of fever (2, 3) are not typical of all fevers, as already observed by Vijayarakṣita. The descriptions of fever by wind, etc. (2, 8-17) are vague and may include a number of infectious diseases, such as enteric fevers and brucellosis. Chakraberty nevertheless equates fever by wind with the cerebrospinal type of pernicious aestivo-autumnal fever (p. 212), fever by bile with the bilious remittent type of subtertian malaria and with blackwater fever, also known as malarial haemoglobinuria (p. 210 and 213), and fever by phlegm with influenza (p. 213). The general picture of fever by concerted action (2, 18-23) is complicated. This *saṃnipātajvara* is often said to be typhoid (Yādavaśarman; Dīnānāth; Chakraberty, p. 215; Chakraberty takes typhoid in such a wide sense that it includes all the eruptive fevers); Filliozat (BSHM 30, 1936, p. 21-29) interprets *saṃnipātajvara* as "les états typhoïdes et comateux", though it has more features in common with louse-borne typhus or a combination of relapsing fever and typhus (the latter two frequently coexist). The many types of fever by concerted action described in the texts (Madhukośa on 2, 18-23 and the notes) are for the greater part not clear, so it is only possible to put forward suggestions as to some of these. The fever called *abhinyāsa* (the "depressing" fever) or *hataujas* (the fever "in which the vital fluid has been damaged") may be viewed as including a.o. uraemic states. A cardio-pulmonary syndrome may be designated by *vibhu* (the "all-pervading" or "powerful" fever), an affection of the lungs and the liver (the pulmonary form of subtertian malaria ?) by *phalgu* (the meaning of this word is not clear : reddish ?, weak ?); *makarī* (named after the *makara*, an aquatic animal, or after the ocean, sometimes called *makarin*) may be some form of cystopyelonephritis; *visphuraka* (the "quivering" fever) is not clear, nor the types called *śīghrakārin* (the "swiftly acting" fever) and *kapphaṇa* (the meaning of this word is not known). In many texts each of the thirteen fevers by concerted action has its own name; though the diseases described escape a reliable identification, it may be useful to add some notes on the meaning of their names. *babhru* is called after the animal bearing this name, which is a mongoose, or after the colour of its coat, which is deep-brown; the meaning of *bhallu* is not clear; *āśukārin* is "quickly acting"; *kampana* means "trembling"; *yāmya* may be connected with Yama, the god of death, and mean "deadly"; *pākala* may be related to *pāka*, "inflammation"; *krakaca* means "saw"; *vaidārika* is the fever that "tears asunder"; *karkoṭaka* is the name of a plant and the fever called thus may derive its appellation from the rough surface of the fruits of this plant; *saṃmohaka* is named thus after one of its symptoms, *saṃmoha*, i.e. "complete mental confusion"; the term *kūṭapākala* suggests a fever with the highest degree (*kūṭa* is the top of a mountain) of inflammation (*pāka*); *śītagātra* designates that the limbs feel cold in this disease; *tandrika* is related to *tandrā*, which means "lassitude", *pralāpaka* and *pralāpin* to *pralāpa*, "confused speech", *raktaṣṭhīvin* to *raktaṣṭhīvana*, "spitting of blood"; *bhugnanetra* and *bhugnadṛś* indicate that the eyes are distorted (*bhugna*); *jihvaka* points to the prominent part of the affection of the tongue (*jihvā*) in the disease described; *saṃdhiga* and *saṃdhika* indicate that the joints (*saṃdhi*) are the main seat of the disease described; *antaka* means "deadly"; *rugdāha* is called thus after the painful (*ruj*) and burning (*dāha*) sensations experienced in this fever; *cittabhrama* points to the important position of mental confusion in the described syndrome; *karṇika* and *karṇaka* point to the ears (*karṇa*) as the special seat of the affection; *kaṇṭhakubja* is a fever in which the throat (*kaṇṭha*) is "crooked" (*kubja*); *kumbhīpāka* may be called thus because inflammation (*pāka*) of a cavity (*kumbha* means a jar), especially the nasal cavity, is present in it; *prorṇunāva* is unclear (the verb *pra-ūrṇu-* means "to cover"); *antardāha* designates a sensation of inner burning as the chief symptom; *daṇḍapāta* is obscure, literally meaning "a blow with a stick"; *eṇīdāha* is a difficult term, connected with the burning sensation (*dāha*) and the feeling as if animals (*hariṇa* can be a synonym of *eṇa*) move about on one's body, occurring as symptoms in this fever; *hāridraka* points to the turmeric-yellow (*hāridra*) colour of the skin, etc. in this disease; *ajaghoṣa* indicates that the patient can only produce sounds (*ghoṣa*) like a he-goat (*aja*); *bhūtahāsa*, meaning "the laughter (*hāsa*) of an evil spirit (*bhūta*)", emphasizes an important feature of the illness; *yantrāpīḍa* is also a descriptive term, meaning "painful oppression (*āpīḍa*) by a mechanical contrivance (*yantra*)"; *saṃnyāsa* usually designates a complete loss of consciousness, but is employed in a different sense to describe the fever called thus; *saṃśoṣin* usually means "completely desiccating", but has a different sense in this fever. The thirteen fevers by concerted action are not uniformly described in the various treatises and in some cases there must have been confusion of particular types. The fever called *krakaca* in the Kāśyapasaṃhitā goes by the name of *pākala* in Vaṅgasena's treatise and the Bhāvaprakāśa; the reverse is true as well; *pākala* of the Kāśyapasaṃhitā corresponds to *krakaca* in Vaṅgasena and the Bhāvaprakāśa.

The swelling at the root of the ear arising at the end of a fever by concerted action (2, 25) may be a parotitis, as Grohmann (Indische Studien 9, p. 398) already observed. Parotitis is frequent as a complication of louse-borne typhus; it may also occur in severe cases of scrub typhus, in louse-borne relapsing fever, etc.

In Indian medicine the concept of irregular fever (*viṣamajvara*) means that a fever which has been present for a certain number of days breaks off to make its reappearance at a later point of time (2, 31cd-32ab). It does not indicate that the fever presents an irregular course; on the contrary, it presents itself, as a rule, at regular intervals of time. *viṣamajvara* should not be translated by malarial fever (Jolly, Medicin, p. 72), nor by malarial remittent fever (Yādavaśarman and Dīnānāth), firstly because not all irregular fevers are malarial in origin and secondly because it is impossible to determine whether the fevers described are of a remittent or intermittent type. Continuous fever (*saṃtatajvara*) (2, 34) lasts for fixed periods of time, a statement which may be based, at least partially, on experience; leptospirosis, also called seven-day fever, is one of the diseases which may be designated in this way, though one or more relapses occur in it. Double quotidian fever (*satataka*) (2, 35) is not a continuous fever (as erroneously indicated by Yādavaśarman); its inclusion in the group of irregular fevers proves that the group as a whole cannot be regarded as forms of malaria. Double quotidian fever may be identified as the typical fever of leishmaniasis (kạla-azar) (Chakraberty p. 211; Sudarśanaśāstrī); the initial fever presents as a rule a double remission in the twenty-four hours. This only occurs in one other tropical fever, subtertian malaria (by Plasmodium falciparum) : a double crisis may occur in this disease, with a drop of temperature — a false crisis — when the fever has attained its apparent fastigium, followed by a fresh rise, which is then succeeded by a true crisis; this phenomenon has been attributed to the presence of two generations of parasites in the blood, one of which matures somewhat later than the other. Quotidian fever (*anyedyuṣka*) (2, 35) is found in malaria and in other diseases. It occurs when there is a double infection with two maturation cycles of Plasmodium vivax or P. ovale; such double infections usually synchronize within a week and then follow the classic tertian pattern. A quotidian fever may also arise in subtertian malaria; in enteric fevers the temperature is sometimes of an intermittent, quotidian type; in many other disorders fever of a quotidian type occurs, resembling malaria : pyelonephritis, cholecystitis, amoebic abscess of the liver, etc. Tertian fever (*tṛtīyaka*) (2, 36) occurs in tertian malaria by Plasmodium vivax or P. ovale. In enteric fevers the temperature may show a perfect tertian periodicity throughout; this has also been seen in meningococcal septicaemia. Quartan fever (*caturthaka*) (2, 36) is found in quartan malaria from Plasmodium malariae. In enteric fevers again there may occur a perfect quartan periodicity, as well as in meningococcal septicaemia. Reversed quartan fever (*caturthakaviparyaya*) (2, 39), usually called double quartan fever (Yādavaśarman; Dīnānāth; Sudarśanaśāstrī) may be seen in multiple infection with Plasmodium malariae; the same applies to reversed tertian fever (*tṛtīyakaviparyaya*) (Madhukośa on 2, 39), sometimes called malignant tertian (Dīnānāth). The type of fever called *vātabalāsaka* (2, 40), incorrectly identified as influenza by Chakraberty (p. 207), looks like a condition that may arise from a number of disorders, e.g. cirrhosis of the liver with advanced hepatic failure and ancyclostomiasis with chronic anaemia. (See about *balāsa* and *vātabalāsaka* : Grohmann, Indische Studien 9, p. 395-401; Filliozat, The classical doctrine, p. 117-119; Jolly, Medicin, p. 72; Karambelkar, p. 214-227; Müller, Wörterheft, nr. 141, p. 119). The fever that goes by the name *pralepaka* (2, 41) may be connected with chronic pulmonary tuberculosis; it has been identified with pneumonia (Jolly, Medicin, p. 73; Chakraberty, p. 206) and is sometimes called hectic fever (Yādavaśarman, Dīnānāth), which is probably inadequate.

The regular course of a fever, with shivering at the beginning, followed by a sensation of warmth, was well known in Indian medicine (2, 45). An aberrant type is also described, in which a peripheral vascular failure develops (2, 46); this occurs in algid malaria, the prognosis of which is bad (2, 46).

The strong fever making partings in the hair of the head (2, 67cd-68ab) may designate a fever with drenching nocturnal sweats, as seen for example in amoebic abscess of the liver.

Chapter 3

The concept of diarrhoea (*atīsāra*) in Āyurveda is theoretically based on an increase of the watery element in the body, leading to a flow (*sāra*) of faecal matter beyond the proper measure (3, 4). In practice this does not work out. The stools need not be liquid in order to classify the disorder as a case of diarrhoea (3, 6). More importance is attached to altered qualities of the stools generally and a raised frequency of their evacuation (3, 7-8). A series of factors is enumerated by which diarrhoea may come about (3, 13). Some of these are really elements furthering the appearance of intestinal disorders : a faultive diet, uncooked food, corrupted water, intestinal parasites, etc. The connection between fear and diarrhoea is well known. Other facts are more difficult of evaluation. The diarrhoea caused by grief, as described in Indian medicine, presents peculiar characteristics. The drinking of a too great quantity of water may have been associated with diarrhoea on account of Indian medical theory. Stagnation of the natural urges as a cause of diarrhoea may refer to the phenomenon that diarrhoea is preceded by constipation in many cases, which was known to the ancient Indian physicians (3, 5).

The frequent evacuation, accompanied by pain, of small amounts of faecal matter (3, 6) usually points to a diarrhoea originating in the colon; this would agree with the Indian view in which the third and last stage of the digestive process is thought to be dominated by wind. The diarrhoea from bile (3, 7ab) is of a composite nature. The diarrhoea from phlegm (3, 7cd) may designate e.g. the various types of the malabsorption syndrome, in which stools of a light colour are evacuated. In the most acute and fulminating forms of bacillary dysentery the mucus in the stools may be mingled with a large amount of altered blood and the evacuations come to resemble "meat washings"; this agrees remarkably well with the severe character of the disease described in 3, 8. The diarrhoea from grief (3, 9-10) is an indistinct entity; the stools resemble *kākaṇantī*, i.e. *guñjā* seeds (the seeds of Abrus precatorius Linn.), which are usually bright scarlet and black. The statement that floating stools are characteristic of maturity (3, 12-13), i.e. of a completed digestive process, is remarkable, because stools of this kind are seen in all disorders associated with steatorrhoea. Many types of diarrhoea were regarded as incurable (3, 14-17); the enumerated characteristics of the stools, considered to indicate a bad prognosis, are not typical of specific diseases; the diarrhoea in which the stools resemble "meat washings" (compare 3, 8) recurs again here; mature *jambū* fruits (Syzygium cumini Skeels) are black and juicy and stools resembling these may point to any disorder in which loss of blood occurs into the gastro-intestinal tract; offensive stools, smelling of decomposing blood, are e.g. evacuated in amoebic dysentery, etc. Diarrhoea caused by some intercurrent disease, e.g. dysentery, has often been the cause of death in patients with a chronic debilitating illness (3, 19).

The bloody diarrhoea, described as related to that caused by bile (3, 20) appears as a secondary development of intestinal disorders, in which bleeding from the distal part of the bowels may occur. The disease, called *pravāhikā*, is usually identified as dysentery (Jolly, Medicin, p. 75; Yādavaśarman; Dīnānāth); the description (3, 21) points to disorders with irritation of the large bowel, including the bacillary dysenteries. In severe cases of diarrhoea, especially in cholera, the secretion of urine may be suppressed; recovery is marked by the passage of some turbid, highly coloured urine, followed by a "critical diuresis" (3, 23).

Chapter 4

The *grahaṇī* disease is a chronic diarrhoea; the term should not be rendered by sprue (Yādavaśarman; Dīnānāth), because a chronic diarrhoea may occur in many disorders. The imaginary organ in which the disease finds its origin is the *grahaṇī*, the seat of the digestive fire (Hariprapanna, Rasayogasāgara, *upodghāta* p. 143, equates it with the mucous membrane of the small intestine, which is not supported by the texts and an inadmissible modern interpretation). An increased frequency of evacuation, accompanied by pain, with varying characters of the stools, is typical of the disease (4, 2-3). Its prodromes mainly consist of signs indicating a faulty digestion (4, 4).

Several disorders may be comprised by the *grahaṇī* disease, such as: tropical sprue, pellagra, ancylostomiasis, amoebic dysentery, chronic bacillary dysentery, tuberculous enteritis, etc. Some of the symptoms enumerated are frequently met with in some of these diseases: fermenting stools (4, 6) in tropical sprue and pellagra, a ravenous appetite (4, 8) in ancylostomiasis, etc.

Chapter 5

Haemorrhoids (*arśas*, pl. *arśāṃsi*) arise from the three anal folds, according to Indian medical tradition (5, 1; Madhukośa; notes). It is not at all clear what is meant by these folds. Hariprapanna (Rasayogasāgara, *upodghāta* p. 144) identifies them as the plicae transversae recti, which disagrees with their description in the texts, because the two or three transverse folds are found higher up in the pars ampullaris recti. Kutumbiah (p. 31) calls them spiral grooves, which again is contradicted by the texts, in which it is distinctly stated that the folds are structures with a lateral elevation. The anulus haemorrhoidalis may be one of the folds, but the number three defies explanation, unless the musculus sphincter ani internus and externus are also regarded as folds. The series of symptoms described as accompanying haemorrhoids and the disorders enumerated as their sequelae (5, 12-15) may really be syndromes in which haemorrhoids can develop secondarily.

Conditions furthering the appearance of haemorrhoids are characterized by an increased hydrostatic pressure in the portal venous system (portal hypertension). The most frequent cause of such a condition in tropical and subtropical countries will be cirrhosis of the liver and primary hepatic carcinoma. Some of the mentioned signs may point to cirrhosis : patients with cirrhosis seem likely to develop tuberculosis and pneumonia (5, 13); cough and shortness of breath occur in cardiac cirrhosis (5, 13); in biliary cirrhosis many patients develop a striking melanotic pigmentation of the skin (5, 14); cirrhosis of the liver leads to splenomegaly (5, 15).

The ancient Indian physicians, unable to discern the underlying causes of the appearance of haemorrhoids, tried to make a classification based on their form and other qualities. Some additional information will help the reader to understand what is said in the text. The fruits of *bimbī* (Coccinia indica Wight et Arn.) are bright scarlet berries; because the lips of women are often compared to them, a synonym of *bimbī* is *oṣṭhopamaphalā*, i.e. (the plant), the fruits of which resemble lips. A *kharjūra* fruit is a date. The fruit of *karkandhū*, as well as of *kola* and *badarī*, is some kind of jujube (the fruit of species of Zizyphus); jujubes are drupes, varying in form, size and colour, with a stone in their interior. The fruits of *kārpāsī* and *vanakārpāsī* (species of Gossypium) are capsules; the seeds are clothed with cotton wool. The form of the flowers of the *kadamba* is explained in the Madhukośa (and in one of my notes). *siddhārthaka* and *sarṣapa* are kinds of mustard seed. *gojihvā* is the name of some plants with prickly leaves (see App. 4). The fruits of *karkoṭa* (Momordica cochinchinensis Spreng.) are cucumber-like, but ovate and pointed, and are covered with conical points.

One of the described syndromes in which haemorrhoids appear (5, 16-18) bears some resemblance to clonorchiasis (an infection with a trematode, Clonorchis sinensis, inhabiting the bile-ducts); in this disease fever occurs and a chronic diarrhoea is established with recurring attacks of jaundice; other hepatic disorders associated with diarrhoea and jaundice may be involved as well.

The signs of haemorrhoids from phlegm (5, 19-23) cannot be attributed to particular diseases with any certainty, though one may think e.g. of lymphogranuloma venereum. The qualities of the haemorrhoids described are clear for the greater part. Some additional remarks may be useful. The fruits of *karīra* (species of Capparis) are fleshy berries, with many seeds, imbedded in pulp. The fruits of *panasa* (Artocarpus integrifolia Linn.f.) are very large; they contain reniform seeds about the size of a nutmeg, enveloped in a thin, smooth, leathery sheath and lodged within the fleshy eatable part of the fruit. A *vaṃśa* sprout is a bamboo sprout. The seeds of *guñjā* (5, 25) (Abrus precatorius Linn.) are bright scarlet and black. The young shoots of the *vaṭa* (5, 25) (Ficus benghalensis Linn.) are pubescent.

Some of the syndromes described suggest carcinoma of the rectum or colon (5, 25-27ab; 5, 27cd-28) and chronic hepatic disorders (5, 29-30).

The ancient Indians regarded haemorrhoids as a manifestation of grave disorders, probably rightly so in many cases, for they were aware of the fact that haemorrhoids may be associated with serious diseases, as appears from the list of prodromes (5, 31-32) and other statements (5. 33-34).

The prognosis of haemorrhoids was thought to be related to their localization (5, 35-37). The conditions in which haemorrhoids have a bad prognosis (5, 39-41) resemble those found in advanced hepatic failure by cardiac cirrhosis, biliary cirrhosis, etc., accompanied by many symptoms caused by the primary disease and by a great number of complications.

The growths occurring on the penis (5, 42), included in the concept of haemorrhoids, may be condylomata acuminata and those arising in the umbilical region (ibid.) mollusca contagiosa.

The polypous growths near the anus, called warts (*carmakīla*), cannot be identified. The disorders mentioned in the Ātaṅkadarpaṇa on 5, 44 are of various kinds; lesions destroying the penis or vulvar region occur in granuloma inguinale.

Chapter 6

In this chapter disturbances of the process of digestion are dealt with, apart from those, associated with a chronic diarrhoea, which belong to the domain of the disease of the *grahaṇī*. The disturbances described first consist of sluggishness of the (transforming) fire (6, 2-3) (*agnimāndya*; Yādavaśarman : dyspepsia; Dīnānāth : anorexia, hypochlorhydria and achylic dyspepsia; Sudarśanaśāstrī : dyspepsia) and other types of inadequacy of the (transforming) fire (6, 2-4), followed by the disorders of the process of disintegration (of the food) (6, 5-14) (*ajīrṇa*; Yādavaśarman : indigestion; Dīnānāth : dyspepsia, indigestion; Sudarśanaśāstrī : indigestion). Nothing definite can be said about the syndromes described; they consist of slight gastro-intestinal disturbances, usually called indigestion or dyspepsia, terms which have no sharply defined meaning, or are symptoms of some more serious disease, which may be of many kinds.

The serious illness called *viśūcī* or *viśūcikā* is usually equated with cholera (see Jolly, Medicin, p. 75; Chakraberty, p. 238; Yādavaśarman; Dīnānāth), though there are insufficient arguments for doing so. From the descriptions of *viśūcī* (6, 16-18) one may deduce that it is a grave disorder, mainly characterized by vomiting and diarrhoea. Many cases of cholera must have been diagnosed as *viśūcī*, but other diseases as well, such as the choleraic form of bacillary dysentery, choleraic and dysenteric forms of subtertian malaria, etc.

Two more syndromes are distinguished: intestinal inertia (6, 19-20) (*alasaka*) and retardation of evacuation (6, 21) (*vilambikā*). The disease called intestinal inertia suggests a variety of disorders, e.g. subacute and chronic colonic obstruction, ascites and peritonitis of whatever origin, etc. Retardation of evacuation points to a chronic obstruction of the bowels, as seen in carcinoma of the colon.

About the secondary affections of *viśūcī* (6, 25) I want to observe that none of these is characteristic of cholera; insomnia is a feature in enteric fevers and dysuria may be a distressing symptom in bacillary dysentery.

Chapter 7

Though the "worms" described in this chapter are mainly parasites, they are called worms in the translation, because the range of the word *kṛmi* or *krimi* by which they are designated is larger than the meaning of the term "parasite"; moreover, the ancient Indians did not clearly distinguish between the several phyla of invertebrates and the developmental stages of many of these animals.

All the texts consulted enumerate twenty kinds of worms, with the exception of the Hāritasaṃhitā, which counts only thirteen different types. External and internal worms are distinguished in Ca., A.h., A.s. and Hā., not in Su. and Bhe. The internal ones are thought to arise from blood, phlegm and faecal matter in Ca., A.h. and A.s., while in Su. all the worms are regarded as arising from these substances. Their classification and names agree to a very large extent in Ca., A.h. and A.s.; Su. adheres to a different scheme. Mādhava follows the lead of A.h. A survey of the classification of the worms and their names is given in the table on page 625.

Some studies have been devoted to the worms in Āyurvedic literature and in the Atharvaveda (R. R. Kashyap, Parasitology in the Atharvaveda, IC 2, 1935-36, p. 93-113; Müller, Indische Würmerkrankheiten, Gesnerus 21, 1964, p. 14-22).

The names of the worms are not always clear, as indicated in the notes, and their identification, in so far as they are no imaginary creatures, proves to be even more difficult. The worms, said in the Suśrutasaṃhitā to arise from faecal matter, are identified by Chakraberty (p. 235) as follows : *ajava*, i.e. slow-moving : *Ascaris lumbricoides*; *vijava*, i.e. agile : flagellates; *kipya*, i.e. creeping : trematodes or flukes; *tripya* (instead of *cipya*), i.e. stealing : hookworms; *gaṇḍūpada*, i.e. knotted feet : species of *Taenia*, tapeworms; *curu*, i.e. thread-like : *Oxyuris vermicularis*, the threadworm; *dvimukha*, i.e. two-mouthed : *Trichuris trichiura*, the whipworm. These identifications, proposed without arguments by Chakraberty, are arbitrary and partly untenable, because flagellates, for example, are invisible to the naked eye. It seems fairly certain that a *yūkā* is a louse; lice are found on the hairs of the head and the clothes (7, 2); so both *Pediculus humanus capitis*, the head-louse, and *P. humanus corporis*, the body-louse, were known. Nits were designated by the term *likṣā*; *pipīlikā*, though commonly used to denote ants, conveys the same sense as *likṣā* in the Carakasaṃhitā (Cakra on Ca.Sū. 19, 4 : *pipīlikā* = *likhyā*). A clear description of the crab-louse (*Phtirus pubis*), chiefly living on the hairs of the genital and inguinal regions, is absent; it may have been known as *cipiṭa*, which means flat or flattened, because it is distinguished from other lice by its broad and flat body. The *matkuṇā* mentioned in the Hārītasaṃhitā may be the bed-bug of the tropics, *Cimex hemipterus* (*rotundatus*).

Ascaris lumbricoides (Linnaeus, 1758), the 'round worm', is probably designated as *udarāveṣṭa* ("throttling the abdomen") or *udarāda* ("eating the abdomen"), for it is said to resemble a *gaṇḍūpada*, i.e. an earthworm (7, 8-9); it may be the *gaṇḍūpada* of Suśruta and the *kiñcukasaṃnibha*, i.e. "resembling an earthworm" of the Hārītasaṃhitā; it is certainly not a tapeworm, as indicated in the dictionaries (PW : Bandwurm; MW : tapeworm).

Tapeworms may have been called *antrāda*, i.e. "bowel-eater", because the latter is said to resemble a broad leather thong (7, 8-9); the proglottides of species of tapeworms of the genus *Taenia* may have been designated as *pṛthumuṇḍa*, i.e. "broad and bald", in the Hārītasaṃhitā.

Enterobius vermicularis (Linnaeus, 1758), formerly called *Oxyuris vermicularis*, the 'threadworm', must have been known, for worms crawling out of the anus and producing itching of the anal region are described (Madhukośa on 7, 13-16); itching of the anus occurs when female threadworms are depositing their eggs in enormous numbers near the anus, as well as on the passage of an ascaris. The name of the threadworm cannot easily be deduced from the descriptions, but it may be the worm called *leliha*, i.e. "constantly licking". *Trichuris trichiura* (Linnaeus, 1771), the 'whipworm', may also have been known, because hyperinfection with these worms eventually results in rectal prolapse, in which the worms may actually be seen attached to the prolapsed bowel. Both the male and the female of this organism have a rather long attenuated anterior portion, which may have given rise to the name *sūcīmukha*, i.e. "having a mouth like a needle", found in the Hārītasaṃhitā.

The term *kuṣṭhaja*, i.e. "arising from *kuṣṭha*" (a skin disease), occurring in the Suśrutasaṃhitā, need not be fanciful. This worm may actually denote the larva of *Chrysomyia bezziana*, a true myiasis-producing fly, never breeding in dead but always in living tissues. It is frequently found in India, where it appears to have a predilection for human beings, the female laying her numerous eggs in the nasal cavity or in tissues from which offensive discharges emanate. Patients with a chronic discharge from nose or ears, and with lepromatous leprosy, are attacked (Manson, p. 767). The fantastic names carried by some worms, e.g. *lomadvīpa* or *romadvīpa*, i.e. "having islands of body-hair", may refer to larvae of flies inhabiting the intestinal canal. Already over twenty species of diptera are recognized the larvae of which have been found in or expelled from the intestinal canal (Manson, p. 769). The commonest is *Calliphora vomitoria*, the larva of which is endowed with circles of little spines (see Manson, p. 769, fig. 231); its name *lomadvīpa* appears very apt.

The symptoms ascribed to the presence of worms are vague; some of them may certainly occur in infections with worms : diarrhoea is common in trichuriasis; intermittent intestinal colic (*śūla*, i.e. "piercing pain") is the most common complaint in ascariasis, etc.; itching of the anal region in infections with *Enterobius vermicularis* has already been referred to.

arising from	Ca.	A.h., A.s., Mādhava	Su.
external impure matter	1) yūkā 2) pipīlikā	1) yūkā 2) likṣā	
phlegm	1) antrāda 2) udarāveṣṭa or udarāda 3) hṛdayāda or hṛdayacara 4) mahāguda 5) curu 6) darbhapuṣpa 7) saugandhika	1) antrāda 2) udarāveṣṭa 3) hṛdayāda 4) mahāguda or mahākuha 5) curu or kuru 6) darbhakusuma 7) sugandha	1) pipīlikā 2) cipiṭa 3) dāruṇa 4) pralūna 5) mahāpuṣpa 6) darbhapuṣpa
blood	1) keśāda 2) lomāda 3) lomadvīpa 4) auḍumbara or audumbara 5) saurasa 6) jantumātṛ	1) keśāda 2) romavidhvaṃsa 3) romadvīpa 4) udumbara 5) saurasa 6) mātṛ or rasamātṛ	1) keśāda 2) romāda 3) dantāda 4) nakhāda 5) kikkiśa 6) kuṣṭhaja 7) parisarpa
faecal matter	1) kakeruka 2) makeruka 3) sausurāda 4) saśūlaka 5) leliha	1) kakeruka 2) makeruka 3) sausurāda 4) saśūla or salūna or sulūna 5) leliha	1) ajava 2) vijava 3) kipya 4) cipya 5) gaṇḍūpada 6) curu 7) dvimukha

The twenty worms enumerated in the Bheḍasaṃhitā are : *majjāja, jarāyuja, lambārūpaka, bahurūpaka, parisarpa, visarpa, gotraja, netraja, romāda, antrāda, ahita, kaṣṭa, dāruṇaka, śiroja, dantaja, śleṣmaja, śakṛdāśraya, lohita, kālaka, śatamātṛka.*

The Hārītasaṃhitā distinguishes seven kinds of external worms and six internal ones; the latter are collectively called *kiñcaka.* The external worms are : *kṛṣṇā yūkā, śvetā yūkā* or *śironivāsinī, carmaṇi sthitā yūkā* or *carmayūkikā, carmayūkā* (the text may also be interpreted thus, that *carmayūkikā* and *carmayūkā* are identical; in that case *śvetā yūkā* and *śironivāsinī* are different types), *yaṣṭikā, bindukī, ṃatkuṇā*; the internal worms are : *pṛthumuṇḍa, kiñcukasaṃnibha, dhānyāṅkuranibha, sūkṣma, aṇu, sūcīmukha.*

Chapter 8

"Morbid pallor" (*pāṇḍuroga*) comprises anaemia, jaundice and other disorders associated with an altered colour or pigmentation of the skin.

It is not correct to translate *pāṇḍuroga* by anaemia, as often occurs (Gulabkunverba translation of the Carakasaṃhitā; Yādavaśarman; Dīnānāth; Sudarśanaśāstrī), and certainly not by jaundice (as in Bhishagratna's translation of the Suśrutasaṃhitā); this has already been pointed out by Müller (Eigenwertungen, p. 36, note 148). Hilgenberg and Kirfel rendered the term by "Bleichsucht" and Hoernle (The Bower Manuscript), correctly, by morbid pallor. The diseases described in the chapter on morbid pallor are at least partially related to the illness called *hariman* in the Atharvaveda (see about *hariman*: Karambelkar, The Atharva-Veda and the Āyur-Veda, p. 205-214; Müller, Die Gelbsucht der Alt-Inder, Janus 34, 1930, p. 177-189).

The syndrome described as morbid pallor caused by wind (8, 4) is rather obscure; it may be related to several disorders: tropical sprue with anaemia, in which the patient is generally dark or muddy in complexion because of a generalized hypermelanosis and complains of dyspeptic distension of the abdomen; many patients with biliary cirrhosis of the liver develop a striking melanotic pigmentation of the skin; in leishmaniasis the skin often acquires a strange earthy-grey colour, which has given rise to the native name, kala-azar, i.e. "the black disease". Morbid pallor from bile (8, 5) suggests jaundice of a non-obstructive type, accompanied by fever, as may occur in a great number of disorders. Morbid pallor from phlegm (8, 6) may represent several syndromes in which a chronic anaemia is found. Morbid pallor arising from the three morbific entities (8, 7) resembles a chronic protein deficiency, associated with hypomelanosis and wasting and easily leading to complications.

Much has been written about the eating of earth (8, 8-10) as a result of or as a habit leading to anaemia. From recent studies it has become clear that the ingestion of earth interferes with the absorption of iron and produces an iron-deficiency anaemia (The Lancet, 18th April 1970, p. 826, where references are given). The eating of earth can be a symptom of ancylostomiasis (Manson, p. 278), which is frequent in India; this infection with hookworms (*Ancylostoma duodenale* and *Necator americanus*) may give rise to severe anaemia.

Anaemia leads to oedema (8, 11) when present to a serious degree;

in ancylostomiasis with chronic anaemia the stools may sometimes contain small flakes of blood-tinged mucus (8, 11).

The disease called *kāmalā* (8, 16-18) is usually equated with jaundice (Jolly, Medicin, p. 87; Hilgenberg and Kirfel; Gulabkunverba translation of the Carakasaṃhitā; Yādavaśarman; Dīnānāth; Sudarśanaśāstrī). Particular forms of jaundice are described as morbid pallor from bile (8, 5), but *kāmalā* is a more pronounced form of it; it may include obstructive jaundice, though the clay-coloured faeces occurring in that syndrome are not mentioned. A more accurate description of obstructive jaundice is found at Ca.Ci. 16, 124cd-128ab (note 39). When *kāmalā* has been present for some time and does not decrease in intensity, it is called *kumbhakāmalā* (8, 19ab); the serious state to which it may give rise (8, 21cd-22ab) is suggestive of advanced hepatic failure caused by cirrhosis or an amoebic liver abscess.

The disease called *halīmaka* (8, 22cd-23) is sometimes interpreted as chlorosis (Yādavaśarman; Dīnānāth; Sudarśanaśāstrī), which is inadequate, because it is a serious illness. Its description may point to a severe chronic anaemia, associated with jaundice; in jaundice the coloration of the skin varies greatly in intensity, from a barely detectable light yellow to a greenish or even brownish colour. Finally it should be mentioned that the best enumeration of the symptoms met with in more serious degrees of anaemia is found in the Carakasaṃhitā (note 19, the generic characteristics of morbid pallor: Ca.Ci. 16, 13-16).

Chapter 9

The disease called "blood-bile" (*raktapitta*) does not fit into any modern medical concept. It comprises all disorders in which loss of blood, or matter supposed to be "blood-bile", occurs through the openings of the body (the eyes and the pores of the hairs are also regarded as openings of the body). It includes haematemesis, haemoptysis, melaena, lower bowel bleeding, anal bleeding, gross haematuria, metrorrhagia and vaginal bleeding, nasal bleeding, loss of blood from the ears and the eyes, generalized bleeding from the gastro-intestinal tract, general disorders with numerous subcutaneous haemorrhages, the discharge of bilious fluid through the mouth, the throwing up of purulent sputum, etc.

Blood-bile from phlegm (9, 5ab) does not seem like a haemorrhage; it may refer to blood-streaked sputum, usually produced by a hard forceful cough. Blood-bile from wind (9, 5cd) may point to the sputum of bacterial pneumonia and to haemoptysis. Blood-bile from bile (9, 6-7ab) may represent haematemesis (blood coming from the stomach may be brown or black) and bilious vomiting (blood-bile resembling the urine of a cow).

The characteristics which indicate a bad prognosis (9, 12) are suggestive of a great variety of disorders; stinking purulent sputum is thrown up e.g. in bronchiectasis and abscesses of the lung; a faecal odour after protracted vomiting indicates low obstruction of the small bowel or peritonitis, etc.

Chapter 10

The disease called *yakṣman*, consumption, or *rājayakṣman*, kingly consumption, was identified as phthisis pulmonalis by Wise (p. 321) and, following his lead, by many others (Yādavaśarman : phthisis, consumption, pulmonary tuberculosis; Dīnānāth : idem; Jolly, Medicin, p. 88, is more critical : Auszehrung und Lungenschwindsucht, i.e. cachexia and phthisis pulmonalis).

The texts make clear that the disease has a much wider range and may be viewed as comprising the whole series of conditions, of whatever origin, between physical exhaustion and cachexia.

A disease of the name *yakṣma* is already referred to in the Atharvaveda (Karambelkar, The Atharva-Veda and the Āyur-Veda, p. 195-200; Müller, yakṣma, MIO 4, 1956, p. 278-313; idem, Die Medizin im Ṛg-Veda, Asia Major 6, 1930, p. 352-357). Müller has repeatedly observed that *(rāja)yakṣma(n)* is not identical with pulmonary tuberculosis and that many disorders are included in the term (see also : Eigenwertungen, p. 24-26), especially in old texts like the Atharvaveda. Filliozat rightly says (The classical doctrine, p. 100) that *rājayakṣma* denotes the cachexia resulting from various consumptive diseases, among which we may recognize pulmonary tuberculosis.

The three cardinal signs of kingly consumption (10, 5) only indicate a disease of the lungs, accompanied by fever. The other symptoms (add. stanza and 10, 6-7) make clear that haemoptysis is a feature of this illness, which may point to pulmonary tuberculosis, but also to a number of other disorders, such as pulmonary infarction, bronchiectasis, mitral stenosis, etc.; the affection of the larynx and the diarrhoea mentioned may occur in tuberculosis.

The disease called "a lesion of the chest" (10, 21-29ab) (*uraḥkṣata*) is sometimes identified as pulmonary cavitation (Yādavaśarman; Dīnānāth), suggesting a tuberculous origin; Jolly (Medicin, p. 88-89) was more prudent, calling it wounds in the chest (Wunden in der Brust. Pneumonie ?). The description of the disorder is not suggestive of pulmonary tuberculosis; the very bad-smelling sputum that is coughed up by the patient rather indicates some other involvement of the lungs.

The states of desiccation (10, 20) (*śoṣa*) and decline (10, 30) (*kṣaya*) represent a wide variety of disorders.

BIBLIOGRAPHY

Aalto, P. — Madyam apeyam. Jñānamuktāvalī, Commemoration Volume in honour of Joh. Nobel, ed. by Claus Vogel, p. 17-37. Sarasvati Vihara Series Nr. 38, 1959.

Ainslie, W. — Materia Indica; or, some account of those articles which are employed by the Hindoos, and other nations, in their medicine, arts, and agriculture; comprising also formulae, with practical observations, names of diseases in various eastern languages, and a copious list of oriental books immediately connected with general science, etc. etc. 2 vols., 2nd ed., London, 1826.

Amarakośa — see : Amarasiṃha.

Amarasiṃha — The Nāmaliṅgānuśāsana of Amarasiṃha with the commentary Ṭīkāsarvasva of Vandyaghaṭīya-Sarvānanda, ed. by T. Gaṇapati Śāstrī. 4 parts, Trivandrum Sanskrit Series Nr. 38 (1911), 43 (1915), 51 (1917), 52 (1917).

Aṣṭāṅgahṛdayasaṃhitā — see : Vāgbhaṭa.

Aṣṭāṅgasaṃgraha — see : Vāgbhaṭa.

Aufrecht, Th. — A catalogue of Sanskrit manuscripts in the Library of Trinity College, Cambridge. Cambridge, 1869.

— Catalogus Catalogorum. An alphabetical register of Sanskrit works and authors. 2 vols. (3 parts). Leipzig, 1891, 1896.

— Florentine Sanskrit Manuscripts (in the Biblioteca Nazionale and the Istituto di Studi Superiori). Leipzig, 1892.

— Zur Handschriftenkunde (Kommentare zum Amarakosha). ZDMG 28, 1874, p. 103-124.

— Bemerkungen. ZDMG 41, 1887, p. 485-493.

Āyurvedaprakāśa — see : Mādhava.

Āyurvedīya Viśva-Kośa, An Encyclopaedical Ayurvedic Dictionary (with full details of Ayurvedic, Unani and Allopathic terms), by Bābū Rāmjīt Siṃh and Bābū Daljīt Siṃh. (in Hindī). 3 vols. 3rd ed., Barālokpur, 1965.

Bagchi, P. C. — A fragment of the Kāśyapa-Saṃhitā in Chinese. IC 9, 1942-43, p. 53-64.

Bāṇa — The Harṣacarita of Bāṇabhaṭṭa, with the commentary Saṃketā of Śaṃkarakavi. Ed. by Kāśīnāth Pāṇḍuraṅg Parab. 7th ed., re-edited by Nārāyaṇ Rām Āchārya. Nirṇaya Sāgar Press, Bombay, 1946.

Barua, B. M. — Bhela-saṃhitā. Its antiquity and importance as a medical treatise. IC 3, 1936-37, p. 190-194.

Bedi, R. — Garlic. P. K. Gode Commemoration Volume, p. 9-14. Poona Oriental Series Nr. 93, 1960.

Bhandarkar, R. G. — Lists of Sanskrit Manuscripts in Private Libraries in the Bombay Presidency. Part 1, Bombay, 1893.

— Report on the search for Sanskrit manuscripts in the Bombay presidency during the year 1883-84. Bombay, 1887.

Bhattacharyya, D. C. — Date and works of Vāgbhaṭa the physician. ABORI 28, 1947, p. 112-127.

— Dates of early historical records of Bengal. IHQ 3, 1927, p. 571-591.

— Gaṅgādāsa and his father Gopāladāsa. IHQ 24, 1948, p. 312-323.

— New light on Vaidyaka literature (from Niścalakara's Ratnaprabhā). IHQ 23, 1947, p. 123-155.

Bhāvamiśra — Bhāvaprakāśa by Bhāvamiśra, with a Hindī-commentary called Vidyotinī, notes, introduction, index etc. by Brahmaśaṅkara Miśra. 2 vols. Kāśī Sanskrit Series Nr. 130. Benares, 1961.

Bhāvaprakāśa — see : Bhāvamiśra.

Bheḍasaṃhitā — see : Bhelasaṃhitā.

Bhelasaṃhitā — ed. by Girijādayālu Śukla. Vidyābhavan Āyurveda Granthamālā Nr. 25. Benares, 1959.

Bhishagratna — see : Suśrutasaṃhitā.

Bhojanakutūhala — see : Raghunātha.

Biswas, K. — Plants of Darjeeling and the Sikkim Himalayas. Vol. 1. Alipore, 1966 (1967).

Bor, N. L. — The grasses of Burma, Ceylon, India and Pakistan (excluding Bambuseae). London, 1960.

Bosch, F. D. K. — De gouden kiem. Inleiding tot de Indische symboliek. Amsterdam and Brussels, 1948.

— The golden germ. The Hague, 1960.

Brandis, D. — Indian Trees, An account of trees, shrubs, woody climbers, bamboos and palms indigenous or commonly cultivated in the British Indian Empire. First published 1906; 5th impr., Dehra Dun, 1971.

Bṛhadyogataraṅgiṇī — see : Trimallabhaṭṭa.

Bṛhatsaṃhitā — see : Varāhamihira.

Brown, G. W. — Prāṇa and apāna. JAOS 39, 1919, p. 104-112.

Bulletin of the Department of History of Medicine, Osmania Medical College, Hyderabad (A. P.) — Vol. 2, 1964, p. 1-12 (Aṣṭāṅgasaṃgraha). Vol. 3, 1965, p. 11-22 (Kalyāṇakāraka); p. 151-160 and p. 210-219 (Toḍarānandāyurvedasaukhya).

Burnell, A. C. — A classified index to the Sanskrit Mss. in the Palace at Tanjore, prepared for the Madras Government. London, 1879-1880.

Burrow, T. — Collected papers on Dravidian linguistics. Annamalai University, Department of linguistics, Publication Nr. 13. Annamalainagar, 1968.

Butterworths Medical Dictionary, ed. by Sir Arthur Salisbury MacNalty. Revised ed., London, 1965.

Cakrapāṇidatta — Cikitsāsārasaṃgrahāparanāmā Cakradattaḥ (Cikitsāsaṃgraha), with the commentary, called Tattvacandrikā, by Śivadāsasena, ed. by Jayadeva Vidyālaṃkāra. Bhāradvāja Press, Lahore, 1928.

— Dravyaguṇa, with a Hindī-translation by Paṇḍit Jvālāprasād Miśra. Lakṣmī-Veṅkaṭeśvar Press, Bombay, 1925.

Caland, W. — Altindisches Zauberritual. Probe einer Uebersetzung der wichtigsten Theile des Kauśika Sūtra. Verhandelingen der Koninklijke Akademie van Wetenschappen te Amsterdam, Afd. Letterkunde, Nieuwe Reeks, Deel 3, Nr. 2. Amsterdam, 1900.

Carakasaṃhitā — The Charakasaṃhitā by Agniveśa, revised by Charaka and Dṛiḍhabala, with the Āyurveda-Dīpikā commentary of Chakrapāṇidatta, ed. by Vaidya Jādavaji Trikamji Āchārya. 3d ed., Nirṇaya Sāgar Press, Bombay, 1941.

— Carakasaṃhitā, with the commentary, called Āyurvedadīpikā, by Cakrapāṇidatta, and the commentary, called Nirantarapadavyākhyā, by Jejjaṭa, ed. by Paṇḍit Haridattaśāstrī. 2 vols. Lahore, 1940-1941.

— Carakasaṃhitā, with the commentary Āyurvedadīpikā by Cakrapāṇidatta, and the commentary Jalpakalpataru by Gaṅgādhara, ed. by Narendranāth Sengupta and Balāīcandra Sengupta. Dhanvantari Steam Press, Calcutta, 1927 (vol. 1), 1928 (vol. 2), 1933 (vol. 3).

— The Charaka Saṃhitā, edited and published in six volumes with translations in Hindi, Gujarati and English by Shree Gulabkunverba Ayurvedic Society. Jamnagar, 1949.

— Carakasaṃhitā. English translation, with notes, by Avinash Chandra Kaviratna, the later parts (after 1905) published by his son, Pareshnath Sarma Kavibhusan. Calcutta, 1890-1914.

Catalogue — Tawney, C. H. and Thomas, F. W., Catalogue of two collections of Sanskrit Manuscripts preserved in the India Office Library (Coll. Jones and Additions). London, 1903.

— Mitra, Rājendralāla, A catalogue of Sanskrit Mss. in the Library of His Highness the Mahārājā of Bikāner. Calcutta, 1880.

— A catalogue of Sanskrit manuscripts in private libraries of the North-Western Provinces, compiled by order of Government. Vol. 1, part 1, Benares, 1874. Vol. 1, part 2, Allahabad, 1877-78.

— Descriptive Catalogue of the Government Collections of Manuscripts deposited at the Bhandarkar Oriental Research Institute, compiled by Dr. Har Dutt Sharma. Vol. 16, part 1, Vaidyaka, Poona, 1939.

— A descriptive catalogue of Sanskrit manuscripts in the Library of the Calcutta Sanskrit College, by Hṛīshikeśa Śāstrī and Śiva Chandra Gui. Vol. 9. Calcutta, 1906.

— Kuppuswami Sastri, S., A descriptive catalogue of the Sanskrit manuscripts in the Government Oriental Manuscripts Library, Madras. Vol. 23, Medicine. Madras, 1918.

— see also : Aufrecht, Bhandarkar, Burnell, Eggeling, Jolly, Krishnamacharya, Raghavan, Peterson, H. Śāstrī.

Chakraberty, C. — An interpretation of ancient Hindu medicine. Calcutta, 1923.

Chakravarti, T. N. — The number five and its association with certain plants and plant products in Bengal. Bhāratīya Vidyā 12, 1951, p. 1-21.

Chakravarty, T. — Food and drink in ancient Bengal. Calcutta, 1959.

Chalam, G. V. and Venkateswarlu, J. — Introduction to agricultural botany in India. Vol. 1. Asia Publishing House, Bombay, etc., 1965.

Chopra, R. N., Chopra, I. C., Handa, K. L. and Kapur, L. D. — Chopra's Indigenous Drugs of India. 2nd ed., revised and largely rewritten by ... Calcutta, 1958.

Chopra, R. N., Nayar, S. L. and Chopra, I. C. — Glossary of Indian medicinal plants. New Delhi, 1956.

Cooke, Th. — The Flora of the Presidency of Bombay. 3 vols. (1901-1903). 2nd reprinted edition. Botanical Survey of India. Calcutta, 1967.

Cordier, P. — Bibliographie (review of J. Jolly : Zur Quellenkunde der indischen Medizin : 1. Vāgbhaṭa). JA, t. 17, 1901, p. 179-187.

— Vāgbhaṭa (étude historique et religieuse). JA, t. 18, 1901, p. 147-181.

— Récentes découvertes de Mss. médicaux sanscrits dans l'Inde (1898-1902). Le Muséon, N.S. 4, 1903, p. 321-352.

Das Gupta, N. N. — A note on the term 'antaraṅga'. IC 1, 1934-35, p. 684-686.

— The Bengali commentators on the Amarakośa. IC 2, 1935-36, p. 261-269.

— The Vaidyaka literature of Bengal in the early mediaeval period. IC 3, 1936-37, p. 153-160.

Dasgupta, S. — History of Indian Philosophy. Vol. 1, London (1922), repr. 1969. Vol. 2, London, (1932), repr. 1968.

Dasgupta, S. N. and De, S. K. — A history of Sanskrit literature. Classical Period. Vol. 1. Calcutta, 1947.

De, S. K. — Sanskrit literature under the Pāla kings of Bengal. NIA 2, 1939-40, p. 263-282.

— Pālakāpya. D. R. Bhandarkar Volume, ed. by Bimala Churn Law, publ. by the Indian Research Institute, p. 73-75. Calcutta, 1940.

Dhanvantarīyanighaṇṭu — Rājanighaṇṭusahito Dhanvantarīyanighaṇṭuḥ. Ed. by Vināyak Gaṇeś Āpṭe. Ānandāśrama Sanskrit Series Nr. 33. 1925.

Dietz, F. R. — Analecta medica ex libris Mss. Fasciculus primus, in quo insunt : 1. Elenchus materiae medicae Ibn Beitharis Malacensis secundum codices Mss. Arabicos Escorialenses, Matritenses, Parisiensem, Hamburgensem. Pars prima. 2. Catalogus codicum de re medica Sanscritorum, qui in palatio societatis negotiatorum Indiae Orientalis (East India House) Londini adservantur. Lipsiae, 1833.

Dravyaguṇamañjūṣā, by Paṇḍit Śivadatta Śukla. Vidyābhavan Āyurveda Granthamālā Nr. 24. Benares, no date.

Dravyaguṇavijñāna, by Yādavaśarman Ācārya (and Bālakṛṣṇaśarman Pāṭhak). 3 vols. 2nd ed., Nirṇaya Sāgar Press, Bombay, 1945-47.

Duthie, J. F. — Flora of the Upper Gangetic Plain and of the adjacent Siwalik and Sub-Himalayan tracts. Vol. 1, Ranunculaceae to Convolvulaceae. (1903). Reprinted under the authority of the Government of India. Botanical Survey of India. Calcutta, 1960.

Dutt, Uday Chand — The materia medica of the Hindus, with a glossary of Indian plants by George King. Revised (2nd) ed., with additions by Kaviraj Binod Lall Sen, Kaviraj Ashutosh Sen and Kaviraj Pulin Krishna Sen. Calcutta, 1922.

— See also : Mādhava(kara), Suśrutasaṃhitā.

Dymock, W. — The vegetable materia medica of Western India. 2nd ed., revised and enlarged. Bombay and London, 1885.

Dymock, W., Warden, C. J. H. and Hooper, D. — Pharmacographia Indica, a history of the principal drugs of vegetable origin met with in British India. 3 vols. in 6 parts. London and Bombay, 1890-1893.

Eggeling, J. — Catalogue of the Sanskrit Manuscripts in the Library of the India Office. Part 5. Sanskrit literature : A. Scientific and technical literature. London, 1896.

Ellerman, J. R. — The Fauna of India including Pakistan, Burma and Ceylon, ed. by M. L. Roonwal. Mammalia (Second Edition), Vol. 3, Rodentia (in two parts), with an Appendix by M. L. Roonwal and B. Biswas. Part 1. Calcutta and Delhi, 1961.

Ellerman, J. R. and Morrison-Scott, T. C. S. — Checklist of Palaearctic and Indian Mammals 1758 to 1946. 2nd ed., London, 1966.

Esser, A.A.M. — Die Ophthalmologie des Bhāvaprakāśa quellenkritisch bearbeitet. Teil 1 : Anatomie und Pathologie. Studien zur Geschichte der Medizin herausgegeben von K. Sudhoff und H. E. Sigerist, Heft 19. Leipzig, 1930.

— Die ophthalmologische Therapie des Bhāvaprakāśa, quellenkritisch bearbeitet. SA 25, 1932, p. 184-213.

Ewing, A. H. — The Hindu conception of the functions of breath. A study in early Hindu psychophysics. JAOS 22, 1901, p. 249-308.

Faddegon, B. — The Vaiçeṣika-System, described with the help of the oldest texts. Verhandelingen der Koninklijke Akademie van Wetenschappen te Amsterdam,

Afd. Letterkunde, Nieuwe Reeks, Deel 18, Nr. 2. (Amsterdam, 1918). Repr., Wiesbaden, 1969.

Filliozat, J. — Liste des manuscrits de la collection Palmyr Cordier conservés à la Bibliothèque Nationale. JA, t. 224, 1934, p. 155-173.

— Un chapitre de la Hārītasaṃhitā sur la rétribution des actes. JA, t. 225, 1934, p. 125-139.

— Les états typhoïdes et comateux dans la médecine et les croyances populaires indiennes. BSHM 30, 1936, p. 21-29.

— Le Kumāratantra de Rāvaṇa et les textes parallèles indiens, tibétains, chinois, cambodgien et arabe. Cahiers de la Société Asiatique, Première Série 4. Paris, 1937.

— Fragments de textes koutchéens de médecine et de magie; texte, parallèles sanskrits et tibétains, traduction et glossaire. Paris, 1948.

—La doctrine classique de la médecine indienne; ses origines et ses parallèles grecs. Paris, 1949. English translation : The classical doctrine of Indian medicine; its origins and its Greek parallels. Translated from the original in French by Ḍev Raj Chanana; with a preface for the English version by J. Filliozat. Delhi, 1964.

Flora — Chavan, A. R. and Oza, G. M., The Flora of Pavagadh (Gujarat State, India). The Maharaja Sayajirao University of Baroda Botanical Memoirs, Nr. 1. Baroda, 1966.

— See also : Biswas, Bor, Brandis, Cooke, Duthie, Hooker, Rechinger, Roxburgh.

Frauwallner, E. — Geschichte der indischen Philosophie. 2. Band — Die naturphilosophischen Schulen und das Vaiśeṣika-System. Das System der Jaina. Der Materialismus. Reihe Wort und Antwort. Band 6/II. Salzburg, 1956.

Garbe, R. — Die indischen Mineralien, ihre Namen und die ihnen zugeschriebenen Kräfte. Narahari's Rājanighaṇṭu, varga 13, Skt. und Deutsch, mit kritischen und erläuternden Anmerkungen herausgegeben von ... Leipzig, 1882.

— Die Sāṃkhya-Philosophie. Eine Darstellung des indischen Rationalismus nach den Quellen. Leipzig, 1894.

— Der Mondschein der Sāṃkhya-Wahrheit, Vācaspatimiśra's Sāṃkhya-tattvakaumudī, in deutscher Übersetzung, nebst einer Einleitung über das Alter und die Herkunft der Sāṃkhya-Philosophie, von R. Garbe. Abhandlungen der philosophisch-philologischen Classe der Königlich Bayerischen Akademie der Wissenschaften. 19. Bd., 1892, p. 519-628.

— Sāṃkhya-pravacana-bhâshya, Vijñânabhikshu's Commentar zu den Sāṃkhyasūtras; aus dem Sanskrit übersetzt und mit Anmerkungen versehen von R. Garbe. Leipzig, 1889.

— See also : Sāṃkhyapravacanabhāṣya.

Ghosh, J. C. — Indigenous drugs of India, their cultivation and manufacture. 2nd ed. (revised and enlarged). Calcutta, 1940.

Glidden, H. W. — The lemon in Asia and Europe. JAOS 57, 1937, p. 381-396.

Gode, P. K. — The nature and contents of a lost medical treatise by Kharanāda or Khāranāḍi. St.I.L.H. 1, p. 112-125 = PO 4, 1939, p. 49-62.

— Antiquity of the lost medical treatise by Khāranāḍi in the light of the leaf of the Khāraṇāda-Nyāsa newly discovered at Gilgit. St.I.L.H. 1, p. 126-131 = ABORI 20, 1938-39, p. 97-102.

— Works and authors mentioned by Candraṭa in his medical compendium Yogaratnasamuccaya (c. A.D. 1000). St.I.L.H. 1, p. 132-137 = Prācyavāṇī 1, 1944, p. 151-155.

— Chronological limits for the commentary of Indu on the Aṣṭāṅgasaṃgraha of Vāgbhaṭa I — Between A.D. 750-1050. St.I.L.H. 1, p. 151-165 = ABORI 25, 1943-44, p. 225-238.

— Vāgbhaṭa, the author of the Aṣṭāṅgahṛdaya and his commentators. St.I.L.H. 1, p. 171-190 = Introduction to the Aṣṭāṅgahṛdayasaṃhitā (p. 1-12) ed. by Hariśāstrī Parāḍkar, 6th ed., Nirṇaya Sāgar Press, Bombay, 1939.

— The chronology of Brahmadeva's commentary on the Siddhayoga of Vṛnda — Between c. A.D. 900 and 1100. St.I.L.H. 1, p. 191-194 = IC 11, 1943-44, p. 36-39.

— Some new evidence from the Rasaratnapradīpa of Rāmarāja on the genealogy of the Ṭākā kings of Kāṣṭhā — Between A.D. 1200 and 1500. St.I.L.H. 1, p. 290-296 = NIA 7, 1944-45, p. 176-180.

— Aruṇadatta and Hemādri, the commentators of the Aṣṭāṅgahṛdaya. St.I.L.H. 1, p. 317-318 = Journal of the University of Bombay 3, part 3, 1936, p. 26-27.

— Date of Vaṅgasena, the author of the Cikitsāsāra-Saṃgraha — before A.D. 1200. St.I.L.H. 1, p. 325-333 = IC 3, 1936-37, p. 535-543.

— Lolimbarāja and his works. St.I.L.H. 2, p. 79-96 = IC 7, 1939-40, p. 327-333 and p. 447-456.

— The history and chronology of a Nāgara Brahmin family of physicians in Gujarāt (A.D. 1275-1475). St.I.L.H. 2, p. 176-181 = Siddha Bhāratī (Dr. Siddheshwar Varma Presentation Volume), part 2, 1950, p. 251-256.

— A topical analysis of the Bhojana-Kutūhala, a work on dietetics, composed by Raghunātha, between A.D. 1675 and 1700. St.I.L.H. 2, p. 380-390 = ABORI 22, 1941, p. 254-263.

— Raghunātha, a protégé of Queen Dīpābāi of Tanjore, and his works — Between A.D. 1675-1712. St.I.L.H. 2, p. 391-403 = Journal of the University of Bombay 10, part 2, 1943, p. 132-140.

— The identification of Raghunātha, the protégé of Queen Dīpābāi of Tanjore and his contact with saint Rāmadāsa — Between A.D. 1648 and 1682. St.I.L.H. 2, p. 404-415 = Journal of the Tanjore Sarasvatī Mahal Library 3, nr. 1, p. 1-12.

— A contemporary manuscript of the Bhojana-Kutūhala of Raghunātha belonging to Śāmjī Nāyak Puṇḍe — Between A.D. 1650 and 1685. St.I.L.H. 2, p. 425-434 = Journal of the University of Bombay 13, part 2, 1946, p. 40-45.

— Studies in the history of dietetics — References to "Avarānna" in the Dharmasūtras of Baudhāyana and Āpastamba and the Gṛhyasūtra of Āpastamba — (Between B.C. 500 and A.D. 500). St.I.L.H. 2, p. 153-160 = PO 12, 1948, p. 1-9.

— Studies in the history of Indian plants — Some notes on the history of caṇaka (Cicer arietinum) — between 500 B.C. and A.D. 1820. St.I.C.H. 1, p. 193-217 = ABORI 27, 1946, p. 56-82.

— Studies in the history of Indian plants — History of caṇaka (gram) as food for horses between c. A.D. 800 and 1870 together with some notes on the import of foreign horses into India in ancient and mediaeval times. St.I.C.H. 2, p. 218-232 = ABORI 26, 1945, p. 89-105.

— Use of caṇaka at an aśvamedha in the Rāmāyaṇa, of caṇakāmla in Rasavidyā (c. A.D. 1000 onwards) and trade in caṇaka (about A.D. 1300). St.I.C.H. 1, p. 233-239 = Adyar Library Bulletin 12, part 1, p. 14-23.

— Studies in the history of Indian plants — The use of caṇaka (gram) as horse-food vouched by five Sanskrit treatises on the Aśvaśāstra. St.I.C.H. 1, p. 240-244 = Prācyavāṇī 3, 1946, p. 35-39.

— Studies in the history of Indian plants — The role of yava and caṇaka (gram) in regimen of Indian horses as disclosed in the Aśvāyurveda of Vāgbhaṭa, the son of Vikrama. St.I.C.H. 1, p. 245-255 = Acharya Dhruva Smāraka Grantha, p. 247 ff.

— Studies in the history of Indian plants — Antiquity of jawār or jondhḷā (Holcus sorghum) (from B.C. 2200 to A.D. 1850). St.I.C.H. 1, p. 266-282 = Dr. B. C. Law Volume, publ. by the Indian Research Institute, Calcutta, 1945, part 1, p. 142-158.

— Date of Yogaratnākara, an anonymous medical compendium — between A.D. 1650 and 1725. Bhāratīya Vidyā 4, part 2, 1943, p. 154-156.

— Quotations from the commentaries of Kārtika or Kārtikakuṇḍa recorded by Ḍallaṇa (c. A.D. 1100), by Vijayarakṣita (c. A.D. 1240) and by Śrīkaṇṭhadatta (c. A.D. 1275). IC 13, 1947, p. 199-208.

— Studies in the history of Indian dietetics — History of the dishes iḍli and dośe — between A.D. 1100 and 1900. Dr. S. K. Chatterji Jubilee Volume (Indian Linguistics 16, 1955), p. 226-231.

Gonda, J. — Ancient-Indian ojas, Latin * augos, and the Indo-European nouns in -es/-os. Utrecht, 1952.

— The savayajñas (Kauśikasūtra 60-68. Translation, Introduction, Commentary). Verhandelingen der Koninklijke Nederlandse Akademie van Wetenschappen, Afd. Letterkunde, Nieuwe Reeks, Deel 71, Nr. 2. Amsterdam, 1965.

Goudriaan, T. — Kāśyapa's book of wisdom. The Hague, 1965.

Grohmann, J. V. — Medicinisches aus dem Atharva-Veda, mit besonderem Bezug auf den Takman. Indische Studien 9, p. 381-423. Leipzig, 1865.

Hariprapanna — Rasayogasāgara. 2 vols. Bombay, 1927, 1930.

Hāritasaṃhitā, with a Hindī-translation by Ravidattaśāstri. Śrīveṅkaṭeśvar Steam Press, Bombay, 1927.

Harṣacarita — see : Bāṇa.

Hilgenberg, L. and Kirfel, W. — see : Vāgbhaṭa.

History and Culture of the Indian People — see : Majumdar, R. C.

Hoernle, A. F. R. — Studies in ancient Indian medicine : I. The commentaries on Suśruta. JRAS, 1906, p. 283-302. II. On some obscure anatomical terms. JRAS, 1906, p. 915-941. IV. The composition of the Caraka Samhita, and the literary methods of the ancient Indian medical writers. (A study in textual criticism). JRAS, 1908, p. 997-1028. V. The composition of the Caraka Samhita in the light of the Bower Manuscript. (An essay in historical and textual criticism). JRAS, 1909, p. 857-893.

— Studies in the medicine of ancient India. Part 1 : Osteology. Oxford, 1907.

— The Bower Manuscript, Facsimile Leaves, Nāgarī Transcript, Romanized Transliteration, and English Translation with Notes, ed. by ... Archaeological Survey of India, New Imperial Series, Vol. 22, Calcutta, 1908.

— See also : Suśrutasaṃhitā.

Hooker, J. D. — The Flora of British India. 7 vols. (1872-1897). Reprinted 1961.

Index — Index Kewensis plantarum phanerogamarum nomina et synonyma omnium generum et specierum a Linnaeo ad annum 1895 complectens nomine recepto auctore patria unicuique plantae subjectis. Sumptibus beati Caroli Roberti Darwin ductu et concilio Josephi D. Hooker confecit D. Daydon Jackson. 4 vols. Oxonii, 1893-1895. Supplementum ... nomina et synonyma omnium generum et specierum ab initio anni 1896 ... nonnulla etiam antea edita complectens. Bruxellis, 1901-....

International Code — International Code of Botanical Nomenclature adopted by the eleventh International Botanical Congress, Seattle, August 1969. Regnum Vegetabile Volume 82. Utrecht, 1972.

The Imperial Gazetteer of India. The Indian Empire. Vol. 1, Descriptive (1909). Vol. 2, Historical (1909). Vol. 3, Economic (1908). Vol. 4, Administrative (1909). New edition, Oxford.

I-Tsing — A record of the Buddhist religion as practised in India and the Malay archipelago (A.D. 671-695), translated by J. Takakusu. Oxford, 1896.

Jaggi, O. P. — Scientists of ancient India and their achievements. New Delhi, etc., 1966.

Jolly, J. — Der Knoblauch in der indischen Medizin. Festgruss an Rudolf von Roth, p. 18-20. Stuttgart, 1893.

— Caraka. WZKM 11, 1897, p. 164-166.

— Medicin. Grundriss der Indo-Arischen Philologie und Altertumskunde, III. Band, 10. Heft. Strassburg, 1901.

— Zur Quellenkunde der indischen Medizin. 3. Ein alter Kommentator zu Suśruta. ZDMG 58, 1904, p. 114-116. 4. Die Cikitsākalikā des Tīsaṭācārya. ZDMG 60, 1906, p. 413-468.

— Die Sanskrit-Handschriften Nr. 287-413 der Königlichen Hof- und Staatsbibliothek in München. 1912.

Kalyāṇakāraka by Ugrāditya — see : Bulletin of the Department of History of Medicine, Hyderabad.

Kangle, R. P. — The Kauṭilīya Arthaśāstra. Part I, A critical edition with a glossary. Bombay, 1960. Part II, An English translation with critical and explanatory notes. Bombay, 1963. Part III, A study. Bombay, 1965. University of Bombay Studies, Sanskrit, Prakrit and Pali, Nr. 1, 2, 3.

Karambelkar, V. W. — The Atharva-Veda and the Āyur-Veda. Nagpur, 1961.

Kashyap, R. R. — Parasitology in the Atharvaveda. IC 2, 1935-36, p. 93-113.

Kāśyapasaṃhitā — The Kāśyapa Saṃhitā (or Vṛddhajīvakīya Tantra) by Vṛddha Jīvaka, revised by Vātsya, with Sanskrit Introduction by Paṇḍit Hemarāja Śarmā, with the Vidyotinī Hindī commentary and Hindī translation of the Sanskrit Introduction by Śrī Satyapāla Bhiṣagācārya. Kāśī Sanskrit Series Nr. 154. Benares, 1953.

Katre, S. L. — Date of Yogaratnākara, an anonymous medical compendium — after 1697 A.C. Bhāratīya Vidyā 12, 1951, p. 59-61.

Kaul Shastri, M. S. — Report on the Gilgit excavation. The Quarterly Journal of the Mythic Society 30, 1939, p. 1-12.

Kauṭilya — see : Kangle, Meyer, Shamasastry.

Keith, A. Berriedale — A history of Sanskrit literature. Reprinted from the first ed. (1920). Oxford University Press, 1966.

Kirfel, W. — Die fünf Elemente, insbesondere Wasser und Feuer. Ihre Bedeutung für den Ursprung altindischer und altmediterraner Heilkunde. Eine medizingeschichtliche Studie. Beiträge zur Sprach- und Kulturgeschichte des Orients, Heft 4. Walldorf-Hessen, 1951.

Kirtikar, K. R., Basu, B. D. and An I, C. S. — Indian Medicinal Plants. Ed., revised, enlarged and mostly rewritten by Blatter, E., Caius, J. F. and Mhaskar, K. S. 2nd ed. (4 vols. text, 4 vols. plates). 1935.

Kohl, J. F. — Einige Bemerkungen zu den Tierlisten des jinistischen Kanons. Asiatica, Festschrift Fr. Weller, p. 365-376. 1954.

Krishnamachariar, M. — History of classical Sanskrit literature. (1937). First reprint, 1970.

Krishnamacharya, V. — Alphabetical Index of Sanskrit Mss. in the Adyar Library. Adyar Library Series Nr. 45, 1944.

Krishnamoorthy, K. — The conception of personality in the Caraka-Saṃhitā and the concept of prajñāparādha. PO 15, 1950, p. 65-89.

Kulkarni, E. D. — Śālihotra of Bhoja, critically ed. by ... Sources of Indo-Aryan Lexicography 11. Poona, 1953.

Kutumbiah, P. — Ancient Indian Medicine; with a foreword by S. Radhakrishnan. Revised ed. Bombay, Calcutta, etc., 1969.

Lacombe, O. — L'Absolu selon le védânta. Les notions de Brahman et d'Atman dans les systèmes de Çankara et Râmânoudja. Paris, 1937.

The Lancet, Nr. 7651, 18 April 1970, p. 826 : Earth-eating and anaemia.

Lévi, S. — Notes sur les Indo-Scythes. JA, t. 8, 1896, p. 444-484.

Losch, H. — Rājadharma. Einsetzung und Aufgabenkreis des Königs im Lichte der Purāṇa's. Bonner Orientalistische Studien, Neue Serie, Band 8. Bonn, 1959.

Lüders, H. — Medizinische Sanskrittexte aus Turkistan. Aus Indiens Kultur, Festschrift für R. Garbe, 1927, p. 148-162 = Lüders, H., Philologica Indica, Göttingen, 1940, p, 579 ff.

— Von indischen Tieren : 1. godhā, 2. parasvat, 3. koka, 4. śiśumāra. ZDMG 96, 1942, p. 23-81.

Madanapālanighaṇṭu, with a Hindī commentary, called Bhāṣātattvaprakāśinī, by Paṇḍit Rāmprasād. Lakṣmī-Veṅkaṭeśvar Steam Press, Bombay, 1954.

Mādhava(kara) — Mādhavanidāna by Mādhavakara, with the commentary Madhukośa by Vijayarakṣita and Śrīkaṇṭhadatta and with extracts from Ātaṅkadarpaṇa by Vācaspati Vaidya, ed. by Vaidya Jādavjī Tricumjī Āchārya. 5th ed. Nirṇaya Sāgar Press, Bombay, 1955.

— Nidāna, a Sanskrit system of pathology. Translated into Bengali by Udoy Chand Dutt. 2nd ed., revised, and with the Sanskrit text added, Calcutta, 1880.

— Mādhava Nidāna, etiology and pathology of Hindu medical science by Mādhava Kara, with commentary Madhukośa by Vijaya Rakṣita and Śrīkaṇṭha Datta, and commentary of Śāradā by Kavirāj Śāradā Caraṇ Sen Kaviratna. 2nd ed., publ. by Kavirāj P. K. Sen Kavirañjan. Benares, 1932.

— The Mādhava Nidāna of Śrī Mādhavakara with the Sudhālaharī comments by Paṇḍit Śrī Umeśānanda Śarmā, ed. with indices and appendices etc. by Paṇḍit Śrī Brahma Śaṅkara Śāstri. Haridās Sanskrit Series Nr. 158. Benares, 1943.

— Mādhavanidāna by Mādhavakara with the commentary, called Madhukośa, by Vijayarakṣita and Śrīkaṇṭhadatta, and the ṭippaṇī, called Yaśovatī, and a Hindī-commentary, called Vikāsinī, by Dīnānāthaśarmaśāstri. 3 vols. Delhi, 1959.

— Mādhavanidāna by Mādhavakara with the commentary Madhukośa by Vijayarakṣita and Śrīkaṇṭhadatta and a Hindī commentary called Vidyotinī and notes by Sudarśanaśāstrī. 2 vols. Kāśī Sanskrit Series Nr. 158. 2nd ed., Benares, 1960.

— Mādhavanidāna by Mādhava with a Hindī commentary by Dattarām. Śrīveṅkaṭeśvar Steam Press, Bombay, 1960.

— Paryāyaratnamāla by Mādhavakara, ed. by Dr. Tarapada Chowdhury. Patna, 1946.

— Āyurvedaprakāśa of Ācārya Śrī Mādhava, ed. with the Arthavidyotinī and Arthaprakāśinī Sanskrit and Hindi commentaries by Śrī Gulrājśarmā Miśra, with introduction by Paṇḍit Śivaśarmā. Vidyābhavan Āyurveda Granthamālā Nr. 37. 2nd ed., Benares, 1962.

Majumdar, G. P. — The history of botany and allied sciences (agriculture, medicine, arbori-horticulture) in ancient India (c. 2000 B.C. to 100 A.D.). Archives internationales d'histoire des sciences 4, 1951, p. 100-133.

Majumdar, R. C. (General Editor) — Bharatiya Vidya Bhavan's History and Culture of the Indian People. Vol. 4 — The age of imperial Kanauj. 1955. Vol. 5 — The struggle for empire. 1957.

— The history of Bengal. Vol. 1 — Hindu Period. 2nd impr., Dacca, 1963.

Majumdar, R. C. — History of ancient Bengal. Calcutta, 1971.

Manson-Bahr, Ph. H. — Manson's Tropical Diseases. A manual of the diseases of warm climates. 16th ed., London, 1966.

Manusmṛti — The Manusmṛti with the commentary Manvarthamuktāvalī of Kullūka, various readings, foot-notes, indices etc. 10th ed., edited with critical and explanatory notes etc., by Nārāyaṇ Rām Āchārya. Nirṇaya Sāgar Press, Bombay, 1946.

Medinikara — Nānārthaśabdakośa or Medinīkośa of Śrī Medinikara, ed. with an Introduction, Index etc. by Paṇḍit Jagannāth Śāstrī Hośiṅg. Kāśī Sanskrit Series Nr. 41. 3rd impr., Benares, 1968.

Mertens, R. — Die Familie der Warane (Varanidae). 3 vols. Abhandlungen der Senckenbergischen Naturforschenden Gesellschaft 462, 465, 466. Frankfurt, 1942.

Meyer, J. J. — Das altindische Buch vom Welt- und Staatsleben. Das Arthaçāstra des Kauṭilya, aus dem Sanskrit übersetzt und mit Einleitung und Anmerkungen versehen von ... Leipzig, 1926.

— Trilogie altindischer Mächte und Feste der Vegetation. Ein Beitrag zur vergleichenden Religions- und Kulturgeschichte, Fest- und Volkskunde. Zürich/Leipzig, 1937.

Meyerhof, M. — 'Alī ibn Rabban aṭ-Ṭabarī, ein persischer Arzt des 9. Jahrhunderts n. Chr. ZDMG 85, 1931, p. 38-68.

— 'Alī aṭ-Ṭabbarī's "Paradise of Wisdom", one of the oldest Arabic Compendiums of Medicine. Isis 16, 1931, p. 6-54.

Monier-Williams, M. — A Sanskrit-English Dictionary, etymologically and philologically arranged with special reference to cognate Indo-European languages. New edition, greatly enlarged and improved, Oxford (1899), reprinted 1951.

Mooss, N. S. — Ayurvedic Flora Medica, with equivalents in Sanskrit and regional languages, medicinal properties and notes on identification. Fasciculus 1, Vaidya Sarathy Series Nr. 12. Vaidya Sarathy Press, Kottayam, 1953.

Müller, A. — Arabische Quellen zur Geschichte der indischen Medizin. ZDMG 34, 1880, p. 465-556.

Müller, R. F. G. — Die Gelbsucht der Alt-Inder. Janus 34, 1930, p. 177-189.

— Die Medizin im Ṛg-Veda. Asia Major 6, 1930, p. 315-376.

— Zum Alter der frühen Fachüberlieferungen der indischen Medizin, der Saṃhitā des Caraka, Suśruta und Vāgbhaṭa. JRAS, 1932, p. 789-814.

— Vom Körperaufbau in der altindischen Medizin. SA 26, 1933, p. 310-317.

— On an origin of the Caraka and Suśruta Saṃhitās. JRAS, 1933, p. 323-327.

— Ueber Pitta oder Galle, unter Bezug zur Tridoṣa-Lehre der altindischen Medizin. Janus 38, 1934, p. 77-106.

— Vom Manas (Geist) und seinen Krankheiten in der altindischen Medizin. Janus 39, 1935, p. 74-93.

— Zu altindischen Anschauungen von den Eingeweiden des Leibes. SA 28, 1935, p. 229-263.

— Die Herz-Lehre der altindischen Aerzte. Janus 41, 1937, p. 261-293.

— Der takman des Atharvaveda (Eine medizin-geschichtliche Skizze). Artibus Asiae 6, 1937, p. 230-242.
— Ueber die Entwicklung von Lehrbüchern indischer Medizin. SA 30, 1937, p. 47-61.
— Ueber die Tridoṣa-Lehre in der altindischen Medizin. SA 32, 1939, p. 290-314.
— Grundlagen altindischer Medizin, NAL, NF Nr. 74, Bd. 11, 1942, p. 3-100.
— Sinneslehre altindischer Medizin unter Beachtung arischer Grundlagen. NAL, NF Nr. 100, Bd. 14, 1944 (1952), p. 27-47.
— Grundsätze altindischer Medizin. Acta historica scientiarum naturalium et medicinalium, edidit Bibliotheca Universitatis Hauniensis, vol. 8. Kopenhagen, 1951.
— Manas und der Geist altindischer Medizin. NAL, NF Nr. 108, Bd. 15, 1952, p. 269-305.
— Zur Feuerwertung in altindischer Medizin. SA 37, 1953, p. 312-319.
— Kannten die altindischen Aerzte die Lunge? (Zur Bedeutung von kloman und phupphusa). SA 39, 1955, p. 134-144.
— yakṣma. MIO 4, 1956, p. 278-313.
— Ueber begriffliche Bewertungen altindischer Aerzte. MIO 4, 1956, p. 368-410.
— Eigenwertungen in altindischer Medizin. NAL, NF Nr. 138, Bd. 20, 1958, p. 1-232.
— Ueber indische Vorstellungen von der Verdauung. MIO 7, 1959-60, p. 198-223.
— Dhātu (eine Ausdrucksbestimmung in der indischen Medizin). PHMA, Heft 7, 1961, p. 3-23.
— Wörterheft zu einigen Ausdrücken indischer Medizin. MIO 8, 1961, p. 64-159 (Wörterheft Nr. 222).
— Eine Wind-Lehre der Bheḷasaṃhitā. WZKSOA 6, 1962, p. 29-39.
— Die vermeintlichen "Temperamente" in den indischen wundärztlichen Lehren. Janus 51, 1964, p. 184-192.
— Indische Würmerkrankheiten. Gesnerus 21, 1964, p. 14-22.
— Ueber indische Bewertungen der Sinne. WZKSOA 9, 1965, p. 39-47.
— Ueber verschiedene Ergebnisse indischer Textuntersuchungen durch Sprachwissenschaftler oder einen Medizingeschichtler. Rocznik Orientalistyczny 30, 1967, p. 95-113.

Mukhopādhyāya, Girindranāth — History of Indian Medicine, containing notices, biographical and bibliographical, of the Ayurvedic physicians and their works on medicine, from the earliest ages to the present time; with a foreword by Sir Asutosh Mookerjee. Vol. 1, Calcutta, 1923. Vol. 2, Calcutta, 1926. Vol. 3, Calcutta, 1929.

Nadkarni, A. K. — Dr. K. M. Nadkarni's Indian Materia Medica. 3d ed., revised and enlarged by A. K. Nadkarni. 2 vols. Bombay, 1954.

New Catalogus Catalogorum — see : Raghavan.

Nicholson, R. A. — A literary history of the Arabs. Cambridge, 1962.

Nighaṇṭu Ādarśa, by Bāpālāl G. Vaidya. Vidyābhavan Āyurveda Granthamālā Nr. 54, Vol. 1. Benares, 1968.

Nobel, J. — Ein alter medizinischer Sanskrit-Text und seine Deutung. JAOS, Suppl. Nr. 11, 1951, p. 1-35.

Nyāyasūtra — Die Nyāyasūtra's. Text, Uebersetzung, Erläuterung und Glossar von W. Ruben. Abhandlungen für die Kunde der Morgenlandes. Bd. 18, Nr. 2. (Leipzig, 1928). Reprint 1966.

Om Prakash — Food and drinks in ancient India (from earliest times to c. 1200 A.D.), with a foreword by B. Ch. Chhabra. Delhi, 1961.

Pālakāpya — Hastyāyurveda. Ed. by Śivadattaśarman. Publ. by Mahādeva Cimaṇājī

Āpṭe. Ānandāśrama Sanskrit Series Nr. 26. 1894.

Pāṇini — Pāṇini's Grammatik, herausgegeben, übersetzt, erläutert und mit verschiedenen Indices versehen von C. Böhtlingk. Reprografischer Nachdruck der Ausgabe Leipzig 1887. Hildesheim, 1964.

Paryāyamuktāvalī by Haricaraṇasena, ed. by Dr. Tarapada Chowdhury. Patna, 1947.

Peters, J. L. — Check-list of the birds of the world. Vol. 3, Columbiformes, Psittaciformes. Vol. 5, Trochili, Coliiformes, Trogoniformes. (Harvard University Press, 1937). Reprinted by the Museum of Comparative Zoology, Cambridge, Mass., 1961.

Petersburg Dictionary — see : Sanskrit-Wörterbuch.

Peterson, P. — A sixth Report of operations in search of Sanscrit Mss. in the Bombay circle. April 1895-March 1898. Bombay, 1899.

Pharmacognosy of Ayurvedic drugs, published by the Central Research Institute, University of Travancore, Trivandrum. Series 1, Nr. 2 (1953), 3 (1957), 4 (1960) 5 (1962), 6 (1963), 7 (1963), 8 (1964) and 9 (1966).

Platts, J. T. — A dictionary of Urdū, classical Hindī, and English. Reprinted from the fifth (1930) impression. Oxford, 1960.

Prater, S. H. — The book of Indian animals. 3d (revised) ed. Publ. by the Bombay Natural History Society. Bombay, 1971.

Purseglove, J, W. — Tropical crops. Dicotyledons. 2 vols. 2nd impr. London, 1969,

Radhakrishnan, S. — Indian Philosophy. 2 vols. First published 1923; repr., London 1951.

Raghavan, Dr. V. — New Catalogus Catalogorum. An alphabetical register of Sanskrit and allied works and authors. Vols. 1-6. Madras, 1967-71.

Raghunātha — Bhojanakutūhala by Raghunātha, publ. by Śūranāṭ Kuñjan Pillai. Vol. 1. Trivandrum Sanskrit Series Nr. 178. Trivandrum, 1956.

Rājanighaṇṭu — see : Dhanvantarīyanighaṇṭu.

Rājavallabhanighaṇṭu, with a Hindī commentary, ed. by Śāligrāmavaiśya. Śrī Veṅkaṭeśvar Press, Bombay, 1895.

Rau, W. — Lotusblumen. Asiatica, Festschrift Fr. Weller, 1954, p. 505-513.

Rāy, P. — History of chemistry in ancient and medieval India, incorporating the History of Hindu Chemistry by Ācārya Prafulla Candra Rāy. Calcutta, 1956.

Rechinger, K. H. — Flora Iranica. Flora des iranischen Hochlandes und der umrahmenden Gebirge : Persien, Afghanistan, Teile von West-Pakistan, Nord-Iraq, Azerbaidjan, Turkmenistan. Graz, 1963- ....

Renou, L. and Filliozat, J. — L'Inde Classique. Manuel d'études indiennes. Tome 2. Bibliothèques de l'École Française d'Extrême-Orient, vol. 3. Paris, 1953.

Robyns, A. — Contribution à l'étude monographique du genre Bombax s.l. Taxon 10, 1961, p. 156-160.

— Essai de monographie du genre Bombax s.l. Bruxelles, 1963.

Roth, R. — Madanapāla. Indische Studien 14, 1876, p. 398-401.

— Reviews (Anzeigen) : ZDMG 48, 1894, p. 138-140.

Rotter, J. — Die Warane (Varanidae). Die Neue Brehm-Bücherei Nr. 325. Wittenberg, 1963.

Roxburgh, W. — Flora Indica; or, Descriptions of Indian plants. Reprinted literatim from Carey's Edition of 1832. New Delhi, 1971.

Śabdakalpadruma or an encyclopaedic dictionary of Sanskrit words, etc. ... by Rājā Rādhā Kānta Deva. 5 vols. Chowkhamba Sanskrit Series Nr. 93, 3d ed., Benares, 1967.

Sachau, E. C. — Alberuni's India, an account of the religion, philosophy, literature, geography, chronology, astronomy, customs, laws and astrology of India about A.D. 1030, edited with notes and indices, by ... First Indian Reprint, Delhi, etc., 1964.

Sādhanamālā, ed. by Benoytosh Bhattacharya. Gaekwad's Oriental Series Nr. 26 (vol. 1) and Nr. 41 (vol. 2). 2nd ed. (repr.). Oriental Institute, Baroda, 1968.

Saduktikarṇāmṛta — see : Śrīdharadāsa.

Sálim Ali and S. Dillon Ripley — Handbook of the birds of India and Pakistan together with those of Nepal, Sikkim, Bhutan and Ceylon. Vol. 3, Stone curlews to owls, 1969. Vol. 4, Frogmouths to pittas, 1970. Oxford University Press, Bombay-London-New-York.

Sāṃkhya — see also : Garbe, R.

Sāṃkhyakārikā — The Sāṃkhya Kārikā of Mahāmuni Śrī Īśvarakṛṣṇa, with the commentary Sārabodhinī of Paṇḍit Śivanārāyaṇa Śāstrī, with the Sāṃkhya Tattvakaumudī of Vācaspaṭi Miśra, published by Pāṇḍurang Jāwaji, Nirṇaya Sāgar Press, Bombay, 1940.

Sāṃkhyapravacanabhāṣya — The Sāṃkhya-pravacana-bhāṣya or commentary on the exposition of the Sāṃkhya philosophy by Vijñānabhikṣu, ed. by R. Garbe. Harvard Oriental Series, vol. 2. 2nd printing. Cambridge, Mass., 1943.

Sāṃkhyasūtra — The Sāṃkhya aphorisms of Kapila, with illustrative extracts from the commentaries; translated by J. R. Ballantyne. Chowkhamba Sanskrit Studies Vol. 34. 4th ed., Benares, 1963.

Sanskrit-Wörterbuch herausgegeben von der Kaiserlichen Akademie der Wissenschaften, bearbeitet von Otto Böhtlingk und Rudolf Roth. Nachdruck der Ausgabe St. Petersburg 1855-1875. 7 vols. Osnabrück/Wiesbaden, 1966.

Sanyal, D. — Vegetable drugs of India. Calcutta, 1924.

Śārṅgadharasaṃhitā — The Śārṅgadhara-Saṃhitā by Paṇḍit Śārṅgadharācārya, son of Paṇḍit Dāmodara, with Āḍhamalla's Dīpikā and Kāśirāma's Gūḍhārtha-Dīpikā, ed. with foot-notes (and introduction) by Paṇḍit Paraśurāma Śāstrī. 2nd ed. Nirṇaya Sāgar Press, Bombay, 1931.

Śāstrī, Haraprasād — Report on the search of Sanskrit Manuscripts during the years 1895-1900. Calcutta, 1901.

— Contributions of Bengal to Hindu civilization. I. The first contribution : Taming and treatment of elephants. JBORS 5, 1919, p. 307-313.

Schmidt, R. — Beiträge zur Flora Sanscritica, III. Der Lotus in der Sanskrit-Literatur. ZDMG 67, 1913, p. 462-470. IV. Arekanusz und Betelpfeffer. ZDMG 67, 1913, p. 653-659.

Seal, B. N. — The positive sciences of the ancient Hindus. (reprinted), Delhi, etc., 1958.

Shamasastry, R. — Kauṭilya's Arthaśāstra, translated by ... 7th ed. Mysore, 1961.

Siddhayoga — see : Vṛnda.

Siddiqi, M. Z. — India as known to the ancient Arabs. Indo-Asian Culture 5, 1957, p. 277-281.

— Indian medical science among the ancient Arabs. Indo-Asian Culture 5, 1957, p. 374-378.

Siggel, A. — Die indischen Bücher aus dem Paradies der Weisheit über die Medizin des 'Alī ibn Sahl Rabban aṭ-Ṭabarī, übersetzt und erläutert von ... Akademie der Wissenschaften und der Literatur—Abhandlungen der Geistes- und Sozialwissenschaftlichen Klasse, Jahrgang 1950, Nr. 14. Wiesbaden, 1951.

Sinh Jee, Bhagvat, Maharaja of Gondal — A short history of Aryan medical science. 2nd ed. Gondal, 1927.

Śrīdharadāsa — Saduktikarṇāmṛta of Śrīdharadāsa, critically edited by S. Ch. Banerji. Calcutta, 1965.

Śrīpati — Gaṇitatilaka by Śrīpati with the commentary of Siṃhatilaka Sūri. Critically edited with introduction und appendices by H. R. Kāpadiā. Gaekwad's Oriental Series Nr. 78. Baroda, 1937.

Srivastava, G. P. — History of Indian Pharmacy. vol. 1. 2nd ed., Calcutta, 1954.

Stein, M. A. — Kalhaṇa's Rājataraṅgiṇī, a chronicle of the kings of Kaśmīr. Translated with an introduction, commentary, and appendices by ... 2 vols. Westminster, 1900.

Steinegger, E. und Hänsel, R. — Lehrbuch der Pharmakognosie auf phytochemischer Grundlage. Zweite neubearbeite Auflage. Berlin, etc., 1968.

Stenzler, A. — Beitrag zur Beantwortung von Prof. Flügel's Fragen über Indische Mediciner. ZDMG 11, 1857, p. 327.

Suśrutasaṃhitā — The Suśrutasaṃhitā of Suśruta, with the Nibandhasaṃgraha commentary of Śrī Ḍalhaṇāchārya and the Nyāyachandrikā Pañjikā of Śrī Gayadāsāchārya on Nidānasthāna. Revised third edition, edited from the beginning to the 9th Adhyāya of Cikitsāsthāna by Vaidya Jādavji Trikamjī Āchārya and the rest by Nārāyaṇ Rām Āchārya "Kāvyatīrtha". Nirṇaya Sāgar Press, Bombay, 1938.

— Suśrutasaṃhitā with a Sanskrit commentary, called Suśrutārthasaṃdīpana, by Hārāṇacandra. Nidānasthāna, 1908; Sūtrasthāna, 1910; Śārīrasthāna, 1910; Kalpasthāna and Uttaratantra ch. 1-38, 1917.

— Suśrutas Āyurvedas, id est medicinae systema a venerabili Dhanvantare demonstratum a Suśruta discipulo compositum. Nunc primum ex Sanskrita in Latinum sermonem vertit, introductionem, annotationes et rerum indicarum adjecit Franciscus Hessler. 3 vols. Erlangae, 1844, 1847, 1850.

— The Suśruta-Saṃhitā, The Hindu System of Medicine according to Suśruta, translated from the original Sanskrit by Udoy Chānd Dutt. Fasc. 2. Bibliotheca Indica, New Series, Nr. 500. Calcutta, 1883.

— The Suśruta-Saṁhitā, The Hindu System of Medicine according to Suśruta, translated from the original Sanskrit by Aughorechunder Chattopadhyaya. Fasc. 3, Bibliotheca Indica, New Series, Nr. 802. Calcutta, 1891.

— The Suçruta-Saṃhitā or The Hindū System of Medicine according to Suçruta, translated from the original Sanskrit by A. F. R Hoernle. Fasc. 1 (Sūtrasthāna, ch. 1-14). Bibliotheca Indica, New Series, Nr. 911. Calcutta, 1897.

— An English translation of the Sushruta Samhita, based on the original Sanskrit text, with a full and comprehensive introduction, additional texts, different readings, glossary and plates (in three volumes), translated and edited by Kaviraj Kunjalal Bhishagratna. Chowkhamba Sanskrit Studies, vol. 30. 2nd ed., Benares, 1963.

Tawney-Penzer — The ocean of story being C. H. Tawney's translation of Somadeva's Kathā Sarit Sāgara (or ocean of streams of story). Now edited with introductions, fresh explanatory notes and terminal essay by N. M. Penzer. 10 vols. (2nd revised and enlarged ed., 1924-28). Indian reprint, Delhi, etc., 1968.

Toḍara — see : Bulletin of the Department of History of Medicine, Hyderabad.

Trimallabhaṭṭa — Bṛdhadyogataraṅgiṇī by Trimallabhaṭṭa. Publ. by Hari Nārāyaṇa Āpṭe. 2 vols. Ānandāśrama Sanskrit Series Nr. 71. 1913, 1914.

Ullmann, M. — Die Medizin im Islam. Handbuch der Orientalistik, Ergänzungsband VI, 1. Abschnitt. Leiden, 1970.

Vāgbhaṭa — Aṣṭāṅgahṛdayasaṃhitā of Vāgbhaṭa, with the commentaries (Sarvāṅgasundarā) of Aruṇadatta and (Āyurvedarasāyana) of Hemādri, collected by Aṇṇā Moreśvar Kuṇṭe and Kṛṣṇaśāstrī Navre, edited by Parāḍkar Hariśāstrī; introduction by P. K. Gode. 6th ed. Nirṇaya Sāgar Press, Bombay, 1939.

— Aṣṭāṅgahṛdayasaṃhitā, with the commentaries of Aruṇadatta, Candranandana and Hemādri. Vol. 1, Sūtrasthāna, with ṭippaṇī by Paṇḍit Rāmprasādjī Śarmā; foreword by Shiv Sharma. Śrīveṅkaṭeśvar Steam Press, Bombay, 1928.

— Aṣṭāṅgahṛdaya of Vāhaṭa, with the commentary Hṛdayabodhikā of Śrīdāsapaṇḍita. Part 2 (Sūtrasthāna ch. 16-30); ed. by P. K. Narayana Pillai. Trivandrum Sanskrit Series Nr. 155. Trivandrum, 1950. Part 3 (Śārīrasthāna and Nidānasthāna); ed. by K. Raghavan Pillai. Trivandrum Sanskrit Series Nr. 201. Trivandrum, 1962.

— Aṣṭāṅgahṛdaya by Vāhaṭa. Uttarasthāna with the "Kairalī" commentary. Vaidyasarathy Series Nr. 1. Vaidyasarathy Press, Kottayam, 1952.

— Vāgbhaṭa's Aṣṭāṅgahṛdayasaṃhitā, ein altindisches Lehrbuch der Heilkunde, aus dem Sanskrit ins Deutsche übertragen mit Einleitung, Anmerkungen und Indices von Luise Hilgenberg und Willibald Kirfel. Leiden, 1941.

— Aṣṭāṅgasaṃgraha by Vāgbhaṭa, with Hindī translation and commentary by Atrideva Gupta. Part 1. Introduction (in Sanskrit) by Nandakiśorśarmā. Nirṇaya Sāgar Press, Bombay, 1951. Part 2. Benares Hindu University Press, Benares, 1962.

— Aṣṭāṅgasaṃgraha by Vāgbhaṭa, with the commentary (Śaśilekhā) of Indu. Nidānasthāna. Ed. by Rāmacandraśāstrī Kiñjavaḍekar. Āyurvedakalpataru Nr. 3. Citraśālā Press, Poona, 1940.

— Rasaratnasamuccaya by Vāgbhaṭa, with a Hindī commentary, called Suratnojjvalā, by Ambikādatta Śāstrī. Haridās Sanskrit Series Nr. 91. 3d ed., Benares, 1961.

— See also : C. Vogel.

Vaidyakaśabdasindhu or a comprehensive lexicon of Hindu medical terms and names of drugs (with their synonyms in Latin, Sanskrit, Hindi, Telugu, Bengali, etc.) with copious references to, and quotations from, standard works, compiled by Kavirāja Umeśachandra Gupta Kaviratna. Calcutta, 1894.

Vaiśeṣikasūtra — see : Faddegon.

Vākpati — The Gaüḍavaho. A Prakrit historical poem by Vākpati, originally edited by Shankar Pandurang Pandit, re-edited for the second edition by Narayan Bapuji Utgikar. Bombay Sanskrit and Prakrit Series Nr. 34. Poona, 1927.

Vallauri, M. — Saggio di versione del "Mādhavanidāna". GSAI 26, 1913-14, p. 253-290.

Vanauṣadhicandrodaya (An encyclopaedia of Indian botany and drugs) (in Hindī) by Śrīcandrarāja Bhaṇḍārī 'Viśārada'. Kāśī Sanskrit Series Nr. 161. 10 parts. 4th impr., Benares, 1956-1968.

Vaṅgasena — Vaṅgasena's Cikitsāsārasaṃgraha, with a Hindī translation by Lālāśāligrāma. Śrīveṅkaṭeśvar Press, Bombay, 1924.

Varāhamihira — Varāhamihira's Bṛhatsaṃhitā with an English translation and notes by Panditabhushana V. Subrahmanya Sastri and Vidwan M. Ramakrishna Bhat. Bangalore, 1947.

Viennot, O. — Le culte de l'arbre dans l'Inde ancienne. Annales du Musée Guimet, 59. Paris, 1954.

Vogel, C. — Vāgbhaṭa's Aṣṭāṅgahṛdayasaṃhitā; the first five chapters of its Tibetan version, edited and rendered into English along with the original Sanskrit, accompanied by a literary introduction and a running commentary on the Tibetan translating-technique. Abhandlungen für die Kunde des Morgenlandes, XXXVII, 2. Wiesbaden, 1965.

Vogel, J. Ph. — Errors in Sanskrit dictionaries. BSOAS 20, 1957, p. 561-567.

Vṛnda — Vṛndamādhava or Siddhayoga, by Vṛnda — with Śrīkaṇṭhadatta's commentary, called Kusumāvalī. Ānandāśrama Sanskrit Series Nr. 27. 2nd ed., 1943.

Watt, G. — The commercial products of India, being an abridgment of "The dictionary of the economic products of India". (London, 1908). Reprint edition, New Delhi, 1966.

Wealth of India, The — A dictionary of Indian raw materials and industrial products. Publ. by the Council of Scientific and Industrial Research, New Delhi. Raw Materials, vols. 1-3, New Delhi, 1948, 1950, 1952.

Winternitz, M. — Geschichte der indischen Literatur. 3 vols. Unveränderte Nachdruck der Auflage von 1908 (vol. 1), 1920 (vols. 2, 3). Stuttgart, 1968.

Wise, T. A. — Commentary on the Hindu System of Medicine. Calcutta, 1845; repr. London, 1860 and 1900.

Yogaratnākara, with Hindī commentary, called Vidyotinī, by Lakṣmīpati Śāstrī. Ed. by Brahmaśaṅkara Śāstrī. Kāśī Sanskrit Series Nr. 160. Benares, 1955.

Yogasūtra — Patanjala Darshana or The System of Yoga Philosophy by Maharshi Kapila, with the commentary of Vyasa and the gloss of Vachaspati Mishra, edited and published by Pandit Jibananda Vidyasagara. 3rd ed., Calcutta, 1940.

— The Yoga-System of Patañjali or The ancient Hindu doctrine of concentration of mind, embracing the mnemonic rules, called Yoga-sūtras, of Patañjali and the comment, called Yoga-Bhāshya, attributed to Veda-Vyāsa and the explanations, called Tattva-Vaiçāradī, of Vāchaspati-Miçra, translated from the original Sanskrit by J. H. Woods. Harvard Oriental Series Vol. 17. 3rd ed., Delhi, 1966.

Zachariae, Th. — Die indischen Wörterbücher (Kośa). Grundriss der Indo-Arischen Philologie und Altertumskunde, I. Band, Heft 3, B. 1897.

Addenda :

Encyclopaedia of Islam, The — New Edition. Vol. III, 1965-71.

Sezgin, F. — Geschichte des arabischen Schrifttums. Bd. III, Medizin-Pharmazie, Zoologie-Tierheilkunde. Leiden, 1971.

SANSKRIT INDEX

Words from other Indian languages between brackets

INDEX OF BOTANICAL NAMES OF PLANTS

INDEX OF ZOOLOGICAL NAMES OF ANIMALS

GENERAL INDEX